Philosophic Classics, 2nd Edition

FROM PLATO TO NIETZSCHE

FORREST E. BAIRD, EDITOR
Whitworth College

WALTER KAUFMANN
Late, of Princeton University

Prentice Hall, Upper Saddle River, New Jersey 07458

Library of Congress Cataloging-in-Publication Data

Philosophic classics: from Plato to Nietzsche / Forrest E. Baird,
    Walter Kaufmann, editor[s].—2nd ed.
        p.   cm.
    Includes bibliographical references.
    ISBN 0–13–237355–6
    1. Philosophy, European.   I. Baird, Forrest E.   II. Kaufmann,
Walter Arnold.
    B21.P394   1997
    190—dc20   96-9092
                                                            CIP

Acquisitions editor: Angela Stone
Editorial/production supervision: Linda Pawelchak
Interior design: Tom Nery
Cover design: Jayne Conte
Copy editing: Stephen Hopkins
Proofreading: Maine Proofreading Services
Cover photo: Raphael, *School of Athens*. Detail of Plato and
    Aristotle. Vatican Palace, Stanza Della Segnatura. Erich Lessins/Art Resource.
Photo editor: Lori Morris-Nantz
Photo research: Page Poore Kidder
Manufacturing buyer: Nick Sklitsis

This book was set in 10/11 Times Roman by The Clarinda Company and
was printed and bound by RR Donnelley & Sons Company. The cover was
printed by Phoenix Color Corp.

Printed in the United States of America
10   9   8   7   6   5   4   3   2   ʼ

ISBN 0-13-237355-6

Prentice-Hall International (UK) Limited, *London*
Prentice-Hall of Australia Pty. Limited, *Sydney*
Prentice-Hall Canada Inc., *Toronto*
Prentice-Hall Hispanoamericana, S.A., *Mexico*
Prentice-Hall of India Private Limited, *New Delhi*
Prentice-Hall of Japan, Inc., *Tokyo*
Simon & Schuster Asia Pte. Ltd., *Singapore*
Editora Prentice-Hall do Brasil, Ltda., *Rio de Janeiro*

Contents

PREFACE   xi

ANCIENT GREEK PHILOSOPHY   1

PLATO   3

Euthyphro   7
Apology   20
Crito   38
Phaedo (72c–82e; 112e–end)   47
Meno   60
Republic (Book III, 412b–417b; Book IV, 427c–448e; Book V, complete: 448e–480a; Books VI–VII, 502c–521b)   85
Parmenides (127–135)   147

ARISTOTLE   154

    Categories (Chapters 1–5)   157
    Physics (Book II, complete)   162
    Metaphysics (Book I, 1–4, 6, 9, Book XII, 6–9)   173
    On the Soul (Book II, 1–3; Book III, 4–5)   189
    Nichomachean Ethics (Books I–II; Book III, 1–5; Books VI–VII;
      Book X, 6–8)   195

HELLENISTIC PHILOSOPHY   267

EPICURUS   270

    Letter to Menoeceus   272
    Principal Doctrines   276

EPICTETUS   279

    Encheiridion (Manual)   280

PLOTINUS   293

    Enneads (Ennead I, Tractate 6)   294

CHRISTIANITY AND EARLY
MEDIEVAL PHILOSOPHY   301

AUGUSTINE   305

    Confessions (Book XI)   308
    City of God (Book XII, 1–9; Book XIX, 11–17)   322

BOETHIUS   341

    The Consolation of Philosophy (Book V, 6)   343

JOHN SCOTUS ERIUGENA   347

    The Division of Nature (Periphyseon) (Book I, 1–7, 14)   349

ANSELM (AND GAUNILO)   353

    Proslogion (Chapters 2–4)   355
    Gaunilo and Anselm: Debate   356

MOSES MAIMONIDES   362

    The Guide for the Perplexed (Part II)   364

THOMAS AQUINAS   368

    Summa Theologica (Part I, Questions 1–2)   372
    The Principles of Nature   388

LATE MEDIEVAL PHILOSOPHY   399

JOHN DUNS SCOTUS   402

    A Treatise on God as First Principle (Chapter 3)   403

WILLIAM OF OCKHAM   409

    Summa Logicae (Part I, 14–16)   411

NICHOLAS CUSANAS   417

    On Learned Ignorance (Chapters 1–4, 26)   418

MODERN PHILOSOPHY   425

RENÉ DESCARTES   427

   Meditations on the First Philosophy   431

THOMAS HOBBES   471

   Leviathan (selections from Chapters 1–3, 6, 9, 12–15,
       17–18, 21)   474

BARUCH SPINOZA   513

   Ethics (Sections 1–2)   515

JOHN LOCKE   567

   An Essay Concerning Human Understanding (in part)   569

GOTTFRIED LEIBNIZ   633

   Discourse on Metaphysics   636
   Theodicy   663
   The Monadology   670

GEORGE BERKELEY   679

   Three Dialogues Between Hylas and Philonous   682

DAVID HUME   740

   An Enquiry Concerning Human Understanding   743

IMMANUEL KANT   821

   Prolegomena to Any Future Metaphysics   824
   Foundation for the Metaphysics of Morals   896

NINETEENTH-CENTURY PHILOSOPHY   941

G.W.F. Hegel   943

Phenomenology of Spirit (B, IV, A)   946
Who Thinks Abstractly?   952
Reason in History (Chapters 1–3)   955

John Stuart Mill   986

Utilitarianism   989
On Liberty (Chapter 3)   1027

Søren Kierkegaard   1039

Fear and Trembling (Problema I)   1043
Concluding Unscientific Postscript (selections from Section I,
  Chapter 2; Section II, Chapter 2)   1051

Karl Marx   1070

Economic and Philosophical Manuscripts (in part)   1074
Manifesto of the Communist Party (with Friedrich Engels)
  (Chapters 1, 2, 4)   1093
A Contribution to the Critique of Political Economy
  (Preface)   1104

Friedrich Nietzsche   1105

The Birth of Tragedy (Chapters 1–3, 15, 25)   1109
On the Genealogy of Morality (first essay)   1119
Thus Spoke Zarathustra (Part I, 1–3)   1136
Twilight of the Idols (in part)   1138
The Anti-Christ (First Book, 1–7, 62)   1143

Preface

There is no better introduction to philosophy than to read some of the great philosophers. But few books are more difficult to read than Aristotle's *Metaphysics* or Spinoza's *Ethics*. Even works that are less puzzling are sometimes like snippets of a conversation that you overhear on entering a room: What is said is clear, only you cannot be sure you understand the point because you do not know what has gone just before. A slight point may be crucial to refute some earlier suggestion, and a seemingly pointless remark may contain a barbed allusion. As a result of this difficulty, some students of philosophy cry out for a simple summary of the "central doctrines" of the great philosophers. Yet carving up great books to excerpt essential doctrines is one of the greatest sins against the spirit of philosophy. If the reading of a whole Platonic dialogue leaves one more doubtful and less sure of oneself than the perusal of a brief summary, so much the better. It is part of the point of philosophy to make us a little less sure about things. After all, Socrates himself insisted that what distinguished him from other persons was not that he knew all, or even most, answers, but rather that he recognized his ignorance.

Still, one need not despair of joining this ongoing conversation. In the first place, you can get in near its beginning by starting with Plato and moving on from there. Given that they are over two thousand years old, his early dialogues are surprisingly easy to follow. The later Platonic dialogues, Aristotle, and much that follows will be more difficult, but by that point you will have some idea of what the conversation is about.

Second, the structure of this book is designed to make this philosophical conversation accessible. There are section introductions and introductions to the individual philosophers. The latter are divided into three parts: (1) biographical (a glimpse of the individual's life), (2) philosophical (a résumé of the philosopher's thought), and (3) bibliographical (suggestions for further reading). To give a sense of the development of ideas, there are short representative passages from some of the less important, but transitional, thinkers. To make all the works more readable, most footnotes treating textual matters (variant readings, etc.) have been omitted and all Greek words have been transliterated and put within angle brackets. My goal throughout this volume is to be unobtrusive and allow you to hear, and perhaps join in, the ongoing conversation that is Western philosophy.

In putting together this combined volume, I have tried to follow the same three principles I used in the individual volumes of the *Philosophic Classics* series: (1) to use complete works or, where more appropriate, complete sections of works (2) in clear translations (3) of texts central to the thinker's philosophy or widely accepted as part of the "canon." Those who use this volume in a one-term introduction to philosophy or history of philosophy course will find more material here than can easily fit in a normal semester. But this embarrassment of riches gives teachers some choice and, for those who offer the same course year after year, an opportunity to change the menu.

Since the publication of the last edition, Prentice Hall has acquired the Macmillan Publishing Company. This fortuitous occurrence has made available a number of new translations, including those from the acclaimed Library of the Liberal Arts series. The following readings are now given in a new translation: Plato, *Euthyphro* and *Republic;* Aristotle, *Nichomachean Ethics;* Epicurus, *Letter to Menoeceus* and *Principal Doctrines;* Boethius, *The Consolation of Philosophy;* John Scotus Eriugena, *The Division of Nature (Periphyseon);* René Descartes, *Meditations on the First Philosophy;* Gottfried Leibniz, *The Monadology;* Immanuel Kant, *Prolegomena to Any Future Metaphysics* and *Foundation for the Metaphysics of Morals;* G.W.F. Hegel, *Phenomenology of Spirit* and *Reason in History: A General Introduction to the Philosophy of History;* and Friedrich Nietzsche, *The Genealogy of Morals.*

In addition to these new translations, I have made the following revisions in this edition:

Additions: Plato, *Republic* (addition of Book III, 412b–417b); Aristotle, *On the Soul* (Book II, 1–3; Book III, 4–5); John Locke, *An Essay Concerning Human Understanding* (about double the material); John Stuart Mill, *On Liberty* (Chapter 3); Karl Marx, *Economic and Philosophical Manuscripts* (added "Alienated Labor" in place of "Introduction" to *A Contribution to the Critique of Political Economy*); Karl Marx and Friedrich Engels, *Manifesto of the Communist Party* (Chapters 1, 2, 4); and Nietzsche, *Twilight of the Idols* ("'Reason' in Philosophy" and "Morality as Anti-Nature").

Changes: Aristotle, *Metaphysics* (changed to Book I, Chapters 1–4, 6, 9; and Book XII, 6–9); Thomas Aquinas, *The Principles of Nature* (in place of *Concerning Being and Essence*); Friedrich Nietzsche, *Thus Spoke Zarathustra* (First Part, 1–3; in place of *The Gay Science* No. 125); three new section introductions; and a newly expanded introduction to Christianity and Early Medieval Philosophy.

*   *   *

I would like to thank the many people who assisted me in this volume, including the library staff of Whitworth College, especially Hans Bynagle, Gail Fielding, and Jeanette Langston; my colleagues, F. Dale Bruner, who made helpful suggestions on all the introductions; Barbara Filo, who helped make selections for the artwork; and Corliss Slack and John Yoder, who provided historical context; Stephen Davis, Claremont McKenna College; Jerry H. Gill, College of St. Rose; Rex Hollowell, Spokane Falls Community College; Arthur F. Holmes, Wheaton College; Stanley Obitts, Westmont

College; Wayne Pomerleau, Gonzaga University; Timothy A. Robinson, College of St. Benedict; Glenn Ross, Franklin and Marshall College; and Charles Young, Claremont Graduate School, who each read some of the introductions and gave helpful advice; my secretary, Michelle Seefried; my development editor, Susan G. Alkana; my production editor, Linda Pawelchak; my acquisitions editor, Angela Stone; and Ted Bolen, formerly of Prentice Hall. I would also like to acknowledge the following reviewers: James W. Allard, Montana State University; Robert W. Beard; Florida State University; Robert C. Bennett, El Centro College; Herbert L. Carson, Ferris State University; Mary T. Clark, Manhattanville College; Sandra S. Edwards, University of Arkansas; Keith W. Krasemann, College of Dupage; Helen S. Lang, Trinity College; Scott MacDonald, University of Iowa; Angel Medina, Georgia State University; Katherine Rogers, University of Delaware; Stephen Scott, Eastern Washington University; Daniel C. Shartin, Worcester State College; Walter G. Scott, Oklahoma State University; Thomas Sheehan, Loyola University; Howard N. Tuttle, University of New Mexico; Richard J. Van Iten, Iowa State University; and Donald Phillip Verene, Emory University.

I am especially thankful to my wife, Joy Lynn Fulton Baird, and to our children, Whitney Jaye, Sydney Tev, and Soren David, who have supported me throughout this enterprise.

Finally, I would like to thank my dear friend and mentor, Jack B. Rogers, to whom this volume is dedicated.

Forrest E. Baird
Professor of Philosophy
Whitworth College
Spokane, WA 99251
fbaird@eve.whitworth.edu

Philosophers in This Volume

400 B.C.	200 B.C.	0	A.D. 200	A.D. 400	A.D. 600	A.D. 800

Socrates
Plato
Aristotle
Epicurus
Epictetus
Plotinus
Augustine
Boethius

Other Important Figures

Pyrrho
Alexander the Great
Zeno of Citium
Cleanthes
Sextus Empiricus
Porphyry
Pseudo-Dionysius Areopagite
Mohammed
Charlemagne
Julius Caesar
Lucretius
Philo of Alexandria
Jesus
Paul
Justin Martyr
Marcus Aurelius
Ptolemy (astronomer)
Clement of Alexandria
Tertullian
Origen

A Sampling of Major Events

Death of Socrates
Punic Wars and rise of Rome
Wall of China
Jerusalem Temple destroyed
Furthest extent of the Roman Empire
Council of Nicea
Roman Empire divided
Fall of Rome
School of Philosophy
in Athens closed
by Justinian
Buddhism introduced
in Japan
Muslim conquest
of Northern Africa
and Spain
Peak of
Mayan
civilization in
Central
America

400 B.C.	200 B.C.	0	A.D. 200	A.D. 400	A.D. 600	A.D. 800

John Scotus Eriugena
Anselm

Moses Maimonides
Thomas Aquinas
Duns Scotus
William of Ockham
Nicholas Cusanas
Rene Descartes
Thomas Hobbes
Baruch
Spinoza

John Locke
Gottfried Leibniz
George Berkeley
George Berkeley
David Hume
Immanuel Kant
G.W.F. Hegel
John Stuart Mill
Søren Kierkegaard
Karl Marx
Friedrich
Nietzsche

Avicenna
Peter Abelard
Hildegard of Bingen
Averroës
Chu Hsi
Genghis Khan
Francis of Assisi
Roger Bacon
Bonaventure
Marco Polo
Meister Eckhart
Dante Alighieri

Catherine of Siena
da Vinci
Copernicus
Martin Luther
John Calvin
Giordano Bruno
Francis Bacon
Galileo
Shakespeare
Rembrandt
Pascal

Louis XIV
Isaac Newton
Giovanni Battista Vico
J.S. Bach
Voltaire
Thomas Reid
J.W. Goethe
Mozart
Mary Wollstonecraft
Napolean Bonaparte
Beethoven
Simón Bolívar
Queen Victoria

First Crusade
Construction of Romanesque Cathedrals
Construction of Gothic Cathedrals
Paris University founded
Magna Carta
Bubonic Plague
Ming Dynasty in China
Gutenberg invents moveable-type printing
Columbus sails to America
Luther begins Protestant Reformation
English defeat Spanish Armada
Manchu Dynasty in China
Charles I of England executed
English "Glorious Revolution"
Declaration of Independence
French Revolution
Chaka founds
Zulu empire
Brazil, Colombia,
and Ecuador
achieve
independence
American
Civil War

ANCIENT GREEK PHILOSOPHY

Something unusual happened in Greece and in the Greek colonies of the Aegean Sea some 2,500 years ago. Whereas the previous great cultures of the Mediterranean had used mythological stories of the gods to explain the operations of the world and of the self, some of the Greeks began to discover new ways of explaining these phenomena. Instead of reading their ideas into, or out of, ancient scriptures or poems, they began to use reason, contemplation, and sensory observation to make sense of reality.

The story as we know it began with the Greeks living on the coast of Asia Minor (present-day Turkey). Colonists there, such as Thales, tried to find the one common element in the diversity of nature. Subsequent thinkers, such as Anaximenes, sought not only to find this one common element, but also to find the process by which one form changes into another. Other thinkers, such as Pythagoras, turned to the nature of form itself rather than the basic stuff that takes on a particular form.

With Socrates, the pursuit of knowledge turned inward as he sought not to understand the world, but himself. His call to "know thyself," together with his uncompromising search for truth, inspired generations of thinkers. With the writings of Plato and Aristotle, ancient Greek thought reached its zenith. These giants of human thought developed all-embracing systems that explained both the nature of the universe and the humans who inhabit it.

All these lovers of wisdom, or *philosophers,* came to different conclusions and often spoke disrespectfully of one another. Some held the universe to be one single entity, whereas others insisted that it must be made of many parts. Some believed that human knowledge was capable of understanding virtually everything about the world and the self, whereas others thought that it was not possible to have any knowledge at all. But despite all their differences, there is a thread of continuity, a continuing focus among them: the *human* attempt to understand the world and the self, using *human* reason. This fact distinguishes these philosophers from the great minds that preceded them.

The philosophers of ancient Greece have fascinated thinking persons for centuries, and their writings have been one of the key influences on the development of Western civilization. The works of Plato and Aristotle, especially, have defined the questions and suggested many of the answers for subsequent generations. As the great Greek statesman Pericles sagely predicted, "Future ages will wonder at us, as the present age wonders at us now."

*　*　*

For a comprehensive, yet readable, work on Greek philosophy, see W.K.C. Guthrie's authoritative *The History of Greek Philosophy,* six vols. (Cambridge: Cambridge University Press, 1962–1981). W.T. Jones, *The Classical Mind* (New York: Harcourt, Brace & World, 1969); Frederick Copleston, *A History of Philosophy: Volume I, Greece & Rome* (Garden City, NY: Doubleday, 1962); Friedo Ricken, *Philosophy of the Ancients,* translated by Eric Watkins (Notre Dame, IN: University of Notre Dame Press, 1991); and J.V. Luce, *An Introduction to Greek Philosophy* (New York: Thames and Hudson, 1992) provide basic introductions. Robert S. Brumbaugh, *The Philosophers of Greece* (Albany, NY: SUNY Press, 1981) is an accessible introduction with pictures, charts, and maps.

SOCRATES
470–399 B.C.

PLATO
428/7–348/7 B.C.

Socrates has fascinated and inspired men and women for over two thousand years. All five of the major "schools" of ancient Greece (Academics, Peripatetics, Epicureans, Stoics, and Cynics) were influenced by his thought. Some of the early Christian thinkers, such as Justin Martyr, considered him a "proto-Christian," while others, such as St. Augustine (who rejected this view) still expressed deep admiration for Socrates' ethical life. More recently, existentialists have found in Socrates' admonition "know thyself" an encapsulation of their thought, and opponents of unjust laws have seen in Socrates' trial a blueprint for civil disobedience. In short, Socrates is one of the most admired men who ever lived.

The Athens into which Socrates was born in 470 B.C. was a city still living in the flush of its epic victory over the Persians, and it was bursting with new ideas. The playwrights Euripides and Sophocles were young boys, and Pericles, the great Athenian democrat, was still a young man. The Parthenon's foundation was laid when Socrates was twenty-two, and its construction completed fifteen years later.

Socrates was the son of Sophroniscus, a sculptor, and of Phaenarete, a midwife. As a boy, Socrates received a classical Greek education in music, gymnastics, and grammar (or the study of language), and he decided early on to become a sculptor like his father. Tradition says he was a gifted artist who fashioned impressively simple statues of the Graces. He married a woman named Xanthippe, and together they had three children. He took an early interest in the developing science of the Milesians, and then he served for a time in the army.

When he was a middle-aged man, Socrates' friend, Chaerephon, asked the oracle at Delphi "if there was anyone wiser than Socrates." For once the mysterious oracle gave an unambiguous answer: "None." When Socrates heard of the incident, he was confused. He knew that he was not a wise man. So he set out to find a wiser man as "an excuse for going back and cross-examining the oracle." Socrates later described the method and results of his mission:

> So I examined this man—there's no need for me to mention his name, let's just say he was a politician—and the result of my examination . . . and of my conversations with him, was this. I decided that although the man seemed to many people, and above all to himself, to be wise, in reality he was not wise. I tried to demonstrate to him that he thought he was wise, but actually was not, and as a result I made an enemy of him, and of many of those present. To myself, as I left him, I reflected, "Here is *one* man less wise than I. In all probability neither of us knows anything worth knowing; but he *thinks* he knows when he doesn't, whereas I, given that I don't in fact know, am at least *aware* I don't know. Apparently, therefore, I am wiser than him in just this one small detail, that when I don't know something, I don't *think* I know it either." From him I went to another man, one of those who seemed wiser than the first. I came to exactly the same conclusion, and made an enemy of him and of many others besides. (*Apology* 21c)

As Socrates continued his mission by interviewing the politicians, poets, and artisans of Athens, young men would follow along. They enjoyed seeing the authority figures humiliated by Socrates' intense questioning. Those in authority, however, were not amused. Athens was no longer the powerful, self-confident city of 470 B.C., the year of Socrates' birth. An exhausting succession of wars with Sparta (the Peloponnesian Wars) and an enervating series of political debacles had left the city narrow in vision and suspicious of new ideas and of dissent. In 399 B.C. Meletus and Anytus brought an indictment of "impiety and corrupting the youth" against Socrates. As recorded in the *Apology,* the Athenian assembly found him guilty by a vote of 280 to 220 and sentenced him to death. His noble death is described incomparably in the closing pages of the *Phaedo* by Plato.

Socrates wrote nothing, and our knowledge of his thought comes exclusively from the report of others. The playwright Aristophanes (455–375 B.C.) satirized Socrates in his comedy *The Clouds.* His caricature of Socrates as a cheat and charlatan was apparently so damaging that Socrates felt compelled to offer a rebuttal before the Athenian assembly (see the *Apology,* following). The military general Xenophon (ca. 430–350 B.C.) honored his friend Socrates in his *Apology of Socrates,* his *Symposium,* and, later, in his *Memorabilia* ("Recollections of Socrates"). In an effort to defend his dead friend's memory, Xenophon's writings illumine Socrates' life and character. Though born fifteen years after the death of Socrates, Aristotle (384–322 B.C.) left many fascinating allusions to Socrates in his philosophic works, as did several later Greek philosophers. But the primary source of our knowledge of Socrates comes from one of those young men who followed him: Plato.

*   *   *

Plato was probably born in 428/7 B.C. He had two older brothers, Adeimantus and Glaucon, who appear in Plato's *Republic,* and a sister, Potone. Though he may have known Socrates since childhood, Plato was probably nearer twenty when he came under the intellectual spell of Socrates. The death of Socrates made an enormous impression on Plato and contributed to his call to bear witness to posterity of "the best, . . . the wisest and most just" person that he knew (*Phaedo,* 118).

Though Plato was from a distinguished family and might have followed his relatives into politics, he chose philosophy.

Following Socrates' execution, the twenty-eight-year-old Plato left Athens and traveled for a time. He is reported to have visited Egypt and Cyrene—though some scholars doubt this. During this time he wrote his early dialogues on Socrates' life and teachings. He also visited Italy and Sicily, where he became the friend of Dion, a relative of Dionysius, the tyrant of Syracuse, Sicily.

On returning to Athens from Sicily, Plato founded a school, which came to be called the Academy. One might say it was the world's first university, and it endured as a center of higher learning for nearly one thousand years, until the Roman emperor Justinian closed it in A.D. 529. Except for two later trips to Sicily, where he unsuccessfully sought to institute his political theories, Plato spent the rest of his life at the Athenian Academy. Among his students was Aristotle. Plato died at eighty in 348/7 B.C.

Plato's influence was best described by the twentieth-century philosopher Alfred North Whitehead when he said, "The safest general characterization of the European philosophical tradition is that it consists of a series of footnotes to Plato."

* * *

It is difficult to separate the ideas of Plato from those of his teacher, Socrates. In virtually all of Plato's dialogues, Socrates is the main character, and it is possible that in the early dialogues Plato is recording his teacher's actual words. But in the later dialogues "Socrates" gives Plato's views—views that, in some cases, in fact, the historical Socrates denied.

The first four dialogues presented in this text describe the trial and death of Socrates and are arranged in narrative order. The first, the *Euthyphro,* takes place as Socrates has just learned of the indictment against him. He strikes up a conversation with a "theologian" so sure of his piety that he is prosecuting his own father for murder. The dialogue moves on, unsuccessfully, to find a definition of piety. Along the way, Socrates asks a question that has vexed philosophers and theologians for centuries: Is something good because the gods say it is, or do the gods say it is good because it is? This dialogue is given in the F.J. Church translation.

The next dialogue, the *Apology,* is generally regarded as one of Plato's first, and as eminently faithful to what Socrates said at his trial on charges of impiety and corruption of youth. The speech was delivered in public and heard by a large audience; Plato has Socrates mention that Plato was present; and there is no need to doubt the historical veracity of the speech, at least in essentials. There are two breaks in the narrative: one after Socrates' defense (during which the Athenians vote "guilty") and one after Socrates proposes an alternative to the death penalty (during which the Athenians decide on death). This dialogue includes Socrates' famous characterization of his mission and purpose in life.

In the *Crito,* Plato has Crito visit Socrates in prison to assure him that his escape from Athens has been well prepared and to persuade him to consent to leave. Socrates argues that one has an obligation to obey the state even when it orders one to suffer wrong. That Socrates, in fact, refused to leave is certain; that he used the arguments Plato ascribes to him is less certain. In any case, anyone who has read the *Apology* will agree that after his speech Socrates could not well escape.

The moving account of Socrates' death is given at the end of the *Phaedo,* the last of our group of dialogues. There is common agreement that this dialogue was written much later than the other three and that the earlier part of the dialogue, with its Platonic doctrine of Forms and immortality, uses "Socrates" as a vehicle for Plato's own ideas.

The *Apology, Crito,* and the selections from the *Phaedo* are all given in new translations by Tom Griffith. These translations capture the conversational nature of the dialogues while maintaining their literary quality and philosophical depth.

Like the *Phaedo,* the *Meno, Symposium,* and the *Republic* were written during Plato's "middle period," when he had returned from Sicily to Athens and had established the Academy. The *Meno* gives a fine and faithful picture of Socrates practicing the art of dialogue; it also marks the point at which Plato moves beyond his master. This dialogue answers the question, "Can virtue be taught?," and treats the issues of knowledge and belief. The *Meno* is given in W.K.C. Guthrie's authoritative translation.

There are few books in Western civilization that have had the impact of Plato's *Republic*—aside from the Bible, perhaps none. Like the Bible there are also few books whose interpretation and evaluation have differed so widely. Apparently it is a description of Plato's ideal society: a utopian vision of the just state, possible only if philosophers were kings. But some (see the following suggested readings) claim that its purpose is not to give a model of the ideal state, but to show the impossibility of such a state and to convince aspiring philosophers to shun politics. Evaluations of the *Republic* have also varied widely: from the criticisms of Karl Popper, who denounced the *Republic* as totalitarian, to the admiration of more traditional interpreters, such as Francis MacDonald Cornford and Gregory Vlastos.

Given the importance of this work and the diversity of opinions concerning its points and value, it was extremely difficult to decide which sections of the *Republic* to include in this series. I chose to include the descriptions of the guardians and of the "noble lie" from Book III, the discussions of the virtues and the soul in Book IV, the presentations of the guardians' qualities and lifestyles in Book V, and the key sections on knowledge (including the analogy of the line and the myth of the cave) from the end of Book VI and the beginning of Book VII. I admit that space constraints have forced me to exclude important sections. Ideally, the selections chosen will whet the student's appetite to read the rest of this classic. I am pleased to be able to use the new Robin Waterfield translation.

The *Parmenides* marks a move in the development of Plato's thought—from positive philosophy to critical issues. The *Parmenides* is remarkable for the honesty with which Plato attacks the problems with his own doctrine of Forms. The *Parmenides* is given in the Cornford translation. The marginal page numbers are those of all scholarly editions, Greek, English, German, or French.

*   *   *

For studies of Socrates, see the classic A.E. Taylor, *Socrates: The Man and His Thought* (London: Methuen, 1933); the second half of Volume III of W.K.C. Guthrie, *The History of Greek Philosophy* (Cambridge: Cambridge University Press, 1969); and Hugh H. Benson, *Essays on the Philosophy of Socrates* (Oxford: Oxford University Press, 1992). For collections of essays, see Gregory Vlastos, ed., *The Philosophy of Socrates* (Garden City, NY: Doubleday, 1971), and Hugh H. Benson, ed., *Essays on the Philosophy of Socrates* (Oxford: Oxford University Press, 1992). For discussions of the similarities and differences between the historical Socrates and the "Socrates" of the Platonic dialogues, see Gregory Vlastos, *Socrates: Ironist and Moral Philosopher* (Ithaca, NY: Cornell

University Press, 1991), especially Chapters 2 and 3, and Thomas C. Brickhouse and Nicholas D. Smith, *Plato's Socrates* (Oxford: Oxford University Press, 1994).

Books about Plato are legion. Once again the work of W.K.C. Guthrie is sensible, comprehensive, yet readable. See Volumes IV and V of his *The History of Greek Philosophy* (Cambridge: Cambridge University Press, 1975 and 1978). Paul Shorey, *What Plato Said* (Chicago: Chicago University Press, 1933), and G.M.A. Grube, *Plato's Thought* (London: Methuen, 1935) are classic treatments of Plato, while Robert Brumbaugh, *Plato for a Modern Age* (New York: Macmillan, 1964), I.M. Crombie, *An Examination of Plato's Doctrines,* two vols. (New York: Humanities Press, 1963–1969), R.M. Hare, *Plato* (Oxford: Oxford University Press, 1982), and David J. Melling, *Understanding Plato* (Oxford: Oxford University Press, 1987) are more recent studies. For collections of essays, see Gregory Vlastos, ed., *Plato: A Collection of Critical Essays,* two vols. (Garden City, NY: Doubleday, 1971) and Richard Kraut, ed., *The Cambridge Companion to Plato* (Cambridge: Cambridge University Press, 1991). For further reading on the *Republic,* see Nicholas P. White, *A Companion to Plato's Republic* (Indianapolis, IN: Hackett, 1979), and Julia Annas, *An Introduction to Plato's Republic* (Oxford: Clarendon Press, 1981). Terence Irwin, *Plato's Ethics* (Oxford: Oxford University Press, 1995) examines several dialogues while thoroughly exploring Plato's ethical thought. Finally, for unusual interpretations of Plato and his work, see Werner Jaeger, *Paideia,* Vols. II and III, translated by Gilbert Highet (New York: Oxford University Press, 1939–1943); Karl R. Popper, *The Open Society and Its Enemies: Volume I: The Spell of Plato* (Princeton, NJ: Princeton University Press, 1962); and Allan Bloom's interpretive essay in Plato, *Republic,* translated by Allan Bloom (New York: Basic Books, 1968).

EUTHYPHRO

Characters

Socrates
Euthyphro
Scene—The Hall of the King*

EUTHYPHRO: What in the world are you doing here in the king's hall, Socrates? Why have you left your haunts in the Lyceum? You surely cannot have a suit before him, as I have.

SOCRATES: The Athenians, Euthyphro, call it an indictment, not a suit.

EUTHYPHRO: What? Do you mean that someone is prosecuting you? I cannot believe that you are prosecuting anyone yourself.

2

b

*The anachronistic title "king" was retained by the magistrate who had jurisdiction over crimes affecting the state religion.

Plato, *Euthyphro, Apology, Crito,* translated by F.J. Church (New York: Macmillan/Library of the Liberal Arts, 1963).

a.

b.

c.

d.

The Acropolis and the Parthenon

a. The *Parthenon*, Athens, built 477–438 B.C. The Parthenon, dedicated to
Athena, patron deity of Athens, was at one period rededicated to the Christian
Virgin Mary and then later became a Turkish mosque. In 1687 a gunpowder
explosion created the ruin we see today. The Doric shell remains as a
monument to ancient architectural engineering expertise and to a sense of
classical beauty and order. (*Greek National Tourist Office Photo*).

b. Restored plan of the Acropolis, 400 B.C. The history of the Acropolis is as
varied as the style and size of the temples and buildings constructed atop the
ancient site.

c. This model of the Acropolis of Athens recreates the complexity of fifth
century B.C. public space, which included centers for worship, public forum,
and entertainment. (*Royal Ontario Museum, Toronto*)

d. Doric, Ionic, and Corinthian columns with their characteristic capitals.
(*Library of Congress*)

SOCRATES: Certainly I am not.
EUTHYPHRO: Then is someone prosecuting you?
SOCRATES: Yes.
EUTHYPHRO: Who is he?
SOCRATES: I scarcely know him myself, Euthyphro; I think he must be some un-
known young man. His name, however, is Meletus, and his district Pitthis, if you can
call to mind any Meletus of that district—a hook-nosed man with lanky hair and rather
a scanty beard.

EUTHYPHRO: I don't know him, Socrates. But tell me, what is he prosecuting you for?

SOCRATES: What for? Not on trivial grounds, I think. It is no small thing for so young a man to have formed an opinion on such an important matter. For he, he says, knows how the young are corrupted, and who are their corrupters. He must be a wise man who, observing my ignorance, is going to accuse me to the state, as his mother, of corrupting his friends. I think that he is the only one who begins at the right point in his political reforms; for his first care is to make the young men as good as possible, just as a good farmer will take care of his young plants first, and, after he has done that, of the others. And so Meletus, I suppose, is first clearing us away who, as he says, corrupt the young men growing up; and then, when he has done that, of course he will turn his attention to the older men, and so become a very great public benefactor. Indeed, that is only what you would expect when he goes to work in this way.

EUTHYPHRO: I hope it may be so, Socrates, but I fear the opposite. It seems to me that in trying to injure you, he is really setting to work by striking a blow at the foundation of the state. But how, tell me, does he say that you corrupt the youth?

SOCRATES: In a way which sounds absurd at first, my friend. He says that I am a maker of gods; and so he is prosecuting me, he says, for inventing new gods and for not believing in the old ones.

EUTHYPHRO: I understand, Socrates. It is because you say that you always have a divine guide. So he is prosecuting you for introducing religious reforms; and he is going into court to arouse prejudice against you, knowing that the multitude are easily prejudiced about such matters. Why, they laugh even at me, as if I were out of my mind, when I talk about divine things in the assembly and tell them what is going to happen; and yet I have never foretold anything which has not come true. But they are resentful of all people like us. We must not worry about them; we must meet them boldly.

SOCRATES: My dear Euthyphro, their ridicule is not a very serious matter. The Athenians, it seems to me, may think a man to be clever without paying him much attention, so long as they do not think that he teaches his wisdom to others. But as soon as they think that he makes other people clever, they get angry, whether it be from resentment, as you say, or for some other reason.

EUTHYPHRO: I am not very anxious to test their attitude toward me in this matter.

SOCRATES: No, perhaps they think that you are reserved, and that you are not anxious to teach your wisdom to others. But I fear that they may think that I am; for my love of men makes me talk to everyone whom I meet quite freely and unreservedly, and without payment. Indeed, if I could I would gladly pay people myself to listen to me. If then, as I said just now, they were only going to laugh at me, as you say they do at you, it would not be at all an unpleasant way of spending the day—to spend it in court, joking and laughing. But if they are going to be in earnest, then only prophets like you can tell where the matter will end.

EUTHYPHRO: Well, Socrates, I dare say that nothing will come of it. Very likely you will be successful in your trial, and I think that I shall be in mine.

SOCRATES: And what is this suit of yours, Euthyphro? Are you suing, or being sued?

EUTHYPHRO: I am suing.

SOCRATES: Whom?

EUTHYPHRO: A man whom people think I must be mad to prosecute.

SOCRATES: What? Has he wings to fly away with?

EUTHYPHRO: He is far enough from flying; he is a very old man.

SOCRATES: Who is he?

EUTHYPHRO: He is my father.

SOCRATES: Your father, my good man?

EUTHYPHRO: He is indeed.

SOCRATES: What are you prosecuting him for? What is the accusation?

EUTHYPHRO: Murder, Socrates.

b   SOCRATES: Good heavens, Euthyphro! Surely the multitude are ignorant of what is right. I take it that it is not everyone who could rightly do what you are doing; only a man who was already well advanced in wisdom.

EUTHYPHRO: That is quite true, Socrates.

SOCRATES: Was the man whom your father killed a relative of yours? But, of course, he was. You would never have prosecuted your father for the murder of a stranger?

EUTHYPHRO: You amuse me, Socrates. What difference does it make whether the murdered man were a relative or a stranger? The only question that you have to ask is, did the murderer kill justly or not? If justly, you must let him alone; if unjustly, you

c   must indict him for murder, even though he share your hearth and sit at your table. The pollution is the same if you associate with such a man, knowing what he has done, without purifying yourself, and him too, by bringing him to justice. In the present case the murdered man was a poor laborer of mine, who worked for us on our farm in Naxos. While drunk he got angry with one of our slaves and killed him. My father therefore bound the man hand and foot and threw him into a ditch, while he sent to Athens to ask the priest what he should do. While the messenger was gone, he entirely neglected the man, thinking that he was a murderer, and that it would be no great matter, even if he were to die. And that was exactly what happened; hunger and cold and

d   his bonds killed him before the messenger returned. And now my father and the rest of my family are indignant with me because I am prosecuting my father for the murder of this murderer. They assert that he did not kill the man at all; and they say that, even if he had killed him over and over again, the man himself was a murderer, and that I ought not to concern myself about such a person because it is impious for a son to pros-

e   ecute his father for murder. So little, Socrates, do they know the divine law of piety and impiety.

SOCRATES: And do you mean to say, Euthyphro, that you think that you understand divine things and piety and impiety so accurately that, in such a case as you have stated, you can bring your father to justice without fear that you yourself may be doing something impious?[7]

EUTHYPHRO: If I did not understand all these matters accurately, Socrates, I

5   should not be worth much—Euthyphro would not be any better than other men.

SOCRATES: Then, my dear Euthyphro, I cannot do better than become your pupil and challenge Meletus on this very point before the trial begins. I should say that I had always thought it very important to have knowledge about divine things; and that now, when he says that I offend by speaking carelessly about them, and by introducing re-

b   forms, I have become your pupil. And I should say, "Meletus, if you acknowledge Euthyphro to be wise in these matters and to hold the correct belief, then think the same of me and do not put me on trial; but if you do not, then bring a suit, not against me, but against my master, for corrupting his elders—namely, myself whom he corrupts by his teaching, and his own father whom he corrupts by admonishing and punishing him." And if I did not succeed in persuading him to release me from the suit or to indict you in my place, then I could repeat my challenge in court.

EUTHYPHRO: Yes, by Zeus! Socrates, I think I should find out his weak points if

c   he were to try to indict me. I should have a good deal to say about him in court long before I spoke about myself.

SOCRATES: Yes, my dear friend, and knowing this I am anxious to become your pupil. I see that Meletus here, and others too, seem not to notice you at all, but he sees through me without difficulty and at once prosecutes me for impiety. Now, therefore, please explain to me what you were so confident just now that you knew. Tell me what are righteousness and sacrilege with respect to murder and everything else. I suppose   d that piety is the same in all actions, and that impiety is always the opposite of piety, and retains its identity, and that, as impiety, it always has the same character, which will be found in whatever is impious.

EUTHYPHRO: Certainly, Socrates, I suppose so.

SOCRATES: Tell me, then, what is piety and what is impiety?

EUTHYPHRO: Well, then, I say that piety means prosecuting the unjust individual who has committed murder or sacrilege, or any other such crime, as I am doing now, whether he is your father or your mother or whoever he is; and I say that impiety means   e not prosecuting him. And observe, Socrates, I will give you a clear proof, which I have already given to others, that it is so, and that doing right means not letting off unpunished the sacrilegious man, whosoever he may be. Men hold Zeus to be the best and the most just of the gods; and they admit that Zeus bound his own father, Cronos, for   6 wrongfully devouring his children; and that Cronos, in his turn, castrated his father for similar reasons. And yet these same men are incensed with me because I proceed against my father for doing wrong. So, you see, they say one thing in the case of the gods and quite another in mine.

SOCRATES: Is not that why I am being prosecuted, Euthyphro? I mean, because I find it hard to accept such stories people tell about the gods? I expect that I shall be found at fault because I doubt those stories. Now if you who understand all these matters so well agree in holding all those tales true, then I suppose that I must yield to your authority.   b What could I say when I admit myself that I know nothing about them? But tell me, in the name of friendship, do you really believe that these things have actually happened?

EUTHYPHRO: Yes, and more amazing things, too, Socrates, which the multitude do not know of.

SOCRATES: Then you really believe that there is war among the gods, and bitter ha-   c treds, and battles, such as the poets tell of, and which the great painters have depicted in our temples, notably in the pictures which cover the robe that is carried up to the Acropolis at the great Panathenaic festival? Are we to say that these things are true, Euthyphro?

EUTHYPHRO: Yes, Socrates, and more besides. As I was saying, I will report to you many other stories about divine matters, if you like, which I am sure will astonish you when you hear them.

SOCRATES: I dare say. You shall report them to me at your leisure another time. At present please try to give a more definite answer to the question which I asked you just now. What I asked you, my friend, was, What is piety? and you have not explained it to me to my satisfaction. You only tell me that what you are doing now, namely, prosecut-   d ing your father for murder, is a pious act.

EUTHYPHRO: Well, that is true, Socrates.

SOCRATES: Very likely. But many other actions are pious, are they not, Euthyphro?

EUTHYPHRO: Certainly,

SOCRATES: Remember, then, I did not ask you to tell me one or two of all the many pious actions that there are; I want to know what is characteristic of piety which makes all pious actions pious. You said, I think, that there is one characteristic which   e makes all pious actions pious, and another characteristic which makes all impious actions impious. Do you not remember?

EUTHYPHRO: I do.

SOCRATES: Well, then, explain to me what is this characteristic, that I may have it to turn to, and to use as a standard whereby to judge your actions and those of other men, and be able to say that whatever action resembles it is pious, and whatever does not, is not pious.

EUTHYPHRO: Yes, I will tell you that if you wish, Socrates.

SOCRATES: Certainly I do.

7   EUTHYPHRO: Well, then, what is pleasing to the gods is pious, and what is not pleasing to them is impious.

SOCRATES: Fine, Euthyphro. Now you have given me the answer that I wanted. Whether what you say is true, I do not know yet. But, of course, you will go on to prove that it is true.

EUTHYPHRO: Certainly.

SOCRATES: Come, then, let us examine our statement. The things and the men that are pleasing to the gods are pious, and the things and the men that are displeasing to the gods are impious. But piety and impiety are not the same; they are as opposite as possible—was not that what we said?

EUTHYPHRO: Certainly.

SOCRATES: And it seems the appropriate statement?

b   EUTHYPHRO: Yes, Socrates, certainly.

SOCRATES: Have we not also said, Euthyphro, that there are quarrels and disagreements and hatreds among the gods?

EUTHYPHRO: We have.

SOCRATES: But what kind of disagreement, my friend, causes hatred and anger? Let us look at the matter thus. If you and I were to disagree as to whether one number were more than another, would that make us angry and enemies? Should we not settle such a dispute at once by counting?

EUTHYPHRO: Of course.

SOCRATES: And if we were to disagree as to the relative size of two things, we should measure them and put an end to the disagreement at once, should we not?

EUTHYPHRO: Yes.

SOCRATES: And should we not settle a question about the relative weight of two things by weighing them?

EUTHYPHRO: Of course.

SOCRATES: Then what is the question which would make us angry and enemies if we disagreed about it, and could not come to a settlement? Perhaps you have not an answer ready; but listen to mine. Is it not the question of the just and unjust, of the honorable and the dishonorable, of the good and the bad? Is it not questions about these matters which make you and me and everyone else quarrel, when we do quarrel, if we differ about them and can reach no satisfactory agreement?

EUTHYPHRO: Yes, Socrates, it is disagreements about these matters.

SOCRATES: Well, Euthyphro, the gods will quarrel over these things if they quarrel at all, will they not?

EUTHYPHRO: Necessarily.

e   SOCRATES: Then, my good Euthyphro, you say that some of the gods think one thing just, the others another; and that what some of them hold to be honorable or good, others hold to be dishonorable or evil. For there would not have been quarrels among them if they had not disagreed on these points, would there?

EUTHYPHRO: You are right.

SOCRATES: And each of them loves what he thinks honorable, and good, and just; and hates the opposite, does he not?

EUTHYPHRO: Certainly.

SOCRATES: But you say that the same action is held by some of them to be just, and by others to be unjust; and that then they dispute about it, and so quarrel and fight   8 among themselves. Is it not so?

EUTHYPHRO: Yes.

SOCRATES: Then the same thing is hated by the gods and loved by them; and the same thing will be displeasing and pleasing to them.

EUTHYPHRO: Apparently.

SOCRATES: Then, according to your account, the same thing will be pious and impious.

EUTHYPHRO: So it seems.

SOCRATES: Then, my good friend, you have not answered my question. I did not ask you to tell me what action is both pious and impious; but it seems that whatever is pleasing to the gods is also displeasing to them. And so, Euthyphro, I should not be sur-   b prised if what you are doing now in punishing your father is an action well pleasing to Zeus, but hateful to Cronos and Uranus, and acceptable to Hephaestus, but hateful to Hera; and if any of the other gods disagree about it, pleasing to some of them and displeasing to others.

EUTHYPHRO: But on this point, Socrates, I think that there is no difference of opinion among the gods: they all hold that if one man kills another unjustly, he must be punished.

SOCRATES: What, Euthyphro? Among mankind, have you never heard disputes   c whether a man ought to be punished for killing another man unjustly, or for doing some other unjust deed?

EUTHYPHRO: Indeed, they never cease from these disputes, especially in courts of justice. They do all manner of unjust things; and then there is nothing which they will not do and say to avoid punishment.

SOCRATES: Do they admit that they have done something unjust, and at the same time deny that they ought to be punished, Euthyphro?

EUTHYPHRO: No, indeed, that they do not.

SOCRATES: Then it is not the case that there is nothing which they will not do and say. I take it, they do not dare to say or argue that they must not be punished if they have done something unjust. What they say is that they have not done anything unjust, is it   d not so?

EUTHYPHRO: That is true.

SOCRATES: Then they do not disagree over the question that the unjust individual must be punished. They disagree over the question, who is unjust, and what was done and when, do they not?

EUTHYPHRO: That is true.

SOCRATES Well, is not exactly the same thing true of the gods if they quarrel about justice and injustice, as you say they do? Do not some of them say that the others are doing something unjust, while the others deny it? No one, I suppose, my dear friend, whether god or man, dares to say that a person who has done something unjust must not   e be punished.

EUTHYPHRO: No, Socrates, that is true, by and large.

SOCRATES: I take it, Euthyphro, that the disputants, whether men or gods, if the gods do disagree, disagree over each separate act. When they quarrel about any act, some of them say that it was just, and others that it was unjust. Is it not so?

EUTHYPHRO: Yes.

SOCRATES: Come, then, my dear Euthyphro, please enlighten me on this point.   9 What proof have you that all the gods think that a laborer who has been imprisoned for murder by the master of the man whom he has murdered, and who dies from his imprisonment before the master has had time to learn from the religious authorities what he should do, dies unjustly? How do you know that it is just for a son to indict his father and to prosecute him for the murder of such a man? Come, see if you can make it clear

b   to me that the gods necessarily agree in thinking that this action of yours is just; and if you satisfy me, I will never cease singing your praises for wisdom.

EUTHYPHRO: I could make that clear enough to you, Socrates; but I am afraid that it would be a long business.

SOCRATES: I see you think that I am duller than the judges. To them, of course, you will make it clear that your father has committed an unjust action, and that all the gods agree in hating such actions.

EUTHYPHRO: I will indeed, Socrates, if they will only listen to me.

c   SOCRATES: They will listen if they think that you are a good speaker. But while you were talking, it occurred to me to ask myself this question: suppose that Euthyphro were to prove to me as clearly as possible that all the gods think such a death unjust, how has he brought me any nearer to understanding what piety and impiety are? This particular act, perhaps, may be displeasing to the gods, but then we have just seen that piety and impiety cannot be defined in that way; for we have seen that what is displeasing to the gods is also

d   pleasing to them. So I will let you off on this point, Euthyphro; and all the gods shall agree in thinking your father's action wrong and in hating it, if you like. But shall we correct our definition and say that whatever all the gods hate is impious, and whatever they all love is pious; while whatever some of them love, and others hate, is either both or neither? Do you wish us now to define piety and impiety in this manner?

EUTHYPHRO: Why not, Socrates?

SOCRATES: There is no reason why I should not, Euthyphro. It is for you to consider whether that definition will help you to teach me what you promised.

e   EUTHYPHRO: Well, I should say that piety is what all the gods love, and that impiety is what they all hate.

SOCRATES: Are we to examine this definition, Euthyphro, and see if it is a good one? Or are we to be content to accept the bare statements of other men or of ourselves without asking any questions? Or must we examine the statements?

EUTHYPHRO: We must examine them. But for my part I think that the definition is right this time.

SOCRATES: We shall know that better in a little while, my good friend. Now con-

10   sider this question. Do the gods love piety because it is pious, or is it pious because they love it?

EUTHYPHRO: I do not understand you, Socrates.

SOCRATES: I will try to explain myself: we speak of a thing being carried and carrying, and being led and leading, and being seen and seeing; and you understand that all such expressions mean different things, and what the difference is.

EUTHYPHRO: Yes, I think I understand.

SOCRATES: And we talk of a thing being loved, of a thing loving, and the two are different?

EUTHYPHRO: Of course.

b   SOCRATES: Now tell me, is a thing which is being carried in a state of being carried because it is carried, or for some other reason?

EUTHYPHRO: No, because it is carried.

SOCRATES: And a thing is in a state of being led because it is led, and of being seen because it is seen?

EUTHYPHRO: Certainly.

SOCRATES: Then a thing is not seen because it is in a state of being seen: it is in a state of being seen because it is seen; and a thing is not led because it is in a state of being led: it is in a state of being led because it is led; and a thing is not carried because it is in a state of being carried: it is in a state of being carried because it is carried. Is my meaning clear now, Euthyphro? I mean this: if anything becomes or is affected, it does not become because it is in a state of becoming: it is in a state of becoming because it   c becomes; and it is not affected because it is in a state of being affected: it is in a state of being affected because it is affected. Do you not agree?

EUTHYPHRO: I do.

SOCRATES: Is not that which is being loved in a state either of becoming or of being affected in some way by something?

EUTHYPHRO: Certainly.

SOCRATES: Then the same is true here as in the former cases. A thing is not loved by those who love it because it is in a state of being loved; it is in a state of being loved because they love it.

EUTHYPHRO: Necessarily.

SOCRATES: Well, then, Euthyphro, what do we say about piety? Is it not loved by   d all the gods, according to your definition?

EUTHYPHRO: Yes.

SOCRATES: Because it is pious, or for some other reason?

EUTHYPHRO: No, because it is pious.

SOCRATES: Then it is loved by the gods because it is pious; it is not pious because it is loved by them?

EUTHYPHRO: It seems so.

SOCRATES: But, then, what is pleasing to the gods is pleasing to them, and is in a state of being loved by them, because they love it?

EUTHYPHRO: Of course.

SOCRATES: Then piety is not what is pleasing to the gods, and what is pleasing to the gods is not pious, as you say, Euthyphro. They are different things.

EUTHYPHRO: And why, Socrates?   e

SOCRATES: Because we are agreed that the gods love piety because it is pious, and that it is not pious because they love it. Is not this so?

EUTHYPHRO: Yes.

SOCRATES: And that what is pleasing to the gods because they love it, is pleasing to them by reason of this same love, and that they do not love it because it is pleasing to them.

EUTHYPHRO: True.

SOCRATES: Then, my dear Euthyphro, piety and what is pleasing to the gods are different things. If the gods had loved piety because it is pious, they would also have   11 loved what is pleasing to them because it is pleasing to them; but if what is pleasing to them had been pleasing to them because they loved it, then piety, too, would have been piety because they loved it. But now you see that they are opposite things, and wholly different from each other. For the one is of a sort to be loved because it is loved, while the other is loved because it is of a sort to be loved. My question, Euthyphro, was, What is piety? But it turns out that you have not explained to me the essential character of   b piety; you have been content to mention an effect which belongs to it—namely, that all the gods love it. You have not yet told me what its essential character is. Do not, if you please, keep from me what piety is; begin again and tell me that. Never mind whether the gods love it, or whether it has other effects: we shall not differ on that point. Do your best to make clear to me what is piety and what is impiety.

EUTHYPHRO: But, Socrates, I really don't know how to explain to you what is in my mind. Whatever statement we put forward always somehow moves round in a circle, and will not stay where we put it.

SOCRATES I think that your statements, Euthyphro, are worthy of my ancestor c Daedalus.* If they had been mine and I had set them down, I dare say you would have made fun of me, and said that it was the consequence of my descent from Daedalus that the statements which I construct run away, as his statues used to, and will not stay where they are put. But, as it is, the statements are yours, and the joke would have no point. You yourself see that they will not stay still.

EUTHYPHRO: Nay, Socrates, I think that the joke is very much in point. It is not my fault that the statement moves round in a circle and will not stay still. But you are the Daedalus, I think; as far as I am concerned, my statements would have stayed put.

SOCRATES: Then, my friend, I must be a more skillful artist than Daedalus; he only used to make his own works move, while I, you see, can make other people's works move, too. And the beauty of it is that I am wise against my will. I would rather that our statements had remained firm and immovable than have all the wisdom of Daedalus and all the riches of Tantalus to boot. But enough of this. I will do my best to help you to explain to me what piety is, for I think that you are lazy. Don't give in yet. Tell me, do you not think that all piety must be just?

12   EUTHYPHRO: I do.

SOCRATES: Well, then, is all justice pious, too? Or, while all piety is just, is a part only of justice pious, and the rest of it something else?

EUTHYPHRO: I do not follow you, Socrates.

SOCRATES: Yet you have the advantage over me in your youth no less than your wisdom. But, as I say, the wealth of your wisdom makes you complacent. Exert yourself, my good friend: I am not asking you a difficult question. I mean the opposite of what the poet [Stasinus] said, when he wrote:

b   "You shall not name Zeus the creator, who made all things: for where there is fear there also is reverence."

Now I disagree with the poet. Shall I tell you why?

EUTHYPHRO: Yes.

SOCRATES: I do not think it true to say that where there is fear, there also is reverence. Many people who fear sickness and poverty and other such evils seem to me to have fear, but no reverence for what they fear. Do you not think so?

EUTHYPHRO: I do.

c   SOCRATES: But I think that where there is reverence there also is fear. Does any man feel reverence and a sense of shame about anything, without at the same time dreading and fearing the reputation of wickedness?

EUTHYPHRO: No, certainly not.

SOCRATES: Then, though there is fear wherever there is reverence, it is not correct to say that where there is fear there also is reverence. Reverence does not always accompany fear; for fear, I take it, is wider than reverence. It is a part of fear, just as the odd is a part of number, so that where you have the odd you must also have number, though where you have number you do not necessarily have the odd. Now I think you follow me?

EUTHYPHRO: I do.

---

*Daedalus' statues were reputed to have been so lifelike that they came alive.

SOCRATES: Well, then, this is what I meant by the question which I asked you. Is   d
there always piety where there is justice? Or, though there is always justice where there
is piety, yet there is not always piety where there is justice, because piety is only a part
of justice? Shall we say this, or do you differ?

EUTHYPHRO: No, I agree. I think that you are right.

SOCRATES: Now observe the next point. If piety is a part of justice, we must find
out, I suppose, what part of justice it is? Now, if you had asked me just now, for instance, what part of number is the odd, and what number is an odd number, I should
have said that whatever number is not even is an odd number. Is it not so?   e

EUTHYPHRO: Yes.

SOCRATES: Then see if you can explain to me what part of justice is piety, that I
may tell Meletus that now that I have been adequately instructed by you as to what actions are righteous and pious, and what are not, he must give up prosecuting me unjustly
for impiety.

EUTHYPHRO: Well, then, Socrates, I should say that righteousness and piety are
that part of justice which has to do with the careful attention which ought to be paid to
the gods; and that what has to do with the careful attention which ought to be paid to
men is the remaining part of justice.   13

SOCRATES: And I think that your answer is a good one, Euthyphro. But there is
one little point about which I still want to hear more. I do not yet understand what the
careful attention is to which you refer. I suppose you do not mean that the attention
which we pay to the gods is like the attention which we pay to other things. We say, for
instance, do we not, that not everyone knows how to take care of horses, but only the
trainer of horses?

EUTHYPHRO: Certainly.

SOCRATES: For I suppose that the skill that is concerned with horses is the art of
taking care of horses.

EUTHYPHRO: Yes.

SOCRATES: And not everyone understands the care of dogs, but only the huntsman.   b

EUTHYPHRO: True.

SOCRATES: For I suppose that the huntsman's skill is the art of taking care of dogs.

EUTHYPHRO: Yes.

SOCRATES: And the herdsman's skill is the art of taking care of cattle.

EUTHYPHRO: Certainly.

SOCRATES: And you say that piety and righteousness are taking care of the gods,
Euthyphro?

EUTHYPHRO: I do.

SOCRATES: Well, then, has not all care the same object? Is it not for the good and
benefit of that on which it is bestowed? For instance, you see that horses are benefited and
improved when they are cared for by the art which is concerned with them. Is it not so?

EUTHYPHRO: Yes, I think so.

SOCRATES: And dogs are benefited and improved by the huntsman's art, and cat-   c
tle by the herdsman's, are they not? And the same is always true. Or do you think care
is ever meant to harm that which is cared for?

EUTHYPHRO: No, indeed; certainly not.

SOCRATES: But to benefit it?

EUTHYPHRO: Of course.

SOCRATES: Then is piety, which is our care for the gods, intended to benefit the
gods, or to improve them? Should you allow that you make any of the gods better when
you do a pious action?

EUTHYPHRO: No indeed; certainly not.

SOCRATES: No, I am quite sure that that is not your meaning, Euthyphro. It was
d for that reason that I asked you what you meant by the careful attention which ought to
be paid to the gods. I thought that you did not mean that.

EUTHYPHRO: You were right, Socrates. I do not mean that.

SOCRATES: Good. Then what sort of attention to the gods will piety be?

EUTHYPHRO: The sort of attention, Socrates, slaves pay to their masters.

SOCRATES: I understand; then it is a kind of service to the gods?

EUTHYPHRO: Certainly.

SOCRATES: Can you tell me what result the art which serves a doctor serves to
produce? Is it not health?

EUTHYPHRO: Yes.

e   SOCRATES: And what result does the art which serves a ship-wright serve to produce?

EUTHYPHRO: A ship, of course, Socrates.

SOCRATES: The result of the art which serves a builder is a house, is it not?

EUTHYPHRO: Yes.

SOCRATES: Then tell me, my good friend: What result will the art which serves
the gods serve to produce? You must know, seeing that you say that you know more
about divine things than any other man.

EUTHYPHRO: Well, that is true, Socrates.

SOCRATES: Then tell me, I beg you, what is that grand result which the gods use
our services to produce?

EUTHYPHRO: There are many notable results, Socrates.

14   SOCRATES: So are those, my friend, which a general produces. Yet it is easy to see
that the crowning result of them all is victory in war, is it not?

EUTHYPHRO: Of course.

SOCRATES: And, I take it, the farmer produces many notable results; yet the principal result of them all is that he makes the earth produce food.

EUTHYPHRO: Certainly.

SOCRATES: Well, then, what is the principal result of the many notable results
which the gods produce?

EUTHYPHRO: I told you just now, Socrates, that accurate knowledge of all these
b matters is not easily obtained. However, broadly I say this: if any man knows that his
words and actions in prayer and sacrifice are acceptable to the gods, that is what is pious; and it preserves the state, as it does private families. But the opposite of what is acceptable to the gods is sacrilegious, and this it is that undermines and destroys everything.

SOCRATES: Certainly, Euthyphro, if you had wished, you could have answered
c my main question in far fewer words. But you are evidently not anxious to teach me.
Just now, when you were on the very point of telling me what I want to know, you
stopped short. If you had gone on then, I should have learned from you clearly enough
by this time what piety is. But now I am asking you questions, and must follow wherever you lead me; so tell me, what is it that you mean by piety and impiety? Do you not
mean a science of prayer and sacrifice?

EUTHYPHRO: I do.

SOCRATES: To sacrifice is to give to the gods, and to pray is to ask of them, is it not?

EUTHYPHRO: It is, Socrates.

SOCRATES: Then you say that piety is the science of asking of the gods and giving
d to them?

EUTHYPHRO: You understand my meaning exactly, Socrates.

SOCRATES: Yes, for I am eager to share your wisdom, Euthyphro, and so I am all attention; nothing that you say will fall to the ground. But tell me, what is this service of the gods? You say it is to ask of them, and to give to them?

EUTHYPHRO: I do.

SOCRATES: Then, to ask rightly will be to ask of them what we stand in need of from them, will it not?

EUTHYPHRO: Naturally.

SOCRATES: And to give rightly will be to give back to them what they stand in   e need of from us? It would not be very skillful to make a present to a man of something that he has no need of.

EUTHYPHRO: True, Socrates.

SOCRATES: Then piety, Euthyphro, will be the art of carrying on business between gods and men?

EUTHYPHRO: Yes, if you like to call it so.

SOCRATES: But I like nothing except what is true. But tell me, how are the gods benefited by the gifts which they receive from us? What they give is plain enough. Every good thing that we have is their gift. But how are they benefited by what we give   15 them? Have we the advantage over them in these business transactions to such an extent that we receive from them all the good things we possess, and give them nothing in return?

EUTHYPHRO: But do you suppose, Socrates, that the gods are benefited by the gifts which they receive from us?

SOCRATES: But what *are* these gifts, Euthyphro, that we give the gods?

EUTHYPHRO: What do you think but honor and praise, and, as I have said, what is acceptable to them.

SOCRATES: Then piety, Euthyphro, is acceptable to the gods, but it is not prof-   b itable to them nor loved by them?

EUTHYPHRO: I think that nothing is more loved by them.

SOCRATES: Then I see that piety means that which is loved by the gods.

EUTHYPHRO: Most certainly.

SOCRATES: After that, shall you be surprised to find that your statements move about instead of staying where you put them? Shall you accuse me of being the Daedalus that makes them move, when you yourself are far more skillful than Daedalus was, and make them go round in a circle? Do you not see that our statement has come round to where it was before? Surely you remember that we have already seen that piety   c and what is pleasing to the gods are quite different things. Do you not remember?

EUTHYPHRO: I do.

SOCRATES: And now do you not see that you say that what the gods love is pious? But does not what the gods love come to the same thing as what is pleasing to the gods?

EUTHYPHRO: Certainly.

SOCRATES: Then either our former conclusion was wrong or, if it was right, we are wrong now.

EUTHYPHRO: So it seems.

SOCRATES: Then we must begin again and inquire what piety is. I do not mean to give in until I have found out. Do not regard me as unworthy; give your whole mind to   d the question, and this time tell me the truth. For if anyone knows it, it is you; and you are a Proteus whom I must not let go until you have told me. It cannot be that you would ever have undertaken to prosecute your aged father for the murder of a laboring man unless you had known exactly what piety and impiety are. You would have feared to risk the anger of the gods, in case you should be doing wrong, and you would have been e afraid of what men would say. But now I am sure that you think that you know exactly what is pious and what is not; so tell me, my good Euthyphro, and do not conceal from me what you think.

EUTHYPHRO: Another time, then, Socrates. I am in a hurry now, and it is time for me to be off.

SOCRATES: What are you doing, my friend! Will you go away and destroy all my hopes of learning from you what is pious and what is not, and so of escaping Meletus?
16 I meant to explain to him that now Euthyphro has made me wise about divine things, and that I no longer in my ignorance speak carelessly about them or introduce reforms. And then I was going to promise him to live a better life for the future.

APOLOGY

17 Well, I don't know what effect the prosecution has had on you, men of Athens. As far as I'm concerned, they made me all but forget the position I am in, they spoke so plausibly. And yet, to all intents and purposes, there was not a word of truth in what they said.

Of their many lies, one in particular filled me with amazement. They said you should be careful to avoid being led astray by my "skill in speaking." They were not in the least embarrassed at the prospect of being immediately proved wrong by my actual
b performance, when it becomes clear that I am not in the least skilled in speaking. That was what I found the most shameless thing about their behaviour—unless of course they call "skilled in speaking" someone who merely speaks the truth. If *that's* what they mean, then I would agree that I am in a different class from them as an orator.

As I say, they have told you little or nothing that was true, whereas from me you will hear the whole truth—certainly not a piece of polished rhetoric like theirs, men of
c Athens, with its words and phrases so cleverly arranged. No, the speech you are going to hear from me will use everyday language, arranged in a straightforward way—after all, I have confidence in the justice of what I have to say—so I hope no–one is expecting anything different. And I shall tell the truth, because it wouldn't be appropriate to appear before you at my age making up stories like a schoolboy.

However, there is one important request and concession I am going to ask of you, men of Athens. If you hear me making my defence in the same language I generally use in the city, among people doing business—where many of you have heard me—and elsewhere, do not be surprised on that account, or start interrupting. The reason for it is this. This is the first time I have ever appeared in court, though I am now seventy years
d of age. The kind of speaking practised here is, quite simply, foreign to me. Imagine I really were a foreigner; you wouldn't hold it against me, presumably, if I spoke in the di-
18 alect and manner in which I had been brought up. In the same way now, I make this request—justified, in my view—that you pay no attention to the manner in which I speak, be it inferior or superior. Please consider one point only, and focus your attention on that. Is there any justice in what I have to say, or not? That, after all, is the function of a member of the jury; the speaker's task is to tell the truth.

First of all, then, men of Athens, I am entitled to defend myself against the earliest false accusations made against me, and against my earliest accusers; after that against the more recent falsehoods, and my present accusers. After all, there have been many people, over the years, making accusations about me to you, and speaking not a word of truth. I fear them more than I fear Anytus and his supporters, dangerous though   b
they are as well. But the earlier ones are more dangerous, gentlemen. They took you in hand from childhood, for the most part, and tried to win you over, making accusations every bit as false as these today; they told you there was this man Socrates, an intellectual, a thinker about the heavens, an expert on everything under the earth, a man who could make the weaker argument the stronger.

These people, men of Athens, the ones who have saddled me with this reputation, are my most dangerous accusers, because those who listen to them think that students of   c
these subjects do not recognise the gods. What's more, there are a great many of these accusers, and they have been accusing me for a long time now. And thirdly, they were speaking to you at the age when you were most likely to believe them, when many of you were children and adolescents. Quite simply, they were prosecuting in an uncontested case, since there was no-one there to answer their charges.

What is particularly unfair is that I cannot even know, or tell you, their names—unless maybe one of them is a writer of comedies. But all those who tried to influence   d
you, out of spite and malice, together with those who were trying to influence others because they were genuinely convinced themselves—all these accusers are very hard to deal with. It is not possible to call any of them as a witness here, or cross-examine them; I just have to make my defence like someone shadow-boxing, and conduct my cross-examination with no-one there to answer.

So I hope you will accept my claim that I have two sets of accusers—the ones   e
who have just now brought this case against me, and the ones from way back, the ones I have been telling you about. Please believe also that I must make my defence against this second set first; after all, you heard their accusations at an earlier age, and on many more occasions, than you heard the later ones.

Very well. I must make my defence, men of Athens, and try to remove from your minds, in the very brief time available, the prejudice which you have so long held. I   19
hope that is how things will turn out, provided it really *is* the best outcome for you and for me, and that I shall achieve something by my defence. But I think it is difficult, and I am well aware of the magnitude of the task. Still, let it turn out as god wills, I must obey the law, and make my defence.

Let us go back to the beginning, then, and see what the accusation is which has   b
created this prejudice against me—the prejudice which Meletus was presumably counting on when he brought this case against me. What exactly did the originators of this prejudice say? We ought really to read out a sworn statement from them, just like the prosecution's. "Socrates is guilty of being a busybody. He enquires into things under the earth and in the heavens, and makes the weaker argument the stronger, and he teaches these same things to other people." That's roughly how it goes. You saw it for your-   c
selves in Aristophanes' comedy; you saw a Socrates there, swinging round and round, claiming he was walking on air, and spouting a whole lot of other drivel on subjects about which I make not the slightest claim to knowledge. Not that I have anything against knowledge of this kind, if anyone is an expert on such subjects; I hope Meletus will never bring enough cases against me to reduce me to that. No, it's just that I myself have no share in such knowledge.

Once again, I can call most of you as witnesses. I'm sure you can make the position clear to one another, and explain, those of you who have ever heard me talking—   d and a lot of you come in that category. Tell one another then, if any of you has ever heard me breathe so much as a word on such topics. That will help you to see that the rest of what is generally said about me has as little foundation.

No, there is no truth in these stories. And if anyone has told you that I undertake
e   to educate people, or that I make money out of it, there is equally little truth in that either. Mind you, if anyone *can* educate people—as Gorgias from Leontini can, or Prodicus from Ceos, or Hippias from Elis—then that seems to me to be a fine thing. Any of these men, gentlemen, can go to any city and persuade the young men, who are at liberty to spend their time, free of charge, with whichever of their fellow-citizens they
20   choose, to abandon the company of those fellow-citizens and spend time with him instead—*and* pay money to do so, *and* be grateful into the bargain.

Come to that, there is even one of them here, a wise man from Paros. I found out he was living in Athens when I ran into Callias, the son of Hipponicus, the man who has paid more money to these teachers than everyone else put together. I asked him—you
b   know he has two sons—"Callias," I said, "if your sons were colts or calves, we would be able to find and employ someone to look after them, someone who would turn them into outstanding examples of their particular species; and this person would be a trainer or farmer of some kind. But they aren't colts or calves; they are men. Whom do you propose to find to look after them? Who is an expert in this kind of excellence—the excellence of a human being and a citizen? I imagine, since you have sons, you must have thought about this question. Is there someone," I asked him, "or not?"

"There certainly is," he said.

"Who is he?" I said. "Where is he from? What does he charge?"

"Evenus," he said. "He is from Paros, Socrates, and he charges 500 drachmas."

I took my hat off to Evenus, if he really did have this ability, and yet taught for so
c   reasonable a fee. I wouldn't. I'd start giving myself airs, and become extremely choosy, if I had this kind of knowledge. But I don't have it, men of Athens.

I can imagine one of you interrupting me, and saying, "That's all very well, Socrates; but what *do* you do? Where have all these prejudices against you come from? I take it all this gossip and rumour about you is not the result of your behaving just like anyone else. You must be doing *something* out of the ordinary. Tell us what it is, so we
d   can avoid jumping to conclusions about you." This seems to me to be a valid point, so I'll try and explain to you what it is that has given me my reputation and created the prejudice against me. Give me a hearing. It may seem to some of you that I am not being serious, but I promise you, every word I say will be the truth.

I have gained this reputation, men of Athens, as a direct result of a kind of wisdom. What sort of wisdom? The sort we might perhaps call human wisdom. In fact, if
e   we are talking about this kind of wisdom, I probably *am* wise. The men I mentioned just now may well be wise with some more-than-human wisdom; I don't know how else to describe it. It's not a wisdom *I* know anything about. Anyone who says I do is lying, and trying to increase the prejudice against me.

Please do not interrupt me, men of Athens, even if you find what I say a little bit boastful. The claim I'm about to make is not *my* claim; I shall appeal to a reliable authority. I shall call the god at Delphi to give evidence to you about my wisdom; he can tell you if I really do possess any, and what it is like.

You remember Chaerephon, I imagine. He was a friend of mine, from an early
21   age, and a friend of most of you. He shared your recent exile, and returned from exile with you. You know what Chaerephon was like, how impetuous he was when he set about something. And sure enough, he went to Delphi one day, and went so far as to put this question to the oracle—I repeat, please do not interrupt, gentlemen—he asked if

there was anyone wiser than me; and the priestess of Apollo replied that there was no-one wiser. His brother here will give evidence to you about this, since Chaerephon himself is dead.

Let me remind you of my reason for telling you this. I am trying to show you the origin of the prejudice against me. When I heard the priestess's reply, my reaction was this: "What on earth is the god saying? What is his hidden meaning? I'm well aware that I have no wisdom, great or small. So what can he mean by saying that I am so wise? He can't be lying; he's not allowed to." I spent a long time wondering what he could mean. Finally, with great reluctance, I decided to verify his claim. What I did was this: I approached one of those who seemed to be wise, thinking that there, if anywhere, I could prove the reply wrong, and say quite clearly to the oracle, "This man is wiser than I am, whereas you said that I was the wisest." b

So I examined this man—there's no need for me to mention his name, let's just say he was a politician—and the result of my examination, men of Athens, and of my conversations with him, was this. I decided that although the man seemed to many people, and above all to himself, to be wise, in reality he was not wise. I tried to demonstrate to him that he thought he was wise, but actually was not, and as a result I made an enemy of him, and of many of those present. To myself, as I left him, I reflected: "Here is *one* man less wise than I. In all probability neither of us knows anything worth knowing; but he *thinks* he knows when he doesn't, whereas I, given that I don't in fact know, am at least *aware* I don't know. Apparently, therefore, I am wiser than him in just this one small detail, that when I don't know something, I don't *think* I know it either." From him I went to another man, one of those who seemed wiser than the first. I came to exactly the same conclusion, and made an enemy of him and of many others besides. d

After that I began approaching people in a systematic way. I could see, with regret and alarm, that I was making enemies, yet I thought it was essential to take the god seriously. So on I had to go, in my enquiry into the meaning of the oracle, to everyone who seemed to have any knowledge. And I swear to you, men of Athens—after all, I am bound to tell you the truth—what I found was this. Those with the highest reputations seemed to me to be pretty nearly the most useless, if I was trying to find out the meaning of what the god had said, whereas others, who appeared of less account, were a much better bet when it came to thinking sensibly. 22

I can best give an account of my quest by likening it to a set of labours—and all, as it turned out, to satisfy myself of the accuracy of the oracle. After the politicians I went to the writers—writers of plays, and songs, and the rest of them. That would be an open-and-shut case, I thought. I should easily show myself up as less wise than them. So I took to reading their works, the ones which struck me as showing the greatest skill in composition, and asking them what they meant; I hoped to learn from them. b

Well, I'm embarrassed to tell you the truth, gentlemen; but I must tell you. Practically anyone present could have given a better account than they did of the works they had themselves written. As a result, I quickly came to a decision about the writers too, in their turn. I realised that their achievements are not the result of wisdom, but of natural talent and inspiration, like fortune-tellers and clairvoyants, who also say many striking things, but have no idea at all of the meaning of what they say. Writers, I felt, were clearly in the same position. Moreover, I could see that their works encouraged them to think that they were the wisest of men in other areas where they were not wise. So I left them too feeling that I had got the better of them, in the same way as I had got the better of the politicians. c

Finally I went to the craftsmen. I was well aware that I knew virtually nothing, and confident that I would find much fine knowledge in them. Nor was I disappointed. d

They *did* know things which I didn't know; in this respect they were wiser than I was. However, our good friends the skilled workmen seemed also to me, men of Athens, to have the same failing as the writers. Each one, because of his skill in practising his craft,

e   thought himself extremely wise in other matters of importance as well; and this presumptuousness of theirs seemed to me to obscure the wisdom they did have. So I asked myself, on behalf of the oracle, whether I should accept being the way I was—without any of their wisdom, or any of their foolishness—or whether I ought to possess both the qualities they possessed. The answer I gave myself and the oracle was that it was best for me to remain as I was.

This survey, men of Athens, has aroused much hostility against me, of the most

23   damaging and serious kind. The result has been a great deal of prejudice, and in particular, this description of me as being "wise." That is because the people who were present on such occasions think that I am an expert myself on those subjects in which I demolish the claims of others. The truth probably is, gentlemen, that in reality god is wise, and that what he means by his reply to Chaerephon is that human wisdom is of little or no value. When he refers to the man here before you—to Socrates—and goes out of his

b   way to use my name, he is probably using me as an example, as if he were saying "That man is the wisest among you, mortals, who realises, as Socrates does, that he doesn't really amount to much when it comes to wisdom."

That's why, to this day, I go round investigating and enquiring, as the god would have me do, if I think anyone—Athenian or foreigner—is wise. And when I find he is not, then, in support of the god, I demonstrate that he is not wise. My preoccupation with this task has left me no time worth speaking of to take any part in public life or family life. Instead I live in extreme poverty as a result of my service to the god.

c   Another problem is that young people follow me—the ones with the most time at their disposal, the sons of the rich—of their own free will; they love listening to people being cross-examined. They often imitate me themselves, and have a go at cross-examining others. Nor do I imagine they have any difficulty in finding people who think they know something, when in fact they know little or nothing. The result is that the victims of their cross-examination are angry with me, rather than themselves; they

d   say Socrates is some sort of criminal, and that he has a bad influence on the young. When you ask them what I do and what I teach that makes me a criminal, they can't answer; they don't know. But since they don't want to lose face, they come out with the standard accusations made against all philosophers, the stuff about "things in heaven and things under the earth," and "not recognising the gods" and "making the weaker argument stronger." The truth, I think, they would refuse to admit, which is that they have been shown up as pretenders to knowledge who really know nothing. Since,

e   therefore, they are ambitious and energetic, and there are a lot of them, and since they speak forcibly and persuasively about me, they have been filling your ears for some time now, and most vigorously, with their attacks on me.

That is what Meletus relied on when he brought this charge against me, with Anytus and Lycon—Meletus feeling offended as one of the poets, Anytus as one of the craftsmen and politicians, Lycon as one of the orators. The result, as I said at the beginning, is that it would surprise me if I were able to remove from your minds, in

24   so short a time, a prejudice which has grown so strong. This is the truth, I assure you, men of Athens. I speak with absolutely no concealment or reservation. I'm pretty sure it's this way of speaking which makes me unpopular. My unpopularity is the proof that I am speaking the truth, that this *is* the prejudice against me, and these *are* the

b   reasons for it. You can enquire into these matters—now or later—and you will find them to be so.

So much for the accusations made by my first group of accusers. I hope you'll find what I've said a satisfactory defence against them. Now let me try and defend myself against Meletus, that excellent patriot (as he claims) and my more recent accusers. Let's treat them as a separate prosecution, and consider in its turn the charge brought by them. It runs something like this: it says that Socrates is guilty of being a bad influence on the young, and of not recognising the gods whom the state recognises, but practising a new religion of the supernatural.

That's what the charge consists of. Let's examine this charge point by point. He   c
says I am guilty of having a bad influence on the young. But *I* claim, men of Athens, that Meletus is guilty of playing games with what is deadly serious; he is too quick to bring people to trial, pretending to be serious and care about things to which he has never given a moment's thought. That this is the truth, I will try to prove to you as well. Come now, Meletus, tell me this. I take it you regard the well-being of the young as of the ut-   d
most importance?

MELETUS: I do.

SOCRATES: In that case, please tell these people who it is who is a good influence on the young. Obviously you must know, since you're so concerned about it. You've tracked down, so you say, the man who is a bad influence—me—and are bringing me here before these people and accusing me. So come on, tell them who is a good influence; point out to them who it is.

You see, Meletus? You are silent; you have nothing to say. Don't you think that's a disgrace, and a sufficient proof of what I am saying—that you haven't given it any thought? Tell us, my friend, who is a good influence?

MELETUS: The laws.   e

SOCRATES: Brilliant! But that's not what I'm asking. The question is what *man*— who will of course start off with just this knowledge, the laws.

MELETUS: These men, Socrates, the members of the jury.

SOCRATES: Really, Meletus? These men are capable of educating the young and being a good influence on them?

MELETUS: They certainly are.

SOCRATES: All of them? Or are some capable, and others not?

MELETUS: All of them.

SOCRATES: How remarkably fortunate—no shortage of benefactors there, then.   25
What about the spectators in court? Do they have a good influence, or not?

MELETUS: Yes, they do, as well.

SOCRATES: What about the members of the council?

MELETUS: Yes, the members of the council also.

SOCRATES: But surely, Meletus, the people in the assembly—the citizens meeting *as* the assembly—surely they don't have a bad influence on the young? Don't they too—all of them—have a good influence?

MELETUS: Yes, they do too.

SOCRATES: Apart from me, then, the entire population of Athens, as it appears, makes the young into upright citizens. I alone am a bad influence. Is that what you mean?

MELETUS: Yes, that's exactly what I mean.

SOCRATES: That's certainly a great misfortune to charge me with. Answer me this,   b
though: do you think the situation is the same with horses as well? Do the people who are good for them make up the entire population, and is there just one person who has a harmful effect on them? Isn't it the exact opposite? Isn't there just one person, or very few people—trainers—capable of doing them any good? Don't most people, if they spend time

with horses, or have anything to do with them, have a harmful effect on them? Isn't that the situation, Meletus, both with horses and with all other living creatures?

It certainly is, whether you and Anytus deny it or admit it. After all, it would be a piece of great good fortune for the young, if only one person has a bad influence on them, and everyone else has a good influence. No, Meletus. You show quite clearly that

c you have never cared in the slightest for the young; you reveal your own lack of interest quite plainly, since you've never given a moment's thought to the things you're prosecuting me for.

Another point. Tell us honestly, Meletus, is it better to live with good fellow-citizens, or with bad? Answer, can't you? It's not a difficult question. Isn't it true that bad citizens do some harm to those who are their neighbours at any particular time, while good citizens do some good?

MELETUS: Yes, of course.

SOCRATES: That being so, does anyone choose to be harmed by those close to him

d rather than be helped by them? Answer, there's a good fellow. Besides, the law requires you to answer. Is there anyone who chooses to be harmed?

MELETUS: No, of course not.

SOCRATES: Well, then. You bring me to court for being a bad influence on the young, and making them worse people. Are you saying I do this deliberately, or without realising it?

MELETUS: Deliberately, I'm sure of it.

SOCRATES: Really, Meletus? How odd. Are you, at your age, so much wiser than me at mine? Are *you* aware that bad people generally have a harmful effect on those

e they come into contact with, and that good people have a good effect? And have *I* reached such a height of stupidity as not even to realise that if I make one of my neighbours a worse man, I'm likely to come to some harm at his hands? And is the result that I deliberately do such great damage as you describe? On this point I don't believe you, Meletus; and nor, I think, does anyone else. No. Either I'm not a bad influence on the

26 young, or if I do have a bad influence, I do so without realising it. Either way you are wrong. And if I have a bad influence without realising it, it's not our custom to bring people here to court for errors of this sort, but to take them on one side, and instruct them privately, pointing out their mistakes. Obviously, if I'm taught, I shall stop doing what I don't at the moment realise I *am* doing. But you avoided spending time with me and instructing me; you refused to do it. Instead you bring me here to court, where it is our custom to bring those who need punishment, not those who need to learn.

I needn't go on, men of Athens. It must now be clear, as I've said, that Meletus has never given the slightest thought to these matters. All the same, Meletus, tell us this:

b *in what way* do you claim I'm a bad influence on the young? Isn't it obvious I do it in the way described in the charge you've brought against me—by teaching them not to recognise the gods the city recognises, but to practise this new religion of the supernatural instead? Isn't that your claim, that it's by teaching them these things that I have a bad influence?

MELETUS: Yes, that certainly is exactly what I claim.

SOCRATES: Well then, Meletus, in the name of these gods we are now talking

c about, make yourself a little clearer, both to me and to these gentlemen here, since *I* at least cannot understand you. Do you mean I teach them to accept that there are *some* gods—not the gods the state accepts, but other gods? In that case I myself must also accept that there are gods, so I am not a complete atheist, and am not guilty on that count. Is this what you charge me with, accepting other gods? Or are you saying that I don't myself recognise any gods at all, and that I teach the same beliefs to others?

MELETUS: Yes, that's what I am saying. You don't recognise any gods at all.

SOCRATES: Meletus, you are beyond belief. What can possess you to say that?   d
Don't I accept that the sun and moon are gods, in the same way as everyone else does?

MELETUS: Good heavens, no, men of the jury. He says the sun is a stone, and the moon is made of earth.

SOCRATES: Is it Anaxagoras you think you're accusing, my dear Meletus? Do you have such contempt for these men here? Do you think them so illiterate as to be unaware that the works of Anaxagoras of Clazomenae are stuffed full of speculations of that sort? And do the young really learn these things from me, when there are often books on sale, for a drachma at the very most, in the Orchestra, in the Agora? They can laugh at Socrates if he claims these views as his own—especially such eccentric views.   e
However, as god is your witness, is that your view of me? Do I not accept the existence of any god at all?

MELETUS: No, in god's name, no god at all.

SOCRATES: What you say is unbelievable, Meletus—even, I think to yourself. This man here, men of Athens, strikes me as an arrogant lout; his prosecution of me is prompted entirely by arrogance, loutishness, and youth. It's as if he were setting a trick question, to test me: "Will Socrates the wise realise that I'm playing with words and   27 contradicting myself, or will I deceive him and the others who hear it?" He certainly seems to me to contradict himself, in his accusation. He might as well say "Socrates is guilty of not recognising the gods, but recognising the gods instead." And that is not a serious proposition.

Please join me, gentlemen, in examining the reasons why I think this is what his accusation amounts to. You, Meletus, answer us. And you *(to the jurymen),* as I asked you at the beginning, remember not to interrupt me if I construct my argument in my   b usual way.

Is there anyone in the world, Meletus, who accepts the existence of human activity, but not of human beings? He must answer, gentlemen. Don't allow him to keep making all these interruptions. Is there anyone who denies horses, but accepts equine activity? Or denies the existence of flute-players, but accepts flute-playing? No, my very good friend, there isn't. If you refuse to answer, then I'll say it—to you and everyone else present here. But do answer my next question: is there anyone who accepts the   c activity of the supernatural, but denies supernatural beings?

MELETUS: No, there isn't.

SOCRATES: How kind of you—forced to answer, against your will, by these people here. Very well, then. You claim that I practise and teach a religion of the supernatural—whether of a new or conventional kind—so I do at least, on your own admission, accept the existence of the supernatural. You even swore to it, on oath, in your indictment. But if I accept the supernatural, it follows, I take it, that I must necessarily admit the existence of supernatural beings, must I not? I must; I take your silence for agreement. And don't we regard supernatural beings as either gods or the children of gods?   d Yes or no?

MELETUS: We certainly do.

SOCRATES: In that case, if I accept supernatural beings—as you admit—and if supernatural beings are gods of some sort, then you can see what I mean when I say that you are setting trick questions, and playing with words, claiming first that I do *not* believe in gods, and then again claiming that I *do* believe in gods, since I do believe in supernatural beings. If, on the other hand, supernatural beings are some form of illegitimate children of gods—born of nymphs or of some of the other mothers they are said to be born from—who on earth could believe that there are children of gods, but no gods?

e   It would be as absurd as saying you believed there were such things as mules, the off-spring of horses and donkeys, but didn't believe there were horses and donkeys.

No, Meletus, the only possible explanation for your bringing this accusation against me is that you wanted to test us—or that you didn't have any genuine offence to charge me with. There's no conceivable way you could persuade anyone in the world
28   with a grain of intelligence that belief in the supernatural and the divine does not imply belief in supernatural beings, divine beings and heroes.

So much for that, men of Athens. I don't think it takes much of a defence to show that in the terms of Meletus' indictment I am not guilty. What I have said so far should be enough. There remains what I said in the earlier part of my speech, that there is strong and widespread hostility towards me. Be in no doubt that this is true. It is this
b   which will convict me, if it does convict me—not Meletus, not Anytus, but the prejudice and malice of the many. What has convicted many other good men before me will, I think, convict me too. There's no danger of its stopping at me.

That being so, you might ask "Well, Socrates, aren't you ashamed of living a life which has resulted in your now being on trial for your life?" I would answer you, quite justifiably, "You are wrong, sir, if you think that a man who is worth anything at all should take into account the chances of life and death. No, the only thing he should think about, when he acts, is whether he is acting rightly or wrongly, and whether this is
c   the behaviour of a good man or a bad man. After all, if we accept your argument, those of the demigods who died at Troy would have been sorry creatures—and none more so than Achilles, the son of Thetis. Compared with the threat of dishonour, he regarded danger as of no importance at all. When he was eager to kill Hector, his mother, who was a goddess, said something like this to him, I imagine: 'My son, if you avenge the death of your friend Patroclus, and kill Hector, you will yourself be killed, since death awaits you immediately after Hector.' When Achilles heard this, he gave no thought to death or danger; what he feared much more was living as a coward, and not avenging
d   his friends. 'Let me die immediately,' he said, 'after making the wrong-doer pay the penalty, rather than remain here by the curved ships, a laughing-stock, like a clod of earth.' You don't imagine *he* gave any thought to death or danger."

That's the way of things, men of Athens, it really is. Where a man takes up his position—in the belief that it is the best position—or is told to take up a position by his commanding officer, there he should stay, in my view, regardless of danger. He should
e   not take death into account, or anything else apart from dishonour. As for me, when the commanders whom you chose to command me told me to take up position at Potidaea and Amphipolis and Delium, on those occasions I stayed where they posted me, just like anyone else, and risked death. Would it not have been very illogical of me, when *god* deployed me, as I thought and believed, to live my life as a philosopher, examining myself and others, then to be afraid of death—or anything else at all—and abandon my post?
29   It would indeed be illogical, and in that case you would certainly be completely justified in bringing me to court for not accepting the existence of the gods, since I disobey their oracle, and am afraid of death, and think I am wise when I am not. After all, the fear of death is just that, gentlemen—thinking one is wise when one is not—since it's a claim to know what one doesn't know. For all anyone knows, death may in fact be the best thing in the world that can happen to a man; yet men fear it as if they had certain knowledge that it is the greatest of all evils. This is without doubt the most reprehensible folly—the folly
b   of thinking one knows what one does not know.

As for me, gentlemen, perhaps here too I *am* different from most people, in this one particular; and if I did claim to be in any way wiser than anyone else, it would be in this, that lacking any certain knowledge of what happens after death, I am also aware that I have no knowledge. But that it is evil and shameful to do wrong, and disobey one's superiors, divine or human, that I *do* know. Compared therefore with the evils which I know to be evils, I shall never fear, or try to avoid, what for all I know may turn out to be good.

Suppose you now acquit me, rejecting Anytus' argument that either this case   c
should not have been brought in the first place, or, since it *had* been brought, that it was out of the question not to put me to death. He told you that if I got away with it, your sons would all start putting Socrates' teachings into practice, and be totally overwhelmed by my bad influence. And suppose your response were to say to me: "Socrates, on this occasion we will not do what Anytus wants. We acquit you—on this condition, however, that you give up spending your time in this enquiry, and give up the search for wisdom. If you are caught doing it again, you will be put to death."

Even if, then, to repeat, you were to acquit me on these conditions, I would say to   d
you, "Men of Athens, I have the highest regard and affection for you, but I will obey god rather than you. While I have breath and strength, I will not give up the search for wisdom. I will carry on nagging at you, and pointing out your errors to those of you I meet from day to day. I shall say, in my usual way, 'My very good sir, you are a citizen of Athens, a city which is the greatest and most renowned for wisdom and power. Aren't you ashamed to care about money, and how to make as much of it as possible, and about reputation and public recognition, whereas for wisdom and truth, and making your soul as good as it can possibly be, you do not care, and give no thought to these things at   e
all?' And if any of you objects, and says he does care, I shall not just let him go, or walk away and leave him. No, I shall question him, cross-examine him, try to prove him wrong. And if I find he has not achieved a state of excellence, but still claims he has, then I shall accuse him of undervaluing what is most important, and paying too much   30
attention to what is less important.

"That is what I shall do for anyone I meet, young or old, foreigner or citizen—but especially for my fellow-citizens, since you are more closely related to me. That is what god tells me to do, I promise you, and I believe that this service of mine to god is the most valuable asset you in this city have ever yet possessed. I spend my whole time going round trying to persuade both the young and old among you not to spend your time or energy in caring about your bodies or about money, but rather in making your souls   b
as good as possible. I tell you, 'Money cannot create a good soul, but a good soul can turn money—and everything else in private life and public life—into a good thing for men.' If saying things like this is a bad influence on the young, then things like this must be harmful. But if anyone claims I say anything different from this, he is wrong. With that in mind, Athenians," I would say, "either do what Anytus wants, or don't do it; either acquit me, or don't, knowing that I will not behave differently even if I am to be put to death a thousand times over."

Don't interrupt, men of Athens. Please stick to what I asked you to do, which was   c
not to interrupt what I say, but to give me a hearing. It will be in your interest, I think, to hear me. I have some more things to say which you could object to quite violently. Please don't, however

I have just described the kind of man I am. Take my word for it, if you put me to death, you will harm yourselves more than you will harm me. As for me, no harm can come to me from Meletus or Anytus, who *cannot* injure me, since I do not think   d
god ever allows a better man to be injured by a worse. Yes, I know he might put me to death, possibly, or send me into exile, or deprive me of citizen rights. And perhaps *he* regards these as great evils—as I suppose others may too. However, *I* do not. I regard

it as a much greater evil to act as he is acting now, attempting to put a man to death unjustly.

It follows, men of Athens, that in this trial I am not by any means defending myself, as you might think. No, I am defending you. I don't want you to fail to recognise god's gift to you, and find me guilty. If you put me to death, you will not easily find another like me. I have, almost literally, settled on the city at god's command. It's as if the city, to use a slightly absurd simile, were a horse—a large horse, high-mettled, but which because of its size is somewhat sluggish, and needs to be stung into action by some kind of horsefly. I think god has caused me to settle on the city as this horsefly, the sort that never stops, all day long, coming to rest on every part of you, stinging each one of you into action, and persuading and criticising each one of you.

Another like me will not easily come your way, gentlemen, so if you take my advice you will spare me. You may very likely get annoyed with me, as people do when they are dozing and somebody wakes them up. And you might then swat me, as Anytus wants you to, and kill me, quite easily. Then you could spend the rest of your lives asleep, unless god cared enough for you to send you someone else.

To convince yourselves that someone like me really is a gift from god to the city, look at things this way. Behaviour like mine does not seem to be natural. I have completely neglected my own affairs, and allowed my family to be neglected, all these years, while I devoted myself to looking after your interests—approaching each one of you individually, like a father or elder brother, and trying to persuade you to consider the good of your soul.

If I made anything out of it, and charged a fee for this advice, there'd be some sense in my doing it. As it is, you can see for yourselves that although the prosecution accused me, in their unscrupulous way, of everything under the sun, there was one point on which they were not so unscrupulous as to produce any evidence. They didn't claim that I ever made any money, or asked for any. I can produce convincing evidence, I think, that I am telling the truth—namely my poverty.

It may perhaps seem odd that in my private life I go round giving people advice like this, and interfering, without having the courage, in public life, to come forward before you, the people, and give advice on matters of public interest. The reason for this is what you have often heard me talking about, in all sorts of places, the kind of divine or supernatural sign that comes to me. This must have been what Meletus was making fun of when he wrote out the charge against me. It started when I was a child, a kind of voice which comes to me, and when it comes, always stops me doing what I'm just about to do; it never tells me what I *should* do. It's this which opposes my taking part in politics, and rightly opposes it, in my opinion. You can be sure, men of Athens, that if I had tried, at any time in the past, to go into politics, I would have been dead long ago, and been no use at all either to you or to myself.

Please don't be annoyed with me for speaking the truth. There is no-one in the world who can get away with deliberately opposing you—or any other popular assembly— or trying to put a stop to all the unjust and unlawful things which are done in politics; it is essential that the true fighter for justice, if he is to survive even for a short time, should remain a private individual, and not go into public life.

I shall give you compelling evidence for this—not words, but what you value, actions. Listen to things which have actually happened to me, and you will realise that I would never obey anyone if it was wrong to do so, simply through fear of dying. No, I would refuse to obey, even if it meant my death. What I am going to say now is the kind of boasting you often hear in the lawcourts; but it is true, for all that.

I have never, men of Athens, held any public office in the city, apart from being a member of the Council. It turned out that our tribe, Antiochis, formed the standing committee when you decided, by a resolution of the Council, to put on trial collectively the ten generals who failed to pick up the survivors from the sea battle. This was unconstitutional, as you afterwards all decided. On that occasion I was the only member of the standing committee to argue against you. I told you not to act unconstitutionally, and voted against you. The politicians were all set to bring an immediate action against me, and have me arrested on the spot, and you were encouraging them to do so, and shouting your approval, but still I thought I ought to take my chance on the side of law and justice, rather than side with you, through fear of imprisonment or death, when you   c
were proposing to act unjustly.

That was when the city was still a democracy. When the oligarchy came to power, the junta in its turn sent for me, with four others, and gave me the task of bringing Leon of Salamis from his home in Salamis to the Council chamber, so he could be put to death. They often gave orders of this kind, to all sorts of people; they wanted to impli-   d
cate as many people as possible in their crimes. Again I demonstrated—by what I did this time, rather than what I said—that my fear of death was, if you will pardon my saying so, negligible; what I was afraid of, more than anything, was acting without regard for justice or religion. I was not intimidated by the junta's power—great though it was—into acting unjustly. When we left the Council chamber, the other four went off to Salamis and fetched Leon, but I left, and went home. I might perhaps have been put to death for that, if their power hadn't soon after been brought to an end. Of these events   e
any number of people will give evidence to you.

Do you think I would have survived all these years if I had taken part in public life, and played the part a good man should play, supporting what was just, and attaching the highest importance to it, as is right? Don't you believe it, men of Athens. Nor would anyone else in the world have survived. As for me, it will be clear that, throughout my life, if I have done anything at all in public life, my character is as I have described—and in private life the same. I was never at any time prepared to tolerate injustice in anyone at all—certainly not in any of the people my critics say were   33
my pupils.

I have never been anyone's teacher. Equally, I never said no to anyone, young or old, who wanted to listen to me talking and pursuing my quest. Nor do I talk if I am paid, and not talk if I am not paid. I make myself available to rich and poor alike, so they can question me and listen, if anyone feels like it, to what I say in reply. And if any   b
of these people turns out well or badly, I cannot legitimately be held responsible; I neither promised any knowledge, ever, to any of them, nor did I teach them. If anyone ever claims to have learnt or heard anything from me privately, beyond what anyone else learnt or heard, I can assure you he is lying.

Why then do some people like spending so much of their time with me? You have   c
heard the answer to that, men of Athens; I have told you the whole truth. They like hearing the cross-examination of those who think they are wise when they are not. After all, it is quite entertaining. For me, as I say, this is a task imposed by god, through prophecies and dreams and in every way in which divine destiny has ever imposed any task on a man.

All this is the truth, men of Athens, and easily tested. If I really am a bad influence on some of the young, and have been a bad influence on others in the past, and if some   d
of them, as they have grown older, have realised that I gave them bad advice at some point when they were young, they ought to come forward now, I'd have thought, to ac-

cuse me and punish me. And if they weren't prepared to do so themselves, some of the
members of their families—fathers, brothers, or other close relatives—ought now to re-
e   member, if those close to them came to some harm at my hands, and want to punish me.
Certainly I can see plenty of them here today—Crito there, for a start, my contemporary
and fellow-demesman, the father of Critobulus, who's here too. Then there's Lysanias
from the deme of Sphettos, the father of Aeschines here; or indeed Antiphon over there,
from Cephisus, the father of Epigenes.

Then there are the ones whose brothers have spent their time in my company:
34   Nicostratus the son of Theozotides, the brother of Theodotus—Theodotus of course is
dead, so he couldn't have put any pressure on his brother; and I can see Paralius, the son
of Demodocus, whose brother was Theages. Then there's Adeimantus I can see, the son
of Ariston, whose brother is Plato here; or Aiantodorus, whose brother Apollodorus is
present also.

There are plenty more I could name for you. Ideally, Meletus would have called
some of them himself to give evidence during his speech. However, in case he forgot at
the time, let him call them now—I give up my place to him—and let him say if he has
any evidence of that kind.

It's the exact opposite, gentlemen. You'll find they're all on my side—although
b   I'm a bad influence, although I harm their relatives, as Meletus and Anytus claim. I can
see why the actual victims of my influence might have some reason to be on my side;
but those who have not been influenced, the older generation, their relatives, what reason do they have for being on my side, other than the correct and valid reason that they
know Meletus is lying, and I am telling the truth?

Well, there we are, gentlemen. That, and perhaps a bit more along the same lines,
c   is roughly what I might have to say in my defence. There may possibly be those among
you who find it irritating, when you remember your own experience; you may, in a trial
less important than this one, have begged and pleaded with the jury, with many tears,
bringing your own children, and many others among your family and friends, up here to
arouse as much sympathy as possible; whereas I refuse to do any of these things—even
though I am, as it probably seems to you, in the greatest danger of all.

d   Thoughts like this could make some of you feel a little antagonistic towards me.
For just this reason, you might get angry, and let anger influence your vote. If any of you
does feel like this—I am sure you don't, but if you did—I think I might fairly say to
you: "Of course I too have a family, my good friend. I do not come, in Homer's famous
words, 'from oak or rock.' No, I was born of men, so I do have a family, and sons, men
of Athens, three of them. One is not quite grown-up, the other two still boys. All the
same, I am not going to bring any of them up here and beg you to acquit me."

e   Why will I not do any of these things? Not out of obstinacy, men of Athens, nor
out of contempt for you. And whether or not I am untroubled by the thought of death is
beside the point. No, it's a question of what is fitting—for me, for you, and for the
whole city. I don't think it's right for me to do any of these things, at my age and with
35   the reputation I have. It may be justified or unjustified, but there's a prevailing belief
that Socrates is in some way different from other people.

If those of you who seem to be outstanding in wisdom or courage, or any other
quality, were to behave like this, it would be deplorable. Yet this is just the way I *have*
seen men behaving when they are brought to trial. They may seem to be men of some
distinction, but still they act in the most extraordinary way; they seem to think it will
be a terrible disaster for them if they are put to death—as if they'd be immortal if you
didn't put them to death. I think they bring disgrace on the city. A visitor to our country might imagine that in Athens people of outstanding character, those whom the Athe-

nians themselves single out from among themselves for positions of office and other   b
distinctions—that these men are no better than women.

Such behaviour, men of Athens, is not right for those of you with any kind of reputation at all; and if we who are on trial behave like that, you should not let us get away
with it. You should make one thing absolutely clear, which is that you are much more
ready to convict a defendant who stages one of these hysterical scenes, and makes our
city an object of ridicule, than a defendant who behaves with decorum.

Quite apart from what is fitting, gentlemen, I think there is no justice, either, in
begging favours from the jury, or being acquitted by begging; justice requires instruc-   c
tion and persuasion. The juryman does not sit there for the purpose of handing out justice as a favour; he sits there to decide what justice is. He has not taken an oath to do a
favour to anyone he takes a fancy to, but rather to reach a verdict in accordance with the
laws. So *we* should not encourage in you the habit of breaking your oath, nor should *you*
allow the habit to develop. If we did, we should neither of us be showing any respect for
the gods.

Do not ask me, therefore, men of Athens, to conduct myself towards you in a way
which I regard as contrary to right, justice and religion—least of all, surely, when I am   d
being accused of impiety by Meletus here. After all, if I did persuade you and coerce
you, by my begging, despite your oath, then clearly I *would* be teaching you to deny the
existence of the gods; my whole defence would simply amount to accusing myself of
not recognising the gods. And that is far from being the case. I do recognise them, men
of Athens, as none of my accusers does, and I entrust to you and to god the task of
reaching a verdict in my case in whatever way will be best both for me and for you.

*   *   *

If I am not upset, men of Athens, at what has just happened—your finding me guilty—   e
there are a number of reasons. In particular, the result was not unexpected; in fact, I'm
surprised by the final number of votes on either side. Personally, I was expecting a large   36
margin, not a narrow one; as it is, if only thirty votes had gone the other way, apparently
I would have been acquitted. Indeed, on Meletus' charge, as I see it, I *have* been acquitted, even as things are. And not just acquitted; it's clear to anyone that if Anytus had not
come forward, with Lycon, to accuse me, Meletus would have incurred a fine of a thousand drachmas for not receiving twenty percent of the votes.   b

So the man proposes the death penalty for me. Very well. What counter-proposal
am I to make to you, men of Athens? What I deserve, obviously. And what is that? What
do I deserve to suffer or pay, for . . . for what? For not keeping quiet all through my
life, for neglecting the things most people devote their lives to: business, family life,
holding office—as general, or as leader of the assembly, or in some other capacity—or
the alliances and factions which occur in political life. I thought, quite honestly, that my
sense of right and wrong would not allow me to survive in politics; so I did not pursue   c
a course in which I should have been no use either to you or to myself, but rather one in
which I could give help to each one of you privately—the greatest help possible, as I
claim. That is the direction I took. I tried to persuade each of you not to give any
thought at all to his own affairs until he had first given some thought to himself, and
tried to make himself as good and wise as possible; not to give any thought to the affairs
of the city without first giving some thought to the city itself; and to observe the same
priorities in other areas as well.

What then do I deserve for behaving like this? Something good, men of Athens, if   d
I am really supposed to make a proposal in accordance with what I deserve. And what's

more, a good of a kind which is some use to me. What then *is* of use to a poor man, your benefactor, who needs free time in which to advise you? There can't be anything more useful to a man of this sort, men of Athens, than to be given free meals at the public expense; this is much more use to him than it is to any Olympic victor among you, if one of you wins the horse race, or the two-horse or four-horse chariot race. The Olympic winner makes you *seem* to be happy; I make you really happy. He doesn't need the food; I do need it. So if I must propose a penalty based on justice, on what I deserve, then that's what I propose—free meals at the public expense.

Here again, I suppose, in the same sort of way as when I was talking about appeals to pity and pleas for mercy, you may think I speak as I do out of sheer obstinacy. But it's not obstinacy, men of Athens; it's like this. I myself am convinced that I don't knowingly do wrong to anyone in the world, but I can't persuade you of that; we haven't had enough time to talk to one another. Mind you, if it were the custom here, as it is in other places, to decide cases involving the death penalty over several days rather than in one day, I believe you would have been persuaded. As it is, it was not easy in a short time to overcome the strong prejudice against me.

But if I am convinced that I don't do wrong to anyone else, I am certainly not going to do wrong to myself, or speak against myself—saying I deserve something bad, and proposing some such penalty for myself. Why should I? Through fear of undergoing the penalty Meletus proposes, when I claim not to know whether it is good or bad? Should I, in preference to that, choose one of the things I know perfectly well to be bad, and propose that as a penalty?

Imprisonment? What is the point of living in prison, and being the slave of those in the prison service at any particular time? A fine? And be imprisoned until I pay? That's the same as the first suggestion, since I haven't any money to pay a fine. Should I propose exile? I suppose you might accept that. But I'd have to be very devoted to life, men of Athens, to lose the power of rational thought so completely, and not be able to work out what would happen. If you, my fellow-citizens, couldn't stand my talk and my conversation, if you found them too boring and irritating, which is why you now want to be rid of them, will people in some other country find it any easier to put up with them? Don't you believe it, men of Athens.

A fine life I should lead in exile, a man of my age—moving and being driven from city to city. I've no doubt that wherever I go, the young will listen to me, the way they do here. If I tell them to go away, they will send me into exile of their own accord, bringing pressure to bear on their elders; if I don't tell them to go away, their fathers and relatives will exile me, out of concern for them.

I can imagine someone saying, "How about keeping your mouth shut, Socrates, and leading a quiet life? Can't you please go into exile, and live like that?" Of all things, this is the hardest point on which to convince some of you. If I say that it is disobeying god, and that for this reason I can't lead a quiet life, you won't believe me—you'll think I'm using that as an excuse. If on the other hand I say that really the greatest good in a man's life is this, to be each day discussing human excellence and the other subjects you hear me talking about, examining myself and other people, and that the unexamined life isn't worth living—if I say this, you will believe me even less.

All the same, the situation is as I describe it, gentlemen—hard though it is to convince you. Equally, for myself, I can't get used to the idea that I deserve anything bad. If I had any money, I would propose as large a fine as I could afford; that wouldn't do me any harm. As it is, I have no money, unless you are willing to have me propose an amount I *could* afford. I suppose I could pay you something like a hundred drachmas of silver, if you like. So that is the amount I propose.

Despite refuting his accusers (as recorded in the *Apology*), Socrates was found
guilty of impiety toward the gods and of corrupting the youth. He was
sentenced to die by drinking the poison hemlock. (*The Bettmann Archive*)

Plato here, men of Athens—and Crito and Critobulus and Apollodorus—tell me
to propose a penalty of 3,000 drachmas; they say they guarantee it. I propose that
amount, therefore, and they will offer full security to you for the money.

*   *   *

For just a small gain in time, men of Athens, you will now have the reputation and re-   c
sponsibility, among those who want to criticise the city, of having put to death Socrates,
that wise man—they will *say* I am wise, the people who want to blame you, even
though I am not. If you'd waited a little, you could have had what you wanted without
lifting a finger. You can see what age I am—far advanced in years, and close to death.

I say that not to all of you, but to those who voted for the death penalty. And I
have something else to say to the same people. You may think, men of Athens, that I   d
have lost my case through inability to make the kind of speech I *could* have used to persuade you, had I thought it right to do and say absolutely anything to secure my acquittal. Far from it. I have lost my case, not for want of a speech, but for want of effrontery
and shamelessness, for refusing to make to you the kind of speech you most enjoy listening to. You'd like to have heard me lamenting and bewailing, and doing and saying
all sorts of other things which are beneath my dignity, in my opinion—the kind of   e
things you've grown used to hearing from other people.

I did not think it right, when I was speaking, to demean myself through fear of
danger, nor do I now regret conducting my defence in the way I did. I had much rather
defend myself like this, and be put to death, than behave in the way I have described,

and go on living. Neither in the courts, nor in time of war, is it right—either for me or
for anyone else—to devote one's efforts simply to avoiding death at all costs.

In battle it is often clear that death can be escaped, by dropping your weapons and
throwing yourself on the mercy of your pursuers—and in any kind of danger there are all
sorts of other devices for avoiding death, if you can bring yourself not to mind what you
do or say. There's no difficulty in *that,* gentlemen, in escaping death. What is much harder
is avoiding wickedness, since wickedness runs faster than death. So now, not surprisingly, I, who am old and slow, have been overtaken by the slower of the two. My accusers, being swift and keen, have been overtaken by the faster, by wickedness. Now I am
departing, to pay the penalty of death inflicted by you. But they have already incurred the
penalty, inflicted by truth, for wickedness and injustice. I accept my sentence, as they do
theirs. I suppose that's probably how it was bound to turn out—and I have no complaints.

Having dealt with that, I now wish to make you a prophecy, those of you who
voted for my condemnation. I am at that point where people are most inclined to make
prophecies—which is when they are just about to die. To you gentlemen who have put
me to death, I say that retribution will come to you, directly after my death—retribution
far worse, god knows, than the death penalty which you have inflicted on me.

You have acted as you have today in the belief that you will avoid having to submit your lives to examination, but you will find the outcome is just the opposite; that is
my prediction. There will be more people now to examine you—the ones I have so far
been keeping in check without your realising it. They will be harder to deal with, being
so much younger, and you will be more troubled by them. If you think that by putting
men to death you can stop people criticising you for not living your lives in the right
way, you are miscalculating badly. As a way of escape, this is neither effective nor cred-
itable; the best and simplest way lies not in weeding out other people, but in making
oneself as good a person as possible.

That is my prophecy to you who voted for my condemnation, and now I am prepared to let you go. To those who voted for my acquittal I'd like to make a few remarks
about what has just happened, while the magistrates get on with the formalities, and it is
not yet time for me to go where I must go to die. Please keep me company, gentlemen,
for this little time; there's no reason why we shouldn't talk to one another while it is permitted. I regard you as my friends, and so to you I am prepared to explain the significance of today's outcome.

Gentlemen of the jury—since you I properly *can* call jurymen—a remarkable
thing has happened to me. The prophetic voice I have got so used to, my supernatural
voice, has always in the past been at my elbow, opposing me even in matters of little importance, if I was about to take a false step. You can see for yourselves the situation I'm
now in. You might think—and this is how it is generally regarded—it was the ultimate
misfortune. Yet the sign from god did not oppose my leaving home this morning, nor
my appearance here in court, nor was there any point in my speech when it stopped me
saying what I was just about to say.

Often in the past, when I have been talking, the sign has stopped me in full flow;
this time it has not opposed me at any stage in the whole proceedings—either in what I
have done or in what I have said. What do I take to be the reason for this? I'll tell you.
The chances are that what has happened to me here is a good thing, and that it is impossible for those of us who think death is an evil to understand it correctly. I have strong
evidence for this. The sign I know so well would unquestionably have opposed me, if
things had not been going to turn out all right for me.

There is another reason for being confident that death is a good thing. Look at it
like this. Death is one of two things; either it is like the dead person being nothing at all,

and having no consciousness of anything at all; or, as we are told, it is actually some sort of change, a journey of the soul from this place to somewhere different. Suppose it is a total absence of consciousness—like sleep, when the sleeper isn't even dreaming. Then death would be a marvellous bonus. At least, I certainly think that if a man had to   d choose the night on which he slept so soundly that he did not even dream, and if he had to compare all the other nights and days of his life with that night, if he had to think carefully about it, and then say how many days and nights he had spent in his life that were better and more enjoyable than that night—I think that not just a private individual, but even the great king of Persia could count these dreamless nights on the fingers   e of one hand compared with the other days and nights. If death is something like that, I call it a bonus. After all, the whole of time, seen in this way, seems no longer than a single night.

If, on the other hand, death is a kind of journey from here to somewhere different, and what we're told about all the dead being there is true, what greater good could there be than that, gentlemen of the jury? Imagine arriving in the other world, getting away   41 from the people here who claim to be judges, and finding real judges, the ones who are said to decide cases there—Minos, Rhadamanthys, Aeacus, Triptolemus, and others of the demigods who acted with justice in their own lives. Wouldn't that be a worthwhile journey?

Or again, what would any of you give to join Orpheus and Musaeus, Hesiod and Homer? Personally, I am quite prepared to die many times over, if these stories are true. For me at least, time spent there would be wonderful—I'd keep meeting people like   b Palamedes, or Aias the son of Telamon, or any other of the ancients who died as a result of an unjust verdict; I could compare my own experience with theirs. That would be entertaining, I imagine. Best of all, I could spend my time questioning and examining people there, just as I do people here, to find out which of them is wise, and which thinks he is wise but isn't.

What would you give, men of the jury, to interview the man who led the great expedition to Troy—or Odysseus, or Sisyphus, or thousands of others one could mention,   c men and women? It would be an unimaginable pleasure to talk to them there, to enjoy their company, and question them. They certainly can't put you to death there for asking questions. They are better off than us in many ways—and not least because they are now immune to death for the rest of time, if what we are told is true.

You too, men of the jury, must not be apprehensive about death. You must regard one thing at least as certain—that no harm can come to a good man either in his life or after his death; what happens to him is not a matter of indifference to the gods. Nor has   d my present situation arisen purely by chance; it is clear to me that it was better for me to die now and be released from my task. That's why my sign didn't at any point dissuade me, and why I am not in the least angry with those who voted against me, or with my accusers. Admittedly that wasn't their reason for voting against me, and accusing me; they thought they were doing me some harm. We *can* blame them for that.

However, I do have one request to make. It concerns my sons. When they grow up, gentlemen, get your own back on them, if you think they are more interested in   e money—or in anything else—than in goodness, by annoying them in exactly the same way as I annoyed you. If they think they amount to something when they don't, then criticise them, as I criticised you. Tell them they are not giving any thought to the things that matter, and that they think they amount to something when they are worth nothing. If you do this, I shall myself have been fairly treated by you—and so will my sons.   42

I must stop. It is time for us to go—me to my death, you to your lives. Which of us goes to the better fate, only god knows.

CRITO

43   SOCRATES: What are you doing here at this time, Crito? Isn't it still early?

CRITO: Yes, it is.

SOCRATES: How early, exactly?

CRITO: It's not yet started to get light.

SOCRATES: I'm surprised the warder didn't refuse to answer your knock.

CRITO: He's become something of a friend of mine, Socrates, what with my coming here so often. Besides, I've done him a bit of a favour.

SOCRATES: Have you just arrived, or have you been here some time?

CRITO: Quite some time.

b   SOCRATES: Then why on earth didn't you wake me up? What were you doing just sitting there beside me in silence?

CRITO: I wouldn't have dreamt of it, Socrates. For my part, I wouldn't choose to be in this state of sleeplessness and misery; and for some time now it has astonished me to see how soundly you sleep. I deliberately didn't wake you because I wanted you to enjoy your rest. It has often struck me in the past, throughout my life in fact, how lucky you are in your temperament—and it strikes me much more forcibly in your present misfortune. You bear it so easily and calmly.

SOCRATES: Yes, Crito, I do. It wouldn't make much sense for a man my age to get upset at the prospect of dying.

c   CRITO: Other people your age, Socrates, find themselves in similar predicaments; *their* age doesn't stop them getting upset at their misfortune.

SOCRATES: That's true. Anyway, why *have* you come so early?

CRITO: To bring news, Socrates, bad news. Not bad for you, as far as I can see, but for me and all your friends it is bad and hard to bear; and I think I shall find it as hard to bear as anybody.

d   SOCRATES: What sort of news? Has the boat from Delos arrived—the one my execution has been waiting for?

CRITO: It hasn't actually arrived, but I think it will today, judging by the reports of some people who've just come from Sunium. It was there when they left. It's clear from what they said that it will arrive today, and so tomorrow, Socrates, you will be forced to end your life.

SOCRATES: Well, Crito, if that is how the gods want it, I hope it will all turn out for the best. All the same, I don't think it will come today.

44   CRITO: What is that based on?

SOCRATES: I'll tell you. My death, I assume, is to take place on the day after the ship arrives.

CRITO: Yes. At least, that's what the prison authorities say.

SOCRATES: Then I think it will come tomorrow, not today. That's based on a dream I had last night, just before I woke up. So perhaps it was lucky you didn't wake me.

CRITO: What was the dream?

SOCRATES: I saw a woman, fair and beautiful, in a white cloak. She came up to
b   me, and called my name. "Socrates," she said, "On the third day shall you come to fertile Phthia."

CRITO: A strange dream, Socrates.

SOCRATES: Clear enough, though, I think, Crito.

CRITO: Only too clear, I'm afraid. Now listen, Socrates, it's not too late, even now, to do as I say and escape. For me, if you are put to death, it is a double disaster. Quite apart from losing a friend such as I shall never find again, there will also be many who will think, those who don't know the two of us well, that I had the chance to save you if I'd been prepared to spend some money, and that I wasn't interested in doing so.

Can you think of a worse reputation than being thought to value money more highly than friends? Most people will never believe that it was you yourself who refused to leave here, and that we strongly encouraged you to do so.

SOCRATES: Really, Crito, why should we care so much about what "most people" believe? The best people, who are the ones we should worry about more, will realise that things were done in the way they actually were done.

CRITO: Yet you can see that we have no choice, Socrates, but to care about what most people think as well. The present situation is a clear example of how the many can injure us in ways which are not trivial, but just about as great as can be, if they are given the wrong impression about someone.

SOCRATES: If only the many *could* do us the greatest injuries, Crito. That would mean they were capable of doing us the greatest good as well, which would be excellent. As it is, they're incapable of doing either. They have no power to make a man either wise or foolish; nor do they care what effect they have.

CRITO: I dare say you are right. But tell me something, Socrates. Are you worried about me and the rest of your friends? Do you think, if you leave here, that we shall get into trouble with the people who make a living out of bringing private prosecutions, because we smuggled you out of here? Do you think we shall be forced to forfeit all our property, or pay a very large fine, and possibly undergo some further penalty in addition?

If something like that is what you are afraid of, don't give it another thought. We are in duty bound to run this risk to save you—that goes without saying—and even greater risks, if need be. Listen to me. Don't say "no."

SOCRATES: It *is* something I worry about, Crito. That, and many other things besides.

CRITO: Well then, do not be afraid on that score. There are people prepared, for not a very large sum of money, to save you and get you out of here. And apart from them, can't you see how easily bought they are, the men who make their living out of prosecutions? It wouldn't need a lot of money to take care of them. You have my resources at your disposal; that should be plenty, I imagine. And if you're worried about me, and feel you shouldn't spend my money, look at the people we've got here who are not Athenians, who are ready to spend theirs. One of them, Simmias the Theban, has actually brought enough money for just this purpose; Cebes too is fully prepared, and so are many others.

So as I say, you should not let these fears stop you saving yourself; and do not let it be an objection, as you claimed in court, that you would not know what to do with yourself if you went into exile. There are lots of places you can go where they'll be glad to see you; if you want to go to Thessaly, for example, my family has friends there who will be delighted to see you, and who will give you sanctuary. Nobody in Thessaly will give you any trouble.

Apart from that, Socrates, it is actually wrong, in my opinion, to sacrifice yourself, as you are proposing to do, when you could escape. You seem to be voluntarily choosing for yourself the kind of fate your enemies would have chosen for you—and *did* choose for you when they were trying to destroy you. Worse still, I think, is the bed trayal of your own sons, when there is nothing to stop you bringing them up and educating them—and yet you are going to go away and leave them, and for all you care they can turn out how they will. They will have, in all probability, the kind of life orphans generally have when they lose their parents.

No. Either you shouldn't have children, or you should play your part, and go through with the labour of raising and educating them. You seem to me to be taking the easy way out. What you should do is choose what a decent and courageous man would
e choose—you who claim to have been concerned with human goodness all your life. Personally, I am ashamed both for you and for those of us who are your friends. I think this whole business of yours will be thought to be the result of some lack of resolution on our part—first of all the fact that the case came to court when it needn't have done, then the
46 actual conduct of the case in court, and now this, as the final absurdity of the whole affair, that we shall be thought to have missed the opportunity—through our own cowardice and lack of resolution, since we didn't save you, nor did you save yourself, though it was possible, and within your power, with even a modest amount of help from us. Don't let all this be a humiliation, Socrates, both for you and for us, in addition to being an evil.

Think it over—or rather, the time for thinking it over is past, you should by now have thought it over—there is only one course of action. The whole thing must be done this coming night. If we wait any longer, it will be impossible; it will not be an option any longer. I cannot urge you too strongly, Socrates. Listen to me. Do as I say.

SOCRATES: My dear Crito, your enthusiasm is most commendable, so long as there is some justification for it. Otherwise, the greater your enthusiasm, the more out of
b place it is. We'd better look into whether this is the right thing to do or not. It has been my practice, not just now but always, to trust, of all the guides at my disposal, only the principle which on reflection seems most appropriate. I cannot now throw overboard principles which I have put forward in the past, simply because of what has happened to me. They still seem to me very much the same as they always did; I still give pride of place to, and value, the same principles as before. Unless we can find some better principle than these to put forward on this occasion, you can be quite sure I am not going
c to agree with you, however many bugbears the power of the many produces to scare us with—as if we were children—letting loose on us its imprisonments, its death sentences, and its fines.

What then is the best way of looking into this question? Why don't we start by going back to the argument you put forward based on what people will think? Were we right or wrong, all those times, when we said we should listen to some opinions, but not to others? Or were we right before I was sentenced to death, only for it now to become clear that it was a waste of breath, spoken simply for the sake of having something to
d say, and that it was really juvenile fantasy? Personally, Crito, I should very much like to carry out a joint enquiry with you, to see whether the principle will seem rather different to me, now that I am in this situation, or whether it will seem the same—and whether we are going to forget about it, or follow it.

The principle so often put forward, I think, by those among us who thought they knew what they were talking about, was the one I referred to just now—that of the opin-
e ions held by men, we should regard some as important, and others not. Seriously, Crito, don't you think this is a sound principle? You are, barring accidents, not in the position
47 of having to die tomorrow, so you shouldn't be influenced by the present situation. Examine the question. Don't you think it a sound principle that we should not value all human opinions equally, but should value some highly, and others not? And the same with the people who hold the opinions. We should not value all of them, but should value some, and not others. What do you think? Isn't this is a sound principle?

CRITO: Yes, it is.

SOCRATES: We should value the good opinions, but not the bad ones?

CRITO: Yes.

SOCRATES: Aren't good opinions the opinions of the wise, whereas bad opinions are those of the foolish?

CRITO: Obviously.

SOCRATES: Well then, what was the kind of analogy we used to employ? If a man b is taking physical exercise, and this is what he is interested in, does he listen to the praise and criticism and opinion of just anyone, or only of one person—the person who is in fact a medical expert or a physical training instructor?

CRITO: Only of one person.

SOCRATES: So he should worry about the criticisms, and welcome the praises, of this one person, but not those of the many?

CRITO: Clearly he should.

SOCRATES: In what he does, then—in the exercise he takes, in what he eats and drinks—he should be guided by the one man, the man in charge, the expert, rather than by everyone else.

CRITO: That is so.

SOCRATES: All right. If he defies the one man, and doesn't value his opinion and c his recommendations, but does value those of the many, those who are not experts, won't he do himself some harm?

CRITO: Of course he will.

SOCRATES: What is this harm? What is its extent? What part of the man who defies the expert does it attack?

CRITO: His body, obviously. That is what it damages.

SOCRATES: Quite right. Well then, is it the same also in other situations, Crito, to save us going through all the examples—and especially with right and wrong, foul and fair, good and bad, the things we are now discussing? Should we follow the opinion of d the many, and fear that, or the opinion of the one man, if we can find an expert on the subject? Should we respect and fear this one man more than all the rest put together? And if we don't follow his advice, we shall injure and do violence to that part which we have often agreed improves with justice and is damaged by injustice. Or is this all wrong?

CRITO: No, I think it is right, Socrates.

SOCRATES: Very well. Take that part of us which improves with health, and is damaged by disease. If we ruin it by following advice other than that of the experts, is life worth living once that part is injured? This is the body, of course, isn't it? e

CRITO: Yes.

SOCRATES: Is life worth living, then, if our body is in poor condition and injured?

CRITO: Certainly not.

SOCRATES: How about the part of us which is attacked by injustice, and helped by justice? Is life worth living when that is injured? Or do we regard it as less important than the body, this part of us—whichever of our faculties it is—the part to which justice 48 and injustice belong?

CRITO: No, we certainly don't.

SOCRATES: More important, then?

CRITO: Much more important.

SOCRATES: In that case, my dear friend, we should not pay the slightest attention, as you suggested we should, to what most people will say about us. We should listen only to the expert on justice and injustice, to the one man, and to the truth itself. So you were wrong, for a start, in one of your recommendations—when you proposed that we should be concerned about the opinion of the many on the subject of justice, right, good, and their opposites. "Ah!" you might say, "but the many are liable to put us to death."

b   CRITO: That too is obviously true. You might well say that, Socrates. You are quite right.

SOCRATES: All the same, my learned friend, I think the principle we have elaborated still has the same force as it did. And what about this second principle? Tell me, does our belief—that the important thing is not being alive, but living a good life—still hold good, or not?

CRITO: It does still hold good.

SOCRATES: And that when we're talking about a life, good, right, and just are one and the same thing—does that still hold good, or not?

CRITO: It does.

c   SOCRATES: Well then, in the light of the points we have agreed, we must look into the question whether it is right, or not right, for me to attempt to leave here without the permission of the Athenians. If it appears to be right, let us make the attempt; otherwise let us forget about it. As for the considerations you raise—questions of expense, public opinion, the upbringing of children—I suspect that these, Crito, are really the concerns of those who readily put people to death, and would as readily bring them back to life again, if they could—for absolutely no reason. I am, of course, talking about the many.

For us, though, the thing is to follow where the argument leads us, and I rather think the only question we need ask is the one we asked just now: shall we act rightly if

d   we give our money, and our thanks, to those who will arrange my escape from here? Shall we ourselves be acting rightly in arranging the escape, and allowing it to be arranged? Or shall we in fact be acting wrongly if we do all these things? If this is clearly the wrong way for us to behave, then I'm pretty sure that compared with the danger of acting wrongly, we should not take into account the certainty either of being put to death if we stay put and accept things quietly, or of suffering anything else at all.

CRITO: I am sure you are right, Socrates. You decide what we should do.

SOCRATES: Let us look into it together, my friend. And if you want to raise an objection at any point while I'm talking, then raise it, and I will listen to you. Otherwise, my fine friend, stop repeating the same thing over and over again—that I should leave here in defiance of the wishes of the Athenians. I attach great importance to acting with your agreement, rather than against your wishes.

Now, think about the starting-point of our enquiry. Do you regard it as satisfac-

49   tory? And when you answer the question, mind you say what you really think.

CRITO: I will try.

SOCRATES: Do we agree that we should never deliberately do wrong, or should we sometimes do wrong, and sometimes not? Is wrong-doing absolutely contrary to what is good and fine, as has often been agreed among us in the past? Or have all those things we once agreed on become, in these last few days, so much water under the

b   bridge? Did we, grown men and at the age we were, Crito, discuss things so enthusiastically with one another, without realising we were no better than children? Or is what we said then more true now than ever? Whether "most people" agree or not, and whether we have to undergo hardships more severe even than these—or possibly less severe—isn't wrongdoing in fact, for the person who does it, wholly evil and bad? Is this what we say, or not?

CRITO: It is.

SOCRATES: A man should never do wrong, then.

CRITO: No, he should not.

SOCRATES: So even if he is wronged, he should not do wrong in return, as most people think, since he ought not *ever* to do wrong.

CRITO: Apparently not.   c

SOCRATES: What about harming people, Crito? Should a man do that, or not?

CRITO: I suppose not, Socrates.

SOCRATES: How about harming people in retaliation, if he is injured by them first—which is what most people say he should do? Is that right or wrong?

CRITO: Completely wrong.

SOCRATES: And that, I imagine, is because injuring people is the same thing as doing them wrong.

CRITO: That is right.

SOCRATES: So he should not do wrong to anyone or injure them, in retaliation, no matter how he has been treated by them. And if you say "yes" to that, Crito, make sure you are not saying "yes" against what you really think. I realise not many people accept   d
this view—or ever will accept it. As a result, there is no common ground between those who do accept it and those who do not; each side necessarily regards the opinions of the other side with contempt. So you too must think very hard about it. Are you on our side?   e
Do you agree with us in accepting this view, and shall we base our argument on the premise that it is never legitimate to do wrong to people, nor do them wrong in retaliation, nor, if one is injured, defend oneself by harming them in return? Or do you disagree? Do you reject the original premise? Personally, I have held this view a long time, and I still hold it now. If you have been holding some other view, tell me; instruct me. But if you stand by what we said earlier, then listen to what follows from it.

CRITO: I do stand by it, and I do agree with you. Tell me what follows.

SOCRATES: Very well, I will tell you. Or rather, I'll ask you. If a man makes an agreement—a fair agreement—with someone, should he fulfil his side of the agreement, or should he try to get out of it?

CRITO: He should fulfil it.

SOCRATES: Then see what follows from that. If we leave here without persuading the city to change its mind, are we doing harm to anyone or anything—those we have   50
least cause to injure—or not? Are we standing by our agreement—our fair agreement—or not?

CRITO: I can't answer your question, Socrates. I don't understand it.

SOCRATES: Look at it like this. Imagine that, just as we were about to run away, or whatever we are supposed to call it, from here, the laws of Athens and the state of Athens appeared before us, and said: "Tell me, Socrates, what are you trying to do? Aren't you simply trying, by this action you are embarking on, to destroy both us, the   b
laws, and the entire city, as far as lies within your power? Do you think it possible for a city to continue to exist, and not sink without trace, if the verdicts of its courts have no force, if they are rendered invalid, and nullified, by private citizens?"

What shall we say, Crito, to these questions and others like them? There's a lot that could be said, especially by the public advocate, in defence of this law we are trying to do away with—the law which lays down that verdicts arrived at in the courts should be binding. Shall we say to the laws, "The city wronged us. It did not reach its   c
verdict fairly?" Shall we say that, or what?

CRITO: Yes, we most emphatically should say that, Socrates.

SOCRATES: Suppose then the laws say, "Was *that* what was agreed between us and you, Socrates? Or was it to abide by the verdicts the city arrives at in its courts?" And if we expressed surprise at their question, they might add: "Do not be surprised by our question, Socrates. Answer it. You have had enough practice at question-and-answer.   d

Come on, then. What principle do you appeal to, against us and the city, to allow you to try and destroy us? Did we not bring you into existence, for a start? Was it not through us that your father married your mother, and fathered you? Tell us, then, those of us who are the laws governing marriage, have you some criticism of us? Is there something wrong with us?"

e   "I have no criticism," I should have to reply.

"All right, then. How about your upbringing and education after you were born? How about the laws to do with those? Did we not give your father the right instructions—those of us whose job it is to attend to this—when we told him to educate you by means of the arts and physical training?"

"No, they were the right instructions," I would say.

"Very well. Since you were born, and brought up, and educated, under our protection, you were our offspring and our slave—both you yourself and your parents. Can you deny that, for a start? And if that is so, do you think that justice gives equivalent rights to you and to us? If we decide to do something to you, do you think you have the right to do it to us in return?

51   "There was no equality of rights as between you and your father or your master, if you had one, entitling you to do to him in retaliation what he did to you—to answer him back if he spoke abusively to you, or beat him in retaliation if he beat you, or anything else like that. Will it then be legitimate for you to retaliate against your country and its laws? And is the result that if we decide to destroy you, because we think it right to do so, you in your turn, to the best of your ability, will set about destroying us, the laws, and your country, in retaliation? Will you claim that in acting like this you are doing what is right, you who are truly so concerned about human excellence? Are you so clever that you fail

b   to realise that your country is an object of greater value, an object of greater respect and reverence, and altogether more important, both among gods and among men, if they have any sense, than your mother and your father and all the rest of your ancestors put together? That you should revere your country, submit to it, mollify it when it is angry with you—more than you would your father—and either persuade it to change its mind, or do what it tells you? That you should quietly accept whatever treatment it ordains you

c   should receive—beating, perhaps, or imprisonment—or if it takes you to war, to be wounded or killed, that is what you should do, and that is what is right? That you should not give way, or retreat, or abandon your position, that in war, in the lawcourts, or anywhere else, you should do what your city and your country tells you, or else convince it where justice naturally lies? And that the use of force, against a mother or a father, is against god's law—still more so the use of force against your country?"

What are we going to say in answer to this, Crito? Shall we say the laws are right, or not?

CRITO: Well, *I* think they are right.

SOCRATES: "Consider, then, Socrates," the laws might perhaps say, "Are we right in saying that you are not justified in embarking on the actions against us which you are

d   now embarking on? We fathered you, brought you up, educated you, gave you and every other citizen a share in every good thing it was in our power to give. And even then, if there is any Athenian who reaches the age of majority, takes a look at his city's constitution, and at us, the laws, and finds we are not to his satisfaction, then by granting him permission we make a public declaration to anyone who wishes that he may take what is his, and go wherever he pleases. If a man chooses to go to one of your colonies, because we and the city are not to his liking, or to leave, emigrate to some other place, and go wherever he wants, with no loss of property, not one of us laws stands in his way, or forbids him.

"To those of you who stay, aware of our way of reaching verdicts in the courts, and of making our other political arrangements, we say that you have now entered into a formal agreement with us, to do what we tell you, and we say that the man who disobeys us is doing wrong in three ways: he is disobeying us who fathered him; he is disobeying those who brought him up; and having made an agreement to obey us, he neither obeys, nor tries to make us change our minds, if we are doing something which is not right. When we make him a fair offer, not harshly demanding that he do whatever we order, but allowing him a straight choice, either to make us change our minds, or to do as we say, he does neither. These are the charges, Socrates, to which we claim that you too will render yourself liable, if you do what you are proposing to do—you in particular, more than any of the Athenians."

If I asked them why me in particular, they might perhaps have a justifiable complaint against me in that I, as much as any of the Athenians, really have entered into this agreement with them. They could say, "Socrates, we have convincing evidence to suggest that we and the city *were* to your liking. You could not possibly have spent more of your time living here in Athens than any other Athenian if the place had not been particularly to your liking; you would not have refused ever to leave the city to see famous places—except Corinth, once—or go anywhere else, unless it was to go somewhere on military service; you never went abroad, as other people do, nor were you seized with a desire to know any other city, or any other laws. No, you were satisfied with us, and with our city. In fact, so strongly did you choose us, and agree to live your life as a citizen under us, that you even produced children in the city. You would not have done that if it had not been to your liking.

"Even at your trial, it was open to you to propose a penalty of exile, if you chose, and do then, with the city's permission, what you are now proposing to do without it. On that occasion you put a brave face on it; you said you didn't mind if you had to die; you preferred, so you said, death to exile. Do not those words now make you feel ashamed? Have you no feeling for us, the laws, as you set about destroying us, and do what the meanest slave might do, trying to run away in breach of the contract and agreement by which you agreed to live your life as a citizen? Answer us this question, for a start: are we right in saying that you have agreed—not just verbally, but by your behaviour—to live your life as a citizen under us? Or are we wrong?"

What are we going to say to this, Crito? Can we do anything but agree?

CRITO: We have no choice, Socrates.

SOCRATES: "Aren't you simply breaking," they might say, "contracts and agreements which you have with us? You did not enter into them under compulsion or false pretences. You were not forced to make up your mind on the spur of the moment, but over a period of seventy years, during which you were at liberty to leave, if we were not to your liking, or if you thought the agreement was unfair. You did not choose Sparta or Crete instead, places which you have always described as well-governed; nor did you choose any other city, inside or outside Greece. Even people who are lame, or blind, or crippled in other ways, spend more time away from Athens than you did. *That* is an indication, quite clearly, of how you, more than any of the Athenians, found the city, and us the laws, to your liking. After all, who could find a city to his liking, and not like its laws? And do you now not stand by what you agreed? You will if you take our advice, Socrates. That way you will avoid making yourself ridiculous by leaving the city.

"Think about it. If you break this agreement, and put yourself in the wrong in this way, what good will you do yourself or your friends? That your friends will probably have to go into exile as well, be cut off from their city, and forfeit their property, is reasonably clear. And you? Well for a start, if you go to one of the cities nearby, say Thebes

or Megara, both of which have good laws, you will come to them, Socrates, as an enemy of their constitution; those who care for their city will look at you with suspicion,
c   believing you to be a subverter of the laws. You will also reinforce the opinion of the
jury about you. They will decide they did reach the right verdict. After all, there is a
strong presumption that a man who subverts the laws will be a corrupting influence on
people who are young and foolish.

"Will you then keep away from cities with good laws, and the most civilised part
of mankind? If you do, will it be worth your while remaining alive? Or will you spend
your time with them? And will you have the nerve, in your conversations with them—
d   what sort of conversations, Socrates? The ones you had here, about human excellence
and justice being the most valuable things for mankind, together with custom and the
laws? Don't you think the whole idea of Socrates will be clearly seen to be a disgrace?
You certainly should.

"Or will you leave this part of the world and go to Thessaly, to Crito's family
friends? Up there you will find all sorts of anarchy and self-indulgence. I am sure they
would be entertained by the amusing story of your running away from prison in some
costume or other—wearing a leather jerkin, perhaps, or one of the other disguises
e   favoured by people running away—and altering your appearance. That an old man, in
all probability with a small span of life remaining to him, could bring himself to cling to
life in this limpet-like way, by transgressing the most important of the laws—will there
be no-one who will say this? Perhaps not, if you can manage not to annoy anyone. Otherwise, Socrates, you will have to listen to a lot of unflattering comments about yourself. Are you going to spend your life ingratiating yourself with everyone, being a slave
to them? Oh, yes, you will have a whale of a time up there in Thessaly, as if you had em-
54   igrated out to dinner in Thessaly. But what, please tell us, will become of all those conversations about justice and other forms of human excellence?

"Or do you want to remain alive for your children's sake, so that you can bring
them up and educate them? How do you feel about taking them to Thessaly, and bringing them up and educating them there, turning them into foreigners, so you can give
them that privilege as well? If not, if they are brought up here, will they be any better
brought up and educated because you are alive and separated from them? Your friends
will be looking after them. Will they look after them if you go to Thessaly to live, and
b   not look after them if you go to the next world? If those who claim to be your friends are
any use at all, of course they will not.

"No, Socrates, obey us who brought you up. Do not regard your children, or life,
or anything at all, as more important than justice; you do not want, when you come to
the other world, to have to defend yourself on these charges to the rulers there. Neither
in this world does it seem to be better, or more just or more godfearing, for you or any
of your friends, if you behave like this; nor, when you come to the next world, will it be
c   better for you there. As it is, you go there, if you do go, as one wronged—not by us, the
laws, but by men. If on the other hand you depart, after so shamefully returning wrong
for wrong, and injury for injury, breaking your own agreement and contract with us, and
injuring those whom you had least cause to injure—yourself, your friends, your country, and us—then we shall be angry with you while you are alive, and in the next world
our brothers, the laws in Hades, will not receive you kindly, since they will know that
d   you tried, to the best of your ability, to destroy us. So do not let Crito persuade you to
follow his advice rather than ours."

That, I assure you, Crito, my very dear friend, is what I think I hear them saying,
just as those gripped by religious fervour think they hear the pipes; the sound of their
words rings in my head, and stops me hearing anything else. Be in no doubt. As far as I

can see at the moment, if you disagree with them, you will speak in vain. All the same, though, if you think it will do any good, then speak.

CRITO: Socrates, I have nothing to say.

SOCRATES: Then forget about it, Crito. Let us act in the way god points out   e
to us.

PHAEDO (in part)

"My dear Cebes, suppose everything which can share in life were to die, and that   72ᶜ
dead things, when they died, were to remain in that state, and not come to life again.
Isn't it inevitable that in the end everything would be dead, and nothing would be   d
alive? If living things came from somewhere other than the dead, and if living things
did die, what is to stop everything being used up, and finishing up dead?"

"Nothing, I think, Socrates," said Cebes. "I entirely agree with you."

"Yes, Cebes, in my opinion it is as true as anything can be, and we are not mistaken in our agreement on this point. There really is such a thing as coming to life
again; the living really are born from the dead; and the souls of the dead really do go   e
on existing."

"And what's more," put in Cebes, "it necessarily follows, I take it, Socrates, both
from the argument you have often used in the past, assuming it's true—that learning for
us is in fact simply recollection, or being reminded—and also from this argument this
morning, that we must have learnt at some earlier time the things we now recollect, or
are reminded of. But this is impossible unless our soul existed somewhere before being
born in this human shape; so this too seems to point to the soul being something im-   73
mortal."

At this point Simmias intervened. "What are the proofs of that argument, Cebes?
Remind me. I can't quite remember them just at the moment."

"One very convincing argument is that when you ask people questions, if you ask
them in the right way, they can give completely accurate answers of their own accord—
though if the knowledge and the correct answer were not in fact present in them, they
would be incapable of doing this. Secondly, the use of diagrams or visual examples of
that kind provides an absolutely clear indication that the theory is true."   b

"And if you don't find that convincing, Simmias," said Socrates, "see if you agree
when you look at it in a slightly different way. Are you dubious about what we call
learning in fact being recollection?"

"Not exactly dubious. It's just that I need the thing itself, this recollection we are
talking about. I can more or less remember from hearing the way Cebes set about the
proof, so I am convinced really. All the same, I wouldn't mind hearing how you set
about it."

"Like this. I imagine we agree that if you are reminded of something, you must   c
have known it at some time in the past."

"Yes."

"Well then, do we also agree that when knowledge comes to us in a particular way, it is recollection, or being reminded? What way do I mean? I'll tell you. If seeing something, or hearing it, or receiving some other perception of it, not only makes you recognise that thing, but also gives you the idea of something else—something the knowledge of which is different—aren't we justified in saying you have been reminded

d of the second thing you had an idea of?"

"What do you mean?"

"Something like this. Knowing a man is not the same thing as knowing a lyre."

"Of course not."

"Right. You know what lovers are like, when they see a lyre or cloak or anything at all their boyfriend generally uses. They recognise the lyre, and along with that knowledge they get a picture of the boy the lyre belongs to. That is what being reminded is. When you see Simmias, for example, you are often reminded of Cebes. I'm sure you could find thousands of examples of the same kind."

"Yes, thousands," said Simmias.

"So is that kind of thing some sort of recollection? Particularly when it happens

e with things which the passage of time—and not seeing them—has made you forget about?"

"Yes, it certainly is."

"What about seeing a picture of a horse, or a picture of a lyre, and being reminded of a man? Or a picture of Simmias, and being reminded of Cebes? Is that possible?"

"Very much so."

74   "And also, presumably, seeing a picture of Simmias, and being reminded of Simmias himself?"

"That is certainly possible."

"Doesn't it turn out, in all these examples, that the recollection can arise either from things which are similar, or from things which are dissimilar?"

"Yes, it does."

"When you are reminded of something by what is similar, doesn't something else inevitably happen as well? Don't you decide whether or not it falls short at all, in point of similarity, of the object you were reminded of?"

"Yes. Inevitably."

"See if the next step is valid. I take it we are prepared to talk about equality. I don't mean a stick being equal to a stick, or a stone equal to a stone, or anything of that sort. I mean something else, apart from all these, equality itself. Should we say there is such a thing, or no such thing?"

b "We should unquestionably say there is," said Simmias. "Most emphatically."

"Do we know just what it is?"

"We certainly do."

"Where did we get our knowledge of it from? Wasn't it from what we were talking about just now—from seeing sticks or stones or other things which were equal? Wasn't it from those that we formed an idea of equality itself, although it is different from them? Or doesn't it seem to you to be different? Look at it like this. Take sticks and stones which are equal. Don't they sometimes, although they don't change, seem to be both equal (to one thing) and unequal (to some other thing)?"

"They certainly do."

c "What about the elements which make up absolute equality? Do you think they are ever unequal? Do you think equality is ever inequality?"

"No, Socrates, never."

"So the particular examples of equal things are not the same as equality itself."

"Not at all the same, I think, Socrates."

"Yet it was from these particular examples, although they are different from that true equality, that you nonetheless conceived and derived a knowledge of it?"

"That is quite true."

"And the equal is either like the particulars, or unlike?"

"Yes."

"In fact it makes no difference. Provided you see one thing, and from seeing that form a conception of another—whether like it or unlike it—then that, without question,   d
is recollection."

"Yes. That's right."

"What about the equality in sticks, and the examples we were talking about a moment ago? Do we find something like this? Do they strike us as being equal in the same way as equality itself? Do they to some extent fall short of it, in their resemblance to the equal? Or do they not fall short at all?"

"They fall a long way short," he said.

"All right, then. Sometimes the sight of something can make you think, 'What I am now seeing is trying to be like some other existing thing, but it falls short of it, and cannot be quite like it, only an inferior version.' Do we agree that when you think this, it necessarily follows that you have in fact previously known the thing you say this ob-   e
ject resembles, though it falls short of it?"

"Yes, necessarily."

"And what about us? Is this what we find with the particular equal things and equality itself, or isn't it?"

"Yes, that's exactly what we find."

"It must follow, then, that we knew about equality before the time when seeing the particular equal things first gave us the idea that they were all striving to be like   75
equality, but falling short of it."

"That is true."

"We also agree on one further point. We did not get this idea, nor *could* we have got it, from anything other than sight, or touch, or one of the other senses. I count all the senses as the same."

"They are the same, Socrates—for the purposes of this argument, at any rate."

"But of course it must be from the senses that we get the idea that all the objects of our senses are striving after that equality which is really equal, and falling short of it.   b
Is that what we are saying?"

"Yes."

"So before we ever started to see, or hear, or use our other senses, we must in fact have gained from somewhere a knowledge of what equality itself really is. Otherwise we could not have referred to it the particular examples of equality derived from the senses, or decided that they were all doing their best to be like it, but falling short of it."

"That necessarily follows from the earlier steps in the argument, Socrates."

"Well then, were we able to see and hear, and did we possess our other senses, as soon as we were born?"

"Of course."

"But we must, didn't we say, have gained our knowledge of equality before our   c
ability to perceive?"

"Yes."

"Before we were born, apparently. That must necessarily be when we gained it."

"Apparently."

"If, in that case, we acquired the knowledge before birth, and were born with it, then did we have the knowledge—both before we were born, and the moment we were born—not only of equality, and of greater and smaller, but also of all other things of the same kind? After all, our present argument is not just about equality. It is also about beauty itself, and good itself, and justice and holiness—in fact everything, as I say, to

d   which we could attach this label 'itself' when we ask our questions or give our answers. We must necessarily, therefore, have acquired our knowledge of all these things before we were born."

"That is true."

"Then if, each time we gain this knowledge, we don't forget it, we must always be born possessing it, and must continue to possess it throughout our lives. After all, knowing something is merely to have acquired the knowledge, and not lost it. Isn't that what we call forgetting, Simmias—the loss of knowledge?"

e   "Exactly that, I think, Socrates."

"The other possibility, I imagine, is that we acquired it before we were born, but then lost it at birth, and only later, through the use of our senses directed towards particular examples, recovered our former knowledge, the knowledge we had once possessed in the past. If that is what happens, wouldn't what we call learning be the recovery of knowledge which is already ours? And would we be justified in calling this recovery recollection, or being reminded?"

"We certainly would."

"Yes, because earlier on we did establish that it was possible, when we perceive

76   something—either by seeing it, or hearing it, or receiving some other perception— to form from it by association an idea of something else which we had forgotten, something which the first thing reminded us of by its dissimilarity or similarity. So as I say, we have two alternatives: either we are all born with this knowledge, and go on possessing it throughout our lives, or else people are simply reminded of it later, when we say they are learning. Learning would then be this reminding, or recollection."

"That is exactly the position, Socrates."

"Which alternative are you going to choose, then, Simmias? Are we born pos-

b   sessing this knowledge, or are we subsequently reminded of things we once had a knowledge of in the past?"

"I don't know how to decide, Socrates, just at the moment."

"How about a different choice? What is your view on this? If a man knows something, could he give an explanation of what he knows, or not?"

"He must necessarily be able to, Socrates."

"And do you think everyone can give an explanation of the things we've just been discussing?"

"If only they could. But I'm very much afraid that this time tomorrow there will be nobody left in the world capable of doing so properly."

c   "Then you don't think everyone has a knowledge of them, Simmias?"

"By no means."

"So people *are* reminded of what they once learnt in the past?"

"They must be."

"When did our souls acquire this knowledge? Clearly not after we are born as human beings."

"Clearly not."

"So it must have been before that."

"Yes."

❘ "In that case, Simmias, our souls did exist even before their existence in human shape, separate from our bodies, and they did possess the power of thought." ❘

"Unless of course we gain the knowledge of these things at the actual moment of birth, Socrates. That period of time still remains a possibility."

"Fair enough, my friend. But our loss of this knowledge, when does that happen   d
if not at birth? We're not born with it—we've just agreed that. Or do we lose it at the precise moment we acquire it? Or is there some other period of time you can suggest?"

"No, Socrates. I didn't realise I was talking nonsense."

"So is this the position we have reached so far, Simmias? If the originals we keep talking about do exist—a beautiful and a good, and every reality of that kind—if it is to this reality that we refer all particulars derived from the senses, finding it readily available and already in our possession, and if we compare the particulars with this reality, it must follow that just as the originals exist, so too our souls must exist even before we are born. And if they don't exist, the argument we have constructed so far will have   e
been a waste of time, won't it? Is that the position? Does the existence of our souls before we were born depend on the existence of those originals? So that if the originals did not exist, then our souls can't have existed either?"

"I think it is overwhelmingly clear, Socrates," said Simmias, "that the one does depend on the other. Luckily for us, the argument comes down to the fact that our soul's existence before we are born is as sure as the reality you are now describing. For my part, I find it as clear as anything can be that the existence of all the things of this type— beauty and goodness and everything else you mentioned just now—is as certain as can   77
be. In my opinion at least, the proof is satisfactory."

"And what about Cebes? We must convince Cebes as well."

"He finds it satisfactory," said Simmias, "at least, I *think* he does, though he's the hardest man in the world when he starts being sceptical about an argument. I think he's fully convinced that our soul existed before we were born. That it will continue to exist even after we die does not seem, even to me, Socrates, to have been proved. Cebes's objection of a short while ago still stands—the common fear that the soul may vanish into   b
thin air when a man dies, and that this may be the end of its existence. After all, what is to stop it coming into being from somewhere other than from the dead, coalescing and existing before its arrival in a human body, and when it does arrive, and is separated from the body, then itself dying and being destroyed as well?"

"I agree, Simmias," said Cebes. "We seem to have proved half of what we had to   c
prove, by showing that our soul existed before we were born. For the proof to be complete, we must now show also that it will go on existing even after we die, just as much as before we were born."

"We *have* shown that already, Simmias and Cebes," said Socrates, "if you care to combine the argument we have just completed with the one before it, which we all accepted—that everything living comes into being from what is dead. After all, if the soul does exist even before birth, and if, when it enters life and is born, the only place it can possibly come from is death, and from being dead, the inescapable conclusion must be that it goes on existing after it dies as well, given that it has to be born again. So the   d
proof you want has been given already. All the same, I suspect you and Simmias would be glad to deal with this argument too in greater detail. I think you have the fear children have, that when the soul leaves the body, the force of the wind really may blow it away in all directions, and cause it to disintegrate—especially if you're unlucky enough to die when there's a strong wind blowing, and not on a nice calm day."

"Cebes laughed. "Assuming we *are* afraid, Socrates, try and reassure us. Or rather,   e
not that *we* are afraid, but perhaps somewhere, even in us, there is a child who does

have fears of this kind. Try and make *him* change his mind, and not fear death as some sort of bogeyman."

"You will have to use enchantments. Sing them to him every day, until you have charmed the fears out of him."

78   "All right, Socrates. But where will we find an enchanter who is any good at dealing with fears of this kind, now that you are leaving us?"

"Greece is a large place, Cebes. There must surely be men who are some good living in it. And there are all the nations of non-Greeks as well. You must investigate all these people in your search for this charmer you want. Don't worry about the expense or the work involved; there's no better investment you could make. You should look for him also in your own conversations with one another; after all, it's quite possible you won't easily find anyone better at it than you are."

b   "Consider it done," said Cebes. "But can we go back to the point where we left off, if you have no objection?"

"Of course I have no objection. Why should I?"

"Good."

"Shouldn't we then," said Socrates, "ask ourselves questions like these? What kind of object is liable to have this happen to it—this process of disintegration? For what kind of object can we be afraid that this *might* happen to it? And what kind of object is not liable? After that shouldn't we look into which kind of object the soul is, and, depending on the answer, be optimistic or apprehensive about our soul?"

"Yes. We should."

c   "Well then, isn't something which is compound, or whose nature is composite, liable to have this happen to it, this separation into the elements of which it is composed? And isn't something which is not composite the one object, if any, which is not liable to have this happen to it?"

"I think it is," said Cebes.

"And things that are always constant and unchanging are most likely not composite, while those that vary from one time to another, and are never constant, are most likely to be composite."

"I think so."

"Take the things we were talking about in the previous argument. Is the actual re-
d   ality whose existence we are defining by our questions and answers always unchanging and constant, or does it vary from one time to another? Surely equality itself, beauty itself, what any given thing in itself is, what is real, surely these don't admit of the slightest change? Since the reality of each of them, taken by itself, has a single form, isn't it always unchanging and constant, never anywhere, in any way, admitting any alteration at all?"

"It must necessarily be unchanging and constant, Socrates."

"What about the many particular examples of beautiful things—such as men, or horses, or clothes, or anything else of the same sort—or the particular examples of equal things, or any of the particulars which go by the same names as the realities we were talking about? Are they constant, or are they just the opposite of those realities? Are they vir-
e   tually never in any way constant, either in relation to themselves, or to each other?"

"You are right about them, too. They are never constant."

"You can touch the particular examples, can't you, or see them, or perceive them with the other senses, whereas you cannot possibly grasp the things which are constant
79   with any faculty other than rational thought? Things of this kind cannot be seen, can they? They are not visible."

"You are absolutely right," he said.

"So do you want us to say there are two classes of object—one visible, the other unseen?"

"Yes."

"Shall we say the unseen is always constant, and the visible never constant?"

"Yes, let's say that as well."

"Well then, isn't one part of us our body, and the other part our soul?" b

"Yes."

"To which class of objects, then, do we say the body would be more similar, and more closely related?"

"It's obvious to anyone that it is more similar to the visible class."

"What about the soul? Is that something visible, or something unseen?"

"Well, it's certainly not visible by men, Socrates."

"Surely when we talked of things being 'visible' and 'invisible,' we meant to human eyes. Or did you think we were talking about some other eyes?"

"No. Human eyes."

"All right, then. What is our view of the soul? Do we regard it as something visible, or something invisible?"

"Something invisible."

"Unseen, in fact?"

"Yes."

"So the soul is more similar than the body to what is unseen, while the body is c
more similar to what is visible."

"They must necessarily be, Socrates."

"Well then, did we also say, a little while back, that when the soul makes use of the body for the purpose of looking into something, by means of sight, or hearing, or one of the other senses—after all, examining something using the body simply means examining it using the senses—it is dragged by the body into the realm of things that are never constant? That it becomes erratic, confused and dizzy, as if it had had too much to drink, because of its contact with objects which have these qualities?"

"We did."

"On the other hand, when it looks at things all by itself, the soul goes to the home d
of what is pure, everlasting, immortal and unchanging. Because of their close kinship, it stays there with it all the time—when it is all by itself, that is, and it is allowed to. Its wanderings are over, and when it is with the objects in that realm it remains all the time constant and unchanging, because of its contact with objects which have these qualities. Don't we call this state of the soul wisdom?"

"You are right, Socrates. Absolutely right."

"Once again, then, on the strength of our previous discussion and of this present discussion, which class of objects do you think the soul more closely resembles, and is e
more closely related to?"

"On this line of argument, Socrates, I think anyone would agree—however slow on the uptake—that in every way possible the soul more closely resembles the class which is always constant than the class which is not."

"What about the body?"

"The body is more like the other class."

"Now for a third argument. When the soul and body are united, nature ordains that the body should serve and be subject, the soul rule and be master. This being so, 80
again, which of them do you think is like what is divine, and which like what is mortal? Don't you think what is divine is a natural ruler and leader, and what is mortal a natural subject and servant?"

"Yes, I do."

"Which of them, then, is the soul like?"

"Obviously, Socrates, the soul is like what is divine, the body like what is mortal."

"What do you think, Cebes? Is the conclusion of our whole discussion so far that the soul most resembles what is divine, immortal, susceptible to thought, unvarying in shape, indestructible, and always remaining constant and true to itself? And that the

b   body, on the other hand, most resembles what is human, mortal, varying in shape, not susceptible to thought, destructible, and never remaining true to itself? Have we any objection to this account of things, my dear Cebes?"

"No, we haven't."

"All right, then. If this is how things are, isn't the body liable to be easily destroyed, while the soul, by contrast, is liable to be altogether indestructible—or very nearly so?"

c   "Of course."

"Think about what happens when a man dies. The visible part of him, his body, which is located in the visible world, and which we call the corpse, is liable to destruction, decay and dissolution. All the same, though, these things do not start happening to it straight away. The corpse is likely to last for a reasonable while, even if a man's body is in the peak of condition when he dies, and he is in the prime of life; and it *can* last for a very long time. If the body is reduced and embalmed, the way people are embalmed in

d   Egypt, it can remain more or less complete for an incredible time; and even if the body decays, still some parts of it—bones, sinews, things like that—are virtually everlasting, aren't they?"

"Yes."

"What about the soul, then, the unseen part of him, which goes to a different place, a place like itself—noble, pure and invisible, the house of Hades in the true sense of the word—to the good and wise god, which is where, god willing, my soul too is shortly going to have to make its way? Does this soul of ours, whose character and nature are as we have described, get blown in all directions and destroyed as soon as it is released from the body, as most people say? Don't you believe it, my dear Cebes and Simmias.

e   "No, what really happens is much more like this. Either the soul is released in a state of purity, unencumbered by any part of the body, since it had no more to do with the body in its life than it could help; it avoided it and kept itself to itself, since this moment was what it spent all its time rehearsing for. Its life amounted simply to the pursuit of wisdom in the right way, and a genuine rehearsal for dying without regret.

81   Or wouldn't this be a rehearsal for death?"

"It certainly would."

"Does a soul of this type, then, go to the place which is like it, to what is invisible—the divine, the everlasting, the realm of thought? When it gets there, does it have the chance to be happy, now that it has been released from its wandering and folly, its fears and wild desires, and from the rest of the evils men are subject to? Does it, as they say of those who have been initiated, truly spend the rest of time in the company of the gods? Should that be our view, Cebes? Or something different?"

"That, most emphatically."

b   "Alternatively, I imagine, the soul may be in a polluted state, and unpurified, when it is released from the body; it may have spent all its time in the company of the body, serving it, in love with it, bewitched by it and by its desires and pleasures. As a result, only what is corporeal seems real to it—things it can touch, or see, or drink, or eat, or use for sexual enjoyment. What is hidden from the eyes and invisible, what can be thought or grasped by philosophy, this it has come to hate and fear and avoid. Do you believe a soul of this type will get away all by itself, pure and unalloyed?"

"Impossible."

"Yes. I should imagine it will have patches of what is corporeal, won't it, which have been grafted on to it by the fellowship and company of the body, through their constant association, and through the habits of a lifetime?"

"It certainly will."

"Yes. And we should regard what is corporeal as being a burden, my friend—as heavy, earthbound, and visible. A soul of this type, with this corporeal element, is weighed down and dragged back to the visible world by fear of the invisible and of Hades, so the stories go. It haunts tombstones and graves. That is where the shadowy phantoms of souls are actually seen, the kind of apparitions produced by souls of this type, souls which have not been set free in a pure state, but still have some element of what is visible—which is why they can be seen."

"Quite likely, Socrates."

"Extremely likely, Cebes. And it won't be the souls of the good, but those of the wicked, that are compelled to wander round places of that sort, paying the penalty for their previous evil life. They go on wandering up to the point when their desire for the element which accompanies them, the corporeal, causes them to go back and be chained to a body again. They are chained, as you would expect, to characters matching their actual habits during their life."

"What sort of characters do you mean, Socrates?"

"Well, for example, if they have made a habit of gluttony, lust and drunkenness, rather than avoiding them, they will probably be born in the guise of donkeys, or some animal like that. Don't you think so?"

"Very probably."

"And those who have set the highest value on injustice, tyranny and robbery, in the guise of wolves, or hawks, or kites. Where else can we say souls like this go?"

"Naturally," said Cebes, "that's the kind of form they will take."

"Is it obvious, then," he said, "that the destination of every other class of soul will depend on how appropriate it is to its previous way of life?"

"Yes, it is obvious. Of course it is."

"The most fortunate among them, then, and the ones who go to the best home, aren't they those who have made a habit of excellence in public and political life—what is known as self-control and justice—when these are the result of their disposition or way of life, but not of philosophy and reason?"

"In what way the most fortunate?"

"Because they will probably return as members of an organised and civilised species like themselves—bees, I should think, or wasps, or ants—and from those back again to the same, human, species, to become decent men."

"They probably will."

"But to join the company of the gods is not granted to the man who has not practised philosophy, and departed this life in a state of perfect purity—only to the lover of wisdom. That is why, my dear Simmias and Cebes, true philosophers abstain from all bodily desires; they stand firm, and do not give in to them. It is not because they have some fear of losing the family fortune, and being poor, as most people have, in their obsession with money. Nor again do they abstain from bodily pleasures through fear of notoriety or the reputation of living an evil life, like those who are eager for public office or public recognition."

"No, that would not be the right motive, Socrates," said Cebes.

"Indeed it would not. That is why those who care at all for their own soul, and do not spend their life moulding it to fit the body, forget about all these people. They regard them as not knowing where they are going, and so they themselves set out by a different route. They believe they must not oppose philosophy, or the release and purification it brings; and so, in their pursuit of it, they follow the direction in which it leads."

"How do they do that, Socrates?"

e   "I'll tell you. Philosophers realise that philosophy finds their soul literally imprisoned in the body, and glued to it, unable to look at reality all by itself, but compelled to look at it through the body, as if through prison bars; philosophy finds the soul wallowing in total ignorance. It can see that the cleverness of the prison is the way it uses desire to make the prisoner, as far as possible, his own jailer. . . ."

*   *   *

112E—END*

112e   "There are many rivers, large and varied. And among these many rivers there are four in particular, of which the greatest, which flows in a circle round the perimeter, is the river called Oceanus. Diametrically opposite to this, flowing in the opposite direction, is the river Acheron, which flows through barren countryside, and then flowing underground

113   comes out into the Acherusian lake. This is where the souls of the dead come to, most of them, and after waiting their appointed time—some longer, some shorter—are sent back again to be born as living creatures.

"The third river issues from a point between these first two. Near its source it flows into a vast expanse blazing all over with fire; there it creates a lake bigger than our sea, a boiling mixture of water and mud. From there it comes round in a circle, foul and muddy, and as it winds itself round inside the earth, it passes a number of places, among

b   them the margin of the Acherusian lake, though it does not mingle with the water. And when it has wound itself round many times, it emerges underground at a lower point in Tartarus. This is the river they call Pyriphlegethon; its streams belch forth fragments at various places on the earth's surface.

"Opposite this river, in turn, issues the fourth river—into a land which in the first place is strange and wild, as the story goes, and which is entirely the colour of lapis

c   lazuli. They call this the Stygian land, and the lake created by the river's outflow they call the Styx. The water of the river, in its descent, acquires strange properties; finally it disappears below the ground, and winds about, flowing in the opposite direction to Pyriphlegethon, and meets it at the Acherusian lake, coming from the other side. Nor does the water of this river mingle with any other, but it too goes round in a circle and comes out into Tartarus opposite Pyriphlegethon. The name of this river, according to the poets, is Cocytus.

"That is the nature of the landscape there. When the dead arrive at the place to

d   which the spirit conveys each one, they first submit themselves to judgment—those who have lived a good and holy life, and those who have not. Those who are found to have lived a middling sort of life make their way to the river Acheron. Using the transport which is available to them, of course, they travel to the lake. There they dwell, and are absolved from their wrongdoings by being purified and paying the penalty for them,

e   those who have done any wrong, while for their good deeds they gain reward, each in proportion to his deserts.

"Those who are judged to be beyond redemption because of the enormity of their crimes—those who are guilty of wholesale robbery from holy places, or of numerous unjust and unlawful killings, or other crimes which are really the equivalent of these—

---

*Socrates is giving his imaginative description of the afterlife of the Underworld.

meet the fate they deserve. They are hurled into Tartarus, whence they nevermore emerge.

"Those who are found guilty of crimes which, though great, are redeemable—for example committing an act of violence in a fit of anger against a father or mother, but then living out one's life in a state of repentance; or becoming a killer in some similar way— these too must of necessity be thrown into Tartarus. But after they have been thrown in and remained there a year, the flood washes them back again, those guilty of homicide down Cocytus, those who have killed a father or mother down Pyriphlegethon. And when in their journey they pass the Acherusian lake, there they shout and call out, some to those they have killed, others to those they have treated with violence. They call out beseeching them, begging them to let them escape into the lake, and to accept them. If they can persuade them, they do escape, and are released from their punishment; otherwise they are borne once more to Tartarus, and from there back again to the rivers. This goes on happening to them until they do persuade those they have wronged, since this is the penalty assigned to them by the judges.

"Those whose lives are judged to have been distinguished by their sanctity are the ones who are released and set free from these places below the ground, as if from prison. They rise, and come to the pure dwelling-place, where they live above the ground. Of this group, those who have been fully cleansed by philosophy live entirely without their bodies for all time thereafter, and they come to dwellings finer still than those I have mentioned; it is not easy to give you a clear idea of them, nor is there time just at the moment. But for the reasons we have described, we should do everything we can, Simmias, to share in human excellence and wisdom while we are alive. The reward is a good one, and our hopes high.

"No sensible man would think it right to state dogmatically that the underworld is exactly as I have described it; but to say that either this or something like it is how things are for our souls and their dwellings, since the soul is clearly something immortal, that I do think is right—and worth taking a chance on, for the man who thinks that is how things are, since there is every chance of being proved right. He should recite to himself stories of the kind we have just told, like enchantments; and this, of course, is why I have been giving this account at such length.

"Those are the grounds for optimism about his soul, for anyone who in his life has rejected, as alien to him, the pleasures of the body and the ways of making it beautiful, believing they do more harm than good. Instead he will have taken seriously the pleasures of learning; he will have beautified his soul with beauties which are its own, and not alien: self-control, justice, courage, freedom and truth. Thus prepared, he now awaits his journey to the underworld. You, Simmias and Cebes, and the rest of you, will all journey there at some time in the future. As for me, my destiny is even now calling me, as the character in the play says, and it's about time for me to be thinking about a bath. I'm sure it's better to have a bath before drinking the poison, and save the women the trouble of washing the corpse."

When he said this, Crito asked him, "Well, Socrates, what instructions do you want to give these people here, or me—about your children, or anything else? What can we do for you that will be most welcome to you?"

"The same as I always say, Crito. Nothing unfamiliar. Take care of yourselves, and whatever you do will be welcome to me, to my family, and to you yourselves, even if you make no promises here and now. If you don't care for yourselves, and refuse to spend your lives on the trail of the things we've been talking about today and in the past, then however many solemn promises you make today, it will get you nowhere."

"We'll try our hardest, then," said Crito, "to do as you say. What about burying you? How do you want us to do that?"

"However you like. Provided you can catch me, that is, and I don't get away from you." He glanced at us, laughing to himself, and said, "Gentlemen, I cannot convince Crito that I am Socrates, here, the person discussing things with you and setting out all these arguments. He thinks I am the body he is shortly going to see, and asks how I

d   would like him to bury me. This whole argument I have spent so much time putting together, to show that when I drink the poison I shall not remain with you, but depart—leaving I trust for that happy region of the blessed—all this encouragement, both of you and of myself, was I think wasted on him. So you must give Crito the opposite undertaking, on my behalf, to the one he wanted to give the jury. His was that I would certainly remain. Yours must be that I shall certainly *not* remain, when I die, but depart and

e   go away. Then Crito will be able to bear it more easily, and will not grieve for me when he sees my body being burnt or buried, as if something terrible were happening to me; he won't say, at my funeral, that he is laying out Socrates, or carrying him out, or burying him.

"Take my word for it, my good friend Crito, saying what is wrong is not only disturbing in itself, but is also damaging to the soul. You must cheer up. Tell yourself you are burying my body, and bury it in a way which is pleasing to you, and which you be-

116   lieve to be most in keeping with tradition."

With these words he got up, and went into a room to take a bath. Crito followed him, telling us to stay where we were. We waited, discussing the arguments among ourselves, examining them closely, and then again repeating to ourselves the great misfortune which had befallen us. We thought, quite simply, that we were losing a father, and that we would be spending the rest of our lives as orphans.

After he had had his bath, his children were taken in to him—he had two young

b   sons, and one fully grown—and the women of his household (you probably know them) went in. He spoke to them in Crito's presence, telling them his last wishes, then told the women and children to leave, and himself came back to us.

It was now close to sunset. He had spent a long time inside. He came and sat down, fresh from his bath. There was not much conversation after this. The officer of

c   the prison authorities came and stood close to him. "Socrates," he said, "I am sure I shall not have the same complaint against you that I often have against others. They get angry with me, and curse me when I tell them to drink the poison, though I am only carrying out the orders of the magistrates. But you, I have come to realise during your time here, are altogether the most generous man, the most gentle, and the best, of all those who have ever come here. And now in particular, I am sure you are angry, not with me, since you know the people responsible, but with them. So now, since you know what I

d   have come to say, farewell, and try to endure what must be as willingly as possible." With this he burst into tears, turned, and left us.

Socrates looked after him. "Farewell to you too. We will do as you say." And then to us, "What a charming man. He has kept coming to see me all this time, and sometimes he has stopped to chat; in fact, he has been altogether the best of men. See how generously now he sheds tears for me. Come, Crito, let us do as he tells us. Let someone bring in the poison, if it has been ground. Otherwise, let the man get on with grinding it."

e   "If you ask me, Socrates," Crito said, "there is still sun on the mountain-tops; it has not set yet. Besides, I know of people who have drunk the poison long after they were told to. They have had dinner, and plenty to drink; some of them have even had sex with the people they most wanted. There is no hurry. We still have some time."

"They have their reasons, Crito, the people you are talking about, for acting

117   as they do. They think they gain something by it. And I have my reasons for not

acting like that, since I do not think I shall gain anything by drinking the poison a little later—apart from making myself ridiculous in my own eyes by clutching on to life, and trying to save the last drops when the cup is already empty. Go on. Believe me. Do as I say."

Crito, hearing this, nodded to his slave who was standing nearby. The slave went out, and after quite a while came back with the man who was going to administer the poison; he brought it, already ground, in a cup. When Socrates saw the man, he said, "Well, my good fellow, you know about these things. What do we have to do?"

"Just drink it and walk about," he replied, "until you feel a heaviness in your legs. Then lie down. If you do that, it will work of its own accord." As he said this, he handed the cup to Socrates.

He took it quite cheerfully, Echecrates, with no hesitation, and no change in his colour or facial expression. Then he gave the man one of his usual quizzical looks, and asked him, "What is your policy about this drink—I mean about pouring a libation to someone? Is it permitted, or not?"

"Socrates, we grind only what we think is the right amount for the person to drink."

"I understand. But a prayer to the gods, I take it, is both permitted and right. Let us hope the move from this world to the next may be a good one. That is what I am praying for, and may that be how it turns out."

Saying this he raised the cup to his lips and drained it, quite unperturbed and with every appearance of enjoyment. Most of us, up to that point, had been reasonably successful in controlling our tears, but when we saw him drinking, saw that he had drunk, we could do so no longer. I found the tears coming despite myself, in a flood, so that I covered my face and wept—not for him, but for my own misfortune, and for the kind of man I was losing as a friend.

Crito collapsed sooner than I did. Unable to hold back his tears any longer, he got up and left. Apollodorus had been crying incessantly even before this, but now he started roaring aloud, upsetting us and making us all break down—apart from Socrates himself.

"Really! What an extraordinary way to behave!" he said. "The main reason I sent the women away was so they would not disturb us like this. I have heard it said that one should die in silence. So keep quiet, and be brave."

When we heard this, we were ashamed, and stopped crying. He walked around, and then, when he said his legs were getting heavy, lay down on his back, as the man had told him to. As he did so, the man who had given him the poison put his hands on him, and after a little time tried his feet and legs; then he squeezed his foot hard, and asked him if he could feel it. He said he could not. After that, again, the man tried his shins. Moving his hand up, he showed us that he was getting cold and stiff. Then the man touched him, and said that when the coldness reached his heart, at that point he would be gone.

The chill had just about reached his abdomen when he uncovered his face—he had covered it up—and said, and these were the last words he uttered, "Crito, we owe a cock to Asclepius. Pay the debt. Don't forget."*

"It shall be done," Crito replied. "Is there anything else you want to say?"

To this question Socrates made no reply, but shortly afterwards he gave a start, and the man uncovered his face. His eyes were fixed. Seeing this, Crito pressed his lips and eyelids together.

---

*[Asclepius was the Greek god of healing. When one recovered from an illness it was customary to offer a cock as a sacrifice, so Socrates' last words imply that death is a kind of healing.]

The Death of Socrates, 1787, by Jacques-Louis David (1748–1825). The Metropolitan Museum of Art, Wolfe Fund, 1931. Catharine Lorillard Wolfe Collection. [31.45])

That, Echecrates, was the death of our friend. Of the men of his time that we knew, he was the best, we would claim, and in general the wisest and most just.

MENO

PERSONS OF THE DIALOGUE:

Meno
A Slave of Meno
Socrates
Anytus

70   MENO: Can you tell me Socrates—is virtue something that can be taught? Or does it come by practice? Or is it neither teaching nor practice that gives it to a man but natural aptitude or something else?

From *Protagoras and Meno,* translated with an introduction by W.K.C. Guthrie (Harmondsworth, Middlesex, England: Penguin Classics, 1956). Reprinted by permission of Penguin Books Ltd.

SOCRATES: Well Meno, in the old days the Thessalians had a great reputation among the Greeks for their wealth and their horsemanship. Now it seems they are philosophers as well—especially the men of Larissa, where your friend Aristippus comes from. It is Gorgias who has done it. He went to that city and captured the hearts of the foremost of the Aleuadae for his wisdom (among them your own admirer Aristippus), not to speak of other leading Thessalians. In particular he got you into the habit of answering any question you might be asked, with the confidence and dignity appropriate to those who know the answers, just as he himself invites questions of every kind from anyone in the Greek world who wishes to ask, and never fails to answer them. But here at Athens, my dear Meno, it is just the reverse. There is a dearth of wisdom, and it looks as if it had migrated from our part of the country to yours. At any rate, if you put your question to any of our people, they will all alike laugh and say: "You must think I am singularly fortunate, to know whether virtue can be taught or how it is acquired. The fact is that far from knowing whether it can be taught, I have no idea what virtue itself is."

That is my own case. I share the poverty of my fellow-countrymen in this respect, and confess to my shame that I have no knowledge about virtue at all. And how can I know a property of something when I don't even know what it is? Do you suppose that somebody entirely ignorant who Meno is could say whether he is handsome and rich and well-born or the reverse? Is that possible, do you think?

MENO: No. But is this true about yourself, Socrates, that you don't even know what virtue is? Is this the report that we are to take home about you?

SOCRATES: Not only that; you may say also that, to the best of my belief, I have never yet met anyone who did know.

MENO: What! Didn't you meet Gorgias when he was here?

SOCRATES: Yes.

MENO: And you still didn't think he knew?

SOCRATES: I'm a forgetful sort of person, and I can't say just now what I thought at the time. Probably he did know, and I expect you know what he used to say about it. So remind me what it was, or tell me yourself if you will. No doubt you agree with him.

MENO: Yes I do.

SOCRATES: Then let's leave him out of it, since after all he isn't here. What do you yourself say virtue is? I do ask you in all earnestness not to refuse me, but to speak out. I shall be only too happy to be proved wrong if you and Gorgias turn out to know this, although I said I had never met anyone who did.

MENO: But there is no difficulty about it. First of all, if it is manly virtue you are after, it is easy to see that the virtue of a man consists in managing the city's affairs capably, and so that he will help his friends and injure his foes while taking care to come to no harm himself. Or if you want a woman's virtue, that is easily described. She must be a good housewife, careful with her stores and obedient to her husband. Then there is another virtue for a child, male or female, and another for an old man, free or slave as you like; and a great many more kinds of virtue, so that no one need be at a loss to say what it is. For every act and every time of life, with reference to each separate function, there is a virtue for each one of us, and similarly, I should say, a vice.

SOCRATES: I seem to be in luck. I wanted one virtue and I find that you have a whole swarm of virtues to offer. But seriously, to carry on this metaphor of the swarm, suppose I asked you what a bee is, what is its essential nature, and you replied that bees were of many different kinds; what would you say if I went on to ask: "And is it in being bees that they are many and various and different from one another? Or would you agree that it is not in this respect that they differ, but in something else, some other quality like size or beauty?"

MENO: I should say that in so far as they are bees, they don't differ from one another at all.

SOCRATES: Suppose I then continued: "Well, this is just what I want you to tell me. What is that character in respect of which they don't differ at all, but are all the same?" I presume you would have something to say?

MENO: I should.

SOCRATES: Then do the same with the virtues. Even if they are many and various, yet at least they all have some common character which makes them virtues. That is what ought to be kept in view by anyone who answers the question: "What is virtue?" Do you follow me?

MENO: I think I do, but I don't yet really grasp the question as I should wish.

SOCRATES: Well, does this apply in your mind only to virtue, that there is a different one for a man and a woman and the rest? Is it the same with health and size and strength, or has health the same character everywhere, if it is health, whether it be in a man or any other creature?

MENO: I agree that health is the same in a man or in a woman.

SOCRATES: And what about size and strength? If a woman is strong, will it be the same thing, the same strength, that makes her strong? My meaning is that in its character as strength, it is no different, whether it be in a man or in a woman. Or do you think it is?

MENO: No.

SOCRATES: And will virtue differ, in its character as virtue, whether it be in a child or an old man, a woman or a man?

MENO: I somehow feel that this is not on the same level as the other cases.

SOCRATES: Well then, didn't you say that a man's virtue lay in directing the city well, and a woman's in directing her household well?

MENO: Yes.

SOCRATES: And is it possible to direct anything well—city or household or anything else—if not temperately and justly?

MENO: Certainly not.

SOCRATES: And that means with temperance and justice?

MENO: Of course.

SOCRATES: Then both man and woman need the same qualities, justice and temperance, if they are going to be good.

MENO: It looks like it.

SOCRATES: And what about your child and old man? Could they be good if they were incontinent and unjust?

MENO: Of course not.

SOCRATES: They must be temperate and just?

MENO: Yes.

SOCRATES: So everyone is good in the same way, since they become good by possessing the same qualities.

MENO: So it seems.

SOCRATES: And if they did not share the same virtue, they would not be good in the same way.

MENO: No.

SOCRATES: Seeing then that they all have the same virtue, try to remember and tell me what Gorgias, and you who share his opinion, say it is.

MENO: It must be simply the capacity to govern men, if you are looking for one quality to cover all the instances.

SOCRATES: Indeed I am. But does this virtue apply to a child or a slave? Should a slave be capable of governing his master, and if he does, is he still a slave?

MENO: I hardly think so.

SOCRATES: It certainly doesn't sound likely. And here is another point. You speak of "capacity to govern." Shall we not add "justly but not otherwise"?

MENO: I think we should, for justice is virtue.

SOCRATES: Virtue, do you say, or *a* virtue?   e

MENO: What do you mean?

SOCRATES: Something quite general. Take roundness, for instance. I should say that it is a shape, not simply that it is shape, my reason being that there are other shapes as well.

MENO: I see your point, and I agree that there are other virtues besides justice.

SOCRATES: Tell me what they are. Just as I could name other shapes if you told   74
me to, in the same way mention some other virtues.

MENO: In my opinion, then, courage is a virtue and temperance and wisdom and dignity and many other things.

SOCRATES: This puts us back where we were. In a different way we have discovered a number of virtues when we were looking for one only. This single virtue, which permeates each of them, we cannot find.

MENO: No, I cannot yet grasp it as you want, a single virtue covering them all, as   b
I do in other instances.

SOCRATES: I'm not surprised, but I shall do my best to get us a bit further if I can. You understand, I expect, that the question applies to everything. If someone took the example I mentioned just now, and asked you: "What is shape?" and you replied that roundness is shape, and he then asked you as I did, "Do you mean it is shape or *a* shape?" you would reply of course that it is *a* shape.

MENO: Certainly.

SOCRATES: Your reason being that there are other shapes as well.   c

MENO: Yes.

SOCRATES: And if he went on to ask you what they were, you would tell him.

MENO: Yes.

SOCRATES: And the same with colour—if he asked you what it is, and on your replying "White," took you up with: "Is white colour or *a* colour?" you would say that it is *a* colour, because there are other colours as well.

MENO: I should.

SOCRATES: And if he asked you to, you would mention other colours which are   d
just as much colours as white is.

MENO: Yes.

SOCRATES: Suppose then he pursued the question as I did, and objected: "We always arrive at a plurality, but that is not the kind of answer I want. Seeing that you call these many particulars by one and the same name, and say that every one of them is a shape, even though they are the contrary of each other, tell me what this is which embraces round as well as straight, and what you mean by shape when you say that   e
straightness is a shape as much as roundness. You do say that?"

MENO: Yes.

SOCRATES: "And in saying it, do you mean that roundness is no more round than straight, and straightness no more straight than round?"

MENO: Of course not.

SOCRATES: "Yet you do say that roundness is no more a shape than straightness, and the other way about."

MENO: Quite true.

SOCRATES: "Then what is this thing which is called 'shape'? Try to tell me." If
when asked this question either about shape or colour you said: "But I don't understand
what you want, or what you mean," your questioner would perhaps be surprised and
say: "Don't you see that I am looking for what is the same in all of them?" Would you
even so be unable to reply, if the question was: "What is it that is common to roundness
and straightness and the other things which you call shapes?"

Do your best to answer, as practice for the question about virtue.

MENO: No, you do it, Socrates.

SOCRATES: Do you want me to give in to you?

MENO: Yes.

SOCRATES: And will you in your turn give me an answer about virtue?

MENO: I will.

SOCRATES: In that case I must do my best. It's in a good cause.

MENO: Certainly.

SOCRATES: Well now, let's try to tell you what shape is. See if you accept this definition. Let us define it as the only thing which always accompanies colour. Does that
satisfy you, or do you want it in some other way? I should be content if your definition
of virtue were on similar lines.

MENO: But that's a naïve sort of definition, Socrates.

SOCRATES: How?

MENO: Shape, if I understand what you say, is what always accompanies colour.
Well and good—but if somebody says that he doesn't know what colour is, but is no
better off with it than he is with shape, what sort of answer have you given him, do you
think?

SOCRATES: A true one; and if my questioner were one of the clever, disputatious
and quarrelsome kind, I should say to him: "You have heard my answer. If it is wrong,
it is for you to take up the argument and refute it." However, when friendly people, like
you and me, want to converse with each other, one's reply must be milder and more
conducive to discussion. By that I mean that it must not only be true, but must employ
terms with which the questioner admits he is familiar. So I will try to answer you like
that. Tell me therefore, whether you recognize the term "end"; I mean limit or boundary—all these words I use in the same sense. Prodicus might perhaps quarrel with us,
but I assume you speak of something being bounded or coming to an end. That is all I
mean, nothing subtle.

MENO: I admit the notion, and believe I understand your meaning.

SOCRATES: And again, you recognize "surface" and "solid," as they are used in
geometry?

MENO: Yes.

SOCRATES: Then with these you should by this time understand my definition of
shape. To cover all its instances, I say that shape is that in which a solid terminates, or
more briefly, it is the limit of a solid.

MENO: And how do you define colour?

SOCRATES: What a shameless fellow you are, Meno. You keep bothering an old
man to answer, but refuse to exercise your memory and tell me what was Gorgias's definition of virtue.

MENO: I will, Socrates, as soon as you tell me this.

SOCRATES: Anyone talking to you could tell blindfolded that you are a handsome
man and still have your admirers.

MENO: Why so?

SOCRATES: Because you are forever laying down the law as spoilt boys do, who act the tyrant as long as their youth lasts. No doubt you have discovered that I can never   c resist good looks. Well, I will give in and let you have your answer.

MENO: Do by all means.

SOCRATES: Would you like an answer *à la* Gorgias, such as you would most readily follow?

MENO: Of course I should.

SOCRATES: You and he believe in Empedocles's theory of effluences, do you not?

MENO: Whole-heartedly.

SOCRATES: And passages to which and through which the effluences make their way?

MENO: Yes.

SOCRATES: Some of the effluences fit into some of the passages, whereas others   d are too coarse or too fine.

MENO: That is right.

SOCRATES: Now you recognize the term "sight"?

MENO: Yes.

SOCRATES: From these notions, then, "grasp what I would tell," as Pindar says. Colour is an effluence from shapes commensurate with sight and perceptible by it.

MENO: That seems to me an excellent answer.

SOCRATES: No doubt it is the sort you are used to. And you probably see that it provides a way to define sound and smell and many similar things.

MENO: So it does.   e

SOCRATES: Yes, it's a high-sounding answer, so you like it better than the one on shape.

MENO: I do.

SOCRATES: Nevertheless, son of Alexidemus, I am convinced that the other is better; and I believe you would agree with me if you had not, as you told me yesterday, to leave before the mysteries, but could stay and be initiated.*

MENO: I would stay, Socrates, if you gave me more answers like this.   77

SOCRATES: You may be sure I shan't be lacking in keenness to do so, both for your sake and mine; but I'm afraid I may not be able to do it often. However, now it is your turn to do as you promised, and try to tell me the general nature of virtue. Stop making many out of one, as the humorists say when somebody breaks a plate. Just leave virtue whole and sound and tell me what it is, as in the examples I have given you.   b

MENO: It seems to me then, Socrates, that virtue is, in the words of the poet, "to rejoice in the fine and have power," and I define it as desiring fine things and being able to acquire them.

SOCRATES: When you speak of a man desiring fine things, do you mean it is good things he desires?

MENO: Certainly.

SOCRATES: Then do you think some men desire evil and others good? Doesn't everyone, in your opinion, desire good things?   c

---

*Evidently the Athenians are about to celebrate the famous rites of the Eleusinian Mysteries, but Meno has to return to Thessaly before they fall due. Plato frequently plays upon the analogy between religious initiation, which bestows a revelation of divine secrets, and the insight that comes from initiation into the truths of philosophy.

MENO: No.

SOCRATES: And would you say that the others suppose evils to be good, or do they still desire them although they recognize them as evil?

MENO: Both, I should say.

SOCRATES: What? Do you really think that anyone who recognizes evils for what they are, nevertheless desires them?

MENO: Yes.

SOCRATES: Desires in what way? To possess them?

MENO: Of course.

d SOCRATES: In the belief that evil things bring advantage to their possessor, or harm?

MENO: Some in the first belief, but some also in the second.

SOCRATES: And do you believe that those who suppose evil things bring advantage understand that they are evil?

MENO: No, that I can't really believe.

SOCRATES: Isn't it clear then that this class, who don't recognize evils for what they are, don't desire evil but what they think is good, though in fact it is evil; those who through ignorance mistake bad things for good obviously desire the good.

MENO: For them I suppose that is true.

SOCRATES: Now as for those whom you speak of as desiring evils in the belief that they do harm to their possessor, these presumably know that they will be injured by them?

MENO: They must.

78 SOCRATES: And don't they believe that whoever is injured is, in so far as he is injured, unhappy?

MENO: That too they must believe.

SOCRATES: And unfortunate?

MENO: Yes.

SOCRATES: Well, does anybody want to be unhappy and unfortunate?

MENO: I suppose not.

SOCRATES: Then if not, nobody desires what is evil; for what else is unhappiness but desiring evil things and getting them?

b MENO: It looks as if you are right, Socrates, and nobody desires what is evil.

SOCRATES: Now you have just said that virtue consists in a wish for good things plus the power to acquire them. In this definition the wish is common to everyone, and in that respect no one is better than his neighbour.

MENO: So it appears.

SOCRATES: So if one man is better than another, it must evidently be in respect of

c the power, and virtue, according to your account, is the power of acquiring good things.

MENO: Yes, my opinion is exactly as you now express it.

SOCRATES: Let us see whether you have hit the truth this time. You may well be right. The power of acquiring good things, you say, is virtue?

MENO: Yes.

SOCRATES: And by good do you mean such things as health and wealth?

MENO: I include the gaining both of gold and silver and of high and honourable office in the State.

SOCRATES: Are these the only classes of goods that you recognize?

MENO: Yes, I mean everything of that sort.

d SOCRATES: Right. In the definition of Meno, hereditary guest-friend of the Great King, the acquisition of gold and silver is virtue. Do you add "just and righteous" to the word "acquisition," or doesn't it make any difference to you? Do you call it virtue all the same even if they are unjustly acquired?

MENO: Certainly not.

SOCRATES: Vice then?

MENO: Most certainly.

SOCRATES: So it seems that justice or temperance or piety, or some other part of virtue, must attach to the acquisition. Otherwise, although it is a means to good things, it will not be virtue.   e

MENO: No, how could you have virtue without these?

SOCRATES: In fact lack of gold and silver, if it results from failure to acquire it—either for oneself or another—in circumstances which would have made its acquisition unjust, is itself virtue.

MENO: It would seem so.

SOCRATES: Then to have such goods is no more virtue than to lack them. Rather we may say that whatever is accompanied by justice is virtue, whatever is without qual-   79 ities of that sort is vice.

MENO: I agree that your conclusion seems inescapable.

SOCRATES: But a few minutes ago we called each of these—justice, temperance, and the rest—a part of virtue?

MENO: Yes, we did.

SOCRATES: So it seems you are making a fool of me.

MENO: How so, Socrates?

SOCRATES: I have just asked you not to break virtue up into fragments, and given you models of the type of answer I wanted, but taking no notice of this you tell me that virtue consists in the acquisition of good things with justice; and justice, you agree, is a   b part of virtue.

MENO: True.

SOCRATES: So it follows from your own statements that to act with a part of virtue is virtue, if you call justice and all the rest parts of virtue. The point I want to make is that whereas I asked you to give me an account of virtue as a whole, far from telling me what it is itself you say that every action is virtue which exhibits a part of virtue, as if you had already told me what the whole is, so that I should recognize it even if you chop   c it up into bits. It seems to me that we must put the same old question to you, my dear Meno—the question: "What is virtue?"—if every act becomes virtue when combined with a part of virtue. That is, after all, what it means to say that every act performed with justice is virtue. Don't you agree that the same question needs to be put? Does anyone know what a part of virtue is, without knowing the whole?

MENO: I suppose not.

SOCRATES: No, and if you remember, when I replied to you about shape just now,   d I believe we rejected the type of answer that employs terms which are still in question and not yet agreed upon.

MENO: We did, and rightly.

SOCRATES: Then please do the same. While the nature of virtue as a whole is still under question, don't suppose that you can explain it to anyone in terms of its parts, or by any similar type of explanation. Understand rather that the same question remains to be answered; you say this and that about virtue, but what *is* it? Does this seem nonsense   e to you?

MENO: No, to me it seems right enough.

SOCRATES: Then go back to the beginning and answer my question. What do you and your friend say that virtue is?

80 Meno: Socrates, even before I met you they told me that in plain truth you are a perplexed man yourself and reduce others to perplexity. At this moment I feel you are exercising magic and witchcraft upon me and positively laying me under your spell until I am just a mass of helplessness. If I may be flippant, I think that not only in outward appearance but in other respects as well you are exactly like

b the flat stingray that one meets in the sea. Whenever anyone comes into contact with it, it numbs him, and that is the sort of thing that you seem to be doing to me now. My mind and my lips are literally numb, and I have nothing to reply to you. Yet I have spoken about virtue hundreds of times, held forth often on the subject in front of large audiences, and very well too, or so I thought. Now I can't even say what it is. In my opinion you are well advised not to leave Athens and live abroad. If you behaved like this as a foreigner in another country, you would most likely be arrested as a wizard.

Socrates: You're a real rascal, Meno. You nearly took me in.

Meno: Just what do you mean?

c Socrates: I see why you used a simile about me.

Meno: Why, do you think?

Socrates: To be compared to something in return. All good-looking people, I know perfectly well, enjoy a game of comparisons. They get the best of it, for naturally handsome folk provoke handsome similes. But I'm not going to oblige you. As for myself, if the stingray paralyses others only through being paralysed itself, then the comparison is just, but not otherwise. It isn't that, knowing the answers myself, I perplex other people. The truth is rather that I infect them also with the perplexity

d I feel myself. So with virtue now. I don't know what it is. You may have known before you came into contact with me, but now you look as if you don't. Nevertheless I am ready to carry out, together with you, a joint investigation and inquiry into what it is.

Meno: But how will you look for something when you don't in the least know what it is? How on earth are you going to set up something you don't know as the object of your search? To put it another way, even if you come right up against it, how will you know that what you have found is the thing you didn't know?

e Socrates: I know what you mean. Do you realize that what you are bringing up is the trick argument that a man cannot try to discover either what he knows or what he does not know? He would not seek what he knows, for since he knows it there is no need of the inquiry, nor what he does not know, for in that case he does not even know what he is to look for.

81 Meno: Well, do you think it a good argument?

Socrates: No.

Meno: Can you explain how it fails?

Socrates: I can. I have heard from men and women who understand the truths of religion—

[Here he presumably pauses to emphasize the solemn change of tone that the dialogue undergoes at this point.]

Meno: What did they say?

Socrates: Something true, I thought, and fine.

Meno: What was it, and who were they?

SOCRATES: Those who tell it are priests and priestesses of the sort who make
it their business to be able to account for the functions which they perform. Pindar   b
speaks of it too, and many another of the poets who are divinely inspired. What
they say is this—see whether you think they are speaking the truth. They say that
the soul of man is immortal: At one time it comes to an end—that which is
called death—and at another is born again, but is never finally exterminated. On
these grounds a man must live all his days as righteously as possible. For those from
whom

> Persephone receives requital for ancient doom,
> In the ninth year she restores again
> Their souls to the sun above.
> From whom rise noble kings
> And the swift in strength and greatest in wisdom;   c
> And for the rest of time
> They are called heroes and sanctified by men.*

Thus the soul, since it is immortal and has been born many times, and has seen
all things both here and in the other world, has learned everything that is. So we need
not be surprised if it can recall the knowledge of virtue or anything else which, as we
see, it once possessed. All nature is akin, and the soul has learned everything, so that   d
when a man has recalled a single piece of knowledge—*learned* it, in ordinary language—there is no reason why he should not find out all the rest, if he keeps a stout
heart and does not grow weary of the search; for seeking and learning are in fact nothing but recollection.

We ought not then to be led astray by the contentious argument you quoted. It
would make us lazy, and is music in the ears of weaklings. The other doctrine produces   e
energetic seekers after knowledge; and being convinced of its truth, I am ready, with
your help, to inquire into the nature of virtue.

MENO: I see, Socrates. But what do you mean when you say that we don't
learn anything, but that what we call learning is recollection? Can you teach me that it
is so?

SOCRATES: I have just said that you're a rascal, and now you ask me if I can teach
you, when I say there is no such thing as teaching, only recollection. Evidently you   82
want to catch me contradicting myself straight away.

MENO: No, honestly, Socrates, I wasn't thinking of that. It was just habit. If you
can in any way make clear to me that what you say is true, please do.

SOCRATES: It isn't an easy thing, but still I should like to do what I can since you
ask me. I see you have a large number of retainers here. Call one of them, anyone you   b
like, and I will use him to demonstrate it to you.

MENO: Certainly. *(to a slave-boy)* Come here.

SOCRATES: He is a Greek and speaks our language?

MENO: Indeed yes—born and bred in the house.

SOCRATES: Listen carefully then, and see whether it seems to you that he is learning from me or simply being reminded.

MENO: I will.

SOCRATES: Now boy, you know that a square is a figure like this?

---

*The quotation is from Pindar.

[Socrates begins to draw figures in the sand at his feet. He points to the square ABCD.]

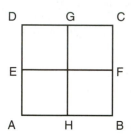

BOY: Yes.

c   SOCRATES: It has all these four sides equal?

BOY: Yes.

SOCRATES: And these lines which go through the middle of it are also equal? *(The lines* EF *and* GH.*)*

BOY: Yes.

SOCRATES: Such a figure could be either larger or smaller, could it not?

BOY: Yes.

SOCRATES: Now if this side is two feet long, and this side the same, how many feet will the whole be? Put it this way. If it were two feet in this direction and only one in that, must not the area be two feet taken once?

BOY: Yes.

d   SOCRATES: But since it is two feet this way also, does it not become twice two feet?

BOY: Yes.

SOCRATES: And how many feet is twice two? Work it out and tell me.

BOY: Four.

SOCRATES: Now could one draw another figure double the size of this, but similar, that is, with all its sides equal like this one?

BOY: Yes.

SOCRATES: It is on this line then, according to you, that we shall make the eight-foot square, by taking four of the same length?

BOY: Yes.

SOCRATES: How many feet will its area be?

BOY: Eight.

SOCRATES: Now then, try to tell me how long each of its sides will be.
e   The present figure has a side of two feet. What will be the side of the double-sized one?

BOY: It will be double, Socrates, obviously.

SOCRATES: You see, Meno, that I am not teaching him anything, only asking. Now he thinks he knows the length of the side of the eight-foot square.

MENO: Yes.

SOCRATES: But does he?

BOY: Of course not.

c   SOCRATES: So doubling the side has given us not a double but a fourfold figure?

BOY: True.

SOCRATES: And four times four are sixteen, are they not?

BOY: Yes.

SOCRATES: Then how big is the side of the eight-foot figure? This one has given us four times the original area, hasn't it?

BOY: Yes.

SOCRATES: And a side half the length gave us a square of four feet?

BOY: Yes.

SOCRATES: Good. And isn't a square of eight feet double this one and half that?

BOY: Yes.

SOCRATES: Will it not have a side greater than this one but less than that?

d   BOY: I think it will.

SOCRATES: Right. Always answer what you think. Now tell me: was not this side two feet long, and this one four?

BOY: Yes.

SOCRATES: Then the side of the eight-foot figure must be longer than two feet but shorter than four?

BOY: It must.

e   SOCRATES: Try to say how long you think it is.

BOY: Three feet.

SOCRATES: If so, shall we add half of this bit *(BO, half of* BJ*)* and make it three feet? Here are two, and this is one, and on this side similarly we have two plus one; and here is the figure you want.

[Socrates completes the square AOPQ.*]*

BOY: Yes.

SOCRATES: If it is three feet this way and three that, will the whole area be three times three feet?

BOY: It looks like it.

SOCRATES: And that is how many?

BOY: Nine.

SOCRATES: Whereas the square double our first square had to be how many?

BOY: Eight.

SOCRATES: But we haven't yet got the square of eight feet even from a three-foot side?

BOY: No.

84   SOCRATES: Then what length will give it? Try to tell us exactly. If you don't want to count it up, just show us on the diagram.

BOY: It's no use, Socrates, I just don't know.

SOCRATES: Observe, Meno, the stage he has reached on the path of recollection. At the beginning he did not know the side of the square of eight feet. Nor indeed does he know it now, but then he thought he knew it and answered boldly, as was appropriate—he felt no perplexity. Now however he does feel perplexed. Not only does he not know the answer; he doesn't even think he knows.

b   MENO: Quite true.

SOCRATES: Isn't he in a better position now in relation to what he didn't know?

MENO: I admit that too.

MENO: Certainly not.

SOCRATES: He thinks it is twice the length of the other.

MENO: Yes.

SOCRATES: Now watch how he recollects things in order—the proper way to recollect.

You say that the side of double length produces the double-sized figure? Like this I mean, not long this way and short that. It must be equal on all sides like the first figure, only twice its size, that is eight feet. Think a moment whether you still expect to get it from doubling the side.   83

BOY: Yes, I do.

SOCRATES: Well now, shall we have a line double the length of this (AB) if we add another the same length at this end (BJ)?

BOY: Yes.

SOCRATES: It is on this line then, according to you, that we shall make the eight-foot square, by taking four of the same length?

BOY: Yes.

SOCRATES: Let us draw in four equal lines *(that is, counting* AJ, *and adding* JK, KL, *and* LA *made complete by drawing in its second half* LD*),* using the first as a base.   b Does this not give us what you call the eight-foot figure?

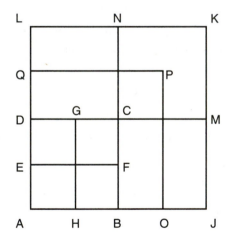

BOY: Certainly.

SOCRATES: But does it contain these four squares, each equal to the original four-foot one?

[Socrates has drawn in the lines CM, CN *to complete the squares that he wishes to point out.]*

BOY: Yes.

SOCRATES: How big is it then? Won't it be four times as big?

BOY: Of course.

SOCRATES: And is four times the same as twice?

SOCRATES: So in perplexing him and numbing him like the stingray, have we done him any harm?

MENO: I think not.

SOCRATES: In fact we have helped him to some extent towards finding out the right answer, for now not only is he ignorant of it but he will be quite glad to look for it. Up to now, he thought he could speak well and fluently, on many occasions and before large audiences, on the subject of a square double the size of a given square, maintaining that it must have a side of double the length.

c

MENO: No doubt.

SOCRATES: Do you suppose then that he would have attempted to look for, or learn, what he thought he knew (though he did not), before he was thrown into perplexity, became aware of his ignorance, and felt a desire to know?

MENO: No.

SOCRATES: Then the numbing process was good for him?

MENO: I agree.

SOCRATES: Now notice what, starting from this state of perplexity, he will discover by seeking the truth in company with me, though I simply ask him questions without teaching him. Be ready to catch me if I give him any instruction or explanation instead of simply interrogating him on his own opinions.

d

[Socrates here rubs out the previous figures and starts again.]

Tell me, boy, is not this our square of four feet? *(ABCD.)* You understand?

BOY: Yes.

SOCRATES: Now we can add another equal to it like this? *(BCEF.)*

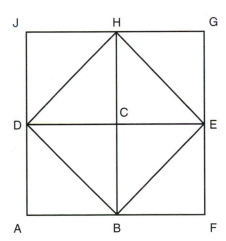

BOY: Yes.

SOCRATES: And a third here, equal to each of the others? *(CEGH.)*

BOY: Yes.

SOCRATES: And then we can fill in this one in the corner? *(DCHJ.)*

BOY: Yes.

SOCRATES: Then here we have four equal squares?

BOY: Yes.

e   SOCRATES: And how many times the size of the first square is the whole?

BOY: Four times.

SOCRATES: And we want one double the size. You remember?

BOY: Yes.

85   SOCRATES: Now does this line going from corner to corner cut each of these squares in half?

BOY: Yes.

SOCRATES: And these are four equal lines enclosing this area? *(BEHD.)*

BOY: They are.

SOCRATES: Now think. How big is this area?

BOY: I don't understand.

SOCRATES: Here are four squares. Has not each line cut off the inner half of each of them?

BOY: Yes.

SOCRATES: And how many such halves are there in this figure? *(BEHD.)*

BOY: Four.

SOCRATES: And how many in this one? *(ABCD.)*

BOY: Two.

b   SOCRATES: And what is the relation of four to two?

BOY: Double.

SOCRATES: How big is this figure then?

BOY: Eight feet.

SOCRATES: On what base?

BOY: This one.

SOCRATES: The line which goes from corner to corner of the square of four feet?

BOY: Yes.

SOCRATES: The technical name for it is "diagonal"; so if we use that name, it is your personal opinion that the square on the diagonal of the original square is double its area.

BOY: That is so, Socrates.

SOCRATES: What do you think, Meno? Has he answered with any opinions that
c   were not his own?

MENO: No, they were all his.

SOCRATES: Yet he did not know, as we agreed a few minutes ago.

MENO: True.

SOCRATES: But these opinions were somewhere in him, were they not?

MENO: Yes.

SOCRATES: So a man who does not know has in himself true opinions on a subject without having knowledge.

MENO: It would appear so.

SOCRATES: At present these opinions, being newly aroused, have a dream-like quality. But if the same questions are put to him on many occasions and in different
d   ways, you can see that in the end he will have a knowledge on the subject as accurate as anybody's.

MENO: Probably.

SOCRATES: This knowledge will not come from teaching but from questioning. He will recover it for himself.

MENO: Yes.

SOCRATES: And the spontaneous recovery of knowledge that is in him is recollection, isn't it?

MENO: Yes.

SOCRATES: Either then he has at some time acquired the knowledge which he now has, or he has always possessed it. If he always possessed it, he must always have known; if on the other hand he acquired it at some previous time, it cannot have been in this life, unless somebody has taught him geometry. He will behave in the same way with all geometrical knowledge, and every other subject. Has anyone taught him all these? You ought to know, especially as he has been brought up in your household.   e

MENO: Yes, I know that no one ever taught him.

SOCRATES: And has he these opinions, or hasn't he?

MENO: It seems we can't deny it.

SOCRATES: Then if he did not acquire them in this life, isn't it immediately clear that he possessed and had learned them during some other period?   86

MENO: It seems so.

SOCRATES: When he was not in human shape?

MENO: Yes.

SOCRATES: If then there are going to exist in him, both while he is and while he is not a man, true opinions which can be aroused by questioning and turned into knowledge, may we say that his soul has been forever in a state of knowledge? Clearly he always either is or is not a man.

MENO: Clearly.

SOCRATES: And if the truth about reality is always in our soul, the soul must be   b immortal, and one must take courage and try to discover—that is, to recollect—what one doesn't happen to know, or (more correctly) remember, at the moment.

MENO: Somehow or other I believe you are right.

SOCRATES: I think I am. I shouldn't like to take my oath on the whole story, but one thing I am ready to fight for as long as I can, in word and act: that is, that we shall be better, braver, and more active men if we believe it right to look for what we don't know than if we believe there is no point in looking because what we don't know we   c can never discover.

MENO: There too I am sure you are right.

SOCRATES: Then, since we are agreed that it is right to inquire into something that one does not know, are you ready to face with me the question: what is virtue?

MENO: Quite ready. All the same, I would rather consider the question as I put it at the beginning, and hear your views on it; that is, are we to pursue virtue as something that can be taught, or do men have it as a gift of nature or how?   d

SOCRATES: If I were your master as well as my own, Meno, we should not have inquired whether or not virtue can be taught until we had first asked the main question—what it is; but not only do you make no attempt to govern your own actions—you prize your freedom, I suppose—but you attempt to govern mine. And you succeed too, so I shall let you have your way. There's nothing else for it, and it seems we must inquire into a single property of something about whose essential nature we are still in the dark. Just   e grant me one small relaxation of your sway, and allow me, in considering whether or not it can be taught, to make use of a hypothesis—the sort of thing, I mean, that geometers often use in their inquiries. When they are asked, for example, about a given area, whether it is possible for this area to be inscribed as a triangle in a given circle, they will probably re-   87 ply: "I don't know yet whether it fulfils the conditions, but I think I have a hypothesis which will help us in the matter. It is this. If the area is such that, when one has applied it *[e.g., as a rectangle]* to the given line *[i.e., the diameter]* of the circle, it is deficient by another rectangle similar to the one which is applied, then, I should say, one result follows; if not, the result is different. If you ask me, then, about the inscription of the figure in   b the circle—whether it is possible or not—I am ready to answer you in this hypotheti-cal way."*

Let us do the same about virtue. Since we don't know what it is or what it resem-bles, let us use a hypothesis in investigating whether it is teachable or not. We shall say: "What attribute of the soul must virtue be, if it is to be teachable or otherwise?" Well, in the first place, if it is anything else but knowledge, is there a possibility of anyone teach-ing it—or, in the language we used just now, reminding someone of it? We needn't
c   worry about which name we are to give to the process, but simply ask: will it be teach-able? Isn't it plain to everyone that a man is not taught anything except knowledge?

MENO: That would be my view.

SOCRATES: If on the other hand virtue is some sort of knowledge, clearly it could be taught.

MENO: Certainly.

SOCRATES: So that question is easily settled; I mean, on what condition virtue would be teachable.

MENO: Yes.

d   SOCRATES: The next point then, I suppose, is to find out whether virtue is knowl-edge or something different.

MENO: That is the next question, I agree.

SOCRATES: Well then, do we assert that virtue is something good? Is that assump-tion a firm one for us?

MENO: Undoubtedly.

SOCRATES: That being so, if there exists any good thing different from, and not associated with, knowledge, virtue will not necessarily be any form of knowledge. If on the other hand knowledge embraces everything that is good, we shall be right to suspect that virtue is knowledge.

MENO: Agreed.

e   SOCRATES: First then, is it virtue which makes us good?

MENO: Yes.

SOCRATES: And if good, then advantageous. All good things are advantageous, are they not?

MENO: Yes.

SOCRATES: So virtue itself must be something advantageous?

MENO: That follows also.

SOCRATES: Now suppose we consider what are the sort of things that profit us. Take them in a list. Health, we may say, and strength and good looks, and wealth—these and their like we call advantageous, you agree?

MENO: Yes.

88   SOCRATES: Yet we also speak of these things as sometimes doing harm. Would you object to that statement?

MENO: No, it is so.

SOCRATES: Now look here: what is the controlling factor which determines whether each of these is advantageous or harmful? Isn't it right use which makes them advantageous, and lack of it, harmful?

MENO: Certainly.

---

*[It is very difficult to understand the geometrical illustration Socrates is giving here.] Sir Thomas Heath in his *History of Greek Mathematics* (1921), Vol. i, p. 298, says that C. Blass, writing in 1861, already knew of thirty different interpretations, and that many more had appeared since then. Fortunately it is not nec-essary to understand the example in order to grasp the hypothetical method Socrates is expounding.

SOCRATES: We must also take spiritual qualities into consideration. You recognize such things as temperance, justice, courage, quickness of mind, memory, nobility of character and others?

MENO: Yes of course I do.

SOCRATES: Then take any such qualities which in your view are not knowledge b but something different. Don't you think they may be harmful as well as advantageous? Courage for instance, if it is something thoughtless, is just a sort of confidence. Isn't it true that to be confident without reason does a man harm, whereas a reasoned confidence profits him?

MENO: Yes.

SOCRATES: Temperance and quickness of mind are no different. Learning and discipline are profitable in conjunction with wisdom, but without it harmful.

MENO: That is emphatically true.

SOCRATES: In short, everything that the human spirit undertakes or suffers will c lead to happiness when it is guided by wisdom, but to the opposite, when guided by folly.

MENO: A reasonable conclusion.

SOCRATES: If then virtue is an attribute of the spirit, and one which cannot fail to be beneficial, it must be wisdom; for all spiritual qualities in and by themselves are neither advantageous nor harmful, but become advantageous or harmful by the presence d with them of wisdom or folly. If we accept this argument, then virtue, to be something advantageous, must be a sort of wisdom.

MENO: I agree.

SOCRATES: To go back to the other class of things, wealth and the like, of which we said just now that they are sometimes good and sometimes harmful, isn't it the same with them? Just as wisdom when it governs our other psychological impulses turns them to advantage, and folly turns them to harm, so the mind by its right use and control of these material assets makes them profitable, and by wrong use renders them e harmful.

MENO: Certainly.

SOCRATES: And the right user is the mind of the wise man, the wrong user the mind of the foolish.

MENO: That is so.

SOCRATES: So we may say in general that the goodness of non-spiritual assets depends on our spiritual character, and the goodness of that on wisdom. This argument shows that the advantageous element must be wisdom; and virtue, we agree, is advantageous, so that amounts to saying that virtue, either in whole or in part, is wisdom.   89

MENO: The argument seems to me fair enough.

SOCRATES: If so, good men cannot be good by nature.

MENO: I suppose not.

SOCRATES: There is another point. If they were, there would probably be experts b among us who could recognize the naturally good at an early stage. They would point them out to us, and we should take them and shut them away safely in the Acropolis, sealing them up more carefully than bullion to protect them from corruption and ensure that when they came to maturity they would be of use to the State.

MENO: It would be likely enough.

SOCRATES: Since then goodness does not come by nature, is it got by learning? c

MENO: I don't see how we can escape the conclusion. Indeed it is obvious on our assumption that, if virtue is knowledge, it is teachable.

SOCRATES: I suppose so. But I wonder if we were right to bind ourselves to that.

MENO: Well, it seemed all right just now.

SOCRATES: Yes, but to be sound it has got to seem all right not only "just now" but at this moment and in the future.

d   MENO: Of course. But what has occurred to you to make you turn against it and suspect that virtue may not be knowledge?

SOCRATES: I'll tell you. I don't withdraw from the position that if it is knowledge, it must be teachable; but as for its being knowledge, see whether you think my doubts on this point are well founded. If anything—not virtue only—is a possible subject of instruction, must there not be teachers and students of it?

MENO: Surely.

e   SOCRATES: And what of the converse, that if there are neither teachers nor students of a subject, we may safely infer that it cannot be taught?

MENO: That is true. But don't you think there are teachers of virtue?

SOCRATES: All I can say is that I have often looked to see if there are any, and in spite of all my efforts I cannot find them, though I have had plenty of fellow-searchers, the kind of men especially whom I believe to have most experience in such matters. But look, Meno, here's a piece of luck. Anytus has just sat down beside us. We couldn't do

90   better than make him a partner in our inquiry. In the first place, he is the son of Anthemion, a man of property and good sense, who didn't get his money out of the blue or as a gift—like Ismenias of Thebes who has just come into the fortune of a Croesus—but earned it by his own brains and hard work. Besides this, he shows himself a decent, modest citizen with no arrogance or bombast or offensiveness about him. Also he brought up his son well and had him properly educated, as the Athenian people appreci-

b   ate: look how they elect him into the highest offices in the State. This is certainly the right sort of man with whom to inquire whether there are any teachers of virtue, and if so who they are.

Please help us, Anytus—Meno, who is a friend of your family, and myself—to find out who may be the teachers of this subject. Look at it like this. If we wanted Meno

c   to become a good doctor, shouldn't we send him to the doctors to be taught?

ANYTUS: Of course.

SOCRATES: And if we wanted him to become a shoemaker, to the shoemakers?

ANYTUS: Yes.

SOCRATES: And so on with other trades?

ANYTUS: Yes.

SOCRATES: Now another relevant question. When we say that to make Meno a

d   doctor we should be right in sending him to the doctors, have we in mind that the sensible thing is to send him to those who profess the subject rather than to those who don't, men who charge a fee as professionals, having announced that they are prepared to teach whoever likes to come and learn?

ANYTUS: Yes.

SOCRATES: The same is surely true of flute-playing and other accomplishments. If

e   you want to make someone a performer on the flute it would be very foolish to refuse to send him to those who undertake to teach the art and are paid for it, but to go and bother other people instead and have him try to learn from them—people who don't set up to be teachers or take any pupils in the subject which we want our young man to learn. Doesn't that sound very unreasonable?

ANYTUS: Sheer stupidity I should say.

SOCRATES: I agree. And now we can both consult together about our visitor

91   Meno. He has been telling me all this while that he longs to acquire the kind of wisdom and virtue which fits men to manage an estate or govern a city, to look after their par-

ents, and to entertain and send off guests in proper style, both their own countrymen and foreigners. With this in mind, to whom would it be right to send him? What we have just said seems to show that the right people are those who profess to be teachers of virtue   b and offer their services freely to any Greek who wishes to learn, charging a fixed fee for their instruction.

ANYTUS: Whom do you mean by that, Socrates?

SOCRATES: Surely you know yourself that they are the men called Sophists.

ANYTUS: Good heavens, what a thing to say! I hope no relative of mine or any of   c my friends, Athenian or foreign, would be so mad as to go and let himself be ruined by those people. That's what they are, the manifest ruin and corruption of anyone who comes into contact with them.

SOCRATES: What, Anytus? Can they be so different from other claimants to useful knowledge that they not only don't do good, like the rest, to the material that one puts in their charge, but on the contrary spoil it—and have the effrontery to take money for doing so? I for one find it difficult to believe you. I know that one of them alone, Pro-tagoras, earned more money from being a Sophist than an outstandingly fine craftsman   d like Phidias and ten other sculptors put together. A man who mends old shoes or restores coats couldn't get away with it for a month if he gave them back in worse condition than he received them; he would soon find himself starving. Surely it is incredible that Pro-tagoras took in the whole of Greece, corrupting his pupils and sending them away worse   e than when they came to him, for more than forty years. I believe he was nearly seventy when he died, and had been practising for forty years, and all that time—indeed to this very day—his reputation has been consistently high; and there are plenty of others be-sides Protagoras, some before his time and others still alive. Are we to suppose from   92 your remark that they consciously deceive and ruin young men, or are they unaware of it themselves? Can these remarkably clever men—as some regard them—be mad enough for that?

ANYTUS: Far from it, Socrates. It isn't they who are mad, but rather the young men who hand over their money; and those responsible for them, who let them get into the Sophists' hands, are even worse. Worst of all are the cities who allow them in, or   b don't expel them, whether it be a foreigner or one of themselves who tries that sort of game.

SOCRATES: Has one of the Sophists done you a personal injury, or why are you so hard on them?

ANYTUS: Heavens, no! I've never in my life had anything to do with a single one of them, nor would I hear of any of my family doing so.

SOCRATES: So you've had no experience of them at all?

ANYTUS: And don't want any either.

SOCRATES: You surprise me. How can you know what is good or bad in some-   c thing when you have no experience of it?

ANYTUS: Quite easily. At any rate I know *their* kind, whether I've had experience or not.

SOCRATES: It must be second sight, I suppose; for how else you know about them, judging from what you tell me yourself, I can't imagine. However, we are not asking whose instruction it is that would ruin Meno's character. Let us say that   d those are the Sophists if you like, and tell us instead about the ones we want. You can do a good turn to a friend of your father's house if you will let him know to whom in our great city he should apply for proficiency in the kind of virtue I have just described.

ANYTUS: Why not tell him yourself?

SOCRATES: Well, I did mention the men who in my opinion teach these things, but apparently I was talking nonsense. So you say, and you may well be right. Now it is your turn to direct him; mention the name of any Athenian you like.

ANYTUS: But why mention a particular individual? Any decent Athenian gentleman whom he happens to meet, if he follows his advice, will make him a better man than the Sophists would.

93   SOCRATES: And did these gentlemen get their fine qualities spontaneously— self-taught, as it were, and yet [they are] able to teach this untaught virtue to others?

ANYTUS: I suppose they in their turn learned it from forebears who were gentlemen like themselves. Would you deny that there have been many good men in our city?

SOCRATES: On the contrary, there are plenty of good statesmen here in Athens, and have been as good in the past. The question is, have they also been good teachers of their own virtue? That is the point we are discussing now—not whether or not there are good men in Athens or whether there have been in past times, but whether virtue can be taught. It amounts to the question whether the good men of this and former times have known how to hand on to someone else the goodness that was in themselves, or whether on the contrary it is not something that can be handed over, or that one man can receive from another. That is what Meno and I have long been puzzling over. Look at it from your own point of view. You would say that Themistocles was a good man?

ANYTUS: Yes, none better.

SOCRATES: And that he, if anyone, must have been a good teacher of his own virtue?

ANYTUS: I suppose so, if he wanted to be.

SOCRATES: But don't you think he must have wanted others to become worthy men—above all, surely, his own son? Do you suppose he grudged him this and purposely didn't pass on his own virtue to him? You must have heard that he had his son Cleophantus so well trained in horsemanship that he could stand upright on horseback and throw a javelin from that position; and many other wonderful accomplishments the young man had, for his father had him taught and made expert in every skill that a good instructor could impart. You must have heard this from older people?

ANYTUS: Yes.

SOCRATES: No one, then, could say that there was anything wrong with the boy's natural powers?

ANYTUS: Perhaps not.

SOCRATES: But have you ever heard anyone, young or old, say that Cleophantus the son of Themistocles was a good and wise man in the way that his father was?

ANYTUS: Certainly not.

SOCRATES: Must we conclude then that Themistocles' aim was to educate his son in other accomplishments, but not to make him any better than his neighbours in his own type of wisdom—that is, supposing that virtue could be taught?

ANYTUS: I hardly think we can.

SOCRATES: So much then for Themistocles as a teacher of virtue, whom you yourself agree to have been one of the best men of former times. Take another example, Aristides, son of Lysimachus. You accept him as a good man?

ANYTUS: Surely.

SOCRATES: He too gave his son Lysimachus the best education in Athens, in all subjects where a teacher could help; but did he make him a better man than his neighbour? You know him, I think, and can say what he is like. Or again there is Pericles, that great and wise man. He brought up two sons, Paralus and Xanthippus, and had them taught riding, music, athletics, and all the other skilled pursuits till they were as good as any in Athens. Did he then not want to make them good men? Yes, he wanted that, no doubt, but I am afraid it is something that cannot be done by teaching. And in case you should think that only very few, and those the most insignificant, lacked this power, consider that Thucydides also had two sons, Melesias and Stephanus, to whom he gave an excellent education. Among other things they were the best wrestlers in Athens, for he gave one to Xanthias to train and the other to Eudoxus—the two who, I understand, were considered the finest wrestlers of their time. You remember?

ANYTUS: I have heard of them.

SOCRATES: Surely then he would never have had his children taught these expensive pursuits and yet refused to teach them to be good men—which would have cost nothing at all—if virtue could have been taught? You are not going to tell me that Thucydides was a man of no account, or that he had not plenty of friends both at Athens and among the allies? He came of an influential family and was a great power both here and in the rest of Greece. If virtue could have been taught, he would have found the man to make his sons good, either among our own citizens or abroad, supposing his political duties left him no time to do it himself. No, my dear Anytus, it looks as if it cannot be taught.

ANYTUS: You seem to me, Socrates, to be too ready to run people down. My advice to you, if you will listen to it, is to be careful. I dare say that in all cities it is easier to do a man harm than good, and it is certainly so here, as I expect you know yourself.

SOCRATES: Anytus seems angry, Meno, and I am not surprised. He thinks I am slandering our statesmen, and moreover he believes himself to be one of them. He doesn't know what slander really is: if he ever finds out he will forgive me.

However, tell me this yourself: are there not similar fine characters in your country?

MENO: Yes, certainly.

SOCRATES: Do they come forward of their own accord to teach the young? Do they agree that they are teachers and that virtue can be taught?

MENO: No indeed, they don't agree on it at all. Sometimes you will hear them say that it can be taught, sometimes that it cannot.

SOCRATES: Ought we then to class as teachers of it men who are not even agreed that it can be taught?

MENO: Hardly, I think.

SOCRATES: And what about the Sophists, the only people who profess to teach it? Do you think they do?

MENO: The thing I particularly admire about Gorgias, Socrates, is that you will never hear him make this claim; indeed he laughs at the others when he hears them do so. In his view his job is to make clever speakers.

SOCRATES: So you too don't think the Sophists are teachers?

MENO: I really can't say. Like most people I waver—sometimes I think they are and sometimes I think they are not.

SOCRATES: Has it ever occurred to you that you and our statesmen are not alone in this? The poet Theognis likewise says in one place that virtue is teachable and in another that it is not.

MENO: Really? Where?

SOCRATES: In the elegiacs in which he writes:

Eat, drink, and sit with men of power and weight,
Nor scorn to gain the favour of the great.
For fine men's teaching to fine ways will win thee:
Low company destroys what wit is in thee.

e   There he speaks as if virtue can be taught, doesn't he?

MENO: Clearly.

SOCRATES: But elsewhere he changes his ground a little:

Were mind by art created and instilled
Immense rewards had soon the pockets filled

of the people who could do this. Moreover

No good man's son would ever worthless be,
Taught by wise counsel. But no teacher's skill
96   Can turn to good what is created ill.

Do you see how he contradicts himself?

MENO: Plainly.

SOCRATES: Can you name any other subject, in which the professed teachers are not only not recognized as teachers of others, but are thought to have no understanding of it themselves, and to be no good at the very subject they profess to teach; whereas
b   those who are acknowledged to be the best at it are in two minds whether it can be taught or not? When people are so confused about a subject, can you say that they are in a true sense teachers?

MENO: Certainly not.

SOCRATES: Well, if neither the Sophists nor those who display fine qualities themselves are teachers of virtue, I am sure no one else can be, and if there are no teachers,
c   there can be no students either.

MENO: I quite agree.

SOCRATES: And we have also agreed that a subject of which there were neither teachers nor students was not one which could be taught.

MENO: That is so.

SOCRATES: Now there turn out to be neither teachers nor students of virtue, so it would appear that virtue cannot be taught.

d   MENO: So it seems, if we have made no mistake; and it makes me wonder, Socrates, whether there are in fact no good men at all, or how they are produced when they do appear.

SOCRATES: I have a suspicion, Meno, that you and I are not much good. Our masters Gorgias and Prodicus have not trained us properly. We must certainly take ourselves in hand, and try to find someone who will improve us by hook or by crook. I say
e   this with our recent discussion in mind, for absurdly enough we failed to perceive that it is not only under the guidance of knowledge that human action is well and rightly conducted. I believe that may be what prevents us from seeing how it is that men are made good.

MENO: What do you mean?

SOCRATES: This: We were correct, were we not, in agreeing that good men must be profitable or useful? It cannot be otherwise, can it?

MENO: No.

SOCRATES: And again that they will be of some use if they conduct our affairs
97   aright—that also was correct?

MENO: Yes.

SOCRATES: But in insisting that knowledge was a *sine qua non* for right leadership, we look like being mistaken.

MENO: How so?

SOCRATES: Let me explain. If someone knows the way to Larissa, or anywhere else you like, then when he goes there and takes others with him he will be a good and capable guide, you would agree?

MENO: Of course.

SOCRATES: But if a man judges correctly which is the road, though he has never   b
been there and doesn't know it, will he not also guide others aright?

MENO: Yes, he will.

SOCRATES: And as long as he has a correct opinion on the points about which the other has knowledge, he will be just as good a guide, believing the truth but not knowing it.

MENO: Just as good.

SOCRATES: Therefore true opinion is as good a guide as knowledge for the purpose of acting rightly. That is what we left out just now in our discussion of the nature of virtue, when we said that knowledge is the only guide to right action. There was also,   c
it seems, true opinion.

MENO: It seems so.

SOCRATES: So right opinion is something no less useful than knowledge.

MENO: Except that the man with knowledge will always be successful, and the man with right opinion only sometimes.

SOCRATES: What? Will he not always be successful so long as he has the right opinion?

MENO: That must be so, I suppose. In that case, I wonder why knowledge should be so much more prized than right opinion, and indeed how there is any difference be-   d
tween them.

SOCRATES: Shall I tell you the reason for your surprise, or do you know it?

MENO: No, tell me.

SOCRATES: It is because you have not observed the statues of Daedalus. Perhaps you don't have them in your country.

MENO: What makes you say that?

SOCRATES: They too, if no one ties them down, run away and escape. If tied, they   e
stay where they are put.

MENO: What of it?

SOCRATES: If you have one of his works untethered, it is not worth much: it gives you the slip like a runaway slave. But a tethered specimen is very valuable, for they are magnificent creations. And that, I may say, has a bearing on the matter of true opinions. True opinions are a fine thing and do all sorts of good so long as they stay in their place; but they will not stay long. They run away from a man's mind, so they are not worth   98
much until you tether them by working out the reason. That process, my dear Meno, is recollection, as we agreed earlier. Once they are tied down, they become knowledge, and are stable. That is why knowledge is something more valuable than right opinion. What distinguishes one from the other is the tether.

MENO: It does seem something like that, certainly.

SOCRATES: Well of course, I have only been using an analogy myself, not knowl-   b
edge. But it is not, I am sure, a mere guess to say that right opinion and knowledge are different. There are few things that I should claim to know, but that at least is among them, whatever else is.

MENO: You are quite right.

SOCRATES: And is this right too, that true opinion when it governs any course of action produces as good a result as knowledge?

MENO: Yes, that too is right, I think.

c   SOCRATES: So that for practical purposes right opinion is no less useful than knowledge, and the man who has it is no less useful than the one who knows.

MENO: That is so.

SOCRATES: Now we have agreed that the good man is useful.

MENO: Yes.

SOCRATES: To recapitulate then: assuming that there are men good and useful to the community, it is not only knowledge that makes them so, but also right opinion, and
d   neither of these comes by nature but both are acquired—or do you think either of them *is* natural?

MENO: No.

SOCRATES: So if both are acquired, good men themselves are not good by nature.

MENO: No.

SOCRATES: That being so, the next thing we inquired was whether their goodness was a matter of teaching, and we decided that it would be, if virtue were knowledge, and conversely, that if it could be taught, it would be knowledge.

MENO: Yes.

e   SOCRATES: Next, that if there were teachers of it, it could be taught, but not if there were none.

MENO: That was so.

SOCRATES: But we have agreed that there are no teachers of it, and so that it cannot be taught and is not knowledge.

MENO: We did.

SOCRATES: At the same time we agreed that it is something good, and that to be useful and good consists in giving right guidance.

MENO: Yes.

99   SOCRATES: And that these two, true opinion and knowledge, are the only things which direct us aright and the possession of which makes a man a true guide. We may except chance, because what turns out right by chance is not due to human direction, and say that where human control leads to right ends, these two principles are directive, true opinion and knowledge.

MENO: Yes, I agree.

SOCRATES: Now since virtue cannot be taught, we can no longer believe it to be
b   knowledge, so that one of our two good and useful principles is excluded, and knowledge is not the guide in public life.

MENO: No.

SOCRATES: It is not then by the possession of any wisdom that such men as Themistocles, and the others whom Anytus mentioned just now, became leaders in their cities. This fact, that they do not owe their eminence to knowledge, will explain why they are unable to make others like themselves.

MENO: No doubt it is as you say.

SOCRATES: That leaves us with the other alternative, that it is well-aimed conjec-
c   ture which statesmen employ in upholding their countries' welfare. Their position in relation to knowledge is no different from that of prophets and tellers of oracles, who under divine inspiration utter many truths, but have no knowledge of what they are saying.

MENO: It must be something like that.

SOCRATES: And ought we not to reckon those men divine who with no conscious thought are repeatedly and outstandingly successful in what they do or say?

MENO: Certainly.

SOCRATES: We are right therefore to give this title to the oracular priests and the
d   prophets that I mentioned, and to poets of every description. Statesmen too, when by

their speeches they get great things done yet know nothing of what they are saying, are to be considered as acting no less under divine influence, inspired and possessed by the divinity.

MENO: Certainly.

SOCRATES: Women, you know, Meno, do call good men "divine," and the Spartans too, when they are singing a good man's praises, say "He is divine."

MENO: And it looks as if they are right—though our friend Anytus may be annoyed with you for saying so.   e

SOCRATES: I can't help that. We will talk to him some other time. If all we have said in this discussion, and the questions we have asked, have been right, virtue will be acquired neither by nature nor by teaching. Whoever has it gets it by divine dispensation without taking thought, unless he be the kind of statesman who can create another like himself. Should there be such a man, he would be among the living practically what   100
Homer said Tiresias was among the dead, when he described him as the only one in the underworld who kept his wits—"the others are mere flitting shades." Where virtue is concerned such a man would be just like that, a solid reality among shadows.

MENO: That is finely put, Socrates.

SOCRATES: On our present reasoning then, whoever has virtue gets it by divine dispensation. But we shall not understand the truth of the matter until, before asking how men get virtue, we try to discover what virtue is in and by itself. Now it is time for me to go; and my request to you is that you will allay the anger of your friend Anytus by convincing him that what you now believe is true. If you succeed, the Athenians may have cause to thank you.

REPUBLIC (in part)

BOOK III

*   *   *

"So much for our educational principles. I mean, we don't have to describe in detail the   412ᵇ
guardians' dances, hunts, sporting competitions, and horse-races: it's fairly obvious that these activities must conform to the same principles, and their elucidation shouldn't cause any problems now."

"No, I suppose they shouldn't," he said.

"All right," I said. "What do we have to decide about next? Shouldn't we decide which members of this particular class will be the rulers and which will be the subjects?"

"Of course."   c

"It's obvious that the older ones should be the rulers and the younger ones the subjects, isn't it?"

Plato, *Republic* (Book III, 412b–417b; Book IV, 427c–448e; Book V, complete: 448e–480a; Books VI–VII, 502c–521b, translated by Robin Waterfield (Oxford: Oxford University Press, 1993). Reprinted by permission of Oxford University Press.

"Yes."

"And only the best of the older ones?"

"Yes, that's obvious too."

"Now, the best farmers are the most accomplished farmers, aren't they?"

"Yes."

"And in the present case, since we're after the best guardians, they must be those who are particularly good at safeguarding the community, mustn't they?"

"Yes."

"They not only have to have the intelligence and the competence for the job, but they also have to care for the community, wouldn't you say?"

d   "Yes."

"Now, you care most for things that happen to be dear to you."

"Inevitably."

"And something is particularly dear to you if you regard your interests and its interests as identical, and if you think that your success and failure follow from its success and failure."

"Yes," he said.

"It follows that we should select from among the guardians men who particularly
e   strike us, on investigation, as being the type to devote their whole lives to wholeheartedly doing what they regard as advantageous to the community, and to completely refusing to do anything they regard as disadvantageous to it."

"Yes, they would make suitable rulers," he said.

"I think we'll have to watch them at every stage of their lives, then, to make sure that they're good at safeguarding this idea and aren't magically or forcibly induced to shed and forget the notion that it's essential to do what's best for the community."

"What do you mean by this shedding?" he asked.

"I'll explain," I said. "It seems to me that the departure of an idea from a person's mind can be either intentional or unintentional. It's intentional if the idea is false and the
413   person learns better, and unintentional whenever the idea is true."

"I understand intentional loss," he said, "but I still don't understand unintentional loss."

"But don't you think that the loss of good things is unintentional, while the loss of bad things is intentional?" I asked. "And don't you think that being deceived about the truth is a bad thing, while having a grasp of the truth is good? And don't you think that having a grasp of the truth is having a belief that matches the way things are?"

"Yes, you're right," he said. "I agree that the loss of a true belief is unintentional."

b   "So when this happens, it's the result of robbery, magic, or brute force, wouldn't you say?"

"I don't understand again," he said.

"I suppose I am talking pompously," I said. "When I talk of a person being robbed of a belief, I mean that he's persuaded by an argument to change his mind, or time causes him to forget it: in either case, he doesn't notice the departure of the belief. I should think you understand now, don't you?"

"Yes."

"And when I talk of a person being forced out of a belief, I mean that pain or suffering makes him change his mind."

"Yes, I understand that too," he said, "and you're right."

c   "And I'm sure you'd agree that anyone who changes his mind because he's been beguiled by pleasure or terrified by threats has had magic used on him."

"Yes," he said, "any deception is a form of magic, I suppose."

"As I was starting to say a moment ago, then, we must try to discover which of our guardians are particularly good at safe-guarding within themselves the belief that they should only ever pursue courses of action which they think are in the community's best interests. We must watch them from childhood onwards, and set them tasks which maximize the possibility of their forgetting a belief like this and being misled; those who bear the belief in mind and prove hard to mislead are the ones we should select, while excluding the others. Do you agree?"   d

"Yes."

"And we should also set them tough and painful assignments and ordeals, and watch for exactly the same things."

"Right," he said.

"Now, we'll have to invent a selection procedure for our third category, magic, as well," I said, "and observe how they perform. People test a foal's nervousness by introducing it to noise and commotion, and in the same way we must bring our guardians, while they're young, face to face with fear and then shift them into facing pleasure. People use fire to test gold, but our test must be far more thorough, and must show us how   e well they resist magic and whether they remain graceful whatever the situation, keep themselves and their cultural education intact, and display rhythm and harmony throughout; if they're capable of doing this, their value to themselves and to the community will be very high. Anyone who emerges without impurities from every single test—as a child, as a young man, and as an adult—should be made a ruler and guardian of our community,   414 and should be honoured in life and in death, in the sense of being awarded the most privileged of funerals and tombs. Anyone who gets corrupted, however, should be excluded. So, Glaucon," I concluded, "I think that this is how we should select and appoint our rulers and guardians. These are just guidelines, though: I haven't gone into details."

"I agree," he said. "It must be something like this."

"And we really and truly could hardly go wrong if we reserved the term   b 'guardian' in its fullest sense for these people, who ensure that neither the desire nor the capacity for harming the community arises, whether from external enemies or from internal friends. As for the young men we've been calling guardians up to now, we should strictly call them auxiliaries and assistants of the guardians and their decision making, don't you think?"

"Yes, I do," he said.

"Now," I said, "can we devise one of those lies—the kind which crop up as the occasion demands, which we were talking about not long ago—so that with a single noble lie we can indoctrinate the rulers themselves, preferably, but at least the rest of the   c community?"

"What sort of lie?" he asked.

"Nothing too outlandish," I replied, "just a tall story about something which happened all over the place in times past (at least, that's what the poets claim and have persuaded us to believe), but which hasn't happened in our lifetimes and I'm not sure it could, and people would need a great deal of convincing about it."

"You seem reluctant to tell us the story," he remarked.

"And you'll see that my reluctance was well founded," I said, "when I do tell you it."

"Don't worry," he said. "Just talk."

"What I'm saying is . . . I'm not sure where to find the gall or the words to tell   d the story . . . I'll be trying above all to convince the rulers themselves and the military,

and secondarily the rest of the community, that all the nurture and education we provided happened to them in a kind of dream-world; in actual fact, they were at that time
being formed and nurtured deep inside the earth, and their weaponry and their equip-
e   ment in general were also being made there. When they were finished products, the
earth, their mother, sent them up above ground; and now in their policy-making they
must regard the country they find themselves in as their mother and their nurse, they
must defend her against invasion, and they should think of the rest of the inhabitants of
the community as their earth-born brothers."

   "I'm not surprised you were ashamed to tell us the lie before," he remarked.
415   "I had good reason," I said. "All the same, do please listen to the rest of the story
as well. 'Although all of you citizens are brothers,' we'll continue the tale by telling
them, 'nevertheless, during the kneading phase, God included gold in the mixture when
he was forming those of you who have what it takes to be rulers (which is why the rulers
have the greatest privileges), silver when he was forming the auxiliaries, and iron and
copper when he was forming the farmers and other workers. Now, despite the fact that
in general your offspring will be similar in kind to yourselves, nevertheless, because
you're all related, sometimes a silver child might be born to a gold parent, a gold one to
b   a silver parent, and so on: any of them might be produced by any of the others. Therefore, of all his instructions to the rulers, there is none that God stresses more than this:
there is no aspect of their work as guardians which they shall be so good at or dedicated
to as watching over the admixture of elements in the minds of the children of the community. If one of their own children is born with a nature tinged with copper or iron,
c   they shall at all costs avoid feeling sorry for it: They shall assign it the status appropriate to its nature and banish it to the workers or the farmers. On the other hand, if a child
born to a worker or a farmer has a nature tinged with gold or silver, they shall honour it
and elevate it to the rank of either guardian or auxiliary, because of an oracle which
states that the community will be destroyed when it has a copper or iron guardian.' Can
you think of any tactics to make them believe this story?"

d   "No, not for this particular lot, anyway," he said, "but I can for the immediately
succeeding generations and all the generations to follow."

   "I've got a pretty good idea of what you're getting at," I said.

   "It would help them care even more for the community and for one another. But
the future of all this will be decided by popular consensus, not by us."

   "What we can do, however, is arm these earth-born men and mobilize them under
the leadership of their rulers. They must go and look for the best location within the
e   community for their barracks, a location from where they can control any disobedience
to the laws on the part of the internal inhabitants, and repel the assault of an external enemy who falls on the community like a wolf on a flock of sheep. When they've occupied the site, they must sacrifice to the appropriate gods and construct shelters, don't
you think?"

   "Yes," he said.

   "And these shelters should provide adequate protection whatever the weather?"

   "Of course," he said. "I mean, these are their living-quarters you're talking about,
I think."

   "Yes," I said, "but military quarters, not places of business."
416   "*Now* what distinction are you getting at?" he asked.

   "I'll try to explain," I answered. "Consider, for example, the dogs which shepherds train to act as their auxiliaries, to help them look after their flocks: there could be
nothing more dreadful or despicable than for these dogs, thanks to their nature or thanks

to the shepherds' training, to be capable of being influenced by indiscipline or hunger or some other bad habit to try to harm the sheep and behave like wolves rather than sheep-dogs."

"It goes without saying that this would be dreadful," he said.

"So we must do everything possible to guard against the possibility of our auxil-   b
iaries treating the inhabitants of our community like that and using their greater power to behave like brutal despots rather than well-intentioned allies."

"Yes, we must," he said.

"Wouldn't a really excellent education have equipped them to take the maximum amount of care?"

"But they did receive an excellent education," he said.

"That's not something we should stake our lives on, my dear Glaucon," I said. "But we should stand firmly by our present position, that whatever constitutes a proper   c
education, it is the chief factor in the guardians' treating themselves and their wards in a civilized fashion."

"That's right," he said.

"Now, doesn't it make sense to say that this education isn't all they need? That in addition their living-quarters and their property in general should be designed not to interfere with their carrying out their work as guardians as well as possible or to encourage them to commit crimes against their fellow citizens?"   d

"Yes, it does."

"I wonder if they'd turn out as we want if their lifestyle and living-quarters were somewhat as follows," I said. "See what you think. In the first place, none of them is to have any private property, except what is absolutely indispensable. In the second place, none of them is to have living-quarters and storerooms which are not able to be entered by anyone who wants to. Their provisions (which should be suitable in quantity for self-controlled and courageous warriors) are to be their stipend, paid by their   e
fellow citizens for their guarding, the amount being fixed so that, at the end of a year, there is no excess or shortfall. There will be shared mess-halls for them to go to, and their lives will be communal, as if they were on campaign. We'll tell them that the permanent presence in their minds of divine gold and silver, which they were granted by the gods, means that they have no need of earthly gold and silver as well; and we'll add that it is sacrilegious for them to adulterate and contaminate that heavenly possession by owning the earthly variety, because in the past this earthly variety, which is accepted as currency by the masses, has provoked many acts of desecration, whereas theirs is   417
untainted. So, unlike any of their fellow citizens, they are not permitted to have any contact or involvement with gold and silver: they are not to come under the same roof as gold and silver, or wear them on their bodies, or drink from gold and silver cups. These precepts will guarantee not only their own integrity, but also the integrity of the community which is in their safekeeping. If they do come to own land and homes and money, they will be estate-managers and farmers instead of guardians; they will become despots, and enemies rather than allies of the inhabitants of the community; they   b
will spend their lives hating and being hated, plotting and being plotted against; they will have internal enemies to fear more, and more intensely, than their external enemies. With private property, they will be racing ever closer to the ruin of themselves and the whole community. All this confirms the importance of our stated arrangements for the guardians' living-quarters and so on," I concluded, "so shall we enshrine them in law, or not?"

"We certainly must," said Glaucon.

BOOK IV

*   *   *

427c   "So there you are, Adeimantus," I said. "Your community seems to have been founded.
d   The next thing for you to do is to get hold of a bright enough light and explore the community—you should invite your brother and Polemarchus and the rest of us to join
you—to see if we can locate morality and immorality within it, discover how they differ from each other, and find out which of them is a prerequisite for happiness, whether
or not its possession is hidden from the eyes of gods and men."

"Rubbish," said Glaucon. "You promised you'd do the investigating, on the
e   grounds that it was sacrilegious for you not to do everything you could to assist morality."

"You're right," I said. "Thanks for the reminder. But you should still help me
while I do so."

"We will," he said.

"I think I know how we'd better conduct the search," I said. "I assume that if the
community has been founded properly, it has everything it takes to be good."

"Necessarily," he replied.

"Obviously, then, it has wisdom, courage, self-discipline, and morality."

"Obviously."

"And clearly, as we go about our search, we'll discover some of these elements
and there'll be some we have yet to discover."

428   "Of course."

"Now, imagine any set of four things, and imagine we're exploring something for
one of the four. Either we'd recognize it straight away and that would do the job, or we
would recognize the one we're looking for by first recognizing the other three, in the
sense that whatever is left is bound to be the one we're looking for."

"Right," he said.

"Well, we're faced with a set of four things here, so the principles of exploration
are the same. Yes?"

"Obviously."

b   "Now, the first thing which I think is visible here is wisdom. And there's a peculiarity in its case."

"What?" he asked.

"Well, I do think that the community we've described really is wise. I mean, it's
resourceful, isn't it?"

"Yes."

"And this thing, resourcefulness, is obviously a kind of knowledge. I mean, it's
not ignorance which makes people resourceful; it's knowledge."

"Obviously."

"Now, there are many branches of knowledge in our community, of all different
kinds."

"Naturally."

"So is it the knowledge its carpenters have which makes the community deserve
to be described as wise and resourceful?"

c   "No, that only entitles us to call it good at carpentry," he replied.

"It shouldn't be called wise, then, because of its knowledge of carpentry and because it is resourceful at ensuring the excellence of its furniture."

"Certainly not."

"Because it knows how to make metal implements, then, or anything like that?"

"Definitely not that either," he said.

"And the fact that it knows how to grow crops only entitles us to describe it as good at agriculture."

"That's what I think."

"All right," I said. "Is there a branch of knowledge which some of the inhabitants of the community we've just founded have, which enables it to think resourcefully   d
about the whole community, not just some element of it, and about enhancing the whole community's domestic and foreign policies?"

"There certainly is."

"What is it?" I asked. "And which of the citizens have it?"

"It is guardianship," he replied, "and the people who have it are those rulers—the ones we not long ago called guardians in the strict sense of the word."

"And what description does this branch of knowledge earn the community, in your opinion?"

"Resourceful and genuinely wise," he answered.

"Now, do you think that in our community metalworkers will outnumber these true guardians, or the other way round?" I asked.   e

"There'll be far more metalworkers," he said.

"And wouldn't these guardians be outnumbered by any of the other acknowledged categories of experts?" I asked.

"Yes, by a long way."

"So when a community is founded on natural principles, the wisdom it has as a whole is due to the smallest grouping and section within it and to the knowledge possessed by this group, which is the authoritative and ruling section of the community. And we also find that this category, which is naturally the least numerous, is the one which inherently possesses the only branch of knowledge which deserves to be called wisdom."   429

"You're absolutely right," he said.

"So we've somehow stumbled across one of the four qualities we were looking for and found whereabouts in the community it is located."

"*I* think it's clear enough, anyway," he said.

"Now, it's not too hard to spot courage and to see which section of the community possesses it and enables the community to be described as courageous."

"Why?"

"The only feature of a community which might justify describing it as either cow-   b
ardly or courageous," I answered, "is its defensive and military arm."

"Yes, that's the only one," he agreed.

"The point is," I went on, "that whether the rest of its inhabitants are cowardly or brave wouldn't affect the nature of the community either way, I imagine."

"No, it wouldn't."

"Again, then, it is a section of a community that earns it the right to be called courageous. This section possesses the ability to retain under all circumstances the notion that the things and kinds of things to be feared are precisely those things and kinds   c
of things which during their education the legislator pronounced fearful. Isn't this what you call courage?"

"I haven't understood your point," he said. "Please could you repeat it."

"I'm saying that courage is a sort of retention," I explained.

"What do you mean, retention?"

"I mean the retention of the notion, which has been inculcated by law through the agency of education, about what things and what kinds of things are to be feared. And d   by its retention 'under all circumstances' I meant keeping it intact and not losing it whether one is under the influence of pain or pleasure, desire or aversion. I can tell you what strikes me as analogous, if you like."

"Yes, please."

"Well," I said, "you know how when dyers want to dye wool purple, they first select something which is naturally white, rather than any other colour; then they subject it to a lengthy preparatory treatment designed to ensure that the colour will take as well

e   as possible; and when it's in the required condition, they dye it. Anything dyed in this way holds its colour, and the colour can't be washed out, whether or not one uses solvent. But you know what happens to anything which isn't dyed in this way, when something of another colour is dyed, or when something white is dyed without having been treated first."

"Yes," he said. "The dye washes out and they look ridiculous."

"So I want you to imagine," I said, "that we too were doing our best to achieve something similar, when we selected our militia and put them through their cultural and

430   physical education. You should assume that the educational programme was designed for one purpose only: to indoctrinate them so thoroughly that the laws take in them like a dye, so that their notions about what is to be feared and about everything else hold fast (which requires a suitable character as well as a suitable upbringing), with the dye being incapable of being washed out by those solvents which are so frighteningly good at scouring—pleasure, which is a more efficient cleanser than any soda and lye, and

b   pain and aversion and desire, which outclass any solvent. So this ability to retain under all circumstances a true and lawful notion about what is and is not to be feared is what I'm calling courage. That's how I'll use the term, unless you have an alternative suggestion."

"No, I don't," he said. "I mean, I think your idea is that any true notion about these matters which is formed in an animal or a slave without the benefit of education is not really lawful, and I suppose you'd find some other name for it, not courage."

c   "You're quite right," I said.

"I accept your definition of courage, then."

"Accept it by all means," I said, "but as a definition of the kind of courage a community has; then your acceptance will be all right. We'll go into the subject more thoroughly later, if you want; you see, at the moment our quarry is morality, not courage, which I think we've explored enough."

"That's fine by me," he said.

"Well, we've still got two qualities to detect in the community," I said, "self-

d   discipline and the purpose of the whole enquiry, morality."

"Quite so."

"Can we somehow locate morality and not bother any more about self-discipline?"

"I don't know if we can," he said, "and anyway I wouldn't like morality to be discovered first if that entails dropping the search for self-discipline. I'd be grateful if you'd look for self-discipline before morality."

e   "Then it's my duty to do so, of course," I said.

"Go on, then," he said.

"All right," I said. "From my point of view, we're faced here with a closer similarity to some kind of harmony and attunement than we were before."

"Why?"

"To be self-disciplined," I replied, "is somehow to order and control the pleasures and desires. Hence the opaque expression 'self-mastery'; and there are other expressions which hint at its nature. Yes?"

"Absolutely," he said.

"Isn't the phrase 'self-mastery' absurd? I mean, anyone who is his own master is also his own slave, of course, and vice versa, since it's the same person who is the subject in all these expressions."

431

"Of course."

"What this expression means, I think," I continued, "is that there are better and worse elements in a person's mind, and when the part which is naturally better is in control of the worse part, then we use this phrase 'self-mastery' (which is, after all, complimentary). But when, as a result of bad upbringing or bad company, the smaller better part is defeated by the superior numbers of the worse part, then we use critical and deprecatory language and describe someone in this state as lacking self-mastery and discipline."

b

"That sounds plausible," he said.

"Have a look at our new community, then," I said, "and you'll find that the first of these alternatives is attributable to it. I mean, you must admit the justice of describing it as having self-mastery, since anything whose better part rules its worse part should be described as having self-discipline and self-mastery."

"Yes, I can see the truth of what you're saying," he said.

"Now, children, women, slaves, and (among so-called freemen), the rabble who constitute the majority of the population, are the ones who evidently experience the greatest quantity and variety of forms of desire, pleasure, and pain."

c

"Yes."

"Whereas simple and moderate forms, which are guided by the rational mind with its intelligence and true beliefs, are encountered only in those few people who have been endowed with excellence by their nature and their education."

"True," he said.

"And is it clear to you that this is a property of your community, where the desires of the common majority are controlled by the desires and the intelligence of the minority of better men?"

d

"It is," he said.

"So if any community deserves to be described as having mastered pleasure and desire, and as having self-mastery, it is this one."

"Without the slightest doubt," he said.

"So it also deserves to be called self-disciplined, doesn't it?"

"Yes, indeed," he said.

"Moreover it is in this community, more than in any other conceivable community, that the rulers and their subjects agree on who the rulers should be, don't you think?"

e

"Definitely," he said.

"In a situation like this, then, is it the rulers or the subjects of the community who, in your opinion, possess self-discipline?"

"Both," he replied.

"Is it clear to you, then," I asked, "that our recent conjecture that self-discipline resembles a kind of attunement wasn't bad?"

"Why?"

"Because unlike courage and wisdom, both of which imbued the community with their respective qualities while being properties of only a part of the community, self-discipline literally spans the whole octaval spread of the community, and makes the weakest, the strongest, and the ones in between all sing in unison, whatever criterion you choose in order to assess their relative strengths—intelligence, physical strength, numerical quantity, wealth, and so on. And the upshot is that we couldn't go wrong if

432

we claimed that self-discipline was this unanimity, a harmony between the naturally worse and naturally better elements of society as to which of them should rule both in a community and in every individual."

b　　"I certainly agree," he said.

"All right," I said. "We've detected three of the qualities in our community, as far as we can tell. But there's one final way in which a community achieves goodness. What precisely is morality? I mean, morality is this missing type of goodness, clearly."

"Clearly."

"We must now imitate hunters surrounding a thicket, Glaucon, and make sure that morality doesn't somehow elude us and disappear into obscurity. I mean, we know it's

c　somewhere round here. Keep your eyes peeled and try to spot it. If you see it before I do, let me know where it is."

"I wish I could," he said. "But in fact it would be more realistic of you to regard me as someone who follows in your footsteps and can see things only when they're pointed out to him."

"Follow me, then," I said, "and pray for success."

"I will," he said. "You have only to lead on."

"Now, we're in a rather rugged and overcast spot, it seems," I said. "At any rate, it's gloomy and hunting won't be easy. Still, we must carry on."

d　　"Yes, we must," he said.

I caught a glimpse of something and shouted, "Hurray! Glaucon, I believe we're on its trail! I don't think it will get clean away from us."

"That's good news," he said.

"What a stupid state to find ourselves in!" I exclaimed.

"What do you mean?"

"It looks as though it's been curled up at our feet all the time, right from the beginning, my friend, and we didn't see it, but just made absolute fools of ourselves. You know how people sometimes go in search of something they're holding in their hands all the time? That's what we've been like. We've been looking off into the distance

e　somewhere, instead of at our quarry, and that was why we didn't notice it, I suppose."

"What do you mean?"

"I'll tell you," I said. "I think it's been the subject of our discussion all along and we just didn't appreciate that we were in a sense talking about it."

"What a long preamble," he said, "when I'm so keen to hear what you're getting at!"

433　　"All right," I said. "See if you think there's anything in what I say. From the outset, when we first started to found the community, there's a principle we established as a universal requirement—and this, or some version of it, is in my opinion morality. The principle we established, and then repeated time and again, as you'll remember, is that every individual has to do just one of the jobs relevant to the community, the one for which his nature has best equipped him."

"Yes, that's what we said."

"Furthermore, the idea that morality is doing one's own job and not intruding

b　elsewhere is commonly voiced, and we ourselves have often said it."

"Yes we have."

"So Glaucon," I said, "it seems likely that this is in a sense what morality is—doing one's own job. Do you know what makes me think so?"

"No," he answered. "Please tell me."

"We've examined self-discipline, courage, and wisdom," I said, "and it occurs to me that this principle is what is left in the community because it is the principle which

makes it possible for all those other qualities to arise in the community, and its contin- c
ued presence allows them to flourish in safety once they have arisen. And we did in fact
say that if we found the other three, then whatever was left would be morality."

"Yes, that's necessarily so," he said.

"But if we had to decide which of these qualities it was whose presence is chiefly
responsible for the goodness of the community," I said, "it would be hard to decide
whether it's the unanimity between rulers and subjects, or the militia's retention of the
lawful notion about what is and is not to be feared, or the wise guardianship which is an d
attribute of the rulers, or the fact that it is an attribute of every child, woman, slave, free
person, artisan, ruler, and subject that each individual does his own job without intruding elsewhere, that is chiefly responsible for making it good."

"Yes, of course that would be a difficult decision," he said.

"When it comes to contributing to a community's goodness, then, there's apparently a close contest between the ability of everyone in a community to do their own
jobs and its wisdom, self-discipline, and courage."

"There certainly is," he said.

"And wouldn't you say that anything which rivals these qualities in contributing
towards a community's goodness must be morality?" e

"Absolutely."

"See if you also agree when you look at it from this point of view. Won't you be
requiring the rulers to adjudicate when lawsuits occur in the community?"

"Of course."

"And won't their most important aim in doing so be to ensure that people don't
get hold of other people's property and aren't deprived of their own?"

"Yes."

"Because this is right?"

"Yes."

"So from this point of view too we are agreed that morality is keeping one's own
property and keeping to one's own occupation." 434

"True."

"See if you agree with me on this as well: if a joiner tried to do a shoemaker's job,
or a shoemaker a carpenter's, or if they swapped tools or status, or even if the same person tried to do both jobs, with all the tools and so on of both jobs switched around, do
you think that much harm would come to the community?"

"Not really," he said.

"On the other hand, when someone whom nature has equipped to be an artisan or
to work for money in some capacity or other gets so puffed up by his wealth or popu- b
larity or strength or some such factor that he tries to enter the military class, or when a
member of the militia tries to enter the class of policy-makers and guardians when he's
not qualified to do so, and they swap tools and status, or when a single person tries to do
all these jobs simultaneously, then I'm sure you'll agree that these interchanges and in-
trusions are disastrous for the community."

"Absolutely."

"There's nothing more disastrous for the community, then, than the intrusion of
any of the three classes into either of the other two, and the interchange of roles among c
them, and there could be no more correct context for using the term 'criminal.'"

"Indubitably."

"And when someone commits the worst crimes against his own community,
wouldn't you describe this as immorality?"

"Of course."

"Then this is what immorality is. Here's an alternative way of putting it: Isn't it the case (to put it the other way round) that when each of the three classes—the one that works for a living, the auxiliaries, and the guardians—performs its proper function and does its own job in the community, then this is morality and makes the community a moral one?"

d   "Yes, I think that's exactly right," he said.

"Let's not be too inflexible about it yet," I warned. "If we also conclude that this type of thing constitutes morality in the case of individual human beings as well, then we'll have no reservations. I mean, how could we under those circumstances? However, if we find that it doesn't apply to humans as well, then we'll have to take the enquiry into new areas. So let's now wind up that aspect of the enquiry which is based on the idea we had that it would be easier to detect the nature of morality in an individual human being if we first tried to observe it in something larger and to watch its operation

e   there. We decided that the larger thing was a community, and so we founded as good a community as we could, because we were well aware that it would have to be a good community for morality to exist in it. What we have to do now is apply the results we found in the case of the community to an individual. If there's a match, that will be fine; but if we find something different in the case of an individual, then we'll return to the

435   community to test the new result. With luck, the friction of comparing the two cases will enable morality to flare up from these fire-sticks, so to speak, and once it's become visible we'll make it more of a force in our own lives."

"That's a viable notion," he said. "We should do as you suggest."

"Well," I said, "if a single property is predicated of two things of different sizes, then in so far as it's the same predicate, is it in fact dissimilar or similar in the two instances?"

"Similar," he said.

b   "So in respect of the actual type of thing morality is, a moral person will be no different from a moral community, but will resemble it."

"Yes," he said.

"Now, we decided that a community was moral when each of the three natural classes that exist within it did its own job, and also that certain other states and conditions of the same three classes made it self-disciplined and courageous and wise."

"True."

"It follows, my friend, that we should expect an individual to have the same three

c   classes in himself, and that the same conditions make him liable to the same predicates as the community receives."

"That's absolutely inevitable," he said.

"Glaucon," I said, "now we're faced with another simple enquiry, to see whether or not the mind contains these three features."

"It hardly seems to me to be a simple one," he remarked. "But then it's probably a true saying, Socrates, that anything fine is difficult."

"I think that's right," I said. "In fact, I have to tell you, Glaucon, that in my opin-

d   ion we'll never completely understand this issue by relying on the kinds of methods we've employed so far in our discussion: a longer and fuller approach is needed. Still, we can hope to come up with something which is in keeping with what we've already said in the earlier stages of our enquiry."

"Shouldn't we be content with that?" he asked. "I for one would be satisfied with that for the time being."

"And it'll do perfectly well for me too," I said.

"No flagging, then," he said. "On with the enquiry."

"Well, here's something we're bound to agree on, aren't we?" I asked. "That we   e
do contain the same kinds of features and characteristics as the community. I mean,
where else could it have got them from? When the general population of a community
consists of people who are reputedly passionate—Thracians and Scythians, for example, and almost any northerner—it would be absurd to think that passion arises in this
community from any other source. And the same goes for love of knowledge, for which
our country has a strong reputation; and being mercenary might be claimed to be a par-   436
ticular characteristic of Phoenicians and Egyptians."

"Certainly."

"This is a matter of fact, then," I said, "and it wasn't hard to discover."

"No."

"But here's a hard one: is there just a single thing which we use for doing everything, or are there three and we use different things for different tasks? Do we learn with
one of our aspects, get worked up with another, and with a third desire the pleasures of
eating, sex, and so on, or do we use the whole of our mind for every task we actually get
going on? These questions won't be easy to answer satisfactorily."   b

"I agree," he said.

"Well, let's approach an answer by trying to see whether these aspects are the
same as one another or are different."

"How?"

"It's clear that the same one thing cannot simultaneously either act or be acted on
in opposite ways in the same respect and in the same context. And consequently, if we
find this happening in the case of these aspects of ourselves, we'll know that there are
more than one of them."

"All right."   c

"What about this, then?"

"What?"

"Is it possible for the same thing to be simultaneously at rest and in motion in the
same respect?" I asked.

"Of course not."

"Let's take a closer look before agreeing, otherwise we'll start arguing later. My
assumption is that if someone claims that a person who is standing still, but moving his
hands and head, is the same person simultaneously being still and moving, we won't approve of this way of putting it, as opposed to saying that one part of him is still, and another part of him is moving. Yes?"   d

"Yes."

"So even if the advocate of the claim were to get even more subtle and ingeniously maintain that when a top is spinning round with its peg fixed in place, then this
is definitely a case of something simultaneously being still and moving as a whole, or
that the same goes for anything else which spins round on one spot, we wouldn't accept
this assertion. We'll say that in this situation these objects are not still and moving in the   e
same respects. We'll point out that they include an axis and a circumference, and that
they may be still in respect of their axes (in the sense that they're not tipping over at all),
but they have circular motion in respect of their circumferences; and we'll add that
when one of these objects tips its upright to the right or left or front or back while simultaneously spinning round, then it has no stillness in any respect."

"Yes, that's right," he said.

"No assertion of this kind will put us off, then, or make us in the slightest inclined
to believe that the same thing could ever simultaneously be acted on or exist or act in   437
opposite ways in the same respect and in the same context."

"I won't be put off, anyway," he said.

"That's as may be," I said. "But let's not feel compelled to have all the bother of going through every single one of these arguments and proving them false. Let's assume that we're right and carry on, with the understanding that if we ever turn out to have been mistaken, all the conclusions we draw on the basis of this assumption will be invalidated."

"Yes, that's what we'd better do," he said.

b   "Wouldn't you count assent and dissent," I asked, "seeking and avoidance, and liking and disliking, as all pairs of opposites? It'll make no difference whether you think of them as ways of acting or of being acted on."

"Yes, they're opposites," he answered.

"What about thirst and hunger and the desires generally," I went on, "and what about wishing and wanting? Wouldn't you say that all these things belong somewhere

c   among the sets we've just mentioned? For example, won't you describe the mind of anyone who is in a state of desire as seeking to fulfil his desires, or as liking whatever the desired object is? Or again, to the extent that it wants to get hold of something, don't you think it is internally assenting to this thing, as if in response to a question, and is longing for it to happen?"

"Yes, I do."

"And what about the states of antipathy, reluctance, or unwillingness? Won't we put these states in the opposite category, which includes dislike and aversion?"

d   "Of course."

"Under these circumstances, then, won't we say that there is a category which consists of the desires, and that the most conspicuous desires are the ones called thirst and hunger?"

"Yes," he said.

"And the one is desire for drink, the other desire for food?"

"Yes."

"Now, is thirst, in itself, the mental desire for anything more than the object we mentioned? For example, is thirst thirst for a hot drink or a cold one, a lot of drink or a little, or in short for any particular kind of drink at all? Doesn't it take heat in addition to thirst to give it the extra feature of being desire for something cold, and cold to make

e   it desire for something hot? Doesn't it take a thirst which has been aggravated into becoming strong to produce the desire for a lot of drink; and doesn't it take a weak thirst to produce the desire for a little drink? The actual state of being thirsty, however, cannot possibly be desire for anything other than its natural object, which is just drink; and the same goes for hunger and food."

"Yes," he said. "Each desire is for its natural object only, and the desire for an object of this or that type is a result of some addition."

438   "It should be quite impossible, then," I said, "for anyone to catch us unawares and rattle us with the claim that no one desires drink, but a good drink, and no one desires food, but good food. Everyone desires good, they say, so if thirst is a desire, it must be desire for a good drink or whatever; and so on for the other desires."

"There might seem to be some plausibility to the claim," he remarked.

"But there are only two categories of things whose nature it is to be relative," I said. "The first category consists, in my opinion, of things which have particular qual-

b   ities and whose correlates have particular qualities; the second category consists of things which are just what they are and whose correlates are just what they are."

"I don't understand," he said.

"Don't you realize," I said, "that anything which is greater is greater than something?"

"Yes."

"Than something smaller?"

"Yes."

"Whereas anything which is a lot greater is relative to something which is a lot smaller. Agreed?"

"Yes."

"And anything which was once greater (or will be) is relative to something which was once smaller (or will be), isn't it?"

"Of course," he said.

"And the same goes for more in relation to less, and double in relation to half (and   c
all similar numerical relations); also for heavier in relation to lighter, quicker in relation to slower, and moreover hot in relation to cold, and so on and so forth, don't you think?"

"Yes."

"And what about the branches of knowledge? Isn't it the same story? Knowledge in itself is knowledge of information in itself (or whatever you choose to call the object of knowledge), but a particular branch of knowledge, knowledge qualified, is knowledge of a particular qualified kind of thing. Here's an example: When the knowledge of   d
making houses was developed, didn't it differ from the rest of the branches of knowledge and consequently gain its own name, building?"

"Of course."

"And didn't it do so by virtue of the fact that it is a particular kind of knowledge, a kind which none of the other branches of knowledge is?"

"Yes."

"And wasn't it when its object came into being as a particular kind of thing that it too came into being as a particular kind of knowledge? And doesn't the same go for all the other branches of expertise and knowledge?"

"Yes, it does."

"I wonder if you've grasped my meaning now," I said. "You should think of this as the point I was trying to make before, when I said that there are two categories of things whose nature it is to be relative: some are only themselves and are related to objects which are only themselves; others have particular qualities and are related to objects with particular qualities. I don't mean to imply that their quality is the same   e
as the quality of their objects—that knowledge of health and illness is itself healthy and ill, and knowledge of evil and good is itself evil and good. I mean that when knowledge occurs whose object is not the unqualified object of knowledge, but an object with a particular quality (say, health and illness), then the consequence is that the knowledge itself also acquires a particular quality, and this is why it is no longer called just plain knowledge: the qualification is added, and it is called medical knowledge."

"I do understand," he said, "and I agree as well."

"As for thirst, then," I said, "don't you think it finds its essential place among rel-   439
ative things? And what it essentially is, of course, is thirst . . ."

". . . for drink," he said. "Yes, I agree."

"So for drink of a particular kind there is also thirst of a particular kind; but thirst in itself is not thirst for a lot of drink or a little drink, or a beneficial drink or a harmful drink, or in short for drink of any particular kind. Thirst in itself is essentially just thirst for drink in itself."

"Absolutely."

"When someone is thirsty, then, the only thing—in so far as he is thirsty—that his mind wants is to drink. This is what it longs for and strives for."   b

"Clearly."

"So imagine an occasion when something is making it resist the pull of its thirst: isn't this bound to be a different part of it from the thirsty part, which is impelling it towards drink as if it were an animal? I mean, we've already agreed that the same one thing cannot thanks to the same part of itself simultaneously have opposite effects in the same context."

"No, it can't."

"As an analogy, it isn't in my opinion right to say that an archer's hands are simultaneously pushing the bow away and pulling it closer. Strictly, one hand is pushing it away and the other is pulling it close."

c   "I quite agree," he said.

"Now, do we know of cases where thirsty people are unwilling to drink?"

"Certainly," he said. "It's a common occurrence."

"What could be the explanation for these cases?" I asked "Don't we have to say that their mind contains a part which is telling them to drink, and a part which is telling them not to drink, and that this is a different part and overcomes the part which is telling them to drink?"

"I think so," he said.

"And those occasions when thirst and so on are countermanded occur thanks to d   rationality, whereas the pulls and impulses occur thanks to afflictions and diseased states, don't they?"

"I suppose so."

"So it wouldn't be irrational of us to expect that these are two separate parts," I said, "one of which we can describe as rational, and the other as irrational and desirous. The first is responsible for the mind's capacity to think rationally, and the second—which is an ally of certain satisfactions and pleasures—for its capacity to feel lust, hunger, and thirst, and in general to be stirred by desire."

e   "No, it wouldn't be irrational," he said. "This would be a perfectly reasonable view for us to hold."

"Let's have these, then," I said, "as two distinct aspects of our minds. What about the passionate part, however, which is responsible for the mind's capacity for passion? Is it a third part, or might it be interchangeable with one of the other two?"

"I suppose it might be the same as the desirous part," he said.

"But there's a story I once heard which seems to me to be reliable," I said, "about how Leontius the son of Aglaeon was coming up from the Piraeus, outside the North Wall but close to it, when he saw some corpses with the public executioner standing near by. On the one hand, he experienced the desire to see them, but at the same time he felt disgust and averted his gaze. For a while, he struggled and kept his hands over his 440   eyes, but finally he was overcome by the desire; he opened his eyes wide, ran up to the corpses, and said, 'There you are, you wretches! What a lovely sight! I hope you feel satisfied!'"

"Yes, I've heard the story too," he said.

"Now, what it suggests," I said, "is that it's possible for anger to be at odds with the desires, as if they were different things."

"Yes, it does," he agreed.

"And that's far from being an isolated case, isn't it?" I asked. "It's not at all un-b   common to find a person's desires compelling him to go against his reason, and to see him cursing himself and venting his passion on the source of the compulsion within him. It's as if there were two warring factions, with passion fighting on the side of reason. But I'm sure you wouldn't claim that you had ever, in yourself or in anyone else, met a case of passion siding with the desires against the rational mind, when the rational mind prohibits resistance."

"No, I certainly haven't," he said.

"And what about when you feel you're in the wrong?" I asked. "If someone who in your opinion has a right to do so retaliates by inflicting on you hunger and cold and so on, then isn't it the case that, in proportion to your goodness of character, you are incapable of getting angry at this treatment and your passion, as I say, has no inclination to get worked up against him?"

"True," he said.

"But suppose you feel you're being wronged. Under these circumstances, your passion boils and rages, and fights for what you regard as right. Then hunger, cold, and other sufferings make you stand firm and conquer them, and only success or death can stop it fighting the good fight, unless it is recalled by your rational mind and calmed down, as a dog is by a shepherd."

"That's a very good simile," he said. "And in fact the part we've got the auxiliaries to play in our community is just like that of dogs, with their masters being the rulers, who are, as it were, the shepherds of the community."

"Yes, you've got it," I said. "That's exactly what I mean. But there's something else here too, and I wonder if you've noticed it as well."

"What is it?"

"That we're getting the opposite impression of the passionate part from what we did before. Previously, we were thinking that it was an aspect of the desirous part, but now that seems to be way off the mark, and we're saying that when there's mental conflict, it is far more likely to fight alongside reason."

"Absolutely," he said.

"Is it different from the rational part, then, or is it a version of it, in which case there are two, not three, mental categories—the rational and the desirous? Or will the analogy with the community hold good? Three classes constituted the community— the one which works for a living, the auxiliaries, and the policy-makers—so is there in the mind as well a third part, the passionate part, which is an auxiliary of the rational part, unless it is corrupted by bad upbringing?"

"It must be a third part," he said.

"Yes," I said, "*if* we find that it's as distinct from the rational part as it is from the desirous part."

"But that's easy," he said. "Just look at children. It's evident that from the moment of their birth they have a copious supply of passion, but I'm not convinced that some of them ever acquire reason, and it takes quite a time for most of them to do so."

"Yes, you've certainly put that well," I said. "And animals provide further evidence of the truth of what you're saying. Moreover, we can adduce the passage from Homer we quoted earlier: 'He struck his breast and spoke sternly to his heart.' Clearly, Homer here has one distinct part rebuking another distinct part—the part which has thought rationally about what is better and worse rebuking the part whose passion is irrationally becoming aroused."

"You're absolutely right," he said.

"It's not been easy," I said, "but we've made it to the other shore: we've reached the reasonable conclusion that the constituent categories of a community and of any individual's mind are identical in nature and number."

"Yes, they are."

"Isn't it bound to follow that the manner and cause of a community's and an individual's wisdom are identical?"

"Naturally."

"And that the manner and cause of a community's and an individual's courage are identical, and that the same goes for every other factor which contributes in both cases towards goodness?"

"Inevitably."

"So no doubt, Glaucon, we'll also be claiming that human morality is the same in kind as a community's morality."

"Yes, that's absolutely inevitable too."

"We can't have forgotten, however, that a community's morality consists in each of its three constituent classes doing its own job."

"No, I'm sure we haven't," he said.

e   "So we should impress upon our minds the idea that the same goes for human beings as well. Where each of the constituent parts of an individual does its own job, the individual will be moral and will do *his* own job."

"Yes, we certainly should do that," he said.

"Since the rational part is wise and looks out for the whole of the mind, isn't it right for it to rule, and for the passionate part to be its subordinate and its ally?"

"Yes."

"Now—to repeat—isn't it the combination of culture and exercise which will make them attuned to each other? The two combined provide fine discussions and stud-

442 ies to stretch and educate the rational part, and music and rhythm to relax, calm, and soothe the passionate part."

"Absolutely."

"And once these two parts have received this education and have been trained and conditioned in their true work, then they are to be put in charge of the desirous part, which is the major constituent of an individual's mind and is naturally insatiably greedy for things. So they have to watch over it and make sure that it doesn't get so saturated with physical pleasures (as they are called) that in its bloated and strengthened state it

b   stops doing its own job, and tries to dominate and rule over things which it is not equipped by its hereditary status to rule over, and so plunges the whole of everyone's life into chaos."

"Yes, indeed," he said.

"Moreover, these two are perfect for guarding the entire mind and the body against external enemies, aren't they?" I asked. "The rational part will do the planning, and the passionate part the fighting. The passionate part will obey the ruling part and employ its courage to carry out the plans."

"True."

"I imagine, then, that it is the passionate part of a person which we are taking into

c   consideration when we describe him as courageous: we're saying that neither pain nor pleasure stops his passionate part retaining the pronouncements of reason about what is and is not to be feared."

"That's right," he agreed.

"And the part we take into consideration when we call him wise is that little part—his internal ruler, which made these pronouncements—which knows what is advantageous for each of the three parts and for their joint unity."

"Yes."

"And don't we call him self-disciplined when there's concord and attunement between these same parts—that is, when the ruler and its two subjects unanimously agree

d   on the necessity of the rational part being the ruler and when they don't rebel against it?"

"Yes, that's exactly what self-discipline is, in both a community and an individual," he said.

"And we're not changing our minds about the manner and cause of morality."

"Absolutely not."

"Well," I said, "have we blunted the edge of our notion of morality in any way? Do we have any grounds for thinking that our conclusions about its nature in a community don't apply in this context?"

"I don't think so," he replied.

"If there's still any doubt in our minds," I said, "we can eradicate it completely by   e checking our conclusion against everyday cases."

"What cases?"

"Take this community of ours and a person who resembles it by virtue of both his nature and his upbringing, and suppose, for instance, we had to state whether, in our opinion, a person of this type would steal money which had been deposited with him. Is it conceivable to you that anyone would think our man capable of this, rather than any   443 other type of person?"

"No one could think that," he said.

"And he could have nothing to do with temple-robbery, theft, and betrayal either of his personal friends or, on a public scale, of his country, could he?"

"No, he couldn't."

"Moreover, nothing could induce him to break an oath or any other kind of agreement."

"No, nothing."

"And he's the last person you'd expect to find committing adultery, neglecting his parents, and failing to worship the gods."

"Yes, of course," he said.

"And isn't the reason for all of this the fact that each of his constituent parts does   b its own job as ruler or subject?"

"Yes, that's the only reason."

"Do you need to look any further for morality, then? Don't you think it can only be the capacity we've come up with, which enables both people and communities to be like this?"

"I for one certainly don't need to look any further," he said.

"Our dream has finally come true, then. We said we had a vague impression that we had probably—with the help of some god—stumbled across the origin and some kind of outline of morality right at the start of our foundation of the commu-   c nity."

"Absolutely."

"It turns out, then, Glaucon—and this is why it was so useful—that the idea that a person who has been equipped by nature to be a shoemaker or a joiner or whatever should make shoes or do joinery or whatever was a dreamt image of morality."

"So it seems."

"And we've found that in real life morality is the same kind of property, apparently, though not in the field of external activities. Its sphere is a person's inner activity: it is really a matter of oneself and the parts of oneself. Once he has stopped his   d mental constituents doing any job which is not their own or intruding on one another's work; once he has set his own house in order, which is what he really should be concerned with; once he is his own ruler, and is well regulated, and has internal concord; once he has treated the three factors as if they were literally the three defining notes of an octave—low, high, and middle—and has created a harmony out of them and however many notes there may be in between; once he has bound all the factors together   e and made himself a perfect unity instead of a plurality, self-disciplined and internally attuned; then and only then does he act—if he acts—to acquire property or look after his body or play a role in government or do some private business. In the course of this activity, it is conduct which preserves and promotes this inner condition of his that he regards as moral and describes as fine, and it is the knowledge which oversees this conduct that he regards as wisdom; however, it is any conduct which disperses this condition that he regards as immoral, and the thinking which oversees this conduct that he regards as stupidity."

"You're absolutely right, Socrates," he said.

"All right," I said. "I imagine that we'd regard as no more than the truth the claim that we had found out what it is to be a moral person and a moral community, and had discovered what morality actually is when it occurs in them."

"Yes, we certainly would," he said.

"Shall we make the claim, then?"

"Yes."

"So be it," I said. "Next, I suppose, we should consider immorality."

"Obviously."

"Isn't it bound to involve these three factors being in conflict, intruding into one another's work, and exchanging roles, and one part rebelling against the mind as a whole in an improper attempt to usurp rulership—improper because its natural function is to be dominated, unless it belongs to the ruling class? Our position, I'm sure, will be that it is disruption and disorder of the three parts along these lines that constitutes not only immorality, but also indiscipline, cowardice, and stupidity—in a word, badness of any kind."

"Precisely," he said.

"Now that morality and immorality are in plain view, doesn't that mean that wrong-doing and immoral conduct, and right conduct too, are as well?" I asked.

"Why?"

"Because their role in the mind happens to be identical to that of healthy or unhealthy factors in the body," I said.

"In what sense?"

"Healthy factors engender health, and unhealthy ones illness."

"Yes."

"Well, doesn't moral behaviour engender morality, while immoral behaviour engenders immorality?"

"Inevitably."

"But you create health by making the components of a body control and be controlled as nature intended, and you create disease by subverting this natural order."

"Yes."

"Doesn't it follow," I said, "that you create morality by making the components of a mind control and be controlled as nature intended, and immorality by subverting this natural order?"

"Absolutely," he said.

"Goodness, then, is apparently a state of mental health, bloom, and vitality; badness is a state of mental sickness, deformity, and infirmity."

"That's right."

"Isn't it the case, therefore, that goodness is a consequence of good conduct, badness of bad conduct?"

"Necessarily."

"Now we come to what is, I suppose, the final topic. We have to consider whether moral conduct, fine behaviour, and being moral (whether or not the person is known to be moral) are rewarding, or whether it is wrong-doing and being immoral (provided that the immoral person doesn't have to pay for his crimes and doesn't become a better person as a result of being punished)."

"It seems to me that it would be absurd to consider that topic now, Socrates," he said. "Life isn't thought to be worth living when the natural constitution of the body is ruined, even if one has all the food and drink and wealth and power in the world. So how could it be worth living when the natural constitution of the very life-force within us is disrupted and ruined? How could life be worth living if a person's chosen course   b
of action is to avoid the path which will lead him away from badness and immorality and towards the possession of morality and goodness, given the evident accuracy of our descriptions of both of these states?"

"Yes, it is absurd," I agreed. "All the same, since we've reached a point which affords the clearest possible view of the truth of these matters, we shouldn't give up now."

"I couldn't agree more," he said. "Giving up should be the last thing on our minds."

"Come and join me here, then," I said, "and you'll see, I think, all the types of   c
badness there are—at least, the ones that are worth seeing.'

"I'm coming," he said. "You have only to tell me."

"Well," I said, "the impression I get from the vantage-point we've reached at this point of our discussion is that while there's only one kind of goodness, there are countless types of badness, of which four are worth mentioning."

"What do you mean?" he asked.

Black-figure lekythos (oil-jug) attributed to the potter Amasis (sixth century B.C.). The women on the left are hand spinning thread while those in the center are weaving wool. Given that Greek women generally remained at home fulfilling such domestic occupations, Plato's suggestions in the *Republic* were quite revolutionary. Though he claims that women are "the weaker sex in all respects," Plato's character, Socrates, concludes "Therefore, my friend, there's no administrative job in a community which belongs to a woman *qua* woman, or to a man *qua* man. . . . Innate qualities have been distributed equally between the two sexes, and women can join in every occupation just as much as men." (*The Metropolitan Museum of Art*)

"There are probably as many types of character," I said, "as there are identifiable forms of political system."

"And how many is that?"

d   "There are five types of political system," I replied, "and five types of character."

"Please tell me what they are," he said.

"All right," I said. "One of the forms of political system would be the one we've described. There are two possible ways of referring to it, however: if a single outstanding individual arises within the ruling class, it's called a kingship; but if there is a plurality of rulers, it's called an aristocracy."

"True," he said.

"This is the first of the types of political system I had in mind," I said. "The point is that whether there is a single ruler in the community, or whether there are more than

e   one, they won't disturb any of the community's important laws, since they'll have been brought up and educated in the manner we've explained."

"No, it's implausible to think that they will," he said.

BOOK V

449   "So that's the kind of community and political system—and the kind of person—I'm calling good and right. Given the rightness of this community, I'm describing all the others as bad and flawed: not only are their political systems wrong, but they also influence individuals' characters incorrectly. And I see them as falling into four categories."

"What four categories?" he asked.

I was on the point of listing them and explaining how, in my opinion, each in turn

b   evolved out of the preceding one, when Polemarchus (who was sitting just beyond Adeimantus) reached out and got hold of Adeimantus' cloak high up, by his shoulder. He drew Adeimantus towards himself, leaned forward and whispered something with his mouth to his ear, so that all we heard of his words was: "Shall we let it drop or what?"

"Of course not," Adeimantus replied—this was out loud.

"What aren't you going to let drop?" I asked.

"You," he said.

c   "What have I done?" I asked.

"We think you're being lazy," he said. "We think you're doing us out of a whole aspect of the discussion, and a not unimportant aspect at that, so that you don't have to spell out the details. You seem to think you can get away with casually saying, as if it were obvious to everyone, that where wives and children are concerned 'friends share.'"

"But that's right, isn't it, Adeimantus?" I asked.

"Yes," he replied. "But it still needs explaining, just as you've explained everything else. What makes this sharing right? I mean, there are all sorts of ways it could

d   happen, so don't leave us guessing as to which one you have in mind. For a long time now we've been patiently expecting you to make some mention of their approach to procreation and how they'll bring up their children, and to discuss the whole issue of the sharing of wives and children, which is a subject you raised, because in our opinion, as far as society is concerned, a great deal—no, everything—hinges on whether or not it happens in the right way. That is why, when you were starting to criticize another type of political system before you'd adequately discussed this issue, we made the decision 450 you overheard—not to let you go on until you'd discussed this whole topic as well."

"You should know that I share his view," said Glaucon. "This decision gets my vote too."

"In fact, you'd better count us as unanimous about this decision, Socrates," said Thrasymachus.

"If only you knew what you'd done, laying into me like this," I said. "You're touching off a huge discussion about the constitution of our community; it'll be like starting again from the beginning. And I was so pleased that I'd finished describing it, and so happy that the description I'd given had been found acceptable and allowed to stand! You've no idea how massive a swarm of arguments you're stirring up now with b your appeals. It's because I noticed its size that I did nothing about it, to avoid all the bother it would cause us."

"Do you think it's gold fever that's brought these people here?" demanded Thrasymachus. "Don't you suppose they've come to hear arguments?"

"Yes," I replied, "but not endless ones."

"Anyone with any sense lets only death put an end to this kind of discussion," Glaucon said. "Please don't spare us a thought: just persevere and explain your views on the matters we're asking about. How will our guardians share children and wives? c What upbringing will they provide for young children between birth and schooling, which is regarded as the most difficult period? Please try to explain it to us."

"It's not an easy matter to go into, Glaucon," I said. "There are plenty of reasons for misgivings—even more than in the matters we've already discussed. I mean, one might doubt the viability of the proposal, and even granting its viability, there'll be room for doubting whether it's the best course of action. That, my dear friend, is why I'm rather hesitant about addressing the topic: I'm scared of my ideas being thought to d be wishful thinking."

"Don't worry," he said. "You won't be faced with an audience of dunces or sceptics or grumblers."

"Was that remark supposed to raise my morale, Glaucon?" I asked.

"Yes," he answered.

"Well, it's having exactly the opposite effect," I said. "If I was sure I knew what I was talking about, then your attempt at encouragement would go down well. I mean, there's no danger or uncertainty when someone who knows the truth speaks among intelligent friends about crucial matters which are close to their hearts, but when someone e who is vacillating and who still hasn't formed any definite conclusions does the talking, as I am, it's a cause for alarm and caution. My worry is not that I might make a fool of 451 myself: that would be a childish worry. But I'm frightened of dragging my friends down with me when I stumble and fall short of the truth in matters where uncertainty is the last thing one wants. I humbly beg Nemesis, Glaucon, to pardon what I'm about to say. You see, I'm sure that deceiving people about customs which are truly good and moral is more of a sin than accidentally killing someone. That is why it's preferable to take this risk when one is in the company of enemies rather than friends—and that's why I really appreciated your encouragement!" b

Glaucon smiled and said, "Socrates, if anything nasty happens to us as a result of what you say, we'll acquit you of murder, so to speak, and find you free of all taint of deceit. So you can talk with confidence."

"Well, it's true that in homicide cases there's a law guaranteeing that anyone who has been acquitted is free of the taint of pollution," I said, "so I suppose the same rule applies here too."

"Then there's nothing to stop you getting on with the discussion," he said.

"We'd better backtrack, then," I said. "The proper time for the discussion may have been earlier, but we'll have to have it now. It'll probably be all right this way, though—to proceed with the women's business now that the men's business is completed and done, especially since that's what you're asking me to do. It is my opinion that there is only one correct way for people with the character and education we've described to have and deal with their children and wives, and that is if they continue in the direction we gave them at the outset. What we tried to do, as you know, was make the men in theory like guardians of a flock."

"Yes."

"So let's keep to the same path and have the women born and brought up in a closely similar way, and see whether or not it turns out right for us."

"How?" he asked.

"Well, should female guard-dogs share with the males the guarding and hunting and whatever other duties the males might have, do you think? Or should they stay indoors, incapacitated by their bearing and rearing of whelps, while the males work and do all the overseeing of the flocks?"

"They should share in everything," he said. "The only qualification is that we're dealing with a physically weaker sex: the males are stronger."

"Can you employ any two creatures for the same purposes if you haven't given them the same upbringing and education?" I asked.

"No."

"Therefore, if we're going to use the women for the same purposes as the men, we have to educate them in the same way."

"Yes."

"Now, the men were set cultural studies and physical exercise."

"Yes."

"So these two subjects had better be set the women too. Then there's the military training: we ought to put them through exactly what we put the men through."

"That's a reasonable deduction from what you're saying," he said.

"I suppose a lot of our suggestions would seem ludicrous and outlandish if they became practical realities," I said.

"No doubt," he said.

"Which of them do you think would be the most ludicrous?" I asked. "Isn't it obviously the idea of having women exercising naked in the gymnasia along with the men—and not only young women, but older ones as well? I mean, there are old men who come to the gymnasia and are still fond of exercise despite their wrinkled flesh and ugly appearance."

"Good heavens, yes!" he said. "That would certainly be thought ludicrous, as things stand today."

"Well," I said, "we've chosen the course of our argument, so we shouldn't let sarcastic jibes worry us. People would crack lots of jokes of all kinds if they were faced in practice with changes of this nature in physical and cultural education, let alone in how armour was worn and horses were ridden."

"You're right," he said.

"We've started out on this argument, however, so we must take the legislative rough with the smooth. We'll ask those wits not to do what they usually do, but to be serious for a change, and we'll remind them that until quite recently the Greeks used to regard it as shocking and ludicrous for *men* to be seen naked—in fact, in most foreign countries this is still the case. The Cretans were the first to exercise naked (followed by the Spartans), and when they started to do so, it was an opportunity for the wags of the day to make fun of it all, don't you think?"   d

"Yes."

"But when experience proved the superiority of nakedness to clothing in all these kinds of contexts, then superficial mockery waned in the light of what reasoned argument revealed to be best. It was shown to be inane to think anything ludicrous except badness, to try to raise a laugh by regarding as absurd the spectacle of anything except foolishness and badness, and also to seriously hold any standard of beauty except good-   e
ness."

"Absolutely," he said.

"The first thing we have to reach agreement on, then, is whether or not these proposals are viable, isn't it? And shouldn't we allow that there is room for doubting—whether the doubt is expressed humorously or seriously—whether women do have the   453
natural ability to co-operate with men in all their jobs, or in none, or in some but not others (in which case there's the further question of which category warfare belongs to)? Don't you think that this would be the best way for us to make a start and would probably lead to the best conclusion?"

"By far the best," he said.

"Shall we voice their doubts between ourselves, then, on their behalf," I asked, "so that the opposite point of view is not left to fend for itself?"

"Why not?" he replied.   b

"So let's have them say, 'You don't need external sceptics, Socrates and Glaucon. You yourselves asserted, right at the start of the founding of your community, that everyone had to do the one job for which his nature had equipped him.'"

"Yes, I should say so. Of course we did."

"'And doesn't a woman's nature differ a great deal from a man's?'"

"Of course it does."

"'So the members of each sex should properly be assigned different work—work which suits their particular nature—shouldn't they?'"   c

"Of course."

"'So your current proposal is bound to be incorrect, and you're contradicting yourselves with the claim that men and women should do the same jobs, despite the enormous differences between their natures.' Can you defend our proposals against this accusation, Glaucon?"

"Hardly," he replied, "not without some preparation. What I'd do is ask *you* to come up with the response for us—so that's what I am doing."

"I foresaw this accusation a long time ago, Glaucon," I said, "and plenty of other similar criticisms too. That's why I was afraid and didn't really want to get involved   d
with regulations about what to do with wives and how to bring up children."

"No, it certainly doesn't seem to be an easy task," he remarked.

"No, it isn't," I said. "But it's like this: it makes no difference whether you fall into a little pool or into the middle of the largest ocean—you're still swimming."

"Yes."

"So we'd better try swimming to safety out of this sea of argument, hoping for some improbable rescue like a dolphin picking us up."

"I suppose so," he said.   e

"Let's see if we can find a way out, then," I continued. "We maintain that different natures should do different work, and that men and women do have different natures; and now we're claiming that these different natures should do the same work. Is this what we're accused of?"

"Exactly."

454   "You know, Glaucon, skill at disputation is a splendid thing," I said.

"Why?"

"Because a lot of people, I think," I replied, "find themselves unconsciously se-
duced by it: they think they're practising dialectic, not eristic. The reason for this is their
inability to conduct the enquiry by dividing the subject-matter into its various aspects.
Instead their goal is the contradiction of statements at the purely verbal level, and they
converse with one another eristically, not dialectically."

"Yes," he said, "that's a common phenomenon. But does it have any relevance to
our current situation?"

b   "Nothing could be more relevant," I answered. "At any rate, we're in danger of
unconsciously resorting to disputation."

"How?"

"We're pursuing the idea that different natures should get different occupations
with considerable vigour and eristic force at the verbal level, but we haven't spent any
time at all enquiring precisely what type of inherent difference and identity we meant
when we assigned different occupations to different natures and identical occupations
to identical natures, and whether context makes any difference to what we said."

"No, we haven't looked into that," he said.

c   "By the same token," I said, "we might as well ask ourselves, apparently, whether
bald men and men with hair have the same nature or completely different natures. And
suppose we agreed that they have completely different natures, then we might have bald
shoemakers, and make hair disqualify people from being shoemakers, or vice versa."

"Which would be absurd," he said.

"And the reason it would be absurd," I said, "is because earlier we weren't talking
about identity or difference of nature in any absolute sense. We had in mind only that
d   type of difference or similarity which is relevant to identity of occupation, didn't we?
We meant, for example, that a man with a medical mind and a woman with a medical
mind have the same nature. Don't you agree?"

"I do."

"Whereas a male doctor and a male joiner have different natures?"

"Absolutely."

"So if either the male or the female gender turns out to be better than the other
gender at some profession or occupation, then we'll claim that this is an occupation
which ought to be assigned to that gender. But if the only difference turns out to be that
e   females bear offspring, while males mount females, then we'll say that this doesn't yet
bring us any closer at all to proving that men and women are different in the context
we're talking about, and we'll continue to think that our guardians and their women
should have the same occupations."

"Right," he said.

"This is exactly what we'll require our opponent to explain to us next, then—for
455   which of the professions or occupations which bear on the organization of a community
are there inherent differences between men and women?"

"Yes, that would be a fair question."

"And he might well copy what you said a few moments ago, and reply that it's
hard to come up with an adequate response on the spur of the moment, but that research
would make it easy."

"Yes, he might."

"Shall we ask our disputatious friend to accompany us, then, to see if we can
b   prove to him that there is no occupation which bears on the administration of a community which belongs especially to women or to men?"

"Yes."

"'All right, then,' we'll say to him, 'here's a question for you: When you distinguish people as naturally competent or incompetent in a particular context, don't you mean that some people find it easy to learn that subject, while others find it hard? And that some people start to do their own broadly speaking original work in the subject after only a little study, while others can't even retain what they've learnt after even a lot of study and care? And that some people's bodies are sufficiently subservient to their minds, while others' are obstructive? Aren't these the features—there are more too—which enable you to define some people as naturally competent, and others as naturally incompetent?'"   c

"Indisputably," he said.

"'Well, do you know of any subject on earth in which men do not outclass women in all these respects?' Anyway, do we need to extend the conversation by discussing sewing, looking after pancakes, and boiling vegetables, which women are supposed to be good at, and where defeat makes them the most ridiculous creatures in the world?"   d

"You're right," he said. "The one gender is far superior to the other in just about every sphere. It may be that many women are better than many men at many things, but by and large it is as you say."

"Therefore, my friend, there's no administrative job in a community which belongs to a woman *qua* woman, or to a man *qua* man," I said. "Innate qualities have been distributed equally between the two sexes, and women can join in every occupation just as much as men, although they are the weaker sex in all respects."   e

"Yes."

"So shall we assign the men all the work and leave the women nothing?"

"Definitely not."

"The point being that some women may be good at medicine or music, even if others aren't. That's what we'll say, I suppose."

"Of course."

"And isn't it the case that some women may be good at sports or warfare, while   456
others aren't?"

"I should say so."

"And philosophically inclined or disinclined too? And some may be passionate, while others aren't?"

"Again, yes."

"Some women may make good guardians, then, while others won't, since these were the innate qualities we selected as the marks of men who would make good guardians, weren't they?"

"They were."

"Both women and men, then, have the same natural ability for guarding a community, and it's just that women are innately weaker than men."

"I suppose so."

"These are the women, then, who should be selected to live with the male   b
guardians and to join them in guardianship. They are endowed with the natural ability to do so, and they are from the same stock as the male guardians."

"Quite."

"And the same occupations should be assigned to people with the same natures, shouldn't they?"

"Yes."

"So we've come full circle back to where we were before. We're agreed that it isn't unnatural for the wives of our guardians to be set cultural studies and physical exercise."

"Absolutely."

"Our regulations were viable, then, and weren't just wishful thinking, since
they're compatible with nature. In fact, it is current practice, which contravenes this,
which is apparently more likely to be unnatural."

"So it seems."

"Now, we were trying to discover whether our proposals were viable and for the
best, weren't we?"

"Yes."

"And we've concluded that they're viable, haven't we?"

"Yes."

"So next we need to reach agreement on whether they're for the best, don't we?"

"Obviously."

"Well, in order to make women good at guarding, we won't be providing them
with a different education from the one that works for men, will we? After all, it's the
same nature the educational system takes on in both cases."

"Yes, it is."

"Now, I wonder what you think about this idea."

"Which one?"

"The notion that some men are better than others. Perhaps you think they're all
the same?"

"Definitely not."

"In the community we're founding, then, do you think the guardians or the shoemakers will prove to be the better people, when the guardians have been educated in the
way we've described and the shoemakers have been educated in their craft?"

"I'm not going to treat that as a serious question," he said.

"I see," I said. "And what about the rest of the citizen body? Will the guardians be
the best?"

"By far the best."

"And won't the women we're talking about be better than all the rest of the
women?"

"Again, by a long way," he said.

"Is anything better for a community than for it to engender women and men who
are exceptionally good?"

"No."

"And this is the effect of cultural studies and physical education when they're employed as we have described, isn't it?"

"Of course."

"In addition to being viable, then, the regulation we were making for our community was for the best as well."

"Yes."

"So the wives of the guardians ought to strip off; they'll be protected by goodness
rather than clothes. They'll take part in warfare and whatever else guarding the community involves, and this will be their one and only occupation. However, they will receive
lighter duties than the men, because of the weakness of their sex. Any man who treats
the fact that women are exercising naked with goodness as their goal as a reason for
laughter is 'plucking laughter unripe'; we now appreciate that he has no awareness of
what he's laughing at or what he's doing, since it's impossible, and will remain impossible, to improve on the idea that anything beneficial is commendable, and anything
harmful is deplorable."

"Absolutely."

"So may we now claim to have escaped this first wave, as it were? We've discussed what legislation to enact where women are concerned and managed to avoid being completely swamped while decreeing that our male and female guardians have to share all their occupations. In fact, the argument was internally consistent in its claim   c
that the proposals were both viable and beneficial."

"It's a pretty sizeable wave you're escaping," he remarked.

"You'll be saying it's pretty insignificant when you see the next one," I said.

"I won't see it unless you tell me about it," he said.

"It's legislation which follows from what we've just enacted and from all the laws we made earlier too, I think," I said.

"But what is it?"

"That there's to be no such thing as private marriage between these women and these men: all the women are to be shared among all the men. And that the children are   d
also to be shared, with no parent knowing which child is his, or child knowing his parent."

"This is a far bigger wave than the first one," he said, "and its viability and value are far more likely to be doubted."

"I don't see how its advantages can be called into question," I said. "If the sharing of wives and children is feasible, it's bound to be extremely valuable. I should think that most of the doubt will be concentrated upon whether or not it's viable."

"No, there are plenty of reasons to be sceptical about both aspects," he said.   e

"You mean I can't separate the two arguments?" I said. "I was hoping I'd escape from one of them, by securing your agreement to the idea's advantages, and that I'd only be left with discussing its viability."

"But you were caught escaping," he said, "and you have to justify both aspects."

"I must pay the penalty," I said, "but I ask for a little bit of leniency: please let me   458
indulge in some lazy thinking, as someone out for a solitary stroll might well do. You know how someone like that doesn't bother with the prior question of how to fulfil his desires. He doesn't want to exhaust himself wondering whether or not their fulfilment is viable, so he just imagines that they've been fulfilled and then sorts everything else out and happily details the kinds of things he's going to do when they are realized—and so makes a mind that was already lazy even lazier. Now, I'm feeling enervated myself at   b
the moment, and I'd like to delay investigating the proposals' viability until later. On the assumption that they are viable, I'll now—with your permission—look into how the rulers will sort them out in practice and prove that nothing could be more advantageous to the community and to the guardians than their enactment. This is what we'll try to investigate together first, if you approve of my suggestion, and then we'll tackle the other issue later."

"That's all right by me," he said. "Go ahead."

"Well, in my opinion," I said, "if the rulers and their auxiliaries live up to their names, then the auxiliaries will be prepared to carry out instructions, and the rulers will   c
be prepared to give them instructions. These instructions will sometimes be in direct conformity with law, but sometimes—where we've left the possibility—they'll simply reflect our legal principles."

"That sounds reasonable," he said.

"Now, you are their legislator," I said, "and once the women have been through the same selection procedure as the men, you'll send the ones who match the men's innate qualities as closely as possible to join them. Since they share living-quarters and mess-halls and since none of them has any private property of this kind, they will coexist and commingle during their exercises and their educational programme in general,   d and consequently their instincts are bound to lure them into having sex with one another. Don't you think that's bound to happen?"

"I don't think it's logically necessary," he replied, "but the imperative is coming from the sex drive, and I suppose most people find the proddings of the sex drive far more influential and compelling than those of logic!"

"They certainly do," I said. "The next point, Glaucon, is that in a community which is to be happy, undisciplined sex (or undisciplined anything else, for that matter) is a profanity, and the rulers won't allow it."

"That's because it's wrong," he said.

"So obviously our next task is to ensure that marriages are as far removed from profanity as possible—which will happen if they contribute as much as possible towards the community's welfare."

"Absolutely."

"So we need to ask how to maximize this contribution of theirs. Now, Glaucon, I've seen lots of hunting dogs and fine birds in your house, so I wonder whether you've noticed a particular aspect of their mating and procreation."

"What?" he asked.

"The main point is this. Isn't it true that although they're all pedigree creatures, some of them prove to be exceptionally good?"

"Yes."

"So do you breed from all of them indiscriminately, or do you take care to choose the outstanding ones as much as possible?"

"I choose the outstanding ones."

"And of these, do you choose the youngest ones or the oldest ones or, wherever feasible, the ones in their prime?"

"The ones in their prime."

"And wouldn't you expect the result of failure to follow this breeding programme to be the deterioration of your strain of birds and dogs?"

"Yes," he said.

"Does a different principle apply to horses and other creatures, do you think?" I asked.

"It would be odd if it did," he said.

"My dear Glaucon!" I exclaimed. "We're going to need really exceptional rulers if the same principle applies to humans too."

"Well, it does," he said. "What do you make of it?"

"That they'll be compelled to rely a great deal on medicines," I said. "As you know, we regard treating people whose bodies don't require medicine, but who are prepared to follow a diet, as within the competence of a less accomplished doctor; when medicines are called for, however, a more courageous doctor is evidently required."

"This is true, but what are you driving at?"

"That the rulers will probably have to rely a lot on falsehood and deceit," I said, "to help their subjects. You'll remember our claim that lies and so on are useful as a type of medicine."

"Yes, and there's nothing wrong with using them like that," he said.

"Well, it occurs to me that this usage is particularly important in the domain of mating and procreation."

"Why?"

"It follows from our conclusions so far that sex should preferably take place between men and women who are outstandingly good, and should occur as little as possible between men and women of a vastly inferior stamp. It also follows that the offspring of the first group should be brought up, while the offspring of the second group shouldn't. This is how to maximize the potential of our flock. And the fact that all this is happening should be concealed from everyone except the rulers themselves, if the herd of guardians is to be as free as possible from conflict."

"You're quite right," he said.

"So what we, as legislators, have to do is institute certain holidays and religious ceremonies, during which we'll bring the brides and the grooms together; and we'll have our poets compose suitable wedding-odes for them. We'll leave the quantity of marriages up to the rulers: they'll want to keep the number of men in the community more or less constant, bearing in mind wars and epidemics and so on, so as to do their best to avoid increasing or decreasing the community's size."

"Right," he said.

"We'd better set up a subtle lottery, then, so that those inferior men we spoke of blame chance and not the rulers every mating-time."

"Definitely," he said.

"And the main privilege and reward that any young men who are good at fighting or at some other activity ought to receive is the right to sleep with the women more frequently, so that as many as possible of the children are fathered by this kind of person, and there is at the same time a plausible reason for this happening."

"Right."

"Now, the officials whose job it is to take charge of any children who are born— and they could be men, women, or some of each, since positions of authority are open to both men and women equally, of course . . ."

"Yes."

"Well, I suppose they'll take the children of good parents to the crèche and hand them over to nurses (who live in a separate section of the community); and they'll find some suitable way of hiding away in some secret and secluded spot the children of worse parents and any handicapped children of good parents."

"Otherwise our breed of guardians will become tainted," he said.

"And they'll take care of the children's feeding by bringing the mothers to the crèche when their breasts are full of milk, although they'll devise all sorts of stratagems to make sure that no mother recognizes her own child. If the mothers' supply of milk is inadequate, they'll bring in other women to supplement it. They'll take care that the mothers don't breast-feed for too long, and they'll assign sleepless nights and all the hard work to wet-nurses and nannies."

"You're making child-bearing very easy for the wives of the guardians," he remarked.

"Which is only right and proper," I said. "But let's get on with the next item of our proposals. We said that the children's parents should be in their prime, didn't we?"

"True."

"Do you agree that a woman is in her prime for twenty years or so, and a man for thirty years or so?"

"Which twenty or thirty years?" he asked.

"A woman can serve the community by producing children between the ages of twenty and forty, a man by fathering children from when he passes his peak as a runner until the age of fifty-five."

"Yes, in both cases this is the period when they're in their physical and intellectual prime," he said.

"Therefore, if the production of children for the community is encroached on by anyone too old or too young, we'll say that he has sinned against both gods and men by fathering a child who (if the matter goes unnoticed and the child is born) will not have been affected by the rites and prayers which the priestesses and priests and the whole community pray at each wedding-festival—for every generation of children to improve

b   on their parents' goodness and value—but will instead have been born under the influence of darkness and dire lack of self-control."

"Right," he said.

"And even if a man's age doesn't exclude him from procreation," I said, "the same regulation will apply if he has sex with a woman of the right age when a ruler has not paired them. We'll declare the child he's trying to foist on the community a bastard, without standing or sanction."

"Quite right," he said.

"When the men and women get past the age for procreation, I imagine we'll release them and allow them the freedom to have sex with anyone they want—except that

c   a man is forbidden to have sex with a daughter and her female offspring, and a mother and her female precursors, and a woman is forbidden to have sex with a son, a father, and their male descendants and precursors. But before we release them, we'll impress upon them the importance of trying their best to abort absolutely every pregnancy that occurs, and of ensuring that any baby born despite their efforts is not brought up."

"Yes, that's a sensible proposal," he said. "But how are they to tell who are whose

d   fathers and daughters and so on?"

"They won't be able to," I said. "However, a man will call any child born in the tenth month, and in the seventh month of course, after he participated in one of the wedding-ceremonies a son (if the child is male) or daughter (if female); they'll call him father and their children will be his grandchildren, who'll regard his generation as grandfathers and grandmothers, and who'll count anyone born in the period when their mothers and fathers were producing children as their sisters and brothers. The result

e   will be what we were just saying: they'll avoid sex with one another. However, the law will allow brothers and sisters to sleep together, if the lottery turns out that way and the Delphic oracle has no objection."

"You're quite right," he said.

"So this is how your community's guardians will share women and children, Glaucon. We next need to have the argument confirm that this is basically in keeping with the constitution and that it is by far the best course of action. Isn't that the thing to do?"

462   "Definitely," he said.

"Shouldn't we initiate the enquiry by asking ourselves which factor, in our opinion, makes the most important positive contribution towards the organization of a community—and this is the factor a legislator has to aim for when he's making his laws—and which factor does the most harm? Then we should try to see whether these new proposals of ours match the traces of the good factor and not of the harmful one."

"Absolutely."

"Could we describe anything as worse for a community, do you think, than some-

b   thing which tears it apart and destroys its unity? And could we describe anything as better for a community than something which binds it together and unifies it?"

"No, we couldn't."

"And isn't it the sharing of feelings of pleasure and distress which binds a community together—when (in so far as it is feasible) the whole citizen body feels more or less the same pleasure or distress at the same gains and losses?"

"Absolutely," he said.

"And isn't it, on the other hand, the non-sharing of these feelings which causes disintegration—when something happens to the community or some of its members and the attendant feelings range from depression to delight?"   c

"Naturally."

"And doesn't this privatization of feelings happen when the members of a community are out of tune with one another when they use expressions like 'mine' and 'not mine,' and likewise when they identify something as foreign?"

"Absolutely."

"So the best-run community is the one in which as many people as possible use these expressions, 'mine' and 'not mine,' to refer to the same things in the same respects. Yes?"

"Definitely."

"And the one which approximates as much as possible to a single human being? I mean, when someone's finger is hurt, the whole federation, which encompasses body and mind in its span and forms a single organized system under its ruling part, is aware of the pain and feels it, as a whole, along with the injured part, and that's   d why we say that the person has hurt his finger. And the same principle applies to any other part of a person, whether it's experiencing the discomfort of pain or the relief of pleasure."

"Yes, I agree," he said. "And, to answer your question, yes—the more closely a community's organization approximates to this situation, the better run that community is."

"So in this kind of community, any experience—whether good or bad—of any of its members will in all likelihood be regarded as its own experience, and the community   e as a whole will share the affected member's feelings of pleasure or pain."

"Yes, that's bound to be the case in a well-regulated community," he said.

"Now would be a good time," I said, "for us to return to our community, and see whether it is the pre-eminent example of a community with the qualities we've just formulated, or whether some other community surpasses it."

"Yes, we ought to do that," he said.

"All right. Now, our community—like every community—contains both rulers   463 and commoners, doesn't it?"

"Yes."

"Who all refer to one another as fellow citizens?"

"Of course."

"But in other communities the commoners call the rulers something else besides 'fellow citizens,' don't they?"

"Yes, in most communities they call them 'masters,' and in democracies they call them just that—'rulers.'"

"What about in our community? How will the general populace think of the rulers, apart from thinking of them as fellow citizens?"

"As their protectors and defenders," he said.   b

"And how will *they* regard the general populace?"

"As their paymasters and quartermasters."

"In other communities how do rulers regard the general populace?"

"As slaves," he said.

"And one another?"

"As fellow rulers," he said.

"How do our rulers regard one another?"

"As fellow guardians."

"Would you say that in other communities a ruler might regard some of his fellow rulers as friends and others as strangers?"

"Yes, that commonly happens."

c   "And he regards and describes his friends as belonging to his circle, and the strangers as nothing to do with him?"

"Yes."

"What about the guardians in your community? Could any of them regard or refer to a fellow guardian as a stranger?"

"Certainly not," he said. "He'll be regarding everyone he meets as a brother or a sister, a father or a mother, a son or a daughter, a grandchild or a grandparent."

"Excellently put," I said. "But here's another question for you. As legislator, will you be obliging them only to label one another relatives, or also to make all their be-
d   haviour conform to these labels? Take their fathers, for instance: will they have to show their fathers all the usual respect and care and obedience due to parents, or else have both gods and men think the worse of them for their unjust and immoral behaviour? Will these be the traditions which every single citizen of your community will din into the ears of the children from their earliest years about the people they are told to regard as fathers and about all their other relatives, or will you have different traditions?"

e   "No, I'll have the ones you've mentioned," he said. "It would be ridiculous for them only to mouth these family labels without it affecting their behaviour."

"So there's no community in which it's more likely that, when one of its members does well or badly, people will be in tune with one another in using the expression we mentioned, and will say, 'The success is mine' or 'The failure is mine.'"

"That's absolutely true," he said.

464   "Well, didn't we say that when people hold this belief and use this expression they start to share feelings of pleasure and distress?"

"We did, and we were right."

"Isn't it above all the members of our community, then, who will genuinely share and refer to the same thing as 'mine'? And because they share in this way, they'll share feelings of pleasure and distress more than anyone else, won't they?"

"Much more."

"And, apart from the general constitution of the community, it's the fact that the guardians share their women and children that is responsible for this, isn't it?"

"Yes, that's by far the most important factor," he said.

b   "Now, our conclusion was that there is nothing better for a community than this sharing of feelings. We compared a well-run community to a body, and pointed out what a body does in relation to the pleasure and pain of its parts."

"Yes, and the conclusion was right," he said.

"So we've demonstrated that the community's greatest benefit is due to the fact that its defenders share their women and children."

"We certainly have," he said.

"Moreover, this conclusion goes with what we were saying earlier. I mean, we did
c   say that genuine guardians shouldn't own houses or land or anything, but should be given their food by others, as payment for their guarding, and should all eat together."

"Right," he said.

"Isn't it the case, as I say, that both our earlier proposals and the current ones increase the likelihood of their being genuine guardians, and prevent them tearing the community apart by using the expression 'mine' to refer not to the same thing, but to various things? Different people call different things 'mine' when they each have their
d   own houses into which they pull anything they can keep out of the hands of others, and

when they each have their own wife and children; and this situation introduces into the community the personal pleasures and pains of private individuals. Aren't they more likely to be genuine guardians if they all regard the same things as within their circle of interest, tend in the same direction, and feel pleasure and pain, as much as possible, under the same circumstances?"

"Absolutely," he said.

"And won't trials and lawsuits against one another be almost non-existent, since they'll own nothing except their bodies and share everything else? And consequently they'll be free of all the conflict that arises when people have money or children and relatives."   e

"That's more or less inevitable," he said.

"Lawsuits for assault or bodily harm won't be part of their moral code either, because we'll make it a moral obligation for people in any given age-group to defend themselves against their peers, which will force them to take care of their bodies."

"Right," he said.

"There's something else that makes this regulation right too," I said. "If an angry   465 person satisfies his rage like this, he's less likely to escalate the matter into a major conflict."

"Yes."

"Now, we'll have given older people authority over younger ones and made them responsible for disciplining them."

"Obviously."

"And it's unlikely that younger people will ever try to assault or strike their elders (unless ordered to do so by the rulers), or show them disrespect in any other way. There are two guardians whose presence is enough to stop them—fear and respect. Respect will stop them laying hands on their parents, and they'll be afraid of all the help any vic-   b tim would get from people who regard themselves as his sons or brothers or fathers."

"Yes, that's what would happen," he said.

"So thanks to our legislation they'll live together in perfect peace, don't you think?"

"Definitely."

"And because of their freedom from in-fighting, there is no danger of a rift ever forming between them and the rest of the community or within the rest of the community."

"No, there isn't."

"For fear of sounding a discordant note, I hardly like even to mention the trivial mischiefs they'll avoid. There's how poor people have to flatter the rich; there are all the   c problems and worries they suffer while they're having their children educated, and because in order to support a household they're forced to raise money by borrowing, by refusing to pay back debts, by doing whatever it takes to make an income—only to hand the accumulated money over to their wives and servants to spend on housekeeping. There are a number of different burdens one finds in this context, but they're too obvious and demeaning to be worth mentioning."

"Yes, even a blind man could see them," he said.   d

"So they'll avoid all these troubles, and they'll live more happily than any Olympic victor."

"Why?"

"The happiness which people attribute to Olympic victors is due to a tiny fraction of what our guardians have. The guardians' victory is more splendid, and their upkeep by the general populace is more thorough-going. The fruit of their victory is the preservation of the whole community, their prize the maintenance of themselves and their children with food and all of life's essentials. During their lifetimes they are honoured by their community, and when they die they are buried in high style."

"These are excellent prizes," he said.

"Do you remember," I asked, "that earlier someone or other criticized us for failing to make the guardians happy because, although they could take possession of the property of everyone in the community, they actually had nothing? We said we'd look into the matter later, if it was convenient, and that for the time being we were making our guardians guardians and making our community as happy as we could, and that it wasn't our intention to single out one particular group within the community and devise happiness just for them."

"I remember," he said.

"Well, since we now think that our auxiliaries live a far better and more rewarding life than any Olympic victor, we're hardly going to place it at the same level as the life of a shoemaker or any of our other urban or rural workers, are we?"

"I don't think so," he answered.

"Nevertheless, the comment I made at the time is also fair in this context. If a guardian aims for the kind of happiness which is incompatible with his being a guardian—if the moderate, secure, and outstanding lifestyle we've described is not enough for him and, under the influence of some idiotic and immature conception of happiness, he sets about exploiting his power to appropriate all the community's assets for himself, he'll start to appreciate how wise Hesiod was when he said that in a sense 'half is more than a whole.'"

"I'd recommend him to keep to the guardian's life," he said.

"Do you agree, then," I said, "that the best course is for the men and women to receive the same education, share children, and co-operate in the guarding of the rest of their fellow citizens, as we've described? And do you agree that whether it involves staying within the community or going out to war, the women should help in the guarding and hunting, as female dogs do? They should share in everything as much as they can, and this will not only be the best course of action for them, but is also not incompatible with their nature, as compared with masculinity, and is the kind of partnership which nature intended for the two sexes?"

"Yes, I agree," he said.

"Well, we still have to decide," I said, "whether in fact, and under what circumstances, this sharing is viable among humans, as it is among other species."

"I was just about to take you up on that very point," he said, "but you got in first."

"Because it's obvious what they'll do about warfare, I suppose," I said.

"What?" he asked.

"Men and women will campaign together, and they'll also take any sturdy children with them to war, so that they see the work they'll have to do when they become adults, just as the children of other kinds of workmen do. But the children won't just watch: they'll also act as apprentices and servants in all aspects of war, and look after their fathers and mothers. I mean, you must have noticed what happens in the case of other occupations—how the children of potters, say, spend a long time as apprentices and observers before getting involved in any actual pottery."

"Yes, I know."

"And should potters take more care than the guardians over educating their children by familiarizing them and letting them observe their duties?"

"That would be ridiculous," he said.

"Moreover, every creature fights better, anyway, when its offspring are around."

"True. But Socrates, aren't they running quite a risk? If they fail, which is always a possibility in war, then they'll be responsible for their children being killed as well as themselves, and for the rest of the community finding it impossible to recover."

"You're right," I said. "But the main point is: do you think they should be provided with a risk-free life?"

"Certainly not."

"Well, if they have to face danger, shouldn't it be when the result of success will be an improvement in their conditions?"

"Obviously."

"And do you think it hardly matters—not enough to compensate for the danger— whether or not the children who are to become soldiers when they're adults observe warfare and all it entails?" c

"No, it does make a difference, in the sense you're talking about."

"It'll be best, then, if our primary objective is having the children observe warfare, but we also find ways to keep them safe. Right?"

"Yes."

"Well, the chief point," I said, "is that their fathers will know all that can humanly be known about warfare, and will therefore be able to distinguish risky military ventures from safe ones." d

"That's likely," he said.

"So they'll take them to the one kind and steer clear of the others."

"Right."

"And they'll not be putting second-rate supervisors in charge of them, but people who thanks to their experience and their age are qualified to act as guides and attendants."

"Yes, that's the right thing to do."

"Still, we're agreed that the unexpected often occurs."

"Yes."

"And that is why we'd better equip our children with wings from an early age, my friend, so that they can escape by flying away, if they have to."

"I don't understand," he said. e

"We have to put them on horseback," I explained, "from the earliest possible age, and they can go and watch campaigns only when they've been taught to ride. The horses they go on won't be excitable or aggressive, but will be the fastest and most manageable ones available. That's the best way for them to take stock of their work, and they'll have no difficulty in following the older people who are their guides to safety if necessary."

"I think you're right," he said.

"What about warfare?" I asked. "What attitudes do you want your soldiers to have towards themselves and towards the enemy? Do you think my ideas are correct or not?" 468

"Tell me them," he said.

"Shouldn't anyone who deserts or discards his weapons or does anything cowardly like that be made an artisan or a farmer?" I asked.

"Yes."

"And anyone who is taken alive by the enemy should be presented to his captors, and they can treat this catch of theirs in any way they choose."

"Absolutely." b

"What about someone who distinguishes himself for outstanding bravery? Shouldn't he first, before returning home from the campaign, be crowned with chaplets by each of his comrades-in-arms—the young men and the children—one by one? Is that a good idea, do you think, or not?"

"I think so."

"And should they take him by the hand?"

"Yes, that too."

"But I don't think you'll go so far as to agree with my next idea," I said.

"What is it?"

"That he should kiss and be kissed by each of his comrades."

c   "That's very important indeed," he said. "In fact, I'll add a rider to your regulation: for the duration of that campaign, no one he wants to kiss is allowed to refuse. This will make anyone who happens to be in love with a male or female comrade try harder to win the prize for bravery."

"That's an excellent idea," I said, "because we've already said that a good man will be allowed to participate in a greater number of marriage ceremonies than others and that it will invariably be a good man rather than anyone else who is selected for them, so that as many children as possible are fathered by men of this type."

"Yes, I remember," he said.

"Moreover, Homer too approved of rewarding young men for their goodness. He

d   said that for distinguishing himself in battle Ajax 'was awarded the whole length of the chine'—this being an appropriate reward for vigour and valour because it's simultaneously a source of strength as well as a reward."

"You're quite right," he said.

"We'll let Homer be our guide in this matter, then," I said. "I mean, we too will use religious rites and so on as occasions for rewarding anyone who has displayed virtue not only with odes and the privileges we've been talking about, but also 'with the seat of honour, with the best cuts of meat, and with goblets full of wine,' so that we simultaneously give our virtuous men and women an opportunity for training as well as a

e   reward."

"That's an exceptionally good idea," he said.

"All right. Now, what about those who die during the course of a campaign? In the first place, we must count anyone who dies a glorious death as a member of the golden caste, mustn't we?"

"Definitely."

"And we'll believe Hesiod when he says that after people of this kind die 'they

469   become pure deities attached to the earth, who in their goodness guard mortal men and keep them from harm.' Right?"

"Yes, we will."

"So won't we consult Apollo to find out how to lay to rest men of superhuman stature and what special things to do, and then bury them in the way he prescribes?"

"Of course."

"And thereafter we'll regard their tombs as the tombs of deities, and we'll tend to

b   them and worship there, won't we? And don't you think we should institute the same custom whenever anyone who during his lifetime was acknowledged to be exceptionally good dies of old age or whatever?"

"Yes, that's the right thing to do," he said.

"Now, what attitude will our soldiers have towards their enemies?"

"In what sense?"

"Take enslavement first. Do you think it's right for communities of Greeks to enslave other Greeks? Shouldn't they do their best to prevent any other community from enslaving Greeks and make it the norm to spare anyone of Greek stock, for fear of

c   themselves being enslaved by non-Greeks?"

"It's absolutely crucial that they spare Greeks," he said.

"Not only should they not own Greek slaves themselves, then, but they should also advise other Greeks to follow their example."

"Yes," he said. "That should encourage them to concentrate on non-Greeks and leave one another alone."

"And what about the victors despoiling the dead? Taking their weapons is all right, but otherwise is it a good practice? I mean, doesn't it provide an excuse for cowards not to advance against an enemy who is still fighting, because they can make out that they're doing their duty by poking around among the corpses? This sort of looting has often in the past been the ruin of armies." d

"I quite agree."

"Plundering corpses seems mean and mercenary, don't you think? And treating the body of a dead person as an enemy, when the hostile element has flown off and only the instrument it once used for fighting remains, seems to indicate a womanly, petty mind. I mean, do you think there's any difference between this behaviour and that of e dogs who, if they're hit with stones, get annoyed at the stones, but don't go anywhere near the person who threw them?"

"That's an absolutely perfect analogy," he replied.

"So we'd better avoid the practice of plundering corpses and also preventing our opponents from recovering the bodies of their dead, don't you think?"

"Yes, we certainly should," he said.

"And we won't be taking arms and armour to our temples as trophies either, especially if they came from Greeks, if we're the slightest bit interested in being on good 470 terms with other Greeks. We're more likely to be afraid of the possible pollution involved in robbing our kin of their weapons and taking them to a sacred site, except when the practice is divinely sanctioned."

"You're quite right," he said.

"What about devastating the land and burning the homes of Greeks? How will your troops behave towards their enemies?"

"I'd be glad to hear what you have to say about this," he said.

"Well, I think they'll avoid both practices," I said, "and only steal the annual harvest. Shall I tell you why?" b

"Yes, please."

"I think that the fact that there are these two separate terms, war and conflict, is indicative of the existence of two things with separate distinguishing features. One of the two is an internal affair, within a single domain; the other is an external affair, crossing borders. 'Conflict' refers to the hostility of an internal element, 'war' to that of an external element."

"No one could fault what you're saying in the slightest," he said.

"I wonder if you'll find the next point just as sound. I maintain that Greeks are c bonded to one another by internal ties of blood and kinship, but interact with non-Greeks as people who are foreign and live outside their domain."

"That's right," he said.

"When Greeks and non-Greeks fight, then, we'll describe this as warfare, and claim that they are natural enemies and that the term 'war' should refer to this type of hostility. But when Greeks get involved in this kind of thing with other Greeks, we'll claim that they are natural friends, and that in a situation like this, Greece is diseased and in conflict, and we'll maintain that the term 'conflict' should refer to this type of hostility." d

"I for one agree with your view," he said.

"Now that we've agreed what conflict is," I said, "imagine it happening, imagine a community divided against itself, and you'll see that, if each side devastates the other side's land and burns their homes, conflict comes across as an abomination and neither side can be regarded as patriotic, since if they were, they would stop short of ravaging their nurse and their mother. However, it seems reasonable for the winners to take the

e   losers' crops, and it smacks of aiming for reconciliation rather than perpetual warfare."

"Yes, there's far more compassion in this aim," he said.

"Well, this community you're founding is going to be Greek, isn't it?" I asked.

"Of course," he answered.

"And its members will be good, compassionate people, won't they?"

"Certainly."

"Won't they feel warmth for their fellow Greeks? Won't they regard Greece as their own land and join all other Greeks in their common religious rites?"

"They certainly will."

471   "Then they'll regard any dissension between themselves and Greeks as conflict, since Greeks are their own people, and they won't even use the term 'war' in this context, will they?"

"No."

"So in times of dissension they'll be looking for reconciliation, won't they?"

"Yes."

"So they won't be motivated by hatred, but by wanting to bring their opponents to their senses. As disciplinarians, then, rather than enemies, they won't punish their opponents with enslavement or death."

"That's right," he said.

"And as Greeks, they won't ravage Greece either, or burn homes, or conclude that the whole population of a given community—men, women, and children—is hostile to them, but only those few hostile people who were responsible for the dissension. All

b   these reasons will make them unwilling to ravage their opponents' land or demolish their houses, since the majority of the population will be their friends; instead, they will see the dispute through until the point is reached when those who are innocent have suffered enough and they force the guilty few to pay for what they've done."

"I agree that this is the attitude the members of our community ought to have towards their opponents," he said. "And they'll reserve for non-Greeks the treatment Greeks currently give one another."

c   "Shall we include this rule among our regulations for the guardians, then—that they are not to devastate land or burn houses?"

"Yes," he said, "and let's add that it and our earlier regulations are all good."

"I get the impression, though, Socrates, that this is the kind of topic where, if no one interrupts you, you'll forget that it is all a digression from a previous topic—that is, whether this political system is viable, and if so, how. I accept that all these practices, if realized, would be good for any community they were practised in, and I can supplement your account: they are highly likely to fight well against enemy forces, in so far as

d   they are highly unlikely to abandon one another, since they regard one another as brothers, fathers, sons, and call one another by these names; if women joined them on a campaign (whether their task was to fight alongside the men or to support them in the rear), they'd have the effect of terrifying the enemy and could come up as reinforcements in an emergency, and I'm sure this would make our militia completely invincible; and I

e   can see all the domestic benefits they'd bring which you haven't mentioned. You can take for granted my agreement that the realization of the constitution would result in all these advantages and innumerable others as well; so you don't have to talk about the actual constitution any more. Let's just try now to convince ourselves that it is viable and to find out how it is viable, and let's not bother with anything else."

"I wasn't expecting you to ambush my argument like this," I said. "Can't you   472
sympathize with my procrastination? Perhaps you don't realize that it was hard enough
for me to escape from the first two waves, and now you're invoking the largest and most
problematic of the set of three waves. When you see it and hear it, then you'll sympathize with me and see that it was perfectly realistic of me to have misgivings and qualms
about proposing such a paradoxical idea for investigation."

"The more you say this kind of thing," he said, "the less likely we are to let you
off discussing how this political system might be realized. Please don't waste any more   b
time: just get on with it."

"Well, the first thing we have to do," I said, "is remember that it's our search for
the nature of morality and immorality that has brought us here."

"All right," he said. "So what?"

"Nothing really. It's just that if we do discover what morality is, will we expect a
moral man to be indistinguishable from it, and to be a perfect image of morality? Or   c
will we be satisfied if he resembles it as closely as possible and participates in it more
thoroughly than anyone else?"

"Yes, we'll be happy with that," he said.

"Therefore," I said, "it's because we need a paradigm that we're trying to find out
what morality is, and are asking whether a perfectly moral man could exist and, if so,
what he would be like (and likewise for immorality and an immoral man). We want to
be able to look at these men, to see how they stand as regards happiness and misery, and
to face the inevitable conclusion about ourselves, that the more we resemble these exemplars, the more our condition will resemble their condition. In other words, the pur-   d
pose of our enquiry is not to try to prove that perfect morality or immorality could ever
actually exist."

"True," he said.

"Do you doubt an artist's competence if he paints a paradigmatically good-looking
human being, and portrays everything perfectly well in the painting, but can't prove that a
person like that could actually exist?"

"I certainly do not," he protested.

"Well, aren't we saying that we're trying to construct a theoretical paradigm of a
good community?"

"Yes."   e

"Then do you doubt our competence as theoreticians in this context if we can't
prove that a community with our theoretical constitution could actually exist?"

"Of course not," he said.

"So that's how matters really stand," I said. "However, if for your sake I also have
to apply myself to proving how and under what circumstances it might get as close as
possible to viability, then although this is a different kind of argument, I must ask you to
make the same concession as before."

"What concession?"

"Is it possible for anything actual to match a theory? Isn't any actual thing bound   473
to have less contact with truth than a theory, however much people deny it? Do you
agree or not?"

"I do," he said.

"So please don't force me to point to an actual case in the material world which
conforms in all respects to our theoretical construct. If we can discover how a community's administration could come very close to our theory, then let's say that we've fulfilled your demands and discovered how it's all viable. I mean, won't you be satisfied if   b
we get that close? I would."

"I would too," he said.

"Next, then, I suppose we should try to discover and show what the flaw is in current political systems which stops communities being governed as well as we've described, and what the smallest change is which could enable a community to achieve this type of constitution. By the smallest change, I mean preferably a single change, but if that's impossible, then two changes, or at any rate as few as possible and the least drastic ones possible."

c   "Absolutely," he said.

"Well," I said, "I think there is a single change which can be shown to bring about the transformation. It's not a small change, however, or easy to achieve, but it is feasible."

"What is it?" he asked.

"I'm now about to confront the difficulty which, in our image, is the largest wave," I said. "Still, it must be voiced, even if it's going to swamp us, exactly like a wave, with scornful and contemptuous laughter. Are you ready for me to speak?"

"Go ahead," he said.

"Unless communities have philosophers as kings," I said, "or the people who are
d   currently called kings and rulers practise philosophy with enough integrity—in other words, unless political power and philosophy coincide, and all the people with their diversity of talents who currently head in different directions towards either government or philosophy have those doors shut firmly in their faces—there can be no end to political troubles, my dear Glaucon, or even to human troubles in general, I'd say, and our
e   theoretical constitution will be stillborn and will never see the light of day. Now you can appreciate what made me hesitate to speak before: I saw how very paradoxical it would sound, since it is difficult to realize that there is no other way for an individual or a community to achieve happiness."

"What a thing to say, Socrates!" Glaucon said in response. "This is quite an idea! Now that it's out in the open, you'd better expect hordes of people—and not second-rate
474   people either—to fling off their clothes (so to speak), pick up the nearest weapon, and rush naked at you with enough energy to achieve heroic feats. And if you don't come up with an argument to keep them at bay while you make your escape, then your punishment will be to discover what scorn really is."

"And it'll all be your fault, won't it?" I said.

"I've no regrets," he replied. "But that doesn't mean I'll desert you: I'll defend you to the best of my ability. Goodwill and encouragement are my arsenal, and my an-
b   swers probably suit you more than someone else's might. You can count on this assistance, so please try to win the sceptics round to your point of view."

"You're providing such major support that I must make the effort," I said. "Now, in my opinion, we'll never escape from the people you mentioned unless we offer them a definition of a philosopher so that it is clear what we mean by our rash claim that philosophers should have political power. When there's no doubt about what it is to be
c   a philosopher, then a defence becomes possible, if we can show that some people are made to practise philosophy and to be political leaders, while others shouldn't engage in philosophy and should follow a leader."

"The definition would be timely," he remarked.

"All right. I wonder if this route leads to any kind of adequate clarification. Why don't you join me, and we'll see?"

"Lead on," he said.

"I'm sure you're aware, without me having to remind you," I said, "that if the claim that someone loves something is to be accurate, he must undeniably love that thing as a whole, not just some aspects of it."

"You've got to remind me, apparently," he said, "because I don't quite under-   d
stand."

"I'd have expected someone else to say that, Glaucon, not you," I said. "It's unlike an expert in love to forget that an amorous lover finds some pretext for being smit-
ten and unhinged by every single alluring boy. They all seem to deserve his attention
and devotion. I mean, isn't this how you and others like you behave towards good-
looking young men? Don't you compliment a snub nose by calling it 'pert,' describe a
hooked nose as 'regal,' and call one which falls between these two extremes 'perfectly   e
proportioned'? Don't you call swarthy young men 'virile' and pallid ones 'children of
the gods'? And who do you think invented the term 'honey coloured'? It could only
have been some lover glossing over and making light of a sallow complexion, because
its possessor was in the alluring period of adolescence. In short, you come up with
every conceivable excuse and all kinds of terms to ensure that you can give your ap-   475
proval to every alluring lad."

"If you insist on trying out your ideas of how lovers behave on me," he said, "you
can have my assent, because I don't want to jeopardize the argument."

"And haven't you seen people who are fond of drinking behave in exactly the
same way?" I went on. "They make all kinds of excuses for their devotion to wine of
every kind."

"Yes."

"And I'm sure you've noticed that if ambitious people can't get the command of
a whole army, they take a company; and if they can't win the respect of important and   b
high-powered people, they're happy to be respected by lesser people. It's status in general which they desire."

"Absolutely."

"So tell me where you stand on this question. If in our opinion someone desires
something, are we to say that he desires that type of thing as a whole, or only some aspects of it?"

"The whole of it," he replied.

"So the same goes for a philosopher too: we're to say that what he desires is the
whole of knowledge, not just some aspects of it. True?"

"True."

"If someone fusses about his lessons, then, especially when he's still young and
without rational understanding of what is and isn't good for him, we can't describe him   c
as a lover of knowledge, a philosopher, just as we can't describe someone who is fuss-
ing about his food as hungry, as desiring food, and don't call him a gourmand, but a
poor eater."

"Yes, it would be wrong to call him anything else."

"On the other hand, if someone is glad to sample every subject and eagerly sets
about his lessons with an insatiable appetite, then we'd be perfectly justified in calling
him a philosopher, don't you think?"

"Then a motley crowd of people will be philosophers," Glaucon said. "For in-   d
stance, sightseers all do what they do because they enjoy learning, I suppose; and it
would be very odd to count theatre-goers as philosophers, when they'd never go oftheir
own accord to hear a lecture or spend time over anything like that, but they rush around
the festivals of Dionysus to hear every theatrical troupe, as if they were getting paid for
the use of their ears, and never miss a single festival, whether it's being held in town or
out of town. Are we to describe all these people and the disciples of other amusements
as philosophers? And what about students of trivial branches of expertise?"   e

"No," I replied, "they're not philosophers, but they resemble philosophers."

"Who are the true philosophers you have in mind?" he asked.

"Sightseers of the truth," I answered.

"That must be right, but what exactly does it mean?" he asked.

"It wouldn't be easy to explain to anyone else," I said. "But you'll grant me this, surely."

"What?"

"Since beautiful is the opposite of ugly, they are two things."

476   "Of course."

"In so far as they are two, each of them is single?"

"Yes."

"And the same principle applies to moral and immoral, good and bad, and every-thing of any type: in itself, each of them is single, but each of them has a plurality of manifestations because they appear all over the place, as they become associated with actions and bodies and one another."

"You're right," he said.

"Well," I continued, "this is what enables me to distinguish the sightseers (to bor-row your term) and the ones who want to acquire some expertise or other and the men
b   of action from the people in question, the ones who are philosophers in the true sense of the term."

"What do you mean?" he asked.

"Theatre-goers and sightseers are devoted to beautiful sounds and colours and shapes, and to works of art which consist of these elements, but their minds are consti-tutionally incapable of seeing and devoting themselves to beauty itself."

"Yes, that's certainly right," he said.

"However, people with the ability to approach beauty itself and see beauty as it actually is are bound to be few and far between, aren't they?"

c   "Definitely."

"So does someone whose horizon is limited to beautiful things, with no concep-tion of beauty itself, and who is incapable of following guidance as to how to gain knowledge of beauty itself, strike you as living in a dream-world or in the real world? Look at it this way. Isn't dreaming precisely the state, whether one is asleep or awake, of taking something to be the real thing, when it is actually only a likeness?"

"Yes, that's what I'd say dreaming is," he said.

"And what about someone who does the opposite—who does think that there is
d   such a thing as beauty itself, and has the ability to see it as well as the things which par-take in it, and never gets them muddled up? Do you think he's living in the real world or in a dream-world?"

"Definitely in the real world," he said.

"So wouldn't we be right to describe the difference between their mental states by saying that while this person has knowledge, the other one has beliefs?"

"Yes."

"Now, suppose this other person—the one we're saying has beliefs, not knowledge—were to get cross with us and query the truth of our assertions. Will we be
e   able to calm him down and gently convince him of our point of view, while keeping him in the dark about the poor state of his health?"

"We really ought to," he said.

"All right, but what shall we say to him, do you think? Perhaps this is what we should ask him. We'll tell him that we don't resent any knowledge he might have—indeed, we'd be delighted to see that he does know something—and then we'll say, 'But can you tell us, please, whether someone with knowledge knows something or nothing?' You'd better answer my questions for him."

"My answer will be that he knows something," he said.

"Something real or something unreal?"

"Real. How could something unreal be known?"   477

"We could look at the matter from more angles, but we're happy enough with the idea that something completely real is completely accessible to knowledge, and something utterly unreal is entirely inaccessible to knowledge. Yes?"

"Perfectly happy."

"All right. But if something is in a state of both reality and unreality, then it falls between that which is perfectly real and that which is utterly unreal, doesn't it?"

"Yes."

"So since the field of knowledge is reality, and since it must be incomprehension whose field is unreality, then we need to find out if there is in fact something which falls between incomprehension and knowledge, whose field is this intermediate, don't we?"   b

"Yes."

"Now, we acknowledge the existence of belief, don't we?"

"Of course."

"Is it a different faculty from knowledge, or is it the same?"

"Different."

"Every faculty has its own distinctive abilities, so belief and knowledge must have different domains."

"Yes."

"Now, since the natural field of knowledge is reality—its function is to know reality as reality. . . . Actually, I think there's something else we need to get clear about first."

"What?"

"Shall we count as a distinct class of things the faculties which give human beings   c
and all other creatures their abilities? By 'faculties' I mean things like sight and hearing. Do you understand the type of thing I have in mind?"

"Yes, I do," he said.

"Let me tell you something that strikes me about them. I can't distinguish one faculty from another the way I commonly distinguish other things, by looking at their colours or shapes or anything like that, because faculties don't have any of those sorts of qualities for me to look at. The only aspect of a faculty I can look at is its field, its effect.   d
This is what enables me to identify each of them as a particular faculty. Where I find a single domain and a single effect, I say there is a single faculty; and I distinguish faculties which have different fields and different effects. What about you? What do you do?"

"The same as you," he said.

"Let's go back to where we were before, then, Glaucon," I said.

"Do you think that knowledge is a faculty, or does it belong in your opinion to some other class?"

"I think it belongs to that class," he said, "and is the most powerful of all the faculties."

"And shall we classify belief as a faculty, or what?"   e

"As a faculty," he said. "Belief is precisely that which enables us to entertain beliefs."

"Not long ago, however, you agreed that knowledge and belief were different."

"Of course," he said. "One is infallible and the other is fallible, so anyone with any sense would keep them separate."

"Good," I said. "There can be no doubt of our position: Knowledge and belief are different."

"Yes."

"Since they're different faculties, then, they have different natural fields, don't they?"

"Necessarily."

"The field of knowledge is reality, isn't it? Its function is to know the reality of anything real?"

"Yes."

"And the function of belief, we're saying, is to entertain beliefs?"

"Yes."

"Does it entertain beliefs about the same thing which knowledge knows? Will what is accessible to knowledge and what is accessible to belief be identical? Or is that out of the question?"

b   "It's ruled out by what we've already agreed," he said. "If different faculties naturally have different fields, and if both knowledge and belief are faculties, and different faculties too, as we said, then it follows that it is impossible for what is accessible to knowledge and what is accessible to belief to be identical."

"So if it is reality that is accessible to knowledge, then it is something else, not reality, that is accessible to belief, isn't it?"

"Yes."

"Does it entertain beliefs about what is unreal? Or is it also impossible for that to happen? Think about this: isn't it the case that someone who is entertaining a belief is bringing his believing mind to bear on something? I mean, is it possible to have a belief, and to be believing nothing?"

"That's impossible."

"In fact, someone who has a belief has some single thing in mind, doesn't he?"

"Yes."

"But the most accurate way to refer to something unreal would be to say that it is nothing, not that it is a single thing, wouldn't it?"

c   "Yes."

"Didn't we find ourselves forced to relate incomprehension to unreality and knowledge to reality?"

"That's right," he said.

"So the field of belief is neither reality nor unreality?"

"No."

"Belief can't be incomprehension or knowledge, then?"

"So it seems."

"Well, does it lie beyond their limits? Does it shed more light than knowledge or spread more obscurity than incomprehension?"

"It does neither."

"Alternatively, does belief strike you as more opaque than knowledge and more lucid than incomprehension?"

"Considerably more," he said.

d   "It lies within their limits?"

"Yes."

"Then belief must fall between them."

"Absolutely."

"Now, didn't we say earlier that something which is simultaneously real and unreal (were such a thing to be shown to exist) would fall between the perfectly real and the wholly unreal, and wouldn't be the field of either knowledge or incomprehension, but of an intermediate (again, if such a thing were shown to exist) between incomprehension and knowledge?"

"Right."

"And now we've found that what we call belief is such an intermediate, haven't we?"

"We have."

"So the only thing left for us to discover, apparently, is whether there's anything   e
which partakes of both reality and unreality, and cannot be said to be perfectly real or perfectly unreal. If we were to come across such a thing, we'd be fully justified in describing it as the field of belief, on the principle that extremes belong together, and so do intermediates. Do you agree?"

"Yes."

"Let's return, on this basis, to the give and take of conversation with that fine fellow who doesn't acknowledge the existence of beauty itself or think that beauty itself   479
has any permanent and unvarying character, but takes the plurality of beautiful things as his norm—that sightseer who can't under any circumstances abide the notion that beauty, morality, and so on are each a single entity. What we'll say to him is, 'My friend, is there one beautiful thing, in this welter of beautiful things, which won't turn out to be ugly? Is there one moral deed which won't turn out to be immoral? Is there one just act which won't turn out to be unjust?'"

"No, there isn't," he said. "It's inevitable for these things to turn out to be both   b
beautiful and ugly, in a sense, and the same goes for all the other qualities you mentioned in your question."

"And there are doubles galore—but they turn out to be halves just as much as doubles, don't they?"

"Yes."

"And do things which are large, small, light, and heavy deserve these attributes any more than they deserve the opposite attributes?"

"No, each of them is bound to have both qualities," he said.

"So isn't it the case, then, that any member of a plurality no more *is* whatever it is said to be than it *is not* whatever it is said to be?"

"This is like those *double-entendres* one hears at parties," he said, "or the riddle children tell about the eunuch and his hitting a bat—they make a riddle by asking what   c
he hit it with and what it was on—in the sense that the members of the plurality are also ambiguous: it is impossible to form a stable conception of any of them as either being what it is, or not being what it is, or being both, or being neither."

"How are you going to cope with them, then?" I asked. "Can you find a better place to locate them than between real being and unreality? I mean, they can't turn out to be more opaque and unreal than unreality, or more lucid and real than reality."   d

"True," he said.

"So there we are. We've discovered that the welter of things which the masses conventionally regard as beautiful and so on mill around somewhere between unreality and perfect reality."

"Yes, we have."

"But we have a prior agreement that were such a thing to turn up, we'd have to call it the field of belief, not of knowledge, since the realm which occupies some uncertain intermediate point must be accessible to the intermediate faculty."

"Yes, we do."

"What shall we say about those spectators, then, who can see a plurality of beau-   e
tiful things, but not beauty itself, and who are incapable of following if someone else tries to lead them to it, and who can see many moral actions, but not morality itself, and so on? That they only ever entertain beliefs, and do not *know* any of the things they believe?"

"That's what we have to say," he said.

"As for those who can see each of these things in itself, in its permanent and unvarying nature, we'll say they have knowledge and are not merely entertaining beliefs, won't we?"

"Again, we have to."

480   "And won't our position be that they're devoted to and love the domain of knowledge, as opposed to the others, who are devoted to and love the domain of belief? I mean, surely we haven't forgotten our claim that these others love and are spectators of beautiful sounds and colours and so on, but can't abide the idea that there is such a thing as beauty itself?"

"No, we haven't forgotten."

"They won't think us nasty if we refer to them as 'lovers of belief' rather than as philosophers, who love knowledge, will they? Are they going to get very cross with us if we say that now?"

"Not if they listen to me," he replied. "It's not right to get angry at the truth."

"But the term 'believers' is inappropriate for those who are devoted to everything that is real: they should be called 'philosophers,' shouldn't they?"

"Absolutely."

Book VI

*   *   *

502ᶜ   "Well, it was quite a struggle, but we've completed that topic. Next we'd better go on to
d   the remaining issues. What will it take—what studies and practices—for these preservers of our political system to be a possibility? And at what ages should they undertake the various subjects to be studied?"

"Yes, we ought to discuss these issues," he agreed.

"So I gained nothing," I said, "when earlier I cleverly delayed the awkward matter of their marital arrangements, and the topics of procreation and what rulers to appoint. I was aware that the whole truth about what rulers to appoint would arouse resentment and anger. It didn't make any difference, though, because now I'm up against
e   the necessity of discussing these matters anyway. There's nothing more to say about women and children, but I've got to start all over again, more or less, in exploring the
503   question of the rulers. I'm sure you remember our claim that they have to demonstrate love of their community while being tested in both pleasant and painful circumstances, and make it clear that they won't shed this patriotism whatever ordeals or fears they meet with, or whatever changing situations they endure. Anyone who is incapable of retaining it is to be excluded, whereas anyone who emerges from every test without impurities (like gold tested in fire) is to be made a ruler and given privileges and rewards in life and in death. We spoke along those lines, but the discussion was starting to devi-
b   ate and hide itself, because it was afraid of broaching the matter we're now facing."

"Yes, I remember," he said. "You're quite right."

"I was too scared to make the reckless assertions that have now been expressed," I said, "but now the presumptuous statement that 'if we are to have absolutely authentic guardians, then we must appoint philosophers,' is out in the open."

"Yes, it is," he said.

"Do you realize how few they'll be, in all likelihood? Consider the nature which, in our account, they have to have and how rare it is for its various parts to coalesce into a single entity: it usually ends up in bits and pieces."

"What do you mean?" he asked.   c

"People who are quick at learning, have good memories, and are astute and smart and so on, tend—as you know—not to combine both energy and broadness of mental vision with the ability to live an orderly, peaceful, and stable life. Instead, their quickness carries them this way and that, and stability plays no part at all in their lives."

"You're right," he said.

"On the other hand, a sound and stable character, which makes people more dependable and slow to respond to frightening situations in battle, also makes them approach their studies in the same way. They're as slow to respond and to learn as if they'd been drugged, and they're constantly dozing off and yawning when they're asked to do anything intellectually arduous."   d

"True," he said.

"But our claim is that a good and sufficient helping of both sets of qualities is a prerequisite for anyone to be allowed to take part in an authentic educational programme or to be awarded political office and power."

"Right," he said.

"So it'll be a rare phenomenon, don't you think?"

"Of course it will."

"It's not just a matter of testing someone in the ways we've already mentioned,   e
then—by means of ordeals and fear and pleasure. There's a further point we omitted before, but are including now: we must give him plenty of intellectual exercise as well, so that we can see whether he is capable of enduring fundamental intellectual work, or whether he'll cut and run as cowards do in other spheres."   504

"Yes, we certainly ought to try to find that out," he said. "But what do you mean by fundamental intellectual work?"

"I'm sure you remember when, as a result of distinguishing three aspects within the mind, we defined morality, self-discipline, courage, and wisdom," I said.

"If I didn't," he said, "then we might as well stop right now."

"Do you also remember how we prefaced our discussion of those qualities?"

"How?"

"We said that it would take a different route, a longer one, to reach the best possible vantage-point and that they would be plainly visible to anyone who went that way,   b
but that it was possible to come up with arguments which were in keeping with the kinds of discussions we'd already been having. You said that would do, and we proceeded at the time on that basis. I think the argument was defective, in terms of precision, but it's up to you to say whether you were happy with it."

"Yes, I was happy enough with it," he said, "and so was everyone else."

"But in these sorts of matters, my friend," I said, "anything which misses the truth   c
by even a tiny amount is nowhere near 'enough.' Anything less than perfect is not up to the mark at all, though people occasionally think it's adequate and that they don't need to look any further."

"Yes, a great many people feel this," he said, "because they're lazy."

"But it's a completely inappropriate feeling for a guardian of a community and its laws to have," I said.

"I suppose so," he said.

"Then a guardian had better take the longer route, Adeimantus," I said, "and put   d
just as much effort into his intellectual work as his physical exercise. Otherwise, as we

said a moment ago, he'll never see that fundamental field of study through to the end—and it's not just fundamental, but particularly appropriate for him."

"Are you implying that morality and the other qualities we discussed are not the most important things there are—that there's something even more fundamental than them?" he asked.

"It's not only more fundamental," I said, "but it's exactly the kind of thing which requires viewing as a completely finished product, without skimping and looking merely at an outline, as we did just now. I mean, wouldn't it be absurd to devote extremes of energy and effort to getting as precise and clear a picture as possible of insignificant matters, and then not to think that the most important matters deserve the utmost precision too?"

"An excellent sentiment," he said. "But surely you don't expect to get away without being asked what this fundamental field of study of yours is, and what it is concerned with?"

"No, I don't," I answered. "Go ahead and ask your questions. In actual fact, you've not infrequently been told what it is, but it's either slipped your mind for the moment, or you're intending to make trouble for me by attacking my position. I incline towards the latter alternative, since you've often been told that the most important thing to try to understand is the character of goodness, because this is where anything which is moral (or whatever) gets its value and advantages from. It can hardly have escaped your notice that this is my position, and you must know what I'm going to add: that our knowledge of goodness is inadequate. And you appreciate, I'm sure, that there's absolutely no point in having expert knowledge of everything else, but lacking knowledge of goodness, just as there isn't in having anything else either, unless goodness comes with it. I mean, do you think there's any advantage in owning everything in the world except good things, or in understanding everything else except goodness, and therefore failing to understand anything worthwhile and good?"

"I certainly don't," he said.

"Now, it can't have escaped your notice either that the usual view of goodness is that it's pleasure, while there's also a more ingenious view around, that it's knowledge."

"Of course it hasn't."

"As you also know, however, my friend, the people who hold the latter view are incapable of explaining exactly *what* knowledge constitutes goodness, but are forced ultimately to say that it is knowledge of goodness."

"And so to make complete fools of themselves," he remarked.

"Of course they do," I said. "First they tell us off for not knowing what goodness is, then they talk to us as if we did know what it is. I mean, to say it's knowledge of goodness is to assume that we understand what they're saying when they use the term 'goodness.'"

"You're absolutely right," he said.

"What about the definition of goodness as pleasure? Aren't its proponents just as thoroughly misguided as the others? I mean, they too are forced to make a concession, in this case that there are bad pleasures, aren't they?"

"Certainly."

"So their position ends up being that it is possible for a single thing to be both good and bad, doesn't it?"

"Naturally."

"It's clear, therefore, that there's plenty of scope for serious disagreement where goodness is concerned. Yes?"

"Of course."

"Well, isn't it also clear that whereas (whether it's a matter of doing something, or owning something, or having a certain reputation) people usually prefer the appearance of morality and right, even if there's no reality involved, yet no one is content with any possession that is only apparently good? It's the reality of goodness they want; no one thinks at all highly of mere appearance in this sphere."

"Yes, that's perfectly clear," he said.

"So here we have something which everyone, whatever their temperament, is after, and which is the goal of all their activities. They have an inkling of its existence, but they're confused about it and can't adequately grasp its nature or be as certain and as confident about it as they can about other things, and consequently they fail to derive any benefit even from those other activities. When something of this kind and this importance is involved, can we allow the best members of our community, the ones to whom we're going to entrust everything, to be equally in the dark?"

"Certainly not," he protested.

"Anyway," I said, "I imagine that anyone who is ignorant about the goodness of moral and right conduct would make a second-rate guardian of morality and right, and I suspect that no one will fully understand them until he knows about their relation to goodness."

"Your suspicion is right," he said.

"So the constitution and organization of our community will be perfect only if they are overseen by the kind of guardian who has this knowledge, won't they?"

"Necessarily," he said. "But Socrates, do *you* identify goodness with knowledge or pleasure, or with something else?"

"Just listen to him!" I exclaimed. "It's been perfectly obvious all along that other people's views on the matter weren't going to be enough for you."

"That's because I don't think it's right, Socrates," he said, "for someone who's devoted so much time to the matter to be in a position to state others' beliefs, but not his own."

"But do you think it's right," I responded, "for someone to talk as if he knew what he doesn't know?"

"Of course not," he said. "Not as if he knew, but as if he'd formed opinions—he should be prepared to say what he thinks."

"But aren't ideas which aren't based on knowledge always defective, in your experience?" I asked. "The best of them are blind. I mean, don't people who have a correct belief, but no knowledge, strike you as exactly like blind people who happen to be taking the right road?"

"Yes," he said.

"Well, do you want to see things which are defective, blind, and deformed," I asked, "when you could be getting lucid, correct views from elsewhere?"

"Socrates," said Glaucon, "please don't back away from the finishing-line, so to speak. We'd be happy with the kind of description of goodness that you gave of morality, self-discipline, and so on."

"So would I, Glaucon," I said, "very happy. But I'm afraid it'll be more than I can manage, and that my malformed efforts will make me ridiculous. What I suggest, my friends, is that we forget about trying to define goodness itself for the time being. You see, I don't at the moment think that our current impulse is enough to take us to where I'd like to see us go. However, I am prepared to talk about something which seems to me to be the child of goodness and to bear a very strong resemblance to it. Would you like me to do that? If not, we can just forget it."

"Please do," he said. "You can settle your account by discussing the father another time."

507   "I hope I can make the repayment," I said, "and you can recover the debt, rather than just the interest, as you are now. Anyway, as interest on your account, here's an account of the child of goodness. But please be careful that I don't cheat you—not that I intend to—by giving you a counterfeit description of the child."

"We'll watch out for that as best we can," he replied. "Just go ahead, please."

"First I want to make sure that we're not at cross purposes," I said, "and to remind you of something that came up earlier, though you've often heard it on other occasions as well."

b   "What?" he asked.

"As we talk," I said, "we mention and differentiate between a lot of beautiful things and a lot of good things and so on."

"Yes, we do."

"And we also talk about beauty itself, goodness itself, and so on. All the things we refer to as a plurality on those occasions, we also conversely count as belonging to a single class by virtue of the fact that they have a single particular character, and we say that the *x* itself is 'what really is.'"

"True."

"And we say that the first lot is visible rather than intelligible, whereas characters are intelligible rather than visible."

"Absolutely."

c   "With what aspect of ourselves do we see the things we see?"

"With our sight," he replied.

"And we use hearing for the things we hear, and so on, for all the other senses and the things we perceive. Yes?"

"Of course."

"Well, have you ever stopped to consider," I asked, "how generous the creator of the senses was when he created the domain of seeing and being seen?"

"No, not really," he said.

"Look at it this way. Are hearing and sound deficient? Do they need an extra

d   something to make the one hear and the other be heard—some third thing without which hearing won't hear and sound won't be heard?"

"No," he answered.

"And in my opinion," I went on, "the same goes for many other domains, if not all: they don't need anything like this. Or can you point to one that does?"

"*I* can't," he said.

"But do you realize that sight and the visible realm *are* deficient?"

"How?"

"Even if a person's eyes are capable of sight, and he's trying to use it, and what he's trying to look at is coloured, the sight will see nothing and the colours will remain

e   unseen, surely, unless there is also present an extra third thing which is made specifically for this purpose."

"What is this thing you're getting at?" he asked.

"It's what we call light," I said.

"You're right," he said.

"So if light has value, then, because it links the sense of sight and the ability to be

508   seen, it is far and away the most valuable link there is."

"Well, it certainly does have value," he said.

"Which of the heavenly gods would you say is responsible for this? Whose light makes it possible for our sight to see and for the things we see to be seen?"

"My reply will be no different from what yours or anyone else's would be," he said. "I mean, you're obviously expecting the answer, 'the sun.'"

"Now, there are certain conclusions to be drawn from comparing sight to this god."

"What?"

"Sight and the sun aren't to be identified: neither the sense itself nor its location—   b
which we call the eye—is the same as the sun."

"True."

"Nevertheless, there's no sense-organ which more closely resembles the sun, in my opinion, than the eye."

"The resemblance is striking."

"Moreover, the eye's ability to see has been bestowed upon it and channeled into it, as it were, by the sun."

"Yes."

"So the sun is not to be identified with sight, but is responsible for sight and is itself within the visible realm. Right?"

"Yes," he said.

"The sun is the child of goodness I was talking about, then," I said. "It is a counterpart to its father, goodness. As goodness stands in the intelligible realm to intelligence and the things we know, so in the visible realm the sun stands to sight and the   c
things we see."

"I don't understand," he said. "I need more detail, please."

"As you know," I explained, "when our eyes are directed towards things whose colours are no longer bathed in daylight, but in artificial light instead, then they're less effective and seem to be virtually blind, as if they didn't even have the potential for seeing clearly."

"Certainly," he said.

"But when they're directed towards things which are lit up by the sun, then they see clearly and obviously do have that potential."   d

"Of course."

"Well, here's how you can think about the mind as well. When its object is something which is lit up by truth and reality, then it has—and obviously has—intelligent awareness and knowledge. However, when its object is permeated with darkness (that is, when its object is something which is subject to generation and decay), then it has beliefs and is less effective, because its beliefs chop and change, and under these circumstances it comes across as devoid of intelligence."

"Yes, it does."

"Well, what I'm saying is that it's goodness which gives the things we know   e
their truth and makes it possible for people to have knowledge. It is responsible for knowledge and truth, and you should think of it as being within the intelligible realm, but you shouldn't identify it with knowledge and truth, otherwise you'll be wrong: for all their value, it is even more valuable. In the other realm, it is right to re-   509
gard light and sight as resembling the sun, but not to identify either of them with the sun; so in this realm it is right to regard knowledge and truth as resembling goodness, but not to identify either of them with goodness, which should be rated even more highly."

"You're talking about something of inestimable value," he said, "if it's not only the source of knowledge and truth, but is also more valuable than them. I mean, you certainly don't seem to be identifying it with pleasure!"

"How could you even think it?" I exclaimed. "But we can take our analogy even further."

"How?"   b

"I think you'll agree that the ability to be seen is not the only gift the sun gives to the things we see. It is also the source of their generation, growth, and nourishment, although it isn't actually the process of generation."

"Of course it isn't."

"And it isn't only the known-ness of the things we know which is conferred upon them by goodness, but also their reality and their being, although goodness isn't actually the state of being, but surpasses being in majesty and might."

c "It's way beyond human comprehension, all right," was Glaucon's quite amusing comment.

"It's your fault for forcing me to express my views on the subject," I replied.

"Yes, and please don't stop," he said. "If you've left anything out of your explanation of the simile of the sun, then the least you could do is continue with it."

"There are plenty of omissions, in fact," I said.

"Don't leave any gaps," he said, "however small."

"I think I'll have to leave a lot out," I said, "but I'll try to make it as complete as I can at the moment."

"All right," he said.

d "So bear in mind the two things we've been talking about," I said, "one of which rules over the intelligible realm and its inhabitants, while the other rules over the visible realm—I won't say over the heavens in case you think I'm playing clever word-games. Anyway, do you understand this distinction between visible things and intelligible things?"

"Yes."

"Well, picture them as a line cut into two unequal sections and, following the same proportion, subdivide both the section of the visible realm and that of the intelli-

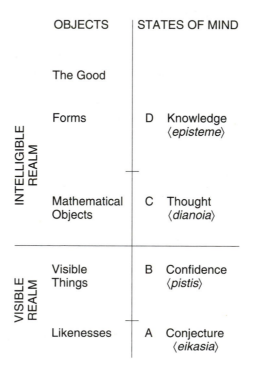

	OBJECTS	STATES OF MIND
	The Good	
INTELLIGIBLE REALM	Forms	D Knowledge ⟨*episteme*⟩
	Mathematical Objects	C Thought ⟨*dianoia*⟩
VISIBLE REALM	Visible Things	B Confidence ⟨*pistis*⟩
	Likenesses	A Conjecture ⟨*eikasia*⟩

gible realm. Now you can compare the sections in terms of clarity and unclarity. The first section in the visible realm consists of likenesses, by which I mean a number of things: shadows, reflections (on the surface of water or on anything else which is inherently compact, smooth, and bright), and so on. Do you see what I'm getting at?" e 510

"I do."

"And you should count the other section of the visible realm as consisting of the things whose likenesses are found in the first section: all the flora and fauna there are in the world, and every kind of artifact too."

"All right."

"I wonder whether you'd agree," I said, "that truth and lack of truth have been the criteria for distinguishing these sections, and that the image stands to the original as the realm of beliefs stands to the realm of knowledge?"

"Yes," he said, "I certainly agree." b

"Now have a look at how to subdivide the section which belongs to the intelligible realm."

"How?"

"Like this. If the mind wants to explore the first subdivision, it can do so only by using those former originals as likenesses and by taking things for granted on its journey, which leads it to an end-point, rather than to a starting-point. If it wants to explore the second subdivision, however, it takes things for granted in order to travel to a starting-point where nothing needs to be taken for granted, and it has no involvement with likenesses, as before, but makes its approach by means of types alone, in and of themselves."

"I don't quite understand what you're saying," he said.

"You will if I repeat it," I said, "because this preamble will make it easier to understand. I'm sure you're aware that practitioners of geometry, arithmetic, and so on take for granted things like numerical oddness and evenness, the geometrical figures, the three kinds of angle, and any other things of that sort which are relevant to a given subject. They act as if they know about these things, treat them as basic, and don't feel any further need to explain them either to themselves or to anyone else, on the grounds that there is nothing unclear about them. They make them the starting-points for their subsequent investigations, which end after a coherent chain of reasoning at the point they'd set out to reach in their research." c

d

"Yes, I'm certainly well aware of this," he said.

"So you must also be aware that in the course of their discussions they make use of visible forms, despite the fact that they're not interested in visible forms as such, but in the things of which the visible forms are likenesses: that is, their discussions are concerned with what it is to be a square, and with what it is to be a diagonal (and so on), rather than with the diagonal (and so on) which occurs in their diagrams. They treat their models and diagrams as likenesses, when these things have likenesses themselves, in fact (that is, shadows and reflections on water); but they're actually trying to see squares and so on in themselves, which only thought can see." e

511

"You're right," he said.

"So it was objects of this type that I was describing as belonging to the intelligible realm, with the rider that the mind can explore them only by taking things for granted, and that its goal is not a starting-point, because it is incapable of changing direction and rising above the things it is taking for granted. And I went on to say that it used as likenesses those very things which are themselves the originals of a lower order of likenesses, and that relative to the likenesses, the originals command respect and admiration for their distinctness."

b   "I see," he said. "You're talking about the objects of geometry and related occupations."

"Now, can you see what I mean by the second subdivision of the intelligible realm? It is what reason grasps by itself, thanks to its ability to practise dialectic. When it takes things for granted, it doesn't treat them as starting-points, but as basic in the strict sense—as platforms and rungs, for example. These serve it until it reaches a point where nothing needs to be taken for granted, and which is the starting-point for everything. Once it has grasped this starting-point, it turns around and by a process of depending on the things which depend from the starting-point, it descends to an end-point.
c   It makes absolutely no use of anything perceptible by the senses: it aims for types by means of types alone, in and of themselves, and it ends its journey with types."

"I don't quite understand," he said. "I mean, you're talking about crucial matters here, I think. I do understand, however, that you want to mark off that part of the real and intelligible realm which is before the eyes of anyone who knows how to practise dialectic as more clear than the other part, which is before the eyes of practitioners of the various branches of expertise, as we call them. The latter make the things they take for granted their starting-points, and although they inevitably use thought, not the senses, to
d   observe what they observe, yet because of their failure to ascend to a starting-point—because their enquiries rely on taking things for granted—you're saying that they don't understand these things, even though they are intelligible, when related to a starting-point. I take you to be describing what geometers and so on do as thinking rather than knowing, on the grounds that thinking is the intermediate state between believing and knowing."

"There's nothing wrong with your understanding," I said. "And you should appreciate that there are four states of mind, one for each of the four sections. There's knowledge for the highest section and thought for the second one; and you'd better as-
e   sign confidence to the third one and conjecture to the final one. You can make an orderly progression out of them, and you should regard them as possessing as much clarity as their objects possess truth."

"I see," he said. "That's fine with me: I'll order them in the way you suggest."

BOOK VII

514   "Next," I said, "here's a situation which you can use as an analogy for the human condition—for our education or lack of it. Imagine people living in a cavernous cell down under the ground; at the far end of the cave, a long way off, there's an entrance open to the outside world. They've been there since childhood, with their legs and necks tied
b   up in a way which keeps them in one place and allows them to look only straight ahead, but not to turn their heads. There's firelight burning a long way further up the cave behind them, and up the slope between the fire and the prisoners there's a road, beside which you should imagine a low wall has been built—like the partition which conjurors place between themselves and their audience and above which they show their tricks."

"All right," he said.

"Imagine also that there are people on the other side of this wall who are carrying
c   all sorts of artifacts. These artifacts, human statuettes, and animal models carved in
515   stone and wood and all kinds of materials stick out over the wall; and as you'd expect, some of the people talk as they carry these objects along, while others are silent."

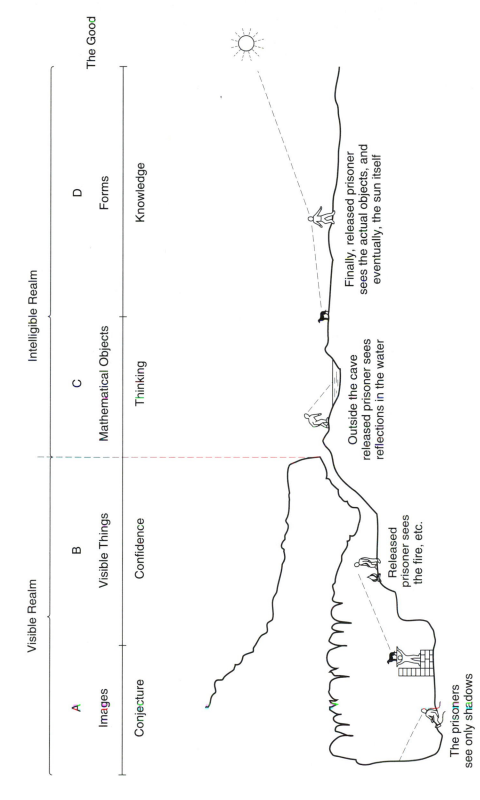

Visible Realm

A	B
Images	Visible Things
Conjecture	Confidence

Intelligible Realm

C	D
Mathematical Objects	Forms
Thinking	Knowledge

The Good

The prisoners
see only shadows

Released
prisoner sees
the fire, etc.

Outside the cave
released prisoner sees
reflections in the water

Finally, released prisoner
sees the actual objects, and
eventually, the sun itself

Adapted from N. Jordan, *Western Philosophy: From Antiquity to the Middle Ages* (New York: Macmillan, 1987), p. 95.

"This is a strange picture you're painting," he said, "with strange prisoners."

"They're no different from us," I said. "I mean, in the first place, do you think they'd see anything of themselves and one another except the shadows cast by the fire on to the cave wall directly opposite them?"

b   "Of course not," he said. "They're forced to spend their lives without moving their heads."

"And what about the objects which were being carried along? Won't they only see their shadows as well?"

"Naturally."

"Now, suppose they were able to talk to one another: Don't you think they'd assume that their words applied to what they saw passing by in front of them?"

"They couldn't think otherwise."

"And what if sound echoed off the prison wall opposite them? When any of the passers-by spoke, don't you think they'd be bound to assume that the sound came from a passing shadow?"

"I'm absolutely certain of it," he said.

c   "All in all, then," I said, "the shadows of artifacts would constitute the only reality people in this situation would recognize."

"That's absolutely inevitable," he agreed.

"What do you think would happen, then," I asked, "if they were set free from their bonds and cured of their inanity? What would it be like if they found that happening to them? Imagine that one of them has been set free and is suddenly made to stand up, to turn his head and walk, and to look towards the firelight. It hurts him to do all this and he's too dazzled to be capable of making out the objects whose shadows he'd formerly been looking at. And suppose someone tells him that what he's been seeing all this time

d   has no substance, and that he's now closer to reality and is seeing more accurately, because of the greater reality of the things in front of his eyes—what do you imagine his reaction would be? And what do you think he'd say if he were shown any of the passing objects and had to respond to being asked what it was? Don't you think he'd be bewildered and would think that there was more reality in what he'd been seeing before than in what he was being shown now?"

"Far more," he said.

e   "And if he were forced to look at the actual firelight, don't you think it would hurt his eyes? Don't you think he'd turn away and run back to the things he could make out, and would take the truth of the matter to be that these things are clearer than what he was being shown?"

"Yes," he agreed.

"And imagine him being dragged forcibly away from there up the rough, steep slope," I went on, "without being released until he's been pulled out into the sunlight.

516   Wouldn't this treatment cause him pain and distress? And once he's reached the sunlight, he wouldn't be able to see a single one of the things which are currently taken to be real, would he, because his eyes would be overwhelmed by the sun's beams?"

"No, he wouldn't," he answered, "not straight away."

"He wouldn't be able to see things up on the surface of the earth, I suppose, until he'd got used to his situation. At first, it would be shadows that he could most easily make out, then he'd move on to the reflections of people and so on in water, and later he'd be able to see the actual things themselves. Next, he'd feast his eyes on the heavenly bodies and the heavens themselves, which would be easier at night: he'd look at

b   the light of the stars and the moon, rather than at the sun and sunlight during the daytime."

"Of course."

"And at last, I imagine, he'd be able to discern and feast his eyes on the sun—not the displaced image of the sun in water or elsewhere, but the sun on its own, in its proper place."

"Yes, he'd inevitably come to that," he said.

"After that, he'd start to think about the sun and he'd deduce that it is the source of the seasons and the yearly cycle, that the whole of the visible realm is its domain, and that in a sense everything which he and his peers used to see is its responsibility."   c

"Yes, that would obviously be the next point he'd come to," he agreed.

"Now, if he recalled the cell where he'd originally lived and what passed for knowledge there and his former fellow prisoners, don't you think he'd feel happy about his own altered circumstances, and sorry for them?"

"Definitely."

"Suppose that the prisoners used to assign prestige and credit to one another, in the sense that they rewarded speed at recognizing the shadows as they passed, and the ability to remember which ones normally come earlier and later and at the same time as which other ones, and expertise at using this as a basis for guessing which ones would arrive next. Do you think our former prisoner would covet these honours and would   d envy the people who had status and power there, or would he much prefer, as Homer describes it, 'being a slave labouring for someone else—someone without property,' and would put up with anything at all, in fact, rather than share their beliefs and their life?"

"Yes, I think he'd go through anything rather than live that way," he said.   e

"Here's something else I'd like your opinion about," I said. "If he went back underground and sat down again in the same spot, wouldn't the sudden transition from the sunlight mean that his eyes would be overwhelmed by darkness?"

"Certainly," he replied.

"Now, the process of adjustment would be quite long this time and suppose that before his eyes had settled down and while he wasn't seeing well, he had once again to   517 compete against those same old prisoners at identifying those shadows. Wouldn't he make a fool of himself? Wouldn't they say that he'd come back from his upward journey with his eyes ruined, and that it wasn't even worth trying to go up there? And wouldn't they—if they could—grab hold of anyone who tried to set them free and take them up there and kill him?"

"They certainly would," he said.

"Well, my dear Glaucon," I said, "you should apply this allegory, as a whole, to what we were talking about before. The region which is accessible to sight should   b be equated with the prison cell, and the firelight there with the light of the sun. And if you think of the upward journey and the sight of things up on the surface of the earth as the mind's ascent to the intelligible realm, you won't be wrong—at least, *I* don't think you'd be wrong, and it's my impression that you want to hear. Only God knows if it's actually true, however. Anyway, it's my opinion that the last thing to be seen— and it isn't easy to see either—in the realm of knowledge is goodness; and the sight   c of the character of goodness leads one to deduce that it is responsible for everything that is right and fine, whatever the circumstances, and that in the visible realm it is the progenitor of light and of the source of light, and in the intelligible realm it is the source and provider of truth and knowledge. And I also think that the sight of it is a prerequisite for intelligent conduct either of one's own private affairs or of public business."

"I couldn't agree more," he said.

"All right, then," I said. "I wonder if you also agree with me in not finding it strange that people who've traveled there don't want to engage in human business: there's nowhere else their minds would ever rather be than in the upper region—which is hardly surprising, if our allegory has got this aspect right as well."

"No, it's not surprising," he agreed.

"Well, what about this?" I asked. "Imagine someone returning to the human world and all its misery after contemplating the divine realm. Do you think it's surprising if he seems awkward and ridiculous while he's still not seeing well, before he's had time to adjust to the darkness of his situation, and he's forced into a contest (in a law-court or wherever) about the shadows of morality or the statuettes which cast the shadows, and into a competition whose terms are the conceptions of morality held by people who have never seen morality itself?"

"No, that's not surprising in the slightest," he said.

"In fact anyone with any sense," I said, "would remember that the eyes can become confused in two different ways, as a result of two different sets of circumstances: it can happen in the transition from light to darkness, and also in the transition from darkness to light. If he took the same facts into consideration when he also noticed someone's mind in such a state of confusion that it was incapable of making anything out, his reaction wouldn't be unthinking ridicule. Instead, he'd try to find out whether this person's mind was returning from a mode of existence which involves greater lucidity and had been blinded by the unfamiliar darkness, or whether it was moving from relative ignorance to relative lucidity and had been overwhelmed and dazzled by the increased brightness. Once he'd distinguished between the two conditions and modes of existence, he'd congratulate anyone he found in the second state, and feel sorry for anyone in the first state. If he did choose to laugh at someone in the second state, his amusement would be less absurd than when laughter is directed at someone returning from the light above."

"Yes," he said, "you're making a lot of sense."

"Now, if this is true," I said, "we must bear in mind that education is not capable of doing what some people promise. They claim to introduce knowledge into a mind which doesn't have it, as if they were introducing sight into eyes which are blind."

"Yes, they do," he said.

"An implication of what we're saying at the moment, however," I pointed out, "is that the capacity for knowledge is present in everyone's mind. If you can imagine an eye that can turn from darkness to brightness only if the body as a whole turns, then our organ of understanding is like that. Its orientation has to be accompanied by turning the mind as a whole away from the world of becoming, until it becomes capable of bearing the sight of real being and reality at its most bright, which we're saying is goodness. Yes?"

"Yes."

"That's what education should be," I said, "the art of orientation. Educators should devise the simplest and most effective methods of turning minds around. It shouldn't be the art of implanting sight in the organ, but should proceed on the understanding that the organ already has the capacity, but is improperly aligned and isn't facing the right way."

"I suppose you're right," he said.

"So although the mental states which are described as good generally seem to resemble good physical states, in the sense that habituation and training do in fact implant them where they didn't use to be, yet understanding (as it turns out) is undoubtedly a property of something which is more divine: it never loses its power, and it is useful and beneficial, or useless and harmful, depending on its orientation. For example, surely you've noticed how the petty minds of those who are acknowledged to be bad, but clever, are sharp-eyed and perceptive enough to gain insights into matters they direct their attention towards. It's not as if they weren't sharp-sighted, but their minds are forced to serve evil, and consequently the keener their vision is, the greater the evil they accomplish."

519

"Yes, I've noticed this," he said.

"However," I went on, "if this aspect of that kind of person is hammered at from an early age, until the inevitable consequences of incarnation have been knocked off it—the leaden weights, so to speak, which are grafted on to it as a result of eating and similar pleasures and indulgences and which turn the sight of the mind downwards—if it sheds these weights and is reoriented towards the truth, then (and we're talking about the same organ and the same people) it would see the truth just as clearly as it sees the objects it faces at the moment."

b

"Yes, that makes sense," he said.

"Well, doesn't this make sense as well?" I asked. "Or rather, isn't it an inevitable consequence of what we've been saying that uneducated people, who have no experience of truth, would make incompetent administrators of a community, and that the same goes for people who are allowed to spend their whole lives educating themselves? The first group would be no good because their lives lack direction: they've got no single point of reference to guide them in all their affairs, whether private or public. The second group would be no good because their hearts wouldn't be in the business: they think they've been transported to the Isles of the Blessed even while they're still alive."

c

"True," he said.

"Our job as founders, then," I said, "is to make sure that the best people come to that fundamental field of study (as we called it earlier): we must have them make the ascent we've been talking about and see goodness. And afterwards, once they've been up there and had a good look, we mustn't let them get away with what they do at the moment."

d

"Which is what?"

"Staying there," I replied, "and refusing to come back down again to those prisoners, to share their work and their rewards, no matter whether those rewards are trivial or significant."

"But in that case," he protested, "we'll be wronging them: we'll be making the quality of their lives worse and denying them the better life they could be living, won't we?"

"You're again forgetting, my friend," I said, "that the point of legislation is not to make one section of a community better off than the rest, but to engineer this for the community as a whole. Legislators should persuade or compel the members of a community to mesh together, should make every individual share with his fellows the benefit which he is capable of contributing to the common welfare, and should ensure that the community does contain people with this capacity; and the purpose of all this is not for legislators to leave people to choose their own directions, but for them to use people to bind the community together."

e

520

"Yes, you're right," he said. "I was forgetting."

"I think you'll also find, Glaucon," I said, "that we won't be wronging any philosophers who arise in our community. Our remarks, as we force them to take care of their fellow citizens and be their guardians, will be perfectly fair. We'll tell them that it's b   reasonable for philosophers who happen to occur in other communities not to share the work of those communities, since their occurrence was spontaneous, rather than planned by the political system of any of the communities in question, and it's fair for anything which arises spontaneously and doesn't owe its nurture to anyone or anything to have no interest in repaying anyone for having provided its nourishment. 'We've bred *you*, however,' we'll say, 'to act, as it were, as the hive's leaders and kings, for your own good as well as that of the rest of the community. You've received a better and more thorough education than those other philosophers, and you're more capable of

c   playing a part in both spheres. So each of you must, when your time comes, descend to where the rest of the community lives, and get used to looking at things in the dark. The point is that once you become acclimatized, you'll see infinitely better than the others there; your experience of genuine right, morality, and goodness will enable you to iden-tify every one of the images and recognize what it is an image of. And then the admin-istration of our community—ours as well as yours—will be in the hands of people who are awake, as distinct from the norm nowadays of communities being governed by peo-ple who shadow-box and fall out with one another in their dreams over who should rule,

d   as if that were a highly desirable thing to do. No, the truth of the matter is this: the less keen the would-be rulers of a community are to rule, the better and less divided the ad-ministration of that community is bound to be, but where the rulers feel the opposite, the administration is bound to be the opposite.'"

"Yes," he said.

"And do you think our wards will greet these views of ours with scepticism and will refuse to join in the work of government when their time comes, when they can still spend most of their time living with one another in the untainted realm?"

e   "No, they couldn't," he answered. "They're fair-minded people, and the instruc-tions we're giving them are fair. However, they'll undoubtedly approach rulership as an inescapable duty—an attitude which is the opposite of the one held by the people who have power in communities at the moment."

"You're right, Glaucon," I said. "You'll only have a well-governed community if

521 you can come up with a way of life for your prospective rulers that is preferable to rul-ing! The point is that this is the only kind of community where the rulers will be gen-uinely well off (not in material terms, but they'll possess the wealth which is a prereq-uisite of happiness—a life of virtue and intelligence), whereas if government falls into the hands of people who are impoverished and starved of any good things of their own, and who expect to wrest some good for themselves from political office, a well-governed community is an impossibility. I mean, when rulership becomes something to fight for, a domestic and internal war like this destroys not only the perpetrators, but also the rest of the community."

"You're absolutely right," he said.

b   "Apart from the philosophical life," I said, "is there any way of life, in your opin-ion, which looks down on political office?"

"No, definitely not," he answered.

"In fact, political power should be in the hands of people who aren't enamoured of it. Otherwise their rivals in love will fight them for it."

"Of course."

"There's no one you'd rather force to undertake the guarding of your community, then, than those who are experts in the factors which contribute towards the good gov-ernment of a community, who don't look to politics for their rewards, and whose life is better than the political life. Agreed?"

"Yes," he said.

PARMENIDES (in part)

According to Antiphon, then, this was Pythodorus' account. Zeno and Parmenides once 127
came to Athens for the Great Panathenaea. Parmenides was a man of distinguished ap- b
pearance. By that time he was well advanced in years, with hair almost white; he may
have been sixty-five. Zeno was nearing forty, a tall and attractive figure. It was said that
he had been Parmenides' favourite. They were staying with Pythodorus outside the
walls in the Ceramicus. Socrates and a few others came there, anxious to hear a reading c
of Zeno's treatise, which the two visitors had brought for the first time to Athens.
Socrates was then quite young. Zeno himself read it to them; Parmenides at the moment
had gone out. The reading of the arguments was very nearly over when Pythodorus
himself came in, accompanied by Parmenides and Aristoteles, the man who was after- d
wards one of the Thirty; so they heard only a small part of the treatise. Pythodorus himself, however, had heard it read by Zeno before.

When Zeno had finished, Socrates asked him to read once more the first hypothesis of the first argument. He did so, and Socrates asked: "What does this statement
mean, Zeno? 'If things are many,' you say, 'they must be both like and unlike. But that
is impossible: unlike things cannot be like, nor like things unlike.' That is what you say, e
isn't it?"

Yes, replied Zeno.

And so, if unlike things cannot be like or like things unlike, it is also impossible
that things should be a plurality; if many things did exist, they would have impossible
attributes. Is this the precise purpose of your arguments—to maintain, against everything that is commonly said, that things are not a plurality? Do you regard every one of
your arguments as evidence of exactly that conclusion, and so hold that, in each argument in your treatise, you are giving just one more proof that a plurality does not exist? 128
Is that what you mean, or am I understanding you wrongly?

No, said Zeno, you have quite rightly understood the purpose of the whole treatise.

I see, Parmenides, said Socrates, that Zeno's intention is to associate himself with
you by means of his treatise no less intimately than by his personal attachment. In a
way, his book states the same position as your own; only by varying the form he tries to
delude us into thinking that his thesis is a different one. You assert, in your poem, that b
the All is one; and for this you advance admirable proofs. Zeno, for his part, asserts that
it is not a plurality; and he too has many weighty proofs to bring forward. You assert
unity, he asserts no plurality; each expresses himself in such a way that your arguments
seem to have nothing in common, though really they come to very much the same thing.
That is why your exposition and his seem to be rather over the heads of outsiders like
ourselves.

Yes, Socrates, Zeno replied, but you have not quite seen the real character of my c
book. True, you are as quick as a Spartan hound to pick up the scent and follow the trail
of the argument; but there is a point you have missed at the outset. The book makes no
pretence of disguising from the public the fact that it was written with the purpose you
describe, as if such deception were something to be proud of. What you have pointed
out is only incidental; the book is in fact a sort of defence of Parmenides' argument

d   against those who try to make fun of it by showing that his supposition, that there is a One, leads to many absurdities and contradictions. This book, then, is a retort against those who assert a plurality. It pays them back in the same coin with something to spare, and aims at showing that, on a thorough examination, their own supposition that there is a plurality leads to even more absurd consequences than the hypothesis of the One. It was written in that controversial spirit in my young days; and someone copied it surreptitiously, so that I had not even the chance to consider whether it should see the light

e   or not. That is where you are mistaken Socrates; you imagine it was inspired, not by a youthful eagerness for controversy, but by the more dispassionate aims of an older man; though, as I said, your description of it was not far wrong.

       I accept that, said Socrates, and I have no doubt it is as you say. But tell me this.
129   Do you not recognise that there exists, just by itself, a Form of Likeness and again another contrary Form, Unlikeness itself, and that of these two Forms you and I and all the things we speak of as "many" come to partake? Also, that things which come to partake of Likeness come to be alike in that respect and just in so far as they do come to partake of it, and those that come to partake of Unlikeness come to be unlike, while those which come to partake of both come to be both? Even if all things come to partake of both, contrary as they are, and by having a share in both are at once like and unlike one an-

b   other, what is there surprising in that? If one could point to things which are simply "alike" or "unlike" proving to be unlike or alike, that no doubt would be a portent; but when things which have a share in both are shown to have both characters, I see nothing strange in that, Zeno; nor yet in a proof that all things are one by having a share in Unity and at the same time many by sharing in Plurality. But if anyone can prove that what is simply Unity itself is many or that Plurality itself is one, then I shall begin to be

c   surprised.

       And so in all other cases; if the kinds or Forms themselves were shown to have these contrary characters among themselves, there would be good ground for astonishment; but what is there surprising in someone pointing out that I am one thing and also many? When he wants to show that I am many things, he say that my right side is a different thing from my left, my front from my back, my upper parts from my lower, since no doubt I do partake of Plurality. When he wants to prove that I am one thing,

d   he will say that I am one person among the seven of us, since I partake also of Unity. So both statements are true. Accordingly, if anyone sets out to show about things of this kind—sticks and stones, and so on—that the same thing is many and one, we shall say that what he is proving is that *something* is many and one, not that Unity is many or that Plurality is one; he is not telling us anything wonderful, but only what we should all admit. But, as I said just now, if he begins by distinguishing the Forms apart just by

e   themselves—Likeness, for instance, and Unlikeness, Plurality and Unity, Rest and Motion, and all the rest—and then shows that these Forms among themselves can be combined with, or separate from, one another, then, Zeno, I should be filled with admiration. I am sure you have dealt with this subject very forcibly; but, as I say, my

130   admiration would be much greater if anyone could show that these same perplexities are everywhere involved in the Forms themselves—among the objects we apprehend in reflection, just as you and Parmenides have shown them to be involved in the things we see.

       While Socrates was speaking, Pythodorus said he was expecting every moment that Parmenides and Zeno would be annoyed; but they listened very attentively and kept on exchanging glances and smiles in admiration of Socrates. When he ended, Parmenides expressed this feeling.

b   Socrates, he said, your eagerness for discussion is admirable. And now tell me: have you yourself drawn this distinction you speak of and separated apart on the one side Forms themselves and on the other the things that share in them? Do you believe that there is such a thing as Likeness itself apart from the likeness that we possess, and so on with Unity and Plurality and all the terms in Zeno's argument that you have just been listening to?

Certainly I do, said Socrates.

And also in cases like these, asked Parmenides: is there, for example, a Form of Rightness or of Beauty or of Goodness, and of all such things?

Yes.

And again, a Form of Man, apart from ourselves and all other men like us—a c Form of Man as something by itself? Or a Form of Fire or of Water?

I have often been puzzled about those things, Parmenides, whether one should say that the same thing is true in their case or not.

Are you also puzzled, Socrates, about cases that might be thought absurd, such as hair or mud or dirt or any other trivial and undignified objects? Are you doubtful whether or not to assert that each of these has a separate Form distinct from things like those we handle? d

Not at all, said Socrates; in these cases, the things are just the things we see; it would surely be too absurd to suppose that they have a Form. All the same, I have sometimes been troubled by a doubt whether what is true in one case may not be true in all. Then, when I have reached that point, I am driven to retreat, for fear of tumbling into a bottomless pit of nonsense. Anyhow, I get back to the things which we were just now speaking of as having Forms, and occupy my time with thinking about them.

That, replied Parmenides, is because you are still young, Socrates, and philoso- e phy has not yet taken hold of you so firmly as I believe it will some day. You will not despise any of these objects then; but at present your youth makes you still pay attention to what the world will think. However that may be, tell me this. You say you hold that there exist certain Forms, of which these other things come to partake and so to be called after their names: by coming to partake of Likeness or Largeness or Beauty or 131 Justice, they become like or large or beautiful or just?

Certainly, said Socrates.

Then each thing that partakes receives as its share either the Form as a whole or a part of it? Or can there be any other way of partaking besides this?

No, how could there be?

Do you hold, then, that the Form as a whole, a single thing, is in each of the many, or how?

Why should it not be in each, Parmenides?

If so, a Form which is one and the same will be at the same time, as a whole, in a b number of things which are separate, and consequently will be separate from itself.

No, it would not, replied Socrates, if it were like one and the same day, which is in many places at the same time and nevertheless is not separate from itself. Suppose any given Form is in them all at the same time as one and the same thing in that way.

I like the way you make out that one and the same thing is in many places at once, Socrates. You might as well spread a sail over a number of people and then say that the one sail as a whole was over them all. Don't you think that is a fair analogy?

Perhaps it is.

Then would the sail as a whole be over each man, or only a part over one, another c part over another?

Only a part.

In that case, Socrates, the Forms themselves must be divisible into parts, and the things which have a share in them will have a part for their share. Only a part of any given Form, and no longer the whole of it, will be in each thing.

Evidently, on that showing.

Are you, then, prepared to assert that we shall find the single Form actually being divided? Will it still be one?

Certainly not.

No, for consider this. Suppose it is Largeness itself that you are going to divide into parts, and that each of the many large things is to be large by virtue of a part of Largeness which is smaller than Largeness itself. Will not that seem unreasonable?

It will indeed.

And again, if it is Equality that a thing receives some small part of, will that part, which is less than Equality itself, make its possessor equal to something else?

No, that is impossible.

Well, take Smallness. Is one of us to have a portion of Smallness, and is Smallness to be larger than that portion, which is a part of it? On this supposition again Smallness itself will be larger, and anything to which the portion taken is added will be smaller, and larger, than it was before.

That cannot be so.

Well then, Socrates, how are the other things going to partake of your Forms, if they can partake of them neither in part nor as wholes?

Really, said Socrates, it seems no easy matter to determine in any way.

Again, there is another question.

What is that?

How do you feel about this? I imagine your ground for believing in a single Form in each case is this. When it seems to you that a number of things are large, there seems, I suppose, to be a certain single character which is the same when you look at them all; hence you think that Largeness is a single thing.

True, he replied.

But now take Largeness itself and the other things which are large. Suppose you look at all these in the same way in your mind's eye, will not yet another unity make its appearance—a Largeness by virtue of which they all appear large?

So it would seem.

If so, a second Form of Largeness will present itself, over and above Largeness itself and the things that share in it; and again, covering all these, yet another, which will make all of them large. So each of your Forms will no longer be one, but an indefinite number.

But, Parmenides, said Socrates, may it not be that each of these Forms is a thought, which cannot properly exist anywhere but in a mind. In that way each of them can be one and the statements that have just been made would no longer be true of it.

Then, is each Form one of these thoughts and yet a thought of nothing?

No, that is impossible.

So it is a thought of something?

Yes.

Of something that is, or of something that is not?

Of something that is.

In fact, of some one thing which that thought observes to cover all the cases, as being a certain single character?

Yes.

Then will not this thing that is thought of as being one and always the same in all cases be a Form?

That again seems to follow.

And besides, said Parmenides, according to the way in which you assert that the other things have a share in the Forms, must you not hold either that each of those things consists of thoughts, so that all things think, or else that they are thoughts which nevertheless do not think?

That too is unreasonable, replied Socrates. But, Parmenides, the best I can make of the matter is this: that these Forms are as it were patterns fixed in the nature of things; the other things are made in their image and are likenesses; and this participation they come to have in the Forms is nothing but their being made in their image.

Well, if a thing is made in the image of the Form, can that Form fail to be like the image of it, in so far as the image was made in its likeness? If a thing is like, must it not be like something that is like it?

It must.

And must not the thing which is like share with the thing that is like it in one and the same thing [character]?

Yes.

And will not that in which the like things share, so as to be alike, be just the Form itself that you spoke of?

Certainly.

If so, nothing can be like the Form, nor can the Form be like anything. Otherwise a second Form will always make its appearance over and above the first Form; and if that second Form is like anything, yet a third; and there will be no end to this emergence of fresh Forms, if the Form is to be like the thing that partakes of it.

Quite true.

It follows that the other things do not partake of Forms by being like them; we must look for some other means by which they partake.

So it seems.

You see then, Socrates, said Parmenides, what great difficulties there are in asserting their existence as Forms just by themselves?

I do indeed.

I assure you, then, you have as yet hardly a notion of how great they will be, if you are going to set up a single Form for every distinction you make among things.

How so?

The worst difficulty will be this, though there are plenty more: Suppose someone should say that the Forms, if they are such as we are saying they must be, cannot even be known. One could not convince him that he was mistaken in that objection, unless he chanced to be a man of wide experience and natural ability, and were willing to follow one through a long and remote train of argument. Otherwise there would be no way of convincing a man who maintained that the Forms were unknowable.

Why so, Parmenides?

Because, Socrates, I imagine that you or anyone else who asserts that each of them has a real being "just by itself," would admit, to begin with, that no such real being exists in our world.

True; for how could it then be just by itself?

Very good, said Parmenides. And further, those Forms which are what they are with reference to one another, have their being in such references among themselves, not with reference to those likenesses, or whatever we are to call them, in our world, which we possess and so come to be called by their several names. And, on the other hand, these things in our world which bear the same names as the Forms are related among themselves, not to the Forms; and all the names of that sort that they bear have reference to one another, not to the Forms.

How do you mean? asked Socrates.

Suppose, for instance, one of us is master or slave of another; he is not, of course, the slave of Master itself, the essential Master, nor, if he is a master, is he master of

Slave itself, the essential Slave, but, being a man, is master or slave of another man; whereas Mastership itself is what it is [mastership] of Slavery itself, and Slavery itself is slavery to Mastership itself. The significance of things in our world is not with reference to things in that other world, nor have these their significance with reference to us; but as I say, the things in that world are what they are with reference to one another and towards one another; and so likewise are the things in our world. You see what I mean?

Certainly I do.

And similarly Knowledge itself, the essence of Knowledge, will be knowledge of that Reality itself, the essentially real.

Certainly.

And again any given branch of Knowledge in itself will be knowledge of some department of real things as it is in itself, will it not?

Yes.

Whereas the knowledge in our world will be knowledge of the reality in our world; and it will follow again that each branch of knowledge in our world must be knowledge of some department of things that exist in our world.

Necessarily.

But, as you admit, we do not possess the Forms themselves, nor can they exist in our world.

No.

And presumably the Forms, just as they are in themselves, are known by the Form of Knowledge itself?

Yes.

The Form which we do not possess.

True.

Then, none of the Forms is known by us, since we have no part in Knowledge itself.

Apparently not.

So Beauty itself or Goodness itself and all the things we take as Forms in themselves, are unknowable to us.

I am afraid that is so.

Then here is a still more formidable consequence for you to consider.

What is that?

You will grant, I suppose, that if there is such a thing as a Form, Knowledge itself, it is much more perfect than the knowledge in our world; and so with Beauty and all the rest.

Yes.

And if anything has part in this Knowledge itself, you would agree that a god has a better title than anyone else to possess the most perfect knowledge?

Undoubtedly.

Then will the god, who possesses Knowledge itself, be able to know the things in our world?

Why not?

Because we have agreed that those Forms have no significance with reference to things in our world, nor have things in our world any significance with reference to them. Each set has it only among themselves.

Yes, we did.

Then if this most perfect Mastership and most perfect Knowledge are in the gods' world, the gods' Mastership can never be exercised over us, nor their Knowledge know us or anything in our world. Just as we do not rule over them by virtue of rule as it exists in our world and we know nothing that is divine by our knowledge, so they, on the same principle, being gods, are not our masters nor do they know anything of human concerns.

But surely, said Socrates, an argument which would deprive the gods of knowledge, would be too strange.

And yet, Socrates, Parmenides went on, these difficulties and many more besides are inevitably involved in the Forms, if these characters of things really exist and one is going to distinguish each Form as a thing just by itself. The result is that the hearer is perplexed and inclined either to question their existence, or to contend that, if they do exist, they must certainly be unknowable by our human nature. Moreover, there seems to be some weight in these objections, and, as we were saying, it is extraordinarily difficult to convert the objector. Only a man of exceptional gifts will be able to see that a Form, or essence just by itself, does exist in each case; and it will require someone still more remarkable to discover it and to instruct another who has thoroughly examined all these difficulties.

I admit that, Parmenides; I quite agree with what you are saying.

But on the other hand, Parmenides continued, if, in view of all these difficulties and others like them, a man refuses to admit that Forms of things exist or to distinguish a definite Form in every case, he will have nothing on which to fix his thought, so long as he will not allow that each thing has a character which is always the same; and in so doing he will completely destroy the significance of all discourse. But of that consequence I think you are only too well aware.

True.

What are you going to do about philosophy, then? Where will you turn while the answers to these questions remain unknown?

I can see no way out at the present moment.

That is because you are undertaking to define "Beautiful," "Just," "Good," and other particular Forms, too soon, before you have had a preliminary training. I noticed that the other day when I heard you talking here with Aristoteles. Believe me, there is something noble and inspired in your passion for argument; but you must make an effort and submit yourself, while you are still young, to a severer training in what the world calls idle talk and condemns as useless. Otherwise, the truth will escape you.

ARISTOTLE
384–322 B.C.

Aristotle was born in Stagira, on the border of Macedonia. His mother, Phaestis, was from a family of doctors, and his father, Nicomachus, was the court physician to the king of Macedonia. At seventeen Aristotle was sent to Athens. There he studied in Plato's Academy for two decades, but, as he later wrote, he loved the truth more than he loved Plato, and so he had no mind to remain a mere disciple. In 347 B.C., after Plato's death, he left Athens and spent the next four years conducting zoological investigations on the islands of Assos and Lesbos.

About 343 B.C. he was called to Macedonia by King Philip to tutor the king's son—the future Alexander the Great. Upon Alexander's ascension to the throne seven years later, Aristotle returned to Athens to set up the Lyceum, a rival to the Academy. Aristotle did much of his teaching walking up and down the colonnades with advanced students. As a result, his school and philosophy came to be called by the Greek word for walking around: *peripatetikos,* from which we get our word "peripatetic." Tradition has it that as Alexander the Great moved east, conquering Persia and moving into India, he would send back biological specimens for Aristotle's school. Although most scholars doubt this popular story, it is nevertheless clear that under Alexander's patronage, the Lyceum flourished.

However, the connection to Alexander proved a liability in the end. On Alexander's death in 323 B.C., the Athenians went on a rampage against any and all associated with him. Indicted on charges of impiety, Aristotle fled Athens, "lest," as he put it, "the Athenians sin twice against philosophy" (referring, of course, to the unjust trial and death of Socrates). Aristotle died a year later. A popular but again highly questionable story says he drowned investigating marine life.

There is no doubt that after Plato, Aristotle is the most influential philosopher of all time. In the early Middle Ages his thought was preserved and commented upon by the great Arab philosophers. He dominated later medieval philosophy to such an extent that St. Thomas referred to him simply as *philosophus,* the "philosopher." Logic, as taught until about the time of the Second World War, was essentially Aristotle's logic. His *Poetics* is still a classic of literary criticism, and his dicta on tragedy are widely accepted even today. Criticism of Aristotle's metaphysical and epistemological views has spread ever since Bacon and Descartes inaugurated modern philosophy; but for all that, the problems Aristotle saw, the distinctions he introduced, and the terms he defined are still central in many, if not most, philosophical discussions. His influence and prestige, like Plato's, are international and beyond all schools.

*   *   *

Aristotle found Plato's theory of Forms unacceptable. Like Plato, he wanted to discover universals, but he did not believe they existed apart from particulars. The form of a chair, for instance, can be thought of apart from the matter out of which the chair is made, but the form does not subsist as a separate invisible entity. The universal of "chairness" exists only in particular chairs—there is no other-worldly "Form of Chairness." Accordingly, Aristotle began his philosophy not with reflection on or dialogue about eternal Forms but with observations of particular objects.

In observing the world, Aristotle saw four "causes" that are responsible for making an object what it is: the material, formal, efficient, and final. In the case of a chair, for example, the chair's material cause would be its wood and cloth, its formal cause would be the structure or form given in its plan or blueprint, its efficient cause would be the worker who made it, and its final cause would be sitting. The material cause, then, is that *out of which* a thing is made, the formal cause is that *into which* a thing is made, the efficient cause is that *by which* a thing is made, and the final cause is that *for which* a thing is made. It is the last of these, the final cause, that Aristotle held to be most important, for it determined the other three. The "goal" or "end" (*telos* in Greek), the final cause, of any given substance is the key to its understanding. This means that all nature is to be understood in terms of final causes or purposes. This is known as a "teleological" explanation of reality.

As Aristotle applied these insights to human beings, he asked what the *telos* of a person could be. By observing what is unique to persons and what they, in fact, do seek, Aristotle came to the conclusion that the highest good or end for humans is *eudaimonia.* While this word is generally translated as "happiness," one must be careful to acknowledge that Aristotle's understanding of "happiness" is rather different from ours. *Eudaimonia* happiness is not a feeling of euphoria—in fact, it is not a feeling at all. It is rather "activity in accordance with virtue." Much of the material from the *Nicomachean Ethics* presented here is devoted both to clarifying the word and to discovering how this kind of "happiness" is to be achieved.

*   *   *

Aristotle's extant works lack the literary grace of Plato's. Like Plato, Aristotle is said to have written popular dialogues—the "exoteric" writings intended for those who were not students at the Lyceum—but they have not survived. What we have instead are the difficult "esoteric" works: lecture notes for classes at school. According to some scholars, these are not even Aristotle's notes, but the notes of students collected by editors. In any case, the writings as we have them contain much overlapping, repetition, and apparent contradiction.

The first five chapters of the *Categories,* with which we begin, help clear up a number of questions about Aristotle's conception of substance. Written as a treatise on language, the *Categories* makes clear why Aristotle rejected Plato's approach to knowledge of the Forms.

The *Physics* deals with some of the main questions of physical science. In Book II, reprinted here (complete), Aristotle makes a distinction between physics and mathematics and discusses the four causes. This work is translated by R.P. Hardie and R.K. Gaye.

The *Metaphysics* probably consists of several independent treatises. Book I *(Alpha)* of this collection develops Aristotle's four causes and reviews the history of philosophy to his time. Book XII *(Lambda)* employs many of the concepts previously introduced, such as substance, actuality, and potency, and then moves to Aristotle's theology of the Unmoved Mover. The work concludes with Aristotle's rejection of Platonic Forms as separate, mathematical entities. Apparently Aristotle was responding to Plato's successors, who emphasized the mathematical nature of the Forms. W.D. Ross is the translator.

The first part of the selection presented from Aristotle's *On the Soul (De Anima)* gives a definition of the soul and distinguishes its faculties. The second part discusses the passive and the active mind. As this selection makes clear, Aristotle rejected Plato's view of a soul separate from the body. The selection is given in the translation by J.A. Smith.

Our final selection, the *Nicomachean Ethics,* is still considered one of the greatest works in ethics. Named for Aristotle's son, Nicomachus, it discusses the nature of the good and of moral and intellectual virtues, as well as investigating specific virtues. The lengthy selection presented here (about one-half of the complete work) reflects this vast range of topics and includes discussions of the subject matter and nature of ethics; of the good for an individual; of moral virtue; of the mean; of the conditions of responsibility for an action; of pride, vanity, humility, and the great-souled man (Aristotle's ideal); of the superiority of loving over being loved; and finally, of human happiness. The translation is Martin Ostwald's.

The marginal page numbers, with their "a" and "b," are those of all scholarly editions—Greek, English, German, French, and others.

*   *   *

Timothy A. Robinson, *Aristotle in Outline* (Indianapolis, IN: Hackett, 1995) provides an excellent short introduction for the beginning student. W.K.C. Guthrie, *A History of Greek Philosophy, VI: Aristotle: An Encounter* (Cambridge: Cambridge University Press, 1981) and the classic W.D. Ross, *Aristotle* (1923; reprinted in New York: Meridian Books, 1959) are more advanced studies. John Herman Randall, Jr., *Aristotle* (New York: Columbia University Press, 1960); Marjorie Grene, *A Portrait of Aristotle* (Chicago: University of Chicago Press, 1963); J.L. Ackrill, *Aristotle the Philosopher* (Oxford: Oxford University Press, 1981); Jonathan Barnes, *Aristotle* (Oxford: Oxford University Press, 1982); Jonathan Lear, *Aristotle: The Desire to Understand* (Cambridge: Cambridge University Press, 1988); Terence Irwin, *Aristotle's First Principles* (Oxford: Oxford

University Press, 1988); and Jonathan Barnes, ed., *The Cambridge Companion to Aristotle* (Cambridge: Cambridge University Press, 1995) also provide helpful overviews of Aristotle's life and thought. For general collections of essays, see R. Bambrough, ed., *New Essays on Plato and Aristotle* (London: Routledge & Kegan Paul, 1965); J.M.E. Moravcsik, ed., *Aristotle: A Collection of Critical Essays* (New York: Anchor Doubleday, 1967); and J. Barnes, M. Schofield, and R. Sorabji, eds., *Articles on Aristotle,* four vols. (London: Duckworth, 1979). For help with specific works (besides the *Nicomachean Ethics*), see Lindsay Judson, *Aristotle's Physics: A Collection of Essays* (Oxford: Oxford University Press, 1991); Helen S. Lang, *Aristotle's Physics and Its Medieval Varieties* (Albany: SUNY Press, 1992); and Martha C. Nussbaum and Amelie O. Rorty, eds., *Essays on Aristotle's De Anima* (Oxford: Oxford University Press, 1992). The *Nichomachean Ethics* has been such an influential book that many commentaries and essays have been written about it. Among these are H.H. Joachim, *Aristotle: The Nicomachean Ethics,* edited by D.A. Rees (Oxford: Clarendon Press, 1951); W.F.R. Hardie, *Aristotle's Ethical Theory,* 2nd edition (Oxford: Oxford University Press, 1980); Amelie O. Rorty, ed., *Essays on Aristotle's Ethics* (Berkeley: University of California Press, 1980); J.O. Urmson, *Aristotle's Ethics* (Oxford: Basil Blackwell, 1988); Sarah Brodie, *Ethics with Aristotle* (Oxford: Oxford University Press, 1991); and Francis Sparshott, *Taking Life Seriously: A Study of the Argument of the Nichomachean Ethics* (Toronto: University of Toronto Press, 1994). Alasdair C. MacIntyre's pair of books, *After Virtue: A Study in Moral Theory* (Notre Dame, IN: University of Notre Dame Press, 1981) and *Whose Justice? Which Rationality?* (Notre Dame, IN: University of Notre Dame Press, 1988) are interesting examples of recent attempts to apply Aristotle's ethics to contemporary moral problems.

CATEGORIES (in part)

1. When things have only a name in common and the definition of being which corresponds to the name is different, they are called *homonymous.* Thus, for example, both a man and a picture are animals. These have only a name in common and the definition of being which corresponds to the name is different; for if one is to say what being an animal is for each of them, one will give two distinct definitions.   5

When things have the name in common and the definition of being which corresponds to the name is the same, they are called *synonymous.* Thus, for example, both a man and an ox are animals. Each of these is called by a common name, "animal," and the definition of being is also the same; for if one is to give the definition of each—what   10
being an animal is for each of them—one will give the same definition.

When things get their name from something, with a difference of ending, they are called *paronymous.* Thus, for example, the grammarian gets his name from grammar, the brave get theirs from bravery.   15

1ª

Aristotle, *Categories,* Chapters 1–5 from *Aristotle's Categories and De Interpretatione,* translated by J.L. Ackrill (Oxford: Oxford University Press, 1963). Reprinted by permission of Oxford University Press.

Diskobolos, by Myron. A Roman copy after a bronze original of ca. 450 B.C. Myron's athlete epitomizes the ideal Olympian goals of godlike perfection and rational beauty. (*Museo del Terme, Rome*)

2. Of things that are said, some involve combination while others are said without combination. Examples of those involving combination are "man runs," "man wins"; and of those without combination "man," "ox," "runs," "wins."

20 Of things there are: *(a)* some are *said of* a subject but are not *in* any subject. For example, man is said of a subject, the individual man, but is not in any subject. *(b)* Some are in a subject but are not said of any subject. (By "in a subject" I mean what is in something, not as a part, and cannot exist separately from what it is in.) For ex-
25 ample, the individual knowledge-of-grammar is in a subject, the soul, but is not said of any subject; and the individual white is in a subject, the body (for all colour is in a body), but is not said of any subject. *(c)* Some are both said of a subject and in a sub-
1ᵇ ject. For example, knowledge is in a subject, the soul, and is also said of a subject, knowledge-of-grammar. *(d)* Some are neither in a subject nor said of a subject, for ex-
5 ample, the individual man or individual horse—for nothing of this sort is either in a subject or said of a subject. Things that are individual and numerically one are, without exception, not said of any subject, but there is nothing to prevent some of them from being in a subject—the individual knowledge-of-grammar is one of the things in a subject.

3. Whenever one thing is predicated of another as of a subject, all things said of what is   10
predicated will be said of the subject also. For example, man is predicated of the individual man, and animal of man; so animal will be predicated of the individual man   15
also—for the individual man is both a man and an animal.

  The differentiae of genera which are different and not subordinate one to the
other are themselves different in kind. For example, animal and knowledge: footed,
winged, aquatic, two-footed, are differentiae of animal, but none of these is a differen-   20
tia of knowledge; one sort of knowledge does not differ from another by being
two-footed. However, there is nothing to prevent genera subordinate one to the
other from having the same differentiae. For the higher are predicated of the genera
below them, so that all differentiae of the predicated genus will be differentiae of the
subject also.

4. Of things said without any combination, each signifies either substance or quantity or   25
qualification or a relative or where or when or being-in-a-position or having or doing or
being-affected. To give a rough idea, examples of substance are man, horse; of quantity:
four-foot, five-foot; of qualification: white, grammatical; of a relative: double, half,   2ᵃ
larger; of where: in the Lyceum, in the market-place; of when: yesterday, last-year; of
being-in-a-position: is-lying, is-sitting; of having: has-shoes-on, has-armour-on; of doing: cutting, burning; of being-affected: being-cut, being-burned.

  None of the above is said just by itself in any affirmation, but by the combination   5
of these with one another an affirmation is produced. For every affirmation, it seems, is
either true or false; but of things said without any combination none is either true or
false (e.g. "man," "white," "runs," "wins").   10

5. A *substance*—that which is called a substance most strictly, primarily, and most of
all—is that which is neither said of a subject nor in a subject, e.g. the individual man or   15
the individual horse. The species in which the things primarily called substances are,
are called *secondary substances,* as also are the genera of these species. For example,
the individual man belongs in a species, man, and animal is a genus of the species; so
these—both man and animal—are called secondary substances.

  It is clear from what has been said that if something is said of a subject both its
name and its definition are necessarily predicated of the subject. For example, man is   20
said of a subject, the individual man, and the name is of course predicated (since you
will be predicating man of the individual man), and also the definition of man will be   25
predicated of the individual man (since the individual man is also a man). Thus both the
name and the definition will be predicated of the subject. But as for things which are in
a subject, in most cases neither the name nor the definition is predicated of the subject.
In some cases there is nothing to prevent the name from being predicated of the subject,   30
but it is impossible for the definition to be predicated. For example, white, which is in a
subject (the body), is predicated of the subject; for a body is called white. But the definition of white will never be predicated of the body.

  All the other things are either said of the primary substances as subjects or in   35
them as subjects. This is clear from an examination of cases. For example, animal is
predicated of man and therefore also of the individual man; for were it predicated of
none of the individual men it would not be predicated of man at all. Again, colour is in
body and therefore also in an individual body; for were it not in some individual body it   2ᵇ
would not be in body at all. Thus all the other things are either said of the primary substances as subjects or in them as subjects. So if the primary substances did not exist it   5
would be impossible for any of the other things to exist.

Of the secondary substances the species is more a substance than the genus, since it is nearer to the primary substance. For if one is to say of the primary substance what it is,
10 it will be more informative and apt to give the species than the genus. For example, it would be more informative to say of the individual man that he is a man than that he is an animal (since the one is more distinctive of the individual man while the other is more general); and more informative to say of the individual tree that it is a tree than that it is a
15 plant. Further, it is because the primary substances are subjects for all the other things and all the other things are predicated of them or are in them, that they are called substances most of all. But as the primary substances stand to the other things, so the species stands
20 to the genus: the species is a subject for the genus (for the genera are predicated of the species but the species are not predicated reciprocally of the genera). Hence for this reason too the species is more a substance than the genus.

But of the species themselves—those which are not genera—one is no more a substance than another: it is no more apt to say of the individual man that he is a man
25 than to say of the individual horse that it is a horse. And similarly of the primary substances one is no more a substance than another: the individual man is no more a substance than the individual ox.

It is reasonable that, after the primary substances, their species and genera should
30 be the only other things called (secondary) substances. For only they, of things predicated, reveal the primary substance. For if one is to say of the individual man what he is, it will be in place to give the species or the genus (though more informative to give man than animal); but to give any of the other things would be out of place—for exam-
35 ple, to say "white" or "runs" or anything like that. So it is reasonable that these should be the only other things called substances. Further, it is because the primary substances are subjects for everything else that they are called substances most strictly. But as the
3ᵃ primary substances stand to everything else, so the species and genera of the primary substances stand to all the rest: all the rest are predicated of these. For if you will call the individual man grammatical it follows that you will call both a man and an animal
5 grammatical; and similarly in other cases.

It is a characteristic common to every substance not to be in a subject. For a pri-
10 mary substance is neither said of a subject nor in a subject. And as for secondary substances, it is obvious at once that they are not in a subject. For man is said of the individual man as subject but is not in a subject: man is not *in* the individual man. Similarly,
15 animal also is said of the individual man as subject but animal is not in the individual man. Further, while there is nothing to prevent the name of what is in a subject from being sometimes predicated of the subject, it is impossible for the definition to be predicated. But the definition of the secondary substances, as well as the name, is predicated
20 of the subject: you will predicate the definition of man of the individual man, and also that of animal. No substance, therefore, is in a subject.

This is not, however, peculiar to substance; the differentia also is not in a subject.
25 For footed and two-footed are said of man as subject but are not in a subject; neither two-footed nor footed is *in* man. Moreover, the definition of the differentia is predicated of that of which the differentia is said. For example, if footed is said of man the definition of footed will also be predicated of man; for man is footed.
30 We need not be disturbed by any fear that we may be forced to say that the parts of a substance, being in a subject (the whole substance), are not substances. For when we spoke of things *in a subject* we did not mean things belonging in something as *parts*.

It is a characteristic of substances and differentiae that all things called from them
35 are so called synonymously. For all the predicates from them are predicated either of the individuals or of the species. (For from a primary substance there is no predicate, since

it is said of no subject; and as for secondary substances, the species is predicated of the individual, the genus both of the species and of the individual. Similarly, differentiae too are predicated both of the species and of the individuals.) And the primary substances admit the definition of the species and of the genera, and the species admits that of the genus; for everything said of what is predicated will be said of the subject also. Similarly, both the species and the individuals admit the definition of the differentiae. But synonymous things were precisely those with both the name in common and the same definition. Hence all the things called from substances and differentiae are so called synonymously.

Every substance seems to signify a certain "this." As regards the primary substances, it is indisputably true that each of them signifies a certain "this"; for the thing revealed is individual and numerically one. But as regards the secondary substances, though it appears from the form of the name—when one speaks of man or animal—that a secondary substance likewise signifies a certain "this," this is not really true; rather, it signifies a certain qualification, for the subject is not, as the primary substance is, one, but man and animal are said of many things. However, it does not signify simply a certain qualification, as white does. White signifies nothing but a qualification, whereas the species and the genus mark off the qualification of substance—they signify substance of a certain qualification. (One draws a wider boundary with the genus than with the species, for in speaking of animal one takes in more than in speaking of man.)

Another characteristic of substances is that there is nothing contrary to them. For what would be contrary to a primary substance? For example, there is nothing contrary to an individual man, nor yet is there anything contrary to man or to animal. This, however, is not peculiar to substance but holds of many other things also, for example, of quantity. For there is nothing contrary to four-foot or to ten or to anything of this kind—unless someone were to say that many is contrary to few or large to small; but still there is nothing contrary to any *definite* quantity.

Substance, it seems, does not admit of a more and a less. I do not mean that one substance is not more a substance than another (we have said that it is), but that any given substance is not called more, or less, than that which it is. For example, if this substance is a man, it will not be more a man or less a man either than itself or than another man. For one man is not more a man than another, as one pale thing is more pale than another and one beautiful thing more beautiful than another. Again, a thing is called more, or less, such-and-such than itself; for example, the body that is pale is called more pale now than before, and the one that is hot is called more, or less, hot. Substance, however, is not spoken of thus. For a man is not called more a man now than before, nor is anything else that is a substance. Thus substance does not admit of a more and a less.

It seems most distinctive of substance that what is numerically one and the same is able to receive contraries. In no other case could one bring forward anything, numerically one, which is able to receive contraries. For example, a colour which is numerically one and the same will not be black and white, nor will numerically one and the same action be bad and good; and similarly with everything else that is not substance. A substance, however, numerically one and the same, is able to receive contraries. For example, an individual man—one and the same—becomes pale at one time and dark at another, and hot and cold, and bad and good.

Nothing like this is to be seen in any other case, unless someone might object and say that statements and beliefs are like this. For the same statement seems to be both true and false. Suppose, for example, that the statement that somebody is sitting is true; after he has got up this same statement will be false. Similarly with beliefs. Suppose you believe truly that somebody is sitting; after he has got up you will believe falsely if you hold the same belief about him. However, even if we were to grant this, there is still a difference in the way contraries are received. For in the case of substances it is by themselves changing that they are able to receive contraries. For what has become cold instead of hot, or dark instead of pale, or good instead of bad, has changed (has altered); similarly in other cases too it is by itself undergoing change that each thing is able to receive contraries. Statements and beliefs, on the other hand, themselves remain completely unchangeable in every way; it is because the *actual thing* changes that the contrary comes to belong to them. For the statement that somebody is sitting remains the same; it is because of a change in the actual thing that it comes to be true at one time and false at another. Similarly with beliefs. Hence at least the *way* in which it is able to receive contraries—through a change in itself—would be distinctive of substance, even if we were to grant that beliefs and statements are able to receive contraries. However, this is not true. For it is not because they themselves receive anything that statements and beliefs are said to be able to receive contraries, but because of what has happened to something else. For it is because the actual thing exists or does not exist that the statement is said to be true or false, not because it is able itself to receive contraries. No statement, in fact, or belief is changed at all by anything. So, since nothing happens in them, they are not able to receive contraries. A substance, on the other hand, is said to be able to receive contraries because it itself receives contraries. For it receives sickness and health, and paleness and darkness; and because it itself receives the various things of this kind it is said to be able to receive contraries. It is, therefore, distinctive of substance that what is numerically one and the same is able to receive contraries. This brings to an end our discussion of substance.

PHYSICS (in part)

BOOK II

1. Of things that exist, some exist by nature, some from other causes. By nature the animals and their parts exist, and the plants and the simple bodies (earth, fire, air, water)—for we say that these and the like exist by nature.

All the things mentioned plainly differ from things which are *not* constituted by nature. For each of them has within itself a principle of motion and of stationariness (in respect of place, or of growth and decrease, or by way of alteration). On the other hand, a bed and a coat and anything else of that sort, *qua* receiving these designations—i.e. in so far as they are products of art—have no innate impulse to change. But in so far as they happen to be composed of stone or of earth or of a mixture of the two, they *do* have such an impulse, and just to that extent which seems to indicate that nature is a princi-

Aristotle, *Physics,* Book II, translated by R.P. Hardie and R.K. Gaye from *Complete Works of Aristotle,* edited by Jonathan Barnes (Princeton, NJ: Princeton University Press, 1984). Copyright © 1984 by PUP. Reprinted by permission of Princeton University Press.

ple or cause of being moved and of being at rest in that to which it belongs primarily, in virtue of itself and not accidentally.

I say "not accidentally," because (for instance) a man who is a doctor might himself be a cause of health to himself. Nevertheless it is not in so far as he is a patient that he possesses the art of medicine: it merely has happened that the same man is doctor and patient—and that is why these attributes are not always found together. So it is with all other artificial products. None of them has in itself the principle of its own production. But while in some cases (for instance houses and the other products of manual labour) that principle is in something else external to the thing, in others—those which may cause a change in themselves accidentally—it lies in the things themselves (but not in virtue of what they are).

Nature then is what has been stated. Things have a nature which have a principle of this kind. Each of them is a substance; for it is a subject, and nature is always in a subject.

The term "according to nature" is applied to all these things and also to the attributes which belong to them in virtue of what they are, for instance the property of fire to be carried upwards—which is not a nature nor has a nature but is by nature or according to nature.

What nature is, then, and the meaning of the terms "by nature" and "according to nature," has been stated. *That* nature exists, it would be absurd to try to prove; for it is obvious that there are many things of this kind, and to prove what is obvious by what is not is the mark of a man who is unable to distinguish what is self-evident from what is not. (This state of mind is clearly possible. A man blind from birth might reason about colours.) Presumably therefore such persons must be talking about words without any thought to correspond.

Some identify the nature or substance of a natural object with that immediate constituent of it which taken by itself is without arrangement, e.g. the wood is the nature of the bed, and the bronze the nature of the statue.

As an indication of this Antiphon points out that if you planted a bed and the rotting wood acquired the power of sending up a shoot, it would not be a bed that would come up, but *wood* which shows that the arrangement in accordance with the rules of the art is merely an accidental attribute, whereas the substance is the other, which, further, persists continuously through the process.

But if the material of each of these objects has itself the same relation to something else, say bronze (or gold) to water, bones (or wood) to earth and so on, *that* (they say) would be their nature and substance. Consequently some assert earth, others fire or air or water or some or all of these, to be the nature of the things that are. For whatever any one of them supposed to have this character—whether one thing or more than one thing—this or these he declared to be the whole of substance, all else being its affections, states, or dispositions. Every such thing they held to be eternal (for it could not pass into anything else), but other things to come into being and cease to be times without number.

This then is one account of nature, namely that it is the primary underlying matter of things which have in themselves a principle of motion or change.

Another account is that nature is the shape or form which is specified in the definition of the thing.

For the word "nature" is applied to what is according to nature and the natural in the same way as "art" is applied to what is artistic or a work of art. We should not say in the latter case that there is anything artistic about a thing, if it is a bed only potentially, not yet having the form of a bed; nor should we call it a work of art. The same is true of

25

30

35

193ᵃ

5

10

15

20

25

30

35

193ᵇ natural compounds. What is potentially flesh or bone has not yet its own nature, and does not exist by nature, until it receives the form specified in the definition, which we name in defining what flesh or bone is. Thus on the second account of nature, it would

5 be the shape or form (not separable except in statement) of things which have in themselves a principle of motion. (The combination of the two, e.g. man, is not nature but by nature.)

The form indeed is nature rather than the matter; for a thing is more properly said to be what it is when it exists in actuality than when it exists potentially. Again man is born from man but not bed from bed. That is why people say that the shape is not the na-

10 ture of a bed, but the wood is—if the bed sprouted, not a bed but wood would come up. But even if the shape *is* art, then on the same principle the shape of man is his nature. For man is born from man.

Again, nature in the sense of a coming-to-be proceeds towards nature. For it is not like doctoring, which leads not to the art of doctoring but to health. Doctoring must start

15 from the art, not lead to it. But it is not in this way that nature is related to nature. What grows *qua* growing grows from something into something. Into what then does it grow? Not into that from which it arose but into that to which it tends. The shape then is nature.

Shape and nature are used in two ways. For the privation too is in a way form. But

20 whether in unqualified coming to be there is privation, i.e. a contrary, we must consider later.

2. We have distinguished, then, the different ways in which the term "nature" is used.

The next point to consider is how the mathematician differs from the student of nature; for natural bodies contain surfaces and volumes, lines and points, and these are

25 the subject-matter of mathematics.

Further, is astronomy different from natural science or a department of it? It seems absurd that the student of nature should be supposed to know the nature of sun or moon, but not to know any of their essential attributes, particularly as the writers on na-

30 ture obviously do discuss their shape and whether the earth and the world are spherical or not.

Now the mathematician, though he too treats of these things, nevertheless does not treat of them as the limits of a natural body; nor does he consider the attributes indicated as the attributes of such bodies. That is why he separates them, for in thought they are separable from motion, and it makes no difference, nor does any falsity result, if

35 they are separated. The holders of the theory of Forms do the same, though they are not aware of it; for they separate the objects of natural science, which are less separable

194ᵃ than those of mathematics. This becomes plain if one tries to state in each of the two cases the definitions of the things and of their attributes. Odd and even, straight and curved, and likewise number, line, and figure, do not involve motion; not so flesh and

5 bone and man—*these* are defined like snub nose, not like curved.

Similar evidence is supplied by the more natural of the branches of mathematics, such as optics, harmonics, and astronomy. These are in a way the converse of geometry.

10 While geometry investigates natural lines but not *qua* natural, optics investigates mathematical lines, but *qua* natural, not *qua* mathematical.

Since two sorts of thing are called nature, the form and the matter, we must investigate its objects as we would the essence of snubness, that is neither independently of matter nor in terms of matter only. Here too indeed one might raise a difficulty. Since

15 there are two natures, with which is the student of nature concerned? Or should he investigate the combination of the two? But if the combination of the two, then also each

severally. Does it belong then to the same or to different sciences to know each severally?

If we look at the ancients, natural science would seem to be concerned with the *matter*. (It was only very slightly that Empedocles and Democritus touched on form and   20 essence.)

But if on the other hand art imitates nature, and it is the part of the same discipline to know the form and the matter up to a point (e.g. the doctor has a knowledge of health and also of bile and phlegm, in which health is realized and the builder both of the form of the house and of the matter, namely that it is bricks and beams, and so forth): if this   25 is so, it would be the part of natural science also to know nature in both its senses.

Again, that for the sake of which, or the end, belongs to the same department of knowledge as the means. But the nature is the end or that for the sake of which. For if a thing undergoes a continuous change toward some end, that last stage is actually that for   30 the sake of which. (That is why the poet was carried away into making an absurd statement when he said "he has the end for the sake of which he was born." For not every stage that is last claims to be an end, but only that which is best.)

For the arts make their material (some simply make it, others make it serviceable), and we use everything as if it was there for our sake. (We also are in a sense an   35 end. "That for the sake of which" may be taken in two ways, as we said in our work *On Philosophy*.) The arts, therefore, which govern the matter and have knowledge are two,   194ᵇ namely the art which uses the product and the art which directs the production of it. That is why the using art also is in a sense directive; but it differs in that it knows the form, whereas the art which is directive as being concerned with production knows the matter. For the helmsman knows and prescribes what sort of form a helm should have,   5 the other from what wood it should be made and by means of what operations. In the products of art, however, we make the material with a view to the function, whereas in the products of nature the matter is there all along.

Again, matter is a relative thing—for different forms there is different matter.

How far then must the student of nature know the form or essence? Up to a point,   10 perhaps, as the doctor must know sinew or the smith bronze (i.e. until he understands the purpose of each); and the student of nature is concerned only with things whose forms are separable indeed, but do not exist apart from matter. Man is begotten by man and by the sun as well. The mode of existence and essence of the separable it is the busi-   15 ness of first philosophy to define.

3. Now that we have established these distinctions, we must proceed to consider causes, their character and number. Knowledge is the object of our inquiry, and men do not think they know a thing till they have grasped the "why" of it (which is to grasp its pri-   20 mary cause). So clearly we too must do this as regards both coming to be and passing away and every kind of natural change, in order that, knowing their principles, we may try to refer to these principles each of our problems.

In one way, then, that out of which a thing comes to be and which persists, is called a cause, e.g. the bronze of the statue, the silver of the bowl, and the genera of   25 which the bronze and the silver are species.

In another way, the form or the archetype, i.e. the definition of the essence, and its genera, are called causes (e.g. of the octave the relation of 2:1, and generally number), and the parts in the definition.

Again, the primary source of the change or rest; e.g. the man who deliberated is a   30 cause, the father is cause of the child, and generally what makes of what is made and what changes of what is changed.

Again, in the sense of end or that for the sake of which a thing is done, e.g. health is the cause of walking about. ("Why is he walking about?" We say: "To be healthy," and, having said that, we think we have assigned the cause.) The same is true also of all the intermediate steps which are brought about through the action of something else as means towards the end, e.g. reduction of flesh, purging, drugs, or surgical instruments are means towards health. All these things are for the sake of the end, though they differ from one another in that some are activities, others instruments.

This then perhaps exhausts the number of ways in which the term "cause" is used.

As things are called causes in many ways, it follows that there are several causes of the same thing (not merely accidentally), e.g. both the art of the sculptor and the bronze are causes of the statue. These are causes of the statue *qua* statue, not in virtue of anything else that it may be—only not in the same way, the one being the material cause, the other the cause whence the motion comes. Some things cause each other reciprocally, e.g. hard work causes fitness and *vice versa,* but again not in the same way, but the one as end, the other as the principle of motion. Further the same thing is the cause of contrary results. For that which by its presence brings about one result is sometimes blamed for bringing about the contrary by its absence. Thus we ascribe the wreck of a ship to the absence of the pilot whose presence was the cause of its safety.

All the causes now mentioned fall into four familiar divisions. The letters are the causes of syllables, the material of artificial products, fire and the like of bodies, the parts of the whole, and the premises of the conclusion, in the sense of "that from which." Of these pairs the one set are causes in the sense of what underlies, e.g. the parts, the other set in the sense of essence—the whole and the combination and the form. But the seed and the doctor and the deliberator, and generally the maker, are all sources whence the change or stationariness originates, which the others are causes in the sense of the end or the good of the rest; for that for the sake of which tends to be what is best and the end of the things that lead up to it. (Whether we call it good or apparently good makes no difference.)

Such then is the number and nature of the kinds of cause.

Now the modes of causation are many, though when brought under heads they too can be reduced in number. For things are called causes in many ways and even within the same kind one may be prior to another: e.g. the doctor and the expert are causes of health, the relation 2:1 and number of the octave, and always what is inclusive to what is particular. Another mode of causation is the accidental and its genera, e.g. in one way Polyclitus, in another a sculptor is the cause of a statue, because being Polyclitus and a sculptor are accidentally conjoined. Also the classes in which the accidental attribute is included; thus a man could be said to be the cause of a statue or, generally, a living creature. An accidental attribute too may be more or less remote, e.g. suppose that a pale man or a musical man were said to be the cause of the statue.

All causes, both proper and accidental, may be spoken of either as potential or as actual; e.g. the cause of a house being built is either a house-builder or a house-builder building.

Similar distinctions can be made in the things of which the causes are causes, e.g. of this statue or of a statue or of an image generally, of this bronze or of bronze or of material generally. So too with the accidental attributes. Again we may use a complex expression for either and say, e.g. neither "Polyclitus" nor a "sculptor" but "Polyclitus, the sculptor."

All these various uses, however, come to six in number, under each of which again the usage is twofold. It is either what is particular or a genus, or an accidental attribute or a genus of that, and these either as a complex or each by itself; and all either as actual or as potential. The difference is this much, that causes which are actually at work and particular exist and cease to exist simultaneously with their effect, e.g. this healing person with this being-healed person and that housebuilding man with that being-built house; but this is not always true of potential causes—the house and the housebuilder do not pass away simultaneously. 20

In investigating the cause of each thing it is always necessary to seek what is most precise (as also in other things): thus a man builds because he is a builder, and a builder builds in virtue of his art of building. This last cause then is prior; and so generally. 25

Further, generic effects should be assigned to generic causes, particular effects to particular causes, e.g. statue to sculptor, this statue to this sculptor; and powers are relative to possible effects, actually operating causes to things which are actually being effected.

This must suffice for our account of the number of causes and the modes of causation. 30

4. But chance and spontaneity are also reckoned among causes: many things are said both to be and to come to be as a result of chance and spontaneity. We must inquire therefore in what manner chance and spontaneity are present among the causes enumerated, and whether they are the same or different, and generally what chance and spontaneity are. 35

Some people even question whether there are such things or not. They say that nothing happens by chance, but that everything which we ascribe to chance or spontaneity has some definite cause, e.g. coming by chance into the market and finding there a man whom one wanted but did not expect to meet is due to one's wish to go and buy in the market. Similarly, in other so-called cases of chance it is always possible, they maintain, to find something which is the cause; but not chance, for if chance were real, it would seem strange indeed, and the question might be raised, why on earth none of the wise men of old in speaking of the causes of generation and decay took account of chance; whence it would seem that they too did not believe that anything is by chance. But there is a further circumstance that is surprising. Many things both come to be and are by chance and spontaneity, and although all know that each of them can be ascribed to some cause (as the old argument said which denied chance), nevertheless they all speak of some of these things as happening by chance and others not. For this reason they ought to have at least referred to the matter in some way or other. 196ᵃ 5 10 15

Certainly the early physicists found no place for chance among the causes which they recognized—love, strife, mind, fire, or the like. This is strange, whether they supposed that there is no such thing as chance or whether they thought there is but omitted to mention it—and that too when they sometimes used it, as Empedocles does when he says that the air is not always separated into the highest region, but as it may chance. At any rate he says in his cosmogony that "it happened to run that way at that time, but it often ran otherwise." He tells us also that most of the parts of animals came to be by chance. 20

There are some who actually ascribe this heavenly sphere and all the worlds to spontaneity. They say that the vortex arose spontaneously, i.e. the motion that separated and arranged the universe in its present order. This statement might well cause surprise. For they are asserting that chance is not responsible for the existence or generation of animals and plants, nature or mind or something of the kind being the cause of them (for it is not any chance thing that comes from a given seed but an olive from one kind and a man from another); and yet at the same time they assert that the heavenly sphere and the divinest of visible things arose spontaneously, having no such cause as is assigned 25 30

35   to animals and plants. Yet if this is so, it is a fact which deserves to be dwelt upon, and
     something might well have been said about it. For besides the other absurdities of the
196ᵇ statement, it is the more absurd that people should make it when they see nothing com-
     ing to be spontaneously in the heavens, but much happening by chance among the
     things which as they say are not due to chance; whereas we should have expected ex-
     actly the opposite.

5   Others there are who believe that chance is a cause, but that it is inscrutable to hu-
     man intelligence, as being a divine thing and full of mystery.

         Thus we must inquire what chance and spontaneity are, whether they are the same
     or different, and how they fit into our division of causes.

10   5. First then we observe that some things always come to pass in the same way, and oth-
     ers for the most part. It is clearly of neither of these that chance, or the result of chance,
     is said to be the cause—neither of that which is by necessity and always, nor of that
     which is for the most part. But as there is a third class of events besides these two—
15   events which all say are by chance—it is plain that there is such a thing as chance and
     spontaneity; for we know that things of this kind are due to chance and that things due
     to chance are of this kind.

         Of things that come to be, some come to be for the sake of something, others not.
     Again, some of the former class are in accordance with intention, others not, but both
     are in the class of things which are for the sake of something. Hence it is clear that even
20   among the things which are outside what is necessary and what is for the most part,
     there are some in connexion with which the phrase "for the sake of something" is ap-
     plicable. (Things that are for the sake of something include whatever may be done as a
     result of thought or of nature.) Things of this kind, then, when they come to pass acci-
25   dentally are said to be by chance. For just as a thing is something either in virtue of it-
     self or accidentally, so may it be a cause. For instance, the housebuilding faculty is in
     virtue of itself a cause of a house, whereas the pale or the musical is an accidental cause.
     That which is *per se* cause is determinate, but the accidental cause is indeterminable; for
     the possible attributes of an individual are innumerable. As we said, then, when a thing
30   of this kind comes to pass among events which are for the sake of something, it is said
     to be spontaneous or by chance. (The distinction between the two must be made later—
     for the present it is sufficient if it is plain that both are in the sphere of things done for
     the sake of something.)

         Example: A man is engaged in collecting subscriptions for a feast. He would have
     gone to such and such a place for the purpose of getting the money, if he had known. He
35   actually went there for another purpose, and it was only accidentally that he got his
     money by going there; and this was not due to the fact that he went there as a rule or
197ᵃ necessarily, nor is the end effected (getting the money) a cause present in himself—it
     belongs to the class of things that are objects of choice and the result of thought. It is
     when these conditions are satisfied that the man is said to have gone by chance. If he
     had chosen and gone for the sake of this—if he always or normally went there when he
5   was collecting payments—he would not be said to have gone by chance.

         It is clear then that chance is an accidental cause in the sphere of those actions for
     the sake of something which involves choice. Thought, then, and chance are in the same
     sphere, for choice implies thought.

         It is necessary, no doubt, that the causes of what comes to pass by chance be in-
     definite; and that is why chance is supposed to belong to the class of the indefinite and
10   to be inscrutable to man, and why it might be thought that, in a way, nothing occurs by
     chance. For all these statements are correct, as might be expected. Things *do,* in a way,

occur by chance, for they occur accidentally and chance is an accidental cause. But it is not the cause without qualification of anything; for instance, a housebuilder is the cause of a house; accidentally, a fluteplayer may be so.   15

And the causes of the man's coming and getting the money (when he did not come for the sake of that) are innumerable. He may have wished to see somebody or been following somebody or avoiding somebody, or may have gone to see a spectacle. Thus to say that chance is unaccountable is correct. For an account is of what holds always or for the most part, whereas chance belongs to a third type of event. Hence, since   20 causes of this kind are indefinite, chance too is indefinite. (Yet in some cases one might raise the question whether *any* chance fact might be the cause of the chance occurrence, e.g. of health the fresh air or the sun's heat may be the cause, but having had one's hair cut *cannot;* for some accidental causes are more relevant to the effect than others.)

Chance is called good when the result is good, evil when it is evil. The terms   25 "good fortune" and "ill fortune" are used when either result is of considerable magnitude. Thus one who comes within an ace of some great evil or great good is said to be fortunate or unfortunate. The mind affirms the presence of the attribute, ignoring the hair's breadth of difference. Further, it is with reason that good fortune is regarded as   30 unstable; for chance is unstable, as none of the things which result from it can hold always or for the most part.

Both are then, as I have said, accidental causes—both chance and spontaneity— in the sphere of things which are capable of coming to pass not simply, nor for the most part and with reference to such of these as might come to pass for the sake of some-   35 thing.

6. They differ in that spontaneity is the wider. Every result of chance is from what is spontaneous, but not everything that is from what is spontaneous is from chance.

Chance and what results from chance are appropriate to agents that are capable of   197^b good fortune and of action generally. Therefore necessarily chance is in the sphere of actions. This is indicated by the fact that good fortune is thought to be the same, or nearly the same, as happiness, and happiness to be a kind of action, since it is well-   5 doing. Hence what is not capable of action cannot do anything by chance. Thus an inanimate thing or a beast or a child cannot do anything by chance, because it is incapable of choice; nor can good fortune or ill fortune be ascribed to them, except metaphorically, as Protarchus, for example, said that the stones of which altars are made are for-   10 tunate because they are held in honour, while their fellows are trodden under foot. Even these things, however, can in a way be affected by chance, when one who is dealing with them does something to them by chance, but not otherwise.

The spontaneous on the other hand is found both in the beasts and in many inanimate objects. We say, for example, that the horse came spontaneously, because, though   15 his coming saved him, he did not come for the sake of safety. Again, the tripod fell spontaneously, because, though it stood on its feet so as to serve for a seat, it did not fall so as to serve for a seat.

Hence it is clear that events which belong to the general class of things that may come to pass for the sake of something, when they come to pass not for the sake of what actually results, and have an external cause, may be described by the phrase "from   20 spontaneity." These spontaneous events are said to be from chance if they have the further characteristics of being the objects of choice and happening to agents capable of choice. This is indicated by the phrase "in vain," which is used when one thing which is for the sake of another, does not result in it. For instance, taking a walk is for the sake of evacuation of the bowels; if this does not follow after walking, we say that we have

25 walked in vain and that the walking was vain. This implies that what is naturally for the sake of an end is in vain, when it does not effect the end for the sake of which it was the natural means—for it would be absurd for a man to say that he had bathed in vain because the sun was not eclipsed, since the one was not done for the sake of the other. Thus the spontaneous is even according to its derivation the case in which the thing itself happens in vain. The stone that struck the man did not fall for the sake of striking

30 him; therefore it fell spontaneously, because it might have fallen by the action of an agent and for the sake of striking. The difference between spontaneity and what results by chance is greatest in things that come to be by nature; for when anything comes to be contrary to nature, we do not say that it came to be by chance, but by spontaneity. Yet

35 strictly this too is different from the spontaneous proper; for the cause of the latter is external, that of the former internal.

198ᵃ   We have now explained what chance is and what spontaneity is, and in what they differ from each other. Both belong to the mode of causation "source of change," for either some natural or some intelligent agent is always the cause; but in this sort of causation the number of possible causes is infinite.

5   Spontaneity and chance are causes of effects which, though they might result from intelligence or nature, have in fact been caused by something accidentally. Now since nothing which is accidental is prior to what is *per se*, it is clear that no accidental

10 cause can be prior to a cause *per se*. Spontaneity and chance, therefore, are posterior to intelligence and nature. Hence, however true it may be that the heavens are due to spontaneity, it will still be true that intelligence and nature will be prior causes of this universe and of many things in it besides.

7. It is clear then that there are causes, and that the number of them is what we have

15 stated. The number is the same as that of the things comprehended under the question "why." The "why" is referred ultimately either, in things which do not involve motion, e.g. in mathematics, to the "what" (to the definition of straight line or commensurable or the like); or to what initiated a motion, e.g. "why did they go to war?—because there

20 had been a raid"; or we are inquiring "for the sake of what?"—"that they may rule"; or in the case of things that come into being, we are looking for the matter. The causes, therefore, are these and so many in number.

Now, the causes being four, it is the business of the student of nature to know about them all, and if he refers his problems back to all of them, he will assign the "why" in the way proper to his science—the matter, the form, the mover, that for the

25 sake of which. The last three often coincide; for the what and that for the sake of which are one, while the primary source of motion is the same in species as these. For man generates man—and so too, in general, with all things which cause movement by being themselves moved; and such as are not of this kind are no longer inside the province of natural science, for they cause motion not by possessing motion or a source of motion in themselves, but being themselves incapable of motion. Hence there are three

30 branches of study, one of things which are incapable of motion, the second of things in motion, but indestructible, the third of destructible things.

The question "why," then, is answered by reference to the matter, to the form, and to the primary moving cause. For in respect of coming to be it is mostly in this last way that causes are investigated—"what comes to be after what? what was the primary

35 agent or patient?" and so at each step of the series.

Now the principles which cause motion in a natural way are two, of which one is

198ᵇ not natural, as it has no principle of motion in itself. Of this kind is whatever causes movement, not being itself moved, such as that which is completely unchangeable, the

primary reality, and the essence of a thing, i.e. the form; for this is the end or that for the sake of which. Hence since nature is for the sake of something, we must know this cause also. We must explain the "why" in all the senses of the term, namely, that from   5
this that will necessarily result ("from this" either without qualification or for the most part); that this must be so if that is to be so (as the conclusion presupposes the premises); that this was the essence of the thing; and because it is better thus (not without qualification, but with reference to the substance in each case).

8. We must explain then first why nature belongs to the class of causes which act for the   10
sake of something; and then about the necessary and its place in nature, for all writers ascribe things to this cause, arguing that since the hot and the cold and the like are of such and such a kind, therefore certain things *necessarily* are and come to be—and if they mention any other cause (one friendship and strife, another mind), it is only to   15
touch on it, and then good-bye to it.

A difficulty presents itself: why should not nature work, not for the sake of something, nor because it is better so, but just as the sky rains, not in order to make the corn grow, but of necessity? (What is drawn up must cool, and what has been cooled must become water and descend, the result of this being that the corn grows.) Similarly if a   20
man's crop is spoiled on the threshing-floor, the rain did not fall for the sake of this—in order that the crop might be spoiled—but that result just followed. Why then should it not be the same with the parts in nature, e.g. that our teeth should come up of necessity—the front teeth sharp, fitted for tearing, the molars broad and useful for   25
grinding down the food—since they did not arise for this end, but it was merely a coincident result; and so with all other parts in which we suppose that there is purpose? Wherever then all the parts came about just what they would have been if they had come to be for an end, such things survived, being organized spontaneously in a fitting   30
way; whereas those which grew otherwise perished and continue to perish, as Empedocles says his "man-faced ox-progeny" did.

Such are the arguments (and others of the kind) which may cause difficulty on this point. Yet it is impossible that this should be the true view. For teeth and all other natural things either invariably or for the most part come about in a given way; but of not one of   35
the results of chance or spontaneity is this true. We do not ascribe to chance or mere coincidence the frequency of rain in winter, but frequent rain in summer we do; nor heat in   199a
summer but only if we have it in winter. If then, it is agreed that things are either the result of coincidence or for the sake of something, and these cannot be the result of coincidence or spontaneity, it follows that they must be for the sake of something; and that such things   5
are all due to nature even the champions of the theory which is before us would agree. Therefore action for an end is present in things which come to be and are by nature.

Further, where there is an end, all the preceding steps are for the sake of that. Now surely as in action, so in nature; and as in nature, so it is in each action, if nothing interferes. Now action is for the sake of an end; therefore the nature of things also is so. Thus   10
if a house, e.g. had been a thing made by nature, it would have been made in the same way as it is now by art; and if things made by nature were made not only by nature but also by art, they would come to be in the same way as by nature. The one, then, is for   15
the sake of the other; and generally art in some cases completes what nature cannot bring to a finish, and in others imitates nature. If, therefore, artificial products are for the sake of an end, so clearly also are natural products. The relation of the later to the earlier items is the same in both.

This is most obvious in the animals other than man: they make things neither by   20
art nor after inquiry or deliberation. That is why people wonder whether it is by intelli-

gence or by some other faculty that these creatures work,—spiders, ants, and the like. By gradual advance in this direction we come to see clearly that in plants too that is produced which is conducive to the end—leaves, e.g. grow to provide shade for the fruit. If then it is both by nature and for an end that the swallow makes its nest and the spider its web, and plants grow leaves for the sake of the fruit and send their roots down (not up) for the sake of nourishment, it is plain that this kind of cause is operative in things which come to be and are by nature. And since nature is twofold, the matter and the form, of which the latter is the end, and since all the rest is for the sake of the end, the form must be the cause in the sense of that for the sake of which.

Now mistakes occur even in the operations of art: the literate man makes a mistake in writing and the doctor pours out the wrong dose. Hence clearly mistakes are possible in the operations of nature also. If then in art there are cases in which what is rightly produced serves a purpose, and if where mistakes occur there was a purpose in what was attempted, only it was not attained, so must it be also in natural products, and monstrosities will be failures in the purposive effort. Thus in the original combinations the "ox-progeny," if they failed to reach a determinate end must have arisen through the corruption of some principle, as happens now when the seed is defective.

Further, seed must have come into being first, and not straightway the animals: what was "undifferentiated first" was seed.

Again, in plants too we find that for the sake of which, though the degree of organization is less. Were there then in plants also olive-headed vine-progeny, like the "man-headed ox-progeny," or not? An absurd suggestion; yet there must have been, if there were such things among animals.

Moreover, among the seeds anything must come to be at random. But the person who asserts this entirely does away with nature and what exists by nature. For those things are natural which, by a continuous movement originated from an internal principle, arrive at some end: the same end is not reached from every principle; nor any chance end, but always the tendency in each is towards the same end, if there is no impediment.

The end and the means towards it may come about by chance. We say, for instance, that a stranger has come by chance, paid the ransom, and gone away, when he does so as if he had come for that purpose, though it was not for that that he came. This is accidental, for chance is an accidental cause, as I remarked before. But when an event takes place always or for the most part, it is not accidental or by chance. In natural products the sequence is invariable, if there is no impediment.

It is absurd to suppose that purpose is not present because we do not observe the agent deliberating. Art does not deliberate. If the ship-building art were in the wood, it would produce the same results by nature. If, therefore, purpose is present in art, it is present also in nature. The best illustration is a doctor doctoring himself: nature is like that.

It is plain then that nature is a cause, a cause that operates for a purpose.

9. As regards what is of necessity, we must ask whether the necessity is hypothetical, or simple as well. The current view places what is of necessity in the process of production, just as if one were to suppose that the wall of a house necessarily comes to be because what is heavy is naturally carried downwards and what is light to the top, so that the stones and foundations take the lowest place, with earth above because it is lighter, and wood at the top of all as being the lightest. Whereas, though the wall does not come to be *without* these, it is not *due* to these, except as its material cause: it comes to be for the sake of sheltering and guarding certain things. Similarly in all other things which involve that for the sake of which: the product cannot come to be without things which have a necessary nature, but it is not due to these (except as its material); it comes to be

for an end. For instance, why is a saw such as it is? To effect so-and-so and for the sake   10
of so-and-so. This end, however, cannot be realized unless the saw is made of iron. It is,
therefore, necessary for it to be of iron, if we are to have a saw and perform the operation of sawing. What is necessary then, is necessary on a hypothesis, not as an end. Necessity is in the matter, while that for the sake of which is in the definition.

Necessity in mathematics is in a way similar to necessity in things which come to   15
be through the operation of nature. Since a straight line is what it is, it is necessary that the
angles of a triangle should equal two right angles. But not conversely; though if the angles are *not* equal to two right angles, then the straight line is not what it is either. But in   20
things which come to be for an end, the reverse is true. If the end is to exist or does exist,
that also which precedes it will exist or does exist; otherwise just as there, if the conclusion is not true, the principle will not be true, so here the end or that for the sake of which
will not exist. For this too is itself a principle, but of the reasoning, not of the action. (In
mathematics the principle is the principle of the reasoning only, as there is no action.) If   25
then there is to be a house, such-and-such things must be made or be there already or exist, or generally the matter relative to the end, bricks and stones if it is a house. But the end
is not due to these except as the matter, nor will it come to exist because of them. Yet if
they do not exist at all, neither will the house, or the saw—the former in the absence of
stones, the latter in the absence of iron—just as in the other case the principles will not be   30
true, if the angles of the triangle are not equal to two right angles.

The necessary in nature, then, is plainly what we call by the name of matter, and
the changes in it. Both causes must be stated by the student of nature, but especially the
end; for that is the cause of the matter, not *vice versa;* and the end is that for the sake of
which, and the principle starts from the definition or essence: as in artificial products,   200^b
since a house is of such-and-such a kind, certain things must *necessarily* come to be or
be there already, or since health is this, these things must necessarily come to be or be
there already, so too if man is this, then these; if these, then those. Perhaps the necessary
is present also in the definition. For if one defines the operation of sawing as being a   5
certain kind of dividing, then this cannot come about unless the saw has teeth of a certain kind; and these cannot be unless it is of iron. For in the definition too there are some
parts that stand as matter.

METAPHYSICS (in part)

BOOK I

1. All men by nature desire to know. An indication of this is the delight we take in our   980^a
senses; for even apart from their usefulness they are loved for themselves; and above all
others the sense of sight. For not only with a view to action, but even when we are not   25
going to do anything, we prefer sight to almost everything else. The reason is that this,

Aristotle, *Metaphysics,* Book I, 1–4, 6, 9; and Book XII, 6–9, translated by W.D. Ross from *The Works of
Aristotle,* translated into English under the editorship of W.D. Ross (Oxford: Clarendon Press, 1908–1952).
Reprinted by permission of Oxford University Press.

most of all the senses, makes us know and brings to light many differences between things.

980^b

By nature animals are born with the faculty of sensation, and from sensation memory is produced in some of them, though not in others. And therefore the former are more intelligent and apt at learning than those which cannot remember; those which are incapable of hearing sounds are intelligent though they cannot be taught, e.g. the bee, and any other race of animals that may be like it; and those which besides memory have this sense of hearing, can be taught.

25

The animals other than man live by appearances and memories, and have but little of connected experience; but the human race lives also by art and reasonings. And from memory experience is produced in men; for many memories of the same thing produce finally the capacity for a single experience. Experience seems to be very similar to science and art, but really science and art come to men *through* experience; for "experience made art," as Polus says, "but inexperience luck." And art arises, when from many notions gained by experience one universal judgement about similar objects is produced. For to have a judgement that when Callias was ill of this disease this did him good, and similarly in the case of Socrates and in many individual cases, is a matter of experience; but to judge that it has done good to all persons of a certain constitution, marked off in one class, when they were ill of this disease, e.g. to phlegmatic or bilious people when burning with fever,—this is a matter of art.

981^a

5

10

With a view to action experience seems in no respect inferior to art, and we even see men of experience succeeding more than those who have theory without experience. The reason is that experience is knowledge of individuals, art of universals, and actions and productions are all concerned with the individual; for the physician does not cure a man, except in an incidental way, but Callias or Socrates or some other called by some such individual name, who happens to be a man. If, then, a man has theory without experience, and knows the universal but does not know the individual included in this, he will often fail to cure; for it is the individual that is to be cured. But yet we think that *knowledge* and *understanding* belong to art rather than to experience, and we suppose artists to be wiser than men of experience (which implies that wisdom depends in all cases rather on knowledge); and this because the former know the cause, but the latter do not. For men of experience know that the thing is so, but do not know why, while the others know the "why" and the cause. Hence we think that the master-workers in each craft are more honourable and know in a truer sense and are wiser than the manual workers, because they know the causes of the things that are done (we think the manual workers are like certain lifeless things which act indeed, but act without knowing what they do, as fire burns,—but while the lifeless things perform each of their functions by a natural tendency, the labourers perform them through habit); thus we view them as being wiser not in virtue of being able to act, but of having the theory for themselves and knowing the causes. And in general it is a sign of the man who knows, that he can teach, and therefore we think art more truly knowledge than experience is; for artists can teach, and men of mere experience cannot.

15

20

25

30

981^b

5

Again, we do not regard any of the senses as wisdom; yet surely these give the most authoritative knowledge of particulars. But they do not tell us the "why" of anything—e.g. why fire is hot; they only say that it is hot.

10

At first he who invented any art that went beyond the common perceptions of man was naturally admired by men, not only because there was something useful in the inventions, but because he was thought wise and superior to the rest. But as more arts were invented, and some were directed to the necessities of life, others to its recreation, the inventors of the latter were always regarded as wiser than the inventors of the for-

15

mer, because their branches of knowledge did not aim at utility. Hence when all such   20
inventions were already established, the sciences which do not aim at giving pleasure or
at the necessities of life were discovered, and first in the places where men first began to
have leisure. This is why the mathematical arts were founded in Egypt; for there the
priestly caste was allowed to be at leisure.

We have said in the *Ethics* what the difference is between art and science and the   25
other kindred faculties; but the point of our present discussion is this, that all men suppose what is called wisdom to deal with the first causes and the principles of things.
This is why, as has been said before, the man of experience is thought to be wiser than   30
the possessors of any perception whatever, the artist wiser than the men of experience,
the master-worker than the mechanic, and the theoretical kinds of knowledge to be
more of the nature of wisdom than the productive. Clearly then wisdom is knowledge   982ª
about certain causes and principles.

2. Since we are seeking this knowledge, we must inquire of what kind are the causes
and the principles, the knowledge of which is wisdom. If we were to take the notions we   5
have about the wise man, this might perhaps make the answer more evident. We suppose first, then, that the wise man knows all things, as far as possible, although he has
not knowledge of each of them individually; secondly, that he who can learn things that   10
are difficult, and not easy for man to know, is wise (sense-perception is common to all,
and therefore easy and no mark of wisdom); again, he who is more exact and more capable of teaching the causes is wiser, in every branch of knowledge; and of the sciences,
also, that which is desirable on its own account and for the sake of knowing it is more   15
of the nature of wisdom than that which is desirable on account of its results, and the superior science is more of the nature of wisdom than the ancillary; for the wise man must
not be ordered but must order, and he must not obey another, but the less wise must
obey *him*.

Such and so many are the notions, then, which we have about wisdom and the   20
wise. Now of these characteristics that of knowing all things must belong to him who
has in the highest degree universal knowledge; for he knows in a sense all the subordinate objects. And these things, the most universal, are on the whole the hardest for men
to know; for they are furthest from the senses. And the most exact of the sciences are   25
those which deal most with first principles; for those which involve fewer principles are
more exact than those which involve additional principles, e.g. arithmetic [is more exact than] than geometry. But the science which investigates causes is also more capable
of reaching, for the people who teach are those who tell the causes of each thing. And   30
understanding and knowledge pursued for their own sake are found most in the knowledge of that which is most knowable; for he who chooses to know for the sake of knowing will choose most readily that which is most truly knowledge, and such is the knowledge of that which is most knowable; and the first principles and the causes are most   982ᵇ
knowable; for by reason of these, and from these, all other things are known, but these
are not known by means of the things subordinate to them. And the science which
knows to what end each thing must be done is the most authoritative of the sciences,   5
and more authoritative than any ancillary science; and this end is the good in each class,
and in general the supreme good in the whole of nature. Judged by all the tests we have
mentioned, then, the name in question falls to the same science; this must be a science
that investigates the first principles and causes; for the good, i.e. that for the sake of
which, is one of the causes.   10

That it is not a science of production is clear even from the history of the earliest
philosophers. For it is owing to their wonder that men both now begin and at first began

to philosophize; they wondered originally at the obvious difficulties, then advanced lit-
15   tle by little and stated difficulties about the greater matters, e.g. about the phenomena of
the moon and those of the sun and the stars, and about the genesis of the universe. And
a man who is puzzled and wonders thinks himself ignorant (whence even the lover of
20   myth is in a sense a lover of wisdom, for myth is composed of wonders); therefore since
they philosophized in order to escape from ignorance, evidently they were pursuing science in order to know, and not for any utilitarian end. And this is confirmed by the facts;
for it was when almost all the necessities of life and the things that make for comfort
25   and recreation were present, that such knowledge began to be sought. Evidently then we
do not seek it for the sake of any other advantage; but as the man is free, we say, who
exists for himself and not for another, so we pursue this as the only free science, for it
alone exists for itself.

Hence the possession of it might be justly regarded as beyond human power; for
30   in many ways human nature is in bondage, so that according to Simonides "God alone
can have this privilege," and it is unfitting that man should not be content to seek the
knowledge that is suited to him. If, then, there is something in what the poets say, and
983ᵃ   jealousy is natural to the divine power, it would probably occur in this case above all,
and all who excelled in this knowledge would be unfortunate. But the divine power cannot be jealous (indeed, according to the proverb, "bards tell many a lie"), nor should any
5   science be thought more honourable than one of this sort. For the most divine science is
also most honourable; and this science alone is, in two ways, most divine. For the science which it would be most meet for God to have is a divine science, and so is any science that deals with divine objects; and this science alone has both these qualities; for
God is thought to be among the causes of all things and to be a first principle, and such
10   a science either God alone can have, or God above all others. All the sciences, indeed,
are more necessary than this, but none is better.

Yet the acquisition of it must in a sense end in something which is the opposite of
our original inquiries. For all men begin, as we said, by wondering that the matter is so
15   (as in the case of automatic marionettes or the solstices or the incommensurability of
the diagonal of a square with the side; for it seems wonderful to all men who have not
yet perceived the explanation that there is a thing which cannot be measured even by
the smallest unit). But we must end in the contrary and, according to the proverb, the
better state, as is the case in these instances when men learn the cause; for there is noth-
20   ing which would surprise a geometer so much as if the diagonal turned out to be commensurable.

We have stated, then, what is the nature of the science we are searching for, and
what is the mark which our search and our whole investigation must reach.

3. Evidently we have to acquire knowledge of the original causes (for we say we know
25   each thing only when we think we recognize its first cause), and causes are spoken of in
four senses. In one of these we mean the substance, i.e. the essence (for the "why" is referred finally to the formula, and the ultimate "why" is a cause and principle); in another
30   the matter or substratum, in a third the source of the change, and in a fourth the cause
opposed to this, that for the sake of which and the good (for this is the end of all generation and change). We have studied these causes sufficiently in our work on nature, but
983ᵇ   yet let us call to our aid those who have attacked the investigation of being and philosophized about reality before us. For obviously they too speak of certain principles and
causes; to go over their views, then, will be of profit to the present inquiry, for we shall
5   either find another kind of cause, or be more convinced of the correctness of those
which we now maintain.

Of the first philosophers, most thought the principles which were of the nature of matter were the only principles of all things; that of which all things that are consist, and from which they first come to be, and into which they are finally resolved (the substance remaining, but changing in its modifications), this they say is the element and the principle of things, and therefore they think nothing is either generated or destroyed, since this sort of entity is always conserved, as we say Socrates neither comes to be absolutely when he comes to be beautiful or musical, nor ceases to be when he loses these characteristics, because the substratum, Socrates himself, remains. So they say nothing else comes to be or ceases to be; for there must be some entity—either one or more than one—from which all other things come to be, it being conserved.

Yet they do not all agree as to the number and the nature of these principles. Thales, the founder of this school of philosophy, says the principle is water (for which reason he declared that the earth rests on water), getting the notion perhaps from seeing that the nutriment of all things is moist, and that heat itself is generated from the moist and kept alive by it (and that from which they come to be is a principle of all things). He got his notion from this fact, and from the fact that the seeds of all things have a moist nature, and that water is the origin of the nature of moist things.

Some think that the ancients who lived long before the present generation, and first framed accounts of the gods, had a similar view of nature; for they made Ocean and Tethys the parents of creation, and described the oath of the gods as being by water, which they themselves call Styx; for what is oldest is most honourable, and the most honourable thing is that by which one swears. It may perhaps be uncertain whether this opinion about nature is primitive and ancient, but Thales at any rate is said to have declared himself thus about the first cause. Hippo no one would think fit to include among these thinkers, because of the paltriness of his thought.

Anaximenes and Diogenes make air prior to water, and the most primary of the simple bodies, while Hippasus of Metapontium and Heraclitus of Ephesus say this of fire, and Empedocles says it of the four elements, adding a fourth—earth—to those which have been named; for these, he says, always remain and do not come to be, except that they come to be more or fewer, being aggregated into one and segregated out of one.

Anaxagoras of Clazomenae, who, though older than Empedocles, was later in his philosophical activity, says the principles are infinite in number; for he says almost all the things that are homogeneous are generated and destroyed (as water or fire is) only by aggregation and segregation, and are not in any other sense generated or destroyed, but remain eternally.

From these facts one might think that the only cause is the so-called material cause; but as men thus advanced, the very facts showed them the way and joined in forcing them to investigate the subject. However true it may be that all generation and destruction proceed from some one or more elements, why does this happen and what is the cause? For at least the substratum itself does not make itself change; e.g. neither the wood nor the bronze causes the change of either of them, nor does the wood manufacture a bed and the bronze a statue, but something else is the cause of the change. And to seek this is to seek the second cause, as *we* should say,—that from which comes the beginning of movement. Now those who at the very beginning set themselves to this kind of inquiry, and said the substratum was one, were not at all dissatisfied with themselves; but some at least of those who maintain it to be one—as though defeated by this search for the second cause—say the one and nature as a whole is unchangeable not only in respect of generation and destruction (for this is an ancient belief, and all agreed in it), but also of all other change; and this view is peculiar to them. Of those who said the uni-

verse was one, none succeeded in discovering a cause of this sort, except perhaps Parmenides, and he only insomuch that he supposes that there is not only one but in some
5   sense two causes. But for those who make more elements it is more possible to state the second cause, e.g. for those who make hot and cold, or fire and earth, the elements; for they treat fire as having a nature which fits it to move things, and water and earth and such things they treat in the contrary way.

When these men and the principles of this kind had had their day, as the latter were found inadequate to generate the nature of things, men were again forced by the truth it-
10   self, as we said, to inquire into the next kind of cause. For surely it is not likely either that fire or earth or any such element should be the reason why things manifest goodness and beauty both in their being and in their coming to be, or that those thinkers should have supposed it was; nor again could it be right to ascribe so great a matter to spontaneity and
15   luck. When one man said, then, that reason was present—as in animals, so throughout nature—as the cause of the world and of all its order, he seemed like a sober man in contrast with the random talk of his predecessors. We know that Anaxagoras certainly adopted these views, but Hermotimus of Clazomenae is credited with expressing them earlier.
20   Those who thought thus stated that there is a principle of things which is at the same time the cause of beauty, and that sort of cause from which things acquire movement.

4. One might suspect that Hesiod was the first to look for such a thing or some one else who put love or desire among existing things as a principle, as Parmenides does; for he,
25   in constructing the genesis of the universe, says:

Love first of all the Gods she planned.

And Hesiod says:

First of all things was chaos made, and then
Broad-breasted earth, and love that foremost is
Among all the immortals,

30   which implies that among existing things there must be a cause which will move things and bring them together. How these thinkers should be arranged with regard to priority of discovery let us be allowed to decide later; but since the contraries of the various forms of good were also perceived to be present in nature—not only order and the beautiful, but also disorder and the ugly, and bad things in greater number than good, and ig-
985ᵃ   noble things than beautiful, therefore another thinker introduced friendship and strife, each of the two the cause of one of these two sets of qualities. For if we were to follow out the view of Empedocles, and interpret it according to its meaning and not to its lisp-
5   ing expression, we should find that friendship is the cause of good things, and strife of bad. Therefore, if we said that Empedocles in a sense both mentions, and is the first to mention, the bad and the good as principles, we should perhaps be right, since the cause
10   of all goods is the good itself.

These thinkers, as we say, evidently got hold up to a certain point of two of the causes which we distinguished in our work on nature—the matter and the source of the movement,—vaguely, however, and with no clearness, but as untrained men behave in
15   fights; for they go round their opponents and often strike fine blows, but they do not fight on scientific principles, and so these thinkers do not seem to know what they say; for it is evident that, as a rule, they make no use of their causes except to a small extent. For Anaxagoras uses reason as a *deus ex machina* for the making of the world, and
20   when he is at a loss to tell for what cause something necessarily is, then he drags reason

in, but in all other cases ascribes events to anything rather than to reason. And Empedocles, though he uses the causes to a greater extent than this, neither does so sufficiently
nor attains consistency in their use. At least, in many cases he makes friendship segre-
gate things, and strife aggregate them. For when the universe is dissolved into its ele-   25
ments by strife, fire is aggregated into one, and so is each of the other elements; but
when again under the influence of friendship they come together into one, the parts
must again be segregated out of each element.

Empedocles, then, in contrast with his predecessors, was the first to introduce this
cause in a divided form, not positing one source of movement, but different and con-   30
trary sources. Again, he was the first to speak of four material elements; yet he does not
use four, but treats them as two only; he treats fire by itself, and its opposites—earth, air,   985^b
and water—as one kind of thing. We may learn this by study of his verses.

This philosopher then, as we say, spoke of the principles in this way, and made
them of this number. Leucippus and his associate Democritus say that the full and the   5
empty are the elements, calling the one being and the other non-being—the full and
solid being, the empty non-being (that is why they say that what is is no more than what
is not, because body no more is than the void); and they make these the material causes
of things. And as those who make the underlying substance one generate all other things   10
by its modifications, supposing the rare and the dense to be the sources of the modifications, in the same way these philosophers say the differences in the elements are the
causes of all other qualities. These differences, they say, are three—shape and order and   15
position. For they say that what is is differentiated only by "rhythm" and "inter-contact"
and "turning"; and of these rhythm is shape, inter-contact is order, and turning is position; for A differs from N in shape, AN from NA in order, ⊐ from H in position. The
question of movement—whence or how it belongs to things—these thinkers, like the
others, lazily neglected.

Regarding the two causes, then, as we say, the inquiry seems to have been pushed   20
thus far by the early philosophers.

*   *   *

6. After the systems we have named came the philosophy of Plato, which in most re-   30
spects followed these thinkers, but had peculiarities that distinguished it from the philosophy of the Italians. For, having in his youth first become familiar with Cratylus and
with the Heraclitean doctrines (that all sensible things are ever in a state of flux and
there is no knowledge about them), these views he held even in later years. Socrates,
however, was busying himself about ethical matters and neglecting the world of nature   987^b
as a whole but seeking the universal in these ethical matters, and fixed thought for the
first time on definitions; Plato accepted his teaching, but held that the problem applied
not to any sensible thing but to entities of another kind—for this reason, that the com-   5
mon definition could not be a definition of any sensible thing, as they were always
changing. Things of this other sort, then, he called Ideas, and sensible things, he said,
were apart from these, and were all called after these; for the multitude of things which
have the same name as the Form exist by participation in it. Only the name "participa-   10
tion" was new; for the Pythagoreans say that things exist by imitation of numbers, and
Plato says they exist by participation, changing the name. But what the participation or
the imitation of the Forms could be they left an open question.

Further, besides sensible things and Forms he says there are the objects of mathematics, which occupy an intermediate position, differing from sensible things in being   15
eternal and unchangeable, from Forms in that there are many alike, while the Form itself is in each case unique.

20   Since the Forms are the causes of all other things, he thought their elements were the elements of all things. As matter, the great and the small were principles; as substance, the One; for from the great and the small, by participation in the One, come the numbers.

But he agreed with the Pythagoreans in saying that the One is substance and not a predicate of something else; and in saying that the numbers are the causes of the sub-
25   stance of other things, he also agreed with them; but positing a dyad and constructing the infinite out of great and small, instead of treating the infinite as one, is peculiar to him; and so is his view that the numbers exist apart from sensible things, while *they* say that the things themselves are numbers, and do not place the objects of mathematics be-tween Forms and sensible things. His divergence from the Pythagoreans in making the
30   One and the numbers separate from things, and his introduction of the Forms, were due to his inquiries in the region of definitory formulae (for the earlier thinkers had no tinc-ture of dialectic), and his making the other entity besides the One a dyad was due to the belief that the numbers, except those which were prime, could be neatly produced out of the dyad as out of a plastic material.

988ª   Yet what happens is the contrary; the theory is not a reasonable one. For they make many things out of the matter, and the form generates only once, but what we ob-serve is that one table is made from one matter, while the man who applies the form,
5   though he is one, makes many tables. And the relation of the male to the female is sim-ilar; for the latter is impregnated by one copulation, but the male impregnates many fe-males; yet these are imitations of those first principles.

Plato, then, declared himself thus on the points in question; it is evident from what has been said that he has used only two causes, that of the essence and the mater-
10   ial cause (for the Forms are the cause of the essence of all other things, and the One is the cause of the essence of the Forms); and it is evident what the underlying matter is, of which the Forms are predicated in the case of sensible things, and the One in the case of Forms, viz. that this is a dyad, the great and the small. Further, he has assigned the
15   cause of good and that of evil to the elements, one to each of the two, as we say some of his predecessors sought to do, e.g. Empedocles and Anaxagoras.

*   *   *

9. Let us leave the Pythagoreans for the present; for it is enough to have touched on them as much as we have done. But as for those who posit the Ideas as causes, firstly, in
990ᵇ   seeking to grasp the causes of the things around us, they introduced others equal in number to these, as if a man who wanted to count things thought he could not do it while they were few, but tried to count them when he had added to their number. For the Forms are practically equal to or not fewer than the things, in trying to explain which
5   these thinkers proceeded from them to the Forms. For to each set of substances there an-swers a Form which has the same name and exists apart from the substances, and so also in the case of all other groups in which there is one character common to many things, whether the things are in this changeable world or are eternal.

Further, of the ways in which we prove that the Forms exist, none is convincing;
10   for from some no inference necessarily follows, and from some it follows that there are Forms of things of which we think there are no Forms.

For according to the arguments from the existence of the sciences there will be Forms of all things of which there are sciences, and according to the argument that there is one attribute common to many things there will be Forms even of negations, and according to the argument that there is an object for thought even when the thing has perished, there will be Forms of perishable things; for we can have an image of these.

Further, of the more accurate arguments, some lead to Ideas of relations, of which   15
we say there is no independent class, and others involve the difficulty of the "third
man."

And in general the arguments for the Forms destroy the things for whose existence we are more anxious than for the existence of the Ideas; for it follows that not the
dyad but number is first, i.e. that the relative is prior to the absolute—besides all the   20
other points on which certain people by following out the opinions held about the Ideas
have come into conflict with the principles of the theory.

Further, according to the assumption on which our belief in the Ideas rests, there
will be Forms not only of substances but also of many other things (for the concept is
single not only in the case of substances but also in the other cases, and there are sci-   25
ences not only of substance but also of other things, and a thousand other such conclusions also follow). But according to the necessities of the case and the opinions held
about the Forms, if they can be shared there must be Ideas of substances only. For they
are not shared incidentally, but a thing must share in its Form as in something not pred-   30
icated of a subject (e.g. if a thing shares in double itself, it shares also in eternal, but incidentally; for eternal happens to be predicable of the double). Therefore the Forms will
be substance; and the same terms indicate substance in this and in the ideal world (or   991ᵃ
what will be the meaning of saying that there is something apart from the particulars—
the one over many?). And if the Ideas and the particulars that share them have the same
Form, there will be something common to these; for why should 2 be one and the same
in the perishable 2's or in those which are many but eternal, and not the same in the 2 it-   5
self as in the particular 2? But if they have not the same Form, they must have only the
name in common, and it is as if one were to call both Callias and a wooden image a
man, without observing any community between them.

Above all one might discuss the question what on earth the Forms contribute to
sensible things, either to those that are eternal or to those that come into being and cease   10
to be. For they cause neither movement nor any change in them. But again they help in
no way towards the *knowledge* of the other things (for they are not even the substance
of these, else they would have been in them), nor towards their being, if they are not *in*
the particulars which share in them; though if they were, they might be thought to be
causes, as white causes whiteness in that with which it is mixed. But this argument,   15
which first Anaxagoras and later Eudoxus and certain others used, is too easily upset;
for it is not difficult to collect many insuperable objections to such a view.

But further all other things cannot come from the Forms in any of the usual senses   20
of "from." And to say that they are patterns and the other things share them is to use
empty words and poetical metaphors. For what is it that works, looking to the Ideas?
Anything can either be, or become, like another without being copied from it, so that
whether Socrates exists or not a man might come to be like Socrates; and evidently this   25
might be so even if Socrates were eternal. And there will be several patterns of the same
thing, and therefore several Forms, e.g. animal and two-footed and also man himself
will be Forms of man. Again, the Forms are patterns not only of sensible things, but of
themselves too, e.g. the Form of genus will be a genus of Forms; therefore the same   30
thing will be pattern and copy.

Again it must be held to be impossible that the substance and that of which it is   991ᵇ
the substance should exist apart; how, therefore, can the Ideas, being the substances of
things, exist apart?

In the *Phaedo* the case is stated in this way—that the Forms are causes both of being and of becoming; yet when the Forms exist, still the things that share in them do not
come into being, unless there is some efficient cause; and many other things come into   5
being (e.g. a house or a ring), of which we say there are no Forms. Clearly, therefore,

even the other things can both be and come into being owing to such causes as produce the things just mentioned.

Again, if the forms are numbers, how can they be causes? Is it because existing things are other numbers, e.g. one number is man, another is Socrates, another Callias? Why then are the one set of numbers causes of the other set? It will not make any difference even if the former are eternal and the latter are not. But if it is because things in this sensible world (e.g. harmony) are ratios of numbers, evidently there is some one class of things of which they are ratios. If, then, this—the matter—is some definite thing, evidently the numbers themselves too will be ratios of something to something else. E.g. if Callias is a numerical ratio between fire and earth and water and air, his Idea also will be a number of certain other underlying things; and the Idea of man, whether it is a number in a sense or not, will still be a numerical ratio of certain things and not a number proper, nor will it be a number merely because it is a numerical ratio.

Again, from many numbers one number is produced, but how can one Form come from many Forms? And if the number comes not from the many numbers themselves but from the units in them, e.g. in 10,000, how is it with the units? If they are specifically alike, numerous absurdities will follow, and also if they are not alike (neither the units in the same number being like one another nor those in different numbers being all like to all); for in what will they differ, as they are without quality? This is not a plausible view, nor can it be consistently thought out. Further, they must set up a second kind of number (with which arithmetic deals), and all the objects which are called intermediate by some thinkers; and how do these exist or from what principles do they proceed? Or why must they be intermediate between the things in this sensible world and the things-in-themselves? Further, the units in 2 must each come from a prior 2; but this is impossible. Further, why is a number, when taken all together, one? Again, besides what has been said, if the units are *diverse* they should have spoken like those who say there are four, or two, elements; for each of these thinkers gives the name of element not to that which is common, e.g. to body, but to fire and earth, whether there is something common to them, viz. body, or not. But in fact they speak as if the One were homogeneous like fire or water; and if this is so, the numbers will not be substances. Evidently, if there is a One-in-itself and this is a first principle, "one" is being used in more than one sense; for otherwise the theory is impossible.

When we wish to refer substances to their principles, we state that lines come from the short and long (i.e. from a kind of small and great), and the plane from the broad and narrow, and the solid from the deep and shallow. Yet how then can the plane contain a line, or the solid a line or a plane? For the broad and narrow is a different class of things from the deep and shallow. Therefore, just as number is not present in these, because the many and few are different from these, evidently no other of the higher classes will be present in the lower. But again the broad is not a genus which includes the deep, for then the solid would have been a species of plane. Further, from what principle will the presence of the points in the line be derived? Plato even used to object to this class of things as being a geometrical fiction. He called the indivisible lines the principle of lines—and he used to lay this down often. Yet these must have a limit; therefore the argument from which the existence of the line follows proves also the existence of the point.

In general, though philosophy seeks the cause of perceptible things, we have given this up (for we say nothing of the cause from which change takes its start), but while we fancy we are stating the substance of perceptible things, we assert the existence of a second class of substances, while our account of the way in which they are the substances of perceptible things is empty talk; for sharing, as we said before, means nothing. Nor have the Forms any connexion with that which we see to be the cause in

the case of the sciences, and for whose sake mind and nature produce all that they do   30
produce,—with this cause we assert to be one of the first principles; but mathematics
has come to be the whole of philosophy for modern thinkers, though they say that it
should be studied for the sake of other things. Further, one might suppose that the substance which according to them underlies as matter is too mathematical, and is a predi-   992ᵇ
cate and differentia of the substance, i.e. of the matter, rather than the matter itself; i.e.
the great and the small are like the rare and the dense which the natural philosophers
speak of, calling these the primary differentiae of the substratum; for these are a kind of   5
excess and defect. And regarding movement, if the great and the small are to *be* movement, evidently the Forms will be moved; but if they are not, whence did movement
come? If we cannot answer this the whole study of nature has been annihilated.

And what is thought to be easy—to show that all things are one—is not done; for   10
by "exposition" all things do not come to be one but there comes to be a One-in-itself,
if we grant all the assumptions. And not even this follows, if we do not grant that the
universal is a class; and this in some cases it cannot be.

Nor can it be explained either how the lines and planes and solids that come after
the numbers exist or can exist, or what meaning they have; for these can neither be   15
Forms (for they are not numbers), nor the intermediates (for those are the objects of
mathematics), nor the perishable things. This is evidently a distinct fourth class.

In general, if we search for the elements of existing things without distinguishing
the many senses in which things are said to exist, we cannot succeed, especially if the
search for the elements of which things are made is conducted in this manner. For it is   20
surely impossible to discover what acting or being acted on, or the straight, is made of,
but if elements can be discovered at all, it is only the elements of substances; therefore to
seek the elements of all existing things or to think one has them is incorrect. And how
could we *learn* the elements of all things? Evidently we cannot start by knowing something before. For as he who is learning geometry, though he may know other things be-   25
fore, knows none of the things with which the science deals and about which he is to
learn, so is it in all other cases. Therefore if there is a science of all things, as some maintain, he who is learning this will know nothing before. Yet all learning is by means of   30
premises which are (either all or some of them) known before,—whether the learning be
by demonstration or by definitions; for the elements of the definition must be known before and be familiar; and learning by induction proceeds similarly. But again, if the sci-   993ᵃ
ence is innate, it is wonderful that we are unaware of our possession of the greatest of sciences. Again, how is one to *know* what all things are made of, and how is this to be made
evident? This also affords a difficulty; for there might be a conflict of opinion, as there is
about certain syllables; some say *za* is made out of *s* and *d* and *a,* while others say it is a   5
distinct sound and none of those that are familiar. Further, how could we know the objects
of sense without having the sense in question? Yet we should, if the elements of which all   10
things consist, as complex sounds consist of their proper elements, are the same.

BOOK XII

*   *   *

6. Since there were three kinds of substance, two of them natural and one unmovable,
regarding the latter we must assert that it is necessary that there should be an eternal unmovable substance. For substances are the first of existing things, and if they are all de-   5

structible, all things are destructible. But it is impossible that movement should either come into being or cease to be; for it must always have existed. Nor can time come into being or cease to be; for there could not be a before and an after if time did not exist. Movement also is continuous, then, in the sense in which time is; for time is either the same thing as movement or an attribute of movement. And there is no continuous movement except movement in place, and of this only that which is circular is continuous.

But if there is something which is capable of moving things or acting on them, but is not actually doing so, there will not be movement; for that which has a capacity need not exercise it. Nothing, then, is gained even if we suppose eternal substances, as the believers in the Forms do, unless there is to be in them some principle which can cause movement; and even this is not enough, nor is another substance besides the Forms enough; for if it does not *act*, there will be no movement. Further, even if it acts, this will not be enough, if its substance is potentiality; for there will not be *eternal* movement; for that which is potentially may possibly not be. There must, then, be such a principle, whose very substance is actuality. Further, then, these substances must be without matter; for they must be eternal, at least if anything else is eternal. Therefore they must be actuality.

Yet there is a difficulty; for it is thought that everything that acts is able to act, but that not everything that is able to act acts, so that the potentiality is prior. But if this is so, nothing at all will exist; for it is possible for things to be capable of existing but not yet to exist. Yet if we follow the mythologists who generate the world from night, or the natural philosophers who say that all things were together, the same impossible result ensues. For how will there be movement, if there is no actual cause? Matter will surely not move itself—the carpenter's art must act on it; nor will the menstrual fluids nor the earth set themselves in motion, but the seeds and the semen must act on them.

This is why some suppose eternal actuality—e.g. Leucippus and Plato; for they say there is always movement. But why and what this movement is they do not say, nor, if the world moves in this way or that, do they tell us the cause of its doing so. Now nothing is moved at random, but there must always be something present, e.g. as a matter of fact a thing moves in one way by nature, and in another by force or through the influence of thought or something else. Further, what sort of movement is primary? This makes a vast difference. But again Plato, at least, cannot even say what it is that he sometimes supposes to be the source of movement—that which moves itself; for the *soul* is later, and simultaneous with the heavens, according to his account. To suppose potentiality prior to actuality, then, is in a sense right, and in a sense not; and we have specified these senses.

That actuality is prior is testified by Anaxagoras (for his thought is actuality) and by Empedocles in his doctrine of love and strife, and by those who say that there is always movement, e.g. Leucippus.

Therefore chaos or night did not exist for any infinite time, but the same things have always existed (either passing through a cycle of changes or in some other way), since actuality is prior to potentiality. If, then, there is a constant cycle, something must always remain, acting in the same way. And if there is to be generation and destruction, there must be something else which is always acting in different ways. This must, then, act in one way in virtue of itself, and in another in virtue of something else—either of a third agent, therefore, or of the first. But it must be in virtue of the first. For otherwise this again causes the motion both of the third agent and of the second. Therefore it is better to say the first. For it was the cause of eternal movement; and something else is the cause of variety, and evidently both together are the cause of eternal variety. This, accordingly, is the character which the motions actually exhibit. What need then is there to seek for other principles?

7. Since this is a possible account of the matter, and if it were not true, the world would have proceeded out of night and "all things together" and out of non-being, these difficulties may be taken as solved. There is, then, something which is always moved with an unceasing motion, which is motion in a circle; and this is plain not in theory only but in fact. Therefore the first heavens must be eternal. There is therefore also something which moves them. And since that which is moved and moves is intermediate, there is a mover which moves without being moved, being eternal, substance, and actuality. And the object of desire and the object of thought move in this way; they move without being moved. The primary objects of desire and of thought are the same. For the apparent good is the object of appetite, and the real good is the primary object of wish. But desire is consequent on opinion rather than opinion on desire; for the thinking is the starting-point. And thought is moved by the object of thought, and one side of the list of opposites is in itself the object of thought; and in this, substance is first, and in substance, that which is simple and exists actually. (The one and the simple are not the same; for "one" means a measure, but "simple" means that the thing itself has a certain nature.) But the good, also, and that which is in itself desirable are on this same side of the list; and the first in any class is always best, or analogous to the best.

That that for the sake of which is found among the unmovables is shown by making a distinction; for that for the sake of which is both that *for* which and that *towards* which, and of these the one is unmovable and the other is not. Thus it produces motion by being loved, and it moves the other moving things. Now if something is moved it is capable of being otherwise than as it is. Therefore if the actuality of the heavens is primary motion, then in so far as they are in motion, in *this* respect they are capable of being otherwise,—in place, even if not in substance. But since there is something which moves while itself unmoved, existing actually, this can in no way be otherwise than as it is. For motion in space is the first of the kinds of change, and motion in a circle the first kind of spatial motion; and this the first mover *produces*. The first mover, then, of necessity exists; and in so far as it is necessary, it is good, and in this sense a first principle. For the necessary has all these senses—that which is necessary perforce because it is contrary to impulse, that without which the good is impossible, and that which cannot be otherwise but is *absolutely* necessary.

On such a principle, then, depend the heavens and the world of nature. And its life is such as the best which we enjoy, and enjoy for but a short time. For it is ever in this state (which we cannot be), since its actuality is also pleasure. (And therefore waking, perception, and thinking are most pleasant, and hopes and memories are so because of their reference to these.) And thought in itself deals with that which is best in itself, and that which is thought in the fullest sense with that which is best in the fullest sense. And thought thinks itself because it shares the nature of the object of thought; for it becomes an object of thought in coming into contact with and thinking its objects, so that thought and object of thought are the same. For that which is *capable* of receiving the object of thought, i.e. the substance, is thought. And it is active when it *possesses* this object. Therefore the latter rather than the former is the divine element which thought seems to contain, and the act of contemplation is what is most pleasant and best. If, then, God is always in that good state in which we sometimes are, this compels our wonder; and if in a better this compels it yet more. And God *is* in a better state. And life also belongs to God; for the actuality of thought is life, and God is that actuality; and God's essential actuality is life most good and eternal. We say therefore that God is a living being, eternal, most good, so that life and duration continuous and eternal belong to God; for this *is* God.

Those who suppose, as the Pythagoreans and Speusippus do, that supreme beauty and goodness are not present in the beginning, because the beginnings both of plants

1073ª

and of animals are *causes,* but beauty and completeness are in the *effects* of these, are wrong in their opinion. For the seed comes from other individuals which are prior and complete, and the first thing is not seed but the complete being, e.g. we must say that before the seed there is a man,—not the man produced from the seed, but another from whom the seed comes.

It is clear then from what has been said that there is a substance which is eternal and unmovable and separate from sensible things. It has been shown also that this substance cannot have any magnitude, but is without parts and indivisible. For it produces movement through infinite time, but nothing finite has infinite power. And, while every magnitude is either infinite or finite, it cannot, for the above reason, have finite magnitude, and it cannot have infinite magnitude because there is no infinite magnitude at all. But it is also clear that it is impassive and unalterable; for all the other changes are posterior to change of place. It is clear, then, why the first mover has these attributes.

8. We must not ignore the question whether we have to suppose one such substance or more than one, and if the latter, how many; we must also mention, regarding the opinions expressed by others, that they have said nothing that can even be clearly stated about the number of the substances. For the theory of Ideas has no special discussion of the subject; for those who believe in Ideas say the Ideas are numbers, and they speak of numbers now as unlimited, now as limited by the number 10; but as for the reason why there should be just so many numbers, nothing is said with any demonstrative exactness.

We however must discuss the subject, starting from the presuppositions and distinctions we have mentioned. The first principle or primary being is not movable either in itself or accidentally, but produces the primary eternal and single movement. And since that which is moved must be moved by something, and the first mover must be in itself unmovable, and eternal movement must be produced by something eternal and a single movement by a single thing, and since we see that besides the simple spatial movement of the universe, which we say the first and unmovable substance produces, there are other spatial movements—those of the planets—which are eternal (for the body which moves in a circle is eternal and unresting; we have proved these points in the *Physics*), each of these movements also must be caused by a substance unmovable in itself and eternal. For the nature of the stars is eternal, being a kind of substance, and the mover is eternal and prior to the moved, and that which is prior to a substance must be a substance. Evidently, then, there must be substances which are of the same number as the movements of the stars, and in their nature eternal, and in themselves unmovable, and without magnitude, for the reason before mentioned.

1073ᵇ

That the movers are substances, then, and that one of these is first and another second according to the same order as the movements of the stars, is evident. But in the number of movements we reach a problem which must be treated from the standpoint of that one of the mathematical sciences which is most akin to philosophy—viz. of astronomy; for this science speculates about substance which is perceptible but eternal, but the other mathematical sciences, i.e. arithmetic and geometry, treat of no substance. That the movements are more numerous than the bodies that are moved, is evident to those who have given even moderate attention to the matter; for each of the planets has more than one movement. But as to the actual number of these movements, we now—to give some notion of the subject—quote what some of the mathematicians say, that our thought may have some definite number to grasp; but, for the rest, we must partly investigate for ourselves, partly learn from other investigators, and if those who study this subject form an opinion contrary to what we have now stated, we must esteem both parties indeed, but follow the more accurate.

Eudoxus supposed that the motion of the sun or of the moon involves, in either case, three spheres, of which the first is the sphere of the fixed stars, and the second moves in the circle which runs along the middle of the zodiac, and the third in the circle which is inclined across the breadth of the zodiac; but the circle in which the moon moves is inclined at a greater angle than that in which the sun moves. And the motion of the planets involves, in each case, four spheres, and of these also the first and second are the same as the first two mentioned above (for the sphere of the fixed stars is that which moves all the other spheres, and that which is placed beneath this and has its movement in the circle which bisects the zodiac is common to all), but the *poles* of the third sphere of each planet are in the circle which bisects the zodiac, and the motion of the fourth sphere is in the circle which is inclined at an angle to the equator of the third sphere; and the poles of the third spheres are different for the other planets, but those of Venus and Mercury are the same.

Callippus made the position of the spheres the same as Eudoxus did, but while he assigned the same number as Eudoxus did to Jupiter and to Saturn, he thought two more spheres should be added to the sun and two to the moon, if we were to explain the phenomena, and one more to each of the other planets.

But it is necessary, if all the spheres combined are to explain the phenomena, that for each of the planets there should be other spheres (one fewer than those hitherto assigned) which counteract those already mentioned and bring back to the same position the first sphere of the star which in each case is situated below the star in question; for only thus can all the forces at work produce the motion of the planets. Since, then, the spheres by which the planets themselves are moved are eight and twenty-five, and of these only those by which the lowest-situated planet is moved need not be counteracted, the spheres which counteract those of the first two planets will be six in number, and the spheres which counteract those of the next four planets will be sixteen, and the number of all the spheres—those which move the planets and those which counteract these— will be fifty-five. And if one were not to add to the moon and to the sun the movements we mentioned, all the spheres will be forty-nine in number.

Let this then be taken as the number of the spheres, so that the unmovable substances and principles may reasonably be taken as just so many; the assertion of *necessity* must be left to more powerful thinkers.

If there can be no spatial movement which does not conduce to the moving of a star, and if further every being and every substance which is immune from change and in virtue of itself has attained to the best must be considered an end, there can be no other being apart from these we have named, but this must be the number of the substances. For if there are others, they will cause change as being an end of movement; but there *cannot* be other movements besides those mentioned. And it is reasonable to infer this from a consideration of the bodies that are moved; for if everything that moves is for the sake of that which is moved, and every movement belongs to something that is moved, no movement can be for the sake of itself or of another movement, but all movements must be for the sake of the stars. For if a movement is to be for the sake of a movement, this latter also will have to be for the sake of something else; so that since there cannot be an infinite regress, the end of every movement will be one of the divine bodies which move through the heaven.

Evidently there is but one heaven. For if there are many heavens as there are many men, the moving principles, of which each heaven will have one, will be one in form but in number many. But all things that are many in number have matter. (For one and the same formula applies to *many* things, e.g. the formula of man; but Socrates is *one*.) But the primary essence has not matter; for it is fulfillment. So the unmovable first mover is one both in formula and in number; therefore also that which is moved always and continuously is one alone; therefore there is one heaven alone.

1074^b

Our forefathers in the most remote ages have handed down to us their posterity a tradition, in the form of a myth, that these substances are gods and that the divine encloses the whole of nature. The rest of the tradition has been added later in mythical form with a view to the persuasion of the multitude and to its legal and utilitarian expediency; they say these gods are in the form of men or like some of the other animals, and they say other things consequent on and similar to these which we have mentioned. But if we were to separate the first point from these additions and take it alone—that they thought the first substances to be gods—we must regard this as an inspired utterance, and reflect that, while probably each art and science has often been developed as far as possible and has again perished, these opinions have been preserved like relics until the present. Only thus far, then, is the opinion of our ancestors and our earliest predecessors clear to us.

5

10

15 9. The nature of the divine thought involves certain problems; for while thought is held to be the most divine of phenomena, the question what it must be in order to have that character involves difficulties. For if it thinks nothing, what is there here of dignity? It is just like one who sleeps. And if it thinks, but this depends on something else, then (as that which is its substance is not the act of thinking, but a capacity) it cannot be the best substance; for it is through thinking that its value belongs to it. Further, whether its substance is the faculty of thought or the act of thinking, what does it think? Either itself or something else; and if something else, either the same always or something different. Does it matter, then, or not, whether it thinks the good or any chance thing? Are there not some things about which it is incredible that it should think? Evidently, then, it thinks that which is most divine and precious, and it does not change; for change would be change for the worse, and this would be already a movement. First, then, if it is not the act of thinking but a capacity, it would be reasonable to suppose that the continuity of its thinking is wearisome to it. Secondly, there would evidently be something else more precious than thought, viz. that which is thought. For both thinking and the act of thought will belong even to one who has the worst of thoughts. Therefore if this ought to be avoided (and it ought, for there are even some things which it is better not to see than to see), the act of thinking cannot be the best of things. Therefore it must be itself that thought thinks (since it is the most excellent of things), and its thinking is a thinking on thinking.

20

25

30

35 But evidently knowledge and perception and opinion and understanding have always something else as their object, and themselves only by the way. Further, if thinking and being thought are different, in respect of which does goodness belong to thought? For being an act of thinking and being an object of thought are not the same.

1075^a We answer that in some cases the knowledge is the object. In the productive sciences (if we abstract from the matter) the substance in the sense of essence, and in the theoretical sciences the formula or the act of thinking, is the object. As, then, thought and the object of thought are not different in the case of things that have not matter, they will be the same, i.e. the thinking will be one with the object of its thought.

A further question is left—whether the object of the thought is composite; for if it were, thought would change in passing from part to part of the whole. We answer that everything which has not matter is indivisible. As human thought, or rather the thought of composite objects, is in a certain period of time (for it does not possess the good at this moment or at that, but its best, being something different from it, is attained only in a whole period of time), so throughout eternity is the thought which has *itself* for its object.

ON THE SOUL (in part)

BOOK II

1. Let the foregoing suffice as our account of the views concerning the soul which have been handed on by our predecessors; let us now make as it were a completely fresh start, endeavouring to answer the question, What is soul? i.e. to formulate the most general possible account of it. 412^a

We say that substance is one kind of what is, and that in several senses: in the sense of matter or that which in itself is not a this, and in the sense of form or essence, which is that precisely in virtue of which a thing is called a this, and thirdly in the sense of that which is compounded of both. Now matter is potentiality, form actuality; and actuality is of two kinds, one as e.g. knowledge, the other as e.g. reflecting.

Among substances are by general consent reckoned bodies and especially natural bodies; for they are the principles of all other bodies. Of natural bodies some have life in them, others not; by life we mean self-nutrition and growth and decay. It follows that every natural body which has life in it is a substance in the sense of a composite.

Now given that there are bodies of such and such a kind, viz. having life, the soul cannot be a body; for the body is the subject or matter, not what is attributed to it. Hence the soul must be a substance in the sense of the form of a natural body having life potentially within it. But substance is actuality, and thus soul is the actuality of a body as above characterized. Now there are two kinds of actuality corresponding to knowledge and to reflecting. It is obvious that the soul is an actuality like knowledge; for both sleeping and waking presuppose the existence of soul, and of these waking corresponds to reflecting, sleeping to knowledge possessed but not employed, and knowledge of something is temporally prior.

That is why the soul is an actuality of the first kind of a natural body having life potentially in it. The body so described is a body which is organized. The parts of plants in spite of their extreme simplicity are organs; e.g. the leaf serves to shelter the pericarp, the pericarp to shelter the fruit, while the roots of plants are analogous to the mouth of animals, both serving for the absorption of food. If, then, we have to give a general formula applicable to all kinds of soul, we must describe it as an actuality of the first kind of a natural organized body. That is why we can dismiss as unnecessary the question whether the soul and the body are one: it is as though we were to ask whether the wax and its shape are one, or generally the matter of a thing and that of which it is the matter. Unity has many senses (as many as "is" has), but the proper one is that of actuality. 412^b

5

10

15

20

25

5

Aristotle, *On the Soul,* Book II, 1–3; III, 4–5, translated by J.A. Smith from *Complete Works of Aristotle,* edited by Jonathan Barnes. Copyright © 1984 by PUP. Reprinted by permission of Princeton University Press.

10   We have now given a general answer to the question, What is soul? It is substance in the sense which corresponds to the account of a thing. That means that it is what it is to be for a body of the character just assigned. Suppose that a tool, e.g. an axe, were a *natural* body, then being an axe would have been its essence, and so its soul; if this dis-

15   appeared from it, it would have ceased to be an axe, except in name. As it is, it is an axe; for it is not of a body of that sort that what it is to be, i.e. its account, is a soul, but of a natural body of a particular kind, viz. one having in itself the power of setting itself in movement and arresting itself. Next, apply this doctrine in the case of the parts of the living body. Suppose that the eye were an animal—sight would have been its soul, for

20   sight is the substance of the eye which corresponds to the account, the eye being merely the matter of seeing; when seeing is removed the eye is no longer an eye, except in name—no more than the eye of a statue or of a painted figure. We must now extend our consideration from the parts to the whole living body; for what the part is to the part, that the whole faculty of sense is to the whole sensitive body as such.

25   We must not understand by that which is potentially capable of living what has lost the soul it had, but only what still retains it; but seeds and fruits are bodies which are potentially of that sort. Consequently, while waking is actuality in a sense corresponding to the cutting and the seeing, the soul is actuality in the sense corresponding to

413ᵃ   sight and the power in the tool; the body corresponds to what is in potentiality; as the pupil *plus* the power of sight constitutes the eye, so the soul *plus* the body constitutes the animal.

     From this it is clear that the soul is inseparable from its body, or at any rate that

5   certain parts of it are (if it has parts)—for the actuality of some of them is the actuality of the parts themselves. Yet some may be separable because they are not the actualities of any body at all. Further, we have no light on the problem whether the soul may not be the actuality of its body in the sense in which the sailor is the actuality of the ship.

10   This must suffice as our sketch or outline of the nature of soul.

     2. Since what is clear and more familiar in account emerges from what in itself is con-

15   fused but more observable by us, we must reconsider our results from this point of view. For it is not enough for a definitional account to express as most now do the mere fact; it must include and exhibit the cause also. At present definitions are given in a form analogous to the conclusion of an argument; e.g. What is squaring? The construction of an equilateral rectangle equal to a given oblong rectangle. Such a definition is in form equivalent to a conclusion. One that tells us that squaring is the discovery of a mean

20   proportional discloses the cause of what is defined.

     We resume our inquiry from a fresh starting-point by calling attention to the fact that what has soul in it differs from what has not in that the former displays life. Now this word has more than one sense, and provided any one alone of these is found in a thing we say that thing is living—viz. thinking or perception or local movement and rest, or move-

25   ment in the sense of nutrition, decay and growth. Hence we think of plants also as living, for they are observed to possess in themselves an originative power through which they increase or decrease in all spatial directions; they do not grow up but not down—they grow alike in both, indeed in all, directions; and that holds for everything which is con-

30   stantly nourished and continues to live, so long as it can absorb nutriment.

     This power of self-nutrition can be separated from the other powers mentioned, but not they from it—in mortal beings at least. The fact is obvious in plants; for it is the only psychic power they possess.

413ᵇ   This is the originative power the possession of which leads us to speak of things as *living* at all, but it is the possession of sensation that leads us for the first time to speak of living things as *animals;* for even those beings which possess no power of local movement but do possess the power of sensation we call animals and not merely living things.

The primary form of sense is touch, which belongs to all animals. Just as the power of self-nutrition can be separated from touch and sensation generally, so touch   5 can be separated from all other forms of sense. (By the power of self-nutrition we mean that part of the soul which is common to plants and animals: all animals whatsoever are observed to have the sense of touch.) What the explanation of these two facts is, we must discuss later. At present we must confine ourselves to saying that soul is the source   10 of these phenomena and is characterized by them, viz. by the powers of self-nutrition, sensation, thinking, and movement.

Is each of these a soul or a part of a soul? And if a part, a part merely distinguishable by definition or a part distinct in local situation as well? In the case of certain of   15 these powers, the answers to these questions are easy, in the case of others we are puzzled what to say. Just as in the case of plants which when divided are observed to continue to live though separated from one another (thus showing that in *their* case the soul of each individual plant was actually one, potentially many), so we notice a similar result in other varieties of soul, i.e. in insects which have been cut in two; each of the seg-   20 ments possesses both sensation and local movement; and if sensation, necessarily also imagination and appetition; for, where there is sensation, there is also pleasure and pain, and, where these, necessarily also desire.

We have no evidence as yet about thought or the power of reflexion; it seems to   25 be a different kind of soul, differing as what is eternal from what is perishable; it alone is capable of being separated. All the other parts of soul, it is evident from what we have said, are, in spite of certain statements to the contrary, incapable of separate existence though, of course, distinguishable by definition. If opining is distinct from perceiving, to be capable of opining and to be capable of perceiving must be dis-   30 tinct, and so with all the other forms of living above enumerated. Further, some animals possess all these parts of soul, some certain of them only, others one only (this is what enables us to classify animals); the cause must be considered later. A similar arrangement is found also within the field of the senses; some classes of animals have   414ᵃ all the senses, some only certain of them, others only one, the most indispensable, touch.

Since the expression "that whereby we live and perceive" has two meanings, just like the expression "that whereby we know"—that may mean either knowledge or the   5 soul, for we can speak of knowing *by* either, and similarly that whereby we are in health may be either health or the body or some part of the body; and since of these knowledge or health is a form, essence, or account, or if we so express it an activity of a recipient matter—knowledge of what is capable of knowing, health of what is capa-   10 ble of being made healthy (for the activity of that which is capable of originating change seems to take place in what is changed or altered); further, since it is the soul by which primarily we live, perceive, and think:—it follows that the soul must be an account and essence, not matter or a subject. For, as we said, the word substance has three meanings—form, matter, and the complex of both—and of these matter is poten-   15 tiality, form actuality. Since then the complex here is the living thing, the body cannot be the actuality of the soul; it is the soul which is the actuality of a certain kind of body. Hence the rightness of the view that the soul cannot *be* without a body, while it cannot   20 be a body; it is not a body but something relative to a body. That is why it is *in* a body, and a body of a definite kind. It was a mistake, therefore, to do as former thinkers did, merely to fit it into a body without adding a definite specification of the kind or char-

25   acter of that body, although evidently one chance thing will not receive another. It comes about as reason requires: the actuality of any given thing can only be realized in what is already potentially that thing, i.e. in a matter of its own appropriate to it. From all this it is plain that soul is an actuality or account of something that possesses a potentiality of being such.

3. Of the psychic powers above enumerated some kinds of living things, as we have
30   said, possess all, some less than all, others one only. Those we have mentioned are the nutritive, the appetitive, the sensory, the locomotive, and the power of thinking. Plants have none but the first, the nutritive, while another order of living things has
414ᵇ   this *plus* the sensory. If any order of living things has the sensory, it must also have the appetitive; for appetite is the genus of which desire, passion, and wish are the species; now all animals have one sense at least, viz. touch, and whatever has a sense has the capacity for pleasure and pain and therefore has pleasant and painful objects
5   present to it, and wherever these are present, there is desire, for desire is appetition of what is pleasant. Further, all animals have the sense for food (for touch is the sense for food); the food of all living things consists of what is dry, moist, hot, cold, and these are the qualities apprehended by touch; all other sensible qualities are
10   apprehended by touch only indirectly. Sounds, colours, and odours contribute nothing to nutriment; flavours fall within the field of tangible qualities. Hunger and thirst are forms of desire, hunger a desire for what is dry and hot, thirst a desire for what is cold and moist; flavour is a sort of seasoning added to both. We must later clear
15   up these points, but at present it may be enough to say that all animals that possess the sense of touch have also appetition. The case of imagination is obscure; we must examine it later. Certain kinds of animals possess in addition the power of locomotion, and still others, i.e. man and possibly another order like man or superior to him, the
20   power of thinking and thought. It is now evident that a single definition can be given of soul only in the same sense as one can be given of figure. For, as in that case there is no figure apart from triangle and those that follow in order, so here there is no soul apart from the forms of soul just enumerated. It is true that a common definition can be given for figure which will fit all figures without expressing the peculiar nature
25   of any figure. So here in the case of soul and its specific forms. Hence it is absurd in this and similar cases to look for a common definition which will not express the peculiar nature of anything that is and will not apply to the approriate indivisible species, while at the same time omitting to look for an account which will. The cases of figure and soul are exactly parallel; for the particulars subsumed under the common
30   name in both cases—figures and living beings—constitute a series, each successive term of which potentially contains its predecessor, e.g. the square the triangle, the sensory power the self-nutritive. Hence we must ask in the case of each order of living things, What is its soul, i.e. What is the soul of plant, man, beast? Why the terms are
415ᵃ   related in this serial way must form the subject of examination. For the power of perception is never found apart from the power of self-nutrition, while—in plants—the lat-
5   ter is found isolated from the former. Again, no sense is found apart from that of touch, while touch *is* found by itself; many animals have neither sight, hearing, nor smell. Again, among living things that possess sense some have the power of locomotion, some not. Lastly, certain living beings—a small minority—possess calculation and thought, for (among mortal beings) those which possess calculation have all the other
10   powers above mentioned, while the converse does not hold—indeed some live by imagination alone, while others have not even imagination. Reflective thought presents a different problem.

It is evident that the way to give the most adequate definition of soul is to seek in the case of *each* of its forms for the most appropriate definition.

⁂   ⁂   ⁂

BOOK III

*   *   *

4. Turning now to the part of the soul with which the soul knows and (whether this is separable from the others in definition only, or spatially as well) we have to inquire what differentiates this part, and how thinking can take place. 429^a 10

If thinking is like perceiving, it must be either a process in which the soul is acted upon by what is capable of being thought, or a process different from but analogous to that. The thinking part of the soul must therefore be, while impassible, capable of receiving the form of an object; that is, must be potentially identical in character with its object without being the object. Thought must be related to what is thinkable, as sense is to what is sensible. 15

Therefore, since everything is a possible object of thought, mind in order, as Anaxagoras says, to dominate, that is, to know, must be pure from all admixture; for the co-presence of what is alien to its nature is a hindrance and a block: it follows that it can have no nature of its own, other than that of having a certain capacity. Thus that in the soul which is called thought (by thought I mean that whereby the soul thinks and judges) is, before it thinks, not actually any real thing. For this reason it cannot reasonably be regarded as blended with the body: if so, it would acquire some quality, e.g. warmth or cold, or even have an organ like the sensitive faculty: as it is, it has none. It was a good idea to call the soul "the place of forms," though this description holds only of the thinking soul, and even this is the forms only potentially, not actually. 20 25

Observation of the sense-organs and their employment reveals a distinction between the impassibility of the sensitive faculty and that of the faculty of thought. After strong stimulation of a sense we are less able to exercise it than before, as e.g. in the case of a loud sound we cannot hear easily immediately after, or in the case of a bright colour or a powerful odour we cannot see or smell, but in the case of thought thinking about an object that is highly thinkable renders it more and not less able afterwards to think of objects that are less thinkable: the reason is that while the faculty of sensation is dependent upon the body, thought is separable from it. 30 429^b 5

When thought has become each thing in the way in which a man who actually knows is said to do so (this happens when he is now able to exercise the power on his own initiative), its condition is still one of potentiality, but in a different sense from the potentiality which preceded the acquisition of knowledge by learning or discovery; and thought is then able to think of itself.

Since we can distinguish between a magnitude and what it is to be a magnitude, and between water and what it is to be water, and so in many other cases (though not in all; for in certain cases the thing and its form are identical), flesh and what it is to be flesh are discriminated either by different faculties, or by the same faculty in two different states; for flesh necessarily involves matter and is like what is snub-nosed, a *this* in a *this*. Now it is by means of the sensitive faculty that we discriminate the hot and the 10

15 cold, i.e. the factors which combined in a certain ratio constitute flesh: the essential character of flesh is apprehended by something different either wholly separate from the sensitive faculty or related to it as a bent line to the same line when it has been straightened out.

Again in the case of abstract objects what is straight is analogous to what is snub-nosed; for it necessarily implies a continuum: its constitutive essence is different, if we may distinguish between straightness and what is straight: let us take it to be two-ness. It must be apprehended, therefore, by a different power or by
20 the same power in a different state. To sum up, in so far as the realities it knows are capable of being separated from their matter, so it is also with the powers of thought.

The problem might be suggested: if thinking is a passive affection, then if thought is simple and impassible and has nothing in common with anything else, as Anaxagoras
25 says, how can it come to think at all? For interaction between two factors is held to require a precedent community of nature between the factors. Again it might be asked, is thought a possible object of thought to itself? For if thought is thinkable *per se* and what is thinkable is in kind one and the same, then either thought will belong to everything, or it will contain some element common to it with all other realities which makes them all thinkable.

30 Have not we already disposed of the difficulty about interaction involving a common element, when we said that thought is in a sense potentially whatever is thinkable, though actually it is nothing until it has thought? What it thinks must be in it just as
430ª characters may be said to be on a writing-table on which as yet nothing actually stands written: this is exactly what happens with thought.

Thought is itself thinkable in exactly the same way as its objects are. For in the case of objects which involve no matter, what thinks and what is thought are identical;
5 for speculative knowledge and its object are identical. (Why thought is not always thinking we must consider later.) In the case of those which contain matter each of the objects of thought is only potentially present. It follows that while they will not have thought in them (for thought is a potentiality of them only in so far as they are capable of being disengaged from matter) thought may yet be thinkable.

10 5. Since in every class of things, as in nature as a whole, we find two factors involved, a matter which is potentially all the particulars included in the class, a cause which is productive in the sense that it makes them all (the latter standing to the former, as e.g. an art to its material), these distinct elements must likewise be found within the soul.

And in fact thought, as we have described it, is what it is by virtue of becoming all
15 things, while there is another which is what it is by virtue of making all things: this is a sort of positive state like light; for in a sense light makes potential colours into actual colours.

Thought in this sense of it is separable, impassible, unmixed, since it is in its essential nature activity (for always the active is superior to the passive factor, the originating force to the matter).

20 Actual knowledge is identical with its object: in the individual, potential knowledge is in time prior to actual knowledge, but absolutely it is not prior even in time. It does not sometimes think and sometimes not think. When separated it is alone just what it is, and this above is immortal and eternal (we do not remember because, while this is impossible, passive thought is perishable); and without this
25 nothing thinks.

NICHOMACHEAN ETHICS (in part)

BOOK I

1. The Good as the Aim of Action

Every art or applied science and every systematic investigation, and similarly   1094ᵃ
every action and choice, seem to aim at some good; the good, therefore, has been well
defined as that at which all things aim.* But it is clear that there is a difference in the
ends at which they aim: in some cases the activity is the end, in others the end is some
product beyond the activity. In cases where the end lies beyond the action the product is   5
naturally superior to the activity.

Since there are many activities, arts, and sciences, the number of ends is correspondingly large: of medicine the end is health, of shipbuilding a vessel, of strategy,
victory, and of household management, wealth. In many instances several such pursuits
are grouped together under a single capacity: the art of bridle-making, for example, and   10
everything else pertaining to the equipment of a horse are grouped together under
horsemanship; horsemanship in turn, along with every other military action, is grouped
together under strategy; and other pursuits are grouped together under other capacities.
In all these cases the ends of the master sciences are preferable to the ends of the subor-   15
dinate sciences, since the latter are pursued for the sake of the former. This is true
whether the ends of the actions lie in the activities themselves or, as is the case in the
disciplines just mentioned, in something beyond the activities.

2. Politics as the Master Science of the Good

Now, if there exists an end in the realm of action which we desire for its own
sake, an end which determines all our other desires; if, in other words, we do not make
all our choices for the sake of something else—for in this way the process will go on   20
infinitely so that our desire would be futile and pointless—then obviously this end will
be the good, that is, the highest good. Will not the knowledge of this good, consequently, be very important to our lives? Would it not better equip us, like archers who
have a target to aim at, to hit the proper mark? If so, we must try to comprehend in outline at least what this good is and to which branch of knowledge or to which capacity   25
it belongs.

This good, one should think, belongs to the most sovereign and most comprehensive master science, and politics** clearly fits this description. For it determines
which sciences ought to exist in states, what kind of sciences each group of citizens

*We do not know who first gave this definition of the good. It is certainly implied in the Platonic dia-
logues, especially in *Republic,* Book VI; but the most likely candidate for the formulation here is Eudoxus.

**Politikē* is the science of the city-state, the *polis,* and its members, not merely in our narrow "polit-
ical" sense of the word but also in the sense that a civilized human existence is, according to Plato and Aristotle, only possible in the *polis.* Thus *politikē* involves not only the science of the state, "politics," but of our
concept of "society" as well.

Aristotle, *The Nichomachean Ethics,* Book I–II; Book III, 1–5; Book IV, 3; Books VI–VII; Book X, 6–8,
translated by Martin Ostwald (New York: Macmillan/Library of the Liberal Arts, 1962).

1094^b must learn, and what degree of proficiency each must attain. We observe further that the most honored capacities, such as strategy, household management, and oratory, are contained in politics. Since this science uses the rest of the sciences, and since, more-

5   over, it legislates what people are to do and what they are not to do, its end seems to embrace the ends of the other sciences. Thus it follows that the end of politics is the good for man. For even if the good is the same for the individual and the state, the good of the state clearly is the greater and more perfect thing to attain and to safeguard. The

10   attainment of the good for one man alone is, to be sure, a source of satisfaction; yet to secure it for a nation and for states is nobler and more divine. In short, these are the aims of our investigation, which is in a sense an investigation of social and political matters.

3. The Limitations of Ethics and Politics

Our discussion will be adequate if it achieves clarity within the limits of the sub-ject matter. For precision cannot be expected in the treatment of all subjects alike, any more than it can be expected in all manufactured articles. Problems of what is noble

15   and just, which politics examines, present so much variety and irregularity that some people believe that they exist only by convention and not by nature. The problem of the good, too, presents a similar kind of irregularity, because in many cases good things bring harmful results. There are instances of men ruined by wealth, and others by courage. Therefore, in a discussion of such subjects, which has to start from a basis of

20   this kind, we must be satisfied to indicate the truth with a rough and general sketch: when the subject and the basis of a discussion consist of matters that hold good only as a general rule, but not always, the conclusions reached must be of the same order. The various points that are made must be received in the same spirit. For a well-schooled man is one who searches for that degree of precision in each kind of study

25   which the nature of the subject at hand admits: it is obviously just as foolish to accept arguments of probability from a mathematician as to demand strict demonstrations from an orator.

Each man can judge competently the things he knows, and of these he is a good

1095^a judge. Accordingly, a good judge in each particular field is one who has been trained in it, and a good judge in general, a man who has received an all-round schooling. For that reason, a young man is not equipped to be a student of politics; for he has no experience in the actions which life demands of him, and these actions form the basis and subject matter of the discussion. Moreover, since he follows his emotions, his study will be

5   pointless and unprofitable, for the end of this kind of study is not knowledge but action. Whether he is young in years or immature in character makes no difference; for his de-ficiency is not a matter of time but of living and of pursuing all his interests under the influence of his emotions. Knowledge brings no benefit to this kind of person, just as it

10   brings none to the morally weak. But those who regulate their desires and actions by a rational principle* will greatly benefit from a knowledge of this subject. So much by way of a preface about the student, the limitations which have to be accepted, and the objective before us.

---

*The fundamental meaning of *Logos* is "speech," "statement," in the sense of a coherent and rational arrangement of words; but it can apply to a rational principle underlying many things, and may be translated in different contexts by "rational account," "explanation," "argument," "treatise," or "discussion." In Chap-ters 7 and 13 below, *Logos* is used in a normative sense, describing the human faculty which comprehends and formulates rational principles and thus guides the conduct of a good and reasonable man.

4. Happiness Is the Good, but Many Views Are Held About It

To resume the discussion: since all knowledge and every choice is directed toward some good, let us discuss what is in our view the aim of politics, i.e., the highest good attainable by action. As far as its name is concerned, most people would probably agree: for both the common run of people and cultivated men call it happiness, and understand by "being happy" the same as "living well" and "doing well." But when it comes to defining what happiness is, they disagree, and the account given by the common run differs from that of the philosophers. The former say it is some clear and obvious good, such as pleasure, wealth, or honor; some say it is one thing and others another, and often the very same person identifies it with different things at different times: when he is sick he thinks it is health, and when he is poor he says it is wealth; and when people are conscious of their own ignorance, they admire those who talk above their heads in accents of greatness. Some thinkers used to believe that there exists over and above these many goods another good, good in itself and by itself, which also is the cause of good in all these things. An examination of all the different opinions would perhaps be a little pointless, and it is sufficient to concentrate on those which are most in evidence or which seem to make some sort of sense.

Nor must we overlook the fact that arguments which proceed from fundamental principles are different from arguments that lead up to them. Plato, too, rightly recognized this as a problem and used to ask whether the discussion was proceeding from or leading up to fundamental principles, just as in a race course there is a difference between running from the judges to the far end of the track and running back again.* Now, we must start with the known. But this term has two connotations: "what is known to us" and "what is known" pure and simple. Therefore, we should start perhaps from what is known to us. For that reason, to be a competent student of what is right and just, and of politics generally, one must first have received a proper upbringing in moral conduct. The acceptance of a fact as a fact is the starting point, and if this is sufficiently clear, there will be no further need to ask why it is so. A man with this kind of background has or can easily acquire the foundations from which he must start. But if he neither has nor can acquire them, let him lend an ear to Hesiod's words:

> That man is all-best who himself works out every problem. . . .
> That man, too, is admirable who follows one who speaks well.
> He who cannot see the truth for himself, nor, hearing it from others,
>   store it away in his mind, that man is utterly useless.

5. Various Views on the Highest Good

But to return to the point from which we digressed. It is not unreasonable that men should derive their concept of the good and of happiness from the lives which they lead. The common run of people and the most vulgar identify it with pleasure, and for that reason are satisfied with a life of enjoyment. For the most notable kinds of life are three: the life just mentioned, the political life, and the contemplative life.

The common run of people, as we saw, betray their utter slavishness in their preference for a life suitable to cattle; but their views seem plausible because many people

15

20

25

30

1095ᵇ

5

10

15

20

---

*A Greek race course was U-shaped with the starting line at the open end, which is also where the judges would have their place. The race was run around a marker set up toward the opposite end of the U, and back again to the starting line.

in high places share the feelings of Sardanapallus.* Cultivated and active men, on the other hand, believe the good to be honor, for honor, one might say, is the end of the political life. But this is clearly too superficial an answer: for honor seems to depend on those who confer it rather than on him who receives it, whereas our guess is that the good is a man's own possession which cannot easily be taken away from him. Furthermore, men seem to pursue honor to assure themselves of their own worth; at any rate, they seek to be honored by sensible men and by those who know them, and they want to be honored on the basis of their virtue or excellence.** Obviously, then, excellence, as far as they are concerned, is better than honor. One might perhaps even go so far as to consider excellence rather than honor as the end of political life. However, even excellence proves to be imperfect as an end: for a man might possibly possess it while asleep or while being inactive all his life, and while, in addition, undergoing the greatest suffering and misfortune. Nobody would call the life of such a man happy, except for the sake of maintaining an argument. But enough of this: the subject has been sufficiently treated in our publications addressed to a wider audience. In the third place there is the contemplative life, which we shall examine later on. As for the money-maker, his life is led under some kind of constraint: clearly, wealth is not the good which we are trying to find, for it is only useful, i.e., it is a means to something else. Hence one might rather regard the aforementioned objects as ends, since they are valued for their own sake. But even they prove not to be the good, though many words have been wasted to show that they are. Accordingly, we may dismiss them.

6. Plato's View of the Good

But perhaps we had better examine the universal good and face the problem of its meaning, although such an inquiry is repugnant, since those who have introduced the doctrine of Forms*** are dear to us. But in the interest of truth, one should perhaps think a man, especially if he is a philosopher, had better give up even [theories that once were] his own and in fact must do so. Both are dear to us, but it is our sacred duty to honor truth more highly [than friends].

The proponents of this theory did not make Forms out of those classes within which they recognized an order involving priority and posteriority; for that reason they made no provision, either, for a Form comprising all numbers.† However, the term "good" is used in the categories of substance, of quality, and of relatedness alike; but a thing-as-such, i.e., a substance, is by nature prior to a relation into which it can enter: relatedness is, as it were, an offshoot or logical accident of substance. Consequently, there cannot be a Form common to the good-as-such and the good as a relation.

---

*Sardanapallus is the Hellenized name of the Assyrian king Ashurbanipal (669–626 B.C.). Many stories about his sensual excesses were current in antiquity.

**Aretē denotes the functional excellence of any person, animal, or thing—that quality which enables the possessor to perform his own particular function well. Thus the aretai (plural) of man in relation to other men are his qualities which enable him to function well in society. The translation "virtue" often seems too narrow, and accordingly "excellence" and "goodness," or a combination of these, will also be used.

***The reference is of course to Plato's theory of eidē or ideai and especially the Form of the Good, which is Aristotle's chief target here.

†Since for Plato and his followers the Forms are absolute being, in which there is no room for becoming or any kind of development, they do not recognize a Form of a developing series, in which each successive member implies the preceding members of the same series. But, as Aristotle proceeds to show, the term "good" belongs to such a developing series: if we call a certain quality, e.g., blueness, "good," we have to assume first that there is such a thing as blueness; i.e., we have to predicate it in the category of substance before we can predicate it in the category of quality.

Secondly, the term "good" has as many meanings as the word "is": it is used to describe substances, e.g., divinity and intelligence are good; qualities, e.g., the virtues are good; quantities, e.g., the proper amount is good; relatedness, e.g., the useful is good; time, e.g., the right moment is good; place, e.g., a place to live is good; and so forth. It is clear, therefore, that the good cannot be something universal, common to all cases, and single; for if it were, it would not be applicable in all categories but only in one.

Thirdly, since the things which are included under one Form are the subject matter of a single science, there should be a single science dealing with all good things. But in actual fact there are many sciences dealing even with the goods that fall into a single category. To take, for example, the right moment: in war it is the proper concern of strategy, whereas in treating a disease it is part of the study of medicine. Or to take the proper amount: in food it is the subject of medicine; in physical training, of gymnastics.

One might even [go further and] raise the question what exactly they mean by a "thing-as-such"; for the selfsame definition of "man" applies to both "man-as-such" and a particular man. For inasmuch as they refer to "man," there will be no difference between the two; and if this is true, there will be no difference, either, between "good-as-such" and "good," since both are good. Nor indeed will the "good-as-such" be more of a good because it is everlasting: after all, whiteness which lasts for a long time is no whiter than whiteness which lasts only for a day.

The argument of the Pythagoreans on this point seems to be more convincing. They give unity a place in the column of goods; and indeed even Speusippus* seems to follow them. But more about this elsewhere.

An objection might be raised against what we have said on the ground that the [Platonic] doctrine does not refer to every kind of good, and that only things which are pursued and loved for their own sake are called "good" by reference to one single Form. That which produces good or somehow guarantees its permanence, [the Platonists argue,] or that which prevents the opposite of a good from asserting itself is called "good" because it is conducive to the intrinsically good and in a different sense. Now, the term "good" has obviously two different meanings: (1) things which are intrinsically good, and (2) things which are good as being conducive to the intrinsically good. Let us, therefore, separate the intrinsically good things from the useful things and examine whether they are called "good" by reference to a single Form.

What sort of things could be called intrinsically good? Are they the goods that are pursued without regard to additional benefits, such as thought, sight, certain pleasures and honors? For even if we pursue these also for the sake of something else, one would still classify them among things intrinsically good. Or is nothing good except the Form of Good? If that is the case, the Form will be pointless. But if, on the contrary, thought, sight, etc. also belong to the group of intrinsically good things, the same definition of "good" will have to be manifested in all of them, just as, for example, the definition of whiteness is the same in snow and in white paint. But in actual fact, the definitions of "good" as manifested in honor, thought, and pleasure are different and distinct. The good, therefore, is not some element common to all these things as derived from one Form.

What, then, is the meaning of "good" [in these different things]? Surely, it is not that they merely happen to have the same name. Do we call them "good" because they are derived from a single good, or because they all aim at a single good? Or do we rather

---

*Speusippus was Plato's nephew and disciple who succeeded him a head of the Academy from 347–339 B.C.

call them "good" by analogy, e.g., as sight is good in the body, so intelligence is good in the soul, and so other things are good within their respective fields?

30   But perhaps this subject should be dismissed for the present, because a detailed discussion of it belongs more properly to a different branch of philosophy, [namely, first philosophy]. The same applies to the Form [of the Good]: for, assuming that there is some single good which different things possess in common, or that there exists a good absolutely in itself and by itself, it evidently is something which cannot be realized in action or attained by man. But the good which we are now seeking must be attainable.

35
1097ª   Perhaps one may think that the recognition of an absolute good will be advantageous for the purpose of attaining and realizing in action the goods which can be attained and realized. By treating the absolute good as a pattern, [they might argue,] we shall gain a better knowledge of what things are good for us, and once we know that, we can achieve them. This argument has, no doubt, some plausibility; however, it does not

5   tally with the procedure of the sciences. For while all the sciences aim at some good and seek to fulfill it, they leave the knowledge of the absolute good out of consideration. Yet if this knowledge were such a great help, it would make no sense that all the craftsmen are ignorant of it and do not even attempt to seek it. One might also wonder what benefit a weaver or a carpenter might derive in the practice of his own art from a knowledge of the absolute Good, or in what way a physician who has contemplated the Form of the

10   Good will become more of a physician or a general more of a general. For actually, a physician does not even examine health in this fashion; he examines the health of man, or perhaps better, the health of a particular man, for he practices his medicine on particular cases. So much for this.

7. The Good Is Final and Self-Sufficient; Happiness Is Defined

15   Let us return again to our investigation into the nature of the good which we are seeking. It is evidently something different in different actions and in each art: it is one thing in medicine, another in strategy, and another again in each of the other arts. What, then, is the good of each? Is it not that for the sake of which everything else is done? That means it is health in the case of medicine, victory in the case of strategy, a house in

20   the case of building, a different thing in the case of different arts, and in all actions and choices it is the end. For it is for the sake of the end that all else is done. Thus, if there is some one end for all that we do, this would be the good attainable by action; if there are several ends, they will be the goods attainable by action.

        Our argument has gradually progressed to the same point at which we were be-
25   fore, and we must try to clarify it still further. Since there are evidently several ends, and since we choose some of these—e.g., wealth, flutes, and instruments generally—as a means to something else, it is obvious that not all ends are final. The highest good, on the other hand, must be something final. Thus, if there is only one final end, this will be the good we are seeking; if there are several, it will be the most final and perfect of

30   them. We call that which is pursued as an end in itself more final than an end which is pursued for the sake of something else; and what is never chosen as a means to something else we call more final than that which is chosen both as an end in itself and as a means to something else. What is always chosen as an end in itself and never as a means to something else is called final in an unqualified sense. This description seems to apply

1097ᵇ   to happiness above all else: for we always choose happiness as an end in itself and never for the sake of something else. Honor, pleasure, intelligence, and all virtue we choose partly for themselves—for we would choose each of them even if no further advantage would accrue from them—but we also choose them partly for the sake of happiness, because we assume that it is through them that we will be happy. On the other hand, no one chooses happiness for the sake of honor, pleasure, and the like, nor as a means to anything at all.

We arrive at the same conclusion if we approach the question from the standpoint of self-sufficiency. For the final and perfect good seems to be self-sufficient. However, we define something as self-sufficient not by reference to the "self" alone. We do not mean a man who lives his life in isolation, but a man who also lives with parents, children, a wife, and friends and fellow citizens generally, since man is by nature a social and political being. But some limit must be set to these relationships; for if they are extended to include ancestors, descendants, and friends of friends, they will go on to infinity. However, this point must be reserved for investigation later. For the present we define as "self-sufficient" that which taken by itself makes life something desirable and deficient in nothing. It is happiness, in our opinion, which fits this description. Moreover, happiness is of all things the one most desirable, and it is not counted as one good thing among many others. But if it were counted as one among many others, it is obvious that the addition of even the least of the goods would make it more desirable; for the addition would produce an extra amount of good, and the greater amount of good is always more desirable than the lesser. We see then that happiness is something final and self-sufficient and the end of our actions.

To call happiness the highest good is perhaps a little trite, and a clearer account of what it is, is still required. Perhaps this is best done by first ascertaining the proper function of man. For just as the goodness and performance of a flute player, a sculptor, or any kind of expert, and generally of anyone who fulfills some function or performs some action, are thought to reside in his proper function, so the goodness and performance of man would seem to reside in whatever is his proper function. Is it then possible that while a carpenter and a shoemaker have their own proper functions and spheres of action, man as man has none, but was left by nature a good-for-nothing without a function? Should we not assume that just as the eye, the hand, the foot, and in general each part of the body clearly has its own proper function, so man too has some function over and above the functions of his parts? What can this function possibly be? Simply living? He shares that even with plants, but we are now looking for something peculiar to man. Accordingly, the life of nutrition and growth must be excluded. Next in line there is a life of sense perception. But this, too, man has in common with the horse, the ox, and every animal. There remains then an active life of the rational element. The rational element has two parts: one is rational in that it obeys the rule of reason, the other in that it possesses and conceives rational rules. Since the expression "life of the rational element" also can be used in two senses, we must make it clear that we mean a life determined by the activity, as opposed to the mere possession, of the rational element. For the activity, it seems, has a greater claim to be the function of man.

The proper function of man, then, consists in an activity of the soul in conformity with a rational principle or, at least, not without it. In speaking of the proper function of a given individual we mean that it is the same in kind as the function of an individual who sets high standards for himself: the proper function of a harpist, for example, is the same as the function of a harpist who has set high standards for himself. The same applies to any and every group of individuals: the full attainment of excellence must be added to the mere function. In other words, the function of the harpist is to play the harp; the function of the harpist who has high standards is to play it well. On these assumptions, if we take the proper function of man to be a certain kind of life, and if this kind of life is an activity of the soul and consists in actions performed in conjunction with the rational element, and if a man of high standards is he who performs these actions well and properly, and if a function is well performed when it is performed in accordance with the excellence appropriate to it; we reach the conclusion that the good of man is an activity of the soul in conformity with excellence or virtue, and if there are several virtues, in conformity with the best and most complete.

But we must add "in a complete life." For one swallow does not make a spring, nor does one sunny day; similarly, one day or a short time does not make a man blessed* and happy.

This will suffice as an outline of the good: for perhaps one ought to make a general sketch first and fill in the details afterwards. Once a good outline has been made, anyone, it seems, is capable of developing and completing it in detail, and time is a good inventor or collaborator in such an effort. Advances in the arts, too, have come about in this way, for anyone can fill in gaps. We must also bear in mind what has been said above, namely that one should not require precision in all pursuits alike, but in each field precision varies with the matter under discussion and should be required only to the extent to which it is appropriate to the investigation. A carpenter and a geometrician both want to find a right angle, but they do not want to find it in the same sense: the former wants to find it to the extent to which it is useful for his work, the latter, wanting to see truth, tries to ascertain what it is and what sort of thing it is. We must, likewise, approach other subjects in the same spirit, in order to prevent minor points from assuming a greater importance than the major tasks. Nor should we demand to know a causal explanation in all matters alike; in some instances, e.g., when dealing with fundamental principles, it is sufficient to point out convincingly that such-and-such is in fact the case. The fact here is the primary thing and the fundamental principle. Some fundamental principles can be apprehended by induction, others by sense perception, others again by some sort of habituation,** and others by still other means. We must try to get at each of them in a way naturally appropriate to it, and must be scrupulous in defining it correctly, because it is of great importance for the subsequent course of the discussion. Surely, a good beginning is more than half the whole, and as it comes to light, it sheds light' on many problems.

8. Popular Views About Happiness Confirm Our Position

We must examine the fundamental principle with which we are concerned, [happiness,] not only on the basis of the logical conclusion we have reached and on the basis of the elements which make up its definition, but also on the basis of the views commonly expressed about it. For in a true statement, all the facts are in harmony; in a false statement, truth soon introduces a discordant note.

Good things are commonly divided into three classes: (1) external goods, (2) goods of the soul, and (3) goods of the body. Of these, we call the goods pertaining to the soul goods in the highest and fullest sense. But in speaking of "soul," we refer to our soul's actions and activities. Thus, our definition tallies with this opinion which has

---

*The distinction Aristotle seems to observe between *makarios,* "blessed" or "supremely happy," and *eudaimōn,* "happy," is that the former describes happiness insofar as it is god-given, while the latter describes happiness as attained by man through his own efforts.

**This, according to Aristotle, is the way in which the fundamental principles of ethics are learned, and for that reason a person must be mature in order to be able to study ethics properly. Aristotle is not trying to persuade his listener of the truth of these principles, but takes it for granted that the listener has learned them at home.

been current for a long time and to which philosophers subscribe. We are also right in defining the end as consisting of actions and activities; for in this way the end is included among the goods of the soul and not among external goods.

Also the view that a happy man lives well and fares well fits in with our definition: for we have all but defined happiness as a kind of good life and well-being.

Moreover, the characteristics which one looks for in happiness are all included in our definition. For some people think that happiness is virtue, others that it is practical wisdom, others that it is some kind of theoretical wisdom; others again believe it to be all or some of these accompanied by, or not devoid of, pleasure; and some people also include external prosperity in its definition.* Some of these views are expressed by many people and have come down from antiquity, some by a few men of high prestige, and it is not reasonable to assume that both groups are altogether wrong; the presumption is rather that they are right in at least one or even in most respects.

Now, in our definition we are in agreement with those who describe happiness as virtue or as some particular virtue, for our term "activity in conformity with virtue" implies virtue. But it does doubtless make a considerable difference whether we think of the highest good as consisting in the possession or in the practice of virtue, viz., as being a characteristic or an activity. For a characteristic may exist without producing any good result, as for example, in a man who is asleep or incapacitated in some other respect. An activity, on the other hand, must produce a result: [an active person] will necessarily act and act well. Just as the crown at the Olympic Games is not awarded to the most beautiful and the strongest but to the participants in the contests—for it is among them that the victors are found—so the good and noble things in life are won by those who act rightly.

The life of men active in this sense is also pleasant in itself. For the sensation of pleasure belongs to the soul, and each man derives pleasure from what he is said to love: a lover of horses from horses, a lover of the theater from plays, and in the same way a lover of justice from just acts, and a lover of virtue in general from virtuous acts. In most men, pleasant acts conflict with one another because they are not pleasant by nature, but men who love what is noble derive pleasure from what is naturally pleasant. Actions which conform to virtue are naturally pleasant, and, as a result, such actions are not only pleasant for those who love the noble but also pleasant in themselves. The life of such men has no further need of pleasure as an added attraction, but it contains pleasure within itself. We may even go so far as to state that the man who does not enjoy performing noble actions is not a good man at all. Nobody would call a man just who does not enjoy acting justly, nor generous who does not enjoy generous actions, and so on. If this is true, actions performed in conformity with virtue are in themselves pleasant.

Of course it goes without saying that such actions are good as well as noble, and they are both in the highest degree, if the man of high moral standards displays any right judgment about them at all; and his judgment corresponds to our description. So we see that happiness is at once the best, noblest, and most pleasant thing, and these qualities are not separate, as the inscription at Delos makes out:

> The most just is most noble, but health is the best, and to
> win what one loves is pleasantest.

*The view that virtue alone constitutes happiness was espoused by Antisthenes and the Cynics (and later by the Stoics); the doctrine that all virtues are forms of *phronēsis* or "practical wisdom" is attributed to Socrates; theoretical wisdom as virtue may perhaps be attributed to Anaxagoras and his doctrine of *Nous;* the view that pleasure must be added to virtue and wisdom is that of Plato; and the ancient commentators on this passage identify Xenocrates, Plato's pupil and later head of the Academy, as regarding external goods as essential for the good life.

For the best activities encompass all these attributes, and it is in these, or in the best one
30   of them, that we maintain happiness consists.

Still, happiness, as we have said, needs external goods as well. For it is impossible or at least not easy to perform noble actions if one lacks the wherewithal. Many ac-
1099ᵇ   tions can only be performed with the help of instruments, as it were: friends, wealth,
and political power. And there are some external goods the absence of which spoils
supreme happiness, e.g., good birth, good children, and beauty: for a man who is
very ugly in appearance or ill-born or who lives all by himself and has no children
5   cannot be classified as altogether happy; even less happy perhaps is a man whose
children and friends are worthless, or one who has lost good children and friends
through death. Thus, as we have said, happiness also requires well-being of this kind,
and that is the reason why some classify good fortune with happiness, while others
link it to virtue.

9. How Happiness Is Acquired

10   This also explains why there is a problem whether happiness is acquired by
learning, by discipline, or by some other kind of training, or whether we attain it by
reason of some divine dispensation or even by chance. Now, if there is anything at all
which comes to men as a gift from the gods, it is reasonable to suppose that happiness
above all else is god-given; and of all things human it is the most likely to be god-
given, inasmuch as it is the best. But although this subject is perhaps more appropriate
to a different field of study, it is clear that happiness is one of the most divine things,
even if it is not god-sent but attained through virtue and some kind of learning or train-
15   ing. For the prize and end of excellence and virtue is the best thing of all, and it is
something divine and blessed. Moreover, if happiness depends on excellence, it will be
shared by many people; for study and effort will make it accessible to anyone whose
20   capacity for virtue is unimpaired. And if it is better that happiness is acquired in this
way rather than by chance, it is reasonable to assume that this is the way in which it is
acquired. For, in the realm of nature, things are naturally arranged in the best way possible—and the same is also true of the products of art and of any kind of causation, especially the highest. To leave the greatest and noblest of things to chance would hardly
be right.
25   A solution of this question is also suggested by our earlier definition, according to
which the good of man, happiness, is some kind of activity of the soul in conformity
with virtue. All the other goods are either necessary prerequisites for happiness, or are
by nature co-workers with it and useful instruments for attaining it. Our results also
tally with what we said at the outset: for we stated that the end of politics is the best of
30   ends; and the main concern of politics is to engender a certain character in the citizens
and to make them good and disposed to perform noble actions.

We are right, then, when we call neither a horse nor an ox nor any other animal
1100ᵃ   happy, for none of them is capable of participating in an activity of this kind. For
the same reason, a child is not happy, either; for, because of his age, he cannot yet
perform such actions. When we do call a child happy, we do so by reason of the hopes
we have for his future. Happiness, as we have said, requires completeness in virtue
5   as well as a complete lifetime. Many changes and all kinds of contingencies befall
a man in the course of his life, and it is possible that the most prosperous man will
encounter great misfortune in his old age, as the Trojan legends tell about Priam.
When a man has met a fate such as his and has come to a wretched end, no one calls
him happy.

10. Can a Man Be Called "Happy" During His Lifetime?

Must we, then, apply the term "happy" to no man at all as long as he is alive? Must we, as Solon would have us do, wait to see his end?* And, on this assumption, is it also true that a man is actually happy after he is dead? Is this not simply absurd, especially for us who define happiness as a kind of activity? Suppose we do not call a dead man happy, and interpret Solon's words to mean that only when a man is dead can we safely say that he has been happy, since he is now beyond the reach of evil and misfortune—this view, too, is open to objection. For it seems that to some extent good and evil really exist for a dead man, just as they may exist for a man who lives without being conscious of them, for example, honors and disgraces, and generally the successes and failures of his children and descendants. This presents a further problem. A man who has lived happily to his old age and has died as happily as he lived may have many vicissitudes befall his descendants: some of them may be good and may be granted the kind of life which they deserve, and others may not. It is, further, obvious that the descendants may conceivably be removed from their ancestors by various degrees. Under such circumstances, it would be odd if the dead man would share in the vicissitudes of his descendants and be happy at one time and wretched at another. But it would also be odd if the fortunes of their descendants did not affect the ancestors at all, not even for a short time.

But we must return to the problem raised earlier, for through it our present problem perhaps may be solved. If one must look to the end and praise a man not as being happy but as having been happy in the past, is it not paradoxical that at a time when a man actually is happy this attribute, though true, cannot be applied to him? We are unwilling to call the living happy because changes may befall them and because we believe that happiness has permanence and is not amenable to changes under any circumstances, whereas fortunes revolve many times in one person's lifetime. For obviously, if we are to keep pace with a man's fortune, we shall frequently have to call the same man happy at one time and wretched at another and demonstrate that the happy man is a kind of chameleon, and that the foundations [of his life] are unsure. Or is it quite wrong to make our judgment depend on fortune? Yes, it is wrong, for fortune does not determine whether we fare well or ill, but is, as we said, merely an accessory to human life; activities in conformity with virtue constitute happiness, and the opposite activities constitute its opposite.

The question which we have just discussed further confirms our definition. For no function of man possesses as much stability as do activities in conformity with virtue: these seem to be even more durable than scientific knowledge. And the higher the virtuous activities, the more durable they are, because men who are supremely happy spend their lives in these activities most intensely and most continuously, and this seems to be the reason why such activities cannot be forgotten.

The happy man will have the attribute of permanence which we are discussing, and he will remain happy throughout his life. For he will always or to the highest degree both do and contemplate what is in conformity with virtue; he will bear the vicissitudes of fortune most nobly and with perfect decorum under all circumstances, inasmuch as he is truly good and "four-square beyond reproach."

But fortune brings many things to pass, some great and some small. Minor instances of good and likewise of bad luck obviously do not decisively tip the scales of

*This is one of the main points made by Solon, Athenian statesman and poet of the early sixth century B.C., in his conversation with the Lydian king, Croesus.

life, but a number of major successes will make life more perfectly happy; for, in the first place, by their very nature they help to make life attractive, and secondly, they afford the opportunity for noble and good actions. On the other hand, frequent reverses can crush and mar supreme happiness in that they inflict pain and thwart many activi-
30   ties. Still, nobility shines through even in such circumstances, when a man bears many great misfortunes with good grace not because he is insensitive to pain but because he is noble and high-minded.

35   If, as we said, the activities determine a man's life, no supremely happy man can ever become miserable, for he will never do what is hateful and base. For in our opin-
1101ᵃ   ion, the man who is truly good and wise will bear with dignity whatever fortune may bring, and will always act as nobly as circumstances permit, just as a good general makes the most strategic use of the troops at his disposal, and a good shoemaker makes
5   the best shoe he can from the leather available, and so on with experts in all other fields. If this is true, a happy man will never become miserable; but even so, supreme happiness will not be his if a fate such as Priam's befalls him. And yet, he will not be
10   fickle and changeable; he will not be dislodged from his happiness easily by any misfortune that comes along, but only by great and numerous disasters such as will make it impossible for him to become happy again in a short time; if he recovers his happiness at all, it will be only after a long period of time, in which he has won great distinctions.

Is there anything to prevent us, then, from defining the happy man as one whose
15   activities are an expression of complete virtue, and who is sufficiently equipped with external goods, not simply at a given moment but to the end of his life? Or should we add that he must die as well as live in the manner which we have defined? For we cannot foresee the future, and happiness, we maintain, is an end which is absolutely final and complete in every respect. If this be granted, we shall define as "supremely happy"
20   those living men who fulfill and continue to fulfill these requirements, but blissful only as human beings. So much for this question.

11. Do the Fortunes of the Living Affect the Dead?

That the fortunes of his descendants and of all those near and dear to him do not affect the happiness of a dead man at all, seems too unfeeling a view and contrary to the prevailing opinions. Many and different in kind are the accidents that can befall us, and
25   some hit home more closely than others. It would, therefore, seem to be a long and endless task to make detailed distinctions, and perhaps a general outline will be sufficient. Just as one's own misfortunes are sometimes momentous and decisive for one's life and
30   sometimes seem comparatively less important, so the misfortunes of our various friends affect us to varying degrees. In each case it makes a considerable difference whether those who are affected by an event are living or dead; much more so than it matters in a tragedy whether the crimes and horrors have been perpetrated before the opening of the play or are part of the plot. This difference, too, must be taken into account and perhaps
35   still more the problem whether the dead participate in any good or evil. These consider-
1101ᵇ   ations suggest that even if any good or evil reaches them at all, it must be something weak and negligible (either intrinsically or in relation to them), or at least something too small and insignificant to make the unhappy happy or to deprive the happy of their bliss.
5   The good as well as the bad fortunes of their friends seem, then, to have some effect upon the dead, but the nature and magnitude of the effect is such as not to make the happy unhappy or to produce any similar changes.

12. The Praise Accorded to Happiness

Now that we have settled these questions, let us consider whether happiness is to   10
be classified among the things which we praise or rather among those which we honor;
for it is clear that it is not a potential [but an actual good].

The grounds on which we bestow praise on anything evidently are its quality and
the relation in which it stands to other things. In other words, we praise a just man, a
courageous man, and in general any good man, and also his virtue or excellence, on the   15
basis of his actions and achievements; moreover, we praise a strong man, a swift runner,
and so forth, because he possesses a certain natural quality and stands in a certain relation to something good and worth while. Our feelings about praising the gods provide a
further illustration of this point. For it is ridiculous to refer the gods to our standards;
but this is precisely what praising them amounts to, since praise, as we said, entails a   20
reference to something else. But if praise is appropriate only for relative things, it is
clear that the best things do not call for praise but for something greater and better, as
indeed is generally recognized: for we call the gods "blessed" and "happy" and use
these terms also for the most godlike man. The same is true of good things: no one   25
praises happiness in the same sense in which he praises justice, but he exalts its bliss as
something better and more nearly divine.

Eudoxus, too, seems to have used the right method for advocating that pleasure is
the most excellent, for he took the fact that pleasure, though a good, is not praised as an
indication of its superiority to the things that are praised, as god and the good are, for   30
they are the standards to which we refer everything else.

Praise is proper to virtue or excellence, because it is excellence that makes men
capable of performing noble deeds. Eulogies, on the other hand, are appropriate for
achievements of the body as well as of the mind. However, a detailed analysis of this
subject is perhaps rather the business of those who have made a study of eulogies. For
our present purposes, we may draw the conclusion from the preceding argument that   35
happiness is one of the goods that are worthy of honor and are final. This again seems to   1102ᵃ
be due to the fact that it is a starting point or fundamental principle, since for its sake all
of us do everything else. And the source and cause of all good things we consider as
something worthy of honor and as divine.

13. The Psychological Foundations
of the Virtues

Since happiness is a certain activity of the soul in conformity with perfect virtue,   5
we must now examine what virtue or excellence is. For such an inquiry will perhaps
better enable us to discover the nature of happiness. Moreover, the man who is truly
concerned about politics seems to devote special attention to excellence, since it is his
aim to make the citizens good and law-abiding. We have an example of this in the law-   10
givers of Crete and Sparta and in other great legislators. If an examination of virtue is
part of politics, this question clearly fits into the pattern of our original plan.

There can be no doubt that the virtue which we have to study is human virtue. For
the good which we have been seeking is a human good and the happiness a human hap-   15
piness. By human virtue we do not mean the excellence of the body, but that of the soul,
and we define happiness as an activity of the soul. If this is true, the student of politics
must obviously have some knowledge of the workings of the soul, just as the man who
is to heal eyes must know something about the whole body. In fact, knowledge is all the   20
more important for the former, inasmuch as politics is better and more valuable than

medicine, and cultivated physicians devote much time and trouble to gain knowledge about the body. Thus, the student of politics must study the soul, but he must do so with his own aim in view, and only to the extent that the objects of his inquiry demand: to go into it in greater detail would perhaps be more laborious than his purposes require.

Some things that are said about the soul in our less technical discussions are adequate enough to be used here, for instance, that the soul consists of two elements, one irrational and one rational. Whether these two elements are separate, like the parts of the body or any other divisible thing, or whether they are only logically separable though in reality indivisible, as convex and concave are in the circumference of a circle, is irrelevant for our present purposes.

Of the irrational element, again, one part seems to be common to all living things and vegetative in nature: I mean that part which is responsible for nurture and growth. We must assume that some such capacity of the soul exists in everything that takes nourishment, in the embryonic stage as well as when the organism is fully developed; for this makes more sense than to assume the existence of some different capacity at the latter stage. The excellence of this part of the soul is, therefore, shown to be common to all living things and is not exclusively human. This very part and this capacity seem to be most active in sleep. For in sleep the difference between a good man and a bad is least apparent—whence the saying that for half their lives the happy are no better off than the wretched. This is just what we would expect, for sleep is an inactivity of the soul in that it ceases to do things which cause it to be called good or bad. However, to a small extent some bodily movements do penetrate to the soul in sleep, and in this sense the dreams of honest men are better than those of average people. But enough of this subject: we may pass by the nutritive part, since it has no natural share in human excellence or virtue.

In addition to this, there seems to be another integral element of the soul which, though irrational, still does partake of reason in some way. In morally strong and morally weak men we praise the reason that guides them and the rational element of the soul, because it exhorts them to follow the right path and to do what is best. Yet we see in them also another natural strain different from the rational, which fights and resists the guidance of reason. The soul behaves in precisely the same manner as do the paralyzed limbs of the body. When we intend to move the limbs to the right, they turn to the left, and similarly, the impulses of morally weak persons turn in the direction opposite to that in which reason leads them. However, while the aberration of the body is visible, that of the soul is not. But perhaps we must accept it as a fact, nevertheless, that there is something in the soul besides the rational element, which opposes and reacts against it. In what way the two are distinct need not concern us here. But, as we have stated, it too seems to partake of reason; at any rate, in a morally strong man it accepts the leadership of reason, and is perhaps more obedient still in a self-controlled and courageous man, since in him everything is in harmony with the voice of reason.

Thus we see that the irrational element of the soul has two parts: the one is vegetative and has no share in reason at all, the other is the seat of the appetites and of desire in general and partakes of reason insofar as it complies with reason and accepts its leadership; it possesses reason in the sense that we say it is "reasonable" to accept the advice of a father and of friends, not in the sense that we have a "rational" understanding of mathematical propositions. That the irrational element can be persuaded by the rational is shown by the fact that admonition and all manner of rebuke and exhortation are possible. If it is correct to say that the appetitive part, too, has reason, it follows that the rational element of the soul has two subdivisions: the one possesses reason in the strict sense, contained within itself, and the other possesses reason in the sense that it listens to reason as one would listen to a father.

Virtue, too, is differentiated in line with this division of the soul. We call some virtues "intellectual" and others "moral": theoretical wisdom, understanding, and prac-   5 tical wisdom are intellectual virtues, generosity and self-control moral virtues. In speaking of a man's character, we do not describe him as wise or understanding, but as gentle or self-controlled; but we praise the wise man, too, for his characteristic, and praiseworthy characteristics are what we call virtues.   10

Book II

1. Moral Virtue as the Result of Habits

Virtue, as we have seen, consists of two-kinds, intellectual virtue and moral virtue. Intellectual virtue or excellence owes its origin and development chiefly to   15 teaching, and for that reason requires experience and time. Moral virtue, on the other hand, is formed by habit, *ethos,* and its name, *ēthikē,* is therefore derived, by a slight variation, from *ethos.* This shows, too, that none of the moral virtues is implanted in us by nature, for nothing which exists by nature can be changed by habit. For example, it   20 is impossible for a stone, which has a natural downward movement, to become habituated to moving upward, even if one should try ten thousand times to inculcate the habit by throwing it in the air; nor can fire be made to move downward, nor can the direction of any nature-given tendency be changed by habituation. Thus, the virtues are implanted in us neither by nature nor contrary to nature: we are by nature equipped with the ability to receive them, and habit brings this ability to completion and fulfillment.   25

Furthermore, of all the qualities with which we are endowed by nature, we are provided with the capacity first, and display the activity afterward. That this is true is shown by the senses: it is not by frequent seeing or frequent hearing that we acquired our senses, but on the contrary we first possess and then use them; we do not acquire them by use. The virtues, on the other hand, we acquire by first having put them into ac-   30 tion, and the same is also true of the arts. For the things which we have to learn before we can do them we learn by doing: men become builders by building houses, and harpists by playing the harp. Similarly, we become just by the practice of just actions,   1103[b] self-controlled by exercising self-control, and courageous by performing acts of courage.

This is corroborated by what happens in states. Lawgivers make the citizens good by inculcating [good] habits in them, and this is the aim of every lawgiver; if he does not succeed in doing that, his legislation is a failure. It is in this that a good constitution   5 differs from a bad one.

Moreover, the same causes and the same means that produce any excellence or virtue can also destroy it, and this is also true of every art. It is by playing the harp that men become both good and bad harpists, and correspondingly with builders and all the other craftsmen: a man who builds well will be a good builder, one who builds badly a   10 bad one. For if this were not so, there would be no need for an instructor, but everybody would be born as a good or a bad craftsman. The same holds true of the virtues: in our transactions with other men it is by action that some become just and others unjust, and   15 it is by acting in the face of danger and by developing the habit of feeling fear or confidence that some become brave men and others cowards. The same applies to the appetites and feelings of anger: by reacting in one way or in another to given circum-

20   stances some people become self-controlled and gentle, and others self-indulgent and short-tempered. In a word, characteristics develop from corresponding activities. For that reason, we must see to it that our activities are of a certain kind, since any variations in them will be reflected in our characteristics. Hence it is no small matter whether one habit or another is inculcated in us from early childhood; on the contrary, it makes a

25   considerable difference, or, rather, all the difference.

2. Method in the Practical Sciences

The purpose of the present study is not, as it is in other inquiries, the attainment of theoretical knowledge: we are not conducting this inquiry in order to know what virtue is, but in order to become good, else there would be no advantage in studying it. For that reason, it becomes necessary to examine the problem of actions, and to ask how they

30   are to be performed. For, as we have said, the actions determine what kind of character-istics are developed.

That we must act according to right reason is generally conceded and may be as-sumed as the basis of our discussion. We shall speak about it later and discuss what right reason is and examine its relation to the other virtues. But let us first agree that any dis-

1104ᵃ   cussion on matters of action cannot be more than an outline and is bound to lack preci-sion; for as we stated at the outset, one can demand of a discussion only what the sub-ject matter permits, and there are no fixed data in matters concerning action and questions of what is beneficial, any more than there are in matters of health. And if this

5   is true of our general discussion, our treatment of particular problems will be even less precise, since these do not come under the head of any art which can be transmitted by precept, but the agent must consider on each different occasion what the situation de-

10   mands, just as in medicine and in navigation. But although such is the kind of discus-sion in which we are engaged, we must do our best.

First of all, it must be observed that the nature of moral qualities is such that they are destroyed by defect and by excess. We see the same thing happen in the case of strength and of health, to illustrate, as we must, the invisible by means of visible ex-

15   amples: excess as well as deficiency of physical exercise destroys our strength, and similarly, too much and too little food and drink destroys our health; the proportionate amount, however, produces, increases, and preserves it. The same applies to self-

20   control, courage, and the other virtues: the man who shuns and fears everything and never stands his ground becomes a coward, whereas a man who knows no fear at all and goes to meet every danger becomes reckless. Similarly, a man who revels in every pleasure and abstains from none becomes self-indulgent, while he who avoids every

25   pleasure like a boor becomes what might be called insensitive. Thus we see that self-control and courage are destroyed by excess and by deficiency and are preserved by the mean.

Not only are the same actions which are responsible for and instrumental in the origin and development of the virtues also the causes and means of their destruction, but they will also be manifested in the active exercise of the virtues. We can see the truth of

30   this in the case of other more visible qualities, e.g., strength. Strength is produced by consuming plenty of food and by enduring much hard work, and it is the strong man who is best able to do these things. The same is also true of the virtues: by abstaining

35   from pleasures we become self-controlled, and once we are self-controlled we are best
1104ᵇ   able to abstain from pleasures. So also with courage: by becoming habituated to despise and to endure terrors we become courageous, and once we have become courageous we will best be able to endure terror.

3. Pleasure and Pain as the Test of Virtue

An index to our characteristics is provided by the pleasure or pain which follows upon the tasks we have achieved. A man who abstains from bodily pleasures and enjoys   5
doing so is self-controlled; if he finds abstinence troublesome, he is self-indulgent; a man who endures danger with joy, or at least without pain, is courageous; if he endures it with pain, he is a coward. For moral excellence is concerned with pleasure and pain; it is pleasure that makes us do base actions and pain that prevents us from doing noble   10
actions. For that reason, as Plato says, men must be brought up from childhood to feel pleasure and pain at the proper things; for this is correct education.

Furthermore, since the virtues have to do with actions and emotions, and since pleasure and pain are a consequence of every emotion and of every action, it follows   15
from this point of view, too, that virtue has to do with pleasure and pain. This is further indicated by the fact that punishment is inflicted by means of pain. For punishment is a kind of medical treatment and it is the nature of medical treatments to take effect through the introduction of the opposite of the disease.* Again, as we said just now, every characteristic of the soul shows its true nature in its relation to and its concern   20
with those factors which naturally make it better or worse. But it is through pleasures and pains that men are corrupted, i.e., through pursuing and avoiding pleasures and pains either of the wrong kind or at the wrong time or in the wrong manner, or by going wrong in some other definable respect. For that reason some people define the virtues as states of freedom from emotion and of quietude. However, they make the mistake of us-   25
ing these terms absolutely and without adding such qualifications as "in the right man-ner," "at the right or wrong time," and so forth. We may, therefore, assume as the basis of our discussion that virtue, being concerned with pleasure and pain in the way we have described, makes us act in the best way in matters revolving pleasure and pain, and that vice does the opposite.

The following considerations may further illustrate that virtue is concerned with pleasure and pain. There are three factors that determine choice and three that determine   30
avoidance: the noble, the beneficial, and the pleasurable, on the one hand, and on the other their opposites: the base, the harmful, and the painful. Now a good man will go right and a bad man will go wrong when any of these, and especially when pleasure is involved. For pleasure is not only common to man and the animals, but also accompa-   35
nies all objects of choice: in fact, the noble and the beneficial seem pleasant to us. More-   1105ᵃ
over, a love of pleasure has grown up with all of us from infancy. Therefore, this emo-tion has come to be ingrained in our lives and is difficult to erase. Even in our actions we use, to a greater or smaller extent, pleasure and pain as a criterion. For this reason,   5
this entire study is necessarily concerned with pleasure and pain; for it is not unimpor-tant for our actions whether we feel joy and pain in the right or the wrong way. Again, it is harder to fight against pleasure than against anger, as Heraclitus says; and both virtue and art are always concerned with what is harder, for success is better when it is hard to achieve. Thus, for this reason also, every study both of virtue and of politics must deal   10
with pleasures and pains, for if a man has the right attitude to them, he will be good; if the wrong attitude, he will be bad.

We have now established that virtue or excellence is concerned with pleasures and pains; that the actions which produce it also develop it and, if differently performed,   15
destroy it; and that it actualizes itself fully in those activities to which it owes its origin.

---

*The idea here evidently is that the pleasure of wrongdoing must be cured by applying its opposite, i.e., pain.

4. Virtuous Action and Virtue

However, the question may be raised what we mean by saying that men become just by performing just actions and self-controlled by practicing self-control. For if they perform just actions and exercise self-control, they are already just and self-controlled, in the same way as they are literate and musical if they write correctly and practice music.

But is this objection really valid, even as regards the arts? No, for it is possible for a man to write a piece correctly by chance or at the prompting of another: but he will be literate only if he produces a piece of writing in a literate way, and that means doing it in accordance with the skill of literate composition which he has in himself.

Moreover, the factors involved in the arts and in the virtues are not the same. In the arts, excellence lies in the result itself, so that it is sufficient if it is of a certain kind. But in the case of the virtues an act is not performed justly or with self-control if the act itself is of a certain kind, but only if in addition the agent has certain characteristics as he performs it: first of all, he must know what he is doing; secondly, he must choose to act the way he does, and he must choose it for its own sake; and in the third place, the act must spring from a firm and unchangeable character. With the exception of knowing what one is about, these considerations do not enter into the mastery of the arts; for the mastery of the virtues, however, knowledge is of little or no importance, whereas the other two conditions count not for a little but are all-decisive, since repeated acts of justice and self-control result in the possession of these virtues. In other words, acts are called just and self-controlled when they are the kind of acts which a just or self-controlled man would perform; but the just and self-controlled man is not he who performs these acts, but he who also performs them in the way just and self-controlled men do.

Thus our assertion that a man becomes just by performing just acts and self-controlled by performing acts of self-control is correct; without performing them, nobody could even be on the way to becoming good. Yet most men do not perform such acts, but by taking refuge in argument they think that they are engaged in philosophy and that they will become good in this way. In so doing, they act like sick men who listen attentively to what the doctor says, but fail to do any of the things he prescribes. That kind of philosophical activity will not bring health to the soul any more than this sort of treatment will produce a healthy body.

5. Virtue Defined: The Genus

The next point to consider is the definition of virtue or excellence. As there are three kinds of things found in the soul: (1) emotions, (2) capacities, and (3) characteristics, virtue must be one of these. By "emotions" I mean appetite, anger, fear, confidence, envy, joy, affection, hatred, longing, emulation, pity, and in general anything that is followed by pleasure or pain; by "capacities" I mean that by virtue of which we are said to be affected by these emotions, for example, the capacity which enables us to feel anger, pain, or pity; and by "characteristics" I mean the condition, either good or bad, in which we are, in relation to the emotions: for example, our condition in relation to anger is bad, if our anger is too violent or not violent enough, but if it is moderate, our condition is good; and similarly with our condition in relation to the other emotions.

Now the virtues and vices cannot be emotions, because we are not called good or bad on the basis of our emotions, but on the basis of our virtues and vices. Also, we are neither praised nor blamed for our emotions: a man does not receive praise for being frightened or angry, nor blame for being angry pure and simple, but for being angry in a certain way. Yet we are praised or blamed for our virtues and vices. Furthermore, no choice is involved when we experience anger or fear, while the virtues are some kind of choice or at least involve choice. Moreover, with regard to our emotions we are said to be "moved," but with regard to our virtues and vices we are not said to be "moved" but to be "disposed" in a certain way.

1106ª

5

For the same reason, the virtues cannot be capacities, either, for we are neither called good or bad nor praised or blamed simply because we are capable of being affected. Further, our capacities have been given to us by nature, but we do not by nature develop into good or bad men. We have discussed this subject before. Thus, if the virtues are neither emotions nor capacities, the only remaining alternative is that they are characteristics. So much for the genus of virtue.

10

6. Virtue Defined: The Differentia

It is not sufficient, however, merely to define virtue in general terms as a characteristic: we must also specify what kind of characteristic it is. It must, then, be remarked that every virtue or excellence (1) renders good the thing itself of which it is the excellence, and (2) causes it to perform its function well. For example, the excellence of the eye makes both the eye and its function good, for good sight is due to the excellence of the eye. Likewise, the excellence of a horse makes it both good as a horse and good at running, at carrying its rider, and at facing the enemy. Now, if this is true of all things, the virtue or excellence of man, too, will be a characteristic which makes him a good man, and which causes him to perform his own function well. To some extent we have already stated how this will be true; the rest will become clear if we study what the nature of virtue is.

15

20

25

Of every continuous entity that is divisible into parts it is possible to take the larger, the smaller, or an equal part, and these parts may be larger, smaller, or equal either in relation to the entity itself, or in relation to us. The "equal" part is something median between excess and deficiency. By the median of an entity I understand a point equidistant from both extremes, and this point is one and the same for everybody. By the median relative to us I understand an amount neither too large nor too small, and this is neither one nor the same for everybody. To take an example: if ten is many and two is few, six is taken as the median in relation to the entity, for it exceeds and is exceeded by the same amount, and is thus the median in terms of arithmetical proportion. But the median relative to us cannot be determined in this manner: if ten pounds of food is much for a man to eat and two pounds little, it does not follow that the trainer will prescribe six pounds, for this may in turn be much or little for him to eat; it may be little for Milo* and much for someone who has just begun to take up athletics. The same applies to running and wrestling. Thus we see that an expert in any field avoids excess and deficiency, but seeks the median and chooses it—not the median of the object but the median relative to us.

30

35

1106ᵇ

5

If this, then, is the way in which every science perfects its work, by looking to the median and by bringing its work up to that point—and this is the reason why it is usually said of a successful piece of work that it is impossible to detract from it or to add to it, the implication being that excess and deficiency destroy success while the mean safeguards it (good craftsmen, we say, look toward this standard in the performance of their

10

---

*Milo of Croton, said to have lived in the second half of the sixth century B.C., was a wrestler famous for his remarkable strength.

work)—and if virtue, like nature, is more precise and better than any art, we must conclude that virtue aims at the median. I am referring to moral virtue: for it is moral virtue
that is concerned with emotions and actions, and it is in emotions and actions that excess, deficiency, and the median are found. Thus we can experience fear, confidence,
desire, anger, pity, and generally any kind of pleasure and pain either too much or too
little, and in either case not properly. But to experience all this at the right time, toward
the right objects, toward the right people, for the right reason, and in the right manner—
that is the median and the best course, the course that is a mark of virtue.

Similarly, excess, deficiency, and the median can also be found in actions. Now
virtue is concerned with emotions and actions; and in emotions and actions excess and
deficiency miss the mark, whereas the median is praised and constitutes success. But
both praise and success are signs of virtue or excellence. Consequently, virtue is a mean
in the sense that it aims at the median. This is corroborated by the fact that there are
many ways of going wrong, but only one way which is right—for evil belongs to the indeterminate, as the Pythagoreans imagined, but good to the determinate. This, by the
way, is also the reason why the one is easy and the other hard: it is easy to miss the target but hard to hit it. Here, then, is an additional proof that excess and deficiency characterize vice, while the mean characterizes virtue: for "bad men have many ways, good
men but one."

We may thus conclude that virtue or excellence is a characteristic involving
choice, and that it consists in observing the mean relative to us, a mean which is defined
by a rational principle, such as a man of practical wisdom would use to determine it. It
is the mean by reference to two vices: the one of excess and the other of deficiency. It is,
moreover, a mean because some vices exceed and others fall short of what is required in
emotion and in action, whereas virtue finds and chooses the median. Hence, in respect

According to Aristotle, virtue or excellence "is the mean by reference to two
vices: the one of excess and the other of deficiency." In this drawing, the
person on the left has an excess of confidence and hence is reckless. The
person on the right is deficient in confidence and so is cowardly. In terms of
fear, the person on the left has a defect and the person on the right an excess.
In both these cases we should seek to rationally chose the "Golden Mean" of
the person in the middle: courage.

of its essence and the definition of its essential nature virtue is a mean, but in regard to goodness and excellence it is an extreme.

Not every action nor every emotion admits of a mean. There are some actions and emotions whose very names connote baseness, e.g., spite, shamelessness, envy; and among actions, adultery, theft, and murder. These and similar emotions and actions imply by their very names that they are bad; it is not their excess nor their deficiency which is called bad. It is, therefore, impossible ever to do right in performing them: to perform them is always to do wrong. In cases of this sort, let us say adultery, rightness and wrongness do not depend on committing it with the right woman at the right time and in the right manner, but the mere fact of committing such action at all is to do wrong. It would be just as absurd to suppose that there is a mean, an excess, and a deficiency in an unjust or a cowardly or a self-indulgent act. For if there were, we would have a mean of excess and a mean of deficiency, and an excess of excess and a deficiency of deficiency. Just as there cannot be an excess and a deficiency of self-control and courage—because the intermediate is, in a sense, an extreme—so there cannot be a mean, excess, and deficiency in their respective opposites: their opposites are wrong regardless of how they are performed; for, in general, there is no such thing as the mean of an excess or a deficiency, or the excess and deficiency of a mean.

7. Examples of the Mean
in Particular Virtues

However, this general statement is not enough; we must also show that it fits particular instances. For in a discussion of moral actions, although general statements have a wider range of application, statements on particular points have more truth in them: actions are concerned with particulars and our statements must harmonize with them. Let us now take particular virtues and vices from the following table.

In feelings of fear and confidence courage is the mean. As for the excesses, there is no name that describes a man who exceeds in fearlessness—many virtues and vices have no name; but a man who exceeds in confidence is reckless, and a man who exceeds in fear and is deficient in confidence is cowardly.

In regard to pleasures and pains—not all of them and to a lesser degree in the case of pains—the mean is self-control and the excess self-indulgence. Men deficient in regard to pleasure are not often found, and there is therefore no name for them, but let us call them "insensitive."

In giving and taking money, the mean is generosity, the excess and deficiency are extravagance and stinginess. In these vices excess and deficiency work in opposite ways: an extravagant man exceeds in spending and is deficient in taking, while a stingy man exceeds in taking and is deficient in spending. For our present purposes, we may rest content with an outline and a summary, but we shall later define these qualities more precisely.

There are also some other dispositions in regard to money: magnificence is a mean (for there is a difference between a magnificent and a generous man in that the former operates on a large scale, the latter on a small); gaudiness and vulgarity are excesses, and niggardliness a deficiency. These vices differ from the vices opposed to generosity. But we shall postpone until later a discussion of the way in which they differ.

As regards honor and dishonor, the mean is high-mindedness, the excess is what we might call vanity, and the deficiency small-mindedness. The same relation which, as we said, exists between magnificence and generosity, the one being distinguished from the other in that it operates on a small scale, exists also between high-mindedness and another virtue: as the former deals with great, so the latter deals with small honors. For it is possible to desire honor as one should or more than one should or less than one should: a man who exceeds in his desires is called ambitious, a man who is deficient unambitious,

30   but there is no name to describe the man in the middle. There are likewise no names for the corresponding dispositions except for the disposition of an ambitious man which is called ambition. As a result, the men who occupy the extremes lay claim to the middle position. We ourselves, in fact, sometimes call the middle person ambitious and sometimes

1108ᵃ   unambitious; sometimes we praise an ambitious and at other times an unambitious man. The reason why we do that will be discussed in the sequel; for the present, let us discuss the rest of the virtues and vices along the lines we have indicated.

In regard to anger also there exists an excess, a deficiency, and a mean. Although

5   there really are no names for them, we might call the mean gentleness, since we call a man who occupies the middle position gentle. Of the extremes, let the man who exceeds be called short-tempered and his vice a short temper, and the deficient man apathetic and his vice apathy.

There are, further, three other means which have a certain 10 similarity with one

10   another, but differ nonetheless one from the other. They are all concerned with human relations in speech and action, but they differ in that one of them is concerned with truth in speech and action and the other two with pleasantness: *(a)* pleasantness in amusement and *(b)* pleasantness in all our daily life. We must include these, too, in our dis-

15   cussion, in order to see more clearly that the mean is to be praised in all things and that the extremes are neither praiseworthy nor right, but worthy of blame. Here, too, most of the virtues and vices have no name, but for the sake of clarity and easier comprehension we must try to coin names for them, as we did in earlier instances.

To come to the point; in regard to truth, let us call the man in the middle position

20   truthful and the mean truthfulness. Pretense in the form of exaggeration is boastfulness and its possessor boastful, while pretense in the form of understatement is self-depreciation and its possessor a self-depreciator.

Concerning pleasantness in amusement, the man in the middle position is witty and

25   his disposition wittiness; the excess is called buffoonery and its possessor a buffoon; and the deficient man a kind of boor and the corresponding characteristic boorishness.

As far as the other kind of pleasantness is concerned, pleasantness in our daily life, a man who is as pleasant as he should be is friendly and the mean is friendliness. A man who exceeds is called obsequious if he has no particular purpose in being pleasant, but if he is acting for his own material advantage, he is a flatterer. And a man who is deficient

30   and unpleasant in every respect is a quarrelsome and grouchy kind of person.

A mean can also be found in our emotional experiences and in our emotions. Thus, while a sense of shame is not a virtue, a bashful or modest man is praised. For even in these matters we speak of one kind of person as intermediate and of another as exceeding if he is terror-stricken and abashed at everything. On the other hand, a man

35   who is deficient in shame or has none at all is called shameless, whereas the intermediate man is bashful or modest.

1108ᵇ   Righteous indignation is the mean between envy and spite, all of these being concerned with the pain and pleasure which we feel in regard to the fortunes of our neighbors. The righteously indignant man feels pain when someone prospers undeservedly; an envious man exceeds him in that he is pained when he sees anyone prosper; and a

5   spiteful man is so deficient in feeling pain that he even rejoices [when someone suffers undeservedly].

But we shall have an opportunity to deal with these matters again elsewhere. After that, we shall discuss justice; since it has more than one meaning, we shall distin-

10   guish the two kinds of justice and show in what way each is a mean.

8. The Relation Between the Mean and Its Extremes

There are, then, three kinds of disposition: two are vices (one marked by excess and one by deficiency), and one, virtue, the mean. Now, each of these dispositions is, in a sense, opposed to both the others: the extremes are opposites to the middle as well as to one another, and the middle is opposed to the extremes. Just as an equal amount is larger in relation to a smaller and smaller in relation to a larger amount, so, in the case   15
both of emotions and of actions, the middle characteristics exceed in relation to the deficiencies and are deficient in relation to the excesses. For example, a brave man seems reckless in relation to a coward, but in relation to a reckless man he seems cowardly.   20
Similarly, a self-controlled man seems self-indulgent in relation to an insensitive man and insensitive in relation to a self-indulgent man, and a generous man extravagant in relation to a stingy man and stingy in relation to an extravagant man. This is the reason why people at the extremes each push the man in the middle over to the other extreme: a coward calls a brave man reckless and a reckless man calls a brave man a coward, and   25
similarly with the other qualities.

However, while these three dispositions are thus opposed to one another, the extremes are more opposed to one another than each is to the median; for they are further apart from one another than each is from the median, just as the large is further removed from the small and the small from the large than either one is from the equal. Moreover,   30
there appears to be a certain similarity between some extremes and their median, e.g., recklessness resembles courage and extravagance generosity; but there is a very great dissimilarity between the extremes. But things that are furthest removed from one another are defined as opposites, and that means that the further things are removed from   35
one another the more opposite they are.

In some cases it is the deficiency and in others the excess that is more opposed to   1109ª
the median. For example, it is not the excess, recklessness, which is more opposed to courage, but the deficiency, cowardice; while in the case of self-control it is not the defect, insensitivity, but the excess, self-indulgence which is more opposite. There are two causes for this. One arises from the nature of the thing itself: when one of the extremes   5
is closer and more similar to the median, we do not treat it but rather the other extreme as the opposite of the median. For instance, since recklessness is believed to be more similar and closer to courage, and cowardice less similar, it is cowardice rather than recklessness which we treat as the opposite of courage. For what is further removed   10
from the middle is regarded as being more opposite. So much for the first cause which arises from the thing itself. The second reason is found in ourselves: the more we are naturally attracted to anything, the more opposed to the median does this thing appear to be. For example, since we are naturally more attracted to pleasure we incline more   15
easily to self-indulgence than to a disciplined kind of life. We describe as more opposed to the mean those things toward which our tendency is stronger; and for that reason the excess, self-indulgence, is more opposed to self-control than is its corresponding deficiency.

9. How to Attain the Mean

Our discussion has sufficiently established (1) that moral virtue is a mean and in what sense it is a mean; (2) that it is a mean between two vices, one of which is marked   20
by excess and the other by deficiency; and (3) that it is a mean in the sense that it aims at the median in the emotions and in actions. That is why it is a hard task to be good; in

25   every case it is a task to find the median: for instance, not everyone can find the middle of a circle, but only a man who has the proper knowledge. Similarly, anyone can get angry—that is easy—or can give away money or spend it; but to do all this to the right person, to the right extent, at the right time, for the right reason, and in the right way is no longer something easy that anyone can do. It is for this reason that good conduct is rare, praiseworthy, and noble.

30   The first concern of a man who aims at the median should, therefore, be to avoid the extreme which is more opposed to it, as Calypso advises: "Keep clear your ship of yonder spray and surf." For one of the two extremes is more in error than the other, and since it is

35   extremely difficult to hit the mean, we must, as the saying has it, sail in the second best
1109ᵇ   way and take the lesser evil; and we can best do that in the manner we have described.

Moreover, we must watch the errors which have the greatest attraction for us personally. For the natural inclination of one man differs from that of another, and we each come to recognize our own by observing the pleasure and pain produced in us [by the different extremes]. We must then draw ourselves away in the opposite direction, for by

5   pulling away from error we shall reach the middle, as men do when they straighten warped timber. In every case we must be especially on our guard against pleasure and what is pleasant, for when it comes to pleasure we cannot act as unbiased judges. Our

10   attitude toward pleasure should be the same as that of the Trojan elders was toward Helen, and we should repeat on every occasion the words they addressed to her. For if we dismiss pleasure as they dismissed her, we shall make fewer mistakes.

In summary, then, it is by acting in this way that we shall best be able to hit the median. But this is no doubt difficult, especially when particular cases are concerned.

15   For it is not easy to determine in what manner, with what person, on what occasion, and for how long a time one ought to be angry. There are times when we praise those who are deficient in anger and call them gentle, and other times when we praise violently angry persons and call them manly. However, we do not blame a man for slightly deviating from the course of goodness, whether he strays toward excess or toward deficiency,

20   but we do blame him if his deviation is great and cannot pass unnoticed. It is not easy to determine by a formula at what point and for how great a divergence a man deserves blame; but this difficulty is, after all, true of all objects of sense perception: determinations of this kind depend upon particular circumstances, and the decision rests with our [moral] sense.

This much, at any rate, is clear: that the median characteristic is in all fields the

25   one that deserves praise, and that it is sometimes necessary to incline toward the excess and sometimes toward the deficiency. For it is in this way that we will most easily hit upon the median, which is the point of excellence.

BOOK III

1. Actions Voluntary and Involuntary

30   Virtue or excellence is, as we have seen, concerned with emotions and actions. When these are voluntary we receive praise and blame; when involuntary, we are pardoned and sometimes even pitied. Therefore, it is, I dare say, indispensable for a student of virtue to differentiate between voluntary and involuntary actions, and useful also for lawgivers, to help them in meting out honors and punishments.

It is of course generally recognized that actions done under constraint or due to ignorance are involuntary. An act is done under constraint when the initiative or source of motion comes from without. It is the kind of act in which the agent or the person acted upon contributes nothing. For example, a wind might carry a person somewhere he did not want to go, or men may do so who have him in their power. But a problem arises in regard to actions that are done through fear of a greater evil or for some noble purpose, for instance, if a tyrant were to use a man's parents or children as hostages in ordering him to commit a base deed, making their survival or death depend on his compliance or refusal. Are actions of this kind voluntary or involuntary? A similar problem also arises when a cargo is jettisoned in a storm. Considering the action itself, nobody would voluntarily throw away property; but when it is a matter of saving one's own life and that of his fellow passengers, any sensible man would do so. Actions of this kind are, then, of a mixed nature, although they come closer to being voluntary than to being involuntary actions. For they are desirable at the moment of action; and the end for which an action is performed depends on the time at which it is done. Thus the terms "voluntary" and "involuntary" are to be used with reference to the moment of action. In the cases just mentioned, the agent acts voluntarily, because the initiative in moving the parts of the body which act as instruments rests with the agent himself; and where the source of motion is within oneself, it is in one's power to act or not to act. Such actions, then, are voluntary, although in themselves they are perhaps involuntary, since nobody would choose to do any one of them for its own sake.

[That actions of this kind are considered as voluntary is also shown by the fact that] sometimes people are even praised for doing them, for example, if they endure shameful or painful treatment in return for great and noble objectives. If the opposite is the case, reproach is heaped upon them, for only a worthless man would endure utter disgrace for no good or reasonable purpose. There are some instances in which such actions elicit forgiveness rather than praise, for example, when a man acts improperly under a strain greater than human nature can bear and which no one could endure. Yet there are perhaps also acts which no man can possibly be compelled to do, but rather than do them he should accept the most terrible sufferings and death. Thus, the circumstances that compel Alcmaeon in Euripides' play to kill his own mother are patently absurd.* In making a choice, it is sometimes hard to decide what advantages and disadvantages should be weighed against one another, and what losses we should endure to gain what we want; but it is even harder to abide by a decision once it is made. For as a rule, what we look forward to is painful and what we are forced to do is base. It is because of this difficulty that praise or blame depends on whether or not a man successfully resists compulsion.

What kind of actions can we say, then, are done under constraint? To state the matter without qualification, are all actions done under constraint of which the cause is external and to which the agent contributes nothing? On the other hand, actions which are in themselves involuntary, yet chosen under given circumstances in return for certain benefits and performed on the initiative of the agent—although such actions are involuntary considered in themselves, they are nonetheless voluntary under the circumstances, and because benefits are expected in return. In fact, they have a greater

35
1110ᵃ

5

10

15

20

25

30

1110ᵇ

5

---

*Euripides' play has not come down to us. According to the myth, Alcmaeon killed his mother, Eriphyle, to avenge the death of his father, Amphiaraus. Amphiaraus, foreknowing through his gift of prophecy that he would be doomed if he joined the expedition of the Seven against Thebes, refused to join it until compelled to do so by his wife, who had been bribed by the gift of a necklace to make him join. An ancient commentator on this passage tells us that Alcmaeon's motive for killing his mother in Euripides' play was to escape the curse of his father.

resemblance to voluntary actions. For actions belong among particulars, and the particular act is here performed voluntarily. But it is not easy to lay down rules how, in making a choice, two alternatives are to be balanced against one another; there are many differences in the case of particulars.

[There is a conceivable objection to this definition of "voluntary."] Suppose someone were to assert that pleasant and noble acts are performed under constraint be-
10   cause the pleasant and the noble are external to us and have a compelling power. But on this view, all actions would be done under constraint: for every man is motivated by what is pleasant and noble in everything he does. Furthermore, it is painful to act under constraint and involuntarily, but the performance of pleasant and noble acts brings pleasure. Finally, it is absurd to blame external circumstances rather than oneself for falling an easy prey to such attractions, and to hold oneself responsible for noble deeds, while
15   pleasure is held responsible for one's base deeds.

It appears, thus, that an act done under constraint is one in which the initiative or source of motion comes from without, and to which the person compelled contributes nothing.

Turning now to acts due to ignorance, we may say that all of them are non-voluntary, but they are involuntary only when they bring sorrow and regret in their train: a man who has acted due to ignorance and feels no compunction whatsoever for
20   what he has done was not a voluntary agent, since he did not know what he was doing, nor yet was he involuntary, inasmuch as he feels no sorrow. There are, therefore, two distinct types of acts due to ignorance: a man who regrets what he has done is considered an involuntary agent, and a man who does not may be called a non-voluntary agent; for as the two cases are different, it is better to give each its own name.
25   There also seems to be a difference between actions *due to* ignorance and acting *in* ignorance. A man's action is not considered to be due to ignorance when he is drunk or angry, but due to intoxication and anger, although he does not know what he is doing and is in fact acting in ignorance.

Now every wicked man is in a state of ignorance as to what he ought to do and what he should refrain from doing, and it is due to this kind of error that men become
30   unjust and, in general, immoral. But an act can hardly be called involuntary if the agent is ignorant of what is beneficial. Ignorance in moral choice does not make an act involuntary—it makes it wicked; nor does ignorance of the universal, for that invites reproach; rather, it is ignorance of the particulars* which constitute the circumstances and
1111ª   the issues involved in the action. It is on these that pity and pardon depend, for a person who acts in ignorance of a particular circumstance acts involuntarily.

It might, therefore, not be a bad idea to distinguish and enumerate these circumstances. They are: ignorance of (1) who the agent is, (2) what he is doing, (3) what thing
5   or person is affected, and sometimes also (4) the means he is using, e.g., some tool, (5) the result intended by his action, e.g., saving a life, and (6) the manner in which he acts, e.g., gently or violently.

---

*A few remarks ought to be made about the practical syllogism involved in this passage. Reasoning on matters of conduct involves two premises, one major and one minor. The major premise is always universal, e.g., "to remove by stealth another person's property is stealing," and the minor premise particular, e.g., "this horse is another person's property," so that the conclusion would be: "To remove this horse by stealth is stealing." What Aristotle says here is that ignorance of the major premise produces an immoral act, while ignorance of the minor premise produces an involuntary act which may be pitied or pardoned. Thus it is a moral defect for a man not to know that to remove by stealth another person's property is stealing. In an involuntary act, on the other hand, the agent does know the universal premise, but is ignorant of the particular, i.e., that this horse is the property of another. We shall hear more about the practical syllogism later, especially in VII. 3.

Now no one except a madman would be ignorant of all these factors, nor can he obviously be ignorant of (1) the agent; for how could a man not know his own identity? But a person might be ignorant of (2) what he is doing. For example, he might plead that something slipped out of his mouth, or that he did not know that he was divulging a secret, as Aeschylus said when he was accused of divulging the Mysteries;* or again, as a man might do who discharges a catapult, he might allege that it went off accidentally while he only wanted to show it. Moreover, (3) someone might, like Merope, mistake a son for an enemy;** or (4) he might mistake a pointed spear for a foil, or a heavy stone for a pumice stone. Again, (5) someone might, in trying to save a man by giving him something to drink, in fact kill him; or, (6) as in sparring, a man might intend merely to touch, and actually strike a blow.

As ignorance is possible with regard to all these factors which constitute an action, a man who acts in ignorance of any one of them is considered as acting involuntarily, especially if he is ignorant of the most important factors. The most important factors are the thing or person affected by the action and the result. An action upon this kind of ignorance is called involuntary, provided that it brings also sorrow and regret in its train.

Since an action is involuntary when it is performed under constraint or through ignorance, a voluntary action would seem to be one in which the initiative lies with the agent who knows the particular circumstances in which the action is performed.

[This implies that acts due to passion and appetite are voluntary.] For it is perhaps wrong to call involuntary those acts which are due to passion and appetite. For on that assumption we would, in the first place, deny that animals or even children are capable of acting voluntarily. In the second place, do we perform none of the actions that are motivated by appetite and passion voluntarily? Or do we perform noble acts voluntarily and base acts involuntarily? The latter alternative is ridiculous, since the cause in both cases is one and the same. But it is no doubt also absurd to call those things which we ought to desire "involuntary." For in some cases we should be angry and there are some things for which we should have an appetite, as for example, health and learning. Moreover, we think of involuntary actions as painful, while actions that satisfy our appetite are pleasant. And finally, what difference is there, as far as involuntariness is concerned, between a wrong committed after calculation and a wrong committed in a fit of passion? Both are to be avoided; but the irrational emotions are considered no less a part of human beings than reasoning is, and hence, the actions of a man which spring from passion and appetite [are equally a part of him]. It would be absurd, then, to count them as involuntary.

2. Choice

After this definition of voluntary and involuntary actions, our next task is to discuss choice. For choice seems to be very closely related to virtue and to be a more reliable criterion for judging character than actions are.

Choice clearly seems to be something voluntary, but it is not the same as voluntariness; voluntariness is a wider term. For even children and animals have a share in

*The Mysteries were a secret form of religious worship whose doctrines and rites were revealed only to the initiated; Aeschylus was accused before the Areopagus of having divulged some of the secrets of the Eleusinian Mysteries. Aeschylus pleaded that he had not known the matter was secret and was acquitted.

**In a lost play of Euripides, Merope was about to slay her son Cresphontes, believing him to be an enemy.

the voluntary, but not in choice. Also, we can describe an act done on the spur of the
10   moment as a voluntary act, but not the result of choice.

It seems to be a mistake to identify choice, as some people do, with appetite, passion, wish, or some form of opinion. For choice is not shared by irrational creatures,
whereas appetite and passion are. Moreover, the acts of a morally weak person are accompanied by appetite, but not by choice, while a morally strong person acts from
15   choice, but not from appetite. Also, appetite can be opposed to choice, but not appetite to appetite. Again, appetite deals with what is pleasant and painful, while choice
deals neither with the pleasant nor with the painful. The resemblance between choice
and passion is even slighter. For an act due to passion hardly seems to be based on
choice.

Choice is not even the same as wish, although the two seem to be close to one
20   another. For choice does not have the impossible as its object, and if anyone were to
assert that he was *choosing* the impossible, he would be considered a fool. But wish
can be for the impossible, e.g., immortality.* Wish has as its objects also those things
which cannot possibly be attained through our own agency. We might, for instance,
25   wish for the victory of a particular actor or a particular athlete. But no one chooses
such things, for we choose only what we believe might be attained through our own
agency. Furthermore, wish is directed at the end rather than the means, but choice at
the means which are conducive to a given end. For example, we *wish* to be healthy
and *choose* the things that will give us health. Similarly, we say that we *wish* to be
happy and describe this as our wish, but it would not be fitting to say that we *choose*
30   to be happy. In general, choice seems to be concerned with the things that lie within
our power.

Again, choice cannot be identified with opinion. For opinion may refer to any
matter, the eternal and the impossible no less than things within our power. Also, opinions are characterized by their truth or falsity, not by their moral goodness or badness,
as choices are.

Now, perhaps no one identifies choice with opinion in general; but it would not
1112ª   even be correct to identify it with some particular opinion. For our character is determined by our choosing good or evil, not by the opinions we hold. We choose to take or
avoid a good or an evil, but we hold opinions as to what a thing is, whom it will benefit,
5   or how: but [the decision] to take or avoid is by no means an opinion. Also, a choice is
praised for being directed to the proper object or for being correctly made, but opinions
are praised for being true. Moreover, we make a choice of things which we definitely
know to be good, whereas we form opinions about what we do not quite know. Nor does
it seem that the same people make the best choices and also hold the best opinions:
10   some hold rather good opinions, but because of a moral depravity they do not make the
right choice. Whether opinion precedes or follows choice is immaterial; for we are not
concerned with this problem, but only whether choice is to be identified with some form
of opinion.

Since choice, then, is none of the things mentioned, what is it or what kind of
thing? As we have said, it clearly seems to be something voluntary, but not everything
15   voluntary is the object of choice. Could it be the result of preceding deliberation? [This
is probably correct,] for choice involves reason and thought. The very name "choice"
seems to suggest that it is something "chosen before" other things.

---

*This statement should not be regarded as a rejection on Aristotle's part of a doctrine of immortality.
What he is asserting here is merely a reflection of the common Greek distinction between "mortal" men and
"immortal" gods: it is impossible to choose to live forever, but it is possible to wish it.

3. Deliberation

[To turn to deliberation:] do people deliberate about everything? And is everything an object of deliberation? Or are there some things about which one cannot deliberate? Perhaps we ought to say that an object of deliberation is what a sensible man would deliberate about, but not a fool or madman. Now, nobody deliberates about the eternal, such as the order of the universe or the incommensurability of the diagonal and the side of the square. Nor, on the other hand, do we deliberate about things that are in motion if they always occur in the same way, whether by sheer necessity, by nature, or by some other cause: for example, we do not deliberate about solstices and sunrises. Neither do we deliberate about irregular occurrences, such as drought or rain, nor about chance events, such as the discovery of a treasure. We do not even deliberate about anything and everything that concerns man: no Spartan deliberates about what form of government would be best for the Scythians. For none of these things can happen through our agency.

But what we do deliberate about are things that are in our power and can be realized in action; in fact, these are the only things that remain to be considered. For in addition to nature, necessity, and chance, we regard as causal principles intelligence and anything done through human agency. But of course different groups of people deliberate only about what is attainable by their own actions. Also, there can be no deliberation in any science that is exact and self-contained, such as writing the letters of the alphabet: we have no differences of opinion as to how they are to be written. Rather, we deliberate about matters which are done through our own agency, though not always in the same manner, e.g., about questions of medicine or of acquiring wealth. We deliberate more about navigation than about physical training, because navigation is less exact as a discipline. The same principle can also be applied to the other branches of knowledge. But we deliberate more about the arts than about the sciences, since we have more differences of opinion about them. Deliberation, then, operates in matters that hold good as a general rule, but whose outcome is unpredictable, and in cases in which an indeterminate element is involved. When great issues are at stake, we distrust our own abilities as insufficient to decide the matter and call in others to join us in our deliberations.

We deliberate not about ends but about the means to attain ends: no physician deliberates whether he should cure, no orator whether he should be convincing, no statesman whether he should establish law and order, nor does any expert deliberate about the end of his profession. We take the end for granted, and then consider in what manner and by what means it can be realized. If it becomes apparent that there is more than one means by which it can be attained, we look for the easiest and best; if it can be realized by one means only, we consider in what manner it can be realized by that means, and how that means can be achieved in its turn. We continue that process until we come to the first link in the chain of causation, which is the last step in order of discovery. For when a man deliberates, he seems to be seeking something and to be analyzing his problem in the manner described, as he would a geometrical figure: the last step in the analysis is at once the first in constructing the figure. (By the way, it seems that not all investigation is deliberation—mathematical investigation is not—though every deliberation is an investigation.) Moreover, if in the process of investigation we encounter an insurmountable obstacle, for example, if we need money and none can be procured, we abandon our investigation; but if it turns out to be possible, we begin to act. By "possible" I mean those things which can be realized through our own agency: for even what our friends do for us is, in a way, done through our own agency, since the initiative is our own. Sometimes the object of our investigation is to find the instruments we need and

sometimes to discover how to use them. The same is true of other matters, too: some-
30   times we have to find what the means are, and sometimes how they are to be used or
through whom they can be acquired. To sum up our conclusions: (1) man is the source
of his actions; (2) deliberation is concerned with things attainable by human action; and
(3) actions aim at ends other than themselves. For we cannot deliberate about ends but
about the means by which ends can be attained. Nor can we deliberate about particular
1113ª   facts, e.g., whether this is a loaf of bread or whether this loaf of bread has been properly
baked: such facts are the object of sense perception. And if we continue deliberating
each point in turn, we shall have to go on to infinity.

The object of deliberation and the object of choice are identical, except that the
object of choice has already been determined, since it has been decided upon on the ba-
5   sis of deliberation. For every man stops inquiring how he is to act when he has traced
the initiative of action back to himself and to the dominant part of himself: it is this part
that exercises choice. This may be illustrated by the ancient political systems represented in Homer, where the kings would make a choice and then proclaim it to the
people.

Since, then, the object of choice is something within our power which we desire
10   as a result of deliberation, we may define choice as a deliberate desire for things that are
within our power: we arrive at a decision on the basis of deliberation, and then let the
deliberation guide our desire. So much for an outline of choice, its objects, and the fact
that it is concerned with means rather than ends.

4. Wish

15   That wish is concerned with the end has already been stated. Now, some people
think that its object is the good, and others think that it is what seems good. Those who
maintain that it is the good are faced with the conclusion that a man who makes a
wrong choice does not really wish what he wishes: for if it is the object of his wish
it must be good, while in the case in question it is actually bad. On the other hand,
20   those who assert that the object of wish is what seems good must conclude that nothing is by nature the object of wish, but only what seems good to a particular individual. Yet different, and in many instances opposite things seem good to different
individuals.

If these consequences are unacceptable, must we not admit that in an unqualified sense and from the standpoint of truth the object of wish is the good, but that
for each individual it is whatever seems good to him? [This distinction solves the
25   problem.] Thus, what seems good to a man of high moral standards is truly the object of wish, whereas a worthless man wishes anything that strikes his fancy. It is the
same with the human body: people whose constitution is good find those things
wholesome which really are so, while other things are wholesome for invalids, and
similarly their opinions will vary as to what is bitter, sweet, hot, heavy, and so forth.
[Just as a healthy man judges these matters correctly, so in moral questions] a
30   man whose standards are high judges correctly, and in each case what is truly good will
appear to him to be so. Thus, what is good and pleasant differs with different characteristics or conditions, and perhaps the chief distinction of a man of high moral
standards is his ability to see the truth in each particular moral question, since he is, as
it were, the standard and measure for such questions. The common run of people,
1113ᵇ   however, are misled by pleasure. For though it is not the good, it seems to be, so
that they choose the pleasant in the belief that it is good and avoid pain thinking that it
is evil.

5. Man as Responsible Agent

Now, since the end is the object of wish, and since the means to the end are the objects of deliberation and choice, it follows that actions concerned with means are based on choice and are voluntary actions. And the activities in which the virtues find their expression deal with means. Consequently, virtue or excellence depends on ourselves, and so does vice. For where it is in our power to act, it is also in our power not to act, and where we can say "no," we can also say "yes." Therefore, if we have the power to act where it is noble to act, we also have the power not to act where not to act is base; and conversely, if we have the power not to act where inaction is noble, we also have the power to act where action is base. But if we have the power to act nobly or basely, and likewise the power not to act, and if such action or inaction constitutes our being good and evil, we must conclude that it depends on us whether we are decent or worthless individuals. The saying, "No one is voluntarily wicked nor involuntarily happy," seems to be partly false and partly true. That no one is involuntarily happy is true, but wickedness is voluntary. If we do not accept that, we must contradict the conclusions at which we have just arrived, and must deny that man is the source and begetter of his actions as a father is of his children. But if our conclusions are accepted, and if we cannot trace back our actions to starting points other than those within ourselves, then all actions in which the initiative lies in ourselves are in our power and are voluntary actions.

These conclusions are corroborated by the judgment of private individuals and by the practice of lawgivers. They chastise and punish evildoers, except those who have acted under constraint or due to some ignorance for which they are not responsible, but honor those who act nobly; their intention seems to be to encourage the latter and to deter the former. Yet nobody encourages us to perform what is not within our power and what is not voluntary: there would be no point in trying to stop by persuasion a man from feeling hot, in pain, or hungry, and so forth, because we will go on feeling these conditions no less for that.

Even ignorance is in itself no protection against punishment if a person is thought to be responsible for his ignorance. For example, the penalty is twice as high if the offender acted in a state of drunkenness, because the initiative is his own: he had the power not to get drunk, and drunkenness was responsible for his ignorance. Moreover, punishment is inflicted for offenses committed in ignorance of such provisions of the law as the offender ought to have known or might easily have known. It is also inflicted in other cases in which ignorance seems to be due to negligence: it was in the offender's power not to be ignorant, it is argued, and he could have made sure had he wanted to.

But, it might be objected, carelessness may be part of a man's character. We counter, however, by asserting that a man is himself responsible for becoming careless, because he lives in a loose and carefree manner; he is likewise responsible for being unjust or self-indulgent, if he keeps on doing mischief or spending his time in drinking and the like. For a given kind of activity produces a corresponding character. This is shown by the way in which people train themselves for any kind of contest or performance: they keep on practicing for it. Thus, only a man who is utterly insensitive can be ignorant of the fact that moral characteristics are formed by actively engaging in particular actions.

Moreover, it is unreasonable to maintain that a man who acts unjustly or self-indulgently does not wish to be unjust or self-indulgent. If a man is not ignorant of what he is doing when he performs acts which will make him unjust, he will of course become unjust voluntarily; nor again, can wishing any more make him stop being unjust

and become just than it can make a sick man healthy. Let us assume the case of a man
who becomes ill voluntarily through living a dissolute life and disobeying doctors' orders. In the beginning, before he let his health slip away, he could have avoided becoming ill: but once you have thrown a stone and let it go, you can no longer recall it, even
though the power to throw it was yours, for the initiative was within you. Similarly,
since an unjust or a self-indulgent man initially had the possibility not to become unjust
or self-indulgent, he has acquired these traits voluntarily; but once he has acquired them
it is no longer possible for him not to be what he is.

There are some cases in which not only the vices of the soul, but also those of the
body are voluntary and are accordingly criticized. Nobody blames a man for being ugly
by nature; but we do blame those who become ugly through lack of exercise and
through taking no care of their person. The same applies to infirmities and physical
handicaps: every one would pity rather than reproach a man who was blind by nature or
whose blindness is due to disease or accident, but all would blame him if it were caused
by drunkenness or some other form of self-indulgence. In other words, those bodily
vices which depend on ourselves are blamed and those which do not are not blamed.
This being so, we may conclude that other kinds of vice for which we are blamed also
depend upon ourselves.

But someone might argue as follows: "All men seek what appears good to them,
but they have no control over how things appear to them; the end appears different to
different men." If, we reply, the individual is somehow responsible for his own characteristics, he is similarly responsible for what appears to him [to be good]. But if he is not
so responsible, no one is responsible for his own wrongdoing, but everyone does wrong
through ignorance of the proper end, since he believes that his actions will bring him the
greatest good. However, the aim we take for the end is not determined by the choice of
the individual himself, but by a natural gift of vision, as it were, which enables him to
make correct judgments and to choose what is truly good: to be well endowed by nature
means to have this natural gift. For to be well and properly provided by nature with the
greatest and noblest of gifts, a gift which can be got or learned from no one else, but
which is one's possession in the form in which nature has given it: that is the meaning
of being well endowed by nature in the full and true sense of the word.

But if this theory is true, how will virtue be any more voluntary than vice? The
end has been determined for, and appears to, a good man and a bad man alike by nature
or something of that sort; and both will use the end thus determined as the standard for
any actions they may undertake. Thus, whether the end that appears [to be good] to a
particular person, whatever it may be, is not simply given to him by nature but is to
some extent due to himself; or whether, though the end is given by nature, virtue is voluntary in the sense that a man of high moral standards performs the actions that lead up
to the end voluntarily: in either case vice, too, is bound to be no less voluntary than
virtue. For, like the good man, the bad man has the requisite ability to perform actions
through his own agency, even if not to formulate his own ends. If, then, our assertion is
correct, viz., that the virtues are voluntary because we share in some way the responsibility for our own characteristics and because the ends we set up for ourselves are determined by the kind of persons we are, it follows that the vices, too, are voluntary; for
the same is true of them.

To sum up: we have described the virtues in general and have given an outline of
the genus to which they belong, i.e., that they are means and that they are characteristics.
We have stated that they spontaneously tend to produce the same kind of actions as those
to which they owe their existence; that they are in our power and voluntary; and that they
follow the dictates of right reason. However, our actions and our characteristics are not

voluntary in the same sense: we are in control of our actions from beginning to end, insofar as we know the particular circumstances surrounding them. But we control only the beginning of our characteristics: the particular steps in their development are imperceptible, just as they are in the spread of a disease; yet since the power to behave or not to behave in a given way was ours in the first place, our characteristics are voluntary.

1115^a

Let us resume our discussion of the various virtues: what are they? With what sort of thing do they deal? And how do they operate? The answer to these questions will also tell us how many virtues there are.

5

*   *   *

BOOK IV

*   *   *

3. High-Mindedness, Pettiness, and Vanity

High-mindedness, as its very name suggests, seems to be concerned with great and lofty matters. Let us take the nature of these matters as the first point of our discussion. It makes no difference whether we investigate the characteristic or the man who is characterized by it. A man is regarded as high-minded when he thinks he deserves great things and actually deserves them; one who thinks he deserves them but does not is a fool, and no man, insofar as he is virtuous, is either foolish or senseless. This then is the description of a high-minded man. A person who deserves little and thinks he deserves little is not high-minded, but is a man who knows his limitations. For high-mindedness implies greatness, just as beauty implies stature in body: small people may have charm and proportion but not beauty. A man who thinks he deserves great things but does not deserve them is vain, though not everybody who overestimates himself is vain. One who underestimates himself is small-minded regardless of whether his actual worth is great or moderate, or whether it is small and he thinks that it is smaller still. A man of great deserts, it would seem, is most [liable to be small-minded,] for what would he do if his deserts were not as great as they are? Thus, measured by the standard of greatness, the high-minded man is an extreme, but by the standard of what is right he occupies the median; for his claims correspond to his deserts, whereas the others exceed or fall short.

1123^a
35
1123^b

5

10

15

Accordingly, if a high-minded man thinks he deserves and actually does deserve great things, especially the greatest, there is one matter that will be his major concern. "Deserts" is a relative term that refers to external goods; and as the greatest external good, we may posit that which we pay as a tribute to the gods, for which eminent people strive most, and which is the prize for the noblest achievements. Honor fits that description, for it is the greatest of external goods. Consequently, it is in matters of honor and dishonor that a high-minded man has the right attitude. It is an obvious fact, and need not be argued, that the high-minded are concerned with honor. For they regard themselves as worthy of honor above all else, but of an honor that they deserve. A small-minded man falls short both in view of his own deserts and in relation to the claims of a high-minded person, while a vain man exceeds his own deserts but does not exceed the high-minded.

20

25

This means that the high-minded man, inasmuch as he deserves what is greatest, is the best. For the deserts of the better man are always greater, and those of the best man the greatest. It follows that a truly high-minded man must be good. And what is great in each virtue would seem to be the mark of a high-minded person. It would be quite out of character for him to run away in battle with arms swinging or to do wrong to anyone. For what motive does he have to act basely, he to whom nothing is great? If we were to examine [his qualities] one by one, we should see the utter absurdity of thinking of a high-minded man as being anything but good. If he were base, he would not even deserve honor, for honor is the prize of excellence and virtue, and it is reserved as a tribute to the good. High-mindedness thus is the crown, as it were, of the virtues: it magnifies them and it cannot exist without them. Therefore, it is hard to be truly high-minded and, in fact, impossible without goodness and nobility.

A high-minded man is, then, primarily concerned with honor and dishonor. From great honors and those that good men confer upon him he will derive a moderate amount of pleasure, convinced that he is only getting what is properly his or even less. For no honor can be worthy of perfect virtue. Yet he will accept it, because they have no greater tribute to pay to him. But he will utterly despise honors conferred by ordinary people and on trivial grounds, for that is not what he deserves. Similarly, he will despise dishonor, for no dishonor can be justified in his case. A high-minded man, as we have stated, is concerned primarily with honors. But he will of course also have a moderate attitude toward wealth, power, and every manner of good or bad luck that may befall him. He will not be overjoyed when his luck is good, nor will bad luck be very painful to him. For even toward honor, his attitude is that it is not of the greatest moment. Power and wealth are desirable for the honor they bring; at any rate, those who have them wish to gain honor through them. But a person who attaches little importance even to honor will also attach little importance to power and wealth. As a result, he is regarded as haughty.

Gifts of fortune, it is believed, also contribute to high-mindedness. Men of noble birth, of power, or of wealth are regarded as worthy of honor, since they occupy a superior position, and whatever is superior in goodness is held in greater honor. That is why the gifts of fortune make men more high-minded, for they are honored by some people [for having them]. But in truth it is the good man alone that ought to be honored, though a man who has both excellence and good fortune is regarded as still more worthy of honor. Whoever possesses the goods of fortune without possessing excellence or virtue is not justified in claiming great deserts for himself, nor is it correct to call him high-minded, for neither is possible without perfect virtue. Their good fortune notwithstanding, such people become haughty and arrogant, for without virtue it is not easy to bear the gifts of fortune gracefully. Unable to bear them and considering themselves superior, they look down upon others, while they themselves do whatever they please. They imitate the high-minded man wherever they can, but they are not really like him. Thus, they look down upon others, but they do not act in conformity with excellence. A high-minded person is justified in looking down upon others for he has the right opinion of them, but the common run of people do so without rhyme or reason.

A high-minded man does not take small risks and, since there are only a few things which he honors, he is not even fond of risks. But he will face great risks, and in the midst of them he will not spare his life, aware that life at any cost is not worth having. He is the kind of man who will do good, but who is ashamed to accept a good turn, because the former marks a man as superior, the latter as inferior. Moreover, he will requite good with a greater good, for in this way he will not only repay the original benefactor but put him in his debt at the same time by making him the recipient of an added

benefit. The high-minded also seem to remember the good turns they have done, but not those they have received. For the recipient is inferior to the benefactor, whereas a high-minded man wishes to be superior. They listen with pleasure to what good they have done, but with displeasure to what good they have received. That is apparently why   15
Thetis does not mention the good turns she had done to Zeus,* and why the Spartans did not mention theirs to the Athenians, but only the good they had received. It is, further, typical of a high-minded man not to ask for any favors, or only reluctantly, but to offer aid readily. He will show his stature in his relations with men of eminence and fortune, but will be unassuming toward those of moderate means. For to be superior to the former is difficult and dignified, but superiority over the latter is easy. Furthermore, there   20
is nothing ignoble in asserting one's dignity among the great, but to do so among the lower classes is just as crude as to assert one's strength against an invalid. He will not go in for pursuits that the common people value, nor for those in which the first place belongs to others. He is slow to act and procrastinates, except when some great honor or achievement is at stake. His actions are few, but they are great and distinguished. He   25
must be open in hate and open in love, for to hide one's feelings and to care more for the opinion of others than for truth is a sign of timidity. He speaks and acts openly: since he looks down upon others his speech is free and truthful, except when he deliberately de-   30
preciates himself in addressing the common run of people. He cannot adjust his life to another, except a friend, for to do so is slavish. That is, [by the way,] why all flatterers   1125ª
are servile and people from the lower classes are flatterers. He is not given to admiration, for nothing is great to him. He bears no grudges, for it is not typical of a high-minded man to have a long memory, especially for wrongs, but rather to overlook them.   5
He is not a gossip, for he will talk neither about himself nor about others, since he is not interested in hearing himself praised or others run down. Nor again is he given to praise; and for the same reason he does not speak evil of others, not even of his enemies, except to scorn them. When he encounters misfortunes that are unavoidable or insignificant, he will not lament and ask for help. That kind of attitude belongs to someone who takes   10
such matters seriously. He is a person who will rather possess beautiful and profitless objects than objects which are profitable and useful, for they mark him more as self-sufficient.

Further, we think of a slow gait as characteristic of a high-minded man, a deep voice, and a deliberate way of speaking. For a man who takes few things seriously is unlikely to be in a hurry, and a person who regards nothing as great is not one to be ex-   15
citable. But a shrill voice and a swift gait are due to hurry and excitement.

Such, then, is the high-minded man. A man who falls short is small-minded, and one who exceeds is vain. Now here, too, these people are not considered to be bad—for they are not evildoers—but only mistaken. For a small-minded man deprives himself of the good he deserves. What seems to be bad about him is due to the fact that he does not   20
think he deserves good things and that he does not know himself; if he did, he would desire what he deserves, especially since it is good. It is not that such people are regarded as foolish, but rather [that they are looked upon] as retiring. However, a reputation of this sort seems to make them even worse. For while any given kind of man strives to get   25
what he deserves, these people keep aloof even from noble actions and pursuits and from external goods as well, because they consider themselves undeserving.

Vain people, on the other hand, are fools and do not know themselves, and they show it openly. They take in hand honorable enterprises of which they are not worthy,

---

*The reference is to Thetis' intercession with Zeus to help avenge the wrong done her son Achilles by Agamemnon.

and then they are found out. They deck themselves out with clothes and showy gear and that sort of thing, and wish to publicize what fortune has given them. They talk about their good fortune in the belief that that will bring them honor.

Small-mindedness is more opposed to high-mindedness than vanity is, for it occurs more frequently and is worse. Thus, as we have said, high-mindedness is concerned with high honors.

*   *   *

BOOK VI

1. Moral and Intellectual Excellence; the Psychological Foundations of Intellectual Excellence

We stated earlier that we must choose the median, and not excess or deficiency, and that the median is what right reason dictates. Let us now analyze this second point.

In all the characteristics we have discussed, as in all others, there is some target on which a rational man keeps his eye as he bends and relaxes his efforts to attain it. There is also a standard that determines the several means which, as we claim, lie between excess and deficiency, and which are fixed by right reason. But this statement, true though it is, lacks clarity. In all other fields of endeavor in which scientific knowledge is possible, it is indeed true to say that we must exert ourselves or relax neither too much nor too little, but to an intermediate extent and as right reason demands. But if this is the only thing a person knows, he will be none the wiser: he will, for example, not know what kind of medicines to apply to his body, if he is merely told to apply whatever medical science prescribes and in a manner in which a medical expert applies them. Accordingly, in discussing the characteristics of the soul, too, it is not enough that the statement we have made be true. We must also have a definition of what right reason is and what standard determines it.

In analyzing the virtues of the soul we said that some are virtues of character and others excellence of thought or understanding. We have now discussed the moral virtues, [i.e., the virtues of character]. In what follows, we will deal with the others, [i.e., the intellectual virtues,] beginning with some prefatory remarks about the soul. We said in our earlier discussion that the soul consists of two parts, one rational and one irrational. We must now make a similar distinction in regard to the rational part. Let it be assumed that there are two rational elements: with one of these we apprehend the realities whose fundamental principles do not admit of being other than they are, and with the other we apprehend things which do admit of being other. For if we grant that knowledge presupposes a certain likeness and kinship of subject and object, there will be a generically different part of the soul naturally corresponding to each of two different kinds of object. Let us call one the scientific and the other the calculative element. Deliberating and calculating are the same thing, and no one deliberates about objects that cannot be other than they are. This means that the calculative constitutes one element of the rational part of the soul. Accordingly, we must now take up the question which is the best characteristic of each element, since that constitutes the excellence or virtue of each. But the virtue of a thing is relative to its proper function.

2. The Two Kinds of Intellectual Excellence and Their Objects

Now, there are three elements in the soul which control action and truth: sense perception, intelligence, and desire. Of these sense perception does not initiate any action. We can see this from the fact that animals have sense perception but have   20
no share in action.* What affirmation and negation are in the realm of thought, pursuit and avoidance are in the realm of desire. Therefore, since moral virtue is a characteristic involving choice, and since choice is a deliberate desire, it follows that, if the choice is to be good, the reasoning must be true and the desire correct; that is,   25
reasoning must affirm what desire pursues. This then is the kind of thought and the kind of truth that is practical and concerned with action. On the other hand, in the kind of thought involved in theoretical knowledge and not in action or production, the good and the bad state are, respectively, truth and falsehood; in fact, the attainment of truth is the function of the intellectual faculty as a whole. But in intellectual activity concerned with action, the good state is truth in harmony with correct   30
desire.

Choice is the starting point of action: it is the source of motion but not the end for the sake of which we act, i.e., the final cause. The starting point of choice, however, is desire and reasoning directed toward some end. That is why there cannot be choice either without intelligence and thought or without some moral characteristic; for good and bad action in human conduct are not possible without thought   35
and character. Now thought alone moves nothing; only thought which is directed to some end and concerned with action can do so. And it is this kind of thought also   1139^b
which initiates production. For whoever produces something produces it for an end. The product he makes is not an end in an unqualified sense, but an end only in a particular relation and of a particular operation. Only the goal of action is an end in the unqualified sense: for the good life is an end, and desire is directed toward this. Therefore, choice is either intelligence motivated by desire or desire operating through thought, and it is as a combination of these two that man is a starting point   5
of action.

(No object of choice belongs to the past: no one chooses to have sacked Troy. For deliberation does not refer to the past but only to the future and to what is possible; and it is not possible that what is past should not have happened. Therefore, Agathon is right when he says: 10

One thing alone is denied even to god:
to make undone the deeds which have been done.**)

As we have seen, truth is the function of both intellectual parts [of the soul]. Therefore, those characteristics which permit each part to be as truthful as possible will be the virtues of the two parts.

---

*Throughout the *Ethics,* Aristotle uses *praxis* ("action") as equivalent to "moral action," "conduct," and assumes animals are not capable of this.
**Agathon was a tragic poet who flourished in the last quarter of the fifth century B.C. Plato's *Symposium* is set in his house.

3. The Qualities by Which Truth
Is Attained: (a) Pure Science or Knowledge

So let us make a fresh beginning and discuss these characteristics once again. Let
us take for granted that the faculties by which the soul expresses truth by way of affirmation or denial are five in number: art, science, practical wisdom, theoretical wisdom,
and intelligence. Conviction and opinion do not belong here, for they may be false.

What pure science or scientific knowledge is—in the precise sense of the word
and not in any of its wider uses based on mere similarity—will become clear in the following. We are all convinced that what we *know* scientifically cannot be otherwise than
it is; but of facts which can possibly be other than they are we do not know whether or
not they continue to be true when removed from our observation. Therefore, an object
of scientific knowledge exists of necessity, and is, consequently, eternal. For everything
that exists of necessity in an unqualified sense is eternal, and what is eternal is ungener-
ated and imperishable [and hence cannot be otherwise].

Moreover, all scientific knowledge is held to be teachable, and what is scientifically knowable is capable of being learned. All teaching is based on what is already
known, as we have stated in the *Analytics;* some teaching proceeds by induction and
some by syllogism. Now, induction is the starting point [for knowledge], of the universal as well [as the particular], while syllogism proceeds *from* universals. Consequently,
there are starting points or principles from which a syllogism proceeds and which are
themselves not arrived at by a syllogism. It is, therefore, induction that attains them. Accordingly, scientific knowledge is a capacity for demonstration and has, in addition, all
the other qualities which we have specified in the *Analytics.* When a man believes
something in the way there specified, and when the starting points or principles on
which his beliefs rest are known to him, then he has scientific knowledge; unless he
knows the starting points or principles better than the conclusion, he will have scientific
knowledge only incidentally. So much for our definition of scientific knowledge or pure
science.

4. (b) Art or Applied Science

Things which admit of being other than they are include both things made and
things done. Production is different from action—for that point we can rely even on our
less technical discussions. Hence, the characteristic of acting rationally is different from
the characteristic of producing rationally. It also follows that one does not include the
other, for action is not production nor production action. Now, building is an art or applied science, and it is essentially a characteristic or trained ability of rationally producing. In fact, there is no art that is not a characteristic or trained ability of rationally producing, nor is there a characteristic of rationally producing that is not an art. It follows
that art is identical with the characteristic of producing under the guidance of true reason. All art is concerned with the realm of coming-to-be, i.e., with contriving and studying how something which is capable both of being and of not being may come into existence, a thing whose starting point or source is in the producer and not in the thing
produced. For art is concerned neither with things which exist or come into being by necessity, nor with things produced by nature: these have their source of motion within
themselves.

Since production and action are different, it follows that art deals with production
and not with action. In a certain sense, fortune and art are concerned with the same
things, as Agathon says: "Fortune loves art and art fortune." So, as we have said, art is

a characteristic of producing under the guidance of true reason, and lack of art, on the   20
contrary, is a characteristic of producing under the guidance of false reason; and both of
them deal with what admits of being other than it is.

5. (c) Practical Wisdom

We may approach the subject of practical wisdom by studying the persons to
whom we attribute it. Now, the capacity of deliberating well about what is good and ad-   25
vantageous for oneself is regarded as typical of a man of practical wisdom—not deliberating well about what is good and advantageous in a partial sense, for example, what
contributes to health or strength, but what sort of thing contributes to the good life in
general. This is shown by the fact that we speak of men as having practical wisdom in a
particular respect, i.e., not in an unqualified sense, when they calculate well with respect
to some worthwhile end, one that cannot be attained by an applied science or art. It fol-   30
lows that, in general, a man of practical wisdom is he who has the ability to deliberate.

Now no one deliberates about things that cannot be other than they are or about actions that he cannot possibly perform. Since, as we saw, pure science involves demonstration, while things whose starting points or first causes can be other than they are do
not admit of demonstration—for such things too and not merely their first causes can all
be other than they are—and since it is impossible to deliberate about what exists by ne-   35
cessity, we may conclude that practical wisdom is neither a pure science nor an art. It is   1140^b
not a pure science, because matters of action admit of being other than they are, and it is
not an applied science or art, because action and production are generically different.

What remains, then, is that it is a truthful characteristic of acting rationally in matters good and bad for man. For production has an end other than itself, but action does   5
not: good action is itself an end. That is why we think that Pericles* and men like him
have practical wisdom. They have the capacity of seeing what is good for themselves
and for mankind, and these are, we believe, the qualities of men capable of managing   10
households and states.

This also explains why we call "self-control" *sōphrosynē:* it "preserves" our
"practical wisdom." What it preserves is the kind of conviction we have described. For
the pleasant and the painful do not destroy and pervert every conviction we hold—not,
for example, our conviction that a triangle has or does not have the sum of its angles
equal to two right angles—but only the convictions we hold concerning how we should   15
act. In matters of action, the principles or initiating motives are the ends at which our
actions are aimed. But as soon as a man becomes corrupted by pleasure or pain, the goal
no longer appears to him as a motivating principle: he no longer sees that he should
choose and act in every case for the sake of and because of this end. For vice tends to
destroy the principle or initiating motive of action.

Necessarily, then, practical wisdom is a truthful rational characteristic of acting   20
in matters involving what is good for man. Furthermore, whereas there exists such a
thing as excellence in art, it does not exist in practical wisdom.** Also, in art a man
who makes a mistake voluntarily is preferable to one who makes it involuntarily; but
in practical wisdom, as in every virtue or excellence, such a man is less desirable. Thus
it is clear that practical wisdom is an excellence or virtue and not an art. Since there
are two parts of the soul that contain a rational element, it must be the virtue of one of   25

---

*The name of Pericles (ca. 495–429 B.C.) is almost synonymous with the Athenian democracy.

**Because practical wisdom is itself a complete virtue or excellence, while the excellence of art de-
pends on the goodness or badness of its product.

them, namely of the part that forms opinions.* For opinion as well as practical wisdom deals with things that can be other than they are. However, it is not merely a rational characteristic or trained ability. An indication that it is something more may be seen in the fact that a trained ability of that kind can be forgotten, whereas practical wisdom cannot.

6. (d) Intelligence

Since pure science or scientific knowledge is a basic conviction concerning universal and necessary truths, and since everything demonstrable and all pure science begins from fundamental principles (for science proceeds rationally), the fundamental principle or starting point for scientific knowledge cannot itself be the object either of science, of art, or of practical wisdom. For what is known scientifically is demonstrable, whereas art and practical wisdom are concerned with things that can be other than they are. Nor are these fundamental principles the objects of theoretical wisdom: for it is the task of a man of theoretical wisdom to have a demonstration for certain truths.** Now, if scientific knowledge, practical wisdom, theoretical wisdom, and intelligence are the faculties by which we attain truth and by which we are never deceived both in matters which can and in those matters which cannot be other than they are; and if three of these—I am referring to practical wisdom, scientific knowledge, and theoretical wisdom—cannot be the faculty in question, we are left with the conclusion that it is intelligence that apprehends fundamental principles.

7. (e) Theoretical Wisdom

We attribute "wisdom" in the arts to the most precise and perfect masters of their skills: we attribute it to Phidias as a sculptor in marble and to Polycletus as a sculptor in bronze. In this sense we signify by "wisdom" nothing but excellence of art or craftsmanship. However, we regard some men as being wise in general, not in any partial sense or in some other particular respect, as Homer says in the *Margites:*

The gods let him not be a digger or a ploughman nor wise at anything.

It is, therefore, clear, that wisdom must be the most precise and perfect form of knowledge. Consequently, a wise man must not only know what follows from fundamental principles, but he must also have true knowledge of the fundamental principles themselves. Accordingly, theoretical wisdom must comprise both intelligence and scientific knowledge. It is science in its consummation, as it were, the science of the things that are valued most highly.

For it would be strange to regard politics or practical wisdom as the highest kind of knowledge, when in fact man is not the best thing in the universe. Surely, if "healthy" and "good" mean one thing for men and another for fishes, whereas "white" and "straight" always mean the same, "wise" must mean the same for everyone, but "practically wise" will be different. For each particular being ascribes practical wisdom in matters relating to itself to that thing which observes its interests well, and it will entrust

---

*"Opinion" here corresponds to the "calculative element" in Chapter 1: both are defined by reference to contingent facts, those which may be otherwise than they are.

**In other words, the undemonstrable first or fundamental principles cannot be the proper and complete object of theoretical wisdom: as the next chapter shows, they are included within its sphere.

itself to that thing. That is the reason why people attribute practical wisdom even to some animals—to all those which display a capacity of forethought in matters relating to their own life.

It is also evident that theoretical wisdom is not the same as politics. If we are to call "theoretical wisdom" the knowledge of what is helpful to us, there will be many kinds of wisdom. There is no single science that deals with what is good for all living things any more than there is a single art of medicine dealing with everything that is, but a different science deals with each particular good. The argument that man is the best of living things makes no difference. There are other things whose nature is much more divine than man's: to take the most visible example only, the constituent parts of the universe.

Our discussion has shown that theoretical wisdom comprises both scientific knowledge and [apprehension by the] intelligence of things which by their nature are valued most highly. That is why it is said that men like Anaxagoras and Thales have theoretical but not practical wisdom: when we see that they do not know what is advantageous to them, we admit that they know extraordinary, wonderful, difficult, and superhuman things, but call their knowledge useless because the good they are seeking is not human.

Practical wisdom, on the other hand, is concerned with human affairs and with matters about which deliberation is possible. As we have said, the most characteristic function of a man of practical wisdom is to deliberate well: no one deliberates about things that cannot be other than they are, nor about things that are not directed to some end, an end that is a good attainable by action. In an unqualified sense, that man is good at deliberating who, by reasoning, can aim at and hit the best thing attainable to man by action.

Nor does practical wisdom deal only with universals. It must also be familiar with particulars, since it is concerned with action and action has to do with particulars. This explains why some men who have no scientific knowledge are more adept in practical matters, especially if they have experience, than those who do have scientific knowledge. For if a person were to know that light meat is easily digested, and hence wholesome, but did not know what sort of meat is light, he will not produce health, whereas someone who knows that poultry is light and wholesome is more likely to produce health.*

Now, practical wisdom is concerned with action. That means that a person should have both [knowledge of universals and knowledge of particulars] or knowledge of particulars rather [than knowledge of universals]. But here, too, it seems, there is a supreme and comprehensive science involved, [i.e., politics].

8. Practical Wisdom and Politics

Political wisdom and practical wisdom are both the same characteristic, but their essential aspect is not the same. There are two kinds of wisdom concerning the state: the one, which acts as practical wisdom supreme and comprehensive, is the art of legislation; the other, which is practical wisdom as dealing with particular facts, bears the name which, [in everyday speech,] is common to both kinds, politics, and it is concerned with action and deliberation. For a decree, [unlike a law, which lays down gen-

30

1141^b

5

10

15

20

25

---

*The point here is that, in practical matters, a man who knows by experience that poultry is wholesome is likely to be more successful than a man who only has the scientific knowledge that light meat is digestible and therefore wholesome, without knowing the particular fact that poultry is light meat.

eral principles,] is a matter for action, inasmuch as it is the last step [in the deliberative process]. That is why only those who make decrees are said to engage in politics, for they alone, like workmen, "do" things.*

It is also commonly held that practical wisdom is primarily concerned with one's own person, i.e., with the individual, and it is this kind that bears the name "practical wisdom," which properly belongs to others as well. The other kinds are called household management, legislation, and politics, the last of which is subdivided into deliberative and judicial.**

Now, knowing what is good for oneself is, to be sure, one kind of knowledge; but it is very different from the other kinds. A man who knows and concerns himself with his own interests is regarded as a man of practical wisdom, while men whose concern is politics are looked upon as busybodies. Euripides' words are in this vein:

How can I be called "wise," who might have filled a common
soldier's place, free from all care, sharing an equal lot . . . ?
For those who reach too high and are too active. . . .

For people seek their own good and think that this is what they should do. This opinion has given rise to the view that it is such men who have practical wisdom. And yet, surely one's own good cannot exist without household management nor without a political system. Moreover, the problem of how to manage one's own affairs properly needs clarification and remains to be examined.

An indication that what we have said is correct is the following common observation. While young men do indeed become good geometricians and mathematicians and attain theoretical wisdom in such matters, they apparently do not attain practical wisdom. The reason is that practical wisdom is concerned with particulars as well [as with universals], and knowledge of particulars comes from experience. But a young man has no experience, for experience is the product of a long time. In fact, one might also raise the question why it is that a boy may become a mathematician but not a philosopher or a natural scientist. The answer may be that the objects of mathematics are the result of abstraction, whereas the fundamental principles of philosophy and natural science come from experience. Young men can assert philosophical and scientific principles but can have no genuine convictions about them, whereas there is no obscurity about the essential definitions in mathematics.

Moreover, in our deliberations error is possible as regards either the universal principle or the particular fact: we may be unaware either that all heavy water is bad, or that the particular water we are faced with is heavy.

That practical wisdom is not scientific knowledge is [therefore] evident. As we stated, it is concerned with ultimate particulars, since the actions to be performed are ultimate particulars. This means that it is at the opposite pole from intelligence. For the intelligence grasps limiting terms and definitions that cannot be attained by reasoning, while practical wisdom has as its object the ultimate particular fact, of which there is perception but no scientific knowledge. This perception is not the kind with which [each

*I.e., lawgivers and other men who are concerned with political wisdom in the supreme and comprehensive sense are not generally regarded as being engaged in politics. The analogy to workmen represents of course not Aristotle's view, which vigorously distinguishes action from production, but rather reflects a widespread attitude toward politics.

**In Athens, "deliberative" politics referred to matters debated in the Council and the Popular Assembly, and "judicial" politics to matters argued in the lawcourts.

of our five senses apprehends] its proper object, but the kind with which we perceive that in mathematics the triangle is the ultimate figure. For in this direction, too, we shall have to reach a stop. But this [type of mathematical cognition] is more truly perception than practical wisdom, and it is different in kind from the other [type of perception which deals with the objects proper to the various senses]. 30

9. Practical Wisdom and Excellence in Deliberation

There is a difference between investigating and deliberating: to deliberate is to investigate a particular kind of object. We must also try to grasp what excellence in deliberation is: whether it is some sort of scientific knowledge, opinion, shrewd guessing, or something generically different from any of these.

Now, scientific knowledge it is certainly not:* people do not investigate matters they already know. But good deliberation is a kind of deliberation, and when a person 1142ᵇ deliberates he is engaged in investigating and calculating [things not yet decided]. Nor yet is it shrewd guessing. For shrewd guessing involves no reasoning and proceeds quickly, whereas deliberation takes a long time. As the saying goes, the action which follows deliberation should be quick, but deliberation itself should be slow. Furthermore, quickness of mind is not the same as excellence in deliberation: quickness of 5 mind is a kind of shrewd guessing. Nor again is excellence in deliberation any form of opinion at all. But since a person who deliberates badly makes mistakes, while he who deliberates well deliberates correctly, it clearly follows that excellence in deliberation is some kind of correctness. But it is correctness neither of scientific knowledge nor of opinion. There cannot be correctness of scientific knowledge any more than there can 10 be error of scientific knowledge; and correctness of opinion is truth. Moreover, anything that is an object of opinion is already fixed and determined, while deliberation deals with objects which remain to be determined. Still, excellence in deliberation does involve reasoning, and we are, consequently, left with the alternative that it is correctness of a process of thought; for thinking is not yet an affirmation. For while opinion is no longer a process of investigation but has reached the point of affirmation, a person who deliberates, whether he does so well or badly, is still engaged in investigating and cal- 15 culating something [not yet determined].

Good deliberation is a kind of correctness of deliberation. We must, therefore, first investigate what deliberation is and with what objects it is concerned. Since the term "correctness" is used in several different senses, it is clear that not every kind of correctness in deliberation [is excellence in deliberation]. For (1) a morally weak or a bad man will, as a result of calculation, attain the goal which he has proposed to himself as the right goal to attain. He will, therefore, have deliberated correctly, but what he will get out of it will be a very bad thing. But the result of good deliberation is generally re- 20 garded as a good thing. It is this kind of correctness of deliberation which is good deliberation, a correctness that attains what is good.

But (2) it is also possible to attain something good by a false syllogism, i.e., to arrive at the right action, but to arrive at it by the wrong means when the middle term is false. Accordingly, this process, which makes us attain the right goal but not by the right means, is still not good deliberation. 25

*Here, as in most of the following paragraph, Aristotle seems to be taking issue with Plato, who had identified the two, e.g., in *Republic,* Book IV, 428b.

Moreover, (3) it is possible that one man attains his goal by deliberating for a long time, while another does so quickly. Now, long deliberation, too, is not as such good deliberation: excellence in deliberation is correctness in assessing what is beneficial, i.e., correctness in assessing the goal, the manner, and the time.

Again, (4) it is possible for a person to have deliberated well either in general, in an unqualified sense, or in relation to some particular end. Good deliberation in the un-
30   qualified sense of course brings success in relation to what is, in an unqualified sense, the end, [i.e., in relation to the good life]. Excellence in deliberation as directed toward some particular end, however, brings success in the attainment of some particular end.

Thus we may conclude that, since it is a mark of men of practical wisdom to have deliberated well, excellence in deliberation will be correctness in assessing what is conducive to the end, concerning which practical wisdom gives a true conviction.

10. Practical Wisdom
and Understanding

Understanding, i.e., excellence in understanding, the quality which makes us call
1143ᵃ   certain people "men of understanding" and "men of good understanding," is in general not identical with scientific knowledge or with opinion. For [if it were opinion,] everyone would be a man of understanding, [since everyone forms opinions]. Nor is it one of the particular branches of science, in the sense in which medicine, for example, is the science of matters pertaining to health, or geometry the science which deals with magnitudes. For understanding is concerned neither with eternal and unchangeable truth nor
5   with anything and everything that comes into being [and passes away again]. It deals with matters concerning which doubt and deliberation are possible. Accordingly, though its sphere is the same as that of practical wisdom, understanding and practical wisdom are not the same. Practical wisdom issues commands: its end is to tell us what we ought to do and what we ought not to do. Understanding, on the other hand, only passes judgment. [There is no difference between understanding and excellence in un-
10   derstanding:] for excellence in understanding is the same as understanding, and men of understanding are men of good understanding.

Thus understanding is neither possession nor acquisition of practical wisdom. Just as learning is called "understanding" when a man makes use of his faculty of knowledge, so [we speak of "understanding"] when it implies the use of one's faculty of opinion in judging statements made by another person about matters which belong to
15   the realm of practical wisdom—and in judging such statements rightly, for *good* understanding means that the judgment is right. It is from this act of learning or understanding [what someone else says] that the term "understanding" as predicated of "men of good understanding" is derived. For we frequently use the words "learning" and "understanding" synonymously.

11. Practical Wisdom and Good Sense

As for what is called "good sense," the quality which makes us say of a person that he has the sense to forgive others, [i.e., sympathetic understanding], and that he has
20   good sense, this is a correct judgment of what is fair or equitable. This is indicated by the fact that we attribute to an equitable man especially sympathetic understanding and that we say that it is fair, in certain cases, to have the sense to forgive. Sympathetic understanding is a correct critical sense or judgment of what is fair; and a correct judgment is a true one.

All these characteristics, as one would expect, tend toward the same goal. We at- 25
tribute good sense, understanding, practical wisdom, and intelligence to the same persons, and in saying that they have good sense, we imply at the same time that they have
a mature intelligence and that they are men of practical wisdom and understanding. For
what these capacities [have in common is that they are] all concerned with ultimate particular facts. To say that a person has good judgment in matters of practical wisdom im- 30
plies that he is understanding and has good sense or that he has sympathetic understanding; for equitable acts are common to all good men in their relation with someone
else. Now, all matters of action are in the sphere of the particulars and ultimates. Not
only must a man of practical wisdom take cognizance of particulars, but understanding
and good sense, too, deal with matters of action, and matters of action are ultimates. As
for intelligence, it deals with ultimates at both ends of the scale. It is intelligence, not
reasoning, that has as its objects primary terms and definitions as well as ultimate particulars. Intelligence grasps, on the one hand, the unchangeable, primary terms and con- 1143ᵇ
cepts for demonstrations; on the other hand, in questions of action, it grasps the ultimate, contingent fact and the minor premise. For it is particular facts that form the
starting points or principles for [our knowledge of] the goal of action: universals arise
out of particulars. Hence one must have perception of particular facts, and this percep- 5
tion is intelligence.* Intelligence is, therefore, both starting point and end; for demonstrations start with ultimate terms and have ultimate facts as their objects.

That is why these characteristics are regarded as natural endowments and, although no one is provided with theoretical wisdom by nature, we do think that men
have good sense, understanding, and intelligence by nature. An indication of this is that
we think of these characteristics as depending on different stages of life, and that at a
given stage of life a person acquires intelligence and good sense: the implication is that
[human] nature is the cause. Therefore, we ought to pay as much attention to the sayings
and opinions, undemonstrated though they are, of wise and experienced older men as
we do to demonstrated truths. For experience has given such men an eye with which 10
they can see correctly.**

We have now completed our discussion of what practical and theoretical wisdom
are; we have described the sphere in which each operates, and we have shown that each 15
is the excellence of a different part of the soul.

12. The Use of Theoretical and Practical Wisdom

One might raise some questions about the usefulness of these two virtues. Theoretical wisdom, [as we have described it,] will study none of the things that make a man
happy, for it is not at all concerned with the sphere of coming-to-be [but only with un- 20
changing realities]. Practical wisdom, on the other hand, *is* concerned with this sphere,
but for what purpose do we need it? (1) It is true that practical wisdom deals with what
is just, noble, and good for man; and it is doing such things that characterizes a man as
good. But our ability to perform such actions is in no way enhanced by knowing them,
since the virtues are characteristics, [that is to say, fixed capacities for action, acquired
by habit]. The same also applies, after all, to matters of health and well-being (not in the 25
sense of "producing health and well-being" but in the sense of "being healthy and well"

---

*I.e., we can attain the end—happiness—only by discovering the general rules of moral conduct, and
these, in turn, rest on the immediate apprehension by intelligence of particular moral facts.

**The "eye given by experience" is of course *nous,* "intelligence."

as the manifestation of a physical condition or a characteristic): our ability to perform actions [which show that we are healthy and well] is in no way enhanced by a mastery of the science of medicine or of physical training.

(2) But if we are to say that the purpose of practical wisdom is not to *know* what is just, noble, and good, but to *become* just, noble, and good, it would be of no use at all to a man who is already good. Moreover, it is of no use to those who do not have virtue, for it makes no difference whether they have practical wisdom themselves or listen to others who have it. It is quite sufficient to take the same attitude as we take toward health: we want to be healthy, yet we do not study medicine.

(3) In addition, it would seem strange if practical wisdom, though [intrinsically] inferior to theoretical wisdom, should surpass it in authority, because that which produces a thing rules and directs it.

These, then, are the questions we must discuss: so far we have only stated them as problems.

First of all, then, we should insist that both theoretical and practical wisdom are necessarily desirable in themselves, even if neither of them produces anything. For each one of them is the virtue of a different part of the soul.

Secondly, they do in fact produce something: theoretical wisdom produces happiness, not as medicine produces health, but as health itself makes a person healthy. For since theoretical wisdom is one portion of virtue in its entirety, possessing and actualizing it makes a man happy. [For happiness, as we have seen (Book I, 7) consists in the activity of virtue.]

In the third place, a man fulfills his proper function only by way of practical wisdom and moral excellence or virtue: virtue makes us aim at the right target, and practical wisdom makes us use the right means. The fourth part of the soul, the nutritive, does not have a virtue [which makes man fulfill his proper function,] since it does not play any role in the decision to act or not to act.

Finally, the argument has to be met that our ability to perform noble and just acts is in no way enhanced by practical wisdom. We have to begin a little further back and take the following as our starting point. It is our contention that people may perform just acts without actually being just men, as in the case of people who do what has been laid down by the laws but do so either involuntarily or through ignorance or for an ulterior motive, and not for the sake of performing just acts. [Such persons are not just men] despite the fact that they act the way they should, and perform all the actions which a morally good man ought to perform. On the other hand, it seems that it is possible for a man to be of such a character that he performs each particular act in such a way as to make him a good man—I mean that his acts are due to choice and are performed for the sake of the acts themselves. Now, it is virtue which makes our choice right. It is not virtue, however, but a different capacity, which determines the steps which, in the nature of the case, must be taken to implement this choice.

We must stop for a moment to make this point clearer. There exists a capacity called "cleverness," which is the power to perform those steps which are conducive to a goal we have set for ourselves and to attain that goal. If the goal is noble, cleverness deserves praise; if the goal is base, cleverness is knavery. That is why men of practical wisdom are often described as "clever" and "knavish." But in fact this capacity [alone] is not practical wisdom, although practical wisdom does not exist without it. Without virtue or excellence, this eye of the soul, [intelligence,] does not acquire the characteristic of practical wisdom: that is what we have just stated and it is obvious. For the syllogisms which express the principles initiating action run: "Since the end, or the highest good, is such-and-such . . ."—whatever it may be; what it really is does not matter for our present argument. But whatever the true end may be, only a good man can judge it correctly. For wickedness distorts and causes us to be completely mistaken about the fundamental principles of action. Hence it is clear that a man cannot have practical wisdom unless he is good. 35

13. Practical Wisdom and Moral Virtue

Accordingly, we must also re-examine virtue or excellence. Virtue offers a close analogy to the relation that exists between practical wisdom and cleverness. Just as these two qualities are not identical but similar, so we find the same relation between natural virtue and virtue in the full sense. It seems that the various kinds of character inhere in all of us, somehow or other, by nature. We tend to be just, capable of self-control, and to show all our other character traits from the time of our birth. Yet we still seek something more, the good in a fuller sense, and the possession of these traits in another way. For it is true that children and beasts are endowed with natural qualities or characteristics, but it is evident that without intelligence these are harmful. This much, to be sure, we do seem to notice: as in the case of a mighty body which, when it moves without vision, comes down with a mighty fall because it cannot see, so it is in the matter under discussion. If a man acts blindly, i.e., using his natural virtue alone, he will fail; but once he acquires intelligence, it makes a great difference in his action. At that point, the natural characteristic will become that virtue in the full sense which it previously resembled. 1144^b

5

10

Consequently, just as there exist two kinds of quality, cleverness and practical wisdom, in that part of us which forms opinions, [i.e., in the calculative element,] so also there are two kinds of quality in the moral part of us, natural virtue and virtue in the full sense. Now virtue in the full sense cannot be attained without practical wisdom. That is why some people maintain that all the virtues are forms of practical wisdom, and why Socrates' approach to the subject was partly right and partly wrong. He was wrong in believing that all the virtues are forms of wisdom, but right in saying that there is no virtue without wisdom. This is indicated by the fact that all the current definitions of virtue,* after naming the characteristic and its objects, add that it is a characteristic "guided by right reason." Now right reason is that which is determined by practical wisdom. So we see that these thinkers all have some inkling that virtue is a characteristic of this kind, namely, a characteristic guided by practical wisdom. 15

20

25

But we must go a little beyond that. Virtue or excellence is not only a characteristic which is guided by right reason, but also a characteristic which is united with right reason; and right reason in moral matters is practical wisdom.** In other words, while Socrates believed that the virtues *are* rational principles—he said that all of them are forms of knowledge—we, on the other hand, think that they are *united with* a rational principle. 30

Our discussion, then, has made it clear that it is impossible to be good in the full sense of the word without practical wisdom or to be a man of practical wisdom without moral excellence or virtue. Moreover, in this way we can also refute the dialectical argument which might be used to prove that the virtues exist independently of one another. The same individual, it might be argued, is not equally well-endowed by nature for all the virtues, with the result that at a given point he will have acquired one virtue 35

---

*The reference is to the doctrines of Plato's successors in the Academy.

**I.e., right reason is not only an external standard of action, but it also lives in us and makes us virtuous.

but not yet another. In the case of the natural virtues this may be true, but it cannot happen in the case of those virtues which entitle a man to be called good in an unqualified sense. For in the latter case, as soon as he possesses this single virtue of practical wisdom, he will also possess all the rest.

It is now clear that we should still need practical wisdom, even if it had no bearing on action, because it is the virtue of a part of our soul. But it is also clear that [it does have an important bearing on action, since] no choice will be right without practical wisdom and virtue. For virtue determines the end, and practical wisdom makes us do what is conducive to the end.

1145ª

5

Lapith and Centaur, Metope from Parthenon, 477–438 B.C. According to a Greek myth, the Lapiths invited the Centaurs to the wedding feast of their king, Peirthon, as a gesture of good will. Upon seeing the beauty of the Lapiety bride, the Centaurs succumbed to their animal instincts of lust and drunkenness and turned the feast into an abduction attempt and brawl. The Lapith warriors, under the cool wisdom of Apollo, brought a sense of calm to the chaos. The image is a symbolic lesson in its appeal for human reason and order over the lower animal instinct of passion—a lesson also taught by Aristotle in the Nichomachean Ethics. (*Hirmer Fotoarchiv*)

Still, practical wisdom has no authority over theoretical wisdom or the better part of our soul* any more than the art of medicine has authority over health. [Just as medicine does not use health but makes the provisions to secure it, so] practical wisdom does not use theoretical wisdom but makes the provisions to secure it. It issues commands to attain it, but it does not issue them to wisdom itself. To say the contrary would be like   10 asserting that politics governs the gods, because it issues commands about everything in the state, [including public worship].

BOOK VII

1. Moral Strength and Moral Weakness; Their Relation to Virtue and Vice and Current Beliefs About Them

We have to make a fresh start now by pointing out that the qualities of character   15 to be avoided are three in kind: vice, moral weakness, and brutishness. The opposites of two of these are obvious: one is called virtue or excellence and the other moral strength. The most fitting description of the opposite of brutishness would be to say that it is superhuman virtue, a kind of heroic and divine excellence; just as Homer has Priam say   20 about Hector that he was of surpassing excellence:

for he did not seem like one who was child of a mortal man, but of god.

Therefore, if, as is said, an excess of virtue can change a man into a god, the characteristic opposed to brutishness must evidently be something of this sort. For just as vice   25 and virtue do not exist in brute beasts, no more can they exist in a god. The quality of gods is something more worthy of honor than [human] virtue or excellence, and the quality of a brute is generically different from [human] vice.

If it is rare to find a man who is divine—as the Spartans, for example, customarily use the attribute "divine man" to express an exceptionally high degree of admiration for a person—it is just as rare that a brute is found among men. It does happen, particu-   30 larly among barbarians, but in some cases disease and physical disability can make a man brutish. "Brutishness" is also used as a term of opprobrium for those who exceed all other men in vice.

But we must defer until later some mention of this kind of disposition, and vice has already been discussed. We must now discuss moral weakness, softness, and effem-   35 inacy, also moral strength and tenacity. We will do so on the assumption that each of these two sets of characteristics is neither identical with virtue or with wickedness nor generically different from it, but different species respectively of the covering genera,   1145^b [namely, qualities to be sought and qualities to be avoided].

The proper procedure will be the one we have followed in our treatment of other subjects: we must present phenomena, [that is, the observed facts of moral life and the current beliefs about them,] and, after first stating the problems inherent in these, we

---

*That is, the scientific or cognitive part in the soul, the rational element which grasps necessary and permanent truths.

5   must, if possible, demonstrate the validity of all the beliefs about these matters,* and, if
not, the validity of most of them or of the most authoritative. For if the difficulties are resolved and current beliefs are left intact, we shall have proved their validity sufficiently.

Now the current beliefs are as follows: (1) Moral strength and tenacity are qualities of great moral value and deserve praise, while moral weakness and softness are
10   base and deserve blame. (2) A man who is morally strong tends to abide by the results
of his calculation, and a morally weak man tends to abandon them. (3) A morally weak
man does, on the basis of emotion, what he knows to be base, whereas a morally strong
man, knowing that certain appetites are base, refuses to follow them and accepts the
guidance of reason. (4) Though a self-controlled man is called morally strong and tena-
15   cious, some people affirm and others deny [the converse, namely,] that a morally strong
person is self-controlled in every respect; likewise, some people call a self-indulgent
person "morally weak" and a morally weak person "self-indulgent" without discrimi-
nating between the two, while others say that they are different. (5) Sometimes it is said
that a man of practical wisdom cannot possibly be morally weak, and sometimes people
who have practical wisdom and who are clever are said to be morally weak. (6) Finally,
it is said that moral weakness is shown even in anger and in the pursuit of honor and
20   profit. These, then, are the opinions commonly heard.

2. Problems in the Current Beliefs
About Moral Strength and Moral Weakness

The problems we might raise are these. [As to (3):] how can a man be morally
weak in his actions, when his basic assumption is correct [as to what he should do]?
Some people claim that it is impossible for him to be morally weak if he has knowledge
[of what he ought to do]. Socrates, for example, believed that it would be strange if,
when a man possesses knowledge, something else should overpower it and drag it about
25   like a slave. In fact, Socrates was completely opposed to the view [that a man may know
what is right but do what is wrong], and did not believe that moral weakness exists. He
claimed that no one acts contrary to what is best in the conviction [that what he is doing
is bad], but through [ignorance of the fact that it is bad].

Now this theory is plainly at variance with the observed facts, and one ought to
investigate the emotion [involved in the acts of a morally weak man]: if it comes about
through ignorance, what manner of ignorance is it? For evidently a man who is morally
30   weak in his actions does not think [that he ought to act the way he does] before he is in
the grip of emotion.

There are some people** who accept only certain points of Socrates' theory, but
reject others. They agree that nothing is better or more powerful than *knowledge,* but
they do not agree that no one acts contrary to what he *thought* was the better thing to do.
35   Therefore, they say, a [morally weak person] does not have knowledge but opinion
when he is overpowered by pleasures.

However, if it really is opinion and not knowledge, if, in other words, the basic
1146ᵃ   conviction which resists [the emotion] is not strong but weak, as it is when people are in
doubt, we can forgive a man for not sticking to his opinions in the face of strong ap-

---

*"Matters" here translates the Greek word *pathos,* which we usually render as "emotion" or "affect."
Here, however, it is used in a loose and general sense to include the whole class of moral phenomena. In
other words, Aristotle does not mean to deny here that the qualities enumerated above are lasting characteristics.
**I.e., Plato's followers in the Academy.

petites. But we do not forgive wickedness or anything else that deserves blame [as moral weakness does. Hence it must be something stronger than opinion which is overpowered]. But does that mean that it is practical wisdom* which resists [the appetite]? This, after all, is the strongest [kind of conviction]. But that would be absurd: for it would mean that the same man will have practical wisdom and be morally weak at the 5 same time, and there is no one who would assert that it is the mark of a man of practical wisdom to perform voluntarily the basest actions. In addition, it has been shown before that a man of practical wisdom is a man of action he is concerned with ultimate particulars that he possesses the other virtues.

Furthermore, [as regards (4)]: if being a morally strong person involves having strong and base appetites, a self-controlled man will not be morally strong nor a morally 10 strong man self-controlled. It is out of character for a self-controlled person to have excessive or base appetites. Yet a morally strong man certainly must have such appetites: for if the appetites are good, the characteristic which prevents him from following them is bad, and that would mean that moral strength is not always morally good. If, on the other hand, our appetites are weak and not base, there is nothing extraordinary in resist- 15 ing them, nor is it a great achievement if they are base and weak.

Again, [to take (1) and (2),] if moral strength makes a person abide by any and every opinion, it is a bad thing; for example, if it makes him persist in a false opinion. And if moral weakness makes a man abandon any and every opinion, moral weakness will occasionally be morally good, as, for example, in the case of Neoptolemus in Sophocles' *Philoctetes*. Neoptolemus deserves praise when he does not abide by the 20 resolution which Odysseus had persuaded him to adopt, because it gives him pain to tell a lie.

Further, [concerning (1) and (3),] the sophistic argument presents a problem. The Sophists want to refute their opponents by leading them to conclusions which contradict generally accepted facts. Their purpose is to have success bring them the reputation of being clever, and the syllogism which results only becomes a problem or quandary [for their opponents]. For the mind is in chains when, because it is dissatisfied with the con- 25 clusion it has reached, it wishes not to stand still, while on the other hand its inability to resolve the argument makes forward movement impossible. Now, they have one argument which leads to the conclusion that folly combined with moral weakness is virtue. This is the way it runs: [if a man is both foolish and morally weak,] he acts contrary to his conviction because of his moral weakness; but [because of his folly,] his conviction is that good things are bad and that he ought not to do them. Therefore, [acting contrary 30 to his conviction,] he will do what is good and not what is bad.

A further problem [arises from (2) and (4)]. A person who, in his actions, pursues, and prefers what is pleasant, convinced or persuaded [that it is good],** would seem to be better than one who acts the same way not on the basis of calculation, but because of moral weakness. For since he may be persuaded to change his mind, he can be cured more easily. To a morally weak man, on the other hand, applies the proverb, "When water chokes you, what can you wash it down with?" For if he had been persuaded to act 35 the way he does, he would have stopped acting that way when persuaded to change his 1146[b] mind. But as it is, though persuaded that he ought to do one thing, he nevertheless does another.

---

*The point is this: if the kind of conviction a morally weak man has is neither knowledge nor a weak conviction, it must be a strong conviction, and practical wisdom is such a conviction.

**I.e., a self-indulgent person.

Finally, if everything is the province of moral weakness and moral strength, who would be morally weak in the unqualified sense of the word? No one has every form of moral weakness, but we do say of some people that they are morally weak in an unqualified sense.

These are the sort of problems that arise. Some of the conflicting opinions must be removed and others must be left intact. For the solution of a problem is the discovery [of truth].

3. Some Problems Solved: Moral Weakness and Knowledge

Our first step is, then, to examine (1) whether morally weak people act knowingly or not, and, if knowingly, in what sense. Secondly, (2) we must establish the kind of questions with which a morally weak and a morally strong man are concerned. I mean, are they concerned with all pleasure and pain or only with certain distinct kinds of them? Is a morally strong person the same as a tenacious person or are they different? Similar questions must also be asked about all other matters germane to this study.

The starting point of our investigation is the question *(a)* whether the morally strong man and the morally weak man have their distinguishing features in the situations with which they are concerned or in their manner [of reacting to the situation]. What I mean is this: does a morally weak person owe his character to certain situations to [which he reacts], or to the manner [in which he reacts], or to both? Our second question *(b)* is whether or not moral weakness and moral strength are concerned with all [situations and feelings. The answer to both these questions is that] a man who is morally weak in the unqualified sense is not [so described because of his reaction] to every situation, but only to those situations in which also a self-indulgent man may get involved. Nor is he morally weak because of the mere fact of his relationship to these situations, [namely, that he yields to temptation]. In that case moral weakness would be the same as self-indulgence. Instead, his moral weakness is defined by the manner [in which he yields]. For a self-indulgent person is led on by his own choice, since he believes that he should always pursue the pleasure of the moment. A morally weak man, on the other hand, does not think he should, but pursues it, nonetheless.

(1) The contention that it is true opinion rather than knowledge which a morally weak man violates in his actions has no bearing on our argument. For some people have no doubts when they hold an opinion, and think they have exact knowledge. Accordingly, if we are going to say that the weakness of their belief is the reason why those who hold opinion will be more liable to act against their conviction than those who have knowledge, we shall find that there is no difference between knowledge and opinion. For some people are no less firmly convinced of what they believe than others are of what they know: Heraclitus is a case in point.* *(a)* But the verb "to know" has two meanings: a man is said to "know" both when he does not use the knowledge he has and when he does use it. Accordingly, when a man does wrong it will make a difference whether he is not exercising the knowledge he has, [viz., that it is wrong to do what he is doing,] or whether he is exercising it. In the latter case, we would be baffled, but not if he acted without exercising his knowledge.

---

*The reference is not to any specific utterance of Heraclitus, but to the tone of intense conviction with which he asserted all his doctrines, some of which Aristotle finds patently false, and hence examples of opinion rather than knowledge.

Moreover, *(b)* since there are two kinds of premise,* [namely, universal and particular,] it may well happen that a man knows both [major and minor premise of a practical syllogism] and yet acts against his knowledge, because the [minor] premise which 1147ᵃ
he uses is universal rather than particular. [In that case, he cannot apply his knowledge to his action,] for the actions to be performed are particulars. Also, there are two kinds of universal term to be distinguished: one applies to *(i)* the agent, and the other *(ii)* to 5
the thing. For example, when a person knows that dry food is good for all men, [he may also know] *(i)* that he is a man, or *(ii)* that this kind of food is dry. But whether the particular food before him is of this kind is something of which a morally weak man either does not have the knowledge or does not exercise it. So we see that there will be a tremendous difference between these two ways of knowing. We do not regard it as at all strange that a morally weak person "knows" in the latter sense [with one term nonspecific], but it would be surprising if he "knew" in the other sense, [namely with both terms apprehended as concrete particulars].

There is *(c)* another way besides those we have so far described, in which it is 10
possible for men to have knowledge. When a person has knowledge but does not use it, we see that "having" a characteristic has different meanings. There is a sense in which a person both has and does not have knowledge, for example, when he is asleep, mad, or drunk. But this is precisely the condition of people who are in the grip of the emo- 15
tions. Fits of passion, sexual appetites, and some other such passions actually cause palpable changes in the body, and in some cases even produce madness. Now it is clear that we must attribute to the morally weak a condition similar to that of men who are asleep, mad, or drunk. That the words they utter spring from knowledge [as to what is good] is no evidence to the contrary. People can repeat geometrical demonstrations and verses of Empedocles even when affected by sleep, madness, and drink; and beginning students 20
can reel off the words they have heard, but they do not yet know the subject. The subject must grow to be part of them, and that takes time. We must, therefore, assume that a man who displays moral weakness repeats the formulae [of moral knowledge] in the same way as an actor speaks his lines.

Further, *(d)* we may also look at the cause [of moral weakness] from the viewpoint of the science of human nature, in the following way. [In the practical syllogism,] one of the premises, the universal, is a current belief, while the other involves particular facts which 25
fall within the domain of sense perception. When two premises are combined into one, [i.e., when the universal rule is realized in a particular case,] the soul is thereupon bound to affirm the conclusion, and if the premises involve action, the soul is bound to perform this act at once. For example, if [the premises are]: "Everything sweet ought to be tasted" and "This thing before me is sweet" ("this thing" perceived as an individual particular ob- 30
ject), a man who is able [to taste] and is not prevented is bound to act accordingly at once.

*What is involved in this paragraph is the practical syllogism which was briefly explained in the footnote on p. 220. However, a refinement is added here, which requires further explanation. A major premise, Aristotle says, may contain two kinds of universal, e.g., the premise that "dry food is good for all men" makes a universal statement about *(i)* men and *(ii)* about dry food. Accordingly, two kinds of syllogism can be developed from this major premise. The first: "dry food is good for all men"; "I am a man"; therefore, "dry food is good for me" is here neglected by Aristotle, because the agent is obviously always aware of being a person. But the second possible syllogism: "dry food is good for all men"; "this kind of food is dry"; therefore, "this kind of food is good for me," leaves the agent only with the general knowledge that, for example, cereals are good, but the individual will not yet know whether this barley is a cereal. "Knowledge" of this sort will obviously not serve to check a healthy appetite faced with an attractive bowl of porridge.

Now, suppose that there is within us one universal opinion forbidding us to taste [things of this kind], and another [universal] opinion which tells us that everything sweet is pleasant, and also [a concrete perception], determining our activity, that the particular thing before us is sweet; and suppose further that the appetite [for pleasure] happens to be present. [The result is that] one opinion tells us to avoid that thing, while
35 appetite, capable as it is of setting in motion each part of our body, drives us to it. [This is the case we have been looking for, the defeat of reason in moral weakness.] Thus it turns out that a morally weak man acts under the influence of some kind of reasoning and opinion, an opinion which is not intrinsically but only incidentally opposed to right
1147ᵇ reason; for it is not opinion but appetite that is opposed to right reason.* And this explains why animals cannot be morally weak: they do not have conceptions of universals, but have only the power to form mental images and memory of particulars.
5
How is the [temporary] ignorance of a morally weak person dispelled and how does he regain his [active] knowledge [of what is good]? The explanation is the same as it is for drunkenness and sleep, and it is not peculiar to the affect of moral weakness. To get it we have to go to the students of natural science.

The final premise, consisting as it does in an opinion about an object perceived by
10 the senses, determines our action. When in the grip of emotion, a morally weak man either does not have this premise, or he has it not in the sense of knowing it, but in the sense of uttering it as a drunken man may utter verses of Empedocles. [Because he is not in active possession of this premise,] and because the final [concrete] term of his reasoning is not a universal and does not seem to be an object of scientific knowledge in the same way that a universal is, [for both these reasons] we seem to be led to the con-
15 clusion which Socrates sought to establish. Moral weakness does not occur in the presence of knowledge in the strict sense, and it is sensory knowledge, not science, which is dragged about by emotion.

This completes our discussion of the question whether a morally weak person acts with knowledge or without knowledge, and in what sense it is possible for him to act knowingly.

4. More Problems Solved: The Sphere in Which Moral Weakness Operates

20 (2) The next point we have to discuss is whether it is possible for a man to be morally weak in the unqualified sense, or whether the moral weakness of all who have it is concerned with particular situations. If the former is the case, we shall have to see with what kind of situations he is concerned.

Now, it is clearly in their attitude to pleasures and pains that men are morally strong and tenacious and morally weak and soft. There are two sources of pleasure: some are necessary, and others are desirable in themselves but admit of excess. The nec-
25 essary kind are those concerned with the body: I mean sources of pleasure such as food and drink and sexual intercourse, in short, the kind of bodily pleasures which we as-

---

*The point is this: there is a kind of reasoning involved in the actions of a morally weak person: such a person starts out with the opinion that everything sweet is pleasant, finds a particular sweet thing, and knows that the thing is pleasant. But this person also has right reason, which warns not to taste everything sweet. However, the appetite for pleasure, taking hold of the opinion that everything sweet is pleasant, transforms this opinion into the action of tasting. What is contrary to right reason (i.e., contrary to the knowledge that not everything sweet should be tasted) is not the person's opinion (that sweet things are pleasant) but rather the person's appetite for pleasure.

signed to the sphere of self-indulgence and self-control.* By sources of pleasure which are not necessary but desirable in themselves, I mean, for example, victory, honor, wealth, and similar good and pleasant things. Now, *(a)* those who violate the right reason that they possess by excessive indulgence in the second type of pleasures, are not called morally weak in the unqualified sense, but only with a qualification: we call them "morally weak in regard to material goods," or profit, or honor, or anger, but not "morally weak" pure and simple. They are different from the morally weak in the unqualified sense and share the same name only by analogy, as in our example of the man called Man, who won an Olympic victory. In his case there is not much difference between the general definition of man and the definition proper to him alone, and yet there was a difference. [That there is similarly a difference between the two senses of morally weak] is shown by the fact that we blame moral weakness—regardless of whether it is moral weakness in the unqualified sense or moral weakness concerning some particular bodily pleasure—not only as an error, but also as a kind of vice. But we do not blame as vicious those [who are morally weak in matters of material goods, profit, ambition, anger, and so forth].

(b) We now come to those bodily enjoyments which, we say, are the sphere of the self-controlled and the self-indulgent. Here a man who pursues the excesses of things pleasant and avoids excesses of things painful (of hunger, thirst, heat, cold, and of anything we feel by touch or taste), and does so not by choice but against his choice and thinking, is called "morally weak" without the addition of "in regard to such-and-such," e.g., "in regard to feelings of anger," but simply morally weak without qualification. The truth of this is proved by the fact that persons who indulge in bodily pleasures are called "soft," but not persons who indulge in feelings of anger and so forth. For this reason, we class the morally weak man with the self-indulgent, and the morally strong with the self-controlled. But we do not include [in the same category] those who indulge in feelings of anger, because moral weakness and self-indulgence are, in a way, concerned with the same pleasures and pains. That is, they are concerned with the same pleasures and pains but not in the same way. Self-indulgent men pursue the excess by choice, but the morally weak do not exercise choice.

That is why we are probably more justified in calling a person self-indulgent who shows little or no appetite in pursuing an excess of pleasures and in avoiding moderate pains, than a person who is driven by strong appetite [to pursue pleasure and to avoid pain]. For what would the former do, if, in addition, he had the vigorous appetite of youth and felt strong pain at lacking the objects necessary for his pleasure?

Some appetites and desires are generically noble and worth while—[let us remember] our earlier distinction of pleasant things into those which are by nature desirable, the opposite of these, and those which are intermediate between the two—for example, material goods, profit, victory, and honor. Now, people are not blamed for being affected by all these and similar objects of pleasure and by those of the intermediate kind, nor are they blamed for having an appetite or a liking for them; they are blamed only for the manner in which they do so, if they do so to excess. This, by the way, is why [we do not regard as wicked] all those who, contrary to right reason, are overpowered by something that is noble and good by nature, or who pursue it—those, for example, who devote themselves to the pursuit of honor or to their children and parents more than they should. All these things are good, and those who devote themselves to them are praised. And yet even here there is an element of excess, if, like Niobe, one were to fight against the gods [for the sake of one's children], or if one showed the same excessively

*I.e., the sensual pleasures of taste and touch.

1148ᵇ   foolish devotion to his father as did Satyros, nicknamed "the filial."* So we see that there cannot be any wickedness in this area, because, as we stated, each of these things is in itself naturally desirable. But excess in one's attachment to them is base and must be avoided.

5   Similarly, there cannot be moral weakness in this area [of things naturally desirable]. Moral weakness is not only something to be avoided, but it is also something that deserves blame. Still, because there is a similarity in the affect, people do call it "moral weakness," but they add "in regard to [such-and-such]," in the same way as they speak of a "bad" doctor or a "bad" actor without meaning to imply that the person is bad in the unqualified sense. So just as in the case of the doctor and the actor [we do not speak of "badness" in the unqualified sense], because their badness is not vice but only some-
10   thing similar to vice by analogy, so it is clear that, in the other case, we must understand by "moral weakness" and moral strength" only that which operates in the same sphere as self-control and self-indulgence. When we use these terms of anger, we do so only in an analogous sense. Therefore, we add a qualification and say "morally weak in regard to anger," just as we say "morally weak in regard to honor or profit."

5. Moral Weakness and Brutishness

15   (1) Some things are pleasant by nature, partly *(a)* without qualification, and partly *(b)* pleasant for different classes of animals and humans. Then (2) there are things which are not pleasant by nature, but which come to be pleasant *(a)* through physical disability, *(b)* through habit, or *(c)* through an [innate] depravity of nature. We can observe characteristics corresponding to each of the latter group (2), just as [we did in discussing (1), things pleasant by nature]. I mean (2c) characteristics of brutishness, for in-
20   stance, the female who is said to rip open pregnant women and devour the infants; or what is related about some of the savage tribes near the Black Sea, that they delight in eating raw meat or human flesh, and that some of them lend each other their children for a feast; or the story told about Phalaris.**

These are characteristics of brutishness. Another set of characteristics (2a) devel-
25   ops through disease and occasionally through insanity, as, for example, in the case of the man who offered his mother as a sacrifice to the gods and ate of her, or the case of the slave who ate the liver of his fellow slave. Other characteristics are the result of disease or (2b) of habit, e.g., plucking out one's hair, gnawing one's fingernails, or even chewing coal or earth, and also sexual relations between males. These practices are, in
30   some cases, due to nature, but in other cases they are the result of habit, when, for example, someone has been sexually abused from childhood.

When nature is responsible, no one would call the persons affected morally weak any more than one would call women morally weak, because they are passive and not active in sexual intercourse. Nor would we apply the term to persons in a morbid condition as a result of habit. To have one of these characteristics means to be outside the
1149ᵃ   limits of vice, just as brutishness, too, lies outside the limits of vice. To have such char-

---

*Niobe boasted that, with her six (or in some versions, seven) sons and an equal number of daughters, she was at least equal to the goddess Leto, who only had two children, the twins Apollo and Artemis. Apollo and Artemis thereupon killed all her children, and Niobe was turned into stone. Who exactly Satyros was, we do not know. Ancient commentators tell us that he committed suicide when his father died, or that he called his father a god.

**Phalaris, tyrant of Acragas in the second quarter of the sixth century B.C., was said to have built a hollow brazen bull, in which he roasted his victims alive, presumably to eat them afterwards. There were several other stories current in antiquity about his brutality.

acteristics and to master them or be mastered by them does not constitute moral [strength or] weakness in an unqualified sense but only by analogy, just as a person is not to be called morally weak without qualification when he cannot master his anger, but only morally weak in regard to the emotion involved.

For all excessive folly, cowardice, self-indulgence, and ill-temper is either brutish   5
or morbid. When someone is by nature the kind of person who fears everything, even the rustling of a mouse, his cowardice is brutish, while the man's fear of the weasel was due to disease. In the case of folly, those who are irrational by nature and live only by their senses, as do some distant barbarian tribes, are brutish, whereas those whose irra-   10
tionality is due to a disease, such as epilepsy, or to insanity, are morbid.

Sometimes it happens that a person merely possesses one of these characteristics without being mastered by it—I mean, for example, if a Phalaris had restrained his appetite so as not to eat the flesh of a child or so as not to indulge in some perverse form of sexual pleasure. But it also happens that a man not only has the characteristic but is   15
mastered by it. Thus, just as the term "wickedness" refers in its unqualified sense to man alone, while in another sense it is qualified by the addition of "brutish" or "morbid," in precisely the same way it is plain that there is a brutish and a morbid kind of moral weakness [i.e., being mastered by brutishness or disease], but in its unqualified sense the term "moral weakness" refers only to human self-indulgence.   20

It is, accordingly, clear that moral weakness and moral strength operate only in the same sphere as do self-indulgence and self-control, and that the moral weakness which operates in any other sphere is different in kind, and is called "moral weakness" only by extension, not in an unqualified sense.

6. Moral Weakness in Anger

At this point we may observe that moral weakness in anger is less base than moral weakness in regard to the appetites. For (1) in a way, anger seems to listen to   25
reason, but to hear wrong, like hasty servants, who run off before they have heard everything their master tells them, and fail to do what they were ordered, or like dogs, which bark as soon as there is a knock without waiting to see if the visitor is a friend.   30
In the same way, the heat and swiftness of its nature make anger hear but not listen to an order, before rushing off to take revenge. For reason and imagination indicate that an insult or a slight has been received, and anger, drawing the conclusion, as it were, that it must fight against this sort of tiring, simply flares up at once. Appetite, on the other hand, is no sooner told by reason and perception that something is pleasant than   35
it rushes off to enjoy it. Consequently, while anger somehow follows reason, appetite   1149ᵇ
does not. Hence appetite is baser [than anger]. For when a person is morally weak in anger, he is in a sense overcome by reason, but the other is not overcome by reason but by appetite.

Further, (2) it is more excusable to follow one's natural desires, inasmuch as we are also more inclined to pardon such appetites as are common to all men and to the ex-   5
tent that they are common to all. Now anger and ill temper are more natural than are the appetites which make us strive for excess and for what is not necessary. Take the example of the man who was defending himself against the charge of beating his father with the words: "Yes, I did it: my father, too, used to beat his father, and he beat his, and"— pointing to his little boy—"he will beat me when he grows up to be a man. It runs in the   10
family." And the story goes that the man who was being dragged out of the house by his son asked him to stop at the door, on the grounds that he himself had not dragged his father any further than that.

Moreover, (3) the more underhanded a person is, the more unjust he is. Now, a
15   hot-tempered man is not underhanded; nor is anger: it is open. But appetite has the same
attribute as Aphrodite, who is called "weaver of guile on Cyprus born," and as her
"pattern-pierced zone," of which Homer says: "endearment that steals the heart away
even from the thoughtful." Therefore, since moral weakness of this type [which involves the appetite] is more unjust and baser than moral weakness concerning anger, it
is this type which constitutes moral weakness in the unqualified sense and is even a kind
of vice.*

20   Again, (4) no one feels pain when insulting another without provocation, whereas
everyone who acts in a fit of anger acts with pain. On the contrary, whoever unprovoked
insults another, feels pleasure. If, then, acts which justify outbursts of anger are more
unjust than others, it follows that moral weakness caused by appetite [is more unjust
than moral weakness caused by anger], for anger does not involve unprovoked insult.

It is now clear that moral weakness in regard to the appetites is more disgraceful
25   than moral weakness displayed in anger, and also that moral strength and weakness operate in the sphere of the bodily appetites and pleasures. But we must still grasp the distinctions to be made within bodily appetites and pleasures. For, as we stated at the beginning, some pleasures are human, i.e., natural in kind as well as in degree, while
others are brutish, and others again are due to physical disability and disease. It is only
30   with the first group of these, [i.e., the human pleasures,] that self-control and self-
indulgence are concerned. For that reason, we do not call beasts either self-controlled or
self-indulgent; if we do so, we do it only metaphorically, in cases where a general distinction can be drawn between one class of animals and another on the basis of wanton-
ness, destructiveness, and indiscriminate voracity. [This use is only metaphorical] because beasts are incapable of choice and calculation, but [animals of this type] stand
35   outside the pale of their nature, just as madmen do among humans.
1150ᵃ   Brutishness is a lesser evil than vice, but it is more horrifying. For [in a beast]
the better element cannot be perverted, as it can be in man, since it is lacking. [To compare a brute beast and a brutish man] is like comparing an inanimate with an animate
being to see which is more evil. For the depravity of a being which does not possess
the source that initiates its own motion is always less destructive [than the depravity of
5   a being that possesses this source], and intelligence is such a source. A similar comparison can be made between injustice [as such] and an unjust man: each is in some
sense worse than the other, for a bad man can do ten thousand times as much harm as
a beast.

7. Moral Strength and Moral Weakness: Tenacity and Softness

As regards the pleasures, pains, appetites, and aversions that come to us through
10   touch and taste, and which we defined earlier as the sphere of self-indulgence and self-
control, it is possible to be the kind of person who is overcome even by those which
most people master; but it is also possible to master those by which most people are
overcome. Those who are overcome by pleasure or master it are, respectively, morally
weak and morally strong; and in the case of pain, they are, respectively, soft and tena-
15   cious. The disposition which characterizes the majority of men lies between these two,
although they tend more to the inferior characteristics.

---

*But it is not vice in the unqualified sense, for that would involve choice.

Some pleasures are necessary, up to a certain point, and others are not, whereas neither excesses nor deficiencies of pleasure are necessary. The same is also true of appetites and pains. From all this it follows that a man is self-indulgent when he pursues excesses of pleasant things, or when he [pursues necessary pleasures] to excess, by   20
choice, for their own sakes, and not for an ulterior result. A man of this kind inevitably feels no regret, and is as a result incorrigible. For a person who feels no regret is incorrigible. A person deficient [in his pursuit of the necessary pleasures] is the opposite [of self-indulgent], and the man who occupies the middle position is self-controlled. In the same way, a man who avoids bodily pain [is self-indulgent], provided he does so by choice and not because he is overcome by them.

A choice is not exercised either by a person who is driven by pleasure, or by a per-   25
son who is avoiding the pain of [unsatisfied] appetite. There is, accordingly, a difference between indulging by choice and not by choice. Everyone would think worse of a man who would perform some disgraceful act actuated only slightly or not at all by appetite, than of a person who was actuated by a strong appetite. And we would regard as worse a man who feels no anger as he beats another man, than someone who does so in anger. For what would he do, if he were in the grip of emotion when acting? Hence a self-   30
indulgent man is worse than one who is morally weak.

So we see that one of the characteristics described, [viz., the deliberate avoidance of pain,] constitutes rather a kind of softness, while a person possessing the other, [viz., the deliberate pursuit of excessive pleasures,] is self-indulgent.

A morally strong is opposed to a morally weak man, and a tenacious to a soft man. For being tenacious consists in offering resistance, while moral strength consists in mastering. Resistance and mastery are two different things, just as not being defeated   35
differs from winning a victory. Hence, moral strength is more desirable than tenacity. A man who is deficient [in his resistance to pains] which most people withstand   1150^b
successfully is soft and effeminate. For effeminacy is a form of softness. A man of this kind lets his cloak trail, in order to save himself the pain of lifting it up, and plays the invalid without believing himself to be involved in the misery which a true invalid   5
suffers.

The situation is similar in the case of moral strength and moral weakness. If a person is overcome by powerful and excessive pleasures or pains, we are not surprised. In fact, we find it pardonable if he is overcome while offering resistance, as, for example, Theodectes' Philoctetes* does when bitten by the snake, or as Cercyon in Carcinus' *Alope*,** or as people who try to restrain their laughter burst out in one great guffaw, as   10
actually happened to Xenophantus.*** But we are surprised if a man is overcome by and unable to withstand those [pleasures and pains] which most people resist successfully, unless his disposition is congenital or caused by disease, as among the kings of

---

*Theodectes (ca. 375–334 B.C.) spent most of his life at Athens. He studied under Plato, Isocrates, and Aristotle, and in addition to writing tragedies, won a considerable reputation as an orator. An ancient note on this passage tells us that, in Theodectes' tragedy, Philoctetes, after repressing his pain for a long time, finally bursts out: "Cut off my hand!"

**Carcinus was a fourth-century B.C. Athenian tragic poet. According to an ancient commentator, "Cercyon had a daughter Alope. Upon learning that his daughter Alope had committed adultery, he asked her who had perpetrated the deed, and said: 'If you tell me, I will not be grieved at all.' When Alope told him who the adulterer was, Cercyon was so overcome with grief that he could no longer stand life and renounced living."

***The occasion is not known. Xenophantus is said to have been a musician at the court of Alexander the Great (356–323 B.C.). Seneca tells us that when Xenophantus sang, Alexander was so stirred that he seized his weapons in his hands.

15   Scythia, for example, in whom softness is congenital,* and as softness distinguishes the female from the male.

A man who loves amusement is also commonly regarded as being self-indulgent, but he is actually soft. For amusement is relaxation, inasmuch as it is respite from work, and a lover of amusement is a person who goes in for relaxation to excess.

One kind of moral weakness is impetuosity and another is a lack of strength. Peo-
20   ple of the latter kind deliberate but do not abide by the results of their deliberation, because they are overcome by emotion, while the impetuous are driven on by emotion, because they do not deliberate. [If they deliberated, they would not be driven on so easily,]
for as those who have just been tickled are immune to being tickled again, so some people are not overcome by emotion, whether pleasant or painful, when they feel and see it
coming and have roused themselves and their power of reasoning in good time. Keen
25   and excitable persons are the most prone to the impetuous kind of moral weakness.
Swiftness prevents the keen and vehemence the excitable from waiting for reason to
guide them, since they tend to be led by their imagination.

8. Moral Weakness and Self-Indulgence

30   A self-indulgent man, as we stated, is one who feels no regret, since he abides by
the choice he has made. A morally weak person, on the other hand, always feels regret.
Therefore, the formulation of the problem, as we posed it above, does not correspond to
the facts: it is a self-indulgent man who cannot be cured, but a morally weak man is curable. For wickedness is like a disease such as dropsy or consumption, while moral
weakness resembles epilepsy: the former is chronic, the latter intermittent. All in all,
35   moral weakness and vice are generically different from each other. A vicious man is not
aware of his vice, but a morally weak man knows his weakness.
1151ᵃ   Among the morally weak, those who lose themselves in [emotion, i.e., the impetuous,] are better than those who have a rational principle but do not abide by it, [i.e.,
those who lack strength]. For they are overcome by a lesser emotion and do not yield
without previous deliberation, as the impetuous do. A man who has this kind of moral
weakness resembles those who get drunk quickly and on little wine, or on less wine
than most people do.
5   That moral weakness is not a vice [in the strict sense] is now evident, though in a
certain sense it is perhaps one. For moral weakness violates choice, whereas vice is in
accordance with choice. Nevertheless, they are similar in the actions to which they lead,
just as Demodocus said of the Milesians:

The Milesians are no stupid crew,
except that they do what the stupid do.**

10   Similarly, the morally weak are not unjust, but they will act like unjust men.

A morally weak man is the kind of person who pursues bodily pleasures to excess
and contrary to right reason, though he is not persuaded [that he ought to do so]; the
self-indulgent, on the other hand, is persuaded to pursue them because he is the kind of
man who does so. This means that it is the former who is easily persuaded to change his
15   mind, but the latter is not. For virtue or excellence preserves and wickedness destroys

---

*According to the Hippocratic treatise *On Airs, Waters, and Places* 22, horseback riding caused softness among the Scythian aristocracy.
**Demodocus wrote lampooning epigrams in the sixth century B.C.

the initiating motive or first cause [of action], and in actions the initiating motive or first cause is the end at which we aim, as the hypotheses are in mathematics. For neither in mathematics nor in moral matters does reasoning teach us the principles or starting points; it is virtue, whether natural or habitual, that inculcates right opinion about the principle or first premise. A man who has this right opinion is self-controlled, and his   20
opposite is self-indulgent.

But there exists a kind of person who loses himself under the impact of emotion and violates right reason, a person whom emotion so overpowers that he does not act according to the dictates of right reason, but not sufficiently to make him the kind of man who is persuaded that he must abandon himself completely to the pursuit of such pleasures. This is the morally weak man: he is better than the self-indulgent, and he is not bad in the unqualified sense of the word. For the best thing in him is saved: the principle or premise [as to how he should act]. Opposed to him is another kind of man, who   25
remains steadfast and does not lose himself, at least not under the impact of emotion. These considerations make it clear that moral strength is a characteristic of great moral worth, while moral weakness is bad.

9. Steadfastness in Moral Strength and Moral Weakness

Is a man morally strong when he abides by any and every dictate of reason and choice, or only when he abides by the right choice? And is a man morally weak when he   30
does not abide by every choice and dictate of reason, or only when he fails to abide by the rational dictate which is not false and the choice which is right? This is the problem we stated earlier. Or is it true reason and right choice as such, but any other kind of choice incidentally, to which the one remains steadfast and the other does not? [This   35
seems to be the correct answer,] for if a person chooses and pursues the attainment of *a*   1151[b]
by means of *b*, his pursuit and choice are for *a* as such but for *b* incidentally. And by "as such" we mean "in the unqualified sense." Therefore, there is a sense in which the one abides by and the other abandons any and every kind of opinion, but in the unqualified sense, only true opinion.

There are those who remain steadfast to their opinion and are called "obstinate." They are hard to convince and are not easily persuaded to change their mind. They bear   5
a certain resemblance to a morally strong person, just as an extravagant man resembles one who is generous, and a reckless man resembles one who is confident. But they are, in fact, different in many respects. The one, the morally strong, will be a person who does not change under the influence of emotion and appetite, but on occasion he will be   10
persuaded [by argument]. Obstinate men, on the other hand, are not easily persuaded by rational argument; but to appetites they are amenable, and in many cases are driven on by pleasures. The various kinds of obstinate people are the opinionated, the ignorant, and the boorish. The opinionated let themselves be influenced by pleasure and pain: they feel the joy of victory, when someone fails to persuade them to change their mind,   15
and they feel pain when their views are overruled, like decrees that are declared null and void. As a result, they bear a greater resemblance to the morally weak than to the morally strong.

Then there are those who do not abide by their decisions for reasons other than moral weakness, as, for example, Neoptolemus in Sophocles' *Philoctetes*. Granted it was under the influence of pleasure that he did not remain steadfast, but it was a noble pleasure: it was noble in his eyes to be truthful, but he was persuaded by Odysseus to tell a lie. For not anybody who acts under the influence of pleasure is self-indulgent,   20 bad, or morally weak, but only those who do so under the influence of a base pleasure.

There is also a type who feels less joy than he should at the things of the body and, therefore, does not abide by the dictates of reason. The median between this type and the morally weak man is the man of moral strength. For a morally weak person does not abide by the dictates of reason, because he feels more joy than he should [in bodily things], but the man under discussion feels less joy than he should. But a morally strong man remains steadfast and does not change on either account. Since moral strength is good, it follows that both characteristics opposed to it are bad, as they in fact turn out to be. But since one of the two opposites is in evidence only in a few people and on few occasions, moral strength is generally regarded as being the only opposite of moral weakness, just as self-control is thought to be opposed only to self-indulgence.

Since many terms are used in an analogical sense, we have come to speak analogically of the "moral strength" of a self-controlled man. [There is a resemblance between the two] since a morally strong man is the kind of person who does nothing contrary to the dictates of reason under the influence of bodily pleasures, and the same is true of a self-controlled man. But while a morally strong man has base appetites, a self-controlled man does not and is, moreover, a person who finds no pleasure in anything that violates the dictates of reason. A morally strong man, on the other hand, does find pleasure in such things, but he is not driven by them. There is also a similarity between the morally weak and the self-indulgent in that both pursue things pleasant to the body; but they are different in that a self-indulgent man thinks he ought to pursue them, while the morally weak thinks he should not.

10. Moral Weakness and Practical Wisdom

It is not possible for the same person to have practical wisdom and be morally weak at the same time, for it has been shown that a man of practical wisdom is *ipso facto* a man of good character. Moreover, to be a man of practical wisdom, one must not only know [what one ought to do], but he must also be able to act accordingly. But a morally weak man is not able so to act. However, there is no reason why a clever man could not be morally weak. That is why occasionally people are regarded as possessing practical wisdom, but as being morally weak at the same time; it is because cleverness differs from practical wisdom in the way we have described in our first discussion of the subject. They are closely related in that both follow the guidance of reason, but they differ in that [practical wisdom alone] involves moral choice.

Furthermore, a morally weak man does not act like a man who has knowledge and exercises it, but like a man asleep or drunk. Also, even though he acts voluntarily—for he knows in a sense what he is doing and what end he is aiming at—he is not wicked, because his moral choice is good,* and that makes him only half-wicked. He is not unjust, either, for he is no underhanded plotter. [For plotting implies deliberation,] whereas one type of morally weak man does not abide by the results of his deliberation, while the other, the excitable type, does not even deliberate. So we see that a morally weak person is like a state which enacts all the right decrees and has laws of a high moral standard, but does not apply them, a situation which Anaxandrides made fun

---

*I.e., his basic moral purpose is good, even though it is eventually vitiated by appetite.

of: "Thus wills the state, that cares not for its laws."* A wicked man, on the other hand, resembles a state which does apply its laws, but the laws are bad.

In relation to the characteristics possessed by most people, moral weakness and moral strength lie at the extremes. For a morally strong person remains more steadfast and a morally weak person less steadfast than the capacity of most men permits.

The kind of moral weakness displayed by excitable people is more easily cured than the moral weakness of those who deliberate but do not abide by their decisions; and those who are morally weak through habituation are more curable than those who are morally weak by nature. For it is easier to change habit than to change nature. Even habit is hard to change, precisely because it resembles nature, as Euenus says:

> A habit, friend, is of long practice born,
> and practice ends in fashioning man's nature.**

We have now completed our definitions of moral strength, moral weakness, tenacity, and softness, and stated how these characteristics are related to one another.

11. Pleasure: Some Current Views

It is the role of a political philosopher to study pleasure and pain. For he is the supreme craftsman of the end to which we look when we call one particular thing bad and another good in the unqualified sense. Moreover, an examination of this subject is one of the tasks we must logically undertake, since we established that virtue and vice of character are concerned with pains and pleasures, and most people claim that happiness involves pleasure. That is why the word "blessed" is derived from the word "enjoy."

Now, (1) some people believe that no pleasure is good, either in itself or incidentally, since the good and pleasure are not the same thing.*** (2) Others hold that, though some pleasures are good, most of them are bad.† (3) Then there is a third view, according to which it is impossible for pleasure to be the highest good, even if all pleasures are good.‡

[The following arguments are advanced to support (1) the contention that] pleasure is not a good at all: *(a)* All pleasure is a process or coming-to-be leading to the natural state [of the subject] and perceived [by the subject]; but no process is of the same order as its ends, e.g., the building process is not of the same order as a house. Further, *(b)* a self-controlled man avoids pleasures. Again, *(c)* a man of practical wisdom does not pursue the pleasant, but what is free from pain.§ Moreover, *(d)* pleasures are an obstacle to good sense: the greater the joy one feels, e.g., in sexual intercourse, the greater the obstacle; for no one is capable of rational insight while enjoying sexual rela-

25

30

35

1152ᵇ

5

10

15

---

*Anaxandrides (fl. 382–349 B.C.) migrated from his native Rhodes (or Colophon) to Athens, where he gained fame as a poet of the Middle Comedy.

**Euenus of Paros was a famous Sophist, who lived in the late fifth century B.C.

***This view seems to have been propounded by Speusippus, Plato's nephew and disciple, who succeeded him as head of the Academy from 347–339 B.C. A similar view had been espoused by Antisthenes (ca. 455–ca. 360 B.C.), the friend of Socrates and precursor of the Cynic School.

†This is probably a reference to the view stated by Plato in *Philebus* 13b.

‡No particular proponents of this view can be identified, but they are also discussed in Plato's *Philebus* 53c–55c.

§Arguments *(b)* and *(c)* had probably been used by Speusippus and before him perhaps by Antisthenes.

tions.* Also, *(e)* there is no art of pleasure; yet every good is the result of an art. Finally, *(f)* children and beasts pursue pleasures, whereas they do not know what is good.

20   [The arguments for the view (2) that] not all pleasures are good are: *(a)* Some pleasures are disgraceful and cause for reproach; and *(b)* some pleasures are harmful, for there are pleasant things that may cause disease.

[And the argument in favor of (3), the contention that] pleasure is not the highest good, is that it is not an end but a process or coming-to-be. These are roughly the views put forward.

12. The Views Discussed: (1) Is Pleasure a Good Thing?

25   But the following considerations will show that the arguments we have enumerated do not lead us to the conclusion that (1) pleasure is not a good, or (3) that it is not the highest good. In the first place, [to answer argument *(1a)* and (3),] we use the word "good" in two senses: a thing may be good in the unqualified sense, or "good" for a particular person. Hence the term has also two meanings when applied to natural states and characteristics [of persons], and consequently also when applied to their motions and processes. This means that motions and processes which are generally held to be bad
30   are partly bad without qualification, but not bad for a particular person, and even desirable for him; and partly not even desirable for a particular person except on occasion and for a short time, though they are not desirable in an unqualified sense. Others again are not even pleasures, but only appear to be, for example, all processes accompanied by pain and undergone for remedial purposes, such as the processes to which the sick are subjected.

Secondly, the good has two aspects: it is both an activity and a characteristic. Now, the processes which restore us to our natural characteristic condition are only in-
35   cidentally pleasant; but the activity which is at work when our appetites [want to see us restored] is the activity of that part of our characteristic condition and natural state which has been left unimpaired. For that matter, there are pleasures which do not in-
1153ª   volve pain and appetite (e.g., the activity of studying) and we experience them when there is nothing deficient in our natural state. [That processes of restoration are only incidentally pleasant] is shown by the fact that the pleasant things which give us joy while our natural state is being replenished are not the same as those which give us joy once it has been restored. Once restored, we feel joy at what is pleasant in the unqualified
5   sense, but while the replenishment goes on, we enjoy even its opposite: for instance, we enjoy sharp and bitter things, none of which are pleasant either by nature or in the unqualified sense. Consequently, the pleasures [derived from them, too, are not pleasant either by nature or in the unqualified sense], for the difference that exists between various pleasant things is the same as that which is found between the pleasures derived from them.

In the third place, there is no need to believe that there exists something better than pleasure which is different from it, just as, according to some, the end is better than the process which leads to it. For pleasures are not processes, nor do all pleasures in-
10   volve processes: they are activities and an end, and they result not from the process of development we undergo, but from the use we make of the powers we have. Nor do all pleasures have an end other than themselves; that is only true of the pleasures of those

*This argument may come from Archytas, a Pythagorean philosopher, mathematician, ruler of Tarentum, and friend of Plato, in the first half of the fourth century B.C.

who are being led to the perfection of their natural states. For that reason, it is not correct, either, to say that pleasure is a process perceived [by the subject]: one should rather call it an "activity of our characteristic condition as determined by our natural state,"   15
and instead of "perceived" we should call it "unobstructed." (There are some who believe pleasure to be process on the ground that it is good in the true sense of the word, for they think that activity is process, but it is, as a matter of fact, different.)

The argument (2*b*) that pleasures [are bad, because] some pleasant things may cause disease, is like arguing that wholesome things are bad, because some of them are bad for making money. Both pleasant and wholesome things are bad in the relative senses mentioned, but that does not make them bad in themselves: even studying is occasionally harmful to health.   20

Also, (1*d*) neither practical wisdom nor any characteristic is obstructed by the pleasure arising from it, but only by alien pleasures extraneous to it. The pleasures arising from study and learning will only intensify study and learning, [but they will never obstruct it].

The argument (1*e*) that no pleasure is the result of an art makes good sense. For art never produces any activity at all: it produces the capacity for the activity. Nevertheless, the arts of perfume-making as well as of cooking are generally regarded as arts of pleasure.   25

The arguments (1*b*) that a self-controlled person avoids pleasure, (1*c*) that a man of practical wisdom pursues a life free from pain, and (1*f*) that children and beasts pursue pleasure, are all refuted by the same consideration. We have stated in what sense pleasures are good without qualification and in what sense not all pleasures are good.   30
These last mentioned are the pleasures which beasts and children pursue, while a man of practical wisdom wants to be free from the pain which they imply. They are the pleasures that involve appetite and pain, i.e., the bodily pleasures—for they are of this sort—and their excesses, in terms of which a self-indulgent man is self-indulgent. That is why a self-controlled man avoids these pleasures. But there are pleasures even for the   35
self-controlled.

13. The Views Discussed: (3) Is Pleasure the Highest Good?

To continue: there is general agreement that pain is bad and must be avoided. One   1153^b
kind of pain is bad in the unqualified sense, and another kind is bad, because in some way or other it obstructs us. Now, the opposite of a thing to be avoided—in the sense that it must be avoided and is bad—is good. It follows, therefore, necessarily that pleasure is a good. Speusippus tried to solve the question by saying that, just as the greater   5
is opposed both to the less and to the equal, [so pleasure is opposed both to pain and to the good]. But this solution does not come out correctly: surely, he would not say that pleasure is essentially a species of evil.

But (2*a*) even if some pleasures are bad, it does not mean that the highest good cannot be some sort of pleasure, just as the highest good may be some sort of knowledge, even though some kinds of knowledge are bad. Perhaps we must even draw the necessary conclusion that it is; for since each characteristic has its unobstructed activi-   10
ties, the activity of all characteristics or of one of them—depending on whether the former or the latter constitutes happiness—if unobstructed, must be the most desirable of all. And this activity is pleasure. Therefore, the highest good is some sort of pleasure, despite the fact that most pleasures are bad and, if you like, bad in the unqualified sense of the word. It is for this reason that everyone thinks that the happy life is a pleasant life,

15   and links pleasure with happiness. And it makes good sense this way: for no activity is complete and perfect as long as it is obstructed, and happiness is a complete and perfect thing. This is why a happy man also needs the goods of the body, external goods, and the goods of fortune, in order not to be obstructed by their absence.

But those who assert* that a man is happy even on the rack and even when great
20   misfortunes befall him, provided that he is good, are talking nonsense, whether they know it or not. Since happiness also needs fortune, some people regard good fortune as identical with happiness. But that is not true, for even good fortune, if excessive, can be an obstruction; perhaps we are, in that case, no longer justified in calling it "good fortune," for its definition is determined by its relation to happiness.

25   Also, the fact that all beasts and all men pursue pleasure is some indication that it is, in a sense, the highest good:

> There is no talk that ever quite dies down,
> if spread by many men. . . .

But since no single nature and no single characteristic condition is, or is regarded, as the
30   best [for all], people do not all pursue the same pleasure, yet all pursue pleasure. Perhaps they do not even pursue the pleasure which they think or would say they pursue, but they all pursue the same [thing], pleasure. For everything has by nature something divine about it. But the bodily pleasures have arrogated the name "pleasure" unto themselves as their own private possession, because everyone tends to follow them and participates in
35   them more frequently than in any others. Accordingly, since these are the only pleasures with which they are familiar, people think they are the only ones that exist.

1154ª   It is also evident that if pleasure, i.e., the activity [of our faculties], is not good, it will be impossible for a happy man to live pleasantly. For to what purpose would he need pleasure, if it were not a good and if it is possible that a happy man's life is one of
5   pain? For if pain is neither good nor bad, pleasure is not, either: so why should he avoid it? Surely, the life of a morally good man is no pleasanter [than that of anyone else], if his activities are not more pleasant.

14. The Views Discussed: (2) Are Most Pleasures Bad?

The subject of the pleasures of the body demands the attention of the proponents of the view that, though some pleasures—for instance, the noble pleasures—are highly
10   desirable, the pleasures of the body—that is, the pleasures which are the concern of the self-indulgent man—are not. If that is true, why then are the pains opposed to them bad? For bad has good as its opposite. Is it that the necessary pleasures are good in the sense in which anything not bad is good? Or are they good up to a certain point? For all characteristics and motions which cannot have an excess of good cannot have an excess
15   of pleasure, either; but those which can have an excess of good can also have an excess of pleasure. Now, excess is possible in the case of the goods of the body, and it is the pursuit of excess, but not the pursuit of necessary pleasures, that makes a man bad. For all men get some kind of enjoyment from good food, wine, and sexual relations, but not everyone enjoys these things in the proper way. The reverse is true of pain: a bad person does not avoid an excess of it, but he avoids it altogether. For the opposite of an excess
20   is pain only for the man who pursues the excess.

*The Cynics are probably meant.

It is our task not only to say what is true, but also to state what causes error, since that helps carry conviction. For when we can give a reasoned explanation why something which appears to be true is, in fact, not true, it makes us give greater credence to what is true. Accordingly, we must now explain why the pleasures of the body appear to be more desirable.   25

The first reason, then, is that pleasure drives out pain. When men experience an excess of pain, they pursue excessive pleasure and bodily pleasure in general, in the belief that it will remedy the pain. These remedial [pleasures] become very intense—and that is the very reason why they are pursued—because they are experienced in contrast   30 with their opposite.

As a matter of fact, these two reasons which we have stated also explain why pleasure is not regarded as having any moral value: some pleasures are the actions that spring from a bad natural state—either congenitally bad, as in the case of a beast, or bad by habit, as in the case of a bad man—while other pleasures are remedial and indicate a deficient natural state, and to be in one's natural state is better than to be moving toward it. But since the remedial pleasures only arise in the process of reaching the perfected   1154^b state, they are morally good only incidentally.

The second reason is that the pleasures of the body are pursued because of their intensity by those incapable of enjoying other pleasures. Take, for example, those who induce themselves to be thirsty. There is no objection to this practice, if the pleasures are harmless; but if they are harmful, it is bad. For many people have nothing else to   5 give them joy, and because of their nature, it is painful for them to feel neither [pleasure nor pain]. Actually, animal nature is under a constant strain, as the students of natural science attest when they say that seeing and hearing are painful, but [we do not feel the pain because,] as they assert, we have become accustomed to it. Similarly, whereas the   10 growing process [we go through] in our youth puts us into the same [exhilarated] state as that of a drunken man, and [makes] youth the age of pleasure, excitable natures, on the other hand, always need remedial action: as a result of [the excess of black bile in their] constitutional blend, their bodies are exposed to constant gnawing sensations, and they are always in a state of vehement desire. Now, since pain is driven out by the pleasure opposed to it or by any strong pleasure at all, excitable people become self-   15 indulgent and bad.

Pleasures unattended by pain do not admit of excess. The objects of these pleasures are what is pleasant by nature and not what is incidentally pleasant. By "things incidentally pleasant" I mean those that act as remedies. For since it is through some action of that part of us which has remained sound that a cure is effected, the remedy is regarded as being pleasant. But [pleasant by nature it is not]: pleasant by nature are those things which produce the action of an unimpaired natural state.   20

There is no single object that continues to be pleasant forever, because our nature is not simple but contains another natural element, which makes us subject to decay. Consequently, whenever one element does something, it runs counter to the nature of the other; and whenever the two elements are in a state of equilibrium, the act performed seems neither painful nor pleasant. If there is a being with a simple nature, the   25 same action will always be the most pleasant to him. That is why the divinity always enjoys one single and simple pleasure: for there is not only an activity of motion but also an activity of immobility, and pleasure consists in rest rather than in motion. But "change in all things is pleasant," as the poet has it, because of some evil in us. For just as a man who changes easily is bad, so also is a nature that needs to change. The reason   30 is that such a nature is not simple and not [entirely] good.

This completes our discussion of moral strength and moral weakness, and of pleasure and pain. We have stated what each of them is and in what sense some of them are good and some bad. It now remains to talk about friendship.

*   *   *

BOOK X

*   *   *

6. Happiness and Activity

1176ª   Now that we have completed our discussion of the virtues, and of the different
30   kinds of friendship and pleasure, it remains to sketch an outline of happiness, since, as we assert, it is the end or goal of human [aspirations]. Our account will be more concise if we recapitulate what we have said so far.

We stated, then, that happiness is not a characteristic; if it were, a person who
35   passes his whole life in sleep, vegetating like a plant, or someone who experiences the greatest misfortunes could possess it. If, then, such a conclusion is unacceptable, we
1176ᵇ   must, in accordance with our earlier discussion, classify happiness as some sort of activity. Now, some activities are necessary and desirable only for the sake of something else, while others are desirable in themselves. Obviously, happiness must be classed as an activity desirable in itself and not for the sake of something else. For happiness lacks
5   nothing and is self-sufficient. Activities desirable in themselves are those from which we seek to derive nothing beyond the actual exercise of the activity. Actions in conformity with virtue evidently constitute such activities; for to perform noble and good deeds is something desirable for its own sake.

Pleasant amusements, too, [are desirable for their own sake]. We do not choose
10   them for the sake of something else, since they lead to harm rather than good when we become neglectful of our bodies and our property. But most of those who are considered happy find an escape in pastimes of this sort, and this is why people who are well versed in such pastimes find favor at the courts of tyrants; they make themselves pleasant by providing what the tyrants are after, and what they want is amusement. Accordingly,
15   such amusements are regarded as being conducive to happiness, because men who are in positions of power devote their leisure to them. But perhaps such persons cannot be [regarded as] evidence. For virtue and intelligence, which are the sources of morally good activities, do not consist in wielding power. Also, if these men, who have never
20   tasted pure and generous pleasure, find an escape in the pleasures of the body, this is no sufficient reason for thinking that such pleasures are in fact more desirable. For children, too, think that what they value is actually the best. It is, therefore, not surprising that as children apparently do not attach value to the same things as do adults, so bad men do not attach value to the same things as do good men. Accordingly, as we have
25   stated repeatedly, what is valuable and pleasant to a morally good man actually is valuable and pleasant. Each individual considers that activity most desirable which corresponds to his own proper characteristic condition, and a morally good man, of course, so considers activity in conformity with virtue.

Consequently, happiness does not consist in amusement. In fact, it would be strange if our end were amusement, and if we were to labor and suffer hardships all our

life long merely to amuse ourselves. For, one might say, we choose everything for the   30
sake of something else—except happiness; for happiness is an end. Obviously, it is
foolish and all too childish to exert serious efforts and toil for purposes of amusement.
Anacharsis* seems to be right when he advises to play in order to be serious; for amusement is a form of rest, and since we cannot work continuously we need rest. Thus rest is   35
not an end, for we take it for the sake of [further] activity. The happy life is regarded as   1177ᵃ
a life in conformity with virtue. It is a life which involves effort and is not spent in
amusement.

Moreover, we say that what is morally good is better than what is ridiculous and
brings amusement, and the better the organ or man—whichever may be involved in a
particular case—the greater the moral value of the activity. But the activity of the better   5
organ or the better man is in itself superior and more conducive to happiness.

Furthermore, any person at all, even a slave, can enjoy bodily pleasures no less
than the best of men. But no one would grant that a slave has a share in happiness any
more than that he lives a life of his own. For happiness does not consist in pastimes of
this sort, but in activities that conform with virtue, as we have stated earlier.   10

7. Happiness, Intelligence, and the Contemplative Life

Now, if happiness is activity in conformity with virtue, it is to be expected that it
should conform with the highest virtue, and that is the virtue of the best part of us.
Whether this is intelligence or something else which, it is thought, by its very nature
rules and guides us and which gives us our notions of what is noble and divine; whether
it is itself divine or the most divine thing in us; it is the activity of this part [when oper-   15
ating] in conformity with the excellence or virtue proper to it that will be complete happiness. That it is an activity concerned with theoretical knowledge or contemplation has
already been stated.

This would seem to be consistent with our earlier statements as well as the truth.
For this activity is not only the highest—for intelligence is the highest possession we   20
have in us, and the objects which are the concern of intelligence are the highest objects
of knowledge-but also the most continuous: we are able to study continuously more
easily than to perform any kind of action. Furthermore, we think of pleasure as a necessary ingredient in happiness. Now everyone agrees that of all the activities that conform
with virtue activity in conformity with theoretical wisdom is the most pleasant. At any
rate, it seems that [the pursuit of wisdom or] philosophy holds pleasures marvelous in   25
purity and certainty, and it is not surprising that time spent in knowledge is more pleasant than time spent in research. Moreover, what is usually called "self-sufficiency" will
be found in the highest degree in the activity which is concerned with theoretical
knowledge. Like a just man and any other virtuous man, a wise man requires the necessities of life; once these have been adequately provided, a just man still needs people to-   30
ward whom and in company with whom to act justly, and the same is true of a self-
controlled man, a courageous man, and all the rest. But a wise man is able to study even
by himself, and the wiser he is the more is he able to do it. Perhaps he could do it better
if he had colleagues to work with him, but he still is the most self-sufficient of all.
Again, study seems to be the only activity which is loved for its own sake. For while we   1177ᵇ

---

*Anacharsis, who is said to have lived early in the sixth century B.C., was a Scythian whose travels all
over the Greek world brought him a reputation for wisdom. He allegedly met Solon at Athens and was numbered in some ancient traditions among the Seven Wise Men.

derive a greater or a smaller advantage from practical pursuits beyond the action itself, from study we derive nothing beyond the activity of studying. Also, we regard happi-
5   ness as depending on leisure; for our purpose in being busy is to have leisure, and we wage war in order to have peace. Now, the practical virtues are activated in political and military pursuits, but the actions involved in these pursuits seem to be unleisurely. This is completely true of military pursuits, since no one chooses to wage war or foments
10   war for the sake of war; he would have to be utterly bloodthirsty if he were to make en-
emies of his friends simply in order to have battle and slaughter. But the activity of the statesman, too, has no leisure. It attempts to gain advantages beyond political action, advantages such as political power, prestige, or at least happiness for the statesman himself and his fellow citizens, and that is something other than political activity: after all,
15   the very fact that we investigate politics shows that it is not the same [as happiness]. Therefore, if we take as established (1) that political and military actions surpass all other actions that conform with virtue in nobility and grandeur; (2) that they are unleisurely, aim at an end, and are not chosen for their own sake; (3) that the activity of our intelligence, inasmuch as it is an activity concerned with theoretical knowledge, is
20   thought to be of greater value than the others, aims at no end beyond itself, and has a pleasure proper to itself—and pleasure increases activity; and (4) that the qualities of this activity evidently are self-sufficiency, leisure, as much freedom from fatigue as a human being can have, and whatever else falls to the lot of a supremely happy man; it follows that the activity of our intelligence constitutes the complete happiness of man,
25   provided that it encompasses a complete span of life; for nothing connected with happi-
ness must be incomplete.

However, such a life would be more than human. A man who would live it would do so not insofar as he is human, but because there is a divine element within him. This divine element is as far above our composite nature* as its activity is above the active exercise of the other, [i.e., practical,] kind of virtue. So if it is true that intelligence is di-
30   vine in comparison with man, then a life guided by intelligence is divine in comparison with human life. We must not follow those who advise us to have human thoughts, since we are [only] men, and mortal thoughts, as mortals should; on the contrary, we should try to become immortal as far as that is possible and do our utmost to live in accordance
1178ᵃ   with what is highest in us. For though this is a small portion [of our nature], it far sur-
passes everything else in power and value. One might even regard it as each man's true self, since it is the controlling and better part. It would, therefore, be strange if a man chose not to live his own life but someone else's.

Moreover, what we stated before will apply here, too: what is by nature proper to
5   each thing will be at once the best and the most pleasant for it. In other words, a life guided by intelligence is the best and most pleasant for man, inasmuch as intelligence, above all else, is man. Consequently, this kind of life is the happiest.

8. The Advantages of the Contemplative Life

A life guided by the other kind of virtue, [the practical,] is happy in a secondary sense, since its active exercise is confined to man. It is in our dealings with one another
10   that we perform just, courageous, and other virtuous acts, when we observe the proper kind of behavior toward each man in private transactions, in meeting his needs, in all

---

*Human beings, consisting of soul and body, i.e., of form and matter, are composite beings, whereas the divine, being all intelligence, is not.

manner of actions, and in our emotions, and all of these are, as we see, peculiarly human. Moreover, some moral acts seem to be determined by our bodily condition, and virtue or excellence of character seems in many ways closely related to the emotions. There is also a close mutual connection between practical wisdom and excellence of character, since the fundamental principles of practical wisdom are determined by the virtues of character, while practical wisdom determines the right standard for the moral virtues. The fact that these virtues are also bound up with the emotions indicates that they belong to our composite nature, and the virtues of our composite nature are human virtues; consequently, a life guided by these virtues and the happiness [that goes with it are likewise human]. The happiness of the intelligence, however, is quite separate [from that kind of happiness]. That is all we shall say about it here, for a more detailed treatment lies beyond the scope of our present task.

It also seems that such happiness has little need of external trimmings, or less need than moral virtue has. Even if we grant that both stand in equal need of the necessities of life, and even if the labors of a statesman are more concerned with the needs of our body and things of that sort—in that respect the difference between them may be small—yet, in what they need for the exercise of their activities, their difference will be great. A generous man will need money to perform generous acts, and a just man will need it to meet his obligations. For the mere wish to perform such acts is inscrutable, and even an unjust man can pretend that he wishes to act justly. And a courageous man will need strength if he is to accomplish an act that conforms with his virtue, and a man of self-control the possibility of indulgence. How else can he or any other virtuous man make manifest his excellence? Also, it is debatable whether the moral purpose or the action is the more decisive element in virtue, since virtue depends on both. It is clear of course that completeness depends on both. But many things are needed for the performance of actions, and the greater and nobler the actions the more is needed. But a man engaged in study has no need of any of these things, at least not for the active exercise of studying; in fact one might even go so far as to say that they are a hindrance to study. But insofar as he is human and lives in the society of his fellow men, he chooses to act as virtue demands, and accordingly, he will need externals for living as a human being.

A further indication that complete happiness consists in some kind of contemplative activity is this. We assume that the gods are in the highest degree blessed and happy. But what kind of actions are we to attribute to them? Acts of justice? Will they not look ridiculous making contracts with one another, returning deposits, and so forth? Perhaps acts of courage—withstanding terror and taking risks, because it is noble to do so? Or generous actions? But to whom will they give? It would be strange to think that they actually have currency or something of the sort. Acts of self-control? What would they be? Surely, it would be in poor taste to praise them for not having bad appetites. If we went through the whole list we would see that a concern with actions is petty and unworthy of the gods. Nevertheless, we all assume that the gods exist and, consequently, that they are active; for surely we do not assume them to be always asleep like Endymion.* Now, if we take away action from a living being, to say nothing of production, what is left except contemplation? Therefore, the activity of the divinity which surpasses all others in bliss must be a contemplative activity, and the human activity which is most closely akin to it is, therefore, most conducive to happiness.

This is further shown by the fact that no other living being has a share in happiness, since they all are completely denied this kind of activity. The gods enjoy a life

*Supposedly the most beautiful of men, Endymion was loved by the Moon, who cast him into a perpetual sleep that she might descend and embrace him each night.

blessed in its entirety; men enjoy it to the extent that they attain something resembling the divine activity; but none of the other living beings can be happy, because they have no share at all in contemplation or study. So happiness is coextensive with study, and the greater the opportunity for studying, the greater the happiness, not as an incidental effect but as inherent in study; for study is in itself worthy of honor. Consequently, happiness is some kind of study or contemplation.

But we shall also need external well-being, since we are only human. Our nature is not self-sufficient for engaging in study: our body must be healthy and we must have food and generally be cared for. Nevertheless, if it is not possible for a man to be supremely happy without external goods, we must not think that his needs will be great and many in order to be happy; for self-sufficiency and moral action do not consist in an excess [of possessions]. It is possible to perform noble actions even without being ruler of land and sea; a man's actions can be guided by virtue also if his means are moderate. That this is so can be clearly seen in the fact that private individuals evidently do not act less honorably but even more honorably than powerful rulers. It is enough to have moderate means at one's disposal, for the life of a man whose activity is guided by virtue will be happy.

Solon certainly gave a good description of a happy man, when he said that he is a man moderately supplied with external goods, who had performed what he, Solon, thought were the noblest actions, and who had lived with self-control. For it is possible to do what one should even with moderate possessions. Also Anaxagoras, it seems, did not assume that a happy man had to be rich and powerful. He said that he would not be surprised if a happy man would strike the common run of people as strange, since they judge by externals and perceive nothing but externals. So it seems that our account is in harmony with the opinion of the wise.

Now, though such considerations carry some conviction, in the field of moral action truth is judged by the actual facts of life, for it is in them that the decisive element lies. So we must examine the conclusions we have reached so far by applying them to the actual facts of life: if they are in harmony with the facts we must accept them, and if they clash we must assume that they are mere words.

A man whose activity is guided by intelligence, who cultivates his intelligence and keeps it in the best condition, seems to be most beloved by the gods. For if the gods have any concern for human affairs—and they seem to have—it is to be expected that they rejoice in what is best and most akin to them, and that is our intelligence; it is also to be expected that they requite with good those who most love and honor intelligence, as being men who care for what is dear to the gods and who act rightly and nobly. That a wise man, more than any other, has all these qualities is perfectly clear. Consequently, he is the most beloved by the gods, and as such he is, presumably, also the happiest. Therefore, we have here a further indication that a wise man attains a higher degree of happiness than anyone.

HELLENISTIC PHILOSOPHY

Following the death of Alexander the Great in 323 B.C., three of his generals, Ptolemy, Seleucus, and Antigonus, carved up the empire he had created. For the next three centuries, the descendants of these three men ruled the eastern Mediterranean world. By 30 B.C., with the Roman Emperor Octavian's defeat of Anthony and Cleopatra and the annexation of Egypt, the period of Greek rule (known as the "Hellenistic" Period from the word ⟨*hellen*⟩, (or "Greek") was over. Real power in the area had shifted westward to emerging Rome.

This shift from Greek to Roman authority did not happen without social and political turmoil, and the philosophies that developed during this period reflect that turmoil. The emphasis now was not on complete systems of thought, such as those proposed by Plato and Aristotle. In their place were theories focusing on the practical questions of the good life for individuals. In a world that seemed more and more chaotic and uncontrollable, philosophers began to seek personal salvation more than comprehensive theories. Even the Platonic Academy and the Aristotelian Lyceum, which continued for centuries, moved from the constructive doctrines of their founders to more narrowly defined critical issues.

Reviewing the development of Greek philosophy from Socrates to the Stoics and Epicureans, one is struck by the overwhelming concern in the later schools with peace of mind. There is, as a consequence, one quality that classical Greeks possessed preeminently and that Stoics and Epicureans preeminently lacked: enthusiasm.

The last great movement of Greek philosophy was Neoplatonism. The leader of this return to Platonic concepts, Plotinus (A.D. 204–270), did not lack enthusiasm, but he was, nevertheless, more remote from classical Greek attitudes than were the earlier Hellenistic philosophers. He extolled the spirit to the point of saying he was ashamed to have a body; his fervor was entirely mystical; and he longed, to cite his famous words, to attain "the flight of the Alone to the Alone." Thus he perfected the less classical tendencies of Plato's thought, merging those tendencies with Neopythagoreanism and with Oriental notions such as the emanations from the One.

In A.D. 529, Plato's Academy was closed by Emperor Justinian, bringing to an end a millennium of Greek philosophy.

*   *   *

For clear, concise introductions to the Hellenistic and Roman philosophers, see Frederick Copleston, "Post-Aristotelian Philosophy," in his *A History of Philosophy: Volume I, Greece & Rome, Part II* (Garden City, NY: Image Books, 1962), and D.W. Hamlyn, "Greek Philosophy after Aristotle," in D.J. O'Connor, ed., *A Critical History of Western Philosophy* (New York: The Free Press, 1964). Eduard Zeller, *The Stoics, Epicureans, and Sceptics,* translated by Oswald J. Reichel

Laocoön, second century B.C., by Hagesandros, Polydoros, and Athenodoros, all of Rhodes. The Trojan Prince Laocoön protested against bringing the Greeks' wooden horse into the city. According to one version of the legend, he was punished for his interference when Apollo sent two serpents to kill him and his sons. The Hellenistic philosophers sought relief from tortured emotions such as this work depicts. *(Hirmer Fotoarchiv)*

(New York: Russell and Russell, 1962); Émile Bréhier, *The Hellenistic and Roman Age,* translated by Wade Baskin (Chicago: University of Chicago Press, 1965); and A.A. Long, *Hellenistic Philosophy: Stoics, Epicureans, Sceptics* (New York: Scribners, 1974) are all solid histories of the period. A.A. Long and D.N. Sedley, eds., *The Hellenistic Philosophers,* two vols. (Cambridge: Cambridge University Press, 1987), provide source material and discussions, while Jacques Brunschwig, *Papers in Hellenistic Philosophy,* translated by Janet Lloyd (Cambridge: Cambridge University Press, 1994) gives a technical exposition of a number of important issues. For primary sources and helpful introductions, see Whitney J. Oates, *The Stoic and Epicurean Philosophers: The Complete Extant Writings of Epicurus, Epictetus, Lucretius, Marcus Aurelius* (New York: Random House, 1940).

EPICURUS
341–270 B.C.

Epicurus was born on the Greek island of Samos approximately seven years after Plato's death. At eighteen he went to Athens for a year, then joined his father in Colophon, a small city in Asia Minor. Epicurus studied the writings of the Pre-Socratic philosopher Democritus, and eventually set up his own school on the island of Lesbos. From there he moved to the Hellespont and, finally, to Athens in 307 B.C. As he moved from place to place, many of his students followed him. In Athens he established a community known as the "Garden," where he spent the rest of his life teaching and writing.

Epicurus' community welcomed people of all classes and of both sexes. The school required no fee from students, accepting what each individual was able and willing to pay. Epicurus himself was almost worshiped by his disciples, and members of his group had to swear an oath: "I will be faithful to Epicurus in accordance with whom I have made it my choice to live."* Among the later followers of Epicurus' thought, the Roman poet Lucretius (98–55 B.C.) considered him to be a god. Yet Epicurus was not overbearing or authoritarian. According to all accounts, he was kind and generous, treating his followers as friends, not subordinates. While dying in agony from a urinary obstruction, Epicurus wrote a letter that illustrates his gracious spirit. The extant portion includes these words to his friend Idomeneus: "I have a bulwark against all this pain from the joy in my soul at the memory of our conversations together."**

---

*Reported in J.V. Luce, *Introduction to Greek Philosophy* (New York: Thames and Hudson, 1992), p. 140.
**Ibid.

Epicurus wrote over three hundred volumes, but all that has survived are some fragments, three complete letters, and a short treatise summarizing his views. These surviving works provide an understanding of Epicurus' physics and ethics and give some sense of his psychology and theory of knowledge. Epicurus' first letter, *To Herodotus,* explains his atomistic theory. Like Democritus before him, Epicurus asserts that reality is composed of tiny "un-cut-ables" ⟨*atomos*⟩ that move within the "void." These atoms combine in different patterns to form the material objects of the observable world. But unlike Democritus, whose atomism is deterministic, Epicurus broaches the notion that atoms sometimes inexplicably "swerve." As atoms "fell downward" through the void, some of them swerved from their paths and collided with other atoms, setting off a chain reaction that eventually led to the world as we know it.

The second letter, *To Pythocles,* on astronomy and meteorology, is of questionable origin and adds little to our understanding of Epicurus' thought. But the third letter, *To Menoeceus,* together with the short work *Principle Doctrines* explains his central ethical theory. Epicurus declares that pleasure is the highest good, though some pleasures are unnatural and unnecessary. In contrast to the modern understanding of the word "epicurean," Epicurus opposed exotic meals and profuse consumption. Such indulgences never bring permanent pleasure and frequently lead to its opposite: pain. Instead Epicurus advocates enjoying only the "natural" pleasures—those most likely to lead to contentment and repose. Epicurus' ethical works are reprinted here, complete, in the Russel M. Geer translation.

*   *   *

The classic secondary work on Epicurus is Cyril Bailey, *The Greek Atomists and Epicurus* (Oxford: Clarendon Press, 1928). Norman Wentworth De Witt, *Epicurus and His Philosophy* (Minneapolis: University of Minnesota Press, 1954), provides an interesting interpretation—one which John M. Rist, *Epicurus: An Introduction* (Cambridge: Cambridge University Press, 1972), contests. A.E. Taylor, *Epicurus* (1911; reprinted New York: Books for Libraries Press, 1969); G.K. Stradach, *The Philosophy of Epicurus* (Evanston, IL: Northwestern University Press, 1963); and Diskin Clay, *Lucretius and Epicurus* (Ithaca, NY: Cornell University Press, 1983), give helpful overviews. A.J. Festugière, *Epicurus and His Gods,* translated by C.W. Chilton (1955; reprinted London: Russell, 1969), and James H. Nichols, Jr., *Epicurean Political Philosophy* (Ithaca, NY: Cornell University Press, 1976), deal with specific topics.

LETTER TO MENOECEUS

I. INTRODUCTION

Epicurus to Menoeceus, greeting.

Let no young man delay the study of philosophy, and let no old man become weary of it; for it is never too early nor too late to care for the well-being of the soul. The man who says that the season for this study has not yet come or is already past is like the man who says it is too early or too late for happiness. Therefore, both the young and the old should study philosophy, the former so that as he grows old he may still retain the happiness of youth in his pleasant memories of the past, the latter so that although he is old he may at the same time be young by virtue of his fearlessness of the future. We must therefore study the means of securing happiness, since if we have it we have everything, but if we lack it we do everything in order to gain it.

II. BASIC TEACHINGS

A. THE GODS

The gods exist; but it is impious to accept the common beliefs about them. They have no concern with men.

Practice and study without ceasing that which I was always teaching you, being assured that these are the first principles of the good life. After accepting god as the immortal and blessed being depicted by popular opinion, do not ascribe to him anything in addition that is alien to immortality or foreign to blessedness, but rather believe about him whatever can uphold his blessed immortality. The gods do indeed exist, for our perception of them is clear; but they are not such as the crowd imagines them to be, for most men do not retain the picture of the gods that they first receive. It is not the man who destroys the gods of popular belief who is impious, but he who describes the gods in the terms accepted by the many. For the opinions of the many about the gods are not perceptions but false suppositions. According to these popular suppositions, the gods send great evils to the wicked, great blessings to the righteous, for they, being always well disposed to their own virtues, approve those who are like themselves, regarding as foreign all that is different.*

*The ambiguous rendition of the last part of this sentence is intentional. "They" may be the gods, who approve men like themselves, or men, who approve gods.

Epicurus, *Letters, Principal Doctrines, and Vatican Sayings,* translated by Russel M. Geer (New York: Macmillan/Library of the Liberal Arts, 1964).

B. Death

Philosophy, showing that death is the end of all consciousness, relieves us of all fear of death. A life that is happy is better than one that is merely long.

Accustom yourself to the belief that death is of no concern to us, since all good and evil lie in sensation and sensation ends with death. Therefore the true belief that death is nothing to us makes a mortal life happy, not by adding to it an infinite time, but by taking away the desire for immortality. For there is no reason why the man who is thoroughly assured that there is nothing to fear in death should find anything to fear in life. So, too, he is foolish who says that he fears death, not because it will be painful when it comes, but because the anticipation of it is painful; for that which is no burden when it is present gives pain to no purpose when it is anticipated. Death, the most dreaded of evils, is therefore of no concern to us; for while we exist death is not present, and when death is present we no longer exist. It is therefore nothing either to the living or to the dead since it is not present to the living, and the dead no longer are.

But men in general sometimes flee death as the greatest of evils, sometimes long for it as a relief from the evils of life.

The wise man neither renounces life nor fears its end; for living does not offend him, nor does he suppose that not to live is in any way an evil. As he does not choose the food that is most in quantity but that which is most pleasant, so he does not seek the enjoyment of the longest life but of the happiest.

He who advises the young man to live well, the old man to die well, is foolish, not only because life is desirable, but also because the art of living well and the art of dying well are one. Yet much worse is he who says that it is well not to have been born, but once born, be swift to pass through Hades' gates.

If a man says this and really believes it, why does he not depart from life? Certainly the means are at hand for doing so if this really be his firm conviction. If he says it in mockery, he is regarded as a fool among those who do not accept his teaching.

Remember that the future is neither ours nor wholly not ours, so that we may neither count on it as sure to come nor abandon hope of it as certain not to be.

III. The Moral Theory

A. Pleasure as the Motive

The necessary desires are for health of body and peace of mind; if these are satisfied, that is enough for the happy life.

You must consider that of the desires some are natural, some are vain, and of those that are natural, some are necessary, others only natural. Of the necessary desires, some are necessary for happiness, some for the ease of the body, some for life itself. The man who has a perfect knowledge of this will know how to make his every choice or rejection tend toward gaining health of body and peace of mind, since this is the final end of the blessed life. For to gain this end, namely freedom from pain and fear, we do everything. When once this condition is reached, all the storm of the soul is stilled, since the creature need make no move in search of anything that is lacking, nor seek after anything else to make complete the welfare of the soul and the body. For we only feel the lack of pleasure when from its absence we suffer pain; but when we do not suffer pain, we no longer are in need of pleasure. For this reason we say that pleasure is the beginning and the end of the blessed life. We recognize pleasure as the first and natural good; starting from pleasure we accept or reject; and we return to this as we judge every good thing, trusting this feeling of pleasure as our guide.

B. PLEASURES AND PAINS

Pleasure is the greatest good; but some pleasures bring pain, and in choosing, we must consider this.

For the very reason that pleasure is the chief and the natural good, we do not choose every pleasure, but there are times when we pass by pleasures if they are outweighed by the hardships that follow; and many pains we think better than pleasures when a greater pleasure will come to us once we have undergone the long-continued pains. Every pleasure is a good since it has a nature akin to ours; nevertheless, not every pleasure is to be chosen. Just so, every pain is an evil, yet not every pain is of a nature to be avoided on all occasions. By measuring and by looking at advantages and disadvantages, it is proper to decide all these things; for under certain circumstances we treat the good as evil, and again, the evil as good.

C. SELF-SUFFICIENCY

The truly wise man is the one who can be happy with a little.

We regard self-sufficiency as a great good, not so that we may enjoy only a few things, but so that, if we do not have many, we may be satisfied with the few, being firmly persuaded that they take the greatest pleasure in luxury who regard it as least needed, and that everything that is natural is easily provided, while vain pleasures are hard to obtain. Indeed, simple sauces bring a pleasure equal to that of lavish banquets if once the pain due to need is removed; and bread and water give the greatest pleasure when one who is in need consumes them. To be accustomed to simple and plain living is conducive to health and makes a man ready for the necessary tasks of life. It also makes us more ready for the enjoyment of luxury if at intervals we chance to meet with it, and it renders us fearless against fortune.

D. TRUE PLEASURE

The truest happiness does not come from enjoyment of physical pleasures but from a simple life, free from anxiety, with the normal physical needs satisfied.

When we say that pleasure is the end, we do not mean the pleasure of the profligate or that which depends on physical enjoyment—as some think who do not understand our teachings, disagree with them, or give them an evil interpretation—but by pleasure we mean the state wherein the body is free from pain and the mind from anxiety. Neither continual drinking and dancing, nor sexual love, nor the enjoyment of fish and whatever else the luxurious table offers brings about the pleasant life; rather, it is produced by the reason which is sober, which examines the motive for every choice and rejection, and which drives away all those opinions through which the greatest tumult lays hold of the mind.

E. PRUDENCE

Prudence or practical wisdom should be our guide.
Of all this the beginning and the chief good is prudence. For this reason prudence is more precious than philosophy itself. All the other virtues spring from it. It teaches that it is not possible to live pleasantly without at the same time living prudently, nobly, and justly, nor to live prudently, nobly, and justly without living pleasantly; for the virtues have grown up in close union with the pleasant life, and the pleasant life cannot be separated from the virtues.

IV. CONCLUSION

A. PANEGYRIC ON THE PRUDENT MAN

Whom then do you believe to be superior to the prudent man: he who has reverent opinions about the gods, who is wholly without fear of death, who has discovered what is the highest good in life and understands that the highest point in what is good is easy to reach and hold and that the extreme of evil is limited either in time or in suffering, and who laughs at that which some have set up as the ruler of all things, Necessity? He thinks that the chief power of decision lies within us, although some things come about by necessity, some by chance, and some by our own wills; for he sees that necessity is irresponsible and chance uncertain, but that our actions are subject to no power. It is for this reason that our actions merit praise or blame. It would be better to accept the myth about the gods than to be a slave to the determinism of the physicists; for the myth hints at a hope for grace through honors paid to the gods, but the necessity of determinism is inescapable. Since the prudent man does not, as do many, regard chance as a god for the gods do nothing in disorderly fashion or as an unstable cause of all things, he believes that chance does not give man good and evil to make his life happy or miserable, but that it does provide opportunities for great good or evil. Finally, he thinks it better to meet misfortune while acting with reason than to happen upon good fortune while acting senselessly; for it is better that what has been well-planned in our actions should fail than that what has been ill-planned should gain success by chance.

B. FINAL WORDS TO MENOECEUS

Meditate on these and like precepts, by day and by night, alone or with a like-minded friend. Then never, either awake or asleep, will you be dismayed; but you will live like a god among men; for life amid immortal blessings is in no way like the life of a mere mortal.

PRINCIPAL DOCTRINES

I. That which is blessed and immortal is not troubled itself, nor does it cause trouble to another. As a result, it is not affected by anger or favor, for these belong to weakness.

II. Death is nothing to us; for what has been dissolved has no sensation, and what has no sensation is nothing to us.

III. The removal of all that causes pain marks the boundary of pleasure. Wherever pleasure is present and as long as it continues, there is neither suffering nor grieving nor both together.

IV. Continuous bodily suffering does not last long. Intense pain is very brief, and even pain that barely outweighs physical pleasure does not last many days. Long illnesses permit physical pleasures that are greater than the pain.

V. It is impossible to live pleasantly without living prudently, well, and justly, and to live prudently, well, and justly without living pleasantly. Even though a man live well and justly, it is not possible for him to live pleasantly if he lacks that from which stems the prudent life.

VI. Any device whatever by which one frees himself from the fear of others is a natural good.

VII. Some, thinking thus to make themselves safe from men, wished to become famous and renowned. They won a natural good if they made their lives secure; but if their lives were not secure, they did not have that for which, following the rule of nature, they first sought.

VIII. No pleasure is evil in itself; but the means by which certain pleasures are gained bring pains many times greater than the pleasures.

IX. If every pleasure were cumulative, and if this were the case both in time and in regard to the whole or the most important parts of our nature, then pleasures would not differ from each other.

X. If the things that produce the pleasures of the dissolute were able to drive away from their minds their fears about what is above them and about death and pain, and to teach them the limit of desires, we would have no reason to find fault with the dissolute; for they would fill themselves with pleasure from every source and would be free from pain and sorrow, which are evil.

XI. If our dread of the phenomena above us, our fear lest death concern us, and our inability to discern the limits of pains and desires were not vexatious to us, we would have no need of the natural sciences.

XII. It is not possible for one to rid himself of his fears about the most important things if he does not understand the nature of the universe but dreads some of the things he has learned in the myths. Therefore, it is not possible to gain unmixed happiness without natural science.

XIII. It is of no avail to prepare security against other men while things above us and beneath the earth and in the whole infinite universe in general are still dreaded.

XIV. When reasonable security from men has been attained, then the security that comes from peace of mind and withdrawal from the crowd is present, sufficient in strength and most unmixed in well-being.

Epicurus, *Letters, Principal Doctrines, and Vatican Sayings,* translated by Russel M. Geer (New York: Macmillan/Library of the Liberal Arts, 1964).

XV. Natural wealth is limited and easily obtained; the wealth defined by vain fancies is always beyond reach.

XVI. Fortune seldom troubles the wise man. Reason has controlled his greatest and most important affairs, controls them throughout his life, and will continue to control them.

XVII. The just man is least disturbed; the unjust man is filled with the greatest turmoil.

XVIII. When once the pain caused by need has been removed, bodily pleasure will not be increased in amount but only varied in quality. The mind attains its utmost pleasure in reflecting on the very things that used to cause the greatest mental fears and on things like them.

XIX. Time that is unlimited and time that is limited afford equal pleasure if one measures pleasure's extent by reason.

XX. The flesh believes that pleasure is limitless and that it requires unlimited time; but the mind, understanding the end and limit of the flesh and ridding itself of fears of the future, secures a complete life and has no longer any need for unlimited time. It does not, however, avoid pleasure; and when circumstances bring on the end of life, it does not depart as if it still lacked any portion of the good life.

XXI. The man who understands the limits of living knows that it is easy to obtain that which removes the pain caused by want and that which perfects the whole life. Therefore, he has no need of things that involve struggle.

XXII. It is necessary to take into account the real purpose of knowledge and all the evidence of that clear perception to which we refer our opinions. If we do not, all will be full of bad judgment and confusion.

XXIII. If you struggle against all your sensations, you will have no standard of comparison by which to measure even the sensations you judge false.

XXIV. If you reject any sensation, and if you fail to distinguish between conjecture based upon that which awaits confirmation and evidence given by the senses, by the feelings, and by the mental examinations of confirmed concepts, you will confuse the other sensations with unfounded conjecture and thus destroy the whole basis for judgment. If among all opinions you accept as equally valid both those that await confirmation and those that have been confirmed, you will not free yourself from error, since you will have preserved all the uncertainty about every judgment of what is true and what is not true.

XXV. If you do not at all times refer each of your actions to the natural end,* but fall short of this and turn aside to something else in choosing and avoiding, your deeds will not agree with your words.

XXVI. Those desires that do not bring pain if they are not satisfied are not necessary; and they are easily thrust aside whenever to satisfy them appears difficult or likely to cause injury.

XXVII. Of the things that wisdom prepares for insuring lifelong happiness, by far the greatest is the possession of friends.

XXVIII. The same wisdom that permits us to be confident that no evil is eternal or even of long duration also recognizes that in our limited state the security that can be most perfectly gained is that of friendship.

XXIX. Of the desires, some are natural and necessary; some are natural but not necessary; and others are neither natural nor necessary but arise from empty opinion.

---

*That is, to pleasure.

XXX. Among the bodily desires, those rest on empty opinion that are eagerly pursued although if unsatisfied they bring no pain. That they are not got rid of is because of man's empty opinion, not because of their own nature.

XXXI. Natural justice is a compact resulting from expediency by which men seek to prevent one man from injuring others and to protect him from being injured by them.

XXXII. There is no such thing as justice or injustice among those beasts that cannot make agreements not to injure or be injured. This is also true of those tribes that are unable or unwilling to make agreements not to injure or be injured.

XXXIII. There is no such thing as justice in the abstract; it is merely a compact between men in their various relations with each other, in whatever circumstances they may be, that they will neither injure nor be injured.

XXXIV. Injustice is not evil in itself, but only in the fear and apprehension that one will not escape those who have been set up to punish the offense.

XXXV. If a man has secretly violated any of the terms of the mutual compact not to injure or be injured, he cannot feel confident that he will be undetected in the future even if he has escaped ten thousand times in the past; for until his death it will remain uncertain whether he will escape.

XXXVI. In general, justice is the same for all, a thing found useful by men in their relations with each other; but it does not follow that it is the same for all in each individual place and circumstance.

XXXVII. Among the things commonly held just, that which has proved itself useful in men's mutual relationships has the stamp of justice whether or not it be the same for all; if anyone makes a law and it does not prove useful in men's relationships with each other, it is no longer just in its essence. If, however, the law's usefulness in the matter of justice should change and it should meet men's expectations only for a short time, nonetheless during that short time it was just in the eyes of those who look simply at facts and do not confuse themselves with empty words.

XXXVIII. If, although no new circumstances have arisen, those things that were commonly held just in these matters did not in their actual effects correspond with that conception, they were not just. Whenever, as a result of new circumstances, the same things that had been regarded as just were no longer useful, they were just at the time when they were useful for the relations of citizens to each other; but afterwards, when they were no longer useful, they were no longer just.

XXXIX. He who has best controlled his lack of confidence in the face of external forces has, as far as possible, treated these externals as akin to himself or, when that was impossible, at least as not alien. Where he was not able to do even this, he kept to himself and avoided whatever it was best to avoid.

XL. Those who were best able to prepare security for themselves in relation to their neighbors* lived most pleasantly with their neighbors since they had the most perfect assurance; and enjoying the most complete intimacy, they did not lament the death of one who died before his time as if it were an occasion for sorrow.

*That is, those who were most self-sufficient and least dependent upon others.

EPICTETUS
ca. A.D. 50–ca. 130

Epictetus was born a slave in Hierapolis, a small town in Phrygia, Asia Minor (in present-day Turkey). His master was Epaphroditus, a member of Emperor Nero's personal staff in Rome. As was often done at that time, Epaphroditus saw to it that Epictetus had a good education, sending him to study with the Roman Stoic, Rufus. Founded by Zeno of Citium (336–265 B.C.), the Stoic school received its name from the columned "porch" ⟨stoa⟩, where Zeno had taught. The Stoics held that human life should be lived in harmony with nature, regardless of what life may bring: a reassuring doctrine for a slave such as Epictetus. But Epictetus did not remain a slave, gaining his freedom sometime after the death of Nero in A.D. 68. He began to teach until A.D. 89 or 93 when Emperor Domitian expelled all the philosophers from Rome. Domitian seems to have been especially angry with the Stoics for teaching that sovereignty comes from God and is for the benefit of the people. (Epictetus' reported claim that he had the same regard for the emperor as for his water-pot could not have helped.) Epictetus moved to Nicropolis in Epirus (northwestern Greece), where he established a thriving Stoic school and lived a simple life with few material goods. As an old man, he married so that he could adopt a child who otherwise would have been "exposed," that is, left to die. Those whom he taught described him as a humble, charitable man of great moral and religious devotion.

Epictetus never wrote anything, but one of his admiring students, Arrian, composed eight *Discourses* based on Epictetus' lectures, along with a summary of the great man's thought, the *Encheiridion* (or *Manual*). The *Encheiridion,* given here complete in the W.A. Oldfather translation, emphasizes the need for acceptance of what life brings. Epictetus points out that we cannot change events that happen to us, but we can change our attitude toward those events. To accomplish this and achieve the good life, we must go through three stages. First, we must order our desires and overcome our fears. Next, we must perform our duties—in whatever role fate has given us. Finally, we must think clearly and judge accurately. Only then will we be successful in ordering our desires and performing our duties; only then will we gain inner tranquillity.

Despite Emperor Domitian's condemnation, Stoicism had a special appeal to the Roman mind. In the austere moral emphasis of Epictetus, with his concomitant stress on self-control and superiority to pain, the Romans found an ideal for the wise man, whereas the Stoic description of natural law provided a basis for Roman law. One might say that the pillars of republican Rome tended to be Stoical, even if some Romans had never heard of Stoicism.

*   *   *

For general introductions to the Stoics, see E. Vernon Arnold, *Roman Stoicism* (1911; reprinted New York: Humanities Press, 1958); L. Edelstein, *The Meaning of Stoicism* (Cambridge, MA: Harvard University Press, 1966); John M. Rist, *Stoic Philosophy* (Cambridge: Cambridge University Press, 1969); F.H. Sandbach, *The Stoics* (New York: Norton, 1975); and Margaret E. Reeser, *The Nature of Man in Early Stoic Philosophy* (New York: St. Martin's Press, 1989). For comparisons between Stoicism and other Hellenistic schools, see R.M. Wenley, *Stoicism and Its Influence* (1924; reprinted New York: Cooper Square, 1963); Edwin R. Bevan, *Stoics and Sceptics* (Oxford: Clarendon Press, 1913); and R.D. Hicks, *Stoic and Epicurean* (1910; reprinted New York: Russell & Russell, 1962). For collections of essays, consult A.A. Long, ed., *Problems in Stoicism* (London: Athlone Press, 1971), and J.M. Rist, ed., *The Stoics* (Berkeley: University of California Press, 1978). For a volume specifically on Epictetus, see John Bonforte, *The Philosophy of Epictetus* (New York: Philosophical Library, 1955). Iason Xenakis, *Epictetus: Philosopher-Therapist* (The Hague, Netherlands: Martinus Nijhoff, 1969), makes an interesting application of Epictetus; whereas W.A. Oldfather, *Contributions Towards a Bibliography of Epictetus* (Urbana: University of Illinois Press, 1927; supplement, 1952), furnishes a bibliography. For a study of Epictetus' star pupil, see Philip A. Stadter, *Arrian of Nicomedia* (Chapel Hill: University of North Carolina Press, 1980).

ENCHEIRIDION (Manual)

1. Some things are under our control, while others are not under our control. Under our control are conception, choice, desire, aversion, and in a word, everything that is our own doing; not under our control are our body, our property, reputation, office and, in a

Reprinted by permission of the publishers and the Loeb Classical Library from Epictetus, *Encheiridion,* translated by W.A. Oldfather (Cambridge, MA: Harvard University Press, 1928). Copyright © 1928 by Harvard University Press.

word, everything that is not our own doing. Furthermore, the things under our control are by nature free, unhindered, and unimpeded; while the things not under our control are weak, servile, subject to hindrance, and not our own. Remember, therefore, that if what is naturally slavish you think to be free, and what is not your own to be your own, you will be hampered, will grieve, will be in turmoil, and will blame both gods and men; while if you think only what is your own to be your own, and what is not your own to be, as it really is, not your own, then no one will ever be able to exert compulsion upon you, no one will hinder you, you will blame no one, will find fault with no one, will do absolutely nothing against your will, you will have no personal enemy, no one will harm you, for neither is there any harm that can touch you.

With such high aims, therefore, remember that you must bestir yourself with no slight effort to lay hold of them, but you will have to give up some things entirely, and defer others for the time being. But if you wish for these things also, and at the same time for both office and wealth, it may be that you will not get even these latter, because you aim also at the former, and certainly you will fail to get the former, which alone bring freedom and happiness.

Make it, therefore, your study at the very outset to say to every harsh external impression, "You are an external impression and not at all what you appear to be." After that examine it and test it by these rules which you have, the first and most important of which is this: Whether the impression has to do with the things which are under our control, or with those which are not under our control; and, if it has to do with some one of the things not under our control, have ready to hand the answer, "It is nothing to me."

2. Remember that the promise of desire is the attainment of what you desire, that of aversion is not to fall into what is avoided, and that he who fails in his desire is unfortunate, while he who falls into what he would avoid experiences misfortune. If, then, you avoid only what is unnatural among those things which are under your control, you will fall into none of the things which you avoid; but if you try to avoid disease, or death, or poverty, you will experience misfortune. Withdraw, therefore, your aversion from all the matters that are not under our control, and transfer it to what is unnatural among those which are under our control. But for the time being remove utterly your desire; for if you desire some one of the things that are not under our control you are bound to be unfortunate; and, at the same time, not one of the things that are under our control, which it would be excellent for you to desire, is within your grasp. But employ only choice and refusal, and these too but lightly, and with reservations, and without straining.

3. With everything which entertains you, is useful, or of which you are fond, remember to say to yourself, beginning with the very least things, "What is its nature?" If you are fond of a jug, say, "I am fond of a jug"; for when it is broken you will not be disturbed. If you kiss your own child or wife, say to yourself that you are kissing a human being; for when it dies you will not be disturbed.

4. When you are on the point of putting your hand to some undertaking, remind yourself what the nature of that undertaking is. If you are going out of the house to bathe, put before your mind what happens at a public bath—those who splash you with water, those who jostle against you, those who vilify you and rob you. And thus you will set about your undertaking more securely if at the outset you say to yourself, "I want to take a bath, and, at the same time, to keep my moral purpose in harmony with nature." And so do in every undertaking. For thus, if anything happens to hinder you in your bathing, you will be ready to say, "Oh, well, this was not the only thing that I wanted, but I wanted also to keep your moral purpose in harmony with nature; and I shall not so keep it if I am vexed at what is going on."

5. It is not the things themselves that disturb men, but their judgements about these things. For example, death is nothing dreadful, or else Socrates too would have thought so, but the judgement that death is dreadful, *this* is the dreadful thing. When, therefore, we are hindered, or disturbed, or grieved, let us never blame anyone but ourselves, that means, our own judgements. It is the part of an uneducated person to blame others where he himself fares ill; to blame himself is the part of one whose education has begun; to blame neither another nor his own self is the part of one whose education is already complete.

6. Be not elated at any excellence which is not your own. If the horse in his elation were to say, "I am beautiful," it could be endured; but when you say in your elation, "I have a beautiful horse," rest assured that you are elated at something good which belongs to a horse. What then, is your own? The use of external impressions. Therefore, when you are in harmony with nature in the use of external impressions, then be elated; for then it will be some good of your own at which you will be elated.

7. Just as on a voyage, when your ship has anchored, if you should go on shore to get fresh water, you may pick up a small shell-fish or little bulb on the way, but you have to keep your attention fixed on the ship, and turn about frequently for fear lest the captain should call; and if he calls, you must give up all these things, if you would escape being thrown on board all tied up like the sheep. So it is also in life: If there be given you, instead of a little bulb and a small shell-fish, a little wife and child, there will be no objection to that; only, if the Captain calls, give up all these things and run to the ship, without even turning around to look back. And if you are an old man, never even get very far away from the ship, for fear that when He calls you may be missing.

8. Do not seek to have everything that happens happen as you wish, but wish for everything to happen as it actually does happen, and your life will be serene.

9. Disease is an impediment to the body, but not to the moral purpose, unless that consents. Lameness is an impediment to the leg, but not to the moral purpose. And say this to yourself at each thing that befalls you; for you will find the thing to be an impediment to something else, but not to yourself.

10. In the case of everything that befalls you, remember to turn to yourself and see what faculty you have to deal with it. If you see a handsome lad or woman, you will find continence the faculty to employ here; if hard labour is laid upon you, you will find endurance; in this fashion, your external impressions will not run away with you.

11. Never say about anything, "I have lost it," but only "I have given it back." Is your child dead? It has been given back. Is your wife dead? She has been given back. "I have had my farm taken away." Very well, this too has been given back. "Yet it was a rascal who took it away." But what concern is it of yours by whose instrumentality the Giver called for its return? So long as He gives it to you, take care of it as of a thing that is not your own, as travellers treat their inn.

12. If you wish to make progress, dismiss all reasoning of this sort: "If I neglect my affairs, I shall have nothing to live on." "If I do not punish my slave-boy he will turn out bad." For it is better to die of hunger, but in a state of freedom from grief and fear, than to live in plenty, but troubled in mind. And it is better for your slave-boy to be bad than for you to be unhappy. Begin, therefore, with the little things. Your paltry oil gets spilled, your miserable wine stolen; say to yourself, "This is the price paid for a calm spirit, this the price for peace of mind." Nothing is got without a price. And when you call your slave-boy, bear in mind that it is possible he may not heed you, and again, that even if he does heed, he may not do what you want done. But he is not in so happy a condition that your peace of mind depends upon him.

13. If you wish to make progress, then be content to appear senseless and foolish in externals, do not make it your wish to give the appearance of knowing anything; and if some people think you to be an important personage, distrust yourself. For be assured that it is no easy matter to keep your moral purpose in a state of conformity with nature, and, at the same time, to keep externals; but the man who devotes his attention to one of these two things must inevitably neglect the other.

14. If you make it your will that your children and your wife and your friends should live forever, you are silly; for you are making it your will that things not under your control should be under your control, and that what is not your own should be your own. In the same way, too, if you make it your will that your slave-boy be free from faults, you are a fool; for you are making it your will that vice be not vice, but something else. If, however, it is your will not to fail in what you desire, this is in your power. Wherefore, exercise yourself in that which is in your power. Each man's master is the person who has the authority over what the man wishes or does not wish, so as to secure it, or take it away. Whoever, therefore, wants to be free, let him neither wish for anything, nor avoid anything, that is under the control of others; or else he is necessarily a slave.

15. Remember that you ought to behave in life as you would at a banquet. As something is being passed around it comes to you; stretch out your hand and take a portion of it politely. It passes on; do not detain it. Or it has not come to you yet; do not project your desire to meet it, but wait until it comes in front of you. So act toward children, so toward a wife, so toward office, so toward wealth; and then some day you will be worthy of the banquets of the gods. But if you do not take these things even when they are set before you, but despise them, then you will not only share the banquet of the gods, but share also their rule. For it was by so doing that Diogenes and Heracleitus, and men like them, were deservedly divine and deservedly so called.

16. When you see someone weeping in sorrow, either because a child has gone on a journey, or because he has lost his property, beware that you be not carried away by the impression that the man is in the midst of external ills, but straightway keep before you this thought: "It is not what has happened that distresses this man (for it does not distress another), but his judgement about it." Do not, however, hesitate to sympathize with him so far as words go, and, if occasion offers, even to groan with him; but be careful not to groan also in the centre of your being.

17. Remember that you are an actor in a play, the character of which is determined by the Playwright: if He wishes the play to be short, it is short; if long, it is long; if He wishes you to play the part of a beggar, remember to act even this role adroitly; and so if your role be that of a cripple, an official, or a layman. For this is your business, to play admirably the role assigned you; but the selection of that rôle is Another's.

18. When a raven croaks inauspiciously, let not the external impression carry you away, but straightway draw a distinction in your own mind, and say, "None of these portents are for me, but either for my paltry body, or my paltry estate, or my paltry opinion, or my children, or my wife. But for me every portent is favourable, if I so wish; for whatever be the outcome, it is within my power to derive benefit from it."

19. You can be invincible if you never enter a contest in which victory is not under your control. Beware lest, when you see some person preferred to you in honour, or possessing great power, or otherwise enjoying high repute, you are ever carried away by the external impression, and deem him happy. For if the true nature of the good is one of the things that are under our control, there is no place for either envy or jealousy; and you yourself will not wish to be a praetor, or a senator, or a consul, but a free man. Now

Theater at Ephesus, Turkey, built A.D. 41–117. In theaters like this, with a capacity for more than eighteen thousand spectators, Greek playwrights presented all-day festivals of drama on every phase of Greek life from the tragic to the comic. It is not surprising that Epictetus uses the image of the play and the playwright to make his point. (*Gian Berto Vanni/Art Resource*)

there is but one way that leads to this, and that is to despise the things that are not under our control.

20. Bear in mind that it is not the man who reviles or strikes you that insults you, but it is your judgement that these men are insulting you. Therefore, when someone irritates you, be assured that it is your own opinion which has irritated you. And so make it your first endeavour not to be carried away by the external impression; for if once you gain time and delay, you will more easily become master of yourself.

21. Keep before your eyes day by day death and exile, and everything that seems terrible, but most of all death; and then you will never have any abject thought, nor will you yearn for anything beyond measure.

22. If you yearn for philosophy, prepare at once to be met with ridicule, to have many people jeer at you, and say, "Here he is again, turned philosopher all of a sudden," and "Where do you suppose he got that high brow?" But do you not put on a high brow, and do you so hold fast to the things which to you seem best, as a man who has been assigned by God to this post; and remember that if you abide by the same principles, those who formerly used to laugh at you will later come to admire you, but if you are worsted by them, you will get the laugh on yourself twice.

23. If it should ever happen to you that you turn to externals with a view to pleasing someone, rest assured that you have lost your plan of life. Be content, therefore, in everything to be a philosopher, and if you wish also to be taken for one, show to yourself that you are one, and you will be able to accomplish it.

24. Let not these reflections oppress you: "I shall live without honour, and be nobody anywhere." For, if lack of honour is an evil, you cannot be in evil through the instrumentality of some other person, any more than you can be in shame. It is not your business, is it, to get office, or to be invited to a dinner-party? Certainly not. How, then, can this be any longer a lack of honour? And how is it that you will be "nobody anywhere," when you ought to be somebody only in those things which are under your control, wherein you are privileged to be a man of the very greatest honour? But your friends will be without assistance? What do you mean by being "without assistance"? They will not have paltry coin from you, and you will not make them Roman citizens. Well, who told you that these are some of the matters under our control, and not rather things which others do? And who is able to give another what he does not himself have? "Get money, then," says some friend, "in order that we too may have it." If I can get money and at the same time keep myself self-respecting, and faithful, and high-minded, show me the way and I will get it. But if you require me to lose the good things that belong to me, in order that you may acquire the things that are not good, you can see for yourselves how unfair and inconsiderate you are. And which do you really prefer? Money, or a faithful and self-respecting friend? Help me, therefore, rather to this end, and do not require me to do those things which will make me lose these qualities.

"But my country," says he, "so far as lies in me, will be without assistance." Again I ask, what kind of assistance do you mean? It will not have loggias or baths of your providing. And what does that signify? For neither does it have shoes provided by the blacksmith, nor has it arms provided by the cobbler; but it is sufficient if each man fulfil his own proper function. And if you secured for it another faithful and self-respecting citizen, would you not be doing it any good? "Yes." Very well, and then you also would not be useless to it. "What place, then, shall I have in the State?" says he. Whatever place you can have, and at the same time maintain the man of fidelity and self-respect that is in you. But if, through your desire to help the State, you lose these qualities, of what good would you become to it, when in the end you turned out to be shameless and unfaithful?

25. Has someone been honoured above you at a dinner-party, or in salutation, or in being called in to give advice? Now if these matters are good, you ought to be happy that he got them; but if evil, be not distressed because you did not get them; and bear in mind that, if you do not act the same way that others do, with a view to getting things which are not under our control, you cannot be considered worthy to receive an equal share with others. Why, how is it possible for a person who does not haunt some man's door, to have equal shares with the man who does? For the man who does not do escort duty, with the man who does? For the man who does not praise, with the man who does? You will be unjust, therefore, and insatiable, if, while refusing to pay the price for which such things are bought, you want to obtain them for nothing. Well, what is the price for heads of lettuce? An obol, perhaps. If, then, somebody gives up his obol and gets his heads of lettuce, while you do not give your obol, and do not get them, do not imagine that you are worse off than the man who gets his lettuce. For as he has his heads of lettuce, so you have your obol which you have not given away.

Now it is the same way also in life. You have not been invited to somebody's dinner-party? Of course not; for you didn't give the host the price at which he sells his dinner. He sells it for praise; he sells it for personal attention. Give him the price, then, for which it is sold, if it is to your interest. But if you wish both not to give up the one and yet to get the other, you are insatiable and a simpleton. Have you, then, nothing in place of the dinner? Indeed you have; you have not had to praise the man you did not want to praise; you have not had to put up with the insolence of his doorkeepers.

26. What the will of nature is may be learned from a consideration of the points in which we do not differ from one another. For example, when some other person's slave-boy breaks his drinking-cup, you are instantly ready to say. "That's one of the things which happen." Rest assured, then, that when your own drinking-cup gets broken, you ought to behave in the same way that you do when the other man's cup is broken. Apply now the same principle to the matters of greater importance. Some other person's child or wife has died; no one but would say, "Such is the fate of man." Yet when a man's own child dies, immediately the cry is, "Alas! Woe is me!" But we ought to remember how we feel when we hear of the same misfortune befalling others.

27. Just as a mark is not set up in order to be missed, so neither does the nature of evil arise in the universe.

28. If someone handed over your body to any person who met you, you would be vexed; but that you hand over your mind to any person that comes along, so that, if he reviles you, it is disturbed and troubled—are you not ashamed of that?

29. In each separate thing that you do, consider the matters which come first and those which follow after, and only then approach the thing itself. Otherwise, at the start you will come to it enthusiastically, because you have never reflected upon any of the subsequent steps, but later on, when some difficulties appear, you will give up disgracefully. Do you wish to win an Olympic victory? So do I, by the gods! for it is a fine thing. But consider the matters which come before that, and those which follow after, and only when you have done that, put your hand to the task. You have to submit to discipline, follow a strict diet, give up sweet cakes, train under compulsion, at a fixed hour, in heat or in cold; you must not drink cold water, nor wine just whenever you feel like it; you must have turned yourself over to your trainer precisely as you would to a physician. Then when the contest comes on, you have to "dig in" beside your opponent, and sometimes dislocate your wrist, sprain your ankle, swallow quantities of sand, sometimes take a scourging, and along with all that get beaten. After you have considered all these points, go on into the games, if you still wish to do so; otherwise, you will be turning back like children. Sometimes they play wrestlers, again gladiators, again they blow trumpets, and then act a play. So you too are now an athlete, now a gladiator, then a rhetorician, then a philosopher, yet with your whole soul nothing; but like an ape you imitate whatever you see, and one thing after another strikes your fancy. For you have never gone out after anything with circumspection, nor after you had examined it all over, but you act haphazard and half-heartedly.

In the same way, when some people have seen a philosopher and have heard someone speaking like Euphrates (though, indeed, who can speak like him?), they wish to be philosophers themselves. Man, consider first the nature of the business, and then learn your own natural ability, if you are able to bear it. Do you wish to be a contender in the pentathlon, or a wrestler? Look to your arms, your thighs, see what your loins are like. For one man has a natural talent for one thing, another for another. Do you suppose that you can eat in the same fashion, drink in the same fashion, give way to impulse and to irritation, just as you do now? You must keep vigils, work hard, abandon your own people, be despised by a paltry slave, be laughed to scorn by those who meet you, in everything get the worst of it, in honour, in office, in court, in every paltry affair. Look these drawbacks over carefully, if you are willing at the price of these things to secure tranquillity, freedom, and calm. Otherwise, do not approach philosophy; don't act like a child—now a philosopher, later on a tax-gatherer, then a rhetorician, then a procurator of Caesar. These things do not go together. You must be one person, either good or bad; you must labour to improve either your own government principle or externals; you must work hard either on the inner man, or on things outside; that is, play either the rôle of a philosopher or else that of a layman.

30. Our duties are in general measured by our social relationships. He is a father, One is called upon to take care of him, to give way to him in all things, to submit when he reviles or strikes you. "But he is a bad father." Did nature, then, bring you into relationship with a *good* father? No, but simply with a father. "My brother does me wrong." Very well, then, maintain the relation that you have toward him; and do not consider what he is doing, but what you will have to do, if your moral purpose is to be in harmony with nature. For no one will harm you without your consent; you will have been harmed only when you think you are harmed. In this way, therefore, you will discover what duty to expect of your neighbour, your citizen, your commanding officer, if you acquire the habit of looking at your social relations with them.

31. In piety towards the gods, I would have you know, the chief element is this, to have right opinions about them—as existing and as administering the universe well and justly—and to have set yourself to obey them and to submit to everything that happens, and to follow it voluntarily, in the belief that it is being fulfilled by the highest intelligence. For if you act in this way, you will never blame the gods, nor find fault with them for neglecting you. But this result cannot be secured in any other way than by withdrawing your idea of the good and the evil from the things which are not under our control, and placing it in those which are under our control, and in those alone. Because, if you think any of those former things to be good or evil, then, when you fail to get what you want and fall into what you do not want, it is altogether inevitable that you will blame and hate those who are responsible for these results. For this is the nature of every living creature, to flee from and to turn aside from the things that appear harmful, and all that produces them, and to pursue after and to admire the things that are helpful, and all that produces them. Therefore, it is impossible for a man who thinks that he is being hurt to take pleasure in that which he thinks is hurting him, just as it is also impossible for him to take pleasure in the hurt itself. Hence it follows that even a father is reviled by a son when he does not give his child some share in the things that seem to be good; and this it was which made Polyneices and Eteocles enemies of one another, the thought that the royal power was a good thing. That is why the farmer reviles the gods, and so also the sailor, and the merchant, and those who have lost their wives and their children. For where a man's interest lies, there is also his piety. Wherefore, whoever is careful to exercise desire and aversion as he should, is at the same time careful also about piety. But it is always appropriate to make libations, and sacrifices, and to give of the firstfruits after the manner of our fathers, and to do all this with purity, and not in a slovenly or careless fashion, nor, indeed, in a miserly way, nor yet beyond our means.

32. When you have recourse to divination, remember that you do not know what the issue is going to be, but that you have come in order to find this out from the diviner; yet if you are indeed a philosopher, you know, when you arrive, what the nature of it is. For if it is one of the things which are not under our control, it is altogether necessary that what is going to take place is neither good nor evil. Do not, therefore, bring to the diviner desire or aversion, and do not approach him with trembling, but having first made up your mind that every issue is indifferent and nothing to you, but that, whatever it may be, it will be possible for you to turn it to good use, and that no one will prevent this. Go, then, with confidence to the gods as to counsellors; and after that, when some counsel has been given you, remember whom you have taken as counsellors, and whom you will be disregarding if you disobey. But go to divination as Socrates thought that men should go, that is, in cases where the whole inquiry has reference to the outcome,

and where neither from reason nor from any other technical art are means vouchsafed for discovering the matter in question. Hence, when it is your duty to share the danger of a friend or of your country, do not ask of the diviner whether you ought to share that danger. For if the diviner forewarns you that the omens of sacrifice have been unfavourable, it is clear that death is portended, or the injury of some member of your body, or exile; yet reason requires that even at this risk you are to stand by your friend, and share the danger with your country. Wherefore, give heed to the greater diviner, the Pythian Apollo, who cast out of his temple the man who had not helped his friend when he was being murdered.

33. Lay down for yourself, at the outset, a certain stamp and type of character for yourself, which you are to maintain whether you are by yourself or are meeting with people. And be silent for the most part, or else make only the most necessary remarks, and express these in few words. But rarely, and when occasion requires you to talk, talk, indeed, but about no ordinary topics. Do not talk about gladiators, or horse-races, or athletes, or things to eat or drink—topics that arise on all occasions; but above all, do not talk about people, either blaming, or praising, or comparing them. If, then, you can, by your own conversation bring over that of your companions to what is seemly. But if you happen to be left alone in the presence of aliens, keep silence.

Do not laugh much, nor at many things, nor boisterously.

Refuse, if you can, to take an oath at all, but if that is impossible, refuse as far as circumstances allow.

Avoid entertainments given by outsiders and by persons ignorant of philosophy; but if an appropriate occasion arises for you to attend, be on the alert to avoid lapsing into the behaviour of such laymen. For you may rest assured, that, if a man's companion be dirty, the person who keeps close company with him must of necessity get a share of his dirt, even though he himself happens to be clean.

In things that pertain to the body take only as much as your bare need requires, I mean such things as food, drink, clothing, shelter, and household slaves; but cut down everything which is for outward show or luxury.

In your sex-life preserve purity, as far as you can, before marriage, and, if you indulge, take only those privileges which are lawful. However, do not make yourself offensive, or censorious, to those who do indulge, and do not make frequent mention of the fact that you do not yourself indulge.

If someone brings you word that So-and-so is speaking ill of you, do not defend yourself against what has been said, but answer, "Yes, indeed, for he did not know the rest of the faults that attach to me; if he had, these would not have been the only ones he mentioned."

It is not necessary, for the most part, to go to the public shows. If, however, a suitable occasion ever arises, show that your principal concern is for none other than yourself, which means, wish only for that to happen which does happen, and for him only to win who does win; for so you will suffer no hindrance. But refrain utterly from shouting, or laughter at anyone, or great excitement. And after you have left, do not talk a great deal about what took place, except in so far as it contributes to your own improvement; for such behaviour indicates that the spectacle has aroused your admiration.

Do not go rashly or readily to people's public reading, but when you do go, maintain your own dignity and gravity, and at the same time be careful not to make yourself disagreeable.

When you are about to meet somebody, in particular when it is one of those men who are held in very high esteem, propose to yourself the question, "What would Socrates or Zeno have done under these circumstances?" and then you will not be at a loss to make proper use of the occasion. When you go to see one of those men who have great power, propose to yourself the thought that you will not find him at home, that you will be shut out, that the door will be slammed in your face, that he will pay no attention to you. And if, despite all this, it is your duty to go, go and take what comes, and never say to yourself, "It was not worth all the trouble." For this is characteristic of the layman, that is, a man who is vexed at externals.

In your conversation avoid making mention at great length and excessively of your own deeds or dangers, because it is not as pleasant for others to hear about your adventures, as it is for you to call to mind your own dangers.

Avoid also raising a laugh, for this is a kind of behaviour that slips easily into vulgarity, and at the same time is calculated to lessen the respect which your neighbours have of you. It is dangerous also to lapse into foul language. When, therefore, anything of the sort occurs, if the occasion be suitable, go even so far as to reprove the person who has made such a lapse; if, however, the occasion does not arise, at all events show by keeping silence, and blushing, and frowning, that you are displeased by what has been said.

34. When you get an external impression of some pleasure, guard yourself, as with impressions in general, against being carried away by it; nay, let the matter wait upon your leisure, and give yourself a little delay. Next think of the two periods of time, first, that in which you will enjoy your pleasure, and second, that in which, after the enjoyment is over, you will later repent and revile your own self; and set over against these two periods of time how much joy and self-satisfaction you will get if you refrain. However, if you feel that a suitable occasion has arisen to do the deed, be careful not to allow its enticement, and sweetness, and attractiveness to overcome you; but set over against all this the thought, how much better is the consciousness of having won a victory over it.

35. When you do a thing which you have made up your mind ought to be done, never try not to be seen doing it, even though most people are likely to think unfavourably about it. If, however, what you are doing is not right, avoid the deed itself altogether; but if it is right, why fear those who are going to rebuke you wrongly?

36. Just as the propositions, "It is day," and "it is night," are full of meaning when separated, but meaningless if united; so also, granted that for you to take the larger share at a dinner is good for your body, still, it is bad for the maintenance of the proper kind of social feeling. When, therefore, you are eating with another person, remember to regard, not merely the value for your body of what lies before you, but also to maintain your respect for your host.

37. If you undertake a role which is beyond your powers, you both disgrace yourself in that one, and at the same time neglect the role which you might have filled with success.

38. Just as you are careful, in walking about, not to step on a nail or to sprain your ankle, so be careful also not to hurt your governing principle. And if we observe this rule in every action, we shall be more secure in setting about it.

39. Each man's body is a measure for his property, just as the foot is a measure for his shoe. If, then, you abide by this principle, you will maintain the proper measure, but if you go beyond it, you cannot help but fall headlong over a precipice, as it were, in the end. So also in the case of your shoe; if once you go beyond the foot, you get first a gilded shoe, then a purple one, then an embroidered one. For once you go beyond the measure there is no limit.

40. Immediately after they are fourteen, women are called "ladies" by men. And so when they see that they have nothing else but only to be the bedfellows of men, they

begin to beautify themselves, and put all their hopes in that. It is worthwhile for us to take pains, therefore, to make them understand that they are honoured for nothing else but only for appearing modest and self-respecting.

41. It is a mark of an ungifted man to spend a great deal of time in what concerns his body, as in much exercise, much eating, much drinking, much evacuating of the bowels, much copulating. But these things are to be done in passing; and let your whole attention be devoted to the mind.

42. When someone treats you ill or speaks ill of you, remember that he acts or speaks thus because he thinks it is incumbent upon him. That being the case, it is impossible for him to follow what appears good to you, but what appears good to himself; whence it follows that, if he gets a wrong view of things, the man that suffers is the man that has been deceived. For if a person thinks a true composite judgement to be false, the composite judgement does not suffer, but the person who has been deceived. If, therefore, you start from this point of view, you will be gentle with the man who reviles you. For you should say on each occasion, "He thought that way about it."

43. Everything has two handles, by one of which it ought to be carried and by the other not. If your brother wrongs you, do not lay hold of the matter by the handle of the wrong that he is doing, because this is the handle by which the matter ought not to be carried; but rather by the other handle—that he is your brother, that you were brought up together, and then you will be laying hold of the matter by the handle by which it ought to be carried.

44. The following statements constitute a *non sequitur:* "I am richer than you are, therefore I am superior to you"; or, "I am more eloquent than you are, therefore I am superior to you." But the following conclusions are better: "I am richer than you are, therefore my property is superior to yours"; or, "I am more eloquent than you are, therefore my elocution is superior to yours." But *you* are neither property nor elocution.

45. Somebody is hasty about bathing; do not say that he bathes badly, but that he is hasty about bathing. Somebody drinks a good deal of wine; do not say that he drinks badly, but that he drinks a good deal. For until you have decided what judgement prompts him, how do you know that what he is doing is bad? And thus the final result will not be that you receive convincing sense-impressions of some things, but give your assent to others.

46. On no occasion call yourself a philosopher, and do not, for the most part, talk among laymen about your philosophic principles, but do what follows from your principles. For example, at a banquet do not say how people ought to eat, but eat as a man ought. For remember how Socrates had so completely eliminated the thought of ostentation, that people came to him when they wanted him to introduce them to philosophers, and he used to bring them along. So well did he submit to being overlooked. And if talk about some philosophic principle arises among laymen, keep silence for the most part for there is great danger that you will spew up immediately what you have not digested. So when a man tells you that you know nothing, and you, like Socrates, are not hurt, then rest assured that you are making a beginning with the business you have undertaken. For sheep, too, do not bring their fodder to the shepherds and show how much they have eaten, but they digest their food within them, and on the outside produce wool and milk. And so do you, therefore, make no display to the laymen of your philosophical principles, but let them see the results which come from these principles when digested.

47. When you have become adjusted to simple living in regard to your bodily wants, do not preen yourself about the accomplishment; and so likewise, if you are a water-drinker, do not on every occasion say that you are a water-drinker. And if ever

you want to train to develop physical endurance, do it by yourself and not for outsiders to behold; do not throw your arms around statues, but on occasion, when you are very thirsty, take cold water into your mouth, and then spit it out, without telling anybody.

48. This is the position and character of a layman: He never looks for either help or harm from himself, but only from externals. This is the position and character of the philosopher: He looks for all his help or harm from himself.

Signs of one who is making progress are: He censures no one, praises no one, blames no one, finds fault with no one, says nothing about himself as though he were somebody or knew something. When he is hampered or prevented, he blames himself. And if anyone compliments him, he smiles to himself at the person complimenting; while if anyone censures him, he makes no defence. He goes about like an invalid, being careful not to disturb, before it has grown firm, any part which is getting well. He has put away from himself his every desire, and has transferred his aversion to those things only, of what is under our control, which are contrary to nature. He exercises no pronounced choice in regard to anything. If he gives the appearance of being foolish or ignorant he does not care. In a word, he keeps guard against himself as though he were his own enemy lying in wait.

49. When a person gives himself airs because he can understand and interpret the books of Chrysippus, say to yourself, "If Chrysippus had not written obscurely, this man would have nothing about which to give himself airs."

But what is it I want? To learn nature and to follow her. I seek, therefore, someone to interpret her; and having heard that Chrysippus does so, I go to him. But I do not understand what he has written; I seek, therefore, the person who interprets Chrysippus. And down to this point there is nothing to justify pride. But when I find the interpreter, what remains is to put his precepts into practice; this is the only thing to be proud about. If, however, I admire the mere act of interpretation, what have I done but turned into a grammarian instead of a philosopher? The only difference, indeed, is that I interpret Chrysippus instead of Homer. Far from being proud, therefore, when somebody says to me, "Read me Chrysippus," I blush the rather, when I am unable to show him such deeds as match and harmonize with his words.

50. Whatever principles are set before you, stand fast by these like laws, feeling that it would be impiety for you to transgress them. But pay no attention to what somebody says about you, for this is, at length, not under your control.

51. How long will you still wait to think yourself worthy of the best things, and in nothing to transgress against the distinctions set up by the reason? You have received the philosophical principles which you ought to accept, and you have accepted them. What sort of a teacher, then, do you still wait for, that you should put off reforming yourself until he arrives? You are no longer a lad, but already a full-grown man. If you are now neglectful and easy-going, and always making one delay after another, and fixing first one day and then another, after which you will pay attention to yourself, then without realizing it you will make no progress, but, living and dying, will continue to be a layman throughout. Make up your mind, therefore, before it is too late, that the fitting thing for you to do is to live as a mature man who is making progress, and let everything which seems to you to be best be for you a law that must not be transgressed. And if you meet anything that is laborious, or sweet, or held in high repute, or in no repute, remember that now is the contest, and here before you are the Olympic games, and that it is impossible to delay any longer, and that it depends on a single day and a single action, whether progress is lost or saved. This is the way Socrates became what he was, by paying attention to nothing but his reason in everything that he encountered. And even if you are not yet a Socrates, still you ought to live as one who wishes to be a Socrates.

52. The first and most necessary division in philosophy is that which has to do with the application of the principles, as, for example, Do not lie. The second deals with the demonstrations, as, for example, How comes it that we ought not to lie? The third confirms and discriminates between these processes, as, for example, How does it come that this is a proof? For what is a proof, what is logical consequence, what contradiction, what truth, what falsehood? Therefore, the third division is necessary because of the second, and the second because of the first; while the most necessary of all, and the one in which we ought to rest, is the first. But we do the opposite; for we spend our time in the third division, and all our zeal is devoted to it, while we utterly neglect the first. Wherefore, we lie, indeed, but are ready with the arguments which prove that one ought not to lie.

53. Upon every occasion we ought to have the following thoughts at our command:

Lead thou me on, O Zeus, and Destiny,
To that goal long ago to me assigned.
I'll follow and not falter; if my will
Prove weak and craven, still I'll follow on.

–Cleanthes

Whoso has rightly with necessity complied, We count him wise, and skilled in things divine.

—Euripides

Well, O Crito, if so it is pleasing to the gods, so let it be.

—Socrates [*Crito,* 43D]

Anytus and Meletus can kill me, but they cannot hurt me.

—Socrates [*Apology,* 30C]

PLOTINUS
ca. A.D. 204–270

The last great school of Greek philosophy was Neoplatonism, and its most famous representative was Plotinus, born in Lykopolis, Egypt, in A.D. 204. Plotinus studied philosophy in Alexandria for eleven years, then joined an expedition to Persia to learn Persian and Indian wisdom. The trek proved unsuccessful and Plotinus moved to Rome. There he established a school of philosophy and a friendship with the emperor Gallenius. He stayed in Rome, teaching and writing, until the death of the emperor in 268. He then moved to the home of a friend where he died in 270, apparently from leprosy.

Developing Plato's dualistic understanding of reality, Plotinus taught that true reality lies "beyond" the physical world. This "reality beyond reality" has no limits and so cannot be described by words, since words invariably have limits. Plotinus, again borrowing from Plato, calls this ultra-reality the "Good" or the "One." The One/Good has no limits and is so supremely rich that it overflows or "emanates" to produce "Intellectual-Principle" or "Divine Mind" ⟨*nous*⟩. This Intellectual-Principle, in turn, overflows and "Divine-Soul" emanates from it. This process continues as Divine-Soul generates the material world. The lowest level of emanation, at the furthest extreme from the One/Good, is the utter formlessness and unreality of matter.

The goal of philosophy is to awaken individuals to the reality beyond the material world. But philosophy alone cannot take a person to the highest reality of the One. Only in mystical experience can an individual unite with the One. Plotinus himself claimed to have achieved such a union four times during his life.

Plotinus' writings were edited by one of his pupils, Porphyry, in the form of six groups of nine "Tractates" (treatises), published as the so-called *Enneads* (from the Greek word for "nine"). The selection given here, in the A.H. Armstrong translation, is Plotinus' Treatise on Beauty. This Tractate explains how the ascent of the soul to the One/Good is dependent on the beauty of soul, a godlike disposition.

Neoplatonism, with its emphasis on the otherworldly and the need for escape from the physical world, was the perfect philosophy for the chaotic final days of the Roman Empire. Plotinus' thought had a profound influence on Christian thought, especially on St. Augustine. Indeed, if St. Thomas is considered an Aristotelian, St. Augustine may be called a Neoplatonist. Many later thinkers, such as Eckhart, Nicolas of Cusa, Comenius, Boehme, Hegel, and Schelling, also had their philosophy molded by Neoplatonist doctrines.

*   *   *

Joseph Katz, *Plotinus' Search for the Good* (New York: King's Crown Press, 1950), and Émile Bréhier, *The Philosophy of Plotinus,* translated by Joseph Thomas (Chicago: University of Chicago Press, 1958) are good introductions to the study of Plotinus. For more advanced studies, see A.H. Armstrong, *The Architecture of the Intelligible Universe in the Philosophy of Plotinus* (Cambridge: Cambridge University Press, 1940), and J.M. Rist, *Plotinus: The Road to Reality* (Cambridge: Cambridge University Press, 1967). E.R. Dodds, *Select Passages Illustrating Neoplatonism,* translated by E.R. Dodds (New York: Macmillan, 1923), and Dominic J. O'Meara, *Plotinus: An Introduction to the Enneads* (Oxford: Oxford University Press, 1993), provide anthologies of the *Enneads* with discussions of important passages. For discussions of Neoplatonism as a school, see Thomas Whittaker, *The Neo-Platonists* (Cambridge: Cambridge University Press, 1918); Arthur O. Lovejoy's influential book, *The Great Chain of Being* (Cambridge, MA: Harvard University Press, 1936); R.T. Wallis, *Neoplatonism* (London: Duckworth, 1972); and the collection of essays, R. Baine Harris, ed., *The Structure of Being: A Neoplatonic Approach* (Norfolk, VA: International Society for Neoplatonic Studies, 1982).

ENNEADS (in part)

ENNEAD I, TRACTATE 6: BEAUTY

1. Beauty is mostly in sight, but it is to be found too in things we hear, in combinations of words and also in music, and in all music [not only in songs]; for tunes and rhythms are certainly beautiful: and for those who are advancing upwards from sense-perception ways of life and actions and characters and intellectual activities are beautiful, and

there is the beauty of virtue. If there is any beauty prior to these, this discussion will reveal it.

Very well then, what is it which makes us imagine that bodies are beautiful and attracts our hearing to sounds because of their beauty? And how are all the things which depend on soul beautiful? Are they all made beautiful by one and the same beauty or is there one beautifulness in bodies and a different one in other things? And what are they, or what is it? Some things, bodies for instance, are not beautiful from the nature of the objects themselves, but by participation, others are beauties themselves, like the nature of virtue. The same bodies appear sometimes beautiful, sometimes not beautiful, so that their being bodies is one thing, their being beautiful another. What is this principle, then, which is present in bodies? We ought to consider this first. What is it that attracts the gaze of those who look at something, and turns and draws them to it and makes them enjoy the sight? If we find this perhaps we can use it as a stepping-stone and get a sight of the rest. Nearly everyone says that it is good proportion of the parts to each other and to the whole, with the addition of good colour, which produces visible beauty, and that with the objects of sight and generally with everything else, being beautiful is being well-proportioned and measured. On this theory nothing single and simple but only a composite thing will have any beauty. It will be the whole which is beautiful, and the parts will not have the property of beauty by themselves, but will contribute to the beauty of the whole. But if the whole is beautiful the parts must be beautiful too; a beautiful whole can certainly not be composed of ugly parts; all the parts must have beauty. For these people, too, beautiful colours, and the light of the sun as well, since they are simple and do not derive their beautifulness from good proportion, will be excluded from beauty. And how do they think gold manages to be beautiful? And what makes lightning in the night and stars beautiful to see? And in sounds in the same way the simple will be banished, though often in a composition which is beautiful as a whole each separate sound is beautiful. And when, though the same good proportion is there all the time, the same face sometimes appears beautiful and sometimes does not, surely we must say that being beautiful is something else over and above good proportion, and good proportion is beautiful because of something else? But if when these people pass on to ways of life and beautiful expressions of thought they allege good proportion as the cause of beauty in these too, what can be meant by good proportion in beautiful ways of life or laws or studies or branches of knowledge? How can speculations be well-proportioned in relation to each other? If it is because they agree, there can be concord and agreement between bad ideas. The statement that "righteousness is a fine sort of silliness" agrees with and is in tune with the saying that "morality is stupidity"; the two fit perfectly. Again, every sort of virtue is a beauty of the soul, a truer beauty than those mentioned before; but how is virtue well-proportioned? Not like magnitudes or a number. We grant that the soul has several parts, but what is the formula for the composition or mixture in the soul of parts or speculations? And what [on this theory], will the beauty of the intellect alone by itself be?

2. So let us go back to the beginning and state what the primary beauty in bodies really is. It is something which we become aware of even at the first glance; the soul speaks of it as if it understood it, recognises and welcomes it and as it were adapts itself to it. But when it encounters the ugly it shrinks back and rejects it and turns away from it and is out of tune and alienated from it. Our explanation of this is that the soul, since it is by nature what it is and is related to the higher kind of reality in the realm of being, when it sees something akin to it or a trace of its kindred reality, is delighted and thrilled and returns to itself and remembers itself and its own possessions. What likeness, then, is there between beautiful things here and There? If there is a likeness, let us agree that

they are alike. But how are both the things in that world and the things in this beautiful? We maintain that the things in this world are beautiful by participating in form; for every shapeless thing which is naturally capable of receiving shape and form is ugly and outside the divine formative power as long as it has no share in formative power and form. This is absolute ugliness. But a thing is also ugly when it is not completely dominated by shape and formative power, since its matter has not submitted to be completely shaped according to the form. The form, then, approaches and composes that which is to come into being from many parts into a single ordered whole; it brings it into a completed unity and makes it one by agreement of its parts; for since it is one itself, that which is shaped by it must also be one as far as a thing can be which is composed of many parts. So beauty rests upon the material thing when it has been brought into unity, and gives itself to parts and wholes alike. When it comes upon something that is one and composed of like parts it gives the same gift to the whole; as sometimes art gives beauty to a whole house with its parts, and sometimes nature gives beauty to a single stone. So then the beautiful body comes into being by sharing in a formative power which comes from the divine forms.

3. The power ordained for the purpose recognises this, and there is nothing more effective for judging its own subject-matter, when the rest of the soul judges along with it; or perhaps the rest of the soul too pronounces the judgement by fitting the beautiful body to the form in itself and using this for judging beauty as we use a ruler for judging straightness. But how does the bodily agree with that which is before body? How does the architect declare the house outside beautiful by fitting it to the form of house within him? The reason is that the house outside, apart from the stones, is the inner form divided by the external mass of matter, without parts but appearing in many parts. When sense-perception, then, sees the form in bodies binding and mastering the nature opposed to it, which is shapeless, and shape riding gloriously upon other shapes, it gathers into one that which appears dispersed and brings it back and takes it in, now without parts, to the soul's interior and presents it to that which is within as something in tune with it and fitting it and dear to it; just as when a good man sees a trace of virtue in the young, which is in tune with his own inner truth, the sight delights him. And the simple beauty of colour comes about by shape and the mastery of the darkness in matter by the presence of light which is incorporeal and formative power and form. This is why fire itself is more beautiful than all other bodies, because it has the rank of form in relation to the other elements; it is above them in place and is the finest and subtlest of all bodies, being close to the incorporeal. It alone does not admit the others; but the others admit it for it warms them but is not cooled itself; it has colour primarily and all other things take the form of colour from it. So it shines and glitters as if it was a form. The inferior thing which becomes faint and dull by the fire's light, is not beautiful any more, as not participating in the whole form of colour. The melodies in sounds, too, the imperceptible ones which make the perceptible ones, make the soul conscious of beauty in the same way, showing the same thing in another medium. It is proper to sensible melodies to be measured by numbers, not according to any and every sort of formula but one which serves for the production of form so that it may dominate. So much, then, for the beauties in the realm of sense, images and shadows which, so to speak, sally out and come into matter and adorn it and excite us when they appear.

4. But about the beauties beyond, which it is no more the part of sense to see, but the soul sees them and speaks of them without instruments—we must go up to them and contemplate them and leave sense to stay down below. Just as in the case of the beauties of sense it is impossible for those who have not seen them or grasped their beauty—those born blind, for instance,—to speak about them, in the same way only those can

speak about the beauty of ways of life who have accepted the beauty of ways of life and kinds of knowledge and everything else of the sort; and people cannot speak about the splendour of virtue who have never even imagined how fair is the face of justice and moral order; "neither the evening nor the morning star are as fair." But there must be those who see this beauty by that with which the soul sees things of this sort, and when they see it they must be delighted and overwhelmed and excited much more than by those beauties we spoke of before, since now it is true beauty they are grasping. These experiences must occur whenever there is contact with any sort of beautiful thing, wonder and a shock of delight and longing and passion and a happy excitement. One can have these experiences by contact with invisible beauties, and souls do have them, practically all, but particularly those who are more passionately in love with the invisible, just as with bodies all see them, but all are not stung as sharply, but some, who are called lovers, are most of all.

5. Then we must ask the lovers of that which is outside sense "What do you feel about beautiful ways of life, as we call them, and beautiful habits and well-ordered characters and in general about virtuous activities and dispositions and the beauty of souls? What do you feel when you see your own inward beauty? How are you stirred to wild exultation, and long to be with yourselves, gathering your selves together away from your bodies?" For this is what true lovers feel. But what is it which makes them feel like this? Not shape or colour or any size, but soul, without colour itself and possessing a moral order without colour and possessing all the other light of the virtues; you feel like this when you see, in yourself or in someone else, greatness of soul, a righteous life, a pure morality, courage with its noble look, and dignity and modesty advancing in a fearless, calm and unperturbed disposition, and the godlike light of intellect shining upon all this. We love and delight in these qualities, but why do we call them beautiful? They exist and appear to us and he who sees them cannot possibly say anything else except that they are what really exists. What does "really exists" mean? That they exist as beauties. But the argument still requires us to explain why real beings make the soul lovable. What is this kind of glorifying light on all the virtues? Would you like to take the opposites, the uglinesses in soul, and contrast them with the beauties? Perhaps a consideration of what ugliness is and why it appears so will help us to find what we are looking for. Suppose, then, an ugly soul, dissolute and unjust, full of all lusts, and all disturbance, sunk in fears by its cowardice and jealousies by its pettiness, thinking mean and mortal thoughts as far as it thinks at all, altogether distorted, loving impure pleasures, living a life which consists of bodily sensations and finding delight in its ugliness. Shall we not say that its ugliness came to it as a "beauty" brought in from outside, injuring it and making it impure and "mixed with a great deal of evil," with its life and perceptions no longer pure, but by the admixture of evil living a dim life and diluted with a great deal of death, no longer seeing what a soul ought to see, no longer left in peace in itself because it keeps on being dragged out, and down, and to the dark? Impure, I think, and dragged in every direction towards the objects of sense, with a great deal of bodily stuff mixed into it, consorting much with matter and receiving a form other than its own it has changed by a mixture which makes it worse; just as if anyone gets into mud or filth he does not show any more the beauty which he had; what is seen is what he wiped off on himself from the mud and filth; his ugliness has come from an addition of alien matter, and his business, if he is to be beautiful again, is to wash and clean himself and so be again what he was before. So we shall be right in saying that the soul becomes ugly by mixture and dilution and inclination towards the body and matter. This is the soul's ugliness, not being pure and unmixed, like gold, but full of earthiness; if anyone takes the earthy stuff away the gold is left, and is beautiful, when

it is singled out from other things and is alone by itself. In the same way the soul too, when it is separated from the lusts which it has through the body with which it consorted too much, and freed from its other affections, purged of what it gets from being embodied, when it abides alone has put away all the ugliness which came from the other nature.

6. For, as was said in old times, self-control, and courage and every virtue, is a purification, and so is even wisdom itself. This is why the mysteries are right when they say riddlingly that the man who has not been purified will lie in mud when he goes to Hades, because the impure is fond of mud by reason of its badness; just as pigs, with their unclean bodies, like that sort of thing. For what can true self-control be except not keeping company with bodily pleasures, but avoiding them as impure and belonging to something impure? Courage, too, is not being afraid of death. And death is the separation of body and soul; and a man does not fear this if he welcomes the prospect of being alone. Again, greatness of soul is despising the things here and wisdom is an intellectual activity which turns away from the things below and leads the soul to those above. So the soul when it is purified becomes form and formative power, altogether bodiless and intellectual and entirely belonging to the divine, whence beauty springs and all that is akin to it. Soul, then, when it is raised to the level of intellect increases in beauty. Intellect and the things of intellect are its beauty, its own beauty and not another's, since only then [when it is perfectly conformed to intellect] is it truly soul. For this reason it is right to say that the soul's becoming something good and beautiful is its being made like to God, because from Him come beauty and all else which falls to the lot of real beings. Or rather, beautifulness is reality, and the other kind of thing is the ugly, and this same is the primary evil; so for God the qualities of goodness and beauty are the same, or the realities, the good and the beautiful. So we must follow the same line of enquiry to discover beauty and goodness, and ugliness and evil. And first we must posit beauty which is also the good; from this immediately comes intellect, which is beauty; and soul is given beauty by intellect. Everything else is beautiful by the shaping of soul, the beauties in actions and in ways of life. And soul makes beautiful the bodies which are spoken of as beautiful; for since it is a divine thing and a kind of part of beauty, it makes everything it grasps and masters beautiful, as far as they are capable of participation.

7. So we must ascend again to the good, which every soul desires. Anyone who has seen it knows what I mean when I say that it is beautiful. It is desired as good, and the desire for it is directed to good, and the attainment of it is for those who go up to the higher world and are converted and strip off what we put on in our descent; (just as for those who go up to the celebrations of sacred rites there are purifications, and strippings off of the clothes they wore before, and going up naked) until, passing in the ascent all that is alien to the God, one sees with one's self alone That alone, simple, single and pure, from which all depends and to which all look and are and live and think for it is the cause of life and mind and being. If anyone sees it, what passion will he feel, what longing in his desire to be united with it, what a shock of delight! The man who has not seen it may desire it as good, but he who has seen it glories in its beauty and is full of wonder and delight, enduring a shock which causes no hurt, loving with true passion and piercing longing; he laughs at all other loves and despises what he thought beautiful before; it is like the experience of those who have met appearances of gods or spirits and do not any more appreciate as they did the beauty of other bodies. "What then are we to think, if anyone contemplates the absolute beauty which exists pure by itself, uncontaminated by flesh or body, not in earth or heaven, that it may keep its purity?" All these other things are external additions and mixtures and not primary, but derived from it. If then one sees That which provides for all and remains by itself and gives to all but receives nothing into itself, if he abides in the contemplation of this kind of beauty and

rejoices in being made like it, how can he need any other beauty? For this, since it is beauty most of all, and primary beauty, makes its lovers beautiful and lovable. Here the greatest, the ultimate contest is set before our souls; all our toil and trouble is for this, not to be left without a share in the best of visions. The man who attains this is blessed in seeing that "blessed sight," and he who fails to attain it has failed utterly. A man has not failed if he fails to win beauty of colours or bodies, or power or office or kingship even, but if he fails to win this and only this. For this he should give up the attainment of kingship and of rule over all earth and sea and sky, if only by leaving and overlooking them he can turn to That and see.

8. But how shall we find the way? What method can we devise? How can one see the "inconceivable beauty" which stays within in the holy sanctuary and does not come out where the profane may see it? Let him who can, follow and come within, and leave outside the sight of his eyes and not turn back to the bodily splendours which he saw before. When he sees the beauty in bodies he must not run after them; we must know that they are images, traces, shadows, and hurry away to that which they image. For if a man runs to the image and wants to seize it as if it was the reality (like a beautiful reflection playing on the water, which some story somewhere, I think, said riddlingly a man wanted to catch and sank down into the stream and disappeared) then this man who clings to beautiful bodies and will not let them go, will, like the man in the story, but in soul, not in body, sink down into the dark depths where intellect has no delight, and stay blind in Hades, consorting with shadows there and here. This would be truer advice "Let us fly to our dear country." What then is our way of escape, and how are we to find it? We shall put out to sea, as Odysseus did, from the witch Circe or Calypso—as the poet says (I think with a hidden meaning)—and was not content to stay though he had delights of the eyes and lived among much beauty of sense. Our country from which we came is there, our Father is there. How shall we travel to it, where is our way of escape? We cannot get there on foot; for our feet only carry us everywhere in this world, from one country to another. You must not get ready a carriage, either, or a boat. Let all these things go, and do not look. Shut your eyes, and change to and wake another way of seeing, which everyone has but few use.

9. And what does this inner sight see? When it is just awakened it is not at all able to look at the brilliance before it. So that the soul must be trained, first of all to look at beautiful ways of life then at beautiful works, not those which the arts produce, but the works of men who have a name for goodness: then look at the souls of the people who produce the beautiful works. How then can you see the sort of beauty a good soul has? Go back into yourself and look; and if you do not yet see yourself beautiful, then, just as someone making a statue which has to be beautiful cuts away here and polishes there and makes one part smooth and clears another till he has given his statue a beautiful face, so you too must cut away excess and straighten the crooked and clear the dark and make it bright, and never stop "working on your statue" till the divine glory of virtue shines out on you, till you see "self-mastery enthroned upon its holy seat." If you have become this, and see it, and are at home with yourself in purity, with nothing hindering you from becoming in this way one, with no inward mixture of anything else, but wholly yourself, nothing but true light, not measured by dimensions, or bounded by shape into littleness, or expanded to size by unboundedness, but everywhere unmeasured, because greater than all measure and superior to all quantity; when you see that you have become this, then you have become sight; you can trust yourself then; you have already ascended and need no one to show you; concentrate your gaze and see. This alone is the eye that sees the great beauty. But if anyone comes to the sight bleary-eyed with wickedness, and unpurified, or weak and by his cowardice unable to look at what is very bright, he sees nothing, even if someone shows him what is there and

The School of Plato, Roman Mosaic, n.d. The Platonism of late antiquity (and the Middles Ages) was strongly influenced by Plotinus' modification of Plato's thought. (*Art Resource*)

possible to see. For one must come to the sight with a seeing power made akin and like to what is seen. No eye ever saw the sun without becoming sunlike, nor can a soul see beauty without becoming beautiful. You must become first all godlike and all beautiful if you intend to see God and beauty. First the soul will come in its ascent to intellect and there will know the Forms, all beautiful, and will affirm that these, the Ideas, are beauty; for all things are beautiful by these, by the products and essence of intellect. That which is beyond this we call the nature of the Good, which holds beauty as a screen before it. So in a loose and general way of speaking the Good is the primary beauty; but if one distinguishes the intelligibles [from the Good] one will say that the place of the Forms is the intelligible beauty, but the Good is That which is beyond, the "spring and origin" of beauty; or one will place the Good and the primal beauty on the same level. In any case, however, beauty is in the intelligible world.

CHRISTIANITY AND EARLY MEDIEVAL PHILOSOPHY

With only a few exceptions, European medieval thought was deeply imbued with Christian faith. As a result, it is not possible to understand medieval philosophy without at least a rudimentary understanding of Christian beliefs as presented in the Bible. Whether or not today's reader accepts the veracity of the claims put forth in these writings, most medievals did believe them, and that belief formed the foundation of their thought.

Beginning as a Jewish sect, Christianity continued to hold a number of beliefs in common with Judaism, including the following bedrock convictions: that the Old Testament is the revealed Word of God; that God is superior to and distinct from the created world; that the world was created by God at a specific point in time and that the world will come to an end; that God is personal and desires a special relationship with the human race; that humans have sinned against God's Law and are in need of God's forgiveness; that God requires righteousness as a means of a right relationship with God and others; and that God would send the Anointed One ("Messiah" in Hebrew, "Christ" in Greek) to set the people of God free.

But while Christians accepted the foundational beliefs of their Jewish ancestors, they differed on one key point: the identity of the Messiah. Whereas the Jews anticipated a spiritual-political figure to save them from the oppression of their enemies, Christians believed the Christ saved his people mainly from the spiritual oppressors of sin and death. Whereas the Jews believed the Messiah would scrupulously follow the Law, favoring and associating only with those who did likewise, the Christ of the Christians seemed to enjoy a remarkable freedom in relation to several of Israel's most venerable institutions—for example, Sabbath observances, the Temple, and ritual purity—while associating with the "lowlifes" of society. In short, whereas the Jewish people were (and still are) awaiting the Messiah, Christians believed (and still believe) Jesus of Nazareth *was* the Messiah.

Christians held that after his death by crucifixion, Jesus rose from the dead (the Resurrection) and taught his followers for forty days before ascending into heaven. As part of that teaching, Jesus promised that he would return again (the Second Coming ⟨*parousia*⟩) and that in the meantime his followers should spread the Christian faith to all the world.

The basic Christian belief was (and still is) that Jesus is the Son of God who became a human (the Incarnation) to atone for human sin (Redemption). The severed relationship between the Holy God and sinful humanity could be restored only through the sacrifice of one who was consummate righteousness. As the Word ⟨*Logos*⟩ of God made flesh, Jesus was that righteousness, made that sacrifice, and offered that restoration. Through faith, Christians accept this work done on their behalf (Justification) and receive the power of God's spirit to overcome sin and to serve others (Sanctification).

As Christians spread this message throughout the Roman Empire, they encountered resistance and persecution from both Jewish and Roman authorities. Many Jewish leaders objected to the Christian identification of Jesus with God; Roman authorities objected to the Christians' unwillingness to participate in emperor worship. Jews, too, had refused to participate in state religion and had often been persecuted. But Christians posed a unique threat to the Romans because, unlike the Jews, Christians proclaimed a supranational, supraracial, universal Lord—one very much in competition with Caesar. And Christians indefatigably sought converts to their universal Savior. Accordingly, they were persecuted on and off for three centuries.

Despite persecution, Christianity grew steadily in the centuries after Christ. There have been many explanations for that growth. The eighteenth-century historian Edward Gibbon* listed five causes: (1) Christianity's inheritance of the zeal of the Jews; (2) its connection to the philosophical doctrine of the immortality of the soul; (3) its claim of miracles; (4) the virtue of the early Christians; and (5) the organization of the church. Recent historians have pointed to the moral exclusivity of Christians, who demanded deep commitment; the definite and absolute character of Christian belief in an age of uncertainty; and the social dimensions of Christianity, which made it attractive to women, the poor, and the oppressed.**

As Christianity grew, doctrinal disputes inevitably arose. What was true Christianity? The answers tended to reflect deep convictions about two essential issues: the nature of the person and work of Jesus Christ and the relationship between faith and reason. What was the relationship between Jesus and God? Did Jesus have two distinct natures: one divine and one human? Or were they merged into a single unique nature? Moreover, if there is only one God, how could God also be three (Father, Son, and Holy Spirit)? And how could reason resolve issues of faith?

The first issue, the nature of Christ, was resolved at the Council of Nicea, convened and presided over by the first Christian emperor, Constantine, in A.D. 325.

---

*The Decline and Fall of the Roman Empire, Chapter xv.

**Of course, Christians have always claimed that none of these reasons is entirely adequate and that the most acceptable explanation for the rise of Christianity is a supernatural one.

The Council determined that the Son was exactly the same substance, "consubstantial" ⟨>*homoousios*⟩, and not just "of like substance" ⟨*homoiousios*⟩, with God the Father. (The single Greek letter "iota," ι, meant a great deal more than "one iota of difference" to the early church.) By the middle of the first millenium, the "Nicene Creed" was confessed by virtually all Christendom as the orthodox answer to the nature-of-Christ question. The Nicene Creed is still authoritative in Orthodox, Catholic, and Protestant churches.

Even though the Christological question was answered at Nicea, the question of the right relation between faith and reason continued to be argued throughout the medieval period. The early Christians had a simple faith in Jesus as Messiah (if they were Jewish Christians) and as Lord (if they were Gentile Christians), and they believed Jesus had lived, taught, died, and risen for them and all others. But almost immediately that simple faith encountered sophisticated Hellenistic thought throughout the Roman Empire. How much should Christian faith concede to the competence of philosophic reason? What was the relation between sacred writings (i.e., the Bible) and secular writings (e.g., philosophy)? In Acts 17, the Apostle Paul, the early Christian convert, used reason and quoted pagan poets to help him preach the gospel to Epicurean and Stoic philosophers in Athens. Yet later, in Colossians 2:8, he warned, "See to it that no one takes you captive through philosophy and empty deceit. . . ." Some early Church Fathers, such as Justin Martyr, used philosophy to help interpret Christian faith. Other Church Fathers, such as Tertullian, argued that reason could be inimical to faith: "What has Jerusalem to do with Athens?," he asked.

Some in the early church even claimed to have special esoteric knowledge not available to the rabble either in the sacred Scriptures or secular reason. They were known as "Gnostics," from the Greek word for knowledge ⟨*gnosis*⟩. These Gnostics emphasized the Platonic belief in the soul as good and the body as evil, and they sought to free the soul from the body by extreme ascetic practices. Some of the Gnostics taught that Jesus was not *really* a physical person (since the body is evil) and that the Old Testament God, Yahweh, who had created bodies and matter, was really the devil. Manicheaism, which rivaled Christianity in the third and fourth centuries, and for a time claimed Augustine as one of its believers, was based on Gnostic thought.

For the most part, the early medieval philosophers sought to resolve these theological issues within the broad framework of Platonic thought. Augustine (as either the last classical thinker or the first medieval one), Boethius, John Scotus Eriugena, and Anselm all used Neoplatonic concepts. In the early Middle Ages, most of Aristotle's writings were not available in the West. But in the East, Islamic philosophers, such as Ibn-Sīna and Ibn Rushd (or Averroës), and Jewish thinkers, such as Moses Maimonides, read and commented on a wide range of Aristotelian works. These works, along with the Muslim and Jewish commentaries on them, were reintroduced to Western Europe in the late Middle Ages and became the basis for the monumental work of Thomas Aquinas.

*   *   *

For discussions of the interaction between Christianity and its surrounding culture, see A.H. Armstrong and R.A. Markus, *Christian Faith and Greek Philosophy* (New York: Sheed and Ward, 1960); E.R. Dodds, *Pagan and Christian in an Age of Anxiety* (Cambridge: Cambridge University Press, 1965); Jaroslav

Pelikan, *The Christian Tradition: A History of the Development of Doctrine,* five vols. (Chicago: University of Chicago Press, 1971–1989); and R.A. Markus, *Christianity in the Roman World* (London: Thames & Hudson, 1974). For a discussion of Christian beliefs in their historical context, see J.N.D. Kelly, *Early Christian Doctrines,* 5th edition (London: Black, 1978). For basic introductions to traditional Christian beliefs, see John R.W. Stott, *Basic Christianity* (Downers Grove, IL: Inter-Varsity Press, 1971), and Hans Küng, *On Being a Christian,* translated by Edward Quinn (Garden City, NY: Doubleday, 1976).

Étienne Gilson's work, *History of Christian Philosophy in the Middle Ages* (New York: Random House, 1955), is the classic study of this time period, while Armand A. Maurer, *Medieval Philosophy* (New York: Random House, 1962); A.H. Armstrong, ed., *The Cambridge History of Later Greek and Early Medieval Philosophy* (Cambridge: Cambridge University Press, 1967); Michael Haren, *Medieval Thought: The Western Intellectual Tradition from Antiquity to the Thirteenth Century* (New York: St. Martin's Press, 1985); and B.B. Price, *Medieval Thought* (Oxford: Blackwell, 1992) are also useful. Hans-Werner Goetz, *Life in the Middle Ages,* translated by Albert Wimmer (Notre Dame, IN: Notre Dame University Press, 1994) provides historical context. For books specifically on the early medieval period, see Frederick Copleston, *A History of Philosophy, Volume II: Medieval Philosophy,* "Part I: Augustine to Bonaventure" (1950; reprinted Garden City, NY: Image Doubleday, 1962), and John Marenbon, *Early Medieval Philosophy (480–1150): An Introduction* (London: Routledge & Kegan Paul, 1983).

AUGUSTINE
A.D. 354–430

Aurelius Augustinus, Saint Augustine, was born of a Christian mother and a pagan father in Thagaste, a small town in what is now Algeria, North Africa. In many ways his family's mixed religious background represented the crumbling Roman Empire. Even though the influence of Christianity had grown since Emperor Constantine's edict of religious toleration in A.D. 313, there were still many rivals to his mother's faith.

As a boy, Augustine showed intellectual promise, and at seventeen he was sent to Carthage to study rhetoric. While there, Augustine found philosophy, rejected Christianity, took a mistress (who bore him a son), and began to investigate some of the religions of the time. He turned first to the followers of the prophet Mani— the Manichaeans. Mani was a third-century prophet who called himself "the apostle of God." He developed the ancient Persian teaching of Zoroaster (or Zarathushtra), which said that there are two great forces in the world, one good and one evil, and that neither can overcome the other. Living a life of sensual indulgence, Augustine took comfort from the idea that God could no more overcome evil in the universe than Augustine could in his own life.

In 375 Augustine returned to Thagaste to begin teaching rhetoric. When his mother, Monica (later sainted for her perseverance in prayer for her son), discovered that he had become a Manichaean, she expelled him from her house. Finding Thagaste boring, and his mother difficult, Augustine returned to Carthage. Over the next seven years, he grew disenchanted with Manichaeism. In 384 he left Carthage for teaching positions in Rome and finally Milan. In Milan Augustine encountered the writings of Plotinus and was converted to Neoplatonism. At the same time, he came into contact with a group of Christians led by the Bishop of

Milan, Ambrose. Under the influence of this group, Augustine was forced to reconsider his earlier rejection of Christianity, yet he was still unwilling to give up his life of self-gratification. In 386, while sitting in a friend's garden, he heard what he thought was a child's voice saying, "Pick up and read, pick up and read." Augustine later recounted what happened:

> So I hurried back to the place where . . . I had put down the book of the apostle when I got up. I seized it, opened it and in silence read the first passage on which my eyes lit: "Not in riots and drunken parties, not in eroticism and indecencies, not in strife and rivalry, but put on the Lord Jesus Christ and make no provision for the flesh in its lusts" (Rom. 13:13–14). I neither wished nor needed to read further. At once, with the last words of this sentence, it was as if a light of relief from all anxiety flooded into my heart. All the shadows of doubt were dispelled.*

The following year Augustine was baptized and returned to Africa to found a monastic community. Within two years he left the cloister, answering the church's call to priesthood. He served as a priest, and later as bishop, in the African town of Hippo for the rest of his life.

*   *   *

While at Hippo, Augustine wrote voluminously on a variety of theological and philosophical topics. Many of his works sought to define exactly what was and was not "Christian." His doctrinal works, such as *The Trinity,* established Christian essentials; whereas his polemical works, directed against "heresies" (positions unacceptable to the church), outlined what was not admissible. Augustine fought two major heresies: the Pelagian and the Donatist. The Pelagians held that sin had affected only Adam, that the will is free from sin, and that God's grace is given on the basis of human merit. The Donatists maintained that the sacraments were effective only when administered by a priest in a state of grace. Augustine argued passionately that both heresies put too much emphasis on human ability and not enough on God's grace.

Augustine's most famous work, the *Confessions,* invented the genre of introspective autobiography. The *Confessions* are full of both psychological and spiritual insight and so can be read as either devotional tract or philosophical essay. Books I through IX are Augustine's life story from the perspective of Christian conversion (detailed in Book VIII). As Augustine reflects on his life, he sees both his sinfulness and his intellectual aimlessness apart from God's grace. He also gives early glimpses of his mature epistemological position that God must illumine the mind in order for an individual to gain wisdom. Following his conversion, Augustine continued to seek understanding—though now firmly founded on faith. Books X–XII illustrate this "faith seeking understanding," as Augustine examines the questions of memory, time, and creation. Book XI, reprinted here complete, examines the nature of time and God's relation to it. Following a short devotional, Augustine shows how difficult it is to explain what God was doing "before" creation. Augustine proceeds to argue that God must be "outside" time in an eternal present. This view of God as timelessly eternal was developed by Boethius and is still influential today (see the suggested readings that follow). I

---

*Saint Augustine, *Confessions,* Book VIII, translated by Henry Chadwick (Oxford: Oxford University Press, 1991), p. 153.

am pleased to offer this selection in the outstanding new translation by Henry Chadwick.

Of Augustine's many other works, *The City of God* is by far the most influential. During the fourth century, Christianity had become the state religion of the Roman Empire; in 410 Rome fell to the Visigoths, and the eternal city was sacked for the first time. Naturally, many considered the sack of Rome a punishment for the betrayal of the old Roman religion. Augustine wrote *The City of God* to answer this charge and in so doing he developed yet another first: the first Western philosophy of history. Rather than a cycle of repeated events, Augustine described history as being linear—from creation to consummation and final judgment. As history moves from beginning to end, we can observe two cities: the City of God, consisting of those who love God; and the City of Man, those who love self rather than God.

Our first selection, from Book XII, explains the origin of evil and of the City of Man. Augustine begins by insisting, against the Manichaeans, that there is no being capable of opposing God: God is all-powerful. But, despite the presence of evil, God is also all-good and everything God created is good. Evil arises when a moral agent (angel or human) wills to love a lesser good (self) rather than the highest good (God). There is no evil "thing" to choose—there is only evil choosing. This leads to the question of what caused the will to choose evilly—a question Augustine says cannot be answered. Our second selection, from Book XIX, presents Augustine's treatise on peace: both earthly peace and the heavenly peace of the City of God. Both selections have been ably translated by Gerald G. Walsh, Daniel J. Honan, and Grace Monahan.

Augustine's impact has been enormous. Medieval Catholic philosophers, such as Anselm and Thomas Aquinas, as well as Protestant reformers, such as Luther and Calvin, wanted to be Augustine's heirs. Many contemporary Christian thinkers still appeal to Augustine's ideas, such as his defense of grace and his explanation of evil. But Augustine's influence has not been limited to theologians and philosophers of religion. Ludwig Wittgenstein began his *Philosophical Investigations* by examining Augustine's theory of language, and Bertrand Russell claimed Augustine's theory of time superior even to that of Kant. Echoes of Augustine's understanding of history as the unfolding of divine purpose can be heard in the writings of Hegel, whereas Augustine's idea that some kind of faith must precede fruitful understanding has been adapted by thinkers in such fields as the sociology of knowledge and philosophy of science.

*   *   *

The best general account of Augustine's philosophy remains Étienne Gilson, *The Christian Philosophy of Saint Augustine,* translated by L.E.M. Lynch (New York: Random House, 1960); Peter Brown, *Augustine of Hippo: A Biography* (Berkeley: University of California Press, 1967), provides an excellent biography. For brief introductions to Augustine's life and thought, see R.A. Markus, "Augustine," in D.J. O'Connor, ed., *A Critical History of Western Philosophy* (New York: The Free Press, 1964); and Henry Chadwick, *Augustine* (Oxford: Oxford University Press, 1986). For more extensive discussions of Augustine's thought, see Robert E. Meagher, *An Introduction to Augustine* (New York: New York University Press, 1978); and Christopher Kirwan, *Augustine* (London: Routledge, 1989). J.N. Figgis, *The Political Aspects of St. Augustine's City of God* (London: Longmans, Green, 1921); Ronald H. Nash, *The Light of the Mind: St. Augustine's Theory of Knowledge* (Lexington: University Press of Kentucky, 1969); and R.A. Markus, *Saeculum: History and Society in the Theology of St. Augustine* (Cambridge: Cambridge University Press, 1970), deal with the specialized topics indicated by their respective titles. For collections of essays, see M.C. D'Arcy et al., *Saint Augustine* (New York: Meridian, 1957), and R.A. Markus, ed., *Augustine: A Collection of Critical Essays* (Garden City, NY: Anchor, Doubleday, 1972).

CONFESSIONS (in part)

BOOK XI—TIME AND ETERNITY

i (1) Lord, eternity is yours, so you cannot be ignorant of what I tell you. Your vision of occurrences in time is not temporally conditioned. Why then do I set before you an ordered account of so many things? It is certainly not through me that you know them. But I am stirring up love for you in myself and in those who read this, so that we may all say "Great is the Lord and highly worthy to be praised" (Ps. 47:1). I have already affirmed this and will say it again: I tell my story for love of your love. We pray, and yet the truth says "Your Father knows what you need before you ask him" (Matt. 6:8). Therefore I lay bare my feelings towards you, by confessing to you my miseries and your mercies to us (Ps. 32:22), so that the deliverance you have begun may be complete. So I may cease to be wretched in myself and may find happiness in you. For you have called us to be "poor in spirit," meek, mournful, hungering and thirsting for righteousness, merciful, pure in heart, and peacemakers (Matt. 5:3–9).

See, the long story I have told to the best of my ability and will responds to your prior will that I should make confession to you, my Lord God. For "you are good, for your mercy is for ever" (Ps. 117:1).

ii (2) But when shall I be capable of proclaiming by "the tongue of my pen" (Ps. 44:2) all your exhortations and all your terrors and consolations and directives, by which you brought me to preach your word and dispense your sacrament to your people? And if I have the capacity to proclaim this in an ordered narrative, yet the drops of time are too precious to me. For a long time past I have been burning to meditate in your law (Ps. 38:4) and confess to you what I know of it and what lies beyond my powers—the first elements granted by your illumination and the remaining areas of darkness in my understanding—until weakness is swallowed up by strength. I am reluctant to expend on any other subject those hours which I find free of the necessities for restoring the body, of intellectual work, and of the service which we owe to people or that which we render to them when under no obligation.

(3) Lord my God, "hear my prayer" (Ps. 60:2), may your mercy attend to my longing which burns not for my personal advantage but desires to be of use in love to the brethren. You see in my heart that this is the case. Let me offer you in sacrifice the

Saint Augustine, *Confessions,* Book XI, translated by Henry Chadwick (Oxford: Oxford University Press, 1991). Reprinted by permission of Oxford University Press.

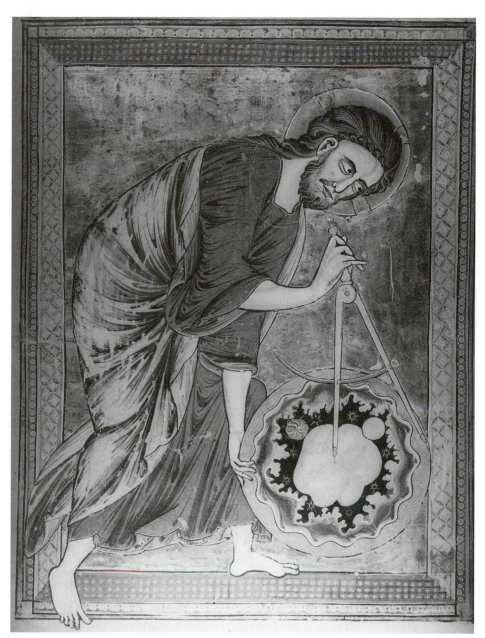

God in Act of Creation, from a thirteenth-century French Bible. In the *Confessions*, Augustine argues that God created the world *ex nihilo* (out of nothing) and that God is outside of time. (*The Bettmann Archive*)

service of my thinking and my tongue, and grant that which I am to offer, "for I am poor and needy" (Ps. 65:15; 85:1). You are "rich to all who call upon you" (Rom. 10:12). You have no cares but take care of us. Circumcise my lips (cf. Exod. 6:12), inwardly and outwardly, from all rashness and falsehood. May your scriptures be my pure delight, so that I am not deceived in them and do not lead others astray in interpreting them. "Lord, listen and have mercy" (Ps. 26:7; 85:3), Lord my God, light of the blind and strength of the weak—and constantly also light of those who can see and strength of the mighty: Listen to my soul and hear it crying from the depth. For if your ears are not present also in the depth, where shall we go? To whom shall we cry? "The day is yours and the night is yours" (Ps. 73:16). At your nod the moments fly by. From them grant us space for our meditations on the secret recesses of your law, and do not close the gate to us as we knock. It is not for nothing that by your will so many pages of scripture are opaque and obscure. These forests are not without deer which recover their strength in them and re-store themselves by walking and feeding, by resting and ruminating (Ps. 28:9). O Lord, bring me to perfection (Ps. 16:5) and reveal to me the meaning of these pages. See, your voice is my joy, your voice is better than a wealth of pleasures (Ps. 118:22). Grant what I love; for I love it, and that love was your gift. Do not desert your gifts, and do not de-spise your plant as it thirsts. Let me confess to you what I find in your books. "Let me hear the voice of praise" (Ps. 25:7) and drink you, and let me consider "wonderful things out of your law" (Ps. 118:18)—from the beginning in which you made heaven and earth until the perpetual reign with you in your heavenly city (Rev. 5:10; 21:2).

(4) "Lord have mercy upon me and listen to my desire" (Ps. 26:7). For I do not think my longing is concerned with earthly things, with gold and silver and precious stones, or with fine clothes or honours and positions of power or fleshly pleasures or even with the body's necessities in this life of our pilgrimage. They are all things added to us as we seek your kingdom and your righteousness (Matt. 6:33). My God, look upon the object of my desire (cf. Ps. 9:14). "The wicked have told me of delights, but they are not allowed by your law, Lord" (Ps. 118:85). See Father: look and see and give your ap-proval. May it please you that in the sight of your mercy (Ps. 18:15) I may find grace be-fore you, so that to me as I knock (Matt. 7:7) may be opened the hidden meaning of your words. I make my prayer through our Lord Jesus Christ your Son, "the man of your right hand, the Son of man whom you have strengthened" (Ps. 79:18) to be medi-ator between yourself and us. By him you sought us when we were not seeking you (Rom. 10:20). But you sought us that we should seek you, your Word by whom you made all things including myself, your only Son by whom you have called to adoption the people who believe (Gal. 4:5), myself among them. I make my prayer to you through him "who sits at your right hand and intercedes to you for us" (Rom. 8:34). "In him are hidden all the treasures of wisdom and knowledge" (Col. 2:3). For those trea-sures I search in your books. Moses wrote of him (John 5:46). He himself said this; this is the declaration of the Truth.

iii (5) May I hear and understand how in the beginning you made heaven and earth (Gen. 1:1). Moses wrote this. He wrote this and went his way, passing out of this world from you to you. He is not now before me, but if he were, I would clasp him and ask him and through you beg him to explain to me the creation. I would concentrate my bodily ears to hear the sounds breaking forth from his mouth. If he spoke Hebrew, he would in vain make an impact on my sense of hearing, for the sounds would not touch my mind at all. If he spoke Latin, I would know what he meant. Yet how would I know whether or not he was telling me the truth? If I did know this, I could not be sure of it from him. Within me, within the lodging of my thinking, there would speak a truth which is neither Hebrew nor Greek nor Latin nor any barbarian tongue and which uses neither mouth nor tongue as instruments and utters no audible syllables. It would say: "What he is saying is true." And I being forthwith assured would say with confidence to the man possessed by you. "What you say is true." But since I cannot question him, I ask you who filled him when he declared what is true; you my God I ask. "Spare my sins" (Job 14:16). You have granted to your servant to utter these things; grant also to me the power to understand them.

iv (6) See, heaven and earth exist, they cry aloud that they are made, for they suffer change and variation. But in anything which is not made and yet is, there is nothing which previously was not present. To be what once was not the case is to be subject to change and variation. They also cry aloud that they have not made themselves: "The manner of our existence shows that we are made. For before we came to be, we did not exist to be able to make ourselves." And the voice with which they speak is self-evidence. You, Lord, who are beautiful, made them for they are beautiful. You are good, for they are good. You are, for they are. Yet they are not beautiful or good or possessed of being in the sense that you their Maker are. In comparison with you they are deficient in beauty and goodness and being. Thanks to you, we know this; and yet our knowledge is ignorance in comparison with yours.

v (7) How did you make heaven and earth, and what machine did you use for so vast an operation? You were not like a craftsman who makes one physical object out of another by an act of personal choice in his mind, which has the power to impose the form which by an inner eye it can see within itself. This capacity it has only because you have so made it. He imposes form on what already exists and possesses being, such as earth or stone or wood or gold or any material of that sort. And these materials exist only because you had first made them. By your creation the craftsman has a body, a mind by which he commands its members, material out of which he makes something, a skill by which he masters his art and sees inwardly what he is making outwardly. From your creation come the bodily senses which he uses to translate his mental concept into the material objects he is making, and to report back to the mind what has been made, so that the mind within may deliberate with the truth presiding over it to consider whether the work has been well done. All these praise you, the creator of everything. But how do you make them? The way, God, in which you made heaven and earth was not that you made them either in heaven or on earth. Nor was it in air or in water, for these belong to heaven and earth. Nor did you make the universe within the framework of the universe. There was nowhere for it to be made before it was brought into existence. Nor did you have any tool in your hand to make heaven and earth. How could you obtain anything you had not made as a tool for making something? What is it for something to be unless it is because you are? Therefore you spoke and they were made, and by your word you made them (Ps. 32:9,6).

vi (8) But how did you speak? Surely not in the way a voice came out of the cloud saying, "This is my beloved Son" (Matt. 17:5). That voice is past and done with; it began and is ended. The syllables sounded and have passed away, the second after the first, the third after the second, and so on in order until, after all the others, the last one came, and after the last silence followed. Therefore it is clear and evident that the utterance came through the movement of some created thing, serving your eternal will but itself temporal. And these your words, made for temporal succession, were reported by the external ear to the judicious mind whose internal ear is disposed to hear your eternal word. But that mind would compare these words, sounding in time, with your eternal word in silence, and say: "It is very different, the difference is enormous. The sounds are far inferior to me, and have no being, because they are fleeting and transient. But the word of my God is superior to me and abides for ever" (Isa. 40:8). If therefore it was with words which sound and pass away that you said that heaven and earth should be made, and if this was how you made heaven and earth, then a created entity belonging to the physical realm existed prior to heaven and earth; and that utterance took time to deliver, and involved temporal changes. However, no physical entity existed before heaven and earth; at least if any such existed, you had made it without using a transient utterance, which could then be used as a basis for another transient utterance, declaring that heaven and earth be made. Whatever it might have been which became the basis for such an utterance, unless it was created by you, it could not exist. Therefore for the creation of a physical entity to become the basis for those words, what kind of word would you have used?

vii (9) You call us, therefore, to understand the Word, God who is with you God (John 1:1). That word is spoken eternally, and by it all things are uttered eternally. It is not the case that what was being said comes to an end, and something else is then said, so that everything is uttered in a succession with a conclusion, but everything is said in the simultaneity of eternity. Otherwise time and change would already exist, and there would not be a true eternity and true immortality. This I know, my God, and give thanks. I know and confess it to you, Lord, and everyone who is not ungrateful for assured truth knows it with me and blesses you. We know this, Lord, we know. A thing dies and comes into being inasmuch as it is not what it was and becomes what it was not. No element of your word yields place or succeeds to something else, since it is truly immortal and eternal. And so by the Word coeternal with yourself, you say all that you say in simultaneity and eternity, and whatever you say will come about does come about. You do not cause it to exist other than by speaking. Yet not all that you cause to exist by speaking is made in simultaneity and eternity.

viii (10) Why, I ask, Lord my God? In some degree I see it, but how to express it I do not know, unless to say that everything which begins to be and ceases to be begins and ends its existence at that moment when, in the eternal reason where nothing begins or ends, it is known that it is right for it to begin and end. This reason is your Word, which is also the Beginning in that it also speaks to us. Thus in the gospel the Word speaks through the flesh, and this sounded externally in human ears, so that it should be believed and sought inwardly, found in the eternal truth where the Master who alone is good (Matt. 19:16) teaches all his disciples. There, Lord, I hear your voice speaking to me, for one who teaches us speaks to us, but one who does not teach us, even though he may speak, does not speak to us. Who is our teacher except the reliable truth? Even when we are instructed through some mutable creature, we are led to reliable truth when we are learning truly by standing still and listening to him. We then "rejoice with joy because of the voice of the bridegroom" (John 3:29), and give ourselves to the source whence we have our being. And in this way he is the Beginning because, unless he were constant, there would be no fixed point to which we could return. But when we return from error, it is by knowing that we return. He teaches us so that we may know; for he is the Beginning, and he speaks to us.

ix (11) In this Beginning, God, you made heaven and earth, in your Word, in your Son, in your power, in your wisdom, in your truth speaking in a wonderful way and making in a wonderful way. Who can comprehend it? Who will give an account of it in words? What is the light which shines right through me and strikes my heart without hurting? It fills me with terror and burning love: with terror inasmuch as I am utterly other than it, with burning love in that I am akin to it. Wisdom, wisdom it is which shines right through me, cutting a path through the cloudiness which returns to cover me as I fall away under the darkness and the load of my punishments. For "my strength is weakened by poverty" (Ps. 30:11), so that I cannot maintain my goodness until you,

Lord, who "have become merciful to all my iniquities, also heal all my sicknesses." You will redeem my life from corruption and crown me with mercy and compassion, and satisfy my longing with good things, in that my youth will be renewed like an eagle's (Ps. 102:3–5). For "by hope we are saved," and we await your promises in patience (Rom. 8:24–5). Let the person who can hear you speaking within listen. Confident on the ground of your inspired utterance, I will cry out: "How magnificent are your works, Lord, you have made all things in wisdom" (Ps. 103:24). Wisdom is the beginning, and in that beginning you made heaven and earth.

x (12) See how full of old errors are those who say to us: "What was God doing before he made heaven and earth? If he was unoccupied," they say, "and doing nothing, why does he not always remain the same for ever, just as before creation he abstained from work? For if in God any new development took place and any new intention, so as to make a creation which he had never made before, how then can there be a true eternity in which a will, not there previously, comes into existence? For God's will is not a creature, but is prior to the created order, since nothing would be created unless the Creator's will preceded it. Therefore God's will belongs to his very substance. If in the substance of God anything has come into being which was not present before, that substance cannot truthfully be called eternal. But if it was God's everlasting will that the created order exist, why is not the creation also everlasting?"

xi (13) People who say this do not yet understand you, O wisdom of God, light of minds. They do not yet understand how things were made which came to be through you and in you. They attempt to taste eternity when their heart is still flitting about in the realm where things change and have a past and future; it is still "vain" (Ps. 5:10). Who can lay hold on the heart and give it fixity, so that for some little moment it may be stable, and for a fraction of time may grasp the splendour of a constant eternity? Then it may compare eternity with temporal successiveness which never has any constancy, and will see there is no comparison possible. It will see that a long time is long only because constituted of many successive movements which cannot be simultaneously extended. In the eternal, nothing is transient, but the whole is present. But no time is wholly present. It will see that all past time is driven backwards by the future, and all future time is the consequent of the past, and all past and future are created and set on their course by that which is always present. Who will lay hold on the human heart to make it still, so that it can see how eternity, in which there is neither future nor past, stands still and dictates future and past times? Can my hand have the strength for this? (Gen. 31:29). Can the hand of my mouth by mere speech achieve so great a thing?

xii (14) This is my reply to anyone who asks: "What was God doing before he made heaven and earth?" My reply is not that which someone is said to have given as a joke to evade the force of the question. He said: "He was preparing hells for people who inquire into profundities." It is one thing to laugh, another to see the point at issue, and this reply I reject. I would have preferred him to answer "I am ignorant of what I do not know" rather than reply so as to ridicule someone who has asked a deep question and to win approval for an answer which is a mistake.

No, I say that you, our God, are the Creator of every created being, and assuming that by "heaven and earth" is meant every created thing I boldly declare: Before God made heaven and earth, he was not making anything. If he was making anything, it could only be something created. I only wish that other useful matters which I long to be sure about I could know with an assurance equal to that with which I know that no created being was made before any creature came into being.

xiii (15) If, however, someone's mind is flitting and wandering over images of past times, and is astonished that you, all powerful, all creating, and all sustaining God, artificer of heaven and earth, abstained for unnumbered ages from this work before you actually made it, he should wake up and take note that his surprise rests on a mistake. How would innumerable ages pass, which you yourself had not made? You are the originator and creator of all ages. What times existed which were not brought into being by you? Or how could they pass if they never had existence? Since, therefore, you are the cause of all times, if any time existed before you made heaven and earth, how can anyone say that you abstained from working? You have made time itself. Time could not elapse before you made time. But if time did not exist before heaven and earth, why do people ask what you were then doing? There was no "then" when there was no time.

(16) It is not in time that you precede times. Otherwise you would not precede all times. In the sublimity of an eternity which is always in the present, you are before all things past and transcend all things future, because they are still to come, and when they have come they are past. "But you are the same and your years do not fail" (Ps. 101:28). Your "years" neither go nor come. Ours come and go so that all may come in succession. All your "years" subsist in simultaneity, because they do not change; those going away are not thrust out by those coming in. But the years which are ours will not all be until all years have ceased to be. Your "years" are "one day" (Ps. 89:4; 2 Pet. 3:8), and your "day" is not any and every day but Today, because your Today does not yield to a tomorrow, nor did it follow on a yesterday. Your Today is eternity. So you begat one coeternal with you, to whom you said: "Today I have begotten you" (Ps. 2:7; Heb. 5:5). You created all times and you exist before all times. Nor was there any time when time did not exist.

xiv (17) There was therefore no time when you had not made something, because you made time itself. No times are coeternal with you since you are permanent. If they were permanent, they would not be times.

What is time? Who can explain this easily and briefly? Who can comprehend this even in thought so as to articulate the answer in words? Yet what do we speak of, in our familiar everyday conversation, more than of time? We surely know what we mean when we speak of it. We also know what is meant when we hear someone else talking about it. What then is time? Provided that no one asks me, I know. If I want to explain it to an inquirer, I do not know. But I confidently affirm myself to know that if nothing passes away, there is no past time, and if nothing arrives, there is no future time, and if nothing existed there would be no present time. Take the two tenses, past and future. How can they "be" when the past is not now present and the future is not yet present? Yet if the present were always present, it would not pass into the past: it would not be time but eternity. If then, in order to be time at all, the present is so made that it passes into the past, how can we say that this present also "is"? The cause of its being is that it will cease to be. So indeed we cannot truly say that time exists except in the sense that it tends towards non-existence.

xv (18) Nevertheless we speak of "a long time" and "a short time," and it is only of the past or the future that we say this. Of the past we speak of "a long time," when, for example, it is more than a hundred years ago. "A long time" in the future may mean a hundred years ahead. By "a short time ago" we would mean, say, ten days back, and "a short time ahead" might mean "in ten days' time." But how can something be long or short which does not exist? For the past now has no existence and the future is not yet. So we ought not to say of the past "It is long," but "it was long," and of the future "it will be long." My Lord, my light, does not your truth mock humanity at this point? This time past which was long, was it long when it was past or when it was still present? It could be long only when it existed to be long. Once past, it no longer was. Therefore it could not be long if it had entirely ceased to exist.

Therefore let us not say "The time past was long." For we cannot discover anything to be long when, after it has become past, it has ceased to be. But let us say "That time once present was long" because it was long at the time when it was present. For it had not yet passed away into non-existence. It existed so as to be able to be long. But after it had passed away, it simultaneously ceased to be long because it ceased to be.

(19) Human soul, let us see whether present time can be long. To you the power is granted to be aware of intervals of time, and to measure them. What answer will you give me? Are a hundred years in the present a long time? Consider first whether a hundred years can be present. For if the first year of the series is current, it is present, but ninety-nine are future, and so do not yet exist. If the second year is current, one is already past, the second is present, the remainder lie in the future. And so between the extremes, whatever year of this century we assume to be present, there will be some years before it which lie in the past, some in the future to come after it. It follows that a century could never be present.

Consider then whether if a single year is current, that can be present. If in this year the first month is current, the others lie in the future; if the second, then the first lies in the past and the rest do not yet exist. Therefore even a current year is not entirely present; and if it is not entirely present, it is not a year which is present. A year is twelve months, of which any month which is current is present; the others are either past or future. Moreover, not even a month which is current is present, but one day. If the first day, the others are future; if the last day, the others are past; any intermediary day falls between past and future.

(20) See—present time, which alone we find capable of being called long, is contracted to the space of hardly a single day. But let us examine that also; for not even one day is entirely present. All the hours of night and day add up to twenty-four. The first of them has the others in the future, the last has them in the past. Any hour between these has past hours before it, future hours after it. One hour is itself constituted of fugitive moments. Whatever part of it has flown away is past. What remains to it is future. If we can think of some bit of time which cannot be divided into even the smallest instantaneous moments, that alone is what we can call "present." And this time flies so quickly from future into past that it is an interval with no duration. If it has duration, it is divisible into past and future. But the present occupies no space.

Where then is the time which we call long? Is it future? We do not really mean "It is long," since it does not yet exist to be long, but we mean it will be long. When will it be long? If it will then still lie in the future, it will not be long, since it will not yet exist to be long. But if it will be long at the time when, out of the future which does not yet exist, it begins to have being and will become present fact, so that it has the potentiality to be long, the present cries out in words already used that it cannot be long.

xvi (21) Nevertheless, Lord, we are conscious of intervals of time, and compare them with each other, and call some longer, others shorter. We also measure how much longer or shorter one period is than another, and answer that the one is twice or three times as much as the other, or that the two periods are equal. Moreover, we are measuring times which are past when our perception is the basis of measurement. But who can measure the past which does not now exist or the future which does not yet exist, unless perhaps someone dares to assert that he can measure what has no existence? At the moment when time is passing, it can be perceived and measured. But when it has passed and is not present, it cannot be.

xvii (22) I am investigating, Father, not making assertions. My God, protect me and rule me (Ps. 22:1; 27:9). Who will tell me that there are not three times, past, present, and future, as we learnt when children and as we have taught children, but only the present, because the other two have no existence? Or do they exist in the sense that, when the present emerges from the future, time comes out of some secret store, and then recedes into some secret place when the past comes out of the present? Where did those who sang prophecies see these events if they do not yet exist? To see what has no existence is impossible. And those who narrate past history would surely not be telling a true story if they did not discern events by their soul's insight. If the past were non-existent, it could not be discerned at all. Therefore both future and past events exist.

xviii (23) Allow me, Lord, to take my investigation further. My hope, let not my attention be distracted. If future and past events exist, I want to know where they are. If I have not the strength to discover the answer, at least I know that wherever they are, they are not there as future or past, but as present. For if there also they are future, they will not yet be there. If there also they are past, they are no longer there. Therefore, wherever they are, whatever they are, they do not exist except in the present. When a true narrative of the past is related, the memory produces not the actual events which have passed away but words conceived from images of them, which they fixed in the mind like imprints as they passed through the senses. Thus my boyhood, which is no longer, lies in past time which is no longer. But when I am recollecting and telling my story, I am looking on its image in present time, since it is still in my memory. Whether a similar cause is operative in predictions of the future, in the sense that images of realities which do not yet exist are presented as already in existence, I confess, my God, I do not know. At least I know this much: we frequently think out in advance our future actions, and that premeditation is in the present; but the action which we premeditate is not yet in being because it lies in the future. But when we have embarked on the action and what we were premeditating begins to be put into effect, then that action will have existence, since then it will be not future but present.

(24) Whatever may be the way in which the hidden presentiment of the future is known, nothing can be seen if it does not exist. Now that which already exists is not future but present. When therefore people speak of knowing the future, what is seen is not events which do not yet exist (that is, they really are future), but perhaps their causes or signs which already exist. In this way, to those who see them they are not future but present, and that is the basis on which the future can be conceived in the mind and made the subject of prediction.

Again, these concepts already exist, and those who predict the future see these concepts as if already present to their minds.

Among a great mass of examples, let me mention one instance. I look at the dawn. I forecast that the sun will rise. What I am looking at is present, what I am forecasting is future. It is not the sun which lies in the future (it already exists) but its rise, which has not yet arrived. Yet unless I were mentally imagining its rise, as now when I am speaking about it, I could not predict it. But the dawn glow which I see in the sky is not sunrise, which it precedes, nor is the imagining of sunrise in my mind the actuality. These are both discerned as present so that the coming sunrise may be foretold.

So future events do not yet exist, and if they are not yet present, they do not exist; and if they have no being, they cannot be seen at all. But they can be predicted from present events which are already present and can be seen.

xix (25) Governor of your creation, what is the way by which you inform souls what lies in the future? For you instructed your prophets. By what method then do you give information about the future—you to whom nothing is future? Is it rather that you inform how to read the future in the light of the present? What does not exist, certainly cannot be the subject of information. This method is far beyond my power of vision. "It is too mighty for me, I cannot attain it" (Ps. 138:6). But it would be in my power with your help if you granted it, sweet light of my uncomprehending eyes.

xx (26) What is by now evident and clear is that neither future nor past exists, and it is inexact language to speak of three times—past, present, and future. Perhaps it would be exact to say: there are three times, a present of things past, a present of things present, a present of things to come. In the soul there are these three aspects of time, and I do not see them anywhere else. The present considering the past is the memory, the present considering the present is immediate awareness, the present considering the future is expectation. If we are allowed to use such language, I see three times, and I admit they are three. Moreover, we may say, There are three times, past, present, and future. This customary way of speaking is incorrect, but it is common usage. Let us accept the usage. I do not object and offer no opposition or criticism, as long as what is said is being understood, namely that neither the future nor the past is now present. There are few usages of everyday speech which are exact, and most of our language is inexact. Yet what we mean is communicated.

xxi (27) A little earlier I observed that we measure past periods of time so that we can say that one period is twice as long as another or equal to it, and likewise of other periods of time which we are capable of measuring and reporting. Therefore, as I was saying, we measure periods of time as they are passing, and if anyone says to me "How do you know?" I reply: I know it because we do measure time and cannot measure what has no being; and past and future have none. But how do we measure present time when it has no extension? It is measured when it passes, but not when it has passed, because then there will be nothing there to measure.

When time is measured, where does it come from, by what route does it pass, and where does it go? It must come out of the future, pass by the present, and go into the past; so it comes from what as yet does not exist, passes through that which lacks extension, and goes into that which is now non-existent. Yet what do we measure but time over some extension? When we speak of lengths of time as single, duple, triple, and equal, or any other temporal relation of this kind, we must be speaking of periods of time possessing extension. In what extension then do we measure time as it is passing? Is it in the future out of which it comes to pass by? No, for we do not measure what does not yet exist. Is it in the present through which it passes? No, for we cannot measure that which has no extension. Is it in the past into which it is moving? No, for we cannot measure what now does not exist.

xxii (28) My mind is on fire to solve this very intricate enigma. Do not shut the door, Lord my God. Good Father, through Christ I beg you, do not shut the door on my longing to understand these things which are both familiar and obscure. Do not prevent me, Lord, from penetrating them and seeing them illuminated by the light of your mercy. Whom shall I ask about them? And to whom but you shall I more profitably confess my incompetence? You are not irritated by the burning zeal with which I study your scriptures. Grant what I love. For I love, and this love was your gift. Grant it, Father. You truly know how to give good gifts to your children (Matt. 7:11). Grant it, since I have undertaken to acquire understanding and "the labour is too much for me" (Ps. 72:16) until you open the way. Through Christ I beg you, in the name of him who is the holy of holy ones, let no one obstruct my inquiry. "I also have believed, and therefore speak" (Ps. 115:1; 2 Cor. 4:13). This is my hope. For this I live "that I may contemplate the delight of the Lord" (Ps. 26:4). "Behold you have made my days subject to ageing" (Ps. 38:6). They pass away, and how I do not know. And we repeatedly speak of time and time, of times and times: "How long ago did he say this?" "How long ago did he do this?" "For how long a time did I fail to see that?" And "These syllables take twice the time of that single, short syllable." We speak in this way, and hear people saying this, and we are understood and we understand. These usages are utterly commonplace and everyday. Yet they are deeply obscure and the discovery of the solution is new.

xxiii (29) I have heard a learned person say that the movements of sun, moon, and stars in themselves constitute time. But I could not agree. Why should not time consist rather of the movement of all physical objects? If the heavenly bodies were to cease and a potter's wheel were revolving, would there be no time by which we could measure its gyrations, and say that its revolutions were equal; or if at one time it moved more slowly and at another time faster, that some rotations took longer, others less? And when we utter these words do not we also speak in time? In our words some syllables are long, others short, in that the sounding of the former requires a longer time, whereas the latter are shorter.

God grant to human minds to discern in a small thing universal truths valid for both small and great matters. There are stars and heavenly luminaries to be "for signs and for times, and for days and for years" (Gen. 1:14). But I would not say that a revolution of that wooden wheel is a day; and that learned friend could not assert that its rotation was not a period of time.

(30) I desire to understand the power and the nature of time, which enables us to measure the motions of bodies and to say that, for instance, this movement requires twice as long as that. I have this question to raise: the word "day" is used not only of the interval of time when the sun is up over the earth, so that day is one thing, night another, but also of the sun's entire circuit from east to west, as when we say "so many days have passed" where "so many days" includes the nights, and the periods of night-time are not counted separately. So a complete day is marked by the movement and circuit of the sun from east to west. My question then is whether the sun's movement itself constitutes the day? or the actual interval of time during which it is accomplished? or both?

In the first instance, it would still be a day even if the sun completed its course in the space of a single hour. In the second case, it would not be a day if from one sunrise to the next so short an interval as one hour passed, but only if the sun completed a day of twenty-four hours. In the third case—a day being both the circuit and the time taken—it could not be called a day if the sun completed its entire circuit in an hour, nor if the sun ceased to move and the length of time passed were the twenty-four hours normally taken by the sun in completing its entire course from sunrise to sunrise. I will not, therefore, now investigate what it is which we call a day, but the nature of time by which we can measure the sun's circuit and by which we might say that, if all was accomplished in twelve hours, the sun had completed its course in half the usual time. I ask what time is when we make a comparison and say that one interval is single and another double, even if the sun were to make its transit from east to west sometimes in single time, sometimes in twice the time.

Let no one tell me then that time is the movements of heavenly bodies. At a man's prayer the sun stood still, so that a battle could be carried through to victory (Josh. 10:12 ff.): the sun stopped but time went on. That battle was fought and completed in its own space of time such as was sufficient for it. I therefore see that time is some kind of extension. But do I really see that? Or do I imagine that I see? You, light and truth, will show me.

xxiv (31) Do you command me to concur if someone says time is the movement of a physical entity? You do not. For I learn that no body can be moved except in time. You tell me so, but I do not learn that the actual movement of a body constitutes time. That is not what you tell me. For when a body is moved, it is by time that I measure the duration of the movement, from the moment it begins until it ends. Unless I have observed the point when it begins, and if its movement is continuous so that I cannot observe when it ceases, I am unable to measure except for the period from the beginning to the end of my observation. If my observing lasts for a considerable time, I can only report that a long time passed, but not precisely how much. When we say how much, we are making a comparison—as, for example, "This period was of the same length as that," or "This period was twice as long as that," or some such relationship.

If, however, we have been able to note the points in space from which and to which a moving body passes, or the parts of a body when it is spinning on its axis, then we can say how much time the movement of the body or its parts required to move from one point to another. It follows that a body's movement is one thing, the period by which we measure is another. It is self-evident which of these is to be described as time. Moreover, a body may at one point be moving, at another point at rest. We measure by time and say "It was standing still for the same time that it was in movement," or "It was still for two or three times as long as it was in movement," or any other measurement we may make, either by precise observation or by a rough estimate (we customarily say "more or less"). Therefore time is not the movement of a body.

xxv (32) I confess to you, Lord, that I still do not know what time is, and I further confess to you, Lord, that as I say this I know myself to be conditioned by time. For a long period already I have been speaking about time, and that long period can only be an interval of time. So how do I know this, when I do not know what time is? Perhaps what I do not know is how to articulate what I do know. My condition is not good if I do not even know what it is I do not know. See, my God, "before you I do not lie" (Gal. 1:21). As I speak, so is my heart. You, Lord, "will light my lamp." Lord, my God, "you will lighten my darkness" (Ps. 17:29).

xxvi (33) My confession to you is surely truthful when my soul declares that times are measured by me. So my God, I measure, and do not know what I am measuring. I measure the motion of a body by time. Then am I not measuring time itself? I could not measure the movement of a body, its period of transit and how long it takes to go from A to B, unless I were measuring the time in which this movement occurs. How then do I measure time itself? Or do we use a shorter time to measure a longer time, as when, for example, we measure a transom by using a cubit length? So we can be seen to use the length of a short syllable as a measure when we say that a long syllable is twice its length. By this method we measure poems by the number of lines, lines by the number of feet, feet by the number of syllables, and long vowels by short, not by the number of pages (for that would give us a measure of space, not of time). The criterion is the time words occupy in recitation, so that we say "That is a long poem, for it consists of so many lines. The lines are long, for they consist of so many feet. The feet are long for they extend over so many syllables. The syllable is long, for it is double the length of a short one."

Nevertheless, even so we have not reached a reliable measure of time. It may happen that a short line, if pronounced slowly, takes longer to read aloud than a longer line taken faster. The same principle applies to a poem or a foot or a syllable. That is why I have come to think that time is simply a distension. But of what is it a distension? I do not know, but it would be surprising if it is not that of the mind itself. What do I measure, I beg you, my God, when I say without precision "This period is longer than that," or with precision "This is twice as long as that"? That I am measuring time I know. But I am not measuring the future which does not yet exist, nor the present which has no extension, nor the past which is no longer in being. What then am I measuring? Time as it passes but not time past? That is what I affirmed earlier.

xxvii (34) Stand firm, my mind, concentrate with resolution. "God is our help, he has made us and not we ourselves" (Ps. 61:9; 99:3). Concentrate on the point where truth is beginning to dawn. For example, a physical voice begins to sound. It sounds. It continues to sound, and then ceases. Silence has now come, and the voice is past. There is now no sound. Before it sounded it lay in the future. It could not be measured because it did not exist; and now it cannot be measured because it has ceased to be. At the time when it was sounding, it was possible because at that time it existed to be measured. Yet even then it had no permanence. It came and went. Did this make it more possible to measure? In process of passing away it was extended through a certain space of time by which it could be measured, since the present occupies no length of time. Therefore during that transient process it could be measured. But take, for example, another voice. It begins to sound and continues to do so unflaggingly without any interruption. Let us measure it while it is sounding; when it has ceased to sound, it will be past and will not exist to be measurable. Evidently we may at that stage measure it by saying how long it lasted. But if it is still sounding, it cannot be measured except from the starting moment when it began to sound to the finish when it ceased. What we measure is the actual interval from the beginning to the end. That is why a sound which has not yet ended cannot be measured: one cannot say how long or how short it is, nor that it is equal to some other length of time or that in relation to another it is single or double or any such proportion. But when it has come to an end, then it will already have ceased to be. By what method then can it be measured?

Nevertheless we do measure periods of time. And yet the times we measure are not those which do not yet exist, nor those which already have no existence, nor those which extend over no interval of time, nor those which reach no conclusions. So the times we measure are not future nor past nor present nor those in process of passing away. Yet we measure periods of time.

(35) "God, Creator of all things"—*Deus Creator omnium*—the line consists of eight syllables, in which short and long syllables alternate. So the four which are short (the first, third, fifth, and seventh) are single in relation to the four long syllables (the second, fourth, sixth, and eighth). Each of the long syllables has twice the time of the short. As I recite the words, I also observe that this is so, for it is evident to sense-perception. To the degree that the sense-perception is unambiguous, I measure the long syllable by the short one, and perceive it to be twice the length. But when one syllable sounds after another, the short first, the long after it, how shall I keep my hold on the short, and how use it to apply a measure to the long, so as to verify that the long is twice as much? The long does not begin to sound unless the short has ceased to sound. I can hardly measure the long during the presence of its sound, as measuring becomes possible only after it has ended. When it is finished, it has gone into the past. What then is it which I measure? Where is the short syllable with which I am making my measurement? Where is the long which I am measuring? Both have sounded; they have flown away; they belong to the past. They now do not exist. And I offer my measurement and declare as confidently as a practised sense-perception will allow, that the short is single, the long double—I mean in the time they occupy. I can do this only because they are past and gone. Therefore it is not the syllables which I am measuring, but something in my memory which stays fixed there.

(36) So it is in you, my mind, that I measure periods of time. Do not distract me; that is, do not allow yourself to be distracted by the hubbub of the impressions being made upon you. In you, I affirm, I measure periods of time. The impression which passing events make upon you abides when they are gone. That present consciousness is what I am measuring, not the stream of past events which have caused it. When I measure periods of time, that is what I am actually measuring. Therefore, either this is what time is, or time is not what I am measuring.

What happens when we measure silences and say that a given period of silence lasted as long as a given sound? Do we direct our attention to measuring it as if a sound occurred, so that we are enabled to judge the intervals of the silences within the space of time concerned? For without any sound or utterance we mentally recite poems and lines and speeches, and we assess the lengths of their movements and the relative amounts of time they occupy, no differently from the way we would speak if we were actually making sounds. Suppose someone wished to utter a sound lasting a long time, and decided in advance how long that was going to be. He would have planned that space of time in silence. Entrusting that to his memory he would begin to utter the sound which continues until it has reached the intended end. It would be more accurate to say the utterance has sounded and will sound. For the part of it which is complete has sounded, but what remains will sound, and so the action is being accomplished as present attention transfers the future into the past. The future diminishes as the past grows, until the future has completely gone and everything is in the past.

xxviii (37) But how does this future, which does not yet exist, diminish or become consumed? Or how does the past, which now has no being, grow, unless there are three processes in the mind which in this is the active agent? For the mind expects and attends and remembers, so that what it expects passes through what has its attention to what it remembers. Who therefore can deny that the future does not yet exist? Yet already in the mind there is an expectation of the future. Who can deny that the past does not now exist? Yet there is still in the mind a memory of the past. None can deny that present time lacks any extension because it passes in a flash. Yet attention is continuous, and it is through this that what will be present progresses towards being absent. So the future, which does not exist, is not a long period of time. A long future is a long expectation of the future. And the past, which has no existence, is not a long period of time. A long past is a long memory of the past.

(38) Suppose I am about to recite a psalm which I know. Before I begin, my expectation is directed towards the whole. But when I have begun, the verses from it which I take into the past become the object of my memory. The life of this act of mine is stretched two ways, into my memory because of the words I have already said and into my expectation because of those which I am about to say. But my attention is on what is present: by that the future is transferred to become the past. As the action advances further and further, the shorter the expectation and the longer the memory, until all expectation is consumed, the entire action is finished, and it has passed into the memory. What occurs in the psalm as a whole occurs in its particular pieces and its individual syllables. The same is true of a longer action in which perhaps that psalm is a part. It is also valid of the entire life of an individual person, where all actions are parts of a whole, and of the total history of "the sons of men" (Ps. 30:20) where all human lives are but parts.

xxix (39) "Because your mercy is more than lives" (Ps. 62:4), see how my life is a distension in several directions. "Your right hand upheld me" (Ps. 17:36; 62:9) in my Lord, the Son of man who is mediator between you the One and us the many, who live in a multiplicity of distractions by many things; so "I might apprehend him in whom also I am apprehended" (Phil. 3:12–14), and leaving behind the old days I might be gathered to follow the One, "forgetting the past" and moving not towards those future things which are transitory but to "the things which are before" me, not stretched out in distraction but extended in reach, not by being pulled apart but by concentration. So I "pursue the prize of the high calling" where I "may hear the voice of praise" and "contemplate your delight" (Ps. 25:7; 26:4) which neither comes nor goes. But now "my years pass in groans" (Ps. 30:11) and you, Lord, are my consolation. You are my eternal Father, but I am scattered in times whose order I do not understand. The storms of incoherent events tear to pieces my thoughts, the inmost entrails of my soul, until that day when, purified and molten by the fire of your love, I flow together to merge into you.

xxx (40) Then shall I find stability and solidity in you, in your truth which imparts form to me. I shall not have to endure the questions of people who suffer from a disease which brings its own punishment and want to drink more than they have the capacity to hold. They say "What was God doing before he made heaven and earth?," or "Why did he ever conceive the thought of making something when he had never made anything before?" Grant them, Lord, to consider carefully what they are saying and to make the discovery that where there is no time, one cannot use the word "never." To say that God has never done something is to say that there is no time when he did it. Let them therefore see that without the creation no time can exist, and let them cease to speak that vanity (Ps. 143:8). Let them also be "extended" towards "those things which are before" (Phil. 3:13), and understand that before all times you are eternal Creator of all time. Nor are any times or created thing coeternal with you, even if there is an order of creation which transcends time.

xxxi (41) Lord my God, how deep is your profound mystery, and how far away from it have I been thrust by the consequences of my sins. Heal my eyes and let me rejoice with your light. Certainly if there were a mind endowed with such great knowledge and prescience that all things past and future could be known in the way I know a very familiar psalm, this mind would be utterly miraculous and amazing to the point of inducing awe. From such a mind nothing of the past would be hidden, nor anything of what remaining ages have in store, just as I have full knowledge of that psalm I sing. I know by heart what and how much of it has passed since the beginning, and what and how much remains until the end. But far be it from you, Creator of the universe, creator of souls and bodies, far be it from you to know all future and past events in this kind of sense. You know them in a much more wonderful and much more mysterious way. A person singing or listening to a song he knows well suffers a distension or stretching in feeling and in sense-perception from the expectation of future sounds and the memory of past sound. With you it is otherwise. You are unchangeably eternal, that is the truly eternal Creator of minds. Just as you knew heaven and earth in the beginning without that bringing any variation into your knowing, so you made heaven and earth in the beginning without that meaning a tension between past and future in your activity. Let the person who understands this make confession to you. Let him who fails to understand it make confession to you. How exalted you are, and the humble in heart are your house (Ps. 137:6; 145:8). You lift up those who are cast down (Ps. 144:14; 145:8), and those whom you raise to that summit which is yourself do not fall.

CITY OF GOD (in part)

BOOK XII

CHAPTER 1

In the previous book we saw something of the beginning of the two cities, so far as angels are concerned. In the same way, we must now proceed to the creation of men and see the beginning of the cities so far as it concerns the kind of rational creatures who are mortal. First, however, a few remarks about the angels must be made in order to make it

St. Augustine, *City of God,* Book XII, 1–9; Book XIX, 11–17, from *Fathers of the Church; Writings of Saint Augustine; Saint Augustine: City of God,* translated by Gerald G. Walsh, Daniel J. Honan, and Grace Monahan (Washington, DC: The Catholic University of America Press, 1952, 1954). Reprinted by permission.

as clear as I can how there is no real difficulty or impropriety in speaking of a single society composed of both men and angels; and why, therefore, it is right to say that there are not four cities or societies, namely, two of angels and two of men, but only two, one of them made up of the good—both angels and men—and the other of those who are evil.

There is no reason to doubt that the contrary dispositions which have developed among these good and bad angels are due, not to different natures and origins, for God the Author and Creator of all substances has created them both, but to the dissimilar choices and desires of these angels themselves. Some, remaining faithful to God, the common good of all, have lived in the enjoyment of His eternity, truth, and love, while others, preferring the enjoyment of their own power, as though they were their own good, departed from the higher good and common blessedness for all and turned to goods of their own choosing.

Preferring the pomp of pride to this sublimity of eternity, the craftiness of vanity to the certainty of truth, and the turmoil of dissension to the union of love, they became proud, deceitful, and envious.

Since the happiness of all angels consists in union with God, it follows that their unhappiness must be found in the very contrary, that is, in not adhering to God. To the question: "Why are the good angels happy?" the right answer is: "Because they adhere to God." To the question: "Why are the others unhappy?" the answer is: "Because they do not adhere to God." In fact, there is no other good which can make any rational or intellectual creature happy except God. Not every creature has the potentialities for happiness. Beasts, trees, stones, and such things neither acquire nor have the capacity for this gift. However, every creature which has this capacity receives it, not from itself, since it has been created out of nothing, but from its Creator. To possess Him is to be happy; to lose Him is to be in misery. And, of course, that One whose beatitude depends upon Himself as His own good and not on any other good can never be unhappy since He can never lose Himself.

Thus, there can be no unchangeable good except our one, true, and blessed God. All things which He has made are good because made by Him, but they are subject to change because they were made, not out of Him, but out of nothing. Although they are not supremely good, since God is a greater good than they, these mutable things are, none the less, highly good by reason of their capacity for union with and, therefore, beatitude in the Immutable Good which is so completely their good that, without this good, misery is inevitable.

But it does not follow that other creatures in the universe are better off merely because they are incapable of misery. That would be like saying that other members of the body are better than the eyes because they can never become blind. A sentient nature even in pain is better than a stone that cannot suffer. In the same way, a rational nature even in misery is higher than one which, because it lacks reason or sensation, cannot suffer misery.

This being the case, it is nothing less than a perversion of the nature of the angels if they do not adhere to God. For, remember, their nature is so high in the order of creation that, mutable as it is, it can attain beatitude by adhering to the immutable and supreme Good, which is God, and that, unless it achieves beatitude, this nature fails to satisfy its inmost exigencies, and, finally, that nothing but God can satisfy these needs of the angelic nature.

Now, this perversion, like every imperfection in a nature, harms nature and, therefore, is contrary to the nature. It follows, therefore, that what makes the wicked angels differ from the good ones is not their nature but a perversion or imperfection; and this very blemish is a proof of how highly to be esteemed is the nature itself. Certainly, no blemish in a thing ought to be blamed unless we are praising the thing as a whole, for the whole point of blaming the blemish is that it mars the perfection of something we would like to see praised.

For example, when we say that blindness is a defect of the eyes, we imply that it is the very nature of the eyes to see, and when we say that deafness is a malady of the ears, we are supposing that it is their nature to hear. So, too, when we say that it is a failure in an angel not to attain union with God, we openly proclaim that they were meant by nature to be one with God.

Of course, no one can fully comprehend or properly express the ineffable union of being one with God in His life, in His wisdom, in His joy, and all this without a shadow of death or darkness or disturbance. One thing is certain. The very failure of the bad angels to cling to God—a desertion that damaged their nature like a disease—is itself proof enough that the nature God gave them was good—so good that not to be one with God was for them a disaster.

CHAPTER 2

This explanation just given seemed to me necessary to forestall the objection that the apostate spirits might have received from some principle other than God a nature different from that of the other angels. The malice of this mistake can be more easily and speedily removed the more clearly one grasps what God meant by the words, "I AM WHO AM" (Exod. 3:14), spoken through the medium of an angel at the time when Moses was being sent to the children of Israel.

Since God is supreme being, that is, since He supremely is and, therefore, is immutable, it follows that He gave "being" to all that He created out of nothing; not, however, absolute being. To some things He gave more of being and to others less and, in this way, arranged an order of natures in a hierarchy of being. (This noun, "being," is derived from the verb "to be," just as "wisdom" is from the verb "to be wise." In Latin, *essentia,* "being," is a new word, not used by the ancient writers, recently adopted in order to find an equivalent of the Greek ⟨*ousía*⟩, of which *essentia* is the exact translation.)

Consequently, no nature—except a non-existent one—can be contrary to the nature which is supreme and which created whatever other natures have being. In other words, nonentity stands in opposition to that which is. Therefore, there is no being opposed to God who is the Supreme Being and Source of all beings without exception.

CHAPTER 3

In Scripture, those who oppose God's rule, not by nature but by sin, are called His enemies. They can do no damage to Him, but only to themselves; their enmity is not a power to harm, but merely an inclination to oppose Him. In any case, God is immutable and completely invulnerable. Hence, the malice by which His so-called enemies oppose God is not a menace to Him, but merely bad for themselves—an evil because what is good in their nature is wounded. It is not their nature, but the wound in their nature, that is opposed to God—as evil is opposed to good.

No one will deny that God is supremely good. Thus, any lack of goodness is opposed to God as evil is opposed to good. At the same time, the nature itself is not less good because the lack of goodness is evil and, therefore, the evil of lacking some goodness is opposed to this good, which is the goodness of the nature. Note that in respect to God the contrast is merely that of evil to good, but in respect to the nature which suffers a lack of something good, the lack is not only evil but also harmful. No evils, of course, can be harmful to God, but only to mutable and corruptible natures—and, even then, the harm done bears witness to the goodness of the natures which suffer, for, unless they were good, they could not suffer the wounds of a lack of goodness.

Just consider the harm done by these wounds—the loss of integrity, of beauty, of health, of virtue, or of any other natural good which can be lost or lessened by sin or sickness. If a nature has nothing of goodness to lose, then there is no harm done by lacking this nothing and, consequently, there is nothing wrong. For, there is no such thing as something wrong that does no harm.

The conclusion is that, although no defect can damage an unchangeable good, no nature can be damaged by a defect unless that nature itself is good—for the simple reason that a defect exists only where harm is done. To put the matter in another way: a defect can never be found in the highest good, nor ever apart from some kind of good.

Thus, good things without defects can sometimes be found; absolutely bad things, never—for even those natures that were vitiated at the outset by an evil will are only evil in so far as they are defective, while they are good in so far as they are natural. And when a vitiated nature is being punished, in addition to the good of being what it is, it is a good for it not to go unpunished, since this is just and whatever is just is certainly good. No one is punished for natural defects, but only for deliberate faults. And even for a vice to develop, by force of habit and overindulgence, into a strong natural defect, the vice must have begun in the will. But here, of course, I am speaking of the vices of that nature which has a mind illumined by an immaterial light in virtue of which it can distinguish what is just from what is unjust.

CHAPTER 4

Of course, in the case of beasts, trees, and other mutable and mortal creatures which lack not merely an intellect, but even sensation or life itself, it would be ridiculous to condemn in them the defects which destroy their corruptible nature. For, it was by the will of the Creator that they received that measure of being whereby their comings and goings and fleeting existences should contribute to that special, if lowly, loveliness of our earthly seasons which chimes with the harmony of the universe. For, there was never any need for the things of earth either to rival those of heaven or to remain uncreated merely because the latter are better.

It is, in fact, the very law of transitory things that, here on earth where such things are at home, some should be born while others die, the weak should give way to the strong and the victims should nourish the life of the victors. If the beauty of this order fails to delight us, it is because we ourselves, by reason of our mortality, are so enmeshed in this corner of the cosmos that we fail to perceive the beauty of a total pattern in which the particular parts, which seem ugly to us, blend in so harmonious and beautiful a way. That is why, in those situations where it is beyond our power to understand the providence of God, we are rightly commanded to make an act of faith rather than allow the rashness of human vanity to criticize even a minute detail in the masterpiece of our Creator.

Although these defects in the things of earth are involuntary and unpunishable, yet, like voluntary ones, when properly contemplated, they reveal the excellence in the natures themselves, all of which have God for their Author and Creator. For, in both cases, what we dislike is the lack by defect of something which we like in the nature as a whole. Sometimes, of course, natures themselves are displeasing to men because they happen to be harmful. It is a case of regarding only their utility, not the things themselves, as with the plague of frogs and flies which scourged the pride of the Egyptians. But, with such reasoning, fault could be found even with the sun, since criminals and debtors have sometimes been judicially condemned to solar exposure. It is not by our comfort or inconvenience, but by the nature considered in itself, that glory is given to its Creator. So, even the nature of unquenchable fire is, without doubt, worthy of praise, although it is to serve as a punishment for the damned. Is there anything, in fact, more beautiful than a leaping, luminous flame of fire? Or anything more useful, when it warms us, heals us, cooks our food? Yet, nothing is more painful when it burns us. Thus, the same thing applied in one way is harmful, but when properly used is extremely beneficial. It is all but impossible to enumerate all the good uses to which fire is put throughout the world.

We should pay no attention to those who praise fire for its light but condemn its heat—on the principle that a thing should be judged not by its nature, but by our comfort or inconvenience. They like to see it, but hate to be burnt. What they forget is that the same light which they like is injurious and unsuitable for weak eyes, and that the heat which they hate is, for some animals, the proper condition for a healthy life.

CHAPTER 5

All natures, then, are good simply because they exist and, therefore, have each its own measure of being, its own beauty, even, in a way, its own peace. And when each is in the place assigned by the order of nature, it best preserves the full measure of being that was given to it. Beings not made for eternal life, changing for better or for worse according as they promote the good and improvement of things to which, by the law of the Creator, they serve as means, follow the direction of Divine Providence and tend toward the particular end which forms a part of the general plan for governing the universe. This means that the dissolution which brings mutable and mortal things to their death is not so much a process of annihilation as a progress toward something they were designed to become.

The conclusion from all this is that God is never to be blamed for any defects that offend us, but should ever be praised for all the perfection we see in the natures He has made. For God is Absolute Being and, therefore, all other being that is relative was made by Him. No being that was made from nothing could be on a par with God, nor could it even be at all, were it not made by Him.

CHAPTER 6

It follows that the true cause of the good angels' beatitude lies in their union with Absolute Being. And if we seek the cause of the bad angels' misery, we are right in finding it in this, that they abandoned Him whose Being is absolute and turned to themselves whose being is relative—a sin that can have no better name than pride. "For pride is the beginning of all sin" (Eccli. 10:15). They refused to reserve their strength for Him. They might have had more of being if they had adhered to Him whose Being is supreme, but, by preferring themselves to Him, they preferred what was less in the order of being.

Such was the first defect, the first lack, the first perversion of that nature which, being created, could not be absolute, and yet, being created for beatitude, might have rejoiced in Him who is Absolute Being; but which, having turned from Him, was doomed, not to be nothing but to have so much less of being that it was bound to be wretched.

If one seeks for the efficient cause of their evil will, none is to be found. For, what can make the will bad when it is the will itself which makes an action bad? Thus, an evil will is the efficient cause of a bad action, but there is no efficient cause of an evil will. If there is such a cause, it either has or has not a will. If it has, then that will is either good or bad. If good, one would have to be foolish enough to conclude that a good will makes a bad will. In that case, a good will becomes the cause of sin—which is utterly absurd. On the other hand, if the hypothetical cause of a bad will has itself a bad will, I would have to ask what made this will bad, and, to put an end to the inquiry: What made the first bad will bad? Now, the fact is that there was no first bad will that was made bad by any other bad will—it was made bad by itself. For, if it were preceded by a cause that made it evil, that cause came first. But, if I am told that nothing made the will evil but that it always was so, then I ask whether or not it existed in some nature.

If this evil will existed in no nature, then it did not exist at all. If it existed in some nature, then it vitiated, corrupted, injured that nature and, therefore, deprived it of some good. An evil will could not exist in an evil nature but only in a good one, mutable enough to suffer harm from this deprivation. For, if no harm were done, then there was no deprivation and, consequently, no right to call the will evil. But, if harm was done, it was done by destroying or diminishing what was good. Thus, an evil will could not have existed from all eternity in a nature in which a previously existing good had to be eliminated before the evil will could harm the nature. But, if it did not exist from all eternity, who, then, caused this evil will?

The only remaining suggestion is that the cause of the evil will was something which had no will. My next question is whether this "something" was superior, inferior, or equal to the will. If superior, then it was better. So, then, how can it have had no will and not rather a good will? If equal, the case is the same: for, as long as two wills are equally good, one cannot produce an evil will in the other. The supposition remains, then, that it was an inferior thing without a will which produced the evil will of the angelic nature which first sinned.

But that thing itself, whatever it was, even though it was low to the lowest point of earthliness, was, without doubt good since it was a nature and a being having its own character and species in its own genus and order. How, then, can a good thing be the efficient cause of an evil will? How, I ask, can good be the cause of evil? For, when the will, abandoning what is above it, turns itself to something lower, it becomes evil because the very turning itself and not the thing to which it turns is evil. Therefore, an inferior being does not make the will evil but the will itself, because it is a created will, wickedly and inordinately seeks the inferior being.

Take the case of two men whose physical and mental make-up is exactly the same. They are both attracted by the exterior beauty of the same person. While gazing at this loveliness, the will of one man is moved with an illicit desire; the will of the other remains firm in its purity. Why did the will become evil in one case and not in the other? What produced the evil will in the man in whom it began to be evil? The physical beauty of the person could not have been the cause, since that was seen by both in exactly the same way and yet both wills did not become evil. Was the cause the flesh of one of those who looked? Then why not the flesh of the other, also? Or was the cause the mind of one of them? Again, why not the mind of both? For the supposition is that both are equally constituted in mind and body. Must we say, then, that one was tempted by a secret suggestion of the Devil, as if it were not rather by his own will that he consented to this suggestion or enticement or whatever it was?

If so, then what was it in him that was the cause of his consent, of the evil will to follow the evil suggestion? To settle this difficulty, let us suppose that the two men are tempted equally, that one yields and consents to the temptation, that the other remains as he was before. The obvious conclusion is that one was unwilling, the other willing, to fail in chastity. And what else could be the cause of their attitudes but their own wills, since both men have the same constitution and temperament? The beauty which attracted the eyes of both was the same; the secret suggestion by which both were tempted was the same. However carefully they examine the situation, eager to learn what it was that made one of the two evil, no cause is apparent.

For, suppose we say that the man himself made his will evil. Very well, but what was the man himself before he made his will evil? He was a good nature, created by God, the immutable God.

Take a person who says that the one who consents to the temptation and enticement made his own will evil although previously he had been entirely good. Recall the facts. The one consents, while the other does not, to a sinful desire concerning a beautiful person; the beauty was seen by both equally, and before the temptation both men were absolutely alike in mind and body. Now, the person who talks of a man making his own will evil must ask why the man made his will evil, whether because he is a nature or because he is nature made out of nothing? He will learn that the evil arises not from the fact that the man is a nature, but from the fact that the nature was made out of nothing.

For, if a nature is the cause of an evil will, then we are compelled to say that evil springs from good and that good is the cause of evil—since a bad will comes from a good nature. But how can it come about that a good, though mutable, nature, even before its will is evil, can produce something evil, namely, this evil will itself?

CHAPTER 7

No one, therefore, need seek for an efficient cause of an evil will. Since the "effect" is, in fact, a deficiency, the cause should be called "deficient." The fault of an evil will begins when one falls from Supreme Being to some being which is less than absolute. Trying to discover causes of such deficiencies—causes which, as I have said, are not efficient but deficient—is like trying to see darkness or hear silence. True, we have some knowledge of both darkness and silence: of the former only by the eyes; of the latter only by the ears. Nevertheless, we have no sensation but only the privation of sensation.

So there is no point in anyone trying to learn from me what I know I do not know—unless, perhaps, he wants to know how not to know what, as he ought to know, no one can know. For, things we know, not by sensation, but by the absence of sensation, are known—if the word says or means anything—by some kind of "unknowing," so that they are both known and not known at the same time. For example, when the vision of the eye passes from sensation to sensation, it sees darkness only when it begins not to see. So, too, no other sense but the ear can perceive silence, yet silence can only be heard by not being heard.

So, too, it is only the vision of the mind that discerns the *species intelligibilis* when it understands intelligible realities. But, when the realities are no longer intelligible, the mind, too, knows by "unknowing." For "who can understand sins?" (Ps. 18:13).

CHAPTER 8

This I know, that the nature of God can never and nowhere be deficient in anything, while things made out of nothing can be deficient. In regard to these latter, the more they have of being and the more good things they do or make—for then they are doing or making something positive—the more their causes are efficient; but in so far as they fail or are defective and, in that sense, "do evil"—if a "defect" can be "done"—then their causes are "deficient." I know, further, that when a will "is made" evil, what happens would not have happened if the will had not wanted it to happen. That is why the punishment which follows is just, since the defection was not necessary but voluntary. The will does not fall "into sin"; it falls "sinfully." Defects are not mere relations to natures that are evil; they are evil in themselves because, contrary to the order of natures, there is a defection from Being that is supreme to some lesser being.

Thus, greed is not a defect in the gold that is desired but in the man who loves it perversely by falling from justice which he ought to esteem as incomparably superior to gold; nor is lust a defect in bodies which are beautiful and pleasing: it is a sin in the soul of the one who loves corporal pleasures perversely, that is, by abandoning that temperance which joins us in spiritual and unblemishable union with realities far more beautiful and pleasing; nor is boastfulness a blemish in words of praise: it is a failing in the soul of one who is so perversely in love with other peoples' applause that he despises the voice of his own conscience; nor is pride a vice in the one who delegates power, still less a flaw in the power itself: it is a passion in the soul of the one who loves his own power so perversely as to condemn the authority of one who is still more powerful.

In a word, anyone who loves perversely the good of any nature whatsoever and even, perhaps, acquires this good makes himself bad by gaining something good and sad by losing something better.

CHAPTER 9

There is, then, no natural efficient cause of an evil will or, if I may use the word, no essential cause. The reason for this is that it is the evil will itself that starts that evil in mutable spirits, which is nothing but a weakening and worsening of the good in their nature. What "makes" the will evil is, in reality, an "unmaking," a desertion from God. The very defection is deficient—in the sense of having no cause. However, in saying that there is no efficient cause even of a good will, we must beware of believing that the good will of the good angels was uncreated and co-eternal with God. But, if good angels were created, how can we say that their good will was not created? The fact is, it was created; the only question is whether it was created simultaneously with the creation of the angels or whether they first existed without a good will. If simultaneously, then, undoubtedly, it was created by Him who created the angels, so that, as soon as they were created, they adhered to Him who created them by means of that love with which they were created. Thus, the reason why the bad were separated from the society of good angels was that the good persevered in the same good will, whereas the others changed themselves into bad angels by defection from good will. The only thing that "made" their will bad was that they fell away from a will which was good. Nor would they have fallen away, had they not chosen to fall away.

In the hypothesis, however, that the good angels, existing at first without a good will, produced it in themselves without the help of God, they must have made themselves better than what they were when God created them. This is nonsense. For, without a good will, what could they be but evil? Or, if we may not say evil, since their will was not yet evil—for they could hardly fall away from what they had not yet begun to have—at least, they certainly were not good angels—not as good as they were to become when they came to possess a good will.

So much for the hypothesis. Since they could not make themselves better than God made them—for no one can make anything better than God can—then it follows that, without the co-operation of their Creator, they could never have come into possession of that good will which made them better.

Now, it is true that their good will was not only the cause of their turning and adhering to Him, who is Perfect Being, rather than to themselves, whose being was less than perfect, but also the reason why they had more of being than before and could live wisely and happily in union with God. Nevertheless, this merely shows that any will, however good, would have been destitute and destined to remain in hopeless desire, did not He who had created their good nature out of nothing, and had given it a capacity for union with Himself, first awaken in the will a greater longing for this union and then fill the will with some of His very Being in order to make it better.

This raises another issue. For, if the good angels did something themselves to bring about their good will, did they do this with or without a will? If without, then, of course, they were not the agents. If with a will, was it an evil or a good one? If evil, how could it produce a good will? If good, well, then, they had a good will already. And who made this but God Himself who created them with a good will (that is, with the unblemished love by which they could adhere to Him) and who at the same time created their nature and enriched it with grace?

Thus, we are compelled to believe that the holy angels never existed without a good will, that is, without the love of God. But what of those angels who were created good and became evil by their own bad will for which their good nature is not responsible except in so far as there was a deliberate defection from good—for it is never good, but a defection from good, that is the cause of evil? These angels either received less grace of divine love than those who persevered in grace, or, if both were created equally good, then, while the former were falling by bad will, the latter were increasingly aided to reach that plenitude of beatitude which made them certain that they would never fall—a matter which I discussed in the preceding Book.

Thus with our praise to our Creator, we should all proclaim that, not only of holy men, but also of holy angels, it may be said that "the charity of God is poured forth" in them "by the Holy Spirit who has been given" to them (Rom. 5:5). Nor is it the good only of men, but first and foremost that of angels, which is referred to in the words: "It is good for me to adhere to my God" (Ps. 72:28).

And they who share this common good are in a holy communion both with Him to whom they adhere and one with another, and they form a single community, one City of God, which is also His living sacrifice and His living temple.

This ends the discussion of the origin of this City in so far as it concerns the angels. I must now turn to the rise of that part of the City which is made up of mortal men, created by the same God, who will one day be united to the immortal angels and who, at present, are either sojourning on earth or, if dead, are resting in the hidden sanctuaries where the souls of the departed have their abode.

It was from one man, the first whom God created, that the whole human race took its start. This is the faith revealed in Holy Scripture, a faith that has gained marvelous and merited authority throughout the world and among all peoples—as, along with other truths, Scripture itself divinely predicted would be the case.

*   *   *

BOOK XIX

*   *   *

CHAPTER 11

Thus, we may say of peace what we have said of eternal life—that it is our highest good; more particularly because the holy Psalmist was addressing the City of God (the nature of which I am trying, with so much difficulty, to make clear) when he said:

St. Matthew, from the Lindisfarne Gospels, before A.D. 698. (*The British Library/Superstock*)

"Praise the Lord, O Jerusalem; praise thy God, O Zion. Because he hath strengthened the bolts of thy gates, he hath blessed thy children within thee. He hath placed peace in thy borders" (Ps. 146:12–14). For, when the bolts of that city's gates will have been strengthened, none will enter in and none will issue forth. Hence, its borders (fines) must be taken to mean that peace which I am trying to show is our final good. Note, too, that Jerusalem, the mystical name which symbolizes this City, means, as I have already mentioned, "the vision of peace."

However, the word "peace" is so often applied to conditions here on earth, where life is not eternal, that it is better, I think, to speak of "eternal life" rather than of "peace" as the end or supreme good of the City of God. It is in this sense that St. Paul says: "But now being made free from sin, and become servants of God, you have your fruit unto sanctification, and the end life everlasting" (Rom. 6:22).

It would be simplest for all concerned if we spoke of "peace in eternal life," or of "eternal" or of "eternal life in peace," as the end or supreme good of this City. The trouble with the expression "eternal life" is that those unfamiliar with the Scriptures might take this phrase to apply also to the eternal loss of the wicked, either because, as philosophers, they accept the immortality of the soul, or even because, as Christians, they know by faith that the punishment of the wicked has no end and, therefore, that they could not be punished forever unless their life were eternal.

The trouble with "peace" is that, even on the level of earthly and temporal values, nothing that we can talk about, long for, or finally get, is so desirable, so welcome, so good as peace. At any rate, I feel sure that if I linger a little longer on this topic of peace I shall tire very few of my readers. After all, peace is the end of this City which is the theme of this work; besides, peace is so universally loved that its very name falls sweetly on the ear.

CHAPTER 12

Any man who has examined history and human nature will agree with me that there is no such thing as a human heart that does not crave for joy and peace. One has only to think of men who are bent on war. What they want is to win, that is to say, their battles are but bridges to glory and to peace. The whole point of victory is to bring opponents to their knees—this done, peace ensues. Peace, then, is the purpose of waging war; and this is true even of men who have a passion for the exercise of military prowess as rulers and commanders.

What, then, men want in war is that it should end in peace. Even while waging a war every man wants peace, whereas no one wants war while he is making peace. And even when men are plotting to disturb the peace, it is merely to fashion a new peace nearer to the heart's desire; it is not because they dislike peace as such. It is not that they love peace less, but that they love their kind of peace more. And even when a secession is successful, its purpose is not achieved unless some sort of peace remains among those who plotted and planned the rebellion. Take even a band of highwaymen. The more violence and impunity they want in disturbing the peace of other men, the more they demand peace among themselves. Take even the case of a robber so powerful that he dispenses with partnership, plans alone, and single-handed robs and kills his victims. Even he maintains some kind of peace, however shadowy, with those he cannot kill and whom he wants to keep in the dark with respect to his crimes. Certainly in his own home he wants to be at peace with his wife and children and any other members of his household. Of course, he is delighted when his every nod is obeyed; if it is not obeyed, he rages, and scolds, and demands peace in his own home and, if need be, gets it by sheer brutality. He knows that the price of peace in domestic society is to have everyone subject in the home to some head—in this instance, to himself.

Suppose, now, a man of this type were offered the allegiance of a larger society, say of a city or of a nation, with the pledge that he would be obeyed as he looks to be obeyed under his own roof. In this case, he would no longer hide himself away in a darksome robber's den; he would show himself off as a high and mighty king—the same man, however, with all of his old greed and criminality. Thus it is that all men want peace in their own society, and all want it in their own way. When they go to war what they want is to make, if they can, their enemies their own, and then to impose on them the victor's will and call it peace.

Now let us imagine a man like the one that poetry and mythology tell us about, a being so wild and anti-social that it was better to call him half-human than fully a man. He was called Cacus, which is Greek for "bad." His kingdom was the solitude of a dreadful cave and it was his extraordinary wickedness that gave him his name. He had no wife to exchange soft words with him; no tiny children to play with; no bigger ones to keep in order; no friend whose company he could enjoy, not even his father, Vulcan—than whom he was at least this much luckier that he had never begotten a monster like himself! There was no one to whom he would give anything, but whenever and from whomsoever he could he would take whatever he wanted and whenever he wanted it.

Nevertheless, all alone as he was in a cave that was always "warm with the blood of some recent victim," his sole longing was for peace in which no force would do him harm and no fear disturb his rest. Even with his own body he wanted to be at peace, and he was at ease only when peace was there. Even when he was bidding his members to obey him and was seizing, killing, and devouring his victims, his purpose was peace—the speediest possible peace with his mortal nature, driven by its needs to rebellion, and with his hunger, in sedition, clamoring for the breakup of the union of body and soul. Brutal and wild as he was and brutal and wild as were his ways, what he wanted was to have his life and limbs in peace. So much so that, had he been as willing to be at peace with his neighbors as he was active in procuring peace within himself and in his cave, no one would have called him wicked, nor a monster, nor even sub-human; or, at least, despite the shape of his body and the smoke and fire that issued from his mouth and kept all neighbors at a distance, people would have said that what looked like injustice, greed, and savagery were merely means to self-preservation. The truth is, of course, that there never existed any such being, or at least, none just like the foil the poets' fancy invented to glorify Hercules at the expense of Cacus. As is the case with most poetic inventions, we need not believe that any such creature, human or subhuman, ever lived.

I turn now to real wild beasts (from which category the animal part of the so-called half-beast, Cacus, was borrowed). They, too, keep their own particular genus in a kind of peace. Their males and females meet and mate, foster and feed their young, even though many of them by nature are more solitary than gregarious, like lions, foxes, eagles, and owls—as contrasted with deer, pigeons, starlings, and bees. Even a tigress purrs over her cubs and curbs all her fierceness when she fondles them. Even a falcon which seems so lonely when hovering above its prey mates and builds a nest, helps to hatch the eggs and feed the young, and makes every effort to maintain with the mother falcon a peaceful domestic society.

It is even more so with man. By the very laws of his nature, he seems, so to speak, forced into fellowship and, as far as in him lies, into peace with every man. At any rate, even when wicked men go to war they want peace for their own society and would like, if possible, to make all men members of that society, so that every one and every thing might be at the service of one head. Of course, the only means such a conqueror knows is to have all men so fear or love him that they will accept the peace which he imposes. For, so does pride perversely copy God. Sinful man hates the equality of all men under God and, as though he were God, loves to impose his sovereignty on his fellow men. He hates the peace of God which is just and prefers his own peace which is unjust. However, he is powerless not to love peace of some sort. For, no man's sin is so unnatural as to wipe out all traces whatsoever of human nature. Anyone, then, who is rational enough to prefer right to wrong and order to disorder can see that the kind of peace that is based on injustice, as compared with that which is based on justice, does not deserve the name of peace.

Of course, even disorder, in whole or in part, must come to some kind of terms either with the situation in which it finds itself or with the elements out of which it takes its being—otherwise it would have no being at all.

Take a man hanging upside down. Certainly his members are in disorder and the posture of the body as a whole is unnatural. The parts which nature demands should be above and below have become topsy-turvy. Such a position disturbs the peace of the body and is therefore painful. Nevertheless, the soul remains at peace with the body and continues to work for its welfare. Otherwise, the man would not live to feel the agony. And even if the soul is driven from the body by excess of pain, nevertheless, so long as the limbs hold together, some kind of peace among these parts remains. Otherwise, there would be no corpse to go on dangling there. Further, the fact that by gravity the corpse, made out of earth, tends to fall to the ground and pulls at the noose that holds it up proves that there is some order in which it seeks peace, and that its weight is, as it were, crying out for a place where it can rest. Lifeless and insensible though the body now is, it does not renounce that appropriate peace in the order of nature which it either has or seeks to have.

So, too, when a corpse is treated to embalming, to prevent dissolution and decay, there is a kind of peace which holds the parts together while the whole is committed to the earth, its proper resting place, and, therefore, a place with which the body is at peace. If, on the other hand, embalming is omitted and nature is allowed to take its course, the corpse remains a battleground of warring exhalations (that attack our senses with the stench we smell) only until such time as they finally fall in with the elements of this world and, slowly, bit by bit, become indistinguishable in a common peace.

Even afterward, however, the law and ordering of the Creator who is supreme in the whole cosmos and the regulator of its peace are still in control. Even when tiny bacteria spring from the corpse of a larger animal, it is by the same law of the Creator that all these minute bodies serve in peace the organic wholes of which they are parts. Even when the flesh of dead animals is eaten by other animals, there is no change in the universal laws which are meant for the common good of every kind of life, the common good that is effected by bringing like into peace with like. It makes no difference what disintegrating forces are at work, or what new combinations are made, or even what changes or transformations are effected.

CHAPTER 13

The peace, then, of the body lies in the ordered equilibrium of all its parts; the peace of the irrational soul, in the balanced adjustment of its appetites; the peace of the reasoning soul, in the harmonious correspondence of conduct and conviction; the peace of body and soul taken together, in the well-ordered life and health of the living whole. Peace between a mortal man and his Maker consists in ordered obedience, guided by faith, under God's eternal law; peace between man and man consists in regulated fellowship. The peace of a home lies in the ordered harmony of authority and obedience between the members of a family living together. The peace of the political community is an ordered harmony of authority and obedience between citizens. The peace of the heavenly City lies in a perfectly ordered and harmonious communion of those who find their joy in God and in one another in God. Peace, in its final sense, is the calm that comes of order. Order is an arrangement of like and unlike things whereby each of them is disposed in its proper place.

This being so, those who are unhappy, in so far as they are unhappy, are not in peace, since they lack the calm of that Order which is beyond every storm; nevertheless, even in their misery they cannot escape from order, since their very misery is related to responsibility and to justice. They do not share with the blessed in their tranquility, but this very separation is the result of the law of order. Moreover, even the miserable can be momentarily free from anxiety and can reach some measure of adjustment to their surroundings and, hence, some tranquility of order and, therefore, some slender peace. However, the reason why they remain unhappy is that, although they *may* be momentarily free from worry and from pain, they are not in a condition where they *must* be free both from worry and pain. Their condition of misery is worse when such peace as they have is not in harmony with that law which governs the order of nature. Their peace can also be disturbed by pain and in proportion to their pain; yet, some peace will remain, so long as the pain is not too acute and their organism as a whole does not disintegrate.

Notice that there can be life without pain, but no pain without some kind of life. In the same way, there can be peace without any kind of war, but no war that does not suppose some kind of peace. This does not mean that war as war involves peace; but war, in so far as those who wage it or have it waged upon them are beings with organic natures, involves peace—for the simple reason that to be organic means to be ordered and, therefore, to be, in some sense, at peace.

Similarly, there can be a nature without any defect and, even, a nature in which there can be no kind of evil whatever, but there can be no nature completely devoid of good. Even the nature of the Devil, in so far as it is a nature, is not evil; it was perversity—not being true to itself—that made it bad. The Devil did not "stand in the truth" (John 8:44) and, therefore, did not escape the judgment of truth. He did not stand fast in the tranquility of order—nor did he, for all that, elude the power of the Ordainer. The goodness which God gave to his nature does not withdraw him from the justice of God by which that nature is subject to punishment. Yet, even in that punishment, God does not hound the good which He created, but only the evil which the Devil committed. So it is that God does not take back the whole of His original gift. He takes a part and leaves a part; He leaves a nature that can regret what God has taken back. Indeed, the very pain inflicted is evidence of both the good that is lost and the good that is left. For, if there were no good left, there would be no one to lament the good that has been lost.

A man who sins is just that much worse if he rejoices in the loss of holiness; but one who suffers pain, and does not benefit by it, laments, at least, the loss of his health. Holiness and health are both good things and, because the loss of any good is more a cause for grief than for gladness (unless there be some higher compensation—the soul's holiness, to be sure, is preferable to the body's health), it is more in accordance with nature that a sinner grieve over his punishment than that he rejoice over his offense. Consequently, just as a man's happiness in abandoning the good of wrong-doing betrays his bad will, so his sorrowing for the good he has lost when in pain bears witness to the good of his nature. For, anyone who grieves over the loss of peace to his nature does so out of some remnant of that peace wherewith his nature loves itself. This is what happens—deservedly, too—in eternal punishment. In the midst of their agonies the evil and the godless weep for the loss of their nature's goods, knowing, meanwhile, that God whose great generosity they condemned was perfectly just when He took these goods away.

God, the wise Creator and just Ordainer of all natures, has made the mortal race of man the loveliest of all lovely things on earth. He has given to men good gifts suited to their existence here below. Among these is temporal peace, according to the poor limits of mortal life, in health, security, and human fellowship; and other gifts, too, needed to preserve this peace or regain it, once lost—for instance, the blessings that lie all around us, so perfectly adapted to our senses: daylight, speech, air to breathe, water to drink, everything that goes to feed, clothe, cure, and beautify the body. These good gifts are granted, however, with the perfectly just understanding that whoever uses the goods which are meant for the mortal peace of mortal men, as these goods should be used, will receive more abundant and better goods—nothing less than immortal peace and all that goes with it, namely, the glory and honor of enjoying God and one's neighbor in God everlastingly; but that whoever misuses his gifts on earth will both lose what he has and never receive the better gifts of heaven.

CHAPTER 14

In the earthly city, then, temporal goods are to be used with a view to the enjoyment of earthly peace, whereas, in the heavenly City, they are used with a view to the enjoyment of eternal peace. Hence, if we were merely unthinking brutes, we would pursue nothing beyond the orderly interrelationship of our bodily part and the appeasing of our appetites, nothing, that is, beyond the comfort of the flesh and plenty of pleasures, so that the peace of body might contribute to peace of the soul. For, if order in the body be lacking, the peace of an irrational soul is checked, since it cannot attain the satisfaction of its appetites. Both of these forms of peace meanwhile subserve that other form of peace which the body and soul enjoy between them, the peace of life and health in good order.

For, just as brutes show that they love the peace or comfort of their bodies by shunning pain, and the peace of their souls by pursuing pleasure to satisfy their appetites, so, too, by running from death, they make clear enough how much they love the peace which keeps body and soul together.

Because, however, man has a rational soul, he makes everything he shares with brutes subserve the peace of his rational soul, so that he first measures things with his mind before he acts, in order to achieve that harmonious correspondence of conduct and conviction which I called the peace of the rational soul. His purpose in desiring not to be vexed with pain, nor disturbed with desire, nor disintegrated by death is that he may learn something profitable and so order his habits and way of life. However, if the infirmity of his human mind is not to bring him in his pursuit of knowledge to some deadly error, he needs divine authority to give secure guidance, and divine help so that he may be unhampered in following the guidance given.

And because, so long as man lives in his mortal body and is a pilgrim far from the Lord, he walks, not by vision, but by faith. Consequently, he refers all peace of body or soul, or their combination, to that higher peace which unites a mortal man with the immortal God and which I defined as "ordered obedience guided by faith, under God's eternal law."

Meanwhile, God teaches him two chief commandments, the love of God and the love of neighbor. In these precepts man finds three beings to love, namely, God, himself, and his fellow man, and knows that he is not wrong in loving himself so long as he loves God. As a result, he must help his neighbor (whom he is obliged to love as himself) to love God. Thus, he must help his wife, children, servants, and all others whom he can influence. He must wish, moreover, to be similarly helped by his fellow man, in case he himself needs such assistance. Out of all this love he will arrive at peace, as much as in him lies, with every man—at that human peace which is regulated fellowship. Right order here means, first, that he harm no one, and, second, that he help whomever he can. His fundamental duty is to look out for his own home, for both by natural and human law he has easier and readier access to their requirements.

St. Paul says: "But if any does not take care of his own, and especially of his household, he has denied the faith and is worse than an unbeliever" (I Tim. 5:8). From this care arises that peace of the home which lies in the harmonious interplay of authority and obedience among those who live there. For, those who have the care of the others give the orders—a man to his wife, parents to their children, masters to their servants. And those who are cared for must obey—wives their husband, children their parents, servants their masters. In the home of a religious man, however, of a man living by faith and as yet a wayfarer from the heavenly City, those who command serve those whom they appear to rule—because, of course, they do not command out of lust to domineer, but out of a sense of duty—not out of pride like princes but out of solicitude like parents.

CHAPTER 15

This family arrangement is what nature prescribes, and what God intended in creating man: "let them have dominion over the fish of the sea, the birds of the air, the cattle, over all the wild animals and every creature that crawls on the earth" (Gen. 1:26). God wanted rational man, made to His image, to have no dominion except over irrational nature. He meant no man, therefore, to have dominion over man, but only man over beast. So it fell out that those who were holy in primitive times became shepherds over sheep rather than monarchs over men, because God wishes in this way to teach us that the normal hierarchy of creatures is different from that which punishment for sin has made imperative. For, when subjection came, it was merely a condition deservedly imposed on sinful man. So, in Scripture, there is no mention of the word "servant" until holy Noah used it in connection with the curse on his son's wrong-doing. It is a designation that is not natural, but one that was deserved because of sin.

The Latin word for "slave" is *servus* and it is said that this word is derived from the fact that those who, by right of conquest, could have been killed were sometimes kept and guarded, *servabantur,* by their captors and so became slaves and were called *servi*. Now, such a condition of servitude could only have arisen as a result of sin, since whenever a just war is waged the opposing side must be in the wrong, and every victory, even when won by wicked men, is a divine judgment to humble the conquered and to reform or punish their sin. To this truth Daniel, the great man of God, bore witness. When he was languishing in the Babylonian captivity he confessed to God his sins and those of his people and avowed, with pious repentance, that these sins were the cause of the captivity. It is clear, then, that sin is the primary cause of servitude, in the sense of a social status in which one man is compelled to be subjected to another man. Nor does this befall a man, save by the decree of God, who is never unjust and who knows how to impose appropriate punishments on different sinners.

Our heavenly Master says: "everyone who commits sin is a slave of sin" (John 8:34). So it happens that holy people are sometimes enslaved to wicked masters who are, in turn, themselves slaves. For, "by whatever a man is overcome, of this also he is a slave" (II Pet. 2:19). Surely it is better to be the slave of a man than the slave of passion as when, to take but one example, the lust for lordship raises such havoc in the hearts of men. Such, then, as men now are, is the order of peace. Some are in subjection to others, and, while humility helps those who serve, pride harms those in power. But, as men once were, when their nature was as God created it, no man was a slave either to man or to sin. However, slavery is now penal in character and planned by that law which commands the preservation of the natural order and forbids its disturbance. If no crime had ever been perpetrated against this law, there would be no crime to repress with the penalty of enslavement.

It is with this in mind that St. Paul goes so far as to admonish slaves to obey their masters and to serve them so sincerely and with such good will that, if there is no chance of manumission, they may make their slavery a kind of freedom by serving with love and loyalty, free from fear and feigning, until injustice becomes a thing of the past and every human sovereignty and power is done away with, so that God may be all in all.

CHAPTER 16

Our holy Fathers in the faith, to be sure, had slaves, but in the regulation of domestic peace it was only in matters of temporal importance that they distinguished the position of their children from the status of their servants. So far as concerns the worship of God—from whom all must hope for eternal blessings—they had like loving care for all the household without exception. This was what nature demanded, and it was from this kind of behavior that there grew the designation "father of the family," which is so widely accepted that even wicked and domineering men love to be so called.

Those who are true fathers are as solicitous for every one in their households as for their own children to worship and to be worthy of God. They hope and yearn for all to arrive in that heavenly home where there will be no further need of giving orders to other human beings, because there will be no longer any duty to help those who are happy in immortal life. In the meantime, fathers ought to look upon their duty to command as harder than the duty of slaves to obey.

Meanwhile, in case anyone in the home behaves contrary to its peace, he is disciplined by words or whipping or other kind of punishment lawful and licit in human society, and for his own good, to readjust him to the peace he has abandoned. For, there is no more benevolence and helpfulness in bringing about the loss of a greater good than there is innocence and compassion in allowing a culprit to go from bad to worse. It is the duty of a blameless person not just to do no wrong, but to keep others from wrong-doing and to punish it when done, so that the one punished may be improved by the experience and others be warned by the example.

Now, since every home should be a beginning or fragmentary constituent of a civil community, and every beginning related to some specific end, and every part to the whole of which it is a part, it ought to follow that domestic peace has a relation to political peace. In other words, the ordered harmony of authority and obedience between those who live together has a relation to the ordered harmony of authority and obedience between those who live in a city. This explains why a father must apply certain regulations of civil law to the governance of his home, so as to make it accord with the peace of the whole community.

CHAPTER 17

While the homes of unbelieving men are intent upon acquiring temporal peace out of the possessions and comforts of this temporal life, the families which live according to faith look ahead to the good things of heaven promised as imperishable, and use material and temporal goods in the spirit of pilgrims, not as snares or obstructions to block their way to God, but simply as helps to ease and never to increase the burdens of this corruptible body which weighs down the soul. Both types of homes and their masters have this in common, that they must use things essential to this mortal life. But the respective purposes to which they put them are characteristic and very different.

So, too, the earthly city which does not live by faith seeks only an earthly peace, and limits the goal of its peace, of its harmony of authority and obedience among its citizens, to the voluntary and collective attainment of objectives necessary to mortal existence. The heavenly City, meanwhile—or, rather, that part that is on pilgrimage in mortal life and lives by faith—must use this earthly peace until such time as our mortality which needs such peace has passed away. As a consequence, so long as her life in the earthly city is that of a captive and an alien (although she has the promise of ultimate delivery and the gift of the Spirit as a pledge), she has no hesitation about keeping in step with the civil law which governs matters pertaining to our existence here below. For, as mortal life is the same for all, there ought to be common cause between the two cities in what concerns our purely human living.

Now comes the difficulty. The city of this world, to begin with, has had certain "wise men" of its own mold, whom true religion must reject, because either out of their own daydreaming or out of demonic deception these wise men came to believe that a multiplicity of divinities was allied with human life, with different duties, in some strange arrangement, and different assignments: this one over the body, that one over the mind; in the body itself, one over the head, another over the neck, still others, one for each bodily part; in the mind, one over the intelligence, another over learning, another over temper, another over desire; in the realities, related to life, that lie about us, one over flocks and one over wheat, one over wine, one over oil, and another over forests, one over currency, another over navigation, and still another over warfare and victory, one over marriage, a different one over fecundity and childbirth, so on and so on.

The heavenly City, on the contrary, knows and, by religious faith, believes that it must adore one God alone and serve Him with that complete dedication which the Greeks call *latreía* and which belongs to Him alone. As a result, she has been unable to share with the earthly city a common religious legislation, and has had no choice but to dissent on this score and so to become a nuisance to those who think otherwise. Hence, she has had to feel the weight of their anger, hatred, and violence, save in those instances when, by sheer numbers and God's help, which never fails, she has been able to scare off her opponents.

So long, then, as the heavenly City is wayfaring on earth, she invites citizens from all nations and all tongues, and unites them into a single pilgrim band. She takes no issue with that diversity of customs, laws, and traditions whereby human peace is sought and maintained. Instead of nullifying or tearing down, she preserves and appropriates whatever in the diversities of diverse races is aimed at one and the same objective of human peace, provided only that they do not stand in the way of the faith and worship of the one supreme and true God.

Thus, the heavenly City, so long as it is wayfaring on earth, not only makes use of earthly peace but fosters and actively pursues along with other human beings a common platform in regard to all that concerns our purely human life and does not interfere with faith and worship. Of course, though, the City of God subordinates this earthly peace to that of heaven. For this is not merely true peace, but, strictly speaking, for any rational creature, the only real peace, since it is, as I said, "the perfectly ordered and harmonious communion of those who find their joy in God and in one another in God."

When this peace is reached, man will be no longer haunted by death, but plainly and perpetually endowed with life, nor will his body, which now wastes away and weighs down the soul, be any longer animal, but spiritual, in need of nothing, and completely under the control of our will.

This peace the pilgrim City already possesses by faith and it lives holily and according to this faith so long as, to attain its heavenly completion, it refers every good act done for God or for his fellow man. I say "fellow man" because, of course, any community life must emphasize social relationships.

BOETHIUS
ca. A.D. 480–ca. 524

Anicius Manlius Severinus Boethius was the son of a Roman high-government official. Possibly educated in Athens or Alexandria, Boethius had a special interest in the writings of Plato and Aristotle. It was his intention to translate all their works into Latin and provide full commentary. He hoped to show the essential unity between Plato and Aristotle, but he translated only Aristotle's logical works. In 510 Boethius became consul and first minister to King Theodoric, the Ostrogothic ruler of Italy. Boethius served the next twelve years in government, wrote commentaries on Porphyry and Cicero, and began his work on Plato and Aristotle. In 522 Boethius' sons were named consuls, and Boethius was promoted to the important rank of "master of the offices." But within a year, tragedy struck. Boethius was accused of treason, imprisoned, and executed sometime around 524. The specific charges are not known, but religious differences were probably involved. Theodoric followed the teachings of Arius (ca. A.D. 256–336) that Jesus Christ was neither coeternal with God the Father nor of the same substance. Boethius, as a Catholic, accepted the conclusions of the Council of Nicea (A.D. 325), which condemned Arian theology.

While in prison, Boethius wrote his most famous work, *The Consolation of Philosophy*. Written as a dialogue between Boethius and Lady Philosophy, it begins with Boethius protesting innocence and complaining of God's injustice and fortune's caprice. Using arguments rooted in both Stoic and Platonic thought, Lady Philosophy replies that fortune is indeed fickle, but that the highest Good is found not in circumstances but in God. The selection given here, translated by Richard Green, is from the final book of the *Consolation* and examines how God's foreknowledge is compatible with free will. Boethius asks how one could

341

be free to perform an action if God knew *beforehand* what one would do. Using a conception of time similar to Augustine's in Book XI of the *Confessions,* Lady Philosophy explains that God is completely outside time. This means that God "sees all things in his eternal present as you see some things in your temporal present . . . This divine foreknowledge does not change the nature and properties of things; it simply sees things present before it as they will later turn out to be in what we regard as the future." For example, just as I know what my son is doing now even though his action is free, so God can know what I will do tomorrow though I act freely—because for God tomorrow *is* now.

It may seem odd that a devout Catholic presented his final thoughts in Neoplatonic and Stoic terms, without any specifically Christian references. Yet Boethius' *magnum opus* was a source of great comfort to Christians in the Middle Ages for, as Étienne Gilson points out, "even when he is speaking only as a philosopher Boethius thinks as a Christian."

*   *   *

For background work on Boethius, see Howard Rollin Patch, *The Tradition of Boethius: A Study of His Importance in Medieval Culture* (New York: Oxford University Press, 1935), and Helen Marjorie Barrett, *Boethius: Some Aspects of His Times and Work* (Cambridge: Cambridge University Press, 1940). Henry Chadwick, *Boethius: The Consolations of Music, Logic, Theology, and Philosophy* (Oxford: Clarendon Press, 1981), and Edmund Reiss, *Boethius* (Boston: Twayne, 1982), study Boethius' writings, whereas Ralph M. McInerny, *Boethius and Aquinas* (Washington, DC: Catholic University of America Press, 1990), shows his influence on Thomas Aquinas. For collections of essays, see Michael Masi, ed., *Boethius and the Liberal Arts: A Collection of Essays* (Las Vegas, NV: Peter Lang, 1981), and Margaret Gibson, ed., *Boethius, His Life, Thought, and Influence* (Oxford: Blackwell, 1981).

In recent years, there has been renewed interest in the problems posed by Boethius' conception of God's timelessness and foreknowledge. Paul Helm, *Eternal God: A Study of God Without Time* (Oxford: Clarendon Press, 1988), for example, argues in favor of Boethius' position, whereas Richard Swinburne, *The Coherence of Theism* (Oxford: Clarendon Press, 1977), and Stephen T. Davis, *Logic and the Nature of God* (Grand Rapids, MI: Eerdmans, 1983), oppose it. Much of the most interesting work in this area is found only in journals, such as the *Journal of Philosophy* and *Faith and Philosophy.*

Theodoric exiles Boethius from Rome to Padua, 1521, woodcut. Boethius was consul and first minister to King Theodoric, the Ostrogothic ruler of Italy. But in 522 Boethius was accused of treason, imprisoned, and, sometime around 524, executed. The specific charges are not known, but probably involved religious differences between the Catholic Boethius and the Arian Theodoric. (*Library of Congress*)

THE CONSOLATION OF PHILOSOPHY (in part)

BOOK V

CHAPTER 6: PHILOSOPHY SOLVES THE PROBLEM OF PROVIDENCE AND FREE WILL BY DISTINGUISHING BETWEEN SIMPLE AND CONDITIONAL NECESSITY

"Since, as we have shown, whatever is known is known according to the nature of the knower, and not according to its own nature, let us now consider as far as is lawful the nature of the Divine Being, so that we may discover what its knowledge is. The common judgment of all rational creatures holds that God is eternal. Therefore let us consider what eternity is, for this will reveal both the divine nature and the divine knowledge.

"Eternity is the whole, perfect, and simultaneous possession of endless life. The meaning of this can be made clearer by comparison with temporal things. For whatever

Boethius, *The Consolation of Philosophy,* translated by Richard Green (New York: Macmillan/Library of the Liberal Arts, 1962), Book V, Chapter 6.

lives in time lives in the present, proceeding from past to future, and nothing is so constituted in time that it can embrace the whole span of its life at once. It has not yet arrived at tomorrow, and it has already lost yesterday; even the life of this day is lived only in each moving, passing moment. Therefore, whatever is subject to the condition of time, even that which—as Aristotle conceived the world to be—has no beginning and will have no end in a life coextensive with the infinity of time, is such that it cannot rightly be thought eternal. For it does not comprehend and include the whole of infinite life all at once, since it does not embrace the future which is yet to come. Therefore, only that which comprehends and possesses the whole plenitude of endless life together, from which no future thing nor any past thing is absent, can justly be called eternal. Moreover, it is necessary that such a being be in full possession of itself, always present to itself, and hold the infinity of moving time present before itself.

"Therefore, they are wrong who, having heard that Plato held that this world did not have a beginning in time and would never come to an end, suppose that the created world is coeternal with its Creator. For it is one thing to live an endless life, which is what Plato ascribed to the world, and another for the whole of unending life to be embraced all at once as present, which is clearly proper to the divine mind. Nor should God be thought of as older than His creation in extent of time, but rather as prior to it by virtue of the simplicity of His nature. For the infinite motion of temporal things imitates the immediate present of His changeless life and, since it cannot reproduce or equal life, it sinks from immobility to motion and declines from the simplicity of the present into the infinite duration of future and past. And, since it cannot possess the whole fullness of its life at once, it seems to imitate to some extent that which it cannot completely express, and it does this by somehow never ceasing to be. It binds itself to a kind of present in this short and transitory period which, because it has a certain likeness to that abiding, unchanging present, gives everything it touches a semblance of existence. But, since this imitation cannot remain still, it hastens along the infinite road of time, and so it extends by movement the life whose completeness it could not achieve by standing still. Therefore, if we wish to call things by their proper names, we should follow Plato in saying that God indeed is eternal, but the world is perpetual.

"Since, then, every judgment comprehends the subjects presented to it according to its own nature, and since God lives in the eternal present, His knowledge transcends all movement of time and abides in the simplicity of its immediate present. It encompasses the infinite sweep of past and future, and regards all things in its simple comprehension as if they were now taking place. Thus, if you will think about the foreknowledge by which God distinguishes all things, you will rightly consider it to be not a foreknowledge of future events, but knowledge of a never changing present. For this reason, divine knowledge is called providence, rather than prevision, because it resides above all inferior things and looks out on all things from their summit.

"Why then do you imagine that things are necessary which are illuminated by this divine light, since even men do not impose necessity on the things they see? Does your vision impose any necessity upon things which you see present before you?"

"Not at all," I answered.

"Then," Philosophy went on, "if we may aptly compare God's present vision with man's, He sees all things in his eternal present as you see some things in your temporal present. Therefore, this divine foreknowledge does not change the nature and properties of things; it simply sees things present before it as they will later turn out to be in what we regard as the future. His judgment is not confused; with a single intuition of his mind He knows all things that are to come, whether necessarily or not. Just as, when you happen to see simultaneously a man walking on the street and the sun shining in the sky, even though you see both at once, you can distinguish between them and realize that one action is voluntary, the other necessary; so the divine mind, looking down on all things, does not disturb the nature of the things which are present before it but are future with respect to time. Therefore, when God knows that something will happen in the future, and at the same time knows that it will not happen through necessity, this is not opinion but knowledge based on truth.

"If you should reply that whatever God foresees as happening cannot help but happen, and that whatever must happen is bound by necessity—if you pin me down to this word 'necessity'—I grant that you state a solid truth, but one which only a profound theologian can grasp. I would answer that the same future event is necessary with respect to God's knowledge of it, but free and undetermined if considered in its own nature. For there are two kinds of necessity: one is simple, as the necessity by which all men are mortals; the other is conditional, as is the case when, if you know that someone is walking, he must necessarily be walking. For whatever is known, must be as it is known to be; but this condition does not involve that other, simple necessity. It is not caused by the peculiar nature of the person in question, but by an added condition. No necessity forces the man who is voluntarily walking to move forward; but as long as he is walking, he is necessarily moving forward. In the same way, if Providence sees anything as present, that thing must necessarily be, even though it may have no necessity by its nature. But God sees as present those future things which result from free will. Therefore, from the standpoint of divine knowledge these things are necessary because of the condition of their being known by God; but, considered only in themselves, they lose nothing of the absolute freedom of their own natures.

"There is no doubt, then, that all things will happen which God knows will happen; but some of them happen as a result of free will. And, although they happen, they do not, by their existence, lose their proper natures by which, before they happened, they were able not to happen. But, you may ask, what does it mean to say that these events are not necessary, since by reason of the condition of divine knowledge they happen just as if they were necessary? The meaning is the same as in the example I used a while ago of the sun rising and the man walking. At the time they are happening, they must necessarily be happening; but the sun's rising is governed by necessity even before it happens, while the man's walking is not. Similarly, all the things God sees as present will undoubtedly come to pass; but some will happen by the necessity of their natures, others by the power of those who make them happen. Therefore, we quite properly said that these things are necessary if viewed from the standpoint of divine knowledge, but if they are considered in themselves, they are free of the bonds of necessity. In somewhat the same way, whatever is known by the senses is singular in itself, but universal as far as the reason is concerned.

"But, you may say, if I can change my mind about doing something, I can frustrate Providence, since by chance I may change something which Providence foresaw. My answer is this: you can indeed alter what you propose to do, but, because the present truth of Providence sees that you can, and whether or not you will, you cannot frustrate the divine knowledge any more than you can escape the eye of someone who is present and watching you, even though you may, by your free will, vary your actions. You may still wonder, however, whether God's knowledge is changed by your decisions, so that when you wish now one thing, now another, the divine knowledge undergoes corresponding changes. This is not the case. For divine Providence anticipates every future action and converts it to its own present knowledge. It does not change, as you imagine, foreknowing this or that in succession, but in a single instant, without being changed itself, anticipates and grasps your changes. God has this present comprehension and immediate vision of all things not from the outcome of future events, but from the simplicity of his own nature. In this way, the problem you raised a moment ago is settled. You observed that it would be unworthy of God if our future acts were said to be the cause of divine knowledge. Now you see that this power of divine knowledge, comprehending all things as present before it, itself constitutes the measure of all things and is in no way dependent on things that happen later.

"Since this is true, the freedom of the human will remains inviolate, and laws are just since they provide rewards and punishments to human wills which are not controlled by necessity. God looks down from above, knowing all things, and the eternal present of his vision concurs with the future character of our actions, distributing rewards to the good and punishments to the evil. Our hopes and prayers are not directed to God in vain, for if they are just they cannot fail. Therefore, stand firm against vice and cultivate virtue. Lift up your soul to worthy hopes, and offer humble prayers to heaven. If you will face it, the necessity of virtuous action imposed upon you is very great, since all your actions are done in the sight of a Judge who sees all things."

JOHN SCOTUS ERIUGENA
ca. A.D. 810–ca. 877

The collapse of the Western Roman Empire led to a period of economic and social anarchy. Living conditions from the end of the sixth to the middle of the eleventh centuries were so primitive that, according to historians, "one can almost speak of five centuries of camping out."* Government was largely tribal in nature, led by warriors who considered loyalty to one's liege lord the primary virtue. What little social stability there was tended to depend upon exceptional individuals, such as Charlemagne and Alfred the Great. One of the few remaining places for intellectual endeavor was the monastery; and monasteries were often far from population centers, many on the very edges of Europe. It should not be surprising, then, that the one philosopher of note to emerge from this period was a monk from Ireland: John Scotus Eriugena.

John Scotus Eriugena's two last names both mean "from Ireland" (at that time the Irish were called "Scoti," and "Eriugena" means "of the people of Erin [Ireland]"). Eriugena, as he is commonly called, studied Greek in an Irish monastery and eventually became a teacher in the court of the king of the Franks, Charles the Bald. While there he was embroiled in a controversy on the nature of the Eucharist, and one of his books was burned. Apart from these slim data, we know little about Eriugena's life and cannot even say for certain when or how he died (though 877 is the frequently given date).

In the selection from *The Division of Nature* given here, in the Myra L. Uhfelder translation, Eriugena shows his Neoplatonic roots by giving two ways of dividing "nature" (meaning all of reality). In the first method, based on the con-

*Robert E. Lerner et al., *Western Civilizations,* 11th edition (New York: Norton, 1988), p. 278.

347

cepts of creating and being created, Eriugena divides nature into four parts. First is "that which creates and is not created" (i.e., God), then "that which is created and also creates" (i.e., Platonic Forms), then "that which is created and does not create" (i.e., the material world), and finally "that which neither creates nor is created" (God again). The first and fourth divisions turn out to be the Creator, whereas the second and third are the creation (immaterial and material, respectively).

The second, and more basic, division of nature is into "things that are" and "things that are not." It might seem that "things that are not" would be sheer nothingness and so not really a part of "nature" at all. But, Eriugena explains, there are several "things" that do not exist in one mode or another. These include (1) anything beyond our faculties of apprehension, (2) the negation of the superior, (3) potential beings, (4) changing particulars, and (5) the sinful nature of humans (who have lost their essential nature). The first of these modes of nonbeing has the dubious distinction of making God one of the "things that are not." Eriugena asserted that indeed "God is not," but he pointed out that this way of thinking and talking is simply the *via negativa*—the negative way of confessing God. There is also a *via affirmativa*, which allows the affirmation of God's essential properties. So, for example, it is correct (using the *via negativa*) to say that "God is not good," whereas it is also correct (using the *via affirmativa*) to say that "God *is* good." Eriugena resolved this seeming contradiction by claiming that although God is not (literally) good, God is (metaphorically) good—in short, God is "*super*-good."

Eriugena's fourfold division of reality looks a good deal like Plotinus' emanations and seems to put God and God's creation in the same category ("Nature"). Not surprisingly, Eriugena was accused by the Catholic Church of Neoplatonic pantheism, and his work was eventually condemned as heretical in 1225.

*   *   *

In addition to the appropriate chapters in the surveys of medieval philosophy previously listed (page 304), the following studies of Eriugena should be consulted for further reading: Henry Bett, *Johannes Scotus Erigena: A Study in Mediaeval Philosophy* (1925; reprinted New York: Russell and Russell, 1964); John O'Meara, *Eriugena* (Oxford: Clarendon Press, 1988); and Dermot Moran, *The Philosophy of John Scotus Eriugena: A Study of Idealism in the Middle Ages* (Cambridge: Cambridge University Press, 1989). For a collection of essays, see F.X. Martin and J.A. Richmond, eds., *From Augustine to Eriugena: Essays on Neoplatonism and Christianity* (Washington, DC: Catholic University of America Press, 1991) and Bernard McGinn and Willemien Otten, eds., *Eriugena: East and West* (Notre Dame, IN: Notre Dame University Press, 1994).

THE DIVISION OF NATURE (*PERIPHYSEON*) (in part)

CHAPTER 1

TEACHER: Often I investigate as carefully as I can and reflect that of all things which can either be perceived by the mind or surpass its concentrated efforts the first and highest division is into what has and what does not have being. At such times the general designation of them all occurs to me, ⟨*physis*⟩ in Greek and *natura* in Latin. Or don't you agree?

STUDENT: Yes, I do. Although I am just entering upon the path of reasoning, I find that it is so.

TEACHER: As we have just said, then, "nature" is a general name for all things, whether or not they have being.

STUDENT: It certainly is, for we can think of nothing at all to which such a designation does not apply.

TEACHER: Since we have agreed that this is a generic designation, I should like you to tell how it is divided into species by *differentiae*. Or if you prefer, I shall try to establish the divisions first and your task will be to judge them.

STUDENT: Please begin. I am eager and impatient to hear you give a true account about these matters.

[1] TEACHER: The division of nature seems to me to admit of four species through four *differentiae*. The first is the division into what creates and is not created; the second into what is created and creates; the third, into what is created and does not create; the fourth, into what neither creates nor is created. Of these four, two pairs consist of opposites. The third is the opposite of the first, the fourth of the second. But the fourth is among the things which are impossible, and its *differentia* is its inability to be. Does such a division seem to you correct or not?

STUDENT: It surely does, but would you please go over it to clarify the opposition of the species just mentioned?

TEACHER: Unless I'm mistaken, you see the opposition of the third species to the first. The first creates and is not created, and its opposite is that which is created and does not create. Likewise the opposition of the second to the fourth, since the second is created and creates; the fourth, which neither creates nor is created, is contrary to it in every respect.

STUDENT: I see that clearly, but I am quite perplexed about the fourth species which you added. As for the other three, I should not venture to have any misgivings; for I judge that the first is understood in the Cause of all things which have and all which do not have being, the second in the primordial causes, the third in those things known by generation in time and place. I see, therefore, that we must have a more detailed discussion about the individual species.

TEACHER: You are quite right. But I leave it to your judgment to determine our order of reasoning; i.e., to decide which species of nature should be discussed first.

John Scotus Erigena [Eriugena], *Periphyseon: On the Division of Nature,* Book I, Chapters 1–7; Chapter 14, edited and translated by Myra L. Uhfelder, summaries by Jean A. Potter (New York: Macmillan/Library of the Liberal Arts, 1976).

STUDENT: I think that it would be proper, before dealing with the others to say what our insight reveals to us about the first.

[2] TEACHER: All right, but I think that first we must talk briefly about the highest and main division of all which, as we said, is the division into the things which have and those which do not have being.

STUDENT: That is a very sound and judicious idea. I see that our reasoning should begin no other way, not only because that is the first *differentia* of all things, but also because it appears, and is, more obscure than the others.

TEACHER: Well, then, the original distinguishing *differentia* of all things demands clear-cut methods of interpretation.

[3] Of these, the first seems to be the one by which reason persuades us that all things subject to corporeal sense or the perception of intelligence can reasonably be said to have being; but all that, by the excellence of their nature, elude not only the *hylion,* i.e., every sense, but also intellect and reason, properly seem not to have being. They are correctly understood only in God, matter, and the reasons and essences of all things created by Him. And that is as it should be; for He Himself, who alone truly has being, is the essence of all things, according to Dionysius the Areopagite, who says: "The being of all things is Superbeing, Divinity." Gregory the Theologian too affirms by many reasons that intellect or reason cannot grasp what any substance or essence is, whether it belongs to visible or to invisible creation. For just as God Himself, in Himself, beyond all creation is grasped by no intellect, so also *ousia* [*"essentia"* or "being"] considered in the innermost recesses of the creation made by Him and existing in Him, is incomprehensible. Besides, whatever in every creature is either perceived by corporeal sense or considered by the intellect is simply some accident, incomprehensible in itself, as has been said, of an essence. By quality, quantity, form, matter, some *differentia,* place, or time we know not *what* it is, but *that* it is. This, then, is the first and highest method of division of what is said to have and what is said not to have being. I believe, however, that that method which it seems, in a way, possible to introduce, namely the one based on privations of states in reference to substances, as sight and blindness in reference to the eyes, must be utterly rejected. For if something wholly lacks being and cannot be and does not surpass intellect because of the supernal height of its existence, I fail to see how it can fit into the divisions of things; unless, perhaps, one should say that the absences and privations of things with being are not absolutely nothing, but that they are contained by some remarkable natural power of those things of which they are the privations, absences, or opposites, so that, in a certain way, they have being.

[4] Let us grant that the second method of being and not-being is the one considered in the orders and *differentiae* of created natures. Beginning from the most exalted intellectual power stationed closest to God, it descends to the extreme of rational and irrational creation. To speak more clearly, I mean from the highest angel to the lowest part of a rational or irrational soul, the vital principle of nutrition and growth (for when the soul is considered as a genus, the part of the soul which nurtures the body and causes it to grow is the lowest). Here each order, including the bottommost order of bodies with which all division is terminated, can be said in a remarkable way to have and not to have being. What is stated affirmatively of the lower is stated negatively of the higher. Likewise what is stated negatively of the lower is stated affirmatively of the higher. In the same way, what is stated affirmatively of the higher is stated negatively of the lower; and what is stated negatively of the higher will be stated affirmatively of the lower. What is stated affirmatively of a man, that he is still mortal, is stated negatively of an angel. What is stated negatively of a man is stated affirmatively of an angel, and vice versa. For example, if a man is a rational, mortal, visible animal, an angel is surely

not a rational, mortal, visible animal. Similarly, if an angel is an essential motion of the intellect focussing on God and the causes of things, surely man is not an essential motion of the intellect focussing on God and the causes of things. The same rule can be observed in all celestial essences until one reaches the highest order of all which is terminated above by the Supreme Negation. Its negative definition affirms that no creature is higher than It. There are three orders called *homotageis* ("of equal rank"). The first of these consists of Cherubim, Seraphim, and Thrones; the second of Virtues, Powers, and Dominations; the third of Principalities, Archangels, and Angels. In descending order, the lowest group of bodies merely negates or affirms what is higher than itself because it has nothing beneath itself to take away or add since it is preceded by all higher orders and does not precede anything lower than itself. Similarly for this reason, every order of rational and intellectual creature is said to have and not to have being. It has being insofar as it is known by higher creatures or by itself; it lacks being insofar as it does not allow itself to be comprehended by its inferiors.

[5] The third method is fittingly observed in the things with which the fullness of this visible world is made complete, and in their prior causes in the innermost recesses of nature. For whatever of the causes themselves is known by generation in time and place in formed matter is said, by human convention, to have being. Whatever, on the other hand, is still contained within the recesses of nature and does not appear in formed matter or in place, time, or the other accidents, is said, by the same human convention, not to have being. Clear examples of this kind abound, particularly in human nature. For God formed all men together in that single first man whom He made in His own image, but He did not bring them forth at the same time into this visible world. Rather, at set times and places in a sequence known to Himself He brings into visible essence the nature which He had formed together. Thus those who now visibly appear in the world and who have appeared are said to have being. Those who still lie hidden, but are destined to be, are said not to have being. This is the difference between the first and third methods. The first is seen generally in all things made once and together in their causes and effects. The third is seen specifically in the things which partly still lie hidden in their causes and partly are revealed in their effects; and of these the fabric of this world is properly woven. To this method belongs the reason which considers the power of seeds, whether in animals, trees, or grasses. The power of the seeds, while it lies still in the secret recesses of nature, is said not to have being because it does not yet appear. Once it has appeared, however, in the birth and growth of animals, flowers, or the fruits of trees and grasses, it is said to be.

[6] The fourth method, according to the plausible theory of philosophers, states that only those things grasped by the intellect alone truly have being; that whatever things are varied, collected, or dissolved through generation, by the expansion or contraction of matter, and by local and temporal motions—e.g., all bodies, which can be born and destroyed—are truly said not to have being.

[7] The fifth method is the one which reason observes only in human nature. When through sin it abandoned the dignity of the divine image in which it had properly subsisted, it deservedly lost its being and therefore is said not to have being. When it is restored by the grace of God's only-begotten Son to the original condition of its substance in which it was created in God's image, it begins to have being and to be alive in Him who was created in God's image. It is evidently to this method that the following statement of the Apostle relates: "And He calls the things which have no being, just as those which do." [Romans 4:17] That is, God the Father calls those lost in the first man and fallen to a kind of substancelessness to have being through faith in His Son like those already reborn in Christ. This method may also be understood, however, as relat-

ing to those whom God daily calls from the hidden recesses of nature, in which they are thought not to have being, into visible appearance in form, matter, and the other things in which the hidden can appear. Perhaps a keener reason can discover something besides these methods, but I think that enough has been said about these matters for the present, unless you disagree.

STUDENT: Quite enough. . . .

*   *   *

[14] TEACHER: . . . If the divine names mentioned are in direct opposition to other names, then necessarily the things properly signified by them are understood to have contraries. Hence they cannot properly be predicated of God, to whom nothing is opposite, or with whom nothing coeternally different in nature is perceived. Of the names mentioned before and others like them, true reason can find none which does not have another name differing from it, whether in an opposite division or within the same genus. And we must necessarily recognize in things signified what we recognize in their names. But since there are countless terms designating God, which are metaphorically predicated of Him in holy Scripture by transposition from creation to Creator (if indeed anything can be rightly predicated of God, a point to be considered elsewhere), and since they cannot be discovered or collected by our poor rational power, a few designations for the Divine must be stated as an example. God, then, is called *Essence,* but He is not properly essence, for nothing is the opposite of essence. He is rather ⟨*hyperousios*⟩, i.e., "superessential." Likewise He is called *Goodness,* but He is not properly goodness, to which evil is opposite. Instead He is ⟨*hyperagathos*⟩, "More Than Good," and ⟨*hyperagathotes*⟩, i.e., "More Than Goodness." He is called *God,* but He is not properly God. Blindness is the opposite of vision, and the non-seer of the seer. He is therefore ⟨*hypertheos*⟩, "More Than Seer," if ⟨*Theos*⟩ is interpreted as "Seer." But if you resort to another etymology of this name and understand the derivation of ⟨*Theos*⟩, "God," not from ⟨*theoro*⟩, "see," but from ⟨*theo*⟩, "run," the result is similar. The nonrunner is opposite to the runner as slowness is to swiftness. He will then be ⟨*hypertheos*⟩, i.e., "More Than Runner," as recorded in the passage "His word runs quickly." [Psalms 147:15] We understand this passage as relating to God, the Word, who ineffably runs through all things with being in order that they may have being. We should have a similar kind of understanding about truth. Falsehood is the opposite of truth; hence He is not properly truth, but ⟨*hyperalethes*⟩ and ⟨*hyperaletheia*⟩, i.e., "More Than True" and "More Than Truth." The same principle must be observed in regard to all divine names. He is not properly called eternity, since temporality is opposed to eternity. He is, then, ⟨*hyperaionios*⟩ and ⟨*hyperaionia*⟩, "More Than Eternal" and "More Than Eternity." The same principle applies about wisdom also, so that it cannot be judged as properly predicated of God, since the foolish and folly are the opposite of the wise and wisdom. Accordingly, he is correctly and truly called ⟨*hypersophos*⟩, i.e., "More Than Wise" and ⟨*hypersophia*⟩, "More Than Wisdom." Similarly He is More Than Life, since death is opposed to life. We must have the same kind of understanding about "Light," since darkness opposes light. These illustrations of my point are sufficient, I believe.

ANSELM (AND GAUNILO)
1033–1109

Saint Anselm was born to a noble family in Aosta, in what is now Italy. Following a youth of travel and learning, Anselm joined the Benedictine monastery in the town of Bec, Normandy (in modern France). He remained in this monastery for the next thirty-three years, the last fifteen as abbot. During this time, he wrote a number of books on theological and philosophical topics. In 1093, Anselm was coerced into leaving the monastery to become Archbishop of Canterbury. Most of his sixteen years in Canterbury were spent skirmishing with the king of England for control of the church (a pattern that continued for five centuries until Henry VIII severed the English church from Rome entirely in 1534). Anselm died in 1109 and was canonized in 1494.

Anselm's thought can be summed up in the Augustinian phrase, "faith seeking understanding." Anselm was a deeply devoted Christian who began his thinking with the assumption that the doctrines of Christianity are true. And this faith drove him to seek understanding, to find rational explanations for the Christian teachings he already believed. His writings reflected this yearning to understand rationally particular problems in faith; he wrote a number of short treatises on such subjects as the Incarnation and the Trinity. He believed that he could demonstrate the truth of these revealed doctrines.

Anselm's most famous work is his attempt to prove the existence of God in Chapters II–IV of the *Proslogion* (or *Discourse*) known now as the "ontological argument" (from Immanuel Kant's description). The ontological argument attempts to show that if one can conceive of "something-than-which-nothing-greater-can-be-thought," one must also acknowledge that this being exists in reality as well as in the understanding. That is, if God is thought of, then God must exist. Recent scholars have pointed out that there are actually two arguments here: one, in Chapter II, that proves that God exists in reality; and another, in Chapters III–IV, that proves that God's existence is necessary.

Anselm's argument was immediately attacked by a fellow monk named Gaunilo. Anselm's exchange with Gaunilo has been preserved and the key sections are reprinted here, along with *Proslogion,* Chapters II–IV, in the M.J. Charlesworth translation.

Despite the fact that this argument has fascinated thinkers for over nine hundred years, a student's first response to this passage is often one of confusion or simple denial: "He can't do that!" The student is not alone in being confused; the history of the argument is full of misrepresentations and misinterpretations. To be sure, careful thinkers such as Hume and Kant have attacked this argument. But it is notoriously difficult to say exactly what is wrong with Anselm's logic, and many purported refutations have actually been refutations of arguments quite different from Anselm's.

In recent years, there has been renewed interest in the argument, with Charles Hartshorne, Norman Malcom, and Alvin Plantinga claiming that it is successful. There has also been a tradition, beginning with the medieval thinker Bonaventure and continuing through Karl Barth in this century, that claims the *Proslogion,* Chapters II–IV, is not a philosophical argument at all. These theologians are convinced that Anselm is not "proving" anything, that he is simply showing the implications of God's self-revelation.

While the debate continues to rage, one fact is clear: Anselm raised some of the most basic questions in the history of philosophy. Questions about modes of existence, possible beings, necessity and contingency, as well as a range of issues in logic, all emerge in discussions of this provocative passage.

*   *   *

For a study of the complete *Proslogion,* see, M.J. Charlesworth, *St. Anselm's Proslogion* (Oxford: Clarendon Press, 1965). For the rest of Anselm's major works see, Anselm, *Basic Writings,* translated by S.N. Deane (1902; reprinted LaSalle, IL: Open Court, 1962). For a study of Anselm's life and times, see R.W. Southern's books *Saint Anselm and His Biographer* (Cambridge: Cambridge University Press, 1963) and the excellent *Saint Anselm: A Portrait in a Landscape* (Cambridge: Cambridge University Press, 1990). Jasper Hopkins, *A Companion to the Study of St. Anselm* (Minneapolis: University of Minnesota Press, 1972), provides a comprehensive discussion of Anselm and his work.

For further reading on the ontological argument, the best source is John Hick and Arthur C. McGill, eds., *The Many-Faced Argument* (New York: Macmillan, 1967). Charles Hartshorne, *Anselm's Discovery: A Re-Examination of the Ontological Argument for God's Existence* (LaSalle, IL: Open Court, 1965); Alvin Plantinga, *The Nature of Necessity* (Oxford: Clarendon Press, 1974)—and his "simplified" version of this difficult work, Alvin Plantinga, *God, Freedom, and Evil* (Grand Rapids, MI: Eerdmans, 1977); and Richard Campbell, *From Belief to Understanding* (Canberra: Australian National University Press, 1976), all defend the argument. For theological interpretations, see Karl Barth, *Anselm: Fides Quaren Intellectum,* translated by Ian W. Robinson (London: SCM Press, 1960). (Key chapters from this work are included in McGill's *The Many-Faced Argument.*)

PROSLOGION (in part)

CHAPTER 2

That God Truly Exists

Well then, Lord, You who give understanding to faith, grant me that I may under-stand, as much as You see fit, that You exist as we believe You to exist, and that You are what we believe You to be. Now we believe that You are something than which nothing greater can be thought. Or can it be that a thing of such a nature does not exist, since "the Fool has said in his heart, there is no God" (Ps. xiii. 1, lii. 1)? But surely, when this same Fool hears what I am speaking about, namely, "something-than-which-nothing-greater-can-be-thought," he understands what he hears, and what he understands is in his mind, even if he does not understand that it actually exists. For it is one thing for an object to ex-ist in the mind, and another thing to understand that an object actually exists. Thus, when a painter plans beforehand what he is going to execute, he has [the picture] in his mind, but he does not yet think that it actually exists because he has not yet executed it. How-ever, when he has actually painted it, then he both has it in his mind and understands that it exists because he has now made it. Even the Fool, then, is forced to agree that some-thing-than-which-nothing-greater-can-be-thought exists in the mind, since he under-stands this when he hears it, and whatever is understood is in the mind. And surely that-than-which-a-greater-cannot-be-thought cannot exist in the mind alone. For if it exists solely in the mind even, it can be thought to exist in reality also, which is greater. If then that-than-which-a-greater-cannot-be-thought exists in the mind alone, this same that-than-which-a-greater-*cannot*-be-thought is that-than-which-a-greater-*can*-be-thought. But this is obviously impossible. Therefore there is absolutely no doubt that something-than-which-a-greater-cannot-be-thought exists both in the mind and in reality.

CHAPTER 3

That God Cannot Be Thought Not to Exist

And certainly this being so truly exists that it cannot be even thought not to exist. For something can be thought to exist that cannot be thought not to exist, and this is greater than that which can be thought not to exist. Hence, if that-than-which-a-greater-cannot-be-thought can be thought not to exist, then that-than-which-a-greater-cannot-be-thought is not the same as that-than-which-a-greater-cannot-be-thought, which is ab-surd. Something-than-which-a-greater-cannot-be-thought exists so truly then, that it cannot be even thought not to exist. And You, Lord our God, are this being. You exist so truly, Lord my God, that You cannot even be thought not to exist. And this is as it should be, for if some intelligence could think of something better than You, the creature would

From M.J. Charlesworth, *St. Anselm's Proslogion* (Oxford: Oxford University Press, 1965). Reprinted by per-mission of Oxford University Press.

be above its creator and would judge its creator—and that is completely absurd. In fact, everything else there is, except You alone, can be thought of as not existing. You alone, then, of all things most truly exist and therefore of all things possess existence to the highest degree; for anything else does not exist as truly, and so possesses existence to a lesser degree. Why then did "the Fool say in his heart, there is no God" (Ps. xiii. 1, lii. 1) when it is so evident to any rational mind that You of all things exist to the highest degree? Why indeed, unless because he was stupid and a fool?

Chapter 4

How "the Fool Said in his Heart" What Cannot Be Thought

How indeed has he "said in his heart" what he could not think; or how could he not think what he "said in his heart," since to "say in one's heart" and to "think" are the same? But if he really (indeed, since he really) both thought because he "said in his heart" and did not "say in his heart" because he could not think, there is not only one sense in which something is "said in one's heart" or thought. For in one sense a thing is thought when the word signifying it is thought; in another sense when the very object which the thing is is understood. In the first sense, then, God can be thought not to exist, but not at all in the second sense.* No one, indeed, understanding what God is can think that God does not exist, even though he may say these words in his heart either without any [objective] signification or with some peculiar signification. For God is that-than-which-nothing-greater-can-be-thought. Whoever really understands this understands clearly that this same being so exists that not even in thought can it not exist. Thus whoever understands that God exists in such a way cannot think of Him as not existing.

I give thanks, good Lord, I give thanks to You, since what I believed before through Your free gift I now so understand through Your illumination, that if I did not want to *believe* that You existed, I should nevertheless be unable not to *understand* it.

GAUNILO AND ANSELM: DEBATE**

Gaunilo

[5.] That, however, [this nature] necessarily exists in reality is demonstrated to me from the fact that, unless it existed, whatever exists in reality would be greater than it and

---

*Later manuscripts insert the following: "For noone who understands what fire and water are can think that the reality of fire is the reality of water. At the level of words, however, this confusion is possible" (Arthur C. McGill, trans.).

**[I have followed the procedure of John Hick, *Classical and Contemporary Readings in the Philosophy of Religion* (Englewood Cliffs, NJ: Prentice Hall, 1964) and put the main points of Gaunilo's critique together with Anselm's replies. The numbers before each section refer to the paragraph numbers of Gaunilo's *A Reply to the Foregoing by a Certain Writer on Behalf of the Fool* (in Arabic numbers) and Anselm's *Reply to the Foregoing by the Author of the Book in Question* (in Roman numerals).]

consequently it would not be that which is greater than everything that undoubtedly had already been proved to exist in the mind. To this I reply as follows: if something that cannot even be thought in the true and real sense must be said to exist in the mind, then I do not deny that this also exists in my mind in the same way. But since from this one cannot in any way conclude that it exists also in reality, I certainly do not yet concede that it actually exists, until this is proved to me by an indubitable argument. For he who claims that it actually exists because otherwise it would not be that which is greater than everything does not consider carefully enough whom he is addressing. For I certainly do not yet admit this greater [than everything] to be any truly existing thing; indeed I doubt or even deny it. And I do not concede that it exists in a different way from that—if one ought to speak of "existence" here—when the mind tries to imagine a completely unknown thing on the basis of the spoken words alone. How then can it be proved to me on that basis that that which is greater than everything truly exists in reality (because it is evident that it is greater than all others) if I keep on denying and also doubting that this is evident and do not admit that this greater [than everything] is either in my mind or thought, not even in the sense in which many doubtfully real and unreal things are? It must first of all be proved to me then that this same greater than everything truly exists in reality somewhere, and then only will the fact that it is greater than everything make it clear that it also subsists in itself.

ANSELM

[II.] I said further that if a thing exists even in the mind alone, it can be thought to exist also in reality, which is greater. If, then, it (namely, "that-than-which-a-greater-can-not- be-thought") exists in the mind alone, it is something than which a greater can be thought. What, I ask you, could be more logical? For if it exists even in the mind alone, cannot it be thought to exist also in reality? And if it can [be so thought], is it not the case that he who thinks this thinks of something greater than it, if it exists in the mind alone? What, then, could follow more logically than that, if "that-than-which-a-greater-*cannot*-be-thought" exists in the mind alone, it is the same as that-than-which-a-greater-*can*-be-thought? But surely "that-than-which-a-greater-*can*-be-thought" is not for any mind [the same as] "that-than-which-a-greater-*cannot*-be-thought." Does it not follow, then, that "that-than-which-a-greater-*cannot*-be-thought," if it exists in any-one's mind, does not exist in the mind alone? For if it exists in the mind alone, it is that-than-which-a-greater-*can*-be-thought, which is absurd.

*   *   *

[IX.] It is evident, moreover, that in the same way one can think of and understand that which cannot not exist. And one who thinks of this thinks of something greater than one who thinks of what can not exist. When, therefore, one thinks of that-than-which-a-greater-cannot-be-thought, if one thinks of what can not exist, one does not think of that-than-which-a-greater-cannot-be-thought. Now the same thing cannot at the same time be thought of and not thought of. For this reason he who thinks of that-than-which-a-greater-cannot-be-thought does not think of something that can not exist but something that cannot not exist. Therefore what he thinks of exists necessarily, since whatever can not exist is not what he thinks of.

GAUNILO

[6.] They say that there is in the ocean somewhere an island which, because of the difficulty (or rather the impossibility) of finding that which does not exist, some have called the "Lost Island." And the story goes that it is blessed with all manner of priceless riches and delights in abundance, much more even than the Happy Isles, and, having no owner or inhabitant, it is superior everywhere in abundance of riches to all those other lands that men inhabit. Now, if anyone tells me that it is like this, I shall easily understand what is said, since nothing is difficult about it. But if he should then go on to say, as though it were a logical consequence of this: You cannot any more doubt that this island that is more excellent than all other lands truly exists somewhere in reality than you can doubt that it is in your mind; and since it is more excellent to exist not only in the mind alone but also in reality, therefore it must needs be that it exists. For if it did not exist, any other land existing in reality would be more excellent than it, and so this island, already conceived by you to be more excellent than others, will not be more excellent. If, I say, someone wishes thus to persuade me that this island really exists beyond all doubt, I should either think that he was joking, or I should find it hard to decide which of us I ought to judge the bigger fool—I, if I agreed with him, or he, if he thought that he had proved the existence of this island with any certainty, unless he had first convinced me that its very excellence exists in my mind precisely as a thing existing truly and indubitably and not just as something unreal or doubtfully real.

ANSELM

[III.] You claim, however, that this is as though someone asserted that it cannot be doubted that a certain island in the ocean (which is more fertile than all other lands and which, because of the difficulty or even the impossibility of discovering what does not exist, is called the "Lost Island") truly exists in reality since anyone easily understands it when it is described in words. Now, I truly promise that if anyone should discover for me something existing either in reality or in the mind alone—except "that-than-which-a-greater-cannot-be-thought"—to which the logic of my argument would apply, then I shall find that Lost Island and give it, never more to be lost, to that person.

GAUNILO

[7.] If then someone should assert [to the Fool in *Proslogium* III] that this greater [than everything] is such that it cannot be thought not to exist (again without any other proof than that otherwise it would not be greater than everything), then he could make this same reply and say: When have I said that there truly existed some being that is "greater than everything," such that from this it could be proved to me that this same being really existed to such a degree that it could not be thought not to exist? That is why it must first be conclusively proved by argument that there is some higher nature, namely that which is greater and better than all the things that are, so that from this we can also infer everything else which necessarily cannot be wanting to what is greater and better than everything.

ANSELM

[III.] It has already been clearly seen, however, that "that-than-which-a-greater-cannot-be-thought" cannot be thought not to exist, because it exists as a matter of such certain truth. Otherwise it would not exist at all. In short, if anyone says that he thinks that this being does not exist, I reply that, when he thinks of this, either he thinks of something than which a greater cannot be thought, or he does not think of it. If he does not think of it, then he does not think that what he does not think of does not exist. If, however, he does think of it, then indeed he thinks of something which cannot be even thought not to exist. For if it could be thought not to exist, it could be thought to have a beginning and an end—but this cannot be. Thus, he who thinks of it thinks of something that cannot be thought not to exist; indeed, he who thinks of this does not think of it as not existing, otherwise he would think what cannot be thought. Therefore "that-than-which-a-greater-cannot-be-thought" cannot be thought not to exist.

GAUNILO

[7.] When, however, it is said that this supreme being cannot be *thought* not to exist, it would perhaps be better to say that it cannot be *understood* not to exist nor even to be able not to exist. For, strictly speaking, unreal things cannot be *understood,* though certainly they can be *thought* of in the same way as the Fool *thought* that God does not exist. I know with complete certainty that I exist, but I also know at the same time nevertheless that I can not-exist. And I *understand* without any doubt that that which exists to the highest degree, namely God, both exists and cannot not exist. I do not know, however, whether I can *think* of myself as not existing while I know with absolute certainty that I do exist; but if I can, why cannot [I do the same] with regard to anything else I know with the same certainty? If however I cannot, this will not be the distinguishing characteristic of God [namely, to be such that He cannot be thought not to exist].

ANSELM

[IV.] You say, moreover, that when it is said that this supreme reality cannot be *thought* not to exist, it would perhaps be better to say that it cannot be *understood* not to exist or even to be able not to exist. However, it must rather be said that it cannot be *thought.* For if I had said that the thing in question could not be *understood* not to exist, perhaps you yourself (who claim that we cannot understand—if this word is to be taken strictly—things that are unreal) would object that nothing that exists can be understood not to exist. For it is false [to say that] what exists does not exist, so that it is not the distinguishing characteristic of God not to be able to be understood not to exist. But, if any of those things which exist with absolute certainty can be understood not to exist, in the same way other things that certainly exist can be understood not to exist. But, if the matter is carefully considered, this objection cannot be made apropos [the term] "thought." For even if none of those things that exist can be *understood* not to exist, all however can be *thought* as not existing, save that which exists to a supreme degree. For in fact all those things (and they alone) that have a beginning or end or are made up of parts and, as I have already said, all those things that do not exist as a whole in a particular place or at a particular time can be thought as not existing. Only that being in which there is neither beginning nor end nor conjunction of parts, and that thought does

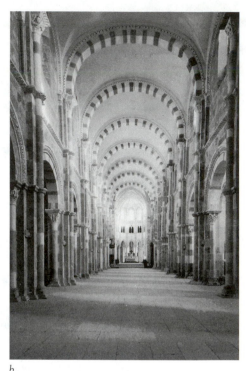

a.   *b.*

The Romanesque Cathedral
a. *Exterior view of the Abbey Church of the Madeleine, Vezelay, France,* built in the twelfth
century. This church typifies the Romanesque style that flourished from about A.D. 1000 to
1200. The rounded arches above the portals are reminiscent of the arches of Roman
construction. The thickness of the stone walls, together with the relatively simple facade, gives
the structure the impression of solidity and solemnity.(*Italian Tourist Office*)
b. *The nave.* The rounded interior arches distribute the weight of the roof outward as well as
downward, necessitating thick stone walls. As a result, only a few small windows are possible in
a Romanesque church—adding to the fortress-like feel of the architecture. (*Scala/Art Resource*)

not discern save as a whole in every place and at every time, cannot be thought as not
existing.

Know then that you can think of yourself as not existing while yet you are absolutely sure that you exist. I am astonished that you have said that you do not know
this. For we think of many things that we know to exist, as not existing; and [we think
of] many things that we know not to exist, as existing—not judging that it is really as
we think but imagining it to be so. We *can,* in fact, think of something as not existing
while knowing that it does exist, since we can [think of] the one and know the other at
the same time. And we *cannot* think of something as not existing if yet we know that it
does exist, since we cannot think of it as existing and not existing at the same time. He,
therefore, who distinguishes these two senses of this assertion will understand that [in
one sense] nothing can be thought as not existing while yet it is known to exist, and that
[in another sense] whatever exists, save that-than-which-a-greater-cannot-be-thought,
can be thought of as not existing even when we know that it does exist. Thus it is that,

on the one hand, it is the distinguishing characteristic of God that He cannot be thought of as not existing [in the one sense], and that, on the other hand, many things, the while they do exist, cannot be thought of as not existing [in the other sense]. In what sense, however, one can say that God can be thought of as not existing I think I have adequately explained in my tract.

MOSES MAIMONIDES
1135–1204

Moses ben Maimon, or Maimonides (referred to by Jewish scholars as "Rambam" for "Rabbi Moses ben Maimon"), was born at 1 P.M. on March 30, 1135, and died on December 13, 1204. The fact that we have such precise dates indicates the esteem with which he was held in his lifetime. As a boy in Córdoba, Spain, he was taught the Torah and the Talmud by his father, along with philosophy and science. At age thirteen, Maimonides and his family were forced to flee Spain after a time of peaceful coexistence between Jews and Muslims came to an end. Following a period of travel, which included a stay in Palestine, Maimonides and his family settled in Cairo, Egypt. There, Maimonides and his brother David became jewel merchants. Within a few years, Maimonides lost both his father and David, the latter killed in a shipwreck in the Indian Ocean during a business trip. Maimonides gave up the jewel business and turned to medicine. His expertise as a doctor eventually led to his appointment as a court physician for the ruler Saladin (the same Saladin who defeated Richard the Lion-Hearted in the Third Crusade). Maimonides' spiritual insights led to his being named the head of the Egyptian Jewish community. While serving both his religion and the state, he still found time to write extensively. His death in 1204 was mourned by Jews throughout the Mediterranean region, and his remains were taken from Cairo to Tiberias, on the Sea of Galilee, where his tomb is still visited today.

Maimonides' philosophical fame rests squarely on his major work, *The Guide for the Perplexed*. This work was written not for the majority of believers, but for those who knew both Jewish Law and Greek philosophy and were perplexed on how to harmonize the two. Though his religion was different, Maimonides was dealing with the same question as his neighboring Muslims and Christians: how to reconcile faith and reason. In the *Guide,* Maimonides asserts that there can be no conflict between faith and reason. Using Aristotle's philosophy (with some Neoplatonic spin), Maimonides believed he could answer a number of philosoph ical questions about the nature of God and of God's creation in a way that was consistent with sacred writings. Apparent disagreements between philosophy and theology were frequently the result of either taking figurative passages in Scripture literally or misunderstanding difficult philosophical arguments. Occasionally, philosophy is simply incapable of answering a given question and one must accept "the authority of Prophecy, which can teach things beyond the reach of human speculation." But even in such cases, philosophy can still provide general reasons for believing Scripture.

The selections given here, in the M. Friedländer translation, present Maimonides' discussion of the nature of God and the basis for his proofs of God's existence. These passages greatly influenced Thomas Aquinas, and echoes of Maimonides' thought can be heard throughout Thomas's writings.

*   *   *

For general surveys of Jewish thought in the Middle Ages, see Isaac Husik, *A History of Mediaeval Jewish Philosophy* (1916; reprinted New York: Atheneum, 1976); and Colette Sirat, *A History of Jewish Philosophy in the Middle Ages* (Cambridge: Cambridge University Press, 1985). For selections from Maimonides' writings, see Jacob Samuel Minkin, *The World of Moses Maimonides, with Selections From His Writings* (New York: T. Yoseloff, 1957), and Moses Maimonides, *Rambam: Readings in the Philosophy of Moses Maimonides,* translated by Lenn Evan Goodman (New York: Viking Press, 1976).

Among the many general introductions to Maimonides' life and thought, recent helpful studies include Abraham Joshua Heschel, *Maimonides: A Biography,* translated by Joachim Neugroschel (New York: Farrar, Straus & Giroux, 1982), and Oliver Leaman, *Moses Maimonides* (London: Routledge, 1990). For more specialized studies, see Carol Klein, *The Credo of Maimonides: A Synthesis* (New York: Philosophical Library, 1958); Jehuda Melber, *The Universality of Maimonides* (New York: Jonathan David, 1968); Menachem Marc Kellner, *Dogma in Medieval Jewish Thought: From Maimonides to Abravanel* (Oxford: Oxford University Press, 1986); and Raymond L. Weiss, *Maimonides' Ethics* (Chicago: University of Chicago Press, 1991). For collections of essays, see Salo Whittmay Baron, ed., *Essays on Maimonides: An Octocennial Volume* (New York: Columbia University Press, 1941); Joseph A. Buijs, ed., *Maimonides: A Collection of Critical Essays* (Notre Dame, IN: University of Notre Dame Press, 1988); and Eric L. Ormsby, ed., *Moses Maimonides and His Time* (Washington, DC: Catholic University of America Press, 1989).

THE GUIDE FOR THE PERPLEXED
(in part)

PART II

INTRODUCTION

Twenty-five of the propositions which are employed in the proof for the existence of God, or in the arguments demonstrating that God is neither corporeal nor a force connected with a material being, or that He is One, have been fully established, and their correctness is beyond doubt. Aristotle and the Peripatetics who followed him have proved each of these propositions. There is, however, one proposition which we do not accept—namely, the proposition which affirms the Eternity of the Universe, but we will admit it for the present, because by doing so we shall be enabled clearly to demonstrate our own theory.

PROPOSITION I: The existence of an infinite magnitude is impossible.

PROPOSITION II: The co-existence of an infinite number of finite magnitudes is impossible.

PROPOSITION III: The existence of an infinite number of causes and effects is impossible, even if these were not magnitudes; if, e.g., one Intelligence were the cause of a second, the second the cause of a third, the third the cause of a fourth, and so on, the series could not be continued ad infinitum.

PROPOSITION IV: Four categories are subject to change:—
    (a.) *Substance.*—Changes which affect the substance of a thing are called genesis and destruction.
    (b.) *Quantity.*—Changes in reference to quantity are increase and decrease.
    (c.) *Quality.*—Changes in the qualities of things are transformations.
    (d.) *Place.*—Change of place is called motion.
    The term "motion" is properly applied to change of place, but is also used in a general sense of all kinds of changes.

PROPOSITION V: Motion implies change and transition from potentiality to actuality.

PROPOSITION VI: The motion of a thing is either essential or accidental; or it is due to an external force, or to the participation of the thing in the motion of another thing. This latter kind of motion is similar to the accidental one. An instance of essential motion may be found in the translation of a thing from one place to another. The accident of a thing, as, e.g., its black color, is said to move when the thing itself changes its place. The upward motion of a stone, owing to a force applied to it in that direction, is an instance of a motion due to an external force. The motion of a nail in a boat may serve to illustrate motion due to the participation of a thing in the motion of another thing; for when the boat moves, the nail is said to move likewise. The same is the case with everything composed of several parts: when the thing itself moves, every part of it is likewise said to move.

PROPOSITION VII: Things which are changeable are, at the same time, divisible. Hence everything that moves is divisible, and consequently corporeal; but that which is indivisible cannot move, and cannot therefore be corporeal.

PROPOSITION VIII: A thing that moves accidentally must come to rest, because it does not move of its own accord; hence accidental motion cannot continue for ever.

PROPOSITION IX: A corporeal thing that sets another corporeal thing in motion can only effect this by setting itself in motion at the time it causes the other thing to move.

PROPOSITION X: A thing which is said to be contained in a corporeal object must satisfy either of the two following conditions: it either exists through that object, as is the case with accidents, or it is the cause of the existence of that object; such is, e.g., its essential property. In both cases it is a force existing in a corporeal object.

PROPOSITION XI: Among the things which exist through a material object, there are some which participate in the division of that object, and are therefore accidentally divisible, as, e.g., its color, and all other qualities that spread throughout its parts. On the other hand, among the things which form the essential elements of an object, there are some which cannot be divided in any way, as, e.g., the soul and the intellect.

PROPOSITION XII: A force which occupies all parts of a corporeal object is finite, that object itself being finite.

PROPOSITION XIII: None of the several kinds of change can be continuous, except motion from place to place, provided it be circular.

PROPOSITION XIV: Locomotion is in the natural order of the several kinds of motion the first and foremost. For genesis and corruption are preceded by transformation, which, in its turn, is preceded by the approach of the transforming agent to the object which is to be transformed. Also, increase and decrease are impossible without previous genesis and corruption.

PROPOSITION XV: Time is an accident that is related and joined to motion in such a manner that the one is never found without the other. Motion is only possible in time, and the idea of time cannot be conceived otherwise than in connection with motion; things which do not move have no relation to time.

PROPOSITION XVI: Incorporeal bodies can only be numbered when they are forces situated in a body; the several forces must then be counted together with substances or objects in which they exist. Hence purely spiritual beings, which are neither corporeal nor forces situated in corporeal objects, cannot be counted, except when considered as causes and effects.

PROPOSITION XVII: When an object moves, there must be some agent that moves it, from without, as, e.g., in the case of a stone set in motion by the hand; or from within, e.g., when the body of a living being moves. Living beings include in themselves, at the same time, the moving agent and the thing moved; when, therefore, a living being dies, and the moving agent, the soul, has left the body, i.e., the thing moved, the body remains for some time in the same condition as before, and yet cannot move in the manner it has moved previously. The moving agent, when included in the thing moved, is hidden from, and imperceptible to, the senses. This circumstance gave rise to the belief that the body of an animal moves without the aid of a moving agent. When we therefore affirm, concerning a thing in motion, that it is its own moving agent, or, as is generally said, that it moves of its own accord, we mean to say that the force which really sets the body in motion exists in that body itself.

PROPOSITION XVIII: Everything that passes over from a state of potentiality to that of actuality, is caused to do so by some external agent; because if that agent existed in the thing itself, and no obstacle prevented the transition, the thing would never be in a state of potentiality, but always in that of actuality. If, on the other hand, while the thing itself contained that agent, some obstacle existed, and at a certain time that obstacle was removed, the same cause which removed the obstacle would undoubtedly be described as the cause of the transition from potentiality to actuality, [and not the force situated within the body]. Note this.

PROPOSITION XIX: A thing which owes its existence to certain causes has in itself merely the possibility of existence; for only if these causes exist, the thing likewise exists. It does not exist if the causes do not exist at all, or if they have ceased to exist, or if there has been a change in the relation which implies the existence of that thing as a necessary consequence of those causes.

PROPOSITION XX: A thing which has in itself the necessity of existence cannot have for its existence any cause whatever.

PROPOSITION XXI: A thing composed of two elements has necessarily their composition as the cause of its present existence. Its existence is therefore not necessitated by its own essence; it depends on the existence of its two component parts and their combination.

PROPOSITION XXII: Material objects are always composed of two elements [at least], and are without exception subject to accidents. The two component elements of all bodies are substance and form. The accidents attributed to material objects are quantity, geometrical form, and position.

PROPOSITION XXIII: Everything that exists potentially, and whose essence includes a certain state of possibility, may at some time be without actual existence.

PROPOSITION XXIV: That which is potentially a certain thing is necessarily material, for the state of possibility is always connected with matter.

PROPOSITION XXV: Each compound substance consists of matter and form, and requires an agent for its existence, viz., a force which sets the substance in motion, and thereby enables it to receive a certain form. The force which thus prepares the substance of a certain individual being, is called the immediate motor. Here the necessity arises of investigating into the properties of motion, the moving agent and the thing moved. But this has already been explained sufficiently; and the opinion of Aristotle may be expressed in the following proposition: Matter does not move of its own accord—an important proposition that led to the investigation of the Prime Motor (the first moving agent)

Of these foregoing twenty-five propositions some may be verified by means of a little reflection and the application of a few propositions capable of proof, or of axioms or theorems of almost the same force, such as have been explained by me. Others require many arguments and propositions, all of which, however, have been established by conclusive proofs partly in the Physics and its commentaries, and partly in the Metaphysics and its commentary. I have already stated that in this work it is not my intention to copy the books of the philosophers or to explain difficult problems, but simply to mention those propositions which are closely connected with our subject, and which we want for our purpose.

To the above propositions one must be added which enunciates that the universe is eternal, and which is held by Aristotle to be true, and even more acceptable than any other theory. For the present we admit it, as a hypothesis, only for the purpose of demonstrating our theory. It is the following proposition:—

PROPOSITION XXVI: Time and motion are eternal, constant, and in actual existence.

In accordance with this proposition, Aristotle is compelled to assume that there exists actually a body with constant motion, viz., the fifth element. He therefore says that the heavens are not subject to genesis or destruction, because motion cannot be generated nor destroyed. He also holds that every motion must necessarily be preceded by another motion, either of the same or of a different kind. The belief that the locomotion of an animal is not preceded by another motion, is not true; for the animal is caused to move, after it had been in rest, by the intention to obtain those very things which bring about that locomotion. A change in its state of health, or some image, or some new idea can produce a desire to seek that which is conducive to its welfare and to avoid that which is contrary. Each of these three causes sets the living being in motion, and each of them is produced by various kinds of motion. Aristotle likewise asserts that everything which is created must, before its actual creation, have existed in potentiâ. By inferences drawn from this assertion he seeks to establish his proposition, viz., The thing that moves is finite, and its path finite; but it repeats the motion in its path an infinite number of times. This can only take place when the motion is circular, as has been stated in Proposition XIII. Hence follows also the existence of an infinite number of things which do not co-exist but follow one after the other.

Aristotle frequently attempts to establish this proposition; but I believe that he did not consider his proofs to be conclusive. It appeared to him to be the most probable and acceptable proposition. His followers, however, and the commentators of his books, contend that it contains not only a probable but a demonstrative proof, and that it has, in fact, been fully established. On the other hand, the Mutakallemim try to prove that the proposition cannot be true, as, according to their opinion, it is impossible to conceive how an infinite number of things could even come into existence successively. They assume this impossibility as an axiom. I, however, think that this proposition is admissible, but neither demonstrative, as the commentators of Aristotle assert, nor, on the other hand, impossible, as the Mutakallemim say. We have no intention to explain here the proofs given by Aristotle, or to show our doubts concerning them, or to set forth our opinions on the creation of the universe. I here simply desire to mention those propositions which we shall require for the proof of the three principles stated above. Having thus quoted and admitted these propositions, I will now proceed to explain what may be inferred from them.

THOMAS AQUINAS
1225–1274

Saint Thomas Aquinas was indisputably the greatest of the medieval philosophers. He was born in his family's castle of Roccasecca near the town of Aquino, about halfway between Rome and Naples. The seventh son of the Count of Aquino, Landolfo, and his wife Teodora, at the age of five Thomas was sent to the Benedictine monastery of Monte Casino, where his uncle was the abbot. His parents hoped he would get a good education at the monastery and perhaps one day become abbot of Monte Casino. However, political struggles between the pope and the emperor of the Holy Roman Empire made the monastery unsafe, and at age fourteen Thomas moved to the Imperial University in Naples.

While at this university, Thomas came under the influence of the Dominicans, a "mendicant," or begging, order of friars. The Dominicans, like their brothers the Franciscans, sought to reverse the secularization of the church. Both these orders lived lives of simple poverty and obedience and were admired by many for their religious commitment. Despite this general admiration, his family was appalled when Thomas (in 1244) announced his plans to join the Dominicans. They considered the Dominicans religious fanatics, virtually a cult, with none of the sophistication, prestige, or power of the long-established Benedictines. At his parents' instigation, Thomas's brothers kidnapped him and held him captive in the family castle. For a year they tried reasoning, shouting, intimidating—even tempting him with a prostitute—but Thomas would not be swayed. He eventually managed to escape and became a Dominican friar.

Thomas went to Paris, where he studied with Albertus Magnus (Albert the Great), an advocate of the newly rediscovered Aristotelian writings, and even followed his teacher to Cologne to continue his study of Aristotle. As a student, Thomas was so stolid and methodical that many of his peers thought he was dull or downright stupid. Given his deliberate manner and his portly build, his classmates dubbed him "the Dumb Ox." But Albertus saw his potential and turned this cruel epithet into a prophecy, saying, "You call him a Dumb Ox; I tell you the Dumb Ox will bellow so loud his bellowing will fill the world." In 1252, Thomas returned to Paris for graduate studies, eventually receiving the magistrate (doctorate) in theology in 1256.

On concluding his studies, it seemed natural that Thomas would join the faculty of the University of Paris. However, scholars from the mendicant orders were held in suspicion by the regular faculty of the university. Along with the great Franciscan friar St. Bonaventure (1217–1274), Thomas was not allowed to teach in Paris until the pope himself intervened.

The rest of Thomas's life was spent teaching in France and Italy and writing extensively on philosophical and theological subjects. His complete works in Latin comprise twenty-five volumes. Thomas was also called upon to intervene in several disputes. In addition to defending his Dominican order, he was forced to articulate a middle position between those who rejected Aristotelian philosophy as anti-Christian and those who accepted Aristotle (or, rather, an interpretation of his work by the Muslim thinker Averroës) too uncritically. Throughout his writings, Thomas negotiated a middle path of critical admiration for Aristotle.

The Benedictine Monastery of Monte Casino. At the age of five, St. Thomas Aquinas was sent here to study. His parents hoped that he might someday become abbot of the monastery, but he chose to join the Dominican order instead. (*The Italian State Tourist Office*)

Like other Christian thinkers, Thomas was concerned with the relation between reason and faith. Using basically Aristotelian categories, Thomas taught that natural reason could establish some of the truths of religion (such as the existence, unity, and goodness of God), but other truths were accessible only through faith. Contrary to some of the Latin Averroists (Western European followers of Averroës), Thomas taught that there was no conflict between the teachings of philosophy and those of theology. To use a later analogy, Thomas believed that "the book of nature" (i.e., the created world) and the "Book of Scripture" were in perfect harmony.

In December 1273, Thomas suddenly stopped writing, apparently the result of a mystical experience. He reported to a friend that "all I have written seems like straw to me." A few months later, he was called to a church council in Lyon, France. On the way there his health forced him to stop at Fossanova (south of Rome) where he died on March 7, 1274, at the age of forty-nine. Three years after his death, several of Thomas's teachings were condemned by the Bishop of Paris. However, the condemnation did not stand long, and in 1323 Saint Thomas Aquinas was canonized. In 1879, Pope Leo XII commended the study of Aquinas's philosophy in an encyclical, *Aeterni Patris.* This papal proclamation did not launch a revival of Thomism, as is often said, but it did lend an enormous prestige to the study of Thomas and his work. The encyclical praises the saint in the highest terms: "As far as man is concerned, reason can now hardly rise higher than she rose, borne up in the flight of Thomas; and Faith can hardly gain more helps from reason than those which Thomas gave her." Despite the encouragement of Leo XII and others, not all Catholic philosophers are by any means Thomists; many twentieth-century Catholic thinkers have shown more interest in existentialism and phenomenology. Today Thomas is studied and admired as much by Protestants and non-Christians as he is by Catholics.

*   *   *

The *Summa Theologica,* Thomas's most famous work, is one of the most comprehensive and systematic works of theology ever written. It has often been likened in its complexity and grandeur to a Gothic cathedral. This monumental classic is divided into four sections that, collectively, include 512 "Questions." Each Question raises a topic or area of investigation and is, in turn, made up of several "Articles" that explore specific concerns. These Articles range from abstract philosophical issues, such as "Whether one can intend two things at the same time," to minutiae of theology, such as "Whether one angel can speak to another in such a way that others will not know what he is saying." Each Article is examined in the same manner, beginning with a question, offering an answer that Thomas considers inadequate, then supporting this answer with several "objections." At this point, a quotation or argument that contradicts the position taken thus far is introduced with the words "On the contrary *(sed contra).*" The dramatic tension between two opposing positions is then resolved by the author's concise and straightforward *Respondeo,* or "I answer that . . . ," which introduces his own view. In presenting his answer, Thomas tries to avoid directly denying the preceding objections, seeing them instead as limited truths that his *Respondeo* supersedes. Finally, Thomas moves on to answer, one by one, each of the initial "objections." (The reader should keep in mind that the *first* things

Thomas says about a subject are the *opposite* of the position he will subsequently defend.)

The selection from the *Summa Theologica* given here includes two Questions from Thomas's "Treatise on God." In Question One, which includes ten Articles, Thomas establishes the nature and limits of the science of sacred doctrine. Question Two's three Articles discuss proofs of God's existence and include the famous "Five Ways" or five arguments for God's existence. The translation is that of the Fathers of the English Dominican Province.

The short work *The Principles of Nature* is given here complete in the Robert P. Goodwin translation. Written in Paris between 1252 and 1256, this treatise includes original metaphysical thinking about the question of existence. It shows that even though Thomas used Aristotelian categories, he was an original thinker, going beyond the work of his ancient Greek predecessor.

* * *

The classic introductions to Thomas Aquinas are F.C. Copleston, *Aquinas* (Baltimore, MD: Penguin Books, 1955), and Étienne Gilson, *The Christian Philosophy of St. Thomas Aquinas* (New York: Random House, 1956). More recent helpful studies include Josef Pieper, *Guide to Thomas Aquinas* (New York: Pantheon, 1962); Ralph McInerny, *St. Thomas Aquinas* (Boston: Twayne, 1977); Anthony Kenny, *Aquinas* (New York: Hill and Wang, 1980); and Brian Davies, *The Thought of Thomas Aquinas* (Oxford: Oxford University Press, 1992). James A. Weisheipl, *Friar Thomas D'Aquino: His Life, Thought, and Works* (Garden City, NY: Doubleday, 1974), offers a biography. G.K. Chesterton's impressionistic study, *St. Thomas Aquinas: The "Dumb Ox"* (1933; reprinted New York: Doubleday Image, 1956), is also a good place to become acquainted with Thomas. For collections of general essays, see Anthony Kenny, ed., *Aquinas: A Collection of Critical Essays* (Garden City, NY: Anchor Doubleday, 1969), and Norman Kretzmann and Eleonore Stump, eds., *The Cambridge Companion to Aquinas* (Cambridge: Cambridge University Press, 1993).

There are many studies on aspects of Thomas's thought. For example, a sampling of works on the "Five Ways" includes A.G.N. Flew, *God and Philosophy* (London: Hutchinson, 1966); Anthony Kenny, *The Five Ways: St. Thomas Aquinas' Proofs of God's Existence* (London: Routledge & Kegan Paul, 1969); Richard Swinburne, *The Existence of God* (Oxford: Clarendon Press, 1979); and J.L. Mackie, *The Miracle of Theism: Arguments for and against the Existence of God* (Oxford: Clarendon Press, 1982).

SUMMA THEOLOGICA (in part)

First Part

Treatise on God

QUESTION 1: THE NATURE AND EXTENT
OF SACRED DOCTRINE (IN TEN ARTICLES)

To place our purpose within proper limits, it is necessary first to investigate the nature and extent of this sacred doctrine. Concerning this there are ten points of inquiry:—

(1) Whether it is necessary? (2) Whether it is a science? (3) Whether it is one or many? (4) Whether it is speculative or practical? (5) How it is compared with other sciences? (6) Whether it is a wisdom? (7) What is its subject-matter? (8) Whether it is a matter of argument? (9) Whether it rightly employs metaphors and similes? (10) Whether the Sacred Scripture of this doctrine may be expounded in different senses?

FIRST ARTICLE

Whether, Besides Philosophy, Any Further Doctrine Is Required?

We Proceed Thus to the First Article:—

Objection 1. It seems that, besides philosophical science we have no need of any further knowledge. For man should not seek to know what is above reason: *Seek not the things that are too high for thee* (Ecclus. iii. 22). But whatever is not above reason is fully treated of in philosophical science. Therefore any other knowledge besides philosophical science is superfluous.

Obj. 2. Further, knowledge can be concerned only with being, for nothing can be known save what is true; and all that is, is true. But everything that is, is treated of in philosophical science—even God Himself, so that there is a part of philosophy called theology, or the divine science, as Aristotle has proved (*Metaph.* vi). Therefore, besides philosophical science, there is no need of any further knowledge.

On the contrary, It is written (2 Tim. iii. 16): *All Scripture inspired of God is profitable to teach, to reprove, to correct, to instruct in justice.* Now Scripture inspired of God is no part of philosophical science, which have been built up by human reason. Therefore it is useful that besides philosophical science there should be other knowledge—i.e., inspired of God.

I answer that, It was necessary for man's salvation that there should be a knowledge revealed by God, besides philosophical science built up by human reason. Firstly, indeed, because man is directed to God as to an end that surpasses the grasp of his rea-

From St. Thomas Aquinas, *Summa Theologica,* "Treatise on God," Part I, Questions 1 & 2, translated by the Fathers of the English Dominican Province (New York: Benziger Brothers, 1947). Reprinted by permission.

son: *The eye hath not seen, O God, besides Thee, what things Thou hast prepared for them that wait for Thee* (Isa. lxvi. 4). But the end must first be known by men who are to direct their thoughts and actions to the end. Hence it was necessary for the salvation of man that certain truths which exceed human reason should be made known to him by divine revelation. Even as regards those truths about God which human reason could have discovered, it was necessary that man should be taught by a divine revelation; because the truth about God such as reason could discover would only be known by a few, and that after a long time, and with the admixture of many errors. Whereas man's whole salvation, which is in God, depends upon the knowledge of this truth. Therefore, in order that the salvation of men might be brought about more fitly and more surely, it was necessary that they should be taught divine truths by divine revelation. It was therefore necessary that, besides philosophical science built up by reason there should be a sacred science learned through revelation.

Reply Obj. 1. Although those things which are beyond man's knowledge may not be sought for by man through his reason, nevertheless, once they are revealed by God they must be accepted by faith. Hence the sacred text continues, *For many things are shown to thee above the understanding of man* (Ecclus. iii. 25). And in this sacred science consists.

Reply Obj. 2. Sciences are differentiated according to the various means through which knowledge is obtained. For the astronomer and the physicist both may prove the same conclusion—that the earth, for instance, is round: the astronomer by means of mathematics (*i.e.,* abstracting from matter), but the physicist by means of matter itself. Hence there is no reason why those things which may be learned from philosophical science, so far as they can be known by natural reason, may not also be taught us by another science so far as they fall within revelation. Hence theology included in sacred doctrine differs in kind from that theology which is part of philosophy.

SECOND ARTICLE

WHETHER SACRED DOCTRINE IS A SCIENCE?

We Proceed Thus to the Second Article:—

Objection 1. It seems that sacred doctrine is not a science. For every science proceeds from self-evident principles. But sacred doctrine proceeds from articles of faith which are not self-evident, since their truth is not admitted by all: *For all men have not faith* (2 Thess. iii. 2). Therefore sacred doctrine is not a science.

Obj. 2. Further, no science deals with individual facts. But this sacred science treats of individual facts, such as the deeds of Abraham, Isaac, and Jacob, and such like. Therefore sacred doctrine is not a science.

On the contrary, Augustine says (*De Trin.* xiv. 1), *to this science alone belongs that whereby saving faith is begotten, nourished, protected, and strengthened.* But this can be said of no science except sacred doctrine. Therefore sacred doctrine is a science.

I answer that, Sacred doctrine is a science. We must bear in mind that there are two kinds of sciences. There are some which proceed from a principle known by the natural light of the intelligence, such as arithmetic and geometry and the like. There are some which proceed from principles known by the light of a higher science: thus the science of perspective proceeds from principles established by geometry, and music from principles established by arithmetic. So it is that sacred doctrine is a science, because it proceeds from principles established by the light of a higher science, namely, the science of God and the blessed. Hence, just as the musician accepts on authority the principles taught him by the mathematician, so sacred science is established on principles revealed by God.

Reply Obj. 1. The principles of any science are either in themselves self-evident, or reducible to the conclusions of a higher science; and such, as we have said, are the principles of sacred doctrine.

Reply Obj. 2. Individual facts are treated of in sacred doctrine, not because it is concerned with them principally: but they are introduced rather both as examples to be followed in our lives (as in moral sciences), and in order to establish the authority of those men through whom the divine revelation, on which this sacred scripture or doctrine is based, has come down to us.

THIRD ARTICLE

WHETHER DOCTRINE IS ONE SCIENCE?

We Proceed Thus to the Third Article:—

Objection 1. It seems that sacred doctrine is not one science; for according to the Philosopher (*Poster.* i) *that science is one which treats only of one class of subjects.* But the creator and the creature, both of whom are treated of in sacred doctrine, cannot be grouped together under one class of subjects. Therefore sacred doctrine is not one science.

Obj. 2. Further, in sacred doctrine we treat of angels, corporeal creatures, and human morality. But these belong to separate philosophical sciences. Therefore sacred doctrine cannot be one science.

On the contrary, Holy Scripture speaks of it as one science: *Wisdom gave him the knowledge [scientiam] of holy things* (Wisd. x. 10).

I answer that, Sacred doctrine is one science. The unity of a faculty or habit is to be gauged by its object, not indeed, in its material aspect, but as regards the precise formality under which it is an object. For example, man, ass, stone agree in the one precise formality of being colored; and color is the formal object of sight. Therefore, because Sacred Scripture considers things precisely under the formality of being divinely revealed, whatever has been divinely revealed possesses the one precise formality of the object of this science; and therefore is included under sacred doctrine as under one science.

Reply Obj. 1. Sacred doctrine does not treat of God and creatures equally, but of God primarily; and of creatures only so far as they are referable to God as their beginning or end. Hence the unity of this science is not impaired.

Reply Obj. 2. Nothing prevents inferior faculties or habits from being differentiated by something which falls under a higher faculty or habit as well; because the higher faculty or habit regards the object in its more universal formality, as the object of the *common sense* is whatever affects the senses, including, therefore, whatever is visible or audible. Hence the *common sense,* although one faculty, extends to all the objects of the five senses. Similarly, objects which are the subject-matter of different philosophical sciences can yet be treated of by this one single sacred science under one aspect precisely so far as they can be included in revelation. So that in this way sacred doctrine bears, as it were, the stamp of the divine science, which is one and simple, yet extends to everything.

FOURTH ARTICLE

WHETHER SACRED DOCTRINE IS A PRACTICAL SCIENCE?

We Proceed Thus to the Fourth Article:—

Objection 1. It seems that sacred doctrine is a practical science; for a practical science is that which ends in action according to the Philosopher (*Metaph.* ii). But sacred doctrine is ordained to action: *Be ye doers of the word, and not hearers only* (Jas. i. 22). Therefore sacred doctrine is a practical science.

Obj. 2. Further, sacred doctrine is divided into the Old and the New Law. But law implies a moral science, which is a practical science. Therefore sacred doctrine is a practical science.

On the contrary, Every practical science is concerned with human operations; as moral science is concerned with human acts, and architecture with buildings. But sacred doctrine is chiefly concerned with God, whose handiwork is especially man. Therefore it is not a practical but a speculative science.

I answer that, Sacred doctrine, being one, extends to things which belong to different philosophical sciences, because it considers in each the same formal aspect, namely so far as they can be known through divine revelation. Hence, although among the philosophical sciences one is speculative and another practical, nevertheless sacred doctrine includes both; as God, by one and the same science, knows both Himself and His works. Still, it is speculative rather than practical, because it is more concerned with divine things than with human acts; though it does treat even of these latter, inasmuch as man is ordained by them to the perfect knowledge of God, in which consists eternal bliss. This is a sufficient answer to the Objections.

FIFTH ARTICLE

WHETHER SACRED DOCTRINE IS NOBLER THAN OTHER SCIENCES?

We Proceed Thus to the Fifth Article:—

Objection 1. It seems that sacred doctrine is not nobler than other sciences; for the nobility of a science depends on the certitude it establishes. But other sciences, the principles of which cannot be doubted, seem to be more certain than sacred doctrine; for its principles—namely, articles of faith—can be doubted. Therefore other sciences seem to be nobler.

Obj. 2. Further, it is the sign of a lower science to depend upon a higher; as music depends upon arithmetic. But sacred doctrine does in a sense depend upon the philosophical sciences; for Jerome observes, in his Epistle to Magnus, *that the ancient doctors so enriched their books with the ideas and phrases of the philosophers, that thou knowest not what more to admire in them, their profane erudition or their scriptural learning.* Therefore sacred doctrine is inferior to other sciences.

On the contrary, Other sciences are called the handmaidens of this one: *Wisdom sent her maids to invite to the tower* (Prov. ix. 3).

I answer that, Since this science is partly speculative and partly practical, it transcends all others speculative and practical. Now one speculative science is said to be nobler than another, either by reason of its greater certitude, or by reason of the higher

worth of its subject-matter. In both these respects this science surpasses other speculative sciences; in point of greater certitude, because other sciences derive their certitude
from the natural light of human reason, which can err; whereas this derives its certitude
from the light of the divine knowledge, which cannot be misled: in point of the higher
worth of its subject-matter, because this science treats chiefly of those things which by
their sublimity transcend human reason; while other sciences consider only those things
which are within reason's grasp. Of the practical sciences, that one is nobler which is
ordained to a further purpose, as political science is nobler than military science; for the
good of the army is directed to the good of the State. But the purpose of this science, in
so far as it is practical, is eternal bliss; to which as to an ultimate end the purposes of
every practical science are directed. Hence it is clear that from every standpoint it is nobler than other sciences.

Reply Obj. 1. It may well happen that what is in itself the more certain may seem
to us the less certain on account of the weakness of our intelligence, "which is dazzled
by the clearest objects of nature; as the owl is dazzled by the light of the sun" (*Metaph.*
ii. lect. i). Hence the fact that some happen to doubt about articles of faith is not due to
the uncertain nature of the truths, but to the weakness of human intelligence; yet the
slenderest knowledge that may be obtained of the highest things is more desirable than
the most certain knowledge obtained of lesser things, as is said in *de Animalibus* xi.

Reply Obj. 2. This science can in a sense depend upon the philosophical sciences,
not as though it stood in need of them, but only in order to make its teaching clearer. For
it accepts its principles not from other sciences; but immediately from God, by revelation. Therefore it does not depend upon other sciences as upon the higher, but makes
use of them as of the lesser, and as handmaidens: even so the master sciences make use
of the sciences that supply their materials, as political of military science. That it thus
uses them is not due to its own defect or insufficiency, but to the defect of our intelligence, which is more easily led by what is known through natural reason (from which
proceed the other sciences), to that which is above reason, such as are the teachings of
this science.

SIXTH ARTICLE

WHETHER THIS DOCTRINE IS THE SAME AS WISDOM?

We Proceed Thus to the Sixth Article:—

Objection 1. It seems that this doctrine is not the same as wisdom. For no doctrine
which borrows its principles is worthy of the name of wisdom; seeing that the wise man
directs, and is not directed (*Metaph.* i). But this doctrine borrows its principles. Therefore this science is not wisdom.

Obj. 2. Further, it is a part of wisdom to prove the principles of other sciences.
Hence it is called the chief of sciences, as is clear in *Ethic.* vi. But this doctrine does not
prove the principles of other sciences. Therefore it is not the same as wisdom.

Obj. 3. Further, this doctrine is acquired by study, whereas wisdom is acquired by
God's inspiration; so that it is numbered among the gifts of the Holy Spirit (Isa. xi. 2).
Therefore this doctrine is not the same as wisdom.

On the contrary, It is written (Deut. iv. 6): *This is your wisdom and understanding
in the sight of nations.*

I answer that, This doctrine is wisdom above all human wisdom; not merely in
any one order, but absolutely. For since it is the part of a wise man to arrange and to

judge, and since lesser matters should be judged in the light of some higher principle, he is said to be wise in any one order who considers the highest principle in that order: thus in the order of building he who plans the form of the house is called wise and architect, in opposition to the inferior laborers who trim the wood and make ready the stones: *As a wise architect I have laid the foundation* (1 Cor. iii. 10). Again, in the order of all human life, the prudent man is called wise, inasmuch as he directs his acts to a fitting end: *Wisdom is prudence to a man* (Prov. x. 23). Therefore he who considers absolutely the highest cause of the whole universe, namely God, is most of all called wise. Hence wisdom is said to be the knowledge of divine things, as Augustine says (*De Trin.* xii. 14). But sacred doctrine essentially treats of God viewed as the highest cause—not only so far as He can be known through creatures just as philosophers knew Him—*That which is known of God is manifest in them* (Rom. i. 19)—but also so far as He is known to Himself alone and revealed to others. Hence sacred doctrine is especially called wisdom.

Reply Obj. 1. Sacred doctrine derives its principles not from any human knowledge, but from the divine knowledge, through which, as through the highest wisdom, all our knowledge is set in order.

Reply Obj. 2. The principles of other sciences either are evident and cannot be proved, or are proved by natural reason through some other science. But the knowledge proper to this science comes through revelation, and not through natural reason. Therefore it has no concern to prove the principles of other sciences, but only to judge of them. Whatsoever is found in other sciences contrary to any truth of this science, must be condemned as false: *Destroying counsels and every height that exalteth itself against the knowledge of God* (2 Cor. x. 4, 5).

Reply Obj. 3. Since judgment appertains to wisdom, the twofold manner of judging produces a twofold wisdom. A man may judge in one way by inclination, as whoever has the habit of a virtue judges rightly of what concerns that virtue by his very inclination towards it. Hence it is the virtuous man, as we read, who is the measure and rule of human acts. In another way, by knowledge, just as a man learned in moral science might be able to judge rightly about virtuous acts, though he had not the virtue. The first manner of judging divine things belongs to that wisdom which is set down among the gifts of the Holy Ghost: *The spiritual man judgeth all things* (1 Cor. ii. 15). And Dionysius says (*Div. Nom.* ii.): *Hierotheus is taught not by mere learning, but by experience of divine things.* The second manner of judging belongs to this doctrine, which is acquired by study, though its principles are obtained by revelation.

SEVENTH ARTICLE

WHETHER GOD IS THE OBJECT OF THIS SCIENCE?

We Proceed Thus to the Seventh Article:—

Objection 1. It seems that God is not the object of this science. For in every science the nature of its object is presupposed. But this science cannot presuppose the essence of God, for Damascene says (*De Fid. Orth.* 1. iv): *It is impossible to define the essence of God.* Therefore God is not the object of this science.

Obj. 2. Further, whatever conclusions are reached in any science must be comprehended under the object of the science. But in Holy Writ we reach conclusions not only concerning God, but concerning many other things, such as creatures and human morality. Therefore God is not the object of this science.

On the contrary, The object of the science is that of which it principally treats. But in this science the treatment is mainly about God; for it is called theology, as treating of God. Therefore God is the object of this science.

I answer that, God is the object of this science. The relation between a science and its object is the same as that between a habit or faculty and its object. Now properly speaking the object of a faculty or habit is the thing under the aspect of which all things are referred to that faculty or habit, as man and stone are referred to the faculty of sight in that they are colored. Hence colored things are the proper objects of sight. But in sacred science all things are treated of under the aspect of God; either because they are God Himself; or because they refer to God as their beginning and end. Hence it follows that God is in very truth the object of this science. This is clear also from the principles of this science, namely, the articles of faith, for faith is about God. The object of the principles and of the whole science must be the same, since the whole science is contained virtually in its principles. Some, however, looking to what is treated of in this science, and not to the aspect under which it is treated, have asserted the object of this science to be something other than God—that is, either things and signs; or the works of salvation; or the whole Christ, as the head and members. Of all these things, in truth, we treat in this science, but so far as they have reference to God.

Reply Obj. 1. Although we cannot know in what consists the essence of God, nevertheless in this science we make use of His effects, either of nature or of grace, in place of a definition, in regard to whatever is treated of in this science concerning God; even as in some philosophical sciences we demonstrate something about a cause from its effect, by taking the effect in place of a definition of the cause.

Reply Obj. 2. Whatever other conclusions are reached in this sacred science are comprehended under God, not as parts or species or accidents, but as in some way related to Him.

EIGHTH ARTICLE

WHETHER SACRED DOCTRINE IS A MATTER OF ARGUMENT?

We Proceed Thus to the Eighth Article:—

Objection 1. It seems this doctrine is not a matter of argument. For Ambrose says (*De Fide,* 1): *Put arguments aside where faith is sought.* But in this doctrine faith especially is sought: *But these things are written that you may believe* (John xx. 31). Therefore sacred doctrine is not a matter of argument.

Obj. 2. Further, if it is a matter of argument, the argument is either from authority or from reason. If it is from authority, it seems unbefitting its dignity, for the proof from authority is the weakest form of proof. But if from reason, this is unbefitting its end, because, according to Gregory (*Homil.* 26), *faith has no merit in those things of which human reason brings its own experience.* Therefore sacred doctrine is not a matter of argument.

On the contrary, The Scripture says that a bishop should *embrace that faithful word which is according to doctrine, that he may be able to exhort in sound doctrine and to convince the gainsayers* (Tit. i. 9).

I answer that, As other sciences do not argue in proof of their principles, but argue from their principles to demonstrate other truths in these sciences: so this doctrine does not argue in proof of its principles, which are the articles of faith, but from them it goes on to prove something else; as the Apostle from the resurrection of Christ argues in proof of the general resurrection (1 Cor. xv). However, it is to be borne in mind, in regard to the philosophical sciences, that the inferior sciences neither prove their principles nor dispute with those who deny them, but leave this to a higher science; whereas the highest of them, viz., metaphysics, can dispute with one who denies its principles, if only the opponent will make some concession; but if he concede nothing, it can have no dispute with him, though it can answer his objections. Hence Sacred Scripture, since it has no science above itself, can dispute with one who denies its principles only if the opponent admits some at least of the truths obtained through divine revelation; thus we can argue with heretics from texts in Holy Writ, and against those who deny one article of faith we can argue from another. If our opponent believes nothing of divine revelation, there is no longer any means of proving the articles of faith by reasoning, but only of answering his objections—if he has any—against faith. Since faith rests upon infallible truth, and since the contrary of a truth can never be demonstrated, it is clear that the arguments brought against faith cannot be demonstrations, but are difficulties that can be answered.

Reply Obj. 1. Although arguments from human reason cannot avail to prove what must be received on faith, nevertheless this doctrine argues from articles of faith to other truths.

Reply Obj. 2. This doctrine is especially based upon arguments from authority, inasmuch as its principles are obtained by revelation: thus we ought to believe on the authority of those to whom the revelation has been made. Nor does this take away from the dignity of this doctrine, for although the argument from authority based on human reason is the weakest, yet the argument from authority based on divine revelation is the strongest. But sacred doctrine makes use even of human reason, not, indeed, to prove faith (for thereby the merit of faith would come to an end), but to make clear other things that are put forward in this doctrine. Since therefore grace does not destroy nature, but perfects it, natural reason should minister to faith as the natural bent of the will ministers to charity. Hence the Apostle says: *Bringing into captivity every understanding unto the obedience of Christ* (2 Cor. x. 5). Hence sacred doctrine makes use also of the authority of philosophers in those questions in which they were able to know the truth by natural reason, as Paul quotes a saying of Aratus: *As some also of your own poets said: For we are also His offspring* (Acts xvii. 28). Nevertheless, sacred doctrine makes use of these authorities as extrinsic and probable arguments; but properly uses the authority of the canonical Scriptures as an incontrovertible proof, and the authority of the doctors of the Church as one that may properly be used, yet merely as probable. For our faith rests upon the revelation made to the apostles and prophets, who wrote the canonical books, and not on the revelations (if any such there are) made to other doctors. Hence Augustine says (*Epist. ad Hieron.* xix. 1): *Only those books of Scripture which are called canonical have I learned to hold in such honor as to believe their authors have not erred in any way in writing them. But other authors I so read as not to deem anything in their works to be true, merely on account of their having so thought and written, whatever may have been their holiness and learning.*

NINTH ARTICLE

WHETHER HOLY SCRIPTURE SHOULD USE METAPHORS?

We Proceed Thus to the Ninth Article:—

Objection 1. It seems that Holy Scripture should not use metaphors. For that which is proper to the lowest science seems not to befit this science, which holds the highest place of all. But to proceed by the aid of various similitudes and figures is proper to poetry, the least of all the sciences. Therefore it is not fitting that this science should make use of such similitudes.

Obj. 2. Further, this doctrine seems to be intended to make truth clear. Hence a reward is held out to those who manifest it: *They that explain me shall have life everlasting* (Ecclus. xxiv. 31). But by such similitudes truth is obscured. Therefore to put forward divine truths by likening them to corporeal things does not befit this science.

Obj. 3. Further, the higher creatures are, the nearer they approach to the divine likeness. If therefore any creature be taken to represent God, this representation ought chiefly to be taken from the higher creatures, and not from the lower; yet this is often found in the Scriptures.

On the contrary, It is written (Osee xii. 10): *I have multiplied visions, and I have used similitudes by the ministry of the prophets.* But to put forward anything by means of similitudes is to use metaphors. Therefore this sacred science may use metaphors.

I answer that, It is befitting Holy Writ to put forward divine and spiritual truths by means of comparisons with material things. For God provides for everything according to the capacity of its nature. Now it is natural to man to attain to intellectual truths through sensible objects, because all our knowledge originates from sense. Hence in Holy Writ spiritual truths are fittingly taught under the likeness of material things. This is what Dionysius says (*Cæl. Hier.* i): *We cannot be enlightened by the divine rays except they be hidden within the covering of many sacred veils.* It is also befitting Holy Writ, which is proposed to all without distinction of persons—*To the wise and to the unwise I am a debtor* (Rom. i. 14)—that spiritual truths be expounded by means of figures taken from corporeal things, in order that thereby even the simple who are unable by themselves to grasp intellectual things may be able to understand it.

Reply Obj. 1. Poetry makes use of metaphors to produce a representation, for it is natural to man to be pleased with representations. But sacred doctrine makes use of metaphors as both necessary and useful.

Reply Obj. 2. The ray of divine revelation is not extinguished by the sensible imagery wherewith it is veiled, as Dionysius says (*Cæl. Hier.* i); and its truth so far remains that it does not allow the minds of those to whom the revelation has been made, to rest in the metaphors, but raises them to the knowledge of truths; and through those to whom the revelation has been made others also may receive instruction in these matters. Hence those things that are taught metaphorically in one part of Scripture, in other parts are taught more openly. The very hiding of truth in figures is useful for the exercise of thoughtful minds, and as a defence against the ridicule of the impious, according to the words *Give not that which is holy to dogs* (Matth. vii. 6).

Reply Obj. 3. As Dionysius says (*loc. cit.*), it is more fitting that divine truths should be expounded under the figure of less noble than of nobler bodies, and this for three reasons. Firstly, because thereby men's minds are the better preserved from error. For then it is clear that these things are not literal descriptions of divine truths, which might have been open to doubt had they been expressed under the figure of nobler bodies, especially for those who could think of nothing nobler than bodies. Secondly, because this is more befitting the knowledge of God that we have in this life. For what He is not is clearer to us than what He is. Therefore similitudes drawn from things farthest away from God form within us a truer estimate that God is above whatsoever we may say or think of Him. Thirdly, because thereby divine truths are the better hidden from the unworthy.

TENTH ARTICLE

WHETHER IN HOLY SCRIPTURE A WORD MAY HAVE SEVERAL SENSES?

We Proceed Thus to the Tenth Article:—

Objection 1. It seems that in Holy Writ a word cannot have several senses, historical or literal, allegorical, tropological or moral, and anagogical. For many different senses in one text produce confusion and deception and destroy all force of argument. Hence no argument, but only fallacies, can be deduced from a multiplicity of propositions. But Holy Writ ought to be able to state the truth without any fallacy. Therefore in it there cannot be several senses to a word.

Obj. 2. Further, Augustine says (*de util. cred.* iii) that *the Old Testament has a fourfold division as to history, etiology, analogy, and allegory.* Now these four seem altogether different from the four divisions mentioned in the first objection. Therefore it does not seem fitting to explain the same word of Holy Writ according to the four different senses mentioned above.

Obj. 3. Further, besides these senses, there is the parabolical, which is not one of these four.

On the contrary, Gregory says (Moral. xx. 1): *Holy Writ by the manner of its speech transcends every science, because in one and the same sentence, while it describes a fact, it reveals a mystery.*

I answer that, The author of Holy Writ is God, in whose power it is to signify His meaning, not by words only (as man also can do), but also by things themselves. So, whereas in every other science things are signified by words, this science has the property, that the things signified by the words have themselves also a signification. Therefore that first signification whereby words signify things belongs to the first sense, the historical or literal. That signification whereby things signified by words have themselves also a signification is called the spiritual sense, which is based on the literal, and presupposes it. Now this spiritual sense has a threefold division. For as the Apostle says (Heb. x. 1) the Old Law is a figure of the New Law, and Dionysius says (*Cæl. Hier.* i) *the New Law itself is a figure of future glory.* Again, in the New Law, whatever our Head has done is a type of what we ought to do. Therefore, so far as the things of the Old Law signify the things of the New Law, there is the allegorical sense; so far as the things done in Christ, or so far as the things which signify Christ, are types of what we ought to do, there is the moral sense. But so far as they signify what relates to eternal glory, there is the anagogical sense. Since the literal sense is that which the author intends, and since the author of Holy Writ is God, Who by one act comprehends all things by His intellect, it is not unfitting, as Augustine says (*Confess.* xii), if, even according to the literal sense, one word in Holy Writ should have several senses.

Reply Obj. 1. The multiplicity of these senses does not produce equivocation or any other kind of multiplicity, seeing that these senses are not multiplied because one word signifies several things; but because the things signified by the words can be themselves types of other things. Thus in Holy Writ no confusion results, for all the senses are founded on one—the literal—from which alone can any argument be drawn, and not from those intended in allegory, as Augustine says (*Epist.* xlviii). Nevertheless, nothing of Holy Scripture perishes on account of this, since nothing necessary to faith is contained under the spiritual sense which is not elsewhere put forward by the Scripture in its literal sense.

Reply Obj. 2. These three—history, etiology, analogy—are grouped under the literal sense. For it is called history, as Augustine expounds (*loc. cit.*), whenever anything is simply related; it is called etiology when its cause is assigned, as when Our Lord gave the reason why Moses allowed the putting away of wives—namely, on account of the hardness of men's hearts; it is called analogy whenever the truth of one text of Scripture is shown not to contradict the truth of another. Of these four, allegory alone stands for the three spiritual senses. Thus Hugh of S. Victor (*Sacram.* iv. 4 *Prolog.*) includes the anagogical under the allegorical sense, laying down three senses only—the historical, the allegorical, and the tropological.

Reply Obj. 3. The parabolical sense is contained in the literal, for by words things are signified properly and figuratively. Nor is the figure itself, but that which is figured, the literal sense. When Scripture speaks of God's arm, the literal sense is not that God has such a member, but only what is signified by this member, namely, operative power. Hence it is plain that nothing false can ever underlie the literal sense of Holy Writ.

QUESTION 2: THE EXISTENCE OF GOD (IN THREE ARTICLES)

Because the chief aim of sacred doctrine is to teach the knowledge of God, not only as He is in Himself, but also as He is the beginning of things and their last end, and especially of rational creatures, as is clear from what has been already said, therefore, in our endeavor to expound this science, we shall treat: (1) Of God; (2) Of the rational creature's advance towards God; (3) Of Christ, Who as man, is our way to God.

In treating of God there will be a threefold division:—

For we shall consider (1) Whatever concerns the Divine Essence; (2) Whatever concerns the distinctions of Persons; (3) Whatever concerns the procession of creatures from Him.

Concerning the Divine Essence, we must consider:—

(1) Whether God exists? (2) The manner of His existence, or, rather, what is *not* the manner of His existence; (3) Whatever concerns His operations—namely, His knowledge, will, power.

Concerning the first, there are three points of inquiry:—

(1) Whether the proposition "God exists" is self-evident? (2) Whether it is demonstrable? (3) Whether God exists?

FIRST ARTICLE

WHETHER THE EXISTENCE OF GOD IS SELF-EVIDENT?

We Proceed Thus to the First Article:—

Objection 1. It seems that the existence of God is self-evident. Now those things are said to be self-evident to us the knowledge of which is naturally implanted in us, as we can see in regard to first principles. But as Damascene says (*De Fid. Orth.* i. 1, 3), *the knowledge of God is naturally implanted in all.* Therefore the existence of God is self-evident.

Obj. 2. Further, those things are said to be self-evident which are known as soon as the terms are known, which the Philosopher (1 *Poster.* iii) says is true of the first principles of demonstration. Thus, when the nature of a whole and of a part is known, it is at once recognized that every whole is greater than its part. But as soon as the signification of the word "God" is understood, it is at once seen that God exists. For by this word is signified that thing than which nothing greater can be conceived. But that which exists actually and mentally is greater than that which exists only mentally. Therefore, since as soon as the word "God" is understood it exists mentally, it also follows that it exists actually. Therefore the proposition "God exists" is self-evident.

Obj. 3. Further, the existence of truth is self-evident. For whoever denies the existence of truth grants that truth does not exist: and if truth does not exist, then the proposition "Truth does not exist" is true: and if there is anything true, there must be truth. But God is truth itself: *I am the way, the truth, and the life* (John xiv. 6). Therefore "God exists" is self-evident.

On the contrary, No one can mentally admit the opposite of what is self-evident; as the Philosopher (*Metaph.* iv., lect. vi) states concerning the first principles of demonstration. But the opposite of the proposition "God is" can be mentally admitted: *The fool said in his heart, There is no God* (Ps. lii. 1). Therefore, that God exists is not self-evident.

I answer that, A thing can be self-evident in either of two ways; on the one hand, self-evident in itself, though not to us; on the other, self-evident in itself, and to us. A proposition is self-evident because the predicate is included in the essence of the subject, as "Man is an animal," for animal is contained in the essence of man. If, therefore the essence of the predicate and subject be known to all, the proposition will be self-evident to all; as is clear with regard to the first principles of demonstration, the terms of which are common things that no one is ignorant of, such as being and non-being, whole and part, and such like. If, however, there are some to whom the essence of the predicate and subject is unknown, the proposition will be self-evident in itself, but not to those who do not know the meaning of the predicate and subject of the proposition. Therefore, it happens, as Boethius says (*Hebdom.,* the title of which is: *"Whether all that is, is good"*), "that there are some mental concepts self-evident only to the learned, as that incorporeal substances are not in space." Therefore I say that this proposition, "God exists," of itself is self-evident, for the predicate is the same as the subject; because God is His own existence as will be hereafter shown (Q. 3, A. 4). Now because we do not know the essence of God, the proposition is not self-evident to us; but needs to be demonstrated by things that are more known to us, though less known in their nature—namely, by effects.

Reply Obj. 1. To know that God exists in a general and confused way is implanted in us by nature, inasmuch as God is man's beatitude. For man naturally desires happiness, and what is naturally desired by man must be naturally known to him. This, however, is not to know absolutely that God exists; just as to know that someone is approaching is not the same as to know that Peter is approaching, even though it is Peter who is approaching; for many there are who imagine that man's perfect good which is happiness, consists in riches, and others in pleasures, and others in something else.

Reply Obj. 2. Perhaps not everyone who hears this word "God" understands it to signify something than which nothing greater can be thought, seeing that some have believed God to be a body. Yet, granted that everyone understands that by this word "God" is signified something than which nothing greater can be thought, nevertheless, it does not therefore follow that he understands that what the word signifies exists actually, but only that it exists mentally. Nor can it be argued that it actually exists, unless it be admitted that there actually exists something than which nothing greater can be thought; and this precisely is not admitted by those who hold that God does not exist.

Reply Obj. 3. The existence of truth in general is self-evident but the existence of a Primal Truth is not self-evident to us.

a.

b.

c.

d.

The Gothic Cathedral
a. The Cathedral of Notre Dame de Chartres, Chartres, France, begun in the 1140s. The word "Gothic" was originally a perjorative term coined by Renaissance thinkers who considered this style to be a barbaric break from classical tradition. The two towers shown here, for example, are not symmetrical. Even though the overall design of the cathedral may not be symmetrical, each of its elements was designed to reflect the harmony and beauty of God's creation. (*Lauros-Giraudon/Art Resource*)
b. Interior, Chartres Cathedral. By using pointed arches, it was possible to make soaring open spaces in the nave (main sanctuary) of the Gothic cathedral. The weight was shifted downward instead of outward. (*Bildarchiv Foto Marburg/Art Resource*)
c. Flying Buttresses at Reims Cathedral, ca. 1230–1235, by Villard De Honnecourt. To leave the interior unencumbered, the remaining outward stresses were often buttressed from outside the building. In some cathedrals exterior buttresses could not be built directly along the outside walls because of side aisles. Instead they were built outside the side aisles and connected to the pillars of the nave by stone ribs. These supporting ribs appear to "fly" over the side aisles. (*Villard de Honnecourt/Giraudon, Art Resource*)
d. The Rose Window, Notre Dame Cathedral, Paris, thirteenth century. By using pointed arches and flying buttresses, the walls of a cathedral did not have to bear the weight of the roof. Instead they could be used as screens for stained glass ornamentation such as this. (*Giraudon-Art Resource*)

SECOND ARTICLE

WHETHER IT CAN BE DEMONSTRATED THAT GOD EXISTS?

We Proceed Thus to the Second Article:—

Objection 1. It seems that the existence of God cannot be demonstrated. For it is an article of faith that God exists. But what is of faith cannot be demonstrated, because a demonstration produces scientific knowledge; whereas faith is of the unseen (Heb. xi. 1). Therefore it cannot be demonstrated that God exists.

Obj. 2. Further, the essence is the middle term of demonstration. But we cannot know in what God's essence consists, but solely in what it does not consist; as Damascene says (*De Fid. Orth.* i. 4). Therefore we cannot demonstrate that God exists.

Obj. 3. Further, if the existence of God were demonstrated, this could only be from His effects. But His effects are not proportionate to Him, since He is infinite and His effects are finite; and between the finite and infinite there is no proportion. Therefore, since a cause cannot be demonstrated by an effect not proportionate to it, it seems that the existence of God cannot be demonstrated.

On the contrary, The Apostle says: *The invisible things of Him are clearly seen, being understood by the things that are made* (Rom. i. 20). But this would not be unless the existence of God could be demonstrated through the things that are made; for the first thing we must know of anything is, whether it exists.

I answer that, Demonstration can be made in two ways: One is through the cause, and is called *a priori,* and this is to argue from what is prior absolutely. The other is through the effect, and is called a demonstration *a posteriori;* this is to argue from what is prior relatively only to us. When an effect is better known to us than its cause, from the effect we proceed to the knowledge of the cause. And from every effect the existence of its proper cause can be demonstrated, so long as its effects are better known to us; because since every effect depends upon its cause, if the effect exists, the cause must pre-exist. Hence the existence of God, in so far as it is not self-evident to us, can be demonstrated from those of His effects which are known to us.

Reply Obj. 1. The existence of God and other like truths about God, which can be known by natural reason, are not articles of faith, but are preambles to the articles; for faith presupposes natural knowledge, even as grace presupposes nature, and perfection supposes something that can be perfected. Nevertheless, there is nothing to prevent a man, who cannot grasp a proof, accepting, as a matter of faith, something which in itself is capable of being scientifically known and demonstrated.

Reply Obj. 2. When the existence of a cause is demonstrated from an effect, this effect takes the place of the definition of the cause in proof of the cause's existence. This is especially the case in regard to God, because, in order to prove the existence of anything, it is necessary to accept as a middle term the meaning of the word, and not its essence, for the question of its essence follows on the question of its existence. Now the names given to God are derived from His effects; consequently, in demonstrating the existence of God from His effects, we may take for the middle term the meaning of the word "God."

Reply Obj. 3. From effects not proportionate to the cause no perfect knowledge of that cause can be obtained. Yet from every effect the existence of the cause can be clearly demonstrated, and so we can demonstrate the existence of God from His effects; though from them we cannot perfectly know God as He is in His essence.

THIRD ARTICLE

WHETHER GOD EXISTS?

We Proceed Thus to the Third Article:—

Objection 1. It seems that God does not exist; because if one of two contraries be infinite, the other would be altogether destroyed. But the word "God" means that He is infinite goodness. If, therefore, God existed, there would be no evil discoverable; but there is evil in the world. Therefore God does not exist.

Obj. 2. Further, it is superfluous to suppose that what can be accounted for by a few principles has been produced by many. But it seems that everything we see in the world can be accounted for by other principles, supposing God did not exist. For all natural things can be reduced to one principle, which is nature; and all voluntary things can be reduced to one principle, which is human reason, or will. Therefore there is no need to suppose God's existence.

On the contrary, It is said in the person of God: *I am Who am* (Exod. iii. 14).

I answer that, The existence of God can be proved in five ways.

The first and more manifest way is the argument from motion. It is certain, and evident to our senses, that in the world some things are in motion. Now whatever is in motion is put in motion by another, for nothing can be in motion except it is in potentiality to that towards which it is in motion; whereas a thing moves inasmuch as it is in act. For motion is nothing else than the reduction of something from potentiality to actuality. But nothing can be reduced from potentiality to actuality, except by something in a state of actuality. Thus that which is actually hot, as fire, makes wood, which is potentially hot, to be actually hot, and thereby moves and changes it. Now it is not possible that the same thing should be at once in actuality and potentiality in the same respect, but only in different respects. For what is actually hot cannot simultaneously be potentially hot; but it is simultaneously potentially cold. It is therefore impossible that in the same respect and in the same way a thing should be both mover and moved, *i.e.*, that it should move itself. Therefore, whatever is in motion must be put in motion by another. If that by which it is put in motion be itself put in motion, then this also must needs be put in motion by another, and that by another again. But this cannot go on to infinity, because then there would be no first mover, and, consequently, no other mover; seeing that subsequent movers move only inasmuch as they are put in motion by the first mover; as the staff moves only because it is put in motion by the hand. Therefore it is necessary to arrive at a first mover, put in motion by no other; and this everyone understands to be God.

The second way is from the nature of the efficient cause. In the world of sense we find there is an order of efficient causes. There is no case known (neither is it, indeed, possible) in which a thing is found to be the efficient cause of itself; for so it would be prior to itself, which is impossible. Now in efficient causes it is not possible to go on to infinity, because in all efficient causes following in order, the first is the cause of the intermediate cause, and the intermediate is the cause of the ultimate cause, whether the intermediate cause be several, or one only. Now to take away the cause is to take away the effect. Therefore if there be no first cause among efficient causes, there will be no ultimate, nor any intermediate cause. But if in efficient causes it is possible to go on to infinity, there will be no first efficient cause, neither will there be an ultimate effect, nor any intermediate efficient causes; all of which is plainly false. Therefore it is necessary to admit a first efficient cause, to which everyone gives the name of God.

The third way is taken from possibility and necessity, and runs thus. We find in nature things that are possible to be and not to be, since they are found to be generated, and to corrupt, and consequently, they are possible to be and not to be. But it is impossible for these always to exist, for that which is possible not to be at some time is not. Therefore, if everything is possible not to be, then at one time there could have been nothing in existence. Now if this were true, even now there would be nothing in existence, because that which does not exist only begins to exist by something already existing. Therefore, if at one time nothing was in existence, it would have been impossible for anything to have begun to exist; and thus even now nothing would be in existence—which is absurd. Therefore, not all beings are merely possible, but there must exist something the existence of which is necessary. But every necessary thing either has its necessity caused by another, or not. Now it is impossible to go on to infinity in necessary things which have their necessity caused by another, as has been already proved in regard to efficient causes. Therefore we cannot but postulate the existence of some being having of itself its own necessity, and not receiving it from another, but rather causing in others their necessity. This all men speak of as God.

The fourth way is taken from the gradation to be found in things. Among beings there are some more and some less good, true, noble, and the like. But "more" and "less" are predicated of different things, according as they resemble in their different ways something which is the maximum, as a thing is said to be hotter according as it more nearly resembles that which is hottest; so that there is something which is truest, something best, something noblest, and, consequently, something which is uttermost being; for those things that are greatest in truth are greatest in being, as it is written in *Metaph.* ii. Now the maximum in any genus is the cause of all in that genus; as fire, which is the maximum of heat, is the cause of all hot things. Therefore there must also be something which is to all beings the cause of their being, goodness, and every other perfection; and this we call God.

The fifth way is taken from the governance of the world. We see that things which lack intelligence, such as natural bodies, act for an end, and this is evident from their acting always, or nearly always, in the same way, so as to obtain the best result. Hence it is plain that not fortuitously, but designedly, do they achieve their end. Now whatever lacks intelligence cannot move towards an end, unless it be directed by some being endowed with knowledge and intelligence; as the arrow is shot to its mark by the archer. Therefore some intelligent being exists by whom all natural things are directed to their end; and this being we call God.

Reply Obj. 1. As Augustine says (*Enchir.* xi): *Since God is the highest good, He would not allow any evil to exist in His works, unless His omnipotence and goodness were such as to bring good even out of evil.* This is part of the infinite goodness of God, that He should allow evil to exist, and out of it produce good.

Reply Obj. 2. Since nature works for a determinate end under the direction of a higher agent, whatever is done by nature must needs be traced back to God, as to its first cause. So also whatever is done voluntarily must also be traced back to some higher cause other than human reason or will, since these can change and fail; for all things that are changeable and capable of defect must be traced back to an immovable and self-necessary first principle, as was shown in the body of the *Article*.

THE PRINCIPLES OF NATURE

CHAPTER I. BEING IN POTENCY AND BEING IN ACT

(1) There are certain things which can exist but do not, and others which do exist. Those which can be are said to exist *in potency,* whereas those which are, are said to exist *in act.* Now there are two ways of existing in act: to exist *essentially* or *substantially* (as when a man exists), and to exist *accidentally* (as when a man exists as white). The former is to exist without qualification, whereas the latter is to exist in a qualified way.

(2) Something is in potency to both the ways of existing in act. Sperm and menstrual blood, for example, are in potency to being man, whereas a man is in potency to being white. Both that which is in potency to exist substantially, and that which is in potency to exist accidently, can, like the sperm and the man, respectively, be called matter. They differ, however, in this: the matter that is in potency to exist substantially is called *matter from which,* whereas the matter that is in potency to exist accidentally is called *matter in which.* Likewise, properly speaking, what is in potency to exist substantially is called *prime matter,* whereas what is in potency to exist accidentally is called a *subject.* Accordingly, accidents are said to be in a subject, but substantial form is not spoken of in this way. Wherefore matter differs from subject, inasmuch as a subject does not have an act of existing from that which accrues to it, but is complete with an act of existing in itself; for example, a man does not have an act of existing from whiteness. But matter has an act of existing from what accrues to it, because of itself it exists in-

St. Thomas Aquinas, *Selected Writings of St. Thomas Aquinas,* translated by Robert P. Goodwin (New York: Macmillan/Library of the Liberal Arts, 1965).

completely. Hence, simply put, form makes matter exist, whereas an accident does not make a subject exist. The subject, however, makes an accident exist. Occasionally, however, one term is substituted for the other—that is, matter for subject, and vice versa.

(3) Moreover, just as everything in potency can be called matter, so anything from which something exists, either substantially or accidentally, can be called a form as man, since he is potentially white, becomes actually white through whiteness, and the sperm, since it is potentially man, becomes actually man through the soul. Because form makes something exist actually, it is said to be an act. What makes something exist substantially is called *substantial form,* and what makes something exist accidentally is called *accidental form.*

(4) As generation is a movement to form, there are two kinds of generation corresponding to the two kinds of form: *generation simply* corresponds to substantial form, and *qualified generation* corresponds to accidental form. For when a substantial form is introduced, something is said to have come into being without qualification, as we have said. For example, a man comes into being, or a man is generated. When, however, an accidental form is introduced, something is said not to have come into being, but to have become this. For example, when a man becomes white, we do not say that the man comes into being or is generated without qualification, but rather that the man becomes, or is made, white.

(5) There are two kinds of corruption opposed to these two kinds of generation: *corruption simply* and *qualified corruption.* Generation simply and corruption simply occur only in the genus *substance,* whereas qualified generation and qualified corruption occur in all other genera. Furthermore, as generation is a kind of passage from not-existing to existing, and, conversely, corruption a passage from existing to not-existing, generation does not arise from any nonentity but from a nonentity which is a being in potency. For example, a statue comes from bronze, which is a statue in potency, not in act.

(6) Therefore, three things are required for generation: namely, a being in potency, which is matter; a state of not-existing in act, which is privation; and that through which something comes to be actually, which is form. Thus when a statue is made from bronze, the bronze, which is in potency to the form *statue,* is the matter. The lack of configuration or arrangement is the privation.

(7) The shape from which it gets the name *statue* is the form. This is, however, not a substantial form because the bronze, before the advent of that form, had an act of existing, and its act of existing does not depend upon that shape. It is an accidental form, as are all artificial forms; for art works only on what is already constituted as existing by nature.

CHAPTER II. MATTER, FORM, AND PRIVATION

(8) Therefore, there are three principles of nature: matter, form, and privation. One of these, form, is that toward which generation moves, whereas the other two lie on the side of that from which generation proceeds. Hence, matter and privation refer to the same subject, but according to different aspects. For the very same thing is both bronze and deprived-of-a-certain-shape before the advent of the form. But it is said to be bronze for one reason, and deprived-of-a-shape for another. Wherefore privation is said to be, not an essential principle, but an accidental one, since it coincides with matter.

Thus we say that a physician builds accidentally, for he does not build by virtue of being a physician but because he is a builder; this characteristic resides in the same subject along with his medical skill.

(9) Now accidents are of two kinds: *necessary,* which are not separated from a certain kind of thing, like risibility from man, and *non-necessary,* which are so separated, as is whiteness from man. Accordingly, although privation is an accidental principle, it does not follow that it is unnecessary for generation. For matter is never lacking privation: inasmuch as it is under one form, it is deprived of another, and vice versa. For example, in fire there is the privation of air; in air there is the privation of fire.*

(10) Although generation is from not-existing, one should realize that we maintain, not that negation is a principle, but rather that privation is, for negation does not determine a subject for itself. Lack of sight can be attributed even to nonentities, for example, "Chimeras do not see." Likewise, we can attribute it to beings that are not meant to see, such as a stone. But privation is attributed only to a determinate subject in which the missing perfection is meant to be. For example, blindness is attributed only to those things that were born to see.

(11) Moreover, it is in accordance with the fact that generation does not arise from non-being simply, but from non-being which is in some subject—and not just any subject, but a determined one—that privation is said to be a principle. For not everything which is not-burning will burn, but only those things that are apt to burn. Privation differs, however, from the other principles, which are principles both in being and in becoming. For something to become a statue, bronze and finally the figure of a statue are necessary. Moreover, when the statue does actually exist, both of these exist. Privation, however, is a principle in becoming but not in being, because while the statue is coming into being the statue cannot exist. For if it did already exist, the statue could not come into being, since what comes to be exists only successively, as do time and change. But when the statue exists, no privation of *statue* is present in it. Just as affirmation and negation cannot exist simultaneously, so neither can privation and the form of which it is the privation. Accordingly, privation is an accidental principle, as has previously been explained; the other two are essential principles.

(12) From what has been said it is evident that matter differs by definition from form and privation. For matter is that in which both form and privation are understood, as one shape and the lack of another shape are understood in bronze. Indeed, sometimes matter is given a name which includes a privation and sometimes not. So bronze, when it is the matter of a statue, does not connote a privation, because in saying "bronze" we do not include in our comprehension the lack of an arrangement or shape. But flour, since it is matter with respect to bread, includes the privation of the form of bread, because in saying "flour," one signifies that lack of disposition or ordination which is opposed to the form of bread. And so, because in generation the matter or subject remains but the privation and the composite of matter and privation do not, therefore matter that does not include privation is permanent, whereas matter that does is transient.

---

*Aquinas is using here a very ancient theory of "chemical elements." He elaborates upon his notion of element below, paragraphs 21 and 22. The theory has a long history, dating back at least to the pre-Socratic philosopher Empedocles (ca. 484–424 B.C.), who had claimed that the things of experience are composed in various ways of four opposed and irreducible elements: fire, water, earth, and air. Many subsequent Greek thinkers, including Aristotle, maintained this division, and Aquinas continues in this tradition. Modern chemistry continues this tradition in a modified way, at least in the sense that it, too, sees all physical realities to be made up of, and reducible to, approximately one hundred elements, which are chemically irreducible to one another.

(13) We should realize, however, that some matter includes a form, like the bronze which is the matter of a statue. Bronze itself is a composite of matter and form. Accordingly, since it possesses matter, bronze cannot be called prime matter. Only that matter which is understood without any form or privation, but which is subject to form and privation, is called prime matter, inasmuch as there is no other matter prior to it. It is also called "hyle."*

(14) Since all cognition and every definition are through form, it follows that prime matter can be known or defined, not of itself, but through the composite. Accordingly, we know prime matter as that which is related to all forms and privations, as bronze is related to the form of a statue and to the privation of some shape. It is called *primary* without qualification. Something can be called "prime matter" with respect to a certain genus, as water is prime matter to the genus of liquids. But this is not primary without qualification, because it is a composite of matter and form; hence there is a matter prior to it.

(15) We should note that prime matter, and even form, are neither generated nor corrupted, inasmuch as every generation is from something to something. That from which generation arises is matter; that to which it proceeds is form. If, therefore, matter and form were generated, there would have to be a matter of matter and a form of form *ad infinitum.* Hence, properly speaking, only composites are generated.

(16) We should note also that prime matter is said to be numerically one in all things. Something can be said to be numerically one in two ways. First, it can be numerically one if it has one numerically determinate form, like Socrates. Prime matter is not said to be numerically one in this way, since in itself it does not have any form. Something can be numerically one in another way, that is, if it lacks the dispositions through which numerical differences occur. Prime matter is said to be numerically one in this way, since it is understood without dispositions by which numerical differences occur.

(17) Finally we note that although prime matter does not in itself have any form or privation, as in the nature of bronze there is neither shape nor the lack of shape, nevertheless prime matter never exists without form and privation. Sometimes it is under one form, sometimes it is under another. But matter cannot exist of itself, since of itself it possesses no form. It does not exist in act, since existing in act occurs only through a form, but exists only in potency. Hence whatever exists in act cannot be called prime matter.

CHAPTER III. CAUSES, PRINCIPLES, AND ELEMENTS

(18) From what has been said, it is evident that there are three principles of nature: matter, form, and privation. These alone, however, are not sufficient for generation. For what is in potency cannot reduce itself to act. Bronze, which is in potency to being a statue, does not make itself be a statue, but needs an agent which draws out the form of statue from potency to act. For form cannot draw itself out from potency to act. Here I am speaking of the form of the thing generated, which we have already said is the term of generation. This form exists only when a change is completed, but the agent

---

*The term *hyle* is a transliteration of a Greek word meaning "matter" or "material."

itself exists only during the becoming—that is, while the thing is coming to be. There is required, therefore, besides form and matter, another principle which acts. This is called the *efficient* or *moving cause,* or agent, or that from which the motion begins.

(19) Because, as Aristotle states in Book Two of the *Metaphysics,* everything that acts, acts only when intending something, a fourth principle is required—that is, what is intended by the agent. This is called the *end.* And although every agent, be it natural or voluntary, intends an end, we should realize nevertheless that it does not follow that every agent knows or deliberates about the end. Knowing the end is necessary for those whose actions are not determined, but for whom opposed goals are possible, as is the case for voluntary agents. These, therefore, must know the end, through which knowledge they determine their actions. However, the actions of natural agents are determined; hence, there is no necessity for their choosing the means to their end. Avicenna offers the example of the cithara* player, who need not deliberate as to which notes form a chord by striking each individually, since they are predetermined. If the player did deliberate, there would be a delay between the notes, producing an arpeggio. Furthermore, deliberation is especially apparent in the voluntary agent, as opposed to the natural agent. So an even stronger argument can be made if one sees that if a voluntary agent (whose deliberation is especially evident) does not always deliberate, then, certainly, neither does the natural agent. Therefore, it is possible for a natural agent to intend an end without deliberating about it. To intend in this way is nothing more than to have a natural inclination toward something.

(20) From what has been said it is evident that there are four causes, namely, material, efficient, formal, and final. Moreover, although "principle" and "cause" are said quasi-interchangeably, as is maintained in Book Five of the *Metaphysics,* nevertheless, Aristotle in his *Physics* contends that there are four causes and three principles. Furthermore, he holds that causes are both extrinsic and intrinsic. Matter and form are said to be intrinsic to a thing inasmuch as they are constitutive parts of a thing, whereas the efficient and the final causes are called extrinsic, since they are external to the thing. But he accepts only intrinsic causes as principles. Privation is not included among the causes, for, as has been said, it is an accidental principle. When we speak of four causes, therefore, we mean essential causes. Accidental causes, however, are reduced to essential ones, since everything that is accidental is reduced to that which is essential.

(21) But although Aristotle contends in Book One of the *Physics* that principles are intrinsic causes, nevertheless, as he states in Book Eleven of the *Metaphysics,* principle is properly said to be an extrinsic cause, whereas those causes which are parts of a thing—that is, the intrinsic causes—are called *elements.* However, both can be said to be causes, although sometimes one is taken for the other. For every cause can be said to be a principle, and every principle a cause. But cause appears to connote something more than what is commonly said to be a principle, inasmuch as anything that is prior, whether or not something else follows from it, can be said to be a principle. An artisan is called the principle of a knife, for example, because a knife comes into being as a result of his activity. But when something is changed from black to white, black is said to be the principle of that motion, just as, universally, anything from which change commences is called a principle. Black, however, is not that from which the being of white follows. Something prior is said to be a cause only when the existence of what is posterior follows from it. Hence, a cause is said to be that from whose existing another follows. Accordingly, what is prior by way of being that from which motion starts cannot

---

*An ancient musical instrument resembling a lyre, and a precursor of the zither.

be called an essential cause, even if it is called a principle. This is the reason for including privation among principles, but not among causes. A privation is that from which generation begins. It can, however, be called an accidental cause, inasmuch as it coincides with matter, as was explained above.

(22) *Element* is predicated properly only of those causes which enter into the composition of a thing, and which are properly material; every material cause, moreover, is not properly said to be an element but only that one which is involved in a thing's primary composition. Thus we do not speak of limbs as elements of man, because his limbs are composed of other things. We do claim, however, that earth and water are elements; for these are not composed of other bodies, rather it is from these that the first composition of natural bodies results. Hence Aristotle, in Book Five of his *Metaphysics,* says that an element is "an immanent, specifically irreducible entity of which a thing is primarily composed." The explanation of the phrase, "of which a thing is primarily composed" is clear from what we have already said. The word "immanent" is used to differentiate an element from that other kind of matter which is totally destroyed by generation, like the bread which is the matter of blood. Blood is generated only if bread is destroyed. Bread does not remain in blood, and therefore it cannot be said to be an element of blood. But elements must remain in some way, since they are not entirely destroyed, as is stated in the book *On Generation.* The phrase "specifically irreducible" differentiates the elements from those materials having parts diverse in form—that is, in species-like a hand, whose parts are flesh and bone, which are specifically different. But an element is not divided into specifically diverse parts; any part of the element water, for example, is water. Nor is it necessary for an element to be undivided quantitatively in order to be an element. It suffices that it not be divided specifically. If it is not divided in any way, it is also called an element, as letters are said to be elements of words. From all that we have said it is clear, therefore, that a principle is in some way more than a cause, and a cause more than an element. This is, indeed, what the Commentator [Averroës] contends in his comment on the fifth book of the *Metaphysics.*

CHAPTER IV. THE RELATIONSHIPS BETWEEN CAUSES

(23) Having seen that there are four kinds of cause, it is also necessary to see that it is not impossible for the same thing to have several causes, like a statue, which has both bronze and an artisan as causes. The artisan is the efficient cause, and the bronze the material one. Nor is it impossible for the same thing to be the cause of contraries, as the pilot is the cause of both the safety and the sinking of his ship. He is the cause of the latter by his absence, and of the former by his presence.

(24) It should be understood also that it is possible for the same thing to be a cause and to be caused, with respect to the same thing but in different ways. For example, taking a walk is the efficient cause of health, while health is the final cause of taking a walk, inasmuch as taking a walk is sometimes done for the sake of health. Likewise, the body is the matter of the soul, and the soul is the form of the body. The efficient cause is said to be a cause with respect to the end, since the end does not exist in act unless the agent acts; but the end is said to be the cause of the efficient cause, since the latter does not operate except through the intention of an end. Hence, an efficient cause is the cause of that which is the end, as in the example of taking a walk for one's health. It does not,

however, maké the end be an end, and therefore it is not the cause of the causality of the end—that is, it does not make the end be a final cause. A physician, for example, produces actual health, but he does not establish health as an end. Moreover, the end does not cause that which is the efficient cause, rather, it is a cause of the efficient cause's being an efficient cause. For health—and I mean the health resulting from the physician's ministrations—does not make a physician be a physician; it causes him to be an efficient cause. Hence, the end is the cause of the causality of the efficient cause, for it makes the efficient cause be an efficient cause. Similarly, it makes the matter be matter, and form be form, since matter receives a form only for some end, and a form perfects matter only for an end. Wherefore the end is said to be the cause of causes, inasmuch as it is the cause of the causality of all the causes. Matter is also said to be the cause of a form, inasmuch as a form does not exist except in matter. Similarly, form is the cause of matter, inasmuch as matter does not actually exist except through form. Matter and form are mutually related, as the second book of the *Physics* states. They are related to the composite, as parts are to the whole and as the simple is to the complex.

(25) Every cause, insofar as it is a cause, is naturally prior to what is caused. We should realize, however, that priority can have two forms, as Aristotle says in Book Sixteen of *On Animals.* Accordingly, a thing can be called prior and posterior, and a cause can be called caused, with respect to the same thing. For one thing can be called prior to another in generation and time, or in substance and completeness. Therefore, since the operation of nature proceeds from the imperfect to the perfect and from the incomplete to the complete, the imperfect is prior to the perfect in generation and time, but the perfect is prior to the imperfect in substance. For example, a man can be said to be prior to a boy in substance and completeness, whereas a boy is prior to a man in generation and time. But, although in things generable the imperfect is prior to the perfect, and potency prior to act—considering, in one and the same thing, that what is prior is imperfect rather than perfect, and in potency rather than in act—nevertheless, speaking without qualification, what is in act and perfect must be prior. This follows because what reduces a potency to act is in act, and what perfects the imperfect is itself perfect. Matter, indeed, is prior to form in generation and time, inasmuch as that to which something is added is prior to that which is added. But form is prior to matter in substance and in fully constituted being, because matter has complete existence only through form. Similarly, the efficient cause is prior to the end in generation and time, since the motion to the end comes about by the efficient cause; but the end is prior to the efficient cause as such in substance and completeness, since the action of the efficient cause is completed only through the end. Therefore, the material and the efficient causes are prior by way of generation, whereas form and end are prior by way of perfection.

(26) It should be noted that necessity is of two kinds: *absolute* and *conditional.* Necessity is indeed absolute when it proceeds from causes which are prior by way of generation, that is, from the material and efficient causes. For example, the necessity of death stems from matter—that is, from the disposition of composing contraries; therefore it is said to be absolute because there is no impediment to it. This is also called the necessity of matter. However, conditional necessity proceeds from causes posterior in generation, that is, from form and end. Accordingly, we say that conception must take place if a man is to be generated. This necessity is said to be conditional, because it is not necessary without qualification for some particular woman to conceive. However, conception is necessary under this condition, namely, if a man is to be generated. This is called the necessity of the end.

(27) We should also realize that three of the causes—form, end, and efficient cause—can coincide. The generation of fire offers a clear example of this. Fire gener-

Three Orders of Society, from L'*image du monde,* Franco-Flemish, late thirteenth century. This detail from an illustrated manuscript page shows the hierarchy of medieval society with monk, knight, and peasant. *(British Museum)*

ates fire; therefore fire is an efficient cause, insofar as it generates. Fire is a form, insofar as it makes that which formerly was in potency be in act. Finally, fire is an end, insofar as it is intended by the agent and insofar as the operation of the agent is terminated in it. There are, however, two kinds of ends, namely, the end of the generation process and the end of the thing generated. Both of these ends are evident in producing a knife. The form *knife* is the end of the generating process; but cutting, which is the knife's operation, is the end of the thing generated—that is, the knife.

(28) Sometimes the end of the generating process coincides with the two other above-mentioned causes: form and efficient cause. This occurs when generation proceeds from one thing to another thing that is similar in species to the first, as when a man generates a man, or an olive tree an olive tree. It is not possible, however, for the end of the thing generated to coincide with the form and the efficient cause; yet we should realize that the end and the form are numerically identical, inasmuch as the form of the thing generated and the end of the generation are numerically the same. The end of the generating process and the efficient cause coincide in species, but not in number. For it is impossible for the maker and the thing made to be the same in num-

ber; but they can be the same in species. For example, when a man generates a man, the man generating and the man generated are diverse in number, but the same in species.

(29) Matter does not coincide with any of the other causes, since, by reason of the fact that it is being in potency, matter is by nature imperfect. The other causes, however, since they are in act, have the nature of something perfect. The perfect and the imperfect do not coincide.

CHAPTER V. OTHER DIVISIONS OF THE CAUSES

(30) Wherefore, having seen that there are four causes, namely, efficient, material, formal, and final, we should also realize that each of these causes can be divided in many ways. There exist what are called *prior* and *posterior* causes. For example, both the physician's art and the physician himself are causes of health, but the art is a prior cause and the physician a posterior one. The same division is true of the formal cause and the other causes. Note also that we should always reduce a question to the first cause. If we were to ask, "Why is the man healthy?" we would answer, "Because the physician healed him." Continuing, we would ask, "But by what means did the physician heal?"—"Through the art of healing that he possesses."

(31) Moreover, we must understand that *proximate cause* means the same as *posterior cause,* and *remote cause* the same as *prior cause.* Accordingly, these two divisions of causes—prior and posterior, and remote and proximate—signify the same thing. Furthermore, we should observe that the more universal cause is always called the remote cause, while the more particular cause is called the proximate cause. For example, the proximate form of man is his definition, that is, *rational mortal animal;* but animal is more remote, and substance even further removed. For all superior things are forms of inferior ones. Similarly, the proximate matter of a statue is bronze, while the remote matter is metal, and the more remote is body.

(32) There is likewise another division of causes: into *essential* and *accidental* causes. A cause is called essential when it causes something by reason of its being what it is, as, for example, the builder is the cause of a house, and the wood is the matter of a bench. A cause is called accidental when it happens to coincide with an essential cause. This may be illustrated by a grammarian who builds something. The grammarian is said to be an accidental cause of a building, not insofar as he is a grammarian, but insofar as being a grammarian is accidental to building. The same is true of the other causes.

(33) In addition, certain causes are *simple,* and others *composite.* A cause is called simple when it alone is said to be the cause, be it essential (as when we say that the builder is the cause of the house) or accidental (as when we say that the physician is the cause of the house). However, we would be speaking of a composite cause when both are called the cause, as when we say that the builder-physician is the cause of the house. A simple cause can also be defined, according to Avicenna, as that which causes without being united with another, like bronze which causes the statue without the addition of any other matter. Further illustrations might be the physician who produces health, or the fire that warms. A cause is called composite when many things must unite into being a cause, as not one man, but many, are the cause of the motion of a ship, and not one stone, but many are the matter of the house.

(34) In addition, certain causes are *actual,* and others *potential.* A cause is actual when it is actually causing the thing, like a builder when he builds, or the bronze from which a statue is being made. A potential cause is one which, although not actually causing the thing, nevertheless can cause something, like a builder when he is not building. It should be understood in speaking of actual causes that what causes and what is caused must exist simultaneously, such that if the one exists, the other does also. For if there is an actual builder, he must be building, and if actual building is going on, the builder must be a builder in act. This is not necessary, however, in those causes which are causes only in potency.

(35) Moreover, we should realize that a universal cause is related to a universal effect, while a singular cause is related to a singular effect. For example, the builder is the cause of the house, while *this* builder is the cause of *this* house.

CHAPTER VI. UNITY AND DIVERSITY WITHIN CAUSES

(36) It should be understood that in speaking of the intrinsic principles matter and form, there are a similarity and a difference of principles, according to the similarity and the difference of things resulting from the principles. Certain things are the same numerically, like Socrates (when Socrates is being pointed at) and this man. Others are diverse numerically but the same specifically, like Socrates and Plato, who, although they are the same in human species, nevertheless differ numerically. Further, certain things are different specifically, but the same generically, like a man and an ass, which are the same in the genus *animal.* Still others are diverse generically but the same only according to an analogy, like substance and quantity, which do not agree in any genus but are similar only analogously; for they are alike only in being. Being is not a genus, however, since it is predicated, not univocally, but analogously.

(37) To grasp this one should understand that something can be predicated of many things in three ways: *univocally, equivocally,* and *analogously.* A univocal predication occurs when something is predicated according to the same name and the same nature, that is, definition, as *animal* is predicated both of man and of ass. Each is called an animal and each is an animated substance capable of sensation, which is the definition of an animal. Equivocal predication occurs when something is predicated of several things according to the same name but diverse natures, like *dog,* said of a barking animal and of a stellar constellation. These agree in name only, not in definition or signification, for what is signified by a name is the definition, as is stated in the fourth book of the *Metaphysics.* An analogous predication occurs when something is predicated of several things which have diverse natures, but which are related to some one thing, as *healthy* is predicated of an animal body, of urine, and of medicine, although it does not wholly signify the same thing in all. For *healthy* is predicated of urine as of a sign of health; of a body, as of its subject; of medicine, as of its cause. Nevertheless, each of these is related to the one end, health.

(38) Sometimes things which are similar analogously—that is, through a proportion, a comparison, or an agreement—are such by being related to one end. The example above is an instance of this. At other times things are analogous by being related to one agent. For example, *physician* is predicated of one who heals through his training; of one who heals without training, like a midwife; and even of the instruments used. But it is predicated of all of them in relation to one agency, which in this case is the healing

art. At still other times many things are similar analogously by attribution to one subject, as *being,* is said of substance, quantity, quality, and the other predicaments. Quantity and the others are called being, but not for the same reason that substance is. All the others are called being inasmuch as they are related to substance, which indeed is their subject. Therefore, *being* is said first of substance and only secondarily of the others. Consequently, being is not the genus of substance and quantity, because no genus is predicated of some of its species first, and of others secondarily. Being is predicated analogously; and this is what we meant when we claimed that substance and quantity differ generically but are analogously the same.

(39) Therefore, of those things which are numerically the same, both the matter and the form are numerically the same, as [both matter and form] of Tullius and of Cicero. Of those which are specifically the same but numerically diverse, the matter and the form are not numerically the same, but are specifically the same, as [those] of Socrates and of Plato. Similarly, of those things which are generically the same, their principles are generically the same, like the soul and the body of an ass and of a horse, which differ specifically but are the same generically. Likewise, of those things which are similar only in an analogous way, their principles are only analogously or proportionately similar. For matter and form and privation, or even potency and act, are principles of substance and of the other genera. Nevertheless, the matter of a substance and that of quantity, and likewise the form and the privation, differ generically, but agree only according to a proportion, which consists in this: just as the matter of a substance is related to the substance in the nature of matter, so too is the matter of quantity related to quantity. Accordingly, just as substance is the cause of all the other things, so the principles of substance are the principles of all the others.

LATE MEDIEVAL PHILOSOPHY

Thomas Aquinas lived during a period of relative calm and well-being, but the century and a half following his death was filled with tumult and upheaval. As a part of the often vicious conflict between church and state, Philip IV of France captured Pope Boniface VIII in 1303 and soon thereafter moved the papal court to Avignon, France—the so-called Babylonian Captivity of the Church. Beginning in 1347, the bubonic plague, or Black Death, struck Western Europe. Responses to the plague ranged from fanatical anti-intellectual apocalypticism to self-indulgent hedonism. Some even blamed the plague on intellectuals such as Thomas Aquinas, saying they provoked divine wrath by explaining God's ways rationally; others simply counselled, "Let us eat, drink, and be merry, for tomorrow we die." Many turned to superstition or to scapegoating Jews. At the same time, England and France were involved in the Hundred Years' War (1337–1453), which brought enormous casualties. Because of the plague and the war, in the years from 1300 to 1450, the population of Western Europe was reduced by half—perhaps by as much as two-thirds. In 1378, the Great Schism divided the Catholic Church as the Italians reinstituted the papacy in Rome, while a second pope reigned in Avignon. For over thirty years, rival popes condemned and excommunicated one another. In 1409, an attempt to end the schism with a compromise pope led only to a third pope and thus a third claimant to St. Peter's universal chair. Finally, in 1417, the church united around one pope ruling in Rome. But by now the power and prestige of the papacy had been severely diminished, and a hundred years later, in the Protestant Reformation, the Western church split decisively.

It is common to view the philosophy of this period in the light of these social upheavals, and, indeed, there does seem to be some connection. Thomas had harmonized philosophy and theology in a systematic way reflective of the relative peacefulness of the thirteenth century. Just as social stability—particularly in the relationship between church and state—deteriorated in the centuries following Thomas, so also the philosophies that developed during this period tended to separate reason and faith. In particular, thinkers became more skeptical about natural theology, that is, about the ability of reason to know truths concerning God. John Duns Scotus began this process as he tended to reduce the competence of theology to supernatural revelation alone, dismissing the natural theology of Thomas. William of Ockham took this tendency further, claiming philosophy and theology to be separate realms with separate rules. The transitional thinker Nicholas Cusanas claimed that knowledge was at best mere conjecture and that contradictories are compatible in reality: God, especially, incorporates all contradictions, all opposites, within the divine being. Clearly the coherent, rational synthesis of Thomas had unravelled.

But as Frederick Copleston has pointed out, there are other ways of understanding this transition. Instead of seeing late medieval–early Renaissance philosophy as destructive to a grand synthesis or as reactive to societal chaos, "one can see . . . philosophy being reborn and growing up under the shadow and care of theology, reaching a more or less adult stage and then tending to go its own way and assert its independence" (*A History of Medieval Philosophy*, p. 314). While acknowledging the disintegration of the peculiarly Thomistic approach to synthesis, this view sees the late medieval period as a natural development of Western European thought.

*   *   *

For general surveys of medieval philosophy, which include the later period, see Maurice De Wulf, *History of Mediaeval Philosophy* (New York: Dover, 1952); Étienne Gilson, *History of Christian Philosophy in the Middle Ages* (New York: Random House, 1955); and Armand A. Maurer, *Medieval Philosophy* (New York: Random House, 1962). The following volumes of Frederick Copleston's *A History of Philosophy* deal with this period: *Volume II: Medieval Philosophy, Part II: Albert the Great to Duns Scotus* (1950; reprinted Garden City, NY: Image Doubleday, 1962); *Volume III: Late Medieval and Renaissance Philosophy, Part I: Ockham to the Speculative Mystics* and *Part II: The Revival of Platonism to Suárez* (both 1953; reprinted Garden City, NY: Image Doubleday, 1963); and the later single volume, *A History of Medieval Philosophy* (New York: Harper & Row, 1972). Ray C. Petry, ed., *Late Medieval Mysticism* (Philadelphia: Westminster Press, 1957); Gordon Leff, *The Dissolution of the Medieval Outlook: An Essay on Intellectual and Spiritual Change in the Fourteenth Century* (New York: New York University Press, 1976), and John Marenbon, *Later Medieval Philosophy (1150–1350): An Introduction* (London: Routledge & Kegan Paul, 1987), give surveys of the late medieval period, while Norman Kretzmann et al., eds., *The Cambridge History of Later Medieval Philosophy: From the Rediscovery of Aristotle to the Disintegration of Scholasticism 1100–1600* (Cambridge: Cambridge University Press, 1982), offers thematic essays.

For general studies of Renaissance thought, see Ernst Cassirer, Paul O. Kristeller, and John H. Randall Jr., eds., *The Renaissance Philosophy of Man* (Chicago: University of Chicago Press, 1948); Ernst Cassirer, *The Individual and Cosmos in Renaissance Philosophy,* translated by Mario Domandi (New York:

Harper & Row, 1963); Paul O. Kristeller, *Renaissance Thought and Its Sources* (New York: Columbia University Press, 1979); Charles B. Schmitt, Quentin Skinner, and Eckhard Kessler, eds., *The Cambridge History of Renaissance Philosophy* (Cambridge: Cambridge University Press, 1988); and Brian P. Copenhaver and Charles B. Schmitt, *Renaissance Philosophy,* Vol. 3 of *History of Western Philosophy* (Oxford: Oxford University Press, 1992).

JOHN DUNS SCOTUS
ca. 1265–1308

Not much is known about the early life of John Duns Scotus except that he was born in Scotland. He later became a Franciscan friar and taught at Cambridge, Oxford, and Paris. In 1303, he was banished from Paris because he sided with Pope Boniface VIII against King Philip IV. He was back in Paris within a year, and in 1305 became regent master of theology. Two years later, he was transferred to Cologne, where he died in 1308.

Scotus managed to write a number of books during his short life—twelve Latin volumes in a seventeenth-century edition—though some work, previously thought his, is now believed to be that of his followers. Duns's abstract metaphysical speculations and technical terminology are extremely difficult to understand. It is not surprising, then, that later thinkers called him the "Subtle Doctor." The followers of John Duns Scotus were so intent on following his subtlety that Renaissance thinkers mocked them as "Dunsmen"—from which we get our word "dunce." Despite this epithet, there are those, such as the poet Gerard Manley Hopkins, who have found Scotus's thought penetrating and profound.

Scotus disagreed with Thomas Aquinas on a number of issues, including the doctrine of analogy, the nature of individuation, and the limits of natural theology. But the most important difference between these two thinkers concerned the relative importance of intellect and will. Whereas Thomas saw the various powers of the soul to be functions of the intellect, Duns Scotus claimed that such an explanation is too limiting. The powers of the soul include memory, intellect, and, most important, will.

In the area of metaphysics, Scotus argued that metaphysics was a science dealing primarily with God and the Intelligences that govern the movements of the planets. In the passage from Allan Wolter's translation of *A Treatise on God as First Principle* given here, Scotus develops an argument for God's existence as the "one nature which is simply first."

*   *   *

For years, Charles R.S. Harris's *Duns Scotus,* two vols. (1927; reprinted New York: Humanities Press, 1959), was the standard work, but this study includes material now known to be unauthentic. For more recent work on Duns Scotus, see Efrem Bettoni, *Duns Scotus: The Basic Principles of His Philosophy,* translated by Bernardine Bonansea (Washington, DC: Catholic University of America Press, 1961), and Allan B. Wolter, *The Philosophical Theology of John Duns Scotus* (Ithaca, NY: Cornell University Press, 1990). For a collection of essays, see John K. Ryan and Bernardine M. Bonansea, eds., *John Duns Scotus* (Washington, DC: Catholic University of America Press, 1965). The "Philosophy Series" of the Franciscan Institute Publications, includes several specialized studies on Duns Scotus, though they may prove difficult for the beginning student.

A TREATISE ON GOD AS FIRST PRINCIPLE (in part)

CHAPTER 3

3.1 The triple primacy of the First Principle.

3.2 O Lord, our God, you have proclaimed yourself to be the first and last. Teach your servant to show by reason what he holds with faith most certain, that you are the most eminent, the first efficient cause and the last end.

3.3 We would like to select three of the six essential orders referred to earlier, the two of extrinsic causality and the one of eminence and, if you grant us to do so, to demonstrate that in these three orders there is some one nature which is simply first. I say one "nature" advisedly, since in this third chapter these three ways of being first will be shown to characterize not a unique singular or what is but one in number, but a unique essence or nature. Numerical unity, however, will be discussed later.

3.4 (First conclusion) *Some nature among beings can produce an effect.*

3.5 This is shown to be so because something can be produced and therefore something can be productive. The implication is evident from the nature of correlatives. Proof of the antecedent: (1) Some nature is contingent. It is possible for it to exist after being nonexistent, not of itself, however, or by reason of nothing, for in both these cases a being would exist by reason of what is not a being. Therefore it is producible by an-

Duns Scotus, *A Treatise on God as First Principle,* translated by Allan B. Wolter (Chicago: Franciscan Herald Press, 1969). Reprinted by permission.

other. (2) Some nature too is changeable or mobile, since it can lack some perfection it is able to have. The result of the change then can begin to be and thus be produced.

3.6 In this conclusion, as in some of those which follow, I could argue in terms of the actual thus. Some nature is producing since some nature is produced, because some nature begins to exist, for some nature is contingent and the result of motion. But I prefer to propose conclusions and premises about the possible. For once those about the actual are granted, those about the possible are also conceded, but the reverse is not the case. Also those about the actual are contingent, though evident enough, whereas those about the possible are necessary. The former concern the being as existing whereas the latter can pertain properly to a being considered even in terms of its essentials. The existence of this essence, of which efficiency is now established, will be proved later.

3.7 (Second conclusion) *Something able to produce an effect is simply first, that is to say, it neither can be produced by an efficient cause nor does it exercise its efficient causality in virtue of anything other than itself.*

3.8 It is proved from the first conclusion that something can produce an effect. Call this producer A. If A is first in the way explained, we have immediately what we seek to prove. If it is not such, then it is a posterior agent either because it can be produced by something else or because it is able to produce its effect only in virtue of some agent other than itself. To deny the negation is to assert the affirmation. Let us assume that this being is not first and call it B. Then we can argue of B as we did of A. Either we go on *ad infinitum* so that each thing in reference to what precedes it in the series will be second; or we shall reach something that has nothing prior to it. However, an infinity in the ascending order is impossible; hence a primacy is necessary because whatever has nothing prior is not posterior to anything posterior to itself, for the second conclusion of chapter two does away with a circle in causes.

3.9 An objection is raised here on the grounds that those who philosophize admit that an infinity is possible in an ascending order, as they themselves were wont to assume infinite generators of which none is first but each is second to some other, and still they assume no circle in causes. In ruling out this objection I declare that the philosophers did not postulate the possibility of an infinity in causes essentially ordered, but only in causes accidentally ordered, as is evident from Avicenna's *Metaphysics,* B. VI, chapter five, where he speaks of an infinity of individuals in a species.

3.10 But to show what I have in mind, I will explain what essentially ordered and accidentally ordered causes are. Here recall that it is one thing to speak of incidental causes *(causae per accidens)* as contrasted with those which are intended to cause a given effect *(causae per se).* It is quite another to speak of causes which are ordered to one another essentially or of themselves *(per se)* and those which are ordered only accidentally *(per accidens).* For in the first instance, we have merely a one-to-one comparison, [namely] of the cause to that which is caused. A *per se* cause is one which causes a given effect by reason of its proper nature and not in virtue of something incidental to it. In the second instance, two causes are compared with each other insofar as they are causes of the same thing.

3.11 *Per se* or essentially ordered causes differ from accidentally ordered causes in three respects. The first difference is that in essentially ordered causes, the second depends upon the first precisely in the act of causing. In accidentally ordered causes this is not the case, although the second may depend upon the first for its existence or in some other way. The second difference is that in essentially ordered causes the causality is of another nature and order, inasmuch as the higher cause is the more perfect, which is not the case with accidentally ordered causes. This second difference is a consequence of the first, since no cause in the exercise of its causality is essentially dependent upon a cause of the same nature as itself, for to produce anything one cause of a given kind suffices. A third difference follows, viz. that all essentially ordered causes are simultaneously required to cause the effect, for otherwise some causality essential to the effect would be wanting. In accidentally ordered causes this simultaneity is not required.

3.12 What we intend to show from this is that an infinity of essentially ordered causes is impossible, and that an infinity of accidentally ordered causes is also impossible unless we admit a *terminus* in an essentially ordered series. Therefore there is no way in which an infinity in essentially ordered causes is possible. And even if we deny the existence of an essential order, an infinity of causes is still impossible. Consequently in any case there is something able to produce an effect which is simply first. Here three propositions are assumed. For the sake of brevity, call the first A, the second B and the third C.

3.13 The proof of these: first, A is proved. (1) If the totality of essentially ordered causes were caused, it would have to be by a cause which does not belong to the group, otherwise it would be its own cause. The whole series of dependents then is dependent and upon something which is not one of the group. (2) [If this were not so], an infinity of essentially ordered causes would be acting at the same time (a consequence of the third difference mentioned above). Now no philosopher assumes this. (3) Thirdly, to be prior, according to Bk. V of the *Metaphysics,* a thing must be nearer the beginning. Consequently, where there is no beginning, nothing can be essentially prior to anything else. (4) Fourthly, by reason of the second difference, the higher cause is more perfect in its causality, therefore what is infinitely higher is infinitely more perfect, and hence of infinite perfection in its causing. Therefore it does not cause in virtue of another, because everything of this kind is imperfect in its causality, since it depends upon another to produce its effect. (5) Fifthly, inasmuch as to be able to produce something does not imply any imperfection—a point evident from conclusion eight of chapter two—it follows that this ability can exist in some nature without imperfection. But if every cause depends upon some prior cause, then efficiency would never be found without imperfection. Consequently, an independent power to produce something can exist in some nature and this is simply first. Therefore, such an efficient power is possible and this suffices for now, since we shall prove later from that that it exists in reality. And so A becomes evident from these five arguments.

3.14 Proof of B: If we assume an infinity of accidentally ordered causes, it is clear that these are not concurrent, but one succeeds another so that the second, though it is in some way from the preceding, does not depend upon it for the exercise of its causality. For it is equally effective whether the preceding cause exists or not. A son in turn may beget a child just as well whether his father be dead or alive. But an infinite succession of such causes is impossible unless it exists in virtue of some nature of infinite duration from which the whole succession and every part thereof depends. For no change of form is perpetuated save in virtue of something permanent which is not a part of that succession, since everything of this succession which is in flux is of the same nature. Something essentially prior to the series, then, exists, for everything that is part of the succession depends upon it, and this dependence is of a different order from that by which it depends upon the immediately preceding cause where the latter is a part of the succession. Therefore B is evident.

3.15 Proof of C: From the first conclusion, some nature is able to produce an effect. But if an essential order of agents be denied, then this nature capable of causing does not cause in virtue of some other cause, and even if we assume that in one individual it is caused, nevertheless in some other it will not be caused, and this is what we propose to prove to be true of the first nature. For if we assume that in every individual this nature is caused, then a contradiction follows if we deny the existence of an essential order, since no nature that is caused can be assumed to exist in each individual in such a way that it is included in an accidental order of causes without being at the same time essentially ordered to some other nature. This follows from B.

3.16 (Third conclusion) *If what is able to cause effectively is simply first, then it is itself incapable of being caused, since it cannot be produced and is independently able to produce its effects.*

3.17 This is clear from the second conclusion, for if such a being could cause only in virtue of something else or if it could be produced, then either a process *ad infinitum* or a circle in causes would result, or else the series would terminate in some being which cannot be produced and yet independently is able to produce an effect. This latter being I call "first," and from what you grant, it is clear that anything other than this is not first. Furthermore, it follows that if the first cannot be produced, then it has no causes whatsoever, for it cannot be the result of a final cause (from conclusion two of chapter two)—nor of a material cause (from the sixth conclusion of the same)—nor of a formal cause (from the seventh conclusion there). Neither can it be caused by matter and form together (from the eighth conclusion there).

3.18 (Fourth conclusion) *A being able to exercise efficient causality which is simply first actually exists, and some nature actually existing is capable of exercising such causality.*

3.19 Proof of this: Anything to whose nature it is repugnant to receive existence from something else, exists of itself if it is able to exist at all. To receive existence from something else is repugnant to the very notion of a being which is first in the order of efficiency, as is clear from the third conclusion. And it can exist, as is clear from the second conclusion. Indeed, the fifth argument there which seems to be less conclusive than the others established this much. The other proofs there can be considered in the existential mode—in which case they concern contingent, though manifest facts—or they can be understood of the nature, the quiddity and possibility, in which case the conclusions proceed from necessary premises. From all this it follows that an efficient cause which is first in the unqualified sense of the term can exist of itself, for what does not actually exist of itself is incapable of existing of itself. Otherwise a nonexistent being would cause something to exist; but this is impossible, even apart from the fact that in such a case the thing would be its own cause and hence could not be entirely uncaused. Another way to establish this fourth conclusion would be to argue from the impropriety of a universe that would lack the highest possible degree of being.

3.20 As a corollary of this fourth conclusion, note that not only is such a cause prior to all others, but that it would be contradictory to say that another is prior to it. And insofar as such a cause is first, it exists. This is proved in the same way as was the fourth conclusion. The very notion of such a being implies its inability to be caused. Therefore, if it can exist, owing to the fact that to be is not contradictory to it, then it follows that it can exist of itself and consequently that it does exist of itself.

3.21 (Fifth conclusion) *A being unable to be caused is of itself necessarily existent.*

3.22 Proof: By excluding every cause of existence other than itself, whether it be intrinsic or extrinsic, we make it impossible for it not to be. Proof: Nothing can be nonexistent unless something either positively or privatively incompatible with it can exist, for one of two contradictories is always true. But nothing can be either positively or privatively incompatible with a being which cannot be caused, because it would be either of itself or from another. Not the first way, for then it would exist of itself—from the fourth conclusion,—so that there would be two incompatible things, and for that reason neither would exist, since you admit that the uncausable is nonexistent because of this incompatible element and vice versa. Neither can the incompatible be from another, because nothing caused has a more intense or potent existence from a cause than an uncausable thing has of itself, since the former is dependent in existing whereas the uncausable is not. Furthermore the possibility of the causable being does not entail its actual existence as is the case with the uncausable. Nothing incompatible with what is already a being can come from a cause unless it receive from that cause a being more intense or powerful than is the being of that which is incompatible with it.

3.23 (Sixth conclusion) *It is the characteristic of but one nature to have necessary being of itself.*

3.24 This is proved thus: If two natures of themselves could be necessary being, then this necessity of existing would be a common feature. And this they would share by reason of some essential or generic kind of entity in addition to which they would differ by reason of their ultimate actual formalities. Now two inconsistencies follow from this. To begin with, each will be a necessary being first of all through that common nature which is the less actual, rather than through that distinctive nature which is the more actual. For were it necessary being also by reason of its distinctive nature, then it will be necessary being twice over, because that distinguishing nature does not formally include the common nature, even as a [specific] difference does not include the genus. It seems impossible however, that the less actual be the primary reason why something is necessary, and that it is neither primarily nor *per se* necessary by reason of what is more actual. The second impossibility is that neither of the two would necessarily exist by virtue of that common nature which is presumed to be the primary reason why each is necessary. For that nature is insufficient to account for the existence of either nature, since every nature is what it is by reason of its ultimate formal constituent. But it is precisely what—to the exclusion of all else—accounts for a thing's actual existence, that is the reason for its being necessary. If you say that the common nature suffices for existence apart from the distinguishing natures, then it follows that the common nature of itself exists actually and without any distinguishing features, and therefore cannot be distinguished, since the necessary being already existing is not in potency to being [different kinds of things] in an unqualified sense [in the way] that the generic being in a species is simply that *kind* of thing.

3.25 Besides, two natures included under a common class are unequal. Proof of this is to be found among the different kinds of things into which a genus is divided. But if the two such natures are unequal, one will be of a more perfect being than the other. Nothing however is more perfect than a being having necessary existence of itself.

3.26 Moreover, if there were two natures having necessary being of themselves, neither would depend upon the other for existence and consequently no essential order would exist between them. One of them, therefore, would not belong to this universe, for there is nothing in the universe which is not related by an essential order to the other beings, for the unity of the universe stems from the order of its parts. Here it is objected that inasmuch as each is related to the parts of the universe through the order of eminence, this suffices for unity. To the contrary: One is not so ordered to the other, for a more perfect existence characterizes the more eminent nature. Nothing however is more perfect than a being having necessary existence of itself. What is more, one of two is not ordered to the parts of the universe, because if the universe is one, then it is characterized by a single order and this obtains where there is but one first. Proof: If you assume there are two first natures, since there is a dual term of reference, the nature next to the first has no unique order or dependence and the same is true of each subsequent nature. And thus through the whole universe there will be two orders, and hence two universes.

Or else where will be an order only to one necessary being, but not to the other. If one proceeds reasonably, then, it seems he ought not to postulate anything for no apparent need, or whose entity is not clearly revealed by reason of some order to other things,—for, according to *Physics,* Bk. I, more than one thing should not be postulated where one suffices. Now we show there is a necessary being in the universe from the uncausable, and this in turn from what is first in causing, and the latter from what is caused. But from these effects there is no apparent necessity for assuming several first causing natures; furthermore, this is impossible, as will be shown later in the fifteenth conclusion of this third chapter. Therefore it is not necessary to assume that there are several things which are uncaused and necessarily exist. With reason, then, they are not postulated.

3.27 Concerning the final cause I propose four conclusions similar to the first four in this chapter about a being able to produce an effect. They are also proved in a similar way. The first of these is this: (Seventh conclusion) *Among beings some nature is able to function as final cause.*

3.28 Proof: Since something is producible (from the proof of the first conclusion of this chapter), something is able to be ordered to an end. The implication is clear. . . . That an essential order is involved is even more evident here than in the case of the efficient cause. . . .

3.29 (Eighth conclusion) *Something able to be an end is simply ultimate, that is to say, it can neither be ordained to something else nor exercise its finality in virtue of something else.*

3.30 This is proved by five arguments similar to those advanced for the second conclusion of this third chapter.

3.31 (Ninth conclusion) *Such an ultimate end cannot be caused in any way.*

3.32 This is proved from the fact that it cannot be ordained for another end; otherwise it would not be ultimate. It follows further that it cannot be caused by an efficient cause (from conclusion four of chapter two and also from what was said above in the proof for the third conclusion of the present chapter).

3.33 (Tenth conclusion) *The being which can be an ultimate end actually exists, and that this primacy pertains to some actually existing nature.*

3.34 The proof for this is like that used for the fourth conclusion of chapter three. Corollary: It is first to such an extent that it is impossible that anything should be prior to it. This is proved in the same fashion as the corollary to the fourth conclusion above.

WILLIAM OF OCKHAM
ca. 1285–1349

William of Ockham was born in Ockham, Surrey, near London, between 1280 and 1290. As a young man, he joined the Franciscan order. In 1309 or 1310, he went to Oxford, where his studies included the work of Duns Scotus. Despite his success as a student and, later, as a student lecturer, Ockham was denied a license to teach. The chancellor of the university accused him of heresy, even going to the papal court in Avignon, France, in 1323 to press charges. Ockham was summoned the following year to Avignon by Pope John XXII. The affair dragged on for four years. Meanwhile, Ockham kept writing and came into conflict with the pope again when he joined the general of his Franciscan order in advocating apostolic poverty.

In 1328, Ockham was forced to flee Avignon when the pope was prepared to condemn the Franciscan position on poverty. He eventually found refuge in Munich under the protection of Emperor Ludwig of Bavaria, who was angry with the pope for not recognizing his crown. Ockham reportedly told the emperor, "Defend me with your sword, and I will defend you with my pen."

Over the next twenty years, Ockham did indeed defend the emperor, arguing that imperial power flows from God through the people, not through the pope—a position that anticipated later political theories. Following Ludwig's death in 1347, Ockham sought reconciliation with the pope (now Clement VI), and a document of submission was drawn up. We do not know whether Ockham ever signed the document, for he died in 1349, apparently from the plague.

Ockham is probably best known for his "Law of Parsimony," or "Ockham's Razor." This principle has often been formulated as *entia non sunt multiplicanda praeter necessitatem,* which translates as "entities are not to be multiplied beyond

Plague Victim, from *Das Buch der Cirurgia,* 1497, by Hieronymus Brunschwig.
Beginning in 1347 the bubonic plague, or Black Death, struck Western Europe.
Transmitted by flea bite, the disease was characterized by enormous swelling or
"buboes" in the groin or armpits. The patient in this woodcut has a large buboe
on his armpit—a sure sign that he will be dead within two or three days.
Apparently William of Ockham met such a fate in 1349. *(Library of Congress)*

necessity," though none of Ockham's known works contains that exact phrase.
Essentially this principle holds that we should always seek the simplest explanation, a principle still used by philosophers and scientists. Ockham was not the first
to enunciate this principle: It can be found earlier in the writings of Thomas
Aquinas, Duns Scotus, and even, in embryonic form, in Aristotle. But the skill
with which Ockham wielded this "razor" ensured its association with his name.

Ockham was especially effective in using his razor on the question of universals. Contrary to the moderate realism dominant in his day, Ockham saw no need to posit universals as real entities beyond individual things. This critique is clear in the reading from the *Summa Logicae,* given here in the Michael J. Loux translation. Following some defining of terms, Ockham argues against the realist position and, with great care, against the position of the "Subtle Doctor," Duns Scotus. Ockham asserts that "in a particular substance there is nothing substantial except the particular form, the particular matter, or the composite of the two"—that is, there is no real universal apart from the particular thing. The selection concludes with Ockham's presentation of a position he later rejected and a restatement of his final understanding of universals.

*   *   *

Marilyn McCord Adams, *William Ockham,* two vols. (Notre Dame, IN: University of Notre Dame Press, 1987), is the definitive introduction to Ockham, whereas Meyrick Heath Carré, *Realists and Nominalists* (London: Oxford University Press, 1946), and Gordon Leff, *William of Ockham: The Metamorphosis of Scholastic Discourse* (Manchester: Manchester University Press, 1975), provide helpful overviews. Specialized studies include E.A. Moody, *The Logic of William of Ockham* (1935; reprinted New York: Russell and Russell, 1965); Damascene Webering, *The Theory of Demonstration According to William Ockham* (St. Bonaventure, NY: Franciscan Institute, 1953); Herman Shapiro, *Motion, Time and Place According to William Ockham* (St. Bonaventure, NY: Franciscan Institute, 1957); and Arthur Stephen McGrade, *The Political Thought of William of Ockham: Personal and Institutional Principles* (London: Cambridge University Press, 1974). For an important collection of essays, see Philotheus Bohner, ed., *Collected Articles on Ockham* (St. Bonaventure, NY: Franciscan Institute, 1958).

SUMMA LOGICAE (in part)

PART I

CHAPTER 14: ON THE UNIVERSAL

It is not enough for the logician to have a merely general knowledge of terms; he needs a deep understanding of the concept of a term. Therefore, after discussing some general divisions among terms we should examine in detail the various headings under these divisions.

First, we should deal with terms of second intention and afterwards with terms of first intention. I have said that "universal," "genus," and "species" are examples of

From *Ockham's Theory of Terms: Part I of the Summa Logicae* by William of Ockham, translated by Michael J. Loux. Copyright © 1974 by University of Notre Dame Press. Reprinted by permission.

terms of second intention. We must discuss those terms of second intention which are called the five universals, but first we should consider the common term "universal." It is predicated of every universal and is opposed to the notion of a particular.

First, it should be noted that the term "particular" has two senses. In the first sense a particular is that which is one and not many. Those who hold that a universal is a certain quality residing in the mind which is predicable of many (not suppositing for itself, of course, but for the many of which it is predicated) must grant that, in this sense of the word, every universal is a particular. Just as a word, even if convention makes it common, is a particular, the intention of the soul signifying many is numerically one thing a particular; for although it signifies many things it is nonetheless one thing and not many.

In another sense of the word we use "particular" to mean that which is one and not many and which cannot function as a sign of many. Taking "particular" in this sense no universal is a particular, since every universal is capable of signifying many and of being predicated of many. Thus, if we take the term "universal" to mean that which is not one in number, as many do, then, I want to say that nothing is a universal. One could, of course, abuse the expression and say that a population constitutes a single universal because it is not one but many. But that would be puerile.

Therefore, it ought to be said that every universal is one particular thing and that it is not a universal except in its signification, in its signifying many things. This is what Avicenna means to say in his commentary on the fifth book of the *Metaphysics*. He says, "One form in the intellect is related to many things, and in this respect it is a universal; for it is an intention of the intellect which has an invariant relationship to anything you choose." He then continues, "Although this form is a universal in its relationship to individuals, it is a particular in its relationship to the particular soul in which it resides; for it is just one form among many in the intellect." He means to say that a universal is an intention of a particular soul. Insofar as it can be predicated of many things not for itself but for these many, it is said to be a universal; but insofar as it is a particular form actually existing in the intellect, it is said to be a particular. Thus "particular" is predicated of a universal in the first sense but not in the second. In the same way we say that the sun is a universal cause and, nevertheless, that it is really and truly a particular or individual cause. For the sun is said to be a universal cause because it is the cause of many things (i.e., every object that is generable and corruptible), but it is said to be a particular cause because it is one cause and not many. In the same way the intention of the soul is said to be a universal because it is a sign predicable of many things, but it is said to be a particular because it is one thing and not many.

But it should be noted that there are two kinds of universals. Some things are universal by nature; that is, by nature they are signs predicable of many in the same way that the smoke is by nature a sign of fire; weeping, a sign of grief; and laughter, a sign of internal joy. The intention of the soul, of course, is a universal by nature. Thus, no substance outside the soul, nor any accident outside the soul is a universal of this sort. It is of this kind of universal that I shall speak in the following chapters.

Other things are universals by convention. Thus, a spoken word, which is numerically one quality, is a universal; it is a sign conventionally appointed for the signification of many things. Thus, since the word is said to be common, it can be called a universal. But notice it is not by nature, but only by convention, that this label applies.

CHAPTER 15: THAT THE UNIVERSAL IS NOT A THING OUTSIDE THE MIND

But it is not enough just to state one's position; one must defend it by philosophical arguments. Therefore, I shall set forth some arguments for my view, and then corroborate it by an appeal to the authorities.

That no universal is a substance existing outside the mind can be proved in a number of ways:

No universal is a particular substance, numerically one; for if this were the case, then it would follow that Socrates is a universal; for there is no good reason why one substance should be a universal rather than another. Therefore no particular substance is a universal; every substance is numerically one and a particular. For every substance is either one thing and not many or it is many things. Now, if a substance is one thing and not many, then it is numerically one; for that is what we mean by "numerically one." But if, on the other hand, some substance is several things, it is either several particular things or several universal things. If the first alternative is chosen, then it follows that some substance would be several particular substances; and consequently that some substance would be several men. But although the universal would be distinguished from a single particular, it would not be distinguished from several particulars. If, however, some substance were to be several universal entities, I take one of those universal entities and ask, "Is it many things or is it one and not many?" If the second is the case then it follows that the thing is particular. If the first is the case then I ask, "Is it several particular things or several universal things?" Thus, either an infinite regress will follow or it will be granted that no substance is a universal in a way that would be incompatible with its also being a particular. From this it follows that no substance is a universal.

Again, if some universal were to be one substance existing in particular substances, yet distinct from them, it would follow that it could exist without them; for everything that is naturally prior to something else can, by God's power, exist without that thing; but the consequence is absurd.

Again, if the view in question were true, no individual would be able to be created. Something of the individual would pre-exist it, for the whole individual would not take its existence from nothing if the universal which is in it were already in something else. For the same reason it would follow that God could not annihilate an individual substance without destroying the other individuals of the same kind. If He were to annihilate some individual, he would destroy the whole which is essentially that individual and, consequently, He would destroy the universal which is in that thing and in others of the same essence. Consequently, other things of the same essence would not remain, for they could not continue to exist without the universal which constitutes a part of them.

Again, such a universal could not be construed as something completely extrinsic to the essence of an individual; therefore, it would belong to the essence of the individual; and, consequently, an individual would be composed of universals, so that the individual would not be any more a particular than a universal.

Again, it follows that something of the essence of Christ would be miserable and damned, since that common nature really existing in Christ would be damned in the damned individual; for surely that essence is also in Judas. But this is absurd.

Many other arguments could be brought forth, but in the interests of brevity, I shall dispense with them. Instead, I shall corroborate my account by an appeal to authorities.

First, in the seventh book of the *Metaphysics,* Aristotle is treating the question of whether a universal is a substance. He shows that no universal is a substance. Thus, he says, "it is impossible that substance be something that can be predicated universally."

Again, in the tenth book of the *Metaphysics,* he says, "Thus, if, as we argued in the discussions on substance and being, no universal can be a substance, it is not possible that a universal be a substance in the sense of a one over and against the many."

From these remarks it is clear that, in Aristotle's view, although universals can supposit for substances, no universal is a substance.

Again, the Commentator in his forty-fourth comment on the seventh book of the *Metaphysics* says, "In the individual, the only substance is the particular form and matter out of which the individual is composed."

Again, in the forty-fifth comment, he says, "Let us say, therefore, that it is impossible that one of those things we call universals be the substance of anything, although they do express the substances of things."

And, again, in the forty-seventh comment, "It is impossible that they (universals) be parts of substances existing of and by themselves."

Again, in the second comment on the eighth book of the *Metaphysics,* he says, "No universal is either a substance or a genus."

Again, in the sixth comment on the tenth book, he says, "Since universals are not substances, it is clear that the common notion of being is not a substance existing outside the mind."

Using these and many other authorities, the general point emerges: no universal is a substance regardless of the viewpoint from which we consider the matter. Thus, the viewpoint from which we consider the matter is irrelevant to the question of whether something is a substance. Nevertheless, the meaning of a term is relevant to the question of whether the expression "substance" can be predicated of the term. Thus, if the term "dog" in the proposition "The dog is an animal" is used to stand for the barking animal, the proposition is true; but if it is used for the celestial body which goes by that name, the proposition is false. But it is impossible that one and the same thing should be a substance from one viewpoint and not a substance from another.

Therefore, it ought to be granted that no universal is a substance regardless of how it is considered. On the contrary, every universal is an intention of the mind which, on the most probable account, is identical with the act of understanding. Thus, it is said that the act of understanding by which I grasp men is a natural sign of men in the same way that weeping is a natural sign of grief. It is a natural sign such that it can stand for men in mental propositions in the same way that a spoken word can stand for things in spoken propositions.

That the universal is an intention of the soul is clearly expressed by Avicenna in the fifth book of the *Metaphysics,* in which he comments, "I say, therefore, that there are three senses of 'universal.' For we say that something is a universal if (like 'man') it is actually predicated of many things; and we also call an intention a universal if it could be predicated of many." Then follows the remark, "An intention is also called a universal if there is nothing inconceivable in its being predicated of many."

From these remarks it is clear that the universal is an intention of the soul capable of being predicated of many. The claim can be corroborated by argument. For every one agrees that a universal is something predicable of many, but only an intention of the soul or a conventional sign is predicated. No substance is ever predicated of anything. Therefore, only an intention of the soul or a conventional sign is a universal; but I am not here using the term "universal" for conventional signs, but only for signs that are universals by nature. That substance is not capable of functioning as predicate is clear;

for if it were, it would follow that a proposition would be composed of particular substances; and, consequently, the subject would be in Rome and the predicate in England which is absurd.

Furthermore, propositions occur only in the mind, in speech, or in writing; therefore, their parts can exist only in the mind, in speech, and in writing. Particular substances, however, cannot themselves exist in the mind, in speech, or in writing. Thus, no proposition can be composed of particular substances. Propositions are, however, composed of universals; therefore, universals cannot conceivably be substances.

CHAPTER 16: AGAINST SCOTUS' ACCOUNT OF THE UNIVERSAL

It may be clear to many that a universal is not a substance outside the mind which exists in, but is distinct from, particulars. Nevertheless, some want to claim that the universal is, in some way, outside the soul and in particulars; and while they do not want to say that a universal is really distinct from particulars, they say that it is formally distinct from particulars. Thus, they say that in Socrates there is human nature which is contracted to Socrates by an individual difference which is not really, but only formally, distinct from that nature. Thus, while there are not two things, one is not formally the other.

I do not find this view tenable:

First, in creatures there can never be any distinction outside the mind unless there are distinct things; if, therefore, there is any distinction between the nature and the difference, it is necessary that they really be distinct things. I prove my premise by the following syllogism: the nature is not formally distinct from itself; this individual difference is formally distinct from this nature; therefore, this individual difference is not this nature.

Again, the same entity is not both common and proper, but in their view the individual difference is proper and the universal is common; therefore, no universal is identical with an individual difference.

Again, opposites cannot be attributed to one and the same created thing, but *common* and *proper* are opposites; therefore, the same thing is not both common and proper. Nevertheless, that conclusion would follow if an individual difference and a common nature were the same thing.

Again, if a common nature were the same thing as an individual difference, there would be as many common natures as there are individual differences; and, consequently, none of those natures would be common, but each would be peculiar to the difference with which it is identical.

Again, whenever one thing is distinct from another it is distinguished from that thing either of and by itself or by something intrinsic to itself. Now, the humanity of Socrates is something different from the humanity of Plato; therefore, they are distinguished of and by themselves and not by differences that are added to them.

Again, according to Aristotle things differing in species also differ in number, but the nature of a man and the nature of a donkey differ in species of and by themselves; therefore, they are numerically distinguished of and by themselves; therefore, each of them is numerically one of and by itself.

Again, that which cannot belong to many cannot be predicated of many; but such a nature, if it really is the same thing as the individual difference, cannot belong to many since it cannot belong to any other particular. Thus, it cannot be predicable of many; but, then, it cannot be a universal.

Again, take an individual difference and the nature which it contracts. Either the difference between these two things is greater or less than the difference between two particulars. It is not greater because they do not differ really; particulars, however, do differ really. But neither is it less because then they would admit of one and the same definition, since two particulars, can admit of the same definition. Consequently, if one of them is, by itself, one in number, the other will also be.

Again, either the nature is the individual difference or it is not. If it is the difference I argue as follows: this individual difference is proper and not common; this individual difference is this nature; therefore this nature is proper and not common, but that is what I set out to prove. Likewise, I argue as follows: the individual difference is not formally distinct from the individual difference; the individual difference is the nature; therefore, the nature is not formally distinct from the individual difference. But if it be said that the individual difference is not the nature, my point has been proved; for it follows that if the individual difference is not the nature, the individual difference is not really the nature; for from the opposite of the consequent follows the opposite of the antecedent. Thus, if it is true that the individual difference really is the nature, then the individual difference is the nature. The inference is valid, for from a determinable taken with its determination (where the determination does not detract from or diminish the determinable) one can infer the determinable taken by itself; but "really" does not express a determination that detracts or diminishes. Therefore, it follows that if the individual difference is really the nature, the individual difference is the nature.

Therefore, one should grant that in created things there is no such thing as a formal distinction. All things which are distinct in creatures are really distinct and, therefore, different things. In regard to creatures modes of argument like the following ought never be denied: this is *A;* this is *B;* therefore, *B* is *A;* and this is not *A;* this is *B;* therefore, *B* is not *A.* Likewise, one ought never deny that, as regards creatures, there are distinct things where contradictory notions hold. The only exception would be the case where contradictory notions hold true because of some syncategorematic element or similar determination, but in the same present case this is not so.

Therefore, we ought to say with the philosophers that in a particular substance there is nothing substantial except the particular form, the particular matter, or the composite of the two. And, therefore, no one ought to think that in Socrates there is a humanity or a human nature which is distinct from Socrates and to which there is added an individual difference which contracts that nature. The only thing in Socrates which can be construed as substantial is this particular matter, this particular form, or the composite of the two. And, therefore, every essence and quiddity and whatever belongs to substance, if it is really outside the soul, is just matter, form, or the composite of these or, following the doctrine of the Peripatetics, a separated and immaterial substance.

NICHOLAS CUSANAS
1401–1464

Nicholas Cusanas (or "Nicholas of Cusa") was born in Cusa (or Kues) on the Moselle River in Germany. As a boy, he studied with the Brothers of the Common Life in Deventer, Holland, a group that put special emphasis on piety and humility. He then went on to study philosophy at Heidelberg (1416), canon (or church) law at Padua (1417–1423), and theology at Cologne (1425). He received a doctorate in canon law at Padua and was ordained a priest in 1426. Soon after his ordination, Nicholas became involved in a number of legal matters related to church reform. He first supported the "conciliar" movement, which advocated the primacy of church councils over the pope. But disillusionment with the Council of Basel's inability to reform the church led him to side with the pope. He was sent by the Holy See on various missions, including the (temporarily) successful negotiations on reunification with the Eastern Church in Byzantium. For his efforts, he was made a cardinal in 1448 and given the bishopric of Brixen in 1450, positions he held until his death in 1464.

Nicholas accepted the Neoplatonic belief that there is a faculty of intuition or intelligence that is above reason. The Aristotelian understanding of reason began with the law of noncontradiction: Contradictories cannot be true of the same thing at the same time. But Nicholas claimed that this law is not so; there is a "coincidence of opposites" in all particular entities, but especially in God. Using language that would later be echoed by the German philosopher Hegel (1770–1831), Nicholas claimed that reason cannot grasp the divine Absolute. We need to recognize the "ignorance" of reason and "see incomprehensively" by means of the higher faculty of intuition.

Nicholas developed this idea in his most famous work, *On Learned Ignorance.* In the opening chapters of this work, given here in the Jasper Hopkins translation, Nicholas asserts that God is both Absolute Maximum and Absolute Minimum and draws out the implications of this position. He goes on to say that although God is beyond our reason, we can have an ignorance about God that is "learned" and "sacred." Our selection ends with the last chapter from Book I, in which Nicholas emphasizes the *via negativa,* the way of negation, which gives us incomprehensible truth about God by telling us what God is not.

*   *   *

Henry Bett, *Nicholas of Cusa* (London: Methuen, 1932), provides the classic study of Nicholas, whereas Jasper Hopkins, *A Concise Introduction to the Philosophy of Nicholas of Cusa,* 2nd edition (Minneapolis: University of Minnesota Press, 1980), and Pauline Moffitt Watts, *Nicolaus Cusanus, A Fifteenth-Century Vision of Man* (Leiden, The Netherlands: E.J. Brill, 1982), give more recent interpretations. For specialized studies, see Paul E. Sigmund, *Nicholas of Cusa and Medieval Political Thought* (Cambridge, MA: Harvard University Press, 1963); James E. Biechler, *The Religious Language of Nicholas of Cusa* (Missoula, MT: Scholars Press, 1975); and Ronald Levao, *Renaissance Minds and Their Fictions: Cusanus, Sidney, Shakespeare* (Berkeley: University of California Press, 1985). For a recent collection of essays, see Gerald Christianson and Thomas M. Izbicki, eds., *Nicholas of Cusa, in Search of God and Wisdom* (Leiden, The Netherlands: E.J. Brill, 1991).

ON LEARNED IGNORANCE (in part)

CHAPTER 1: HOW IT IS THAT KNOWING IS NOT-KNOWING.

We see that by the gift of God there is present in all things a natural desire to exist in the best manner in which the condition of each thing's nature permits this. And [we see that all things] act toward this end and have instruments adapted thereto. They have an innate sense of judgment which serves the purpose of knowing. [They have this] in order that their desire not be in vain but be able to attain rest in that [respective] object which is desired by the propensity of each thing's own nature. But if perchance affairs turn out otherwise, this [outcome] must happen by accident—as when sickness misleads taste or an opinion misleads reason. Wherefore, we say that a sound, free intellect knows to be true that which is apprehended by its affectionate embrace. (The intellect insatiably desires to attain unto the true through scrutinizing all things by means of its innate faculty of inference.) Now, that from which no sound mind can withhold assent is, we have no

Reprinted, by permission, from Jasper Hopkins, *Nicholas of Cusa on Learned Ignorance: A Translation and an Appraisal of De Docta Ignorantia,* Chapters 1–4, 26 (Minneapolis, MN: Banning Press, 2nd edition, 2nd printing, 1990).

La Primavera (*"The Allegory of Spring"*), ca. 1482. Botticelli (1445–1510) shows the eternal spring of Venus' garden of Hesperides. Like Nicholas Cusanas, Botticelli was heavily influenced by Neoplatonism and his paintings are usually interpreted in Neoplatonic terms. (For example, there are nine figures in this work just as there are nine Enneads of Plotinus.) (*Alinari/Art Resource*)

doubt, most true. However, all those who make an investigation judge the uncertain proportionally, by means of a comparison with what is taken to be certain. Therefore, every inquiry is comparative and uses the means of comparative relation. Now, when, the things investigated are able to be compared by means of a close proportional tracing back to what is taken to be [certain], our judgment apprehends easily; but when we need many intermediate steps, difficulty arises and hard work is required. These points are recognized in mathematics, where the earlier propositions are quite easily traced back to the first and most evident principles but where later propositions [are traced back] with more difficulty because [they are traced back] only through the mediation of the earlier ones.

Therefore, every inquiry proceeds by means of a comparative relation, whether an easy or a difficult one. Hence, the infinite, qua infinite, is unknown; for it escapes all comparative relation. But since comparative relation indicates an agreement in some one respect and, at the same time, indicates an otherness, it cannot be understood independently of number. Accordingly, number encompasses all things related comparatively. Therefore, number, which is a necessary condition of comparative relation, is present not only in quantity but also in all things which in any manner whatsoever can agree or differ either substantially or accidentally. Perhaps for this reason Pythagoras deemed all things to be constituted and understood through the power of numbers.

Both the precise combinations in corporeal things and the congruent relating of known to unknown surpass human reason—to such an extent that Socrates seemed to himself to know nothing except that he did not know. And the very wise Solomon maintained that all things are difficult and unexplainable in words. And a certain other man of divine spirit says that wisdom and the seat of understanding are hidden from the eyes of all the living. Even the very profound Aristotle, in his First Philosophy, asserts that in things most obvious by nature such difficulty occurs for us as for a night owl which is trying to look at the sun. Therefore, if the foregoing points are true, then since the desire in us is not in vain, assuredly we desire to know that we do not know. If we can fully attain unto this [knowledge of our ignorance], we will attain unto learned ignorance. For a man even one very well versed in learning—will attain unto nothing more perfect than to be found to be most learned in the ignorance which is distinctively his. The more he knows that he is unknowing, the more learned he will be. Unto this end I have undertaken the task of writing a few things about learned ignorance.

CHAPTER 2: PRELIMINARY CLARIFICATION OF WHAT WILL FOLLOW.

Since I am going to discuss the maximum learning of ignorance, I must deal with the nature of Maximality. Now, I give the name "Maximum" to that than which there cannot be anything greater. But fulness befits what is one. Thus, oneness—which is also being—coincides with Maximality. But if such oneness is altogether free from all relation and contraction, obviously nothing is opposed to it, since it is Absolute Maximality. Thus, the Maximum is the Absolute One which is all things. And all things are in the Maximum (for it is the Maximum); and since nothing is opposed to it, the Minimum likewise coincides with it, and hence the Maximum is also in all things. And because it is absolute, it is, actually, every possible being; it contracts nothing from things, all of which [derive] from it. In the first book I shall strive to investigate—incomprehensibly above human reason—this Maximum, which the faith of all nations indubitably believes to be God. [I shall investigate] with the guidance of Him "who alone dwells in inaccessible light."

Secondly, just as Absolute Maximality is Absolute Being, through which all things are that which they are, so from Absolute Being there exists a universal oneness of being which is spoken of as "a maximum deriving from the Absolute [Maximum]"—existing from it contractedly and as a universe. This maximum's oneness is contracted in plurality, and it cannot exist without plurality. Indeed, in its universal oneness this maximum encompasses all things, so that all the things which derive from the Absolute [Maximum] are in this maximum and this maximum is in all [these] things. Nevertheless, it does not exist independently of the plurality in which it is present, for it does not exist without contraction, from which it cannot be freed. In the second book I will add a few points about this maximum, viz., the universe.

Thirdly, a maximum of a third sort will thereafter be exhibited. For since the universe exists-in-plurality only contractedly, we shall seek among the many things the one maximum in which the universe actually exists most greatly and most perfectly as in its goal. Now, such [a maximum] is united with the Absolute [Maximum], which is the universal end; [it is united] because it is a most perfect goal, which surpasses our every capability. Hence, I shall add some points about this maximum, which is both contracted and absolute and which we name *Jesus,* blessed forever. [I shall add these points] according as Jesus Himself will provide inspiration.

However, someone who desires to grasp the meaning must elevate his intellect above the import of the words rather than insisting upon the proper significations of words which cannot be properly adapted to such great intellectual mysteries. Moreover, it is necessary to use guiding illustrations in a transcendent way and to leave behind perceptible things, so that the reader may readily ascend unto simple intellectuality. I have endeavored, for the purpose of investigating this pathway, to explain [matters] to those of ordinary intelligence as clearly as I could. Avoiding all roughness of style, I show at the outset that learned ignorance has its basis in the fact that the precise truth is inapprehensible.

CHAPTER 3: THE PRECISE TRUTH IS INCOMPREHENSIBLE.

It is self-evident that there is no comparative relation of the infinite to the finite. Therefore, it is most clear that where we find comparative degrees of greatness, we do not arrive at the unqualifiedly Maximum; for things which are comparatively greater and lesser are finite; but, necessarily, such a Maximum is infinite. Therefore, if anything is posited which is not the unqualifiedly Maximum, it is evident that something greater can be posited. And since we find degrees of equality (so that one thing is more equal to a second thing than to a third, in accordance with generic, specific, spatial, causal, and temporal agreement and difference among similar things), obviously we cannot find two or more things which are so similar and equal that they could not be progressively more similar *ad infinitum*. Hence, the measure and the measured—however equal they are—will always remain different.

Therefore, it is not the case that by means of likenesses a finite intellect can precisely attain the truth about things. For truth is not something more or something less but is something indivisible. Whatever is not truth cannot measure truth precisely. (By comparison, a noncircle [cannot measure] a circle, whose being is something indivisible.) Hence, the intellect, which is not truth, never comprehends truth so precisely that truth cannot be comprehended infinitely more precisely. For the intellect is to truth as [an inscribed] polygon is to [the inscribing] circle. The more angles the inscribed polygon has the more similar it is to the circle. However, even if the number of its angles is increased ad infinitum, the polygon never becomes equal [to the circle] unless it is resolved into an identity with the circle. Hence, regarding truth, it is evident that we do not know anything other than the following: viz., that we know truth not to be precisely comprehensible as it is. For truth may be likened unto the most absolute necessity (which cannot be either something more or something less than it is), and our intellect may be likened unto possibility. Therefore, the quiddity of things, which is the truth of beings, is unattainable in its purity; though it is sought by all philosophers, it is found by no one as it is. And the more deeply we are instructed in this ignorance, the closer we approach to truth.

CHAPTER 4: THE ABSOLUTE MAXIMUM, WITH WHICH THE MINIMUM COINCIDES, IS UNDERSTOOD INCOMPREHENSIBLY.

Since the unqualifiedly and absolutely Maximum (than which there cannot be a greater) is greater than we can comprehend (because it is Infinite Truth), we attain unto it in no other way than incomprehensibly. For since it is not of the nature of those things which can be comparatively greater and lesser, it is beyond all that we can conceive. For whatsoever things are apprehended by the senses, by reason, or by intellect differ both within themselves and in relation to one another—[differ] in such way that there is no precise equality among them. Therefore, Maximum Equality, which is neither other than nor different from anything, surpasses all understanding. Hence, since the absolutely Maximum is all that which can be, it is altogether actual. And just as there cannot be a greater, so for the same reason there cannot be a lesser, since it is all that which can be. But the Minimum is that than which there cannot be a lesser. And since the Maximum is also such, it is evident that the Minimum coincides with the Maximum. The foregoing [point] will become clearer to you if you contract maximum and minimum to quantity. For maximum quantity is maximally large; and minimum quantity is maximally small. Therefore, if you free *maximum* and *minimum* from *quantity*—by mentally removing *large* and *small*—you will see clearly that maximum and minimum coincide. For *maximum* is a superlative just as *minimum* is a superlative. Therefore, it is not the case that absolute quantity is maximum quantity rather than minimum quantity; for in it the minimum is the maximum coincidingly.

Therefore, opposing features belong only to those things which can be comparatively greater and lesser; they befit these things in different ways; [but they do] not at all [befit] the absolutely Maximum, since it is beyond all opposition. Therefore, because the absolutely Maximum is absolutely and actually all things which can be (and is so free of all opposition that the Minimum coincides with it), it is beyond both all affirmation and all negation. And it is not, as well as is, all that which is conceived to be; and it is, as well as is not, all that which is conceived not to be. But it is a given thing in such way that it is all things; and it is all things in such way that it is no thing; and it is maximally a given thing in such way that it is it minimally. For example, to say "God, who is Absolute Maximality, is light" is [to say] no other than "God is maximally light in such way that He is minimally light." For Absolute Maximality could not be actually all possible things unless it were infinite and were the boundary of all things and were unable to be bounded by any of these things—as, by the graciousness of God, I will explain in subsequent sections. However, the [absolutely Maximum] transcends all our understanding. For our intellect cannot, by means of reasoning, combine contradictories in their Beginning, since we proceed by means of what nature makes evident to us. Our reason falls far short of this infinite power and is unable to connect contradictories, which are infinitely distant. Therefore, we see incomprehensibly, beyond all rational inference, that Absolute Maximality (to which nothing is opposed and with which the Minimum coincides) is infinite. But "maximum" and "minimum," as used in this [first] book, are transcendent terms of absolute signification, so that in their absolute simplicity they encompass—beyond all contraction to quantity of mass or quantity of power—all things.

*   *   *

CHAPTER 26: NEGATIVE THEOLOGY.

The worshipping of God, who is to be worshipped in spirit and in truth, must be based upon affirmations about Him. Accordingly, every religion, in its worshipping, must mount upward by means of affirmative theology. [Through affirmative theology] it worships God as one and three, as most wise and most gracious, as Inaccessible Light, as Life, Truth, and so on. And it always directs its worship by faith, which it attains more truly through learned ignorance. It believes that He whom it worships as one is All-in-one, and that He whom it worships as Inaccessible Light is not light as is corporeal light, to which darkness is opposed, but is infinite and most simple Light, in which darkness is Infinite Light; and [it believes] that Infinite Light always shines within the darkness of our ignorance but [that] the darkness cannot comprehend it. And so, the theology of negation is so necessary for the theology of affirmation that without it God would not be worshipped as the Infinite God but, rather, as a creature. And such worship is idolatry; it ascribes to the image that which befits only the reality itself. Hence, it will be useful to set down a few more things about negative theology.

Sacred ignorance has taught us that God is ineffable. He is so because He is infinitely greater than all nameable things. And by virtue of the fact that [this] is most true, we speak of God more truly through removal and negation—as [teaches] the greatest Dionysius, who did not believe that God is either Truth or Understanding or Light or anything which can be spoken of. (Rabbi Solomon and all the wise follow Dionysius.) Hence, in accordance with this negative theology, according to which [God] is only infinite, He is neither Father nor Son nor Holy Spirit. Now, the Infinite qua Infinite is neither Begetting, Begotten, nor Proceeding. Therefore, when Hilary of Poitiers distinguished the persons, he most astutely used the expressions "Infinity in the Eternal," "Beauty in the Image," and "Value in the Gift." He means that although in eternity we can see only infinity, nevertheless since the infinity which is eternity is negative infinity, it cannot be understood as Begetter but [can] rightly [be understood as] eternity, since "eternity" is affirmative of oneness, or maximum presence. Hence, [Infinity-in-the-Eternal is] the Beginning without beginning. "Beauty in the Image" indicates the Beginning from the Beginning. "Value in the Gift" indicates the Procession from these two.

All these things are very well known through the preceding [discussion]. For although eternity is infinity, so that eternity is not a greater cause of the Father than is infinity: nevertheless, in a manner of considering, eternity is attributed to the Father and not to the Son or to the Holy Spirit; but infinity is not [attributed] to one person more than to another. For according to the consideration of oneness infinity is the Father; according to the consideration of equality of oneness it is the Son; according to the consideration of the union [of the two it is] the Holy Spirit. And according to the simple consideration of itself infinity is neither the Father nor the Son nor the Holy Spirit. Yet, infinity (as also eternity) is each of the three persons, and, conversely, each person is infinity (and eternity)—not, however, according to [the simple] consideration [of itself], as I said. For according to the consideration of infinity God is neither one nor many. Now, according to the theology of negation, there is not found in God anything other than infinity. Therefore, according to this theology [God] is not knowable either in this world or in the world to come (for in this respect every created thing is darkness, which cannot comprehend Infinite Light), but is known only to Himself.

From these [observations] it is clear (1) that in theological matters negations are true and affirmations are inadequate, and (2) that, nonetheless, the negations which remove the more imperfect things from the most Perfect are truer than the others. For example, it is truer that God is not stone than that He is not life or intelligence; and [it is truer that He] is not drunkenness than that He is not virtue. The contrary [holds] for affirmations; for the affirmation which states that God is intelligence and life is truer than [the affirmation that He is] earth or stone or body. All these [points] are very clear from the foregoing. Therefrom we conclude that the precise truth shines incomprehensibly within the darkness of our ignorance. This is the learned ignorance we have been seeking and through which alone, as I explained, [we] can approach the maximum, triune God of infinite goodness—[approach Him] according to the degree of our instruction in ignorance, so that with all our might we may ever praise Him, who is forever blessed above all things, for manifesting to us His incomprehensible self.

MODERN PHILOSOPHY

To a large extent, modern philosophy begins with a rejection of tradition. Whereas medieval philosophers such as Thomas Aquinas had taken great pains to incorporate and reconcile ancient writings, early modern philosophers such as René Descartes encouraged their readers to make a clean sweep of the past. Previous thinkers had been deluded by errors in thinking or had relied too heavily on authority. In the modern age, the wisdom of the past was to be discarded as error-prone. As Descartes observed in his *Meditations,*

> Some years ago I was struck by the large number of falsehoods that I had accepted as true in my childhood, and by the highly doubtful nature of the whole edifice that I had subsequently based on them. I realized that it was necessary, once in the course of my life, to demolish everything completely and start again right from the foundations if I wanted to establish anything at all in the sciences that was stable and likely to last.

This quest to establish a stable intellectual foundation on which to build something "likely to last" characterized seventeenth- and eighteenth-century European philosophy. "British Empiricists," such as Thomas Hobbes, John Locke, and David Hume found such a foundation in sensory experience and developed their thought on that basis. On the other hand, the "Continent Rationalists," philosophers such as Descartes, Baruch Spinoza, and Gottfried Leibniz, thought the senses inadequate for such a task. They considered reason superior to experience and sought to establish their philosophies on the basis of more certain principles. The greatest of the modern philosophers, Immanuel Kant, sought to combine these two approaches and in so doing developed a uniquely influential system of philosophy.

Contemporary thinkers in the West are still trying to come to grips with these modern philosophers. For better or for worse, their ideas have influenced virtually all areas of Euro-American civilization. The subtlety and clarity with which these thinkers wrote continues to demand careful study even in this "post-modern" age.

*   *   *

There are a number of fine introductions to modern philosophy. Among the classics in this area are Étienne Gilson, *Modern Philosophy: Descartes to Kant* (New York: Random House, 1963); the appropriate works from Frederick Copleston, *A History of Philosophy, Volume IV: Descartes to Leibniz, Volume V: Hobbes to Hume,* and *Volume VI: Wolff to Kant* (1960; reprinted New York: Image Double-day, 1959–1960); and W.T. Jones's books, *Hobbes to Hume,* 2nd edition and *Kant and the Nineteenth Century,* 2nd edition, revised (both New York: Harcourt, Brace & World, 1969 and 1975). More recent general surveys include Roger Scruton, *A Short History of Modern Philosophy: From Descartes to Wittgenstein* (London: Routledge, 1984), and Wallace I. Matson, *A New History of Philosophy, Volume II: Modern* (San Diego, CA: Harcourt Brace Jovanovich, 1987). The following is a sampling of the many specialized books on specific topics from this era: Louis E. Loeb, *From Descartes to Hume: Continental Metaphysics and the Development of Modern Philosophy* (Ithaca, NY: Cornell University Press, 1981); Robert C. Solomon, *Continental Philosophy Since 1750: The Rise and Fall of the Self* (Oxford: Oxford University Press, 1988); and Iain Hampshire-Monk, *A History of Modern Political Thought* (Oxford: Blackwell, 1992).

René Descartes
1596–1650

René Descartes was born into the family of a minor noble in the town of La Haye in Touraine, France. At ten, René began a nine-year course of studies at the Royal Jesuit College of La Flèche. There he studied the humanities, theology, and philosophy (which included morals, logic, mathematics, metaphysics, and science). Though he did well in school, he was disillusioned by the uncertainty of his studies and their contradictory conclusions. Like modern students, he felt overwhelmed by the many opinions he encountered. He later wrote in his *Discourse on Method* that upon completion of his course of study, "I found myself embarrassed with so many doubts and errors that it seemed to me that the effort to instruct myself had no effect other than the increasing discovery of my own ignorance."

However, there was one discipline in which he found the certainty he was seeking: mathematics. The truths of mathematics were assured regardless of one's metaphysical or epistemological assumptions: $2 + 2 = 4$ whether one is a Platonist or an Aristotelian; $3 \times 3 = 9$ whether one is a Roman Catholic or a Protestant. Given mathematical certainty, Descartes found it odd that on such a firm basis "no loftier edifice had been reared."

Left a modest inheritance by his father, Descartes spent the rest of his life seeking the certainty not found in college. After receiving a law degree at Poitiers in 1616, he served as a gentleman volunteer in the army of Maurice of Nassau. While soldiering, he began to develop the idea of connecting mathematical certainty with philosophy. In 1619, he had a series of dreams convincing him that the "spirit of truth" was leading him and that he had divine approval for his studies. For the next ten years, while traveling and serving in the army, he developed his ideas. In 1628, he had a debate with Chandoux, a scientist who claimed that science could only be founded on probability. Descartes argued eloquently that knowledge must be based on certainty and that he had a system that provided that basis. Encouraged by others to develop his system, he retired to Holland, where he found a greater degree of intellectual freedom and spent the next twenty years writing and publishing his ideas. His major philosophical works include *Rules for the Direction of the Mind* (written 1628, but not published until 1701), *Discourse on Method* (published in 1637 as a preface to the essays *Geometry, Dioptric,* and *Meteors),* and *Meditations on First Philosophy* (1641). Descartes also published seven sets of *Objections to the Meditations* of such thinkers as Hobbes, Arnauld, and Gassendi, accompanied by his *Reply to Objections.* In addition to his work in philosophy, Descartes made major contributions to the fields of optics, anatomy, physiology, and mathematics (especially analytic geometry in which "Cartesian coordinates" are still used).

Descartes chose to write his works in French as well as Latin in order to reach beyond the academics to a wider audience. His writings did, indeed, reach learned people throughout Europe and that fact, unfortunately, led indirectly to his death. In 1649, Queen Christina of Sweden invited Descartes to join a circle of leading thinkers to instruct her in philosophy. Although he initially resisted the invitation, he finally felt compelled to accept. Upon arriving in Sweden, Descartes discovered that Queen Christina had time to see him only at five each morning. Descartes had been used to lying in bed until late in the morning, reflecting and philosophizing. Within a year, the rigorous new schedule, together with Sweden's harsh weather, led to his death.

*   *   *

Descartes began his philosophy by sweeping away all the "errors of the past" using mathematics, specifically geometry. He began by establishing twenty-one *Rules for the Direction of the Mind.* He would begin by finding knowledge that he could "clearly and evidently intuit, or deduce with certainty." Then he would build from this knowledge deductively, one step at a time. This procedure would parallel the geometrical method of moving with deductive certainty from postulates to axioms. His *Meditations on First Philosophy,* reprinted here (complete) in the latest John Cottingham translation, chronicles this process.

The key was to find the knowledge that he could "clearly and evidently intuit" that could serve as his starting point. Although uncertainty and doubt were the enemies, Descartes hit upon the idea of using doubt as a tool or a weapon. Instead of fighting doubt, he would use it to find certainty. He would use doubt as an acid to pour over every "truth" to see if there was anything that would not be dissolved, any "truth" that could not be doubted. Some of his doubts may seem extreme (such as that the earth may not exist or that I may be dreaming all this), but in order to find one-hundred percent certainty he had to find a starting point with zero percent doubt.

After subjecting all his knowledge to the acid of doubt, he concluded that there was one thing he could not doubt: that he was doubting. The one fact the acid of doubt could not dissolve was doubt itself. This meant there had to be an "I" who was doing the doubting. Even if he were deceived about everything else, he had to exist in order to be deceived. This led Descartes to his famous statement, *Cogito ergo sum,* meaning "I think, therefore I am" (although these exact words do not appear in the *Meditations).* Here was the "clearly and evidently intuited" knowledge, the starting point, that Descartes had been seeking.

Having established that there is an "I," a self, a starting point, Descartes began to explore the nature of this "I":

> But what then am I? A thing that thinks. What is that? A thing that doubts, understands, affirms, denies, is willing, is unwilling, and also imagines and has sensory perceptions.

Among the ideas of this "thinking thing" called the "I" is the idea of a perfect God. Descartes went on to argue that nothing less than God could have caused the idea of God. He therefore concluded with a second certainty: that God exists.

From here Descartes moved to his third certainty: We have a strong tendency to believe in the existence of a reality beyond our consciousness. If there is no such external world, then we are terribly deceived. But a perfect God would not allow us to be unavoidably deceived, since deceit implies imperfection. Accordingly, we can conclude that we are not misled about those natural beliefs, such as

The Anatomy Lesson, 1632, by Rembrandt (1606–1669). Members of the Surgeons and Physicians Guild personify the Age of Observation with their intense scientific inquiry into human anatomy. Descartes was also interested in anatomy, making such important discoveries as that muscles work in opposition to each other. *(Mauritshuis, The Hague)*

the existence of an external world, so long as they can withstand the scrutiny of reason and are not willfully disregarded.

Descartes had now established a basis for accepting the "obvious" truths he had thrown out earlier by his method of doubt. He had at the same time identified the criterion needed to distinguish the foundational truths upon which his knowledge rested, namely, the criterion that a truth must be "clearly and distinctly perceived." An example of his rationalistic dependence upon such intuitions is his claim that the essential nature of a material object can only be known intuitively, not through sense perceptions.

One final point needs to be noted. The "I" that Descartes found at the end of his methodological doubting was "entirely distinct from the body." This "I" was an immaterial mind, a "spiritual" thing. The body is an "extended, non-thinking thing." As such, it is part of the material world, subject to the same laws of motion as a billiard ball. The "I," or the mind, on the other hand, is not bound by physical laws. This Cartesian distinction leads to a problem about the relationship between body and mind with which we still struggle today.

* * *

For a concise treatment of Descartes' thought in its historical context, see Alexandre Koyré, "Introduction," in E. Anscombe and P.T. Geach, eds., *René Descartes' Philosophical Writings* (Edinburgh: Nelson, 1954). Among the best of several excellent general studies of Descartes are Anthony Kenny, *Descartes: A Study of His Philosophy* (New York: Random House, 1968); John Cottingham, *Descartes* (Oxford: Basil Blackwell, 1986); and Stephen Gaukroger, *Descartes: An Intellectual Biography* (Oxford: Oxford University Press, 1995). For discussions of Descartes' *Meditations,* see L.J. Beck, *The Metaphysics of Descartes: A Study of the Meditations* (Oxford: Clarendon Press, 1965); E.M. Curley, *Descartes Against the Skeptics* (Cambridge, MA: Harvard University Press, 1978); and Georges Dicker, *Descartes* (Oxford: Oxford University Press, 1993). R.S. Woolhouse, *Descartes, Spinoza, Leibniz: The Concept of Substance in Seventeeth-Century Metaphysics* (London: Routledge, 1993) provides a comparative study; whereas John Cottingham, *A Descartes Dictionary* (Oxford: Basil Blackwell, 1995) offers a helpful reference work. For collections of essays on Descartes, see Willis Doney, ed., *Descartes: A Collection of Critical Essays* (Garden City, NY: Doubleday, 1967); Michael Hooker, ed., *Descartes: Critical and Interpretive Essays* (Baltimore, MD: Johns Hopkins University Press, 1978); Amelie O. Rorty, ed., *Essays on Descartes' Meditations* (Berkeley: University of California Press, 1986); Georges J.D. Moyal, ed., *René Descartes: Critical Assessments* (London: Routledge, 1991); Vere Chappell, ed., *Essays on Early Modern Philosophers: René Descartes* (Hamden, CT: Garland, 1992); John Cottingham, ed., *The Cambridge Companion to Descartes* (Cambridge: Cambridge University Press, 1992); and Stephen Voss, ed., *Essays on the Philosophy and Science of René Descartes* (Oxford: Oxford University Press, 1993). Gilbert Ryle, *The Concept of Mind* (London: Hutchinson's University Library, 1949) is the classic critique of Descartes' views on body and mind.

MEDITATIONS ON THE FIRST PHILOSOPHY

[Dedicatory Letter to the Sorbonne]

To those most learned and distinguished men, the Dean and Doctors
of the sacred Faculty of Theology at Paris, from René Descartes.

I have a very good reason for offering this book to you, and I am confident that you will have an equally good reason for giving it your protection once you understand the principle behind my undertaking; so much so, that my best way of commending it to you will be to tell you briefly of the goal which I shall be aiming at in the book.

I have always thought that two topics—namely God and the soul—are prime examples of subjects where demonstrative proofs ought to be given with the aid of philosophy rather than theology. For us who are believers, it is enough to accept on faith that the human soul does not die with the body, and that God exists; but in the case of unbelievers, it seems that there is no religion, and practically no moral virtue, that they can be persuaded to adopt until these two truths are proved to them by natural reason. And since in this life the rewards offered to vice are often greater than the rewards of virtue, few people would prefer what is right to what is expedient if they did not fear God or have the expectation of an after-life. It is of course quite true that we must believe in the existence of God because it is a doctrine of Holy Scripture, and conversely, that we must believe Holy Scripture because it comes from God; for since faith is the gift of God, he who gives us grace to believe other things can also give us grace to believe that he exists. But this argument cannot be put to unbelievers because they would judge it to be circular. Moreover, I have noticed both that you and all other theologians assert that the existence of God is capable of proof by natural reason, and also that the inference from Holy Scripture is that the knowledge of God is easier to acquire than the knowledge we have of many created things—so easy, indeed, that those who do not acquire it are at fault. This is clear from a passage in the Book of Wisdom, Chapter 13: "Howbeit they are not to be excused; for if their knowledge was so great that they could value this world, why did they not rather find out the Lord thereof?" And in Romans, Chapter I it is said that they are "without excuse." And in the same place, in the passage "that which is known of God is manifest in them," we seem to be told that everything that may be known of God can be demonstrated by reasoning which has no other source but our own mind. Hence I thought it was quite proper for me to inquire how this may be, and how God may be more easily and more certainly known than the things of this world.

As regards the soul, many people have considered that it is not easy to discover its nature, and some have even had the audacity to assert that, as far as human reasoning goes, there are persuasive grounds for holding that the soul dies along with the body and that the opposite view is based on faith alone. But in its eighth session the Lateran Council held under Leo X condemned those who take this position,* and expressly en-

---

*The Lateran Council of 1513 condemned the Averroist heresy that denied personal immortality.

René Descartes, *Meditations on the First Philosophy with Selections from the Objections and Replies,* translated by John Cottingham (Cambridge: Cambridge University Press, 1986). Reprinted by permission of Cambridge University Press.

joined Christian philosophers to refute their arguments and use all their powers to establish the truth; so I have not hesitated to attempt this task as well.

In addition, I know that the only reason why many irreligious people are unwilling to believe that God exists and that the human mind is distinct from the body is the alleged fact that no one has hitherto been able to demonstrate these points. Now I completely disagree with this: I think that when properly understood almost all the arguments that have been put forward on these issues by the great men have the force of demonstrations, and I am convinced that it is scarcely possible to provide any arguments which have not already been produced by someone else. Nevertheless, I think there can be no more useful service to be rendered in philosophy than to conduct a careful search, once and for all, for the best of these arguments, and to set them out so precisely and clearly as to produce for the future a general agreement that they amount to demonstrative proofs. And finally, I was strongly pressed to undertake this task by several people who knew that I had developed a method for resolving certain difficulties in the sciences—not a new method (for nothing is older than the truth), but one which they had seen me use with some success in other areas; and I therefore thought it my duty to make some attempt to apply it to the matter in hand.

The present treatise contains everything that I have been able to accomplish in this area. Not that I have attempted to collect here all the different arguments that could be put forward to establish the same results, for this does not seem worthwhile except in cases where no single argument is regarded as sufficiently reliable. What I have done is to take merely the principal and most important arguments and develop them in such a way that I would now venture to put them forward as very certain and evident demonstrations. I will add that these proofs are of such a kind that I reckon they leave no room for the possibility that the human mind will ever discover better ones. The vital importance of the cause and the glory of God, to which the entire undertaking is directed, here compel me to speak somewhat more freely about my own achievements than is my custom. But although I regard the proofs as quite certain and evident, I cannot therefore persuade myself that they are suitable to be grasped by everyone. In geometry there are many writings left by Archimedes, Apollonius, Pappus, and others which are accepted by everyone as evident and certain because they contain absolutely nothing that is not very easy to understand when considered on its own, and each step fits in precisely with what has gone before; yet because they are somewhat long, and demand a very attentive reader, it is only comparatively few people who understand them. In the same way, although the proofs I employ here are in my view as certain and evident as the proofs of geometry, if not more so, it will, I fear, be impossible for many people to achieve an adequate perception of them, both because they are rather long and some depend on others, and also, above all, because they require a mind which is completely free from preconceived opinions and which can easily detach itself from involvement with the senses. Moreover, people who have an aptitude for metaphysical studies are certainly not to be found in the world in any greater numbers than those who have an aptitude for geometry. What is more, there is the difference that in geometry everyone has been taught to accept that as a rule no proposition is put forward in a book without there being a conclusive demonstration available; so inexperienced students make the mistake of accepting what is false, in their desire to appear to understand it, more often than they make the mistake of rejecting what is true. In philosophy, by contrast, the belief is that everything can be argued either way; so few people pursue the truth, while the great majority build up their reputation for ingenuity by boldly attacking whatever is most sound.

Hence, whatever the quality of my arguments may be, because they have to do with philosophy I do not expect they will enable me to achieve any very worthwhile results unless you come to my aid by granting me your patronage.* The reputation of your Faculty is so firmly fixed in the minds of all, and the name of the Sorbonne has such authority that, with the exception of the Sacred Councils, no institution carries more weight than yours in matters of faith; while as regards human philosophy, you are thought of as second to none, both for insight and soundness and also for the integrity and wisdom of your pronouncements. Because of this, the results of your careful attention to this book, if you deigned to give it, would be threefold. First, the errors in it would be corrected—for when I remember not only that I am a human being, but above all that I am an ignorant one, I cannot claim it is free of mistakes. Secondly, any passages which are defective, or insufficiently developed or requiring further explanation, would be supplemented, completed and clarified, either by yourselves or by me after you have given me your advice. And lastly, once the arguments in the book proving that God exists and that the mind is distinct from the body have been brought, as I am sure they can be, to such a pitch of clarity that they are fit to be regarded as very exact demonstrations, you may be willing to declare as much, and make a public statement to that effect. If all this were to happen, I do not doubt that all the errors which have ever existed on these subjects would soon be eradicated from the minds of men. In the case of all those who share your intelligence and learning, the truth itself will readily ensure that they subscribe to your opinion. As for the atheists, who are generally posers rather than people of real intelligence or learning, your authority will induce them to lay aside the spirit of contradiction; and, since they know that the arguments are regarded as demonstrations by all who are intellectually gifted, they may even go so far as to defend them, rather than appear not to understand them. And finally, everyone else will confidently go along with so many declarations of assent, and there will be no one left in the world who will dare to call into doubt either the existence of God or the real distinction between the human soul and body. The great advantage that this would bring is something which you, in your singular wisdom, are in a better position to evaluate than anyone; and it would ill become me to spend any more time commending the cause of God and religion to you, who have always been the greatest tower of strength to the Catholic Church.

Preface to Reader

I briefly touched on the topics of God and the human mind in my *Discourse on the method of rightly conducting reason and seeking the truth in the sciences,* which was published in French in 1637. My purpose there was not to provide a full treatment, but merely to offer a sample, and learn from the views of my readers how I should handle these topics at a later date. The issues seemed to me of such great importance that I considered they ought to be dealt with more than once; and the route which I follow in explaining them is so untrodden and so remote from the normal way, that I thought it would not be helpful to give a full account of it in a book written in French and designed to be read by all and sundry, in case weaker intellects might believe that they ought to set out on the same path.

---

*Although the title page of the first edition of the *Meditations* carries the words "with the approval of the learned doctors," Descartes never, in fact, obtained the endorsement from the Sorbonne which he sought.

In the *Discourse* I asked anyone who found anything worth criticizing in what I had written to be kind enough to point it out to me. In the case of my remarks concerning God and the soul, only two objections worth mentioning were put to me, which I shall now briefly answer before embarking on a more precise elucidation of these topics.

The first objection is this. From the fact that the human mind, when directed towards itself, does not perceive itself to be anything other than a thinking thing, it does not follow that its nature or essence consists only in its being a thinking thing, where the word "only" excludes everything else that could be said to belong to the nature of the soul. My answer to this objection is that in that passage it was not my intention to make those exclusions in an order corresponding to the actual truth of the matter (which I was not dealing with at that stage) but merely in an order corresponding to my own perception. So the sense of the passage was that I was aware of nothing at all that I knew belonged to my essence, except that I was a thinking thing, or a thing possessing within itself the faculty of thinking. I shall, however, show below how it follows from the fact that I am aware of nothing else belonging to my essence, that nothing else does in fact belong to it.

The second objection is this. From the fact that I have within me an idea of a thing more perfect than myself, it does not follow that the idea itself is more perfect than me, still less that what is represented by the idea exists. My reply is that there is an ambiguity here in the word "idea." "Idea" can be taken materially, as an operation of the intellect, in which case it cannot be said to be more perfect than me. Alternatively, it can be taken objectively, as the thing represented by that operation; and this thing, even if it is not regarded as existing outside the intellect, can still, in virtue of its essence, be more perfect than myself. As to how, from the mere fact that there is within me an idea of something more perfect than me, it follows that this thing really exists, this is something which will be fully explained below.

Apart from these objections, there are two fairly lengthy essays which I have looked at, but these did not attack my reasoning on these matters so much as my conclusions, and employed arguments lifted from the standard sources of the atheists. But arguments of this sort can carry no weight with those who understand my reasoning. Moreover, the judgement of many people is so silly and weak that, once they have accepted a view, they continue to believe it, however false and irrational it may be, in preference to a true and well-grounded refutation which they hear subsequently. So I do not wish to reply to such arguments here, if only to avoid having to state them. I will only make the general point that all the objections commonly tossed around by atheists to attack the existence of God invariably depend either on attributing human feelings to God or on arrogantly supposing our own minds to be so powerful and wise that we can attempt to grasp and set limits to what God can or should perform. So, provided only that we remember that our minds must be regarded as finite, while God is infinite and beyond our comprehension, such objections will not cause us any difficulty.

But now that I have, after a fashion, taken an initial sample of people's opinions, I am again tackling the same questions concerning God and the human mind; and this time I am also going to deal with the foundations of First Philosophy in its entirety. But I do not expect any popular approval, or indeed any wide audience. On the contrary I would not urge anyone to read this book except those who are able and willing to meditate seriously with me, and to withdraw their minds from the senses and from all preconceived opinions. Such readers, as I well know, are few and far between. Those who do not bother to grasp the proper order of my arguments and the connection between them, but merely try to carp at individual sentences, as is the fashion, will not get much benefit from reading this book. They may well find an opportunity to quibble in many places, but it will not be easy for them to produce objections which are telling or worth replying to.

But I certainly do not promise to satisfy my other readers straightaway on all points, and I am not so presumptuous as to believe that I am capable of foreseeing all the difficulties which anyone may find. So first of all, in the *Meditations,* I will set out the very thoughts which have enabled me, in my view, to arrive at a certain and evident knowledge of the truth, so that I can find out whether the same arguments which have convinced me will enable me to convince others. Next, I will reply to the objections of various men of outstanding intellect and scholarship who had these Meditations sent to them for scrutiny before they went to press. For the objections they raised were so many and so varied that I would venture to hope that it will be hard for anyone else to think of any point—at least of any importance—which these critics have not touched on. I therefore ask my readers not to pass judgement on the *Meditations* until they have been kind enough to read through all these objections and my replies to them.

SYNOPSIS OF FOLLOWING SIX MEDITATIONS

In the First Meditation reasons are provided which give us possible grounds for doubt about all things, especially material things, so long as we have no foundations for the sciences other than those which we have had up till now. Although the usefulness of such extensive doubt is not apparent at first sight, its greatest benefit lies in freeing us from all our preconceived opinions, and providing the easiest route by which the mind may be led away from the senses. The eventual result of this doubt is to make it impossible for us to have any further doubts about what we subsequently discover to be true.

In the Second Meditation, the mind uses its own freedom and supposes the non-existence of all the things about whose existence it can have even the slightest doubt; and in so doing the mind notices that it is impossible that it should not itself exist during this time. This exercise is also of the greatest benefit, since it enables the mind to distinguish without difficulty what belongs to itself, i.e. to an intellectual nature, from what belongs to the body. But since some people may perhaps expect arguments for the immortality of the soul in this section, I think they should be warned here and now that I have tried not to put down anything which I could not precisely demonstrate. Hence the only order which I could follow was that normally employed by geometers, namely to set out all the premises on which a desired proposition depends, before drawing any conclusions about it. Now the first and most important prerequisite for knowledge of the immortality of the soul is for us to form a concept of the soul which is as clear as possible and is also quite distinct from every concept of body; and that is just what has been done in this section. A further requirement is that we should know that everything that we clearly and distinctly understand is true in a way which corresponds exactly to our understanding of it; but it was not possible to prove this before the Fourth Meditation. In addition we need to have a distinct concept of corporeal nature, and this is developed partly in the Second Meditation itself, and partly in the Fifth and Sixth Meditations. The inference to be drawn from these results is that all the things that we clearly and distinctly conceive of as different substances (as we do in the case of mind and body) are in fact substances which are really distinct one from the other; and this conclusion is drawn in the Sixth Meditation. This conclusion is confirmed in the same Meditation by the fact that we cannot understand a body except as being divisible, while by contrast we cannot understand a mind except as being indivisible. For we cannot conceive of half of a mind, while we can always conceive of half of a body, however small; and this leads us to recognize that the natures of mind and body are not only different, but in some way opposite. But I have not pursued this topic any further in this book, first because these arguments are enough to show that the decay of the body does not imply the destruction of the mind, and are hence enough to give mortals the hope of an afterlife, and secondly because the premises which lead to the conclusion that the soul is immortal depend on an account of the whole of physics. This is required for two reasons. First, we need to know that absolutely all substances, or things which must be created by God in order to exist, are by their nature incorruptible and cannot ever cease to exist unless they are reduced to nothingness by God's denying his concurrence* to them. Secondly, we need to recognize that body, taken in the general sense, is a substance, so that it too never perishes. But the human body, in so far as it differs from other bodies, is simply made up of a certain configuration of limbs and other accidents** of this sort; whereas the human mind is not made up of any accidents in this way, but is a pure substance. For even if all the accidents of the mind change, so that it has different objects of the understanding and different desires and sensations, it does not on that account become a different mind; whereas a human body loses its identity merely as a result of a change in the shape of some of its parts. And it follows from this that while the body can very easily perish, the mind*** is immortal by its very nature.

In the Third Meditation I have explained quite fully enough, I think, my principal argument for proving the existence of God. But in order to draw my readers' minds away from the senses as far as possible, I was not willing to use any comparison taken from bodily things. So it may be that many obscurities remain; but I hope they will be completely removed later, in my Replies to the Objections. One such problem, among others, is how the idea of a supremely perfect being, which is in us, possesses so much objective reality that it can come only from a cause which is supremely perfect. In the Replies this is illustrated by the comparison of a very perfect machine, the idea of which is in the mind of some engineer. Just as the objective intricacy belonging to the idea must have some cause, namely the scientific knowledge of the engineer, or of someone else who passed the idea on to him, so the idea of God which is in us must have God himself as its cause.

In the Fourth Meditation it is proved that everything that we clearly and distinctly perceive is true, and I also explain what the nature of falsity consists in. These results need to be known both in order to confirm what has gone before and also to make intelligible what is to come later. (But here it should be noted in passing that I do not deal at all with sin, i.e. the error which is committed in pursuing good and evil, but only with the error that occurs in distinguishing truth from falsehood. And there is no discussion of matters pertaining to faith or the conduct of life, but simply of speculative truths which are known solely by means of the natural light.)

In the Fifth Meditation, besides an account of corporeal nature taken in general, there is a new argument demonstrating the existence of God. Again, several difficulties may arise here, but these are resolved later in the Replies to the Objections. Finally I ex-

*The continuous divine action necessary to maintain things in existence.

**Descartes here uses this scholastic term to refer to those features of a thing which may alter, e.g. the particular size, shape, etc. of a body, or the particular thoughts, desires, etc. of a mind.

***". . . or the soul of man, for I make no distinction between them" (added in French version).

plain the sense in which it is true that the certainty even of geometrical demonstrations depends on the knowledge of God.

Lastly, in the Sixth Meditation, the intellect is distinguished from the imagination; the criteria for this distinction are explained; the mind is proved to be really distinct from the body, but is shown, notwithstanding, to be so closely joined to it that the mind and the body make up a kind of unit; there is a survey of all the errors which commonly come from the senses, and an explanation of how they may be avoided; and, lastly, there is a presentation of all the arguments which enable the existence of material things to be inferred. The great benefit of these arguments is not, in my view, that they prove what they establish—namely that there really is a world, and that human beings have bodies and so on—since no sane person has ever seriously doubted these things. The point is that in considering these arguments we come to realize that they are not as solid or as transparent as the arguments which lead us to knowledge of our own minds and of God, so that the latter are the most certain and evident of all possible objects of knowledge for the human intellect. Indeed, this is the one thing that I set myself to prove in these Meditations. And for that reason I will not now go over the various other issues in the book which are dealt with as they come up.

MEDITATIONS ON FIRST PHILOSOPHY
IN WHICH ARE DEMONSTRATED
THE EXISTENCE OF GOD
AND THE DISTINCTION BETWEEN
THE HUMAN SOUL AND THE BODY

FIRST MEDITATION

What can be called into doubt

Some years ago I was struck by the large number of falsehoods that I had accepted as true in my childhood, and by the highly doubtful nature of the whole edifice that I had subsequently based on them. I realized that it was necessary, once in the course of my life, to demolish everything completely and start again right from the foundations if I wanted to establish anything at all in the sciences that was stable and likely to last. But the task looked an enormous one, and I began to wait until I should reach a mature enough age to ensure that no subsequent time of life would be more suitable for tackling such inquiries. This led me to put the project off for so long that I would now be to blame if by pondering over it any further I wasted the time still left for carrying it out. So today I have expressly rid my mind of all worries and arranged for myself a clear stretch of free time. I am here quite alone, and at last I will devote myself sincerely and without reservation to the general demolition of my opinions.

But to accomplish this, it will not be necessary for me to show that all my opinions are false, which is something I could perhaps never manage. Reason now leads me to think that I should hold back my assent from opinions which are not completely certain and indubitable just as carefully as I do from those which are patently false. So, for the purpose of rejecting all my opinions, it will be enough if I find in each of them at least some reason for doubt. And to do this I will not need to run through them all individually, which would be an endless task. Once the foundations of a building are undermined, anything built on them collapses of its own accord; so I will go straight for the basic principles on which all my former beliefs rested.

Whatever I have up till now accepted as most true I have acquired either from the senses or through the senses. But from time to time I have found that the senses deceive, and it is prudent never to trust completely those who have deceived us even once.

Yet although the senses occasionally deceive us with respect to objects which are very small or in the distance, there are many other beliefs about which doubt is quite impossible, even though they are derived from the senses—for example, that I am here, sitting by the fire, wearing a winter dressing-gown, holding this piece of paper in my hands, and so on again, how could it be denied that these hands or this whole body are mine? Unless perhaps I were to liken myself to madmen, whose brains are so damaged by the persistent vapours of melancholia that they firmly maintain they are kings when they are paupers, or say they are dressed in purple when they are naked, or that their heads are made of earthenware or that they are pumpkins, or made of glass. But such people are insane and I would be thought equally mad if I took anything from them as: model for myself.

A brilliant piece of reasoning! As if I were not a man who sleeps a night, and regularly has all the same experiences while asleep a madmen do when awake—indeed sometimes even more improbable ones. How often, asleep at night, am I convinced of just such familiar events—that I am here in my dressing-gown, sitting by the fire—when in fact I am lying undressed in bed! Yet at the moment my eyes are certainly wide awake when I look at this piece of paper; I shake my head and it is not asleep; as I stretch out and feel my hand I do so deliberately, and I know what I am doing. All this would not happen with such distinctness to someone asleep. Indeed! As if I did not remember other occasions when I have been tricked by exactly similar thoughts while asleep! As I think about this more carefully, I see plainly that there are never any sure signs by means of which being awake can be distinguished from being asleep. The result is that I begin to feel dazed, and this very feeling only reinforces the notion that I may be asleep.

Suppose then that I am dreaming, and that these particulars—that my eyes are open, that I am moving my head and stretching out my hands—are not true. Perhaps, indeed, I do not even have such hands or such a body at all. Nonetheless, it must surely be admitted that the visions which come in sleep are like paintings, which must have been fashioned in the likeness of things that are real, and hence that at least these general kinds of things—eyes, head, hands and the body as a whole—are things which are not imaginary but are real and exist. For even when painters try to create sirens and satyrs with the most extraordinary bodies, they cannot give them natures which are new in all respects; they simply jumble up the limbs of different animals. Or if perhaps they manage to think up something so new that nothing remotely similar has ever been seen before—something which is therefore completely fictitious and unreal—at least the colours used in the composition must be real. By similar reasoning, although these general kinds of things—eyes, head, hands and so on—could be imaginary, it must at least be admitted that certain other even simpler and more universal things are real. These are as it were the real colours from which we form all the images of things, whether true or false, that occur in our thought.

This class appears to include corporeal nature in general, and its extension; the shape of extended things; the quantity, or size and number of these things;

the place in which they may exist, the time through which they may endure, and so on.

So a reasonable conclusion from this might be that physics, astronomy, medicine, and all other disciplines which depend on the study of composite things, are doubtful; while arithmetic, geometry and other subjects of this kind, which deal only with the simplest and most general things, regardless of whether they really exist in nature or not, contain something certain and indubitable. For whether I am awake or asleep, two and three added together are five, and a square has no more than four sides. It seems impossible that such transparent truths should incur any suspicion of being false.

And yet firmly rooted in my mind is the long-standing opinion that there is an omnipotent God who made me the kind of creature that I am. How do I know that he has not brought it about that there is no earth, no sky, no extended thing, no shape, no size, no place, while at the same time ensuring that all these things appear to me to exist just as they do now? What is more, since I sometimes believe that others go astray in cases where they think they have the most perfect knowledge, may I not similarly go wrong every time I add two and three or count the sides of a square, or in some even simpler matter, if that is imaginable? But perhaps God would not have allowed me to be deceived in this way, since he is said to be supremely good. But if it were inconsistent with his goodness to have created me such that I am deceived all the time, it would seem equally foreign to his goodness to allow me to be deceived even occasionally; yet this last assertion cannot be made.

Perhaps there may be some who would prefer to deny the existence of so powerful a God rather than believe that everything else is uncertain. Let us not argue with them, but grant them that everything said about God is a fiction. According to their supposition, then, I have arrived at my present state by fate or chance or a continuous chain of events, or by some other means; yet since deception and error seem to be imperfections, the less powerful they make my original cause, the more likely it is that I am so imperfect as to be deceived all the time. I have no answer to these arguments, but am finally compelled to admit that there is not one of my former beliefs about which a doubt may not properly be raised; and this is not a flippant or ill-considered conclusion, but is based on powerful and well thought-out reasons. So in future I must withhold my assent from these former beliefs just as carefully as I would from obvious falsehoods, if I want to discover any certainty.

But it is not enough merely to have noticed this; I must make an effort to remember it. My habitual opinions keep coming back, and, despite my wishes, they capture my belief, which is as it were bound over to them as a result of long occupation and the law of custom. I shall never get out of the habit of confidently assenting to these opinions, so long as I suppose them to be what in fact they are, namely highly probable opinions—opinions which, despite the fact that they are in a sense doubtful, as has just been shown, it is still much more reasonable to believe than to deny. In view of this, I think it will be a good plan to turn my will in completely the opposite direction and deceive myself, by pretending for a time that these former opinions are utterly false and imaginary. I shall do this until the weight of preconceived opinion is counter-balanced and the distorting influence of habit no longer prevents my judgement from perceiving things correctly. In the meantime, I know that no danger or error will result from my plan, and that I cannot possibly go too far in my distrustful attitude. This is because the task now in hand does not involve action but merely the acquisition of knowledge.

I will suppose therefore that not God, who is supremely good and the source of truth, but rather some malicious demon of the utmost power and cunning has employed all his energies in order to deceive me. I shall think that the sky, the air, the earth, colours, shapes, sounds and all external things are merely the delusions of dreams which he has devised to ensnare my judgement. I shall consider myself as not having hands or eyes, or flesh, or blood or senses, but as falsely believing that I have all these things. I shall stubbornly and firmly persist in this meditation; and, even if it is not in my power to know any truth, I shall at least do what is in my power, that is, resolutely guard against assenting to any falsehoods, so that the deceiver, however powerful and cunning he may be, will be unable to impose on me in the slightest degree. But this is an arduous undertaking, and a kind of laziness brings me back to normal life. I am like a prisoner who is enjoying an imaginary freedom while asleep; as he begins to suspect that he is asleep, he dreads being woken up, and goes along with the pleasant illusion as long as he can. In the same way, I happily slide back into my old opinions and dread being shaken out of them, for fear that my peaceful sleep may be followed by hard labour when I wake, and that I shall have to toil not in the light, but amid the inextricable darkness of the problems I have now raised.

SECOND MEDITATION

The nature of the human mind, and how it is better known than the body

So serious are the doubts into which I have been thrown as a result of yesterday's meditation that I can neither put them out of my mind nor see any way of resolving them. It feels as if I have fallen unexpectedly into a deep whirlpool which tumbles me around so that I can neither stand on the bottom nor swim up to the top. Nevertheless I will make an effort and once more attempt the same path which I started on yesterday. Anything which admits of the slightest doubt I will set aside just as if I had found it to be wholly false; and I will proceed in this way until I recognize something certain, or, if nothing else, until I at least recognize for certain that there is no certainty. Archimedes used to demand just one firm and immovable point in order to shift the entire earth; so I too can hope for great things if I manage to find just one thing, however slight, that is certain and unshakeable.

I will suppose then, that everything I see is spurious. I will believe that my memory tells me lies, and that none of the things that it reports ever happened. I have no senses. Body, shape, extension, movement and place are chimeras. So what remains true? Perhaps just the one fact that nothing is certain.

Yet apart from everything I have just listed, how do I know that there is not something else which does not allow even the slightest occasion for doubt? Is there not a God, or whatever I may call him, who puts into me the thoughts I am now having? But why do I think this, since I myself may perhaps be the author of these thoughts? In that case am not I, at least, something? But I have just said that I have no senses and no body. This is the sticking point: what follows from this? Am I not so bound up with a body and with senses that I cannot exist without them? But I have convinced myself that there is absolutely nothing in the world, no sky, no earth, no minds, no bodies. Does it now follow that I too do not exist? No: if I convinced myself of something then I certainly existed. But there is a deceiver of supreme power and cunning who is deliberately and constantly deceiving me. In that case I too undoubtedly exist, if he is deceiving me; and let him deceive me as much as he can, he will never bring it about that I am nothing so long as I think that I am something. So after considering everything very thoroughly, I must finally conclude that this proposition, *I am, I exist,* is necessarily true whenever it is put forward by me or conceived in my mind.

But I do not yet have a sufficient understanding of what this "I" is, that now necessarily exists. So I must be on my guard against carelessly taking something else to be this "I," and so making a mistake in the very item of knowledge that I maintain is the most certain and evident of all. I will therefore go back and meditate on what I originally believed myself to be, before I embarked on this present train of thought. I will then subtract anything capable of being weakened, even minimally, by the arguments now introduced, so that what is left at the end may be exactly and only what is certain and unshakeable.

What then did I formerly think I was? A man. But what is a man? Shall I say "a rational animal"? No; for then I should have to inquire what an animal is, what rationality is, and in this way one question would lead me down the slope to other harder ones, and I do not now have the time to waste on subtleties of this kind. Instead I propose to concentrate on what came into my thoughts spontaneously and quite naturally whenever I used to consider what I was. Well, the first thought to come to mind was that I had a face, hands, arms and the whole mechanical structure of limbs which can be seen in a corpse, and which I called the body. The next thought was that I was nourished, that I moved about, and that I engaged in sense-perception and thinking; and these actions I attributed to the soul. But as to the nature of this soul, either I did not think about this or else I imagined it to be something tenuous, like a wind or fire or ether, which permeated my more solid parts. As to the body, however, I had no doubts about it, but thought I knew its nature distinctly. If I had tried to describe the mental conception I had of it, I would have expressed it as follows: by a body I understand whatever has a determinable shape and a definable location and can occupy a space in such a way as to exclude any other body; it can be perceived by touch, sight, hearing, taste or smell, and can be moved in various ways, not by itself but by whatever else comes into contact with it. For, according to my judgement, the power of self-movement, like the power of sensation or of thought, was quite foreign to the nature of a body; indeed, it was a source of wonder to me that certain bodies were found to contain faculties of this kind.

But what shall I now say that I am, when I am supposing that there is some supremely powerful and, if it is permissible to say so, malicious deceiver, who is deliberately trying to trick me in every way he can? Can I now assert that I possess even the most insignificant of all the attributes which I have just said belong to the nature of a body? I scrutinize them, think about them, go over them again, but nothing suggests itself; it is tiresome and pointless to go through the list once more. But what about the attributes I assigned to the soul? Nutrition or movement? Since now I do not have a body, these are mere fabrications. Sense-perception? This surely does not occur without a body, and besides, when asleep I have appeared to perceive through the senses many things which I afterwards realized I did not perceive through the senses at all. Thinking? At last I have discovered it—thought; this alone is inseparable from me. I am, I exist—that is certain. But for how long? For as long as I am thinking. For it could be that were I totally to cease from thinking, I should totally cease to exist. At present I am not admitting anything except what is necessarily true. I am, then, in the strict sense only a thing that thinks; that is, I am a mind, or intelligence, or intellect, or reason—words whose meaning I have been ignorant of until now. But for all that I am a thing which is real and which truly exists. But what kind of a thing? As I have just said—a thinking thing.

What else am I? I will use my imagination. I am not that structure of limbs which is called a human body. I am not even some thin vapour which permeates the limbs—a wind, fire, air, breath, or whatever I depict in my imagination; for these are things which I have supposed to be nothing. Let this supposition stand; for all that I am still something. And yet may it not perhaps be the case that these very things which I am supposing to be nothing, because they are unknown to me, are in reality identical with the "I" of which I am aware? I do not know, and for the moment I shall not argue the point, since I can make judgements only about things which are known to me. I know that I exist; the question is, what is this "I" that I know? If the "I" is understood strictly as we have been taking it, then it is quite certain that knowledge of it does not depend on things of whose existence I am as yet unaware; so it cannot depend on any of the things which I invent in my imagination. And this very word "invent" shows me my mistake. It would indeed be a case of fictitious invention if I used my imagination to establish that I was something or other; for imagining is simply contemplating the shape or image of a corporeal thing. Yet now I know for certain both that I exist and at the same time that all such images and, in general, everything relating to the nature of body, could be mere dreams [and chimeras]. Once this point has been grasped, to say "I will use my imagination to get to know more distinctly what I am" would seem to be as silly as saying "I am now awake, and see some truth; but since my vision is not yet clear enough, I will deliberately fall asleep so that my dreams may provide a truer and clearer representation." I thus realize that none of the things that the imagination enables me to grasp is at all relevant to this knowledge of myself which I possess, and that the mind must therefore be most carefully diverted from such things if it is to perceive its own nature as distinctly as possible.

But what then am I? A thing that thinks. What is that? A thing that doubts, understands, affirms, denies, is willing, is unwilling, and also imagines and has sensory perceptions.

This is a considerable list, if everything on it belongs to me. But does it? Is it not one and the same "I" who is now doubting almost everything, who nonetheless understands some things, who affirms that this one thing is true, denies everything else, desires to know more, is unwilling to be deceived, imagines many things even involuntarily, and is aware of many things which apparently come from the senses? Are not all these things just as true as the fact that I exist, even if I am asleep all the time, and even if he who created me is doing all he can to deceive me? Which of all these activities is distinct from my thinking? Which of them can be said to be separate from myself? The fact that it is I who am doubting and understanding and willing is so evident that I see no way of making it any clearer. But it is also the case that the "I" who imagines is the same "I." For even if, as I have supposed, none of the objects of imagination are real, the power of imagination is something which really exists and is part of my thinking. Lastly, it is also the same "I" who has sensory perceptions, or is aware of bodily things as it were through the senses. For example, I am now seeing light, hearing a noise, feeling heat. But I am asleep, so all this is false. Yet I certainly *seem* to see, to hear, and to be warmed. This cannot be false; what is called "having a sensory perception" is strictly just this, and in this restricted sense of the term it is simply thinking.

From all this I am beginning to have a rather better understanding of what I am. But it still appears—and I cannot stop thinking this—that the corporeal things of which images are formed in my thought, and which the senses investigate, are known with much more distinctness than this puzzling "I" which cannot be pictured in the imagination. And yet it is surely surprising that I should have a more distinct grasp of things which I realize are doubtful, unknown and foreign to me, than I have of that which is true and known—my own self. But I see what it is: my mind enjoys wandering off and will not yet submit to being restrained within the bounds of truth. Very well then; just this once let us give it a completely free rein, so that after a while, when it is time to tighten the reins, it may more readily submit to being curbed.

Let us consider the things which people commonly think they understand most distinctly of all; that is, the bodies which we touch and see. I do not mean bodies in general—for general perceptions are apt to be somewhat more confused—but one particular body. Let us take, for example, this piece of wax. It has just been taken from the honeycomb; it has not yet quite lost the taste of the honey; it retains some of the scent of the flowers from which it was gathered; its colour, shape and size are plain to see; it is hard, cold and can be handled without difficulty; if you rap it with your knuckle it makes a sound. In short, it has everything which appears necessary to enable a body to be known as distinctly as possible. But even as I speak, I put the wax by the fire, and look: the residual taste is eliminated, the smell goes away, the colour changes, the shape is lost, the size increases; it becomes liquid and hot; you can hardly touch it, and if you strike it, it no longer makes a sound. But does the same wax remain? It must be admitted that it does; no one denies it, no one thinks otherwise. So what was it in the wax that I understood with such distinctness? Evidently none of the features which I arrived at by means of the senses; for whatever came under taste, smell, sight, touch or hearing has now altered—yet the wax remains.

Perhaps the answer lies in the thought which now comes to my mind; namely, the wax was not after all the sweetness of the honey, or the fragrance of the flowers, or the whiteness, or the shape, or the sound, but was rather a body which presented itself to me in these various forms a little while ago, but which now exhibits different ones. But what exactly is it that I am now imagining? Let us concentrate, take away everything which does not belong to the wax, and see what is left: merely something extended, flexible and changeable. But what is meant here by "flexible" and "changeable"? Is it what I picture in my imagination: that this piece of wax is capable of changing from a round shape to a square shape, or from a square shape to a triangular shape? Not at all; for I can grasp that the wax is capable of countless changes of this kind, yet I am unable to run through this immeasurable number of changes in my imagination, from which it follows that it is not the faculty of imagination that gives me my grasp of the wax as flexible and changeable. And what is meant by "extended"? Is the extension of the wax also unknown? For it increases if the wax melts, increases again if it boils, and is greater still if the heat is increased. I would not be making a correct judgement about the nature of wax unless I believed it capable of being extended in many more different ways than I will ever encompass in my imagination. I must therefore admit that the nature of this piece of wax is in no way revealed by my imagination, but is perceived by the mind alone. (I am speaking of this particular piece of wax; the point is even clearer with regard to wax in general.) But what is this wax which is perceived by the mind alone? It is of course the same wax which I see, which I touch, which I picture in my imagination, in short the same wax which I thought it to be from the start. And yet, and here is the point, the perception I have of it is a case not of vision or touch or imagination—nor has it ever been, despite previous appearances—but of purely mental scrutiny; and this can be imperfect and confused, as it was before, or clear and distinct as it is now, depending on how carefully I concentrate on what the wax consists in.

But as I reach this conclusion I am amazed at how [weak and] prone to error my mind is. For although I am thinking about these matters within myself, silently and without speaking, nonetheless the actual words bring me up short, and I am almost tricked by ordinary ways of talking. We say that we see the wax itself, if it is there before us, not that we judge it to be there from its colour or shape; and this might lead me to conclude without more ado that knowledge of the wax comes from what the eye sees, and not from the scrutiny of the mind alone. But then if I look out of the window and see men crossing the square, as I just happen to have done, I normally say that I see the men

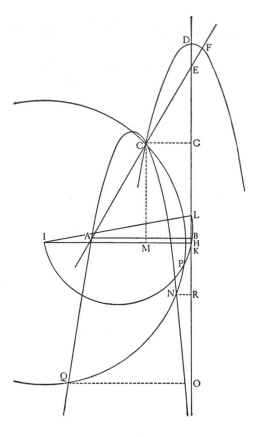

Geometry formula from Descartes' *Geometry* (1637). The X–Y axes in analytic geometry, which Descartes invented, are still called "Cartesian coordinates." (*Library of Congress*)

themselves, just as I say that I see the wax. Yet do I see any more than hats and coats which could conceal automatons? I *judge* that they are men. And so something which I thought I was seeing with my eyes is in fact grasped solely by the faculty of judgement which is in my mind.

However, one who wants to achieve knowledge above the ordinary level should feel ashamed at having taken ordinary ways of talking as a basis for doubt. So let us proceed, and consider on which occasion my perception of the nature of the wax was more perfect and evident. Was it when I first looked at it, and believed I knew it by my external senses, or at least by what they call the "common" sense—that is, the power of imagination? Or is my knowledge more perfect now, after a more careful investigation of the nature of the wax and of the means by which it is known? Any doubt on this issue would clearly be foolish; for what distinctness was there in my earlier perception? Was there anything in it which an animal could not possess? But when I distinguish the wax from its outward forms—take the clothes off, as it were, and consider it naked—then although my judgement may still contain errors, at least my perception now requires a human mind.

But what am I to say about this mind, or about myself? (So far, remember, I am not admitting that there is anything else in me except a mind.) What, I ask, is this "I" which seems to perceive the wax so distinctly? Surely my awareness of my own self is not merely much truer and more certain than my awareness of the wax, but also much more distinct and evident. For if I judge that the wax exists from the fact that I see it, clearly this same fact entails much more evidently that I myself also exist. It is possible that what I see is not really the wax; it is possible that I do not even have eyes with which to see anything. But when I see, or think I see (I am not here distinguishing the two), it is simply not possible that I who am now thinking am not something. By the same token, if I judge that the wax exists from the fact that I touch it, the same result follows, namely that I exist. If I judge that it exists from the fact that I imagine it, or for any other reason, exactly the same thing follows. And the result that I have grasped in the case of the wax may be applied to everything else located outside me. Moreover, if my perception of the wax seemed more distinct after it was established not just by sight or touch but by many other considerations, it must be admitted that I now know myself even more distinctly. This is because every consideration whatsoever which contributes to my perception of the wax, or of any other body, cannot but establish even more effectively the nature of my own mind. But besides this, there is so much else in the mind itself which can serve to make my knowledge of it more distinct, that it scarcely seems worth going through the contributions made by considering bodily things.

I see that without any effort I have now finally got back to where I wanted. I now know that even bodies are not strictly perceived by the senses or the faculty of imagination but by the intellect alone, and that this perception derives not from their being touched or seen but from their being understood; and in view of this I know plainly that I can achieve an easier and more evident perception of my own mind than of anything else. But since the habit of holding on to old opinions cannot be set aside so quickly, I should like to stop here and meditate for some time on this new knowledge I have gained, so as to fix it more deeply in my memory.

THIRD MEDITATION

The existence of God

I will now shut my eyes, stop my ears, and withdraw all my senses. I will eliminate from my thoughts all images of bodily things, or rather, since this is hardly possible, I will regard all such images as vacuous, false and worthless. I will converse with myself and scrutinize myself more deeply; and in this way I will attempt to achieve, little by little, a more intimate knowledge of myself. I am a thing that thinks: that is, a thing that doubts, affirms, denies, understands a few things, is ignorant of many things, is willing, is unwilling, and also which imagines and has sensory perceptions; for as I have noted before, even though the objects of my sensory experience and imagination may have no existence outside me, nonetheless the modes of thinking which I refer to as cases of sensory perception and imagination, in so far as they are simply modes of thinking, do exist within me—of that I am certain.

In this brief list I have gone through everything I truly know, or at least everything I have so far discovered that I know. Now I will cast around more carefully to see whether there may be other things within me which I have not yet noticed. I am certain that I am a thinking thing. Do I not therefore also know what is required for my being certain about anything? In this first item of knowledge there is simply a clear and distinct perception of what I am asserting; this would not be enough to make me certain of the truth of the matter if it could ever turn out that something which I perceived with such clarity and distinctness was false. So I now seem to be able to lay it down as a general rule that whatever I perceive very clearly and distinctly is true.

Yet I previously accepted as wholly certain and evident many things which I after-wards realized were doubtful. What were these? The earth, sky, stars, and everything else that I apprehended with the senses. But what was it about them that I perceived clearly? Just that the ideas, or thoughts, of such things appeared before my mind. Yet even now I am not denying that these ideas occur within me. But there was something else which I used to assert, and which through habitual belief I thought I perceived clearly, although I did not in fact do so. This was that there were things outside me which were the sources of my ideas and which resembled them in all respects. Here was my mistake; or at any rate, if my judgement was true, it was not thanks to the strength of my perception.

But what about when I was considering something very simple and straightfor-ward in arithmetic or geometry, for example that two and three added together make five, and so on? Did I not see at least these things clearly enough to affirm their truth? Indeed, the only reason for my later judgement that they were open to doubt was that it occurred to me that perhaps some God could have given me a nature such that I was de-ceived even in matters which seemed most evident. And whenever my preconceived be-lief in the supreme power of God comes to mind, I cannot but admit that it would be easy for him, if he so desired, to bring it about that I go wrong even in those matters which I think I see utterly clearly with my mind's eye. Yet when I turn to the things themselves which I think I perceive very clearly, I am so convinced by them that I spon-taneously declare: let whoever can do so deceive me, he will never bring it about that I am nothing, so long as I continue to think I am something; or make it true at some fu-ture time that I have never existed, since it is now true that I exist; or bring it about that two and three added together are more or less than five, or anything of this kind in which I see a manifest contradiction. And since I have no cause to think that there is a deceiving God, and I do not yet even know for sure whether there is a God at all, any reason for doubt which depends simply on this supposition is a very slight and, so to speak, metaphysical one. But in order to remove even this slight reason for doubt, as soon as the opportunity arises I must examine whether there is a God, and, if there is, whether he can be a deceiver. For if I do not know this, it seems that I can never be quite certain about anything else.

First, however, considerations of order appear to dictate that I now classify my thoughts into definite kinds, and ask which of them can properly be said to be the bear-ers of truth and falsity. Some of my thoughts are as it were the images of things, and it is only in these cases that the term "idea" is strictly appropriate—for example, when I think of a man, or a chimera, or the sky, or an angel, or God. Other thoughts have vari-ous additional forms: thus when I will, or am afraid, or affirm, or deny, there is always a particular thing which I take as the object of my thought, but my thought includes something more than the likeness of that thing. Some thoughts in this category are called volitions or emotions, while others are called judgements.

Now as far as ideas are concerned, provided they are considered solely in them-selves and I do not refer them to anything else, they cannot strictly speaking be false; for whether it is a goat or a chimera that I am imagining, it is just as true that I imagine the former as the latter. As for the will and the emotions, here too one need not worry about falsity; for even if the things which I may desire are wicked or even non-existent, that does not make it any less true that I desire them. Thus the only remaining thoughts where I must be on my guard against making a mistake are judgements. And the chief and most common mistake which is to be found here consists in my judging that the ideas which are in me resemble, or conform to, things located outside me. Of course, if I considered just the ideas themselves simply as modes of my thought, without referring them to anything else, they could scarcely give me any material for error.

Among my ideas, some appear to be innate, some to be adventitious,* and others to have been invented by me. My understanding of what a thing is, what truth is, and what thought is, seems to derive simply from my own nature. But my hearing a noise, as I do now, or seeing the sun, or feeling the fire, comes from things which are located outside me, or so I have hitherto judged. Lastly, sirens, hippogriffs and the like are my own invention. But perhaps all my ideas may be thought of as adventitious, or they may all be innate, or all made up; for as yet I have not clearly perceived their true origin.

But the chief question at this point concerns the ideas which I take to be derived from things existing outside me: what is my reason for thinking that they resemble these things? Nature has apparently taught me to think this. But in addition I know by experience that these ideas do not depend on my will, and hence that they do not depend simply on me. Frequently I notice them even when I do not want to: now, for example, I feel the heat whether I want to or not, and this is why I think that this sensation or idea of heat comes to me from something other than myself, namely the heat of the fire by which I am sitting. And the most obvious judgement for me to make is that the thing in question transmits to me its own likeness rather than something else.

I will now see if these arguments are strong enough. When I say "Nature taught me to think this," all I mean is that a spontaneous impulse leads me to believe it, not that its truth has been revealed to me by some natural light. There is a big difference here. Whatever is revealed to me by the natural light—for example that from the fact that I am doubting it follows that I exist, and so on—cannot in any way be open to doubt. This is because there cannot be another faculty both as trustworthy as the natural light and also capable of showing me that such things are not true. But as for my natural impulses, I have often judged in the past that they were pushing me in the wrong direction when it was a question of choosing the good, and I do not see why I should place any greater confidence in them in other matters.

Then again, although these ideas do not depend on my will, it does not follow that they must come from things located outside me. Just as the impulses which I was speaking of a moment ago seem opposed to my will even though they are within me, so there may be some other faculty not yet fully known to me, which produces these ideas without any assistance from external things; this is, after all, just how I have always thought ideas are produced in me when I am dreaming.

And finally, even if these ideas did come from things other than myself, it would not follow that they must resemble those things. Indeed, I think I have often discovered a great disparity [between an object and its idea] in many cases. For example, there are two different ideas of the sun which I find within me. One of them, which is acquired as it were from the senses and which is a prime example of an idea which I reckon to come from an external source, makes the sun appear very small. The other idea is based on astronomical reasoning, that is, it is derived from certain notions which are innate in me (or else it is constructed by me in some other way), and this idea shows the sun to be several times larger than the earth. Obviously both these ideas cannot resemble the sun which exists outside me; and reason persuades me that the idea which seems to have emanated most directly from the sun itself has in fact no resemblance to it at all.

All these considerations are enough to establish that it is not reliable judgement but merely some blind impulse that has made me believe up till now that there exist things distinct from myself which transmit to me ideas or images of themselves through the sense organs or in some other way.

---

*". . . foreign to me and coming from outside" (French version).

But it now occurs to me that there is another way of investigating whether some of the things of which I possess ideas exist outside me. In so far as the ideas are [considered] simply [as] modes of thought, there is no recognizable inequality among them: they all appear to come from within me in the same fashion. But in so far as different ideas [are considered as images which] represent different things, it is clear that they differ widely. Undoubtedly, the ideas which represent substances to me amount to something more and, so to speak, contain within themselves more objective reality than the ideas which merely represent modes or accidents. Again, the idea that gives me my understanding of a supreme God, eternal, infinite, [immutable,] omniscient, omnipotent and the creator of all things that exist apart from him, certainly has in it more objective reality than the ideas that represent finite substances.

Now it is manifest by the natural light that there must be at least as much [reality] in the efficient and total cause as in the effect of that cause. For where, I ask, could the effect get its reality from, if not from the cause? And how could the cause give it to the effect unless it possessed it? It follows from this both that something cannot arise from nothing, and also that what is more perfect—that is, contains in itself more reality—cannot arise from what is less perfect. And this is transparently true not only in the case of effects which possess [what the philosophers call] actual or formal reality, but also in the case of ideas, where one is considering only [what they call] objective reality. A stone, for example, which previously did not exist, cannot begin to exist unless it is produced by something which contains, either formally or eminently everything to be found in the stone; similarly, heat cannot be produced in an object which was not previously hot, except by something of at least the same order [degree or kind] of perfection as heat, and so on. But it is also true that the idea of heat, or of a stone, cannot exist in me unless it is put there by some cause which contains at least as much reality as I conceive to be in the heat or in the stone. For although this cause does not transfer any of its actual or formal reality to my idea, it should not on that account be supposed that it must be less real. The nature of an idea is such that of itself it requires no formal reality except what it derives from my thought, of which it is a mode. But in order for a given idea to contain such and such objective reality, it must surely derive it from some cause which contains at least as much formal reality as there is objective reality in the idea. For if we suppose that an idea contains something which was not in its cause, it must have got this from nothing; yet the mode of being by which a thing exists objectively [or representatively] in the intellect by way of an idea, imperfect though it may be, is certainly not nothing, and so it cannot come from nothing.

And although the reality which I am considering in my ideas is merely objective reality, I must not on that account suppose that the same reality need not exist formally in the causes of my ideas, but that it is enough for it to be present in them objectively. For just as the objective mode of being belongs to ideas by their very nature, so the formal mode of being belongs to the causes of ideas—or at least the first and most important ones—by *their* very nature. And although one idea may perhaps originate from another, there cannot be an infinite regress here; eventually one must reach a primary idea, the cause of which will be like an archetype which contains formally [and in fact] all the reality [or perfection] which is present only objectively [or representatively] in the idea. So it is clear to me, by the natural light, that the ideas in me are like [pictures, or] images which can easily fall short of the perfection of the things from which they are taken, but which cannot contain anything greater or more perfect.

The longer and more carefully I examine all these points, the more clearly and distinctly I recognize their truth. But what is my conclusion to be? If the objective reality of any of my ideas turns out to be so great that I am sure the same reality does not reside in me, either formally or eminently, and hence that I myself cannot be its cause, it will necessarily follow that I am not alone in the world, but that some other thing which is the cause of this idea also exists. But if no such idea is to be found in me, I shall have 110 arguments to convince me of the existence of anything apart from myself. For despite a most careful and comprehensive survey, this is the only argument I have so far been able to find.

Among my ideas, apart from the idea which gives me a representation of myself, which cannot present any difficulty in this context, there are ideas which variously represent God, corporeal and inanimate things, angels, animals and finally other men like myself.

As far as concerns the ideas which represent other men, or animals, or angels, I have no difficulty in understanding that they could be put together from the ideas I have of myself, of corporeal things and of God, even if the world contained no men besides me, no animals and no angels.

As to my ideas of corporeal things, I can see nothing in them which is so great [or excellent] as to make it seem impossible that it originated in myself. For if I scrutinize them thoroughly and examine them one by one, in the way in which I examined the idea of the wax yesterday, I notice that the things which I perceive clearly and distinctly in them are very few in number. The list comprises size, or extension in length, breadth and depth; shape, which is a function of the boundaries of this extension; position, which is a relation between various items possessing shape; and motion, or change in position; to these may be added substance, duration and number. But as for all the rest, including light and colours, sounds, smells, tastes, heat and cold and the other tactile qualities, I think of these only in a very confused and obscure way, to the extent that I do not even know whether they are true or false, that is, whether the ideas I have of them are ideas of real things or of non-things. For although, as I have noted before, falsity in the strict sense, or formal falsity, can occur only in judgements, there is another kind of falsity, material falsity, which occurs in ideas, when they represent non-things as things. For example, the ideas which I have of heat and cold contain so little clarity and distinctness that they do not enable me to tell whether cold is merely the absence of heat or vice versa, or whether both of them are real qualities, or neither is. And since there can be no ideas which are not as it were of things, if it is true that cold is nothing but the absence of heat, the idea which represents it to me as something real and positive deserves to be called false; and the same goes for other ideas of this kind.

Such ideas obviously do not require me to posit a source distinct from myself. For on the one hand, if they are false, that is, represent non-things, I know by the natural light that they arise from nothing—that is, they are in me only because of a deficiency and lack of perfection in my nature. If on the other hand they are true, then since the reality which they represent is so extremely slight that I cannot even distinguish it from a non-thing, I do not see why they cannot originate from myself.

With regard to the clear and distinct elements in my ideas of corporeal things, it appears that I could have borrowed some of these from my idea of myself, namely substance, duration, number and anything else of this kind. For example, I think that a stone is a substance, or is a thing capable of existing independently, and I also think that I am a substance. Admittedly I conceive of myself as a thing that thinks and is not extended, whereas I conceive of the stone as a thing that is extended and does not think, so that the two conceptions differ enormously; but they seem to agree with respect to the classification "substance." Again, I perceive that I now exist, and remember that I have existed for some time; moreover, I have various thoughts which I can count; it is in these ways that I acquire the ideas of duration and number which I can then transfer to other things. As for all the other elements which make up the ideas of corporeal things, namely extension, shape, position and movement, these are not formally contained in me, since I am nothing but a thinking thing; but since they are merely modes of a substance, and I am a substance, it seems possible that they are contained in me eminently.

So there remains only the idea of God; and I must consider whether there is anything in the idea which could not have originated in myself. By the word "God" I understand a substance that is infinite, [eternal, immutable,] independent, supremely intelligent, supremely powerful, and which created both myself and everything else (if anything else there be) that exists. All these attributes are such that, the more carefully I concentrate on them, the less possible it seems that they could have originated from me alone. So from what has been said it must be concluded that God necessarily exists.

It is true that I have the idea of substance in me in virtue of the fact that I am a substance; but this would not account for my having the idea of an infinite substance, when I am finite, unless this idea proceeded from some substance which really was infinite.

And I must not think that, just as my conceptions of rest and darkness are arrived at by negating movement and light, so my perception of the infinite is arrived at not by means of a true idea but merely by negating the finite. On the contrary, I clearly understand that there is more reality in an infinite substance than in a finite one, and hence that my perception of the infinite, that is God, is in some way prior to my perception of the finite, that is myself. For how could I understand that I doubted or desired—that is, lacked something—and that I was not wholly perfect, unless there were in me some idea of a more perfect being which enabled me to recognize my own defects by comparison?

Nor can it be said that this idea of God is perhaps materially false and so could have come from nothing, which is what I observed just a moment ago in the case of the ideas of heat and cold, and so on. On the contrary, it is utterly clear and distinct, and contains in itself more objective reality than any other idea; hence there is no idea which is in itself truer or less liable to be suspected of falsehood. This idea of a supremely perfect and infinite being is, I say, true in the highest degree; for although perhaps one may imagine that such a being does not exist, it cannot be supposed that the idea of such a being represents something unreal, as I said with regard to the idea of cold. The idea is, moreover, utterly clear and distinct; for whatever I clearly and distinctly perceive as being real and true, and implying any perfection, is wholly contained in it. It does not matter that I do not grasp the infinite, or that there are countless additional attributes of God which I cannot in any way grasp, and perhaps cannot even reach in my thought; for it is in the nature of the infinite not to be grasped by a finite being like myself. It is enough that I understand the infinite,* and that I judge that all the attributes which I clearly perceive and know to imply some perfection—and perhaps countless others of which I am ignorant—are present in God either formally or eminently. This is enough to make the idea that I have of God the truest and most clear and distinct of all my ideas.

But perhaps I am something greater than I myself understand, and all the perfections which I attribute to God are somehow in me potentially, though not yet emerging or actualized. For I am now experiencing a gradual increase in my knowledge, and I see nothing to prevent its increasing more and more to infinity. Further, I see no reason why

---

*According to Descartes one can know or understand something without fully grasping it "just as we can touch a mountain but not put our arms around it. To grasp something is to embrace it in one's thought; to know something, it suffices to touch it with one's thought" (letter to Mersenne, 26 May 1630).

I should not be able to use this increased knowledge to acquire all the other perfections of God. And finally, if the potentiality for these perfections is already within me, why should not this be enough to generate the idea of such perfections?

But all this is impossible. First, though it is true that there is a gradual increase in my knowledge, and that I have many potentialities which are not yet actual, this is all quite irrelevant to the idea of God, which contains absolutely nothing that is potential; indeed, this gradual increase in knowledge is itself the surest sign of imperfection. What is more, even if my knowledge always increases more and more, I recognize that it will never actually be infinite, since it will never reach the point where it is not capable of a further increase; God, on the other hand, I take to be actually infinite, so that nothing can be added to his perfection. And finally, I perceive that the objective being of an idea cannot be produced merely by potential being, which strictly speaking is nothing, but only by actual or formal being.

If one concentrates carefully, all this is quite evident by the natural light. But when I relax my concentration, and my mental vision is blinded by the images of things perceived by the senses, it is not so easy for me to remember why the idea of a being more perfect than myself must necessarily proceed from some being which is in reality more perfect. I should therefore like to go further and inquire whether I myself, who have this idea, could exist if no such being existed.

From whom, in that case, would I derive my existence? From myself presumably, or from my parents, or from some other beings less perfect than God; for nothing more perfect than God, or even as perfect, can be thought of or imagined.

Yet if I derived my existence from myself, then I should neither doubt nor want, nor lack anything at all; for I should have given myself all the perfections of which I have any idea, and thus I should myself be God. I must not suppose that the items I lack would be more difficult to acquire than those I now have. On the contrary, it is clear that, since I am a thinking thing or substance, it would have been far more difficult for me to emerge out of nothing than merely to acquire knowledge of the many things of which I am ignorant—such knowledge being merely an accident of that substance. And if I had derived my existence from myself, which is a greater achievement, I should certainly not have denied myself the knowledge in question, which is something much easier to acquire, or indeed any of the attributes which I perceive to be contained in the idea of God; for none of them seem any harder to achieve. And if any of them were harder to achieve, they would certainly appear so to me, if I had indeed got all my other attributes from myself, since I should experience a limitation of my power in this respect.

I do not escape the force of these arguments by supposing that I have always existed as I do now, as if it followed from this that there was no need to look for any author of my existence. For a life-span can be divided into countless parts, each completely independent of the others, so that it does not follow from the fact that I existed a little while ago that I must exist now, unless there is some cause which as it were creates me afresh at this moment—that is, which preserves me. For it is quite clear to anyone who attentively considers the nature of time that the same power and action are needed to preserve anything at each individual moment of its duration as would be required to create that thing anew if it were not yet in existence. Hence the distinction between preservation and creation is only a conceptual one, and this is one of the things that are evident by the natural light.

I must therefore now ask myself whether I possess some power enabling me to bring it about that I who now exist will still exist a little while from now. For since I am nothing but a thinking thing—or at least since I am now concerned only and precisely with that part of me which is a thinking thing—if there were such a power in me, I should undoubtedly be aware of it. But I experience no such power, and this very fact makes me recognize most clearly that I depend on some being distinct from myself.

But perhaps this being is not God, and perhaps I was produced either by my parents or by other causes less perfect than God. No; for as I have said before, it is quite clear that there must be at least as much in the cause as in the effect. And therefore whatever kind of cause is eventually proposed, since I am a thinking thing and have within me some idea of God, it must be admitted that what caused me is itself a thinking thing and possesses the idea of all the perfections which I attribute to God. In respect of this cause one may again inquire whether it derives its existence from itself or from another cause. If from itself, then it is clear from what has been said that it is itself God, since if it has the power of existing through its own might, then undoubtedly it also has the power of actually possessing all the perfections of which it has an idea—that is, all the perfections which I conceive to be in God. If, on the other hand, it derives its existence from another cause, then the same question may be repeated concerning this further cause, namely whether it derives its existence from itself or from another cause, until eventually the ultimate cause is reached, and this will be God.

It is clear enough that an infinite regress is impossible here, especially since I am dealing not just with the cause that produced me in the past, but also and most importantly with the cause that preserves me at the present moment.

Nor can it be supposed that several partial causes contributed to my creation, or that I received the idea of one of the perfections which I attribute to God from one cause and the idea of another from another—the supposition here being that all the perfections are to be found somewhere in the universe but not joined together in a single being, God. On the contrary, the unity, the simplicity, or the inseparability of all the attributes of God is one of the most important of the perfections which I understand him to have. And surely the idea of the unity of all his perfections could not have been placed in me by any cause which did not also provide me with the ideas of the other perfections; for no cause could have made me understand the interconnection and inseparability of the perfections without at the same time making me recognize what they were.

Lastly, as regards my parents, even if everything I have ever believed about them is true, it is certainly not they who preserve me; and in so far as I am a thinking thing, they did not even make me; they merely placed certain dispositions in the matter which I have always regarded as containing me, or rather my mind, for that is all I now take myself to be. So there can be no difficulty regarding my parents in this context. Altogether then, it must be concluded that the mere fact that I exist and have within me an idea of a most perfect being, that is, God, provides a very clear proof that God indeed exists.

It only remains for me to examine how I received this idea from God. For I did not acquire it from the senses; it has never come to me unexpectedly, as usually happens with the ideas of things that are perceivable by the senses, when these things present themselves to the external sense organs—or seem to do so. And it was not invented by me either; for I am plainly unable either to take away anything from it or to add anything to it. The only remaining alternative is that it is innate in me, just as the idea of myself is innate in me.

And indeed it is no surprise that God, in creating me, should have placed this idea in me to be, as it were, the mark of the craftsman stamped on his work—not that the mark need be anything distinct from the work itself. But the mere fact that God created me is a very strong basis for believing that I am somehow made in his image and likeness, and that I perceive that likeness, which includes the idea of God, by the same faculty which enables me to perceive myself. That is, when I turn my mind's eye upon myself, I understand that I am a thing which is incomplete and dependent on another and which aspires without limit to ever greater and better things; but I also understand at the same time that he on whom I depend has within him all those greater things, not just indefinitely and potentially but actually and infinitely, and hence that he is God. The whole force of the argument lies in this: I recognize that it would be impossible for me to exist with the kind of nature I have—that is, having within me the idea of God—were it not the case that God really existed. By "God" I mean the very being the idea of whom is within me, that is, the possessor of all the perfections which I cannot grasp, but can somehow reach in my thought, who is subject to no defects whatsoever. It is clear enough from this that he cannot be a deceiver, since it is manifest by the natural light that all fraud and deception depend on some defect.

But before examining this point more carefully and investigating other truths which may be derived from it, I should like to pause here and spend some time in the contemplation of God; to reflect on his attributes, and to gaze with wonder and adoration on the beauty of this immense light, so far as the eye of my darkened intellect can bear it. For just as we believe through faith that the supreme happiness of the next life consists solely in the contemplation of the divine majesty, so experience tells us that this same contemplation, albeit much less perfect, enables us to know the greatest joy of which we are capable in this life.

FOURTH MEDITATION

Truth and falsity

During these past few days I have accustomed myself to leading my mind away from the senses; and I have taken careful note of the fact that there is very little about corporeal things that is truly perceived, whereas much more is known about the human mind, and still more about God. The result is that I now have no difficulty in turning my mind away from imaginable things and towards things which are objects of the intellect alone and are totally separate from matter. And indeed the idea I have of the human mind, in so far as it is a thinking thing, which is not extended in length, breadth or height and has no other bodily characteristics, is much more distinct than the idea of any corporeal thing. And when I consider the fact that I have doubts, or that I am a thing that is incomplete and dependent, then there arises in me a clear and distinct idea of a being who is independent and complete, that is, an idea of God. And from the mere fact that there is such an idea within me, or that I who possess this idea exist, I clearly infer that God also exists, and that every single moment of my entire existence depends on him. So clear is this conclusion that I am confident that the human intellect cannot know anything that is more evident or more certain. And now, from this contemplation of the true God, in whom all the treasures of wisdom and the sciences lie hidden, I think I can see a way forward to the knowledge of other things.

To begin with, I recognize that it is impossible that God should ever deceive me. For in every case of trickery or deception some imperfection is to be found; and although the ability to deceive appears to be an indication of cleverness or power, the will to deceive is undoubtedly evidence of malice or weakness, and so cannot apply to God.

Next, I know by experience that there is in me a faculty of judgement which, like everything else which is in me, I certainly received from God. And since God does not wish to deceive me, he surely did not give me the kind of faculty which would ever enable me to go wrong while using it correctly.

There would be no further doubt on this issue were it not that what I have just said appears to imply that I am incapable of ever going wrong. For if everything that is in me comes from God, and he did not endow me with a faculty for making mistakes, it appears that I can never go wrong. And certainly, so long as I think only of God, and turn my whole attention to him, I can find no cause of error or falsity. But when I turn back to myself, I know by experience that I am prone to countless errors. On looking for the cause of these errors, I find that I possess not only a real and positive idea of God, or a being who is supremely perfect, but also what may be described as a negative idea of nothingness, or of that which is farthest removed from all perfection. I realize that I am, as it were, something intermediate between God and nothingness, or between supreme being and non-being: my nature is such that in so far as I was created by the supreme being, there is nothing in me to enable me to go wrong or lead me astray; but in so far as I participate in nothingness or non-being, that is, in so far as I am not myself the supreme being and am lacking in countless respects, it is no wonder that I make mistakes. I understand, then, that error as such is not something real which depends on God, but merely a defect. Hence my going wrong does not require me to have a faculty specially bestowed on me by God; it simply happens as a result of the fact that the faculty of true judgement which I have from God is in my case not infinite.

But this is still not entirely satisfactory. For error is not a pure negation, but rather a privation or lack of some knowledge which somehow should be in me. And when I concentrate on the nature of God, it seems impossible that he should have placed in me a faculty which is not perfect of its kind, or which lacks some perfection which it ought to have. The more skilled the craftsman the more perfect the work produced by him; if this is so, how can anything produced by the supreme creator of all things not be complete and perfect in all respects? There is, moreover, no doubt that God could have given me a nature such that I was never mistaken; again, there is no doubt that he always wills what is best. Is it then better that I should make mistakes than that I should not do so?

As I reflect on these matters more attentively, it occurs to me first of all that it is no cause for surprise if I do not understand the reasons for some of God's actions; and there is no call to doubt his existence if I happen to find that there are other instances where I do not grasp why or how certain things were made by him. For since I now know that my own nature is very weak and limited, whereas the nature of God is immense, incomprehensible and infinite, I also know without more ado that he is capable of countless things whose causes are beyond my knowledge. And for this reason alone I consider the customary search for final causes to be totally useless in physics; there is considerable rashness in thinking myself capable of investigating the [impenetrable] purposes of God.

It also occurs to me that whenever we are inquiring whether the works of God are perfect, we ought to look at the whole universe, not just at one created thing on its own. For what would perhaps rightly appear very imperfect if it existed on its own is quite perfect when its function as a part of the universe is considered. It is true that, since my decision to doubt everything, it is so far only myself and God whose existence I have been able to know with certainty; but after considering the immense power of God, I cannot deny that many other things have been made by him, or at least could have been made, and hence that I may have a place in the universal scheme of things.

Next, when I look more closely at myself and inquire into the nature of my errors (for these are the only evidence of some imperfection in me), I notice that they depend on two concurrent causes, namely on the faculty of knowledge which is in me, and on the faculty of choice or freedom of the will; that is, they depend on both the intellect and the will simultaneously. Now all that the intellect does is to enable me to perceive the ideas which are subjects for possible judgements; and when regarded strictly in this light, it turns out to contain no error in the proper sense of that term. For although countless things may exist without there being any corresponding ideas in me, it should not, strictly speaking, be said that I am deprived of these ideas, but merely that I lack them, in a negative sense. This is because I cannot produce any reason to prove that God ought to have given me a greater faculty of knowledge than he did; and no matter how skilled I understand a craftsman to be, this does not make me think he ought to have put into every one of his works all the perfections which he is able to put into some of them. Besides, I cannot complain that the will or freedom of choice which I received from God is not sufficiently extensive or perfect, since I know by experience that it is not restricted in any way. Indeed, I think it is very noteworthy that there is nothing else in me which is so perfect and so great that the possibility of a further increase in its perfection or greatness is beyond my understanding. If, for example, I consider the faculty of understanding, I immediately recognize that in my case it is extremely slight and very finite, and I at once form the idea of an understanding which is much greater—indeed supremely great and infinite; and from the very fact that I can form an idea of it, I perceive that it belongs to the nature of God. Similarly, if I examine the faculties of memory or imagination, or any others, I discover that in my case each one of these faculties is weak and limited, while in the case of God it is immeasurable. It is only the will, or freedom of choice, which I experience within me to be so great that the idea of any greater faculty is beyond my grasp; so much so that it is above all in virtue of the will that I understand myself to bear in some way the image and likeness of God. For although God's will is incomparably greater than mine, both in virtue of the knowledge and power that accompany it and make it more firm and efficacious, and also in virtue of its object, in that it ranges over a greater number of items, nevertheless it does not seem any greater than mine when considered as will in the essential and strict sense. This is because the will simply consists in our ability to do or not do something (that is, to affirm or deny, to pursue or avoid); or rather, it consists simply in the fact that when the intellect puts something forward for affirmation or denial or for pursuit or avoidance, our inclinations are such that we do not feel we are determined by any external force. In order to be free, there is no need for me to be inclined both ways; on the contrary, the more I incline in one direction—either because I clearly understand that reasons of truth and goodness point that way, or because of a divinely produced disposition of my inmost thoughts—the freer is my choice. Neither divine grace nor natural knowledge ever diminishes freedom; on the contrary, they increase and strengthen it. But the indifference I feel when there is no reason pushing me in one direction rather than another is the lowest grade of freedom; it is evidence not of any perfection of freedom, but rather of a defect in knowledge or a kind of negation. For if I always saw clearly what was true and good, I should never have to deliberate about the right judgement or choice; in that case, although I should be wholly free, it would be impossible for me ever to be in a state of indifference.

From these considerations I perceive that the power of willing which I received from God is not, when considered in itself, the cause of my mistakes; for it is both extremely ample and also perfect of its kind. Nor is my power of understanding to blame; for since my understanding comes from God, everything that I understand I undoubtedly understand correctly, and any error here is impossible. So what then is the source of my mistakes? It must be simply this: the scope of the will is wider than that of the intellect; but instead of restricting it within the same limits, I extend its use to matters which I do not understand. Since the will is indifferent in such cases, it easily turns aside from what is true and good, and this is the source of my error and sin.

For example, during these past few days I have been asking whether anything in the world exists, and I have realized that from the very fact of my raising this question it follows quite evidently that I exist. I could not but judge that something which I understood so clearly was true; but this was not because I was compelled so to judge by any external force, but because a great light in the intellect was followed by a great inclination in the will, and thus the spontaneity and freedom of my belief was all the greater in proportion to my lack of indifference. But now, besides the knowledge that I exist, in so far as I am a thinking thing, an idea of corporeal nature comes into my mind; and I happen to be in doubt as to whether the thinking nature which is in me, or rather which I am, is distinct from this corporeal nature or identical with it. I am making the further supposition that my intellect has not yet come upon any persuasive reason in favour of one alternative rather than the other. This obviously implies that I am indifferent as to whether I should assert or deny either alternative, or indeed refrain from making any judgement on the matter.

What is more, this indifference does not merely apply to cases where the intellect is wholly ignorant, but extends in general to every case where the intellect does not have sufficiently clear knowledge at the time when the will deliberates. For although probable conjectures may pull me in one direction, the mere knowledge that they are simply conjectures, and not certain and indubitable reasons, is itself quite enough to push my assent the other way. My experience in the last few days confirms this: the mere fact that I found that all my previous beliefs were in some sense open to doubt was enough to turn my absolutely confident belief in their truth into the supposition that they were wholly false.

If, however, I simply refrain from making a judgement in cases where I do not perceive the truth with sufficient clarity and distinctness, then it is clear that I am behaving correctly and avoiding error. But if in such cases I either affirm or deny, then I am not using my free will correctly. If I go for the alternative which is false, then obviously I shall be in error; if I take the other side, then it is by pure chance that I arrive at the truth, and I shall still be at fault since it is clear by the natural light that the perception of the intellect should always precede the determination of the will. In this incorrect use of free will may be found the privation which constitutes the essence of error. The privation, I say, lies in the operation of the will in so far as it proceeds from me, but not in the faculty of will which I received from God, nor even in its operation, in so far as it depends on him.

And I have no cause for complaint on the grounds that the power of understanding or the natural light which God gave me is no greater than it is; for it is in the nature of a finite intellect to lack understanding of many things, and it is in the nature of a created intellect to be finite. Indeed, I have reason to give thanks to him who has never owed me anything for the great bounty that he has shown me, rather than thinking myself deprived or robbed of any gifts he did not bestow.

Nor do I have any cause for complaint on the grounds that God gave me a will which extends more widely than my intellect. For since the will consists simply of one thing which is, as it were, indivisible, it seems that its nature rules out the possibility of anything being taken away from it. And surely, the more widely my will extends, then the greater thanks I owe to him who gave it to me.

Finally, I must not complain that the forming of those acts of will or judgements in which I go wrong happens with God's concurrence. For in so far as these acts depend on God, they are wholly true and good; and my ability to perform them means that there is in a sense more perfection in me than would be the case if I lacked this ability. As for the privation involved—which is all that the essential definition of falsity and wrong consists in this does not in any way require the concurrence of God, since it is not a thing; indeed, when it is referred to God as its cause, it should be called not a privation but simply a negation. For it is surely no imperfection in God that he has given me the freedom to assent or not to assent in those cases where he did not endow my intellect with a clear and distinct perception; but it is undoubtedly an imperfection in me to misuse that freedom and make judgements about matters which I do not fully understand. I can see, however, that God could easily have brought it about that without losing my freedom, and despite the limitations in my knowledge, I should nonetheless never make a mistake. He could, for example, have endowed my intellect with a clear and distinct perception of everything about which I was ever likely to deliberate; or he could simply have impressed it unforgettably on my memory that I should never make a judgement about anything which I did not clearly and distinctly understand. Had God made me this way, then I can easily understand that, considered as a totality, I would have been more perfect than I am now. But I cannot therefore deny that there may in some way be more perfection in the universe as a whole because some of its parts are not immune from error, while others are immune, than there would be if all the parts were exactly alike. And I have no right to complain that the role God wished me to undertake in the world is not the principal one or the most perfect of all.

What is more, even if I have no power to avoid error in the first way just mentioned, which requires a clear perception of everything I have to deliberate on, I can avoid error in the second way, which depends merely on my remembering to withhold judgement on any occasion when the truth of the matter is not clear. Admittedly, I am aware of a certain weakness in me, in that I am unable to keep my attention fixed on one and the same item of knowledge at all times; but by attentive and repeated meditation I am nevertheless able to make myself remember it as often as the need arises, and thus get into the habit of avoiding error.

It is here that man's greatest and most important perfection is to be found, and I therefore think that today's meditation, involving an investigation into the cause of error and falsity, has been very profitable. The cause of error must surely be the one I have explained; for if, whenever I have to make a judgement, I restrain my will so that it extends to what the intellect clearly and distinctly reveals, and no further, then it is quite impossible for me to go wrong. This is because every clear and distinct perception is undoubtedly something, and hence cannot come from nothing, but must necessarily have God for its author. Its author, I say, is God, who is supremely perfect, and who cannot be a deceiver on pain of contradiction; hence the perception is undoubtedly true. So today I have learned not only what precautions to take to avoid ever going wrong, but also what to do to arrive at the truth. For I shall unquestionably reach the truth, if only I give sufficient attention to all the things which I perfectly understand, and separate these from all the other cases where my apprehension is more confused and obscure. And this is just what I shall take good care to do from now on.

FIFTH MEDITATION

The essence of material things, and the existence of God considered a second time

There are many matters which remain to be investigated concerning the attributes of God and the nature of myself, or my mind; and perhaps I shall take these up at another time. But now that I have seen what to do and what to avoid in order to reach the truth, the most pressing task seems to be to try to escape from the doubts into which I fell a few days ago, and see whether any certainty can be achieved regarding material objects.

But before I inquire whether any such things exist outside me, I must consider the ideas of these things, in so far as they exist in my thought, and see which of them are distinct, and which confused.

Quantity, for example, or "continuous" quantity as the philosophers commonly call it, is something I distinctly imagine. That is, I distinctly imagine the extension of the quantity (or rather of the thing which is quantified) in length, breadth and depth. I also enumerate various parts of the thing, and to these parts I assign various sizes, shapes, positions and local motions; and to the motions I assign various durations.

Not only are all these things very well known and transparent to me when regarded in this general way, but in addition there are countless particular features regarding shape, number, motion and so on, which I perceive when I give them my attention. And the truth of these matters is so open and so much in harmony with my nature, that on first discovering them it seems that I am not so much learning something new as remembering what I knew before; or it seems like noticing for the first time things which were long present within me although I had never turned my mental gaze on them before.

But I think the most important consideration at this point is that I find within me countless ideas of things which even though they may not exist anywhere outside me still cannot be called nothing; for although in a sense they can be thought of at will, they are not my invention but have their own true and immutable natures. When, for example, I imagine a triangle, even if perhaps no such figure exists, or has ever existed, anywhere outside my thought, there is still a determinate nature, or essence, or form of the triangle which is immutable and eternal, and not invented by me or dependent on my mind. This is clear from the fact that various properties can be demonstrated of the triangle, for example that its three angles equal two right angles, that its greatest side subtends its greatest angle, and the like; and since these properties are ones which I now clearly recognize whether I want to or not, even if I never thought of them at all when I previously imagined the triangle, it follows that they cannot have been invented by me.

It would be beside the point for me to say that since I have from time to time seen bodies of triangular shape, the idea of the triangle may have come to me from external things by means of the sense organs. For I can think up countless other shapes which there can be no suspicion of my ever having encountered through the senses, and yet I can demonstrate various properties of these shapes, just as I can with the triangle. All these properties are certainly true, since I am clearly aware of them, and therefore they are something, and not merely nothing; for it is obvious that whatever is true is something; and I have already amply demonstrated that everything of which I am clearly aware is true. And even if I had not demonstrated this, the nature of my mind is such that I cannot but assent to these things, at least so long as I clearly perceive them. I also remember that even before, when I was completely preoccupied with the objects of the senses, I always held that the most certain truths of all were the kind which I recognized clearly in connection with shapes, or numbers or other items relating to arithmetic or geometry, or in general to pure and abstract mathematics.

But if the mere fact that I can produce from my thought the idea of something entails that everything which I clearly and distinctly perceive to belong to that thing really does belong to it, is not this a possible basis for another argument to prove the existence of God? Certainly, the idea of God, or a supremely perfect being, is one which I find within me just as surely as the idea of any shape or number. And my understanding that it belongs to his nature that he always exists is no less clear and distinct than is the case when I prove of any shape or number that some property belongs to its nature. Hence, even if it turned out that not everything on which I have meditated in these past days is true, I ought still to regard the existence of God as having at least the same level of certainty as I have hitherto attributed to the truths of mathematics.

At first sight, however, this is not transparently clear, but has some appearance of being a sophism. Since I have been accustomed to distinguish between existence and essence in everything else, I find it easy to persuade myself that existence can also be separated from the essence of God, and hence that God can be thought of as not existing. But when I concentrate more carefully, it is quite evident that existence can no more be separated from the essence of God than the fact that its three angles equal two right angles can be separated from the essence of a triangle, or than the idea of a mountain can be separated from the idea of a valley. Hence it is just as much of a contradiction to think of God (that is, a supremely perfect being) lacking existence (that is, lacking a perfection), as it is to think of a mountain without a valley.

However, even granted that I cannot think of God except as existing, just as I cannot think of a mountain without a valley, it certainly does not follow from the fact that I think of a mountain with a valley that there is any mountain in the world; and similarly, it does not seem to follow from the fact that I think of God as existing that he does exist. For my thought does not impose any necessity on things; and just as I may imagine a winged horse even though no horse has wings, so I may be able to attach existence to God even though no God exists.

But there is a sophism concealed here. From the fact that I cannot think of a mountain without a valley, it does not follow that a mountain and valley exist anywhere, but simply that a mountain and a valley, whether they exist or not, are mutually inseparable. But from the fact that I cannot think of God except as existing, it follows that existence is inseparable from God, and hence that he really exists. It is not that my thought makes it so, or imposes any necessity on any thing; on the contrary, it is the necessity of the thing itself, namely the existence of God, which determines my thinking in this respect. For I am not free to think of God without existence (that is, a supremely perfect being without a supreme perfection) as I am free to imagine a horse with or without wings.

And it must not be objected at this point that while it is indeed necessary for me to suppose God exists, once I have made the supposition that he has all perfections (since existence is one of the perfections), nevertheless the original supposition was not necessary. Similarly, the objection would run, it is not necessary for me to think that all quadrilaterals can be inscribed in a circle; but given this supposition, it will be necessary for me to admit that a rhombus can be inscribed in a circle—which is patently false. Now admittedly, it is not necessary that I ever light upon any thought of God; but whenever I do choose to think of the first and supreme being, and bring forth the idea of God from the treasure house of my mind as it were, it is necessary that I attribute all perfections to him, even if I do not at that time enumerate them or attend to them individually. And this necessity plainly guarantees that, when I later realize that existence is a perfection, I am correct in inferring that the first and supreme being exists. In the same way, it is not necessary for me ever to imagine a triangle; but whenever I do wish to consider a rectilinear figure having just three angles, it is necessary that I attribute to it the properties which license the inference that its three angles equal no more than two right angles, even if I do not notice this at the time. By contrast, when I examine what figures can be inscribed in a circle, it is in no way necessary for me to think that this class includes all quadrilaterals. Indeed, I cannot even imagine this, so long as I am willing to admit only what I clearly and distinctly understand. So there is a great difference between this kind of false supposition and the true ideas which are innate in me, of which the first and most important is the idea of God. There are many ways in which I understand that this idea is not something fictitious which is dependent on my thought, but is an image of a true and immutable nature. First of all, there is the fact that, apart from God, there is nothing else of which I am capable of thinking such that existence belongs to its essence. Second, I cannot understand how there could be two or more Gods of this kind; and after supposing that one God exists, I plainly see that it is necessary that he has existed from eternity and will abide for eternity. And finally, I perceive many other attributes of God, none of which I can remove or alter.

But whatever method of proof I use, I am always brought back to the fact that it is only what I clearly and distinctly perceive that completely convinces me. Some of the things I clearly and distinctly perceive are obvious to everyone, while others are discovered only by those who look more closely and investigate more carefully; but once they have been discovered, the latter are judged to be just as certain as the former. In the case of a right-angled triangle, for example, the fact that the square on the hypotenuse is equal to the square on the other two sides is not so readily apparent as the fact that the hypotenuse subtends the largest angle; but once one has seen it, one believes it just as strongly. But as regards God, if I were not overwhelmed by preconceived opinions, and if the images of things perceived by the senses did not besiege my thought on every side, I would certainly acknowledge him sooner and more easily than anything else. For what is more self-evident than the fact that the supreme being exists, or that God, to whose essence alone existence belongs, exists?

Although it needed close attention for me to perceive this, I am now just as certain of it as I am of everything else which appears most certain. And what is more, I see that the certainty of all other things depends on this, so that without it nothing can ever be perfectly known.

Admittedly my nature is such that so long as I perceive something very clearly and distinctly I cannot but believe it to be true. But my nature is also such that I cannot fix my mental vision continually on the same thing, so as to keep perceiving it clearly; and often the memory of a previously made judgement may come back, when I am no longer attending to the arguments which led me to make it. And so other arguments can now occur to me which might easily undermine my opinion, if I did not possess knowledge of God; and I should thus never have true and certain knowledge about anything, but only shifting and changeable opinions. For example, when I consider the nature of a triangle, it appears most evident to me, steeped as I am in the principles of geometry, that its three angles are equal to two right angles; and so long as I attend to the proof, I cannot but believe this to be true. But as soon as I turn my mind's eye away from the proof, then in spite of still remembering that I perceived it very clearly, I can easily fall into doubt about its truth, if I am without knowledge of God. For I can convince myself that I have a natural disposition to go wrong from time to time in matters which I think I perceive as evidently as can be. This will seem even more likely when I remember that there have been frequent cases where I have regarded things as true and certain, but have later been led by other arguments to judge them to be false.

Now, however, I have perceived that God exists, and at the same time I have understood that everything else depends on him, and that he is no deceiver; and I have drawn the conclusion that everything which I clearly and distinctly perceive is of necessity true. Accordingly, even if I am no longer attending to the arguments which led me to judge that this is true, as long as I remember that I clearly and distinctly perceived it, there are no counter-arguments which can be adduced to make me doubt it, but on the contrary I have true and certain knowledge of it. And I have knowledge not just of this matter, but of all matters which I remember ever having demonstrated, in geometry and so on. For what objections can now be raised? That the way I am made makes me prone to frequent error? But I now know that I am incapable of error in those cases where my understanding is transparently clear. Or can it be objected that I have in the past regarded as true and certain many things which I afterwards recognized to be false? But none of these were things which I clearly and distinctly perceived: I was ignorant of this rule for establishing the truth, and believed these things for other reasons which I later discovered to be less reliable. So what is left to say? Can one raise the objection I put to myself a while ago, that I may be dreaming, or that everything which I am now thinking has as little truth as what comes to the mind of one who is asleep? Yet even this does not change anything. For even though I might be dreaming, if there is anything which is evident to my intellect, then it is wholly true.

Thus I see plainly that the certainty and truth of all knowledge depends uniquely on my knowledge of the true God, to such an extent that I was incapable of perfect knowledge about anything else until I knew him. And now it is possible for me to achieve full and certain knowledge of countless matters, both concerning God himself and other things whose nature is intellectual, and also concerning the whole of that corporeal nature which is the subject-matter of pure mathematics.

SIXTH MEDITATION

The existence of material things, and the real distinction between mind and body

It remains for me to examine whether material things exist. And at least I now know they are capable of existing, in so far as they are the subject-matter of pure mathematics, since I perceive them clearly and distinctly. For there is no doubt that God is capable of creating everything that I am capable of perceiving in this manner; and I have never judged that something could not be made by him except on the grounds that there would be a contradiction in my perceiving it distinctly. The conclusion that material things exist is also suggested by the faculty of imagination, which I am aware of using when I turn my mind to material things. For when I give more attentive consideration to what imagination is, it seems to be nothing else but an application of the cognitive faculty to a body which is intimately present to it, and which therefore exists.

To make this clear, I will first examine the difference between imagination and pure understanding. When I imagine a triangle, for example, I do not merely understand that it is a figure bounded by three lines, but at the same time I also see the three lines with my mind's eye as if they were present before me; and this is what I call imagining. But if I want to think of a chiliagon, although I understand that it is a figure consisting of a thousand sides just as well as I understand the triangle to be a three-sided figure, I do not in the same way imagine the thousand sides or see them as if they were present before me. It is true that since I am in the habit of imagining something whenever I think of a corporeal thing, I may construct in my mind a confused representation of some figure; but it is clear that this is not a chiliagon. For it differs in no way from the representation I should form if I were thinking of a myriagon, or any figure with very many sides. Moreover, such a representation is useless for recognizing the properties which distinguish a chiliagon from other polygons. But suppose I am dealing with a pentagon: I can of course understand the figure of a pentagon, just as I can the figure of a chiliagon, without the help of the imagination; but I can also imagine a pentagon, by applying my mind's eye to its five sides and the area contained within them. And in doing this I notice quite clearly that imagination requires a peculiar effort of mind which is not required for understanding; this additional effort of mind clearly shows the difference between imagination and pure understanding.

Besides this, I consider that this power of imagining which is in me, differing as it does from the power of understanding, is not a necessary constituent of my own essence, that is, of the essence of my mind. For if I lacked it, I should undoubtedly remain the same individual as I now am; from which it seems to follow that it depends on something distinct from myself. And I can easily understand that, if there does exist some body to which the mind is so joined that it can apply itself to contemplate it, as it were, whenever it pleases, then it may possibly be this very body that enables me to imagine corporeal things. So the difference between this mode of thinking and pure understanding may simply be this: when the mind understands, it in some way turns towards itself and inspects one of the ideas which are within it; but when it imagines, it turns towards the body and looks at something in the body which conforms to an idea understood by the mind or perceived by the senses. I can, as I say, easily understand that this is how imagination comes about, if the body exists; and since there is no other equally suitable way of explaining imagination that comes to mind, I can make a probable conjecture that the body exists. But this is only a probability; and despite a careful and comprehensive investigation, I do not yet see how the distinct idea of corporeal nature which I find in my imagination can provide any basis for a necessary inference that some body exists.

But besides that corporeal nature which is the subject-matter of pure mathematics, there is much else that I habitually imagine, such as colours, sounds, tastes, pain and so on—though not so distinctly. Now I perceive these things much better by means of the senses, which is how, with the assistance of memory, they appear to have reached the imagination. So in order to deal with them more fully, I must pay equal attention to the senses, and see whether the things which are perceived by means of that mode of thinking which I call "sensory perception" provide me with any sure argument for the existence of corporeal things.

To begin with, I will go back over all the things which I previously took to be perceived by the senses, and reckoned to be true; and I will go over my reasons for thinking this. Next, I will set out my reasons for subsequently calling these things into doubt. And finally I will consider what I should now believe about them.

First of all then, I perceived by my senses that I had a head, hands, feet and other limbs making up the body which I regarded as part of myself, or perhaps even as my whole self. I also perceived by my senses that this body was situated among many other bodies which could affect it in various favourable or unfavourable ways; and I gauged the favourable effects by a sensation of pleasure, and the unfavourable ones by a sensation of pain. In addition to pain and pleasure, I also had sensations within me of hunger, thirst, and other such appetites, and also of physical propensities towards cheerfulness, sadness, anger and similar emotions. And outside me, besides the extension, shapes and movements of bodies, I also had sensations of their hardness and heat, and of the other tactile qualities. In addition, I had sensations of light, colours, smells, tastes and sounds, the variety of which enabled me to distinguish the sky, the earth, the seas, and all other bodies, one from another. Considering the ideas of all these qualities which presented themselves to my thought, although the ideas were, strictly speaking, the only immediate objects of my sensory awareness, it was not unreasonable for me to think that the items which I was perceiving through the senses were things quite distinct from my thought, namely bodies which produced the ideas. For my experience was that these ideas came to me quite without my consent, so that I could not have sensory awareness of any object, even if I wanted to, unless it was present to my sense organs; and I could not avoid having sensory awareness of it when it was present. And since the ideas perceived by the senses were much more lively and vivid and even, in their own way, more distinct than any of those which I deliberately formed through meditating or which I found impressed on my memory, it seemed impossible that they should have come from within me; so the only alternative was that they came from other things. Since the sole source of my knowledge of these things was the ideas themselves, the supposition that the things resembled the ideas was bound to occur to me. In addition, I remembered that the use of my senses had come first, while the use of my reason came only later; and I saw that the ideas which I formed myself were less vivid than those which I perceived with the senses and were, for the most part, made up of elements of sensory ideas. In this way I easily convinced myself that I had nothing at all in the intellect which I had not previously had in sensation. As for the body which by some special right I called "mine," my belief that this body, more than any other, belonged to me had some justification. For I could never be separated from it, as I could from other bodies; and I felt all my appetites and emotions in, and on account of, this body; and finally, I was aware of pain and pleasurable ticklings in parts of this body, but not in other bodies external to it. But why should that curious sensation of pain give rise to a particular distress of mind; or why should a certain kind of delight follow on a tickling sensation? Again, why should that curious tugging in the stomach which I call hunger tell me that I should eat, or a dryness of the throat tell me to drink, and so on? I was not able to give any explanation of all this, except that nature taught me so. For there is absolutely no connection (at least that I can understand) between the tugging sensation and the decision to take food, or between the sensation of something causing pain and the mental apprehension of distress that arises from that sensation. These and other judgements that I made concerning sensory objects, I was apparently taught to make by nature; for I had already made up my mind that this was how things were, before working out any arguments to prove it.

Later on, however, I had many experiences which gradually undermined all the faith I had had in the senses. Sometimes towers which had looked round from a distance appeared square from close up; and enormous statues standing on their pediments did not seem large when observed from the ground. In these and countless other such cases, I found that the judgements of the external senses were mistaken. And this applied not just to the external senses but to the internal senses as well. For what can be more internal than pain? And yet I had heard that those who had had a leg or an arm amputated sometimes still seemed to feel pain intermittently in the missing part of the body. So even in my own case it was apparently not quite certain that a particular limb was hurting, even if I felt pain in it. To these reasons for doubting, I recently added two very general ones. The first was that every sensory experience I have ever thought I was having while awake I can also think of myself as sometimes having while asleep; and since I do not believe that what I seem to perceive in sleep comes from things located outside me, I did not see why I should be any more inclined to believe this of what I think I perceive while awake. The second reason for doubt was that since I did not know the author of my being (or at least was pretending not to), I saw nothing to rule out the possibility that my natural constitution made me prone to error even in matters which seemed to me most true. As for the reasons for my previous confident belief in the truth of the things perceived by the senses, I had no trouble in refuting them. For since I apparently had natural impulses towards many things which reason told me to avoid, I reckoned that a great deal of confidence should not be placed in what I was taught by nature. And despite the fact that the perceptions of the senses were not dependent on my will, I did not think that I should on that account infer that they proceeded from things distinct from myself, since I might perhaps have a faculty not yet known to me which produced them.

But now, when I am beginning to achieve a better knowledge of myself and the author of my being, although I do not think I should heedlessly accept everything I seem to have acquired from the senses, neither do I think that everything should be called into doubt.

First, I know that everything which I clearly and distinctly understand is capable of being created by God so as to correspond exactly with my understanding of it. Hence the fact that I can clearly and distinctly understand one thing apart from another is enough to make me certain that the two things are distinct, since they are capable of being separated, at least by God. The question of what kind of power is required to bring about such a separation does not affect the judgement that the two things are distinct. Thus, simply by knowing that I exist and seeing at the same time that absolutely nothing else belongs to my nature or essence except that I am a thinking thing, I can infer correctly that my essence consists solely in the fact that I am a thinking thing. It is true that I may have (or, to anticipate, that I certainly have) a body that is very closely joined to me. But nevertheless, on the one hand I have a clear and distinct idea of myself, in so far as I am simply a thinking, non-extended thing; and on the other hand I have a distinct idea of body,* in so far as this is simply an extended, non-thinking thing. And accordingly, it is certain that I am really distinct from my body, and can exist without it.

Besides this, I find in myself faculties for certain special modes of thinking, namely imagination and sensory perception. Now I can clearly and distinctly understand myself as a whole without these faculties; but I cannot, conversely, understand these faculties without me, that is, without an intellectual substance to inhere in. This is because there is an intellectual act included in their essential definition; and hence I perceive that the distinction between them and myself corresponds to the distinction between the modes of a thing and the thing itself. Of course I also recognize that there are other faculties (like those of changing position, of taking on various shapes, and so on) which, like sensory perception and imagination, cannot be understood apart from some substance for them to inhere in, and hence cannot exist without it. But it is clear that these other faculties, if they exist, must be in a corporeal or extended substance and not an intellectual one; for the clear and distinct conception of them includes extension, but does not include any intellectual act whatsoever. Now there is in me a passive faculty of sensory perception, that is, a faculty for receiving and recognizing the ideas of sensible objects; but I could not make use of it unless there was also an active faculty, either in me or in something else, which produced or brought about these ideas. But this faculty cannot be in me, since clearly it presupposes no intellectual act on my part, and the ideas in question are produced without my cooperation and often even against my will. So the only alternative is that it is in another substance distinct from me—a substance which contains either formally or eminently all the reality which exists objectively in the ideas produced by this faculty (as I have just noted). This substance is either a body, that is, a corporeal nature, in which case it will contain formally [and in fact] everything which is to be found objectively [or representatively] in the ideas; or else it is God, or

---

*The Latin term *corpus* as used here by Descartes is ambiguous between "body" (i.e. corporeal matter in general) and "the body" (i.e. this particular body of mine). The French version preserves the ambiguity.

some creature more noble than a body, in which case it will contain eminently whatever is to be found in the ideas. But since God is not a deceiver, it is quite clear that he does not transmit the ideas to me either directly from himself, or indirectly, via some creature which contains the objective reality of the ideas not formally but only eminently. For God has given me no faculty at all for recognizing any such source for these ideas; on the contrary, he has given me a great propensity to believe that they are produced by corporeal things. So I do not see how God could be understood to be anything but a deceiver if the ideas were transmitted from a source other than corporeal things. It follows that corporeal things exist. They may not all exist in a way that exactly corresponds with my sensory grasp of them, for in many cases the grasp of the senses is very obscure and confused. But at least they possess all the properties which I clearly and distinctly understand, that is, all those which, viewed in general terms, are comprised within the subject-matter of pure mathematics.

What of the other aspects of corporeal things which are either particular (for example that the sun is of such and such a size or shape), or less clearly understood, such as light or sound or pain, and so on? Despite the high degree of doubt and uncertainty involved here, the very fact that God is not a deceiver, and the consequent impossibility of there being any falsity in my opinions which cannot be corrected by some other faculty supplied by God, offers me a sure hope that I can attain the truth even in these matters. Indeed, there is no doubt that everything that I am taught by nature contains some truth. For if nature is considered in its general aspect, then I understand by the term nothing other than God himself, or the ordered system of created things established by God. And by my own nature in particular I understand nothing other than the totality of things bestowed on me by God.

There is nothing that my own nature teaches me more vividly than that I have a body, and that when I feel pain there is something wrong with the body, and that when I am hungry or thirsty the body needs food and drink, and so on. So I should not doubt that there is some truth in this.

Nature also teaches me, by these sensations of pain, hunger, thirst and so on, that I am not merely present in my body as a sailor is present in a ship, but that I am very closely joined and, as it were, intermingled with it, so that I and the body form a unit. If this were not so, I, who am nothing but a thinking thing, would not feel pain when the body was hurt, but would perceive the damage purely by the intellect, just as a sailor perceives by sight if anything in his ship is broken. Similarly, when the body needed food or drink, I should have an explicit understanding of the fact, instead of having confused sensations of hunger and thirst. For these sensations of hunger, thirst, pain and so on are nothing but confused modes of thinking which arise from the union and, as it were, intermingling of the mind with the body.

I am also taught by nature that various other bodies exist in the vicinity of my body, and that some of these are to be sought out and others avoided. And from the fact that I perceive by my senses a great variety of colours, sounds, smells and tastes, as well as differences in heat, hardness and the like, I am correct in inferring that the bodies which are the source of these various sensory perceptions possess differences corresponding to them, though perhaps not resembling them. Also, the fact that some of the perceptions are agreeable to me while others are disagreeable makes it quite certain that my body, or rather my whole self, in so far as I am a combination of body and mind, can be affected by the various beneficial or harmful bodies which surround it.

There are, however, many other things which I may appear to have been taught by nature, but which in reality I acquired not from nature but from a habit of making ill-considered judgements; and it is therefore quite possible that these are false. Cases in point are the belief that any space in which nothing is occurring to stimulate my senses must be empty; or that the heat in a body is something exactly resembling the idea of heat which is in me; or that when a body is white or green, the selfsame whiteness or greenness which I perceive through my senses is present in the body; or that in a body which is bitter or sweet there is the selfsame taste which I experience, and so on; or, finally, that stars and towers and other distant bodies have the same size and shape which they present to my senses, and other examples of this kind. But to make sure that my perceptions in this matter are sufficiently distinct, I must more accurately define exactly what I mean when I say that I am taught something by nature. In this context I am taking nature to be something more limited than the totality of things bestowed on me by God. For this includes many things that belong to the mind alone—for example my perception that what is done cannot be undone, and all other things that are known by the natural light; but at this stage I am not speaking of these matters. It also includes much that relates to the body alone, like the tendency to move in a downward direction, and so on; but I am not speaking of these matters either. My sole concern here is with what God has bestowed on me as a combination of mind and body. My nature, then, in this limited sense, does indeed teach me to avoid what induces a feeling of pain and to seek out what induces feelings of pleasure, and so on. But it does not appear to teach us to draw any conclusions from these sensory perceptions about things located outside us without waiting until the intellect has examined the matter. For knowledge of the truth about such things seems to belong to the mind alone, not to the combination of mind and body. Hence, although a star has no greater effect on my eye than the flame of a small light, that does not mean that there is any real or positive inclination in me to believe that the star is no bigger than the light; I have simply made this judgement from childhood onwards without any rational basis. Similarly, although I feel heat when I go near a fire and feel pain when I go too near, there is no convincing argument for supposing that there is something in the fire which resembles the heat, any more than for supposing that there is something which resembles the pain. There is simply reason to suppose that there is something in the fire, whatever it may eventually turn out to be, which produces in us the feelings of heat or pain. And likewise, even though there is nothing in any given space that stimulates the senses, it does not follow that there is no body there. In these cases and many others I see that I have been in the habit of misusing the order of nature. For the proper purpose of the sensory perceptions given me by nature is simply to inform the mind of what is beneficial or harmful for the composite of which the mind is a part; and to this extent they are sufficiently clear and distinct. But I misuse them by treating them as reliable touchstones for immediate judgements about the essential nature of the bodies located outside us; yet this is an area where they provide only very obscure information.

I have already looked in sufficient detail at how, notwithstanding the goodness of God, it may happen that my judgements are false. But a further problem now comes to mind regarding those very things which nature presents to me as objects which I should seek out or avoid, and also regarding the internal sensations, where I seem to have detected errors—e.g. when someone is tricked by the pleasant taste of some food into eating the poison concealed inside it. Yet in this case, what the man's nature urges him to go for is simply what is responsible for the pleasant taste, and not the poison, which his nature knows nothing about. The only inference that can be drawn from this is that his nature is not omniscient. And this is not surprising, since man is a limited thing, and so it is only fitting that his perfection should be limited.

And yet it is not unusual for us to go wrong even in cases where nature does urge us towards something. Those who are ill, for example, may desire food or drink that will shortly afterwards turn out to be bad for them. Perhaps it may be said that they go wrong because their nature is disordered, but this does not remove the difficulty. A sick man is no less one of God's creatures than a healthy one, and it seems no less a contradiction to suppose that he has received from God a nature which deceives him. Yet a clock constructed with wheels and weights observes all the laws of its nature just as closely when it is badly made and tells the wrong time as when it completely fulfils the wishes of the clockmaker. In the same way, I might consider the body of a man as a kind of machine equipped with and made up of bones, nerves, muscles, veins, blood and skin in such a way that, even if there were no mind in it, it would still perform all the same movements as it now does in those cases where movement is not under the control of the will or, consequently, of the mind. I can easily see that if such a body suffers from dropsy, for example, and is affected by the dryness of the throat which normally produces in the mind the sensation of thirst, the resulting condition of the nerves and other parts will dispose the body to take a drink, with the result that the disease will be aggravated. Yet this is just as natural as the body's being stimulated by a similar dryness of the throat to take a drink when there is no such illness and the drink is beneficial. Admittedly, when I consider the purpose of the clock, I may say that it is departing from its nature when it does not tell the right time; and similarly when I consider the mechanism of the human body, I may think that, in relation to the movements which normally occur in it, it too is deviating from its nature if the throat is dry at a time when drinking is not beneficial to its continued health. But I am well aware that "nature" as I have just used it has a very different significance from "nature" in the other sense. As I have just used it, "nature" is simply a label which depends on my thought; it is quite extraneous to the things to which it is applied, and depends simply on my comparison between the idea of a sick man and a badly-made clock, and the idea of a healthy man and a well-made clock. But by "nature" in the other sense I understand something which is really to be found in the things themselves; in this sense, therefore, the term contains something of the truth.

When we say, then, with respect to the body suffering from dropsy, that it has a disordered nature because it has a dry throat and yet does not need drink, the term "nature" is here used merely as an extraneous label. However, with respect to the composite, that is, the mind united with this body, what is involved is not a mere label, but a true error of nature, namely that it is thirsty at a time when drink is going to cause it harm. It thus remains to inquire how it is that the goodness of God does not prevent nature, in this sense, from deceiving us.

The first observation I make at this point is that there is a great difference between the mind and the body, inasmuch as the body is by its very nature always divisible, while the mind is utterly indivisible. For when I consider the mind, or myself in so far as I am merely a thinking thing, I am unable to distinguish any parts within myself; I understand myself to be something quite single and complete. Although the whole mind seems to be united to the whole body, I recognize that if a foot or arm or any other part of the body is cut off, nothing has thereby been taken away from the mind. As for the faculties of willing, of understanding, of sensory perception and so on, these cannot be termed parts of the mind, since it is one and the same mind that wills, and understands and has sensory perceptions. By contrast, there is no corporeal or extended thing that I can think of which in my thought I cannot easily divide into parts; and this very fact makes me understand that it is divisible. This one argument would be enough to show me that the mind is completely different from the body, even if I did not already know as much from other considerations.

My next observation is that the mind is not immediately affected by all parts of the body, but only by the brain, or perhaps just by one small part of the brain, namely

A diagram from Descartes'
Tractatus de Homine (1677)
showing how the pineal gland
(shown here at the back of the
head) connects sensory images
from the eyes to the muscles of
the arm. *(Library of Congress)*

the part which is said to contain the "common" sense. Every time this part of the brain is in a given state, it presents the same signals to the mind, even though the other parts of the body may be in a different condition at the time. This is established by countless observations, which there is no need to review here.

I observe, in addition, that the nature of the body is such that whenever any part of it is moved by another part which is some distance away, it can always be moved in the same fashion by any of the parts which lie in between, even if the more distant part does nothing. For example, in a cord ABCD, if one end D is pulled so that the other end A moves, the exact same movement could have been brought about if one of the intermediate points B or C had been pulled, and D had not moved at all. In similar fashion, when I feel a pain in my foot, physiology tells me that this happens by means of nerves distributed throughout the foot, and that these nerves are like cords which go from the foot right up to the brain. When the nerves are pulled in the foot, they in turn pull on inner parts of the brain to which they are attached, and produce a certain motion in them; and nature has laid it down that this motion should produce in the mind a sensation of pain, as occurring in the foot. But since these nerves, in passing from the foot to the brain, must pass through the calf, the thigh, the lumbar region, the back and the neck, it can happen that, even if it is not the part in the foot but one of the intermediate parts which is being pulled, the same motion will occur in the brain as occurs when the foot is hurt, and so it will necessarily come about that the mind feels the same sensation of pain. And we must suppose the same thing happens with regard to any other sensation.

My final observation is that any given movement occurring in the part of the brain that immediately affects the mind produces just one corresponding sensation; and hence the best system that could be devised is that it should produce the one sensation which, of all possible sensations, is most especially and most frequently conducive to the preservation of the healthy man. And experience shows that the sensations which nature has given us are all of this kind; and so there is absolutely nothing to be found in them that does not bear witness to the power and goodness of God. For example, when the nerves in the foot are set in motion in a violent and unusual manner, this motion, by way of the spinal cord, reaches the inner parts of the brain, and there gives the mind its signal for having a certain sensation, namely the sensation of a pain as occurring in the foot. This stimulates the mind to do its best to get rid of the cause of the pain, which it takes to be harmful to the foot. It is true that God could have made the nature of man such that this particular motion in the brain indicated something else to the mind; it might, for example, have made the mind aware of the actual motion occurring in the brain, or in the foot, or in any of the intermediate regions; or it might have indicated something else entirely. But there is nothing else which would have been so conducive to the continued well-being of the body. In the same way, when we need drink, there arises a certain dryness in the throat; this sets in motion the nerves of the throat, which in turn move the inner parts of the brain. This motion produces in the mind a sensation of thirst, because the most useful thing for us to know about the whole business is that we need drink in order to stay healthy. And so it is in the other cases.

It is quite clear from all this that, notwithstanding the immense goodness of God, the nature of man as a combination of mind and body is such that it is bound to mislead him from time to time. For there may be some occurrence, not in the foot but in one of the other areas through which the nerves travel in their route from the foot to the brain, or even in the brain itself; and if this cause produces the same motion which is generally produced by injury to the foot, then pain will be felt as if it were in the foot. This deception of the senses is natural, because a given motion in the brain must always produce the same sensation in the mind; and the origin of the motion in question is much more often going to be something which is hurting the foot, rather than something existing elsewhere. So it is reasonable that this motion should always indicate to the mind a pain in the foot rather than in any other part of the body. Again, dryness of the throat may sometimes arise not, as it normally does, from the fact that a drink is necessary to the health of the body, but from some quite opposite cause, as happens in the case of the man with dropsy. Yet it is much better that it should mislead on this occasion than that it should always mislead when the body is in good health. And the same goes for the other cases.

This consideration is the greatest help to me, not only for noticing all the errors to which my nature is liable, but also for enabling me to correct or avoid them without difficulty. For I know that in matters regarding the well-being of the body, all my senses report the truth much more frequently than not. Also, I can almost always make use of more than one sense to investigate the same thing; and in addition, I can use both my memory, which connects present experiences with preceding ones, and my intellect, which has by now examined all the causes of error. Accordingly, I should not have any further fears about the falsity of what my senses tell me every day; on the contrary, the exaggerated doubts of the last few days should be dismissed as laughable. This applies especially to the principal reason for doubt, namely my inability to distinguish between being asleep and being awake. For I now notice that there is a vast difference between the two, in that dreams are never linked by memory with all the other actions of life as waking experiences are. If, while I am awake, anyone were suddenly to appear to me and then disappear immediately, as happens in sleep, so that I could not see where he had come from or where he had gone to, it would not be unreasonable for me to judge that he was a ghost, or a vision created in my brain, rather than a real man. But when I distinctly see where things come from and where and when they come to me, and when I can connect my perceptions of them with the whole of the rest of my life without a break, then I am quite certain that when I encounter these things I am not asleep but awake. And I ought not to have even the slightest doubt of their reality if, after calling upon all the senses as well as my memory and my intellect in order to check them, I receive no conflicting reports from any of these sources. For from the fact that God is not a deceiver it follows that in cases like these I am completely free from error. But since the pressure of things to be done does not always allow us to stop and make such a meticulous check, it must be admitted that in this human life we are often liable to make mistakes about particular things, and we must acknowledge the weakness of our nature.

THOMAS HOBBES
1588–1679

Born prematurely when his mother heard of the approach of the Spanish Armada, Thomas Hobbes often quipped that he was born "a twin with fear." Hobbes saw much to fear in his long life. He observed a civil war, the execution of Charles I, and periods of great political and social upheaval. On more than one occasion, he was forced to flee England; and he often feared for his life. It is not surprising, then, that he would develop a political philosophy emphasizing fear of death and the need for security.

Hobbes was born in Malmesbury, Whiltshire, England, the son of a disreputable vicar. His father was forced to leave the Whiltshire area after brawling outside his church. Young Thomas was sent to live with a rich uncle. At the age of fourteen, he went to Oxford University. Like Descartes, he found most of his schooling to be a waste of time. He particularly disliked the Aristotelianism of his college, Magdalen Hall. In 1608, he became the tutor to the son of William Cavendish, Earl of Devonshire. For the rest of his life, Hobbes remained a friend of the Cavendish family and a royalist sympathizer.

Hobbes made several extended visits to the Continent—some voluntary, some a result of running for his life. At home and on the Continent, Hobbes met and conversed with such leading thinkers as Descartes, Galileo, and Bacon. Although he, of course, had differences with them, he nevertheless used each thinker's ideas to refine his own philosophy. From Descartes, he learned to value the geometric method. Descartes used geometry to establish epistemological certainty. Hobbes used geometry to develop a political theory. In opposition to the dominant Aristotelian thesis that rest is the natural state of objects, Galileo had proposed that all bodies are naturally in motion. Hobbes took Galileo's postulate and proceeded to argue that all things in the world, including human beings, are bodies in motion. With Bacon, Hobbes agreed that scientific knowledge was primarily useful for improving the human condition.

In 1628, Hobbes published his first literary work: a translation of Thucydides, by which he hoped to use history to enlighten the English people. In Thucydides' *Peloponnesian War,* democratic Athens had been defeated by monarchical Sparta. Hobbes wanted to warn his fellow citizens of the creeping democracy threatening England. Hobbes was convinced that democracy led to chaos and that a strong central government was essential for national stability. In 1640, Hobbes was forced to flee England for Paris when the Long Parliament supplanted the king. In Paris, Hobbes wrote the book for which he is famous, *Leviathan, or the Matter, Form, and Power of a Commonwealth, Ecclesiastical and Civil.* The book was published between the execution of Charles I (1649) and the Protectorate of Cromwell (1653), a time ripe for political philosophy.

Cromwell permitted Hobbes to return to England in 1652. Although Hobbes had always been a royalist, his argument for the absolute power of the sovereign was not restricted to kings. Thus Cromwell had no reason to consider Hobbes's doctrine seditious—nor did Charles II, whom Hobbes had tutored in Paris, and who was later restored to the monarchy.

Hobbes's later years were spent writing and arguing for his ideas. Although he continued to have enemies, with the king's friendship he managed to stay out of serious trouble. In his early eighties, Hobbes wrote a history of the period 1640–1660, which he called *Behemoth.* When he was eighty-four, Hobbes published his autobiography in Latin verse; at eighty-six, he produced a verse translation of both the *Iliad* and the *Odyssey* (for lack of anything better to do, he commented). He died in 1679 at the age of 91.

*   *   *

The *Leviathan* is known primarily for its political philosophy, but it touches on a number of other issues including epistemology, metaphysics, ethics, and religion. Hobbes begins with a thoroughgoing version of materialism. Everything in the world, including humans, consists of bodies in motion. Knowledge of the world begins in sensation. Bodies in motion outside of a person cause motion within the person. Memories, imagination, and other "mental" phenomena are the aftershocks of sensations—what Hobbes calls "decaying sense." *Willing* is that "beginning of motion" that leads to action when individuals move and so move other bodies.

Using a mechanistic explanation of "voluntary motions," which he calls "endeavors," Hobbes believes that in human life self-interest and the desire for power are the basic motive powers. According to Hobbes, each person is constantly seeking an advantage over everyone else. Yet since all are born equal, there is no inherent reason why one person should give way to another. The result is what Hobbes calls "a war of every man against every man . . . [in which] the notions of right and wrong, justice and injustice, have no place." In such an environment, life is "solitary, poor, nasty, brutish, and short."

To avoid this natural state of anarchy, individuals must enter into a social contract or covenant with all other individuals to give up their power irrevocably to a sovereign: "This is the generation of that great LEVIATHAN, or rather, to speak more reverently, of that 'mortal god,' to which we owe under the 'immortal God,' our peace and defence." This contract is not binding on the sovereign, as the sovereign is not a party to it. Hence there is no legal limitation on the sovereign's power. The sovereign is the essence of the commonwealth, which can be defined as

> one person, of whose acts a great multitude, by mutual covenants one with another, have made themselves every one the author, to the end he may use the strength and means of them all, as he shall think expedient, for their peace and common defence. . . . And he that carries this person, is called SOVEREIGN, and said to have sovereign power; and every one besides, his SUBJECT.

Hobbes believes this sovereign did not have to be a single person—sovereignty could reside in an individual (a monarchy), a small group (an aristocracy), or in the entire population (a democracy)—though he shows a marked preference for monarchy because of its greater stability and efficiency. What matters to Hobbes above all else is that the sovereign has absolute power in order to keep the peace and to guarantee security. To be sure, an absolute sovereign might abuse power, but the only alternative to this possible abuse, Hobbes claims, is an unthinkable anarchy.

*   *   *

Hobbes wrote many books over the course of his long life—the standard Oxford edition of his English works includes eleven volumes with another five volumes of his Latin works—but it is *Leviathan* (1651) that is the basis of his fame. The key sections of this work, from Chapters 1–3, 6, 9, 12, 15, 17–18, and 21, are reprinted here. The spelling has been updated and standardized.

For a general introduction to Hobbes's life and thought, see John Laird, *Hobbes* (London: Ernest Benn, 1934); Richard Peters, *Hobbes* (Baltimore, MD: Penguin Books, 1956); G.C. Robertson, *Hobbes* (New York: AMS Press, 1968); and Tom Sorell, *Hobbes* (London: Routledge, 1986). For discussions of Hobbes's ethical and political thought as developed in *Leviathan,* see Leo Strauss, *The Political Philosophy of Hobbes* (Chicago: University of Chicago Press, 1952); Howard Warrender, *The Political Philosophy of Hobbes: His Theory of Obligation* (Oxford: Clarendon Press, 1957); David P. Gauthier, *The Logic of Leviathan: The Moral and Political Theory of Thomas Hobbes* (Oxford: Clarendon Press, 1969); and Michael Oakeshott, *Hobbes on Civil Association* (Berkeley: University of California Press, 1975). A.P. Martinish, *A Hobbes Dictionary* (Oxford: Basil Blackwell, 1995) provides a helpful reference work. For collections of essays on Hobbes, see Keith Brown, ed., *Hobbes Studies* (Cambridge, MA: Harvard University Press, 1965); G.A.J. Rogers and Alan Ryan, eds., *Perspectives on Thomas Hobbes* (Oxford: Oxford University Press, 1989); and Vere Chappell, ed., *Essays on Early Modern Philosophers: Thomas Hobbes* (Hamden, CT: Garland, 1992).

LEVIATHAN OR THE MATTER, FORM, AND POWER OF A COMMONWEALTH, ECCLESIASTICAL AND CIVIL (in part)

PART I—OF MAN

CHAPTER 1. OF SENSE

Concerning the thoughts of man, I will consider them first singly, and afterwards in train, or dependence upon one another. Singly, they are every one a "representation" or "appearance" of some quality, or other accident of a body without us, which is commonly called an "object." Which object works on the eyes, ears, and other parts of a man's body, and, by diversity of working, produces diversity of appearances.

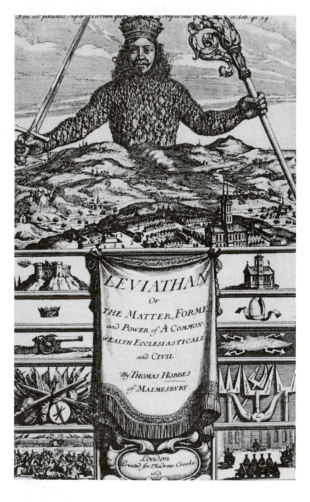

The title page of Hobbes's *Leviathan* (1651). The sovereign in the background, whose body is composed of the people, is supreme. He is shown here holding the symbols of both church and state. (*Library of Congress*)

The original of them all is that which we call "sense," for there is no conception in a man's mind which hath not at first, totally or by parts, been begotten upon the organs of sense. The rest are derived from that original.

To know the natural cause of sense is not very necessary to the business now in hand; and I have elsewhere written of the same at large. Nevertheless, to fill each part of my present method I will briefly deliver the same in this place.

The cause of sense is the external body, or object, which presses the organ proper to each sense, either immediately, as in the taste and touch, or mediately, as in seeing, hearing, and smelling; which pressure, by the mediation of the nerves and other strings and membranes of the body continued inwards to the brain and heart, causes there a resistance, or counter-pressure, or endeavor of the heart to deliver itself, which endeavor, because "outward," seems to be some matter without. And this "seeming" or "fancy" is that which men call "sense" and consists, as to the eye, in a "light" or "color figured"; to the ear, in a "sound"; to the nostril, in an "odor"; to the tongue and palate, in a "savor"; and to the rest of the body, in "heat," "cold," "hardness," "softness," and such other qualities as we discern by "feeling." All which qualities, called "sensible" are in the object that causes them but so many several motions of the matter, by which it presses our organs diversely. Neither in us that are pressed are they anything else but divers motions; for motion produces nothing but motion. But their appearance to us is fancy, the same waking that dreaming. And as pressing, rubbing, or striking the eye, makes us fancy a light, and pressing the ear produces a din, so do the bodies also we see or hear produce the same by their strong, though unobserved, action. For if those colors and sounds were in the bodies, or objects that cause them, they could not be severed from them, as by glasses, and in echoes by reflection, we see they are, where we know the thing we see is in one place, the appearance in another. And though at some certain distance the real and very object seem invested with the fancy it begets in us, yet still the object is one thing, the image or fancy is another. So that sense in all cases is nothing else but original fancy, caused, as I have said, by the pressure, that is by the motion, of external things upon our eyes, ears, and other organs thereunto ordained.

But the philosophy schools through all the universities of Christendom, grounded upon certain texts of Aristotle, teach another doctrine, and say, for the cause of "vision," that the thing seen sends forth on every side a "visible species," in English, a "visible show," "apparition," or "aspect," or "a being seen"; the receiving whereof into the eye is "seeing." And for the cause of "hearing," that the thing heard sends forth an "audible species," that is an "audible aspect," or "audible being seen," which entering at the ear makes "hearing." Nay, for the cause of "understanding" also, they say the thing understood sends forth an "intelligible species," that is, an "intelligible being seen," which, coming into the understanding, makes us understand. I say not this as disproving the use of universities; but, because I am to speak hereafter of their office in a commonwealth. I must let you see on all occasions by the way what things would be amended in them, amongst which the frequency of insignificant speech is one.

CHAPTER 2. OF IMAGINATION

That when a thing lies still, unless somewhat else stir it, it will lie still for ever, is a truth that no man doubts of. But that when a thing is in motion, it will eternally be in motion, unless somewhat else stay it, though the reason be the same, namely that nothing can change itself, is not so easily assented to. For men measure not only other men but all other things, by themselves; and, because they find themselves subject after motion to pain and lassitude, think everything else grows weary of motion, and seeks repose of its own accord; little considering whether it be not some other motion wherein that desire of rest they find in themselves consists. From hence it is that the schools say heavy bodies fall downwards out of an appetite to rest, and to conserve their nature in that place which is most proper for them; ascribing appetite and knowledge of what is good for their conservation, which is more than man has, to things inanimate, absurdly.

When a body is once in motion, it moves, unless something else hinder it, eternally; and whatsoever hinders it cannot in an instant, but in time and by degrees, quite extinguish it; and, as we see in the water though the wind cease the waves give not over rolling for a long time after: so also it happens in that motion which is made in the internal parts of a man, then, when he sees, dreams, etc. For, after the object is removed, or the eye shut, we still retain an image of the thing seen, though more obscure than when we see it. And this is it the Latins call "imagination," from the image made in seeing; and apply the same, though improperly, to all the other senses. But the Greeks call it "fancy," which signifies "appearance," and is as proper to one sense as to another. "Imagination," therefore, is nothing but "decaying sense," and is found in men, and many other living creatures, as well sleeping as waking.

The decay of sense in men waking is not the decay of the motion made in sense, but an obscuring of it in such manner as the light of the sun obscures the light of the stars, which stars do no less exercise their virtue, by which they are visible, in the day than in the night. But because amongst many strokes which our eyes, ears, and other organs, receive from external bodies, the predominant only is sensible; therefore, the light of the sun being predominant, we are not affected with the action of the stars. And any object being removed from our eyes, though the impression it made in us remain, yet other objects more present succeeding and working on us, the imagination of the past is obscured and made weak, as the voice of a man is in the noise of the day. From whence it follows that the longer the time is, after the sight or sense of any object, the weaker is the imagination. For the continual change of man's body destroys in time the parts which in sense were moved; so that distance of time, and of place, hath one and the same effect in us. For as at a great distance of place that which we look at appears dim and without distinction of the smaller parts, and as voices grow weak and inarticulate, so also after great distance of time our imagination of the past is weak; and we lose, for example, of cities we have seen many particular streets, and of actions many particular circumstances. This "decaying sense," when we would express the thing itself, I mean "fancy" itself, we call "imagination," as I said before; but when we would express the decay, and signify that the sense is fading, old, and past, it is called "memory." So that imagination and memory are but one thing, which for divers considerations hath divers names.

Much memory, or memory of many things, is called "experience." Again, imagination being only of those things which have been formerly perceived by sense, either all at once or by parts at several times the former, which is the imagining the whole object as it was presented to the sense, is "simple" imagination, as when one imagines a man, or horse, which he hath seen before. The other is "compounded," as when, from the sight of a man at one time, and of a horse at another, we conceive in our mind a Centaur. So when a man compounds the image of his own person with the image of the actions of another man, as when a man images himself a Hercules or an Alexander, which happens often to them that are much taken with reading of romances, it is a compound imagination, and properly but a fiction of the mind. There be also other imaginations that rise in men, though waking, from the great impression made in sense; as, from gazing upon the sun, the impression leaves an image of the sun before our eyes a long time after; and, from being long and vehemently intent upon geometrical figures, a man shall in the dark, though awake, have the images of lines and angles before his eyes; which kind of fancy hath no particular name, as being a thing that doth not commonly fall into men's discourse.

The imaginations of them that sleep are those we call "dreams." And these also, as also all other imaginations, have been before, either totally or by parcels, in the sense. And, because in sense, the brain and nerves, which are the necessary organs of sense, are so benumbed in sleep as not easily to be moved by the action of external objects, there can happen in sleep no imagination, and therefore no dream, but what proceeds from the agitation of the inward parts of man's body; which inward parts, for the connection they have with the brain and other organs, when they be distempered, do keep the same in motion; whereby the imaginations there formerly made, appear as if a man were waking; saving that the organs of sense being now benumbed, so as there is no new object which can master and obscure them with a more vigorous impression, a dream must needs be more clear in this silence of sense than our waking thoughts. And hence it comes to pass that it is a hard matter, and by many thought impossible, to distinguish exactly between sense and dreaming. For my part, when I consider that in dreams I do not often nor constantly think of the same persons, places, objects, and actions, that I do waking, nor remember so long a train of coherent thoughts, dreaming, as at other times, and because waking I often observe the absurdity of dreams, but never dream of the absurdities of my waking thoughts, I am well satisfied, that, being awake, I know I dream not, though when I dream I think myself awake.

And, seeing dreams are caused by the distemper of some of the inward parts of the body, divers distempers must needs cause different dreams. And hence it is that lying cold breeds dreams of fear, and raises the thought and image of some fearful object, the motion from the brain to the inner parts and from the inner parts to the brain being reciprocal; and that, as anger causes heat in some parts of the body when we are awake, so when we sleep the overheating of the same parts causes anger, and raises up in the brain the imagination of an enemy. In the same manner, as natural kindness, when we are awake, causes desire, and desire makes heat in certain other parts of the body; so also too much heat in those parts, while we sleep, raises in the brain an imagination of some kindness shown. In sum, our dreams are the reverse of our waking imaginations, the motion when we are awake beginning at one end, and when we dream at another.

The most difficult discerning of a man's dream from his waking thoughts is, then, when by some accident we observe not that we have slept: which is easy to happen to a man full of fearful thoughts, and whose conscience is much troubled, and that sleeps without the circumstances of going to bed or putting off his clothes, as one that nods in a chair. For he that takes pains, and industriously lays himself to sleep, in case any uncouth and exorbitant fancy come unto him, cannot easily think it other than a dream. We read of Marcus Brutus (one that had his life given him by Julius Cæsar, and was also his favorite, and notwithstanding murdered him) how at Philippi, the night before he gave battle to Augustus Cæsar, he saw a fearful apparition, which is commonly related by historians as a vision; but, considering the circumstances, one may easily judge to have been but a short dream. For, sitting in his tent, pensive and troubled with the horror of his rash act, it was not hard for him, slumbering in the cold, to dream of that which most frightened him; which fear, as by degrees it made him wake, so also it must needs make the apparition by degrees to vanish; and, having no assurance that he slept, he could have no cause to think it a dream or anything but a vision. And this is no very rare accident; for even they that be perfectly awake, if they be timorous and superstitious, possessed with fearful tales, and alone in the dark, are subject to the like fancies, and believe they see spirits and dead men's ghosts walking in churchyards; whereas it is either their fancy only, or else the knavery of such persons as make use of such superstitious fear to pass disguised in the night to places they would not be known to haunt.

From this ignorance of how to distinguish dreams and other strong fancies from vision and sense, did arise the greatest part of the religion of the Gentiles in time past, that worshipped satyrs, fawns, nymphs, and the like; and now-a-days the opinion that rude people have of fairies, ghosts, and goblins, and of the power of witches. For as for witches, I think not that their witchcraft is any real power; but yet that they are justly punished for the false belief they have that they can do such mischief, joined with their purpose to do it if they can; their trade being nearer to a new religion than to a craft or science. And for fairies and walking ghosts, the opinion of them has, I think, been on purpose either taught, or not confuted, to keep in credit the use of exorcism, of crosses, of holy water, and other such inventions of ghostly men. Nevertheless there is no doubt but God can make unnatural apparitions; but that He does it so often as men need to fear such things more than they fear the stay or change of the course of nature, which He also can stay and change, is no point of Christian faith. But evil men, under pretext that God can do anything, are so bold as to say anything when it serves their turn, though they think it untrue; it is the part of a wise man to believe them no farther than right reason makes that which they say appear credible. If this superstitious fear of spirits were taken away, and with it prognostics from dreams, false prophecies, and many other things depending thereon, by which crafty ambitious persons abuse the simple people, men would be much more fitted than they are for civil obedience.

And this ought to be the work of the schools; but they rather nourish such doctrine. For, not knowing what imagination or the senses are, what they receive they teach; some saying that imaginations rise of themselves and have no cause; others that they rise most commonly from the will, and that good thoughts are blown (inspired) into a man by God, and evil thoughts by the devil; or that good thoughts are poured (infused) into a man by God, and evil ones by the devil. Some say the senses receive the species of things, and deliver them to the common sense, and the common sense delivers them over to the fancy, and the fancy to the memory, and the memory to the judgment, like handling of things from one to another, with many words making nothing understood.

The imagination that is raised in man, or any other creature endowed with the faculty of imagining, by words or other voluntary signs, is that we generally call "understanding," and is common to man and beast. For a dog by custom will understand the call or the rating of his master; and so will many other beasts. That understanding which is peculiar to man, is the understanding of not only his will, but his conceptions and thoughts, by the sequel and contexture of the names of things into affirmations, negations, and other forms of speech; and of this kind of understanding I shall speak hereafter.

CHAPTER 3. OF THE CONSEQUENCE OR TRAIN OF IMAGINATIONS

By "consequence," or "train," of thoughts I understand that succession of one thought to another which is called, to distinguish it from discourse in words, "mental discourse."

When a man thinks on anything whatever, his next thought after is not altogether so casual as it seems to be. Not every thought to every thought succeeds indifferently. But as we have no imagination whereof we have not formerly had sense, in whole or in parts, so we have no transition from one imagination to another whereof we never had the like before in our senses. The reason whereof is this. All fancies are motions within us, relics of those made in the sense, and those motions that immediately succeeded one another in the sense continue also together after sense: in so much as the former coming again to take place, and be predominant, the latter followeth, by coherence of the matter moved, in such manner as water upon a plane table is drawn which way any one part of it is guided by the finger. But because in sense to one and the same thing perceived, sometimes one thing sometimes another, succeeds, it comes to pass in time that in the imagining of anything there is no certainty what we shall imagine next: only this is certain, it shall be something that succeeded the same before, at one time or another.

This train of thoughts, or mental discourse, is of two sorts. The first is "unguided," "without design," and inconstant; wherein there is no passionate thought, to govern and direct those that follow, to itself, as the end and scope of some desire or other passion: in which case the thoughts are said to wander, and seem impertinent one to another as in a dream. Such are commonly the thoughts of men that are not only without company but also without care of anything; though even then their thoughts are as busy as at other times, but without harmony; as the sound which a lute out of tune would yield to any man, or in tune to one that could not play. And yet in this wild ranging of the mind a man may oft-times perceive the way of it, and the dependence of one thought upon another. For in a discourse of our present civil war, what could seem more impertinent than to ask, as one did, what was the value of a Roman penny. Yet the coherence to me was manifest enough. For the thought of the war introduced the thought of the delivering up the king to his enemies, the thought of that brought in the thought of the delivering up of Christ; and that again the thought of the thirty pence, which was the price of that treason; and thence easily followed that malicious question; and all this in a moment of time—for thought is quick.

The second is more constant; as being "regulated" by some desire and design. For the impression made by such things as we desire, or fear, is strong and permanent, or, if it cease for a time, of quick return: so strong it is sometimes as to hinder and break our sleep. From desire arises the thought of some means we have seen produce the like of that which we aim at; and from the thought of that, the thought of means to that mean, and so continually till we come to some beginning within our own power. And because the end, by the greatness of the impression, comes often to mind, in case our thoughts begin to wander, they are quickly again reduced into the way: which observed by one of the Seven Wise Men, made him give men this precept, which is now worn out, *Respice finem;* that is to say, in all your actions look often upon what you would have as the thing that directs all your thoughts in the way to attain it.

The train of regulated thoughts is of two kinds; one, when of an effect imagined we seek the causes or means that produce it; and this is common to man and beast. The other is when imagining anything whatsoever we seek all the possible effects that can by it be produced, that is to say, we imagine what we can do with it when we have it. Of which I have not at any time seen any sign but in man only; for this is a curiosity hardly incident to the nature of any living creature that has no other passion but sensual, such as are hunger, thirst, lust, and anger. In sum, the discourse of the mind, when it is governed by design, is nothing but "seeking," or the faculty of invention, which the Latins called *sagacitas,* and *solertia;* a hunting out of the causes, of some effect, present or past; or of the effects, of some present or past cause. Sometimes a man seeks what he hath lost; and from that place and time wherein he misses it his mind runs back, from place to place, and time to time, to find where and when he had it, that is to say, to find some certain and limited time and place in which to begin a method of seeking. Again, from thence his thoughts run over the same places and times to find what action or other occasion might make him lose it. This we call "remembrance," or calling to mind: the Latins call it *reminiscentia,* as it were a "re-conning" of our former actions.

Sometimes a man knows a place determinate, within the compass whereof he is to seek; and then his thoughts run over all the parts thereof, in the same manner as one would sweep a room to find a jewel, or as a spaniel ranges the field till he find a scent, or as a man should run over the alphabet to start a rhyme.

Sometimes a man desires to know the event of an action; and then he thinks of some like action past, and the events thereof one after another, supposing like events will follow like actions. As he that foresees what will become of a criminal recons what he has seen follow on the like crime before, having this order of thoughts, the crime, the officer, the prison, the judge, and the gallows. Which kind of thoughts is called "foresight," and "prudence," or "providence," and sometimes "wisdom," though such conjecture, through the difficulty of observing all circumstances, be very fallacious. But this is certain: by how much one man has more experience of things past than another, by so much also he is more prudent, and his expectations the seldomer fail him. The "present" only has a being in nature; things "past" have a being in the memory only, but things "to come" have no being at all, the "future" being but a fiction of the mind, applying the sequels of actions past to the actions that are present; which with most certainty is done by him that has most experience, but not with certainty enough. And though it be called prudence, when the event answers our expectation, yet, in its own nature, it is but presumption. For the foresight of things to come, which is providence, belongs only to him by whose will they are to come. From him only, and supernaturally, proceeds prophecy. The best prophet naturally is the best guesser; and the best guesser he that is most versed and studied in the matters he guesses at, for he hath most "signs" to guess by.

A "sign" is the event antecedent of the consequent; and, contrarily, the consequent of the antecedent, when the like consequences have been observed before; and the oftener they have been observed, the less uncertain is the sign. And therefore he that has most experience in any kind of business has most signs whereby to guess at the future time, and consequently is the most prudent; and so much more prudent than he that is new in that kind of business as not to be equalled by any advantage of natural and extemporary wit; though perhaps many young men think the contrary.

Nevertheless it is not prudence that distinguishes man from beast. There be beasts that at a year old observe more, and pursue that which is for their good more prudently than a child can do at ten.

As prudence is a "presumption" of the "future" contracted from the "experience" of time "past," so there is a presumption of things past taken from other things, not future, but past also. For he that hath seen by what courses and degrees a flourishing state hath first come into civil war, and then to ruin, upon the sight of the ruins of any other state will guess the like war and the like courses have been there also. But this conjecture has the same uncertainty almost with the conjecture of the future, both being grounded only upon experience.

There is no other act of man's mind that I can remember naturally planted in him, so as to need no other thing to the exercise of it but to be born a man, and live with the use of his five senses. Those other faculties of which I shall speak by and by, and which seem proper to man only, are acquired and increased by study and industry, and of most men learned by instruction and discipline; and proceed all from the invention of words and speech. For besides sense, and thoughts, and the train of thoughts, the mind of man has no other motion, though by the help of speech and method the same faculties may be improved to such a height as to distinguish men from all other living creatures.

Whatsoever we imagine is "finite." Therefore there is no idea or conception of any thing we call "infinite." No man can have in his mind an image of infinite magnitude, nor conceive infinite swiftness, infinite time, or infinite force, or infinite power. When we say anything is infinite, we signify only that we are not able to conceive the ends and bounds of the things named; having no conception of the thing, but of our own inability. And therefore the name of God is used, not to make us conceive Him, for He is incomprehensible, and His greatness and power are inconceivable, but that we may honor Him. Also because, whatsoever, as I said before, we conceive, has been perceived first by sense, either all at once or by parts; a man can have no thought representing anything not subject to sense. No man therefore can conceive anything but he must conceive it in some place, and endowed with some determinate magnitude, and which may be divided into parts; nor that anything is all in this place and all in another place at the same time; nor that two or more things can be in one and the same place at once: for none of these things ever have or can be incident to sense, but are absurd speeches, taken upon credit, without any signification at all, from deceived philosophers, and deceived or deceiving schoolmen.

*   *   *

CHAPTER 6. OF THE INTERIOR BEGINNINGS OF VOLUNTARY MOTIONS; COMMONLY CALLED THE PASSIONS; AND THE SPEECHES BY WHICH THEY ARE EXPRESSED

There be in animals two sorts of "motions" peculiar to them: one called "vital," begun in generation, and continued without interruption through their whole life, such as are the "course" of the "blood," the "pulse," the "breathing," the "concoction, nutrition, excretion," etc., to which motions there needs no help of imagination: the other is "animal motion," otherwise called "voluntary motion," as to "go," to "speak," to "move" any of our limbs in such manner as is first fancied in our minds. That sense is motion in the organs and interior parts of man's body, caused by the action of the things we see, hear, etc.; and that fancy is but the relics of the same motion, remaining after sense, has been already said in the first and second chapters. And, because "going," "speaking," and the like voluntary motions, depend always upon a precedent thought of "whither," "which way," and "what," it is evident that the imagination is the first internal beginning of all voluntary motion. And, although unstudied men do not conceive any motion at all to be there where the thing moved is invisible, or the space it is moved in is, for the shortness of it, insensible, yet that doth not hinder but that such motions are. For, let a space be never so little, that which is moved over a greater space, whereof that little one is part, must first be moved over that. These small beginnings of motion within the body of man before they appear in walking, speaking, striking, and other visible actions, are commonly called "endeavor."

This endeavor, when it is toward something which causes it, is called "appetite," or "desire," the latter being the general name, and the other oftentimes restrained to signify the desire of food, namely "hunger" and "thirst." And, when the endeavor is fromward something, it is generally called "aversion." These words, "appetite" and "aversion," we have from the Latins—and they both of them signify the motions, one of approaching, the other of retiring. So also do the Greek words for the same, which are ⟨horma⟩ and ⟨aphorma⟩. For Nature itself does often press upon men those truths which afterwards, when they look for somewhat beyond Nature, they stumble at. For the schools find in mere appetite to go, or move, no actual motion at all; but, because some motion they must acknowledge, they call it metaphorical motion, which is but an absurd speech; for though words may be called metaphorical, bodies and motions cannot.

That which men desire they are also said to "love"; and to "hate" those things for which they have aversion. So that desire and love are the same thing, save that by desire we always signify the absence of the object, by love most commonly the presence of the same. So also by aversion we signify the absence, and by hate, the presence of the object.

Of appetites and aversions, some are born with men, as appetite of food, appetite of excretion, and exoneration, which may also and more properly be called aversions from somewhat they feel in their bodies; and some other appetites, not many. The rest, which are appetites of particular things, proceed from experience and trial of their effects upon themselves or other men. For of things we know not at all, or believe not to be, we can have no further desire than to taste and try. But aversion we have for things not only which we know have hurt us, but also that we do not know whether they will hurt us or not.

Those things which we neither desire nor hate we are said to "contemn," "contempt" being nothing else but an immobility or contumacy of the heart in resisting the action of certain things, and proceeding from that the heart is already moved otherwise by other more potent objects, or from want of experience of them.

And, because the constitution of a man's body is in continual mutation, it is impossible that all the same things should always cause in him the same appetites and aversions: much less can all men consent in the desire of almost any one and the same object.

But whatsoever is the object of any man's appetite or desire, that is it which he for his part calls "good"; and the object of his hate and aversion, "evil"; and of his contempt "vile" and "inconsiderable." For these words of good, evil, and contemptible, are ever used with relation to the person that uses them, there being nothing simply and absolutely so; nor any common rule of good and evil, to be taken from the nature of the objects themselves; but from the person of the man, where there is no commonwealth, or, in a commonwealth, from the person that represents it; or from an arbitrator or judge, whom men disagreeing shall by consent set up, and make his sentence the rule thereof.

The Latin tongue has two words whose significations approach to those of good and evil, but are not precisely the same; and those are *pulchrum* and *turpe*. Whereof the former signifies that which by some apparent signs promises good; and the latter that which promises evil. But in our tongue we have not so general names to express them by. But for *pulchrum* we say in some things "fair," in others, "beautiful," or "handsome," or "gallant," or "honorable," or "comely," or "amiable"; and for *turpe*, "foul," "deformed," "ugly," "base," "nauseous," and the like, as the subject shall require; all which words, in their proper places, signify nothing else but the "mien," or countenance, that promises good and evil. So that of good there be three kinds: good in the promise, that is *pulchrum;* good in effect, as the end desired, which is called *jucundum,* "delightful"; and good as the means which is called *utile,* "profitable"; and as many of evil: for "evil" in promise is that they call *turpe;* evil in effect, and end is *molestum,* "unpleasant," "troublesome"; and evil in the means, *inutile,* "unprofitable," "hurtful."

As, in sense, that which is really within us is, as I have said before, only motion caused by the action of external objects but in appearance—to the sight, light and color; to the ear, sound; to the nostril, odor, etc.; so, when the action of the same object is continued from the eyes, ears, and other organs to the heart, the real effect there is nothing but motion or endeavor which consists in appetite, or aversion, to or from the object moving. But the appearance, or sense of that motion, is that we either call "delight" or "trouble of mind."

This motion, which is called appetite, and for the appearance of it "delight" and "pleasure," seems to be a corroboration of vital motion, and a help thereunto; and therefore such things as caused delight were not improperly called *jucunda—juvando,* from helping or fortifying; and the contrary *molesta,* "offensive," from hindering and troubling the motion vital.

"Pleasure," therefore, or "delight," is the appearance or sense of good; and "molestation," or "displeasure," the appearance or sense of evil. And consequently all appetite, desire, and love, is accompanied with some delight more or less; and all hatred and aversion with more or less displeasure and offence.

Of pleasures or delights some arise from the sense of an object present; and those may be called "pleasures of sense," the word "sensual," as it is used by those only that condemn them, having no place till there be laws. Of this kind are all onerations and exonerations of the body, as also all that is pleasant in the "sight," "hearing," "smell," "taste," or "touch." Others arise from the expectation that proceeds from foresight of the end or consequence of things, whether those things in the sense please or displease. And these are "pleasures of the mind" of him that draws those consequences, and are generally called "joy." In the like manner, displeasures are some in the sense, and called "pain"; others in the expectation of consequences, and are called "grief."

These simple passions called "appetite," "desire," "love," "aversion," "hate," "joy," and "grief," have their names for divers considerations diversified. As first, when they one succeed another, they are diversely called from the opinion men have of the likelihood of attaining what they desire. Secondly, from the object loved or hated. Thirdly, from the consideration of many of them together. Fourthly, from the alteration or succession itself.

For "appetite" with an opinion of attaining is called "hope."

The same without such opinion, "despair."

"Aversion" with opinion of "hurt" from the object "fear."

The same with hope of avoiding that hurt by resistance, "courage."

Sudden "courage," "anger."

Constant "hope," "confidence" of ourselves.

Constant "despair," "diffidence" of ourselves.

"Anger" for great hurt done to another, when we conceive the same to be done by injury, "indignation."

"Desire" of good to another, "benevolence," "good will," "charity." If to man generally, "good-nature."

"Desire" of riches, "covetousness," a name used always in signification of blame, because men contending for them are displeased with one another attaining them, though the desire in itself be to be blamed, or allowed, according to the means by which those riches are sought.

"Desire" of office, or precedence, "ambition," a name used also in the worse sense, for the reason before mentioned.

"Desire" of things that conduce but a little to our ends, and fear of things that are but of little hindrance, "pusillanimity."

"Contempt" of little helps and hindrances, "magnanimity."

"Magnanimity" in danger of death or wounds, "valor," "fortitude."

"Magnanimity" in the use of riches, "liberality."

"Pusillanimity" in the same, "wretchedness," "miserableness," or "parsimony," as it is liked or disliked.

"Love" of persons for society, "kindness."

"Love" of persons for pleasing the sense only, "natural lust."

"Love" of the same, acquired from rumination, that is imagination of pleasure past, "luxury."

"Love" of one singularly, with desire to be singularly beloved, "the passion of love." The same, with fear that the love is not mutual, "jealousy."

"Desire," by doing hurt to another, to make him condemn some fact of his own, "revengefulness."

"Desire" to know why and how, "curiosity," such as is in no living creature but "man," so that man is distinguished not only by his reason but also by this singular passion from other "animals," in whom the appetite of food, and other pleasures of sense, by predominance take away the care of knowing causes, which is a lust of the mind, that by a perseverance of delight in the continual and indefatigable generation of knowledge exceeds the short vehemence of any carnal pleasure.

"Fear" of power invisible, feigned by the mind or imagined from tales publicly allowed, "religion," not allowed, "superstition." And when the power imagined is truly such as we imagine, "true religion."

"Fear," without the apprehension of why or what, "panic terror," called so from the fables that make Pan the author of them, whereas in truth there is always in him that so fears, first some apprehension of the cause, though the rest run away by example, every one supposing his fellow to know why. And therefore this passion happens to none but in a throng or multitude of people.

"Joy," from apprehension of novelty "admiration," proper to man, because it excites the appetite of knowing the cause.

"Joy," arising from imagination of a man's own power and ability is that exultation of the mind which is called "glorying," which, if grounded upon the experience of his own former actions, is the same as "confidence," but if grounded on the flattery of others or only supposed by himself for delight in the consequences of it, is called "vain-glory," which name is properly given, because a well-grounded "confidence" begets attempt, whereas the supposing of power does not, and is therefore rightly called "vain."

"Grief" from opinion of want of power is called "dejection of mind."

The "vain-glory" which consists in the feigning or supposing of abilities in ourselves which we know are not is most incident to young men, and nourished by the histories or fictions of gallant persons, and is corrected oftentimes by age and employment.

"Sudden glory" is the passion which makes those "grimaces" called "laughter"; and is caused either by some sudden act of their own that pleases them, or by the apprehension of some deformed thing in another by comparison whereof they suddenly applaud themselves. And it is incident most to them that are conscious of the fewest abilities in themselves; who are forced to keep themselves in their own favor by observing the imperfections of other men. And therefore much laughter at the defects of others is a sign of pusillanimity. For of great minds one of the proper works is to help and free others from scorn and compare themselves only with the most able.

On the contrary, "sudden dejection" is the passion that causes "weeping," and is caused by such accidents as suddenly take away some vehement hope or some prop of their power; and they are most subject to it that rely principally on helps external, such as are women and children. Therefore some weep for the loss of friends, others for their unkindness, others for the sudden stop made to their thoughts of revenge by reconciliation. But in all cases, both laughter and weeping, are sudden motions, custom taking them both away. For no man laughs at old jests, or weeps for an old calamity.

"Grief" for the discovery of some defect of ability is "shame," or the passion that discovers itself in "blushing," and consists in the apprehension of something dishonorable; and in young men is a sign of the love of good reputation, and commendable: in old men it is a sign of the same; but, because it comes too late, not commendable.

The "contempt" of good reputation is called "impudence."

"Grief" for the calamity of another is "pity," and arises from the imagination that the like calamity may befall himself; and therefore is called also "compassion," and in the phrase of this present time a "fellow-feeling"; and therefore for calamity arriving from great wickedness the best men have the least pity; and for the same calamity those have least pity that think themselves least obnoxious to the same.

"Contempt," or little sense of the calamity of others, is that which men call "cruelty," proceeding from security of their own fortune. For, that any man should take pleasure in other men's great harms without other end of his own, I do not conceive it possible.

"Grief" for the success of a competitor in wealth, honor, or other good, if it be joined with endeavor to enforce our own abilities to equal or exceed him, is called "emulation"; but joined with endeavor to supplant or hinder a competitor, "envy."

When in the mind of man, appetites and aversions, hopes and fears, concerning one and the same thing, arise alternately, and divers good and evil consequences of the doing or omitting the thing propounded, come successively into our thoughts, so that sometimes we have an appetite to it, sometimes an aversion from it, sometimes hope to be able to do it, sometimes despair or fear to attempt it, the whole sum of desires, aversions, hopes, and fears, continued till the thing be either done or thought impossible, is that we call "deliberation."

Therefore of things past there is no "deliberation," because manifestly impossible to be changed; nor of things known to be impossible, or thought so, because men know, or think, such deliberation vain. But of things impossible which we think possible we may deliberate, not knowing it is in vain. And it is called "deliberation," because it is a putting an end to the "liberty" we had of doing or omitting according to our own appetite or aversion.

This alternate succession of appetites, aversions, hopes, and fears, is no less in other living creatures than in man; and therefore beasts also deliberate.

Every "deliberation" is then said to "end" when that whereof they deliberate is either done or thought impossible because till then we retain the liberty of doing or omitting according to our appetite or aversion.

In "deliberation," the last appetite, or aversion, immediately adhering to the action, or to the omission thereof, is that we call the "will," the act, not the faculty, of "willing." And beasts that have "deliberation" must necessarily also have "will." The definition of the "will" given commonly by the schools, that it is a "rational appetite," is not good. For if it were, then could there be no voluntary act against reason. For a "voluntary act" is that which proceeds from the "will" and no other. But if instead of a rational appetite we shall say an appetite resulting from a precedent deliberation, then the definition is the same that I have given here. Will, therefore, is the last appetite in deliberating. And, though we say in common discourse a man had a will once to do a thing, that nevertheless he forbore to do, yet that is properly but an inclination, which makes no action voluntary; because the action depends not of it, but of the last inclination or appetite. For if the intervenient appetites make any action voluntary, then by the same reason all intervenient aversions should make the same action involuntary; and so one and the same action should be both voluntary and involuntary.

By this it is manifest that not only actions that have their beginning from covetousness, ambition, lust, or other appetites to the thing propounded, but also those that have their beginning from aversion, or fear of those consequences that follow the omission, are "voluntary actions."

The forms of speech by which the passions are expressed are partly the same, and partly different from those by which we express our thoughts. And, first, generally all passions may be expressed "indicatively," as "I love," "I fear," "I joy," "I deliberate," "I will," "I command," but some of them have particular expressions by themselves, which nevertheless are not affirmations, unless it be when they serve to make other inferences besides that of the passion they proceed from. Deliberation is expressed "subjunctively," which is a speech proper to signify suppositions, with their consequences: as, "if this be done, then this will follow," and differs not from the language of reasoning, save that reasoning is in general words—but deliberation for the most part is of particulars. The language of desire, and aversion, is "imperative," as "do this," "forbear that," which when the party is obliged to do, or forbear, is "command"; otherwise "prayer," or else "counsel." The language of vain-glory, of indignation, pity and revengefulness, "optative," but of the desire to know there is a peculiar expression, called "interrogative," as "what is it?" "when shall it?" "how is it done?" and "why so?" Other language of the passions I find none; for cursing, swearing, reviling, and the like, do not signify as speech, but as the actions of a tongue accustomed.

These forms of speech, I say, are expressions, or voluntary significations of our passions—but certain signs they be not, because they may be used arbitrarily, whether they that use them have such passions or not. The best signs of passions present are either in the countenance, motions of the body, actions, and ends, or aims, which we otherwise know the man to have.

And because in deliberation the appetites and aversions are raised by foresight of the good and evil consequences, and sequels of the action whereof we deliberate, the good or evil effect thereof depends on the foresight of a long chain of consequences of which very seldom any man is able to see to the end. But for so far as a man sees, if the good in those consequences be greater than the evil, the whole chain is that which writers call "apparent" or "seeming good." And, contrarily, when the evil exceeds the good, the whole is "apparent" or "seeming evil," so that he who hath by experience, or reason, the greatest and surest prospect of consequences, deliberates best himself, and is able, when he will, to give the best counsel unto others.

"Continual success" in obtaining those things which a man from time to time desires, that is to say continual prospering, is that men call "felicity"; I mean the felicity of this life. For there is no such thing as perpetual tranquility of mind while we live here, because life itself is but motion, and can never be without desire, nor without fear, no more than without sense. What kind of felicity God hath ordained to them that devoutly honor Him a man shall no sooner know than enjoy, being joys that now are as incomprehensible as the word of schoolmen "beatifical vision" is unintelligible.

The form of speech whereby men signify their opinion of the goodness of anything is "praise." That whereby they signify the power and greatness of anything is "magnifying." And that whereby they signify the opinion they have of a man's felicity is by the Greeks called ⟨makarismos⟩ for which we have no name in our tongue. And thus much is sufficient for the present purpose, to have been said of the "passions."

*   *   *

CHAPTER 9. OF THE SEVERAL SUBJECTS OF KNOWLEDGE

There are of "knowledge" two kinds, whereof one is "knowledge of fact," the other "knowledge of the consequence of one affirmation to another." The former is nothing else but sense and memory, and is "absolute knowledge," as when we see a fact doing or remember it done; and this is the knowledge required in a witness. The latter is called "science," and is "conditional," as when we know that "if the figure shown be a circle, then any straight line through the center shall divide it into two equal parts." And this is the knowledge required in a philosopher, that is to say of him that pretends to reasoning.

The register of "knowledge of fact" is called "history," whereof there be two sorts: one called "natural history," which is the history of such facts or effects of Nature as have no dependence on man's "will," such as are the histories of "metals," "plants," "animals," "regions," and the like. The other is "civil history," which is the history of the voluntary actions of men in commonwealths.

The registers of science are such "books," as contain the "demonstrations" of consequences of one affirmation to another, and are commonly called "books of philosophy," whereof the sorts are many, according to the diversity of the matter, and may be divided in such manner as I have divided them in the . . . table [see following page].

*   *   *

CHAPTER 12. OF RELIGION

Seeing there are no signs nor fruit of "religion" but in man only, there is no cause to doubt but that the seed of "religion" is also only in man—and consists in some peculiar quality or at least in some eminent degree thereof not to be found in other living creatures.

And, first, it is peculiar to the nature of man to be inquisitive into the causes of the events they see, some more, some less; but all men so much as to be curious in the search of the causes of their own good and evil fortune.

Secondly, upon the sight of anything that hath a beginning to think also it had a cause which determined the same to begin, then when it did, rather than sooner or later.

Thirdly, whereas there is no other felicity of beasts but the enjoying of their quotidian food, ease, and lusts, as having little or no foresight of the time to come, for want of observation and memory of the order, consequence, and dependence of the things they see, man observes how one event hath been produced by another, and remembers in them antecedence and consequence; and, when he cannot assure himself of the true causes of things (for the causes of good and evil fortune for the most part are invisible), he supposes causes of them, either such as his own fancy suggests, or trusts the authority of other men, such as he thinks to be his friends and wiser than himself.

The two first make anxiety. For, being assured that there be causes of all things that have arrived hitherto or shall arrive hereafter, it is impossible for a man, who continually endeavors to secure himself against the evil he fears and procure the good he desires, not to be in a perpetual solicitude of the time to come; so that every man, especially those that are over-provident, are in a state like to that of Prometheus. For as Prometheus, which interpreted is "the prudent man," was bound to the hill Caucasus, a place of large prospect, where an eagle feeding on his liver devoured in the day as much as was repaired in the night, so that man, which looks too far before him in the care of

SCIENCE, that is, Knowledge of Consequences; which is called also PHILOSOPHY

- Consequences from the Accidents of Bodies Natural; which is called NATURAL PHILOSOPHY.
  - Consequences from the Accidents common to all Bodies Natural; which are *Quantity*, and *Motion*.
    - Consequences from Quantity, and Motion *indeterminate*; which being the Principles, or first foundation of Philosophy, is called *Philosophia Prima*. → PHILOSOPHIA PRIMA.
    - Consequences from Quantity, and Motion *determined*.
      - Consequences from Quantity, and Motion determined — *Mathematics*,
        - By Figure, ... → GEOMETRY.
        - By Number, .. → ARITHMETIC.
      - Consequences from the Motion, and Quantity of Bodies in *special*.
        - Consequences from the Motion, and Quantity of the great parts of the World, as the *Earth* and *Stars* — *Cosmography*
          - → ASTRONOMY.
          - → GEOGRAPHY.
        - Consequences from the Motion of Special kinds, and Figures of Body,
          - *Mechanics*, Doctrine of *Weight*,
            - Science of ENGINEERS.
            - ARCHITECTURE.
            - NAVIGATION.
          - → METEOROLOGY.
  - PHYSICS, or Consequences from *Qualities*.
    - Consequences from the Qualities of Bodies *Transient*, such as sometimes appear, sometimes vanish, → METEOROLOGY.
    - Consequences from the Qualities of Bodies *Permanent*.
      - Consequences from the Qualities of the *Stars*.
        - Consequences from the *Light* of the Stars. Out of this, and the Motion of the Sun, is made the Science of ...... → SCIOGRAPHY.
        - Consequences from the *Influence* of the Stars, ... → ASTROLOGY.
      - Consequences of the Qualities from *Liquid* Bodies that fill the space between the Stars; such as are the *Air*, or Substance etherial.
      - Consequences from the Qualities of Bodies *Terrestrial*.
        - Consequences from the parts of the Earth, that are *without Sense*.
          - Consequences from the Qualities of *Minerals*, as *Stones, Metals*, & etc.
          - Consequences from the Qualities of *Vegetables*.
        - Consequences from the Qualities of *Animals*.
          - Consequences from the Qualities of *Animals in general*.
            - Consequences from *Vision*. .. → OPTICS.
            - Consequences from *Sounds*, .. → MUSIC.
            - Consequences from the rest of the *Senses*.
          - Consequences from the Qualities of *Men in special*.
            - Consequences from the *Passions* of Men. .... → ETHICS.
            - Consequences from *Speech*,
              - In *Magnifying, Vilifying*, & etc. → POETRY.
              - In *Persuading*, → RHETORIC.
              - In *Reasoning*, → LOGIC.
              - In *Contracting*, → The *Science* of *Just and Unjust*

- Consequences from the Accidents of Politic Bodies; which is called POLITICS, and CIVIL PHILOSOPHY.
  1. Of Consequences from the *Institution* of COMMONWEALTHS, to the *Rights*, and *Duties* of the *Body Politic*, or *Soveraign*.
  2. Of Consequences from the same to the *Duty*, and *Right* of the *Subjects*.

future time, hath his heart all the day long gnawed on by fear of death, poverty, or other calamity, and has no repose nor pause of his anxiety but in sleep.

This perpetual fear, always accompanying mankind in the ignorance of causes, as it were in the dark, must needs have for object something. And therefore, when there is nothing to be seen, there is nothing to accuse, either of their good or evil fortune, but some "power" or agent "invisible" in which sense perhaps it was that some of the old poets said that the gods were at first created by human fear; which spoken of the gods, that is to say of the many gods of the Gentiles, is very true. But the acknowledging of one God, eternal, infinite, and omnipotent, may more easily be derived, from the desire men have to know the causes of natural bodies and their several virtues and operations, than from the fear of what was to befall them in time to come. For he that from any effect he sees come to pass should reason to the next and immediate cause thereof, and from thence to the cause of that cause, and plunge himself profoundly in the pursuit of causes, shall at last come to this, that there must be, as even the heathen philosophers confessed, one first mover, that is, a first and an eternal cause of all things, which is that which men mean by the name of God, and all this without thought of their fortune; the solicitude whereof both inclines to fear and hinders them from the search of the causes of other things, and thereby gives occasion of feigning of as many gods as there be men that feign them.

And, for the matter or substance of the invisible agents so fancied, they could not by natural cogitation fall upon any other conceit, but that it was the same with that of the soul of man; and that the soul of man was of the same substance with that which appears in a dream to one that sleeps or in a looking-glass to one that is awake, which, men not knowing that such apparitions are nothing else but creatures of the fancy, think to be real and external substances, and therefore call them ghosts; as the Latins called them *imagines* and *umbræ,* and thought them spirits, that is thin aerial bodies, and those invisible agents which they feared, to be like them, save that they appear and vanish when they please. But the opinion that such spirits were incorporeal, or immaterial, could never enter into the mind of any man by nature, because, though men may put together words of contradictory signification, as "spirit" and "incorporeal," yet they can never have the imagination of anything answering to them; and therefore men that by their own meditation arrive to the acknowledgment of one infinite, omnipotent, and eternal God chose rather to confess He is incomprehensible and above their understanding than to define His nature by "spirit incorporeal," and then confess their definition to be unintelligible; or, if they give Him such a title, it is not "dogmatically" with intention to make the divine nature understood, but "piously," to honor Him with attributes of significations as remote as they can from the grossness of bodies visible.

Then for the way by which they think these invisible agents wrought their effects, that is to say, what immediate causes they used in bringing things to pass, men that know not what it is that we call "causing," that is almost all men, have no other rule to guess by but by observing and remembering what they have seen to precede the like effect at some other time or times before, without seeing between the antecedent and subsequent event any dependence or connection at all; and therefore from the like things past they expect the like things to come, and hope for good or evil luck, superstitiously, from things that have no part at all in the causing of it: as the Athenians did for their war at Lepanto, demand another Phormio; the Pompeian faction for their war in Africa, another Scipio, and others have done in divers other occasions since. In like manner they attribute their fortune to a stander-by, to a lucky or unlucky place, to words spoken, especially if the name God be amongst them, as charming and conjuring, the liturgy of witches; inasmuch as to believe they have power to turn a stone into bread, bread into a man, or anything into anything.

Thirdly, for the worship which naturally men exhibit to powers invisible, it can be no other but such expressions of their reverence, as they would use towards men; gifts, petitions, thanks, submission of body, considerate addresses, sober behavior, premeditated words, swearing, that is assuring one another of their promises by invoking them. Beyond that, reason suggests nothing, but leaves them either to rest there, or, for further ceremonies, to rely on those they believe to be wiser than themselves.

Lastly, concerning how these invisible powers declare to men the things which shall hereafter come to pass, especially concerning their good or evil fortune in general or good or ill success in any particular undertaking, men are naturally at a stand, save that, using to conjecture of the time to come by the time past, they are very apt not only to take casual things, after one or two encounters, for prognostics of the like encounter ever after, but also to believe the like prognostics from other men of whom they have once conceived a good opinion.

And, in these four things, opinion of ghosts, ignorance of second causes, devotion towards what men fear, and taking of things casual for prognostics, consists the natural seed of "religion," which, by reason of the different fancies, judgments, and passions of several men, hath grown up into ceremonies so different that those which are used by one man are for the most part ridiculous to another.

For these seeds have received culture from two sorts of men. One sort have been they that have nourished and ordered them according to their own invention. The other have done it by God's commandment and direction; but both sorts have done it with a purpose to make those men that relied on them the more apt to obedience, laws, peace, charity and civil society. So that the religion of the former sort is a part of human politics, and teaches part of the duty which earthly kings require of their subjects. And the religion of the latter sort is divine politics, and contains precepts to those that have yielded themselves subjects in the kingdom of God. Of the former sort were all the founders of commonwealths and the lawgivers of the Gentiles; of the latter sort, were Abraham, Moses, and our blessed Savior, by whom have been derived unto us the laws of the kingdom of God.

*   *   *

CHAPTER 13. OF THE NATURAL CONDITION OF MANKIND AS CONCERNING THEIR FELICITY AND MISERY

Nature hath made men so equal in the faculties of the body and mind, as that, though there be found one man sometimes manifestly stronger in body or of quicker mind than another, yet when all is reckoned together the difference between man and man is not so considerable as that one man can thereupon claim to himself any benefit to which another may not pretend as well as he. For, as to the strength of body, the weakest has strength enough to kill the strongest, either by secret machination or by confederacy with others that are in the same danger with himself.

And, as to the faculties of the mind, setting aside the arts grounded upon words and especially that skill of proceeding upon general and infallible rules called science, which very few have and but in few things, as being not a native faculty born with us, nor attained, as prudence, while we look after somewhat else, I find yet a greater equality amongst men than that of strength. For prudence is but experience, which equal time equally bestows on all men in those things they equally apply themselves unto. That which may perhaps make such equality incredible is but a vain conceit of one's own wisdom, which almost all men think they have in a greater degree than the vulgar, that is, than all men but themselves, and a few others whom by fame or for concurring with themselves they approve. For such is the nature of men that, howsoever they may acknowledge many others to be more witty or more eloquent or more learned, yet they will hardly believe there be many so wise as themselves, for they see their own wit at hand and other men's at a distance. But this proves rather that men are in that point equal than unequal. For there is not ordinarily a greater sign of the equal distribution of anything than that every man is contented with his share.

From this equality of ability arises equality of hope in the attaining of our ends. And therefore, if any two men desire the same thing which nevertheless they cannot both enjoy, they become enemies—and, in the way to their end, which is principally their own conservation and sometimes their delectation only, endeavor to destroy or subdue one another. And from hence it comes to pass that, where an invader hath no more to fear than another man's single power, if one plant, sow, build, or possess, a convenient seat others may probably be expected to come prepared with forces united to dispossess and deprive him not only of the fruit of his labor but also of his life or liberty. And the invader again is in the like danger of another.

And from this diffidence of one another there is no way for any man to secure himself so reasonable as anticipation, that is, by force or wiles to master the persons of all men he can so long till he see no other power great enough to endanger him; and this is no more than his own conservation requires and is generally allowed. Also, because there be some that, taking pleasure in contemplating their own power in the acts of conquest, which they pursue farther than their security requires, if others, that otherwise would be glad to be at ease within the modest bounds, should not by invasion increase their power, they would not be able for a long time, by standing only on their defence, to subsist. And by consequence, such augmentation of dominion over men being necessary to a man's conservation, it ought to be allowed him.

Again, men have no pleasure, but on the contrary a great deal of grief, in keeping company where there is no power able to overawe them all. For every man looks that his companion should value him at the same rate he sets upon himself, and, upon all signs of contempt or undervaluing, naturally endeavors as far as he dares (which amongst them that have no common power to keep them in quiet, is far enough to make them destroy each other) to extort a greater value from his condemners by damage, and from others by the example.

So that in the nature of man we find three principal causes of quarrel. First, competition; secondly, diffidence; thirdly, glory.

The first makes man invade for gain; the second, for safety; and the third, for reputation. The first use violence, to make themselves masters of other men's persons, wives, children, and cattle; the second, to defend them; the third, for trifles, as a word, a smile, a different opinion, and any other sign of undervalue, either direct in their persons or by reflection in their kindred, their friends, their nation, their profession, or their name.

Hereby it is manifest that, during the time men live without a common power to keep them all in awe, they are in that condition which is called war, and such a war as is of every man against every man. For "war" consists not in battle only or the act of fighting, but in a tract of time wherein the will to contend by battle is sufficiently known, and therefore the notion of "time" is to be considered in the nature of war, as it is in the nature of weather. For as the nature of foul weather lies not in a shower or two of rain but in an inclination thereto of many days together, so the nature of war consists not in actual fighting but in the known disposition thereto during all the time there is no assurance to the contrary. All other time is "peace."

Whatsoever therefore is consequent to a time of war where every man is enemy to every man, the same is consequent to the time wherein men live without other security than what their own strength and their own invention shall furnish them withal. In such condition there is no place for industry, because the fruit thereof is uncertain, and consequently no culture of the earth, no navigation nor use of the commodities that may be imported by sea, no commodious building, no instruments of moving and removing such things as require much force, no knowledge of the face of the earth; no account of time, no arts, no letters, no society, and, which is worst of all, continual fear and danger of violent death, and the life of man solitary, poor, nasty, brutish, and short.

It may seem strange to some man that has not well weighed these things that Nature should thus dissociate and render men apt to invade and destroy one another; and he may therefore, not trusting to this inference made from the passions, desire perhaps to have the same confirmed by experience. Let him therefore consider with himself, when taking a journey, he arms himself and seeks to go well accompanied; when going to sleep, he locks his doors; when even in his house, he locks his chests; and this when he knows there be laws and public officers armed to revenge all injuries shall be done him; what opinion he has of his fellow-subjects, when he rides armed—of his fellow-citizens, when he locks his doors; and of his children and servants, when he locks his chests. Does he not there as much accuse mankind by his actions as I do by my words? But neither of us accuse man's nature in it. The desires and other passions of man are in themselves no sin. No more are the actions that proceed from those passions, till they know a law that forbids them; which, till laws be made, they cannot know, nor can any law be made till they have agreed upon the person that shall make it.

It may peradventure be thought there was never such a time nor condition of war as this; and I believe it was never generally so over all the world, but there are many places where they live so now. For the savage people in many places of America, except the government of small families the concord whereof depends on natural lust, have no government at all, and live at this day in that brutish manner as I said before. Howsoever, it may be perceived what manner of life there would be where there were no common power to fear, by the manner of life which men that have formerly lived under a peaceful government use to degenerate into, in a civil war. But, though there had never been any time wherein particular men were in a condition of war one against another, yet in all times kings and persons of sovereign authority, because of their independence, are in continual jealousies and in the state and posture of gladiators, having their weapons pointing, and their eyes fixed on one another, that is, their forts, garrisons, and guns, upon the frontiers of their kingdoms, and continual spies upon their neighbors: which is a posture of war. But because they uphold thereby the industry of their subjects, there does not follow from it that misery which accompanies the liberty of particular men.

To this war of every man against every man this also is consequent, that nothing can be unjust. The notions of right and wrong, justice and injustice, have there no place. Where there is no common power, there is no law; where no law, no injustice. Force and fraud are in war the two cardinal virtues. Justice and injustice are none of the faculties neither of the body nor mind. If they were, they might be in a man that were alone in the world, as well as his senses and passions. They are qualities that relate to men in society, not in solitude. It is consequent also to the same condition that there be no propriety, no dominion, no "mine" and "thine" distinct, but only that to be every man's that he can get, and for so long as he can keep it. And thus much for the ill condition which man by mere nature is actually placed in, though with a possibility to come out of it, consisting partly in the passions, partly in his reason.

The passions that incline men to peace are fear of death, desire of such things as are necessary to commodious living, and a hope by their industry to obtain them. And reason suggests convenient articles of peace, upon which men may be drawn to agreement. These articles are they which otherwise are called the Laws of Nature, whereof I shall speak more particularly in the two following chapters.

CHAPTER 14. OF THE FIRST AND SECOND NATURAL LAWS, AND OF CONTRACTS

"The right of Nature," which writers commonly call *jus naturale,* is the liberty each man hath to use his own power as he will himself for the preservation of his own nature, that is to say, of his own life; and consequently of doing anything which in his own judgment and reason he shall conceive to be the aptest means thereunto.

By "liberty" is understood, according to the proper signification of the word, the absence of external impediments which impediments may oft take away part of a man's power to do what he would, but cannot hinder him from using the power left him according as his judgment and reason shall dictate to him.

A "law of Nature," *lex naturalis,* is a precept or general rule found out by reason by which a man is forbidden to do that which is destructive of his life or takes away the means of preserving the same, and to omit that by which he thinks it may be best preserved. For, though they that speak of this subject use to confound *jus* and *lex,* "right" and "law," yet they ought to be distinguished; because "right" consists in liberty to do or to forbear, whereas "law" determines and binds to one of them: so that law and right differ as much as obligation and liberty; which in one and the same matter are inconsistent.

And because the condition of man, as hath been declared in the precedent chapter, is a condition of war of every one against every one, in which case every one is governed by his own reason, and there is nothing he can make use of that may not be a help unto him in preserving his life against his enemies, it follows that in such a condition every man has a right to everything, even to one another's body. And therefore, as long as this natural right of every man to everything endures, there can be no security to any man, how strong or wise soever he be, of living out the time which Nature ordinarily allows men to live. And consequently it is a precept or general rule of reason "that every man ought to endeavor peace as far as he has hope of obtaining it, and, when he cannot obtain it, that he may seek and use all helps and advantages of war." The first branch of which rule contains the first and fundamental law of Nature, which is, "to seek peace, and follow it." The second, the sum of the right of Nature, which is, "by all means we can, to defend ourselves."

From this fundamental law of Nature, by which men are commanded to endeavor peace, is derived this second law, "that a man be willing, when others are so too, as far-forth as for peace and defence of himself he shall think it necessary, to lay down this right to all things, and be contented with so much liberty against other men as he would allow other men against himself." For as long as every man holds this right of doing anything he likes, so long are all men in the condition of war. But if other men will not lay down their right as well as he, then there is no reason for any one to divest himself of his: for that were to expose himself to prey, which no man is bound to, rather than to dispose himself to peace. This is that law of the Gospel: "whatsoever you require that others should do to you, that do ye to them." And that law of all men, *quod tibi fieri non vis, alteri ne feceris.*

To "lay down" a man's "right" to anything is to "divest" himself of the "liberty," of hindering another of the benefit of his own right to the same. For he that renounces or passes away his right gives not to any other man a right which he had not before, because there is nothing to which every man had not right by Nature; but only stands out of his way that he may enjoy his own original right without hindrance from him, not without hindrance from another. So that the effect which redounds to one man, by another man's defect of right, is but so much diminution of impediments to the use of his own right original.

Right is laid aside either by simply renouncing it, or by transferring it to another. By "simply renouncing" when he cares not to whom the benefit thereof redounds. By "transferring," when he intends the benefit thereof to some certain person or persons. And, when a man hath in either manner abandoned or granted away his right, then is he said to be "obliged" or "bound" not to hinder those to whom such right is granted or abandoned from the benefit of it; and that he "ought," and it is his "duty," not to make void that voluntary act of his own; and that such hindrance is "injustice" and "injury" as being *sine jure,* the right being before renounced or transferred. So that "injury" or "injustice," in the controversies of the world, is somewhat like to that which in the disputations of scholars is called "absurdity." For, as it is there called an absurdity to contradict what one maintained in the beginning, so in the world it is called injustice and injury voluntarily to undo that from the beginning he had voluntarily done. The way by which a man either simply renounces or transfers his right is a declaration or signification, by some voluntary and sufficient sign or signs, that he doth so renounce or transfer, or hath so renounced or transferred, the same, to him that accepts it. And these signs are either words only or actions only, or, as it happens most often, both words and actions. And the same are the "bonds" by which men are bound and obliged: bonds that have their strength not from their own nature, for nothing is more easily broken than a man's word, but from fear of some evil consequence upon the rupture.

Whensoever a man transfers his right or renounces it, it is either in consideration of some right reciprocally transferred to himself, or for some other good he hopes for thereby. For it is a voluntary act: and of the voluntary acts of every man the object is some good "to himself." And therefore there be some rights which no man can be understood by any words or other signs to have abandoned or transferred. As first a man cannot lay down the right of resisting them that assault him by force to take away his life, because he cannot be understood to aim thereby at any good to himself. The same may be said of wounds, and chains, and imprisonment, both because there is no benefit consequent to such patience, as there is to the patience of suffering another to be wounded or imprisoned, as also because a man cannot tell when he sees men proceed against him by violence whether they intend his death or not. And lastly the motive and end for which this renouncing and transferring of right is introduced is nothing else but the security of a man's person in his life and in the means of so preserving life as not to be weary of it. And therefore if a man by words or other signs seem to despoil himself of the end for which those signs were intended, he is not to be understood as if he meant it or that it was his will, but that he was ignorant of how such words and actions were to be interpreted.

The mutual transferring of right is that which men call "contract."

* * *

CHAPTER 15. OTHER LAWS OF NATURE

From that law of Nature by which we are obliged to transfer to another such rights as, being retained, hinder the peace of mankind, there follows a third, which is this, "that men perform their covenants made"; without which covenants are in vain, and but empty words: and the right of all men to all things remaining, we are still in the condition of war.

And in this law of Nature consists the fountain and original of "justice." For, where no covenant hath preceded, there hath no right been transferred, and every man hath right to everything; and consequently, no action can be unjust. But when a covenant is made, then to break it is "unjust"; and the definition of "injustice" is no other than "the not performance of covenant." And whatsoever is not unjust is "just."

But because covenants of mutual trust, where there is a fear of not performance on either part, as hath been said in the former chapter, are invalid, though the original of justice be the making of covenants, yet injustice actually there can be none, till the cause of such fear be taken away, which, while men are in the natural condition of war, cannot be done. Therefore, before the names of just and unjust can have place, there must be some coercive power to compel men equally to the performance of their covenants, by the terror of some punishment greater than the benefit they expect by the breach of their covenant; and to make good that propriety which by mutual contract men acquire in recompense of the universal right they abandon; and such power there is none before the erection of a commonwealth. And this is also to be gathered out of the ordinary definition of justice in the schools; for they say that "justice is the constant will of giving to every man his own." And therefore where there is no "own" there is no propriety, there is no injustice; and where there is no coercive power erected, that is, where there is no commonwealth, there is no propriety, all men having right to all things: therefore, where there is no commonwealth, there nothing is unjust. So that the nature of justice consists in keeping of valid covenants; but the validity of covenants begins not with the constitution of a civil power sufficient to compel men to keep them; and then it is also that propriety begins.

The fool hath said in his heart there is no such thing as justice, and sometimes also with his tongue, seriously alleging that every man's conservation and contentment, being committed to his own care, there could be no reason why every man might not do what he thought conduced thereunto; and therefore also to make or not make, keep or not keep, covenants was not against reason when it conduced to one's benefit. He does not therein deny that there be covenants, and that they are sometimes broken, sometimes kept, and that such breach of them may be called injustice, and the observance of them justice; but he questions whether injustice taking away the fear of God, for the same fool hath said in his heart there is no God, may not sometimes stand with that reason which dictates to every man his own good; and particularly then when it conduces to such a benefit as shall put a man in a condition to neglect not only the dispraise and revilings, but also the power, of other men. The kingdom of God is gotten by violence; but what if it could be gotten by unjust violence? Were it against reason so to get it, when it is impossible to receive hurt by it? And, if it be not against reason, it is not against justice, or else justice is not to be approved for good. From such reasoning as this, successful wickedness hath obtained the name of virtue, and some that in all other things have disallowed the violation of faith, yet have allowed it when it is for the getting of a kingdom. And the heathen that believed that Saturn was deposed by his son Jupiter believed nevertheless the same Jupiter to be the avenger of injustice somewhat like to a piece of law in Coke's *Commentaries on Littleton,* where he says, if the right heir of the crown be attainted of treason, yet the crown shall descend to him, and *eo instante* the attainder be void; from which instances a man will be very prone to infer that, when the heir apparent of a kingdom shall kill him that is in possession, though his father, you may call it injustice or by what other name you will, yet it can never be against reason seeing all the voluntary actions of men tend to the benefit of themselves; and those actions are most reasonable that conduce most to their ends. This specious reasoning is nevertheless false.

For the question is not of promises mutual, where there is no security of performance on either side, as when there is no civil power erected over the parties promising, for such promises are no covenants, but either where one of the parties has performed already, or where there is a power to make him perform, there is the question whether it be against reason, that is against the benefit of the other to perform or not. And I say it is not against reason. For the manifestation whereof we are to consider, first that when a man doth a thing which notwithstanding anything can be foreseen and reckoned on tends to his own destruction, howsoever some accident which he could not expect, arriving may turn it to his benefit, yet such events do not make it reasonably or wisely done. Secondly, that, in a condition of war, wherein every man to every man, for want of a common power to keep them all in awe, is an enemy, there is no man who can hope by his own strength or wit to defend himself from destruction without the help of confederates; where every one expects the same defence by the confederation that any one else does; and therefore he which declares he thinks it reason to deceive those that help him can in reason expect no other means of safety than what can be had from his own single power. He therefore that breaks his covenant, and consequently declares that he thinks he may with reason do so, cannot be received into any society that unite themselves for peace and defence but by the error of them that receive him; nor, when he is received, be retained in it without seeing the danger of their error; which errors a man cannot reasonably reckon upon as the means of his security; and therefore, if he be left or cast out of society, he perishes; and if he live in society, it is by the errors of other men which he could not foresee nor reckon upon, and consequently against the reason of his preservation; and so, as all men that contribute not to his destruction, forbear him only out of ignorance of what is good for themselves.

As for the instance of gaining the secure and perpetual felicity of heaven by any way, it is frivolous; there being but one way imaginable; and that is not breaking, but keeping of covenant.

And, for the other instance of attaining sovereignty by rebellion, it is manifest that, though the event follow, yet, because it cannot reasonably be expected, but rather the contrary, and because by gaining it so, others are taught to gain the same in like manner, the attempt thereof is against reason. Justice therefore, that is to say keeping of covenant, is a rule of reason by which we are forbidden to do anything destructive to our life; and consequently a law of Nature.

There be some that proceed further, and will not have the law of Nature to be those rules which conduce to the preservation of man's life on earth, but to the attaining of an eternal felicity after death; to which they think the breach of covenant may conduce; and consequently be just and reasonable; such are they that think it a work of merit to kill or depose or rebel against the sovereign power constituted over them by their own consent. But, because there is no natural knowledge of man's estate after death, much less of the reward that is then to be given to breach of faith, but only a belief grounded upon other men's saying that they know it supernaturally, or that they know those that knew them, that knew others, that knew it supernaturally; breach of faith cannot be called a precept of reason or nature.

Others that allow for a law of Nature the keeping of faith do nevertheless make exception of certain persons as heretics and such as use not to perform their covenant to others; and this also is against reason. For if any fault of a man be sufficient to discharge our covenant made, the same ought in reason to have been sufficient to have hindered the making of it.

The names of just and unjust, when they are attributed to men, signify one thing; and when they are attributed to actions, another. When they are attributed to men they signify conformity or inconformity of manners to reason. But, when they are attributed to actions, they signify the conformity or inconformity to reason, not of manners or manner of life but of particular actions. A just man, therefore, is he that takes all the care he can that his actions may be all just, and an unjust man is he that neglects it. And such men are more often in our language styled by the names of righteous and unrighteous than just and unjust, though the meaning be the same. Therefore a righteous man does not lose that title by one or a few unjust actions that proceed from sudden passion or mistake of things or persons; nor does an unrighteous man lose his character for such actions as he does, or forbears to do, for fear, because his will is not framed by the justice but by the apparent benefit of what he is to do. That which gives to human actions the relish of justice is a certain nobleness or gallantness of courage, rarely found, by which a man scorns to be beholden for the contentment of his life to fraud or breach of promise. This justice of the manners is that which is meant where justice is called a virtue, and injustice a vice.

But the justice of actions denominates men not just, "guiltless"; and the injustice of the same, which is also called injury, gives them but the name of "guilty."

Again, the injustice of manners is the disposition or aptitude to do injury, and is injustice before it proceeds to act, and without supposing any individual person injured. But the injustice of an action, that is to say injury, supposes an individual person injured, namely him to whom the covenant was made; and therefore many times the injury is received by one man when the damage redounds to another. As when the master commands his servant to give money to a stranger: if it be not done, the injury is done to the master, whom he had before covenanted to obey; but the damage redounds to the stranger, to whom he had no obligation, and therefore could not injure him. And so also in commonwealths. Private men may remit to one another their debts, but not robberies or other violences whereby they are endamaged, because the detaining of debt is an injury to themselves, but robbery and violence are injuries to the person of the commonwealth.

Whatsoever is done to a man conformable to his own will signified to the doer is no injury to him. For, if he that does it hath not passed away his original right to do what he please by some antecedent covenant, there is no breach of covenant, and therefore no injury done him. And if he have, then his will to have it done being signified is a release of that covenant, and so again there is no injury done him.

Justice of action is by writers divided into "commutative" and "distributive"; and the former they say consists in proportion arithmetical, the latter in proportion geometrical. Commutative, therefore, they place in the equality of value of the things contracted for—and distributive, in the distribution of equal benefit to men of equal merit. As if it were injustice to sell dearer than we buy, or to give more to a man than he merits. The value of all things contracted for is measured by the appetite of the contractors; and therefore the just value is that which they be contented to give. And merit, besides that which is by covenant, where the performance on one part merits the performance of the other part, and falls under justice commutative not distributive, is not due by justice, but is rewarded of grace only. And therefore this distinction, in the sense wherein it uses to be expounded, is not right. To speak properly, commutative justice is the justice of a contractor; that is, a performance of covenant in buying and selling, hiring and letting to hire, lending and borrowing, exchanging, bartering, and other acts of contract.

And distributive justice, the justice of an arbitrator; that is to say, the act of defining what is just. Wherein, being trusted by them that make him arbitrator, if he perform his trust he is said to distribute to every man his own; and this is indeed just distribution, and may be called, though improperly, distributive justice, but more properly equity, which also is a law of Nature, as shall be shown in due place.

As justice depends on antecedent covenant, so does "gratitude" depend on antecedent grace, that is to say, antecedent free gift; and is the fourth law of Nature; which may be conceived in this form, "that a man, which receives benefit from another of mere grace, endeavor that he which gives it have no reasonable cause to repent him of his good will." For no man gives but with intention of good to himself; because gift is voluntary; and of all voluntary acts the object is to every man his own good, of which, if men see they shall be frustrated, there will be no beginning of benevolence, or trust, nor consequently of mutual help, nor of reconciliation of one man to another; and therefore they are to remain still in the condition of "war," which is contrary to the first and fundamental law of Nature, which commands men to "seek peace." The breach of this law is called "ingratitude," and hath the same relation to grace that injustice hath to obligation by covenant.

A fifth law of Nature, is "complaisance," that is to say, "that every man strive to accommodate himself to the rest." For the understanding whereof, we may consider that there is in men's aptness to society, a diversity of nature, rising from their diversity of affections, not unlike to that we see in stones brought together for building of an edifice. For as that stone which by the asperity and irregularity of figure takes more room from others than itself fills, and for the hardness cannot be easily made plain, and thereby hinders the building, is by the builders cast away as unprofitable and troublesome, so also a man that by asperity of nature will strive to retain those things which to himself are superfluous and to others necessary, and for the stubbornness of his passions cannot be corrected, is to be left or cast out of society as cumbersome thereunto. For seeing every man, not only by right but also by necessity of nature, is supposed to endeavor all he can to obtain that which is necessary for his conversation, he that shall oppose himself against it for things superfluous is guilty of the war that thereupon is to follow; and therefore doth that which is contrary to the fundamental law of Nature, which commands "to seek peace." The observers of this law may be called "sociable"—the Latins call them *commodi;* the contrary, "stubborn," "insociable," "froward," "intractable."

A sixth law of Nature is this, "that, upon caution of the future time, a man ought to pardon the offences past of them that, repenting, desire it." For "pardon" is nothing but granting of peace, which, though granted to them that persevere in their hostility, be not peace but fear; yet not granted to them that give caution of the future time is sign of an aversion to peace, and therefore contrary to the law of Nature.

A seventh is, "that in revenges," that is, retribution of evil for evil, "men look not at the greatness of the evil past but the greatness of the good to follow." Whereby we are forbidden to inflict punishment with any other design than for correction of the offender or direction of others. For this law is consequent to the next before it, that commands pardon, upon security of the future time. Besides, revenge, without respect to the example and profit to come, is a triumph or glorying in the hurt of another tending to no end;

for the end is always somewhat to come; and glorying to no end is vain-glory and contrary to reason, and to hurt without reason tends to the introduction of war, which is against the law of Nature, and is commonly by the name of "cruelty."

*   *   *

PART II—OF COMMONWEALTH

CHAPTER 17. OF THE CAUSES, GENERATION, AND DEFINITION OF A COMMONWEALTH

The final cause, end, or design of men, who naturally love liberty, and dominion over others, in the introduction of that restraint upon themselves, in which we see them live in commonwealths, is the foresight of their own preservation, and of a more contented life thereby; that is to say, of getting themselves out from that miserable condition of war, which is necessarily consequent, as hath been shown in Chapter XIII, to the natural passions of men, when there is no visible power to keep them in awe, and tie them by fear of punishment to the performance of their covenants, and observation of those laws of nature set down in the fourteenth and fifteenth chapters.

For the laws of nature, as "justice," "equity," "modesty," "mercy," and, in sum, "doing to others, as we would be done to," of themselves, without the terror of some power, to cause them to be observed, are contrary to our natural passions, that carry us to partiality, pride, revenge, and the like. And covenants, without the sword, are but words, and of no strength to secure a man at all. Therefore notwithstanding the laws of nature (which every one hath then kept, when he has the will to keep them, when he can do it safely) if there be no power erected, or not great enough for our security; every man will, and may lawfully rely on his own strength and art, for caution against all other men. And in all places, where men have lived by small families, to rob and spoil one another, has been a trade, and so far from being reputed against the law of nature, that the greater spoils they gained, the greater was their honor; and men observed no other laws therein, but the laws of honor; that is, to abstain from cruelty, leaving to men their lives, and instruments of husbandry. And as small families did then; so now do cities and kingdoms which are but greater families, for their own security, enlarge their dominions, upon all pretenses of danger, and fear of invasion, or assistance that may be given to invaders, and endeavor as much as they can, to subdue, or weaken their neighbors, by open force, and secret arts, for want of other caution, justly; and are remembered for it in after ages with honor.

Nor is it the joining together of a small number of men, that gives them this security; because in small numbers, small additions on the one side or the other, make the advantage of strength so great, as is sufficient to carry the victory; and therefore gives encouragement to an invasion. The multitude sufficient to confide in for our security, is not determined by any certain number, but by comparison with the enemy we fear; and is then sufficient, when the odds of the enemy is not of so visible and conspicuous moment, to determine the event of war, as to move him to attempt.

And be there never so great a multitude; yet if their actions be directed according to their particular judgments, and particular appetites, they can expect thereby no de-

The execution of King Charles I of England, 1649, engraving by Wenceslaus Holler (1607–1677). Hobbes considered this event a horrible example of what happens when the sovereign does not have absolute power. (*Library of Congress*)

fence, nor protection, neither against a common enemy, nor against the injuries of one another. For being distracted in opinions concerning the best use and application of their strength, they do not help but hinder one another; and reduce their strength by mutual opposition to nothing: whereby they are easily, not only subdued by a very few that agree together; but also when there is no common enemy, they make war upon each other, for their particular interests. For if we could suppose a great multitude of men to consent in the observation of justice, and other laws of nature, without a common power to keep them all in awe; we might as well suppose all mankind to do the same; and then there neither would be, nor need to be any civil government, or commonwealth at all; because there would be peace without subjection.

Nor is it enough for the security, which men desire should last all the time of their life, that they be governed, and directed by one judgment, for a limited time; as in one battle, or one war. For though they obtain a victory by their unanimous endeavor against a foreign enemy; yet afterwards, when either they have no common enemy, or he that by one part is held for an enemy, is by another part held for a friend, they must needs by the difference of their interests dissolve, and fall again into a war amongst themselves.

It is true that certain living creatures, as bees, and ants, live sociably one with another, which are therefore by Aristotle numbered amongst political creatures; and yet have no other direction, than their particular judgments and appetites; nor speech, whereby one of them can signify to another, what he thinks expedient for the common benefit: and therefore some man may perhaps desire to know, why mankind cannot do the same. To which I answer,

First, that men are continually in competition for honor and dignity, which these creatures are not; and consequently amongst men there arises on that ground, envy and hatred, and finally war; but amongst these not so.

Secondly, that amongst these creatures, the common good differs not from the private; and being by nature inclined to their private, they procure thereby the common benefit. But man, whose joy consists in comparing himself with other men, can relish nothing but what is eminent.

Thirdly, that these creatures, having not, as man, the use of reason, do not see, nor think they see any fault, in the administration of their common business; whereas amongst men, there are very many, that think themselves wiser, and abler to govern the public, better than the rest; and these strive to reform and innovate, one this way, another that way; and thereby bring it into distraction and civil war.

Fourthly, that these creatures, though they have some use of voice, in making known to one another their desires, and other affections; yet they want that art of words, by which some men can represent to others, that which is good, in the likeness of evil; and evil, in the likeness of good; and augment, or diminish the apparent greatness of good and evil; discontenting men, and troubling their peace at their pleasure.

Fifthly, irrational creatures cannot distinguish between "injury," and "damage"; and therefore as long as they be at ease, they are not offended with their fellows: whereas man is then most troublesome, when he is most at ease: for then it is that he loves to shew his wisdom, and control the actions of them that govern the commonwealth.

Lastly, the agreement of these creatures is natural; that of men, is by covenant only, which is artificial: and therefore it is no wonder if there be somewhat else required, besides covenant, to make their agreement constant and lasting; which is a common power, to keep them in awe, and to direct their actions to the common benefit.

The only way to erect such a common power, as may be able to defend them from the invasion of foreigners, and the injuries of one another, and thereby to secure them in such sort, as that by their own industry, and by the fruits of the earth, they may nourish themselves and live contentedly; is, to confer all their power and strength upon one man, or upon one assembly of men, that may reduce all their wills, by plurality of voices, unto one will: which is as much as to say, to appoint one man, or assembly of men, to bear their person; and every one to own, and acknowledge himself to be author of whatsoever he that so bears their person, shall act, or cause to be acted, in those things which concern the common Peace and safety; and therein to submit their wills, every one to his will, and their judgments, to his judgment. This is more than consent, or concord; it is a real unity of them all, in one and the same person, made by covenant of every man with every man, in such manner, as if every man should say to every man, "I authorize and give up my right of governing myself to this man, or to this assembly of men, on this condition, that thou give up thy right to him, and authorize all his actions in like manner." This done, the multitude so united in one person, is called a COMMONWEALTH, in Latin *CIVITAS*. This is the generation of that great LEVIATHAN, or rather, to speak more reverently, of that "mortal god," to which we owe under the "immortal God," our peace and defence. For by this authority, given him by every particular man in the commonwealth, he hath the use of so much power and strength conferred on him, that by terror thereof, he is enabled to form the wills of them all, to peace at home, and mutual aid against their enemies abroad. And in him consists the essence of the commonwealth; which, to define it, "is one person, of whose acts a great multitude, by mutual covenants one with another, have made themselves every one the author, to the end he may use the strength and means of them all, as he shall think expedient, for their peace and common defence."

And he that carries this person, is called SOVEREIGN, and said to have sovereign power; and every one besides, his SUBJECT.

The attaining to this sovereign power, is by two ways. One, by natural force; as when a man makes his children, to submit themselves, and their children to his government, as being able to destroy them if they refuse; or by war subdues his enemies to his will, giving them their lives on that condition. The other, is when men agree amongst themselves, to submit to some man, or assembly of men, voluntarily, on confidence to be protected by him against all others. This latter, may be called a political commonwealth, or commonwealth by "institution"; and the former, a commonwealth by "acquisition." And first, I shall speak of a commonwealth by institution.

CHAPTER 18. OF THE RIGHTS OF SOVEREIGNS BY INSTITUTION

A "commonwealth" is said to be "instituted," when a "multitude" of men do agree, and "covenant, every one, with every one," that to whatsoever "man," or "assembly of men," shall be given by the major part, the "right" to "present" the person of them all, that is to say, to be their "representative"; every one, as well he that "voted for it," as he that "voted against it," shall "authorize" all the actions and judgments, of that man, or assembly of men, in the same manner, as if they were his own, to the end, to live peaceably amongst themselves, and be protected against other men.

From this institution of a commonwealth are derived all the "rights," and faculties of him, or them, on whom the sovereign power is conferred by the consent of the people assembled.

First, because they covenant, it is to be understood, they are not obliged by former covenant to any thing repugnant hereunto. And consequently they that have already instituted a commonwealth, being thereby bound by covenant, to own the actions, and judgments of one, cannot lawfully make a new covenant, amongst themselves, to be obedient to any other, in any thing whatsoever, without his permission. And therefore, they that are subjects to a monarch, cannot without his leave cast off monarchy, and return to the confusion of a disunited multitude; nor transfer their person from him that bears it, to another man, or other assembly of men: for they are bound, every man to every man, to own, and be reputed author of all, that he that already is their sovereign, shall do, and judge fit to be done: so that any one man dissenting, all the rest should break their covenant made to that man, which is injustice: and they have also every man given the sovereignty to him that bears their person; and therefore if they depose him, they take from him that which is his own, and so again it is injustice. Besides, if he that attempts to depose his sovereign, be killed, or punished by him for such attempt, he is author of his own punishment, as being by the institution, author of all his sovereign shall do: and because it is injustice for a man to do any thing, for which he may be punished by his own authority, he is also upon that title, unjust. And whereas some men have pretended for their disobedience to their sovereign, a new covenant, made, not with men, but with God; this also is unjust: for there is no covenant with God, but by mediation of somebody that represents God's person which none doth but God's lieutenant, who hath the sovereignty under God. But this pretence of covenant with God, is so evident a lie, even in the pretenders' own consciences, that it is not only an act of an unjust, but also of a vile, and unmanly disposition.

Secondly, because the right of bearing the person of them all, is given to him they make sovereign, by covenant only of one to another, and not of him to any of them; there can happen no breach of covenant on the part of the sovereign; and consequently none of his subjects, by any pretence of forfeiture, can be freed from his subjection. That he which is made sovereign makes no covenant with his subjects beforehand, is manifest; because either he must make it with the whole multitude, as one party to the covenant; or he must make a several covenant with every man. With the whole, as one party, it is impossible; because as yet they are not one person: and if he make so many several covenants as there be men, those covenants after he hath the sovereignty are void; because what act soever can be pretended by any one of them for breach thereof, is the act both of himself, and of all the rest, because done in the person, and by the right of every one of them in particular. Besides, if any one, or more of them, pretend a breach of the covenant made by the sovereign at his institution; and others, or one other of his subjects, or himself alone, pretend there was no such breach, there is in this case, no judge to decide the controversy; it returns therefore to the sword again; and every man recovers the right of protecting himself by his own strength, contrary to the design they had in the institution. It is therefore in vain to grant sovereignty by way of precedent covenant. The opinion that any monarch receives his power by covenant, that is to say, on condition, proceeds from want of understanding this easy truth, that covenants being but words and breath, have no force to oblige, contain, constrain, or protect any man, but what it has from the public sword; that is, from the untied hands of that man, or assembly of men that hath the sovereignty, and whose actions are avouched by them all, and performed by the strength of them all, in him united. But when an assembly of men is made sovereign; then no man imagines any such covenant to have passed in the institution; for no man is so dull as to say, for example, the people of Rome made a covenant with the Romans, to hold the sovereignty on such or such conditions; which not performed, the Romans might lawfully depose the Roman people. That men see not the reason to be alike in a monarchy, and in a popular government, proceeds from the ambition of some, that are kinder to the government of an assembly, whereof they may hope to participate, than of monarchy, which they despair to enjoy.

Thirdly, because the major part hath by consenting voices declared a sovereign; he that dissented must now consent with the rest—that is, be contented to avow all the actions he shall do, or else justly be destroyed by the rest. For if he voluntarily entered into the congregation of them that were assembled, he sufficiently declared thereby his will, and therefore tacitly covenanted, to stand to what the major part should ordain: and therefore if he refuse to stand thereto, or make protestation against any of their decrees, he does contrary to his covenant, and therefore unjustly. And whether he be of the congregation, or not; and whether his consent be asked, or not, he must either submit to their decrees, or be left in the condition of war he was in before; wherein he might without injustice be destroyed by any man whatsoever.

Fourthly, because every subject is by this institution author of all the actions, and judgments of the sovereign instituted; it follows, that whatsoever he doth, it can be no injury to any of his subjects; nor ought he to be by any of them accused of injustice. For he that doth anything by authority from another, doth therein no injury to him by whose authority he acts: but by this institution of a commonwealth, every particular man is author of all the sovereign doth: and consequently he that complains of injury from his sovereign, complains of that whereof he himself is author, and therefore ought not to accuse any man but himself; no nor himself of injury; because to do injury to one's self, is impossible. It is true that they that have sovereign power may commit iniquity; but not injustice, or injury in the proper signification.

Fifthly, and consequently to that which was said last, no man that hath sovereign power can justly be put to death, or otherwise in any manner by his subject punished. For seeing every subject is author of the actions of his sovereign; he punishes another for the actions committed by himself.

And because the end of this institution, is the peace and defence of them all; and whosoever has right to the end, has right to the means; it belongs of right, to whatsoever man, or assembly that hath the sovereignty, to be judge both of the means of peace and defence, and also of the hindrances, and disturbances of the same; and to do whatsoever he shall think necessary to be done, both beforehand, for the preserving of peace and security, by prevention of discord at home, and hostility from abroad; and, when peace and security are lost, for the recovery of the same. And therefore,

Sixthly, it is annexed to the sovereignty, to be judge of what opinions and doctrines are averse, and what conducing to peace; and consequently, on what occasions, how far, and what men are to be trusted withal, in speaking to multitudes of people; and who shall examine the doctrines of all books before they be published. For the actions of men proceed from their opinions; and in the well-governing of opinions, consists the well-governing of men's actions, in order to their peace, and concord. And though in matter of doctrine, nothing ought to be regarded but the truth; yet this is not repugnant to regulating the same by peace. For doctrine repugnant to peace, can no more be true, than peace and concord can be against the law of nature. It is true, that in a commonwealth, where by the negligence, or unskillfulness of governors, and teachers, false doctrines are by time generally received; the contrary truths may be generally offensive. Yet the most sudden, and rough bustling in of a new truth, that can be, does never break the peace, but only sometimes awake the war. For those men that are so remissly governed, that they dare take up arms to defend, or introduce an opinion, are still in war; and their condition not peace, but only a cessation of arms for fear of one another; and they live, as it were, in the precincts of battle continually. It belongs therefore to him that hath the sovereign power, to be judge, or constitute all judges of opinions and doctrines, as a thing necessary to peace; thereby to prevent discord and civil war.

Seventhly, is annexed to the sovereignty, the whole power of prescribing the rules, whereby every man may know, what goods he may enjoy, and what actions he may do, without being molested by any of his fellow-subjects; and this is it men call "propriety." For before constitution of sovereign power, as hath already been shown, all men had right to all things; which necessarily causes war: and therefore this propriety, being necessary to peace, and depending on sovereign power, is the act of that power, in order to the public peace. These rules of propriety, or *meum* and *tuum,* and of "good," "evil," "lawful," and "unlawful" in the actions of subjects, are the civil laws; that is to say, the laws of each commonwealth in particular; though the name of civil law be now restrained to the ancient civil laws of the city of Rome—which being the head of a great part of the world, her laws at that time were in these parts the civil law.

Eighthly, is annexed to the sovereignty, the right judicature; that is to say, of hearing and deciding all controversies, which may arise concerning law, either civil, or natural; or concerning fact. For without the decision of controversies, there is no protection of one subject, against the injuries of another; the laws concerning *meum* and *tuum* are in vain; and to every man remains, from the natural and necessary appetite of his own conservation, the right of protecting himself by his private strength, which is the condition of war, and contrary to the end for which every commonwealth is instituted.

Ninthly, is annexed to the sovereignty, the right of making war and peace with other nations, and commonwealths; that is to say, of judging when it is for the public good, and how great forces are to be assembled, armed, and paid for that end; and to levy money upon the subjects, to defray the expenses thereof. For the power by which the people are to be defended, consists in their armies; and the strength of an army, in the union of their strength under one command, which command the sovereign instituted, therefore hath; because the command of the "militia," without other institution, makes him that hath it sovereign. And therefore whosoever is made general of an army, he that hath the sovereign power is always generalissimo.

Tenthly, is annexed to the sovereignty, the choosing of all counsellors, ministers, magistrates, and officers, both in peace, and war. For seeing the sovereign is charged with the end, which is the common peace and defence, he is understood to have power to use such means, as he shall think most fit for his discharge.

Eleventhly, to the sovereign is committed the power of rewarding with riches, or honor, and of punishing with corporal or pecuniary punishment, or with ignominy, every subject according to the law he hath formerly made; or if there be no law made, according as he shall judge most to conduce to the encouraging of men to serve the commonwealth, or deterring of them from doing disservice to the same.

Lastly, considering what value men are naturally apt to set upon themselves; what respect they look for from others; and how little they value other men; from whence continually arise amongst them, emulation, quarrels, factions, and at last war, to the destroying of one another, and diminution of their strength against a common enemy; it is necessary that there be laws of honor, and a public rate of the worth of such men as have deserved, or are able to deserve well of the commonwealth; and that there be force in the hands of some or other, to put those laws in execution. But it hath already been shown, that not only the whole "militia," or forces of the commonwealth; but also the judicature of all controversies, is annexed to the sovereignty. To the sovereign therefore it belongs also to give titles of honor; and to appoint what order of place, and dignity, each man shall hold; and what signs of respect, in public or private meetings, they shall give to one another.

These are the rights, which make the essence of sovereignty, and which are the marks, whereby a man may discern in what man, or assembly of men, the sovereign power is placed, and resides. For these are incommunicable, and inseparable. The power to coin money; to dispose of the estate and persons of infant heirs; to have pre-emption in markets; and all other statute prerogatives, may be transferred by the sovereign; and yet the power to protect his subjects be retained. But if he transfer the "militia," he retains the judicature in vain, for want of execution of the laws: or if he grant away the power of raising money; the "militia" is in vain; or if he give away the government of doctrines, men will be frighted into rebellion with the fear of spirits. And so if we consider any one of the said rights, we shall presently see, that the holding of all the rest will produce no effect, in the conservation of peace and justice, the end for which all commonwealths are instituted. And this division is it, whereof it is said, "a kingdom divided in itself cannot stand": for unless this division precede, division into opposite armies can never happen. If there had not first been an opinion received of the greatest part of England, that these powers were divided between the King, and the Lords, and the House of Commons, the people had never been divided and fallen into this civil war; first between those that disagreed in politics; and after between the dissenters about the liberty of religion; which have so instructed men in this point of sovereign right, that there be few now in England that do not see, that these rights are inseparable, and will be so generally acknowledged at the next return of peace; and so continue, till their miseries are forgotten; and no longer, except the vulgar be better taught than they have hitherto been.

And because they are essential and inseparable rights, it follows necessarily, that in whatsoever words any of them seem to be granted away, yet if the sovereign power itself be not in direct terms renounced, and the name of sovereign no more given by the grantees to him that grants them, the grant is void: for when he has granted all he can, if we grant back the sovereignty, all is restored, as inseparably annexed thereunto.

This great authority being indivisible and inseparably annexed to the sovereignty, there is little ground for the opinion of them, that say of sovereign kings, though they be *singulis majores,* of greater power than every one of their subjects, yet they be *universis minores,* of less power than them all together. For if by "all together," they mean not the collective body as one person, then "all together," and "every one," signify the same; and the speech is absurd. But if by "all together," they understand them as one person, which person the sovereign bears, then the power of all together, is the same with the sovereign's power; and so again the speech is absurd: which absurdity they see well enough, when the sovereignty is in an assembly of the people; but in a monarch they see it not; and yet the power of sovereignty is the same in whomsoever it be placed.

And as the power, so also the honor of the sovereign, ought to be greater, than that of any, or all the subjects. For in the sovereignty is the fountain of honor. The dignities of lord, earl, duke, and prince are his creatures. As in the presence of the master, the servants are equal, and without any honor at all; so are the subjects, in the presence of the sovereign. And though they shine some more, some less, when they are out of his sight; yet in his presence, they shine no more than the stars in the presence of the sun.

But a man may here object, that the condition of subjects is very miserable; as being obnoxious to the lusts, and other irregular passions of him, or them that have so unlimited a power in their hands. And commonly they that live under a monarch, think it the fault of monarchy; and they that live under the government of democracy, or other sovereign assembly, attribute all the inconvenience to that form of commonwealth; whereas the power in all forms, if they be perfect enough to protect them, is the same: not considering that the state of man can never be without some incommodity or other; and that the greatest, that in any form of government can possibly happen to the people in general, is scarce sensible in respect of the miseries, and horrible calamities, that accompany a civil war, or that dissolute condition of masterless men, without subjection to laws, and a coercive power to tie their hands from rapine and revenge: nor considering that the greatest pressure of sovereign governors, proceeds not from any delight, or profit they can expect in the damage or weakening of their subjects, in whose vigor, consists their own strength and glory; but in the restiveness of themselves, that unwillingly contributing to their own defence, make it necessary for their governors to draw from them what they can in time of peace, that they may have means on any emergent occasion, or sudden need, to resist, or take advantage on their enemies. For all men are by nature provided of notable multiplying glasses, that is their passions and self-love, through which, every little payment appears a great grievance; but are destitute of those prospective glasses, namely moral and civil science, to see afar off the miseries that hang over them, and cannot without such payments be avoided.

*   *   *

CHAPTER 21. OF THE LIBERTY OF SUBJECTS

LIBERTY, or FREEDOM, signifies, properly, the absence of opposition; by opposition, I mean external impediments of motion; and may be applied no less to irrational, and inanimate creatures, than to rational. For whatsoever is so tied, or environed, as it cannot move but within a certain space, which space is determined by the opposition of some external body, we say it hath not liberty to go further. And so of all living creatures, whilst they are imprisoned, or restrained, with walls, or chains; and of the water whilst it is kept in by banks, or vessels, that otherwise would spread itself into a larger space, we use to say, they are not at liberty, to move in such manner, as without those external impediments they would. But when the impediment of motion, is in the constitution of the thing itself, we use not to say; it wants the liberty; but the power to move; as when a stone lies still, or a man is fastened to his bed by sickness.

And according to this proper, and generally received meaning of the word, a FREEMAN, is he, that in those things, which by his strength and wit he is able to do, is not hindered to do what he has a will to. But when the words "free," and "liberty," are applied to any thing but "bodies," they are abused; for that which is not subject to motion, is not subject to impediment: and therefore, when it is said, for example, the way is free, no liberty of the way is signified, but of those that walk in it without stop. And when we say a gift is free, there is not meant any liberty of the gift but of the giver, that was not bound by any law or covenant to give it. So when we "speak freely," it is not the liberty of voice, or pronunciation, but of the man, whom no law hath obliged to speak otherwise than he did. Lastly, from the use of the word "free-will," no liberty can be inferred of the will, desire, or inclination, but the liberty of the man; which consists in this, that he finds no stop, in doing what he has the will, desire, or inclination to do.

Fear and liberty are consistent; as when a man throws his goods into the sea for "fear" the ship should sink, he doth it nevertheless very willingly, and may refuse to do it if he will: it is therefore the action of one that was "free"; so a man sometimes pays his debt, only for "fear" of imprisonment, which because nobody hindered him from detaining, was the action of a man at "liberty." And generally all actions which men do in commonwealths, for fear of the law, are actions, which the doers had liberty to omit.

"Liberty," and "necessity" are consistent: as in the water, that hath not only "liberty," but a "necessity" of descending by the channel; so likewise in the actions which men voluntarily do: which, because they proceed from their will, proceed from liberty; and yet, because every act of man's will, and every desire, and inclination proceeds from some cause, and that from another cause, in a continual chain, whose first link is in the hand of God the first of all causes, proceed from "necessity." So that to him that could see the connection of those causes, the necessity of all men's voluntary actions, would appear manifest. And therefore God, that sees, and disposes all things, sees also that the "liberty" of man in doing what he will, is accompanied with the "necessity" of doing that which God will, and no more, nor less. For though men may do many things, which God does not command, nor is therefore author of them; yet they can have no passion, nor appetite to any thing, of which appetite God's will is not the cause. And did not his will assure the "necessity" of man's will, and consequently of all that on man's will depends, the "liberty" of men would be a contradiction, and impediment to the omnipotence and "liberty" of God. And this shall suffice, as to the matter in hand, of that natural "liberty," which only is properly called "liberty."

But as men, for the attaining of peace, and conservation of themselves thereby, have made an artificial man, which we call a commonwealth; so also have they made artificial chains, called "civil laws," which they themselves, by mutual covenants, have fastened at one end, to the lips of that man, or assembly, to whom they have given the sovereign power; and at the other end to their own ears. These bonds, in their own nature but weak, may nevertheless be made to hold, by the danger, though not by the difficulty of breaking them.

In relation to these bonds only it is, that I am to speak now, of the "liberty" of "subjects." For seeing there is no commonwealth in the world, wherein there be rules enough set down, for the regulating of all the actions, and words of men; as being a thing impossible: it follows necessarily, that in all kinds of actions by the laws pretermitted, men have the liberty, of doing what their own reasons shall suggest, for the most profitable to themselves. For if we take liberty in the proper sense, for corporal liberty; that is to say, freedom from chains and prison; it were very absurd for men to clamor as they do, for the liberty they so manifestly enjoy. Again, if we take liberty, for an exemption from laws, it is no less absurd, for men to demand as they do, that liberty, by which all other men may be masters of their lives. And yet, as absurd as it is, this is it they demand; not knowing that the laws are of no power to protect them, without a sword in the hands of a man, or men, to cause those laws to be put in execution. The liberty of a subject, lies therefore only in those things, which in regulating their actions, the sovereign hath pretermitted: such as is the liberty to buy, and sell, and otherwise contract with one another; to choose their own abode, their own diet, their own trade of life, and institute their children as they themselves think fit; and the like.

Nevertheless we are not to understand, that by such liberty, the sovereign power of life and death, is either abolished, or limited. For it has been already shown, that nothing the sovereign representative can do to a subject, on what pretence soever, can properly be called injustice, or injury; because every subject is author of every act the sovereign doth; so that he never wants right to any thing, otherwise, than as he himself is the subject of God, and bound thereby to observe the laws of nature. And therefore it may, and doth often happen in commonwealths, that a subject may be put to death, by the command of the sovereign power; and yet neither do the other wrong: as when Jephtha caused his daughter to be sacrificed: in which, and the like cases, he that so dies, had liberty to do the action, for which he is nevertheless, without injury put to death. And the same holds also in a sovereign prince, that puts to death an innocent subject. For though the action be against the law of nature, as being contrary to equity, as was the killing of Uriah, by David; yet it was not an injury to Uriah, but to God. Not to Uriah, because the right to do what he pleased was given him by Uriah himself: and yet to God, because David was God's subject, and prohibited all iniquity by the law of nature: which distinction, David himself, when he repented the fact, evidently confirmed, saying, "To thee only have I sinned." In the same manner, the people of Athens, when they banished the most potent of their commonwealth for ten years, thought they committed no injustice; and yet they never questioned what crime he had done; but what hurt he would do: nay they commanded the banishment of they knew not whom; and every citizen bringing his oystershell into the market place, written with the name of him he desired should be banished, without actually accusing him, sometimes banished an Aristides, for his reputation of justice; and sometimes a scurrilous jester, as Hyperbolus, to make a jest of it. And yet a man cannot say, the sovereign people of Athens wanted right to banish them; or an Athenian the liberty to jest, or to be just.

The liberty, whereof there is so frequent and honorable mention, in the histories, and philosophy of the ancient Greeks, and Romans, and in the writings, and discourse of those that from them have received all their learning in the politics, is not the liberty of particular men; but the liberty of the commonwealth: which is the same with that which every man then should have, if there were no civil laws, nor commonwealth at all. And the effects of it also be the same. For as amongst masterless men, there is perpetual war, of every man against his neighbor; no inheritance, to transmit to the son, nor to expect from the father; no propriety of goods, or lands; no security; but a full and absolute liberty in every particular man: so in states, and commonwealths not dependent on one another, every commonwealth, not every man, has an absolute liberty, to do what it shall judge, that is to say, what that man, or assembly that represents it, shall judge most conducing to their benefit. But withal, they live in the condition of a perpetual war, and upon the confines of battle, with their frontiers armed, and cannons planted against their neighbors round about. The Athenians, and Romans were free; that is, free commonwealths: not that any particular men had the liberty to resist their own representative; but that their representative had the liberty to resist, or invade other people. There is written on the turrets of the city of Lucca in great characters at this day, the word LIBERTAS; yet no man can thence infer, that a particular man has more liberty, or immunity from the service of the commonwealth there, than in Constantinople. Whether a commonwealth be monarchical, or popular, the freedom is still the same.

But it is an easy thing, for men to be deceived, by the specious name of liberty; and for want of judgment to distinguish, mistake that for their private inheritance, and birth-right, which is the right of the public only. And when the same error is confirmed by the authority of men in reputation for their writings on this subject, it is no wonder if it produce sedition, and change of government. In these western parts of the world, we are made to receive our opinions concerning the institution, and rights of commonwealths, from Aristotle, Cicero, and other men, Greeks and Romans, that living under popular states, derived those rights, not from the principles of nature, but transcribed them into their books, out of the practice of their own commonwealths, which were popular; as the grammarians describe the rules of language, out of the practice of the time; or the rules of poetry, out of the poems of Homer and Virgil. And because the Athenians were taught, to keep them from desire of changing their government, that they were freemen, and all that lived under monarchy were slaves; therefore Aristotle puts it down in his *Politics* (lib. 6. cap. ii.): "In democracy, LIBERTY is to be supposed: for it is commonly held, that no man is FREE in any other government." And as Aristotle; so Cicero, and other writers have grounded their civil doctrine, on the opinions of the Romans, who were taught to hate monarchy, at first, by them that having deposed their sovereign, shared amongst them the sovereignty of Rome; and afterwards by their successors. And by reading of these Greek, and Latin authors, men from their childhood have gotten a habit, under a false show of liberty, of favoring tumults, and of licentious controlling the actions of their sovereigns, and again of controlling those controllers; with the effusion of so much blood, as I think I may truly say, there was never any thing so dearly bought, as these western parts have bought the learning of the Greek and Latin tongues.

To come now to the particulars of the true liberty of a subject; that is to say, what are the things, which though commanded by the sovereign, he may nevertheless, without injustice, refuse to do; we are to consider, what rights we pass away, when we make a commonwealth; or, which is all one, what liberty we deny ourselves, by owning all the actions, without exception, of the man, or assembly we make our sovereign. For in the act of our "submission," consists both our "obligation," and our "liberty"; which must therefore be inferred by arguments taken from thence; there being no obligation on any man, which arises not from some act of his own; for all men equally, are by nature free. And because such arguments, must either be drawn from the express words, I "authorize all his actions," or from the intention of him that submits himself to his power, which intention is to be understood by the end for which he so submits; the obligation, and liberty of the subject, is to be derived, either from those words, or others equivalent; or else from the end of the institution of sovereignty, namely, the peace of the subjects within themselves, and their defence against a common enemy.

First therefore, seeing sovereignty by institution, is by covenant of every one to every one; and sovereignty by acquisition, by covenants of the vanquished to the victor, or child to the parent; it is manifest, that every subject has liberty in all those things, the right whereof cannot by covenant be transferred. I have shown before in the 14th chapter, that covenants, not to defend a man's own body, are void. Therefore,

If the sovereign command a man, though justly condemned, to kill, wound, or maim himself; or not to resist those that assault him; or to abstain from the use of food, air, medicine, or any other thing, without which he cannot live; yet hath that man the liberty to disobey.

If a man be interrogated by the sovereign, or his authority, concerning a crime done by himself, he is not bound, without assurance of pardon, to confess it; because no man, as I have shown in the same chapter, can be obliged by covenant to accuse himself.

Again, the consent of a subject to sovereign power, is contained in these words, "I authorize, or take upon me, all his actions"; in which there is no restriction at all, of his own former natural liberty: for by allowing him to "kill me," I am not bound to kill myself when he commands me. It is one thing to say, "kill me, or my fellow, if you please"; another thing to say, "I will kill myself, or my fellow." It follows therefore, that

No man is bound by the words themselves, either to kill himself, or any other man; and consequently, that the obligation a man may sometimes have, upon the command of the sovereign to execute any dangerous, or dishonorable office, depends not on the words of our submission; but on the intention, which is to be understood by the end thereof. When therefore our refusal to obey, frustrates the end for which the sovereignty was ordained; then there is no liberty to refuse: otherwise there is.

Upon this ground, a man that is commanded as a soldier to fight against the enemy, though his sovereign have right enough to punish his refusal with death, may nevertheless in many cases refuse, without injustice; as when he substitutes a sufficient soldier in his place: for in this case he deserts not the service of the commonwealth. And there is allowance to be made for natural timorousness; not only to women, of whom no such dangerous duty is expected, but also to men of feminine courage. When armies fight, there is on one side, or both, a running away; yet when they do it not out of treachery, but fear, they are not esteemed to do it unjustly, but dishonorably. For the same reason, to avoid battle, is not injustice, but cowardice. But he that enrolls himself a soldier, or takes imprest money, takes away the excuse of a timorous nature; and is obliged, not only to go to the battle, but also not to run from it, without his captain's leave. And when the defence of the commonwealth, requires at once the help of all that are able to bear arms, every one is obliged; because otherwise the institution of the commonwealth, which they have not the purpose, or courage to preserve, was in vain.

To resist the sword of the commonwealth, in defence of another man, guilty, or innocent, no man hath liberty; because such liberty, takes away from the sovereign, the means of protecting us; and is therefore destructive of the very essence of government. But in case a great many men together, have already resisted the sovereign power unjustly, or committed some capital crime, for which every one of them expects death, whether have they not the liberty then to join together, and assist, and defend one another? Certainly they have: for they but defend their lives, which the guilty man may as well do, as the innocent. There was indeed injustice in the first breach of their duty; their bearing of arms subsequent to it, though it be to maintain what they have done, is no new unjust act. And if it be only to defend their persons, it is not unjust at all. But the offer of pardon takes from them, to whom it is offered, the plea of self-defence, and makes their perseverance in assisting, or defending the rest, unlawful.

As for other liberties, they depend on the silence of the law. In cases where the sovereign has prescribed no rule, their the subject hath the liberty to do, or forbear, according to his own discretion. And therefore such liberty is in some places more, and in some less; and in some times more, in other times less, according as they that have the sovereignty shall think most convenient. As for example, there was a time, when in England a man might enter into his own land, and dispossess such as wrongfully possessed it, by force. But in aftertimes, that liberty of forcible entry, was taken away by a statute made, by the king, in parliament. And in some places of the world, men have the liberty of many wives: in other places, such liberty is not allowed.

If a subject have a controversy with his sovereign, of debt, or of right of possession of lands or goods, or concerning any service required at his hands, or concerning any penalty, corporal, or pecuniary, grounded on a precedent law; he hath the same liberty to sue for his right, as if it were against a subject; and before such judges, as are appointed by the sovereign. For seeing the sovereign demands by force of a former law, and not by virtue of his power; he declares thereby, that he requires no more, than shall appear to be due by that law. The suit therefore is not contrary to the will of the sovereign; and consequently the subject hath the liberty to demand the hearing of his cause; and sentence, according to that law. But if he demand, or take any thing by pretence of his power; there lies, in that case, no action of law; for all that is done by him in virtue of his power, is done by the authority of every subject, and consequently he that brings an action against the sovereign, brings it against himself.

If a monarch, or sovereign assembly, grant a liberty to all, or any of his subjects, which grant standing, he is disabled to provide for their safety, the grant is void; unless he directly renounce, or transfer the sovereignty to another. For in that he might openly, if it had been his will, and in plain terms, have renounced, or transferred it, and did not; it is to be understood it was not his will, but that the grant proceeded from ignorance of the repugnancy between such a liberty and the sovereign power; and therefore the sovereignty is still retained; and consequently all those powers, which are necessary to the exercising thereof; such as are the power of war, and peace, of judicature, of appointing officers, and councilors, of levying money, and the rest named in the eighteenth chapter.

The obligation of subjects to the sovereign, is understood to last as long, and no longer, than the power lasts, by which he is able to protect them. For the right men have by nature to protect themselves, when none else can protect them, can by no covenant be relinquished. The sovereignty is the soul of the commonwealth which once departed from the body, the members do no more receive their motion from it. The end of obedience is protection; which, wheresoever a man sees it, either in his own, or in another's sword, nature applies his obedience to it, and his endeavor to maintain it. And though sovereignty, in the intention of them that make it, be immortal; yet it is in its own nature, not only subject to violent death, by foreign war; but also through the ignorance, and passions of men, it hath in it, from the very institution, many seeds of a natural mortality, by intestine discord.

If a subject be taken prisoner in war; or his person, or his means of life be within the guards of the enemy, and hath his life and corporal liberty given him, on condition to be subject to the victor, he hath liberty to accept the condition; and having accepted it, is the subject of him that took him; because he had no other way to preserve himself. The case is the same, if he be detained on the same terms, in a foreign country. But if a man be held in prison, or bonds, or is not trusted with the liberty of his body; he cannot be understood to be bound by covenant to subjection; and therefore may, if he can, make his escape by any means whatsoever.

If a monarch shall relinquish the sovereignty, both for himself, and his heirs; his subjects return to the absolute liberty of nature; because, though nature may declare who are his sons, and who are the nearest of his kin; yet it depends on his own will, as hath been said in the precedent chapter, who shall be his heir. If therefore he will have no heir, there is no sovereignty, nor subjection. The case is the same, if he die without known kindred, and without declaration of his heir. For then there can no heir be known, and consequently no subjection be due.

If the sovereign banish his subject; during the banishment, he is not subject. But he that is sent on a message, or hath leave to travel, is still subject; but it is, by contract between sovereigns, not by virtue of the covenant of subjection. For whosoever enters into another's dominion, is subject to all the laws thereof; unless he have a privilege by the amity of the sovereigns, or by special license.

If a monarch subdued by war, render himself subject to the victor; his subjects are delivered from their former obligation, and become obliged to the victor. But if he be held prisoner, or have not the liberty of his own body; he is not understood to have given away the right of sovereignty; and therefore his subjects are obliged to yield obedience to the magistrates formerly placed, governing not in their own name, but in his. For, his right remaining, the question is only of the administration; that is to say, of the magistrates and officers; which, if he have not means to name, he is supposed to approve those, which he himself had formerly appointed.

BARUCH SPINOZA
1632–1677

Except for Socrates himself, it would be difficult to find a philosopher who was a more highly regarded person than Benedict (Baruch) Spinoza. Like Socrates, he was not interested in power or wealth. Like Socrates, he was accused of atheism and was hounded for his unorthodox beliefs. Like Socrates, he was interested in philosophy as a way of life, not as a professional discipline.

Spinoza was born in Amsterdam, the son of Jewish refugees who had fled from Portugal to escape persecution. As a young man, he was trained in Jewish tradition under a celebrated Talmudist, Saul Levi Morteira. He later studied with Manasseh ben Israel, the man who persuaded Cromwell to allow Jews to return to England, and with a Dutch physician, Franz van der Ende.

As a Jew, Spinoza was an outsider in Holland—not even entitled to citizenship because of his faith. As an original thinker, Spinoza soon became an outsider within the Jewish community as well. He was accused of heresy by the synagogue of Amsterdam and required to disavow his teachings. Spinoza refused and was officially excommunicated in 1656, when he was twenty-three years old. (In the twentieth century, the new state of Israel formally revoked the ban.)

With no wish to join any other religious community, Spinoza left Amsterdam and eventually settled in The Hague. He lived very simply, supporting himself by grinding and polishing lenses, a craft he had adopted out of respect for the Jewish tradition, which required scholars to learn a trade.

Spinoza published only two works during his lifetime. His first work was *Principles of Descartes' Philosophy* (1663), which critically examined the presuppositions and structure of Descartes' system. Using what later came to be called "higher criticism," his second book, *Theological-Political Treatise* (1670), subjected Scripture to rational analysis. He concluded that the Bible does not aim at truth but at pious and obedient behavior. Writing soon after the Thirty Years War (1618–1648), he proposed that religion and truth be separated altogether. This separation, he believed, would be the best safeguard against fanaticism. And pious conduct flourishes best in an atmosphere of free speech.

His *Theological-Political Treatise* attracted a great deal of criticism. It also brought an invitation to the chair of philosophy at the University of Heidelberg, Germany. Although the invitation included a guarantee of academic freedom, Spinoza rejected it out of his passion for freedom to speak and write as he saw fit.

The rigor of his simple life, with the glass dust of his trade, hastened his death from consumption at the age of forty-four, two years before Hobbes died at ninety-one. Immediately following his death, Spinoza's other works, including *Political Treatise* (which supports individual liberty, religious tolerance, and democracy), *On the Improvement of the Intellect,* and his masterpiece, *Ethics,* were published.

*   *   *

Whereas Descartes and Hobbes used the geometrical *method,* Spinoza used geometrical *form* as well. The *Ethics* is presented as a geometrical system, developing propositions from axioms and definitions.

In Books I and II of his *Ethics,* reprinted here in the E. Curley translation, Spinoza deals with God and the nature and origin of mind. He begins by accepting Descartes' idea that "infinite substance" is completely independent and necessary. But he claims that Descartes had contradicted himself by allowing for "finite substances" as well. Instead, Spinoza claims that there could only be one substance: God. God exists necessarily and as God is the only substance, what we call "Nature" is also God. This also means that whatever happens is necessary (though individuals are often confused and do not understand the connections).

Although God is the only substance, God has infinite attributes. The only two divine attributes we can know are thought (of which minds are modifications) and extension (of which bodies are modifications). To Spinoza, Descartes was wrong to present mind and body as two separate substances (with all the concomitant problems of interaction). Instead, says Spinoza, body and mind are both attributes of the One substance. Thinking substance and extended substance are really the same substance.

In Books III–V of the *Ethics,* Spinoza argues that we must free ourselves from the tyranny of the passions. The key to this freedom is an understanding of God that allows us to see the necessary, rational structure of reality: "The more this knowledge, that things are necessary, is applied to particular things . . . the greater is the power of the mind over the emotions." The final goal of this knowledge is "blessedness," which consists of intellectual love towards God. This program of overcoming the passions by reason may be difficult, but Spinoza concludes that "all things excellent are as difficult as they are rare" (an apt description of Spinoza's classic).

*   *   *

For a general introduction to Spinoza's life and thought, see Stuart Hampshire, *Spinoza* (Baltimore, MD: Penguin Books, 1952); Henry E. Allison, *Benedict De*

Spinoza (Boston: Twayne, 1975); and Alan Donagan, *Spinoza* (Chicago: University of Chicago Press, 1988). For an interesting study of Spinoza's thought in relation to the other Continental rationalists, see John Cottingham, *The Rationalists* (Oxford: Oxford University Press, 1988). The generally accepted "classic" commentary on the *Ethics* remains Harry Austryn Wolfson, *The Philosophy of Spinoza: Unfolding the Latent Processes of His Reasoning* (1934; reprint New York: Schocken, 1969). For more recent discussions of Spinoza's *Ethics,* see Jonathan Bennett, *A Study of Spinoza's Ethics* (Indianapolis, IN: Hackett, 1984); and Edwin Curley, *Behind the Geometrical Method: A Reading of Spinoza's Ethics* (Princeton, NJ: Princeton University Press, 1988). For collections of essays on Spinoza, see S. Paul Kashap, ed., *Studies in Spinoza* (Berkeley: University of California Press, 1972); Robert W. Shahan and J.I. Biro, eds., *Spinoza: New Perspectives* (Norman, OK: University of Oklahoma Press, 1978); Richard Kennington, ed., *The Philosophy of Baruch Spinoza* (Washington, DC: Catholic University of America Press, 1980); and Vere Chappell, ed., *Essays on Early Modern Philosophers: Baruch De Spinoza* (Hamden, CT: Garland, 1992). Finally, for an interesting discussion of the Jewish character of Spinoza's thought, see Yirmiyahu Yovel's pair of books, *The Marrano of Reason* and *The Adventures of Immanence* (both Princeton, NJ: Princeton University Press, 1991).

ETHICS (in part)

FIRST PART OF THE ETHICS

ON GOD

Definitions

D1: By cause of itself I understand that whose essence involves existence, *or* that whose nature cannot be conceived except as existing.

D2: That thing is said to be finite in its own kind that can be limited by another of the same nature.

For example, a body is called finite because we always conceive another that is greater. Thus a thought is limited by another thought. But a body is not limited by a thought nor a thought by a body.

Baruch Spinoza, *Ethics* from *Collected Works of Spinoza,* Vol. 1, edited and translated by Edwin Curley (Princeton, NJ: Princeton University Press, 1985). © 1985 by Princeton University Press. Reprinted by permission of Princeton University Press. [Material within square brackets is from *De Nagelate Schriften van B.D.S.,* a later edition of the *Ethics,* and is included by Curley in the primary text.]

D3: By substance I understand what is in itself and is conceived through itself, i.e., that whose concept does not require the concept of another thing, from which it must be formed.

D4: By attribute I understand what the intellect perceives of a substance, as constituting its essence.

D5: By mode I understand the affections of a substance, or that which is in another through which it is also conceived.

D6: By God I understand a being absolutely infinite, i.e., a substance consisting of an infinity of attributes, of which each one expresses an eternal and infinite essence.
   Exp: I say absolutely infinite, not infinite in its own kind; for if something is only infinite in its own kind, we can deny infinite attributes of it [(i.e., we can conceive infinite attributes which do not pertain to its nature)]; but if something is absolutely infinite, whatever expresses essence and involves no negation pertains to its essence.

D7: That thing is called free which exists from the necessity of its nature alone, and is determined to act by itself alone. But a thing is called necessary, or rather compelled, which is determined by another to exist and to produce an effect in a certain and determinate manner.

D8: By eternity I understand existence itself, insofar as it is conceived to follow necessarily from the definition alone of the eternal thing.
   Exp: For such existence, like the essence of a thing, is conceived as an eternal truth, and on that account cannot be explained by duration or time, even if the duration is conceived to be without beginning or end.

Axioms

A1: Whatever is, is either in itself or in another.

A2: What cannot be conceived through another, must be conceived through itself.

A3: From a given determinate cause the effect follows necessarily; and conversely, if there is no determinate cause, it is impossible for an effect to follow.

A4: The knowledge of an effect depends on, and involves, the knowledge of its cause.

A5: Things that have nothing in common with one another also cannot be understood through one another, or the concept of the one does not involve the concept of the other.

A6: A true idea must agree with its object.

A7: If a thing can be conceived as not existing, its essence does not involve existence.

P1: *A substance is prior in nature to its affections.*
   Dem.: This is evident from D3 and D5.

P2: *Two substances having different attributes have nothing in common with one another.*

Dem.: This is also evident from D3. For each must be in itself and be conceived through itself, or the concept of the one does not involve the concept of the other.

P3: *If things have nothing in common with one another, one of them cannot be the cause of the other.*

Dem.: If they have nothing in common with one another, then (by A5) they cannot be understood through one another, and so (by A4) one cannot be the cause of the other, q.e.d.*

P4: *Two or more distinct things are distinguished from one another, either by a difference in the attributes of the substances or by a difference in their affections.*

Dem.: Whatever is, is either in itself or in another (by A1), i.e. (by D3 and D5), outside the intellect there is nothing except substances and their affections. Therefore, there is nothing outside the intellect through which a number of things can be distinguished from one another except substances, or what is the same (by D4), their attributes, and their affections, q.e.d.

P5: *In nature there cannot be two or more substances of the same nature or attribute.*

Dem.: If there were two or more distinct substances, they would have to be distinguished from one another either by a difference in their attributes, or by a difference in their affections (by P4). If only by a difference in their attributes, then it will be conceded that there is only one of the same attribute. But if by a difference in their affections, then since a substance is prior in nature to its affections (by P1), if the affections are put to one side and [the substance] is considered in itself, i.e. (by D3 and A6), considered truly, one cannot be conceived to be distinguished from another, i.e. (by P4), there cannot be many, but only one [of the same nature *or* attribute], q.e.d.

P6: *One substance cannot be produced by another substance.*

Dem.: In nature there cannot be two substances of the same attribute (by P5), i.e. (by P2), which have something in common with each other. Therefore (by P3) one cannot be the cause of the other, or cannot be produced by the other, q.e.d.

Cor.: From this it follows that a substance cannot be produced by anything else. For in nature there is nothing except substances and their affections, as is evident from A1, D3, and D5. But it cannot be produced by a substance (by P6). Therefore, substance absolutely cannot be produced by anything else, q.e.d.

Alternatively: This is demonstrated even more easily from the absurdity of its contradictory. For if a substance could be produced by something else, the knowledge of it would have to depend on the knowledge of its cause (by A4). And so (by D3) it would not be a substance.

P7: *It pertains to the nature of a substance to exist.*

*[*quod erat demonstrandum*—"which was to be demonstrated"]

Dem.: A substance cannot be produced by anything else (by P6C); therefore it will be the cause of itself, i.e. (by D1), its essence necessarily involves existence, or it pertains to its nature to exist, q.e.d.

P8: *Every substance is necessarily infinite.*

Dem.: A substance of one attribute does not exist unless it is unique (P5), and it pertains to its nature to exist (P7). Of its nature, therefore, it will exist either as finite or as infinite. But not as finite. For then (by D2) it would have to be limited by something else of the same nature, which would also have to exist necessarily (by P7), and so there would be two substances of the same attribute, which is absurd (by P5). Therefore, it exists as infinite, q.e.d.

Schol. 1: Since being finite is really, in part, a negation, and being infinite is an absolute affirmation of the existence of some nature, it follows from P7 alone that every substance must be infinite. [For if we assumed a finite substance, we would, in part, deny existence to its nature, which (by P7) is absurd.]

Schol. 2: I do not doubt that the demonstration of P7 will be difficult to conceive for all who judge things confusedly, and have not been accustomed to know things through their first causes—because they do not distinguish between the modifications of substances and the substances themselves, nor do they know how things are produced. So it happens that they fictitiously ascribe to substances the beginning which they see that natural things have; for those who do not know the true causes of things confuse everything and without any conflict of mind feign that both trees and men speak, imagine that men are formed both from stones and from seed, and that any form whatever is changed into any other. So also, those who confuse the divine nature with the human easily ascribe human affects to God, particularly so long as they are also ignorant of how those affects are produced in the mind.

But if men would attend to the nature of substance, they would have no doubt at all of the truth of P7. Indeed, this proposition would be an axiom for everyone, and would be numbered among the common notions. For by substance they would understand what is in itself and is conceived through itself, i.e., that the knowledge of which does not require the knowledge of any other thing. But by modifications they would understand what is in another, those things whose concept is formed from the concept of the thing in which they are.

This is how we can have true ideas of modifications which do not exist; for though they do not actually exist outside the intellect, nevertheless their essences are comprehended in another in such a way that they can be conceived through it. But the truth of substances is not outside the intellect unless it is in them themselves, because they are conceived through themselves.

Hence, if someone were to say that he had a clear and distinct, i.e., true, idea of a substance, and nevertheless doubted whether such a substance existed, that would indeed be the same as if he were to say that he had a true idea, and nevertheless doubted whether it was false (as is evident to anyone who is sufficiently attentive). Or if someone maintains that a substance is created, he maintains at the same time that a false idea has become true. Of course nothing more absurd can be conceived. So it must be confessed that the existence of a substance, like its essence, is an eternal truth.

And from this we can infer in another way that there is only one [substance] of the same nature, which I have considered it worth the trouble of showing here. But to do this in order, it must be noted,

  I. that the true definition of each thing neither involves nor expresses anything except the nature of the thing defined.

From which it follows,

  II. that no definition involves or expresses any certain number of individuals,

since it expresses nothing other than the nature of the thing defined. E.g., the definition of the triangle expresses nothing but the simple nature of the triangle, but not any certain number of triangles. It is to be noted,

  III. that there must be, for each existing thing, a certain cause on account of which it exists.

Finally, it is to be noted,

  IV. that this cause, on account of which a thing exists, either must be contained in the very nature and definition of the existing thing (viz. that it pertains to its nature to exist) or must be outside it.

From these propositions it follows that if, in nature, a certain number of individuals exists, there must be a cause why those individuals, and why neither more nor fewer, exist.

For example, if 20 men exist in nature (to make the matter clearer, I assume that they exist at the same time, and that no others previously existed in nature), it will not be enough (i.e., to give a reason why 20 men exist) to show the cause of human nature in general; but it will be necessary in addition to show the cause why not more and not fewer than 20 exist. For (by III) there must necessarily be a cause why each [particular man] exists. But this cause (by II and III) cannot be contained in human nature itself, since the true definition of man does not involve the number 20. So (by IV) the cause why these 20 men exist, and consequently, why each of them exists, must necessarily be outside each of them.

For that reason it is to be inferred absolutely that whatever is of such a nature that there can be many individuals [of that nature] must, to exist, have an external cause to exist. Now since it pertains to the nature of a substance to exist (by what we have already shown in this Scholium), its definition must involve necessary existence, and consequently its existence must be inferred from its definition alone. But from its definition (as we have shown from II and III) the existence of a number of substances cannot follow. Therefore it follows necessarily from this, that there exists only one of the same nature, as was proposed.

P9: *The more reality or being each thing has, the more attributes belong to it.*
  Dem.: This is evident from D4.

P10: *Each attribute of a substance must be conceived through itself.*
  Dem.: For an attribute is what the intellect perceives concerning a substance, as constituting its essence (by D4); so (by D3) it must be conceived through itself, q.e.d.
  Schol.: From these propositions it is evident that although two attributes may be conceived to be really distinct (i.e., one may be conceived without the aid of the other), we still can not infer from that that they constitute two beings, *or* two different sub-

stances. For it is of the nature of a substance that each of its attributes is conceived through itself, since all the attributes it has have always been in it together, and one could not be produced by another, but each expresses the reality, *or* being of substance.

So it is far from absurd to attribute many attributes to one substance. Indeed, nothing in nature is clearer than that each being must be conceived under some attribute, and the more reality, or being it has, the more it has attributes which express necessity, *or* eternity, and infinity. And consequently there is also nothing clearer than that a being absolutely infinite must be defined (as we taught in D6) as a being that consists of infinite attributes, each of which expresses a certain eternal and infinite essence.

But if someone now asks by what sign we shall be able to distinguish the diversity of substances, let him read the following propositions, which show that in Nature there exists only one substance, and that it is absolutely infinite. So that sign would be sought in vain.

P11: *God, or a substance consisting of infinite attributes, each of which expresses eternal and infinite essence, necessarily exists.*

Dem.: If you deny this, conceive, if you can, that God does not exist. Therefore (by A7) his essence does not involve existence. But this (by P7) is absurd. Therefore God necessarily exists, q.e.d.

Alternatively: For each thing there must be assigned a cause, or reason, as much for its existence as for its nonexistence. For example, if a triangle exists, there must be a reason *or* cause why it exists; but if it does not exist, there must also be a reason *or* cause which prevents it from existing, *or* which takes its existence away.

But this reason, *or* cause, must either be contained in the nature of the thing, or be outside it. E.g., the very nature of a square circle indicates the reason why it does not exist, viz. because it involves a contradiction. On the other hand, the reason why a substance exists also follows from its nature alone, because it involves existence (see P7). But the reason why a circle or triangle exists, or why it does not exist, does not follow from the nature of these things, but from the order of the whole of corporeal Nature. For from this [order] it must follow either that the triangle necessarily exists now or that it is impossible for it to exist now.

These things are evident through themselves, but from them it follows that a thing necessarily exists if there is no reason or cause which prevents it from existing. Therefore, if there is no reason or cause which prevents God from existing, or which takes his existence away, it must certainly be inferred that he necessarily exists.

But if there were such a reason, *or* cause, it would have to be either in God's very nature or outside it, i.e., in another substance of another nature. For if it were of the same nature, that very supposition would concede that God exists. But a substance which was of another nature [than the divine] would have nothing in common with God (by P2), and therefore could neither give him existence nor take it away.

Since, then, there can be, outside the divine nature, no reason, *or* cause, which takes away the divine existence, the reason will necessarily have to be in his nature itself, if indeed he does not exist. That is, his nature would involve a contradiction [as in our second Example]. But it is absurd to affirm this of a Being absolutely infinite and supremely perfect. Therefore, there is no cause, *or* reason, either in God or outside God, which takes his existence away. And therefore, God necessarily exists, q.e.d.

Alternatively: To be able not to exist is to lack power, and conversely, to be able to exist is to have power (as is known through itself). So, if what now necessarily exists are only finite beings, then finite beings are more powerful than an absolutely infinite Being. But this, as is known through itself, is absurd. So, either nothing exists or an absolutely infinite Being also exists. But we exist, either in ourselves, or in something else, which necessarily exists (see A1 and P7). Therefore an absolutely infinite Being—i.e. (by D6), God—necessarily exists, q.e.d.

Schol.: In this last demonstration I wanted to show God's existence a posteriori, so that the demonstration would be perceived more easily—but not because God's existence does not follow a priori from the same foundation. For since being able to exist is power, it follows that the more reality belongs to the nature of a thing, the more powers it has, of itself, to exist. Therefore, an absolutely infinite Being, *or* God, has, of himself, an absolutely infinite power of existing. For that reason, he exists absolutely.

Still, there may be many who will not easily be able to see how evident this demonstration is, because they have been accustomed to contemplate only those things that flow from external causes. And of these, they see that those which quickly come to be, i.e., which easily exist, also easily perish. And conversely, they judge that those things to which they conceive more things to pertain are more difficult to do, i.e., that they do not exist so easily. But to free them from these prejudices, I have no need to show here in what manner this proposition—*what quickly comes to be, quickly perishes*—is true, nor whether or not all things are equally easy in respect to the whole of Nature. It is sufficient to note only this, that I am not here speaking of things that come to be from external causes, but only of substances that (by P6) can be produced by no external cause.

For things that come to be from external causes—whether they consist of many parts or of few—owe all the perfection or reality they have to the power of the external cause; and therefore their existence arises only from the perfection of their external cause, and not from their own perfection. On the other hand, whatever perfection substance has is not owed to any external cause. So its existence must follow from its nature alone; hence its existence is nothing but its essence.

Perfection, therefore, does not take away the existence of a thing, but on the contrary asserts it. But imperfection takes it away. So there is nothing of whose existence we can be more certain than we are of the existence of an absolutely infinite, *or* perfect, Being—i.e., God. For since his essence excludes all imperfection, and involves absolute perfection, by that very fact it takes away every cause of doubting his existence, and gives the greatest certainty concerning it. I believe this will be clear even to those who are only moderately attentive.

P12: *No attribute of a substance can be truly conceived from which it follows that the substance can be divided.*

Dem.: For the parts into which a substance so conceived would be divided either will retain the nature of the substance or will not. If the first [viz. they retain the nature of the substance], then (by P8) each part will have to be infinite, and (by P7) its own cause, and (by P5) each part will have to consist of a different attribute. And so many substances will be able to be formed from one, which is absurd (by P6). Furthermore, the parts (by P2) would have nothing in common with their whole, and the whole (by D4 and P10) could both be and be conceived without its parts, which is absurd, as no one will be able to doubt.

But if the second is asserted, viz. that the parts will not retain the nature of substance, then since the whole substance would be divided into equal parts, it would lose the nature of substance, and would cease to be, which (by P7) is absurd.

P13: *A substance which is absolutely infinite is indivisible.*

Dem.: For if it were divisible, the parts into which it would be divided will either retain the nature of an absolutely infinite substance or they will not. If the first, then there will be a number of substances of the same nature, which (by P5) is absurd. But if the second is asserted, then (as above [P12]), an absolutely infinite substance will be able to cease to be, which (by P11) is also absurd.

Cor.: From these [propositions] it follows that no substance, and consequently no corporeal substance, insofar as it is a substance, is divisible.

Schol.: That substance is indivisible, is understood more simply merely from this, that the nature of substance cannot be conceived unless as infinite, and that by a part of substance nothing can be understood except a finite substance, which (by P8) implies a plain contradiction.

P14: *Except God, no substance can be or be conceived.*

Dem.: Since God is an absolutely infinite being, of whom no attribute which expresses an essence of substance can be denied (by D6), and he necessarily exists (by P11), if there were any substance except God, it would have to be explained through some attribute of God, and so two substances of the same attribute would exist, which (by P5) is absurd. And so except God, no substance can be or, consequently, be conceived. For if it could be conceived, it would have to be conceived as existing. But this (by the first part of this demonstration) is absurd. Therefore, except for God no substance can be or be conceived, q.e.d.

Cor. 1: From this it follows most clearly, first, that God is unique, i.e. (by D6), that in Nature there is only one substance, and that it is absolutely infinite (as we indicated in P10S).

Cor. 2: It follows, second, that an extended thing and a thinking thing are either attributes of God, or (by A1) affections of God's attributes.

P15: *Whatever is, is in God, and nothing can be or be conceived without God.*

Dem.: Except for God, there neither is, nor can be conceived, any substance (by P14), i.e. (by D3), thing that is in itself and is conceived through itself. But modes (by D5) can neither be nor be conceived without substance. So they can be in the divine nature alone, and can be conceived through it alone. But except for substances and modes there is nothing (by A1). Therefore, [everything is in God and] nothing can be or be conceived without God, q.e.d.

Schol.: [I.] There are those who feign a God, like man, consisting of a body and a mind, and subject to passions. But how far they wander from the true knowledge of God, is sufficiently established by what has already been demonstrated. Them I dismiss. For everyone who has to any extent contemplated the divine nature denies that God is corporeal. They prove this best from the fact that by body we understand any quantity, with length, breadth, and depth, limited by some certain figure. Nothing more absurd than this can be said of God, viz. of a being absolutely infinite.

But meanwhile, by the other arguments by which they strive to demonstrate this same conclusion they clearly show that they entirely remove corporeal, *or* extended, substance itself from the divine nature. And they maintain that it has been created by God. But by what divine power could it be created? They are completely ignorant of that. And this shows clearly that they do not understand what they themselves say.

At any rate, I have demonstrated clearly enough—in my judgment, at least—that no substance can be produced or created by any other (see P6C and P8S2). Next, we have shown (P14) that except for God, no substance can either be or be conceived, and hence [in P14C2] we have concluded that extended substance is one of God's infinite attributes. But to provide a fuller explanation, I shall refute my opponents' arguments, which all reduce to these.

[II.] *First,* they think that corporeal substance, insofar as it is substance, consists of parts. And therefore they deny that it can be infinite, and consequently, that it can pertain to God. They explain this by many examples, of which I shall mention one or two.

[i] If corporeal substance is infinite, they say, let us conceive it to be divided in two parts. Each part will be either finite or infinite. If the former, then an infinite is composed of two finite parts, which is absurd. If the latter [i.e., if each part is infinite], then there is one infinite twice as large as another, which is also absurd. [ii] Again, if an infinite quantity is measured by parts [each] equal to a foot, it will consist of infinitely many such parts, as it will also, if it is measured by parts [each] equal to an inch. And therefore, one infinite number will be twelve times greater than another [which is no less absurd]. [iii] Finally, if we conceive that from one point of a certain infinite quantity two lines, say AB and AC, are extended to infinity, it is certain that, although in the beginning they are a certain, determinate distance apart, the distance between B and C is continuously increased, and at last, from being determinate, it will become indeterminable.

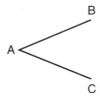

Since these absurdities follow—so they think—from the fact that an infinite quantity is supposed, they infer that corporeal substance must be finite, and consequently cannot pertain to God's essence.

[III.] Their *second* argument is also drawn from God's supreme perfection. For God, they say, since he is a supremely perfect being, cannot be acted on. But corporeal substance, since it is divisible, can be acted on. It follows, therefore, that it does not pertain to God's essence.

[IV.] These are the arguments which I find authors using, to try to show that corporeal substance is unworthy of the divine nature, and cannot pertain to it. But anyone who is properly attentive will find that I have already replied to them, since these arguments are founded only on their supposition that corporeal substance is composed of parts, which I have already (P12 and P13C) shown to be absurd. And then anyone who wishes to consider the matter rightly will see that all those absurdities *(if indeed they are all absurd, which I am not now disputing),* from which they wish to infer that extended substance is finite, do not follow at all from the fact that an infinite quantity is supposed, but from the fact that they suppose an infinite quantity to be measurable and composed of finite parts. So from the absurdities which follow from that they can infer only that infinite quantity is not measurable, and that it is not composed of finite parts. This is the same thing we have already demonstrated above (P12, etc.). So the weapon they aim at us, they really turn against themselves.

If, therefore, they still wish to infer from this absurdity of theirs that extended substance must be finite, they are indeed doing nothing more than if someone feigned that a circle has the properties of a square, and inferred from that the circle has no center, from which all lines drawn to the circumference are equal. For corporeal substance, which cannot be conceived except as infinite, unique, and indivisible (see P8, 5 and 12), they conceive to be composed of finite parts, to be many, and to be divisible, in order to infer that it is finite.

So also others, after they feign that a line is composed of points, know how to invent many arguments, by which they show that a line cannot be divided to infinity. And indeed it is no less absurd to assert that corporeal substance is composed of bodies, or parts, than that a body is composed of surfaces, the surfaces of lines, and the lines, finally, of points.

All those who know that clear reason is infallible must confess this—particularly those who deny that there is a vacuum. For if corporeal substance could be so divided that its parts were really distinct, why, then, could one part not be annihilated, the rest remaining connected with one another as before? And why must they all be so fitted together that there is no vacuum? Truly, of things which are really distinct from one another, one can be, and remain in its condition, without the other. Since, therefore, there is no vacuum in nature (a subject I discuss elsewhere), but all its parts must so concur that there is no vacuum, it follows also that they cannot be really distinguished, i.e., that corporeal substance, insofar as it is a substance, cannot be divided.

[V.] If someone should now ask why we are, by nature, so inclined to divide quantity, I shall answer that we conceive quantity in two ways: abstractly, or superficially, as we [commonly] imagine it, *or* as substance, which is done by the intellect alone [without the help of the imagination]. So if we attend to quantity as it is in the imagination, which we do often and more easily, it will be found to be finite, divisible, and composed of parts; but if we attend to it as it is in the intellect, and conceive it insofar as it is a substance, which happens [seldom and] with great difficulty, then (as we have already sufficiently demonstrated) it will be found to be infinite, unique, and indivisible.

This will be sufficiently plain to everyone who knows how to distinguish between the intellect and the imagination—particularly if it is also noted that matter is everywhere the same, and that parts are distinguished in it only insofar as we conceive matter to be affected in different ways, so that its parts are distinguished only modally, but not really.

For example, we conceive that water is divided and its parts separated from one another—insofar as it is water, but not insofar as it is corporeal substance. For insofar as it is substance, it is neither separated nor divided. Again, water, insofar as it is water, is generated and corrupted, but insofar as it is substance, it is neither generated nor corrupted.

[VI.] And with this I think I have replied to the second argument also, since it is based on the supposition that matter, insofar as it is substance, is divisible, and composed of parts. Even if this [reply] were not [sufficient], I do not know why [divisibility] would be unworthy of the divine nature. For (by P14) apart from God there can be no substance by which [the divine nature] would be acted on. All things, I say, are in God, and all things that happen, happen only through the laws of God's infinite nature and follow (as I shall show) from the necessity of his essence. So it cannot be said in any way that God is acted on by another, or that extended substance is unworthy of the divine nature, even if it is supposed to be divisible, so long as it is granted to be eternal and infinite. But enough of this for the present.

P16: *From the necessity of the divine nature there must follow infinitely many things in infinitely many modes (i.e., everything which can fall under an infinite intellect).*

Dem.: This Proposition must be plain to anyone, provided he attends to the fact that the intellect infers from the given definition of any thing a number of properties that really do follow necessarily from it (i.e., from the very essence of the thing); and that it infers more properties the more the definition of the thing expresses reality, i.e., the more reality the essence of the defined thing involves. But since the divine nature has absolutely infinite attributes (by D6), each of which also expresses an essence infinite in its own kind, from its necessity there must follow infinitely many things in infinite modes (i.e., everything which can fall under an infinite intellect), q.e.d.

Cor. 1: From this it follows that God is the efficient cause of all things which can fall under an infinite intellect.

Cor. 2: It follows, secondly, that God is a cause through himself and not an accidental cause.

Cor. 3: It follows, thirdly, that God is absolutely the first cause.

P17: *God acts from the laws of his nature alone, and is compelled by no one.*

Dem.: We have just shown (P16) that from the necessity of the divine nature alone, or (what is the same thing) from the laws of his nature alone, absolutely infinite things follow, and in P15 we have demonstrated that nothing can be or be conceived without God, but that all things are in God. So there can be nothing outside him by which he is determined or compelled to act. Therefore, God acts from the laws of his nature alone, and is compelled by no one, q.e.d.

Cor. 1: From this it follows, first, that there is no cause, either extrinsically or intrinsically, which prompts God to action, except the perfection of his nature.

Cor. 2: It follows, secondly, that God alone is a free cause. For God alone exists only from the necessity of his nature (by P11 and P14C1), and acts from the necessity of his nature (by P17). Therefore (by D7) God alone is a free cause, q.e.d.

Schol.: [I.] Others think that God is a free cause because he can (so they think) bring it about that the things which we have said follow from his nature (i.e., which are in his power) do not happen or are not produced by him. But this is the same as if they were to say that God can bring it about that it would not follow from the nature of a triangle that its three angles are equal to two right angles; or that from a given cause the effect would not follow—which is absurd.

Further, I shall show later, without the aid of this Proposition, that neither intellect nor will pertain to God's nature. Of course I know there are many who think they can demonstrate that a supreme intellect and a free will pertain to God's nature. For they say they know nothing they can ascribe to God more perfect than what is the highest perfection in us.

Moreover, even if they conceive God to actually understand in the highest degree, they still do not believe that he can bring it about that all the things he actually understands exist. For they think that in that way they would destroy God's power. If he had created all the things in his intellect (they say), then he would have been able to create nothing more, which they believe to be incompatible with God's omnipotence. So they preferred to maintain that God is indifferent to all things, not creating anything except what he has decreed to create by some absolute will.

But I think I have shown clearly enough (see P16) that from God's supreme power, *or* infinite nature, infinitely many things in infinitely many modes, i.e., all things, have necessarily flowed, or always follow, by the same necessity and in the same way as from the nature of a triangle it follows, from eternity and to eternity, that its three angles are equal to two right angles. So God's omnipotence has been actual from eternity and will remain in the same actuality to eternity. And in this way, at least in my opinion, God's omnipotence is maintained far more perfectly.

Indeed—to speak openly—my opponents seem to deny God's omnipotence. For they are forced to confess that God understands infinitely many creatable things, which nevertheless he will never be able to create. For otherwise, if he created everything he understood [to be creatable] he would (according to them) exhaust his omnipotence and render himself imperfect. Therefore to maintain that God is perfect, they are driven to maintain at the same time that he cannot bring about everything to which his power extends. I do not see what could be feigned which would be more absurd than this or more contrary to God's omnipotence.

[II.] Further—to say something here also about the intellect and will which we commonly attribute to God—if will and intellect do pertain to the eternal essence of God, we must of course understand by each of these attributes something different from what men commonly understand. For the intellect and will which would constitute God's essence would have to differ entirely from our intellect and will, and could not agree with them in anything except the name. They would not agree with one another any more than do the dog that is a heavenly constellation and the dog that is a barking animal. I shall demonstrate this.

If intellect pertains to the divine nature, it will not be able to be (like our intellect) by nature either posterior to (as most would have it), or simultaneous with, the things understood, since God is prior in causality to all things (by P16C1). On the contrary, the truth and formal essence of things is what it is because it exists objectively in that way in God's intellect. So God's intellect, insofar as it is conceived to constitute God's essence, is really the cause both of the essence and of the existence of things. This seems also to have been noticed by those who asserted that God's intellect, will and power are one and the same.

Therefore, since God's intellect is the only cause of things (viz. as we have shown, both of their essence and of their existence), he must necessarily differ from them both as to his essence and as to his existence. For what is caused differs from its cause precisely in what it has from the cause [for that reason it is called the effect of such a cause]. E.g., a man is the cause of the existence of another man, but not of his essence, for the latter is an eternal truth. Hence, they can agree entirely according to their essence. But in existing they must differ. And for that reason, if the existence of one perishes, the other's existence will not thereby perish. But if the essence of one could be destroyed, and become false, the other's essence would also be destroyed [and become false].

So the thing that is the cause both of the essence and of the existence of some effect, must differ from such an effect, both as to its essence and as to its existence. But God's intellect is the cause both of the essence and of the existence of our intellect. Therefore, God's intellect, insofar as it is conceived to constitute the divine essence, differs from our intellect both as to its essence and as to its existence, and cannot agree with it in anything except in name, as we supposed. The proof proceeds in the same way concerning the will, as anyone can easily see.

P18: *God is the immanent, not the transitive, cause of all things.*

Dem.: Everything that is, is in God, and must be conceived through God (by P15), and so (by P16C1) God is the cause of [all] things, which are in him. That is the first [thing to be proven]. And then outside God there can be no substance (by P14), i.e. (by D3), thing which is in itself outside God. That was the second. God, therefore, is the immanent, not the transitive cause of all things, q.e.d.

P19: *God is eternal, or all God's attributes are eternal.*

Dem.: For God (by D6) is substance, which (by P11) necessarily exists, i.e. (by P7), to whose nature it pertains to exist, or (what is the same) from whose definition it follows that he exists; and therefore (by D8), he is eternal.

Next, by God's attributes are to be understood what (by D4) expresses an essence of the Divine substance, i.e., what pertains to substance. The attributes themselves, I say, must involve it itself. But eternity pertains to the nature of substance (as I have already demonstrated from P7). Therefore each of the attributes must involve eternity, and so, they are all eternal, q.e.d.

Schol.: This Proposition is also as clear as possible from the way I have demonstrated God's existence (P11). For from that demonstration, I say, it is established that God's existence, like his essence, is an eternal truth. And then I have also demonstrated God's eternity in another way (Descartes' *Principles* IP19), and there is no need to repeat it here.

P20: *God's existence and his essence are one and the same.*

Dem.: God (by P19) and all of his attributes are eternal, i.e. (by D8), each of his attributes expresses existence. Therefore, the same attributes of God which (by D4) explain God's eternal essence at the same time explain his eternal existence, i.e., that itself which constitutes God's essence at the same time constitutes his existence. So his existence and his essence are one and the same, q.e.d.

Cor. 1: From this it follows, first, that God's existence, like his essence, is an eternal truth.

Cor. 2: It follows, secondly, that God, *or* all of God's attributes, are immutable. For if they changed as to their existence, they would also (by P20) change as to their essence, i.e. (as is known through itself), from being true become false, which is absurd.

P21: *All the things which follow from the absolute nature of any of God's attributes have always had to exist and be infinite, or are, through the same attribute, eternal and infinite.*

Dem.: If you deny this, then conceive (if you can) that in some attribute of God there follows from its absolute nature something that is finite and has a determinate existence, *or* duration, e.g., God's idea in thought. Now since thought is supposed to be an attribute of God, it is necessarily (by P11) infinite by its nature. But insofar as it has God's idea, [thought] is supposed to be finite. But (by D2) [thought] cannot be conceived to be finite unless it is determined through thought itself. But [thought can] not [be determined] through thought itself, insofar as it constitutes God's idea, for to that extent [thought] is supposed to be finite. Therefore, [thought must be determined] through thought insofar as it does not constitute God's idea, which [thought] nevertheless (by P11) must necessarily exist. Therefore, there is thought which does not constitute God's idea, and on that account God's idea does not follow necessarily from the nature [of this thought] insofar as it is absolute thought (for [thought] is conceived both as constituting God's idea and as not constituting it). [That God's idea does not follow from thought, insofar as it is absolute thought] is contrary to the hypothesis. So if God's idea in thought, or anything else in any attribute of God (for it does not matter what example is taken, since the demonstration is universal), follows from the necessity of the absolute nature of the attribute itself, it must necessarily be infinite. This was the first thing to be proven.

Next, what follows in this way from the necessity of the nature of any attribute cannot have a determinate [existence, or] duration. For if you deny this, then suppose there is, in some attribute of God, a thing which follows from the necessity of the nature of that attribute—e.g., God's idea in thought—and suppose that at some time [this idea] did not exist or will not exist. But since thought is supposed to be an attribute of God, it must exist necessarily and be immutable (by P11 and P20C2). So beyond the limits of the duration of God's idea (for it is supposed that at some time [this idea] did not exist or will not exist) thought will have to exist without God's idea. But this is contrary to the hypothesis, for it is supposed that God's idea follows necessarily from the given thought. Therefore, God's idea in thought, or anything else which follows necessarily from the absolute nature of some attribute of God, cannot have a determinate duration, but through the same attribute is eternal. This was the second thing [to be proven]. Note that the same is to be affirmed of any thing which, in some attribute of God, follows necessarily from God's absolute nature.

P22: *Whatever follows from some attribute of God insofar as it is modified by a modification which, through the same attribute, exists necessarily and is infinite, must also exist necessarily and be infinite.*

Dem.: The demonstration of this proposition proceeds in the same way as the demonstration of the preceding one.

P23: *Every mode which exists necessarily and is infinite has necessarily had to follow either from the absolute nature of some attribute of God, or from some attribute, modified by a modification which exists necessarily and is infinite.*

Dem.: For a mode is in another, through which it must be conceived (by D5), i.e. (by P15), it is in God alone, and can be conceived through God alone. So if a mode is conceived to exist necessarily and be infinite, [its necessary existence and infinitude] must necessarily be inferred, *or* perceived through some attribute of God, insofar as that attribute is conceived to express infinity and necessity of existence, *or* (what is the same, by D8) eternity, i.e. (by D6 and P19), insofar as it is considered absolutely. Therefore, the mode, which exists necessarily and is infinite, has had to follow from the absolute nature of some attribute of God—either immediately (see P21) or by some mediating modification, which follows from its absolute nature, i.e. (by P22), which exists necessarily and is infinite, q.e.d.

P24: *The essence of things produced by God does not involve existence.*

Dem.: This is evident from D1. For that whose nature involves existence (considered in itself), is its own cause, and exists only from the necessity of its nature.

Cor.: From this it follows that God is not only the cause of things' beginning to exist, but also of their persevering in existing, or (to use a Scholastic term) God is the cause of the being of things. For—whether the things [produced] exist or not—so long as we attend to their essence, we shall find that it involves neither existence nor duration. So their essence can be the cause neither of their existence nor of their duration, but only God, to whose nature alone it pertains to exist [can be the cause] (by P14C1).

P25: *God is the efficient cause, not only of the existence of things, but also of their essence.*

Dem.: If you deny this, then God is not the cause of the essence of things; and so (by A4) the essence of things can be conceived without God. But (by P15) this is absurd. Therefore God is also the cause of the essence of things, q.e.d.

Schol.: This Proposition follows more clearly from P16. For from that it follows that from the given divine nature both the essence of things and their existence must necessarily be inferred; and in a word, God must be called the cause of all things in the same sense in which he is called the cause of himself. This will be established still more clearly from the following corollary.

Cor.: Particular things are nothing but affections of God's attributes, or modes by which God's attributes are expressed in a certain and determinate way. The demonstration is evident from P15 and D5.

P26: *A thing which has been determined to produce an effect has necessarily been determined in this way by God; and one which has not been determined by God cannot determine itself to produce an effect.*

Dem.: That through which things are said to be determined to produce an effect must be something positive (as is known through itself). And so, God, from the necessity of his nature, is the efficient cause both of its essence and of its existence (by P25 and 16); this was the first thing. And from it the second thing asserted also follows very clearly. For if a thing which has not been determined by God could determine itself, the first part of this [proposition] would be false, which is absurd, as we have shown.

P27: *A thing which has been determined by God to produce an effect, cannot render itself undetermined.*

Dem.: This proposition is evident from A3.

P28: *Every singular thing, or any thing which is finite and has a determinate existence, can neither exist nor be determined to produce an effect unless it is determined to exist and produce an effect by another cause, which is also finite and has a determinate existence; and again, this cause also can neither exist nor be determined to produce an effect unless it is determined to exist and produce an effect by another, which is also finite and has a determinate existence, and so on, to infinity.*

Dem.: Whatever has been determined to exist and produce an effect has been so determined by God (by P26 and P24C). But what is finite and has a determinate existence could not have been produced by the absolute nature of an attribute of God; for whatever follows from the absolute nature of an attribute of God is eternal and infinite (by P21). It had, therefore, to follow either from God or from an attribute of God insofar as it is considered to be affected by some mode. For there is nothing except substance and its modes (by A1, D3, and D5) and modes (by P25C) are nothing but affections of God's attributes. But it also could not follow from God, or from an attribute of God, insofar as it is affected by a modification which is eternal and infinite (by P22). It had, therefore, to follow from, or be determined to exist and produce an effect by God or an attribute of God insofar as it is modified by a modification which is finite and has a determinate existence. This was the first thing to be proven.

And in turn, this cause, *or* this mode (by the same reasoning by which we have already demonstrated the first part of this proposition) had also to be determined by another, which is also finite and has a determinate existence; and again, this last (by the same reasoning) by another, and so always (by the same reasoning) to infinity, q.e.d.

Schol.: Since certain things had to be produced by God immediately, viz. those which follow necessarily from his absolute nature, and others (which nevertheless can neither be nor be conceived without God) had to be produced by the mediation of these first things, it follows:

I. That God is absolutely the proximate cause of the things produced immediately by him, and not [a proximate cause] in his own kind, as they say. For God's effects can neither be nor be conceived without their cause (by P15 and P24C).

II. That God cannot properly be called the remote cause of singular things, except perhaps so that we may distinguish them from those things that he has produced immediately, or rather, that follow from his absolute nature. For by a remote cause we under-

The Synagogue, Amsterdam, n.d., by Rembrandt (1606–1669). Spinoza was a member of the Amsterdam Synagogue until he was excommunicated in 1656. (*Musée de la Ville de Paris, Musée du Petit-Palais/Art Resource*)

stand one which is not conjoined in any way with its effect. But all things that are, are in God, and so depend on God that they can neither be nor be conceived without him.

P29: *In nature there is nothing contingent, but all things have been determined from the necessity of the divine nature to exist and produce an effect in a certain way.*

Dem.: Whatever is, is in God (by P15); but God cannot be called a contingent thing. For (by P11) he exists necessarily, not contingently. Next, the modes of the divine nature have also followed from it necessarily and not contingently (by P16)—either insofar as the divine nature is considered absolutely (by P21) or insofar as it is considered to be determined to act in a certain way (by P28). Further, God is the cause of these modes not only insofar as they simply exist (by P24C), but also (by P26) insofar as they are considered to be determined to produce an effect. For if they have not been determined by God, then (by P26) it is impossible, not contingent, that they should determine themselves. Conversely (by P27) if they have been determined by God, it is not contingent, but impossible, that they should render themselves undetermined. So all things have been determined from the necessity of the divine nature, not only to exist, but to exist in a certain way, and to produce effects in a certain way. There is nothing contingent, q.e.d.

Schol.: Before I proceed further, I wish to explain here—or rather to advise [the reader]—what we must understand by *Natura naturans* and *Natura naturata*. For from the preceding I think it is already established that by *Natura naturans* we must understand what is in itself and is conceived through itself, or such attributes of substance as express an eternal and infinite essence, i.e. (by P14C1 and P17C2), God, insofar as he is considered as a free cause.

But by *Natura naturata* I understand whatever follows from the necessity of God's nature, or from any of God's attributes, i.e., all the modes of God's attributes insofar as they are considered as things which are in God, and can neither be nor be conceived without God.

P30: *An actual intellect, whether finite or infinite, must comprehend God's attributes and God's affections, and nothing else.*

Dem.: A true idea must agree with its object (by A6), i.e. (as is known through itself), what is contained objectively in the intellect must necessarily be in nature. But in nature (by P14C1) there is only one substance, viz. God, and there are no affections other than those which are in God (by P15) and which can neither be nor be conceived without God (by P15). Therefore, an actual intellect, whether finite or infinite, must comprehend God's attributes and God's affections, and nothing else, q.e.d.

P31: *The actual intellect, whether finite or infinite, like will, desire, love, etc., must be referred to* Natura naturata, *not to* Natura naturans.

Dem.: By intellect (as is known through itself) we understand not absolute thought, but only a certain mode of thinking, which mode differs from the others, such as desire, love, etc., and so (by D5) must be conceived through absolute thought, i.e. (by P15 and D6), it must be so conceived through an attribute of God, which expresses the eternal and infinite essence of thought, that can neither be nor be conceived without [that attribute]; and so (by P29S), like the other modes of thinking, it must be referred to *Natura naturata,* not to *Natura naturans,* q.e.d.

Schol.: The reason why I speak here of actual intellect is not because I concede that there is any potential intellect, but because, wishing to avoid all confusion, I wanted to speak only of what we perceive as clearly as possible, i.e., of the intellection itself. We perceive nothing more clearly than that. For we can understand nothing that does not lead to more perfect knowledge of the intellection.

P32: *The will cannot be called a free cause, but only a necessary one.*

Dem.: The will, like the intellect, is only a certain mode of thinking. And so (by P28) each volition can neither exist nor be determined to produce an effect unless it is determined by another cause, and this cause again by another, and so on, to infinity. Even if the will be supposed to be infinite, it must still be determined to exist and produce an effect by God, not insofar as he is an absolutely infinite substance, but insofar as he has an attribute that expresses the infinite and eternal essence of thought (by P23). So in whatever way it is conceived, whether as finite or as infinite, it requires a cause by which it is determined to exist and produce an effect. And so (by D7) it cannot be called a free cause, but only a necessary or compelled one, q.e.d.

Cor. 1: From this it follows, first, that God does not produce any effect by freedom of the will.

Cor. 2: It follows, secondly, that will and intellect are related to God's nature as motion and rest are, and as are absolutely all natural things, which (by P29) must be determined by God to exist and produce an effect in a certain way. For the will, like all other things, requires a cause by which it is determined to exist and produce an effect in a certain way. And although from a given will, *or* intellect infinitely many things may follow, God still cannot be said, on that account, to act from freedom of the will, any more than he can be said to act from freedom of motion and rest on account of those things that follow from motion and rest (for infinitely many things also follow from motion and rest). So will does not pertain to God's nature any more than do the other natural things, but is related to him in the same way as motion and rest, and all the other things which, as we have shown, follow from the necessity of the divine nature and are determined by it to exist and produce an effect in a certain way.

P33: *Things could have been produced by God in no other way, and in no other order than they have been produced.*

Dem.: For all things have necessarily followed from God's given nature (by P16), and have been determined from the necessity of God's nature to exist and produce an effect in a certain way (by P29). Therefore, if things could have been of another nature, or could have been determined to produce an effect in another way, so that the order of Nature was different, then God's nature could also have been other than it is now, and therefore (by P11) that [other nature] would also have had to exist, and consequently, there could have been two or more Gods, which is absurd (by P14C1). So things could have been produced in no other way and no other order, etc., q.e.d.

Schol. 1: Since by these propositions I have shown more clearly than the noon light that there is absolutely nothing in things on account of which they can be called contingent, I wish now to explain briefly what we must understand by contingent—but first, what [we must understand] by necessary and impossible.

A thing is called necessary either by reason of its essence or by reason of its cause. For a thing's existence follows necessarily either from its essence and definition or from a given efficient cause. And a thing is also called impossible from these same causes—viz. either because its essence, or definition, involves a contradiction, or because there is no external cause which has been determined to produce such a thing.

But a thing is called contingent only because of a defect of our knowledge. For if we do not know that the thing's essence involves a contradiction, or if we do know very well that its essence does not involve a contradiction, and nevertheless can affirm nothing certainly about its existence, because the order of causes is hidden from us, it can never seem to us either necessary or impossible. So we call it contingent or possible.

Schol. 2: From the preceding it clearly follows that things have been produced by God with the highest perfection, since they have followed necessarily from a given most perfect nature. Nor does this convict God of any imperfection, for his perfection compels us to affirm this. Indeed, from the opposite, it would clearly follow (as I have just shown), that God is not supremely perfect; because if things had been produced by God in another way, we would have to attribute to God another nature, different from that which we have been compelled to attribute to him from the consideration of the most perfect Being.

Of course, I have no doubt that many will reject this opinion as absurd, without even being willing to examine it—for no other reason than because they have been accustomed to attribute another freedom to God, far different from that we have taught (D7), viz. an absolute will. But I also have no doubt that, if they are willing to reflect on the matter, and consider properly the chain of our demonstrations, in the end they will utterly reject the freedom they now attribute to God, not only as futile, but as a great obstacle to science. Nor is it necessary for me to repeat here what I said in P17S.

Nevertheless, to please them, I shall show that even if it is conceded that will pertains to God's essence, it still follows from his perfection that things could have been created by God in no other way or order. It will be easy to show this if we consider, first, what they themselves concede, viz. that it depends on God's decree and will alone that each thing is what it is. For otherwise God would not be the cause of all things. Next, that all God's decrees have been established by God himself from eternity. For otherwise he would be convicted of imperfection and inconstancy. But since, in eternity, there is neither when, nor *before,* nor *after,* it follows, from God's perfection alone, that he can never decree anything different, and never could have, *or* that God was not before his decrees, and cannot be without them.

But they will say that even if it were supposed that God had made another nature of things, or that from eternity he had decreed something else concerning nature and its order, no imperfection in God would follow from that.

Still, if they say this, they will concede at the same time that God can change his decrees. For if God had decreed, concerning nature and its order, something other than what he did decree, i.e., had willed and conceived something else concerning nature, he would necessarily have had an intellect other than he now has, and a will other than he now has. And if it is permitted to attribute to God another intellect and another will, without any change of his essence and of his perfection, why can he not now change his decrees concerning created things, and nevertheless remain equally perfect? For his intellect and will concerning created things and their order are the same in respect to his essence and his perfection, however his will and intellect may be conceived.

Further, all the Philosophers I have seen concede that in God there is no potential intellect, but only an actual one. But since his intellect and his will are not distinguished from his essence, as they all also concede, it follows that if God had had another actual intellect, and another will, his essence would also necessarily be other. And therefore (as I inferred at the beginning) if things had been produced by God otherwise than they now are, God's intellect and his will, i.e. (as is conceded), his essence, would have to be different [from what it now is]. And this is absurd.

Therefore, since things could have been produced by God in no other way, and no other order, and since it follows from God's supreme perfection that this is true, no truly sound reason can persuade us to believe that God did not will to create all the things that are in his intellect, with that same perfection with which he understands them.

But they will say that there is no perfection or imperfection in things; what is in them, on account of which they are perfect or imperfect, and are called good or bad, depends only on God's will. And so, if God had willed, he could have brought it about that what is now perfection would have been the greatest imperfection, and conversely [that what is now an imperfection in things would have been the most perfect]. How would this be different from saying openly that God, who necessarily understands what he wills, can bring it about by his will that he understands things in another way than he does understand them? As I have just shown, this is a great absurdity.

So I can turn the argument against them in the following way. All things depend on God's power. So in order for things to be able to be different, God's will would necessarily also have to be different. But God's will cannot be different (as we have just shown most evidently from God's perfection). So things also cannot be different.

I confess that this opinion, which subjects all things to a certain indifferent will of God, and makes all things depend on his good pleasure, is nearer the truth than that of those who maintain that God does all things for the sake of the good. For they seem to place something outside God, which does not depend on God, to which God attends, as a model, in what he does, and at which he aims, as at a certain goal. This is simply to subject God to fate. Nothing more absurd can be maintained about God, whom we have shown to be the first and only free cause, both of the essence of all things, and of their existence. So I shall waste no time in refuting this absurdity.

P34: *God's power is his essence itself.*

Dem.: For from the necessity alone of God's essence it follows that God is the cause of himself (by P11) and (by P16 and P16C) of all things. Therefore, God's power, by which he and all things are and act, is his essence itself, q.e.d.

P35: *Whatever we conceive to be in God's power, necessarily exists.*

Dem.: For whatever is in God's power must (by P34) be so comprehended by his essence that it necessarily follows from it, and therefore necessarily exists, q.e.d.

P36: *Nothing exists from whose nature some effect does not follow.*

Dem.: Whatever exists expresses the nature, or essence of God in a certain and determinate way (by P25C), i.e. (by P34), whatever exists expresses in a certain and determinate way the power of God, which is the cause of all things. So (by P16), from [everything that exists] some effect must follow, q.e.d.

Appendix

With these [demonstrations] I have explained God's nature and properties: that he exists necessarily; that he is unique; that he is and acts from the necessity alone of his nature; that (and how) he is the free cause of all things; that all things are in God and so depend on him that without him they can neither be nor be conceived; and finally, that all things have been predetermined by God, not from freedom of the will *or* absolute good pleasure, but from God's absolute nature, or infinite power.

Further, I have taken care, whenever the occasion arose, to remove prejudices that could prevent my demonstrations from being perceived. But because many prejudices remain that could, and can, be a great obstacle to men's understanding the connection of things in the way I have explained it, I considered it worthwhile to submit them here to the scrutiny of reason. All the prejudices I here undertake to expose depend on this one: that men commonly suppose that all natural things act, as men do, on account of an end; indeed, they maintain as certain that God himself directs all things to some certain end, for they say that God has made all things for man, and man that he might worship God.

So I shall begin by considering this one prejudice, asking *first* [I] why most people are satisfied that it is true, and why all are so inclined by nature to embrace it. *Then* [II] I shall show its falsity, and *finally* [III] how, from this, prejudices have arisen concerning *good* and *evil, merit* and *sin, praise* and *blame, order* and *confusion, beauty* and *ugliness,* and other things of this kind.

[I.] Of course this is not the place to deduce these things from the nature of the human mind. It will be sufficient here if I take as a foundation what everyone must acknowledge: that all men are born ignorant of the causes of things, and that they all want to seek their own advantage, and are conscious of this appetite.

From these [assumptions] it follows, *first,* that men think themselves free, because they are conscious of their volitions and their appetite, and do not think, even in their dreams, of the causes by which they are disposed to wanting and willing, because they are ignorant of [those causes]. It follows, *secondly,* that men act always on account of an end, viz. on account of their advantage, which they want. Hence they seek to know only the final causes of what has been done, and when they have heard them, they are satisfied, because they have no reason to doubt further. But if they cannot hear them from another, nothing remains for them but to turn toward themselves, and reflect on the ends by which they are usually determined to do such things; so they necessarily judge the temperament of other men from their own temperament.

Furthermore, they find—both in themselves and outside themselves—many means that are very helpful in seeking their own advantage, e.g., eyes for seeing, teeth for chewing, plants and animals for food, the sun for light, the sea for supporting fish [and so with almost all other things whose natural causes they have no reason to doubt]. Hence, they consider all natural things as means to their own advantage. And knowing that they had found these means, not provided them for themselves, they had reason to believe that there was someone else who had prepared those means for their use. For after they considered things as means, they could not believe that the things had made themselves; but from the means they were accustomed to prepare for themselves, they had to infer that there was a ruler, or a number of rulers of nature, endowed with human freedom, who had taken care of all things for them, and made all things for their use.

And since they had never heard anything about the temperament of these rulers, they had to judge it from their own. Hence, they maintained that the Gods direct all things for the use of men in order to bind men to them and be held by men in the highest honor. So it has happened that each of them has thought up from his own temperament different ways of worshipping God, so that God might love them above all the rest, and direct the whole of Nature according to the needs of their blind desire and insatiable greed. Thus this prejudice was changed into superstition, and struck deep roots in their minds. This was why each of them strove with great diligence to understand and explain the final causes of all things.

But while they sought to show that nature does nothing in vain (i.e., nothing which is not of use to men), they seem to have shown only that nature and the Gods are as mad as men. See, I ask you, how the matter has turned out in the end! Among so many conveniences in nature they had to find many inconveniences: storms, earthquakes, diseases, etc. These, they maintain, happen because the Gods [(whom they judge to be of the same nature as themselves)] are angry on account of wrongs done to them by men, or on account of sins committed in their worship. And though their daily experience contradicted this, and though infinitely many examples showed that conveniences and inconveniences happen indiscriminately to the pious and the impious alike, they did not on that account give up their longstanding prejudice. It was easier for them to put this among the other unknown things, whose use they were ignorant of, and so remain in the state of ignorance in which they had been born, than to destroy that whole construction, and think up a new one.

So they maintained it as certain that the judgments of the Gods far surpass man's grasp. This alone, of course, would have caused the truth to be hidden from the human race to eternity, if Mathematics, which is concerned not with ends, but only with the essences and properties of figures, had not shown men another standard of truth. And besides Mathematics, we can assign other causes also (which it is unnecessary to enumerate here), which were able to bring it about that men [—but very few, in relation to the whole human race—] would notice these common prejudices and be led to the true knowledge of things.

[II.] With this I have sufficiently explained what I promised in the first place [viz. why men are so inclined to believe that all things act for an end]. Not many words will be required now to show that Nature has no end set before it, and that all final causes are nothing but human fictions. For I believe I have already sufficiently established it, both by the foundations and causes from which I have shown this prejudice to have had its origin, and also by P16, P32C1 and C2, and all those [propositions] by which I have shown that all things proceed by a certain eternal necessity of nature, and with the greatest perfection.

I shall, however, add this: this doctrine concerning the end turns nature completely upside down. For what is really a cause, it considers as an effect, and conversely [what is an effect it considers as a cause]. What is by nature prior, it makes posterior. And finally, what is supreme and most perfect, it makes imperfect.

For—to pass over the first two, since they are manifest through themselves—as has been established in PP21–23, that effect is most perfect which is produced immediately by God, and the more something requires intermediate causes to produce it, the more imperfect it is. But if the things which have been produced immediately by God had been made so that God would achieve his end, then the last things, for the sake of which the first would have been made, would be the most excellent of all.

Again, this doctrine takes away God's perfection. For if God acts for the sake of an end, he necessarily wants something which he lacks. And though the Theologians and Metaphysicians distinguish between an end of need and an end of assimilation, they nevertheless confess that God did all things for his own sake, not for the sake of the things to be created. For before creation they can assign nothing except God for whose sake God would act. And so they are necessarily compelled to confess that God lacked those things for the sake of which he willed to prepare means, and that he desired them. This is clear through itself.

Nor ought we here to pass over the fact that the Followers of this doctrine, who have wanted to show off their cleverness in assigning the ends of things, have introduced—to prove this doctrine of theirs—a new way of arguing: by reducing things, not to the impossible, but to ignorance. This shows that no other way of defending their doctrine was open to them.

For example, if a stone has fallen from a roof onto someone's head and killed him, they will show, in the following way, that the stone fell in order to kill the man. For if it did not fall to that end, God willing it, how could so many circumstances have concurred by chance (for often many circumstances do concur at once)? Perhaps you will answer that it happened because the wind was blowing hard and the man was walking that way. But they will persist: why was the wind blowing hard at that time? why was the man walking that way at that same time? If you answer again that the wind arose then because on the preceding day, while the weather was still calm, the sea began to toss, and that the man had been invited by a friend, they will press on—for there is no end to the questions which can be asked: but why was the sea tossing? why was the man invited at just that time? And so they will not stop asking for the causes of causes until you take refuge in the will of God, i.e., the sanctuary of ignorance.

Similarly, when they see the structure of the human body, they are struck by a foolish wonder, and because they do not know the causes of so great an art, they infer that it is constructed, not by mechanical, but by divine, or supernatural art, and constituted in such a way that one part does not injure another.

Hence it happens that one who seeks the true causes of miracles, and is eager, like an educated man, to understand natural things, not to wonder at them, like a fool, is generally considered and denounced as an impious heretic by those whom the people honor as interpreters of nature and the Gods. For they know that if ignorance is taken away, then foolish wonder, the only means they have of arguing and defending their authority, is also taken away. But I leave these things, and pass on to what I have decided to treat here in the third place.

[III.] After men persuaded themselves that everything that happens, happens on their account, they had to judge that what is most important in each thing is what is most useful to them, and to rate as most excellent all those things by which they were most pleased. Hence, they had to form these notions, by which they explained natural things: *good, evil, order, confusion, warm, cold, beauty, ugliness.* And because they think themselves free, those notions have arisen: *praise* and *blame, sin* and *merit.* The latter I shall explain after I have treated human nature; but the former I shall briefly explain here.

Whatever conduces to health and the worship of God, they have called *good;* but what is contrary to these, *evil.*

And because those who do not understand the nature of things, but only imagine them, affirm nothing concerning things, and take the imagination for the intellect, they firmly believe, in their ignorance of things and of their own nature, that there is an order in things. For when things are so disposed that, when they are presented to us through the senses, we can easily imagine them, and so can easily remember them, we say that they are well-ordered; but if the opposite is true, we say that they are badly ordered, or confused.

And since those things we can easily imagine are especially pleasing to us, men prefer order to confusion, as if order were anything in nature more than a relation to our imagination. They also say that God has created all things in order, and so, unknowingly attribute imagination to God—unless, perhaps, they mean that God, to provide for human imagination, has disposed all things so that men can very easily imagine them. Nor will it, perhaps, give them pause that infinitely many things are found which far surpass our imagination, and a great many which confuse it on account of its weakness. But enough of this.

The other notions are also nothing but modes of imagining, by which the imagination is variously affected; and yet the ignorant consider them the chief attributes of things, because, as we have already said, they believe all things have been made for their sake, and call the nature of a thing good or evil, sound or rotten and corrupt, as they are affected by it. For example, if the motion the nerves receive from objects presented through the eyes is conducive to health, the objects by which it is caused are called beautiful; those which cause a contrary motion are called ugly. Those which move the sense through the nose, they call pleasant-smelling or stinking; through the tongue, sweet or bitter, tasty or tasteless; through touch, hard or soft, rough or smooth, etc.; and finally, those which move the ears are said to produce noise, sound or harmony. Men have been so mad as to believe that God is pleased by harmony. Indeed there are Philosophers who have persuaded themselves that the motions of the heavens produce a harmony.

All of these things show sufficiently that each one has judged things according to the disposition of his brain; or rather, has accepted affections of the imagination as things. So it is no wonder (to note this, too, in passing) that we find so many controversies to have arisen among men, and that they have finally given rise to Skepticism. For although human bodies agree in many things, they still differ in very many. And for that reason what seems good to one, seems bad to another; what seems ordered to one, seems confused to another; what seems pleasing to one, seems displeasing to another, and so on.

I pass over the [other notions] here, both because this is not the place to treat them at length, and because everyone has experienced this [variability] sufficiently for himself. That is why we have such sayings as "So many heads, so many attitudes," "everyone finds his own judgment more than enough," and "there are as many differences of brains as of palates." These proverbs show sufficiently that men judge things according to the disposition of their brain, and imagine, rather than understand them. For if men had understood them, the things would at least convince them all, even if they did not attract them all, as the example of mathematics shows.

We see, therefore, that all the notions by which ordinary people are accustomed to explain nature are only modes of imagining, and do not indicate the nature of anything, only the constitution of the imagination. And because they have names, as if they were [notions] of beings existing outside the imagination, I call them beings, not of reason, but of imagination. So all the arguments in which people try to use such notions against us can easily be warded off.

For many are accustomed to arguing in this way: if all things have followed from the necessity of God's most perfect nature, why are there so many imperfections in nature? why are things corrupt to the point where they stink? so ugly that they produce nausea? why is there confusion, evil, and sin?

As I have just said, those who argue in this way are easily answered. For the perfection of things is to be judged solely from their nature and power; things are not more or less perfect because they please or offend men's senses, or because they are of use to, or are incompatible with, human nature.

But to those who ask "why God did not create all men so that they would be governed by the command of reason?" I answer only "because he did not lack material to create all things, from the highest degree of perfection to the lowest"; or, to speak more properly, "because the laws of his nature have been so ample that they sufficed for producing all things which can be conceived by an infinite intellect" (as I have demonstrated in P16). These are the prejudices I undertook to note here. If any of this kind still remain, they can be corrected by anyone with only a little meditation. [And so I find no reason to devote more time to these matters, etc.]

SECOND PART OF THE ETHICS

ON THE NATURE AND ORIGIN OF THE MIND

I pass now to explaining those things which must necessarily follow from the essence of God, or the infinite and eternal Being—not, indeed, all of them, for we have demonstrated (IP16) that infinitely many things must follow from it in infinitely many modes, but only those that can lead us, by the hand, as it were, to the knowledge of the human Mind and its highest blessedness.

Definitions

D1: By body I understand a mode that in a certain and determinate way expresses God's essence insofar as he is considered as an extended thing (see IP25C).

D2: I say that to the essence of any thing belongs that which, being given, the thing is [also] necessarily posited and which, being taken away, the thing is necessarily [also] taken away; or that without which the thing can neither be nor be conceived, and which can neither be nor be conceived without the thing.

D3: By idea I understand a concept of the Mind that the Mind forms because it is a thinking thing.

Exp.: *I say concept rather than perception, because the word perception seems to indicate that the Mind is acted on by the object. But concept seems to express an action of the Mind.*

D4: By adequate idea I understand an idea which, insofar as it is considered in itself, without relation to an object, has all the properties, or intrinsic denominations of a true idea.
        Exp.: *I say intrinsic to exclude what is extrinsic, viz. the agreement of the idea with its object.*

D5: Duration is an indefinite continuation of existing.
        Exp.: *I say indefinite because it cannot be determined at all through the very nature of the existing thing, nor even by the efficient cause, which necessarily posits the existence of the thing, and does not take it away.*

D6: By reality and perfection I understand the same thing.

D7: By singular things I understand things that are finite and have a determinate existence. And if a number of Individuals so concur in one action that together they are all the cause of one effect, I consider them all, to that extent, as one singular thing.

Axioms

A1: The essence of man does not involve necessary existence, i.e., from the order of nature it can happen equally that this or that man does exist, or that he does not exist.

A2: Man thinks.

A3: There are no modes of thinking, such as love, desire, or whatever is designated by the word affects of the mind, unless there is in the same Individual the idea of the thing loved, desired, etc. But there can be an idea, even though there is no other mode of thinking.

A4: We feel that a certain body is affected in many ways.

A5: We neither feel nor perceive any singular things [or anything of *natura naturata*], except bodies and modes of thinking.
        See the postulates after P13.

P1: *Thought is an attribute of God, or God is a thinking thing.*
        Dem.: Singular thoughts, or this or that thought, are modes that express God's nature in a certain and determinate way (by IP25C). Therefore (by ID5) there belongs to God an attribute whose concept all singular thoughts involve, and through which they are also conceived. Therefore, Thought is one of God's infinite attributes, which expresses an eternal and infinite essence of God (see ID6), *or* God is a thinking thing, q.e.d.
        Schol.: This Proposition is also evident from the fact that we can conceive an infinite thinking being. For the more things a thinking being can think, the more reality, or perfection, we conceive it to contain. Therefore, a being that can think infinitely many things in infinitely many ways is necessarily infinite in its power of thinking. So since we can conceive an infinite Being by attending to thought alone, Thought (by ID4 and D6) is necessarily one of God's infinite attributes, as we maintained.

P2: *Extension is an attribute of God, or God is an extended thing.*

Dem.: The demonstration of this proceeds in the same way as that of the preceding Proposition.

P3: *In God there is necessarily an idea, both of his essence and of everything that necessarily follows from his essence.*

Dem.: For God (by P1) can think infinitely many things in infinitely many modes, *or* (what is the same, by IP16) can form the idea of his essence and of all the things which necessarily follow from it. But whatever is in God's power necessarily exists (by IP35); therefore, there is necessarily such an idea, and (by IP15) it is only in God, q.e.d.

Schol.: By God's power ordinary people understand God's free will and his right over all things which are, things which on that account are commonly considered to be contingent. For they say that God has the power of destroying all things and reducing them to nothing. Further, they very often compare God's power with the power of Kings.

But we have refuted this in IP32C1 and C2, and we have shown in IP16 that God acts with the same necessity by which he understands himself, i.e., just as it follows from the necessity of the divine nature (as everyone maintains unanimously) that God understands himself, with the same necessity it also follows that God does infinitely many things in infinitely many modes. And then we have shown in IP34 that God's power is nothing except God's active essence. And so it is as impossible for us to conceive that God does not act as it is to conceive that he does not exist.

Again, if it were agreeable to pursue these matters further, I could also show here that that power which ordinary people fictitiously ascribe to God is not only human (which shows that ordinary people conceive God as a man, or as like a man), but also involves lack of power. But I do not wish to speak so often about the same topic. I only ask the reader to reflect repeatedly on what is said concerning this matter in Part I, from P16 to the end. For no one will be able to perceive rightly the things I maintain unless he takes great care not to confuse God's power with the human power or right of Kings.

P4: *God's idea, from which infinitely many things follow in infinitely many modes, must be unique.*

Dem.: An infinite intellect comprehends nothing except God's attributes and his affections (by IP30). But God is unique (by IP14C1). Therefore God's idea, from which infinitely many things follow in infinitely many modes, must be unique, q.e.d.

P5: *The formal being of ideas admits God as a cause only insofar as he is considered as a thinking thing, and not insofar as he is explained by any other attribute. I.e., ideas, both of God's attributes and of singular things, admit not the objects themselves, or the things perceived, as their efficient cause, but God himself, insofar as he is a thinking thing.*

Dem.: This is evident from P3. For there we inferred that God can form the idea of his essence, and of all the things that follow necessarily from it, solely from the fact that God is a thinking thing, and not from the fact that he is the object of his own idea. So the formal being of ideas admits God as its cause insofar as he is a thinking thing.

But another way of demonstrating this is the following. The formal being of ideas is a mode of thinking (as is known through itself), i.e. (by IP25C), a mode that expresses, in a certain way, God's nature insofar as he is a thinking thing. And so (by IP10) it involves the concept of no other attribute of God, and consequently (by IA4) is the effect of no other attribute than thought. And so the formal being of ideas admits God as its cause insofar as he is considered only as a thinking thing, etc., q.e.d.

P6: *The modes of each attribute have God for their cause only insofar as he is considered under the attribute of which they are modes, and not insofar as he is considered under any other attribute.*

Dem.: For each attribute is conceived through itself without any other (by IP10). So the modes of each attribute involve the concept of their own attribute, but not of another one; and so (by IA4) they have God for their cause only insofar as he is considered under the attribute of which they are modes, and not insofar as he is considered under any other, q.e.d.

Cor.: From this it follows that the formal being of things which are not modes of thinking does not follow from the divine nature because [God] has first known the things; rather the objects of ideas follow and are inferred from their attributes in the same way and by the same necessity as that with which we have shown ideas to follow from the attribute of Thought.

P7: *The order and connection of ideas is the same as the order and connection of things.*

Dem.: This is clear from IA4. For the idea of each thing caused depends on the knowledge of the cause of which it is the effect.

Cor.: From this it follows that God's [actual] power of thinking is equal to his actual power of acting. I.e., whatever follows formally from God's infinite nature follows objectively in God from his idea in the same order and with the same connection.

Schol.: Before we proceed further, we must recall here what we showed [in the First Part], viz. that whatever can be perceived by an infinite intellect as constituting an essence of substance pertains to one substance only, and consequently that the thinking substance and the extended substance are one and the same substance, which is now comprehended under this attribute, now under that. So also a mode of extension and the idea of that mode are one and the same thing, but expressed in two ways. Some of the Hebrews seem to have seen this, as if through a cloud, when they maintained that God, God's intellect, and the things understood by him are one and the same.

For example, a circle existing in nature and the idea of the existing circle, which is also in God, are one and the same thing, which is explained through different attributes. Therefore, whether we conceive nature under the attribute of Extension, or under the attribute of Thought, or under any other attribute, we shall find one and the same order, or one and the same connection of causes, i.e., that the same things follow one another.

When I said [before] that God is the cause of the idea, say of a circle, only insofar as he is a thinking thing, and [the cause] of the circle, only insofar as he is an extended thing, this was for no other reason than because the formal being of the idea of the circle can be perceived only through another mode of thinking, as its proximate cause, and that mode again through another, and so on, to infinity. Hence, so long as things are considered as modes of thinking, we must explain the order of the whole of nature, *or* the connection of causes, through the attribute of Thought alone. And insofar as they are considered as modes of Extension, the order of the whole of nature must be explained through the attribute of Extension alone. I understand the same concerning the other attributes.

So of things as they are in themselves, God is really the cause insofar as he consists of infinite attributes. For the present, I cannot explain these matters more clearly.

P8: *The ideas of singular things, or of modes, that do not exist must be comprehended in God's infinite idea in the same way as the formal essences of the singular things, or modes, are contained in God's attributes.*

Dem.: This Proposition is evident from the preceding one, but is understood more clearly from the preceding scholium.

Cor.: From this it follows that so long as singular things do not exist, except insofar as they are comprehended in God's attributes, their objective being, *or* ideas, do not exist except insofar as God's infinite idea exists. And when singular things are said to exist, not only insofar as they are comprehended in God's attributes, but insofar also as they are said to have duration, their ideas also involve the existence through which they are said to have duration.

Schol.: If anyone wishes me to explain this further by an example, I will, of course, not be able to give one which adequately explains what I speak of here, since it is unique. Still I shall try as far as possible to illustrate the matter: the circle is of such a nature that the rectangles formed from the segments of all the straight lines intersecting in it are equal to one another. So in a circle there are contained infinitely many rectangles that are equal to one another. Nevertheless, none of them can be said to exist except insofar as the circle exists, nor also can the idea of any of these rectangles be said to exist except insofar as it is comprehended in the idea of the circle. Now of these infinitely many [rectangles] let two only, viz. [those formed from the segments of lines] D and E, exist.

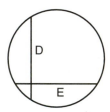

Of course their ideas also exist now, not only insofar as they are only comprehended in the idea of the circle, but also insofar as they involve the existence of those rectangles. By this they are distinguished from the other ideas of the other rectangles.

P9: *The idea of a singular thing which actually exists has God for a cause not insofar as he is infinite, but insofar as he is considered to be affected by another idea of a singular thing which actually exists; and of this [idea] God is also the cause, insofar as he is affected by another third [idea], and so on, to infinity.*

Dem.: The idea of a singular thing which actually exists is a singular mode of thinking, and distinct from the others (by P8C and S), and so (by P6) has God for a cause only insofar as he is a thinking thing. But not (by IP28) insofar as he is a thing thinking absolutely; rather insofar as he is considered to be affected by another [determinate] mode of thinking. And God is also the cause of this mode, insofar as he is affected by another [determinate mode of thinking], and so on, to infinity. But the order and connection of ideas (by P7) is the same as the order and connection of causes. Therefore, the cause of one singular idea is another idea, or God, insofar as he is considered to be affected by another idea; and of this also [God is the cause], insofar as he is affected by another, and so on, to infinity, q.e.d.

Cor.: Whatever happens in the singular object of any idea, there is knowledge of it in God, only insofar as he has the idea of the same object.

Dem.: Whatever happens in the object of any idea, there is an idea of it in God (by P3), not insofar as he is infinite, but insofar as he is considered to be affected by another idea of [an existing] singular thing (by P9); but the order and connection of ideas (by P7) is the same as the order and connection of things; therefore, knowledge of what happens in a singular object will be in God only insofar as he has the idea of the same object, q.e.d.

P10: *The being of substance does not pertain to the essence of man, or substance does not constitute the form of man.*

Dem.: For the being of substance involves necessary existence (by IP7). Therefore, if the being of substance pertained to the essence of man, then substance being given, man would necessarily be given (by D2), and consequently man would exist necessarily, which (by A1) is absurd, q.e.d.

Schol.: This proposition is also demonstrated from IP5, viz. that there are not two substances of the same nature. Since a number of men can exist, what constitutes the form of man is not the being of substance. Further, this proposition is evident from the other properties of substance, viz. that substance is, by its nature, infinite, immutable, indivisible, etc., as anyone can easily see.

Cor.: From this it follows that the essence of man is constituted by certain modifications of God's attributes.

Dem.: For the being of substance does not pertain to the essence of man (by P10). Therefore, it is something (by IP15) which is in God, and which can neither be nor be conceived without God, *or* (by IP25C) an affection, *or* mode, which expresses God's nature in a certain and determinate way.

Schol.: Everyone, of course, must concede that nothing can either be or be conceived without God. For all confess that God is the only cause of all things, both of their essence and of their existence. I.e., God is not only the cause of the coming to be of things, as they say, but also of their being.

But in the meantime many say that anything without which a thing can neither be nor be conceived pertains to the nature of the thing. And so they believe either that the nature of God pertains to the essence of created things, or that created things can be or be conceived without God—or what is more certain, they are not sufficiently consistent.

The cause of this, I believe, was that they did not observe the [proper] order of Philosophizing. For they believed that the divine nature, which they should have contemplated before all else (because it is prior both in knowledge and in nature) is last in the order of knowledge, and that the things that are called objects of the senses are prior to all. That is why, when they contemplated natural things, they thought of nothing less than they did of the divine nature; and when afterwards they directed their minds to contemplating the divine nature, they could think of nothing less than of their first fictions, on which they had built the knowledge of natural things, because these could not assist knowledge of the divine nature. So it is no wonder that they have generally contradicted themselves.

But I pass over this. For my intent here was only to give a reason why I did not say that anything without which a thing can neither be nor be conceived pertains to its nature—viz. because singular things can neither be nor be conceived without God, and nevertheless, God does not pertain to their essence. But I have said that what necessarily constitutes the essence of a thing is that which, if it is given, the thing is posited, and if it is taken away, the thing is taken away, i.e., the essence is what the thing can neither be nor be conceived without, and vice versa, what can neither be nor be conceived without the thing.

P11: *The first thing that constitutes the actual being of a human Mind is nothing but the idea of a singular thing which actually exists.*

Dem.: The essence of man (by P10C) is constituted by certain modes of God's attributes, viz. (by A2) by modes of thinking, of all of which (by A3) the idea is prior in nature, and when it is given, the other modes (to which the idea is prior in nature) must be in the same individual (by A3). And therefore an idea is the first thing that constitutes the being of a human Mind. But not the idea of a thing which does not exist. For then (by P8C) the idea itself could not be said to exist. Therefore, it will be the idea of a thing which actually exists. But not of an infinite thing. For an infinite thing (by IP21 and 22) must always exist necessarily. But (by A1) it is absurd [that this idea should be of a necessarily existing object]. Therefore, the first thing that constitutes the actual being of a human Mind is the idea of a singular thing which actually exists, q.e.d.

Cor.: From this it follows that the human Mind is a part of the infinite intellect of God. Therefore, when we say that the human Mind perceives this or that, we are saying nothing but that God, not insofar as he is infinite, but insofar as he is explained through the nature of the human Mind, *or* insofar as he constitutes the essence of the human Mind, has this or that idea; and when we say that God has this or that idea, not only insofar as he constitutes the nature of the human Mind, but insofar as he also has the idea of another thing together with the human Mind, then we say that the human Mind perceives the thing only partially, *or* inadequately.

Schol.: Here, no doubt, my readers will come to a halt, and think of many things which will give them pause. For this reason I ask them to continue on with me slowly, step by step, and to make no judgment on these matters until they have read through them all.

P12: *Whatever happens in the object of the idea constituting the human Mind must be perceived by the human Mind, or there will necessarily be an idea of that thing in the Mind; i.e., if the object of the idea constituting a human Mind is a body, nothing can happen in that body which is not perceived by the Mind.*

Dem.: For whatever happens in the object of any idea, the knowledge of that thing is necessarily in God (by P9C), insofar as he is considered to be affected by the idea of the same object, i.e. (by P11), insofar as he constitutes the mind of some thing. Therefore, whatever happens in the object of the idea constituting the human Mind, the knowledge of it is necessarily in God insofar as he constitutes the nature of the human Mind, i.e. (by P11C), knowledge of this thing will necessarily be in the Mind, or the Mind will perceive it, q.e.d.

Schol.: This Proposition is also evident, and more clearly understood from P7S, which you should consult.

P13: *The object of the idea constituting the human Mind is the Body, or a certain mode of Extension which actually exists, and nothing else.*

Dem.: For if the object of the human Mind were not the Body, the ideas of the affections of the Body would not be in God (by P9C) insofar as he constituted our Mind, but insofar as he constituted the mind of another thing, i.e. (by P11C), the ideas of the affections of the Body would not be in our Mind; but (by A4) we have ideas of the affections of the body. Therefore, the object of the idea that constitutes the human Mind is the Body, and it (by P11) actually exists.

Next, if the object of the Mind were something else also, in addition to the Body, then since (by IP36) nothing exists from which there does not follow some effect, there would necessarily (by P12) be an idea in our Mind of some effect of it. But (by A5) there is no idea of it. Therefore, the object of our Mind is the existing Body and nothing else, q.e.d.

Cor.: From this it follows that man consists of a Mind and a Body, and that the human Body exists, as we are aware of it.

Schol.: From these [propositions] we understand not only that the human Mind is united to the Body, but also what should be understood by the union of Mind and Body. But no one will be able to understand it adequately, or distinctly, unless he first knows adequately the nature of our Body. For the things we have shown so far are completely general and do not pertain more to man than to other Individuals, all of which, though in different degrees, are nevertheless animate. For of each thing there is necessarily an idea in God, of which God is the cause in the same way as he is of the idea of the human Body. And so, whatever we have said of the idea of the human Body must also be said of the idea of any thing.

However, we also cannot deny that ideas differ among themselves, as the objects themselves do, and that one is more excellent than the other, and contains more reality, just as the object of the one is more excellent than the object of the other and contains more reality. And so to determine what is the difference between the human Mind and the others, and how it surpasses them, it is necessary for us, as we have said, to know the nature of its object, i.e., of the human Body. I cannot explain this here, nor is that necessary for the things I wish to demonstrate. Nevertheless, I say this in general, that in proportion as a Body is more capable than others of doing many things at once, or being acted on in many ways at once, so its Mind is more capable than others of perceiving many things at once. And in proportion as the actions of a body depend more on itself alone, and as other bodies concur with it less in acting, so its mind is more capable of understanding distinctly. And from these [truths] we can know the excellence of one mind over the others, and also see the cause why we have only a completely confused knowledge of our Body, and many other things which I shall deduce from them in the following [propositions]. For this reason I have thought it worthwhile to explain and demonstrate these things more accurately. To do this it is necessary to premise a few things concerning the nature of bodies.

A1': All bodies either move or are at rest.

A2': Each body moves now more slowly, now more quickly.

L1: *Bodies are distinguished from one another by reason of motion and rest, speed and slowness, and not by reason of substance.*

Dem.: I suppose that the first part of this is known through itself. But that bodies are not distinguished by reason of substance is evident both from IP5 and from IP8. But it is more clearly evident from those things which are said in IP15S.

L2: *All bodies agree in certain things.*

Dem.: For all bodies agree in that they involve the concept of one and the same attribute (by D1), and in that they can move now more slowly, now more quickly, and absolutely, that now they move, now they are at rest.

L3: *A body which moves or is at rest must be determined to motion or rest by another body, which has also been determined to motion or rest by another, and that again by another, and so on, to infinity.*

Dem.: Bodies (by D1) are singular things which (by L1) are distinguished from one another by reason of motion and rest; and so (by IP28), each must be de-termined necessarily to motion or rest by another singular thing, viz. (by P6) by another body, which (by A1′) either moves or is at rest. But this body also (by the same reasoning) could not move or be at rest if it had not been determined by another to motion or rest, and this again (by the same reasoning) by another, and so on, to in-finity, q.e.d.

Cor.: From this it follows that a body in motion moves until it is determined by another body to rest; and that a body at rest also remains at rest until it is determined to motion by another.

This is also known through itself. For when I suppose that body A, say, is at rest, and do not attend to any other body in motion, I can say nothing about body A except that it is at rest. If afterwards it happens that body A moves, that of course could not have come about from the fact that it was at rest. For from that nothing else could fol-low but that body A would be at rest.

If, on the other hand, A is supposed to move, then as often as we attend only to A, we shall be able to affirm nothing concerning it except that it moves. If afterwards it happens that A is at rest, that of course also could not have come about from the motion it had. For from the motion nothing else could follow but that A would move. Therefore, it happens by a thing which was not in A, viz. by an external cause, by which [the Body in motion, A] has been determined to rest.

A1″: All modes by which a body is affected by another body follow both from the na-ture of the body affected and at the same time from the nature of the affecting body, so that one and the same body may be moved differently according to differences in the nature of the bodies moving it. And conversely, different bodies may be moved differ-ently by one and the same body.

A2″: When a body in motion strikes against another which is at rest and cannot give way, then it is reflected, so that it continues to move, and the angle of the line of the re-flected motion with the surface of the body at rest which it struck against will be equal to the angle which the line of the incident motion makes with the same surface.

This will be sufficient concerning the simplest bodies, which are distinguished from one another only by motion and rest, speed and slowness. Now let us move up to composite bodies.

Definition: *When a number of bodies, whether of the same or of different size, are so constrained by other bodies that they lie upon one another, or if they so move, whether with the same degree or different degrees of speed, that they communicate their motions to each other in a certain fixed manner, we shall say that those bodies are united with one another and that they all together compose one body or Individual, which is distin-guished from the others by this union of bodies.*

A3″: As the parts of an Individual, or composite body, lie upon one another over a larger or smaller surface, so they can be forced to change their position with more or less difficulty; and consequently the more or less will be the difficulty of bringing it about that the Individual changes its shape. And therefore the bodies whose parts lie upon one another over a large surface, I shall call *hard;* those whose parts lie upon one another over a small surface, I shall call *soft;* and finally those whose parts are in motion, I shall call *fluid.*

L4: *If, of a body, or of an Individual, which is composed of a number of bodies, some are removed, and at the same time as many others of the same nature take their place, the [body, or the] Individual will retain its nature, as before, without any change of its form.*

Dem.: For (by L1) bodies are not distinguished in respect to substance; what constitutes the form of the Individual consists [only] in the union of the bodies (by the preceding definition). But this [union] (by hypothesis) is retained even if a continual change of bodies occurs. Therefore, the Individual will retain its nature, as before, both in respect to substance, and in respect to mode, q.e.d.

L5: *If the parts composing an Individual become greater or less, but in such a proportion that they all keep the same ratio of motion and rest to each other as before, then the Individual will likewise retain its nature, as before, without any change of form.*

Dem.: The demonstration of this is the same as that of the preceding Lemma.

L6: *If certain bodies composing an Individual are compelled to alter the motion they have from one direction to another, but so that they can continue their motions and communicate them to each other in the same ratio as before, the Individual will likewise retain its nature, without any change of form.*

Dem.: This is evident through itself. For it is supposed that it retains everything which, in its definition, we said constitutes its form. [See the Definition before L4.]

L7: *Furthermore, the Individual so composed retains its nature, whether it, as a whole, moves or is at rest, or whether it moves in this or that direction, so long as each part retains its motion, and communicates it, as before, to the others.*

Dem.: This [also] is evident from the definition preceding L4.

Schol.: By this, then, we see how a composite Individual can be affected in many ways, and still preserve its nature. So far we have conceived an Individual which is composed only of bodies which are distinguished from one another only by motion and rest, speed and slowness, i.e., which is composed of the simplest bodies. But if we should now conceive of another, composed of a number of Individuals of a different nature, we shall find that it can be affected in a great many other ways, and still preserve its nature. For since each part of it is composed of a number of bodies, each part will therefore (by L7) be able, without any change of its nature, to move now more slowly, now more quickly, and consequently communicate its motion more quickly or more slowly to the others.

But if we should further conceive a third kind of Individual, composed [of many individuals] of this second kind, we shall find that it can be affected in many other ways, without any change of its form. And if we proceed in this way to infinity, we shall easily conceive that the whole of nature is one Individual, whose parts, i.e., all bodies, vary in infinite ways, without any change of the whole Individual.

If it had been my intention to deal expressly with body, I ought to have explained and demonstrated these things more fully. But I have already said that I intended something else, and brought these things forward only because I can easily deduce from them the things I have decided to demonstrate.

Postulates

I. The human Body is composed of a great many individuals of different natures, each of which is highly composite.

II. Some of the individuals of which the human Body is composed are fluid, some soft, and others, finally are hard.

III. The individuals composing the human Body, and consequently, the human Body itself, are affected by external bodies in very many ways.

IV. The human Body, to be preserved, requires a great many other bodies, by which it is, as it were, continually regenerated.

V. When a fluid part of the human Body is determined by an external body so that it frequently thrusts against a soft part [of the Body], it changes its surface and, as it were, impresses on [the soft part] certain traces of the external body striking against [the fluid part].

VI. The human Body can move and dispose external bodies in a great many ways.

P14: *The human Mind is capable of perceiving a great many things, and is the more capable, the more its body can be disposed in a great many ways.*

Dem.: For the human Body (by Post. 3 and 6) is affected in a great many ways by external bodies, and is disposed to affect external bodies in a great many ways. But the human Mind must perceive everything which happens in the human body (by P12). Therefore, the human Mind is capable of perceiving a great many things, and is the more capable [, as the human Body is more capable], q.e.d.

P15: *The idea that constitutes the formal being [esse] of the human Mind is not simple, but composed of a great many ideas.*

Dem.: The idea that constitutes the formal being of the human Mind is the idea of a body (by P13), which (by Post. 1) is composed of a great many highly composite Individuals. But of each Individual composing the body, there is necessarily (by P8C) an idea in God. Therefore (by P7), the idea of the human Body is composed of these many ideas of the parts composing the Body, q.e.d.

P16: *The idea of any mode in which the human Body is affected by external bodies must involve the nature of the human Body and at the same time the nature of the external body.*

Dem.: For all the modes in which a body is affected follow from the nature of the affected body, and at the same time from the nature of the affecting body (by A1″ [II/99]). So the idea of them (by IA4) will necessarily involve the nature of each body. And so the idea of each mode in which the human Body is affected by an external body involves the nature of the human Body and of the external body, q.e.d.

Cor. 1: From this it follows, first, that the human Mind perceives the nature of a great many bodies together with the nature of its own body.

Cor. 2: It follows, second, that the ideas which we have of external bodies indicate the condition of our own body more than the nature of the external bodies. I have explained this by many examples in the Appendix of Part I.

P17: *If the human Body is affected with a mode that involves the nature of an external body, the human Mind will regard the same external body as actually existing, or as present to it, until the Body is affected by an affect that excludes the existence or presence of that body.*

Dem.: This is evident. For so long as the human Body is so affected, the human Mind (by P12) will regard this affection of the body, i.e. (by P16), it will have the idea of a mode that actually exists, an idea that involves the nature of the external body, i.e., an idea that does not exclude, but posits, the existence or presence of the nature of the external body. And so the Mind (by P16C1) will regard the external body as actually existing, or as present, until it is affected, etc., q.e.d.

Cor.: Although the external bodies by which the human body has once been affected neither exist nor are present, the mind will still be able to regard them as if they were present.

Dem.: While external bodies so determine the fluid parts of the human body that they often thrust against the softer parts, they change (by Post. 5) their surfaces with the result (see A2″ after L3) that they are reflected from it in another way than they used to be before, and still later, when the fluid parts, by their spontaneous motion, encounter those new surfaces, they are reflected in the same way as when they were driven against those surfaces by the external bodies. Consequently, while, thus reflected, they continue to move, they will affect the human Body with the same mode, concerning which the Mind (by P12) will think again, i.e. (by P17), the Mind will again regard the external body as present; this will happen as often as the fluid parts of the human body encounter the same surfaces by their spontaneous motion. So although the external bodies by which the human Body has once been affected do not exist, the Mind will still regard them as present, as often as this action of the body is repeated, q.e.d.

Schol.: We see, therefore, how it can happen (as it often does) that we regard as present things that do not exist. This can happen from other causes also, but it is sufficient for me here to have shown one through which I can explain it as if I had shown it through its true cause; still, I do not believe that I wander far from the true [cause] since all those postulates which I have assumed contain hardly anything that is not established by experience which we cannot doubt, after we have shown that the human Body exists as we are aware of it (see P13C).

Furthermore (from P17C and P16C2), we clearly understand what is the difference between the idea of, say, Peter, which constitutes the essence of Peter's mind, and the idea of Peter which is in another man, say in Paul. For the former directly explains the essence of Peter's body, and does not involve existence, except so long as Peter exists; but the latter indicates the condition of Paul's body more than Peter's nature [see P16C2], and therefore, while that condition of Paul's body lasts, Paul's Mind will still regard Peter as present to itself, even though Peter does not exist.

Next, to retain the customary words, the affections of the human Body whose ideas present external bodies as present to us, we shall call images of things, even if they do not reproduce the [external] figures of things. And when the Mind regards bodies in this way, we shall say that it imagines.

And here, in order to begin to indicate what error is, I should like you to note that the imaginations of the Mind, considered in themselves contain no error, or that the Mind does not err from the fact that it imagines, but only insofar as it is considered to lack an idea that excludes the existence of those things that it imagines to be present to it. For if the Mind, while it imagined nonexistent things as present to it, at the same time knew that those things did not exist, it would, of course, attribute this power of imagining to a virtue of its nature, not to a vice—especially if this faculty of imagining depended only on its own nature, i.e. (by ID7), if the Mind's faculty of imagining were free.

P18: *If the human Body has once been affected by two or more bodies at the same time, then when the Mind subsequently imagines one of them, it will immediately recollect the others also.*

Dem.: The Mind (by P17C) imagines a body because the human Body is affected and disposed as it was affected when certain of its parts were struck by the external body itself. But (by hypothesis) the Body was then so disposed that the Mind imagined two [or more] bodies at once; therefore it will now also imagine two [or more] at once, and when the Mind imagines one, it will immediately recollect the other also, q.e.d.

Schol.: From this we clearly understand what Memory is. For it is nothing other than a certain connection of ideas involving the nature of things which are outside the human Body—a connection that is in the Mind according to the order and connection of the affections of the human Body.

I say, *first,* that the connection is only of those ideas that involve the nature of things which are outside the human Body, but not of the ideas that explain the nature of the same things. For they are really (by P16) ideas of affections of the human Body which involve both its nature and that of external bodies.

I say, *second,* that this connection happens according to the order and connection of the affections of the human Body in order to distinguish it from the connection of ideas which happens according to the order of the intellect, by which the Mind perceives things through their first causes, and which is the same in all men.

And from this we clearly understand why the Mind, from the thought of one thing, immediately passes to the thought of another, which has no likeness to the first: as, for example, from the thought of the word *pomum* a Roman will immediately pass to the thought of the fruit [viz. an apple], which has no similarity to that articulate sound and nothing in common with it except that the Body of the same man has often been affected by these two [at the same time], i.e., that the man often heard the word *pomum* while he saw the fruit.

And in this way each of us will pass from one thought to another, as each one's association has ordered the images of things in the body. For example, a soldier, having seen traces of a horse in the sand, will immediately pass from the thought of a horse to the thought of a horseman, and from that to the thought of war, etc. But a Farmer will pass from the thought of a horse to the thought of a plow, and then to that of a field, etc. And so each one, according as he has been accustomed to join and connect the images of things in this or that way, will pass from one thought to another.

P19: *The human Mind does not know the human Body itself, nor does it know that it exists, except through ideas of affections by which the Body is affected.*

Dem.: For the human Mind is the idea itself, or knowledge of the human Body (by P13), which (by P9) is indeed in God insofar as he is considered to be affected by another idea of a singular thing, or because (by Post. 4) the human Body requires a great many bodies by which it is, as it were, continually regenerated; and [because] the order and connection of ideas is (by P7) the same as the order and connection of causes, this idea will be in God insofar as he is considered to be affected by the ideas of a great many singular things. Therefore, God has the idea of the human Body, or knows the human Body, insofar as he is affected by a great many other ideas, and not insofar as he constitutes the nature of the human Mind, i.e. (by P11C), the human Mind does not know the human Body.

But the ideas of affections of the Body are in God insofar as he constitutes the nature of the human Mind, or the human Mind perceives the same affections (by P12), and consequently (by P16) the human Body itself, as actually existing (by P17).

Therefore to that extent only, the human Mind perceives the human Body itself, q.e.d.

P20: *There is also in God an idea, or knowledge, of the human Mind, which follows in God in the same way and is related to God in the same way as the idea, or knowledge, of the human Body.*

Dem.: Thought is an attribute of God (by P1), and so (by P3) there must necessarily be in God an idea both of [thought] and of all of its affections, and consequently (by P11), of the human Mind also. Next, this idea, *or* knowledge, of the Mind does not follow in God insofar as he is infinite, but insofar as he is affected by another idea of a singular thing (by P9). But the order and connection of ideas is the same as the order and connection of causes (by P7). Therefore, this idea, *or* knowledge, of the Mind follows in God and is related to God in the same way as the idea, *or* knowledge, of the Body, q.e.d.

P21: *This idea of the Mind is united to the Mind in the same way as the Mind is united to the Body.*

Dem.: We have shown that the Mind is united to the Body from the fact that the Body is the object of the Mind (see P12 and 13); and so by the same reasoning the idea of the Mind must be united with its own object, i.e., with the Mind itself, in the same way as the Mind is united with the Body, q.e.d.

Schol.: This proposition is understood far more clearly from what is said in P7S; for there we have shown that the idea of the Body and the Body, i.e. (by P13), the Mind and the Body, are one and the same Individual, which is conceived now under the attribute of Thought, now under the attribute of Extension. So the idea of the Mind and the Mind itself are one and the same thing, which is conceived under one and the same attribute, viz. Thought. The idea of the Mind, I say, and the Mind itself follow in God from the same power of thinking and by the same necessity. For the idea of the Mind, i.e., the idea of the idea, is nothing but the form of the idea insofar as this is considered as a mode of thinking without relation to the object. For as soon as someone knows something, he thereby knows that he knows it, and at the same time knows that he knows that he knows, and so on, to infinity. But more on these matters later.

P22: *The human Mind perceives not only the affections of the Body, but also the ideas of these affections.*

Dem.: The ideas of the ideas of the affections follow in God in the same way and are related to God in the same way as the ideas themselves of the affections (this is demonstrated in the same way as P20). But the ideas of the affections of the Body are in the human Mind (by P12), i.e. (by P11C), in God, insofar as he constitutes the essence of the human Mind. Therefore, the ideas of these ideas will be in God insofar as he has the knowledge, *or* idea, of the human Mind, i.e. (by P21), they will be in the human Mind itself, which for that reason perceives not only the affections of the Body, but also their ideas, q.e.d.

P23: *The Mind does not know itself, except insofar as it perceives the ideas of the affections of the Body.*

Dem.: The idea, *or* knowledge, of the Mind (by P20) follows in God in the same way, and is related to God in the same way as the idea, *or* knowledge, of the body. But since (by P19) the human Mind does not know the human Body itself, i.e. (by P11C), since the knowledge of the human Body is not related to God insofar as he constitutes the nature of the human Mind, the knowledge of the Mind is also not related to God insofar as he constitutes the essence of the human Mind. And so (again by P11C) to that extent the human Mind does not know itself.

Next, the ideas of the affections by which the Body is affected involve the nature of the human Body itself (by P16), i.e. (by P13), agree with the nature of the Mind. So knowledge of these ideas will necessarily involve knowledge of the Mind. But (by P22) knowledge of these ideas is in the human Mind itself. Therefore, the human Mind, to that extent only, knows itself, q.e.d.

P24: *The human Mind does not involve adequate knowledge of the parts composing the human Body.*

Dem.: The parts composing the human Body pertain to the essence of the Body itself only insofar as they communicate their motions to one another in a certain fixed manner (see the Definition after L3C), and not insofar as they can be considered as Individuals, without relation to the human Body. For (by Post. 1) the parts of the human Body are highly composite Individuals, whose parts (by L4) can be separated from the human Body and communicate their motions (see A1" after L3) to other bodies in another manner, while the human Body completely preserves its nature and form. And so the idea, or knowledge, of each part will be in God (by P3), insofar as he is considered to be affected by another idea of a singular thing (by P9), a singular thing which is prior, in the order of nature, to the part itself (by P7). The same must also be said of each part of the Individual composing the human Body. And so, the knowledge of each part composing the human Body is in God insofar as he is affected with a great many ideas of things, and not insofar as he has only the idea of the human Body, i.e. (by P13), the idea that constitutes the nature of the human Mind. And so, by P11C) the human Mind does not involve adequate knowledge of the parts composing the human Body, q.e.d.

P25: *The idea of any affection of the human Body does not involve adequate knowledge of an external body.*

Dem.: We have shown (P16) that the idea of an affection of the human Body involves the nature of an external body insofar as the external body determines the human Body in a certain fixed way. But insofar as the external body is an Individual that is not related to the human Body, the idea, *or* knowledge, of it is in God (by P9) insofar as God is considered to be affected with the idea of another thing which (by P7) is prior in nature to the external body itself. So adequate knowledge of the external body is not in God insofar as he has the idea of an affection of the human Body, *or* the idea of an affection of the human Body does not involve adequate knowledge of the external body, q.e.d.

P26: *The human Mind does not perceive any external body as actually existing, except through the ideas of the affections of its own Body.*

Dem.: If the human Body is not affected by an external body in any way, then (by P7) the idea of the human Body, i.e. (by P13) the human Mind, is also not affected in any way by the idea of the existence of that body, *or* it does not perceive the existence of that external body in any way. But insofar as the human Body is affected by an external body in some way, to that extent [the human Mind] (by P16 and P16C1) perceives the external body, q.e.d.

Cor.: Insofar as the human Mind imagines an external body, it does not have adequate knowledge of it.

Dem.: When the human Mind regards external bodies through ideas of the affections of its own Body, then we say that it imagines (see P17S); and the Mind cannot in any other way (by P26) imagine external bodies as actually existing. And so (by P25), insofar as the Mind imagines external bodies, it does not have adequate knowledge of them, q.e.d.

P27: *The idea of any affection of the human Body does not involve adequate knowledge of the human body itself.*

Dem.: Any idea of any affection of the human Body involves the nature of the human Body insofar as the human Body itself is considered to be affected with a certain definite mode (see P16). But insofar as the human Body is an Individual, which can be affected with many other modes, the idea of this [affection] etc. (See P25D.)

P28: *The ideas of the affections of the human Body, insofar as they are related only to the human Mind, are not clear and distinct, but confused.*

Dem.: For the ideas of the affections of the human Body involve the nature of external bodies as much as that of the human Body (by P16), and must involve the nature not only of the human Body [as a whole], but also of its parts; for the affections are modes (by Post. 3) with which the parts of the human Body, and consequently the whole Body, are affected. But (by P24 and P25) adequate knowledge of external bodies and of the parts composing the human Body is in God, not insofar as he is considered to be affected with the human Mind, but insofar as he is considered to be affected with other ideas. Therefore, these ideas of the affections, insofar as they are related only to the human Mind, are like conclusions without premises, i.e. (as is known through itself), they are confused ideas, q.e.d.

Schol.: In the same way we can demonstrate that the idea that constitutes the nature of the human Mind is not, considered in itself alone, clear and distinct; we can also demonstrate the same of the idea of the human Mind and the ideas of the ideas of the human Body's affections [viz. that are confused], insofar as they are referred to the Mind alone. Anyone can easily see this.

P29: *The idea of the idea of any affection of the human Body does not involve adequate knowledge of the human Mind.*

Dem.: For the idea of an affection of the human Body (by P27) does not involve adequate knowledge of the Body itself, *or* does not express its nature adequately, i.e. (by P13), does not agree adequately with the nature of the Mind; and so (by IA6) the idea of this idea does not express the nature of the human mind adequately, *or* does not involve adequate knowledge of it, q.e.d.

Cor.: From this it follows that so long as the human Mind perceives things from the common order of nature, it does not have an adequate, but only a confused and mutilated knowledge of itself, of its own Body, and of external bodies. For the Mind does not know itself except insofar as it perceives ideas of the affections of the body (by P23). But it does not perceive its own Body (by P19) except through the very ideas themselves of the affections [of the body], and it is also through them alone that it perceives external bodies (by P26). And so, insofar as it has these [ideas], then neither of itself (by P29), nor of its own Body (by P27), nor of external bodies (by P25) does it have an adequate knowledge, but only (by P28 and P28S) a mutilated and confused knowledge, q.e.d.

Schol.: I say expressly that the Mind has, not an adequate, but only a confused [and mutilated] knowledge, of itself, of its own Body, and of external bodies, so long as it perceives things from the common order of nature, i.e., so long as it is determined externally, from fortuitous encounters with things, to regard this or that, and not so long as it is determined internally, from the fact that it regards a number of things at once, to understand their agreements, differences, and oppositions. For so often as it is disposed internally, in this or another way, then it regards things clearly and distinctly, as I shall show below.

P30: *We can have only an entirely inadequate knowledge of the duration of our Body.*

Dem.: Our body's duration depends neither on its essence (by A1), nor even on God's absolute nature (by IP21). But (by IP28) it is determined to exist and produce an effect from such [other] causes as are also determined by others to exist and produce an effect in a certain and determinate manner, and these again by others, and so to infinity. Therefore, the duration of our Body depends on the common order of nature and the constitution of things. But adequate knowledge of how things are constituted is in God, insofar as he has the ideas of all of them, and not insofar as he has only the idea of the human Body (by P9C). So the knowledge of the duration of our Body is quite inadequate in God, insofar as he is considered to constitute only the nature of the human Mind, i.e. (by P11C), this knowledge is quite inadequate in our Mind, q.e.d.

P31: *We can have only an entirely inadequate knowledge of the duration of the singular things which are outside us.*

Dem.: For each singular thing, like the human Body, must be determined by another singular thing to exist and produce effects in a certain and determinate way, and this again by another, and so to infinity (by IP28). But since (in P30) we have demonstrated from this common property of singular things that we have only a very inadequate knowledge of the duration of our Body, we shall have to draw the same conclusion concerning the duration of singular things [outside us], viz. that we can have only a very inadequate knowledge of their duration, q.e.d.

Cor.: From this it follows that all particular things are contingent and corruptible. For we can have no adequate knowledge of their duration (by P31), and that is what we must understand by the contingency of things and the possibility of their corruption (see IP33S1). For (by IP29) beyond that there is no contingency.

P32: *All ideas, insofar as they are related to God, are true.*

Dem.: For all ideas which are in God agree entirely with their objects (by P7C), and so (by IA6) they are all true, q.e.d.

P33: *There is nothing positive in ideas on account of which they are called false.*

Dem.: If you deny this, conceive (if possible) a positive mode of thinking which constitutes the form of error, or falsity. This mode of thinking cannot be in God (by P32). But it also can neither be nor be conceived outside God (by IP15). And so there can be nothing positive in ideas on account of which they are called false, q.e.d.

P34: *Every idea that in us is absolute, or adequate and perfect, is true.*

Dem.: When we say that there is in us an adequate and perfect idea, we are saying nothing but that (by P11C) there is an adequate and perfect idea in God insofar as he constitutes the essence of our Mind, and consequently (by P32) we are saying nothing but that such an idea is true, q.e.d.

P35: *Falsity consists in the privation of knowledge which inadequate, or mutilated and confused, ideas involve.*

Dem.: There is nothing positive in ideas that constitutes the form of falsity (by P33); but falsity cannot consist in an absolute privation (for it is Minds, not Bodies, which are said to err, or be deceived), nor also in absolute ignorance. For to be ignorant and to err are different. So it consists in the privation of knowledge that inadequate knowledge of things, or inadequate and confused ideas, involve, q.e.d.

Schol.: In P17S I explained how error consists in the privation of knowledge. But to explain the matter more fully, I shall give [one or two examples]: men are deceived in that they think themselves free [i.e., they think that, of their own free will, they can either do a thing or forbear doing it], an opinion which consists only in this, that they are conscious of their actions and ignorant of the causes by which they are determined. This, then, is their idea of freedom—that they do not know any cause of their actions. They say, of course, that human actions depend on the will, but these are only words for which they have no idea. For all are ignorant of what the will is, and how it moves the Body; those who boast of something else, who feign seats and dwelling places of the soul, usually provoke either ridicule or disgust.

Similarly, when we look at the sun, we imagine it as about 200 feet away from us, an error that does not consist simply in this imagining, but in the fact that while we imagine it in this way, we are ignorant of its true distance and of the cause of this imagining. For even if we later come to know that it is more than 600 diameters of the earth away from us, we nevertheless imagine it as near. For we imagine the sun so near not because we do not know its true distance, but because an affection of our body involves the essence of the sun insofar as our body is affected by the sun.

P36: *Inadequate and confused ideas follow with the same necessity as adequate, or clear and distinct ideas.*

Dem.: All ideas are in God (by IP15); and, insofar as they are related to God, are true (by P32), and (by P7C) adequate. And so there are no inadequate or confused ideas except insofar as they are related to the singular Mind of someone (see P24 and P28). And so all ideas—both the adequate and the inadequate—follow with the same necessity (by P6C), q.e.d.

P37: *What is common to all things (on this see L2, above) and is equally in the part and in the whole, does not constitute the essence of any singular thing.*

Dem.: If you deny this, conceive (if possible) that it does constitute the essence of some singular thing, say the essence of B. Then (by D2) it can neither be nor be conceived without B. But this is contrary to the hypothesis. Therefore, it does not pertain to the essence of B, nor does it constitute the essence of any other singular thing, q.e.d.

P38: *Those things which are common to all, and which are equally in the part and in the whole, can only be conceived adequately.*

Dem.: Let A be something which is common to all bodies, and which is equally in the part of each body and in the whole. I say that A can only be conceived adequately. For its idea (by P7C) will necessarily be adequate in God, both insofar as he has the idea of the human Body and insofar as he has ideas of its affections, which (by P16, P25, and P27) involve in part both the nature of the human Body and that of external bodies. That is (by P12 and P13), this idea will necessarily be adequate in God insofar as he constitutes the human Mind, *or* insofar as he has ideas that are in the human Mind. The Mind therefore (by P11C) necessarily perceives A adequately, and does so both insofar as it perceives itself and insofar as it perceives its own or any external body. Nor can A be conceived in another way, q.e.d.

Cor.: From this it follows that there are certain ideas, *or* notions, common to all men. For (by L2) all bodies agree in certain things, which (by P38) must be perceived adequately, or clearly and distinctly, by all.

P39: *If something is common to, and peculiar to, the human Body and certain external bodies by which the human Body is usually affected, and is equally in the part and in the whole of each of them, its idea will also be adequate in the Mind.*

Dem.: Let A be that which is common to, and peculiar to, the human Body and certain external bodies, which is equally in the human Body and in the same external bodies, and finally, which is equally in the part of each external body and in the whole. There will be an adequate idea of A in God (by P7C), both insofar as he has the idea of the human Body, and insofar as he has ideas of the posited external bodies. Let it be posited now that the human Body is affected by an external body through what it has in common with it, i.e., by A; the idea of this affection will involve property A (by P16), and so (by P7C) the idea of this affection, insofar as it involves property A, will be adequate in God insofar as he is affected with the idea of the human Body, i.e. (by P13), insofar as he constitutes the nature of the human Mind. And so (by P11C), this idea is also adequate in the human Mind, q.e.d.

Cor.: From this it follows that the Mind is the more capable of perceiving many things adequately as its Body has many things in common with other bodies.

P40: *Whatever ideas follow in the Mind from ideas that are adequate in the mind are also adequate.*

Dem.: This is evident. For when we say that an idea in the human Mind follows from ideas that are adequate in it, we are saying nothing but that (by P11C) in the Divine intellect there is an idea of which God is the cause, not insofar as he is infinite, nor insofar as he is affected with the ideas of a great many singular things, but insofar as he constitutes only the essence of the human Mind [and therefore, it must be adequate].

Schol. 1: With this I have explained the cause of those notions which are called *common,* and which are the foundations of our reasoning.

But some axioms, or notions, result from other causes which it would be helpful to explain by this method of ours. For from these [explanations] it would be established which notions are more useful than the others, and which are of hardly any use; and then, which are common, which are clear and distinct only to those who have no prejudices, and finally, which are ill-founded. Moreover, we would establish what is the origin of those notions they call *Second,* and consequently of the axioms founded on them, and other things I have thought about, from time to time, concerning these matters. But since I have set these aside for another Treatise, and do not wish to give rise to disgust by too long a discussion, I have decided to pass over them here.

But not to omit anything it is necessary to know, I shall briefly add something about the causes from which the terms called *Transcendental* have had their origin—I mean terms like Being, Thing and something. These terms arise from the fact that the human Body, being limited, is capable of forming distinctly only a certain number of

Interior of a House, ca. 1660, by Pieter De Hooch (1629–1684). This Dutch Baroque painting provides a visual metaphor for the precise geometry of Spinoza's Ethics. *(Wallace Collection, London, © Archivi Alinari, 1990/Art Resource)*

images at the same time (I have explained what an image is in P17S). If that number is exceeded, the images will begin to be confused, and if the number of images the Body is capable of forming distinctly in itself at once is greatly exceeded, they will all be completely confused with one another.

Since this is so, it is evident from P17C and P18, that the human Mind will be able to imagine distinctly, at the same time, as many bodies as there can be images formed at the same time in its body. But when the images in the body are completely confused, the Mind also will imagine all the bodies confusedly, without any distinction, and comprehend them as if under one attribute, viz. under the attribute of Being, Thing, etc. This can also be deduced from the fact that images are not always equally vigorous and from other causes like these, which it is not necessary to explain here. For our purpose it is sufficient to consider only one. For they all reduce to this: these terms signify ideas that are confused in the highest degree.

Those notions they call *Universal,* like Man, Horse, Dog, etc., have arisen from similar causes, viz. because so many images (e.g., of men) are formed at one time in the human Body that they surpass the power of imagining—not entirely, of course, but still to the point where the Mind can imagine neither slight differences of the singular [men] (such as the color and size of each one, etc.) nor their determinate number, and imagines distinctly only what they all agree in, insofar as they affect the body. For the body has been affected most [forcefully] by [what is common], since each singular has affected it [by this property]. And [the mind] expresses this by the word *man,* and predicates it of infinitely many singulars. For as we have said, it cannot imagine a determinate number of singulars.

But it should be noted that these notions are not formed by all [men] in the same way, but vary from one to another, in accordance with what the body has more often been affected by, and what the Mind imagines or recollects more easily. For example, those who have more often regarded men's stature with wonder will understand by the word *man* an animal of erect stature. But those who have been accustomed to consider something else, will form another common image of men—e.g., that man is an animal capable of laughter, or a featherless biped, or a rational animal.

And similarly concerning the others—each will form universal images of things according to the disposition of his body. Hence it is not surprising that so many controversies have arisen among the philosophers, who have wished to explain natural things by mere images of things.

Schol. 2: From what has been said above, it is clear that we perceive many things and form universal notions:

I. From singular things which have been represented to us through the senses in a way that is mutilated, confused, and without order for the intellect (see P29C); for that reason I have been accustomed to call such perceptions knowledge from random experience;

II. From signs, e.g., from the fact that, having heard or read certain words, we recollect things, and form certain ideas of them, which are like them, and through which we imagine the things (P18S). These two ways of regarding things I shall henceforth call knowledge of the first kind, opinion or imagination.

III. Finally, from the fact that we have common notions and adequate ideas of the properties of things (see P38C, P39, P39C, and P40). This I shall call reason and the second kind of knowledge.

IV. In addition to these two kinds of knowledge, there is (as I shall show in what follows) another, third kind, which we shall call intuitive knowledge. And this kind of knowing proceeds from an adequate idea of the formal essence of certain attributes of God to the adequate knowledge of the [formal] essence of things.

I shall explain all these with one example. Suppose there are three numbers, and the problem is to find a fourth which is to the third as the second is to the first. Merchants do not hesitate to multiply the second by the third, and divide the product by the first, because they have not yet forgotten what they heard from their teacher without any demonstration, or because they have often found this in the simplest numbers, or from the force of the Demonstration of P7 in Bk. VII of Euclid, viz. from the common property of proportionals. But in the simplest numbers none of this is necessary. Given the numbers 1, 2, and 3, no one fails to see that the fourth proportional number is 6—and we see this much more clearly because we infer the fourth number from the ratio which, in one glance, we see the first number to have the second.

P41: *Knowledge of the first kind is the only cause of falsity, whereas knowledge of the second and of the third kind is necessarily true.*

Dem.: We have said in the preceding scholium that to knowledge of the first kind pertain all those ideas which are inadequate and confused; and so (by P35) this knowledge is the only cause of falsity. Next, we have said that to knowledge of the second and third kinds pertain those which are adequate; and so (by P34) this knowledge is necessarily true.

P42: *Knowledge of the second and third kinds, and not of the first kind, teaches us to distinguish the true from the false.*

Dem.: This Proposition is evident through itself. For he who knows how to distinguish between the true and the false must have an adequate idea of the true and of the false, i.e. (P40S2), must know the true and the false by the second or third kind of knowledge.

P43: *He who has a true idea at the same time knows that he has a true idea, and cannot doubt the truth of the thing.*

Dem.: An idea true in us is that which is adequate in God insofar as he is explained through the nature of the human Mind (by P11C). Let us posit, therefore, that there is in God, insofar as he is explained through the nature of the human Mind, an adequate idea, A. Of this idea there must necessarily also be in God an idea which is related to God in the same way as idea A (by P20, whose demonstration is universal [and can be applied to all ideas]). But idea A is supposed to be related to God insofar as he is explained through the nature of the human Mind; therefore the idea of idea A must also be related to God in the same way, i.e. (by the same P11C), this adequate idea of idea A will be in the Mind itself which has the adequate idea A. And so he who has an adequate idea, *or* (by P34) who knows a thing truly, must at the same time have an adequate idea, *or* true knowledge, of his own knowledge. I.e. (as is manifest through itself), he must at the same time be certain, q.e.d.

Schol.: In P21S I have explained what an idea of an idea is. But it should be noted that the preceding proposition is sufficiently manifest through itself. For no one who has a true idea is unaware that a true idea involves the highest certainty. For to have a true idea means nothing other than knowing a thing perfectly, *or* in the best way. And of course no one can doubt this unless he thinks that an idea is something mute, like a picture on a tablet, and not a mode of thinking, viz. the very [act of] understanding. And I ask, who can know that he understands some thing unless he first understands it? I.e., who can know that he is certain about some thing unless he is first certain about it? What can there be which is clearer and more certain than a true idea, to serve as a standard of truth? As the light makes both itself and the darkness plain, so truth is the standard both of itself and of the false.

By this I think we have replied to these questions: if a true idea is distinguished from a false one, [not insofar as it is said to be a mode of thinking, but] only insofar as it is said to agree with its object, then a true idea has no more reality or perfection than a false one (since they are distinguished only through the extrinsic denomination [and not through the intrinsic denomination])—and so, does the man who has true ideas [have any more reality or perfection] than him who has only false ideas? Again, why do men have false ideas? And finally, how can someone know certainly that he has ideas which agree with their objects?

To these questions, I say, I think I have already replied. For as far as the difference between a true and a false idea is concerned, it is established from P35 that the true is related to the false as being is to nonbeing. And the causes of falsity I have shown most clearly from P19 to P35S. From this it is also clear what is the difference between the man who has true ideas and the man who has only false ideas. Finally, as to the last, viz. how a man can know that he has an idea that agrees with its object? I have just shown, more than sufficiently, that this arises solely from his having an idea that does agree with its object—or that truth is its own standard. Add to this that our Mind, insofar as it perceives things truly, is part of the infinite intellect of God (by P11C); hence, it is as necessary that the mind's clear and distinct ideas are true as that God's ideas are.

P44: *It is of the nature of Reason to regard things as necessary, not as contingent.*

Dem.: It is of the nature of reason to perceive things truly (by P41), viz. (by IA6) as they are in themselves, i.e. (by IP29), not as contingent but as necessary, q.e.d.

Cor. 1: From this it follows that it depends only on the imagination that we regard things as contingent, both in respect to the past and in respect to the future.

Schol.: I shall explain briefly how this happens. We have shown above (by P17 and P17C) that even though things do not exist, the Mind still imagines them always as present to itself, unless causes occur which exclude their present existence. Next, we have shown (P18) that if the human Body has once been affected by two external bodies at the same time, then afterwards, when the Mind imagines one of them, it will immediately recollect the other also, i.e., it will regard both as present to itself unless causes occur which exclude their present existence. Moreover, no one doubts but what we also imagine time, viz. from the fact that we imagine some bodies to move more slowly, or more quickly, or with the same speed.

Let us suppose, then, a child, who saw Peter for the first time yesterday, in the morning, but saw Paul at noon, and Simon in the evening, and today again saw Peter in the morning. It is clear from P18 that as soon as he sees the morning light, he will immediately imagine the sun taking the same course through the sky as he saw on the preceding day, *or* he will imagine the whole day, and Peter together with the morning, Paul with noon, and Simon with the evening. That is, he will imagine the existence of Paul and of Simon with a relation to future time. On the other hand, if he sees Simon in the evening, he will relate Paul and Peter to the time past, by imagining them together with past time. And he will do this more uniformly, the more often he has seen them in this same order.

But if it should happen at some time that on some other evening he sees James instead of Simon, then on the following morning he will imagine now Simon, now James, together with the evening time, but not both at once. For it is supposed that he has seen one or the other of them in the evening, but not both at once. His imagination, therefore, will vacillate and he will imagine now this one, now that one, with the future evening time, i.e., he will regard neither of them as certainly future, but both of them as contingently future.

And this vacillation of the imagination will be the same if the imagination is of things we regard in the same way with relation to past time or to present time. Consequently we shall imagine things as contingent in relation to present time as well as to past and future time.

Cor. 2: It is of the nature of Reason to perceive things under a certain species of eternity.

Dem.: It is of the nature of Reason to regard things as necessary and not as contingent (by P44). And it perceives this necessity of things truly (by P41), i.e. (by IA6), as it is in itself. But (by IP16) this necessity of things is the very necessity of God's eternal nature. Therefore, it is of the nature of Reason to regard things under this species of eternity.

Add to this that the foundations of Reason are notions (by P38) which explain those things that are common to all, and which (by P37) do not explain the essence of any singular thing. On that account, they must be conceived without any relation to time, but under a certain species of eternity, q.e.d.

P45: *Each idea of each body, or of each singular thing which actually exists, necessarily involves an eternal and infinite essence of God.*

Dem.: The idea of a singular thing which actually exists necessarily involves both the essence of the thing and its existence (by P8C). But singular things (by IP15) cannot be conceived without God—on the contrary, because (by P6) they have God for a cause insofar as he is considered under the attribute of which the things are modes, their ideas must involve the concept of their attribute (by IA4), i.e. (by ID6), must involve an eternal and infinite essence of God, q.e.d.

Schol.: By existence here I do not understand duration, i.e., existence insofar as it is conceived abstractly, and as a certain species of quantity. For I am speaking of the very nature of existence, which is attributed to singular things because infinitely many things follow from the eternal necessity of God's nature in infinitely many modes (see IP16). I am speaking, I say, of the very existence of singular things insofar as they are in God. For even if each one is determined by another singular thing to exist in a certain way, still the force by which each one perseveres in existing follows from the eternal necessity of God's nature. Concerning this, see IP24C.

P46: *The knowledge of God's eternal and infinite essence which each idea involves is adequate and perfect.*

Dem.: The demonstration of the preceding Proposition is Universal, and whether the thing is considered as a part or as a whole, its idea, whether of the whole or a part (by P45), will involve God's eternal and infinite essence. So what gives knowledge of an eternal and infinite essence of God is common to all, and is equally in the part and in the whole. And so (by P38) this knowledge will be adequate, q.e.d.

P47: *The human Mind has an adequate knowledge of God's eternal and infinite essence.*

Dem.: The human Mind has ideas (by P22) from which it perceives (by P23) itself, (by P19) its own Body, and (by P16C1 and P17) external bodies as actually existing. And so (by P45 and P46) it has an adequate knowledge of God's eternal and infinite essence, q.e.d.

Schol.: From this we see that God's infinite essence and his eternity are known to all. And since all things are in God and are conceived through God, it follows that we can deduce from this knowledge a great many things which we know adequately, and so can form that third kind of knowledge of which we spoke in P40S2 and of whose excellence and utility we shall speak in Part V.

But that men do not have so clear a knowledge of God as they do of the common notions comes from the fact that they cannot imagine God, as they can bodies, and that they have joined the name *God* to the images of things which they are used to seeing. Men can hardly avoid this, because they are continually affected by bodies.

And indeed, most errors consist only in our not rightly applying names to things. For when someone says that the lines which are drawn from the center of a circle to its circumference are unequal, he surely understands (then at least) by a circle something different from what Mathematicians understand. Similarly, when men err in calculating, they have certain numbers in their mind and different ones on the paper. So if you consider what they have in Mind, they really do not err, though they seem to err because we think they have in their mind the numbers which are on the paper. If this were not so, we would not believe that they were erring, just as I did not believe that he was erring whom I recently heard cry out that his courtyard had flown into his neighbor's hen [although his words were absurd], because what he had in mind seemed sufficiently clear to me [viz. that his hen had flown into his neighbor's courtyard].

And most controversies have arisen from this, that men do not rightly explain their own mind, or interpret the mind of the other man badly. For really, when they contradict one another most vehemently, they either have the same thoughts, or they are thinking of different things, so that what they think are errors and absurdities in the other are not.

P48: *In the Mind there is no absolute, or free, will, but the Mind is determined to will this or that by a cause which is also determined by another, and this again by another, and so to infinity.*

Dem.: The Mind is a certain and determinate mode of thinking (by P11), and so (by IP17C2) cannot be a free cause of its own actions, or cannot have an absolute faculty of willing and not willing. Rather, it must be determined to willing this or that (by IP28) by a cause which is also determined by another, and this cause again by another, etc., q.e.d.

Schol.: In this same way it is also demonstrated that there is in the Mind no absolute faculty of understanding, desiring, loving, etc. From this it follows that these and similar faculties are either complete fictions *or* nothing but Metaphysical beings, or universals, which we are used to forming from particulars. So intellect and will are to this or that idea, or to this or that volition as "stone-ness" is to this or that stone, or man to Peter or Paul.

We have explained the cause of men's thinking themselves free in the Appendix of Part I. But before I proceed further, it should be noted here that by will I understand a faculty of affirming and denying, and not desire. I say that I understand the faculty by which the Mind affirms or denies something true or something false, and not the desire by which the Mind wants a thing or avoids it.

But after we have demonstrated that these faculties are universal notions which are not distinguished from the singulars from which we form them, we must now investigate whether the volitions themselves are anything beyond the very ideas of things. We must investigate, I say, whether there is any other affirmation or negation in the Mind except that which the idea involves, insofar as it is an idea—on this see the following Proposition and also D3—so that our thought does not fall into pictures. For by ideas I understand, not the images that are formed at the back of the eye (and, if you like, in the middle of the brain), but concepts of Thought [or the objective Being of a thing insofar as it consists only in Thought].

P49: *In the Mind there is no volition, or affirmation and negation, except that which the idea involves insofar as it is an idea.*

Dem.: In the Mind (by P48) there is no absolute faculty of willing and not willing, but only singular volitions, viz. this and that affirmation, and this and that negation. Let us conceive, therefore, some singular volition, say a mode of thinking by which the Mind affirms that the three angles of a triangle are equal to two right angles.

This affirmation involves the concept, *or* idea, of the triangle, i.e., it cannot be conceived without the idea of the triangle. For to say that A must involve the concept of B is the same as to say that A cannot be conceived without B. Further, this affirmation (by A3) also cannot be without the idea of the triangle. Therefore, this affirmation can neither be nor be conceived without the idea of the triangle.

Next, this idea of the triangle must involve this same affirmation, viz. that its three angles equal two right angles. So conversely, this idea of the triangle also can neither be nor be conceived without this affirmation.

So (by D2) this affirmation pertains to the essence of the idea of the triangle, and is nothing beyond it. And what we have said concerning this volition (since we have selected it at random), must also be said concerning any volition, viz. that it is nothing apart from the idea, q.e.d.

Cor.: The will and the intellect are one and the same.

Dem.: The will and the intellect are nothing apart from the singular volitions and ideas themselves (by P48 and P48S). But the singular volitions and ideas are one and the same (by P49). Therefore the will and the intellect are one and the same, q.e.d.

Schol.: [I.] By this we have removed what is commonly maintained to be the cause of error. Moreover, we have shown above that falsity consists only in the privation that mutilated and confused ideas involve. So a false idea, insofar as it is false, does not involve certainty. When we say that a man rests in false ideas, and does not doubt them, we do not, on that account, say that he is certain, but only that he does not doubt, or that he rests in false ideas because there are no causes to bring it about that his imagination wavers [or to cause him to doubt them]. On this, see P44S.

Therefore, however stubbornly a man may cling to something false [so that we cannot in any way make him doubt it], we shall still never say that he is certain of it. For by certainty we understand something positive (see P43 and P43S), not the privation of doubt. But by the privation of certainty, we understand falsity.

However, to explain the preceding Proposition more fully, there remain certain things I must warn you of. And then I must reply to the objections that can be made against this doctrine of ours. And finally, to remove every uneasiness, I thought it worthwhile to indicate some of the advantages of this doctrine. Some, I say—for the most important ones will be better understood from what we shall say in Part V.

[II.] I begin, therefore, by warning my Readers, first, to distinguish accurately between an idea, *or* concept, of the Mind, and the images of things that we imagine. And then it is necessary to distinguish between ideas and the words by which we signify things. For because many people either completely confuse these three—ideas, images, and words—or do not distinguish them accurately enough, or carefully enough, they have been completely ignorant of this doctrine concerning the will. But it is quite necessary to know it, both for the sake of speculation and in order to arrange one's life wisely.

Indeed, those who think that ideas consist in images which are formed in us from encounters with [external] bodies, are convinced that those ideas of things [which can make no trace in our brains, or] of which we can form no similar image [in our brain] are not ideas, but only fictions which we feign from a free choice of the will. They look on ideas, therefore, as mute pictures on a panel and preoccupied with this prejudice, do not see that an idea, insofar as it is an idea, involves an affirmation or negation.

And then, those who confuse words with the idea, or with the very affirmation that the idea involves, think that they can will something contrary to what they are aware of, when they only affirm or deny with words something contrary to what they are aware of. But these prejudices can easily be put aside by anyone who attends to the nature of thought, which does not at all involve the concept of extension. He will then understand clearly that an idea (since it is a mode of thinking) consists neither in the image of anything, nor in words. For the essence of words and of images is constituted only by corporeal motions, which do not at all involve the concept of thought.

It should suffice to have issued these few words of warning on this matter, so I pass to objections mentioned above.

[III.A.(i)] The first of these is that they think it clear that the will extends more widely than the intellect, and so is different from the intellect. The reason why they think the will extends more widely than the intellect is that they say they know by experience that they do not require a greater faculty of assenting, or affirming, and denying, than we already have, in order to assent to infinitely many other things which we do not perceive—but they do require a greater faculty of understanding. The will, therefore, is distinguished from the intellect because the intellect is finite and the will is infinite.

[III.A.(ii)] Secondly, it can be objected to us that experience seems to teach nothing more clearly than that we can suspend our judgment so as not to assent to things we perceive. This also seems to be confirmed from the fact that no one is said to be deceived insofar as he perceives something, but only insofar as he assents or dissents. E.g., someone who feigns a winged horse does not on that account grant that there is a winged horse, i.e., he is not on that account deceived unless at the same time he grants that there is a winged horse. Therefore, experience seems to teach nothing more clearly than that the will, *or* faculty of assenting, is free, and different from the faculty of understanding.

[III.A.(iii)] Thirdly, it can be objected that one affirmation does not seem to contain more reality than another, i.e., we do not seem to require a greater power to affirm that what is true, is true, than to affirm that something false is true. But [with ideas it is different, for] we perceive that one idea has more reality, *or* perfection, than another. As some objects are more excellent than others, so also some ideas of objects are more perfect than others. This also seems to establish a difference between the will and the intellect.

[III.A.(iv)] Fourth, it can be objected that if man does not act from freedom of the will, what will happen if he is in a state of equilibrium, like Buridan's ass? Will he perish of hunger and of thirst? If I concede that he will, I would seem to conceive an ass, or a statue of a man, not a man. But if I deny that he will, then he will determine himself, and consequently have the faculty of going where he wills and doing what he wills.

Perhaps other things in addition to these can be objected. But because I am not bound to force on you what anyone can dream, I shall only take the trouble to reply to these objections—and that as briefly as I can.

[III.B.(i)] To the first I say that I grant that the will extends more widely than the intellect, if by intellect they understand only clear and distinct ideas. But I deny that the will extends more widely than perceptions, *or* the faculty of conceiving. And indeed, I do not see why the faculty of willing should be called infinite, when the faculty of sensing is not. For just as we can affirm infinitely many things by the same faculty of willing (but one after another, for we cannot affirm infinitely many things at once), so also we can sense, *or* perceive, infinitely many bodies by the same faculty of sensing (viz. one after another [and not at once]).

If they say that there are infinitely many things which we cannot perceive, I reply that we cannot reach them by any thought, and consequently, not by any faculty of willing. But, they say, if God willed to bring it about that we should perceive them also, he would have to give us a greater faculty of perceiving, but not a greater faculty of willing than he has given us. This is the same as if they said that, if God should will to bring it about that we understood infinitely many other beings, it would indeed be necessary for him to give us a greater intellect, but not a more universal idea of being, in order for us to embrace the same infinity of beings. For we have shown that the will is a universal being, *or* idea, by which we explain all the singular volitions, i.e., it is what is common to them all.

Therefore, since they believe that this common *or* universal idea of all volitions is a faculty, it is not at all surprising if they say that this faculty extends beyond the limits of the intellect to infinity. For the universal is said equally of one, a great many, or infinitely many individuals.

[III.B.(ii)] To the second objection I reply by denying that we have a free power of suspending judgment. For when we say that someone suspends judgment, we are saying nothing but that he sees that he does not perceive the thing adequately. Suspension of judgment, therefore, is really a perception, not [an act of] free will.

To understand this clearly, let us conceive a child imagining a winged horse, and not perceiving anything else. Since this imagination involves the existence of the horse (by P17C), and the child does not perceive anything else that excludes the existence of the horse, he will necessarily regard the horse as present. Nor will he be able to doubt its existence, though he will not be certain of it.

We find this daily in our dreams, and I do not believe there is anyone who thinks that while he is dreaming he has a free power of suspending judgment concerning the things he dreams, and of bringing it about that he does not dream the things he dreams he sees. Nevertheless, it happens that even in dreams we suspend judgment, viz. when we dream that we dream.

Next, I grant that no one is deceived insofar as he perceives, i.e., I grant that the imaginations of the Mind, considered in themselves, involve no error. But I deny that a man affirms nothing insofar as he perceives. For what is perceiving a winged horse other than affirming wings of the horse? For if the Mind perceived nothing else except the winged horse, it would regard it as present to itself, and would not have any cause of doubting its existence, or any faculty of dissenting, unless either the imagination of the winged horse were joined to an idea which excluded the existence of the same horse, or the Mind perceived that its idea of a winged horse was inadequate. And then either it will necessarily deny the horse's existence, or it will necessarily doubt it.

[III.B.(iii)] As for the third objection, I think what has been said will be an answer to it too: viz. that the will is something universal, which is predicated of all ideas, and which signifies only what is common to all ideas, viz. the affirmation, whose adequate essence, therefore, insofar as it is thus conceived abstractly, must be in each idea, and in this way only must be the same in all, but not insofar as it is considered to constitute the idea's essence; for in that regard the singular affirmations differ from one another as much as the ideas themselves do. For example, the affirmation that the idea of a circle involves differs from that which the idea of a triangle involves as much as the idea of the circle differs from the idea of the triangle.

Next, I deny absolutely that we require an equal power of thinking, to affirm that what is true is true, as to affirm that what is false is true. For if you consider the mind, they are related to one another as being to not-being. For there is nothing positive in ideas which constitutes the form of falsity (see P35, P35S, and P47S). So the thing to note here, above all, is how easily we are deceived when we confuse universals with singulars, and beings of reason and abstractions with real beings.

[III.B.(iv)] Finally, as far as the fourth objection is concerned, I say that I grant entirely that a man placed in such an equilibrium (viz. who perceives nothing but thirst and hunger, and such food and drink as are equally distant from him) will perish of hunger and thirst. If they ask me whether such a man should not be thought an ass, rather than a man, I say that I do not know—just as I also do not know how highly we should esteem one who hangs himself, or children, fools, and madmen, etc.

[IV.] It remains now to indicate how much knowledge of this doctrine is to our advantage in life. We shall see this easily from the following considerations:

[A.] Insofar as it teaches that we act only from God's command, that we share in the divine nature, and that we do this the more, the more perfect our actions are, and the more and more we understand God. This doctrine, then, in addition to giving us complete peace of mind, also teaches us wherein our greatest happiness, *or* blessedness, consists: viz. in the knowledge of God alone, by which we are led to do only those things which love and morality advise. From this we clearly understand how far they stray from the true valuation of virtue, who expect to be honored by God with the greatest rewards for their virtue and best actions, as for the greatest bondage—as if virtue itself, and the service of God, were not happiness itself, and the greatest freedom.

[B.] Insofar as it teaches us how we must bear ourselves concerning matters of fortune, or things which are not in our power, i.e., concerning things which do not follow from our nature—that we must expect and bear calmly both good fortune and bad. For all things follow from God's eternal decree with the same necessity as from the essence of a triangle it follows that its three angles are equal to two right angles.

[C.] This doctrine contributes to social life, insofar as it teaches us to hate no one, to disesteem no one, to mock no one, to be angry at no one, to envy no one; and also insofar as it teaches that each of us should be content with his own things, and should be helpful to his neighbor, not from unmanly compassion, partiality, or superstition, but from the guidance of reason, as the time and occasion demand. I shall show this in the Fourth Part.

[D.] Finally, this doctrine also contributes, to no small extent, to the common society insofar as it teaches how citizens are to be governed and led, not so that they may be slaves, but that they may do freely the things that are best.

And with this I have finished what I had decided to treat in this scholium, and put an end to this our Second Part. In it I think that I have explained the nature and properties of the human Mind in sufficient detail, and as clearly as the difficulty of the subject allows, and that I have set out doctrines from which we can infer many excellent things, which are highly useful and necessary to know.

JOHN LOCKE
1632–1704

John Locke was born in Wrington, Somerset, the son of a Puritan lawyer. His father fought on the side of the Parliament against Charles I, and Locke himself was a lifelong defender of the parliamentary system.

As a teenager, Locke attended Westminster School, studying classics under the harsh discipline of the time. He later condemned the English educational system for its brutality and one-sided emphasis on the past. In 1652, he entered Christ Church, Oxford, where he received his B.A. in 1656 and an M.A. in 1658. Again, he found his Oxford education obsessed with the past—in particular the Scholasticism of the late Middle Ages. Hence, he sought knowledge in the emerging sciences. In 1659, he was named a Senior Student at Oxford—a position he held until he lost it for political reasons in 1684.

In 1662, Locke met Lord Ashley, the Earl of Shaftesbury. Locke and Shaftesbury became close friends and in 1667 Locke went to live with Shaftesbury as his personal physician, securing his medical degree and license in 1674. Locke also helped Shaftesbury with several projects, including the writing of a constitution for the colony of Carolina. As a member of Shaftesbury's entourage, Locke traveled extensively and met many of the leading thinkers of his day.

When Shaftesbury became the leader of the parliamentary opposition to the king, Locke's friendship became a liability. Shaftesbury was tried for treason in 1681; and although he was acquitted, he fled to Holland where he died in 1683. Without the backing of his powerful patron, Locke also fled to Holland where he became an advisor to William and Mary of Orange. Following the Glorious Revolution of 1688, which removed Locke's enemy, James II, from the throne, Locke returned home in the company of William and Mary—now king and queen of England.

Following his return to England, Locke published his most important work, *Essay Concerning Human Understanding* (1690). Locke spent the rest of his life writing and serving the new government as Commissioner of Appeals and, later, as Commissioner of Trade and Plantations. He died quietly at the home of a friend in 1704.

*   *   *

Locke begins his *Essay* with several arguments against the Cartesian notion of innate ideas. He claims that the mind is a *tabula rasa,* a blank tablet or "white paper, void of all characters, without any ideas." All ideas come from one source: experience. Experience in turn is of two types: sensation or reflection. Sensations are derived from our sensory perceptions of the external world. Reflection, on the other hand, provides ideas by the mind "reflecting on its own operations within itself."

Having explained the *origin* of ideas, Locke then explains the *nature* of ideas. All ideas are either simple or complex. Simple ideas are uncompounded; that is, they cannot be broken down further, such as the ideas of "sweetness" or "redness." Complex ideas are composed of two or more simple ideas, such as the idea of a red, sweet apple. Locke then classifies simple and complex ideas by sources (sensation, reflection, or both).

Having explained the sources of ideas, Locke next asks if the ideas that come from sensation actually resemble the qualities of the external objects that gave rise to them. He answers first by dividing qualities into primary and secondary. Primary qualities are "utterly inseparable" from external objects regardless of their state—such qualities include solidity, extension, figure, motion, rest, and number. On the other hand, secondary qualities are "nothing in the objects themselves, but powers to produce various sensations in us by their primary qualities." These secondary qualities would include such things as colors, sounds, tastes, and the like. So, for example, the primary qualities of an apple (a solid, being extended in space, etc.) have the power to produce the secondary quality of a sweet taste and a red color. This analysis means that the world *as we experience it* is only a representation of the way the world actually is. The blooming, buzzing, colorful world of our experience is not the real world.

Finally, Locke asks what these primary and secondary qualities are qualities *of.* He argues that there must be "some *substratum* wherein [ideas] do subsist, and from which they do result, which therefore we call *substance*." Although we cannot have any idea of substance, nor can we explain the concept, we must posit substance as a "supporter" of qualities—a "something I know not what," Locke said.

*   *   *

Locke spent twenty years preparing his *Essay Concerning Human Understanding* for publication in 1690. The *Essay* went through several editions while Locke was still living, including an abridgment with his consent. Our selection here is an abridgment by Kaufmann, which I have modified. This abridgment owes much to John Wynne's (1695) editing and to the modern work of A.S. Pringle-Pattison.

In addition to this work, Locke wrote *Two Treatises of Government* (1690), *The Reasonableness of Christianity as Delivered in the Scriptures* (1695), *Vindications of the Reasonableness of Christianity* (1695 and 1697), and several "Letters" concerning toleration.

The best commentary on Locke's thought in general and on the *Essay* in particular is Richard I. Aaron, *John Locke* (Oxford: Clarendon Press, 1971). Also useful as a general overview are D.J. O'Connor, *John Locke* (Harmondsworth, Middlesex: Penguin Books, 1952); John W. Yolton, *Locke and the Way of Ideas* (Oxford: Clarendon Press, 1968); R.S. Woolhouse, *Locke* (Minneapolis: University of Minnesota Press, 1983); and John Dunn, *Locke* (New York: Oxford University Press, 1984)—part of the "Past Masters" series, now reprinted in the combined volume of John Dunn et al., eds., *The British Empiricists* (Oxford: Oxford University Press, 1992). For help with Locke's *Essay,* see John W. Yolton, *Locke and the Compass of Human Understanding: A Selective Commentary on the "Essay"* (London: Cambridge University Press, 1970), and John L. Mackie, *Problems from Locke* (Oxford: Oxford University Press, 1976). For guides to Locke's political thought, see John Dunn, *The Political Thought of John Locke* (Cambridge: Cambridge University Press, 1969), and J.W. Gough, *John Locke's Political Philosophy* (Oxford: Clarendon Press, 1973). John Yolton, *A Locke Dictionary* (Oxford; Basil Blackwell, 1993) provides a useful reference work. For collections of essays on Locke's thought, see C.B. Martin and D.M. Armstrong, eds., *Locke and Berkeley: A Collection of Critical Essays* (Notre Dame, IN: Notre Dame University Press, 1968); John W. Yolton, ed., *John Locke: Problems and Perspectives: A Collection of New Essays* (Cambridge: Cambridge University Press, 1969); and Vere Chappell's trio of books, *Essays on Early Modern Philosophers: John Locke—Theory of Knowledge, John Locke—Political Philosophy* (both Hamden, CT: Garland Press, 1992), and *The Cambridge Companion to Locke* (Cambridge: Cambridge University Press, 1994). For an interesting, if unusual, analysis of Locke's political thought, see Leo Strauss, *Natural Right and History* (Chicago: University of Chicago Press, 1952).

AN ESSAY CONCERNING HUMAN UNDERSTANDING (in part)

INTRODUCTION

1. *An enquiry into the understanding, pleasant and useful.*—Since it is the *understanding* that sets man above the rest of sensible beings, and gives him all the advantage and dominion which he has over them, it is certainly a subject, even for its nobleness, worth our labour to enquire into. The understanding, like the eye, whilst it makes us see and perceive all other things, takes no notice of itself; and it requires art and pains to set it at a distance, and make it its own object. But whatever be the difficulties that lie in the way of this enquiry; whatever it be that keeps us so much in the dark to ourselves; sure I am that all the light we can let in upon our own minds, all the acquaintance we can make with our own understandings, will not only be very pleasant, but bring us great advantage in directing our thoughts in the search of other things.

2. *Design.*—This, therefore, being my purpose, to enquire into the original, certainty, and extent of *human knowledge,* together with the grounds and degrees of *belief, opinion,* and *assent,* I shall not at present meddle with the physical consideration of the mind, or trouble myself to examine wherein its essence consists, or by what motions of our spirits, or alterations of our bodies, we come to have any *sensation* by our organs, or any *ideas* in our understandings; and whether those ideas do, in their formation, any or all of them, depend on matter or no. These are speculations which, however curious and entertaining, I shall decline, as lying out of my way in the design I am now upon. It shall suffice to my present purpose, to consider the discerning faculties of a man as they are employed about the objects which they have to do with: and I shall imagine I have not wholly misemployed myself in the thoughts I shall have on this occasion, if, in this historical, plain method, I can give any account of the ways whereby our understandings come to attain those notions of things we have, and can set down any measures of the certainty of our knowledge, or the grounds of those persuasions which are to be found amongst men, so various, different, and wholly contradictory; and yet asserted somewhere or other with such assurance, and confidence, that he that shall take a view of the opinions of mankind, observe their opposition, and at the same time consider the fondness and devotion wherewith they are embraced, the resolution and eagerness wherewith they are maintained, may perhaps have reason to suspect that either there is no such thing as truth at all, or that mankind hath no sufficient means to attain a certain knowledge of it.

3. *Method.*—It is therefore worth while to search out the bounds between opinion and knowledge, and examine by what measures, in things whereof we have no certain knowledge, we ought to regulate our assent, and moderate our persuasions. In order whereunto, I shall pursue this following method:—

First, I shall enquire into the original of those *ideas,* notions, or whatever else you please to call them, which a man observes, and is conscious to himself he has in his mind; and the ways whereby the understanding comes to be furnished with them.

Secondly, I shall endeavour to show what *knowledge* the understanding hath by those ideas, and the certainty, evidence, and extent of it.

Thirdly, I shall make some enquiry into the nature and grounds of *faith* or *opinion:* whereby I mean that assent which we give to any proposition as true, of whose truth yet we have no certain knowledge. And here we shall have occasion to examine the reasons and degrees of *assent.*

4. *Useful to know the extent of our comprehension.*—If by this enquiry into the nature of the understanding, I can discover the powers thereof, how far they reach, to what things they are in any degree proportionate, and where they fail us, I suppose it may be of use, to prevail with the busy mind of man to be more cautious in meddling with things exceeding its comprehension, to stop when it is at the utmost extent of its tether, and to sit down in a quiet ignorance of those things which, upon examination, are found to be beyond the reach of our capacities. We should not then perhaps be so forward, out of an affection of an universal knowledge, to raise questions, and perplex ourselves and others with disputes about things to which our understandings are not suited, and of which we cannot frame in our minds any clear or distinct perceptions, or whereof (as it has, perhaps, too often happened) we have not any notions at all. If we can find out how far the understanding can extend its view, how far it has faculties to attain certainty, and in what cases it can only judge and guess, we may learn to content ourselves with what is attainable by us in this state.

*   *   *

8. *What "idea" stands for.*—Thus much I thought necessary to say concerning the occasion of this enquiry into human understanding. But, before I proceed on to what I have thought on this subject, I must here, in the entrance, beg pardon of my reader for the frequent use of the word *idea* which he will find in the following treatise. It being that term which, I think, serves best to stand for whatsoever is the *object* of the understanding when a man thinks, I have used it to express whatever is meant by *phantasm, notion, species,* or *whatever it is which the mind can be employed about in thinking;* and I could not avoid frequently using it.

I presume it will be easily granted me, that there are such *ideas* in men's minds; every one is conscious of them in himself, and men's words and actions will satisfy him that they are in others.

Our first enquiry then shall be,—how they come into the mind.

BOOK I. NEITHER PRINCIPLES NOR IDEAS ARE INNATE

CHAPTER 1. NO INNATE PRINCIPLES IN THE MIND

1. *The way shown how we come by any knowledge, sufficient to prove it not innate.*—It is an established opinion amongst some men, that there are in the understanding certain *innate principles;* some primary notions, ⟨*koinai ennoiai*⟩, characters, as it were stamped upon the mind of man, which the soul receives in its very first being, and brings into the world with it. It would be sufficient to convince unprejudiced readers of the falseness of this supposition, if I should only show (as I hope I shall in the following parts of this discourse) how men, barely by the use of their natural faculties, may attain to all the knowledge they have, without the help of any innate impressions; and may arrive at certainty, without any such original notions or principles. For I imagine any one will easily grant, that it would be impertinent to suppose the ideas of colours innate in a creature to whom God hath given sight, and a power to receive them by the eyes from external objects: and no less unreasonable would it be to attribute several truths to the impressions of nature and innate characters, when we may observe in ourselves faculties fit to attain as easy and certain knowledge of them as if they were originally imprinted on the mind.

But because a man is not permitted without censure to follow his own thoughts in the search of truth, when they lead him ever so little out of the common road, I shall set down the reasons that made me doubt of the truth of that opinion, as an excuse for my mistake, if I be in one; which I leave to be considered by those who, with me, dispose themselves to embrace truth wherever they find it.

2. *General assent the great argument.*—There is nothing more commonly taken for granted, than that there are certain *principles,* both *speculative* and *practical* (for they speak of both), universally agreed upon by all mankind; which therefore, they argue, must needs be the constant impressions which the souls of men receive in their first beings and which they bring into the world with them, as necessarily and really as they do any of their inherent faculties.

3. *Universal consent proves nothing innate.*—This argument, drawn from universal consent, has this misfortune in it, that if it were true in matter of fact, that there were certain truths wherein all mankind agreed, it would not prove them innate, if there can

be any other way shown, how men may come to that universal agreement in the things they do consent in; which I presume may be done.

4. *"What is, is,"* and *"It is impossible for the same Thing to be and not to be,"* *not universally assented to.*—But, which is worse, this argument of universal consent which is made use of to prove innate principles, seems to me a demonstration that there are none such: because there are none to which all mankind give an universal assent. I shall begin with the speculative, and instance in those magnified principles of demonstration, "Whatsoever is, is," and "It is impossible for the same thing to be and not to be"; which, of all others, I think have the most allowed title to innate. These have so settled a reputation of maxims universally received, that it will no doubt be thought strange if any one should seem to question it. But yet I take liberty to say, that these propositions are so far from having an universal assent, that there are a great part of mankind to whom they are not so much as known.

5. *Not on the mind naturally imprinted, because not known to children, idiots,* *etc.*—For, first, it is evident, that all children and idiots have not the least apprehension or thought of them. And the want of that is enough to destroy that universal assent, which must needs be the necessary concomitant of all innate truths: it seeming to me near a contradiction to say, that there are truths imprinted on the soul which it perceives or understands not; imprinting, if it signify anything, being nothing else but the making certain truths to be perceived. . . . No proposition can be said to be in the mind which it never yet knew, which it was never yet conscious of. For if any one may, then, by the same reason, all propositions that are true, and the mind is capable ever of assenting to, may be said to be in the mind, and to be imprinted; since if any one can be said to be in the mind, which it never yet knew, it must be only because it is capable of knowing it; and so the mind is of all truths it ever shall know. Nay, thus truths may be imprinted on the mind which it never did, nor ever shall know: for a man may live long, and die at last in ignorance of many truths which his mind was capable of knowing, and that with certainty. So that if the capacity of knowing be the natural impression contended for, all the truths a man ever comes to know will, by this account, be every one of them innate: and this great point will amount to no more, but only to a very high improper way of speaking. But then, to what end such contest for certain innate maxims? If truths can be imprinted on the understanding without being perceived, I can see no difference there can be between any truths the mind is *capable* of knowing in respect of their original: they must all be innate, or all adventitious; in vain shall a man go about to distinguish them. He therefore that talks of innate notions in the understanding, cannot (if he intend thereby any distinct sort of truths) mean such truths to be in the understanding as it never perceived, and is yet wholly ignorant of. For if these words "to be in the understanding" have any propriety, they signify to be understood. If therefore these two propositions: "Whatsoever is, is," and, "It is impossible for the same thing to be, and not to be," are by nature imprinted, children cannot be ignorant of them; infants, and all that have souls, must necessarily have them in their understandings, know the truth of them, and assent to it.

*   *   *

CHAPTER 2. NO INNATE PRACTICAL PRINCIPLES

1. *No moral principles so clear and so generally received as the forementioned* *speculative maxims.*—If those speculative maxims whereof we discoursed in the foregoing chapter have not an actual universal assent from all mankind, as we there proved,

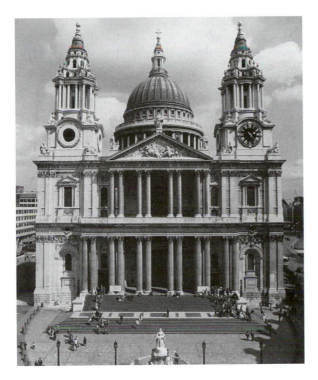

St. Paul's Cathedral, London, facade, built 1675–1710. Like Locke, Sir Chistopher Wren (1632–1723) was interested in science and combining reason and religion. The left turret of the facade he designed for St. Paul's conceals an observatory (opposite the clock in the right turret). (*The British Tourist Authority*)

it is much more visible concerning *practical principles,* that they come short of an universal reception. . . .

2. *Faith and justice not owned as principles by all men.*—Whether there be any such moral principles wherein all men do agree, I appeal to any who have been but moderately conversant in the history of mankind, and looked abroad beyond the smoke of their own chimneys. Where is that practical truth that is universally received without doubt or question, as it must be if innate? *Justice,* and keeping of contracts, is that which most men seem to agree in. This is a principle which is thought to extend itself to the dens of thieves, and the confederacies of the greatest villains; and they who have gone farthest towards the putting off of humanity itself, keep faith and rules of justice one with another. I grant that outlaws themselves do this one amongst another; but it is without receiving these as the innate laws of nature. They practice them as rules of convenience within their own communities: but it is impossible to conceive that he embraces justice as a practical principle who acts fairly with his fellow-highwayman, and at the same plunders or kills the next honest man he meets with.

*   *   *

CHAPTER 3. CONSIDERATIONS ON INNATE PRINCIPLES

8. *Idea of God not innate.*—If any idea can be imagined innate, the idea of *God* may, of all others, for many reasons, be thought so; since it is hard to conceive how there should be innate moral principles without an innate idea of a Deity: without a no-

tion of a lawmaker, it is impossible to have a notion of a law, and an obligation to observe it. Besides the atheists taken notice of amongst the ancients, and left branded upon the records of history, hath not navigation discovered, in these latter ages, whole nations, at the Bay of Soldania, in Brazil, in Boranday, and the Caribbee Islands, etc., amongst whom there was to be found no notion of a God, no religion? . . . Perhaps, if we should with attention mind the lives and discourses of people not so far off, we should have too much reason to fear that many, in more civilized countries, have no very strong and clear impressions of a Deity upon their minds; and that the complaints of atheism made from the pulpit are not without reason. . . .

9. *The name of God not universal or obscure in meaning.*—But had all mankind everywhere a notion of a God (whereof yet history tells us the contrary), it would not from thence follow that the idea of him was innate, . . . especially if it be such an idea as is agreeable to the common light of reason, and naturally deducible from every part of our knowledge, as that of a God is. For the visible marks of extraordinary wisdom and power appear so plainly in all the work of the creation, that a rational creature who will but seriously reflect on them, cannot miss the discovery of a Deity; and the influence that the discovery of such a Being must necessarily have on the minds of all that have but once heard of it, is so great, and carries such a weight of thought and communication with it, that it seems stranger to me that a whole nation of men should be anywhere found so brutish as to want the notion of a God, than that they should be without any notion of numbers, or fire.

*   *   *

BOOK II. OF IDEAS

CHAPTER 1. OF IDEAS IN GENERAL AND THEIR ORIGINAL

1. *Idea is the object of thinking.*—Every man being conscious to himself that he thinks, and that which his mind is applied about whilst thinking being the ideas that are there, it is past doubt that men have in their minds several ideas, such as are those expressed by the words *whiteness, hardness, sweetness, thinking, motion, man, elephant, army, drunkenness,* and others. It is in the first place then to be enquired, How he comes by them?

I know it is a received doctrine, that men have native ideas and original characters stamped upon their minds in their very first being. This opinion I have at large examined already; and, I suppose, what I have said in the foregoing Book will be much more easily admitted, when I have shown whence the understanding may get all the ideas it has, and by what ways and degrees they may come into the mind; for which I shall appeal to every one's own observation and experience.

2. *All ideas come from sensation or reflection.*—Let us then suppose the mind to be, as we say, white paper, void of all characters, without any ideas; how comes it to be furnished? Whence comes it by that vast store, which the busy and boundless fancy of man has painted on it with an almost endless variety? Whence has it all the *materials* of reason and knowledge? To this I answer, in one word, from EXPERIENCE; in that all

our knowledge is founded, and from that it ultimately derives itself. Our observation, employed either about external sensible objects, or about the internal operations of our minds, perceived and reflected on by ourselves, is that which supplies our understandings with all the *materials* of thinking. These two are the fountains of knowledge, from whence all the ideas we have or can naturally have, do spring.

3. *The objects of sensation one source of ideas.*—First, our senses, conversant about particular sensible objects, do convey into the mind several distinct perceptions of things, according to those various ways wherein those objects do affect them; and thus we come by those *ideas* we have of *yellow, white, heat, cold, soft, hard, bitter, sweet,* and all those which we call sensible qualities; which when I say the senses convey into the mind, I mean, they from external objects convey into the mind what produces there those perceptions. This great source of most of the ideas we have, depending wholly upon our senses, and derived by them to the understanding, I call, SENSATION.

4. *The operations of our minds the other source of them.*—Secondly, the other fountain, from which experience furnishes the understanding with ideas, is the perception of the operations of our mind within us, as it is employed about the ideas it has got; which operations, when the soul comes to reflect on and consider, do furnish the understanding with another set of ideas which could not be had from things without: and such are *perception, thinking, doubting, believing, reasoning, knowing, willing,* and all the different actings of our own minds; which we being conscious of, and observing in ourselves, do from these receive into our understanding as distinct ideas, as we do from bodies affecting our senses. This source of ideas every man has wholly in himself: and though it be not sense, as having nothing to do with external objects, yet it is very like it, and might properly enough be called *internal sense.* But as I call the other SENSATION, so I call this REFLECTION, the ideas it affords being such only as the mind gets by reflecting on its own operations within itself. By Reflection, then, in the following part of this discourse, I would be understood to mean that notice which the mind takes of its own operations, and the manner of them, by reason whereof there come to be ideas of these operations in the understanding. These two, I say, viz., external material things as the objects of SENSATION, and the operations of our own minds within as the objects of REFLECTION are, to me, the only originals from whence all our ideas take their beginnings. The term *operations* here, I use in a large sense, as comprehending not barely the actions of the mind about its ideas, but some sort of passions arising sometimes from them, such as is the satisfaction or uneasiness arising from any thought.

5. *All our ideas are of the one or the other of these.*—The understanding seems to me not to have the least glimmering of any ideas which it doth not receive from one of these two. *External objects* furnish the mind with the ideas of sensible qualities, which are all those different perceptions they produce in us; and *the mind* furnishes the understanding with ideas of its own operations. These, when we have taken a full survey of them, and their several modes, combinations, and relations, we shall find to contain all our whole stock of ideas; and that we have nothing in our minds which did not come in one of these two ways. Let any one examine his own thoughts, and thoroughly search into his understanding, and then let him tell me, whether all the original ideas he has there, are any other than of the objects of his senses, or of the operations of his mind considered as objects of his reflection; and how great a mass of knowledge soever he imagines to be lodged there, he will, upon taking a strict view, see that he has not any idea in his mind but what one of these two have imprinted, though perhaps with infinite variety compounded and enlarged by the understanding, as we shall see hereafter.

6. *Observable in children.*—He that attentively considers the state of a child at his first coming into the world, will have little reason to think him stored with plenty of ideas that are to be the matter of his future knowledge. It is *by degrees* he comes to be furnished with them: and though the ideas of obvious and familiar qualities themselves before the memory begins to keep a register of time and order, yet it is often so late before some unusual qualities come in the way, that there are few men that cannot recollect the beginning of their acquaintance with them: and if it were worth while, no doubt a child might be so ordered as to have but a very few even of the ordinary ideas till he were grown up to a man. But all that are born into the world being surrounded with bodies that perpetually and diversely affect them, variety of ideas, whether care be taken about it or no, are imprinted on the minds of children. Light and colours are busy and at hand everywhere when the eye is but open; sounds and some tangible qualities fail not to solicit their proper senses, and force an entrance to the mind; but yet I think it will be granted easily, that if a child were kept in a place where he never saw any other but black and white till he were a man, he would have no more ideas of scarlet or green, than he that from his childhood never tasted an oyster or a pineapple has of those particular relishes.

7. *Men are differently furnished with these according to the different objects they converse with.*—Men then come to be furnished with fewer or more simple ideas from without, according as the objects they converse with afford greater or less variety; and from the operations of their minds within, according as they more or less reflect on them. For, though he that contemplates the operations of his mind cannot but have plain and clear ideas of them; yet, unless he turn his thoughts that way, and considers them *attentively,* he will no more have clear and distinct ideas of all the operations of his mind, and all that may be observed therein, than he will have all the particular ideas of any landscape, or of the parts and motions of a clock, who will not turn his eyes to it, and with attention heed all the parts of it. The picture or clock may be so placed, that they may come in his way every day; but yet he will have but a confused idea of all the parts they are made up of, till he applies himself with attention to consider them each in particular.

8. *Ideas of reflection later, because they need attention.*—And hence we see the reason why it is pretty late before most children get ideas of the operations of their own minds; and some have not any very clear or perfect ideas of the greatest part of them all their lives. Because, though they pass there continually, yet, like floating visions, they make not deep impressions enough to leave in the mind clear, distinct, lasting ideas, till the understanding turns inward upon itself, reflects on its own operations, and makes them the object of its own contemplation. Children, when they come first into it, are surrounded with a world of new things, which, by a constant solicitation of their senses, draw the mind constantly to them, forward to take notice of new, and apt to be delighted with the variety of changing objects. Thus the first years are usually employed and diverted in looking abroad. Men's business in them is to acquaint themselves with what is to be found without; and so, growing up in a constant attention to outward sensations, seldom make any considerable reflection on what passes within them till they come to be of riper years; and some scarce ever at all.

9. *The soul begins to have ideas when it begins to perceive.*—To ask, at what time a man has first any ideas, is to ask when he begins to perceive; having ideas, and perception, being the same thing. I know it is an opinion, that the soul always thinks; and that it has the actual perception of ideas in itself constantly, as long as it exists; and that actual thinking is as inseparable from the soul, as actual extension is from the body: which if true, to enquire after the beginning of a man's ideas is the same as to enquire

after the beginning of his soul. For by this account, soul and its ideas, as body and its extension, will begin to exist both at the same time.

*   *   *

CHAPTER 2. OF SIMPLE IDEAS

1. *Uncompounded appearances.*—The better to understand the nature, manner, and extent of our knowledge, one thing is carefully to be observed concerning the ideas we have; and that is, that some of them are *simple,* and some *complex.*

Though the qualities that affect our senses are, in the things themselves, so united and blended that there is no separation, no distance between them; yet it is plain the ideas they produce in the mind enter by the senses simple and unmixed. For though the sight and touch often take in from the same object at the same time different ideas; as a man sees at once motion and colour, the hand feels softness and warmth in the same piece of wax; yet the simple ideas thus united in the same subject are as perfectly distinct as those that come in by different senses. The coldness and hardness which a man feels in a piece of ice being as distinct ideas in the mind as the smell and whiteness of a lily, or as the taste of sugar and smell of a rose: and there is nothing can be plainer to a man than the clear and distinct perception he has of those simple ideas; which, being each in itself uncompounded, contains in it nothing but *one uniform appearance or conception in the mind,* and is not distinguishable into different ideas.

2. *The mind can neither make nor destroy them.*—These simple ideas, the materials of all our knowledge, are suggested and furnished to the mind only by those two ways above mentioned, viz., sensation and reflection. When the understanding is once stored with these simple ideas, it has the power to repeat, compare, and unite them, even to an almost infinite variety, and so can make at pleasure new complex ideas. But it is not in the power of the most exalted wit or enlarged understanding, by any quickness or variety of thought, to *invent* or *frame* one new simple idea in the mind, not taken in by the ways before mentioned; nor can any force of the understanding *destroy* those that are there. The dominion of man in this little world of his own understanding, being much-what the same as it is in the great world of visible things, wherein his power, however managed by art and skill, reaches no farther than to compound and divide the materials that are made to his hand, but can do nothing towards the making the least particle of new matter, or destroying one atom of what is already in being. The same inability will every one find in himself, who shall go about to fashion in his understanding any simple idea not received in by his senses from external objects, or by reflection from the operations of his own mind about them. I would have any one try to fancy any taste which had never affected his palate, or frame the idea of a scent he had never smelt; and when he can do this, I will also conclude, that a blind man hath ideas of colours, and a deaf man true distinct notions of sounds.

3. *Only the qualities that affect the sense are imaginable.*—This is the reason why, though we cannot believe it impossible to God to make a creature with other organs, and more ways to convey into the understanding the notice of corporeal things than those five, as they are usually counted, which he has given to man—yet I think it is *not possible* for any one to *imagine* any other qualities in bodies, howsoever constituted, whereby they can be taken notice of, besides sounds, tastes, smells, visible and tangible qualities. And had mankind been made with but four senses, the qualities then which are the object of the fifth sense, had been as far from our notice, imagination, and

conception, as now any belonging to a sixth, seventh, or eighth sense, can possibly be: which, whether yet some other creatures, in some other parts of this vast and stupendous universe, may not have, will be a great presumption to deny. He that will not set himself proudly at the top of all things, but will consider the immensity of this fabric, and the great variety that is to be found in this little and inconsiderable part of it which he has to do with, may be apt to think, that in other mansions of it there may be other and different intelligible beings, of whose faculties he has as little knowledge or apprehension, as a worm shut up in one drawer of a cabinet hath of the senses or understanding of a man; such variety and excellency being suitable to the wisdom and power of the Maker. I have here followed the common opinion of man's having but five senses, though perhaps there may be justly counted more, but either supposition serves equally to my present purpose.

CHAPTER 3. OF IDEAS OF ONE SENSE

1. *Division of simple ideas.*—The better to conceive the ideas we receive from sensation, it may not be amiss for us to consider them in reference to the different ways whereby they make their approaches to our minds, and make themselves perceivable by us.

First, then, There are some which come into our minds *by one sense* only.

Secondly. There are others that convey themselves into the mind *by more senses than one.*

Thirdly. Others that are from *reflection only.*

Fourthly. There are some that make themselves way, and are suggested to the mind *by all the ways of sensation and reflection.*

We shall consider them apart under these several heads.

Ideas of one sense. There are some ideas which have admittance only through one sense, which is peculiarly adapted to receive them. Thus light and colours, as white, red, yellow, blue, with their several degrees or shades and mixtures, as green, scarlet, purple, sea-green, and the rest come in only by the eyes; all kinds of noises, sounds, and tones, only by the ears; the several tastes and smells, by the nose and palate. And if these organs, or the nerves which are the conduits to convey them from without to their audience in the brain, the mind's presence-room (as I may so call it), are, any of them, so disordered as not to perform their functions, they have no postern to be admitted by, no other way to bring themselves into view, and be perceived by the understanding.

The most considerable of those belonging to the touch are heat, and cold, and solidity; all the rest, consisting almost wholly in the sensible configuration, as smooth and rough; or else, more or less firm adhesion of the parts, as hard and soft, tough and brittle, are obvious enough.

2. *Few simple ideas have names.*—I think it will be needless to enumerate all the particular simple ideas belonging to each sense. Nor indeed is it possible if we would, there being a great many more of them belonging to most of the senses than we have names for. The variety of smells, which are as many almost, if not more than species of bodies in the world, do most of them want names. Sweet and stinking commonly serve our turn for these ideas, which in effect is little more than to call them pleasing or displeasing; though the smell of a rose and violet, both sweet, are certainly very distinct ideas. Nor are the different tastes that by our palates we receive ideas of, much better provided with names. Sweet, bitter, sour, harsh, and salt, are almost all the epithets we have to denominate that numberless variety of relishes which are to be found distinct,

not only in almost every sort of creatures, but in the different parts of the same plant, fruit, or animal. The same may be said of colours and sounds. I shall therefore, in the account of simple ideas I am here giving, content myself to set down only such as are most material to our present purpose, or are in themselves less apt to be taken notice of, though they are very frequently the ingredients of our complex ideas; amongst which, I think, I may well account solidity, which therefore I shall treat of in the next chapter.

CHAPTER 4. OF SOLIDITY

1. *We receive this idea from touch.*—The idea of solidity we receive by our touch; and it arises from the resistance which we find in body to the entrance of any other body into the place it possesses, till it has left it. There is no idea which we receive more constantly from sensation than solidity. Whether we move or rest, in what posture soever we are, we always feel something under us that supports us, and hinders our farther sinking downwards; and the bodies which we daily handle make us perceive that whilst they remain between them, they do, by an insurmountable force, hinder the approach of the parts of our hands that press them. *That which thus hinders the approach of two bodies, when they are moving one towards another, I call solidity.* I will not dispute whether this acceptation of the word solid be nearer to its original signification than that which mathematicians use it in: it suffices that, I think, the common notion of solidity will allow, if not justify, this use of it; but if any one think it better to call it *impenetrability,* he has my consent. Only I have thought the term solidity the more proper to express this idea, not only because of its vulgar use in that sense, but also because it carries something more of positive in it than impenetrability, which is negative, and is, perhaps, more a consequence of solidity than solidity itself. This, of all other, seems the idea most intimately connected with and essential to body, so as nowhere else to be found or imagined, but only in matter; and though our senses take no notice of it, but in masses of matter, of a bulk sufficient to cause a sensation in us; yet the mind, having once got this idea from such grosser sensible bodies, traces it farther, and considers it, as well as figure, in the minutest particle of matter that can exist, and finds it inseparably inherent in body, wherever or however modified.

2. *Solidity fills Space.*—This is the idea which belongs to body, whereby we conceive it to fill space. The idea of which filling of space is,—that where we imagine any space taken up by a solid substance, we conceive it so to possess it, that it excludes all other solid substances; and will for ever hinder any other two bodies, that move towards one another in a straight line, from coming to touch one another, unless it removes from between them in a line not parallel to that which they move in. This idea of it, the bodies which we ordinarily handle sufficiently furnish us with.

3. *Distinct from space.*—This resistance, whereby it keeps other bodies out of the space which it possesses, is so great, that no force, how great soever, can surmount it. All the bodies in the world, pressing a drop of water on all sides, will never be able to overcome the resistance which it will make, as soft as it is, to their approaching one another, till it be removed out of their way; whereby our idea of solidity is distinguished both from pure space, which is capable neither of resistance nor motion, and from the ordinary idea of hardness. For a man may conceive two bodies at a distance so as they may approach one another without touching or displacing any solid thing till their superficies come to meet; whereby, I think, we have the clear idea of space without solidity. For (not to go so far as annihilation of any particular body) I ask, whether a man cannot have the idea of the motion of one single body alone, without any other suc-

ceeding immediately into its place? I think it is evident he can: the idea of motion in one body no more including the idea of motion in another, than the idea of a square figure in one body includes the idea of a square figure in another. I do not ask, whether bodies do *so exist,* that the motion of one body cannot really be without the motion of another? To determine this either way is to beg the question for or against a *vacuum.* But my question is, whether one cannot have the *idea* of one body moved, whilst others are at rest? And I think this no one will deny: if so, then the place it deserted gives us the idea of pure space without solidity, whereinto another body may enter without either resistance or protrusion of anything. When the sucker in a pump is drawn, the space it filled in the tube is certainly the same, whether any other body follows the motion of the sucker or no; nor does it imply a contradiction that upon the motion of one body, another that is only contiguous to it should not follow it. The necessity of such a motion is built only on the supposition, that the world is full, but no on the distinct *ideas* of space and solidity; which are as different as resistance and not resistance, protrusion and not protrusion. And that men have ideas of space without body, their very disputes a vacuum plainly demonstrate as is showed in another place.

4. *From hardness.*—Solidity is hereby also differenced from hardness, in that solidity consists in repletion, and so an utter exclusion of other bodies out of the space it possesses; but hardness, in a firm cohesion of the parts of matter, making up masses of a sensible bulk, so that the whole does not easily change its figure. And, indeed, hard and soft are names that we give to things only in relation to the constitutions of our own bodies; that being generally called hard by us which will put us to pain sooner than change figure by the pressure of any part of our bodies; and that, on the contrary, soft which changes the situation of its parts upon an easy and unpainful touch.

But this difficulty of changing the situation of the sensible parts amongst themselves, or of the figure of the whole, gives no more solidity to the hardest body in the world than to the softest; nor is an adamant one jot more solid than water. For though the two flat sides of two pieces of marble will more easily approach each other, between there is nothing but water or air, than if there be a diamond between them; yet it is not that the parts of the diamond are more solid than those of water, or resist more, but because the parts of water being more easily separable from each other, they will by a side-motion be more easily removed and give way to the approach of the two pieces of marble: but if they could be kept from making place by that side-motion, they would eternally hinder the approach of these two pieces of marble as much as the diamond. The softest body in the world will as invincibly resist the coming together of any two other bodies, if it be not put out of the way, but remain between them, as the hardest that can be found or imagined. He that shall fill a yielding soft body well with air or water will quickly find its resistance: and he that thinks that nothing but bodies that are hard can keep his hands from approaching one another, may be pleased to make a trial with the air enclosed in a football. The experiment I have been told was made at Florence, with a hollow globe of gold filled with water, and exactly closed, farther shows the solidity of so soft a body as water. For the golden globe thus filled being put into a press which was driven by the extreme force of screws, the water made itself way through the pores of that very close metal, and finding no room for a nearer approach of its particles within, got to the outside, where it rose like a dew, and so fell in drops before the sides of the globe could be made to yield to the violent compression of the engine that squeezed it.

5. *On solidity depend impulse, resistance, and protrusion.*—By this idea of solidity is the extension of body distinguished from the extension of space. The extension of body being nothing but the cohesion or continuity of solid, separable parts; and the extension of space, the continuity of unsolid, inseparable, and immovable parts. Upon the

solidity of bodies also depend their mutual impulse, resistance, and protrusion. Of pure space then, and solidity, there are several (amongst which I confess myself one) who persuade themselves they have clear and distinct ideas; and that they can think on space without anything in it that resists or is protruded by body. This is the idea of pure space, which they think they have as clear as any idea they can have of the extension of body. . . .

6. *What solidity is.*—If any one asks me, *what this solidity is,* I send him to his senses to inform him: let him put a flint or a football between his hands, and then endeavour to join them, and he will know. If he thinks this is not a sufficient explanation of solidity, what it is, and wherein it consists, I promise to tell him what it is, and wherein it consists, when he tells me what thinking is, or wherein it consists; or explains to me what extension or motion is, which perhaps seems much easier. The simple ideas we have are such as experience teaches them us; but if, beyond that, we endeavour by words to make them clearer in the mind, we shall succeed no better than if we went about to clear up the darkness of a blind man's mind by talking, and to discourse into him the ideas of light and colours. The reason of this I shall show in another place.

Chapter 5. Of Simple Ideas of Divers Senses

Ideas received both by seeing and touching.—The ideas we get by more than one sense are of *space* or *extension, figure, rest* and *motion:* for these make perceivable impressions both on the eyes and touch; and we can receive and convey into our minds the ideas of the extension, figure, motion, and rest of bodies, both by seeing and feeling. But having occasion to speak more at large of these in another place, I here only enumerate them.

Chapter 6. Of Simple Ideas of Reflection

1. *Simple ideas are the operations of the mind about its other ideas.*—The mind, receiving the ideas mentioned in the foregoing chapters from without, when it turns its view inward upon itself, and observes its own actions about those ideas it has, takes from thence other ideas, which are as capable to be the objects of its contemplation as any of those it received from foreign things.

2. *The idea of perception, and idea of willing, we have from reflection.*—The two great and principal actions of the mind, which are most frequently considered, and which are so frequent that every one that pleases may take notice of them in himself, are these two:—*Perception* or *Thinking,* and *Volition* or *Willing.* The power of thinking is called the *Understanding* and the power of volition is called the *Will;* and these two powers of abilities in the mind are denominated *faculties.* Of some of the *modes* of these simple ideas of reflection, such as are *remembrance, discerning, reasoning, judging, knowledge, faith, etc.,* I shall have occasion to speak hereafter.

Chapter 7. Of Simple Ideas of Both Sensation and Reflection

1. *Ideas of pleasure and pain.*—There be other simple ideas which convey themselves into the mind by all the ways of sensation and reflection; viz., *pleasure* or *delight,* and its opposite, *pain* or *uneasiness; power; existence; unity.*

2. *Mix with almost all our other ideas.*—Delight or uneasiness, one or other of them, join themselves to almost all our ideas both of sensation and reflection; and there is scarce any affection of our senses from without, any retired thought of our mind within, which is not able to produce in us pleasure or pain. By pleasure and pain, I would be understood to signify whatsoever delights or molests us; whether it arises from the thoughts of our minds, or anything operating on our bodies. For whether we call it satisfaction, delight, pleasure, happiness, etc., on the one side, or uneasiness, trouble, pain, torment, anguish, misery, etc., on the other, they are still but different degrees of the same thing, and belong to the ideas of pleasure and pain, delight or uneasiness; which are the names I shall most commonly use for those two sorts of ideas.

3. *As motives of our actions.*—The infinite wise Author of our being, . . . to excite us to these actions of thinking and motion that we are capable of, has been pleased to join to several thoughts and several sensations a perception of delight. If this were wholly separated from all our outward sensations and inward thoughts, we should have no reason to prefer one thought or action to another, negligence to attention, or motion to rest. And so we should neither stir our bodies, nor employ our minds, but let our thoughts (if I may so call it) run adrift, without any direction or design; and suffer the ideas of our minds, like unregarded shadows, to make their appearances there as it happened, without attending to them. In which state man, however furnished with the faculties of understanding and will, would be a very idle, unactive creature, and pass his time only in a lazy, lethargic dream. . . .

4. *An end and use of pain.*—Pain has the same efficacy and use to set us on work that pleasure has, we being as ready to employ our faculties to avoid that, as to pursue this: only this is worth our consideration, that pain is often produced by the same objects and ideas that produce pleasure in us. . . . Thus heat, that is very agreeable to us in one degree, by a little greater increase of it proves no ordinary torment; and the most pleasant of all sensible objects, light itself, if there be too much of it, if increased beyond a due proportion to our eyes, causes a very painful sensation. Which is wisely and favourably so ordered by nature, that when any object does by the vehemency of its operation disorder the instruments of sensation, whose structures cannot but be very nice and delicate, we might by the pain be warned to withdraw before the organ be quite put out of order, and so be unfitted for its proper functions for the future.

*   *   *

7. *Ideas of existence and unity.*—Existence and unity are two other ideas that are suggested to the understanding by every object without, and every idea within. When ideas are in our minds, we consider them as being actually there, as well as we consider things to be actually without us: which is, that they exist, or have existence. And whatever we can consider as one thing, whether a real being or idea, suggests to the understanding the idea of unity.

8. *Idea of power.*—Power also is another of those ideas which we receive from sensation and reflection. For, observing in ourselves that we do and can think, and that we can at pleasure move several parts of our bodies which were at rest, the effects also that natural bodies are able to produce in one another occurring every moment to our senses, we both these ways get the idea of power.

9. *Idea of succession.*—Besides these there is another idea, which though suggested by our senses yet is more constantly offered us by what passes in our own minds; and that is the idea of succession. For if we look immediately into ourselves,

and reflect on what is observable there, we shall find our ideas always, whilst we are awake or have any thought, passing in train, one going and another coming without intermission.

10. *Simple ideas the materials of all our knowledge.*—These, if they are not all, are at least (as I think) the most considerable of those simple ideas which the mind has, and out of which is made all its other knowledge: all of which it receives only by the two forementioned ways of sensation and reflection.

Nor let any one think these too narrow bounds for the capacious mind of man to expatiate in, which takes its flight farther than the stars, and cannot be confined by the limits of the world. I grant all this, but desire any one to assign any *simple idea* which is not received from one of those inlets before mentioned, or any *complex idea* not made out of those simple ones.

Nor will it be so strange to think these few simple ideas sufficient to employ the quickest thought or largest capacity, and to furnish the materials of all that various knowledge and more various fancies and opinions of all mankind, if we consider how many words may be made out of the various composition of twenty-four letters; or if, going one step farther, we will but reflect on the variety of combinations may be made with barely one of the above-mentioned ideas, viz., number, whose stock is inexhaustible and truly infinite: and what a large and immense field doth extension alone afford the mathematicians?

CHAPTER 8. SOME FURTHER CONSIDERATIONS CONCERNING OUR SIMPLE IDEAS OF SENSATION

1. *Positive ideas from privative causes.*—Concerning the simple ideas of sensation it is to be considered, that whatsoever is so constituted in nature as to be able by affecting our senses to cause any perception in the mind, doth thereby produce in the understanding a simple idea; which, whatever be the external cause of it, when it comes to be taken notice of by our discerning faculty, it is by the mind looked on and considered there to be a real positive idea in the understanding, as much as any other whatsoever; though perhaps the cause of it be but a privation in the subject.

2. *Ideas in the mind distinguished from that in things which gives rise to them.*—Thus the ideas of heat and cold, light and darkness, white and black, motion and rest, are equally clear and positive ideas in the mind; though perhaps some of the causes which produce them are barely privations in those subjects from whence our senses derive those ideas. These the understanding, in its view of them, considers all as distinct positive ideas without taking notice of the causes that produce them: which is an enquiry not belonging to the idea as it is in the understanding, but to the nature of the things existing without us. These are two very different things, and carefully to be distinguished; it being one thing to perceive and know the idea of white or black, and quite another to examine what kind of particles they must be, and how ranged in the superficies, to make any object appear white or black.

3. *We may have ideas when we are ignorant of their physical causes.*—A painter or dyer who never enquired into their causes, hath the ideas of white and black and other colours as clearly, perfectly, and distinctly in his understanding, and perhaps more distinctly than the philosopher who hath busied himself in considering their natures, and thinks he knows how far either of them is in its cause positive or privative; and the idea of black is no less positive in his mind than that of white, however the cause of that colour in the external object may be only a privation.

4. *Why a privative cause in nature may occasion a positive idea.*—If it were the design of my present undertaking to enquire into the natural causes and manner of perception, I should offer this as a reason why a privative cause might, in some cases at least, produce a positive idea, viz., that all sensation being produced in us only by different degrees and modes of motion in our animal spirits, variously agitated by external objects, the abatement of any former motion must as necessarily produce a new sensation as the variation or increase of it; and so introduce a new idea, which depends only on a different motion of the animal spirits in that organ.

5. *Negative names need not be meaningless.*—But whether this be so or no I will not here determine, but appeal to every one's own experience, whether the shadow of a man, though it consists of nothing but the absence of light (and the more the absence of light is, the more discernible is the shadow), does not, when a man looks on it, cause as clear and positive an idea in his mind as a man himself, though covered over with clear sunshine. And the picture of a shadow is a positive thing. Indeed, we have negative names, which stand not directly for positive ideas, but for their absence, such as *insipid, silence, nihil, etc.,* which words denote positive ideas, v.g., *taste, sound, being,* with a signification of their absence.

6. *Whether any ideas are due to causes really privative.*—And thus one may truly be said to see darkness. . . . The privative causes I have here assigned of positive ideas are according to the common opinion; but in truth it will be hard to determine whether there be really any ideas from a privative cause, till it be determined whether rest be any more a privation than motion.

7. *Ideas in the mind, qualities in bodies.*—To discover the nature of our *ideas* the better, and to discourse of them intelligibly, it will be convenient to distinguish them *as they are ideas or perceptions in our minds, and as they are modifications of matter in the bodies that cause such perceptions in us:* that so we may not think (as perhaps usually is done) that they are exactly the images and resemblances of something inherent in the subject; most of those of sensation being in the mind no more the likeness of something existing without us than the names that stand for them are the likeness of our ideas, which yet upon hearing they are apt to excite in us.

8. *Our ideas and the qualities of bodies.*—Whatsoever the mind perceives *in itself,* or is the immediate object of perception, thought, or understanding, that I call *idea;* and the power to produce any idea in our mind, I call *quality* of the subject wherein that power is. Thus a snowball having the power to produce in us the ideas of white, cold, and round, the powers to produce those ideas in us as they are in the snowball, I call qualities; and as they are sensations or perceptions in our understandings, I call them ideas; which *ideas,* if I speak of them sometimes as in the things themselves, I would be understood to mean those qualities in the objects which produce them in us.

9. *Primary qualities of bodies.*—Qualities thus considered in bodies are, *First,* such as are utterly inseparable from the body, in what estate soever it be; such as, in all the alterations and changes it suffers, all the force can be used upon it, it constantly keeps; and such as sense constantly finds in every particle of matter which has bulk enough to be perceived, and the mind finds inseparable from every particle of matter, though less than to make itself singly be perceived by our senses: v.g., take a grain of wheat, divide it into two parts, each part has still solidity, extension, figure, and mobility; divide it again, and it retains still the same qualities: and so divide it on, till the parts become insensible; they must retain still each of them all those qualities. . . . These I call *original* or *primary qualities* of body, which I think we may observe to produce simple ideas in us, viz., solidity, extension, figure, motion or rest, and number.

10. *Secondary qualities of bodies.*—Secondly, such qualities, which in truth are nothing in the objects themselves, but powers to produce various sensations in us by their primary qualities, i.e., by the bulk, figure, texture, and motion of their insensible parts, as colours, sounds, tastes, etc., these I call *secondary qualities.* To these might be added a third sort, which are allowed to be barely powers, though they are as much real qualities in the subject as those which I, to comply with the common way of speaking, call qualities, but, for distinction, secondary qualities. For the power in fire to produce a new colour or consistence in *wax* or *clay* by its primary qualities, is as much a quality in fire as the power it has to produce in *me* a new idea or sensation of warmth or burning, which I felt not before, by the same primary qualities, viz., the bulk, texture, and motion of its insensible parts.

11. *How bodies produce ideas in us.*—The next thing to be considered is, how bodies produce ideas in us; and that is manifestly by impulse, the only way which we can conceive bodies operate in.

12. *By motions, external, and in our organism.*—If, then, external objects be not united to our minds when they produce ideas in it, and yet we perceive these *original* qualities in such of them as singly fall under senses, it is evident that some motion must be thence continued by our nerves or animal spirits, by some parts of our bodies, to the brains or the seat of sensation, there to produce in our minds the particular ideas we have of them. And since the extension, figure, number, and motion of bodies of an observable bigness, may be perceived at a distance by the sight, it is evident some singly imperceptible bodies must come from them to the eyes, and thereby convey to the brain some motion which produces these ideas which we have of them in us.

13. *How secondary qualities produce their ideas.*—After the same manner that the ideas of these original qualities are produced in us, we may conceive that the ideas of *secondary* qualities are also produced, viz., by the operation of insensible particles on our senses. . . . The different motions and figures, bulk and number of such particles, affecting the several organs of our senses, produce in us those different sensations which we have from the colours and smells of bodies; v.g., that a violet, by the impulse of such insensible particle, of matter of peculiar figures and bulks, and in different degrees and modifications of their motions, causes the ideas of the blue colour and sweet scent of that flower to be produced in our minds. It being no more impossible to conceive that God should annex such ideas to such motions with which they have no similitude, than that he should annex the idea of pain to the motion of a piece of steel dividing our flesh, with which that idea hath no resemblance.

14. *They depend on the primary qualities.*—What I have said concerning colours and smells may be understood also of tastes and sounds, and other the like sensible qualities; which, whatever reality we by mistake attribute to them, are in truth nothing in the objects themselves, but powers to produce various sensations in us, and depend on those primary qualities, viz., bulk, figure, texture, and motion of parts, as I have said.

15. *Ideas of primary qualities are resemblances; of secondary, not.*—From whence I think it is easy to draw this observation, that the ideas of primary qualities of bodies are resemblances of them, and their patterns do really exist in the bodies themselves; but the ideas produced in us by these secondary qualities have no resemblance of them at all. There is nothing like our ideas existing in the bodies themselves. They are, in the bodies we denominate from them, only a power to produce those sensations in us: and what is sweet, blue, or warm in idea, is but the certain bulk, figure, and motion of the insensible parts in the bodies themselves, which we call so.

16. *Examples.*—Flame is denominated hot and light; snow, white and cold; and manna, white and sweet, from the ideas they produce in us. Which qualities are com-

monly thought to be the same in those bodies that those ideas are in us, the one the perfect resemblance of the other, as they are in a mirror; and it would by most men be judged very extravagant, if one should say otherwise. And yet he that will consider that the same fire that at one distance produces in us the sensation of warmth, does at a nearer approach produce in us the far different sensation of pain, ought to bethink himself what reason he has to say, that his idea of warmth which was produced in him by the fire, is *actually in the fire;* and his idea of pain which the same fire produced in him the same way is *not* in the fire. Why is whiteness and coldness in snow, and pain not, when it produces the one and the other idea in us, and can do neither, but by the bulk, figure, number, and motion of its solid parts?

17. *The ideas of the primary alone really exist.*—The particular bulk, number, figure, and motion of the parts of fire or snow are really in them, whether any one's senses perceive them or no; and therefore they may be called *real* qualities, because they really exist in those bodies. But light, heat, whiteness, or coldness, are no more really in them than sickness or pain is in manna. Take away the sensation of them; let not the eyes see light or colours, nor the ears hear sounds; let the palate not taste, nor the nose smell; and all colours, tastes, odours, and sounds, *as they are such particular ideas,* vanish and cease, and are reduced to their causes, i.e., bulk, figure, and motion of parts.

18. *Secondary exist only as modes of the primary.*—A piece of manna of a sensible bulk is able to produce in us the idea of a round or square figure; and, by being removed from one place to another, the idea of motion. This idea of motion represents it as it really is in the manna moving; a circle or square are the same, whether in idea or existence, in the mind or in the manna; and this, both motion and figure are really in the manna, whether we take notice of them or no: this everybody is ready to agree to. Besides, manna, by the bulk, figure, texture, and motion of its parts, has a power to produce the sensations of sickness, and sometimes of acute pains or gripings, in us. That these ideas of sickness and pain are not in the manna, but effects of its operations on us, and are nowhere when we feel them not: this also every one readily agrees to. And yet men are hardly to be brought to think that sweetness and whiteness are not really in manna, which are but the effects of the operations of manna by the motion, size, and figure of its particles on the eyes and palate: as the pain and sickness caused by manna are confessedly nothing but the effects of its operations on the stomach. . . . Why the pain and sickness, ideas that are the effects of manna, should be thought to be nowhere when they are not felt; and yet the sweetness and whiteness, effects of the same manna on other parts of the body, by ways equally as unknown, should be thought to exist in the manna, when they are not seen nor tasted, would need some reason to explain.

19. *Examples.*—Let us consider the red and white colours in porphyry: hinder light but from striking on it, and its colours vanish; it no longer produces any such ideas in us. Upon the return of light, it produces these appearances on us again. Can any one think any real alterations are made in the porphyry by the presence or absence of light, and that those ideas of whiteness and redness are really in porphyry in the light, when it is plain *it has no colour in the dark?* It has indeed such a configuration of particles, both night and day, as are apt, by the rays of light rebounding from some parts of that hard stone, to produce in us the idea of redness, and from others the idea of whiteness: but whiteness or redness are not in it at any time, but such a texture that hath the power to produce such a sensation in us.

*   *   *

22. *Excursion into natural philosophy.*—I have, in what just goes before, been engaged in physical enquiries a little farther than perhaps I intended. But it being necessary to make the nature of sensation a little understood, and to make the difference between the *qualities* in bodies and the *ideas* produced by them in the mind to be distinctly conceived, without which it were impossible to discourse intelligibly of them, I hope I shall be pardoned this little excursion into natural philosophy, it being necessary in our present enquiry to distinguish the *primary* and *real* qualities of bodies, which are always in them (viz., solidity, extension, figure, number, and motion or rest, and are sometimes perceived by us, viz., when the bodies they are in are big enough singly to be discerned), from those *secondary* and *imputed* qualities, which are but the powers of several combinations of those primary ones, when they operate without being distinctly discerned: whereby we also may come to know what ideas are, and what are not, resemblances of something really existing in the bodies we denominate from them.

23. *Three sorts of qualities in bodies.*—The qualities then that are in bodies, rightly considered, are of three sorts:

First, the bulk, figure, number, situation, and motion or rest of their solid parts. Those are in them, whether we perceive them or no; and when they are of that size that we can discover them, we have by these an idea of the thing as it is in itself, as is plain in artificial things. These I call *primary qualities.*

Secondly, the power that is in any body, by reason of its insensible primary qualities, to operate after a peculiar manner on any of our senses, and thereby produce in *us* the different ideas of several colours, sounds, smells, tastes, etc. These are usually called *sensible qualities.*

Thirdly, the power that is in any body, by reason of the particular constitution of its primary qualities, to make such a change in the bulk, figure, texture, and motion of *another body,* as to make it operate on our senses differently from what it did before. Thus the sun has a power to make wax white, and fire, to make lead fluid. These are usually called *powers.*

The first of these, as has been said, I think may be properly called real, original, or primary qualities, because they are in the things themselves, whether they are perceived or no: and upon their different modifications it is that the secondary qualities depend.

The other two are only powers to act differently upon other things, which powers result from the different modifications of those primary qualities.

24. *The first are resemblances; the second thought to be resemblances, but are not; the third neither are, nor are thought so.*—But though these two latter sorts of qualities are powers barely, and nothing but powers, relating to several other bodies, and resulting from the different modifications of the original qualities, yet they are generally otherwise thought of . . . . V.g., the idea of heat or light which we receive by our eyes or touch from the sun, are commonly thought real qualities existing in the sun, and something more than mere powers in it. But when we consider the sun in reference to wax, which it melts or blanches, we look upon the whiteness and softness produced in the wax, not as qualities in the sun, but effects produced by powers in it: whereas, if rightly considered, these qualities of light and warmth, which are perceptions in me when I am warmed or enlightened by the sun, are no otherwise in the sun than the changes made in the wax, when it is blanched or melted, are in the sun. They are all of them equally *powers in the sun, depending on its primary qualities* . . . .

25. *Why the secondary are ordinarily taken for real qualities, and not for bare powers.*—The reason why the one are ordinarily taken for real qualities, and the other only for bare powers, seems to be because the ideas we have of distinct colours, sounds,

etc., containing nothing at all in them of bulk, figure, or motion, we are not apt to think them the effects of these primary qualities which appear not to our senses to operate in their production, and with which they have not any apparent congruity, or conceivable connexion. Hence it is that we are so forward to imagine that those ideas are the resemblances of something really existing in the objects themselves. . . . But, in the other case, in the operations of bodies changing the qualities one of another, we plainly discover that the quality produced hath commonly no resemblance with anything in the thing producing it; wherefore we look on it as a bare effect of power. . . .

*   *   *

CHAPTER 9. OF PERCEPTION

1. *Perception the first simple idea of reflection.*—PERCEPTION, as it is the first faculty of the mind exercised about our ideas; so it is the first and simplest idea we have from reflection, and is by some called thinking in general. Though thinking, in the propriety of the English tongue, signifies that sort of operation in the mind about its ideas, wherein the mind is active; where it, with some degree of voluntary attention, considers anything. For in bare naked perception, the mind is, for the most part, only passive; and what it perceives, it cannot avoid perceiving.

2. *Reflection alone can give us the idea of what, perception is.*—What perception is, every one will know better by reflecting on what he does himself, when he sees, hears, feels, etc., or thinks, than by any discourse of mine. Whoever reflects on what passes in his own mind cannot miss it. And if he does not reflect, all the words in the world cannot make him have any notion of it.

3. *Arises in sensation only when the mind notices the organic impression.*—This is certain, that whatever alterations are made in the body, if they reach not the mind; whatever impressions are made on the outward parts, if they are not taken notice of within, there is no perception. Fire may burn our bodies with no other effect than it does a billet, unless the motion be continued to the brain, and there the sense of heat, or idea of pain, produced in the mind; wherein consists actual perception.

4. *Impulse on the organ insufficient.*—How often may a man observe in himself, that whilst his mind is intently employed in the contemplation of some objects, and curiously surveying some ideas that are there, it takes no notice of impressions of sounding bodies made upon the organ of hearing, with the same alteration that uses to be for the producing the idea of sound? A sufficient impulse there may be on the organ; but it not reaching the observation of the mind, there follows no perception: and though the motion that uses to produce the idea of sound be made in the ear, yet no sound is heard. Want of sensation, in this case, is not through any defect in the organ, or that the man's ears are less affected than at other times when he does hear: but that which uses to produce the idea, though conveyed in by the usual organ, not being taken notice of in the understanding, and so imprinting no idea in the mind, there follows no sensation. So that wherever there is sense or perception, there some idea is actually produced, and present in the understanding.

*   *   *

8. *Sensations often changed by the judgment.*—We are further to consider concerning perception, that the ideas we receive by sensation are often, in grown people, al-

tered by the judgment, without our taking notice of it. When we set before our eyes a round globe of any uniform colour, v.g., gold, alabaster, or jet, it is certain that the idea thereby imprinted on our mind is of a flat circle, variously shadowed, with several degrees of light and brightness coming to our eyes. But we having, by use, been accustomed to perceive what kind of appearance convex bodies are wont to make in us; what alterations are made in the reflections of light by the difference of the sensible figures of bodies;—the judgment presently, by an habitual custom, alters the appearances into their causes. So that from that which is truly variety of shadow or colour, collecting the figure, it makes it pass for a mark of figure, and frames to itself the perception of a convex figure and an uniform colour; when the idea we receive from thence is only a plane variously coloured, as is evident in painting. To which purpose I shall here insert a problem of that very ingenious and studious promoter of real knowledge, the learned and worthy Mr. Molyneux, which he was pleased to send me in a letter some months since; and it is this:—"Suppose a man born blind, and now adult, and taught by his touch to distinguish between a cube and a sphere of the same metal, and nighly of the same bigness, so as to tell, when he felt one and the other, which is the cube, which the sphere. Suppose then the cube and sphere placed on a table, and the blind man be made to see: *quære* whether *by his sight, before he touched them,* he could now distinguish and tell which is the globe, which the cube?" To which the acute and judicious proposer answers, "Not. For, though he has obtained the experience of how a globe, how a cube affects his touch, yet he has not yet obtained the experience, that what affects his touch so or so, must affect his sight so or so; or that a protuberant angle in the cube, that pressed his hand unequally, shall appear to his eye as it does in the cube."—I agree with this thinking gentleman, whom I am proud to call my friend, in his answer to this problem; and am of opinion that the blind man, at first sight, would not be able with certainty to say which was the globe, which the cube, whilst he only saw them; though he could unerringly name them by his touch, and certainly distinguish them by the difference of their figures felt. This I have set down, and leave with my reader, as an occasion for him to consider how much he may be beholden to experience, improvement, and acquired notions, where he thinks he had not the least use of, or help from them. And the rather, because this observing gentleman further adds, that "having, upon the occasion of my book, proposed this to divers very ingenious men, he hardly ever met with one that at first gave the answer to it which he thinks true, till by hearing his reasons they were convinced."

*   *   *

CHAPTER 11. OF DISCERNING, AND OTHER OPERATIONS
OF THE MIND

*   *   *

8. *Naming.*—When children have, by repeated sensations, got ideas fixed in their memories, they begin by degrees to learn the use of signs; and when they have got the skill to apply the organs of speech to the framing of articulate sounds, they begin to make use of words to signify their ideas to others. These verbal signs they sometimes borrow from others, and sometimes make themselves, as one may observe among the new and unusual names children often give to things in the first use of language.

9. *Abstraction.*—The use of words, then, being to stand as outward marks of our internal ideas, and those ideas being taken from particular things, if every particular

idea that we take in should have a distinct name, names must be endless. To prevent this, the mind makes the particular ideas received from particular objects to become general; which is done by considering them as they are in the mind, such appearances, separate from all other existences, and the circumstances of real existence, as time, place, or any other concomitant ideas. This is called abstraction, whereby ideas taken from particular beings become general representatives of all of the same kind, and their names general names, applicable to whatever exists conformable to such abstract ideas. Such precise, naked appearances in the mind, without considering how, whence, or with what others they came there, the understanding lays up (with names commonly annexed to them) as the standard to rank real existences into sorts, as they agree with these patterns, and to denominate them accordingly. Thus the same colour being observed to-day in chalk or snow, which the mind yesterday received from milk, it considers that appearance alone makes it a representative of all of that kind; and having given it the name *whiteness,* it by that sound signifies the same quality, wheresoever to be imagined or met with, and thus universals, whether ideas or terms, are made.

10. *Brutes abstract not.*—If it may be doubted whether beasts compound and enlarge their ideas that way to any degree; this, I think, I may be positive in, that the power of abstracting is not at all in them; and that the having of general ideas is that which puts a perfect distinction betwixt man and brutes, and is an excellency which the faculties of brutes do by no means attain to; for it is evident we observe no footsteps in them of making use of general signs for universal ideas; from which we have reason to imagine that they have not the faculty of abstracting, or making general ideas, since they have no use of words, or any other general signs.

*   *   *

CHAPTER 12. OF COMPLEX IDEAS

1. *Made by the mind out of simple ones.*—We have hitherto considered those ideas, in the reception whereof the mind is only passive, which are those simple ones received from sensation and reflection before mentioned, whereof the mind cannot make one to itself, nor have any idea which does not wholly consist of them. [But as the mind is wholly passive in the reception of all its simple ideas, so it exerts several acts of its own, whereby out of its simple ideas, as the materials and foundations of the rest, the other are framed. The acts of the mind wherein it exerts its power over its simple ideas are chiefly these three: (1) Combining several simple ideas into one compound one; and thus all *complex ideas* are made. (2) The second is bringing two ideas, whether simple or complex, together, and setting them by one another, so as to take a view of them at once, without uniting them into one; by which it gets all its *ideas of relations.* (3) The third is separating them from all other ideas that accompany them in their real existence; this is called abstraction: and thus all its *general ideas* are made. This shows man's power and its way of operation to be much the same in the material and intellectual world. For, the materials in both being such as he has no power over, either to make or destroy, all that man can do is either to unite them together, or to set them by one another, or wholly separate them. I shall here begin with the first of these in the consideration of complex ideas, and come to the other two in their due places.] As simple ideas are observed to exist in several combinations united together, so the mind has a power to consider several of them united together as one idea; and that not only as they are united in external objects, but as itself has joined them. Ideas thus made up of several

simple ones put together I call *complex;* such as are beauty, gratitude, a man, an army, the universe; which, though complicated of various simple ideas or complex ideas made up of simple ones, yet are, when the mind pleases, considered each by itself as one entire thing, and signified by one name.

2. *Made voluntarily.*—In this faculty of repeating and joining together its ideas, the mind has great power in varying and multiplying the objects of its thoughts infinitely beyond what sensation or reflection furnished it with: but all this still confined to those simple ideas which it received from those two sources, and which are the ultimate materials of all its compositions. For simple ideas are all from things themselves; and of these the mind can have no more nor other than what are suggested to it. It can have no other ideas of sensible qualities than what come from without by the senses, nor any ideas of other kind of operations of a thinking substance than what it finds in itself: but when it has once got these simple ideas, it is not confined barely to observation, and what offers itself from without; it can, by its own power, put together those ideas it has, and make new complex ones which it never received so united.

3. *Complex ideas are either modes, substances, or relations.*—COMPLEX IDEAS, however compounded and decompounded, though their number be infinite, and the variety endless wherewith they fill and entertain the thoughts of men, yet I think they may be all reduced under these three heads: 1. *Modes.* 2. *Substances.* 3. *Relations.*

4. *Ideas of modes.*—First, *Modes* I call such complex ideas which, however compounded, contain not in them the supposition of subsisting by themselves, but are considered as dependences on, or affections of substances; such as are the ideas signified by the words triangle, gratitude, murder, etc. And if in this I use the word mode in somewhat a different sense from its ordinary signification, I beg pardon; it being unavoidable in discourses differing from the ordinary received notions, either to make new words, or to use old words in somewhat a new signification: the latter whereof, in our present case, is perhaps the more tolerable of the two.

5. *Simple and mixed modes of simple ideas.*—Of these modes there are two sorts which deserve distinct consideration. First, there are some which are only variations or different combinations of the same simple idea, without the mixture of any other, as a dozen, or score; which are nothing but the ideas of so many distinct units added together: and these I call *simple modes,* as being contained within the bounds of one simple idea. Secondly, there are others compounded of simple ideas of several kinds, put together to make one complex one; v.g., beauty, consisting of a certain composition of colour and figure, causing delight in the beholder; theft, which, being the concealed change of the possession of anything, without the consent of the proprietor, contains, as is visible, a combination of several ideas of several kinds: and these I call *mixed modes.*

6. *Ideas of substances, single or collective.*—Secondly, the ideas of *Substances* are such combinations of simple ideas as are taken to represent distinct particular things subsisting by themselves, in which the supposed or confused idea of substance, such as it is, is always the first and chief. Thus, if to substance be joined the simple idea of a certain dull whitish colour, with certain degrees of weight, hardness, ductility, and fusibility, we have the idea of lead; and a combination of the ideas of a certain sort of figure, with the powers of motion, thought, and reasoning, joined to substance, make the ordinary idea of a man. Now of substances also there are two sorts of ideas, one of single substances, as they exist separately, as of a man or a sheep; the other of several of those put together, as an army of men, or flock of sheep; which *collective* ideas of several substances thus put together, are as much each of them one single idea as that of a man or an unit.

7. *Ideas of relation.*—Thirdly, the last sort of complex ideas is that we call *Relation,* which consists in the consideration and comparing one idea with another. Of these several kinds we shall treat in their order.

8. *The abstrusest ideas we can have are all from two sources.*—If we will trace the progress of our minds, and with attention observe how it repeats, adds together, and unites its simple ideas received from sensation or reflection, it will lead us farther than at first perhaps we should have imagined. And I believe we shall find, if we warily observe the originals of our notions, that *even the most abstruse ideas,* how remote soever they may seem from sense, or from any operation of our own minds, are yet only such as the understanding frames to itself, by repeating and joining together ideas that it had either from objects of sense, or from its own operations about them: so that those even large and abstract ideas are *derived from sensation or refection,* being no other than what the mind, by the ordinary use of its own faculties, employed about ideas received from objects of sense, or from the operations it observes in itself about them, may and does attain unto. This I shall endeavour to show in the ideas we have of space, time, and infinity, and some few other, that seem the most remote from those originals.

*   *   *

CHAPTER 21. OF POWER

1. *This idea how got.*—The mind being every day informed, by the senses, of the alteration of those simple ideas it observes in things without; and taking notice how one comes to an end and ceases to be, and another begins to exist which was not before; reflecting also, on what passes within itself, and observing a constant change of its ideas, sometimes by the impression of outward objects on the senses, and sometimes by the determination of its own choice; and concluding from what it has so constantly observed to have been, that the like changes will for the future be made in the same things by like agents, and by the like ways; considers in one thing the possibility of having any of its simple ideas changed, and in another the possibility of making that change; and so comes by that idea which we call *power.* Thus we say, fire has a power to melt gold, i.e., to destroy the consistency of its insensible parts, and consequently its hardness, and make it fluid; and gold has a power to be melted: that the sun has a power to blanch wax; and wax a power to be blanched by the sun, whereby the yellowness is destroyed, and whiteness made to exist in its room. In which and the like cases, the power we consider is in reference to the change of perceivable ideas. For we cannot observe any alteration to be made in, or operation upon, anything, but by the observable change of its sensible ideas: nor conceive any alteration to be made, but by conceiving a change of some of its ideas.

2. *Power, active and passive.*—Power thus considered is twofold, viz., as able to make, or able to receive, any change: the one may be called *active,* and the other *passive,* power. Whether matter be not wholly destitute of active power, as its author, God, is truly above all passive power; and whether the intermediate state of created spirits be not that alone which is capable of both active and passive power, may be worth consideration. I shall not now enter into that enquiry: my present business being not to search into the original of power, but how we come by the *idea* of it. But since active powers make so great a part of our complex ideas of natural substances (as we shall see hereafter), yet they being not, perhaps, so truly active powers as our hasty thoughts are apt to represent them, I judge it not amiss, by this intimation, to direct our minds to the consideration of God and spirits, for the clearest idea of *active* power.

3. *Power includes relation.*—I confess power includes in it some kind of *relation* (a relation to action or change), as indeed, which of our ideas, of what kind soever, when attentively considered, does not? For our ideas of extension, duration, and number, do they not all contain in them a secret relation of the parts? Figure and motion have something relative in them much more visibly: and sensible qualities, as colours and smells, etc., what are they but the powers of different bodies in relation to our perception? And if considered in the things themselves, do they not depend on the bulk, figure, texture, and motion of the parts? All which include some kind of relation in them. Our idea therefore of power, I think, may well have a place amongst other *simple* ideas, and be considered as one of them, being one of those that make a principal ingredient in our complex ideas of substances, as we shall hereafter have occasion to observe.

4. *The clearest idea of active power had from spirit.*—We are abundantly furnished with the idea of *passive* power, by almost all sorts of sensible things. In most of them we cannot avoid observing their sensible qualities, nay, their very substances, to be in a continual flux: and therefore with reason we look on them as liable still to the same change. Nor have we of *active* power (which is the more proper signification of the word power) fewer instances. Since whatever change is observed, the mind must collect a power somewhere, able to make that change, as well as a possibility in the thing itself to receive it. But yet, if we will consider it attentively, bodies by our senses do not afford us so clear and distinct an idea of active power as we have from reflection on the operations of our minds. For all power relating to action, and there being but two sorts of action whereof we have any idea, viz., thinking and motion, let us consider whence we have the clearest ideas of the powers which produce these actions. (1) Of thinking, body affords us no idea at all: it is only from reflection that we have that. (2) Neither have we from body any idea of the beginning of motion. A body at rest affords us no idea of any active power to move; and when it is set in motion itself, that motion is rather a passion than an action in it. For when the ball obeys the stroke of a billiard-stick, it is not any action of the ball, but bare passion. Also when by impulse it sets another ball in motion that lay in its way, it only communicates the motion it had received from another, and loses in itself so much as the other received: which gives us but a very obscure idea of an *active* power of moving in body, whilst we observe it only to *transfer,* but not *produce* any motion. . . . The idea of the *beginning* of motion we have only from reflection on what passes in ourselves, where we find by experience, that, barely by willing it, barely by a thought of the mind, we can move the parts of our bodies which were before at rest. So that it seems to me, we have, from the observation of the operation of bodies by our senses, but a very imperfect, obscure idea of *active* power, since they afford us not any idea in themselves of the power to begin any action, either motion or thought. But if, from the impulse bodies are observed to make one upon another, any one thinks he has a clear idea of power, it serves as well to my purpose, sensation being one of those ways whereby the mind comes by its ideas: only I thought it worth while to consider here by the way, whether the mind doth not receive its idea of active power clearer from reflection on its own operations, than it doth from any external sensation.

5. *Will and understanding two powers in mind or spirit.*—this, at least, I think evident,—That we find in ourselves a power to begin or forbear, continue or end several actions of our minds, and motions of our bodies, barely by a thought or preference of the mind ordering, or as it were commanding, the doing or not doing such or such a particular action. This power which the mind has thus to order the consideration of any idea, or the forbearing to consider it; or to prefer the motion of any part of the body to

its rest, and *vice versa,* in any particular instance, is that which we call the *Will.* The actual exercise of that power, by directing any particular action, or its forbearance, is that which we call *volition* or *willing.* The forbearance of that action, consequent to such order or command of the mind, is called *voluntary.* And whatsoever action is performed without such a thought of the mind, is called *involuntary.* The power of perception is that which we call the *Understanding.* Perception, which we make the act of the understanding, is of three sorts:—1. The perception of ideas in our minds. 2. The perception of the signification of signs. 3. The perception of the connexion or repugnancy, agreement or disagreement, that there is between any of our ideas. All these are attributed to the understanding, or perceptive power, though it be the two latter only that use allows us to say we understand.

*   *   *

7. *Whence the idea of liberty and necessity.*—Everyone, I think, finds in himself a power to begin or forbear, continue or put an end to several actions in himself. From the consideration of the extent of this power of the mind over the actions of the man, which everyone finds in himself, arise the ideas of liberty and necessity.

8. *Liberty, what.*—All the actions that we have any idea of reducing themselves, as has been said, to these two, viz. thinking and motion; so far as a man has power to think or not to think, to move or not to move, according to the preference or direction of his own mind, so far is a man *free.* Wherever any performance or forbearance are not equally in a man's power; wherever doing or not doing will not equally *follow* upon the preference of his mind directing it, there he is not free, though perhaps the action may be voluntary. So, that the idea of *liberty* is, the idea of a power in any agent to do or forbear any particular action, according to the determination or thought of the mind, whereby either of them is preferred to the other: where either of them is not in the power of the agent to be produced by him according to his volition, there he is not at liberty; that agent is under *necessity.* So that liberty cannot be where there is no thought, no volition, no will; but there may be thought, there may be will, there may be volition, where there is no liberty. A little consideration of an obvious instance or two may make this clear.

9. *Supposes understanding and will.*—A tennis-ball, whether in motion by the stroke of a racket, or lying still at rest, is not by any one taken to be a free agent.—If we inquire into the reason, we shall find it is because we conceive not a tennis-ball to think, and consequently not to have any volition, or *preference* of motion to rest, or *vice versa;* and therefore has not liberty, is not a free agent; but all its both motion and rest come under our idea of necessary, and are so called. Likewise a man falling into the water, (a bridge breaking under him,) has not herein liberty, is not a free agent. For though he has volition, though he prefers his not falling to falling; yet the forbearance of that motion not being in his power, the stop or cessation of that motion follows not upon his volition; and therefore therein he is not free. So a man striking himself, or his friend, by a convulsive motion of his arm, which it is not in his power, by volition or the direction of his mind, to stop or forbear, nobody thinks he has in this liberty; every one pities him, as acting by necessity and constraint.

10. *Belongs not to volition.*—Again: suppose a man be carried, whilst fast asleep, into a room where is a person he longs to see and speak with; and be there locked fast in, beyond his power to get out: he awakes, and is glad to find himself in so desirable company, which he stays willingly in, i.e., prefers his stay to going away. I ask, is not this stay voluntary? I think nobody will doubt it: and yet, being locked fast in, it is evi-

dent he is not at liberty not to stay, he has not freedom to be gone. So that liberty is not an idea belonging to volition, or preferring; but to the person having the power of doing, or forbearing to do, according as the mind shall choose or direct. Our idea of liberty reaches as far as that power, and no farther. For wherever restraint comes to check that power, or compulsion takes away that indifferency of ability to act, or to forbear acting, there liberty, and our notion of it, presently ceases.

11. *Voluntary opposed to involuntary, not to necessary.*—We have instances enough, and often more than enough, in our own bodies. A man's heart beats, and the blood circulates, which it is not in his power by any thought or volition to stop; and therefore in respect of these motions, where rest depends not on his choice, nor would follow the determination of his mind, if it should prefer it, he is not a free agent. Convulsive motions agitate his legs, so that though he wills it ever so much, he cannot by any power of his mind stop their motion, (as in that odd disease called *chorea sancti viti*), but he is perpetually dancing; he is not at liberty in this action, but under as much necessity of moving, as a stone that falls, or a tennis-ball struck with a racket. On the other side, a palsy or the stocks hinder his legs from obeying the determination of his mind, if it would thereby transfer his body to another place. In all these there is want of freedom; though the sitting still, even of a paralytic, whilst he prefers it to a removal, is truly voluntary. Voluntary, then, is not opposed to necessary, but to involuntary. For a man may prefer what he can do, to what he cannot do; the state he is in, to its absence or change; though necessity has made it in itself unalterable.

12. *Liberty, what.*—As it is in the motions of the body, so it is in the thoughts of our minds: where any one is such, that we have power to take it up, or lay it by, according to the preference of the mind, there we are at liberty. A waking man, being under the necessity of having some ideas constantly in his mind, is not at liberty to think or not to think; no more than he is at liberty, whether his body shall touch any other or no: but whether he will remove his contemplation from one idea to another is many times in his choice; and then he is, in respect of his ideas, as much at liberty as he is in respect of bodies he rests on; he can at pleasure remove himself from one to another. But yet some ideas to the mind, like some motions to the body, are such as in certain circumstances it cannot avoid, nor obtain their absence by the utmost effort it can use. A man on the rack is not at liberty to lay by the idea of pain, and divert himself with other contemplations: and sometimes a boisterous passion hurries our thoughts, as a hurricane does our bodies, without leaving us the liberty of thinking on other things, which we would rather choose. But as soon as the mind regains the power to stop or continue, begin or forbear, any of these motions of the body without, or thoughts within, according as it thinks fit to prefer either to the other, we then consider the man as a *free agent* again.

13. *Necessity, what.*—Wherever thought is wholly wanting, or the power to act or forbear according to the direction of thought, there necessity takes place. This, in an agent capable of volition, when the beginning or continuation of any action is contrary to that preference of his mind, is called compulsion; when the hindering or stopping any action is contrary to his volition, it is called restraint. Agents that have no thought, no volition at all, are in everything *necessary agents*.

14. *Liberty belongs not to the will.*—If this be so, (as I imagine it is,) I leave it to be considered, whether it may not help to put an end to that long agitated, and, I think, unreasonable, because unintelligible question, viz., *Whether man's will be free or no?* For if I mistake not, it follows from what I have said, that the question itself is altogether improper; and it is as insignificant to ask whether man's *will* be free, as to ask whether his sleep be swift, or his virtue square: liberty being as little applicable to the will, as swiftness of motion is to sleep, or squareness to virtue. Every one would laugh

at the absurdity of such a question as either of these: because it is obvious that the modifications of motion belong not to sleep, nor the difference of figure to virtue; and when any one well considers it, I think he will as plainly perceive that liberty, which is but a power, belongs only to *agents,* and cannot be an attribute or modification of the will, which is also but a power.

15. *Volition.*—Such is the difficulty of explaining and giving clear notions of internal actions by sounds, that I must here warn my reader, that *ordering, directing, choosing, preferring, etc.,* which I have made use of, will not distinctly enough express volition, unless he will reflect on what he himself does when he wills. For example, preferring, which seems perhaps best to express the act of volition, does it not precisely. For though a man would prefer flying to walking, yet who can say he ever wills it? Volition, it is plain, is an act of the mind knowingly exerting that dominion it takes itself to have over any part of the man, by employing it in, or withholding it from, any particular action. And what is the will, but the faculty to do this? And is that faculty anything more in effect than a power; the power of the mind to determine its thought, to the producing, continuing, or stopping any action, as far as it depends on us? For can it be denied that whatever agent has a power to think on its own actions, and to prefer their doing or omission either to other, has that faculty called will? *Will,* then, is nothing but such a power. *Liberty,* on the other side, is the power a *man* has to do or forbear doing any particular action according as its doing or forbearance has the actual preference in the mind; which is the same thing as to say, according as he himself wills it.

16. *Powers, belonging to agents.*—It is plain then that the will is nothing but one power or ability, and *freedom* another power or ability so that, to ask, whether the will has freedom, is to ask whether one power has another power, one ability another ability; a question at first sight too grossly absurd to make a dispute, or need an answer. For, who is it that sees not that powers belong only to agents, and are attributes only of substances, and not of powers themselves? So that this way of putting the question (viz., whether the will be free) is in effect to ask, whether the will be a substance, an agent, or at least to suppose it, since freedom can properly be attributed to nothing else. If freedom can with any propriety of speech be applied to power, it may be attributed to the power that is in a man to produce, or forbear producing, motion in parts of his body, by choice or preference; which is that which denominates him free, and is freedom itself. But if any one should ask, whether freedom were free, he would be suspected not to understand well what he said; and he would be thought to deserve Midas's ears, who, knowing that rich was a denomination for the possession of riches, should demand whether riches themselves were rich.

* * *

21. *But to the agent or man.*—To return, then, to the inquiry about liberty, I think the question is not proper, *whether the will be free,* but *whether a man be free.* Thus, I think.

First, That so far as any one can, by the direction or choice of his mind, preferring the existence of any action to the non-existence of that action, and *vice versa,* make *it* to exist or not exist, so far *he* is free. For if I can, by a thought directing the motion of my finger, make it move when it was at rest, or *vice versa,* it is evident, that in respect of that I am free: and if I can, by a like thought of my mind, preferring one to the other, produce either words or silence, I am at liberty to speak or hold my peace: and as far as this power reaches, of acting or not acting, by the determination of his own thought preferring either, so far is a man free. For how can we think any one freer, than to have the power to do what he will? And so far as any one can, by preferring any action to its not being, or rest to any action, produce that action or rest, so far can he do what he will. For such a preferring of action to its absence, is the willing of it: and we can scarce tell how to imagine any being freer, than to be able to do what he wills. So that in respect of actions within the reach of such a power in him, a man seems as free as it is possible for freedom to make him.

22. *In respect of willing, a man is not free.*—But the inquisitive mind of man, willing to shift off from himself, as far as he can, all thoughts of guilt, though it be by putting himself into a worse state than that of fatal necessity, is not content with this: freedom, unless it reaches further than this, will not serve the turn: and it passes for a good plea, that a man is not free at all, if he be not as *free to will* as he is to *act what he wills*. Concerning a man's liberty, there yet, therefore, is raised this further question, *Whether a man be free to will?* which I think is what is meant, when it is disputed whether the will be free. And as to that I imagine.

23. *How a man cannot be free to will.*—Secondly, That willing, or volition, being an action, and freedom consisting in a power of acting or not acting, a man in respect of willing or the act of volition, when any action in his power is once proposed to his thoughts, as presently to be done, cannot be free. The reason whereof is very manifest. For, it being unavoidable that the action depending on his will should exist or not exist, and its existence or not existence following perfectly the determination and preference of his will, he cannot avoid willing the existence or non-existence of that action; it is absolutely necessary that he will the one or the other; i.e., prefer the one to the other: since one of them must necessarily follow; and that which does follow follows by the choice and determination of his mind; that is, by his willing it: for if he did not will it, it would not be. So that, in respect of the act of willing, a man in such a case is not free: liberty consisting in a power to act or not to act; which, in regard of volition, a man, upon such a proposal, has not. For it is unavoidably necessary to prefer the doing or forbearance of an action in a man's power, which is once so proposed to his thoughts; a man must necessarily will the one or the other of them; upon which preference or volition, the action or its forbearance certainly follows, and is truly voluntary. But the act of volition, or preferring one of the two, being that which he cannot avoid, a man, in respect of that act of willing, is under a necessity, and so cannot be free; unless necessity and freedom can consist together, and a man can be free and bound at once. Besides to make a man free after this manner, by making the action of willing to depend on his will, there must be another antecedent will, to determine the acts of this will, and another to determine that, and so *in infinitum:* for wherever one stops, the actions of the last will cannot be free. Nor is any being, as far I can comprehend beings above me, capable of such a freedom of will, that it can forbear to will, i.e., to prefer the being or not being of anything in its power, which it has once considered as such.

24. *Liberty is freedom to execute what is willed.*—This, then, is evident, That *a man is not at liberty to will, or not to will, anything in his power that he once considers of:* liberty consisting in a power to act or to forbear acting, and in that only. For a man that sits still is said yet to be at liberty; because he can walk if he wills it. A man that walks is at liberty also, not because he walks or moves; but because he can stand still if he wills it. But if a man sitting still has not a power to remove himself, he is not at liberty; so likewise a man falling down a precipice, though in motion, is not at liberty, because he cannot stop that motion if he would. This being so, it is plain that a man that is walking, to whom it is proposed to give off walking, is not at liberty, whether he will determine himself to walk, or give off walking or not: he must necessarily prefer one or the other of them; walking or not walking. And so it is in regard of all other actions in our power so proposed, which are the far greater number. For, considering the vast

number of voluntary actions that succeed one another every moment that we are awake in the course of our lives, there are but few of them that are thought on or proposed to the will, till the time they are to be done; and in all such actions, as I have shown, the mind, in respect of willing, has not a power to act or not to act, wherein consists liberty. The mind, in that case, has not a power to forbear *willing;* it cannot avoid some determination concerning them, let the consideration be as short, the thought as quick as it will, it either leaves the man in the state he was before thinking, or changes it; continues the action, or puts an end to it. Whereby it is manifest, that *it* orders and directs one, in preference to, or with neglect of the other, and thereby either the continuation or change becomes unavoidably voluntary.

25. *The will determined by something without it.*—Since then it is plain that, in most cases, a man is not at liberty, whether he will or no, (for, when an action in his power is proposed to his thoughts, he *cannot* forbear volition; he *must* determine one way or the other); the next thing demanded is,—*Whether a man be at liberty to will which of the two he pleases, motion or rest?* This question carries the absurdity of it so manifestly in itself, that one might thereby sufficiently be convinced that liberty concerns not the will. For, to ask whether a man be at liberty to will either motion or rest, speaking or silence, which he pleases, is to ask whether a man can will what he wills, or be pleased with what he is pleased with? A question which, I think, needs no answer: and they who can make a question of it must suppose one will to determine the acts of another, and another to determine that, and so on *in infinitum.*

26. *The ideas of* liberty *and* volition *must be defined.*—To avoid these and the like absurdities, nothing can be of greater use than to establish in our minds determined ideas of the things under consideration. If the ideas of liberty and volition were well fixed in our understandings, and carried along with us in our minds, as they ought, through all the questions that are raised about them, I suppose a great part of the difficulties that perplex men's thoughts, and entangle their understandings, would be much easier resolved; and we should perceive where the confused signification of terms, or where the nature of the thing caused the obscurity.

27. *Freedom.*—First, then, it is carefully to be remembered, That freedom consists in the dependence of the existence, or not existence of any *action,* upon our *volition* of it; and not in the dependence of any action, or its contrary, on our *preference.* A man standing on a cliff, is at liberty to leap twenty yards downwards into the sea, not because he has a power to do the contrary action, which is to leap twenty yards upwards, for that he cannot do; but he is therefore free, because he has a power to leap or not to leap. But if a greater force than his, either holds him fast, or tumbles him down, he is no longer free in that case; because the doing or forbearance of that particular action is no longer in his power. He that is a close prisoner in a room twenty feet square, being at the north side of his chamber, is at liberty to walk twenty feet southward, because he can walk or not walk it; but is not, at the same time, at liberty to do the contrary, i.e., to walk twenty feet northward.

In this, then, consists freedom, *viz., in our being able to act or not to act, according as we shall choose or will.*

28. *What volition and action mean.*—Secondly, we must remember, that *volition* or *willing* is an act of the mind directing its thought to the production of any action, and thereby exerting its power to produce it. To avoid multiplying of words, I would crave leave here, under the word action, to comprehend the forbearance too of any action proposed: sitting still, or holding one's peace, when walking or speaking are proposed, though mere forbearances, requiring as much the determination of the will, and being as often weighty in their consequences, as the contrary actions, may, on that consideration,

well enough pass for actions too: but this I say, that I may not be mistaken, if (for brevity's sake) I speak thus.

29. *What determines the will.*—Thirdly, the will being nothing but a power in the mind to direct the operative faculties of a man to motion or rest, as far as they depend on such direction; to the question, What is it determines the will? the true and proper answer is, The mind. For that which determines the general power of directing, to this or that particular direction, is nothing but the agent itself exercising the power it has that particular way. If this answer satisfies not, it is plain the meaning of the question, What determines the will? is this,—What moves the mind, in every particular instance, to determine its general power of directing, to this or that particular motion or rest? And to this I answer,—The motive for continuing in the same state or action, is only the present satisfaction in it; the motive to change is always some uneasiness: nothing setting us upon the change of state, or upon any new action, but some uneasiness. This is the great motive that works on the mind to put it upon action, which for shortness' sake we will call determining of the will, which I shall more at large explain.

*   *   *

73. *Recapitulation—liberty of indifferency.*—To conclude this inquiry into *human liberty,* which, as it stood before, I myself from the beginning fearing, and a very judicious friend of mine, since the publication, suspecting to have some mistake in it, though he could not particularly show it me, I was put upon a stricter review of this chapter. Wherein lighting upon a very easy and scarce observable slip I had made, in putting one seemingly indifferent word for another that discovery opened to me this present view, which here, in this second edition, I submit to the learned world, and which, in short, is this: *Liberty* is a power to act or not to act, according as the mind directs. A power to direct the operative faculties to motion or rest in particular instances is that which we call the *will.* That which in the train of our voluntary actions determines the will to any change of operation is *some present uneasiness,* which is, or at least is always accompanied with that of *desire.* Desire is always moved by evil, to fly it: because a total freedom from pain always makes a necessary part of our happiness: but every good, nay, every greater good, does not constantly move desire, because it may not make, or may not be taken to make, any necessary part of our happiness. For all that we desire, is only to be happy. But, though this general desire of happiness operates constantly and invariably, yet the satisfaction of any particular desire *can be suspended* from determining the will to any subservient action, till we have maturely examined whether the particular apparent good which we then desire makes a part of our real happiness, or be consistent or inconsistent with it. The result of our judgment upon that examination is what ultimately determines the man; who could not be *free* if his will were determined by some, is placed in an indifferency of the man; antecedent to the determination of his will. I wish they who lay so much stress on such an antecedent indifferency, as they call it, had told us plainly, whether this supposed indifferency be antecedent to the thought and judgment of the understanding, as well as to the decree of the will. For it is pretty hard to state it between them, i.e., immediately *after* the judgment of the understanding, and *before* the determination of the will: because the determination of the will immediately follows the judgment of the understanding: and to place liberty in an indifferency, antecedent to the thought and judgment of the understanding, seems to me to place liberty in a state of darkness, wherein we can neither see nor say anything of it; at least it places it in a subject incapable of it, no agent being allowed capable of liberty, but in consequence of thought and judgment. I am not nice

about phrases, and therefore consent to say with those that love to speak so, that liberty is placed in indifferency; but it is an indifferency which remains after the judgment of the understanding, yea, even after the determination of the will: and that is an indifferency not of the *man,* (for after he has once judged which is best, viz., to do or forbear, he is no longer indifferent,) but an indifferency of *the operative powers of the man,* which remaining equally able to operate or to forbear operating after as before the decree of the will, are in a state, which, if one pleases, may be called indifferency; and as far as this indifferency reaches, a man is free, and no further: v.g., I have the ability to move my hand, or to let it rest; that operative power is indifferent to move or not to move my hand. I am then, in that respect perfectly free; my will determines that operative power to rest: I am yet free, because the indifferency of that my operative power to act, or not to act, still remains; the power of moving my hand is not at all impaired by the determination of my will, which at present orders rest; the indifferency of that power to act, or not to act, is just as it was before, as will appear, if the will puts it to the trial, by ordering the contrary. But if, during the rest of my hand, it be seized with a sudden palsy, the indifferency of that operative power is gone, and with it my liberty; I have no longer freedom in that respect, but am under a necessity of letting my hand rest. On the other side, if my hand be put into motion by a convulsion, the indifferency of that operative faculty is taken away by that motion; and my liberty in that case is lost, for I am under a necessity of having my hand move. I have added this, to show in what sort of indifferency liberty seems to me to consist, and not in any other, real or imaginary.

74. *Active and passive power, in motions and in thinking.—* . . . Before I close this chapter, it may perhaps be to our purpose, and help to give us clearer conceptions about *power,* if we make our thoughts take a little more exact survey of *action.* I have said above, that we have ideas but of two sorts of action, viz., motion and thinking. These, in truth, though called and counted actions, yet, if nearly considered, will not be found to be always perfectly so. For, if I mistake not, there are instances of both kinds, which, upon due consideration, will be found rather passions than actions; and consequently so far the effects barely of *passive powers* in those subjects, which yet on their accounts are thought agents. For, in these instances, the substance that hath motion or thought receives the impression, whereby it is put into that action, purely from without, and so acts merely by the capacity it has to receive such an impression from some external agent; and such a power is not properly an active power, but a mere passive capacity in the subject. Sometimes the substance or agent puts itself into action by its own power, and this is properly *active power.* Whatsoever modification a substance has, whereby it produces any effect, that is called action: v.g., a solid substance, by motion, operates on or alters the sensible ideas of another substance, and therefore this modification of motion we call action. But yet this motion in that solid substance is, when rightly considered, but a passion, if it received it only from some external agent. So that the active power of motion is in no substance which cannot begin motion in itself or in another substance when at rest. So likewise in thinking, a power to receive ideas or thoughts from the operation of any external substance is called a power of thinking: but this is but a passive power, or capacity. But to be able to bring into view ideas out of sight at one's own choice, and to compare which of them one thinks fit, this is an active power. This reflection may be of some use to preserve us from mistakes about powers and actions, which grammar, and the common frame of languages, may be apt to lead us into. Since what is signified by verbs that grammarians call active, does not always signify action: v.g., this proposition: I *see* the moon, or a star, or I *feel* the heat of the sun, though expressed by a verb active, does not signify any action in me, whereby I operate on those substances, but only the reception of the ideas of light,

The Funeral of Phocion, 1648, by Nicholas Poussin (1594–1665). In this classical-style painting, nature is depicted in geometrical terms that imply a sense of permanence. Locke believed that the complex ideas we have about such scenes are built up out of "a great number of the simple ideas conveyed in by the senses." *(Louvre/Paris)*

roundness, and heat; wherein I am not active, but barely passive, and cannot, in that position of my eyes or body, avoid receiving them. But when I turn my eyes another way, or remove my body out of the sunbeams, I am properly active; because of my own choice, by a power within myself, I put myself into that motion. Such an action is the product of active power.

$$*\quad*\quad*$$

CHAPTER 23. OF OUR COMPLEX IDEAS OF SUBSTANCES

1. *Ideas of particular substances, how made.*—The mind being, as I have declared, furnished with a great number of the simple ideas conveyed in by the senses, as they are found in exterior things, or by reflection on its own operations, takes notice also, that a certain number of these simple ideas go constantly together; which being presumed to belong to one thing, and words being suited to common apprehensions, and made use of for quick dispatch, are called, so united in one subject, by one name; which, by inadvertency, we are apt afterward to talk of and consider as one simple idea, which indeed is a complication of many ideas together: because, as I have said, not imagining how these simple ideas can subsist by themselves, we accustom ourselves to suppose some *substratum* wherein they do subsist, and from which they do result, which therefore we call *substance*.

2. *Our obscure idea of substance in general.*—So that if any one will examine himself concerning his notion of pure substance in general, he will find he has no other idea of it at all, but only a supposition of he knows not what *support* of such qualities which are capable of producing simple ideas in us; which qualities are commonly called accidents. If any one should be asked, what is the subject wherein colour or weight inheres, he would have nothing to say, but the solid extended parts: and if he were demanded, what is it that that solidity and extension inhere in, he would not be in a much better case than the Indian before mentioned, who saying that the world was supported by a great elephant, was asked, what the elephant rested on; to which his answer was, a great tortoise: but being again pressed to know what gave support to the broad-backed tortoise, replied, *something, he knew not what.* And thus here, as in all other cases where we use words without having clear and distinct ideas, we talk like children; who being questioned what such a thing is which they know not, readily give this satisfactory answer, that it is *something;* which in truth signifies no more, when so used, either by children or men, but that they know not what; and that the thing they pretend to know, and talk of, is what they have no distinct idea of at all, and so are perfectly ignorant of it, and in the dark. The idea, then, we have, to which we give the *general* name substance, being nothing but the supposed, but unknown, support of those qualities we find existing, which we imagine cannot subsist *sine re substante,* without something to support them, we call that support *substantia;* which, according to the true import of the word, is, in plain English, standing under, or upholding.

3. *Of the sorts of substances.*—An obscure and relative idea of *substance in general* being thus made, we come to have the ideas of *particular sorts of substances,* by collecting *such* combinations of simple ideas as are, by experience and observation of men's senses, taken notice of to exist together, and are therefore supposed to flow from the particular internal constitution or unknown essence of that substance. Thus we come to have the ideas of a man, horse, gold, water, etc., of which substances, whether any one has any other *clear* idea, farther than of certain simple ideas coexisting together, I appeal to every one's own experience. It is the ordinary qualities observable in iron or a diamond, put together, that make the true complex idea of those substances, which a smith or a jeweller commonly knows better than a philosopher; who, whatever *substantial forms* he may talk of, has no other idea of those substances than what is framed by a collection of those simple ideas which are to be found in them. Only we must take notice, that our complex ideas of substances, besides all these simple ideas they are made up of, have always the confused idea of something to which they belong and in which they subsist. And therefore, when we speak of any sort of substance, we say it is a thing having such or such qualities; as body is a thing that is extended, figured, and capable of motion; a spirit, a thing capable of thinking; and so hardness, friability, and power to draw iron, we say, are qualities to be found in a loadstone. These and the like fashions of speaking intimate that the substance is supposed always *something besides* the extension, figure, solidity, motion, thinking, or other observable ideas, though we know not what it is.

4. *No clear or distinct idea of substance in general.*—Hence, when we talk or think of any particular sort of corporeal substances, as horse, stone, etc., though the idea we have of either of them be but the complication or collection of those several simple ideas of sensible qualities which we use to find united in the thing called horse or stone; yet *because we cannot conceive how they should subsist alone, nor one in another,* we suppose them existing in, and supported by, some common subject; which support we denote by the name substance, though it be certain we have no clear or distinct idea of that thing we suppose a support.

5. *As clear an idea of spiritual substance as of corporeal substance.*—The same happens concerning the operations of the mind, viz., thinking, reasoning, fearing, etc., which we concluding not to subsist of themselves, nor apprehending how they can belong to body, or be produced by it, we are apt to think these the actions of some other *substance,* which we call *spirit;* whereby yet it is evident, that having no other idea or notion of matter, but something wherein those many sensible qualities which affect our senses do subsist; by supposing a substance wherein thinking, knowing, doubting, and a power of moving, etc., do subsist; we have as clear a notion of the substance of spirit as we have of body; the one being supposed to be (without knowing what it is) the *substratum* to those simple ideas we have from without; and the other supposed (with a like ignorance of what it is) to be the *substratum* to those operations which we experiment in ourselves within. It is plain, then, that the idea of *corporeal substance* in matter is as remote from our conceptions and apprehensions as that of *spiritual substance* or spirit; and therefore, from our not having any notion of the substance of spirit, we can no more conclude its nonexistence than we can, for the same reason, deny the existence of body: it being as rational to affirm there is no body, because we have no clear and distinct idea of the substance of matter, as to say there is no spirit, because we have no clear and distinct idea of the substance of a spirit.

6. *Our ideas of particular sorts of substances.*—Whatever therefore be the secret and abstract nature of substance in general, all the ideas we have of particular distinct sorts of substances are nothing but several combinations of simple ideas coexisting in such, though unknown, cause of their union, as makes the whole subsist of itself. It is by such combinations of simple ideas, and nothing else, that we represent particular sorts of substances to ourselves. Such are the ideas we have of their several species in our minds; and such only do we, by their specific names, signify to others, v.g., man, horse, sun, water, iron; upon hearing which words, every one who understands the language frames in his mind a combination of those several simple ideas which he has usually observed or fancied to exist together under that denomination; all which he supposes to rest in, and be, as it were, adherent to, that unknown common subject, which inheres not in anything else. Though in the meantime it be manifest, and every one upon enquiry into his own thoughts will find, that he has no other idea of any substance but what he has barely of those sensible qualities, which he supposes to inhere, with a supposition of such a *substratum,* as gives, as it were, a support to those qualities or simple ideas, which he has observed to exist united together. Thus the idea of the sun, what is it but an aggregate of those several simple ideas, bright, hot, roundish, having a constant regular motion, at a certain distance from us, and perhaps some other? As he who thinks and discourses of the sun, has been more or less accurate in observing those sensible qualities, ideas, or properties, which are in that thing which he calls the sun.

7. *Their active and passive powers a great part of our complex ideas of substances.*—For he has the perfectest idea of any of the particular sorts of substances who has gathered and put together most of those simple ideas which do exist in it, among which are to be reckoned its active powers and passive capacities; which, though not simple ideas, yet in this respect, for brevity's sake, may conveniently enough be reckoned amongst them; . . . We immediately by our senses perceive in fire its heat and colour; which are, if rightly considered, nothing but powers in it to produce those ideas in *us:* we also by our senses perceive the colour and brittleness of charcoal, whereby we come by the knowledge of another power in fire, which it has to change the colour and consistency of *wood.* By the former, fire immediately, by the latter, it mediately discovers to us these several powers; which therefore we look upon to be a part of the qualities

of fire, and so make them a part of the complex idea of it. For all those powers that we take cognizance of, terminating only in the alteration of some sensible qualities in those subjects on which they operate, and so making them exhibit to us new sensible ideas; therefore it is that I have reckoned these powers amongst the simple ideas which make the complex ones of the sorts of substances; though these powers, considered in themselves, are truly complex ideas. . . .

8. *And why.*—Nor are we to wonder that powers make a great part of our complex ideas of substances, since their secondary qualities are those which, in most of them, serve principally to distinguish substances one from another and commonly make a considerable part of the complex idea of the several sorts of them. For our senses failing us in the discovery of the bulk, texture, and figure of the minute parts of bodies, on which their real constitutions and differences depend, we are fain to make use of their secondary qualities as the characteristical notes and marks whereby to frame ideas of them in our minds, and distinguish them one from another. All which secondary qualities, as has been shown, are nothing but bare powers. For the colour and taste of opium are, as well as its soporific or anodyne virtues, mere powers depending on its primary qualities, whereby it is fitted to produce different operations on different parts of our bodies.

9. *Three sorts of ideas make our complex ones of corporeal substances.*—The ideas that make our complex ones of corporeal substances are of these three sorts. First, the ideas of the primary qualities of things which are discovered by our senses, and are in them even when we perceive them not: such are the bulk, figure, number, situation, and motion of the parts of bodies, which are really in them, whether we take notice of them or no. Secondly, the sensible secondary qualities which, depending on these, are nothing but the powers those substances have to produce several ideas in us by our senses; which ideas are not in the things themselves otherwise than as anything is in its cause. Thirdly, the aptness we consider in any substance to give or receive such alterations of primary qualities as that the substance so altered should produce in us different ideas from what it did before; these are called active and passive powers: all which powers, as far as we have any notice or notion of them, terminate only in sensible simple ideas. For whatever alteration a loadstone has the power to make in the minute particles of iron, we should have no notion of any power it had at all to operate on iron, did not its sensible motion discover it; and I doubt not but there are a thousand changes that bodies we daily handle have a power to cause in one another, which we never suspect, because they never appear in sensible effects.

10. *Powers thus make a great part of our complex ideas of particular substances.*—Powers therefore justly make a great part of our complex ideas of substances. He that will examine his complex idea of gold, will find several of its ideas that make it up to be only powers: as the power of being melted, but of not spending itself in the fire, of being dissolved in *aqua regia,* are ideas as necessary to make up our complex idea of gold, as its colour and weight: which, if duly considered, are also nothing but different powers. For to speak truly, yellowness is not actually in gold, but is a power in gold to produce that idea in us by our eyes when placed in a due light: and the heat which we cannot leave out of our idea of the sun, is no more really in the sun than the white colour it introduces into wax. . . .

11. *The now secondary qualities of bodies would disappear, if we could discover the primary ones of their minute parts.*—Had we senses acute enough to discern the minute particles of bodies, and the real constitution on which their sensible qualities depend, I doubt not but they would produce quite different ideas in us, and that which is now the yellow colour of gold would then disappear, and instead of it we should see an

admirable texture of parts of a certain size and figure. This microscopes plainly discover to us: for what to our naked eyes produces a certain colour is, by thus augmenting the acuteness of our senses, discovered to be quite a different thing; and the thus altering, as it were, the proportion of the bulk of the minute parts of a coloured object to our usual sight, produces different ideas from what it did before. Thus sand, or pounded glass, which is opaque and white to the naked eye, is pellucid in a microscope: . . . blood to the naked eye appears all red; but by a good microscope, wherein its lesser parts appear, shows only some few globules of red, swimming in a pellucid liquor; and how these red globules would appear, if glasses could be found that yet could magnify them one thousand or ten thousand times more, is uncertain.

*   *   *

30. *Our idea of spirit and our idea of body compared.*—So that, in short, the idea we have of spirit, compared with the idea we have of body, stands thus: The substance of spirit is unknown to us; and so is the substance of body equally unknown to us. Two primary qualities or properties of body, viz., solid coherent parts and impulse, we have distinct clear ideas of: so likewise we know and have distinct clear ideas of two primary qualities or properties of spirit, viz., thinking, and a power of action; i.e., a power of beginning or stopping several thoughts or motions. We have also the ideas of several qualities inherent in bodies, and have the clear distinct ideas of them: which qualities are but the various modifications of the extension of cohering solid parts and their motion. We have likewise the ideas of the several modes of thinking, viz., believing, doubting, intending, fearing, hoping; all which are but the several modes of thinking. We have also the ideas of willing, and moving the body consequent to it, and with the body itself too; for, as has been showed, spirit is capable of motion.

*   *   *

33. *Our complex idea of God.*—For if we examine the idea we have of the incomprehensible Supreme Being, we shall find, that we come by it the same way; and that the complex ideas we have both of God and separate spirits are made up of the simple ideas we receive from reflection: v.g., having, from what we experiment in ourselves, got the ideas of existence and duration, of knowledge and power, of pleasure and happiness, and of several other qualities and powers which it is better to have than to be without; when we would frame an idea the most suitable we can to the Supreme Being, we enlarge every one of these with our idea of infinity; and so, putting them together, make our complex idea of God. For that the mind has such a power of enlarging some of its ideas, received from sensation and reflection, has been already showed.

*   *   *

35. *God in his own essence incognisable.*—It is infinity which, joined to our ideas of existence, power, knowledge, etc., makes that complex idea whereby we represent to ourselves, the best we can, the Supreme Being. For though in his own essence (which certainly we do not know, not knowing the real essence of a pebble, or a fly, or of our own selves) God be simple and uncompounded; yet, I think, I may say we have no other idea of him but a complex one of existence, knowledge, power, happiness, etc., infinite and eternal: which are all distinct ideas, and some of them being relative are again compounded of others; all which being, as has been shown,

originally got from sensation and reflection, go to make up the idea or notion we have of God.

*   *   *

37. *Recapitulation.*—And thus we have seen what kind of ideas we have of *substances of all kinds,* wherein they consist, and how we come by them. From whence, I think, it is very evident,

First, That all our ideas of the several *sorts* of substances are nothing but collections of simple ideas, with a supposition of *something* to which they belong, and in which they subsist; though of this supposed something we have no clear distinct idea at all.

Secondly, That all the simple ideas that, thus united in one common *substratum,* make up our complex ideas of several *sorts* of substances, are no other but such as we have received from sensation or reflection. . . .

Thirdly, That most of the simple ideas that make up our complex ideas of substances, when truly considered, are only *powers,* however we are apt to take them for positive qualities: v.g., the greatest part of the ideas that make our complex idea of *gold* are yellowness, great weight, ductility, fusibility, and solubility in *aqua regia,* etc., all united together in an unknown *substratum;* all which ideas are nothing else but so many relations to other substances, and are not really in the gold considered barely in itself, though they depend on those real and primary qualities of its internal constitution, whereby it has a fitness differently to operate and be operated on by several other substances.

*   *   *

CHAPTER 27. OF IDENTITY AND DIVERSITY

1. *Wherein identity consists.*—Another occasion the mind often takes of comparing, is the very being of things, when, considering *anything as existing at any determined time and place,* we compare it with *itself existing at another time,* and thereon form the ideas of *identity* and *diversity.* When we see anything to be in any place in any instant of time, we are sure (be it what it will) that it is that very thing, and not another which at that same time exists in another place, how like and undistinguishable soever it may be in all other respects: and in this consists *identity,* when the ideas it is attributed to vary not at all from what they were that moment wherein we consider their former existence, and to which we compare the present. For we never finding, nor conceiving it possible, that two things of the same kind should exist in the same place at the same time, we rightly conclude, that, whatever exists anywhere at any time, excludes all of the same kind, and is there itself alone. When therefore we demand whether anything be the *same* or no, it refers always to something that existed such a time in such a place, which it was certain, at that instant, was the same with itself, and no other. From whence it follows, that one thing cannot have two beginnings of existence, nor two things one beginning; it being impossible for two things of the same kind to be or exist in the same instant, in the very same place; or one and the same thing in different places. That, therefore, that had one beginning, is the same thing; and that which had a different beginning in time and place from that, is not the same, but diverse. That which has made the difficulty about this relation has been the little care and attention used in having precise notions of the things to which it is attributed.

identity of consciousness, wherein if Socrates and the present mayor of Queinborough agree, they are the same person: if the same Socrates waking and sleeping do not partake of the same consciousness, Socrates waking and sleeping are not the same person. And to punish Socrates waking for what Socrates sleeping thought, and waking Socrates was never conscious of, would be no more of right, than to punish one twin for what his brother-twin did, whereof he knew nothing, because their outsides were so alike, that they could not be distinguished; for such twins have been seen.

20. *Absolute oblivion separates what is thus forgotten from the person, but not from the man.*—But yet possibly it will still be objected,—Suppose I wholly lose the memory of some parts of my life, beyond a possibility of retrieving them, so that perhaps I shall never be conscious of them again; yet am I not the same person that did those actions, had those thoughts that I once was conscious of, though I have now forgot them? To which I answer, that we must here take notice what the word *I* is applied to; which, in this case, is the *man* only. And the same man being presumed to be the same person, I is easily here supposed to stand also for the same person. But if it be possible for the same man to have distinct incommunicable consciousness at different times, it is past doubt the same man would at different times make different persons; which, we see, is the sense of mankind in the solemnest declaration of their opinions, human laws not punishing the mad man for the sober man's actions, nor the sober man for what the mad man did,—thereby making them two persons: which is somewhat explained by our way of speaking in English when we say such an one is "not himself," or is "beside himself"; in which phrases it is insinuated, as if those who now, or at least first used them, thought that self was changed; the self-same person was no longer in that man.

*   *   *

22. *Is not a man drunk and sober the same person?*—Why else is he punished for the fact he commits when drunk, though he be never afterwards conscious of it? Just as much the same person as a man that walks, and does other things in his sleep, is the same person, and is answerable for any mischief he shall do in it. Human laws punish both, with a justice suitable to *their* way of knowledge;—because, in these cases, they cannot distinguish certainly what is real, what counterfeit: and so the ignorance in drunkenness or sleep is not admitted as a plea. For, though punishment be annexed to personality, and personality to consciousness, and the drunkard perhaps be not conscious of what he did, yet human judicatures justly punish him; because the fact is proved against him, but want of consciousness cannot be proved for him. But in the Great Day, wherein the secrets of all hearts shall be laid open, it may be reasonable to think, no one shall be made to answer for what he knows nothing of; but shall receive his doom, his conscience accusing or excusing him.

*   *   *

25. *Consciousness unites substances, material or spiritual, with the same personality.*—I agree, that more probable opinion is, that this consciousness is annexed to, and the affection of, one individual immaterial substance.

But let men, according to their diverse hypotheses, resolve of that as they please. This every intelligent being, sensible of happiness or misery, must grant—that there is something that is *himself,* that he is concerned for, and would have happy; that this self has existed in a continued duration more than one instant, and therefore it is possible may exist, as it has done, months and years to come, without any certain bounds to be set to its duration; and may be the same self, by the same consciousness continued on for the future. And thus, by this consciousness he finds himself to be the same self which did such and such an action some years since, by which he comes to be happy or miserable now. In all which account of self, the same numerical substance is not considered as making the same self; but the same continued *consciousness,* in which several substances may have been united, and again separated from it, which, whilst they continued in a vital union with that wherein this consciousness then resided, made a part of that same self. Thus any part of our bodies, vitally united to that which is conscious in us, makes a part of ourselves: but upon separation from the vital union by which that consciousness is communicated, that which a moment since was part of ourselves, is now no more so than a part of another man's self is a part of me: and it is not impossible but in a little time may become a real part of another person. And so we have the same numerical substance become a part of two different persons; and the same person preserved under the change of various substances. Could we suppose any spirit wholly stripped of all its memory or consciousness of past actions, as we find our minds always are of a great part of ours, and sometimes of them all; the union or separation of such a spiritual substance would make no variation of personal identity, any more than that of any particle of matter does. Any substance vitally united to the present thinking being is a part of that very same self which now is; anything united to it by a consciousness of former actions, makes also a part of the same self, which is the same both then and now.

*   *   *

BOOK III. OF WORDS

CHAPTER 2. OF THE SIGNIFICATION OF WORDS

1. *Words are sensible signs, necessary for communication of ideas.*—Man, though he have great variety of thoughts, and such from which others as well as himself might receive profit and delight; yet they are all within his own breast, invisible and hidden from others, nor can of themselves be made to appear. The comfort and advantage of society not being to be had without communication of thoughts, it was necessary that man should find out some external sensible signs, whereof those invisible ideas, which his thoughts are made up of, might be made known to others. For this purpose nothing was so fit, either for plenty or quickness, as those articulate sounds, which with so much ease and variety he found himself able to make. Thus we may conceive how *words,* which were by nature so well adapted to that purpose, came to be made use of by men as the signs of their ideas; not by any natural connexion that there is between particular articulate sounds and certain ideas, for then there would be but one language amongst all men; but by a voluntary imposition, whereby such a word is made arbitrarily the mark of such an idea. The use, then, of words, is to be sensible marks of ideas; and the ideas they stand for are their proper and immediate signification.

*   *   *

3. *Examples of this.*—This is so necessary in the use of language, that in this respect the knowing and the ignorant, the learned and the unlearned, use the words they speak (with any meaning) all alike. They, in every man's mouth, stand for the ideas he has, and which he would express by them. A child having taken notice of nothing in the metal he hears called *gold,* but the bright shining yellow colour, he applies the word gold only to his own idea of that colour, and nothing else; and therefore calls the same colour in a peacock's tail gold. Another that hath better observed, adds to shining yellow great weight: and then the sound gold, when he uses it, stands for a complex idea of a shining yellow and a very weighty substance. Another adds to those qualities fusibility: and then the word gold signifies to him a body, bright, yellow, fusible, and very heavy. Another adds malleability. Each of these uses equally the word gold, when they have occasion to express the idea which they have applied it to: but it is evident that each can apply it only to his own idea; nor can he make it stand as a sign of such a complex idea as he has not.

*   *   *

CHAPTER 3. OF GENERAL TERMS

1. *The greatest part of words are general terms.*—All things that exist being particulars, it may perhaps be thought reasonable that words, which ought to be conformed to things, should be so too,—I mean in their signification: but yet we find quite the contrary. The far greatest part of words that make all languages are general terms: which has not been the effect of neglect or chance, but of reason and necessity.

2. *That every particular thing should have a name for itself is impossible.*—First, It is impossible that every particular thing should have a distinct peculiar name. For, the signification and use of words depending on that connexion which the mind makes between its ideas and the sounds it uses as signs of them, it is necessary, in the application of names to things, that the mind should have distinct ideas of the things, and retain also the particular name that belongs to every one, with its peculiar appropriation to that idea. But it is beyond the power of human capacity to frame and retain distinct ideas of all the particular things we meet with: every bird and beast men saw; every tree and plant that affected the senses, could not find a place in the most capacious understanding. If it be looked on as an instance of a prodigious memory, that some generals have been able to call every soldier in their army by his proper name, we may easily find a reason why men have never attempted to give names to each sheep in their flock, or crow that flies over their heads; much less to call every leaf of plants, or grain of sand that came in their way, by a peculiar name.

3. *And would be useless, if it were possible.*—Secondly, If it were possible, it would yet be useless; because it would not serve to the chief end of language. Men would in vain heap up names of particular things, that would not serve them to communicate their thoughts. Men learn names, and use them in talk with others, only that they may be understood: which is then only done when, by use or consent, the sound I make by the organs of speech, excites in another man's mind who hears it, the idea I apply it to in mine, when I speak it. This cannot be done by names applied to particular things; whereof I alone having the ideas in my mind, the names of them could not be significant or intelligible to another, who was not acquainted with all those very particular things which had fallen under my notice.

4. *A distinct name for every particular thing, not fitted for enlargement of knowledge.*—Thirdly, But yet, granting this also feasible, (which I think is not), yet a distinct

name for every particular thing would not be of any great use for the improvement of knowledge: which, though founded in particular things, enlarges itself by general views; to which things reduced into sorts, under general names, are properly subservient. These, with the names belonging to them, come within some compass, and do not multiply every moment, beyond what either the mind can contain, or use requires. And therefore, in these, men have for the most part stopped: but yet not so as to hinder themselves from distinguishing particular things by appropriated names, where convenience demands it. And therefore in their own species, which they have most to do with, and wherein they have often occasion to mention particular persons, they make use of proper names; and there distinct individuals have distinct denominations.

5. *What things have proper names, and why.*—Besides persons, countries also, cities, rivers, mountains, and other the like distinctions of place have usually found peculiar names, and that for the same reason; they being such as men have often an occasion to mark particularly, and, as it were, set before others in their discourses with them. And I doubt not but, if we had reason to mention particular horses as often as we have to mention particular men, we should have proper names for the one, as familiar as for the other, and Bucephalus would be a word as much in use as Alexander. And therefore we see that, amongst jockeys, horses have their proper names to be known and distinguished by, as commonly as their servants: because, amongst them, there is often occasion to mention this or that particular horse when he is out of sight.

6. *How general words are made.*—The next thing to be considered is,—How general words come to be made. For, since all things that exist are only particulars, how come we by general terms; or where find we those general natures they are supposed to stand for? Words become general by being made the signs of general ideas: and ideas become general, by separating from them the circumstances of time and place, and any other ideas that may determine them to this or that particular existence. By this way of abstraction they are made capable of representing more individuals than one; each of which having in it a conformity to that abstract idea, is (as we call it) of that sort.

7. *Shown by the way we enlarge our complex ideas from infancy.*—But, to deduce this a little more distinctly, it will not perhaps be amiss to trace our notions and names from their beginning, and observe by what degrees we proceed, and by what steps we enlarge our ideas from our first infancy. There is nothing more evident, than that the ideas of the persons children converse with (to instance in them alone) are like the persons themselves, only particular. The ideas of the nurse and the mother are well framed in their minds; and, like pictures of them there, represent only those individuals. The names they first gave to them are confined to these individuals; and the names of *nurse* and *mamma,* the child uses, determine themselves to those persons. Afterwards, when time and a larger acquaintance have made them observe that there are a great many other things in the world, that in some common agreements of shape, and several other qualities, resemble their father and mother, and those persons they have been used to, they frame an idea, which they find those many particulars do partake in; and to that they give, with others, the name *man,* for example. And thus they come to have a general name, and a general idea. Wherein they make nothing new; but only leave out of the complex idea they had of Peter and James, Mary and Jane, that which is peculiar to each, and retain only what is common to them all.

8. *And further enlarge our complex ideas, by still leaving out properties contained in them.*—By the same way that they come by the general name and idea of *man,* they easily advance to more general names and notions. For, observing that several things that differ from their idea of man, and cannot therefore be comprehended under that name, have yet certain qualities wherein they agree with man, by retaining only

those qualities, and uniting them into one idea, they have again another and more general idea, to which having given a name they make a term of a more comprehensive extension: which new idea is made, not by any new addition, but only as before, by leaving out the shape, and some other properties signified by the name man, and retaining only a body, with life, sense, and spontaneous motion, comprehended under the name animal.

9. *General natures are nothing but abstract and partial ideas of more complex ones.*—That this is the way whereby men first formed general ideas, and general names to them, I think is so evident, that there needs no other proof of it but the considering of a man's self, or others, and the ordinary proceedings of their minds in knowledge. And he that thinks *general natures* or *notions* are anything else but such abstract and partial ideas of more complex ones, taken at first from particular existences, will, I fear, be at a loss where to find them. For let any one effect, and then tell me, wherein does his idea of *man* differ from that of *Peter* and *Paul,* or his idea of *horse* from that of *Bucephalus,* but in the leaving out something that is peculiar to each individual, and retaining so much of those particular complex ideas of several particular existences as they are found to agree in? Of the complex ideas signified by the names *man* and *horse,* leaving out but those particulars wherein they differ, and retaining only those wherein they agree, and of those making a new distinct complex idea, and giving the name *animal* to it, one has a more general term, that comprehends with man several other creatures. Leave out of the idea of *animal,* sense and spontaneous motion, and the remaining complex idea, made up of the remaining simple ones of body, life, and nourishment, becomes a more general one, under the more comprehensive term, *vivens.* And, not to dwell longer upon this particular, so evident in itself; by the same way the mind proceeds to *body, substance,* and at last to *being, thing,* and such universal terms, which stand for any of our ideas whatsoever. To conclude: this whole mystery of genera and species, which make such a noise in the schools, and are with justice so little regarded out of them, is nothing else but *abstract ideas,* more or less comprehensive, with names annexed to them. In all which this is constant and unvariable, that every more general term stands for such an idea, and is but a part of any of those contained under it.

10. *Why the genus is ordinarily made use of in definitions.*—This may show us the reason why, in the defining of words, which is nothing but declaring their signification, we make use of the *genus,* or next general word that comprehends it. Which is not out of necessity, but only to save the labour of enumerating the several simple ideas which the next general word or *genus* stands for; or, perhaps, sometimes the shame of not being able to do it. But though defining by *genus* and *differentia* (I crave leave to use these terms of art, though originally Latin, since they most properly suit those notions they are applied to), I say, though defining by the *genus* be the shortest way, yet I think it may be doubted whether it be the best. This I am sure, it is not the only, and so not absolutely necessary. For, definition being nothing but making another understand by words what idea the term defined stands for, a definition is best made by enumerating those simple ideas that are combined in the signification of the term defined: and, if, instead of such an enumeration, men have accustomed themselves to use the next general term, it has not been out of necessity, or for greater clearness, but for quickness and dispatch sake. For I think that, to one who desired to know what idea the word man stood for; if it should be said, that man was a solid extended substance, having life, sense, spontaneous motion, and the faculty of reasoning, I doubt not but the meaning of the term man would be as well understood, and the idea it stands for be at least as clearly made known, as when it is defined to be a rational animal: which, by the several definitions of *animal, vivens,* and *corpus,* resolves itself into those enumerated ideas. I have,

in explaining the term *man,* followed here the ordinary definition of the schools; which, though perhaps not the most exact, yet serves well enough to my present purpose. And one may, in this instance, see what gave occasion to the rule, that a definition must consist of *genus* and *differentia;* and it suffices to show us the little necessity there is of such a rule, or advantage in the strict observing of it. For, definitions, as has been said, being only the explaining of one word by several others, so that the meaning or idea it stands for may be certainly known; languages are not always so made according to the rules of logic, that every term can have its signification exactly and clearly expressed by two others. Experience sufficiently satisfies us to the contrary; or else those who have made this rule have done ill, that they have given us so few definitions conformable to it. But of definitions more in the next chapter.

11. *General and universal are creatures of the understanding, and belong not to the real existence of things.*—To return to general words: it is plain, by what has been said, that *general* and *universal* belong not to the real existence of things; but are the inventions and creatures of the understanding, made by it for its own use, and concern only signs, whether words or ideas. Words are general, as has been said, when used for signs of general ideas, and so are applicable indifferently to many particular things; and ideas are general when they are set up as the representatives of many particular things: but universality belongs not to things themselves, which are all of them particular in their existence, even those words and ideas which in their signification are general. When therefore we quit particulars, the generals that rest are only creatures of our own making; their general nature being nothing but the capacity they are put into, by the understanding, of signifying or representing many particulars. For the signification they have is nothing but a relation that, by the mind of man, is added to them.

12. *Abstract ideas are the essences of genera and species.*—The next thing therefore to be considered is, What kind of signification it is that general words have. For, as it is evident that they do not signify barely one particular thing; for then they would not be general terms, but proper names, so, on the other side, it is as evident they do not signify a plurality; for *man* and *men* would then signify the same; and the distinction of numbers (as the grammarians call them) would be superfluous and useless. That then which general words signify is a *sort* of things; and each of them does that, by being a sign of an abstract idea in the mind; to which idea, as things existing are found to agree, so they come to be ranked under that name, or, which is all one, be of that sort. Whereby it is evident that the *essences* of the sorts, or, if the Latin word pleases better, *species* of things, are nothing else but these abstract ideas. For the having the essence of any species, being that which makes anything to be of that species; and the conformity to the idea to which the name is annexed being that which gives a right to that name; the having the essence, and the having that conformity, must needs be the same thing: since to be of any species, and to have a right to the name of that species, is all one. As, for example, to be a *man,* or of the *species* man, and to have right to the *name* man, is the same thing. Again, to be a man, or of the species man, and have the *essence* of a man, is the same thing. Now, since nothing can be a man, or have a right to the name man, but what has a conformity to the abstract idea the name man stands for, nor anything be a man, or have a right to the species man, but what has the essence of that species; it follows, that the abstract idea for which the name stands, and the essence of the species, is one and the same. From whence it is easy to observe, that the essences of the sorts of things, and, consequently, the sorting of things, is the workmanship of the understanding that abstracts and makes those general ideas.

13. *They are the workmanship of the understanding, but have their foundation in the similitude of things.*—I would not here be thought to forget, much less to deny, that

Nature, in the production of things, makes several of them alike: there is nothing more obvious, especially in the races of animals, and all things propagated by seed. But yet I think we may say, *the sorting of them under names is the workmanship of the understanding, taking occasion, from the similitude it observes amongst them, to make abstract general ideas,* and set them up in the mind, with names annexed to them, as patterns or forms (for, in that sense, the word *form* has a very proper signification) to which as particular things existing are found to agree, so they come to be of that species, have that denomination, or are put into that *classis.* For when we say this is a man, that a horse; this justice, that cruelty; this a watch, that a jack; what do we else but rank things under different specific names, as agreeing to those abstract ideas, of which we have made those names the signs? And what are the essences of those species set out and marked by names, but those abstract ideas in the mind; which are, as it were, the bonds between particular things that exist, and the names they are to be ranked under? And when general names have any connexion with particular beings, these abstract ideas are the medium that unites them: so that the essences of species, as distinguished and denominated by us, neither are nor can be anything but those precise abstract ideas we have in our minds. And therefore the supposed real essences of substances, if different from our abstract ideas, cannot be the essences of the species we rank things into. For two species may be one, as rationally as two different essences be the essence of one species: and I demand what are the alterations [which] may, or may not be made in a *horse* or *lead,* without making either of them to be of another species? In determining the species of things by *our* abstract ideas, this is easy to resolve, but if any one will regulate himself herein by supposed *real* essences, he will, I suppose, be at a loss: and he will never be able to know when anything precisely ceases to be of the species of a *horse* or *lead.*

14. *Each distinct abstract idea is a distinct essence.*—Nor will any one wonder that I say these essences, or abstract ideas (which are the measures of name, and the boundaries of species) are the workmanship of the understanding, who considers that at least the complex ones are often, in several men, different collections of simple ideas; and therefore that is *covetousness* to one man, which is not so to another. Nay, even in substances, where their abstract ideas seem to be taken from the things themselves, they are not constantly the same; no, not in that species which is most familiar to us, and with which we have the most intimate acquaintance: it having been more than once doubted, whether the *fetus* born of a woman were a *man,* even so far as that it hath been debated, whether it were or were not to be nourished and baptized: which could not be, if the abstract idea or essence to which the name man belonged were of nature's making; and were not the uncertain and various collection of simple ideas, which the understanding put together, and then, abstracting it, affixed a name to it. So that, in truth, every distinct abstract idea is a distinct essence; and the names that stand for such distinct ideas are the names of things essentially different. Thus a circle is as essentially different from an oval as a sheep from a goat; and rain is as essentially different from snow as water from earth: that abstract idea which is the essence of one being impossible to be communicated to the other. And thus any two abstract ideas, that in any part vary one from another, with two distinct names annexed to them, constitute two distinct sorts, or, if you please, *species,* as essentially different as any two of the most remote or opposite in the world.

15. *Several significations of the word "essence."*—But since the essences of things are thought by some (and not without reason) to be wholly unknown, it may not be amiss to consider the several significations of the word *essence.*

Real essence.—First, Essence may be taken for the very being of anything, whereby it is what it is. And thus the real internal, but generally (in substances) unknown constitution of things, whereon their discoverable qualities depend, may be called their essence. This is the proper original signification of the word, as is evident from the formation of it; *essentia,* in its primary notation, signifying properly, being. And in this sense it is still used, when we speak of the essence of *particular* things, without giving them any name.

Nominal essences.—Secondly, The learning and disputes of the schools having been much busied about *genus* and *species,* the word *essence* has almost lost its primary signification: and, instead of the real constitution of things, has been almost wholly applied to the artificial constitution of *genus* and *species.* It is true, there is ordinarily supposed a real constitution of the sorts of things; and it is past doubt there must be some real constitution, on which any collection of simple ideas co-existing must depend. But, it being evident that things are ranked under names into sorts or species, only as they agree to certain abstract ideas, to which we have annexed those names, the essence of each *genus,* or sort, comes to be nothing but that abstract idea which the general, or sortal (if I may have leave so to call it from sort, as I do general from genus) name stands for. And this we shall find to be that which the word essence imports in its most familiar use.

These two sorts of essences, I suppose, may not unfitly be termed, the one the *real,* the other *nominal essence.*

*   *   *

BOOK IV. OF KNOWLEDGE AND PROBABILITY

CHAPTER 1. OF KNOWLEDGE IN GENERAL

1. *Our knowledge conversant about our ideas only.*—Since the mind, in all its thoughts and reasonings, hath no other immediate object but its own ideas, which it alone does or can contemplate, it is evident that our knowledge is only conversant about them.

2. *Knowledge is the perception of the agreement or disagreement of two ideas.*— *Knowledge* then seems to me to be nothing but *the perception of the connexion and agreement, or disagreement and repugnancy, of any of our ideas.* In this alone it consists. Where this perception is, there is knowledge; and where it is not, there, though we may fancy, guess, or believe, yet we always come short of knowledge. For when we know that white is not black, what do we else but perceive that these two ideas do not agree? When we possess ourselves with the utmost security of the demonstration that the three angles of a triangle are equal to two right ones, what do we more but perceive, that equality to two right ones does necessarily agree to, and is inseparable from, the three angles of a triangle?

3. *This agreement or disagreement may be any of four sorts.*—But to understand a little more distinctly wherein this agreement or disagreement consists, I think we may reduce it all to these four sorts: (1) *Identity,* or *diversity.* (2) *Relation.* (3) *Coexistence,* or *necessary connexion.* (4) *Real existence.*

4. *Of identity, or diversity in ideas.*—First, As to the first sort of agreement or disagreement, viz., *identity,* or *diversity.* It is the first act of the mind, when it has any sentiments or ideas at all, to perceive its ideas, and, so far as it perceives them, to know

each what it is, and thereby also to perceive their difference, and that one is not another. This is so absolutely necessary, that without it there could be no knowledge, no reasoning, no imagination, no distinct thoughts at all. By this the mind clearly and infallibly perceives each idea to agree with itself, and to be what it is; and all distinct ideas to disagree, i.e., the one not to be the other: and this it does without pains, labour, or deduction; but at first view, by its natural power of perception and distinction. And though men of art have reduced this into those general rules, *What is, is;* and, *It is impossible for the same thing to be and not to be,* for ready application in all cases wherein there may be occasion to reflect on it; yet it is certain that the first exercise of this faculty is about particular ideas. A man infallibly knows, as soon as ever he has them in his mind, that the ideas he calls *white* and *round* are the very ideas they are, and that they are not other ideas which he calls *red* or *square.* Nor can any maxim or proposition in the world make him know it clearer or surer than he did before, and without any such general rule. This then is the first agreement or disagreement which the mind perceives in its ideas; which it always perceives at first sight; and if there ever happen any doubt about it, it will always be found to be about the names, and not the ideas themselves, whose identity and diversity will always be perceived as soon and as clearly as the ideas themselves are, nor can it possibly be otherwise.

5. *Of abstract relations between ideas.—Secondly,* The next sort of agreement or disagreement the mind perceives in any of its ideas may, I think, be called *relative,* and is nothing but the perception of the *relation* between any two ideas, of what kind soever, whether substances, modes, or any other. For, since all distinct ideas must eternally be known not to be the same, and so be universally and constantly denied one of another, there could be no room for any positive knowledge at all, if we could not perceive any relation between our ideas, and find out the agreement or disagreement they have one with another, in several ways the mind takes of comparing them.

6. *Of their necessary coexistence in substances.—Thirdly,* The third sort of agreement or disagreement to be found in our ideas, which the perception of the mind is employed about, is *coexistence,* or *non-coexistence* in the *same subject;* and this belongs particularly to substances. Thus when we pronounce concerning gold that it is fixed, our knowledge of this truth amounts to no more but this, that fixedness, or a power to remain in the fire unconsumed, is an idea that always accompanies and is joined with that particular sort of yellowness, weight, fusibility, malleableness, and solubility in *aqua regia,* which make our complex idea, signified by the word gold.

7. *Of real existence agreeing to any idea.—Fourthly,* The fourth and last sort is that of *actual real existence* agreeing to any idea. Within these four sorts of agreement or disagreement is, I suppose, contained all the knowledge we have or are capable of; for all the enquiries that we can make concerning any of our ideas, all that we know or can affirm concerning any of them, is, that it is or is not the same with some other; that it does or does not always coexist with some other idea in the same subject; that it has this or that relation to some other idea; or that it has a real existence without the mind. Thus, "Blue is not yellow," is of identity. "Two triangles upon equal bases between two parallels are equal," is of relation. "Iron is susceptible of magnetical impressions," is of coexistence. "God is," is of real existence. Though identity and coexistence are truly nothing but relations, yet they are so peculiar ways of agreement or disagreement of our ideas, that they deserve well to be considered as distinct heads, and not under relation in general: since they are so different grounds of affirmation and negation, as will easily appear to any one who will but reflect on what is said in several places of this *Essay.* I should now proceed to examine the several degrees of our knowledge, but that it is necessary first to consider the different acceptations of the word knowledge.

8. *Knowledge is either actual or habitual.*—There are several ways wherein the mind is possessed of truth, each of which is called knowledge.

(1) There is *actual knowledge,* which is the present view the mind has of the agreement or disagreement of any of its ideas, or of the relation they have one to another.

(2) A man is said to know any proposition which having been once laid before his thoughts, he evidently perceived the agreement or disagreement of the ideas whereof it consists; and so lodged it in his memory, that whenever that proposition comes again to be reflected on, he, without doubt or hesitation, embraces the right side, assents to and is certain of the truth of it. This, I think, one may call *habitual knowledge.* . . . For our finite understandings being able to think clearly and distinctly but on one thing at once, if men had no knowledge of any more than what they actually thought on, they would all be very ignorant; and he that knew most would know but one truth, that being all he was able to think on at one time.

9. *Habitual knowledge is of two degrees.*—Of habitual knowledge there are also, vulgarly speaking, two degrees:—

First, The one of such truths laid up in the memory as, whenever they occur to the mind, it *actually perceives the relation is between those ideas.* And this is in all those truths whereof we have an intuitive knowledge, where the ideas themselves, by an immediate view, discover their agreement or disagreement one with another.

Secondly, The other is of such truths, whereof the mind having been convinced, it *retains the memory of the conviction without the proofs.* Thus a man that remembers certainly that he once perceived the demonstration that the three angles of a triangle are equal to two right ones, is certain that he knows it, because he cannot doubt of the truth of it. In his adherence to a truth where the demonstration by which it was at first known is forgot, though a man may be thought rather to believe his memory than really to know, and this way of entertaining a truth seemed formerly to me like something between opinion and knowledge, a sort of assurance which exceeds bare belief, for that relies on the testimony of another; yet, upon a due examination, I find it comes not short of perfect certainty, and is, in effect, true knowledge. That which is apt to mislead our first thoughts into a mistake in this matter is, that the agreement or disagreement of the ideas in this case is not perceived, as it was at first, by an actual view of all the intermediate ideas whereby the agreement or disagreement of those in the proposition was at first perceived; but by other intermediate ideas, that show the agreement or disagreement of the ideas contained in the proposition whose certainty we remember. For example: in this proposition, that "the three angles of a triangle are equal to two right ones," one who has seen and clearly perceived the demonstration of this truth knows it to be true, when that demonstration is gone out of his mind, so that at present it is not actually in view, and possibly cannot be recollected; but he knows it in a different way from what he did before. The agreement of the two ideas joined in that proposition is perceived; but it is by the intervention of other ideas than those which at first produced that perception. He remembers, i.e., he knows (for remembrance is but the reviving of some past knowledge) that he was once certain of the truth of this proposition, that "the three angles of a triangle are equal to two right ones." The immutability of the same relations between the same immutable things is now the idea that shows him, that if the three angles of a triangle were once equal to two right ones, they will always be equal to two right ones. And hence he comes to be certain, that what was once true in the case is always true; what ideas once agreed will always agree: and consequently, what he once knew to be true he will always know to be true, as long as he can remember that he once knew it. Upon this ground it is that particular demonstrations in mathematics afford general knowledge. If then the perception that the same ideas will eternally have the same habitudes and relations be not a sufficient ground of knowledge, there could be no knowledge of general propositions in mathematics; for no mathematical demonstration would be any other than particular and when a man had demonstrated any proposition concerning one triangle or circle, his knowledge would not reach beyond that particular diagram. If he would extend it farther, he must renew his demonstration in another instance, before he could know it to be true in another like triangle, and so on by which means one could never come to the knowledge of any general propositions. Nobody, I think, can deny that Mr. Newton certainly knows any proposition that he now at any time reads in his book to be true, though he has not in actual view that admirable chain of intermediate ideas whereby he at first discovered it to be true. Such a memory as that, able to retain such a train of particulars, may be well thought beyond the reach of human faculties, when the very discovery, perception, and laying together that wonderful connexion of ideas is found to surpass most readers' comprehension. But yet it is evident the author himself knows the proposition to be true, remembering he once saw the connexion of those ideas, as certainly as he knows such a man wounded another, remembering that he saw him run him through. But because the memory is not always so clear as actual perception, and does in all men more or less decay in length of time, this amongst other differences, is one which shows that *demonstrative* knowledge is much more imperfect than *intuitive,* as we shall see in the following chapter.

CHAPTER 2. OF THE DEGREES OF OUR KNOWLEDGE

1. *Of the degree, or differences in clearness, of our knowledge:* I. *Intuitive*—All our knowledge consisting, as I have said, in the view the mind has of its own ideas, which is the utmost light and greatest certainty we, with our faculties and in our way of knowledge, are capable of, it may not be amiss to consider a little the degrees of its evidence. The different clearness of our knowledge seems to me to lie in the different way of perception the mind has of the agreement or disagreement of any of its ideas. For if we will reflect on our own ways of thinking, we shall find that sometimes the mind perceives the agreement or disagreement of two ideas *immediately by themselves,* without the intervention of any other and this, I think, we may call *intuitive knowledge.* For in this the mind is at no pains of proving or examining, but perceives the truth, as the eye doth light, only by being directed towards it. Thus the mind perceives that *white* is not *black,* that a *circle* is not a *triangle,* that *three* are more than *two,* and equal to *one and two.* Such kind of truths the mind perceives at the first sight of the ideas together, by bare intuition, without the intervention of any other idea; and this kind of knowledge is the clearest and most certain that human frailty is capable of. This part of knowledge is irresistible, and like bright sunshine, forces itself immediately to be perceived as soon as ever the mind turns its view that way; and leaves no room for hesitation, doubt, or examination, but the mind is presently filled with the clear light of it. *It is on this intuition that depends all the certainty and evidence of all our knowledge;* which certainty every one finds to be so great, that he cannot imagine, and therefore not require, a greater for a man cannot conceive himself capable of a greater certainty, than to know that any idea in his mind is such as he perceives it to be; and that two ideas wherein he perceives a difference, are different, and not precisely the same. He that demands a greater certainty that this demands he knows not what, and shows only that he has a mind to be a skeptic without being able to be so. Certainty depends so wholly on this intuition, that in the next degree of knowledge, which I call demonstrative, this intuition is necessary in all

the connexions of the intermediate ideas, without which we cannot attain knowledge and certainty.

2. *II. Demonstrative.*—The next degree of knowledge is, where the mind perceives the agreement or disagreement of any ideas, but not immediately. . . . In this case, when the mind cannot so bring its ideas together as, by their immediate comparison and, as it were, juxtaposition or application one to another, to perceive their agreement or disagreement, it is fain, by the intervention of other ideas (one or more, as it happens), to discover the agreement or disagreement which it searches; and this is that which we call *reasoning*. Thus the mind, being willing to know the agreement or disagreement in bigness between the three angles of a triangle and two right ones, cannot, by an immediate view and comparing them, do it: because the three angles of a triangle cannot be brought at once, and be compared with any other one or two angles; and so of this the mind has no immediate, no intuitive knowledge. In this case the mind is fain to find out some other angles, to which the three angles of a triangle have an equality; and finding those equal to two right ones, comes to know their equality to two right ones.

3. *Demonstration depends on clearly perceived proofs.*—Those intervening ideas which serve to show the agreement of any two others, are called *proofs;* and where the agreement or disagreement is by this means plainly and clearly perceived, it is called *demonstration,* it being *shown* to the understanding, and the mind made to see that it is so. A quickness in the mind to find out these intermediate ideas (that shall discover the agreement or disagreement of any other), and to apply them right, is, I suppose, that which is called *sagacity.*

4. *As certain, but not so easy and ready as intuitive knowledge.*—This knowledge by intervening proofs, though it be certain, yet the evidence of it is not altogether so clear and bright, nor the assent so ready, as in intuitive knowledge. For though in demonstration the mind does at last perceive the agreement or disagreement of the ideas it considers, yet it is not without pains and attention: there must be more than one transient view to find it. A steady application and pursuit is required to this discovery: and there must be a progression by steps and degrees before the mind can in this way arrive at certainty. . . .

5. *The demonstrated conclusion not without doubt, precedent to the demonstration.*—Another difference between intuitive and demonstrative knowledge is, that though in the latter all doubt be removed, when by the intervention of the intermediate ideas the agreement or disagreement is perceived; yet before the demonstration there was a doubt; which in intuitive knowledge cannot happen to the mind that has its faculty of perception left to a degree capable of distinct ideas, no more than it can be a doubt to the eye (that can distinctly see white and black), whether this ink and this paper be all of a colour. . . .

6. *Not so clear as intuitive knowledge.*—It is true, the perception produced by demonstration is also very clear; yet it is often with a great abatement of that evident lustre and full assurance that always accompany that which I call intuitive; like a face reflected by several mirrors one to another, where, as long as it retains the similitude and agreement with the object, it produces a knowledge; but it is still, in every successive reflection, with a lessening of that perfect clearness and distinctness which is in the first, till at last, after many removes, it has a great mixture of dimness, and is not at first sight so knowable, especially to weak eyes. Thus it is with knowledge made out by a long train of proofs.

7. *Each step in demonstrated knowledge must have intuitive evidence.*—Now, in every step reason makes in demonstrative knowledge, there is an intuitive knowledge of that agreement or disagreement it seeks with the next intermediate idea, which it uses as

a proof: for it were not so, that yet would need a proof; since without the perception of such agreement or disagreement there is no knowledge produced. . . . This intuitive perception of the agreement or disagreement of the intermediate ideas, in each step and progression of the demonstration, must also be carried exactly in the mind, and a man must be sure that no part is left out: which, because in long deductions, and the use of many proofs, the memory does not always so readily and exactly retain; therefore it comes to pass, that this is more imperfect than intuitive knowledge, and men embrace often falsehood for demonstrations.

8. *Hence the mistake, ex præcognitis et præconcessis.*—The necessity of this intuitive knowledge, in each step of scientifical or demonstrative reasoning, gave occasion, I imagine, to that mistaken axiom, that all reasoning was *ex præcognitis et præconcessis;* which how far it is mistaken, I shall have occasion to show more at large where I come to consider propositions, and particularly those propositions which are called "maxims"; and to show that it is by a mistake that they are supposed to be the foundations of all our knowledge and reasonings.

9. *Demonstration not limited to ideas of mathematical quantity.*—It has been generally taken for granted, that mathematics alone are capable of demonstrative certainty: but to have such an agreement or disagreement as may intuitively be perceived being, as I imagine, not the privilege of the ideas of number, extension, and figure alone, it may possibly be the want of due method and application in us, and not of sufficient evidence in things, that demonstration has been thought to have so little to do in other parts of knowledge, and been scarce so much as aimed at by any but mathematicians. . . .

10. *Why it has been thought to be so limited.*—The reason why it has been generally sought for and supposed to be only in those, I imagine, has been not only the general usefulness of those sciences, but because, in comparing their equality or excess, the modes of numbers have every the least difference very clear and perceivable: and though in extension every the least excess is not so perceptible, yet the mind has found out ways to examine and discover demonstratively the just equality of two angles, or extensions, or figures. . . .

11. *Modes of qualities not demonstrable like modes of quantity.*—But in other simple ideas, whose modes and differences are made and counted by degrees, and not quantity, we have not so nice and accurate a distinction of their differences as to perceive or find ways to measure their just equality or the least differences. For those other simple ideas, being appearances or sensations produced in us by the size, figure, number, and motion of minute corpuscles singly insensible, their different degrees also depend upon the variation of some or all of those causes; which since it cannot be observed by us in particles of matter whereof each is too subtle to be perceived, it is impossible for us to have any exact measures of the different degrees of these simple ideas. . . .

* * *

13. *The secondary qualities of things not discovered by demonstration.*—Not knowing what number of particles, nor what motion of them, is fit to produce any precise degree of whiteness, we cannot demonstrate the certain equality of any two degrees of whiteness; because we have no certain standard to measure them by, nor means to distinguish every the least real difference; the only help we have being from our senses, which in this point fail us. But where the difference is so great as to produce in the mind clearly distinct ideas, whose differences can be perfectly retained, there these ideas of

colours, as we see in different kinds, as blue and red, are as capable of demonstration as ideas of number and extension. What I have here said of whiteness and colours, I think, holds true in all secondary qualities, and their modes.

14. *Sensitive knowledge of the particular existence of finite beings without us.*— These two, viz., intuition and demonstration, are the degrees of our *knowledge;* whatever comes short of one of these, with what assurance soever embraced, is but *faith* or *opinion,* but not knowledge, at least in all general truths. There is, indeed, another perception of the mind employed about *the particular existence of finite beings without us,* which, going beyond bare probability, and yet not reaching perfectly to either of the foregoing degrees of certainty, passes under the name of *knowledge.* There can be nothing more certain, than that the idea we receive from an external object is in our minds; this is intuitive knowledge. But whether there be anything more than barely that idea in our minds, whether we can thence certainly infer the existence of anything without us which corresponds to that idea, is that whereof some men think there may be a question made; because men may have such ideas in their minds when no such thing exists, no such object affects their senses. But yet here, I think, we are provided with an evidence that puts us past doubting; for I ask any one, whether he be not invincibly conscious to himself of a different perception when he looks on the sun by day, and thinks on it by night; when he actually tastes wormwood, or smells a rose, or only thinks on that savour or odour? We as plainly find the difference there is between any idea revived in our minds by our own memory, and actually coming into our minds by our senses, as we do between any two distinct ideas. If any one say, a dream may do the same thing, and all these ideas may be produced in us without any external objects; he may please to dream that I make him this answer: (1) That it is no great matter whether I remove his scruple or no: where all is but dream, reasoning and arguments are of no use, truth and knowledge nothing. (2) That I believe he will allow a very manifest difference between dreaming of being in the fire, and being actually in it. But yet if he be resolved to appear so skeptical as to maintain, that what I call being actually in the fire is nothing but a dream; and that we cannot thereby certainly know that any such thing as fire actually exists without us; I answer, that we certainly finding that pleasure or pain follows upon the application of certain objects to us, whose existence we perceive, or dream that we perceive, by our senses; this certainly is as great as our happiness or misery, beyond which we have no concernment to know or to be. So that, I think, we may add to the two former sorts of knowledge this also, of the existence of particular external objects by that perception and consciousness we have of the actual entrance of ideas from them, and allow these three degrees of knowledge, viz., *intuitive, demonstrative,* and *sensitive:* in each of which there are different degrees and ways of evidence and certainty.

* * *

CHAPTER 3. OF THE EXTENT OF HUMAN KNOWLEDGE

1. *Extent of our knowledge.*—KNOWLEDGE, as has been said, lying in the perception of the agreement or disagreement of any of our ideas, it follows from hence that,

It extends no farther than we have ideas.—First, We can have knowledge no farther than we have ideas.

2. *It extends no farther than we can perceive their agreement or disagreement.*— Secondly, That we can have no knowledge farther than we can have *perception* of that

agreement or disagreement: which perception being, (1) Either by *intuition,* or the immediate comparing any two ideas; or, (2) By *reason,* examining the agreement or disagreement of two ideas by the intervention of some others; or (3) By *sensation,* perceiving the existence of particular things; hence it also follows,

3. *Intuitive knowledge extends itself not to all the relations of all our ideas.*— Thirdly, that we cannot have an *intuitive knowledge* that shall extend itself to all our ideas, and all that we would know about them; because we cannot examine and perceive all the relations they have one to another by juxtaposition, or an immediate comparison one with another. Thus having the ideas of an obtuse and an acute angled triangle, both drawn from equal bases, and between parallels, I can by intuitive knowledge perceive the one not to be the other; but cannot that way know whether they be equal or no: because their agreement or disagreement in equality can never be perceived by an immediate comparing them; the difference of figure makes their parts incapable of an exact immediate application; and therefore there is need of some intervening quantities to measure them by, which is demonstration or rational knowledge.

4. *Nor does demonstrative knowledge.*—Fourthly, It follows also, from what is above observed, that our *rational knowledge* cannot reach to the whole extent of our ideas. Because between two different ideas we would examine, we cannot always find such mediums as we can connect one to another with an intuitive knowledge, in all the parts of the deduction; and wherever that fails, we come short of knowledge and demonstration.

5. *Sensitive knowledge narrower than either.*—Fifthly, *Sensitive knowledge,* reaching no farther than the existence of things actually present to our senses, is yet much narrower than either of the former.

*   *   *

Chapter 9. Of our Threefold Knowledge of Existence

1. *General propositions that are certain concern not existence.*—Hitherto we have only considered the essences of things; which being only abstract ideas, and thereby removed in our thoughts from particular existence, (that being the proper operation of the mind, in abstraction, to consider an idea under no other existence but what it has in the understanding,) gives us no knowledge of real existence at all. Where, by the way, we may take notice, that universal propositions of whose truth or falsehood we can have certain knowledge concern not existence: and further, that all particular affirmations or negations that would not be certain if they were made general, are only concerning existence; they declaring only the accidental union or separation of ideas in things existing, which, in their abstract natures, have no known necessary union or repugnancy.

2. *A threefold knowledge of existence.*—But, leaving the nature of propositions, and different ways of predication to be considered more at large in another place, let us proceed now to inquire concerning our knowledge of the *existence of things,* and how we come by it. I say, then, that we have the knowledge of *our own existence* by intuition; of the existence of *God* by demonstration; and of *other things* by sensation.

3. *Our knowledge of our own existence is intuitive.*—As for our own existence, we perceive it so plainly and so certainly, that it neither needs nor is capable of any proof. For nothing can be more evident to us than our own existence. I think, I reason, I feel pleasure and pain: can any of these be more evident to me than my own existence? If I doubt of all other things, that very doubt makes me perceive my own existence, and

will not suffer me to doubt of that. For if I know I feel pain, it is evident I have as certain perception of my own existence, as of the existence of the pain I feel: or if I know I doubt, I have as certain perception of the existence of the thing doubting, as of that thought which I *call doubt.* Experience then convinces us, that we have an *intuitive knowledge* of our own existence, and an internal infallible perception that we are. In every act of sensation, reasoning, or thinking, we are conscious to ourselves of our own being; and, in this matter, come not short of the highest degree of certainty.

CHAPTER 10. OF OUR KNOWLEDGE OF THE EXISTENCE OF A GOD

1. *We are capable of knowing certainly that there is a God.*—Though God has given us no innate ideas of himself; though he has stamped no original characters on our minds, wherein we may read his being; yet having furnished us with those faculties our minds are endowed with, he hath not left himself without witness: since we have sense, perception, and reason, and cannot want a clear proof of him, as long as we carry *ourselves* about us. Nor can we justly complain of our ignorance in this great point; since he has so plentifully provided us with the means to discover and know him; so far as is necessary to the end of our being, and the great concernment of our happiness. But, though this be the most obvious truth that reason discovers, and though its evidence be (if I mistake not) equal to mathematical certainty: yet it requires thought and attention; and the mind must apply itself to a regular deduction of it from some part of our intuitive knowledge, or else we shall be as uncertain and ignorant of this as of other propositions, which are in themselves capable of clear demonstration. To show, therefore, that we are capable of *knowing,* i.e., *being certain* that there is a God, and *how we may come by* this certainty, I think we need go no further than *ourselves,* and that undoubted knowledge we have of our own existence.

2. *For man knows that he himself exists.*—I think it is beyond question, that man has a clear idea of his own being; he knows certainly he exists, and that he is something. He that can doubt-whether he be anything or no, I speak not to; no more than I would argue with pure nothing, or endeavour to convince nonentity that it were something. If any one pretends to be so sceptical as to deny his own existence, (for really to doubt of it is manifestly impossible,) let him for me enjoy his beloved happiness of being nothing, until hunger or some other pain convince him of the contrary. This, then, I think I may take for a truth, which every one's certain knowledge assures him of, beyond the liberty of doubting, viz., that he is something that actually exists.

3. *He knows also that nothing cannot produce a being; therefore something must have existed from eternity.*—In the next place, man knows, by an intuitive certainty, that bare *nothing can no more produce any real being, than it can be equal to two right angles.* If a man knows not that nonentity, or the absence of all being, cannot be equal to two right angles, it is impossible he should know any demonstration in Euclid. If, therefore, we know there is some real being, and that nonentity cannot produce any real being, it is an evident demonstration, that *from eternity there has been something;* since what was not from eternity had a beginning; and what had a beginning must be produced by something else.

4. *And that eternal Being must be most powerful.*—Next, it is evident, that what had its being and beginning from another, must also have all that which is in and belongs to its being from another too. All the powers it has must be owing to and received from the same source. This eternal source, then, of all being must also be the source and original of all power; and so *this eternal Being must be also the most powerful.*

5. *And most knowing.*—Again, a man finds in *himself* perception and knowledge. We have then got one step further; and we are certain now that there is not only some being, but some knowing, intelligent being in the world. There was a time, then, when there was no knowing being and when knowledge began to be; or else there has been also *a knowing being from eternity.* If it be said, there was a time when no being had any knowledge, when that eternal being was void of all understanding; I reply, that then it was impossible there should ever have been any knowledge: it being as impossible that things wholly void of knowledge, and operating blindly, and without any perception, should produce a knowing being, as it is impossible that a triangle should make itself three angles bigger than two right ones. For it is as repugnant to the idea of senseless matter, that it should put into itself sense, perception, and knowledge, as it is repugnant to the idea of a triangle, that it should put into itself greater angles than two right ones.

6. *And therefore God.*—Thus, from the consideration of ourselves, and what we infallibly find in our own constitutions, our reason leads us to the knowledge of this certain and evident truth,—*That there is an eternal, most powerful, and most knowing Being;* which whether any one will please to call God, it matters not. The thing is evident, and from this idea duly considered, will easily be deduced all those other attributes, which we ought to ascribe to this eternal Being. If, nevertheless, any one should be found so senselessly arrogant, as to suppose man alone knowing and wise, but yet the product of mere ignorance and chance; and that all the rest of the universe acted only by that blind haphazard; I shall leave with him that very rational and emphatical rebuke of Tully, to be considered at his leisure: "What can be more sillily arrogant and misbecoming, than for a man to think that he has a mind and understanding in him, but yet in all the universe beside there is no such thing? Or that those things, which with the utmost stretch of his reason he can scarce comprehend, should be moved and managed without any reason at all?" . . .

From what has been said, it is plain to me we have a more certain knowledge of the existence of a God, than of anything our senses have not immediately discovered to us. Nay, I presume I may say, that we more certainly know that there is a God, than that there is anything else without us. When I say we *know,* I mean there is such a knowledge within our reach which we cannot miss, if we will but apply our minds to that, as we do to several other inquiries.

*   *   *

CHAPTER 11. OF OUR KNOWLEDGE OF THE EXISTENCE OF OTHER THINGS

1. *Knowledge of the existence of other finite beings is to be had only by actual sensation.*—The knowledge of our own being we have by intuition. The existence of a God, reason clearly makes known to us, as has been shown.

The knowledge of the existence of *any other thing* we can have only by sensation: for there being no necessary connexion of real existence with any idea a man hath in his memory; nor of any other existence but that of God with the existence of any particular man: no particular man can know the existence of any other being, but only when, by actual operating upon him, it makes itself perceived by him. For, the having the idea of anything in our mind, no more proves the existence of that thing, than the picture of a man evidences his being in the world, or the visions of a dream make thereby a true history.

2. *Instance: whiteness of this paper.*—It is therefore the *actual receiving* of ideas from without that gives us notice of the existence of other things, and makes us know, that something doth exist at that time without us, which causes that idea in us; though perhaps we neither know nor consider how it does it. For it takes not from the certainty of our senses, and the ideas we receive by them, that we know not the manner wherein they are produced: v.g., whilst I write this, I have, by the paper affecting my eyes, that idea produced in my mind, which, whatever object causes, I call *white;* by which I know that that quality or accident (i.e., whose appearance before my eyes always causes that idea) doth really exist, and hath a being without me. And of this, the greatest assurance I can possibly have, and to which my faculties can attain, is the testimony of my eyes, which are the proper and sole judges of this thing; whose testimony I have reason to rely on as so certain, that I can no more doubt, whilst I write this, that I see white and black, and that something really exists that causes that sensation in me, than that I write or move my hand; which is a certainty as great as human nature is capable of, concerning the existence of anything, but a man's self alone, and of God.

3. *This notice by our senses, though not so certain as demonstration, yet may be called knowledge, and proves the existence of things without us.*—The notice we have by our senses of the existing of things without us, though it be not altogether so certain as our intuitive knowledge, or the deductions of our reason employed about the clear abstract ideas of our own minds; yet it is an assurance that deserves the name of *knowledge.* If we persuade ourselves that our faculties act and inform us right concerning the existence of those objects that affect them, it cannot pass for an ill-grounded confidence: for I think nobody can, in earnest, be so sceptical as to be uncertain of the existence of those things which he sees and feels. At least, he that can doubt so far, (whatever he may have with his own thoughts,) will never have any controversy with me; since he can never be sure I say anything contrary to his own opinion. As to myself, I think God has given me assurance enough of the existence of things without me: since, by their different application, I can produce in myself both pleasure and pain, which is one great concernment of my present state. This is certain: the confidence that our faculties do not herein deceive us, is the greatest assurance we are capable of concerning the existence of material beings. For we cannot act anything but by our faculties; nor talk of knowledge itself, but by the help of those faculties which are fitted to apprehend even what knowledge is.

But besides the assurance we have from our senses themselves, that they do not err in the information they give us of the existence of things without us, when they are affected by them, we are further confirmed in this assurance by other concurrent reasons:—

4. I. *Confirmed by concurrent reasons:—First, because we cannot have ideas of sensation but by the inlet of the senses.*—It is plain those perceptions are produced in us by exterior causes affecting our senses: because those that want the organs of any sense, never can have the ideas belonging to that sense produced in their minds. This is too evident to be doubted: and therefore we cannot but be assured that they come in by the organs of that sense, and no other way. The organs themselves, it is plain, do not produce them: for then the eyes of a man in the dark would produce colours, and his nose smell roses in the winter: but we see nobody gets the relish of a pineapple, till he goes to the Indies, where it is, and tastes it.

5. II. *Secondly, Because we find that an idea from actual sensation, and another from memory, are very distinct perceptions.*—Because sometimes I find that *I cannot avoid the having those ideas produced in my mind.* For though, when my eyes are shut, or windows fast, I can at pleasure recall to my mind the ideas of light, or the sun, which

former sensations had lodged in my memory; so I can at pleasure lay by *that* idea, and take into my view that of the smell of a rose, or taste of sugar. But, if I turn my eyes at noon towards the sun, I cannot avoid the ideas which the light or sun then produces in me. So that there is a manifest difference between the ideas laid up in my memory, (over which, if they were there only, I should have constantly the same power to dispose of them, and lay them by at pleasure,) and those which force themselves upon me, and I cannot avoid having. And therefore it must needs be some exterior cause, and the brisk acting of some objects without me, whose efficacy I cannot resist, that produces those ideas in my mind, whether I will or no. Besides, there is nobody who doth not perceive the difference in himself between contemplating the sun, as he hath the idea of it in his memory, and actually looking upon it: of which two, his perception is so distinct, that few of his ideas are more distinguishable one from another. And therefore he hath certain knowledge that they are not *both* memory, or the actions of his mind, and fancies only within him; but that actual seeing hath a cause without.

6. III. *Thirdly, because pleasure or pain, which accompanies actual sensation, accompanies not the returning of those ideas without the external objects.*—Add to this, that many of those ideas are *produced in us with pain,* which afterwards we remember without the least offence. Thus, the pain of heat or cold, when the idea of it is revived in our minds, gives us no disturbance; which, when felt, was very troublesome; and is again, when actually repeated: which is occasioned by the disorder the external object causes in our bodies when applied to them: and we remember the pains of hunger, thirst, or the headache, without any pain at all; which would either never disturb us, or else constantly do it, as often as we thought of it, were there nothing more but ideas floating in our minds, and appearances entertaining our fancies, without the real existence of things affecting us from abroad. The same may be said of *pleasure,* accompanying several actual sensations. And though mathematical demonstration depends not upon sense, yet the examining them by diagrams gives great credit to the evidence of our sight, and seems to give it a certainty approaching to that of demonstration itself. For, it would be very strange, that a man should allow it for an undeniable truth, that two angles of a figure, which he measures by lines and angles of a diagram, should be bigger one than the other, and yet doubt of the existence of those lines and angles, which by looking on he makes use of to measure that by.

7. IV. *Fourthly, because our senses assist one Another's testimony of the existence of outward things, and enable us to predict.*—Our *senses* in many cases *bear witness to the truth of each other's report,* concerning the existence of sensible things without us. He that *sees* a fire, may, if he doubt whether it be anything more than a bare fancy, *feel* it too; and be convinced, by putting his hand in it. Which certainly could never be put into such exquisite pain by a bare idea or phantom, unless that the pain be a fancy too: which yet he cannot, when the burn is well, by raising the idea of it, bring upon himself again.

Thus I see, whilst I write this, I can change the appearance of the paper; and by designing the letters, tell *beforehand* what new idea it shall exhibit the very next moment, by barely drawing my pen over it: which will neither appear (let me fancy as much as I will) if my hands stand still, or though I move my pen, if my eyes be shut: nor, when those characters are once made on the paper, can I choose afterwards but see them as they are; that is, have the ideas of such letters as I have made. Whence it is manifest, that they are not barely the sport and play of my own imagination, when I find that the characters that were made at the pleasure of my own thoughts, do not obey them; nor yet cease to be, whenever I shall fancy it, but continue to affect my senses constantly and regularly, according to the figures I made them. To which if we will add, that the sight of those shall, from another man, draw such sounds as I beforehand design they shall stand for, there will be little reason left to doubt that those words I write do really exist without me, when they cause a long series of regular sounds to affect my ears, which could not be the effect of my imagination, nor could my memory retain them in that order.

8. *This certainty is as great as our condition needs.*—But yet, if after all this any one will be so sceptical as to distrust his senses, and to affirm that all we see and hear, feel and taste, think and do, during our whole being, is but the series and deluding appearances of a long dream, whereof there is no reality; and therefore will question the existence of all things, or our knowledge of anything: I must desire him to consider, that, if all be a dream, then he doth but dream that he makes the question, and so it is not much matter that a waking man should answer him. But yet, if he pleases, he may dream that I make him this answer, That the certainty of things existing in *rerum natura* when we have the testimony of our senses for it is not only as great as our frame can attain to, but as our condition needs. For, our faculties being suited not to the full extent of being, nor to a perfect, clear, comprehensive knowledge of things free from all doubt and scruple; but to the preservation of us, in whom they are; and accommodated to the use of life: they serve to our purpose well enough, if they will but give us certain notice of those things, which are convenient or inconvenient to us. For he that sees a candle burning, and hath experimented the force of its flame by putting his finger in it, will little doubt that this is something existing without him, which does him harm, and puts him to great pain: which is assurance enough, when no man requires greater certainty to govern his actions by than what is as certain as his actions themselves. And if our dreamer pleases to try whether the glowing heat of a glass furnace be barely a wandering imagination in a drowsy man's fancy, by putting his hand into it, he may perhaps be wakened into a certainty greater than he could wish, that it is something more than bare imagination. So that this evidence is as great as we can desire, being as certain to us as our pleasure or pain, i.e., happiness or misery; beyond which we have no concernment, either of knowing or being. Such an assurance of the existence of things without us is sufficient to direct us in the attaining the good and avoiding the evil which is caused by them, which is the important concernment we have of being made acquainted with them.

9. *But reaches no further than actual sensation.*—In fine, then, when our senses do actually convey into our understandings any idea, we cannot but be satisfied that there doth something *at that time* really exist without us, which doth affect our senses, and by them give notice of itself to our apprehensive faculties, and actually produce that idea which we then perceive: and we cannot so far distrust their testimony, as to doubt that such *collections* of simple ideas as we have observed by our senses to be united together, do really exist together. But this knowledge extends as far as the present testimony of our senses, employed about particular objects that do then affect them, and no further. For if I saw such a collection of simple ideas as is wont to be called *man,* existing together one minute since, and am now alone, I cannot be certain that the same man exists now, since there is no *necessary connexion* of his existence a minute since with his existence now: by a thousand ways he may cease to be, since I had the testimony of my senses for his existence. And if I cannot be certain that the man I saw last to-day is now in being, I can less be certain that he is so who hath been longer removed from my senses, and I have not seen since yesterday, or since the last year: and much less can I be certain of the existence of men that I never saw. And, therefore, though it be highly probable that millions of men do now exist, yet, whilst I am alone, writing this, I have not that certainty of it which we strictly call knowledge; though the great likelihood of

it puts me past doubt, and it be reasonable for me to do several things upon the confidence that there are men (and men also of my acquaintance, with whom I have to do) now in the world: but this is but probability, not knowledge.

10. *Folly to expect demonstration in everything.*—Whereby yet we may observe how foolish and vain a thing it is for a man of a narrow knowledge, who having reason given him to judge of the different evidence and probability of things, and to be swayed accordingly; how vain, I say, it is to expect demonstration and certainty in things not capable of it—and refuse assent to very rational propositions, and act contrary to very plain and clear truths, because they cannot be made out so evident, as to surmount every the least (I will not say reason, but) pretence of doubting. He that, in the ordinary affairs of life, would admit of nothing but direct plain demonstration would be sure of nothing in this world but of perishing quickly. The wholesomeness of his meat or drink would not give him reason to venture on it: and I would fain know what it is he could do upon such grounds as are capable of no doubt, no objection.

11. *Past existence of other things is known by memory.*—As *when our senses are actually employed about any object,* we do know that it does exist; so *by our memory* we may be assured, that heretofore things that affected our senses have existed. And thus we have knowledge of the past existence of several things, whereof our senses having informed us, our memories still retain the ideas; and of this we are past all doubt, so long as we remember well. But this knowledge also reaches no further than our senses have formerly assured us. Thus, seeing water at this instant, it is an unquestionable truth to me that water doth exist: and remembering that I saw it yesterday, it will also be always true, and as long as my memory retains it always an undoubted proposition to me, that water did exist the 10th of July, 1688; as it will also be equally true that a certain number of very fine colours did exist, which at the same time I saw upon a bubble of that water: but, being now quite out of sight both of the water and bubbles too, it is no more certainly known to me that the water doth now exist, than that the bubbles or colours therein do so: it being no more necessary that water should exist to-day, because it existed yesterday, than that the colours or bubbles exist to-day, because they existed yesterday, though it be exceedingly much more probable; because water hath been observed to continue long in existence, but bubbles, and the colours on them, quickly cease to be.

12. *The existence of other finite spirits not knowable, and rests on faith.*—What ideas we have of spirits, and how we come by them, I have already shown. But though we have those ideas in our minds, and know we have them there, the having the ideas of spirits does not make us know that any such things do exist without us, or that there are any finite spirits, or any other spiritual beings, but the Eternal God. We have ground from revelation, and several other reasons, to believe with assurance that there are such creatures: but our senses not being able to discover them, we want the means of knowing their particular existences. For we can no more know that there are finite spirits really existing, by the idea we have of such beings in our minds, than by the ideas any one has of fairies or centaurs, he can come to know that things answering those ideas do really exist.

And therefore concerning the existence of finite spirits, as well as several other things, we must content ourselves with the evidence of faith; but universal, certain propositions concerning this matter are beyond our reach. For however true it may be, v.g., that all the intelligent spirits that God ever created do still exist, yet it can never make a part of our certain knowledge. These and the like propositions we may assent to, as highly probable, but are not, I fear, in this state capable of knowing. We are not, then, to put others upon demonstrating, nor ourselves upon search of universal certainty in all those matters; wherein we are not capable of any other knowledge, but what our senses give us in this or that particular.

13. *Only particular propositions concerning concrete existences are knowable.*—By which it appears that there are two sorts of propositions:—(1) There is one sort of propositions concerning the *existence* of anything answerable to such an idea: as having the idea of an elephant, phoenix, motion, or an angel, in my mind, the first and natural inquiry is, Whether such a thing does anywhere exist? And this knowledge is only of particulars. No existence of anything without us, but only of God, can certainly be known further than our senses inform us. (2) There is another sort of propositions, wherein is expressed the agreement or disagreement of *our abstract ideas,* and their dependence on one another. Such propositions may be universal and certain. So, having the idea of God and myself, of fear and obedience, I cannot but be sure that God is to be feared and obeyed by me: and this proposition will be certain, concerning man in general, if I have made an abstract idea of such a species, whereof I am one particular. But yet this proposition, how certain soever, that "men ought to fear and obey God" proves not to me the *existence* of *men* in the world but will be true of all such creatures, whenever they do exist: which certainty of such general propositions depends on the agreement or disagreement to be discovered in those abstract ideas.

14. *And all general propositions that are known to be true concern abstract ideas.*—In the former case, our knowledge is the consequence of the existence of things, producing ideas in our minds by our senses: in the latter, knowledge is the consequence of the ideas (be they what they will) that are in our minds, producing there general certain propositions. Many of these are called *aeternae veritates,* and all of them indeed are so; not from being written, all or any of them, in the minds of all men; or that they were any of them propositions in any one's mind, till he, having got the abstract ideas, joined or separated them by affirmation or negation. But wheresoever we can suppose such a creature as man is, endowed with such faculties, and thereby furnished with such ideas as we have, we must conclude, he must needs, when he applies his thoughts to the consideration of his ideas, know the truth of certain propositions that will arise from the agreement or disagreement which he will perceive in his own ideas. Such propositions are therefore called *eternal truths,* not because they are eternal propositions actually formed, and antecedent to the understanding that at any time makes them; nor because they are imprinted on the mind from any patterns that are anywhere out of the mind, and existed before: but because, being once made about abstract ideas, so as to be true, they will, whenever they can be supposed to be made again at any time, past or to come, by a mind having those ideas, always actually be true. For names being supposed to stand perpetually for the same ideas, and the same ideas having immutably the same habitudes one to another, propositions concerning any abstract ideas that are once true must needs be *eternal verities.*

GOTTFRIED LEIBNIZ
1646–1716

Gottfried Wilhelm Von Leibniz was born and raised in academe. His father was a professor of moral philosophy at the University of Leipzig and his mother was the daughter of a law professor at the same institution. His advance was prodigious: At fifteen, he began his study of the history of philosophy at the university; at seventeen, after defending his thesis, he proceeded to the University of Jena where he studied mathematics and law; at eighteen, he published his treatise on law; and at twenty, he was ready to present himself as a candidate for the doctor of law degree, but he was declared too young. So he moved to the University of Altdorf, where he not only received his doctoral degree but was offered a professorship. He declined this invitation and settled into a position with Johann Philipp von Schönborn, elector of Mainz.

While in the service of the Mainz court, he lived for a time in Paris, where he made the acquaintance of leading thinkers of his day, such as the physicist Christian Huygens and the philosophers Antoine Arnauld and Nicolas Malebranche. As part of his mission in Paris, Leibniz prepared a plan for invading Egypt for Louis XIV (hoping to deflect Louis from military action in Europe). Though Louis never acted on the plan, many scholars believe that Napoleon used the scheme 120 years later.

In addition to diplomatic initiatives, Leibniz worked extensively on mathematics while he was in Paris. He invented a calculating machine that could add, subtract, multiply, divide, and extract square roots. When he demonstrated his machine in London, he was made a member of the Royal Society (1673). He also discovered differential and integral calculus—though years later there was an unpleasant dispute over whether Leibniz or Newton should get the credit for it. Did one of these great men steal the idea from the other? The Royal Society officially belittled Leibniz's achievement (quite unjustly according to the verdict of subsequent scholarship). It has been said that the dispute "redounded to the discredit of all concerned." It may be best to credit both men with the discovery. Interestingly, Leibniz's notation proved the more convenient and is the system presently used.

In 1676, Leibniz went into the service of the Duke of Brunswick in Hanover, where he remained the rest of his life. He traveled extensively and met such notable people as Spinoza and the chemist Boyle. In 1700, he was elected a foreign member of the French Academy. In the same year, by his inspiration, the *Akademie der Wissenschaften* was founded in Berlin and he was elected its first president. He was a close friend of Sophie Charlotte, the wife of the Elector of Brandenburg (subsequently the first king of Prussia). The only large systematic philosophic work he published, *Theodicy* (1710), grew out of his discussions with Sophie Charlotte.

Despite his accomplishments, Leibniz was not well liked. As Bertrand Russell later commented, "Leibniz was one of the supreme intellects of all time, but he was not admirable." Leibniz's death in 1716 was ignored not only by the Royal Society in London but also by the *Akademie* in Berlin and by the court at Hanover. His secretary is said to have been his only mourner, and an eyewitness reports in his memoirs that Leibniz "was buried more like a robber than what he really was, the ornament of his country."

At his death, he left an enormous number of unpublished letters and manuscripts. One major work was published in 1765: his detailed critique of Locke's *Essay,* entitled *Nouveaux essais sur L'entendement humain.* Leibniz had completed the book in 1704 but withheld it from publication when Locke died the same year. The book greatly stimulated Immanuel Kant, particularly his *Critique of Pure Reason.* In this century, thinkers such as Bertrand Russell and Ernst Cassirer have focused attention on Leibniz's work in logic. The neglect of Leibniz in his lifetime has given way in this century to great admiration for the scope and originality of his thought.

*   *   *

Leibniz's philosophy begins by rejecting the notion that extension is a substance (as Descartes claimed) or an attribute of substance (as in Spinoza). Instead of understanding nature as a collection of discrete extended entities, such as atoms, Leibniz says that the basic substance is a "Monad," or a unit of psychic force. Such Monads are without parts (i.e., simple) and have no interaction with one another. As Leibniz puts it, they have "no windows through which anything may come in or go out." Each Monad has within itself an internal principle of "appetition" that causes it to change. Although there is no causal interaction between Monads, they may *appear* to influence one another. This connection is merely a reflection of the "pre-established harmony" by which God created each of the Monads to "mirror" the others. A Monad's entire past and present are contained within it so that whatever it does, it does so by necessity. If we could know the entire past of a given Monad, we could predict its entire future.

Monads all differ qualitatively and occupy different points of view. This means that each Monad "mirrors" the world in a slightly different way and with different levels of clarity. Rocks and dirt are made of colonies of "low level" Monads that have only dull and confused perceptions as they mirror the world. It might seem odd to talk about rocks as having perceptions at all, but according to Leibniz, *every Monad has some sort of psychic life*: Each Monad has an "internal state [by which it] represent[s] external things." Those Monads whose perceptions are "more distinct and are accompanied by memory" are on a higher level. The dominant Monad of an animal, for example, has distinct perceptions and memory of those perceptions: "If you show a stick to a dog, for instance, it remembers the pain caused by it and howls or runs away." This dominant Monad Leibniz calls a "soul" to distinguish it from lower level or "naked" Monads. Human beings are Monad aggregates of yet a higher degree. Whereas human bodies are colonies of lower Monads, the dominant Monad in a person is a "spirit," because it is capable of performing "reflective acts." Spirits are also capable of knowing the universe and of entering into a relationship with the chief Monad, God.

Leibniz's metaphysics seems to exclude the possibility of freedom. If each Monad has its entire future within it, and if it thus unfolds that future by necessity, how can we, as colonies of a dominant "spirit" Monad and lower "body" Monads, be free? Leibniz's answer to this question turns on his definition of "freedom." To be "free," claims Leibniz, does not mean "liberty of indifference." Instead we are "free" in that our actions flow from our wills and there is no logical contradiction in our willing other than we do. As Leibniz put it, "there is always a prevailing reason which prompts the will to its choice, and for the maintenance of freedom for the will it suffices that this reason should incline without necessitating." Of course, he also claims that our wills are created by God and that God foreknows what we will will ourselves to do. But the action of our wills is not necessary in the sense that willing something else involves a logical contradiction; hence, our wills can be said to be "free."

In creating the world, God considered all possibilities and actualized only those ensuring the greatest perfection. As Leibniz explained in his *Theodicy,* God creates only those substances that will harmonize with other entities to the fullest possible extent. Whereas we may not understand it fully, the world as it actually exists is "the best of all possible worlds." It is this point that is satirized so ruthlessly in Voltaire's *Candide* (1759).

*   *   *

Leibniz never wrote a "magnum opus" that clearly defined his position on philosophical issues. The *Discourse on Metaphysics* (1686), reprinted here (complete) in the Martin and Brown translation, gives his early ideas on metaphysics. *The Monadology* (1714), also reprinted here (complete) in the Paul Schrecker and Anne Martin Schrecker translation, presents his mature position on metaphysics.

After the publication of *Theodicy* in 1710, Leibniz wrote a brief summary of his argument. This summary is presented (complete) in the George M. Duncan translation.

For general introductions to Leibniz's philosophy, see Herbert Wildon Carr, *Leibniz* (Boston: Little, Brown, 1929); Ruth Lydia Saw, *Leibniz* (Baltimore, MD: Penguin Books, 1954); Nicholas Rescher, *The Philosophy of Leibniz* (Englewood Cliffs, NJ: Prentice Hall, 1967); C.D. Broad, *Leibniz: An Introduction,* edited by C. Lewy (Cambridge: Cambridge University Press, 1975); Stuart Brown, *Leibniz* (Minneapolis: University of Minnesota Press, 1984); and Robert Merrihew Adams, *Leibniz: Determinist, Theist, Idealist* (Oxford: Oxford University Press, 1994). For a discussion of the logic and metaphysics of Leibniz, Bertrand Russell,

A Critical Exposition of the Philosophy of Leibniz (London: George Allen & Unwin, 1900), is still a valuable source. For more recent treatments of these issues, see Hidé Ishiguro, *Leibniz's Philosophy of Logic and Language* (Ithaca, NY: Cornell University Press, 1972); Robert McRae, *Leibniz: Perception, Apperception, and Thought* (Toronto: University of Toronto Press, 1976); and Benson Mates, *The Philosophy of Leibniz: Metaphysics and Language* (Oxford: Oxford University Press, 1986). For a commentary on *The Monadology,* see Herbert Wildon Carr, *The Monadology of Leibniz* (Los Angeles: University of Southern California Press, 1930). For an interesting discussion of the *Theodicy,* see John Hick, *Evil and the God of Love* (New York: Harper & Row, 1966). For collections of essays, see Harry G. Frankfurt, ed., *Leibniz: A Collection of Critical Essays* (Garden City, NY: Doubleday, 1972); R.S. Woolhouse, ed., *Leibniz: Metaphysics and Philosophy of Science* (Oxford: Oxford University Press, 1981); Michael Hooker, *Leibniz: Critical and Interpretive Essays* (Minneapolis: University of Minnesota Press, 1984); Vere Chappell, ed., *Essays on Early Modern Philosophers: Gottfried Wilhelm Leibniz* (Hamden, CT: Garland Press, 1992); and Nicholas Jolley, ed., *The Cambridge Companion to Leibniz* (Cambridge: Cambridge University Press, 1995).

DISCOURSE ON METAPHYSICS

1. ON THE DIVINE PERFECTION: GOD DOES EVERYTHING IN THE MOST DESIRABLE WAY.

The most commonly accepted notion of God we have, and the one most full of meaning, is well enough expressed in these terms: God is an absolutely perfect being. Not enough thought, however, is given to its consequences. If we are to make progress, it is relevant to note that in nature there are several entirely different perfections, that God possesses them all together, and that each belongs to Him to the highest degree.

We also need to understand what a perfection is. A sure enough mark of one is that forms or natures not admitting of an ultimate degree are not perfections, as for example the nature of numbers or of shape. For the greatest of all numbers (or rather the number of all numbers), and the greatest of all shapes imply contradictions while omniscience and omnipotence involve no impossibility. Consequently, power and knowledge are perfections, and to the extent that they belong to God, they have no limits.

Hence it follows that since God possesses supreme and infinite wisdom, He acts in the most perfect manner, not only in the metaphysical sense, but also morally speaking. From our point of view we can express ourselves thus: the more we are enlightened and informed about the works of God, the more we shall be disposed to find that they are excellent and satisfactory in every way we could hope.

Gottfried Liebniz, *Discourse on Metaphysics and Related Writings,* edited and translated by R.N.D. Martin and Stuart Brown (Manchester and New York: Manchester University Press, 1988). Reprinted by permission of Manchester University Press.

[Liebniz made minor additions, deletions, and/or changes to virtually every paragraph of this work. I have chosen to reproduce Liebniz's text minus all material deleted by Leibniz.]

2. AGAINST THOSE WHO MAINTAIN THAT THERE IS NO GOODNESS IN THE WORKS OF GOD, OR THAT THE RULES OF GOODNESS AND BEAUTY ARE ARBITRARY.

Thus I am far removed from the opinion of those who maintain that there are no rules of goodness or perfection in the nature of things or in the ideas God has of them, and that the works of God are good only for the formal reason that God made them. For if that were so, since God knew He was their author, He had only to look at them after making them to find them good, in accordance with the testimony of Holy Scripture. But Scripture seems to have made use of this anthropomorphic way of speaking only to make us realise that we recognise the excellence of God's works by considering them by themselves, even when we disregard the purely extrinsic denomination that refers them to their cause. This is all the more true in that it is by considering the works that we can discover the Worker, so that the works must carry His marks in themselves. I confess that the contrary opinion seems to me extremely dangerous, and very close to the way the Spinozists think of goodness and harmony. Their opinion is that the beauty of the universe and the goodness we attribute to the works of God are no more than the chimeras of men who conceive God according to their own way of thinking. Also, if we say that things are good by no rule of goodness beyond the will of God alone, we thoughtlessly destroy, I feel, all the love and glory of God. For why praise Him for what He had done if He would be equally praiseworthy for doing the opposite? Where will His justice and His wisdom be, if all that remains of Him is some kind of a despotic power, if His will takes the place of reason, and if, by the very definition of tyranny, what pleases the Almighty is *ipso facto* just? Besides, it seems that every act of willing presupposes some reason for willing, and that reason is naturally prior to will. That is why I still find altogether strange the expression of Descartes who says that even the eternal truths of metaphysics and geometry, and consequently also the rules of goodness, justice and perfection are no more than the effects of God's will. It seems to me, rather, that they are no more than the consequences of His understanding, which certainly does not depend on His will, any more His essence does.

3. AGAINST THOSE WHO THINK GOD COULD HAVE DONE BETTER.

Neither can I approve the opinion of some scholastics who maintain boldly that what God has done is not absolutely perfect, and that He could have done much better. For it seems to me that the consequences of this opinion are altogether contrary to the glory of God. "Just as the lesser evil contains a proportion of good, so the lesser good contains a proportion of evil." To act with less perfection than one could have done is to act imperfectly. To show that an architect could have done better is to find fault with his work. It also runs counter to the assurance of the goodness of God's works in Holy Scripture. For, since perfections decrease to infinity, however God did his work, it would always be good in comparison with the less perfect, if that were enough. But a thing is not very praiseworthy if it is only so in that way. I also think that a very large number of passages favouring my opinion could be found in the divine Scriptures and the holy Fathers, with scarcely any favouring that of those new scholastics a view unknown, in my opinion, to the whole of antiquity. It is based on our insufficient knowledge of the general harmony of the universe and of the hidden reasons for God's conduct which lead us to the rash judgement that many things could have been done better. Besides, these moderns insist on some subtleties that are not very sound, for they imagine that nothing is so perfect but that there is something that is more perfect, which is a mistake. There is an infinity of regular figures, but one is the most perfect, namely the circle. If a triangle had to be made and there was no further specification of the kind of triangle, God would assuredly make an equilateral triangle because, absolutely speaking, that is the most perfect.

They also think that in this way they are providing for the liberty of God, as if it were not the highest liberty to act in accordance with sovereign reason. For, apart from its apparent impossibility, the belief that God acts in some matter without any reason for His act of will is hardly consistent with His glory. Suppose, for example, that God chooses between A and B, and that He takes A without any reason for preferring it to B; I say that that action of God would at the least not be praiseworthy. For every praise must be based on some reason and here *ex hypothesi* there is none. On the contrary, I hold that God does nothing for which He does not merit being glorified.

4. LOVING GOD DEMANDS COMPLETE SATISFACTION WITH AND ACQUIESCENCE IN WHAT HE DOES, BUT WE DO NOT, ON THAT ACCOUNT, HAVE TO BE QUIETISTS.

The general recognition of this great truth—that God always acts in the most perfect and desirable manner possible—is to my mind the basis of the love we owe to God concerning all things. For he who loves seeks his satisfaction in the happiness or perfection of the loved one and his actions. "True friendship is to want the same and to reject the same." And I think that it is difficult to love God well when not disposed to will what He wills, if changing that were in our power. Indeed those who are not satisfied with what He does seem to me like discontented subjects of a king or of a republic whose intentions are little different from those of rebels.

Hence, in accordance with these principles, I hold that to act in conformity with the love of God it is not enough to be patient under duress. We must be truly satisfied with all that happens to us in consequence of His will. I mean this acquiescence to apply to the past. As far as the future is concerned, we must not be quietists nor wait ridiculously with arms folded for what God will do, in accordance with the sophism the Ancients called ⟨*logon aegon*⟩, lazy reason. On the contrary, we must act in accordance with the presumptive will of God, as far as we can judge it, trying with all our ability to contribute to the general good, especially to the adornment and perfection of what concerns us or is near us, or, so to speak, within our range. For when the outcome shows that God may perhaps not want our good will to have its effect for the present, it does not follow that He does not want us to do what we have done. On the contrary, since He is the best of all masters, He never asks for more than the right intentions, and it is for Him to know the hour and the place for bringing good plans to fruition.

5. WHAT ARE THE RULES OF PERFECTION OF GOD'S CONDUCT; AND THAT THE SIMPLICITY OF MEANS IS BALANCED BY THE RICHNESS OF EFFECTS.

Hence it is enough to have this confidence in God, that He does everything for the best and that nothing can harm those who love him. But to know in detail the reasons that could have moved Him to choose this order of the universe, to allow sins, or to dispense His saving grace in a particular way, is beyond the power of a finite mind, particularly of a finite mind that has not yet attained enjoyment of the sight of God.

Nevertheless, some general remarks can be made on the conduct of Providence in the government of things. Thus it can be said that whatever encloses more reality in less volume is more perfect, that he who acts perfectly is like an excellent geometer who knows how to find the best constructions for a problem; like a good architect who arranges his site and the funds intended for the building in the most advantageous manner, so as to leave nothing that jars or lacks the beauty of which it is capable; like a good householder who uses his property so that nothing is left uncultivated or barren; like a skilled engineer who achieves his result by the least complicated way that could be chosen; like an experienced author who includes as much reality as he is able in the least space. Now the most perfect of all beings, occupying the least volume, in other words, those which hinder the least, are minds, and their perfections are the virtues. That is why we must not doubt that the happiness of minds is the principal objective of God and that He pursues it as much as the general harmony allows. More will be said of this presently.

As for the simplicity of God's ways, that applies properly in respect of means whereas the variety, richness or abundance applies to aims or effects. The one has to be in balance with the other, like the expenses of a building with the size and beauty expected of it. It is true that nothing costs God anything, much less than it costs a philosopher to make hypotheses for the construction of his imaginary world, since God has only to make decrees to bring a real world to birth; but in relation to wisdom, in so far as they are mutually independent, decrees or hypotheses take the place of expenditure, for reason demands that we avoid a multiplicity of hypotheses or principles; in almost the same way the simplest system is always preferred in astronomy.

6. God Does Nothing Out of Order and It Is Not Even Possible to Imagine Events That Are Not Regular.

The decisions or actions of God are commonly divided into ordinary and extraordinary. But it is well to bear in mind that God does nothing out of order. So, whatever passes for extraordinary is only so in relation to some particular order established among creatures. For, in relation to the universal order, everything conforms to it. So true is this, that not only does nothing happen in the world that is absolutely irregular, but such a thing cannot even be imagined. Suppose, for example, that someone puts a number of points on paper completely at random like those who practise the ridiculous art of geomancy, then I say that it is possible to find a geometric line whose notion is constant and uniform according to some rule, so that this line passes through all these points and does so in the same order as they were made by the hand.

And if someone were to draw in one movement a line that was sometimes straight, sometimes circular, and sometimes of some other kind, it is possible to find a notion, a rule, or an equation common to all the points in that line and in virtue of which these same changes had to occur. For example there is no face whose contour is not part of a geometric line and cannot be drawn all in one movement by some rule-governed motion. But when a rule is very complicated, what conforms to it is taken to be irregular.

Thus it can be said that however God might have created the world, it would always have been regular and within some general order. But God chose that world that is the most perfect, i.e. the one that is simultaneously the simplest in hypotheses and richest in phenomena, just as a geometric line might be if its construction was easy but its properties most admirable and extensive. I make use of these comparisons to sketch some kind of imperfect resemblance to the divine wisdom and to say something that could at least raise our minds to conceive in some way what cannot be adequately expressed. But by this I do not claim to explain the great mystery on which the whole universe depends.

7. MIRACLES CONFORM TO THE GENERAL ORDER ALTHOUGH THEY ARE CONTRARY TO SUBALTERN NORMS. WHAT GOD WISHES OR PERMITS BY A GENERAL OR PARTICULAR WILL.

Now, since nothing can take place that is not within the order, it can be said that miracles are just as much within the order as natural operations, are so called because they conform to certain subaltern norms we call the nature of things. For it can be said that this "nature" is no more than a custom of God from which He can exempt Himself in virtue of a stronger reason than the one that moved Him to make use of these norms.

As for the general and particular wills, depending on how we take the matter, it can be said that God does everything in accordance with His most general will, the one in conformity with the most perfect order He chose. But it can also be said that He has particular wills, which are exceptions to the subaltern norms mentioned above; for the most general of the laws of God, by means of which He regulates the whole universe, are without exception.

It can also be said that God wills everything that is an object of His particular will. But as for the objects of His general will, such as the actions of other creatures, particularly of those that are rational, and with which, (i.e. the *actions*) God wishes to concur, we must draw a distinction: if the action is good in itself, it can be said that God wills it and sometimes commands it, even when it does not happen; but if it is evil in itself, and only becomes good by accident, it has to be said that God permits it and not that He wills it, though He concurs in it through the laws of nature established by Him, and because he is able to draw from it greater good. This comes about because the sequence of things, particularly punishment and recompense, corrects its evil nature, and compensates for the evil with interest, so that in the end there is more perfection in all that follows than if none of the evil had happened.

8. IN ORDER TO DISTINGUISH THE ACTIONS OF GOD FROM THOSE OF CREATURES, AN EXPLANATION IS GIVEN OF THE NOTION OF AN INDIVIDUAL SUBSTANCE.

It is rather difficult to distinguish the actions of God from those of creatures as well as the actions and passions of these same creatures. For there are those who think that God does everything, while others imagine that He does no more than conserve the force He has given to creatures. What follows will show how far either of these can be said. Now since, properly speaking, actions belong to individual substances ("actions belong to supposita"), it will be necessary to explain just what such a substance is.

It seems to me that when several predications are attributed to the same subject and this subject is not attributed to any other, this subject is called an individual substance. But that is not enough and such an explanation is merely nominal, so we need to consider what it is to be truly attributed to a particular subject.

Now it is acknowledged that all true predication has some basis in the nature of things, and when a proposition is not an identity, that is, when the predicate is not expressly included in the subject, it must be so included virtually. That is what the Philosophers call *inesse*, when they say that the predicate is in the subject. Thus the subject term must always include that of the predicate, so that whoever understood the notion of the subject perfectly would also judge that the predicate belongs to it.

That being so, we can say that the nature of an individual substance or complete being is to have such a complete notion as to include and entail all the predicates of the subject that notion is attributed to. In contrast, an accident is a being whose notion does not include all that can be attributed to the subject it is attributed to. Thus the circular figure of the ring of Gyges, does not contain everything that makes up the individual notion of this ring. Whereas God sees in it at the same time the foundation and cause for all the predicates that can truly be applied to it, such as that it would be swallowed by a fish and nevertheless returned to its master. I speak here as if this ring were a substance.

9. EACH UNIQUE SUBSTANCE EXPRESSES THE WHOLE UNIVERSE IN ITS OWN WAY, AND INCLUDED IN ITS NOTION ARE ALL THE EVENTS THAT HAPPEN TO IT WITH ALL THEIR CIRCUMSTANCES, AND THE WHOLE SEQUENCE OF EXTERNAL THINGS.

Among several paradoxical conclusions following from this, is that it is not true that two substances are completely alike, differing only numerically, and what St Thomas has to say on this point about angels and intelligences ("in these cases every individual is a lowest species") is true of all substances provided that the specific difference is taken in the way geometers take it in relation to their figures. Likewise, if bodies are substances, their natures cannot possibly consist solely in size, figure and motion: something else is needed. Likewise, a substance can begin only by creation and perish only by annihilation; a substance cannot be divided into two, nor can two substances become one, and so the number of substances does not naturally increase or diminish, though they are frequently transformed.

Moreover every substance is as it were an entire world and a mirror of God, or rather of the whole universe, expressing it in its own way, somewhat as the same town is variously represented according to the different positions of an observer. It can even be said that every substance bears in some way the mark of the infinite wisdom and omnipotence of God, imitating Him as far as it is capable. For it expresses, if only confusedly, all that happens in the universe, past, present and future, and this has some resemblance to an infinite perception or knowledge. And since all other substances in turn express it and are accommodated to it, it can be said to extend its power over all the others in imitation of the omnipotence of the Creator.

10. THERE IS SOME SOUNDNESS TO THE BELIEF IN SUBSTANTIAL FORMS, BUT THESE MAKE NO DIFFERENCE TO THE PHENOMENA, AND SHOULD NOT BE USED TO EXPLAIN PARTICULAR EFFECTS.

It seems that the ancients in distinguishing an *ens per se* from an *ens per accidens* and in introducing substantial forms, as well as the many able people who were accustomed to profound meditations and who taught theology and philosophy centuries ago, many of them praiseworthy for their sanctity, had some knowledge of what we have just said. This is what led them to introduce and uphold the substantial forms so much in disfavour today. But they are neither so far from the truth nor as ridiculous as the common run of our modern philosophers imagine.

I agree that the knowledge of forms is of no use in the details of physics and should not be used for explaining the particulars of phenomena. That is where our scholastics went wrong, and with them the physicians of the past who followed their example, in thinking to account for the properties of bodies by mentioning forms and qualities without taking the trouble to examine their manner of operation. It is as if we were to content ourselves with saying that a clock has the horodictic [time-telling] quality deriving from its form without considering what that consists in. That indeed might be enough for whoever buys the clock, provided he left its maintenance to someone else.

But this shortcoming and misuse of forms should not make us reject something whose knowledge is so necessary in metaphysics that without it, I hold, the first principles cannot be well understood, nor the mind sufficiently raised to the knowledge of incorporeal natures and the wonders of God.

Nevertheless, a geometer has no need to trouble his mind with the famous labyrinth of the composition of the continuum, and neither has any moral philosopher, and still less any legal expert or politician, any need to trouble himself with the great difficulties involved in reconciling the freedom of the will with the providence of God. For the geometer can complete all his demonstrations and the politician conclude all his deliberations without entering into these discussions, important as they are in philosophy and theology. In the same way, a physicist can account for experiments, sometimes by means of simpler experiments carried out before, and sometimes by means of geometrical and mechanical demonstrations, without the need of forms and other general considerations belonging to another sphere. If he employs the extraordinary concurrence of God, or some soul, *arché* or other thing of that nature, he is wandering as far off course as he who tries to introduce the nature of destiny and our liberty into a deliberation about an important practical matter. Men often make this mistake without thinking when they trouble their minds by considering fate, and sometimes they are even diverted from some good resolution or necessary care as a result.

11. THE MEDITATIONS OF THE THEOLOGIANS AND PHILOSOPHERS CALLED "SCHOLASTICS" ARE NOT TO BE DESPISED ENTIRELY.

I know that in claiming in some way to rehabilitate the old philosophy and restore the all but banished substantial forms to which not enough justice has been done to life, I am proposing a big paradox. But I only do this on the supposition that it is possible to speak of bodies as substances. But perhaps I shall not be lightly condemned if it is known that I have long meditated on modern philosophy, and spent much time on physical experiments and geometrical demonstrations, and that I was long persuaded of the vanity of such beings. But I was eventually obliged to take them up again against my will and as if by force. It was as a result of carrying out my own researches that I was made to recognise that our moderns do not do full justice to St Thomas and other great men of those times, and that the opinions of scholastic philosophers and theologians are much more sound than is imagined, as long as they are used appropriately and in their place. I am even convinced that if some exact and reflecting mind took the trouble to clarify and digest their thoughts in the manner of analytical geometry, he would find a treasure store of very important truths which could be demonstrated completely.

12. Notions Defined by Extension Involve Something Imaginary and Cannot Constitute the Essence of Bodies.

But, to take up again the thread of our considerations, I believe that any one who medi-tates on the nature of substance as I have explained it above will find that either bodies are not substances in strict metaphysical rigour (the view indeed of the Platonists), or that the whole nature of body does not consist solely in extension, i.e. in size, shape and motion. On the contrary, something related to souls which is commonly called a "sub-stantial form" has necessarily to be recognised in them, though that makes no more dif-ference to the phenomena than the souls of animals, if they have any. It can even be demonstrated that the notions of size, shape and motion are not so distinct as is imag-ined and that they involve something imaginary and relative to our perceptions, just as colour, heat and other similar qualities also do, (to an even greater extent)—we may doubt that these are truly in the nature of external things. That is why qualities of these kinds could not constitute any substance. And if there were no other principle of iden-tity in body than the one just considered, no body would ever last more than a moment.

Nevertheless, souls and substantial forms of other bodies are very different from intelligent souls, who alone know what they do, and which not only do not naturally perish but even for ever retain the basis of the knowledge of what they are. This makes them liable to punishment and reward, and makes them citizens of the republic of the universe whose monarch is God. It also follows that all other creatures ought to serve them, something we shall discuss more fully presently.

13. Since the Individual Notion of Every Person Includes Once for All Everything That Will Ever Happen to Him, in It Are to be Seen the a Priori Proofs of Each Event, or Rather Why One Happened Rather Than the Other. But Although These Truths are Assured, They Do Not Cease to Be Contingent, Since They Are Based on the Free Will of God or of Creatures. There Are Always Reasons for Their Choices but These Incline Without Necessitating.

But a great difficulty can arise from the foundations laid above, and before proceeding further, we must try to deal with it. We said that the notion of an individual substance includes once for all everything that can ever happen to it, and that by considering this notion, we can see in it everything that can truly be stated about it, just as we can see in the nature of the circle all the properties that can be derived from it. But from that it seems that all events will become fatally necessary that the difference between neces-sary and contingent truths will be destroyed, that all the fate of the Stoics will take the place of liberty, there will no longer be any room for human liberty, and absolute fate will reign over all our actions as well as over all other events in the world. My reply is: we must distinguish between what is certain and what is necessary. Everyone agrees that future contingents are assured since God foresees them, but it is not for all that ad-mitted that they are necessary. But (it will be said) if some conclusion can be infallibly deduced from a definition or notion will be necessary. Now in fact we do maintain that everything that is to happen to a person is already included virtually in his nature or notion, just as the properties of a circle are included in its definition. So the difficulty remains. In order to give a sound answer, I claim that connection or derivation is of two kinds: one is absolutely necessary (its contrary implies a contradiction) and occurs with eternal truths like those of geometry; the other is necessary only *ex hypothesi,* by accident, so to speak, but in itself it is contingent, since its contrary does not imply a contradiction. This connection is based, not on the absolutely pure ideas and God's bare understanding alone, but also on His free decrees and the connection of the universe.

Let us take an example. Since Peter will deny our Lord, that action is included in his notion, for we are supposing it to be in the nature of such a perfect notion to include everything, so that the predicate should be included in it, *ut possit inesse subjecto.* We could say that it is not in virtue of this notion or idea or nature that he must sin, since that only applies to him because God knows everything. But, it will be insisted, his nature or form corresponds to his notion. I reply that it is indeed true and since God imposed this personality on him he must henceforth conform to it. I could reply with the objection of future contingents, for these have as yet no reality outside the understanding and the will, and since God gave them this form in advance, they will have to conform to it all the same.

But I prefer to deal with difficulties than make excuses for them with examples of some other similar difficulties, and what I am going to say will help clarify both. Thus it is here that we must apply the distinction between the kinds of connection. I say that what happens in accordance with these prior conditions is assured, but that it is not necessary; and if he did the opposite, he would be doing nothing impossible in itself though it would be *ex hypothesi* impossible that this should happen. For if someone were capable of completing the whole of the demonstration by virtue of which he proved the connection between the subject Peter and the predicate (namely, his denial), he would show that this fact had its basis in his notion or nature, and that it was reasonable and consequently assured that it should come about; but he would not show that it was necessary in itself, nor that its contrary implied a contradiction. In almost the same way, it is reasonable and assured that God will always do the best, although what is less perfect involves no contradiction in itself.

For it would be found that this demonstration of this predicate of Peter is not as absolute as those of numbers and geometry, but that it supposes the sequence of things freely chosen by God and founded on the first free decree of God, which always leads him to do what is most perfect, as well as on the decree God made (in consequence of the first) concerning human nature, which is that man will always (although freely) do what seems best. Now every truth founded on decrees of this kind is contingent, although certain, since those decrees make no difference to the possibility of things and, as I have already said, although God assuredly always chooses the best, that does not prevent what is less perfect remaining possible in itself, though it does not happen. It is not its impossibility but its imperfection that causes it to be rejected. Nothing is necessary if its contrary is possible.

Hence, we are in a position to meet such difficulties, great as they may appear to be (and indeed they are no less pressing for all others who have ever dealt with this matter,) provided it is fully realised that contingent propositions have reasons for being that way rather than otherwise, or (what comes to the same thing) that there are *a priori* proofs of their truth which make them certain and show that the subject-predicate connection in these propositions has its basis in the nature of each. But these are not necessary demonstrations, since these reasons are only based on the principle of the contingency or of the existence of things, i.e. on what is or seems to be the best of several equally possible things; whereas necessary truths are founded on the principle of contradiction and on the possibility or impossibility of the essences themselves, without regard to the free will of God or of creatures.

14. God Produces Different Substances According
to the Different Views He Has of the Universe.
The Distinctive Nature of Each Substance Ensures,
by the (Mediation) of God, That What Happens to Each
Corresponds to What Happens to All the Others,
Without Them Acting Directly on Each Other.

Having after a fashion come to know what the nature of created substances consists in, we must try to explain their mutual dependence and their actions and passions. Now, in the first place, it is altogether obvious that created substances depend on God who conserves them—and even continually produces them by a kind of emanation, as we do our thoughts. For as God, so to speak, turns on all its sides and in all ways the general system of phenomena which He finds it good to produce to manifest His glory, and as He looks at all the faces of the world in all possible ways—because there is no relation that escapes His omniscience—the result of each view of the universe as if seen from a particular place is a substance expressing the universe in conformity with that view, if God finds it good to make His thought effective and produce this substance. And since the view of God is always true, our perceptions are so too; it is those of our judgements that derive from us that deceive us.

Now we have said above, and it follows from what we have just said, that each substance is like a world on its own, independent of everything else apart from God. Hence all our phenomena, that is, all that can ever happen to us, are consequences of our natures and, since we are free substances, of our wills. Since these phenomena preserve a particular order conforming to our nature or, so to speak, the world within us, so that we are able (to make observations useful for regulating our conduct which are justified by the favourable outcome of future phenomena) and to judge the future by the past without error, this enables us to say that these phenomena are true, without worrying whether they are outside us or whether others perceive them as well. Nevertheless, it is very true that the perceptions or qualities of all substances correspond with each other, so that each, carefully following the particular reasons or laws it has observed, fits in with the other in doing the same, just as when several people agree with each other to be at a particular place at a prearranged day, they can in fact do so if they wish. Now although all express the same phenomena, it does not follow from this that their expressions should be perfectly similar: it is enough that they are proportionate to each other. In the same way several spectators think they have seen the same thing and indeed agree with each other, although each sees and speaks according to his point of view.

Now it is God from whom all substances emanate continually and He sees the universe, not only as they see it, but quite differently from them all as well. He is the only cause of this correspondence between their phenomena, and He alone makes what is peculiar to one public to all, otherwise there would be no connection between them. Hence it can be said in a manner of speaking and in a sense that is good, though remote from ordinary usage that a particular substance never acts on another particular substance and is not acted upon by another either. This follows if we remember that what happens to each is only a consequence of its idea or complete notion alone, since that idea already includes all the predicates or events, and expresses the whole universe. Indeed, nothing can happen to us but thoughts and perceptions, and all our thoughts and our future perceptions are no more than consequences, albeit contingent, of our previous thoughts and perceptions. Hence, if I were capable of considering distinctly everything happening or appearing to me at the present time, I would be able to see therein everything that would ever happen or appear to me. This would not fail, but would happen in any case, if everything outside me were destroyed and only God and myself remained. But as we attribute to other things, as if to causes acting on us, what we perceive in some way in other things, we have to consider the basis of this judgement, and what truth there is in it.

It is above all agreed that if we desire some phenomenon to happen at a certain time and it occurs in the ordinary course of things, we say that we acted and that we were the cause of it, as when I want to, as we say, "move my hand." Also, when it seems to me that by my will something happens to what I call another substance (and that this is the way it would happen as I judge from frequent observation) although it was not willed by it, I judge that this substance is acted upon. I admit this of myself when something happens to me in accordance with the will of another substance. Also, when we will something to happen, and something else follows from it that we did not want, we still say that we did it, provided that we understood how it followed. There are also some phenomena of extension that we attribute to ourselves more particularly and which have their basis *a parte rei* in what is called our body. As everything of importance happening to it (i.e. all the notable changes appearing to us in it) make themselves strongly felt in it, ordinarily at least, we attribute all the passions to this body to ourselves. We do so with very good reason, for even if we did not perceive them at the time, we do not fail to become well aware of the consequences, just as if we had been transported from one place to another while asleep. We also attribute to ourselves the actions of this body, as when we run, hit or fall, and when our body, continuing the motion once begun, has some effect. But I do not attribute to myself what happens to other bodies, because I realise that great changes can happen that I cannot perceive, unless my body is exposed to them in a way I conceive appropriate to that assumption.

So it is quite clear that although all the bodies of the universe belong to us in some way and harmonise with ours, we do not attribute to ourselves what happens to them. For when my body is pushed, I say that I myself have been pushed, but if someone else is pushed, I do not say that I have been pushed, even though I may perceive it and some passion in me may arise from it, since I measure where I am by the place my body is in. And this language is highly reasonable because it is appropriate for clear expression in everyday practice. As for the mind, it can be said briefly that our acts of will and judgements or reasonings are actions while our perceptions or sensations are passions. As for the body, we say that a change that happens to it is an action when it follows from a previous change, but otherwise it is a passion.

In general, to give our terms a meaning that reconciles metaphysics with practice, it can be said that when several powers are affected by the same change the one that passes to a higher degree of perfection or continues in the same acts, while the one that immediately becomes more limited thereby, so that its expressions become more confused, is acted upon.

15. THE ACTION OF ONE FINITE SUBSTANCE ON ANOTHER CONSISTS SOLELY IN THE INCREASE IN THE DEGREE OF ITS EXPRESSION TOGETHER WITH THE DIMINUTION OF THAT OF THE OTHER, IN SO FAR AS GOD HAS MADE THEM CONFORM TO EACH OTHER.

But without getting involved in a long discussion, it is enough for the present to reconcile the language of metaphysics with that of practice by noting that we attribute to ourselves our more clear and distinct perceptions and that we can in general attribute to a substance its more clear and distinct expression and, with reason, the phenomena we express more perfectly, while we attribute to other substances what each best expresses. Thus a substance of infinite extension, in so far as it expresses everything, becomes limited by its more or less perfect manner of expression. Thus in this way it is possible to conceive that substances mutually hinder or limit each other and, consequently, in this sense, to say that they act on each other and, so to speak, are obliged to conform to each other. For it can happen that a change which increases the expression of the one diminishes that of the other. Now, the virtue of a particular substance is to express well the glory of God, and it is there that it is least limited, and everything that exerts its virtue or power, that is when it acts, changes for the better and is extended in so far as it acts. Thus when a change affects several substances (since indeed every change touches all of them), I think that it can be said that the one that thereby passes to a higher degree of perfection or to a more perfect expression exerts its power and acts, while the other one that passes to a lesser degree shows its weakness and is acted upon. So I hold that every action of a substance possessing perception implies some pleasure and every passion some pain, and vice versa. This notwithstanding that it can easily happen that a present advantage is destroyed in what follows. Hence it follows that it is possible to sin by acting or exerting one's power and finding pleasure therein.

16. THE EXTRA ORDINARY CONCURRENCE OF GOD IS INCLUDED
IN THE EXPRESSION OF OUR ESSENCE BECAUSE IT APPLIES
TO EVERYTHING, BUT IT TRANSCENDS THE POWERS OF OUR
NATURE OF DISTINCT EXPRESSION (WHICH IS FINITE
AND FOLLOWS PARTICULAR SUBALTERN NORMS).

All that remains for the present is to explain how it is sometimes possible for God to have influence on men or other substances through an extraordinary or miraculous concurrence, since it seems that everything that has to happen to them is natural in so far as it is a consequence of their substance. But what we said above about miracles in the universe must be remembered: they always conform to the universal laws of the general order, even though these transcend the subordinate norms. And, to the extent that every person or substance is like a little world expressing the great one, it can even be said that this extraordinary concurrence of God is included in the general order of the universe in so far as that is expressed by the nature of this person, but it does not cease to be miraculous and to be beyond the norms. That is why, if everything it expresses is included in our nature, nothing is supernatural with respect to it, for it extends to everything, since an effect always expresses its cause and God is the true cause of substances. But since what our nature expresses more perfectly particularly belongs to it, that is what its power consists in—and since, as I have just explained, it is limited, there are many things that surpass the powers of our natures, and even those of every limited nature. Consequently, to speak more clearly, I say that miracles and the extraordinary acts of God's concurrence have the particular character that they could not be foreseen by the reasoning of any created mind, however enlightened it might be, since the comprehension of the general order surpasses them all, while everything called natural depends on the less general norms creatures can understand. Hence, in order to say nothing of these norms or laws of nature that might cause offence, it would be good to link particular ways of speaking with particular thoughts: whatever includes everything we express could then be called our essence or idea, and since it expresses our union with God, it has no limits and nothing exceeds it. But what is limited in us could be called our nature or power, and in this respect what exceeds the natures of all created substances is supernatural.

17. EXAMPLE OF A SUBALTERN NORM OR LAW OF NATURE;
IN WHICH IT IS SHOWN THAT GOD ALWAYS PRESERVES THE SAME
FORCE, BUT NOT THE SAME QUANTITY OF MOTION . . .
AGAINST THE CARTESIANS AND SOME OTHERS.

I have often mentioned subaltern maxims or laws of nature already, and it would be good to give an example. Our new philosophers commonly make use of that famous rule advanced by Descartes that God always preserves the same quantity of motion in the world. It seems highly plausible indeed, and in the past I held it to be indubitable. But I have since come to recognise wherein lay its error. It is that Descartes and many other able mathematicians thought that the quantity of motion (i.e. the speed times the size of the mobile) was the same thing as the force, or at least expressed it perfectly, or geometrically speaking, that the forces are in compound proportion of the speeds and the bodies. Now it is obvious indeed that the same force should always be preserved in the universe. So, when we attend to the phenomena with care, we see clearly that mechanical perpetual motion does not occur, because then the force of a machine, which is continually being slightly diminished by friction, and must consequently soon cease, would be replaced and so would increase of itself without any new impulsion from outside. We also note that the force of a body is diminished solely to the extent that it gives some of it to neighbouring bodies or to its own parts in so far as these have independent motions.

Thus they thought that what can be said of force could also be said of quantity of motion. But, to show the difference, I suppose that a body falling from a particular height acquires the force needed to climb up again, if its direction of travel should take it that way, unless there are hindrances. For example, a pendulum would rise right back again to the height it had fallen from if the resistance of the air and other small obstacles did not somehow diminish the force acquired.

I suppose also that as much force is needed to raise a body A of one pound a height CD of four fathoms as to raise a body B of four pounds a height EF of one fathom. All this is accepted by our new philosophers.

Hence, it is manifest that body (A), after falling from the height CD has acquired as much force precisely as body (B) after falling from the height EF. For when body (B) has arrived at F and has the force to climb back to E (by the first supposition), it has in consequence the force to carry a body of four pounds, that is its own body, to the height EF of one fathom, and similarly, when body (A) has reached D and has the force to

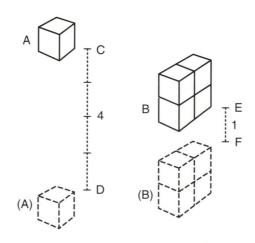

climb back to C, it has the force to carry a body of one pound, that is its own body, to the height CD of four fathoms. Hence (by the second supposition), the forces of the two bodies are equal.

Now let us see whether the quantity of motion is also the same in both cases: but it is here that there will be surprise at finding a very great difference. For it has been demonstrated by Galileo that the speed acquired in the fall CD is twice that acquired in the fall EF, though the height is quadruple. If then, we multiply the body (A), in the proportion 1, by the speed, in the proportion 2, the product or quantity of motion will be as 2, and if on the other hand, we multiply the body (B), which is as 4, by its speed, which is as 1, then the product or quantity of motion will be as 4. Hence the quantity of motion of body (A) at point D is half the quantity of motion of body (B) at point F, though their forces are equal. Hence there is a great difference between the quantity of motion and the force, as was to be proved.

From this it is seen that the force must be measured by the quantity of the effect it can produce, e.g. by the height to which a heavy body of a particular size and kind can be raised, something very different from the speed that can be given it, and that to give it twice the speed more than twice the force is needed.

Nothing is simpler than this proof. Descartes only fell into error here because he trusted too much in his thoughts before they had matured enough with a confidence based on the happy success of some of his thoughts and on his experience of the penetration of his mind, which rendered him rather too rash in the end. But I am astonished that his followers have not recognised this error since, and I fear that little by little they begin to imitate the Peripatetics they so make fun of, and that like them they grow accustomed to consulting the books of their master rather than reason and nature.

18. IMPORTANCE OF THE DISTINCTION BETWEEN FORCE
AND QUANTITY OF MOTION INTER ALIA IN DECIDING THAT WE
MUST HAVE RECOURSE TO METAPHYSICAL CONSIDERATIONS
DISTINCT FROM EXTENSION TO EXPLAIN THE NATURE OF BODIES.

This consideration of the distinction of force from quantity of motion is important enough, not only in physics and mechanics in the discovery of the true laws of nature and rules of motions, and even in the correction of several practical errors that have slipped into the writings of some able mathematicians, but also in metaphysics, in the better understanding of the principles of things. For motion, if its precise formal content only—i.e. change of place—is considered, is not a completely real thing, and when several bodies mutually exchange their places, it is impossible to determine from these changes alone which of them ought to have motion or rest attributed to it, as I could show geometrically if I wanted to dwell on this point now.

But the force or direct cause of these changes is something more real, and there is some basis for attributing it to one body rather than to another, and it is only thereby that we can know which one the motion is best attributed to. Now, this force is something different from size and motion, and it can be concluded from this that what is conceived in bodies does not consist solely in extension and its modifications, contrary to the conviction of our moderns. Hence, too, we are obliged to re-establish some of the beings or forms banished by them. And although all the particular phenomena of corporeal nature can be explained mathematically or mechanically by those who understand them, it nevertheless appears more and more that the general principles of corporeal mechanical nature itself are metaphysical rather than geometrical, belonging to forms or indivisible

natures functioning as causes of the matter or extension rather than to corporeal or extended mass—a reflection capable of reconciling the mechanical philosophy of the
moderns with the circumspection of some intelligent well-intentioned people who fear
quite reasonably that we are moving too far from immaterial beings to the disadvantage
of piety.

19. USEFULNESS OF FINAL CAUSES IN PHYSICS.

As I do not like to judge people's intentions, or only do so favourably if I can, I am not
accusing our new philosophers of impiety when they claim to banish final causes in
physics. Nevertheless I am obliged to admit that I do not recognise their usual intelligence and prudence therein and that the consequences of this opinion seem dangerous
to me, particularly when it is connected with that refuted by me at the beginning of this
discourse, which seems to lead to their removal altogether, as if God never had any aim,
whether good or active, or as if the good were not the object of His will. . . . For my
part, I hold on the contrary that it is just there that we have to seek the principle of all
existences and even of the laws of nature, since God always intends what is best and
most perfect.

I am happy to admit that we are liable to error when we want to determine the
aims and counsels of God, but that is only when we try to restrict them to a particular
plan, in the belief that He has only one single thing in view, whereas in fact He considers everything at once. Thus, when we think that God made the world for us alone, we
are greatly mistaken, although it is true that He made it in its totality for us and that
there is nothing in the world that does not affect us and does not also conform to His
concerns for us, in accordance with the above principles. Thus, when we see some good
effect or perfection happening or resulting from the works of God, we can certainly say
that God intended it, for He does nothing by chance and unlike us does not sometimes
fail to do well. That is why, far from being in an error here, akin to that of the overly political who attribute excessive refinement to the designs of princes, or to that of commentators who search for too much erudition in their authors, we cannot attribute too
many reflections to this infinite Wisdom, and there is no matter in which there is less
danger of error as long as we only affirm and avoid negative propositions here that limit
the plans of God.

Everyone who sees the admirable structure of animals is led to recognise the wisdom of the Author of things, and I advise those with any feeling of piety or even of true
Philosophy to avoid the expression of some would-be tough minds who say that we see
because we happen to have eyes, without noting that the eyes were made to see. If we
are seriously involved in these opinions that assign everything to the necessity of matter or to a particular chance (although both must seem ridiculous to those who understand what we have explained above), we will inevitably fail to recognise an intelligent
Author of nature. For it is ridiculous to introduce a Sovereign Intelligence as the Ordainer of things and not use His wisdom to account for phenomena. As if, in accounting
for the conquest of a great prince in capturing an important position, a historian tried to
say that it was because the particles of the gunpowder liberated by lighting the fuse escaped at a speed capable of pushing a hard heavy body against the walls of the position,
while the branches of the particles composing the copper of the cannon were sufficiently intertwined not to be separated by this speed, instead of showing how the foresight of the victor caused him to choose the appropriate time and means, and how his
power overcame all the obstacles.

20. Remarkable Passage of Socrates in Plato Against Excessively Materialistic Philosophers.

This point reminds me of a fine passage of Socrates in Plato's *Phaedo*. In marvellous agreement with my thoughts on this point, it seems to be written expressly against our excessively materialistic philosophers. So this account made me want to translate it, and though it is rather long, perhaps this sample will give one of us the occasion to share many other fine sound thoughts from the writings of the great man.

"One day," he said, "I heard someone read a book of Anaxagoras, where there were these words 'that an Intelligent Being was the cause of all things, and that He arranged and adorned them.' I was extremely pleased with that, for I thought that if the world was the result of an Intelligence, everything would have been made in the most perfect way possible. That is why I thought that he who wanted to explain why things came to be, perished or subsisted had to search for what suited the perfection of each. Thus man would only have to consider in himself or in some other thing, what was best or most perfect, alone. For he who knew the most perfect would easily decide thereby what was imperfect, since there is only one true knowledge of both.

"In view of all this, I rejoiced to have found a master able to teach the reason of things: whether, for example, the earth was round or flat, and why it was best that way rather than otherwise. . . . Moreover, I expected that when he said that the earth was or was not at the centre of the universe, he would explain to me why that was the most suitable. And when he said the same of the sun, the moon, the stars and their motions. . . . And finally, after showing what was suitable to each thing individually, he would show me what was best in general.

"Full of this hope, I took and skimmed through the books of Anaxagoras with great eagerness, but I was far from my expectation, for I was surprised to see that he made no use of this governing Intelligence, set out in advance, that he spoke no more of the adornment and the perfection of things, and introduced some rather implausible ethereal matters.

"In this he was rather like the man who said that Socrates did things intelligently, but when he came to explaining in particular the causes of his actions, thereupon said that he was sitting here because he had a body composed of bone, flesh and nerves, that the bones were solid, but had gaps and joints, that the nerves could be tensed or relaxed, and that was why the body was flexible and I was sitting. Or if he wanted to explain the present speech, he had recourse to the air, to vocal and aural organs and like things, while forgetting the true causes, that is that the Athenians thought it better to condemn than to acquit me, and I for my part thought it better to sit here than to take flight. For, by my faith, these nerves and these bones would long since be with the Boeotians and the Megarans, if I had not found it more just and more honest for me to suffer the penalty the fatherland wants to impose on me than live elsewhere a wanderer in exile. That is why it is unreasonable to call these bones and nerves and their motions causes.

"It is true that whoever said that I could not do all this without bones and nerves would be right, but the true cause is something else . . . and that is no more than a condition without which the cause could not be the cause. . . .

"People who say no more than, for example, that the motions of the bodies surrounding the earth support the earth where it is, forget that the divine power arranges everything in the finest way, and do not understand that it is the good and the beautiful that join, form and preserve the world. . . ." Thus far Socrates, for the things about ideas or forms that follow in Plato are not less excellent but a bit more difficult.

21. IF THE RULES OF MECHANICS DEPENDED ON GEOMETRY ALONE WITHOUT METAPHYSICS, THE PHENOMENA WOULD BE QUITE DIFFERENT.

Now, since the wisdom of God has always been recognised in the details of the mechanical structures of particular bodies, it is very necessary that it should also be shown in the general set-up of the world and the constitution of the laws of nature. This is so true that the counsels of this Wisdom are observed in the laws of motion in general. For if there were nothing else to bodies but an extended mass and nothing to motion but change of place, and if everything had to and could be deduced from these definitions alone by geometrical necessity, it would follow, as I have shown elsewhere, that the least body would give the same speed as its own to the largest resting body it met without losing any of its own, and many other rules of this sort would have to be accepted, such as are altogether contrary to the construction of a system. But the decree of the divine wisdom to preserve always the same total force and direction has provided for this.

I even find that many natural effects can be demonstrated doubly, i.e. through the efficient cause and separately through the final cause as well, by using for example the decree of God to produce His effect by the simplest and most determinate ways, as I have shown elsewhere in my account of the rules of catoptrics and dioptrics, and I shall say more of it below.

22. RECONCILIATION OF THE TWO WAYS BY FINAL AND EFFICIENT CAUSES IN DEFENCE OF BOTH THOSE WHO EXPLAIN NATURE MECHANICALLY AND THOSE WHO HAVE RECOURSE TO INCORPOREAL NATURES.

It is good to note this point to reconcile those who hope to explain mechanically the formation of the first tissues of an animal and the complete machine of its parts with those who account for the same structure by final causes. Both are good and both can be useful, not only for admiring the artifice of the great Workman, but also in discovering something useful in physics and medicine. Authors who follow these different routes should not be hard on each other.

For I see that those who concentrate on explaining the beauty of divine Anatomy laugh at others who imagine that an apparently fortuitous motion of particular fluids can make such a beautiful variety of members, and call such people rash and profane, while on the other hand the latter call the former simple and superstitious like the ancients who took it that the physicists were impious when they held that it was not Jupiter that thundered but some matter in the clouds. The best thing would be to unite both considerations, for, to use a vulgar comparison, the skill of a workman is recognised and praised not only by showing what designs he had when he made the parts of his machine, but also by explaining the tools he used to make each part, particularly when these tools are simple and ingeniously contrived. *God is skilful enough an artisan* to produce a machine a thousand times still more ingenious than that of our body if that were possible, using only a few simple enough fluids expressly formed so that only the ordinary laws of nature are needed to sort them out as necessary to produce such an admirable effect, but it is also true that this would not happen if God were not the Author of nature.

I find, nevertheless, that the way of efficient causes is while indeed more profound and in one way more direct and *a priori,* on the other hand rather difficult when we get down to details and I think that our Philosophers are most often still rather far from that. In contrast, the way of final causes is easier and is moreover often helpful in guessing important and useful truths that would have been a long time in the searching by the former more physical route, and of this Anatomy can furnish important examples. I also hold that Snell, the first discoverer of the rules of refraction, would have taken a long time to find them if he had tried to find out first how light was formed. But he seems to have followed the method the ancients used in catoptrics, that of final causes in fact. For, in the search for the easiest way of conducting a ray from one given point to another by reflection at a given plane (supposing that this is nature's design), they discovered the equality of the angles of incidence and reflection, as can be seen in a little treatise of Heliodorus of Larissa and elsewhere. That is what in my opinion Snell, and after him (though without knowing anything about him) Fermat, applied more ingeniously to refraction. For when in the same media the rays observe the same proportion of sines which is also that of the resistances of the media, it turns out to be the easiest, or at least the most determinate way of passing from a given point in one medium to a given point in the other. The demonstration Descartes tried to give of this same theorem by the way of efficient causes is far from being as good. At least there are grounds for suspecting that he would never have found it that way if he had not heard something of Snell's discovery in Holland.

23. Returning to Immaterial Substances; the Explanation of How God Acts on the Understanding of Minds and of Whether We Always Have an Idea of What We Think.

I have found it relevant to insist somewhat on these considerations concerning final causes, incorporeal natures and an Intelligent Cause in relation to bodies, to make known their use even in physics and mathematics. On the one hand, this is to purge the mechanical philosophy of the profanity imputed to it. On the other hand it is to raise the minds of our philosophers from mere material considerations to more noble meditations. It is now time to return from bodies to immaterial natures, to minds in particular, and to say something of the ways God uses to illumine them and act on them, for we must not doubt that here too there are laws of nature, a point I could discuss more fully elsewhere. For now, it is enough to touch a little on ideas, on whether we see all things in God, and on how God is our light.

Now, it is relevant to note that several errors are occasioned by the misuse of ideas. For when we reason on something we imagine we have an idea of it, and on that foundation some recent authors have built a demonstration of God that is, rigorously speaking, very imperfect. For, they say, I must have an idea of God or of a perfect being, since I am thinking of Him, and it is impossible to think without an idea. Now the idea of this Being includes all the perfections and existence is one of these, so that consequently He exists. But as we often think of impossible chimerae, such as the ultimate degree of speed or the greatest number or the meeting of the conchoid [a plane curve in geometry] with its base or rule, this reasoning is not enough. Hence in this sense a person can say he has true or false ideas according as the thing in question is possible or not, and it is only when we are assured of its possibility that we can boast of having an idea of the thing. Thus the above argument proves at least that God necessarily exists if He is possible. This is indeed an excellent privilege of the divine nature: to need only its possibility or essence to exist in fact, just what is called an *Ens a se*.

24. JUST WHAT IS CLEAR OR OBSCURE, DISTINCT OR CONFUSED, ADEQUATE AND INTUITIVE OR SUPPOSITIVE KNOWLEDGE, AND WHAT ARE NOMINAL, REAL, CAUSAL AND ESSENTIAL DEFINITIONS.

The better to understand the nature of ideas, we have to touch a little on the varieties of knowledge. When I know only through experience that something is possible, because everything that exists is possible, my knowledge is confused. It is in this way that we know bodies and their qualities. But when I can prove a priori that something is possible, this knowledge is distinct. When I can recognise one thing among others without being able to say in what its *differentiae* or properties consist, my knowledge is confused. Thus it is that we sometimes know *clearly* without being in any doubt at all whether a poem or picture is well or badly made, because there is an I don't know what that satisfies or shocks us. But only when I can explain the marks available to me is my knowledge called *distinct*. Such is the knowledge of the assayer who discerns the true and the false by particular tests or marks comprising the definition of gold.

But there are degrees of distinct knowledge, for the notions that enter the definition would ordinarily themselves need definition and are only confusedly known. But when every thing that enters a definition or distinct item of knowledge is distinctly known right back to the primitive notions, I call this knowledge *adequate,* and when my mind understands all the primitive ingredients of a notion all at once and distinctly, then it has an intuitive knowledge of it, something very rare since most human knowledge is confused or even *suppositive.*

It is also good to distinguish nominal definitions from real ones. I refer to a nominal definition when it is still possible to doubt that the notion defined is possible. Thus, for example, when I say that an endless screw is a solid line whose parts are congruent or can coincide with each other, whoever did not otherwise know what an endless screw was could doubt the possibility of such a line, though indeed it was a reciprocal property of an endless screw, since the other lines whose parts are congruent are planar (the circumference of the circle and the straight line only), that is they can be drawn *in a plane.* This shows that every reciprocal property can be used in a nominal definition, whereas when the property makes known the possibility of the thing, it makes the definition real. As long as we have a mere nominal definition, we could never be sure of the consequences drawn from it, for if it concealed some contradiction or impossibility, contrary conclusions could be drawn from it. That is why truths do not depend on names and are not arbitrary as held by some new philosophers.

25. IN WHAT CASE OUR KNOWLEDGE IS JOINED TO THE CONTEMPLATION OF THE IDEA.

Now it is obvious that we have no idea of a notion when it is impossible. And when our knowledge is merely *suppositive,* when we have the idea we do not contemplate it, for such a notion is known only in the same way as those that are occultly impossible, and if it is possible it is not learned by that method of knowing. For example, when I think of a thousand, or of chiliagon [a group of one thousand things], I often do so without contemplating the idea, as when I say that a thousand is ten times a hundred without putting myself to the trouble of thinking what ten and a hundred are. That is because I *suppose* I know it and see no need for the present to pause to conceive it. Thus it can easily happen, as indeed it does often enough, that I am in error with respect to a notion

I suppose or believe I understand, although in truth it is impossible, or at least incompatible with the others I join it to. Whether or not I am in error, this suppositive way of conceiving remains the same. Hence, it is only when our knowledge of confused things is *clear* or our knowledge of distinct things intuitive, that we contemplate the complete idea of them.

26. We Have All Ideas in Us; Plato's Notion of Reminiscence.

If we are to conceive properly what an idea is, we must avoid an ambiguity. For there are some who take the idea to be the form or way of distinguishing our thoughts. On this view we have the idea in our minds only to the extent that we think of it, and whenever we think of it again, we have ideas of the same thing different from though similar to the previous ones. But it seems that others take the idea to be an immediate object of thought, or some permanent form remaining when we do not contemplate it. Indeed, there is always in our souls the capacity to conceive any nature or form whatever, when the opportunity of thinking of it presents itself. I think that this capacity of our souls, to the extent that it expresses some nature, form or essence, is properly speaking the idea of the thing, in us and always in us, whether we think of it or not. For our soul expresses God and the universe, and all essences as well as all existences.

This follows from my principles, for nothing enters our minds naturally from outside, and it is a bad habit of ours to think as if our souls received some messenger—species or had gates and windows. We have all the forms in our minds, for all time even, because the mind always expresses all its future thoughts, and already thinks confusedly everything it will ever think distinctly. Nothing could be taught us whose idea was not already present in our minds as the matter from which this thought was formed.

That is what Plato understood so well when he put forward his doctrine of reminiscence, which is very sound provided we take it the right way and purge it of the error of pre-existence, and do not imagine that the soul has to have once known and distinctly thought what it is now learning and thinking. He also confirmed his opinion by a beautiful experiment. He introduced a little boy in his dialogue called *Meno* whom he led insensibly into the most difficult geometrical truths concerning incommensurables, without teaching him anything, merely putting relevant questions in order. This shows that our souls have virtual knowledge of everything. They need only attention to know the truths, and consequently have at least the truths on which these truths depend. It can even be said, if the latter are taken for the relations of ideas, that they already possess these truths.

27. In What Sense Our Souls May Be Compared to Empty Tablets, and How Our Notions Come from the Senses.

Aristotle preferred to compare our souls to tablets that were still bare with space for writing on, and he claimed that nothing was in our understanding that did not come from the senses. As is the way with Aristotle, this is more in conformity with popular notions, whereas Plato goes deeper. Nevertheless, such everyday expressions or practical sayings are liable to pass into common usage, almost as with the followers of Copernicus who continue to say that the sun rises and sets. I often find, even, that a good sense can be given to them in accordance with which there is nothing wrong with them. Just as I have already remarked on the way it is possible to say truly that particular substances act on each other, in this same sense it can be said that we receive some knowledge from outside by the ministry of the senses, because some external things contain, or more particularly express, the reasons determining our souls to particular thoughts. But when we are concerned with the accuracy of metaphysical truths, it is important to recognise the extent and independence of our souls. This goes infinitely further than is vulgarly supposed, although in the ordinary course of life only what is more certainly perceived and belongs to us in a particular way is attributed to it, since there is no purpose in going further.

Nevertheless, it would be good to choose special terms for both senses to avoid ambiguity. Hence, expressions in our souls, whether conceived or not, can be called *ideas,* while those we conceive or form can be called *notions* or *concepts.* But however we take it, it is always false to say that all our notions come from the senses called external, since the one I have of myself, and of my thoughts, and consequently of being, substance, action, identity and many others, comes from internal experience.

28. GOD ALONE IS THE IMMEDIATE OBJECT OF OUR PERCEPTIONS EXISTING OUTSIDE US, FOR HE ALONE IS OUR LIGHT.

Now, in the rigour of metaphysical truth, there is no external cause acting on us but God alone, and He alone communicates himself to us directly in virtue of our continual dependence. It follows from this that there is no other external object touching our souls and exciting our perceptions directly. So it is only in virtue of the continual action of God on us that we have in our souls the ideas of everything, i.e. because every effect expresses its cause and hence the essence of our souls is a particular expression, imitation, or image of the essence, thought and will of God and of all the ideas included in Him. Hence, it can be said that God alone is our immediate object outside us, and that it is in Him that we see all things. For example, when we see the sun and the stars, it is God who gave us them and preserves their ideas in us, and in fact determines us to think of them at the time at which our senses are disposed in a particular way, through His ordinary concurrence and in accordance with the laws established by Him. God is the sun and light of souls, "the light enlightening every man born into the world." It is not just today that people are of this opinion. After Holy Scripture and the Fathers—always more for Plato than for Aristotle—I recall noticing once that in the time of the Scholastics some believed that God was the light of the soul and, in their way of speaking, "the active intellect of the rational soul." The Averroists gave this a bad meaning, but others such as, I think, William of St. Amour doctor of the Sorbonne and several mystical theologians, took it in a manner worthy of God and capable of raising the soul to the knowledge of its good.

29. NEVERTHELESS WE THINK DIRECTLY BY OUR OWN IDEAS AND NOT BY THOSE OF GOD.

Nevertheless I am not of the opinion of some able philosophers who seem to maintain that our very ideas are in God, and not at all in us. In my opinion, this comes about because they have still not pondered enough what we have just explained concerning substances, nor the entire extent and independence of our souls (which means that they include everything happening to them and express the essence of God, and with Him all possible and actual beings, like an effect its cause). Also, it is inconceivable that I should think by means of the thoughts of someone else. It is very necessary that an effect should express its cause and it is also very necessary that the soul should be actually affected in a particular way when it thinks of something and that it should have in advance, not only the passive power of being affected in this way, something already determined, but also an active power, in virtue of which there has always been in its nature the marks of the future production of that thought and dispositions to produce it when the time came. All this already includes the idea contained in that thought.

30. HOW GOD INCLINES WITHOUT NECESSITATING; WE HAVE NO RIGHT TO COMPLAIN, AND WE MUST NOT ASK WHY JUDAS SINS SINCE THIS FREE ACTION IS INCLUDED IN HIS NOTION, ONLY WHY JUDAS THE SINNER IS ADMITTED TO EXISTENCE IN PREFERENCE TO OTHER POSSIBLE PERSONS. THE ORIGIN OF EVIL COMES FROM THIS, THE ORIGINAL IMPERFECTION BEFORE SIN, AND THE DEGREES OF GRACE.

Concerning the action of God on the human will, there are many rather difficult questions that would take time to pursue here. Nevertheless, in outline, this is what can be said. When God concurs in our actions, He ordinarily does no more than follow the laws of nature He has established, i.e. He preserves and continually produces our nature, so that the thoughts spontaneously and naturally or freely happen to us in the order carried by the notion of our individual substance, within which they could have been foreseen from all eternity. Moreover, in virtue of the decree that the will should always tend towards the apparent good, and so express or imitate God's will in certain particular respects in respect of which this apparent good always has something of the true, He determines our will to choose what seems the best without nonetheless necessitating it. For, absolutely speaking, in so far as it may be opposed to necessity, our will is indifferent and has the power to do otherwise or to suspend its action altogether, since both are and remain possible.

Hence it falls to the soul to take precautions against the appearances taking it by surprise by means of a firm resolve to reflect and to refuse to act or judge on particular occasions without thorough deliberation. Nevertheless it is true and even certain from all eternity that a particular soul will not use this power on one such occasion. But who could do anything about it or do other than complain about himself? For all complaints after the fact are unjust when they would have been unjust before. Now would this soul, shortly before sinning, be in the right to complain of God, who has not determined him to flee from the sin as if He had determined him to sin? Since God's determinations in these matters are unforeseeable, how does he know himself to be determined to sin, unless in fact he is already actually sinning? It is only a matter of not willing, and God could propose no easier or juster condition. Moreover, any judge stops only to consider how far a man's will is bad without searching for the reasons disposing him to have a bad will. But perhaps it is certain from all eternity that I will sin? Answer yourself· perhaps not. Do not think about what you cannot know and cannot enlighten you, but act in accordance with the duty you know.

But, someone else will ask, whence comes it that that man will certainly do this sin? The answer is easy: otherwise he would not be that man. For God sees for all time that there will be a certain Judas whose notion, or idea God has of him, contains this future free action. Hence the only question that remains is why such a Judas, the traitor, who is merely a possible in the idea of God actually exists. But to that question there is no answer to be expected here below, unless that in general we must say that since God thought it good for him to exist, despite the sin he foresaw this evil must be repaid with interest in the universe, that God will obtain a greater good from it; and that in all He will find this sequence of things including the existence of this sinner the most perfect of all the other possible ones. But to explain in all cases the admirable economy of this choice is not possible while we are travellers in this vale of tears in this world. It is enough to know without understanding it. It is time here to recognise "the height of the riches," the width and depth of the divine wisdom, without seeking a detail involving these infinite considerations.

Nevertheless, it is clear that God is not the cause of evil. For not only did original sin take hold of the soul after the loss of innocence but before then there was a limitation or original imperfection common to the natures of all creatures making them capable of sin or liable to fail. Thus there is no more difficulty with regard to the supralapsarians* than with the others. In my opinion, it is to this that the opinion of St Augustine and other authors that the root of evil is in nothingness should be reduced, i.e. in the privation or the limitation of creatures that God graciously remedies by giving them the degree of perfection it pleases Him to give. Whether ordinary or extraordinary, this grace of God has its degrees and measures, always in itself efficacious in producing a proportionate effect. Moreover it is always sufficient, not only to guarantee us against sin, but to produce salvation, if the man joins himself to it with his will, though it is not always sufficient to surmount human inclinations, otherwise it would depend on nothing more, and that is reserved to the absolutely efficacious grace alone that is always victorious whether by itself or by the congruity of circumstances.

31. THE FOREKNOWLEDGE OF MERIT, THE DISPENSING OF GRACE, THE MOTIVES OF ELECTION, THE MIDDLE KNOWLEDGE, THE ABSOLUTE DECREE; THAT EVERYTHING REDUCES TO THE REASON WHY GOD CHOSE A PARTICULAR POSSIBLE PERSON FOR EXISTENCE, WHOSE NOTION INCLUDES THAT PARTICULAR SEQUENCE OF GRACES AND FREE ACTIONS, SO THAT ALL THE DIFFICULTIES ARE REMOVED AT ONCE.

In the end, the graces of God are graces pure and simple over which creatures have no claim. However, just as when we are giving an account of the action of God in dispensing these graces it is not enough to have recourse to His foresight, whether absolute or conditional, of the future actions of men, so we must not imagine absolute decrees with no reasonable motive. As regards God's foresight of faith and good works, it is very true that God has elected only those whose faith and charity He foresaw, "those He foreknew He would give faith to," but the same question returns: why God will give the grace of faith and good works to some rather than to others. As for this middle knowledge of God's, the foresight, not of good works, but of their matter and predisposition, or of what the man would contribute from his side (since it is true that there is diversity on the human side wherever there is on the side of grace, and since indeed, although man needs to be excited towards the good and converted, it is very necessary that he should also play his part here after the fact) some people think that it could be said that since God sees what man would do without grace or extraordinary assistance, or at least

*[Calvinists who believe that election to heaven or hell was a part of God's original plan.]

what he will have on his side apart from grace, He could resolve to give grace to those whose natural disposition was the best or at any rate the least imperfect or least evil. But if that was the case, it could be said that these natural dispositions, in so far as they are good, are still the effect of an act of grace, even if an ordinary one, since God has advantaged some more than others. And since He well knows that these natural advantages He gives will provide the motive for grace or extraordinary assistance, does it not follow from the doctrine that truly everything in the end reduces to His mercy?

Hence, I believe (since we do not know how much or how God takes account of natural dispositions in dispensing grace) that the most accurate and certain thing to say is, as already noted and in conformity with our principles, that among the possible beings there should be the person of Peter or John whose notion or idea contains the whole sequence of ordinary and extraordinary graces and all the other events along with their circumstances, and that it pleased God to choose him from among an infinity of other equally possible persons for actual existence. After that it seems that there is no more to ask and that all the difficulties disappear.

For, considering this single great question, why it pleased God to choose one from so many other possible persons, we would have to be unreasonable indeed not to be satisfied with the general reasons given, for which the detail is beyond our reach. So, we should not have recourse to an absolute decree, which is unreasonable since there is no reason for it, or to reasons that do not succeed in resolving the difficulty. Instead the best will be to say with St Paul that there are certain grand reasons for this unknown to mortals and founded in the general order whose aim is the greatest perfection of the universe, and that God has observed these. It is to this that the motives of the glory of God and the manifestation of His justice reduce, as well as His mercy and His perfections generally, and finally that immense depth of His riches Paul's soul was enchanted with.

32. USEFULNESS OF THESE PRINCIPLES IN MATTERS OF PIETY AND RELIGION.

For the rest, it seems that the thoughts we have just explained, particularly the grand principle of the perfection of the operations of God and the notion of the substance including all the events with all their circumstances, far from harming religion, serve to confirm it, removing very great difficulties, inflaming souls with a divine love and raising minds to the knowledge of incorporeal substances to a much greater extent than the hypotheses we have seen up to now. For it is clear that just as thoughts depend on our substance, all other substances depend on God, that God is all in all, and that He is intimately united with all creatures (though to the extent of their perfection), and that He alone determines them externally by His influence. And if to act is to determine directly, it can be said in this sense, in the language of metaphysics, that God operates on me and is alone able to do me good or ill, while other substances are nothing but occasional causes, for the reason that as God considers all of them, He distributes His acts of goodness and obliges them to conform to each other. Also, God alone makes the connection and communication of substances, and it is by Him that phenomena of any given substance meet and fit with those of the others, and consequently that there is reality in our perceptions. But in practice action is attributed to particular occasional causes in the sense explained above, because it is not always necessary to mention the universal cause in particular cases.

It is seen also that every substance has a perfect spontaneity (which in intelligent substances becomes liberty): that everything that happens to it is a consequence of its ideas or being, and that it is determined by nothing but God alone. That is why a person of noble mind whose sanctity is greatly revered used to say that the soul must often think as if there were only God and it in the world.

Now nothing makes immortality more completely comprehensible than this independence and extent of the soul. It protects it absolutely from all external things, since it alone constitutes the whole world and, with God, suffices to itself. It is also impossible for it to perish other than by annihilation, and impossible for the world (of which it is a living and perpetual expression) to destroy itself. Hence, it is not possible for the changes in that extended mass called our body to do anything to our soul, or for the disappearance of that body to destroy what is indivisible.

33. EXPLANATION OF THE UNION OF SOUL AND BODY SOMETHING ONCE THOUGHT INEXPLICABLE OR MIRACULOUS, AND THE ORIGIN OF CONFUSED PERCEPTIONS.

Also clear is the unexpected solution of that great mystery of the union of soul and body, i.e. how it happens that the actions and passions of the one are accompanied by the actions and passions, or rather appropriate phenomena, of the other. For there is no way of conceiving any influence of the one on the other, and it is unreasonable simply to have recourse to the extraordinary operation of the universal cause in something ordinary and particular. But here is the true reason. We have said that everything happening to the soul and to every substance is a consequence of its notion. Hence the very idea or essence of the soul makes all its appearances or perceptions arise spontaneously out of its own nature, and just so, that they answer of themselves to what happens in the whole universe, though particularly in the body assigned to it, because in a way and for a time, it is in accordance with the relation of other bodies to its own that the soul expresses the state of the universe. This shows yet again how our bodies belong to us without nevertheless being attached to our essences. I believe that persons able to meditate will see advantage in our principles in just this, that it is easy to see in what exactly the connection between soul and body—apparently inexplicable by any other means—consists.

It can also be seen that the perceptions of our senses, even when they are clear, must necessarily contain some confused sensations. For as all the bodies in the universe are in sympathy, ours receive the impressions of all the others. Although our senses relate to everything, it is not possible for our souls to attend to all individually, and that is why our confused sensations are the result of a variety, altogether infinite, of perceptions. It is almost like the confused murmur heard by those approaching the shores of the sea that arises from the accumulation of the reverberations of innumerable waves. Now if of several perceptions (not coming together to become a single one) none stands out above the others, and if they make almost equally strong impressions, or are equally capable of determining the attention of the soul, it can only register them confusedly.

34. THE EXCELLENCE OF MINDS COMPARED WITH OTHER SUBSTANCES OR SUBSTANTIAL FORMS. THE IMMORTALITY CALLED FOR IMPLIES MEMORY.

One thing I do not propose to decide is whether in metaphysical rigour bodies are substances or are no more than *true* phenomena like the rainbow, nor consequently whether there are substances, souls or substantial forms that are not intelligent. But if we suppose that bodies like man that constitute unities in themselves are substances and have substantial forms, we are obliged to admit that these souls and substantial forms could no more entirely perish than atoms if there are any or ultimate particles of matter can, in the opinion of other philosophers. For though it may become quite different, no substance perishes. Although more imperfectly than minds, they too express the whole universe. But the principal difference is that they do not know what they are nor what they are doing. Consequently, since they have no power of reflection, they are unable to discover necessary and universal truths. It is also for want of reflection on themselves that they have no moral qualities, so that, when we consider how a caterpillar changes into a butterfly through almost a thousand transformations, it comes to the same for morals and practice as saying that they perish, as can indeed be said physically (as we say of bodies that they perish by corruption). But the intelligent soul that knows what it is, and is capable of pronouncing this me which says so much, not only remains the same metaphysically to a greater extent than the others, but it also remains morally the same and constitutes the same personality. For it is the memory and knowledge of this me that makes it liable to punishment and reward. Also, the immortality called for both in morality and religion does not consist merely in that perpetual subsistence proper to all substances. For without the memory of what has been, there would be nothing desirable about it. Let us suppose that some poor wretch suddenly became King of China, but only on condition that he forgot what he had been, as if he had just been reborn: does that not come to the same in practice, or in the effects that could be registered, as if he had to be annihilated and a King of China created at the same instant aNd at the same place? Something this individual has no reason to desire.

35. The Excellence of Minds. God Considers Them in Preference to Other Creatures. Minds Express God Rather Than the World, but Other Substances Express the World Rather Than God.

But to show by natural reasons that God always will preserve not only our substance but also our personality, that is memory and knowledge of what we are although distinct knowledge of that may sometimes by suspended when asleep or unconscious, morality must be joined to Metaphysics. That is, God has not only to be considered as the principle and cause of all substances and all beings, but also as the chief of all persons or intelligent substances and the absolute monarch of the most perfect city or republic, like that of the universe composed of all minds together, since God himself is the most accomplished of all Minds as well as the greatest of all Beings. For assuredly, minds are either the only substances existing in the world if bodies are no more than true phenomena, or else they are at least the most perfect ones. And since the whole nature, end, virtue and function of substances is merely to express God and the universe, as has been sufficiently explained, there are no grounds for doubting that substances expressing Him in the knowledge of what they are doing, and capable of knowing great truths regarding God and the universe, express Him incomparably better than those natures that are either animal and incapable of knowing truths, or altogether destitute of sense and knowledge; and the difference between intelligent substances and those that are not is as great as that between the mirror and he who sees.

And since God Himself is the greatest and wisest of minds, it is easy to conclude that beings with whom He can so to speak enter into conversation or even into fellowship, communicating His thoughts and intentions individually, so that they can know and love their Benefactor, must concern Him infinitely more than all other beings, able only to pass for the tools of minds, just as we can see wise persons taking infinitely more account of a man than of some other thing, however precious that may be. It seems that the greatest satisfaction an otherwise contented soul can have is to see himself loved by others although in respect of God there is this difference that His glory and our worship can add nothing to His satisfaction, since the knowledge of creatures is no more than a consequence of His sovereign and perfect happiness and very far from contributing to the latter or being part of the cause thereof. Nevertheless, what is good and reasonable in finite minds is supremely so in Him and just as we would praise a king who preferred to preserve the life of a man before the most precious and rare of animals, we should not doubt that the most enlightened and just of all Monarchs is of the same opinion.

36. GOD IS THE MONARCH OF THAT MOST PERFECT REPUBLIC
THAT CONSISTS OF ALL MINDS, AND THE HAPPINESS OF THIS
CITY OF GOD IS HIS PRINCIPAL DESIGN.

In fact, minds are the most perfectible of all substances and their perfections have this characteristic that they hinder each other the least, or rather that they assist each other, for only the most virtuous can be the most perfect friends. Hence it manifestly follows that God who always looks to the greatest perfection in general, will have the most care of minds, and will give them, not only generally but to each individually, the greatest perfection the universal harmony can permit.

It can even be said that God, in so far as He is a mind, is the origin of existent things—if there were no will to choose best there would be no reason for one possible thing to exist in preference to others. Hence God's quality of being Himself a mind precedes all other considerations He may have with respect to creatures. Minds only are made in His image, and it is as if they are of His race and children of His house, since they alone can serve Him freely and act consciously in imitation of the divine nature. One mind is worth an entire world, since it does not only express it, but knows it, and governs itself there in the manner of God. So much so that it seems that while every substance expresses the whole universe, other substances express the world rather than God while minds express God rather than the world. And this natural nobility of minds, which brings them as near to the divine as is possible for mere creatures, means that God receives from them infinitely more glory than from other beings, or rather other beings merely give minds matter for glorifying Him.

That is why this moral quality of God that makes Him the Lord and Monarch of Minds, affects Him so to speak personally in a quite special manner. It is in this that He becomes human and is willing to allow human ways of speaking about Him, and enters into fellowship with us like a Prince with his subjects. This consideration is so dear to Him that the happy and flourishing state of His empire, that consists in the greatest possible happiness of the inhabitants, becomes the supreme subaltern law of His conduct. For happiness is to persons what perfection is to beings, and if the first principle of existence of the physical world is the decree giving it the greatest possible perfection, the first principle of existence of the moral world or City of God, the most noble part of the universe, must be to spread as much happiness as possible in it.

Hence it must not be doubted that God so ordained (not only that minds could live forever, which is inevitable, but also that they should conserve forever their moral nature) so that this city should lose no person just as the world loses no substance. And consequently, they will always know what they are, otherwise they would not be liable to reward or punishment, which however is the essence of any republic, above all of one that is the most perfect, in which nothing can be neglected.

Finally, since God is at once the most just and the most good-natured of monarchs, and asks only for good will, provided that it is sincere and serious, His subjects could not hope for better conditions: to make them perfectly happy, He wants only that they love Him.

37. Jesus Christ Has Revealed to Men the Mystery and Admirable Laws of the Kingdom of Heaven and the Greatness of the Supreme Happiness God Prepares for Those Who Love Him.

The ancient philosophers had very little knowledge of these important truths. Jesus Christ alone expressed them divinely well and in such a clear and familiar way, that the most crude minds came to understand them. So His gospel changed the entire face of human affairs. He brought us knowledge of the Kingdom of Heaven or this perfect republic of minds that merits the title "City of God" whose admirable laws he revealed to us, and he alone shows us how much God loves us; the exactness with which He has provided for all that concerns us; that since He cares for sparrows, He will not neglect the reasonable creatures who are infinitely more dear to Him; that all the hairs in our heads are counted; that heaven and earth will pass away before the Word of God and everything belonging to the pattern of our salvation is changed; God has more concern with the least of intelligent souls than with the whole machine of the world; that we must not fear those who can destroy the body but are unable to harm souls, since God alone can make them happy or unhappy; that the just are in His hand protected from all the revolutions of the universe, since nothing can act on them but God alone; that none of our actions is forgotten; that everything is taken into account, right down to unguarded words, and a spoonful of water well used; and finally that all things must result in the greatest good for those that are good; that the just are like suns and that neither our senses nor our minds have ever tasted anything approaching the happiness God prepares for those who love Him.

THEODICY

Abridgement of the Argument Reduced to Syllogistic Form

Some intelligent persons have desired that this supplement be made [to the Theodicy], and I have the more readily yielded to their wishes as in this way I have an opportunity again to remove certain difficulties and to make some observations which were not sufficiently emphasized in the work itself.

I. *Objection.* Whoever does not choose the best is lacking in power, or in knowledge, or in goodness.

God did not choose the best in creating this world.

Therefore, God has been lacking in power, or in knowledge, or in goodness.

Answer. I deny the minor, that is, the second premise of this syllogism; and our opponent proves it by this.

Prosyllogism. Whoever makes things in which there is evil, which could have been made without any evil, or the making of which could have been omitted, does not choose the best.

God has made a world in which there is evil, a world, I say, which could have been made without any evil, or the making of which could have been omitted altogether.

Therefore, God has not chosen the best.

Answer. I grant the minor of this prosyllogism; for it must be confessed that there is evil in this world which God has made, and that it was possible to make a world without evil, or even not to create a world at all, for its creation has depended on the free will of God; but I deny the major, that is, the first of the two premises of the prosyllogism, and I might content myself with simply demanding its proof; but in order to make the matter clearer, I have wished to justify this denial by showing that the best plan is not always that which seeks to avoid evil, since it may happen that *the evil is accompanied by a greater good.* For example, a general of an army will prefer a great victory with a slight wound to a condition without wound and without victory. We have proved this more fully in the large work by making it clear, by instances taken from mathematics and elsewhere, that an imperfection in the part may be required for a greater perfection in the whole. In this I have followed the opinion of St. Augustine, who has said a hundred times, that God has permitted evil in order to bring about good, that is, a greater good; and that of Thomas Aquinas (in libr. II. sent. dist. 32, qu. I, art. 1), that the permitting of evil tends to the good of the universe. I have shown that the ancients called Adam's fall *felix culpa,* a happy sin, because it had been retrieved with immense advantage by the incarnation of the Son of God, who has given to the universe something nobler than anything that ever would have been among creatures except for it. For the sake of a clearer understanding, I have added, following many good authors, that it was in accordance with order and the general good that God allowed to certain creatures the opportunity of exercising their liberty, even when he foresaw that they would turn to evil, but which he could so well rectify; because it was not fitting that, in order to hinder sin, God should always act in an extraordinary manner. To overthrow this objection, therefore, it is sufficient to show that a world with evil might be better than a world without evil; but I have gone even farther, in the work, and have even proved that this universe must be in reality better than every other possible universe.

II. *Objection.* If there is more evil than good in intelligent creatures, then there is more evil than good in the whole work of God.

Now, there is more evil than good in intelligent creatures.

Therefore, there is more evil than good in the whole work of God.

Answer. I deny the major and the minor of this conditional syllogism. As to the major, I do not admit it at all, because this pretended deduction from a part to the whole, from intelligent creatures to all creatures, supposes tacitly and without proof that creatures destitute of reason cannot enter into comparison nor into account with those which possess it. But why may it not be that the surplus of good in the non-intelligent creatures which fill the world, compensates for, and even incomparably surpasses, the surplus of evil in the rational creatures? It is true that the value of the latter is greater; but, in compensation, the others are beyond comparison the more numerous, and it may be that the proportion of number and quantity surpasses that of value and of quality.

As to the minor, that is no more to be admitted; that is, it is not at all to be admitted that there is more evil than good in the intelligent creatures. There is no need even of granting that there is more evil than good in the human race, because it is possible, and in fact very probable, that the glory and the perfection of the blessed are incomparably greater than the misery and the imperfection of the damned, and that here the excellence of the total good in the smaller number exceeds the total evil in the greater number. The blessed approach the Divinity, by means of a Divine Mediator, as near as may suit these creatures, and make such progress in good as is impossible for the damned to make in evil, approach as nearly as they may to the nature of demons. God is infinite, and the devil is limited; the good may and does go to infinity, while evil has its bounds. It is therefore possible, and is credible, that in the comparison of the blessed and the damned, the contrary of that which I have said might happen in the comparison of intelligent and nonintelligent creatures, takes place; namely, it is possible that in the comparison of the happy and the unhappy, the proportion of degree exceeds that of number, and that in the comparison of intelligent and non-intelligent creatures, the proportion of number is greater than that of value. I have the right to suppose that a thing is possible so long as its impossibility is not proved; and indeed that which I have here advanced is more than a supposition.

But in the second place, if I should admit that there is more evil than good in the human race, I have still good grounds for not admitting that there is more evil than good in all intelligent creatures. For there is an inconceivable number of genii, and perhaps of other rational creatures. And an opponent could not prove that in all the City of God, composed as well of genii as of rational animals without number and of an infinity of kinds, evil exceeds good. And although in order to answer an objection, there is no need of proving that a thing is, when its mere possibility suffices; yet, in this work, I have not omitted to show that it is a consequence of the supreme perfection of the Sovereign of the universe, that the kingdom of God is the most perfect of all possible states or governments, and that consequently the little evil there is, is required for the consummation of the immense good which is found there.

III. *Objection.* If it is always impossible not to sin, it is always unjust to punish.

Now, it is always impossible not to sin; or, in other words, every sin is necessary.

Therefore, it is always unjust to punish.

The minor of this is proved thus:

1. *Prosyllogism.* All that is predetermined is necessary.

Every event is predetermined.

Therefore, every event (and consequently sin also) is necessary.

Again this second minor is proved thus:

2. *Prosyllogism.* That which is future, that which is foreseen, that which is involved in the causes, is predetermined.

Every event is such.

Therefore, every event is predetermined.

Answer. I admit in a certain sense the conclusion of the second prosyllogism, which is the minor of the first; but I shall deny the major of the first prosyllogism, namely, that every thing predetermined is necessary; understanding by the necessity of sinning, for example, or by the impossibility of not sinning, or of not performing any action, the necessity with which we are here concerned, that is, that which is essential and absolute, and which destroys the morality of an action and the justice of punishments. For if anyone understood another necessity or impossibility, namely, a necessity which should be only moral, or which was only hypothetical (as will be explained shortly); it is clear that I should deny the major of the objection itself. I might content myself with this answer and demand the proof of the proposition denied; but I have again desired to explain my procedure in this work, in order to better elucidate the matter and to throw more light on the whole subject, by explaining the necessity which ought to be rejected and the determination which must take place. That *necessity* which is contrary to morality and which ought to be rejected, and which would render punishment unjust, is an insurmountable necessity which would make all opposition useless, even if we should wish with all our heart to avoid the necessary action, and should make all possible efforts to that end. Now, it is manifest that this is not applicable to voluntary actions, because we would not perform them if we did not choose to. Also their prevision and predetermination are not absolute, but presuppose the will: if it is certain that we shall perform them, it is not less certain that we shall choose to perform them. These voluntary actions and their consequences will not take place no matter what we do or whether we wish them or not; but, *through* that which we shall do and through that which we shall wish to do, which leads to them. And this is involved in prevision and in predetermination, and even constitutes their ground. And the necessity of such an event is called conditional or hypothetical, or the necessity of consequence, because it supposes the will, and the other *requisites;* whereas the necessity which destroys morality and renders punishment unjust and reward useless, exists in things which will be whatever we may do or whatever we may wish to do, and, in a word, is in that which is essential; and this is what is called an absolute necessity. Thus it is to no purpose, as regards what is absolutely necessary, to make prohibitions or commands, to propose penalties or prizes, to praise or to blame; it will be none the less. On the other hand, in voluntary actions and in that which depends upon them, precepts armed with power to punish and to recompense are very often of use and are included in the order of causes which make an action exist. And it is for this reason that not only cares and labors but also prayers are useful; God having had these prayers in view before he regulated things and having had that consideration for them which was proper. This is why the precept which says *ora et labora* (pray and work), holds altogether good; and not only those who (under the vain pretext of the necessity of events) pretend that the care which business demands may be neglected, but also those who reason against prayer, fall into what the ancients even then called the *lazy sophism.* Thus the predetermination of events by causes is just what contributes to morality instead of destroying it, and causes incline the will, without compelling it. This is why the *determination* in question is not a necessitation—it is certain (to him who knows all) that the effect will follow this inclination; but this effect does not follow by a necessary consequence, that is, one the contrary of which implies contradiction. It is also by an internal inclination such as this that the will is determined, without there being any necessity. Suppose that one has the greatest passion in the world (a great thirst, for example), you will admit to me that the soul can find some reason for resisting it, if it were only that of showing its power. Thus, although one may never be in a perfect indifference of equilibrium and there may be always a preponderance of inclination for the side taken, it, nevertheless, never renders the resolution taken absolutely necessary.

IV. *Objection.* Whoever can prevent the sin of another and does not do so but rather contributes to it although he is well informed of it, is accessory to it.

God can prevent the sin of intelligent creatures; but he does not do so, and rather contributes to it by his concurrence and by the opportunities which he brings about, although he has a perfect knowledge of it.

Hence, etc.

Answer. I deny the major of this syllogism. For it is possible that one could prevent sin, but ought not, because he could not do it without himself committing a sin, or (when God is in question) without performing an unreasonable action. Examples have been given and the application to God himself has been made. It is possible also that we contribute to evil and that sometimes we even open the road to it, in doing things which we are obliged to do; and, when we do our duty or (in speaking of God) when, after thorough consideration, we do that which reason demands, we are not responsible for the results, even when we foresee them. We do not desire these evils; but we are willing to permit them for the sake of a greater good which we cannot reasonably help preferring to other considerations. And this is a *consequent* will, which results from *antecedent* wills by which we will the good. I know that some persons, in speaking of the *antecedent* and consequent will of God, have understood by the antecedent that which wills that all men should be saved; and by the *consequent,* that which wills, in consequence of persistent sin, that some should be damned. But these are merely illustrations of a more general idea, and it may be said for the same reason that God, by his antecedent will, wills that men should not sin; and by his consequent or final and decreeing will (that which is always followed by its effect), he wills to permit them to sin, this permission being the result of superior reasons. And we have the right to say in general that the antecedent will of God tends to the production of good and the prevention of evil, each taken in itself and as if alone (*particulariter et secundum quid,* Thom. I, qu. 19, art. 6), according to the measure of the degree of each good and of each evil; but that the divine consequent or final or total will tends toward the production of as many goods as may be put together, the combination of which becomes in this way determined, and includes also the permission of some evils and the exclusion of some goods, as the best possible plan for the universe demands. Arminius, in his *Anti-perkinsus,* has very well explained that the will of God may be called consequent, not only in relation to the action of the creature considered beforehand in the divine understanding, but also in relation to other anterior divine acts of will. But this consideration of the passage cited from Thomas Aquinas, and that from Scotus (I. dist. 46, qu. XI), is enough to show that they make this distinction as I have done here. Nevertheless, if anyone objects to this use of terms let him substitute *deliberating* will, in place of antecedent, and *final* or decreeing will, in place of consequent. For I do not wish to dispute over words.

V. *Objection.* Whoever produces all that is real in a thing, is its cause.

God produces all that is real in sin.

Hence, God is the cause of sin.

Answer. I might content myself with denying the major or the minor, since the term *real* admits of interpretations which would render these propositions false. But in order to explain more clearly, I will make a distinction. *Real* signifies either that which is positive only, or, it includes also privative beings: in the first case, I deny the major and admit the minor; in the second case, I do the contrary. I might have limited myself to this, but I have chosen to proceed still farther and give the reason for this distinction. I have been very glad therefore to draw attention to the fact that every reality purely positive or absolute is a perfection; and that imperfection comes from limitation, that is, from the privative: for to limit is to refuse progress, or the greatest possible progress. Now God is the cause of all perfections and consequently of all realities considered as purely positive. But limitations or privations result from the original imperfection of creatures, which limits their receptivity. And it is with them as with a loaded vessel, which the river causes to move more or less slowly according to the weight which it carries: thus its speed depends upon the river, but the retardation which limits this speed comes from the load. Thus in the *Theodicy,* we have shown how the creature, in causing sin, is a defective cause; how errors and evil inclinations are born of privation; and how privation is accidentally efficient; and I have justified the opinion of St. Augustine (lib. I. ad Simpl. qu. 2) who explains, for example, how God makes the soul obdurate, not by giving it something evil, but because the effect of his good impression is limited by the soul's resistance and by the circumstances which contribute to this resistance, so that he does not give it all the good which would overcome its evil. *Nec* (inquit) *ab illo erogatur aliquid quo homo fit deterior, sed tantum quo fit melior non erogatur.* But if God had wished to do more, he would have had to make either other natures for creatures or other miracles to change their natures, things which the best plan could not admit. It is as if the current of the river must be more rapid than its fall admitted or that the boats should be loaded more lightly, if it were necessary to make them move more quickly. And the original limitation or imperfection of creatures requires that even the best plan of the universe could not receive more good, and could not be exempt from certain evils, which, however, are to result in a greater good. There are certain disorders in the parts which marvelously enhance the beauty of the whole; just as certain dissonances, when properly used, render harmony more beautiful. But this depends on what has already been said in answer to the first objection.

VI. *Objection.* Whoever punishes those who have done as well as it was in their power to do, is unjust.

God does so.

Hence, etc.

Answer. I deny the minor of this argument. And I believe that God always gives sufficient aid and grace to those who have a good will, that is, to those who do not reject this grace by new sin. Thus I do not admit the damnation of infants who have died without baptism or outside of the church; nor the damnation of adults who have acted according to the light which God has given them. And I believe that if *any one has followed the light which has been given him,* he will undoubtedly receive greater light when he has need of it, as the late M. Hulseman, a profound and celebrated theologian at Leipzig, has somewhere remarked; and if such a man has failed to receive it during his lifetime he will at least receive it when at the point of death.

VII. *Objection.* Whoever gives only to some, and not to all, the means which produces in them effectively a good will and salutary final faith, has not sufficient goodness.

God does this.

Hence, etc.

Answer. I deny the major of this. It is true that God could overcome the greatest resistance of the human heart; and does it, too, sometimes, either by internal grace, or by external circumstances which have a great effect on souls; but he does not always do this. Whence comes this distinction? it may be asked, and why does his goodness seem limited? It is because, as I have already said in answering the first objection, it would not have been in order always to act in an extraordinary manner, and to reverse the connection of things. The reasons of this connection, by means of which one is placed in more favorable circumstances than another, are hidden in the depths of the wisdom of God: they depend upon the universal harmony. The best plan of the universe, which God could not fail to choose, made it so. We judge from the event itself; since God has made it, it was not possible to do better. Far from being true that this conduct is contrary to goodness, it is supreme goodness which led him to it. This objection with its solution might have been drawn from what was said in regard to the first objection; but it seemed useful to touch upon it separately.

VIII. *Objection.* Whoever cannot fail to choose the best, is not free.

God cannot fail to choose the best.

Hence, God is not free.

Answer. I deny the major of this argument; it is rather true liberty, and the most perfect, to be able to use one's free will for the best, and to always exercise this power, without ever being turned aside either by external force or by internal passions, the first of which causes slavery of the body, the second, slavery of the soul. There is nothing less servile, and nothing more in accordance with the highest degree of freedom, than to be always led toward the good, and always by one's own inclination, without any constraint and without any displeasure. And to object therefore that God had need of external things, is only a sophism. He created them freely; but having proposed to himself an end, which is to exercise his goodness, wisdom has determined him to choose the means best fitted to attain this end. To call this a need, is to take that term in an unusual sense which frees it from all imperfection, just as when we speak of the wrath of God.

Seneca has somewhere said that God commanded but once but that he obeys always, because he obeys laws which he willed to prescribe to himself: *semel jussit, semper paret.* But he might better have said that God always commands and that he is always obeyed; for in willing, he always follows the inclination of his own nature, and all other things always follow his will. And as this will is always the same, it cannot be said that he obeys only that will which he formerly had. Nevertheless, although his will is always infallible and always tends toward the best, the evil, or the lesser good, which he rejects, does not cease to be possible in itself; otherwise the necessity of the good would be geometrical (so to speak), or metaphysical, and altogether absolute; the contingency of things would be destroyed, and there would be no choice. But this sort of necessity, which does not destroy the possibility of the contrary, has this name only by analogy; it becomes effective, not by the pure essence of things, but by that which is outside of them, above them, namely, by the will of God. This necessity is called moral, because, to the sage, *necessity* and *what ought to be* are equivalent things; and when it always has its effect, as it really has in the perfect sage, that is, in God, it may be said that it is a happy necessity. The nearer creatures approach to it, the nearer they approach to perfect happiness. Also this kind of necessity is not that which we try to avoid and which destroys morality, rewards and praise. For that which it brings, does not happen whatever we may do or will, but because we will it so. And a will to which it is natural to choose well, merits praise so much the more; also it carries its reward with it, which is sovereign happiness. And as this constitution of the divine nature gives entire satisfaction to him who possesses it, it is also the best and the most desirable for the creatures who are all dependent on God. If the will of God did not have for a rule the principle of the best, it would either tend toward evil, which would be the worst; or it would be in some way indifferent to good and to evil, and would be guided by chance: but a will which would allow itself always to act by chance, would not be worth more for the government of the universe than the fortuitous concourse of atoms, without there being any divinity therein. And even if God should abandon himself to chance only in some cases and in a certain way (as he would do, if he did not always work entirely for the best and if he were capable of preferring a lesser work to a greater, that is, an evil to a good, since that which prevents a greater good is an evil), he would be imperfect, as well as the object of his choice; he would not merit entire confidence; he would act without reason in such a case, and the government of the universe would be like certain games, equally divided between reason and chance. All this proves that this objection which is made against the choice of the best, perverts the notions of the free and of the necessary, and represents to us the best even as evil: which is either malicious or ridiculous.

THE MONADOLOGY

1. The object of this discourse, the *monad,* is nothing else than a simple substance, which enters into the composites; *simple* meaning, which has no parts.

2. And there must be simple substances, since there are composites; for the composite is nothing else than an accumulation or aggregate of the simples.

3. But where there are no parts, neither extension, nor figure, nor divisibility is possible. Thus, these monads are the veritable atoms of nature, and, in one word, the elements of all things.

4. Hence no dissolution is to be feared for them, and a simple substance cannot perish naturally in any conceivable manner.

5. For the same reason, no simple substance can come into being naturally, since it cannot be formed by composition.

6. Thus it may be maintained that monads cannot begin or end otherwise than instantaneously, that is, they can begin only by creation, and end only by annihilation; while what is complete begins and ends through and in its parts.

7. It is impossible also to explain how a monad can be altered, that is, internally changed, by any other creature. For there is nothing in it which might be transposed, nor can there be conceived in it any internal movement which could be excited, directed, or diminished. In composites this is possible, since the parts can interchange place. The monads have no windows through which anything could come in or go out.

8. Nevertheless, the monads must have some qualities, otherwise they would not even be beings. And if the simple substances did not differ through their qualities, there would be no means at all of perceiving any change in things. For what is in the composites can come only from the ingredient simples. So the monads, if they were without qualities, would be indistinguishable the one from the other, since they do not differ in quantity either. The plenum being presupposed, no space, consequently, could ever receive through movement anything but the equivalent of what has been in it, and one state of things would be indiscernible from another.

9. Each monad must even be different from every other. For in nature there are never two beings which are perfectly like one another, and between which it would not be possible to find an internal difference, that is, a difference founded on an intrinsic denomination.

10. I take it also for granted that all created beings, consequently the created monads as well, are subject to change, and that this change is even continual in each one.

11. In consequence of what has been said, the natural changes of the monads must result from an *internal principle,* since no external cause could influence their interior.

12. But besides the principle of change, there must be a *particular trait of what is changing,* which produces, so to speak, the specification and variety of the simple substances.

13. This particular must comprehend a multiplicity in the unity, that is, in the simple. For since all natural change proceeds by degrees, something changes and some-

Gottfried Wilhelm Von Leibniz, *Monadology and Other Philosophical Essays,* translated by Paul Schrecker and Anne Martin Schrecker (New York: Macmillan/Library of the Liberal Arts, 1965).

thing remains. Consequently, there must be in the simple substance a plurality of affections and relations, though it has no parts.

14. The passing state which comprehends and represents a multiplicity in the unity or simple substance is nothing but what is called *perception;* it must be clearly distinguished from apperception or consciousness, as will become clear later on. On this point the Cartesian doctrine has been very defective, since it has entirely neglected those perceptions which are not apperceived; the same failure to distinguish has made the Cartesians believe that only spirits are monads, and that there are neither animal souls nor other entelechies. Therefore, they, like the unlearned, have confused a long swoon with death, strictly speaking, and yielded to the scholastic prejudice that there are entirely separated souls. The same error has even confirmed unsound minds in the opinion that souls are mortal.

15. The action of the internal principle which produces change, that is, the passage from one perception to another, may be called *appetition.* It is true that appetition may not always entirely attain the whole perception toward which it tends, but it always obtains something and arrives at new perceptions.

16. We ourselves experience a multiplicity in the simple substance, when we observe that the least thought which we apperceive in ourselves comprehends a variety in its object. Thus, all those who recognize that the soul is a simple substance must recognize this multiplicity in the monad. Pierre Bayle should not have found a difficulty in this theory, as he indeed did in the article "Rorarius" of his *Dictionary.*

17. Moreover, it must be avowed that *perception* and what depends upon it *cannot possibly be explained by mechanical reasons,* that is, by figure and movement. Suppose that there be a machine, the structure of which produces thinking, feeling, and perceiving; imagine this machine enlarged but preserving the same proportions, so that you could enter it as if it were a mill. This being supposed, you might visit its inside; but what would you observe there? Nothing but parts which push and move each other, and never anything that could explain perception. This explanation must therefore be sought in the simple substance, not in the composite, that is, in the machine. However, there is nothing else to be found in the simple substance but perceptions and their changes. In this alone can consist all the *internal actions* of simple substances.

18. The name *entelechies* would fit all the simple substances or created monads. For they have in themselves a certain perfection *[echousi to enteles],* and they are endowed with a self-sufficiency *[autarkeia]* which makes them the sources of their own actions and, so to speak, incorporeal automata.

19. If we want to call *soul* all that has perception and appetition, in the general sense explained above, we might give the name soul to all simple substances or created monads. But since sensation is something more than a simple perception, I agree that the general name monad or entelechy may suffice for those simple substances which have nothing but perception and appetition; the name souls may then be reserved for those having perception that is more distinct and is accompanied by memory.

20. Indeed, we experience in ourselves a state in which we remember nothing and have no distinct perception at all, e.g., when we faint or are overcome by a deep and dreamless sleep. In this state the soul is not noticeably different from a simple monad. However, since this state does not last, the soul being able to pull itself out of it, the soul is more than a simple monad.

21. Besides, it does not follow at all that in such a state the simple substance entirely lacks perception. For the reasons propounded a while ago, this lack is not possible; for the monad cannot perish, nor can it subsist without some affection, which is nothing but its perception. But when there is a great multitude of minute perceptions

lacking distinctness, one becomes dizzy: for example, when you turn around several consecutive times, you get a vertigo which may make you faint and leave you without any distinct perception. Death may throw animals into such a state for a time.

22. The present state of a simple substance is the natural result of its precedent state, so much so that the present is pregnant with the future.

23. Therefore, since on awakening from such a swoon, you apperceive your perceptions, it follows that you must have had some perceptions immediately before, though you did not apperceive them. For a perception cannot come naturally except from another perception, just as movement cannot come naturally except from another movement.

24. Hence it is evident that if in our perceptions there were nothing distinct nor anything, so to speak, in relief and of a more marked taste, we would always be in a swoon. And that is the state of the mere naked monads.

25. We see indeed that nature has given distinct perceptions to the animals, for care has been taken to provide them with organs which collect several light rays or several air waves, to unite them and thereby give them greater effect. Something similar occurs in scent, taste, and touch, and perhaps in many other senses unknown to us. I shall explain soon how what occurs in the soul represents what occurs in the sense organs.

26. Memory provides the souls with a sort of *consistency* which imitates reason but has to be distinguished from it. For we see that animals, perceiving something which impresses them and of which they have previously had a resembling perception, are brought by the representation of their memory to expect what has been associated with this perception in the past and are moved to feelings similar to those they had then. If you show a stick to a dog, for instance, it remembers the pain caused by it and howls or runs away.

27. The vividness of the imagination which strikes and moves animals comes from either the strength or the frequency of preceding perceptions. For often one strong impression produces at once the effect of a long *habit* or of many reiterated impressions of minor strength.

28. Men act like animals in so far as the succession of their perceptions is brought about by the principle of memory. In this they resemble medical empiricists whose practice is not backed by theory. In fact, we are mere empiricists in three quarters of all our actions. If you expect, for instance, that the sun will rise tomorrow because up to now it has always happened, you act as an empiricist. The astronomer alone judges by reason.

29. Knowledge of necessary and eternal truths, however, distinguishes us from mere animals and grants us *reason* and the sciences, elevating us to the knowledge of ourselves and of God. This possession is what is called our reasonable soul or *spirit.*

30. By this knowledge of necessary truths and by the abstractions made possible through them, we also are raised to *acts of reflection* which enable us to think of the so-called *self* and to consider this or that to be in us. Thinking thus about ourselves, we think of being, substance, the simple and the composite, the immaterial, and even of God, conceiving what is limited in us as without limit in him. These acts of reflection furnish the principal objects of our reasoning.

31. Our reasoning is founded on two great principles: The first is the principle of *contradiction,* by virtue of which we consider as false what implies a contradiction and as true what is the opposite of the contradictory or false.

32. The second is the principle of *sufficient reason,* by virtue of which we hold that no fact can be true or existing and no statement truthful without a sufficient reason

for its being so and not different; albeit these reasons most frequently must remain unknown to us.

33. There are also two kinds of *truths:* those of *reason,* which are necessary and of which the opposite is impossible, and those of *fact,* which are contingent and of which the opposite is possible. When a truth is necessary, the reasons for it can be found through analysis, that is, by resolving it into simpler ideas and truths until one comes to primitives.

34. Thus the mathematicians, using the analytical method, reduce the speculative *theorems* and the practical *canons* to *definitions, axioms,* and *postulates.*

35. In the end, there are *simple ideas* of which no definition can be given. Moreover, there are axioms and postulates, in short, *primitive principles,* which cannot be demonstrated and do not need demonstration. They are *identical propositions,* the opposite of which contains an express contradiction.

36. A *sufficient reason,* however, must also exist for *contingent truths* or *truths of fact,* that is, for the series of things comprehended in the universe of creatures. Here the resolution into particular reasons could be continued without limit; for the variety of natural things is immense, and bodies are infinitely divided. There is an infinity of figures and movements, past and present, which contribute to the efficient cause of my presently writing this. And there is an infinity of minute inclinations and dispositions of my soul, which contribute to the final cause of my writing.

37. Now, all of this detail implies previous or more particular contingents, each of which again stands in need of a similar analysis to be accounted for, so that nothing is gained by such an analysis. The sufficient or ultimate reason must therefore exist outside the succession or series of contingent particulars, infinite though this series may be.

38. Consequently, the ultimate reason of all things must subsist in a necessary substance, in which all particular changes may exist only virtually as in its source: this substance is what we call *God.*

39. Now, this substance is the sufficient reason for all this particular existence which is, moreover, interconnected throughout. Hence, there is but one God, and this God suffices.

40. This Supreme Substance is unique, universal, and necessary. There is nothing existing apart from it which would be independent of it, and the existence of this being is a simple consequence of its possibility. It follows that this substance does not admit of any limitation and must contain as much reality as is possible.

41. God, therefore, is absolutely perfect, *perfection* meaning the quantity of positive reality. In things which have limits, that is, in finite things, this perfection has to be strictly interpreted, namely as the quantity of positive reality within their given limits. But where there are no limits, namely in God, perfection is absolutely infinite.

42. It follows that creatures owe their perfections to the divine influence, but their imperfections to their proper nature, which is incapable of being without limits. For it is in this that they are distinguished from God. The created things' *original imperfection* manifests itself through the *natural inertia* of all bodies.

43. Moreover, it is true that in God is the source not only of all existence, but also of all essence endowed with reality, that is, the source of what is real in the possibles. For the divine understanding is the region of the eternal truths and of the ideas on which they depend, and without him there would not be anything real in the possibles; that is, without him there would not only be nothing existing, but even nothing possible.

44. Indeed, if there is to be any reality in the essences or possibles, that is, in the necessary truths, this reality must be founded on the existence of the necessary being

whose essence implies its existence, that is, to which it suffices to be possible in order to be actual.

45. Thus God alone (or the necessary being) has the privilege of existing necessarily, provided only he be possible. Now, since nothing can hinder the possibility of the substance which contains no limits, no negation, and hence no contradiction, this provides a sufficient reason for the knowledge *a priori* of God's existence. Besides, we have proved it by the reality of the eternal truths. In addition, we also have proved this existence *a posteriori* by the existence of contingent beings. For the sufficient and ultimate reason of these can lie only in the necessary being which has in itself the reason of its existence.

46. It must not be imagined, however, as certain authors have imagined, that since the eternal truths depend upon God, they are arbitrary and depend upon his will. Descartes seems to have thought so, and after him Poiret. This is true only of the contingent truths which are based on the principle of fitness, that is, the choice of the best possible; while the necessary truths depend only on his understanding, of which they are the internal object.

47. Thus God is the only primitive unit or the only original simple substance, of which all the created or derivative monads are the products, born, so to speak, every moment by continual fulgurations from the divinity, and limited by the capacities of creatures, to which limitation is essential.

48. In God there are his *power* which is the source of everything, his *knowledge* which contains the particulars of the ideas, and finally his *will* which is the source of change or production and acts according to the principle of the best possible. Corresponding to these divine attributes, there is in the created monads the subject or basis, namely, the faculty of perception and the faculty of appetition. In God, however, these attributes are absolutely infinite and perfect, whereas in the created monads or *entelechies* (Hermolaus Barbarus translated this word into Latin by *perfectihabies*) these attributes are only likenesses, possessed by the monads in proportion to their perfections.

49. Creatures are said to *act* outwardly in so far as they have perfection, and to *suffer* from other creatures in so far as they are imperfect. Thus *activity* has to be attributed to the monad in so far as it has distinct perceptions, and passivity in so far as it has confused perceptions.

50. One creature is more perfect than another, in so far as there is found in the former a reason to account *a priori* for what is happening in the latter; this is why one says that the former acts upon the latter.

51. But in the simple substances this influence of one monad upon the other is but *ideal* and can take effect only through the intervention of God; in the ideas of God, indeed, any monad reasonably requires that in his ruling of all others, God, from the beginning, take that monad into consideration. For since no created monad can exercise a physical influence upon the interior of any other, this is the only means by which the one can depend upon the other.

52. By this means actions and passions among creatures are mutual. For when God compares two simple substances, he finds in either one reasons which oblige him to adjust the other to it. What appears as active in certain respects, consequently appears as passive from another point of view: it appears as *active* in so far as what is distinctly known in one monad serves to account for what happens in another; it appears as passive in so far as the reason for what happens in it is to be found in what is distinctly known in another.

53. Now, since in the divine ideas there is an infinity of possible universes of which only one can exist, the choice made by God must have a sufficient reason which determines him to the one rather than to another.

54. This reason can be found only in fitness, that is, in the degree of perfection contained in these worlds. For each possible has a right to claim existence in proportion to the perfection it involves. Thus nothing is entirely arbitrary.

55. This is the cause for the existence of the best, which is disclosed to him by his wisdom, determines his choice by his goodness, and is produced by his power.

56. This *connection* of all created things with every single one of them and their adaptation to every single one, as well as the connection and adaptation of every single thing to all others, has the result that every single substance stands in relations which express all the others. Whence every single substance is a perpetual living mirror of the universe.

57. Just as the same city regarded from different sides offers quite different aspects, and thus appears multiplied *by the perspective,* so it also happens that the infinite multitude of simple substances creates the appearance of as many different universes. Yet they are but perspectives of a single universe, varied according to the *points of view,* which differ in each monad.

58. This is the means of obtaining the greatest possible variety, together with the greatest possible order; in other words, it is the means of obtaining as much perfection as possible.

59. Only by this hypothesis (which I dare to call demonstrated) can the greatness of God be exalted as it ought to be. Pierre Bayle has recognized this when he objected to the hypothesis in the article "Rorarius" of his *Dictionary.* In that passage he was inclined to believe that I attributed to God too much, and even more than is possible. But he was unable to adduce any reason why this universal harmony, due to which every substance exactly expresses all the others through the relations it has with them, should be impossible.

60. In what I have just stated, there can also be discerned reasons a priori why things could not be different. For God, legislating the whole, has considered every part and particularly every monad. And since the nature of every monad is representative, there is nothing which could limit it to representing only a part of all things. It is true, however, that this representation is but confused concerning the particulars of the whole universe and can be distinct concerning only a small part of all things, namely those which are either the nearest or the largest in respect to each of the monads. For otherwise every monad would be a deity. It is not in the objects of their knowledge, but in the modes of this knowledge that the monads are limited. All of them have a confused knowledge of the infinite, that is, of the whole; but they are limited and distinguished by the degrees of distinct perception.

61. The composite substances are in this respect symbols of the simples. For since all is a plenum, all matter is connected and all movement in the plenum produces some effect on the distant bodies, in proportion to the distance. Hence every body is affected not only by those with which it is in contact, and thus feels in some way everything that happens to them; but through them it also feels those that touch the ones with which it is in immediate contact. Hence it follows that this communication extends over any distance whatever. Consequently, every body experiences everything that goes on in the universe, so much so that he who sees everything might read in any body what is happening anywhere, and even what has happened or will happen. He would be able to observe in the present what is remote in both time and space: *[sumpnoia panta],* as Hippocrates stated. A soul, however, can read in itself only what is distinctly represented in it; it is unable to unfold all at once all its folds; for these go on into infinity.

62. Thus, every created monad represents the whole universe; nevertheless, it represents more distinctly the body which is particularly attached to it and of which it is the entelechy. And since this body expresses the whole universe through the intercon-

nection of all the matter in the plenum, the soul, too, represents the whole universe by representing this body which in a particular manner belongs to it.

63. The body belonging to a monad which is its entelechy or its soul constitutes, together with this entelechy, what may be called a *living unit,* and together with this soul what may be called an *animal.* This body of a living being or of an animal is always an organism. For since every monad is, in its way, a mirror of the universe, and since the universe is ruled in a perfect order, there must also be an order in the representing, that is, in the perceptions of the soul, and consequently in the body. The representation of the universe in the body evinces this order.

64. Thus every body of a living being is a sort of divine machine or natural automaton, which infinitely surpasses all artificial automata. For a machine made by human art is not a machine in all its parts. The cog on a brass wheel, for instance, has parts or fragments which for us are no longer artificial things, and are no longer proper to the machine with respect to the purpose for which the wheel was designed. The machines of nature (namely, the living bodies) are, on the contrary, machines even in their smallest parts without any limit. Herein lies the difference between nature and art, that is, between divine and human art.

65. The author of nature, indeed, has been able to practice this divine and infinitely marvellous art because any portion of matter is not only infinitely divisible, as the ancients recognized, but also actually subdivided *ad infinitum:* every part having parts each of which has its own particular movement. For otherwise it would be impossible for every portion of matter to express the whole universe.

66. Hence it can be seen that in the smallest portion of matter there is a world of creatures, living beings, animals, entelechies, and souls.

67. Thus every portion of matter can be conceived as a garden full of plants or as a pond full of fish. But every branch of the plant, every limb of the animal, every drop of its humors, is again such a garden or such a pond.

68. And though the soil and the air in the intervals between the plants of the garden is not a plant, nor the water between the fishes a fish, yet these intervals contain again plants or fishes. But these living beings most frequently are so minute that they remain imperceptible to us.

69. Thus there is nothing uncultured, sterile or dead in the universe, no chaos, no disorder, though this may be what appears. It would be about the same with a pond seen from a distance: you would perceive a confused movement, a squirming of fishes, if I may say so, without discerning the single fish.

70. Hence it becomes clear that every living body has a dominant entelechy which in an animal is its soul. But the limbs of this living body are full of other living beings, plants or animals, each of which again has its entelechy or its dominant soul.

71. But you must not imagine—like some authors who have misinterpreted my thought—that each soul has a mass or portion of matter forever belonging or attached to it and that, consequently, it owns other living, though inferior, beings forever destined to serve it. For all bodies are, like rivers, in a perpetual flux; small parts enter and leave them continually.

72. Thus the soul changes its body bit by bit, and by degrees, so that it never is deprived all at once of all its organs; in animals there is frequently metamorphosis. Never, however, is there metempsychosis nor transmigration of souls. Nor are there any totally separate *souls,* nor *genii* without body. God alone is entirely bodiless.

73. This also proves that, strictly speaking, there never is either complete generation or perfect death, which would consist in the separation of the soul. What we call

generation consists in developments and growths, just as what we call *death* consists in involutions and diminutions.

74. Philosophers formerly have been very perplexed concerning the origin of forms, entelechies, or souls. Today, however, it has been discovered through precise observations made on plants, insects, and animals that the organized bodies of nature are never produced out of a chaos or putrefaction, but always out of seeds, in which doubtless there has been some *preformation.* Hence it has been concluded, not only that the organized body was already in the seed before conception, but also that there was a soul in this body, and, in short, the animal itself. Through the conception, furthermore, the animal has only been disposed to a great transformation, namely to become an animal of a different species. Something similar can even be observed outside generation, as, for instance, when worms become flies, or caterpillars butterflies.

75. Those animals among which some are elevated by means of the conception to the grade of larger animals, may be called *spermatic;* while those among them which remain within their species, that is, the majority, are born, multiply, and are destroyed like the large animals. Only a small number of elect pass on to a greater stage.

76. This, so far, has been but half the truth. Therefore I have concluded that if it be true that the animal never begins naturally, it will not end naturally either, and that consequently there will be, strictly speaking, neither generation nor entire destruction, that is, death. These arguments made a posteriori and drawn from experience agree perfectly with my principles deduced *a priori* a while ago.

77. Thus it may be said that not only the soul (mirror of an indestructible universe) is indestructible, but also that the animal itself is indestructible, albeit its machine often partly perishes, and casts off or takes on organic accretions.

78. These principles have enabled me to propose a natural explanation for the union or conformity of the soul and the organized body. The soul follows its own laws, and so does the body. They meet by virtue of the *pre-established harmony* prevailing among all substances, since they all are representations of one and the same universe.

79. The souls act according to the laws of final causes, through appetitions, ends, and means. The bodies act according to the laws of efficient causes, that is, of motion. And the two realms, that of efficient causes and that of final causes, are in mutual harmony.

80. Descartes has recognized that souls cannot impart force to bodies, because there is always the same quantity of force in matter. He believed, however, that the soul was able to change the directions of bodies. For at his time it was unknown yet that there is a law of nature according to which the total direction of matter is equally conserved. If he had been aware of this, he would have hit upon my system of pre-established harmony.

81. This system maintains that bodies act as though there were no souls (assuming the impossible); and that souls act as though there were no bodies; and that both act as though the one influenced the other.

82. As to *spirits* or reasonable souls, I find that essentially all the living beings and animals have the same nature, as I have said before, namely that the animal and the soul begin with the world and end no more than the world. Nevertheless, the reasonable souls have this in particular, that their little spermatic animals have only ordinary or sensitive souls, as long as they remain undeveloped. As soon, however, as those who, so to speak, are elected attain human nature through an actual conception, their sensitive souls are promoted to the rank of human nature and to the prerogative of spirits.

83. Among other differences existing between ordinary souls and spirits, some of which I have already pointed out, there is also this one, that souls in general are living mirrors or images of the created universe, while the spirits are in addition the images of the Deity itself or of the author of nature himself. They are capable of knowing the system of the universe and of imitating some of it by architectonic specimens, each spirit being like a small deity in his field.

84. This is the reason why the spirits are capable of entering a kind of society with God, and why with respect to them he is not only as an inventor is to his machine (this being the relation of God to the other creatures), but also as a prince to his subjects and even as a father to his children.

85. Hence it may easily be concluded that the assemblage of all the spirits must compose the City of God, that is, the most perfect city possible, under the most perfect monarch possible.

86. This City of God, this truly universal monarchy, is a moral world within the natural world; it is among the works of God the most exalted and the most divine. In it consists veritably the glory of God: for he would be without glory unless his greatness and goodness were recognized and admired by the spirits. Properly speaking, his goodness is directed toward this divine City, while his wisdom and power manifest themselves everywhere.

87. We have established above the perfect harmony between two natural realms, that of efficient causes and the other of final causes. To this we must add here still another harmony, namely, between the physical realm of nature and the moral realm of grace, that is, between God considered as the architect of the machine of the universe, and God considered as the monarch of the divine city of the spirits.

88. This harmony has the result that events lead to grace through the very processes of nature, and that our globe, for instance, must be destroyed and repaired through natural processes at the moments when the government of the spirits so demands, to chastise some and to reward others.

89. One may add that God as the architect satisfies in all respects God as the legislator. Thus sin must entail punishment according to the order of nature and as the very result of the mechanical structure of the universe; and, analogously, good actions will attract their rewards through machinelike corporeal processes. Of course, these results cannot be and ought not always to be obtained as an immediate consequence.

90. Finally, under this perfect government, no good action will remain without its reward, no evil action without its punishment. All events in this city conspire to the advantage of the good people, that is, of those who are not discontented in this great State; who, once they have fulfilled their duties, trust in providence and duly love and imitate the author of all good; who enjoy the contemplation of his perfections as required by the nature of the true *pure love,* which consists in taking pleasure in the felicity of the beloved. This pure love makes the wise and virtuous people work at everything that seems conformable to the divine will, presumed or antecedent, and yet renders them contented with any event that God actually brings about through his secret, consequent, and decisive will. They realize that, could we only understand sufficiently the order of the universe, we should find that this order surpasses all the wishes of the wisest and that it is impossible to improve it; that it is the best not only for the whole in general, but also for ourselves in particular. For ourselves, that is, provided we are duly attached to the author of all things, not only as to the architect and efficient cause of our being, but also as to the master and to the final cause who ought to provide the sole goal of our will and who alone can give us happiness.

GEORGE BERKELEY
1685–1753

George Berkeley was born near Kilkenny, Ireland, and, although an Anglican of English descent, he emphatically considered himself to be Irish. He studied at Kilkenny College and in 1700 went on to Trinity College, Dublin. There he read Descartes, Newton, and Locke. In 1707, he became a Fellow of the College and was ordained in the Anglican church. The next six years were to be the most philosophically productive in his life. In 1709, he published his *New Theory of Vision,* and in the following year his most important philosophic work, *A Treatise Concerning the Principles of Human Knowledge.* In 1711, he wrote *Discourse on Passive Obedience.* Two years later, he published a more popular exposition of the doctrine of his *Principles* in the form of *Three Dialogues Between Hylas and Philonous.*

For the next eleven years, Berkeley traveled widely, visiting with many of the great thinkers of his day. He became Dean of Derry in 1724, though most of his energy at this time seems to have been given to the founding of a college in the Bermudas. With promises of financial support, he sailed for Rhode Island in 1728 to establish farms for supplying his future college with food. Berkeley spent two and a half years in Rhode Island with his new wife and friends, waiting for the £20,000 the government had promised. When the funds never arrived, he finally gave up and returned to London.

In 1733, he published *Alciphron,* or *The Minute Philosopher,* against the freethinkers (agnostics), and in the following year *The Analyst,* a criticism of Newton. That same year, he was made Bishop of Cloyne. For the next eighteen years, he energetically served his remote, poor diocese. Among the works he wrote during this period are *The Querist* (1737), which used questions to propose public works and education as remedies to the crushing poverty he observed, and *Siris* (1744), an unusual work dealing with the medicinal value of tar water. In 1751, he lost his eldest son, and the next year he moved to Oxford, where another son was beginning his studies. On January 14, 1753, Berkeley died suddenly and he was buried at Christ Church, Oxford.

*   *   *

Like Locke before him, Berkeley accepted the empiricist doctrine that all we can know are ideas and that ideas come from perception or reflection. But Berkeley saw a problem in Locke's assertion of an external world of material "substances" giving rise to perceptions. If all we can know are ideas, how can we *know* there is a world "out there" giving rise to our ideas? Locke had said that the primary qualities of an "external object" (such as extension and solidity) are "utterly inseparable" from the objects themselves; whereas, this is not the case with secondary qualities (such as color, taste, etc.). But again, asked Berkeley, how can Locke know this? He cannot get "outside himself" to see which of his perceptions are actually a part of objects "out there." Berkeley concluded that Locke's philosophy will lead to skepticism, whereby we must admit that we cannot really know *anything* about the world "out there."

To avoid this skepticism, Berkeley made the radical claim that there is no "out there," or, more precisely, there is no *matter.* Berkeley's position, which is called "idealism," can be summed up in his famous phrase *"esse* is *percipi"*: to be is to be perceived. What we call "bodies," or physical objects, are simply stable collections of perceptions to which we give names such as "apples," "trees," and so on. These collections of perceptions have no existence apart from a perceiving mind. The answer to the famous conundrum "If a tree falls in the forest and no one hears it, does it make a sound?" is that if no one is perceiving it, it not only does *not* make a sound, the tree does not even exist!

Does this mean that trees go out of existence when no one is left in the forest to perceive them and that they come back into existence when someone enters the forest to perceive them again? It would seem that Berkeley must accept this odd conclusion were it not for one important point: God never leaves the forest and God is *always* perceiving the trees. By always holding all collections of perceptions in the divine mind, God ensures their continued existence and the perceived regularity in what we call "nature." This point has been classically formulated in the following limericks:

> There was a young man who said, "God,
> Must think it exceedingly odd
>   If he finds that this tree
>   Continues to be
> When there's no one about in the Quad."

> REPLY:
> "Dear Sir: Your astonishment's odd:
> *I* am always about in the Quad.
>   And that's why the tree
>   Continues to be,
> Since observed by, Yours faithfully, God."

Berkeley saw his philosophy as a common-sense attack on the metaphysical excesses of medieval Scholastics, Continental Rationalists, and even fellow empiricists such as Hobbes and Locke. Although Berkeley understood his philosophy to be common sense, his readers came to different conclusions. One prominent physician of his day claimed Berkeley was insane. The great Dr. Samuel Johnson dismissed Berkeley's ideas with his famous "I refute Berkeley *thus*" and then he kicked a rock. Of course, this did not refute Berkeley at all. It only proved Johnson had not understood Berkeley's point. Berkeley did not claim the non-existence of stones or that kicking a stone will not produce sensation. He claimed the rock did not exist apart from the perception of its solidity or the perception of pain when struck, and so on. An oft-repeated epitaph summarizes the general reaction to Berkeley: "His arguments produce no conviction, though they cannot be refuted."

*   *   *

In Berkeley's *Three Dialogues Between Hylas and Philonous,* reprinted here complete, Hylas argues for materialism, whereas Philonous presents Berkeley's own position. The dialogue form allows Berkeley to expound his own philosophy while meeting various anticipated objections.

For general introductions to Berkeley, see G.J. Warnock, *Berkeley* (Harmondsworth, Middlesex: Penguin Books, 1953); Harry M. Bracken, *Berkeley* (New York: St. Martin's Press, 1974); J.O. Urmson, *Berkeley* (Oxford: Oxford University Press, 1982)—part of the Past Masters series, now reprinted in the combined volume John Dunn et al., eds., *The British Empiricists* (Oxford: Oxford University Press, 1992); and David Berman, *George Berkeley: Idealism and the Man* (Oxford: Oxford University Press, 1994). For interesting but difficult discussions of Berkeley's arguments, see George Pitcher, *Berkeley* (London: Routledge, 1977) or Kenneth Winkler, *Berkeley: An Interpretation* (Oxford: Oxford University Press, 1989). For collections of essays, see Gale W. Engle and Gabriele Taylor, eds., *Berkeley's Principles of Human Knowledge* (Belmont, CA: Wadsworth, 1968); Colin M. Turbayne, ed., *Berkeley: Critical and Interpretive Essays* (Minneapolis: University of Minnesota Press, 1982); John Foster and Howard Robinson, eds., *Essays on Berkeley: A Tercentennial Celebration* (Oxford: Oxford University Press, 1985); and D.M. Armstrong and C.B. Martin, *Berkeley: A Collection of Critical Essays* (Hamden, CT: Garland, 1992)—a reprint of the second half of *Locke and Berkeley: A Collection of Critical Essays* (Garden City, NY: Doubleday, 1968).

THREE DIALOGUES BETWEEN HYLAS AND PHILONOUS, IN OPPOSITION TO SCEPTICS AND ATHEISTS

THE FIRST DIALOGUE

PHILONOUS: Good morrow, Hylas: I did not expect to find you abroad so early.

HYLAS: It is indeed something unusual; but my thoughts were so taken up with a subject I was discoursing of last night, that finding I could not sleep, I resolved to rise and take a turn in the garden.

PHILONOUS: It happened well, to let you see what innocent and agreeable pleasures you lose every morning. Can there be a pleasanter time of the day, or a more delightful season of the year? That purple sky, those wild but sweet notes of birds, the fra-

Fruits and Dishes on the Table, by Jan Davids de Heem (1606–1683). The underlying theme of *Vanitas* in Dutch still life presents a dual message in the arrangement of fine and rare objects. On the one hand the objects represent the joy of possessions and the good life, yet the half-eaten pie and the peeled fruit cause reflection on the brevity of human existence and the fleeting nature of material objects. Berkeley takes this a step further by denying material substance and claiming that such objects do not exist apart from a perceiving mind. *(Lauros-Giraudon/Art Resource)*

grant bloom upon the trees and flowers, the gentle influence of the rising sun, these and a thousand nameless beauties of nature inspire the soul with secret transports; its faculties too being at this time fresh and lively, are fit for those meditations, which the solitude of a garden and tranquillity of the morning naturally dispose us to. But I am afraid I interrupt your thoughts: for you seemed very intent on something.

HYLAS: It is true, I was, and shall be obliged to you if you will permit me to go on in the same vein; not that I would by any means deprive myself of your company, for my thoughts always flow more easily in conversation with a friend, than when I am alone: but my request is, that you would suffer me to impart my reflexions to you.

PHILONOUS: With all my heart, it is what I should have requested myself if you had not prevented me.

HYLAS: I was considering the odd fate of those men who have in all ages, through an affectation of being distinguished from the vulgar, or some unaccountable turn of thought, pretended either to believe nothing at all, or to believe the most extravagant things in the world. This however might be borne, if their paradoxes and scepticism did not draw after them some consequences of general disadvantage to mankind. But the mischief lies here; that when men of less leisure see them who are supposed to have spent their whole time in the pursuits of knowledge professing an entire ignorance of all things, or advancing such notions as are repugnant to plain and commonly received principles, they will be tempted to entertain suspicions concerning the most important truths, which they had hitherto held sacred and unquestionable.

PHILONOUS: I entirely agree with you, as to the ill tendency of the affected doubts of some philosophers, and fantastical conceits of others. I am even so far gone of late in this way of thinking, that I have quitted several of the sublime notions I had got in their schools for vulgar opinions. And I give it you on my word; since this revolt from metaphysical notions to the plain dictates of nature and common sense, I find my understanding strangely enlightened, so that I can now easily comprehend a great many things which before were all mystery and riddle.

HYLAS: I am glad to find there was nothing in the accounts I heard of you.

PHILONOUS: Pray, what were those?

HYLAS: You were represented, in last night's conversation, as one who maintained the most extravagant opinion that ever entered into the mind of man, to wit, that there is no such thing as *material substance* in the world.

PHILONOUS: That there is no such thing as what philosophers call *material substance,* I am seriously persuaded: but, if I were made to see anything absurd or sceptical in this, I should then have the same reason to renounce this that I imagine I have now to reject the contrary opinion.

HYLAS: What! Can anything be more fantastical, more repugnant to common sense, or a more manifest piece of scepticism, than to believe there is no such thing as *matter?*

PHILONOUS: Softly, good Hylas. What if it should prove that you, who hold there is, are, by virtue of that opinion, a greater *sceptic,* and maintain more paradoxes and repugnances to common sense, than I who believe no such thing?

HYLAS: You may as soon persuade me, the part is greater than the whole, as that, in order to avoid absurdity and scepticism, I should ever be obliged to give up my opinion in this point.

PHILONOUS: Well then, are you content to admit that opinion for true, which upon examination shall appear most agreeable to common sense, and remote from scepticism?

HYLAS: With all my heart. Since you are for raising disputes about the plainest things in nature, I am content for once to hear what you have to say.

PHILONOUS: Pray, Hylas, what do you mean by a *sceptic?*

HYLAS: I mean what all men mean—one that doubts of everything.

PHILONOUS: He then who entertains no doubts concerning some particular point, with regard to that point cannot be thought a *sceptic.*

HYLAS: I agree with you.

PHILONOUS: Whether does doubting consist in embracing the affirmative or negative side of a question?

HYLAS: In neither; for whoever understands English cannot but know that doubting signifies a suspense between both.

PHILONOUS: He then that denies any point, can no more be said to doubt of it, than he who affirms it with the same degree of assurance.

HYLAS: True.

PHILONOUS: And, consequently, for such his denial is no more to be esteemed a *sceptic* than the other.

HYLAS: I acknowledge it.

PHILONOUS: How comes it to pass then, Hylas, that you pronounce me a *sceptic,* because I deny what you affirm, to wit the existence of matter? Since, for aught you can tell I am as peremptory in my denial, as you in your affirmation.

HYLAS: Hold, Philonous, I have been a little out in my definition; but every false step a man makes in discourse is not to be insisted on. I said indeed that a sceptic was one who doubted of everything; but I should have added, or who denies the reality and truth of things.

PHILONOUS: What things? Do you mean the principles and theorems of sciences? But these you know are universal intellectual notions, and consequently independent of matter. The denial therefore of this does not imply the denying of them.

HYLAS: I grant it. But are there no other things? What think you of distrusting the senses, of denying the real existence of sensible things, or pretending to know nothing of them. Is not this sufficient to denominate a man a *sceptic?*

PHILONOUS: Shall we therefore examine which of us it is that denies the reality of sensible things, or professes the greatest ignorance of them; since, if I take you rightly, he is to be esteemed the greatest *sceptic?*

HYLAS: That is what I desire.

PHILONOUS: What mean you by Sensible Things?

HYLAS: Those things which are perceived by the senses. Can you imagine that I mean anything else?

PHILONOUS: Pardon me, Hylas, if I am desirous clearly to apprehend your notions, since this may much shorten our inquiry. Suffer me then to ask you this farther question. Are those things only perceived by the senses which are perceived immediately? Or, may those things properly be said to be *sensible* which are perceived mediately, or not without the intervention of others?

HYLAS: I do not sufficiently understand you.

PHILONOUS: In reading a book, what I immediately perceive are the letters; but mediately, or by means of these, are suggested to my mind the notions of God, virtue, truth, &c. Now, that the letters are truly sensible things, or perceived by sense, there is no doubt: but I would know whether you take the things suggested by them to be so too.

HYLAS: No, certainly: it were absurd to think *God* or *virtue* sensible things; though they may be signified and suggested to the mind by sensible marks, with which they have an arbitrary connexion.

PHILONOUS: It seems then, that by *sensible things* you mean those only which can be perceived immediately by sense?

HYLAS: Right.

PHILONOUS: Does it not follow from this, that though I see one part of the sky red, and another blue, and that my reason does thence evidently conclude there must be some cause of that diversity of colours, yet that cause cannot be said to be a sensible thing, or perceived by the sense of seeing?

HYLAS: It does.

PHILONOUS: In like manner, though I hear variety of sounds, yet I cannot be said to hear the causes of those sounds?

HYLAS: You cannot.

PHILONOUS: And when by my touch I perceive a thing to be hot and heavy, I cannot say, with any truth or propriety, that I feel the cause of its heat or weight?

HYLAS: To prevent any more questions of this kind, I tell you once for all, that by *sensible things* I mean those only which are perceived by sense; and that in truth the senses perceive nothing which they do not perceive immediately: for they make no inferences. The deducing therefore of causes or occasions from effects and appearances, which alone are perceived by sense, entirely relates to reason.

PHILONOUS: This point then is agreed between us—That *sensible things are those only which are immediately perceived by sense.* You will farther inform me, whether we immediately perceive by sight anything beside light, and colours, and figures; or by hearing, anything but sounds; by the palate, anything beside tastes; by the smell, beside odours; or by the touch, more than tangible qualities.

HYLAS: We do not.

PHILONOUS: It seems, therefore, that if you take away all sensible qualities, there remains nothing sensible?

HYLAS: I grant it.

PHILONOUS: Sensible things therefore are nothing else but so many sensible qualities, or combinations of sensible qualities?

HYLAS: Nothing else.

PHILONOUS: Heat then is a sensible thing?

HYLAS: Certainly.

PHILONOUS: Does the reality of sensible things consist in being perceived? Or, is it something distinct from their being perceived, and that bears no relation to the mind?

HYLAS: To *exist* is one thing, and to be *perceived* is another.

PHILONOUS: I speak with regard to sensible things only. And of these I ask, whether by their real existence you mean a subsistence exterior to the mind, and distinct from their being perceived?

HYLAS: I mean a real absolute being, distinct from, and without any relation to, their being perceived.

PHILONOUS: Heat therefore, if it be allowed a real being, must exist without the mind?

HYLAS: It must.

PHILONOUS: Tell me, Hylas, is this real existence equally compatible to all degrees of heat, which we perceive; or is there any reason why we should attribute it to some, and deny it to others? And if there be, pray let me know that reason.

HYLAS: Whatever degree of heat we perceive by sense, we may be sure the same exists in the object that occasions it.

PHILONOUS: What! The greatest as well as the least?

HYLAS: I tell you, the reason is plainly the same in respect of both. They are both perceived by sense; nay, the greater degree of heat is more sensibly perceived, and consequently, if there is any difference, we are more certain of its real existence than we can be of the reality of a lesser degree.

PHILONOUS: But is not the most vehement and intense degree of heat a very great pain?

HYLAS: No one can deny it.

PHILONOUS: And is any unperceiving thing capable of pain or pleasure?

HYLAS: No, certainly.

PHILONOUS: Is your material substance a senseless being, or a being endowed with sense and perception?

HYLAS: It is senseless without doubt.

PHILONOUS: It cannot therefore be the subject of pain?

HYLAS: By no means.

PHILONOUS: Nor consequently of the greatest heat perceived by sense, since you acknowledge this to be no small pain?

HYLAS: I grant it.

PHILONOUS: What shall we say then of your external object; is it a material substance, or no?

HYLAS: It is a material substance with the sensible qualities inhering in it.

PHILONOUS: How then can a great heat exist in it, since you own it cannot in a material substance? I desire you would clear this point.

HYLAS: Hold, Philonous, I fear I was out in yielding intense heat to be a pain. It should seem rather, that pain is something distinct from heat, and the consequence or effect of it.

PHILONOUS: Upon putting your hand near the fire, do you perceive one simple uniform sensation, or two distinct sensations?

HYLAS: But one simple sensation.

PHILONOUS: Is not the heat immediately perceived?

HYLAS: It is.

PHILONOUS: And the pain?

HYLAS: True.

PHILONOUS: Seeing therefore they are both immediately perceived at the same time, and the fire affects you only with one simple or uncompounded idea, it follows that this same simple idea is both the intense heat immediately perceived, and the pain; and, consequently, that the intense heat immediately perceived is nothing distinct from a particular sort of pain.

HYLAS: It seems so.

PHILONOUS: Again, try in your thoughts, Hylas, if you can conceive a vehement sensation to be without pain or pleasure.

HYLAS: I cannot.

PHILONOUS: Or can you frame to yourself an idea of sensible pain or pleasure in general, abstracted from every particular idea of heat, cold, tastes, smells? &c.

HYLAS: I do not find that I can.

PHILONOUS: Does it not therefore follow, that sensible pain is nothing distinct from those sensations or ideas, in an intense degree?

HYLAS: It is undeniable; and, to speak the truth, I begin to suspect a very great heat cannot exist but in a mind perceiving it.

PHILONOUS: What! Are you then in that *sceptical* state of suspense, between affirming and denying?

HYLAS: I think I may be positive in the point. A very violent and painful heat cannot exist without the mind.

PHILONOUS: It hath not therefore, according to you, any real being?

HYLAS: I own it.

PHILONOUS: Is it therefore certain, that there is no body in nature really hot?

HYLAS: I have not denied there is any real heat in bodies. I only say, there is no such thing as an intense real heat.

PHILONOUS: But, did you not say before that all degrees of heat were equally real; or, if there was any difference, that the greater were more undoubtedly real than the lesser?

HYLAS: True: but it was because I did not then consider the ground there is for distinguishing between them, which I now plainly see. And it is this: because intense heat is nothing else but a particular kind of painful sensation; and pain cannot exist but in a perceiving being; it follows that no intense heat can really exist in an unperceiving corporeal substance. But this is no reason why we should deny heat in an inferior degree to exist in such a substance.

PHILONOUS: But how shall we be able to discern those degrees of heat which exist only in the mind from those which exist without it?

HYLAS: That is no difficult matter. You know the least pain cannot exist unperceived; whatever, therefore, degree of heat is a pain exists only in the mind. But, as for all other degrees of heat, nothing obliges us to think the same of them.

PHILONOUS: I think you granted before that no unperceiving being was capable of pleasure, any more than of pain.

HYLAS: I did.

PHILONOUS: And is not warmth, or a more gentle degree of heat than what causes uneasiness, a pleasure?

HYLAS: What then?

PHILONOUS: Consequently, it cannot exist without the mind in an unperceiving substance, or body.

HYLAS: So it seems.

PHILONOUS: Since, therefore, as well those degrees of heat that are not painful, as those that are, can exist only in a thinking substance; may we not conclude that external bodies are absolutely incapable of any degree of heat whatsoever?

HYLAS: On second thoughts, I do not think it so evident that warmth is a pleasure as that a great degree of heat is a pain.

PHILONOUS: I do not pretend that warmth is as great a pleasure as heat is a pain. But, if you grant it to be even a small pleasure, it serves to make good my conclusion.

HYLAS: I could rather call it an *indolence*. It seems to be nothing more than a privation of both pain and pleasure. And that such a quality or state as this may agree to an unthinking substance, I hope you will not deny.

PHILONOUS: If you are resolved to maintain that warmth, or a gentle degree of heat, is no pleasure, I know not how to convince you otherwise than by appealing to your own sense. But what think you of cold?

HYLAS: The same that I do of heat. An intense degree of cold is a pain; for to feel a very great cold, is to perceive a great uneasiness: it cannot therefore exist without the mind; but a lesser degree of cold may, as well as a lesser degree of heat.

PHILONOUS: Those bodies, therefore, upon whose application to our own, we perceive a moderate degree of heat, must be concluded to have a moderate degree of heat or warmth in them—and those, upon whose application we feel a like degree of cold, must be thought to have cold in them.

HYLAS: They must.

PHILONOUS: Can any doctrine be true that necessarily leads a man into an absurdity?

HYLAS: Without doubt it cannot.

PHILONOUS: Is it not an absurdity to think that the same thing should be at the same time both cold and warm?

HYLAS: It is.

PHILONOUS: Suppose now one of your hands hot, and the other cold, and that they are both at once put into the same vessel of water, in an intermediate state; will not the water seem cold to one hand, and warm to the other?

HYLAS: It will.

PHILONOUS: Ought we not therefore, by your principles, to conclude it is really both cold and warm at the same time, that is, according to your own concession, to believe an absurdity?

HYLAS: I confess it seems so.

PHILONOUS: Consequently, the principles themselves are false, since you have granted that no true principle leads to an absurdity.

HYLAS: But, after all, can anything be more absurd than to say, *there is no heat in the fire?*

PHILONOUS: To make the point still clearer; tell me whether, in two cases exactly alike, we ought not to make the same judgment?

HYLAS: We ought.

PHILONOUS: When a pin pricks your finger, does it not rend and divide the fibres of your flesh?

HYLAS: It does.

PHILONOUS: And when a coal burns your finger, does it any more?

HYLAS: It does not.

PHILONOUS: Since, therefore, you neither judge the sensation itself occasioned by the pin, nor anything like it to be in the pin; you should not, conformably to what you have now granted, judge the sensation occasioned by the fire, or anything like it, to be in the fire.

HYLAS: Well, since it must be so, I am content to yield this point, and acknowledge that heat and cold are only sensations existing in our minds. But there still remain qualities enough to secure the reality of external things.

PHILONOUS: But what will you say, Hylas, if it shall appear that the case is the same with regard to all other sensible qualities, and that they can no more be supposed to exist without the mind, than heat and cold?

HYLAS: Then indeed you will have done something to the purpose; but that is what I despair of seeing proved.

PHILONOUS: Let us examine them in order. What think you of tastes—do they exist without the mind, or no?

HYLAS: Can any man in his senses doubt whether sugar is sweet, or wormwood bitter?

PHILONOUS: Inform me, Hylas. Is a sweet taste a particular kind of pleasure or pleasant sensation, or is it not?

HYLAS: It is.

PHILONOUS: And is not bitterness some kind of uneasiness or pain?

HYLAS: I grant it.

PHILONOUS: If therefore sugar and wormwood are unthinking corporeal substances existing without the mind, how can sweetness and bitterness, that is, pleasure and pain, agree to them?

HYLAS: Hold, Philonous, I now see what it was deluded me all this time. You asked whether heat and cold, sweetness and bitterness, were not particular sorts of pleasure and pain; to which I answered simply, that they were. Whereas I should have thus distinguished:—those qualities, as perceived by us, are pleasures or pains; but not as existing in the external objects. We must not therefore conclude absolutely, that there is no heat in the fire, or sweetness in the sugar, but only that heat or sweetness, as perceived by us, are not in the fire or sugar. What say you to this?

PHILONOUS: I say it is nothing to the purpose. Our discourse proceeded altogether concerning sensible things, which you defined to be, the things we *immediately perceive by our senses.* Whatever other qualities, therefore, you speak of as distinct from these, I know nothing of them, neither do they at all belong to the point in dispute. You may, indeed, pretend to have discovered certain qualities which you do not perceive, and assert those insensible qualities exist in fire and sugar. But what use can be made of this to your present purpose, I am at a loss to conceive. Tell me then once more, do you acknowledge that heat and cold, sweetness and bitterness (meaning those qualities which are perceived by the senses), do not exist without the mind?

HYLAS: I see it is to no purpose to hold out, so I give up the cause as to those mentioned qualities. Though I profess it sounds oddly, to say that sugar is not sweet.

PHILONOUS: But, for your farther satisfaction, take this along with you: that which at other times seems sweet, shall, to a distempered palate, appear bitter. And, nothing can be plainer than that divers persons perceive different tastes in the same food; since that which one man delights in, another abhors. And how could this be, if the taste was something really inherent in the food?

HYLAS: I acknowledge I know not how.

PHILONOUS: In the next place, *odours* are to be considered. And, with regard to these, I would fain know whether what hath been said of tastes does not exactly agree to them? Are they not so many pleasing or displeasing sensations?

HYLAS: They are.

PHILONOUS: Can you then conceive it possible that they should exist in an unperceiving thing?

HYLAS: I cannot.

PHILONOUS: Or, can you imagine that filth and ordure affect those brute animals that feed on them out of choice, with the same smells which we perceive in them?

HYLAS: By no means.

PHILONOUS: May we not therefore conclude of smells, as of the other forementioned qualities, that they cannot exist in any but a perceiving substance or mind?

HYLAS: I think so.

PHILONOUS: Then as to *sounds,* what must we think of them: are they accidents really inherent in external bodies, or not?

HYLAS: That they inhere not in the sonorous bodies is plain from hence: because a bell struck in the exhausted receiver of an air-pump sends forth no sound. The air, therefore, must be thought the subject of sound.

PHILONOUS: What reason is there for that, Hylas?

HYLAS: Because, when any motion is raised in the air, we perceive a sound greater or lesser, according to the air's motion; but without some motion in the air, we never hear any sound at all.

PHILONOUS: And granting that we never hear a sound but when some motion is produced in the air, yet I do not see how you can infer from thence, that the sound itself is in the air.

HYLAS: It is this very motion in the external air that produces in the mind the sensation of *sound*. For, striking on the drum of the ear, it causes a vibration, which by the auditory nerves being communicated to the brain, the soul is thereupon affected with the sensation called *sound*.

PHILONOUS: What! Is sound then a sensation?

HYLAS: I tell you, as perceived by us, it is a particular sensation in the mind.

PHILONOUS: And can any sensation exist without the mind?

HYLAS: No, certainly.

PHILONOUS: How then can sound, being a sensation, exist in the air, if by the *air* you mean a senseless substance existing without the mind?

HYLAS: You must distinguish, Philonous, between sound as it is perceived by us, and as it is in itself; or (which is the same thing) between the sound we immediately perceive, and that which exists without us. The former, indeed, is a particular kind of sensation, but the latter is merely a vibrative or undulatory motion in the air.

PHILONOUS: I thought I had already obviated that distinction, by the answer I gave when you were applying it in a like case before. But, to say no more of that, are you sure then that sound is really nothing but motion?

HYLAS: I am.

PHILONOUS: Whatever therefore agrees to real sound, may with truth be attributed to motion?

HYLAS: It may.

PHILONOUS: It is then good sense to speak of *motion* as of a thing that is *loud, sweet, acute,* or *grave.*

HYLAS: I see you are resolved not to understand me. Is it not evident those accidents or modes belong only to sensible sound, or *sound* in the common acceptation of the word, but not to *sound* in the real and philosophic sense; which, as I just now told you, is nothing but a certain motion of the air?

PHILONOUS: It seems then there are two sorts of sound—the one vulgar, or that which is heard, the other philosophical and real?

HYLAS: Even so.

PHILONOUS: And the latter consists in motion?

HYLAS: I told you so before.

PHILONOUS: Tell me, Hylas, to which of the senses, think you, the idea of motion belongs? To the hearing?

HYLAS: No, certainly; but to the sight and touch.

PHILONOUS: It should follow then, that, according to you, real sounds may possibly be *seen* or *felt,* but never *heard.*

HYLAS: Look you, Philonous, you may, if you please, make a jest of my opinion, but that will not alter the truth of things. I own, indeed, the inferences you draw me into sound something oddly, but common language, you know, is framed by, and for the use of the vulgar: we must not therefore wonder if expressions adapted to exact philosophic notions seem uncouth and out of the way.

PHILONOUS: Is it come to that? I assure you, I imagine myself to have gained no small point, since you make so light of departing from common phrases and opinions; it being a main part of our inquiry, to examine whose notions are widest of the common road, and most repugnant to the general sense of the world. But, can you think it no more than a philosophical paradox, to say that *real sounds are never heard,* and that the idea of them is obtained by some other sense? And is there nothing in this contrary to nature and the truth of things?

HYLAS: To deal ingenuously, I do not like it. And, after the concessions already made, I had as well grant that sounds too have no real being without the mind.

PHILONOUS: And I hope you will make no difficulty to acknowledge the same of colours.

HYLAS: Pardon me: the case of colours is very different. Can anything be plainer than that we see them on the objects?

PHILONOUS: The objects you speak of are I suppose, corporeal substances existing without the mind?

HYLAS: They are.

PHILONOUS: And have true and real colours inhering in them?

HYLAS: Each visible object hath that colour which we see in it.

PHILONOUS: How! Is there anything visible but what we perceive by sight?

HYLAS: There is not.

PHILONOUS: And, do we perceive anything by sense which we do not perceive immediately?

HYLAS: How often must I be obliged to repeat the same thing? I tell you, we do not.

PHILONOUS: Have patience, good Hylas; and tell me once more, whether there is anything immediately perceived by the senses, except sensible qualities. I know you asserted there was not; but I would now be informed, whether you still persist in the same opinion.

HYLAS: I do.

PHILONOUS: Pray, is your corporeal substance either a sensible quality, or made up of sensible qualities?

HYLAS: What a question that is! Who ever thought it was?

PHILONOUS: My reason for asking was, because in saying, *each visible object hath that colour which we see in it,* you make visible objects to be corporeal substances; which implies either that corporeal substances are sensible qualities, or else that there is something besides sensible qualities perceived by sight: but, as this point was formerly agreed between us, and is still maintained by you, it is a clear consequence, that your corporeal substance is nothing distinct from sensible qualities.

HYLAS: You may draw as many absurd consequences as you please, and endeavour to perplex the plainest things; but you shall never persuade me out of my senses. I clearly understand my own meaning.

PHILONOUS: I wish you would make me understand it too. But, since you are unwilling to have your notion of corporeal substance examined, I shall urge that point no farther. Only be pleased to let me know, whether the same colours which we see exist in external bodies, or some other.

HYLAS: The very same.

PHILONOUS: What! Are then the beautiful red and purple we see on yonder clouds really in them? Or do you imagine, they have in themselves any other form than that of a dark mist or vapour?

HYLAS: I must own, Philonous, those colours are not really in the clouds as they seem to be at this distance. They are only apparent colours.

PHILONOUS: *Apparent* call you them? How shall we distinguish these apparent colours from real?

HYLAS: Very easily. Those are to be thought apparent which, appearing only at a distance, vanish upon a nearer approach.

PHILONOUS: And those, I suppose, are to be thought real which are discovered by the most near and exact survey.

HYLAS: Right.

PHILONOUS: Is the nearest and exactest survey made by the help of a microscope, or by the naked eye?

HYLAS: By a microscope, doubtless.

PHILONOUS: But a microscope often discovers colours in an object different from those perceived by the unassisted sight. And, in case we had microscopes magnifying to any assigned degree, it is certain that no object whatsoever, viewed through them, would appear in the same colour which it exhibits to the naked eye.

HYLAS: And what will you conclude from all this? You cannot argue that there are really and naturally no colours on objects: because by artificial managements they may be altered, or made to vanish.

PHILONOUS: I think it may evidently be concluded from your own concessions, that all the colours we see with our naked eyes are only apparent as those on the clouds, since they vanish upon a more close and accurate inspection which is afforded us by a microscope. Then, as to what you say by way of prevention: I ask you whether the real and natural state of an object is better discovered by a very sharp and piercing sight, or by one which is less sharp?

HYLAS: By the former without doubt.

PHILONOUS: Is it not plain from *Dioptrics* that microscopes make the sight more penetrating, and represent objects as they would appear to the eye in case it were naturally endowed with a most exquisite sharpness?

HYLAS: It is.

PHILONOUS: Consequently the microscopical representation is to be thought that which best sets forth the real nature of the thing, or what it is in itself. The colours, therefore, by it perceived are more genuine and real than those perceived otherwise.

HYLAS: I confess there is something in what you say.

PHILONOUS: Besides, it is not only possible but manifest, that there actually are animals whose eyes are by nature framed to perceive those things which by reason of their minuteness escape our sight. What think you of those inconceivably small animals perceived by glasses? Must we suppose they are all stark blind? Or, in case they see, can it be imagined their sight hath not the same use in preserving their bodies from injuries, which appears in that of all other animals? And if it hath, is it not evident they must see particles less than their own bodies; which will present them with a far different view in each object from that which strikes our senses? Even our own eyes do not always represent objects to us after the same manner. In the jaundice every one knows that all things seem yellow. Is it not therefore highly probable those animals in whose eyes we discern a very different texture from that of ours, and whose bodies abound with different humors, do not see the same colours in every object that we do? From all which, should it not seem to follow that all colours are equally apparent, and that none of those which we perceive are really inherent in any outward object?

HYLAS: It should.

PHILONOUS: The point will be past all doubt, if you consider that, in case colours were real properties or affections inherent in external bodies, they could admit of no alteration without some change wrought in the very bodies themselves: but, is it not evident from what hath been said that, upon the use of microscopes, upon a change happening in the humors of the eye, or a variation of distance, without any manner of real alteration in the thing itself, the colours of any object are either changed, or totally disappear? Nay, all other circumstances remaining the same, change but the situation of some objects, and they shall present different colours to the eye. The same thing happens upon viewing an object in various degrees of light. And what is more known than that the same bodies appear differently coloured by candle-light from what they do in the open day? Add to these the experiment of a prism which, separating the heterogeneous rays of light, alters the colour of any object, and will cause the whitest to appear of a deep blue or red to the naked eye. And now tell me whether you are still of opinion that every body hath its true real colour inhering in it; and, if you think it hath, I would fain know farther from you, what certain distance and position of the object, what peculiar texture and formation of the eye, what degree or kind of light is necessary for ascertaining that true colour, and distinguishing it from apparent ones.

HYLAS: I own myself entirely satisfied, that they are all equally apparent, and that there is no such thing as colour really inhering in external bodies, but that it is altogether in the light. And what confirms me in this opinion is, that in proportion to the light colours are still more or less vivid; and if there be no light, then are there no colours perceived. Besides, allowing there are colours on external objects, yet, how is it possible for us to perceive them? For no external body affects the mind, unless it acts first on our organs of sense. But the only action of bodies is motion; and motion cannot be communicated otherwise than by impulse. A distant object therefore cannot act on the eye, nor consequently make itself or its properties perceivable to the soul. Whence it plainly follows that it is immediately some contiguous substance, which, operating on the eye, occasions a perception of colours: and such is light.

PHILONOUS: How! Is light then a substance?

HYLAS: I tell you, Philonous, external light is nothing but a thin fluid substance, whose minute particles being agitated with a brisk motion, and in various manners reflected from the different surfaces of outward objects to the eyes, communicate different motions to the optic nerves; which, being propagated to the brain, cause therein various impressions; and these are attended with the sensations of red, blue, yellow, &c.

PHILONOUS: It seems then the light does no more than shake the optic nerves.

HYLAS: Nothing else.

PHILONOUS: And consequent to each particular motion of the nerves, the mind is affected with a sensation, which is some particular colour.

HYLAS: Right.

PHILONOUS: And these sensations have no existence without the mind.

HYLAS: They have not.

PHILONOUS: How then do you affirm that colours are in the light; since by light you understand a corporeal substance external to the mind?

HYLAS: Light and colours, as immediately perceived by us, I grant cannot exist without the mind. But in themselves they are only the motions and configurations of certain insensible particles of matter.

PHILONOUS: Colours then, in the vulgar sense, or taken for the immediate objects of sight, cannot agree to any but a perceiving substance.

HYLAS: That is what I say.

PHILONOUS: Well then, since you give up the point as to those sensible qualities which are alone thought colours by all mankind beside, you may hold what you please with regard to those invisible ones of the philosophers. It is not my business to dispute about them; only I would advise you to bethink yourself, whether, considering the inquiry we are upon, it be prudent for you to affirm—*the red and blue which we see are not real colours, but certain unknown motions and figures which no man ever did or can see are truly so.* Are not these shocking notions, and are not they subject to as many ridiculous inferences, as those you were obliged to renounce before in the case of sounds?

HYLAS: I frankly own, Philonous, that it is in vain to stand out any longer. Colours, sounds, tastes, in a word all those termed *secondary qualities,* have certainly no existence without the mind. But by this acknowledgment I must not be supposed to derogate anything from the reality of matter, or external objects; seeing it is no more than several philosophers maintain, who nevertheless are the farthest imaginable from denying matter. For the clearer understanding of this, you must know sensible qualities are by philosophers divided into *primary* and *secondary.* The former are extension, figure, solidity, gravity, motion, and rest; and these they hold exist really in bodies. The latter are those above enumerated; or, briefly, all sensible qualities beside the primary; which they assert are only so many sensations or ideas existing nowhere but in the mind. But all this, I doubt not, you are apprised of. For my part, I have been a long time sensible there was such an opinion current among philosophers, but was never thoroughly convinced of its truth until now.

PHILONOUS: You are still then of opinion that extension and figures are inherent in external unthinking substances?

HYLAS: I am.

PHILONOUS: But what if the same arguments which are brought against secondary qualities will hold good against these also?

HYLAS: Why then I shall be obliged to think, they too exist only in the mind.

PHILONOUS: Is it your opinion the very figure and extension which you perceive by sense exist in the outward object or material substance?

HYLAS: It is.

PHILONOUS: Have all other animals as good grounds to think the same of the figure and extension which they see and feel?

HYLAS: Without doubt, if they have any thought at all.

PHILONOUS: Answer me, Hylas. Think you the senses were bestowed upon all animals for their preservation and well-being in life? Or were they given to men alone for this end?

HYLAS: I make no question but they have the same use in all other animals.

PHILONOUS: If so, is it not necessary they should be enabled by them to perceive their own limbs, and those bodies which are capable of harming them?

HYLAS: Certainly.

PHILONOUS: A mite therefore must be supposed to see his own foot, and things equal or even less than it, as bodies of some considerable dimension, though at the same time they appear to you scarce discernible, or at best as so many visible points?

HYLAS: I cannot deny it.

PHILONOUS: And to creatures less than the mite they will seem yet larger?

HYLAS: They will.

PHILONOUS: Insomuch that what you can hardly discern will to another extremely minute animal appear as some huge mountain?

HYLAS: All this I grant.

PHILONOUS: Can one and the same thing be at the same time in itself of different dimensions?

HYLAS: That were absurd to imagine.

PHILONOUS: But, from what you have laid down it follows that both the extension by you perceived, and that perceived by the mite itself, as likewise all those perceived by lesser animals, are each of them the true extension of the mite's foot; that is to say, by your own principles you are led into an absurdity.

HYLAS: There seems to be some difficulty in the point.

PHILONOUS: Again, have you not acknowledged that no real inherent property of any object can be changed without some change in the thing itself?

HYLAS: I have.

PHILONOUS: But, as we approach to or recede from an object, the visible extension varies, being at one distance ten or a hundred times greater than another. Does it not therefore follow from hence likewise that it is not really inherent in the object?

HYLAS: I own I am at a loss what to think.

PHILONOUS: Your judgment will soon be determined, if you will venture to think as freely concerning this quality as you have done concerning the rest. Was it not admitted as a good argument, that neither heat nor cold was in the water, because it seemed warm to one hand and cold to the other?

HYLAS: It was.

PHILONOUS: Is it not the very same reasoning to conclude, there is no extension or figure in an object, because to one eye it shall seem little, smooth, and round, when at the same time it appears to the other, great, uneven, and regular?

HYLAS: The very same. But does this latter fact ever happen?

PHILONOUS: You may at any time make the experiment, by looking with one eye bare, and with the other through a microscope.

HYLAS: I know not how to maintain it; and yet I am loath to give up *extension,* I see so many odd consequences following upon such a concession.

PHILONOUS: Odd, say you? After the concessions already made, I hope you will stick at nothing for its oddness. But, on the other hand, should it not seem very odd, if the general reasoning which includes all other sensible qualities did not also include extension? If it be allowed that no idea, nor anything like an idea, can exist in an unperceiving substance, then surely it follows that no figure, or mode of extension, which we can either perceive, or imagine, or have any idea of, can be really inherent in matter; not to mention the peculiar difficulty there must be in conceiving a material substance, prior to and distinct from extension to be the *substratum* of extension. Be the sensible quality what it will—figure, or sound, or colour, it seems alike impossible it should subsist in that which does not perceive it.

HYLAS: I give up the point for the present, reserving still a right to retract my opinion, in case I shall hereafter discover any false step in my progress to it.

PHILONOUS: That is a right you cannot be denied. Figures and extension being dispatched, we proceed next to *motion.* Can a real motion in any external body be at the same time very swift and very slow?

HYLAS: It cannot.

PHILONOUS: Is not the motion of a body swift in a reciprocal proportion to the time it takes up in describing any given space? Thus a body that describes a mile in an hour moves three times faster than it would in case it described only a mile in three hours.

HYLAS: I agree with you.

PHILONOUS: And is not time measured by the succession of ideas in our minds?

HYLAS: It is.

PHILONOUS: And is it not possible ideas should succeed one another twice as fast in your mind as they do in mine, or in that of some spirit of another kind?

HYLAS: I own it.

PHILONOUS: Consequently the same body may to another seem to perform its motion over any space in half the time that it does to you. And the same reasoning will hold as to any other proportion: that is to say, according to your principles (since the motions perceived are both really in the object) it is possible one and the same body shall be really moved the same way at once, both very swift and very slow. How is this consistent either with common sense, or with what you just now granted?

HYLAS: I have nothing to say to it.

PHILONOUS: Then as for *solidity;* either you do not mean any sensible quality by that word, and so it is beside our inquiry: or if you do, it must be either hardness or resistance. But both the one and the other are plainly relative to our senses: it being evident that what seems hard to one animal may appear soft to another, who hath greater force and firmness of limbs. Nor is it less plain that the resistance I feel is not in the body.

HYLAS: I own the very sensation of resistance, which is all you immediately perceive, is not in the *body;* but the cause of that sensation is.

PHILONOUS: But the causes of our sensations are not things immediately perceived, and therefore are not sensible. This point I thought had been already determined.

HYLAS: I own it was; but you will pardon me if I seem a little embarrassed: I know not how to quit my old notions.

PHILONOUS: To help you out, do but consider that if extension be once acknowledged to have no existence without the mind, the same must necessarily be granted of motion, solidity, and gravity; since they all evidently suppose extension. It is therefore superfluous to inquire particularly concerning each of them. In denying extension, you have denied them all to have any real existence.

HYLAS: I wonder, Philonous, if what you say be true, why those philosophers who deny the secondary qualities any real existence should yet attribute it to the primary. If there is no difference between them, how can this be accounted for?

PHILONOUS: It is not my business to account for every opinion of the philosophers. But, among other reasons which may be assigned for this, it seems probable that pleasure and pain being rather annexed to the former than the latter may be one. Heat and cold, tastes and smells, have something more vividly pleasing or disagreeable than the ideas of extension, figure, and motion affect us with. And, it being too visibly absurd to hold that pain or pleasure can be in an unperceiving substance, men are more easily weaned from believing the external existence of the secondary than the primary qualities. You will be satisfied there is something in this, if you recollect the difference you made between an intense and more moderate degree of heat; allowing the one a real existence, while you denied it to the other. But, after all, there is no rational ground for that distinction; for, surely an indifferent sensation is as truly a *sensation* as one more pleasing or painful; and consequently should not any more than they be supposed to exist in an unthinking subject.

HYLAS: It is just come into my head, Philonous, that I have somewhere heard of a distinction between absolute and sensible extension. Now, though it be acknowledged that *great* and *small,* consisting merely in the relation which other extended beings have to the parts of our own bodies, do not really inhere in the substances themselves; yet nothing obliges us to hold the same with regard to *absolute extension,* which is something abstracted from *great* and *small,* from this or that particular magnitude or figure. So likewise as to motion; *swift* and *slow* are altogether relative to the succession of ideas in our own minds. But, it does not follow, because those modifications of motion exist not without the mind, that therefore absolute motion abstracted from them does not.

PHILONOUS: Pray what is it that distinguishes one motion, or one part of extension, from another? Is it not something sensible, as some degree of swiftness or slowness, some certain magnitude or figure peculiar to each?

HYLAS: I think so.

PHILONOUS: These qualities, therefore, stripped of all sensible properties, are without all specific and numerical differences, as the schools call them.

HYLAS: They are.

PHILONOUS: That is to say, they are extension in general, and motion in general.

HYLAS: Let it be so.

PHILONOUS: But it is a universally received maxim that *Everything which exists is particular.* How then can motion in general, or extension in general, exist in any corporeal substance?

HYLAS: I will take time to solve your difficulty.

PHILONOUS: But I think the point may be speedily decided. Without doubt you can tell whether you are able to frame this or that idea. Now I am content to put our dispute on this issue. If you can frame in your thoughts a distinct abstract idea of motion or extension, divested of all those sensible modes, as swift and slow, great and small, round and square, and the like, which are acknowledged to exist only in the mind, I will then yield the point you contend for. But if you cannot, it will be unreasonable on your side to insist any longer upon what you have no notion of.

HYLAS: To confess ingenuously, I cannot.

PHILONOUS: Can you even separate the ideas of extension and motion from the ideas of all those qualities which they who make the distinction term *secondary?*

HYLAS: What! Is it not an easy matter to consider extension and motion by themselves, abstracted from all other sensible qualities? Pray how do the mathematicians treat of them?

PHILONOUS: I acknowledge, Hylas, it is not difficult to form general propositions and reasonings about those qualities, without mentioning any other; and, in this sense, to consider or treat of them abstractedly. But, how does it follow that, because I can pronounce the word *motion* by itself, I can form the idea of it in my mind exclusive of body? Or, because theorems may be made of extension and figures, without any mention of *great* or *small,* or any other sensible mode or quality, that therefore it is possible such an abstract idea of extension, without any particular size or figure, or sensible quality, should be distinctly formed, and apprehended by the mind? Mathematicians treat of quantity, without regarding what other sensible qualities it is attended with, as being altogether indifferent to their demonstrations. But, when laying aside the words, they contemplate the bare ideas, I believe you will find, they are not the pure abstracted ideas of extension.

HYLAS: But what say you to *pure intellect?* May not abstracted ideas be framed by that faculty?

PHILONOUS: Since I cannot frame abstract ideas at all, it is plain I cannot frame them by the help of *pure intellect;* whatsoever faculty you understand by those words. Besides, not to inquire into the nature of pure intellect and its spiritual objects, as *virtue, reason, God,* or the like, thus much seems manifest—that sensible things are only to be perceived by sense, or represented by the imagination. Figures, therefore, and extension, being originally perceived by sense, do not belong to pure intellect: but, for your farther satisfaction, try if you can frame the idea of any figure, abstracted from all particularities of size, or even from other sensible qualities.

HYLAS: Let me think a little—I do not find that I can.

PHILONOUS: And can you think it possible that should really exist in nature which implies a repugnancy in its conception?

HYLAS: By no means.

PHILONOUS: Since therefore it is impossible even for the mind to disunite the ideas of extension and motion from all other sensible qualities, does it not follow, that where the one exist there necessarily the other exist likewise?

HYLAS: It should seem so.

PHILONOUS: Consequently, the very same arguments which you admitted as conclusive against the secondary qualities are, without any farther application of force, against the primary too. Besides, if you will trust your senses, is it not plain all sensible qualities coexist, or to them appear as being in the same place? Do they ever represent a motion, or figure, as being divested of all other visible and tangible qualities?

HYLAS: You need say no more on this head. I am free to own, if there be no secret error or oversight in our proceedings hitherto, that all sensible qualities are alike to be denied existence without the mind. But, my fear is that I have been too liberal in my former concessions, or overlooked some fallacy or other. In short, I did not take time to think.

PHILONOUS: For that matter, Hylas, you may take what time you please in reviewing the progress of our inquiry. You are at liberty to recover any slips you might have made, or offer whatever you have omitted which makes for your first opinion.

HYLAS: One great oversight I take to be this—that I did not sufficiently distinguish the *object* from the *sensation*. Now though this latter may not exist without the mind, yet it will not thence follow that the former cannot.

PHILONOUS: What object do you mean? The object of the senses?

HYLAS: The same.

PHILONOUS: It is then immediately perceived?

HYLAS: Right.

PHILONOUS: Make me to understand the difference between what is immediately perceived and a sensation.

HYLAS: The sensation I take to be an act of the mind perceiving; besides which, there is something perceived, and this I call the *object*. For example, there is red and yellow on that tulip. But then the act of perceiving those colours is in me only, and not in the tulip.

PHILONOUS: What tulip do you speak of? Is it that which you see?

HYLAS: The same.

PHILONOUS: And what do you see beside colour, figure, and extension?

HYLAS: Nothing.

PHILONOUS: What you would say then is that the red and yellow are coexistent with the extension; is it not?

HYLAS: That is not all; I would say they have a real existence without the mind, in some unthinking substance.

PHILONOUS: That the colours are really in the tulip which I see is manifest. Neither can it be denied that this tulip may exist independent of your mind or mine; but, that any immediate object of the senses—that is, any idea, or combination of ideas—should exist in an unthinking substance, or exterior to all minds, is in itself an evident contradiction. Nor can I imagine how this follows from what you said just now, to wit, that the red and yellow were on the tulip *you saw,* since you do not pretend to see that unthinking substance.

HYLAS: You have an artful way, Philonous, of diverting our inquiry from the subject.

PHILONOUS: I see you have no mind to be pressed that way. To return then to your distinction between *sensation* and *object;* if I take you right, you distinguish in every perception two things, the one an action of the mind, the other not.

HYLAS: True.

PHILONOUS: And this action cannot exist in, or belong to, any unthinking thing; but, whatever beside is implied in a perception may?

HYLAS: That is my meaning.

PHILONOUS: So that if there was a perception without any act of the mind, it were possible such a perception should exist in an unthinking substance?

HYLAS: I grant it. But it is impossible there should be such a perception.

PHILONOUS: When is the mind said to be active?

HYLAS: When it produces, puts an end to, or changes, anything.

PHILONOUS: Can the mind produce, discontinue, or change anything, but by an act of the will?

HYLAS: It cannot.

PHILONOUS: The mind therefore is to be accounted active in its perceptions so far forth as volition is included in them?

HYLAS: It is.

PHILONOUS: In plucking this flower I am *active;* because I do it by the motion of my hand, which was consequent upon my *volition;* so likewise in applying it to my nose. But is either of these smelling?

HYLAS: No.

PHILONOUS: I act too in drawing the air through my nose; because my breathing so rather than otherwise is the effect of my volition. But neither can this be called *smelling:* for, if it were, I should smell every time I breathed in that manner?

HYLAS: True.

PHILONOUS: Smelling then is somewhat consequent to all this?

HYLAS: It is.

PHILONOUS: But I do not find my will concerned any farther. Whatever more there is—as that I perceive such a particular smell, or any smell at all—this is independent of my will, and therein I am altogether passive. Do you find it otherwise with you, Hylas?

HYLAS: No, the very same.

PHILONOUS: Then, as to seeing, is it not in your power to open your eyes, or keep them shut; to turn them this or that way?

HYLAS: Without doubt.

PHILONOUS: But does it in like manner depend on your will that in looking on this flower you perceive *white* rather any other colour? Or, directing your open eyes towards yonder part of the heaven, can you avoid seeing the sun? Or is light or darkness the effect of your volition?

HYLAS: No, certainly.

PHILONOUS: You are then in these respects altogether passive?

HYLAS: I am.

PHILONOUS: Tell me now, whether *seeing* consists in perceiving light and colours, or in opening and turning the eyes?

HYLAS: Without doubt, in the former.

PHILONOUS: Since therefore you are in the very perception of light and colours altogether passive, what is become of that action you were speaking of as an ingredient in every sensation? And, does it not follow from your own concessions, that the perception of light and colours, including no action in it, may exist in an unperceiving substance? And is not this a plain contradiction?

HYLAS: I know not what to think of it.

PHILONOUS: Besides, since you distinguish the *active* and *passive* in every perception, you must do it in that of pain. But how is it possible that pain, be it as little active as you please, should exist in an unperceiving substance? In short, do but consider the point, and then confess ingenuously, whether light and colours, tastes, sounds, &c. are not all equally passions or sensations in the soul. You may indeed call them *external objects,* and give them in words what subsistence you please. But, examine your own thoughts, and then tell me whether it be not as I say?

HYLAS: I acknowledge, Philonous, that, upon a fair observation of what passes in my mind I can discover nothing else but that I am a thinking being, affected with variety of sensations; neither is it possible to conceive how a sensation should exist in an unperceiving substance.—But then, on the other hand, when I look on sensible things in a different view, considering them as so many modes and qualities, I find it necessary to suppose a *material* substratum, without which they cannot be conceived to exist.

PHILONOUS: *Material substratum* call you it? Pray, by which of your senses came you acquainted with that being?

HYLAS: It is not itself sensible; its modes and qualities only being perceived by the senses.

PHILONOUS: I presume then it was by reflexion and reason you obtained the idea of it?

HYLAS: I do not pretend to any proper positive idea of it. However, I conclude it exists, because qualities cannot be conceived to exist without a support.

PHILONOUS: It seems then you have only a relative notion of it, or that you conceive it not otherwise than by conceiving the relation it bears to sensible qualities?

HYLAS: Right.

PHILONOUS: Be pleased therefore to let me know wherein that relation consists.

HYLAS: Is it not sufficiently expressed in the term *substratum,* or *substance?*

PHILONOUS: If so, the word *substratum* should import that it is spread under the sensible qualities or accidents?

HYLAS: True.

PHILONOUS: And consequently under extension?

HYLAS: I own it.

PHILONOUS: It is therefore somewhat in its own nature entirely distinct from extension?

HYLAS: I tell you, extension is only a mode, and matter is something that supports modes. And is it not evident the thing supported is different from the thing supporting?

PHILONOUS: So that something distinct from, and exclusive of, extension is supposed to be the substratum of extension?

HYLAS: Just so.

PHILONOUS: Answer me, Hylas. Can a thing be spread without extension? or is not the idea of extension necessarily included in *spreading?*

HYLAS: It is.

PHILONOUS: Whatsoever therefore you suppose spread under anything must have in itself an extension distinct from the extension of that thing under which it is spread?

HYLAS: It must.

PHILONOUS: Consequently, every corporeal substance, being the *substratum* of extension, must have in itself another extension, by which it is qualified to be a *substratum:* and so on to infinity. And I ask whether this be not absurd in itself, and repugnant to what you granted just now, to wit, that the *substratum* was something distinct from and exclusive of extension?

HYLAS: Aye but, Philonous, you take me wrong. I do not mean that matter is *spread* in a gross literal sense under extension. The word *substratum* is used only to express in general the same thing with *substance.*

PHILONOUS: Well then, let us examine the relation implied in the term *substance*. Is it not that it stands under accidents?

HYLAS: The very same.

PHILONOUS: But, that one thing may stand under or support another, must it not be extended?

HYLAS: It must.

PHILONOUS: Is not therefore this supposition liable to the same absurdity with the former?

HYLAS: You still take things in a strict literal sense. That is not fair, Philonous.

PHILONOUS: I am not for imposing any sense on your words: you are at liberty to explain them as you please. Only, I beseech you, make me understand something by them. You tell me matter supports or stands under accidents. How! is it as your legs support your body?

HYLAS: No; that is the literal sense.

PHILONOUS: Pray let me know any sense, literal or not literal, that you understand it in.—How long must I wait for an answer, Hylas?

HYLAS: I declare I know not what to say. I once thought I understood well enough what was meant by matter's supporting accidents. But now, the more I think on it the less can I comprehend it: in short I find that I know nothing of it.

PHILONOUS: It seems then you have no idea at all, neither relative nor positive, of matter; you know neither what it is in itself, nor what relation it bears to accidents?

HYLAS: I acknowledge it.

PHILONOUS: And yet you asserted that you could not conceive how qualities or accidents should really exist, without conceiving at the same time a material support of them?

HYLAS: I did.

PHILONOUS: That is to say, when you conceive the real existence of qualities, you do withal conceive something which you cannot conceive?

HYLAS: It was wrong, I own. But still I fear there is some fallacy or other. Pray what think you of this? It is just come into my head that the ground of all our mistake lies in your treating of each quality by itself. Now, I grant that each quality cannot singly subsist without the mind. Colour cannot without extension, neither can figure without some other sensible quality. But, as the several qualities united or blended together form entire sensible things, nothing hinders why such things may not be supposed to exist without the mind.

PHILONOUS: Either, Hylas, you are jesting, or have a very bad memory. Though indeed we went through all the qualities by name one after another, yet my arguments or rather your concessions, nowhere tended to prove that the secondary qualities did not subsist each alone by itself; but, that they were not *at all* without the mind. Indeed, in treating of figure and motion we concluded they could not exist without the mind, because it was impossible even in thought to separate them from all secondary qualities, so as to conceive them existing by themselves. But then this was not the only argument made use of upon that occasion. But (to pass by all that hath been hitherto said, and reckon it for nothing, if you will have it so) I am content to put the whole upon this issue. If you can conceive it possible for any mixture or combination of qualities, or any sensible object whatever, to exist without the mind, then I will grant it actually to be so.

HYLAS: If it comes to that the point will soon be decided. What more easy than to conceive a tree or house existing by itself, independent of, and unperceived by, any mind whatsoever? I do at this present time conceive them existing after that manner.

PHILONOUS: How say you, Hylas, can you see a thing which is at the same time unseen?

HYLAS: No, that were a contradiction.

PHILONOUS: Is it not as great a contradiction to talk of *conceiving* a thing which is *unconceived?*

HYLAS: It is.

PHILONOUS: The tree or house therefore which you think of is conceived by you?

HYLAS: How should it be otherwise?

PHILONOUS: And what is conceived is surely in the mind?

HYLAS: Without question, that which is conceived is in the mind.

PHILONOUS: How then came you to say, you conceived a house or tree existing independent and out of all minds whatsoever?

HYLAS: That was I own an oversight; but stay, let me consider what led me into it.—It is a pleasant mistake enough. As I was thinking of a tree in a solitary place, where no one was present to see it, methought that was to conceive a tree as existing unperceived or unthought of; not considering that I myself conceived it all the while. But now I plainly see that all I can do is to frame ideas in my own mind. I may indeed conceive in my own thoughts the idea of a tree, or a house, or a mountain, but that is all. And this is far from proving that I can conceive them *existing out of the minds of all spirits.*

PHILONOUS: You acknowledge then that you cannot possibly conceive how any one corporeal sensible thing should exist otherwise than in the mind?

HYLAS: I do.

PHILONOUS: And yet you will earnestly contend for the truth of that which you cannot so much as conceive?

HYLAS: I profess I know not what to think, but still there are some scruples remain with me. Is it not certain I *see* things at a distance? Do we not perceive the stars and moon, for example, to be a great way off? Is not this, say, manifest to the senses?

PHILONOUS: Do you not in a dream too perceive those or the like objects?

HYLAS: I do.

PHILONOUS: And have they not then the same appearance of being distant?

HYLAS: They have.

PHILONOUS: But you do not thence conclude the apparitions in a dream to be without the mind?

HYLAS: By no means.

PHILONOUS: You ought not therefore to conclude that sensible objects are without the mind, from their appearance, or manner wherein they are perceived.

HYLAS: I acknowledge it. But does not my sense deceive me in those cases?

PHILONOUS: By no means. The idea or thing which you immediately perceive, neither sense nor reason informs you that it actually exists without the mind. By sense you only know that you are affected with such certain sensations of light and colours, &c. And these you will not say are without the mind.

HYLAS: True: but, beside all that, do you not think the sight suggests something of *outness* or *distance?*

PHILONOUS: Upon approaching a distant object, do the visible size and figure change perpetually, or do they appear the same at all distances?

HYLAS: They are in a continual change.

PHILONOUS: Sight therefore does not suggest, or any way inform you, that the visible object you immediately perceive exists at a distance, or will be perceived when you advance farther onward; there being a continued series of visible objects succeeding each other during the whole time of your approach.

HYLAS: It does not; but still I know, upon seeing an object, what object I shall perceive after having passed over a certain distance: no matter whether it be exactly the same or no: there is still something of distance suggested in the case.

PHILONOUS: Good Hylas, do but reflect a little on the point, and then tell me whether there be any more in it than this: from the ideas you actually perceive by sight, you have by experience learned to collect what other ideas you will (according to the standing order of nature) be affected with, after such a certain succession of time and motion.

HYLAS: Upon the whole, I take it to be nothing else.

PHILONOUS: Now, is it not plain that if we suppose a man born blind was on a sudden made to see, he could at first have no experience of what may be suggested by sight?

HYLAS: It is.

PHILONOUS: He would not then, according to you, have any notion of distance annexed to the things he saw; but would take them for a new set of sensations, existing only in his mind?

HYLAS: It is undeniable.

PHILONOUS: But, to make it still more plain: is not *distance* a line turned endwise to the eye?

HYLAS: It is.

PHILONOUS: And can a line so situated be perceived by sight?

HYLAS: It cannot.

PHILONOUS: Does it not therefore follow that distance is not properly and immediately perceived by sight?

HYLAS: It should seem so.

PHILONOUS: Again, is it your opinion that colours are at a distance?

HYLAS: It must be acknowledged they are only in the mind.

PHILONOUS: But do not colours appear to the eye as coexisting in the same place with extension and figures?

HYLAS: They do.

PHILONOUS: How can you then conclude from sight that figures exist without, when you acknowledge colours do not; the sensible appearance being the very same with regard to both?

HYLAS: I know not what to answer.

PHILONOUS: But, allowing that distance was truly and immediately perceived by the mind, yet it would not thence follow it existed out of the mind. For, whatever is immediately perceived is an idea: and can any *idea* exist out of the mind?

HYLAS: To suppose that were absurd: but, inform me, Philonous, can we perceive or know nothing beside our ideas?

PHILONOUS: As for the rational deducing of causes from effects, that is beside our inquiry. And, by the senses you can best tell whether you perceive anything which is not immediately perceived. And I ask you, whether the things immediately perceived are other than your own sensations or ideas? You have indeed more than once, in the course of this conversation, declared yourself on those points; but you seem, by this last question, to have departed from what you then thought.

HYLAS: To speak the truth, Philonous, I think there are two kinds of objects:—the one perceived immediately, which are likewise called *ideas;* the other are real things or external objects, perceived by the mediation of ideas, which are their images and representations. Now, I own ideas do not exist without the mind; but the latter sort of objects do. I am sorry I did not think of this distinction sooner; it would probably have cut short your discourse.

PHILONOUS: Are those external objects perceived by sense or by some other faculty?

HYLAS: They are perceived by sense.

PHILONOUS: How! Is there any thing perceived by sense which is not immediately perceived?

HYLAS: Yes, Philonous, in some sort there is. For example when I look on a picture or statue of Julius Caesar, I may be said after a manner to perceive him (though not immediately) by my senses.

PHILONOUS: It seems then you will have our ideas, which alone are immediately perceived, to be pictures of external things: and that these also are perceived by sense, inasmuch as they have a conformity or resemblance to our ideas?

HYLAS: That is my meaning.

PHILONOUS: And, in the same way that Julius Caesar, in himself invisible, is nevertheless perceived by sight; real things, in themselves imperceptible, are perceived by sense.

HYLAS: In the very same.

PHILONOUS: Tell me, Hylas, when you behold the picture of Julius Caesar, do you see with your eyes any more than some colours and figures, with a certain symmetry and composition of the whole?

HYLAS: Nothing else.

PHILONOUS: And would not a man who had never known anything of Julius Caesar see as much?

HYLAS: He would.

PHILONOUS: Consequently he hath his sight, and the use of it, in as perfect a degree as you?

HYLAS: I agree with you.

PHILONOUS: Whence comes it then that your thoughts are directed to the Roman emperor, and his are not? This cannot proceed from the sensations or ideas of sense by you then perceived; since you acknowledge you have no advantage over him in that respect. It should seem therefore to proceed from reason and memory: should it not?

HYLAS: It should.

PHILONOUS: Consequently, it will not follow from that instance that anything is perceived by sense which is not immediately perceived. Though I grant we may, in one acceptation, be said to perceive sensible things mediately by sense: that is, when, from a frequently perceived connexion, the immediate perception of ideas by one sense suggests to the mind others, perhaps belonging to another sense, which are wont to be connected with them. For instance, when I hear a coach drive along the streets, immediately I perceive only the sound; but, from the experience I have had that such a sound is connected with a coach, I am said to hear the coach. It is nevertheless evident that, in truth and strictness, nothing can be *heard* but *sound;* and the coach is not then properly perceived by sense, but suggested from experience. So likewise when we are said to see a red-hot bar of iron; the solidity and heat of the iron are not the objects of sight, but suggested to the imagination by the colour and figure which are properly perceived by that sense. In short, those things alone are actually and strictly perceived by any sense, which would have been perceived in case that same sense had then been first conferred on us. As for other things, it is plain they are only suggested to the mind by experience, grounded on former perceptions. But, to return to your comparison of Caesar's picture, it is plain, if you keep to that, you must hold the real things, or archetypes of our ideas, are not perceived by sense, but by some internal faculty of the soul, as reason or memory. I would therefore fain know what arguments you can draw from reason for the existence of what you call real *things* or *material objects.* Or, whether you remember to have seen them formerly as they are in themselves; or, if you have heard or read of any one that did.

HYLAS: I see, Philonous, you are disposed to raillery; but that will never convince me.

PHILONOUS: My aim is only to learn from you the way to come at the knowledge of *material beings.* Whatever we perceive is perceived immediately or mediately: by sense, or by reason and reflexion. But, as you have excluded sense, pray show me what reason you have to believe their existence; or what *medium* you can possibly make use of to prove it, either to mine or your own understanding.

HYLAS: To deal ingenuously, Philonous, now I consider the point, I do not find I can give you any good reason for it. But, thus much seems pretty plain, that it is at least possible such things may really exist. And, as long as there is no absurdity in supposing them, I am resolved to believe as I did, till you bring good reasons to the contrary.

PHILONOUS: What! Is it come to this, that you only believe the existence of material objects, and that your belief is founded barely on the possibility of its being true? Then you will have me bring reasons against it: though another would think it reasonable the proof should lie on him who holds the affirmative. And, after all, this very point which you are now resolved to maintain, without any reason, is in effect what you have more than once during this discourse seen good reason to give up. But, to pass over all this; if I understand you rightly, you say our ideas do not exist without the mind, but that they are copies, images, or representations, of certain originals that do?

HYLAS: You take me right.

PHILONOUS: They are then like external things?

HYLAS: They are.

PHILONOUS: Have those things a stable and permanent nature, independent of our senses; or are they in a perpetual change, upon our producing any motions in our bodies—suspending, exerting, or altering, our faculties or organs of sense?

HYLAS: Real things, it is plain, have a fixed and real nature, which remains the same notwithstanding any change in our senses, or in the posture and motion of our bodies; which indeed may affect the ideas in our minds, but it were absurd to think they had the same effect on things existing without the mind.

PHILONOUS: How then is it possible that things perpetually fleeting and variable as our ideas should be copies or images of anything fixed and constant? Or, in other words, since all sensible qualities, as size, figure, colour, &c., that is, our ideas, are continually changing, upon every alteration in the distance, medium, or instruments of sensation; how can any determinate material objects be properly represented or painted forth by several distinct things, each of which is so different from and unlike the rest? Or, if you say it resembles some one only of our ideas, how shall we be able to distinguish the true copy from all the false ones?

HYLAS: I profess, Philonous, I am at a loss. I know not what to say to this.

PHILONOUS: But neither is this all. Which are material objects in themselves—perceptible or imperceptible?

HYLAS: Properly and immediately nothing can be perceived but ideas. All material things, therefore, are in themselves insensible, and to be perceived only by our ideas.

PHILONOUS: Ideas then are sensible, and their archetypes or originals insensible?

HYLAS: Right.

PHILONOUS: But how can that which is sensible be like that which is insensible? Can a real thing, in itself *invisible,* be like a *colour;* or a real thing, which is not *audible,* be like a *sound?* In a word, can anything be like a sensation or idea, but another sensation or idea?

HYLAS: I must own, I think not.

PHILONOUS: Is it possible there should be any doubt on the point? Do you not perfectly know your own ideas?

HYLAS: I know them perfectly; since what I do not perceive or know can be no part of my idea.

PHILONOUS: Consider, therefore, and examine them, and then tell me if there be anything in them which can exist without the mind: or if you can conceive anything like them existing without the mind.

HYLAS: Upon inquiry, I find it is impossible for me to conceive or understand how anything but an idea can be like an idea. And it is most evident that *no idea can exist without the mind.*

PHILONOUS: You are therefore, by your principles, forced to deny the reality of sensible things; since you made it to consist in an absolute existence exterior to the mind. That is to say, you are a downright *sceptic.* So I have gained my point, which was to show your principles led to scepticism.

HYLAS: For the present I am, if not entirely convinced, at least silenced.

PHILONOUS: I would fain know what more you would require in order to a perfect conviction. Have you not had the liberty of explaining yourself all manner of ways? Were any little slips in discourse laid hold and insisted on? Or were you not allowed to retract or reinforce anything you had offered, as best served your purpose? Hath not everything you could say been heard and examined with all the fairness imaginable? In a word, have you not in every point been convinced out of your own mouth? And, if you can at present discover any flaw in any of your former concessions, or think of any remaining subterfuge, any new distinction, colour, or comment whatsoever, why do you not produce it?

HYLAS: A little patience, Philonous. I am at present so amazed to see myself ensnared, and as it were imprisoned in the labyrinths you have drawn me into, that on the sudden it cannot be expected I should find my way out. You must give me time to look about me and recollect myself.

PHILONOUS: Hark; is not this the college bell?

HYLAS: It rings for prayers.

PHILONOUS: We will go in then, if you please, and meet here again tomorrow morning. In the meantime, you may employ your thoughts on this morning's discourse, and try if you can find any fallacy in it, or invent any new means to extricate yourself.

HYLAS: Agreed.

THE SECOND DIALOGUE

HYLAS: I beg your pardon, Philonous, for not meeting you sooner. All this morning my head was so filled with our late conversation that I had not leisure to think of the time of the day, or indeed of anything else.

PHILONOUS: I am glad you were so intent upon it, in hopes if there were any mistakes in your concessions, or fallacies in my reasonings from them, you will now discover them to me.

HYLAS: I assure you I have done nothing ever since I saw you but search after mistakes and fallacies, and, with that view, have minutely examined the whole series of yesterday's discourse: but all in vain, for the notions it led me into, upon review, appear still more clear and evident; and, the more I consider them, the more irresistibly do they force my assent.

PHILONOUS: And is not this, think you, a sign that they are genuine, that they proceed from nature, and are conformable to right reason? Truth and beauty are in this alike, that the strictest survey sets them both off to advantage; while the false lustre of error and disguise cannot endure being reviewed, or too nearly inspected.

HYLAS: I own there is a great deal in what you say. Nor can any one be more entirely satisfied of the truth of those odd consequences, so long as I have in view the reasonings that lead to them. But, when these are out of my thoughts, there seems, on the other hand, something so satisfactory, so natural and intelligible, in the modern way of explaining things that, I profess, I know not how to reject it.

PHILONOUS: I know not what way you mean.

HYLAS: I mean the way of accounting for our sensations or ideas.

PHILONOUS: How is that?

HYLAS: It is supposed the soul makes her residence in some part of the brain, from which the nerves take their rise, and are thence extended to all parts of the body; and that outward objects, by the different impressions they make on the organs of sense, communicate certain vibrative motions to the nerves; and these being filled with spirits propagate them to the brain or seat of the soul, which, according to the various impressions or traces thereby made in the brain, is variously affected with ideas.

PHILONOUS: And call you this an explication of the manner whereby we are affected with ideas?

HYLAS: Why not, Philonous? Have you anything to object against it?

PHILONOUS: I would first know whether I rightly understand your hypothesis. You make certain traces in the brain to be the causes or occasions of our ideas. Pray tell me whether by the brain you mean any sensible thing.

HYLAS: What else think you I could mean?

PHILONOUS: Sensible things are all immediately perceivable; and those things which are immediately perceivable are ideas; and these exist only in the mind. Thus much you have, if I mistake not, long since agreed to.

HYLAS: I do not deny it.

PHILONOUS: The brain therefore you speak of, being a sensible thing, exists only in the mind. Now, I would fain know whether you think it reasonable to suppose that one idea or thing existing in the mind occasions all other ideas. And, if you think so, pray how do you account for the origin of that primary idea or brain itself?

HYLAS: I do not explain the origin of our ideas by that brain which is perceivable to sense—this being itself only a combination of sensible ideas—but by another which I imagine.

PHILONOUS: But are not things imagined as truly *in the mind as* things perceived?

HYLAS: I must confess they are.

PHILONOUS: It comes therefore, to the same thing; and you have been all this while accounting for ideas by certain motions or impressions of the brain; that is, by some alterations in an idea, whether sensible or imaginable it matters not.

HYLAS: I begin to suspect my hypothesis.

PHILONOUS: Besides spirits, all that we know or conceive are our own ideas. When, therefore, you say all ideas are occasioned by impressions in the brain, do you conceive this brain or no? If you do, then you talk of ideas imprinted in an idea causing that same idea, which is absurd. If you do not conceive it, you talk unintelligibly, instead of forming a reasonable hypothesis.

HYLAS: I now clearly see it was a mere dream. There is nothing in it.

PHILONOUS: You need not be much concerned at it; for after all, this way of explaining things, as you called it, could never have satisfied any reasonable man. What connexion is there between a motion in the nerves, and the sensations of sound or colour in the mind? Or how is it possible these should be the effect of that?

HYLAS: But I could never think it had so little in it as now it seems to have.

PHILONOUS: Well then, are you at length satisfied that no sensible things have a real existence; and that you are in truth an arrant *sceptic?*

HYLAS: It is too plain to be denied.

PHILONOUS: Look! Are not the fields covered with a delightful verdure? Is there not something in the woods and groves, in the rivers and clear springs, that soothes, that delights, that transports the soul? At the prospect of the wide and deep ocean, or some huge mountain whose top is lost in the clouds, or of an old gloomy forest, are not our minds filled with a pleasing horror? Even in rocks and deserts is there not an agreeable wildness? How sincere a pleasure is it to behold the natural beauties of the earth! To preserve and renew our relish for them, is not the veil of night alternately drawn over her face, and does she not change her dress with the seasons? How aptly are the elements disposed! What variety and use in the meanest productions of nature! What delicacy, what beauty, what contrivance, in animal and vegetable bodies! How exquisitely are all things suited, as well to their particular ends, as to constitute opposite parts of the whole! And, while they mutually aid and support, do they not also set off and illustrate each other? Raise now your thoughts from this ball of earth to all those glorious luminaries that adorn the high arch of heaven. The motion and situation of the planets, are they not admirable for use and order? Were those (miscalled *erratic*) globes once known to stray, in their repeated journeys through the pathless void? Do they not measure areas round the sun ever proportioned to the times? So fixed, so immutable are the laws by which the unseen author of nature actuates the universe. How vivid and radiant is the lustre of the fixed stars! How magnificent and rich that negligent profusion with which they appear to be scattered throughout the whole azure vault! Yet, if you take the telescope, it brings into your sight a new host of stars that escape the naked eye. Here they seem contiguous and minute, but to a nearer view immense orbs of light at various distances, far sunk in the abyss of space. Now you must call imagination to your aid. The feeble narrow sense cannot descry innumerable worlds revolving round the central fires and in those worlds the energy of an all-perfect mind displayed in endless forms. But, neither sense nor imagination are big enough to comprehend the boundless extent, with all its glittering furniture. Though the labouring mind exert and strain each power to its utmost reach, there still stands out ungrasped a surplusage immeasurable. Yet all the vast bodies that compose this mighty frame, how distant and remote soever, are by some secret mechanism, some divine art and force, linked in a mutual dependence and intercourse with each other; even with this earth, which was almost slipt from my thoughts and lost in the crowd of worlds. Is not the whole system immense, beautiful, glorious beyond expression and beyond thought! What treatment, then, do those philosophers deserve, who would deprive these noble and delightful scenes of all reality? How should those principles be entertained that lead us to think all the visible beauty of the creation a false imaginary glare? To be plain, can you expect this scepticism of yours will not be thought extravagantly absurd by all men of sense?

HYLAS: Other men may think as they please; but for your part you have nothing to reproach me with. My comfort is, you are as much a *sceptic* as I am.

PHILONOUS: There, Hylas, I must beg leave to differ from you.

HYLAS: What! Have you all along agreed to the premises, and do you now deny the conclusion, and leave me to maintain those paradoxes by myself which you led me into? This surely is not fair.

PHILONOUS: I deny that I agreed with you in those notions that led to scepticism. You indeed said the *reality* of sensible things consisted in an *absolute existence* out of the minds of spirits, or distinct from their being perceived. And pursuant to this notion of reality, you are obliged to deny sensible things any real existence: that is, according to your own definition, you profess yourself a *sceptic*. But I neither said nor thought the reality of sensible things was to be defined after that manner. To me it is evident for the reasons you allow of, that sensible things cannot exist otherwise than in a mind or spirit. Whence I conclude, not that they have no real existence, but that, seeing they depend not on my thought, and have an existence distinct from being perceived by me, *there must be some other mind wherein they exist.* As sure, therefore, as the sensible world really exists, so sure is there an infinite omnipresent spirit who contains and supports it.

HYLAS: What! This is no more than I and all Christians hold; nay, and all others too who believe there is a God, and that he knows and comprehends all things.

PHILONOUS: Aye, but here lies the difference. Men commonly believe that all things are known or perceived by God, because they believe the being of a God; whereas I, on the other side, immediately and necessarily conclude the being of a God, because all sensible things must be perceived by him.

HYLAS: But, so long as we all believe the same thing, what matter is it how we come by that belief?

PHILONOUS: But neither do we agree in the same opinion. For philosophers, though they acknowledge all corporeal beings to be perceived by God, yet they attribute to them an absolute subsistence distinct from their being perceived by any mind whatever; which I do not. Besides, is there no difference between saying, *There is a God, therefore he perceives all things;* and saying, *Sensible things do really exist; and, if they really exist, they are necessarily perceived by an infinite mind: therefore there is an infinite mind or God?* This furnishes you with a direct and immediate demonstration, from a most evident principle, of the *being of a God.* Divines and philosophers had proved beyond all controversy, from the beauty and usefulness of the several parts of the creation, that it was the workmanship of God. But that—setting aside all help of astronomy and natural philosophy, all contemplation of the contrivance, order, and adjustment of things—an infinite mind should be necessarily inferred from the bare *existence* of the sensible world, is an advantage to them only who have made this easy reflexion: that the sensible world is that which we perceive by our several senses; and that nothing is perceived by the senses beside ideas; and that no idea or archetype of an idea can exist otherwise than in a mind. You may now, without any laborious search into the sciences, without any subtlety of reason, or tedious length of discourse, oppose and baffle the most strenuous advocate for Atheism. Those miserable refuges, whether in an eternal succession of unthinking causes and effects, or in a fortuitous concourse of atoms; those wild imaginations of Vanini, Hobbes, and Spinoza: in a word, the whole system of Atheism, is it not entirely overthrown, by this single reflexion on the repugnancy included in supposing the whole, or any part, even the most rude and shapeless, of the visible world, to exist without a mind? Let any one of those abettors of impiety but look into his own thoughts, and there try if he can conceive how so much as a rock, a desert, a chaos, or confused jumble of atoms; how anything at all, either sensible or imaginable, can exist independent of a mind, and he need go no farther to be convinced of his folly. Can anything be fairer than to put a dispute on such an issue, and leave it to a man himself to see if he can conceive, even in thought, what he holds to be true in fact, and from a notional to allow it a real existence?

HYLAS: It cannot be denied there is something highly serviceable to religion in what you advance. But do you not think it looks very like a notion entertained by some eminent moderns, of *seeing all things in God?*

PHILONOUS: I would gladly know that opinion: pray explain it to me.

HYLAS: They conceive that the soul, being immaterial, is incapable of being united with material things, so as to perceive them in themselves; but that she perceives them by her union with the substance of God, which, being spiritual, is therefore purely intelligible, or capable of being the immediate object of a spirit's thought. Besides the divine essence contains in it perfections correspondent to each created being; and which are, for that reason, proper to exhibit or represent them to the mind.

PHILONOUS: I do not understand how our ideas, which are things altogether passive and inert, can be the essence, or any part (or like any part) of the essence or substance of God, who is an impassive, indivisible, pure, active being. Many more difficulties and objections there are which occur at first view against this hypothesis; but I shall only add that it is liable to all the absurdities of the common hypothesis, in making a created world exist otherwise than in the mind of a spirit. Besides all which it hath this peculiar to itself; that it makes that material world serve to no purpose. And, if it pass for a good argument against other hypotheses in the sciences, that they suppose nature, or the divine wisdom, to make something in vain, or do that by tedious roundabout methods which might have been performed in a much more easy and compendious way, what shall we think of that hypothesis which supposes the whole world made in vain?

HYLAS: But what say you? Are not you too of opinion that we see all things in God? If I mistake not, what you advance comes near it.

PHILONOUS: Few men think; yet all have opinions. Hence men's opinions are superficial and confused. It is nothing strange that tenets which in themselves are ever so different, should nevertheless be confounded with each other, by those who do not consider them attentively. I shall not therefore be surprised if some men imagine that I run into the enthusiasm of Malebranche; though in truth I am very remote from it. He builds on the most abstract general ideas, which I entirely disclaim. He asserts an absolute external world, which I deny. He maintains that we are deceived by our senses, and know not the real natures or the true forms and figures of extended beings; of all which I hold the direct contrary. So that upon the whole there are no principles more fundamentally opposite than his and mine. It must be owned that I entirely agree with what the Holy Scripture says, "That in God we live and move and have our being" [Acts 17:28]. But that we see things in His essence, after the manner above set forth, I am far from believing. Take here in brief my meaning:—It is evident that the things I perceive are my own ideas, and that no idea can exist unless it be in a mind: nor is it less plain that these ideas or things by me perceived, either themselves or their archetypes, exist independently of my mind, since I know myself not to be their author, it being out of my power to determine at pleasure what particular ideas I shall be affected with upon opening my eyes or ears: they must therefore exist in some other mind, whose will it is they should be exhibited to me. The things, I say, immediately perceived are ideas or sensations, call them which you will. But how can any idea or sensation exist in, or be produced by, anything but a mind or spirit? This indeed is inconceivable. And to assert that which is inconceivable is to talk nonsense: is it not?

HYLAS: Without doubt.

PHILONOUS: But, on the other hand, it is very conceivable that they should exist in and be produced by a spirit; since this is no more than I daily experience in myself, inasmuch as I perceive numberless ideas; and, by an act of my will, can form a great variety of them, and raise them up in my imagination: though, it must be confessed, these creatures of the fancy are not altogether so distinct, so strong, vivid, and permanent, as those perceived by my senses—which latter are called *real things*. From all which I conclude, *there is a mind which affects me every moment with all the sensible impressions I perceive*. And, from the variety, order, and manner of these, I conclude the author of them to be *wise, powerful, and good, beyond comprehension*. Mark it well; I do not say, I see things by perceiving that which represents them in the intelligible substance of God. This I do not understand; but I say, the things by me perceived are known by the understanding, and produced by the will of an infinite spirit. And is not all this most plain and evident? Is there any more in it than what a little observation in our own minds, and that which passes in them, not only enables us to conceive, but also obliges us to acknowledge.

HYLAS: I think I understand you very clearly; and own the proof you give of a deity seems no less evident than it is surprising. But, allowing that God is the supreme and universal cause of all things, yet, may there not be still a third nature besides spirits and ideas? May we not admit a subordinate and limited cause of our ideas? In a word, may there not for all that be *matter?*

PHILONOUS: How often must I inculcate the same thing? You allow the things immediately perceived by sense to exist nowhere without the mind; but there is nothing perceived by sense which is not perceived immediately: therefore there is nothing sensible that exists without the mind. The matter, therefore, which you still insist on is something intelligible, I suppose; something that may be discovered by reason, and not by sense.

HYLAS: You are in the right.

PHILONOUS: Pray let me know what reasoning your belief of matter is grounded on; and what this matter is, in your present sense of it.

HYLAS: I find myself affected with various ideas, whereof I know I am not the cause; neither are they the cause of themselves, or of one another, or capable of subsisting by themselves, as being altogether inactive, fleeting, dependent beings. They have therefore some cause distinct from me and them: of which I pretend to know no more than that it is *the cause of my ideas*. And this thing, whatever it be, I call matter.

PHILONOUS: Tell me, Hylas, hath every one a liberty to change the current proper signification attached to a common name in any language? For example, suppose a traveler should tell you that in a certain country men pass unhurt through the fire; and, upon explaining himself, you found he meant by the word *fire* that which others call *water.* Or, if he should assert that there are trees that walk upon two legs, meaning men by the term *trees.* Would you think this reasonable?

HYLAS: No; I should think it very absurd. Common custom is the standard of propriety in language. And for any man to affect speaking improperly is to pervert the use of speech, and can never serve to a better purpose than to protract and multiply disputes where there is no difference in opinion.

PHILONOUS: And does not *matter,* in the common current acceptation of the word, signify an extended, solid, moveable, unthinking, inactive substance?

HYLAS: It does.

PHILONOUS: And, has it not been made evident that no such substance can possibly exist? And, though it should be allowed to exist, yet how can that which is *inactive* be a cause; or that which is *unthinking* be a *cause of thought?* You may, indeed, if you please, annex to the word *matter* a contrary meaning to what is vulgarly received; and tell me you understand by it, an unextended, thinking, active being, which is the cause of our ideas. But what else is this than to play with words, and run into that very fault you just now condemned with so much reason? I do by no means find fault with your reasoning, in that you collect a cause from the *phenomena:* but I deny that the cause deducible by reason can properly be termed matter.

HYLAS: There is indeed something in what you say. But I am afraid you do not thoroughly comprehend my meaning. I would by no means be thought to deny that God, or an infinite spirit, is the supreme cause of all things. All I contend for is, that, subordinate to the supreme agent, there is a cause of a limited and inferior nature, which concurs in the production of our ideas, not by any act of will, or spiritual efficiency, but by that kind of action which belongs to matter, *viz.* motion.

PHILONOUS: I find you are at every turn relapsing into your old exploded conceit, of a moveable, and consequently an extended, substance, existing without the mind. What! Have you already forgotten you were convinced; or are you willing I should repeat what has been said on that head? In truth this is not fair dealing in you, still to suppose the being of that which you have so often acknowledged to have no being. But, not to insist farther on what has been so largely handled, I ask whether all your ideas are not perfectly passive and inert, including nothing of action in them.

HYLAS: They are.

PHILONOUS: And are sensible qualities anything else but ideas?

HYLAS: How often have I acknowledged that they are not.

PHILONOUS: But is not motion a sensible quality?

HYLAS: It is.

PHILONOUS: Consequently it is no action?

HYLAS: I agree with you. And indeed it is very plain that when I stir my finger, it remains passive; but my will which produced the motion is active.

PHILONOUS: Now, I desire to know, in the first place, whether motion being allowed to be no action, you can conceive any action besides volition: and, in the second place, whether to say something and conceive nothing be not to talk nonsense: and, lastly, whether, having considered the premises, you do not perceive that to suppose any efficient or active cause of our ideas, other than *spirit,* is highly absurd and unreasonable?

HYLAS: I give up the point entirely. But, though matter may not be a cause, yet what hinders its being an *instrument,* subservient to the supreme agent in the production of our ideas?

PHILONOUS: An instrument say you; pray what may be the figure, springs, wheels, and motions, of that instrument?

HYLAS: Those I pretend to determine nothing of, both the substance and its qualities being entirely unknown to me.

PHILONOUS: What? You are then of opinion it is made up of unknown parts, that it hath unknown motions, and an unknown shape?

HYLAS: I do not believe that it hath any figure or motion at all, being already convinced, that no sensible qualities can exist in an unperceiving substance.

PHILONOUS: But what notion is it possible to frame of an instrument void of all sensible qualities, even extension itself?

HYLAS: I do not pretend to have any notion of it.

PHILONOUS: And what reason have you to think this unknown, this inconceivable somewhat does exist? Is it that you imagine God cannot act as well without it; or that you find by experience the use of some such thing, when you form ideas in your own mind?

HYLAS: You are always teasing me for reasons of my belief. Pray what reasons have you not to believe it?

PHILONOUS: It is to me a sufficient reason not to believe the existence of anything, if I see no reason for believing it. But, not to insist on reasons for believing, you will not so much as let me know what it is you would have me believe; since you say you have no manner of notion of it. After all, let me entreat you to consider whether it be like a philosopher, or even like a man of common sense, to pretend to believe you know not what, and you know not why.

HYLAS: Hold, Philonous. When I tell you matter is an *instrument,* I do not mean altogether nothing. It is true I know not the particular kind of instrument; but, however, I have some notion of *instrument in general,* which I apply to it.

PHILONOUS: But what if it should prove that there is something, even in the most general notion of *instrument,* as taken in a distinct sense from *cause,* which makes the use of it inconsistent with the divine attributes?

HYLAS: Make that appear and I shall give up the point.

PHILONOUS: What mean you by the general nature or notion of instrument?

HYLAS: That which is common to all particular instruments composes the general notion.

PHILONOUS: Is it not common to all instruments, that they are applied to the doing those things only which cannot be performed by the mere act of our wills? Thus, for instance, I never use an instrument to move my finger, because it is done by a volition. But I should use one if I were to remove part of a rock, or tear up a tree by the roots. Are you of the same mind? Or, can you show any example where an instrument is made use of in producing an effect immediately depending on the will of the agent?

HYLAS: I own I cannot.

PHILONOUS: How therefore can you suppose that an all-perfect spirit, on whose will all things have an absolute and immediate dependence, should need an instrument in his operations, or, not needing it, make use of it? Thus it seems to me that you are obliged to own the use of a lifeless inactive instrument to be incompatible with the infinite perfection of God; that is, by your own confession, to give up the point.

HYLAS: It does not readily occur what I can answer you.

PHILONOUS: But, methinks you should be ready to own the truth, when it has been fairly proved to you. We indeed, who are beings of finite powers, are forced to make use of instruments. And the use of an instrument shows the agent to be limited by rules of another's prescription, and that he cannot obtain his end but in such a way, and by such conditions. Whence it seems a clear consequence, that the supreme unlimited agent uses no tool or instrument at all. The will of an omnipotent spirit is no sooner exerted than executed, without the application of means; which, if they are employed by inferior agents, it is not upon account of any real efficacy that is in them, or necessary aptitude to produce any effect, but merely in compliance with the laws of nature, or those conditions prescribed to them by the first cause, who is himself above all limitation or prescription whatsoever.

HYLAS: I will no longer maintain that matter is an instrument. However, I would not be understood to give up its existence neither; since, notwithstanding what hath been said, it may still be an *occasion.*

PHILONOUS: How many shapes is your matter to take? Or, how often must it be proved not to exist, before you are content to part with it? But, to say no more of this (though by all the laws of disputation I may justly blame you for so frequently changing the signification of the principal term)—I would fain know what you mean by affirming that matter is an occasion, having already denied it to be a cause. And, when you have shown in what sense you understand *occasion,* pray, in the next place be pleased to show me what reason induces you to believe there is such an occasion of our ideas?

HYLAS: As to the first point: by *occasion* I mean an inactive unthinking being, at the presence whereof God excites ideas in our minds.

PHILONOUS: And what may be the nature of that inactive unthinking being?

HYLAS: I know nothing of its nature.

PHILONOUS: Proceed then to the second point, and assign some reason why we should allow an existence to this inactive, unthinking, unknown thing.

HYLAS: When we see ideas produced in our minds, after an orderly and constant manner, it is natural to think they have some fixed and regular occasions, at the presence of which they are excited.

PHILONOUS: You acknowledge then God alone to be the cause of our ideas, and that he causes them at the presence of those occasions.

HYLAS: That is my opinion.

PHILONOUS: Those things which you say are present to God, without doubt he perceives.

HYLAS: Certainly; otherwise they could not be to him an occasion of acting.

PHILONOUS: Not to insist now on your making sense of this hypothesis, or answering all the puzzling questions and difficulties it is liable to: I only ask whether the order and regularity observable in the series of our ideas, or the course of nature, be not sufficiently accounted for by the wisdom and power of God; and whether it does not derogate from those attributes, to suppose he is influenced, directed, or put in mind, when and what he is to act, by an unthinking substance? And, lastly, whether, in case I granted all you contend for, it would make anything to your purpose; it not being easy to conceive how the external or absolute existence of an unthinking substance, distinct from its being perceived, can be inferred from my allowing that there are certain things perceived by the mind of God, which are to him the occasion of producing ideas in us?

HYLAS: I am perfectly at a loss what to think, this notion of occasion seeming now altogether as groundless as the rest.

PHILONOUS: Do you not at length perceive that in all these different acceptations of *matter,* you have been only supposing you know not what, for no manner of reason, and to no kind of use?

HYLAS: I freely own myself less fond of my notions since they have been so accurately examined. But still, methinks, I have some confused perception that there is such a thing as *matter.*

PHILONOUS: Either you perceive the being of matter immediately or mediately. If immediately, pray inform me by which of the senses you perceive it. If mediately, let me know by what reasoning it is inferred from those things which you perceive immediately. So much for the perception. Then for the matter itself, I ask whether it is object, *substratum,* cause, instrument, or occasion? You have already pleaded for each of these, shifting your notions, and making matter to appear sometimes in one shape, then in another. And what you have offered hath been disapproved and rejected by yourself. If you have anything new to advance I would gladly hear it.

HYLAS: I think I have already offered all I had to say on those heads. I am at a loss what more to urge.

PHILONOUS: And yet you are loath to part with your old prejudice. But, to make you quit it more easily, I desire that, beside what has been hitherto suggested, you will farther consider whether, upon supposition that matter exists, you can possibly conceive how you should be affected by it. Or, supposing it did not exist, whether it be not evident you might for all that be affected with the same ideas you now are, and consequently have the very same reasons to believe its existence that you now can have.

HYLAS: I acknowledge it is possible we might perceive all things just as we do now, though there was no matter in the world; neither can I conceive, if there be matter, how it should produce any idea in our minds. And, I do farther grant you have entirely satisfied me that it is impossible there should be such a thing as matter in any of the foregoing acceptations. But still I cannot help supposing that there is *matter* in some sense or other. What that is I do not indeed pretend to determine.

PHILONOUS: I do not expect you should define exactly the nature of that unknown being. Only be pleased to tell me whether it is a substance; and if so, whether you can suppose a substance without accidents; or, in case you suppose it to have accidents or qualities, I desire you will let me know what those qualities are, at least what is meant by matter's supporting them?

HYLAS: We have already argued on those points. I have no more to say to them. But, to prevent any farther questions, let me tell you I at present understand by *matter* neither substance nor accident, thinking nor extended being, neither cause, instrument, nor occasion, but something entirely unknown, distinct from all these.

PHILONOUS: It seems then you include in your present notion of matter nothing but the general abstract idea of *entity.*

HYLAS: Nothing else; save only that I superadd to this general idea the negation of all those particular things, qualities, or ideas, that I perceive, imagine, or in anywise apprehend.

PHILONOUS: Pray where do you suppose this unknown matter to exist?

HYLAS: Oh Philonous! Now you think you have entangled me, for, if I say it exists in place, then you will infer that it exists in the mind, since it is agreed that place or extension exists only in the mind. But I am not ashamed to own my ignorance. I know not where it exists; only I am sure it exists not in place. There is a negative answer for you. And you must expect no other to all the questions you put for the future about matter.

PHILONOUS: Since you will not tell me where it exists, be pleased to inform me after what manner you suppose it to exist, or what you mean by its *existence?*

HYLAS: It neither thinks nor acts, neither perceives nor is perceived.

PHILONOUS: But what is there positive in your abstracted notion of its existence?

HYLAS: Upon a nice observation, I do not find I have any positive notion or meaning at all. I tell you again, I am not ashamed to own my ignorance. I know not what is meant by its *existence,* or how it exists.

PHILONOUS: Continue, good Hylas, to act the same ingenuous part, and tell me sincerely whether you can frame a distinct idea of Entity in general, prescinded from and exclusive of all thinking and corporeal beings, all particular things whatsoever.

HYLAS: Hold, let me think a little—I profess, Philonous I do not find that I can. At first glance, methought I had some dilute and airy notion of pure entity in abstract; but, upon closer attention, it hath quite vanished out of sight. The more I think on it, the more am I confirmed in my prudent resolution of giving none but negative answers, and not pretending to the least degree of any positive knowledge or conception of matter, its *where,* its *how,* its *entity,* or anything belonging to it.

PHILONOUS: When, therefore, you speak of the existence of matter, you have not any notion in your mind?

HYLAS: None at all.

PHILONOUS: Pray tell me if the case stands not thus: At first, from a belief of material substance, you would have it that the immediate objects existed without the mind; then that they are archetypes; then causes; next instruments; then occasions: lastly *something in general,* which being interpreted proves *nothing.* So matter comes to nothing. What think you, Hylas, is not this a fair summary of your whole proceeding?

HYLAS: Be that as it will, yet I still insist upon it, that our not being able to conceive a thing is no argument against its existence.

PHILONOUS: That from a cause, effect, operation, sign, or other circumstance, there may reasonably be inferred the existence of a thing not immediately perceived; and that it were absurd for any man to argue against the existence of that thing, from his having no direct and positive notion of it, I freely own. But, where there is nothing of all this; where neither reason nor revelation induces us to believe the existence of a thing; where we have not even a relative notion of it; where an abstraction is made from perceiving and being perceived, from spirit and idea: lastly, where there is not so much as the most inadequate or faint idea pretended to—I will not indeed thence conclude against the reality of any notion, or existence of anything; but my inference shall be, that you mean nothing at all; that you employ words to no manner of purpose, without any design or signification whatsoever. And I leave it to you to consider how mere jargon should be treated.

HYLAS: To deal frankly with you, Philonous, your arguments seem in themselves unanswerable; but they have not so great an effect on me as to produce that entire conviction, that hearty acquiescence, which attends demonstration. I find myself relapsing into an obscure surmise of I know not what, *matter.*

PHILONOUS: But, are you not sensible, Hylas, that two things must concur to take away all scruple, and work a plenary assent in the mind? Let a visible object be set in never so clear a light, yet, if there is any imperfection in the sight, or if the eye is not directed towards it, it will not be distinctly seen. And though a demonstration be never so well grounded and fairly proposed, yet, if there is withal a stain of prejudice, or a wrong bias on the understanding, can it be expected on a sudden to perceive clearly, and adhere firmly to the truth? No; there is need of time and pains: the attention must be awakened and detained by a frequent repetition of the same thing placed oft in the same, oft in different lights. I have said it already, and find I must still repeat and inculcate, that it is an unaccountable licence you take, in pretending to maintain you know not what, for you know not what reason, to you know not what purpose. Can this be paralleled in any art or science, any sect or profession of men? Or is there anything so barefacedly groundless and unreasonable to be met with even in the lowest of common conversation? But, perhaps you will still say, matter may exist; though at the same time you neither know what is meant by *matter,* or by its *existence.* This indeed is surprising, and the more so because it is altogether voluntary, you not being led to it by any one reason; for I challenge you to show me that thing in nature which needs matter to explain or account for it.

HYLAS: The reality of things cannot be maintained without supposing the existence of matter. And is not this, think you, a good reason why I should be earnest in its defence?

PHILONOUS: The reality of things! What things, sensible or intelligible?

HYLAS: Sensible things.

PHILONOUS: My glove for example?

HYLAS: That, or any other thing perceived by the senses.

PHILONOUS: But to fix on some particular thing. Is it not a sufficient evidence to me of the existence of this *glove,* that I see it, and feel it, and wear it? Or, if this will not do, how is it possible I should be assured of the reality of this thing, which I actually see in this place, by supposing that some unknown thing, which I never did or can see, exists after an unknown manner, in an unknown place, or in no place at all? How can the supposed reality of that which is intangible be a proof that anything tangible really exists? Or, of that which is invisible, that any visible thing, or, in general of anything which is imperceptible, that a perceptible exists? Do but explain this and I shall think nothing too hard for you.

HYLAS: Upon the whole, I am content to own the existence of matter is highly improbable, but the direct and absolute impossibility of it does not appear to me.

PHILONOUS: But granting matter to be possible, yet, upon that account merely, it can have no more claim to existence than a golden mountain, or a centaur.

HYLAS: I acknowledge it; but still you do not deny it is possible; and that which is possible, for aught you know, may actually exist.

PHILONOUS: I deny it to be possible; and have, if I mistake not, evidently proved, from your own concessions, that it is not. In the common sense of the word *matter,* is there any more implied than an extended, solid, figured, movable substance, existing without the mind? And have not you acknowledged, over and over, that you have seen evident reason for denying the possibility of such a substance?

HYLAS: True, but that is only one sense of the term matter.

PHILONOUS: But is it not the only proper genuine received sense? And, if matter, in such a sense, be proved impossible, may it not be thought with good grounds absolutely impossible? Else how could anything be proved impossible? Or, indeed, how could there be any proof at all one way or other, to a man who takes the liberty to unsettle and change the common signification of words?

HYLAS: I thought philosophers might be allowed to speak more accurately than the vulgar, and were not always confined to the common acceptation of a term.

PHILONOUS: But this now mentioned is the common received sense among philosophers themselves. But, not to insist on that, have you not been allowed to take matter in what sense you pleased? And have you not used this privilege in the utmost extent; sometimes entirely changing, at others leaving out, or putting into the definition of it whatever, for the present, best served your design, contrary to all the known rules of reason and logic? And hath not this shifting, unfair method of yours spun out our dispute to an unnecessary length; matter having been particularly examined, and by your own confession refuted in each of those senses? And can any more be required to prove the absolute impossibility of a thing, than the proving it impossible in every particular sense that either you or any one else understands it in?

HYLAS: But I am not so thoroughly satisfied that you have proved the impossibility of matter, in the last most obscure abstracted and indefinite sense.

PHILONOUS: When is a thing shown to be impossible?

HYLAS: When a repugnancy is demonstrated between the ideas comprehended in its definition.

PHILONOUS: But where there are no ideas, there no repugnancy can be demonstrated between ideas?

HYLAS: I agree with you.

PHILONOUS: Now, in that which you call the obscure indefinite sense of the word matter, it is plain, by your own confession, there was included no idea at all, no sense except an unknown sense; which is the same thing as none. You are not, therefore, to expect I should prove a repugnancy between ideas, where there are no ideas; or the impossibility of matter taken in an *unknown* sense, that is, no sense at all. My business was only to show you meant *nothing;* and this you were brought to own. So that, in all your various senses, you have been showed either to mean nothing at all, or, if anything, an absurdity. And if this be not sufficient to prove the impossibility of a thing, I desire you will let me know what is.

HYLAS: I acknowledge you have proved that matter is impossible; nor do I see what more can be said in defence of it. But, at the same time that I give up this, I suspect all my other notions. For surely none could be more seemingly evident than this once was: and yet it now seems as false and absurd as ever it did true before. But I think we have discussed the point sufficiently for the present. The remaining part of the day I would willingly spend in running over in my thoughts the several heads of this morning's conversation, and tomorrow shall be glad to meet you here again about the same time.

PHILONOUS: I will not fail to attend you.

THE THIRD DIALOGUE

PHILONOUS: Tell me, Hylas, what are the fruits of yesterday's meditation? Has it confirmed you in the same mind you were in at parting? or have you since seen cause to change your opinion?

HYLAS: Truly my opinion is that all our opinions are alike vain and uncertain. What we approve today, we condemn tomorrow. We keep a stir about knowledge, and spend our lives in the pursuit of it, when, alas! we know nothing all the while: nor do I think it possible for us ever to know anything in this life. Our faculties are too narrow and too few. Nature certainly never intended us for speculation.

PHILONOUS: What! Say you we can know nothing, Hylas?

HYLAS: There is not that single thing in the world whereof we can know the real nature, or what it is in itself.

PHILONOUS: Will you tell me I do not really know what fire or water is?

HYLAS: You may indeed know that fire appears hot, and water fluid; but this is no more than knowing what sensations are produced in your own mind, upon the application of fire and water to your organs of sense. Their internal constitution, their true and real nature, you are utterly in the dark as to *that*.

PHILONOUS: Do I not know this to be a real stone that I stand on, and that which I see before my eyes to be a real tree?

HYLAS: Know? No, it is impossible you or any man alive should know it. All you know is, that you have such a certain idea or appearance in your own mind. But what is this to the real tree or stone? I tell you that colour, figure, and hardness, which you perceive, are not the real natures of those things, or in the least like them. The same may be said of all other real things, or corporeal substances, which compose the world. They have none of them anything of themselves, like those sensible qualities by us perceived. We should not therefore pretend to affirm or know anything of them, as they are in their own nature.

PHILONOUS: But surely, Hylas, I can distinguish gold, for example, from iron: and how could this be, if I knew not what either truly was?

HYLAS: Believe me, Philonous, you can only distinguish between your own ideas. That yellowness, that weight, and other sensible qualities, think you they are really in the gold? They are only relative to the senses, and have no absolute existence in nature. And in pretending to distinguish the species of real things, by the appearances in your mind, you may perhaps act as wisely as he that should conclude two men were of a different species, because their clothes were not of the same colour.

PHILONOUS: It seems, then, we are altogether put off with the appearances of things, and those false ones too. The very meat I eat, and the cloth I wear, have nothing in them like what I see and feel.

HYLAS: Even so.

PHILONOUS: But is it not strange the whole world should be thus imposed on, and so foolish as to believe their senses? And yet I know not how it is, but men eat, and drink, and sleep, and perform all the offices of life, as comfortably and conveniently as if they really knew the things they are conversant about.

HYLAS: They do so: but you know ordinary practice does not require a nicety of speculative knowledge. Hence the vulgar retain their mistakes, and for all that make a shift to bustle through the affairs of life. But philosophers know better things.

PHILONOUS: You mean, they know that they *know nothing.*

HYLAS: That is the very top and perfection of human knowledge.

PHILONOUS: But are you all this while in earnest, Hylas; and are you seriously persuaded that you know nothing real in the world? Suppose you are going to write, would you not call for pen, ink, and paper, like another man; and do you not know what it is you call for?

HYLAS: How often must I tell you, that I know not the real nature of any one thing in the universe? I may indeed upon occasion make use of pen, ink, and paper. But what any one of them is in its own true nature, I declare positively I know not. And the same is true with regard to every other corporeal thing. And, what is more, we are not only ignorant of the true and real nature of things, but even of their existence. It cannot be denied that we perceive such certain appearances or ideas; but it cannot be concluded from thence that bodies really exist. Nay, now I think on it, I must, agreeably to my former concessions, farther declare that it is impossible any real corporeal thing should exist in nature.

PHILONOUS: You amaze me. Was ever anything more wild and extravagant than the notions you now maintain: and is it not evident you are led into all these extravagances by the belief of *material substance?* This makes you dream of those unknown natures in everything. It is this occasions your distinguishing between the reality and sensible appearances of things. It is to this you are indebted for being ignorant of what everybody else knows perfectly well. Nor is this all: you are not only ignorant of the true nature of everything, but you know not whether anything really exists, or whether there are any true natures at all; forasmuch as you attribute to your material beings an absolute or external existence, wherein you suppose their reality consists. And, as you are forced in the end to acknowledge such an existence means either a direct repugnancy, or nothing at all, it follows that you are obliged to pull down your own hypothesis of material substance, and positively to deny the real existence of any part of the universe. And so you are plunged into the deepest and most deplorable *scepticism* that ever man was. Tell me, Hylas, is it not as I say?

HYLAS: I agree with you. *Material substance* was no more than an hypothesis; and a false and groundless one too. I will no longer spend my breath in defence of it. But whatever hypothesis you advance, or whatsoever scheme of things you introduce in its stead, I doubt not it will appear every whit as false: let me but be allowed to question you upon it. That is, suffer me to serve you in your own kind, and I warrant it shall conduct you through as many perplexities and contradictions, to the very same state of scepticism that I myself am in at present.

PHILONOUS: I assure you, Hylas, I do not pretend to frame any hypothesis at all. I am of a vulgar cast, simple enough to believe my senses, and leave things as I find them. To be plain, it is my opinion that the real things are those very things I see, and feel, and perceive by my senses. These I know; and, finding they answer all the necessities and purposes of life, have no reason to be solicitous about any other unknown beings. A piece of sensible bread, for instance, would stay my stomach better than ten thousand times as much of that insensible, unintelligible, real bread you speak of. It is likewise my opinion that colours and other sensible qualities are on the objects. I cannot for my life help thinking that snow is white, and fire hot. You indeed, who by *snow* and *fire* mean certain external, unperceived, unperceiving substances, are in the right to deny whiteness or heat to be affections inherent in them. But I, who understand by those words the things I see and feel, am obliged to think like other folks. And, as I am no sceptic with regard to the nature of things, so neither am I as to their existence. That a thing should be really perceived by my senses, and at the same time not really exist, is to me a plain contradiction; since I cannot prescind or abstract, even in thought, the existence of a sensible thing from its being perceived. Wood, stones, fire, water, flesh, iron, and the like things, which I name and discourse of, are things that I know. And I should not have known them but that I perceived them by my senses; and things perceived by the senses are immediately perceived; and things immediately perceived are ideas; and ideas cannot exist without the mind, their existence therefore consists in being perceived; when, therefore, they are actually perceived there can be no doubt of their existence. Away then with all that scepticism, all those ridiculous philosophical doubts. What a jest is it for a philosopher to question the existence of sensible things, till he hath it proved to him from the veracity of God; or to pretend our knowledge in this point falls short of intuition or demonstration! I might as well doubt of my own being, as of the being of those things I actually see and feel.

HYLAS: Not so fast, Philonous: you say you cannot conceive how sensible things should exist without the mind. Do you not?

PHILONOUS: I do.

HYLAS: Supposing you were annihilated, cannot you conceive it possible that things perceivable by sense may still exist?

PHILONOUS: I can, but then it must be in another mind. When I deny sensible things an existence out of the mind, I do not mean my mind in particular, but all minds. Now, it is plain they have an existence exterior to my mind, since I find them by experience to be independent of it. There is therefore some other mind wherein they exist, during the intervals between the times of my perceiving them: as likewise they did before my birth, and would do after my supposed annihilation. And, as the same is true with regard to all other finite created spirits, it necessarily follows there is an *omnipresent eternal mind,* which knows and comprehends all things, and exhibits them to our view in such a manner, and according to such rules, as he himself hath ordained, and are by us termed the *laws of nature.*

HYLAS: Answer me, Philonous. Are all our ideas perfectly inert beings? Or have they any agency included in them?

PHILONOUS: They are altogether passive and inert.

HYLAS: And is not God an agent, a being purely active?

PHILONOUS: I acknowledge it.

HYLAS: No idea therefore can be like unto, or represent the nature of God?

PHILONOUS: It cannot.

HYLAS: Since therefore you have no idea of the mind of God, how can you conceive it possible that things should exist in His mind? Or, if you can conceive the mind of God, without having an idea of it, why may not I be allowed to conceive the existence of matter, notwithstanding I have no idea of it?

PHILONOUS: As to your first question: I own I have properly no idea, either of God or any other spirit; for these being active, cannot be represented by things perfectly inert, as our ideas are. I do nevertheless know that I, who am a spirit or thinking substance, exist as certainly as I know my ideas exist. Farther, I know what I mean by the terms *I* and *myself;* and I know this immediately or intuitively, though I do not perceive it as I perceive a triangle, a colour, or a sound. The mind, spirit, or soul is that indivisible unextended thing which thinks, acts, and perceives. I say *indivisible,* because *unextended;* and unextended, because extended, figured, movable things are ideas; and that which perceives ideas, which thinks and wills, is plainly itself no idea, nor like an idea. Ideas are things inactive, and perceived. And spirits a sort of beings altogether different from them. I do not therefore say my soul is an idea, or like an idea. However, taking the word *idea* in a large sense, my soul may be said to furnish me with an idea, that is, an image or likeness of God—though indeed extremely inadequate. For, all the notion I have of God is obtained by reflecting on my own soul, heightening its powers, and removing its imperfections. I have, therefore, though not an inactive idea, yet in *myself* some sort of an active thinking image of the Deity. And, though I perceive him not by sense, yet I have a notion of him, or know him by reflexion and reasoning. My own mind and my own ideas I have an immediate knowledge of; and, by the help of these, do mediately apprehend the possibility of the existence of other spirits and ideas. Farther, from my own being, and from the dependency I find in myself and my ideas, I do, by an act of reason, necessarily infer the existence of a God, and of all created things in the mind of God. So much for your first question. For the second: I suppose by this time you can answer it yourself. For you neither perceive matter objectively, as you do an inactive being or idea; nor know it, as you do yourself, by a reflex act, neither do you mediately apprehend it by similitude of the one or the other; nor yet collect it by reasoning from that which you know immediately. All which makes the case of *matter* widely different from that of the *Deity.*

HYLAS: You say your own soul supplies you with some sort of an idea or image of God. But, at the same time, you acknowledge you have, properly speaking, no idea of your own soul. You even affirm that spirits are a sort of beings altogether different from ideas. Consequently that no idea can be like a spirit. We have therefore no idea of any spirit. You admit nevertheless that there is spiritual substance, although you have no idea of it; while you deny there can be such a thing as material substance, because you have no notion or idea of it. Is this fair dealing? To act consistently, you must either admit matter or reject spirit. What say you to this?

PHILONOUS: I say, in the first place, that I do not deny the existence of material substance, merely because I have no notion of it, but because the notion of it is inconsistent; or, in other words, because it is repugnant that there should be a notion of it. Many things, for aught I know, may exist, whereof neither I nor any other man hath or can have any idea or notion whatsoever. But then those things must be possible, that is, nothing inconsistent must be included in their definition. I say, secondly, that, although we believe things to exist which we do not perceive, yet we may not believe that any particular thing exists, without some reason for such belief: but I have no reason for believing the existence of matter. I have no immediate intuition thereof: neither can I immediately from my sensations, ideas, notions, actions, or passions, infer an unthinking, unperceiving, inactive substance—either by probable deduction, or necessary consequence. Whereas the being of my Self, that is, my own soul, mind, or thinking principle, I evidently know by reflexion. You will forgive me if I repeat the same things in answer to the same objections. In the very notion or definition of *material substance,* there is included a manifest repugnance and inconsistency. But this cannot be said of the notion of spirit. That ideas should exist in what does not perceive or be produced by what does not act, is repugnant. But, it is no repugnancy to say that a perceiving thing should be the subject of ideas, or an active thing the cause of them. It is granted we have neither an immediate evidence nor a demonstrative knowledge of the existence of other finite spirits; but it will not thence follow that such spirits are on a foot with material substances: if to suppose the one be inconsistent, and it be not inconsistent to suppose the other; if the one can be inferred by no argument, and there is a probability for the other; if we see signs and effects indicating distinct finite agents like ourselves, and see no sign or symptom whatever that leads to a rational belief of matter. I say, lastly, that I have a notion of spirit, though I have not, strictly speaking, an idea of it. I do not perceive it as an idea, or by means of an idea, but know it by reflexion.

HYLAS: Notwithstanding all you have said, to me it seems that, according to your own way of thinking, and in consequence of your own principles, it should follow that you are only a system of floating ideas, without any substance to support them. Words are not to be used without a meaning. And, as there is no more meaning in *spiritual substance* than in *material substance,* the one is to be exploded as well as the other.

PHILONOUS: How often must I repeat, that I know or am conscious of my own being; and that *I myself* am not my ideas, but somewhat else, a thinking, active principle that perceives, knows, wills, and operates about ideas I know that I, one and the same self, perceive both colours and sounds: that a colour cannot perceive a sound, nor a sound a colour: that I am therefore one individual principle, distinct from colour and sound, and, for the same reason, from all other sensible things and inert ideas. But, I am not in like manner conscious either of the existence or essence of matter. On the contrary, I know that nothing inconsistent can exist, and that the existence of matter implies an inconsistency. Farther, I know what I mean when I affirm that there is a spiritual substance or support of ideas, that is, that a spirit knows and perceives ideas. But, I do not know what is meant when it is said that an unperceiving substance hath inherent in it and supports either ideas or the archetypes of ideas. There is therefore upon the whole no parity of case between spirit and matter.

HYLAS: I own myself satisfied in this point. But, do you in earnest think the real existence of sensible things consists in their being actually perceived? If so; how comes it that all mankind distinguish between them? Ask the first man you meet, and he shall tell you, *to be perceived* is one thing, and *to exist* is another.

PHILONOUS: I am content, Hylas, to appeal to the common sense of the world for the truth of my notion. Ask the gardener why he thinks yonder cherry-tree exists in the garden, and he shall tell you, because he sees and feels it; in a word, because he perceives it by his senses. Ask him why he thinks an orange-tree not to be there, and he shall tell you, because he does not perceive it. What he perceives by sense, that he terms a real being, and says it *is* or *exists;* but, that which is not perceivable, the same, he says, has no being.

HYLAS: Yes, Philonous, I grant the existence of a sensible thing consists in being perceivable, but not in being actually perceived.

PHILONOUS: And what is perceivable but an idea? And can an idea exist without being actually perceived? These are points long since agreed between us.

HYLAS: But, be your opinion never so true, yet surely you will not deny it is shocking, and contrary to the common sense of men. Ask the fellow whether yonder tree hath an existence out of his mind: what answer think you he would make?

PHILONOUS: The same that I should myself, to wit, that it does exist out of his mind. But then to a Christian it cannot surely be shocking to say, the real tree, existing without his mind, is truly known and comprehended by (that is *exists in*) the infinite mind of God. Probably he may not at first glance be aware of the direct and immediate proof there is of this; inasmuch as the very being of a tree, or any other sensible thing, implies a mind wherein it is. But the point itself he cannot deny. The question between the materialists and me is not, whether things have a real existence out of the mind of this or that person, but whether they have an absolute existence, distinct from being per-ceived by God, and exterior to all minds. This indeed some heathens and philosophers have affirmed, but whoever entertains notions of the Deity suitable to the Holy Scrip-tures will be of another opinion.

HYLAS: But, according to your notions, what difference is there between real things, and chimeras formed by the imagination, or the visions of a dream—since they are all equally in the mind?

PHILONOUS: The ideas formed by the imagination are faint and indistinct; they have, besides, an entire dependence on the will. But the ideas perceived by sense, that is, real things, are more vivid and clear; and, being imprinted on the mind by a spirit dis-tinct from us, have not the like dependence on our will. There is therefore no danger of confounding these with the foregoing; and there is as little of confounding them with the visions of a dream, which are dim, irregular, and confused. And, though they should happen to be never so lively and natural, yet, by their not being connected, and of a piece with the preceding and subsequent transactions of our lives, they might easily be distinguished from realities. In short, by whatever method you distinguish *things* from *chimeras* on your scheme, the same, it is evident, will hold also upon mine. For, it must be, I presume, by some perceived difference; and I am not for depriving you of any one thing that you perceive.

HYLAS: But still, Philonous, you hold, there is nothing in the world but spirits and ideas. And this, you must needs acknowledge, sounds very oddly.

PHILONOUS: I own the word *idea,* not being commonly used for *thing,* sounds something out of the way. My reason for using it was, because a necessary relation to the mind is understood to be implied by that term; and it is now commonly used by philosophers to denote the immediate objects of the understanding. But, however oddly the proposition may sound in words, yet it includes nothing so very strange or shocking in its sense, which in effect amounts to no more than this, to wit, that there are only things perceiving, and things perceived; or that every unthinking being is necessarily, and from the very nature of its existence, perceived by some mind; if not by a finite cre-ated mind, yet certainly by the infinite mind of God, in whom "we live, and move, and have our being." Is this as strange as to say, the sensible qualities are not on the objects: or that we cannot be sure of the existence of things, or know any thing of their real natures—though we both see and feel them, and perceive them by all our senses?

HYLAS: And, in consequence of this, must we not think there are no such things as physical or corporeal causes; but that a spirit is the immediate cause of all the phe-nomena in nature? Can there be anything more extravagant than this?

PHILONOUS: Yes, it is infinitely more extravagant to say—a thing which is inert operates on the mind, and which is unperceiving is the cause of our perceptions, with-out any regard either to consistency, or the old known axiom: *Nothing can give to an-other that which it hath not itself.* Besides, that which to you, I know not for what rea-son, seems so extravagant is no more than the Holy Scriptures assert in a hundred places. In them God is represented as the sole and immediate author of all those effects which some heathens and philosophers are wont to ascribe to nature, matter, fate, or the like unthinking principle. This is so much the constant language of Scripture that it were needless to confirm it by citations.

HYLAS: You are not aware Philonous, that in making God the immediate author of all the motions in nature, you make him the author of murder, sacrilege, adultery, and the like heinous sins.

PHILONOUS: In answer to that, I observe, first, that the imputation of guilt is the same, whether a person commits an action with or without an instrument. In case therefore you suppose God to act by the mediation of an instrument or occasion, called *matter,* you as truly make him the author of sin as I, who think him the immediate agent in all those operations vulgarly ascribed to nature. I farther observe that sin or moral turpitude does not consist in the outward physical action or motion, but in the internal deviation of the will from the laws of reason and religion. This is plain, in that the killing an enemy in a battle, or putting a criminal legally to death, is not thought sinful; though the outward act be the very same with that in the case of murder. Since therefore, sin does not consist in the physical action, the making God an immediate cause of all such actions is not making him the author of sin. Lastly, I have nowhere said that God is the only agent who produces all the motions in bodies. It is true I have denied there are any other agents besides spirits, but this is very consistent with allowing to thinking rational beings, in the production of motions, the use of limited powers, ultimately indeed derived from God, but immediately under the direction of their own wills which is sufficient to entitle them to all the guilt of their actions.

HYLAS: But the denying matter, Philonous, or corporeal substance; there is the point. You can never persuade me that this is not repugnant to the universal sense of mankind. Were our dispute to be determined by most voices, I am confident you would give up the point, without gathering the votes.

PHILONOUS: I wish both our opinions were fairly stated and submitted to the judgment of men who had plain common sense, without the prejudices of a learned education. Let me be represented as one who trusts his senses, who thinks he knows the things he sees and feels, and entertains no doubts of their existence, and you fairly set forth with all your doubts, your paradoxes, and your scepticism about you, and I shall willingly acquiesce in the determination of any indifferent person. That there is no substance wherein ideas can exist beside spirit is to me evident. And that the objects immediately perceived are ideas, is on all hands agreed. And that sensible qualities are objects immediately perceived no one can deny. It is therefore evident there can be no *substratum* of those qualities but spirit; in which they exist, not by way of mode or property, but as a thing perceived in that which perceives it. I deny therefore that there is any unthinking *substratum* of the objects of sense, and in that acceptation that there is any material substance. But if by *material substance* is meant only sensible body—that which is seen and felt (and the unphilosophical part of the world, I dare say, mean no more)—then I am more certain of matter's existence than you or any other philosopher pretend to be. If there be anything which makes the generality of mankind averse from the notions I espouse: it is a misapprehension that I deny the reality of sensible things. But, as it is you who are guilty of that, and not I, it follows that in truth their aversion is against your notions and not mine. I do therefore assert that I am as certain as of my own being, that there are bodies or corporeal substances (meaning the things I perceive by my senses); and that, granting this, the bulk of mankind will take no thought about, nor think themselves at all concerned in the fate of those unknown natures, and philosophical quiddities, which some men are so fond of.

HYLAS: What say you to this? Since, according to you, men judge of the reality of things by their senses, how can a man be mistaken in thinking the moon a plain lucid surface, about a foot in diameter; or a square tower, seen at a distance, round; or an oar, with one end in the water, crooked?

PHILONOUS: He is not mistaken with regard to the ideas he actually perceives, but in the inference he makes from his present perceptions. Thus, in the case of the oar, what he immediately perceives by sight is certainly crooked; and so far he is in the right. But if he thence conclude that upon taking the oar out of the water he shall perceive the same crookedness; or that it would affect his touch as crooked things are wont to do: in that he is mistaken. In like manner, if he shall conclude from what he perceives in one station, that, in case he advances towards the moon or tower, he should still be affected with the like ideas, he is mistaken. But his mistake lies not in what he perceives immediately, and at present, (it being a manifest contradiction to suppose he should err in respect of that) but in the wrong judgment he makes concerning the ideas he apprehends to be connected with those immediately perceived: or, concerning the ideas that, from what he perceives at present, he imagines would be perceived in other circumstances. The case is the same with regard to the Copernican system. We do not here perceive any motion of the earth: but it were erroneous thence to conclude, that, in case we were placed at as great a distance from that as we are now from the other planets, we should not then perceive its motion.

HYLAS: I understand you; and must needs own you say things plausible enough. But, give me leave to put you in mind of one thing. Pray, Philonous, were you not formerly as positive that matter existed, as you are now that it does not?

PHILONOUS: I was. But here lies the difference. Before, my positiveness was founded, without examination, upon prejudice; but now, after inquiry, upon evidence.

HYLAS: After all, it seems our dispute is rather about words than things. We agree in the thing, but differ in the name. That we are affected with ideas from without is evident, and it is no less evident that there must be (I will not say archetypes, but) Powers without the mind, corresponding to those ideas. And, as these Powers cannot subsist by themselves, there is some subject of them necessarily to be admitted; which I call *matter,* and you call *spirit.* This is all the difference.

PHILONOUS: Pray, Hylas, is that powerful being, or subject of powers, extended?

HYLAS: It hath not extension; but it hath the power to raise in you the idea of extension.

PHILONOUS: It is therefore itself unextended?

HYLAS: I grant it.

PHILONOUS: Is it not also active?

HYLAS: Without doubt. Otherwise, how could we attribute powers to it?

PHILONOUS: Now let me ask you two questions: *First,* whether it be agreeable to the usage either of philosophers or others to give the name *matter* to an unextended active being? And, *secondly,* whether it be not ridiculously absurd to misapply names contrary to the common use of language?

HYLAS: Well then, let it not be called matter, since you will have it so, but some *third nature* distinct from matter and spirit. For what reason is there why you should call it spirit? Does not the notion of spirit imply that it is thinking, as well as active and unextended?

PHILONOUS: My reason is this: because I have a mind to have some notion of meaning in what I say: but I have no notion of any action distinct from volition, neither can I conceive volition to be anywhere but in a spirit: therefore, when I speak of an active being, I am obliged to mean a spirit. Beside, what can be plainer than that a thing which hath no ideas in itself cannot impart them to me, and, if it hath ideas, surely it must be a spirit. To make you comprehend the point still more clearly if it be possible, I assert as well as you that, since we are affected from without, we must allow powers to be without, in a being distinct from ourselves. So far we are agreed. But then we differ as to the kind of this powerful being. I will have it to be spirit, you matter, or I know not what (I may add too, you know not what) third nature. Thus, I prove it to be spirit. From the effects I see produced, I conclude there are actions; and, because actions, volitions; and, because there are volitions, there must be a will. Again, the things I perceive must have an existence, they or their archetypes, out of my mind: but, being ideas, neither they nor their archetypes can exist otherwise than in an understanding, there is therefore an understanding. But will and understanding constitute in the strictest sense a mind or spirit. The powerful cause, therefore, of my ideas is in strict propriety of speech a *spirit*.

HYLAS: And now I warrant you think you have made the point very clear, little suspecting that what you advance leads directly to a contradiction. Is it not an absurdity to imagine any imperfection in God?

PHILONOUS: Without a doubt.

HYLAS: To suffer pain is an imperfection?

PHILONOUS: It is.

HYLAS: Are we not sometimes affected with pain and uneasiness by some other being?

PHILONOUS: We are.

HYLAS: And have you not said that being is a spirit, and is not that spirit God?

PHILONOUS: I grant it.

HYLAS: But you have asserted that whatever ideas we perceive from without are in the mind which affects us. The ideas, therefore, of pain and uneasiness are in God; or, in other words, God suffers pain: that is to say, there is an imperfection in the divine nature: which, you acknowledged, was absurd. So you are caught in a plain contradiction.

PHILONOUS: That God knows or understands all things, and that he knows, among other things, what pain is, even every sort of painful sensation, and what it is for His creatures to suffer pain, I make no question. But, that God, though he knows and sometimes causes painful sensations in us, can himself suffer pain, I positively deny. We, who are limited and dependent spirits, are liable to impressions of sense, the effects of an external agent, which, being produced against our wills, are sometimes painful and uneasy. But God, whom no external being can affect, who perceives nothing by sense as we do; whose will is absolute and independent, causing all things, and liable to be thwarted or resisted by nothing: it is evident, such a being as this can suffer nothing, nor be affected with any painful sensation, or indeed any sensation at all. We are chained to a body: that is to say, our perceptions are connected with corporeal motions. By the law of our nature, we are affected upon every alteration in the nervous parts of our sensible body; which sensible body, rightly considered, is nothing but a complexion of such qualities or ideas as have no existence distinct from being perceived by a mind. So that this connexion of sensations with corporeal motions means no more than a correspondence in the order of nature, between two sets of ideas, or things immediately perceivable. But God is a pure spirit, disengaged from all such sympathy, or natural ties. No corporeal motions are attended with the sensations of pain or pleasure in His mind. To know everything knowable, is certainly a perfection; but to endure or suffer, or feel anything by sense, is an imperfection. The former, I say, agrees to God, but not the latter. God knows, or hath ideas; but His ideas are not conveyed to him by sense, as ours are. Your not distinguishing, where there is so manifest a difference, makes you fancy you see an absurdity where there is none.

HYLAS: But, all this while you have not considered that the quantity of matter has been demonstrated to be proportioned to the gravity of bodies. And what can withstand demonstration?

PHILONOUS: Let me see how you demonstrate that point.

HYLAS: I lay it down for a principle, that the moments or quantities of motion in bodies are in a direct compounded reason of the velocities and quantities of matter contained in them. Hence, where the velocities are equal, it follows the moments are directly as the quantity of matter in each. But it is found by experience that all bodies (bating the small inequalities, arising from the resistance of the air) descend with an equal velocity; the motion therefore of descending bodies, and consequently their gravity, which is the cause or principle of that motion, is proportional to the quantity of matter; which was to be demonstrated.

PHILONOUS: You lay it down as a self-evident principle that the quantity of motion in any body is proportional to the velocity and *matter* taken together: and this is made use of to prove a proposition from whence the existence of *matter* is inferred. Pray is not this arguing in a circle?

HYLAS: In the premise I only mean that the motion is proportional to the velocity, jointly with the extension and solidity.

PHILONOUS: But, allowing this to be true, yet it will not thence follow that gravity is proportional to *matter,* in your philosophic sense of the word, except you take it for granted that unknown *substratum,* or whatever else you call it, is proportional to those sensible qualities; which to suppose is plainly begging the question. That there is magnitude and solidity, or resistance, perceived by sense, I readily grant, as likewise, that gravity may be proportional to those qualities I will not dispute. But that either these qualities as perceived by us, or the powers producing them, do exist in a *material substratum;* this is what I deny, and you indeed affirm, but, notwithstanding your demonstration, have not yet proved.

HYLAS: I shall insist no longer on that point. Do you think, however, you shall persuade me the natural philosophers have been dreaming all this while? Pray what becomes of all their hypotheses and explications of the *phenomena,* which suppose the existence of matter?

PHILONOUS: What mean you, Hylas, by the *phenomena?*

HYLAS: I mean the appearances which I perceive by my senses.

PHILONOUS: And the appearances perceived by sense, are they not ideas?

HYLAS: I have told you so a hundred times.

PHILONOUS: Therefore, to explain the phenomena, is, to show how we come to be affected with ideas, in that manner and order wherein they are imprinted on our senses. Is it not?

HYLAS: It is.

PHILONOUS: Now, if you can prove that any philosopher has explained the production of any one idea in our minds by the help of *matter,* I shall for ever acquiesce, and look on all that hath been said against it as nothing; but, if you cannot, it is vain to urge the explication of *phenomena.* That a being endowed with knowledge and will should produce or exhibit ideas is easily understood. But that a being which is utterly destitute of these faculties should be able to produce ideas, or in any sort to affect an intelligence, this I can never understand. This I say, though we had some positive conception of matter, though we knew its qualities, and could comprehend its existence, would yet be so far from explaining things, that it is itself the most inexplicable thing in the world. And yet, for all this, it will not follow that philosophers have been doing nothing; for, by observing and reasoning upon the connexion of ideas, they discover the laws and methods of nature, which is a part of knowledge both useful and entertaining.

HYLAS: After all, can it be supposed God would deceive all mankind? Do you imagine he would have induced the whole world to believe the being of matter, if there was no such thing?

PHILONOUS: That every epidemical opinion, arising from prejudice, or passion, or thoughtlessness, may be imputed to God, as the author of it, I believe you will not affirm. Whatsoever opinion we father on him, it must be either because he has discovered it to us by supernatural revelation; or because it is so evident to our natural faculties, which were framed and given us by God, that it is impossible we should withhold our assent from it. But where is the revelation? Or where is the evidence that extorts the belief of matter? Nay, how does it appear, that matter, taken for something distinct from what we perceive by our senses, is thought to exist by all mankind; or indeed, by any except a few philosophers, who do not know what they would be at? Your question supposes these points are clear; and, when you have cleared them, I shall think myself obliged to give you another answer. In the meantime, let it suffice. That I tell you, I do not suppose God has deceived mankind at all.

HYLAS: But the novelty, Philonous, the novelty! There lies the danger. New notions should always be discountenanced; they unsettle men's minds, and nobody knows where they will end.

PHILONOUS: Why the rejecting a notion that has no foundation, either in sense, or in reason, or in divine authority, should be thought to unsettle the belief of such opinions as are grounded on all or any of these, I cannot imagine. That innovations in government and religion are dangerous, and ought to be discountenanced, I freely own. But is there the like reason why they should be discouraged in philosophy? The making anything known which was unknown before is an innovation in knowledge: and, if all such innovations had been forbidden, men would have made a notable progress in the arts and sciences. But it is none of my business to plead for novelties and paradoxes. That the qualities we perceive are not on the objects: that we must not believe our senses: that we know nothing of the real nature of things, and can never be assured even of their existence: that real colours and sounds are nothing but certain unknown figures and motions: that motions are in themselves neither swift nor slow: that there are in bodies absolute extensions, without any particular magnitude or figure: that a thing stupid, thoughtless, and inactive, operates on a spirit: that the least particle of a body contains innumerable extended parts:—these are the novelties, these are the strange notions which shock the genuine uncorrupted judgment of all mankind; and being once admitted, embarrass the mind with endless doubts and difficulties. And it is against these and the like innovations I endeavour to vindicate common sense. It is true, in doing this, I may perhaps be obliged to use some *ambages,* and ways of speech not common. But, if my notions are once thoroughly understood, that which is most singular in them will, in effect, be found to amount to no more than this:—that it is absolutely impossible, and a plain contradiction, to suppose any unthinking being should exist without being perceived by a mind. And, if this notion be singular, it is a shame it should be so, at this time of day, and in a Christian country.

HYLAS: As for the difficulties other opinions may be liable to, those are out of the question. It is your business to defend your own opinion. Can anything be plainer than that you are for changing all things into ideas? You, I say, who are not ashamed to charge me with *scepticism.* This is so plain, there is no denying it.

PHILONOUS: You mistake me. I am not for changing things into ideas, but rather ideas into things; since those immediate objects of perception, which, according to you, are only appearances of things, I take to be the real things themselves.

HYLAS: Things! You may pretend what you please; but it is certain you leave us nothing but the empty forms of things, the outside only which strikes the senses.

PHILONOUS: What you call the empty forms and outside of things seem to me the very things themselves. Nor are they empty or incomplete, otherwise than upon your supposition—that matter is an essential part of all corporeal things. We both, therefore, agree in this, that we perceive only sensible forms: but herein we differ—you will have them to be empty appearances, I real beings. In short, you do not trust your senses, I do.

HYLAS: You say you believe your senses; and seem to applaud yourself that in this you agree with the vulgar. According to you, therefore, the true nature of a thing is discovered by the senses. If so, whence comes that disagreement? Why is not the same figure, and other sensible qualities, perceived all manner of ways? And why should we use a microscope the better to discover the true nature of a body, if it were discoverable to the naked eye?

PHILONOUS: Strictly speaking, Hylas, we do not see the same object that we feel; neither is the same object perceived by the microscope which was by the naked eye. But, in case every variation was thought sufficient to constitute a new kind of individual, the endless number of confusion of names would render language impracticable. Therefore, to avoid this, as well as other inconveniences which are obvious upon a little thought, men combine together several ideas, apprehended by divers senses, or by the same sense at different times, or in different circumstances, but observed, however, to have some connexion in nature, either with respect to co-existence or succession; all which they refer to one name, and consider as one thing. Hence it follows that when I examine, by my other senses, a thing I have seen, it is not in order to understand better the same object which I had perceived by sight, the object of one sense not being perceived by the other senses. And, when I look through a microscope, it is not that I may perceive more clearly what I perceived already with my bare eyes; the object perceived by the glass being quite different from the former. But, in both cases, my aim is only to know what ideas are connected together; and the more a man knows of the connexion of ideas, the more he is said to know of the nature of things. What, therefore, if our ideas are variable; what if our senses are not in all circumstances affected with the same appearances. It will not thence follow they are not to be trusted; or that they are inconsistent either with themselves or anything else: except it be with your preconceived notion of (I know not what) one single, unchanged, unperceivable, real nature, marked by each name. Which prejudice seems to have taken its rise from not rightly understanding the common language of men, speaking of several distinct ideas as united into one thing by the mind. And, indeed, there is cause to suspect several erroneous conceits of the philosophers are owing to the same original: while they began to build their schemes not so much on notions as on words, which were framed by the vulgar, merely for conveniency and dispatch in the common actions of life, without any regard to speculation.

HYLAS: Methinks I apprehend your meaning.

PHILONOUS: It is your opinion the ideas we perceive by our senses are not real things, but images or copies of them. Our knowledge, therefore, is no farther real than as our ideas are the true representations of those originals. But, as these supposed originals are in themselves unknown, it is impossible to know how far our ideas resemble them; or whether they resemble them at all. We cannot, therefore, be sure we have any real knowledge. Farther, as our ideas are perpetually varied, without any change in the supposed real things, it necessarily follows they cannot all be true copies of them: or, if some are and others are not, it is impossible to distinguish the former from the latter. And this plunges us yet deeper in uncertainty. Again, when we consider the point, we cannot conceive how any idea, or anything like an idea, should have an absolute existence out of a mind: nor consequently, according to you, how there should be any real thing in nature. The result of all which is that we are thrown into the most hopeless and abandoned *scepticism*. Now, give me leave to ask you, *first,* whether your referring ideas to certain absolutely existing unperceived substances, as their originals, be not the source of all this *scepticism? Secondly,* whether you are informed, either by sense or reason, of the existence of those unknown originals? And, in case you are not, whether it be not absurd to suppose them? *Thirdly,* whether, upon inquiry, you find there is anything distinctly conceived or meant by the *absolute or external existence of unperceiving substances? Lastly,* whether, the premises considered, it be not the wisest way to follow nature, trust your senses, and, laying aside all anxious thought about unknown natures or substances, admit with the vulgar those for real things which are perceived by the senses?

HYLAS: For the present, I have no inclination to the answering part. I would much rather see how you can get over what follows. Pray are not the objects perceived by the senses of one, likewise perceivable to others present? If there were a hundred more here, they would all see the garden, the trees, and flowers, as I see them. But they are not in the same manner affected with the ideas I frame in my imagination. Does not this make a difference between the former sort of objects and the latter?

PHILONOUS: I grant it does. Nor have I ever denied a difference between the objects of sense and those of imagination. But what would you infer from thence? You cannot say that sensible objects exist unperceived, because they are perceived by many.

HYLAS: I own I can make nothing of that objection: but it hath led me into another. Is it not your opinion that by our senses we perceive only the ideas existing in our minds?

PHILONOUS: It is.

HYLAS: But the same idea which is in my mind cannot be in yours, or in any other mind. Does it not therefore follow, from your principles, that no two can see the same thing? And is not this highly absurd?

PHILONOUS: If the term *same* be taken in the vulgar acceptation, it is certain (and not at all repugnant to the principles I maintain) that different persons may perceive the same thing; or the same thing or idea exist in different minds. Words are of arbitrary imposition, and since men are used to apply the word *same* where no distinction or variety is perceived, and I do not pretend to alter their perceptions, it follows that, as men have said before, *several saw the same thing,* so they may, upon like occasions, still continue to use the same phrase, without any deviation either from propriety of language, or the truth of things. But, if the term *same* be used in the acceptation of philosophers, who pretend to an abstracted notion of identity, then, according to their sundry definitions of this notion (for it is not yet agreed wherein that philosophic identity consists), it may or may not be possible for divers persons to perceive the same thing. But whether philosophers shall think fit to call a thing the *same* or no, is, I conceive, of small importance. Let us suppose several men together, all endued with the same faculties, and consequently affected in like sort by their senses, and who had yet never known the use of language; they would, without question, agree in their perceptions. Though perhaps, when they came to the use of speech, some regarding the uniformness of what was perceived, might call it the *same* thing: others, especially regarding the diversity of persons who perceived, might choose the denomination of *different* things. But who sees not that all the dispute is about a word? To wit, whether what is perceived by different persons may yet have the term *same* applied to it? Or, suppose a house, whose walls or outward shell remaining unaltered, the chambers are all pulled down, and new ones built in their place; and that you should call this the *same,* and I should say it was not the *same* house:—would we not, for all this, perfectly agree in our thoughts of the house, considered in itself? And would not all the difference consist in a sound? If you should say, We differed in our notions; for that you superadded to your idea of the house the simple abstracted idea of identity, whereas I did not; I would tell you, I know not what you mean by the *abstracted idea of identity;* and should desire you to look into your own thoughts, and be sure you understood yourself.—Why so silent, Hylas? Are you not yet satisfied men may dispute about identity and diversity, without any real difference in their thoughts and opinions, abstracted from names? Take this farther reflexion with you— that whether matter be allowed to exist or no, the case is exactly the same as to the point in hand. For the materialists themselves acknowledge what we immediately perceive by our senses to be our own ideas. Your difficulty, therefore, that no two see the same thing, makes equally against the materialists and me.

HYLAS: But they suppose an external archetype, to which referring their several ideas they may truly be said to perceive the same thing.

PHILONOUS: And (not to mention your having discarded those archetypes) so may you suppose an external archetype on my principles; *external,* I mean, to your own mind: though indeed it must be supposed to exist in that mind which comprehends all things; but then, this serves all the ends of identity, as well as if it existed out of a mind. And I am sure you yourself will not say it is less intelligible.

HYLAS: You have indeed clearly satisfied me—either that there is no difficulty at bottom in this point; or, if there be, that it makes equally against both opinions.

PHILONOUS: But that which makes equally against two contradictory opinions can be a proof against neither.

HYLAS: I acknowledge it. But, after all, Philonous, when I consider the substance of what you advance against *scepticism,* it amounts to no more than this:—We are sure that we really see, hear, feel; in a word, that we are affected with sensible impressions.

PHILONOUS: And how are we concerned any farther? I see this *cherry,* I feel it, I taste it: and I am sure *nothing* cannot be seen, or felt, or tasted: it is therefore *real.* Take away the sensations of softness, moisture, redness, tartness, and you take away the *cherry,* since it is not a being distinct from sensations. A *cherry,* I say, is nothing but a congeries of sensible impressions, or ideas perceived by various senses: which ideas are united into one thing (or have one name given them) by the mind, because they are observed to attend each other. Thus, when the palate is affected with such a particular taste, the sight is affected with a red colour, the touch with roundness, softness, &c. Hence, when I see, and feel, and taste, in such sundry certain manners, I am sure the *cherry* exists, or is real; its reality being in my opinion nothing abstracted from those sensations. But if by the word *cherry* you mean an unknown nature, distinct from all those sensible qualities, and by its existence something distinct from its being perceived; then, indeed, I own, neither you nor I, nor any one else, can be sure it exists.

HYLAS: But, what would you say, Philonous, if I should bring the very same reasons against the existence of sensible things in a mind, which you have offered against their existing in a material *substratum?*

PHILONOUS: When I see your reasons, you shall hear what I have to say to them.

HYLAS: Is the mind extended or unextended?

PHILONOUS: Unextended, without doubt.

HYLAS: Do you say the things you perceive are in your mind?

PHILONOUS: They are.

HYLAS: Again, have I not heard you speak of sensible impressions?

PHILONOUS: I believe you may.

HYLAS: Explain to me now, O Philonous! how it is possible there should be room for all those trees and houses to exist in your mind. Can extended things be contained in that which is unextended? Or, are we to imagine impressions made on a thing void of all solidity? You cannot say objects are in your mind, as books in your study: or that things are imprinted on it, as the figure of a seal upon wax. In what sense, therefore, are we to understand those expressions? Explain me this if you can: and I shall then be able to answer all those queries you formerly put to me about my *substratum.*

PHILONOUS: Look you, Hylas, when I speak of objects as existing in the mind, or imprinted on the senses, I would not be understood in the gross literal sense, as when bodies are said to exist in a place, or a seal to make an impression upon wax. My meaning is only that the mind comprehends or perceives them; and that it is affected from without, or by some being distinct from itself. This is my explication of your difficulty; and how it can serve to make your tenet of an unperceiving material substratum intelligible, I would fain know.

HYLAS: Nay, if that be all, I confess I do not see what use can be made of it. But are you not guilty of some abuse of language in this?

PHILONOUS: None at all. It is no more than common custom, which you know is the rule of language, hath authorised: nothing being more usual, than for philosophers to speak of the immediate objects of the understanding as things existing in the mind. Nor is there anything in this but what is conformable to the general analogy of language; most part of the mental operations being signified by words borrowed from sensible things; as is plain in the terms *comprehend, reflect, discourse,* &c., which, being applied to the mind, must not be taken in their gross, original sense.

HYLAS: You have, I own, satisfied me in this point. But there still remains one great difficulty, which I know not how you will get over. And, indeed, it is of such importance that if you could solve all others, without being able to find a solution for this, you must never expect to make me a proselyte to your principles.

PHILONOUS: Let me know this mighty difficulty.

HYLAS: The Scripture account of the creation is what appears to me utterly irreconcilable with your notions. Moses tells us of a creation: a creation of what? Of ideas? No, certainly, but of things, of real things, solid corporeal substances. Bring your principles to agree with this, and I shall perhaps agree with you.

PHILONOUS: Moses mentions the sun, moon, and stars, earth and sea, plants and animals. That all these do really exist, and were in the beginning created by God, I make no question. If by *ideas* you mean fictions and fancies of the mind, then these are no ideas. If by *ideas* you mean immediate objects of the understanding, or sensible things, which cannot exist unperceived, or out of a mind, then these things are ideas. But whether you do or do not call them *ideas,* it matters little. The difference is only about a name. And, whether that name be retained or rejected, the sense, the truth, and reality of things continues the same. In common talk, the objects of our senses are not termed *ideas,* but *things.* Call them so still: provided you do not attribute to them any absolute external existence, and I shall never quarrel with you for a word. The creation, therefore, I allow to have been a creation of things, of *real* things. Neither is this in the least inconsistent with my principles, as is evident from what I have now said; and would have been evident to you without this, if you had not forgotten what had been so often said before. But as for solid corporeal substances, I desire you to show where Moses makes any mention of them; and, if they should be mentioned by him, or any other inspired writer, it would still be incumbent on you to show those words were not taken in the vulgar acceptation, for things falling under our senses, but in the philosophic acceptation, for matter, or an unknown quiddity, with an absolute existence. When you have proved these points, then (and not till then) may you bring the authority of Moses into our dispute.

HYLAS: It is in vain to dispute about a point so clear. I am content to refer it to your own conscience. Are you not satisfied there is some peculiar repugnancy between the Mosaic account of the creation and your notions?

PHILONOUS: If all possible sense which can be put on the first chapter of Genesis may be conceived as consistently with my principles as any other, then it has no peculiar repugnancy with them. But there is no sense you may not as well conceive, believing as I do. Since, besides spirits, all you conceive are ideas; and the existence of these I do not deny. Neither do you pretend they exist without the mind.

HYLAS: Pray let me see any sense you can understand it in.

PHILONOUS. Why, I imagine that if I had been present at the creation, I should have seen things produced into being—that is become perceptible—in the order prescribed by the sacred historian. I never before believed the Mosaic account of the creation, and now find no alteration in my manner of believing it. When things are said to begin or end their existence, we do not mean this with regard to God, but His creatures. All objects are eternally known by God, or, which is the same thing, have an eternal existence in His mind: but when things, before imperceptible to creatures, are, by a decree of God, perceptible to them, then are they said to begin a relative existence, with respect to created minds. Upon reading therefore the Mosaic account of the creation, I understand that the several parts of the world became gradually perceivable to finite spirits, endowed with proper faculties; so that, whoever such were present, they were in truth perceived by them. This is the literal obvious sense suggested to me by the words of the Holy Scripture: in which is included no mention, or no thought, either of *substratum,* instrument, occasion, or absolute existence. And, upon inquiry, I doubt not it will be found that most plain honest men, who believe the creation, never think of those things any more than I. What metaphysical sense you may understand it in, you only can tell.

HYLAS: But, Philonous, you do not seem to be aware that you allow created things, in the beginning, only a relative, and consequently hypothetical being: that is to say, upon supposition there were men to perceive them; without which they have no actuality of absolute existence, wherein creation might terminate. Is it not, therefore, according to you, plainly impossible the creation of any inanimate creatures should precede that of man? And is not this directly contrary to the Mosaic account?

PHILONOUS: In answer to that, I say, *first,* created beings might begin to exist in the mind of other created intelligences, beside men. You will not therefore be able to prove any contradiction between Moses and my notions, unless you first show there was no other order of finite created spirits in being, before man. I say farther, in case we conceive the creation, as we should at this time, a parcel of plants or vegetables of all sorts produced, by an invisible Power, in a desert where nobody was present—that this way of explaining or conceiving it is consistent with my principles, since they deprive you of nothing, either sensible or imaginable; that it exactly suits with the common, natural, and undebauched notions of mankind; that it manifests the dependence of all things on God; and consequently hath all the good effect or influence, which it is possible that important article of our faith should have in making men humble, thankful, and resigned to their great creator. I say, moreover, that, in this naked conception of things, divested of words, there will not be found any notion of what you call the *actuality of absolute existence.* You may indeed raise a dust with those terms, and so lengthen our dispute to no purpose. But I entreat you calmly to look into your own thoughts, and then tell me if they are not a useless and unintelligible jargon.

HYLAS: I own I have no very clear notion annexed to them. But what say you to this? Do you not make the existence of sensible things consist in their being in a mind? And were not all things eternally in the mind of God? Did they not therefore exist from all eternity, according to you? And how could that which was eternal be created in time? Can anything be clearer or better connected than this?

PHILONOUS: And are not you too of opinion, that God knew all things from eternity?

HYLAS: I am.

PHILONOUS: Consequently they always had a being in the divine intellect.

HYLAS: This I acknowledge.

PHILONOUS: By your own confession, therefore, nothing is new, or begins to be, in respect of the mind of God. So we are agreed in that point.

HYLAS: What shall we make then of the creation?

PHILONOUS: May we not understand it to have been entirely in respect of finite spirits; so that things, with regard to us, may properly be said to begin their existence, or be created, when God decreed they should become perceptible to intelligent creatures, in that order and manner which he then established, and we now call the laws of nature? You may call this a *relative,* or *hypothetical existence* if you please. But, so long as it supplies us with the most natural, obvious, and literal sense of the Mosaic history of the creation; so long as it answers all the religious ends of that great article; in a word, so long as you can assign no other sense or meaning in its stead; why should we reject this? Is it to comply with a ridiculous sceptical humour of making everything nonsense and unintelligible? I am sure you cannot say it is for the glory of God. For, allowing it to be a thing possible and conceivable that the corporeal world should have an absolute existence extrinsical to the mind of God, as well as to the minds of all created spirits; yet how could this set forth either the immensity or omniscience of the Deity, or the necessary and immediate dependence of all things on him? Nay, would it not rather seem to derogate from those attributes?

HYLAS: Well, but as to this decree of God's, for making things perceptible, what say you, Philonous? Is it not plain, God did either execute that decree from all eternity or at some certain time began to will what he had not actually willed before, but only designed to will? If the former, then there could be no creation, or beginning of existence, in finite things. If the latter, then we must acknowledge something new to befall the Deity; which implies a sort of change: and all change argues imperfection.

PHILONOUS: Pray consider what you are doing. Is it not evident this objection concludes equally against a creation in any sense; nay, against every other act of the Deity, discoverable by the light of nature? None of which can we conceive, otherwise than as performed in time, and having a beginning. God is a being of transcendent and unlimited perfections: His nature, therefore, is incomprehensible to finite spirits. It is not, therefore, to be expected that any man, whether *materialist* or *immaterialist,* should have exactly just notions of the Deity, His attributes, and ways of operation. If then you would infer anything against me, your difficulty must not be drawn from the inadequateness of our conceptions of the divine nature, which is unavoidable on any scheme; but from the denial of matter, of which there is not one word, directly or indirectly, in what you have now objected.

HYLAS: I must acknowledge the difficulties you are concerned to clear are such only as arise from the non-existence of matter, and are peculiar to that notion. So far you are in the right. But I cannot by any means bring myself to think there is no such peculiar repugnancy between the creation and your opinion; though indeed where to fix it, I do not distinctly know.

PHILONOUS: What would you have? Do I not acknowledge a twofold state of things—the one ectypal or natural, the other archetypal and eternal? The former was created in time; the latter existed from everlasting in the mind of God. Is not this agreeable to the common notions of divines? or, is any more than this necessary in order to conceive the creation? But you suspect some peculiar repugnancy, though you know not where it lies. To take away all possibility of scruple in the case, do but consider this one point. Either you are not able to conceive the creation on any hypothesis whatsoever; and, if so, there is no ground for dislike or complaint against any particular opinion on that score: or you are able to conceive it; and, if so, why not on my principles, since thereby nothing conceivable is taken away? You have all along been allowed the full scope of sense, imagination, and reason. Whatever, therefore, you could before apprehend, either immediately or mediately by your senses, or by ratiocination from your senses; whatever you could perceive, imagine, or understand, remains still with you. If, therefore, the notion you have of the creation by other principles be intelligible, you have it still upon mine; if it be not intelligible, I conceive it to be no notion at all; and so there is no loss of it. And indeed it seems to me very plain that the supposition of matter, that is a thing perfectly unknown and inconceivable, cannot serve to make us conceive anything. And, I hope it need not be proved to you that if the existence of matter does not make the creation conceivable, the creation's being without it inconceivable can be no objection against its non-existence.

HYLAS: I confess, Philonous, you have almost satisfied me in this point of the creation.

PHILONOUS: I would fain know why you are not quite satisfied. You tell me indeed of a repugnancy between the Mosaic history and immaterialism: but you know not where it lies. Is this reasonable, Hylas? Can you expect I should solve a difficulty without knowing what it is? But, to pass by all that, would not a man think you were assured there is no repugnancy between the received notions of materialists and the inspired writings?

HYLAS: And so I am.

PHILONOUS: Ought the historical part of Scripture to be understood in a plain obvious sense, or in a sense which is metaphysical and out of the way?

HYLAS: In the plain sense, doubtless.

PHILONOUS: When Moses speaks of herbs, earth, water, &c. as having been created by God; think you not the sensible things commonly signified by those words are suggested to every unphilosophical reader?

HYLAS: I cannot help thinking so.

PHILONOUS: And are not all ideas, or things perceived by sense, to be denied a real existence by the doctrine of the materialist?

HYLAS: This I have already acknowledged.

PHILONOUS: The creation, therefore, according to them, was not the creation of things sensible, which have only a relative being, but of certain unknown natures, which have an absolute being, wherein creation might terminate?

HYLAS: True.

PHILONOUS: Is it not therefore evident the assertors of matter destroy the plain obvious sense of Moses, with which their notions are utterly inconsistent; and instead of it obtrude on us I know not what; something equally unintelligible to themselves and me?

HYLAS: I cannot contradict you.

PHILONOUS: Moses tells us of a creation. A creation of what? of unknown quiddities, of occasions, or *substratum?* No, certainly; but of things obvious to the senses. You must first reconcile this with your notions, if you expect I should be reconciled to them.

HYLAS: I see you can assault me with my own weapons.

PHILONOUS: Then as to *absolute existence;* was there ever known a more jejune notion than that? Something it is so abstracted and unintelligible that you have frankly owned you could not conceive it, much less explain anything by it. But allowing matter to exist, and the notion of absolute existence to be clear as light; yet, was this ever known to make the creation more credible? Nay, hath it not furnished the atheists and infidels of all ages with the most plausible arguments against a creation? That a corporeal substance, which hath an absolute existence without the minds of spirits, should be produced out of nothing, by the mere will of a spirit, hath been looked upon as a thing so contrary to all reason, so impossible and absurd, that not only the most celebrated among the ancients, but even divers modern and Christian philosophers have thought matter co-eternal with the Deity. Lay these things together, and then judge you whether materialism disposes men to believe the creation of things.

HYLAS: I own, Philonous, I think it does not. This of the *creation* is the last objection I can think of; and I must needs own it hath been sufficiently answered as well as the rest. Nothing now remains to be overcome but a sort of unaccountable backwardness that I find in myself towards your notions.

PHILONOUS: When a man is swayed, he knows not why, to one side of the question, can this, think you, be anything else but the effect of prejudice, which never fails to attend old and rooted notions? And indeed in this respect I cannot deny the belief of matter to have very much the advantage over the contrary opinion, with men of a learned education.

HYLAS: I confess it seems to be as you say.

PHILONOUS: As a balance, therefore, to this weight of prejudice, let us throw into the scale the great advantages that arise from the belief of immaterialism, both in regard to religion and human learning. The being of a God, and incorruptibility of the soul, those great articles of religion, are they not proved with the clearest and most immediate evidence? When I say the being of a *God,* I do not mean an obscure general cause of things, whereof we have no conception, but *God,* in the strict and proper sense of the word. A being whose spirituality, omnipresence, providence, omniscience, infinite power and goodness, are as conspicuous as the existence of sensible things, of which (nothwithstanding the fallacious pretences and affected scruples of *sceptics*) there is no more reason to doubt than of our own being. Then, with relation to human sciences. In natural philosophy, what intricacies, what obscurities, what contradictions hath the belief of matter led men into! To say nothing of the numberless disputes about its extent, continuity, homogeneity, gravity, divisibility, &c.—do they not pretend to explain all things by bodies operating on bodies, according to the laws of motion? And yet, are they able to comprehend how one body should move another? Nay, admitting there was no difficulty in reconciling the notion of an inert being with a cause, or in conceiving how an accident might pass from one body to another; yet, by all their strained thoughts and extravagant suppositions, have they been able to reach the mechanical production of any one animal or vegetable body? Can they account, by the laws of motion, for sounds, tastes, smells, or colours; or for the regular course of things? Have they accounted, by physical principles, for the aptitude and contrivance even of the most inconsiderable parts of the universe? But, laying aside matter and corporeal causes, and admitting only the efficiency of an all-perfect mind, are not all the effects of nature easy and intelligible? If the *phenomena* are nothing else but *ideas;* God is a *spirit,* but matter an unintelligent, unperceiving being. If they demonstrate an unlimited power in their cause; God is active and omnipotent, but matter an inert mass. If they order regularity, and usefulness of them can never be sufficiently admired; God is infinitely wise and provident, but matter destitute of all contrivance and design. These surely are great advantages in *physics.* Not to mention that the apprehension of a distant Deity naturally disposes men to a negligence in their *moral* actions; which they would be more cautious of, in case they thought him immediately present, and acting on their minds, without the interposition of matter, or unthinking second causes. Then in *metaphysics:* what difficulties concerning entity in abstract, substantial forms, hylarchic principles, plastic natures, substance and accident, principle of individuation, possibility of matter's thinking, origin of ideas, the manner how two independent substances so widely different as *spirit* and *matter,* should mutually operate on each other? What difficulties, I say, and endless disquisitions, concerning these and innumerable other the like points, do we escape, by supposing only spirits and ideas? Even the *mathematics* themselves, if we take away the absolute existence of extended things, become much more clear and easy; the most shocking paradoxes and intricate speculations in those sciences depending on the infinite divisibility of finite extension; which depends on that supposition. But what need is there to insist on the particular sciences? Is not that opposition to all science whatsoever, that frenzy of the ancient and modern *sceptics,* built on the same foundation? Or can you produce so much as one argument against the reality of corporeal things, or in behalf of that avowed utter ignorance of their natures, which does not suppose their reality to consist in an external absolute existence? Upon this supposition, indeed, the objections from the change of colours in a pigeon's neck, or the appearance of the broken oar in the water, must be allowed to have weight. But these and the like objections vanish, if we do not maintain the being of absolute external originals, but place the reality of things in ideas, fleeting indeed, and changeable; however, not changed at random, but according to the fixed order of nature. For, herein consists that constancy and truth of things which secures all the concerns of life, and distinguishes that which is *real* from the irregular visions of the fancy.

HYLAS: I agree to all you have now said, and must own that nothing can incline me to embrace your opinion more than the advantages I see it is attended with. I am by nature lazy; and this would be a mighty abridgment in knowledge. What doubts, what hypotheses, what labyrinths of amusement, what fields of disputation, what an ocean of false learning, may be avoided by that single notion of *immaterialism!*

PHILONOUS: After all, is there anything farther remaining to be done? You may remember you promised to embrace that opinion which upon examination should appear most agreeable to common sense and remote from *scepticism.* This, by your own confession, is that which denies matter, or the absolute existence of corporeal things. Nor is this all; the same notion has been proved several ways, viewed in different lights, pursued in its consequences, and all objections against it cleared. Can there be a greater evidence of its truth? Or is it possible it should have all the marks of a true opinion and yet be false?

HYLAS: I own myself entirely satisfied for the present in all respects. But, what security can I have that I shall still continue the same full assent to your opinion, and that no unthought-of objection or difficulty will occur hereafter?

PHILONOUS: Pray, Hylas, do you in other cases, when a point is once evidently proved, withhold your consent on account of objections or difficulties it may be liable to? Are the difficulties that attend the doctrine of incommensurable quantities, of the angle of contact, of the asymptotes to curves, or the like, sufficient to make you hold out against mathematical demonstration? Or will you disbelieve the Providence of God, because there may be some particular things which you know not how to reconcile with it? If there are difficulties attending *immaterialism,* there are at the same time direct and evident proofs of it. But for the existence of matter there is not one proof, and far more numerous and insurmountable objections lie against it. But where are those mighty difficulties you insist on? Alas! you know not where or what they are; something which may possibly occur hereafter. If this be a sufficient pretence for withholding your full assent, you should never yield it to any proposition, how free soever from exceptions, how clearly and solidly soever demonstrated.

HYLAS: You have satisfied me, Philonous.

PHILONOUS: But, to arm you against all future objections, do but consider: That which bears equally hard on two contradictory opinions can be proof against neither. Whenever, therefore, any difficulty occurs, try if you can find a solution for it on the hypothesis of the *materialists.* Be not deceived by words; but sound your own thoughts.

And in case you cannot conceive it easier by the help of *materialism,* it is plain it can be no objection against *immaterialism.* Had you proceeded all along by this rule, you would probably have spared yourself abundance of trouble in objecting; since of all your difficulties I challenge you to show one that is explained by matter: nay, which is not more unintelligible with than without that supposition; and consequently makes rather *against* than *for* it. You should consider, in each particular, whether the difficulty arises from the *non-existence of matter.* If it does not, you might as well argue from the infinite divisibility of extension against the divine prescience, as from such a difficulty against *immaterialism.* And yet, upon recollection, I believe you will find this to have been often, if not always, the case. You should likewise take heed not to argue on a *petitio principii.* One is apt to say, the unknown substances ought to be esteemed real things, rather than the ideas in our minds: and who can tell but the unthinking external substance may concur, as a cause or instrument, in the productions of our ideas? But is not this proceeding on a supposition that there are such external substances? And to suppose this is it not begging the question? But, above all things, you should beware of imposing on yourself by that vulgar sophism which is called *ignoratio elenchi.* You talked often as if you thought I maintained the non-existence of Sensible Things. Whereas in truth no one can be more thoroughly assured of their existence than I am. And it is you who doubt; I should have said, positively deny it. Everything that is seen, felt, heard, or any way perceived by the senses, is, on the principles I embrace, a real being; but not on yours. Remember, the matter you contend for is an unknown somewhat (if indeed it may be termed *somewhat*), which is quite stripped of all sensible qualities, and can neither be perceived by sense, nor apprehended by the mind. Remember I say, that it is not any object which is hard or soft, hot or cold, blue or white, round or square, &c. For all these things I affirm do exist. Though indeed I deny they have an existence distinct from being perceived; or that they exist out of all minds whatsoever. Think on these points; let them be attentively considered and still kept in view. Otherwise you will not comprehend the state of the question; without which your objections will always be wide of the mark, and, instead of mine, may possibly be directed (as more than once they have been) against your own notions.

HYLAS: I must needs own, Philonous, nothing seems to have kept me from agreeing with you more than this same *mistaking the question.* In denying matter, at first glimpse I am tempted to imagine you deny the things we see and feel: but, upon reflexion, find there is no ground for it. What think you, therefore, of retaining the name *matter,* and applying it to sensible things? This may be done without any change in your sentiments: and, believe me, it would be a means of reconciling them to some persons who may be more shocked at an innovation in words than in opinion.

PHILONOUS: With all my heart: retain the word *matter,* and apply it to the objects of sense, if you please; provided you do not attribute to them any subsistence distinct from their being perceived. I shall never quarrel with you for an expression. *Matter,* or *material substance,* are terms introduced by philosophers; and, as used by them, imply a sort of independency, or a subsistence distinct from being perceived by a mind: but are never used by common people; or, if ever, it is to signify the immediate objects of sense. One would think, therefore, so long as the names of all particular things, with the terms *sensible, substance, body, stuff,* and the like, are retained, the word *matter* should be never missed in common talk. And in philosophical discourses it seems the best way to leave it quite out: since there is not, perhaps, any one thing that hath more favoured and strengthened the depraved bent of the mind towards Atheism than the use of that general confused term.

HYLAS: Well but, Philonous, since I am content to give up the notion of an unthinking substance exterior to the mind, I think you ought not to deny me the privilege of using the word *matter* as I please, and annexing it to a collection of sensible qualities subsisting only in the mind. I freely own there is no other substance, in a strict sense, than *spirit*. But I have been so long accustomed to the term *matter* that I know not how to part with it: to say, there is no matter in the world, is still shocking to me. Whereas to say, there is no *matter*, if by that term be meant an unthinking substance existing without the mind; but if by matter is meant some sensible thing, whose existence consists in being perceived, then there is matter: this distinction gives it quite another turn; and men will come into your notions with small difficulty, when they are proposed in that manner. For, after all, the controversy about *matter* in the strict acceptation of it, lies altogether between you and the philosophers: whose principles, I acknowledge, are not near so natural, or so agreeable to the common sense of mankind, and Holy Scripture, as yours. There is nothing we either desire or shun but as it makes, or is apprehended to make, some part of our happiness or misery. But what has happiness or misery, joy or grief, pleasure or pain, to do with absolute existence; or with unknown entities, abstracted from all relation to us? It is evident, things regard us only as they are pleasing or displeasing: and they can please or displease only so far forth as they are perceived. Farther, therefore, we are not concerned, and thus far you leave things as you found them. Yet still there is something new in this doctrine. It is plain, I do not now think with the philosophers; nor yet altogether with the vulgar. I would know how the case stands in that respect; precisely, what you have added to, or altered in my former notions.

PHILONOUS: I do not pretend to be a setter-up of new notions. My endeavours tend only to unite, and place in a clearer light, that truth which was before shared between the vulgar and the philosophers:—the former being of opinion, that *those things they immediately perceive are the real things;* and the latter, that *the things immediately perceived are ideas, which exist only in the mind.* Which two notions put together, do, in effect, constitute the substance of what I advance.

HYLAS: I have been a long time distrusting my senses: methought I saw things by a dim light and through false glasses. Now the glasses are removed and a new light breaks in upon my understanding. I am clearly convinced that I see things in their native forms, and am no longer in pain about their *unknown natures* or *absolute existence.* This is the state I find myself in at present; though, indeed, the course that brought me to it I do not yet thoroughly comprehend. You set out upon the same principles that Academics, Cartesians, and the like sects usually do; and for a long time it looked as if you were advancing their philosophical *scepticism:* but, in the end, your conclusions are directly opposite to theirs.

PHILONOUS: You see, Hylas, the water of yonder fountain, how it is forced upwards, in a round column, to a certain height; at which it breaks, and falls back into the basin from whence it rose: its ascent, as well as descent, proceeding from the same uniform law or principle of *gravitation.* Just so, the same principles which, at first view, lead to *scepticism,* pursued to a certain point, bring men back to common sense.

DAVID HUME
1711–1776

David Hume was born in Edinburgh, Scotland, in 1711. His father, a lawyer, died before David was two years old. He was raised by his mother, a deeply religious woman, on a pleasant, but modest, family estate at Ninewells, near Berwick in southern Scotland. Young David was very religious as a boy, often making lists of his sins so that he could seek forgiveness. But shortly after beginning his studies at the University of Edinburgh, at age twelve, he seems to have lost his faith.

Although the family was not poor, there was not enough wealth to provide a comfortable life of study for David, the youngest child. His family decided, therefore, that Hume should follow his father into law. This was not to be, however, for as Hume later wrote, "I found an unsurmountable aversion to everything but the pursuit of philosophy and general learning."

In 1729, when he was only eighteen, Hume had a breakthrough, discovering what he called "a new Science of Thought." He gave up all pretense of becoming a lawyer and applied his energies to his new insight. To conserve his limited finances, he moved to a small town in France, La Flèche, where Descartes had studied. There he completed his first work, *A Treatise of Human Nature, Being an Attempt to Introduce the Experimental Method of Reasoning into Moral Subjects,* published in 1739 and 1740. Hume hoped this work would give him his "love of literary fame"—while putting him in a more comfortable financial situation. But, as he later said, the work "fell dead-born from the press, without reaching such distinction as even to excite a murmur among the zealots."

For the next thirteen years, Hume held a variety of positions, including tutor to a mad marquess and secretary to a general. During this time, Hume wrote and published his *Essays, Moral and Political* (1741–1742). The success of this work led him to rewrite Book I of his earlier *Treatise,* this time titled as *An Enquiry Concerning Human Understanding* (1748). He added chapters on miracles, free will, and the argument from design, which he had left out of the earlier work, and he omitted many of his psychological speculations. This book enjoyed some success, though its antireligious nature may have contributed to Hume's rejected applications for two different chairs of philosophy. In 1751, he also recast Book III of the earlier *Treatise,* under the title *Enquiry Concerning the Principles of Morals.*

Hume was appointed Librarian to the Faculty of Advocates in Edinburgh in 1752. In this post, he wrote a multivolume history of England. He also managed to infuriate the library curators with his selections, and in 1757 he was forced to resign when he refused to remove books the curators considered obscene. In the same year, he published *Four Dissertations,* including "The Natural History of Religion," "Of the Passions" (a truncated version of Book II of the *Treatise*), "Of Tragedy," and "Of the Standard of Taste." By now Hume's works had become well known on the Continent, and when he returned to France in 1763 as part of the British ambassador's staff, he was lionized by French intellectual society. Hume was a favorite at French soirées: Sociable and witty, he was called "le bon David" by his French friends.

When Hume returned to England in 1766, he found that his works had finally brought him the literary fame at home that he had so long desired. In 1767, he took another government post, but two years later he resigned and retired to Edinburgh. There he spent his last years quietly, until his death, probably from cancer, in 1776. His *Dialogues Concerning Natural Religion,* written in the 1750s, was published posthumously in 1779.

* * *

Hume's philosophy, as developed in the *Enquiry,* begins with a rejection of the "abstruse speculations" and "superstitions" of contemporary thought. With Locke, Hume agrees that there are no such things as innate ideas; all knowledge comes through sensory experience. Yet as he worked out the implications of these convictions, he came to conclusions quite different from those of his predecessor.

According to Hume, all the perceptions of the mind may be divided into "impressions" and "ideas." Using an empirical distinction, Hume believes impressions to be "more lively" than ideas. These impressions and ideas are then divided into simple and complex, impressions of sensation and impressions of reflection, and so on. The source of impressions cannot be known empirically, so Hume does not address this question. Simple ideas, on the other hand, must come from impressions. In fact, for an idea to have any meaning whatever, it must be derived from an impression or from a combination of impressions. If I have the idea of a gold mountain, for instance, it is because I have previously had impressions that gave rise to the ideas of "gold" and "mountain" that I am now associating. Using this empirical criterion of meaning, it becomes clear that ideas such as "substance," "God," or even "the self" are without a clear meaning. So according to Hume, Locke's idea of an eternal world of "substances" and Berkeley's idea of an all-perceiving God are without meaning.

Hume then considers the association between ideas and argues that there are "only three principles of connexion among ideas, namely, *Resemblance, Contiguity* in time or place, and *Cause* or *Effect.*" These associations of ideas are really nothing more than habit or "custom" and so do not necessarily reflect the "real world." Take causality, for example. One could imagine Pavlov's dogs hearing the bell, getting the food, hearing the bell, getting the food, hearing the bell . . . and after a period of time concluding, "bells cause food." But there is obviously no *necessary* relation between cause and effect in this case. There is no *logical* reason why the bell might not sound and yet no food appear. Hume argues that all supposed instances of cause and effect are of this kind. We get so used to seeing two events joined that we conclude that one *caused* the other. Thus, according to Hume, Locke's claim that the "external world" *causes* sensations and the Thomistic First-Cause argument for God's existence are without empirical foundation. It also means that the "laws of nature" are founded only on past experience and that we have no *a priori* evidence that tomorrow will be the same as today.

The remainder of the *Enquiry* develops the implications of Hume's radical empiricism and deals with the skepticism arising from it. He acknowledges that his own practice does not always reflect his philosophical position. Hume recognizes that despite his causal skepticism, it would not be wise to "throw himself out at the window." As he wrote early on in this work, we must "be modest in our pretensions; and even to discover the difficulty ourselves before it is objected to us. By this means, we may make a kind of merit of our very ignorance."

*   *   *

Philosophers differ in their appraisals of Hume's two greatest works, the *Treatise* and its reworking, the *Enquiry*. Many consider the *Enquiry* more mature; others think the *Treatise* more brilliant. Hume himself said that the *Enquiry,* not the *Treatise,* contained his "philosophical sentiments and principles." The *Enquiry* is reprinted here (complete).

For a comprehensive biography of Hume, including interesting material from his letters, see Ernest Campbell Mossner, *The Life of David Hume* (Oxford: Clarendon Press, 1954, 1980). The classic studies of Hume's thought are Charles William Hendel, *Studies in the Philosophy of David Hume* (Princeton, NJ: Princeton University Press, 1925), and, especially, Norman Kemp Smith, *The Philosophy of David Hume* (London: Macmillan, 1941). A short, clear overview of his thought is A.J. Ayer, *Hume* (New York: Oxford University Press, 1981)—part of the "Past Masters" series, now reprinted in a combined volume, John Dunn et al., eds., *The British Empiricists* (Oxford: Oxford University Press, 1992). For studies in specific areas of Hume's thought, see Tom L. Beauchamp, *Hume and the Problem of Causation* (New York: Oxford University Press, 1981); Robert J. Fogelin, *Hume's Skepticism in the Treatise of Human Nature* (London: Routledge, 1985); and David Pears, *Hume's System* (Oxford: Oxford University Press, 1991), for epistemology and philosophy of mind; Jonathan Harrison, *Hume's Moral Epistemology* (Oxford: Clarendon Press, 1976); and J.L. Mackie, *Hume's Moral Theory* (London: Routledge & Kegan Paul, 1980), for ethics; and Antony Flew, *Hume's Philosophy of Belief* (London: Routledge & Kegan Paul; New York: Humanities Press, 1961); J.C.A. Gaskin, *Hume's Philosophy of Religion* (New York: Barnes & Noble, 1978); and Keith E. Yandell, *Hume's "Inexplicable Mystery": His Views on Religion* (Philadelphia: Temple University Press, 1990), for philosophy of religion. For collections of essays, see David Pears, ed., *David Hume: A Symposium* (London: St. Martin's Press, 1963); A. Sesonke and N. Fleming, eds.,

Human Understanding: Studies in the Philosophy of David Hume (Belmont, CA: Wadsworth, 1965); and the excellent V.C. Chappell, ed., *Hume: A Collection of Critical Essays* (Notre Dame, IN: Notre Dame University Press, 1968).

AN ENQUIRY CONCERNING HUMAN UNDERSTANDING

SECTION I. OF THE DIFFERENT SPECIES OF PHILOSOPHY

Moral philosophy, or the science of human nature, may be treated after two different manners; each of which has its peculiar merit, and may contribute to the entertainment, instruction, and reformation of mankind. The one considers man chiefly as born for action; and as influenced in his measures by taste and sentiment; pursuing one object, and avoiding another, according to the value which these objects seem to possess, and according to the light in which they present themselves. As virtue, of all objects, is allowed to be the most valuable, this species of philosophers paint her in the most amiable colours; borrowing all helps from poetry and eloquence, and treating their subject in an easy and obvious manner, and such as is best fitted to please the imagination, and engage the affections. They select the most striking observations and instances from common life; place opposite characters in a proper contrast; and alluring us into the paths of virtue by the views of glory and happiness, direct our steps in these paths by the soundest precepts and most illustrious examples. They make us *feel* the difference between vice and virtue; they excite and regulate our sentiments; and so they can but bend our hearts to the love of probity and true honour, they think, that they have fully attained the end of all their labours.

The other species of philosophers consider man in the light of a reasonable rather than an active being, and endeavour to form his understanding more than cultivate his manners. They regard human nature as a subject of speculation; and with a narrow scrutiny examine it, in order to find those principles, which regulate our understanding, excite our sentiments, and make us to approve or blame any particular object, action, or behaviour. They think it a reproach to all literature, that philosophy should not yet have fixed, beyond controversy, the foundation of morals, reasoning, and criticism; and should for ever talk of truth and falsehood, vice and virtue, beauty and deformity, without being able to determine the source of these distinctions. While they attempt this arduous task, they are deterred by no difficulties; but proceeding from particular instances to general principles, they still push on their enquiries to principles more general, and rest not satisfied till they arrive at those original principles, by which, in every science, all human curiosity must be bounded. Though their speculations seem abstract, and even unintelligible to common readers, they aim at the approbation of the learned and the wise; and think themselves sufficiently compensated for the labour of their whole lives, if they can discover some hidden truths, which may contribute to the instruction of posterity.

It is certain that the easy and obvious philosophy will always, with the generality of mankind, have the preference above the accurate and abstruse; and by many will be recommended, not only as more agreeable, but more useful than the other. It enters more into common life; moulds the heart and affections; and, by touching those principles which actuate men, reforms their conduct, and brings them nearer to that model of perfection which it describes. On the contrary, the abstruse philosophy, being founded on a turn of mind, which cannot enter into business and action, vanishes when the philosopher leaves the shade, and comes into open day; nor can its principles easily retain any influence over our conduct and behaviour. The feelings of our heart, the agitation of our passions, the vehemence of our affections, dissipate all its conclusions, and reduce the profound philosopher to a mere plebeian.

This also must be confessed, that the most durable, as well as justest fame, has been acquired by the easy philosophy, and that abstract reasoners seem hitherto to have enjoyed only a momentary reputation, from the caprice or ignorance of their own age, but have not been able to support their renown with more equitable posterity. It is easy for a profound philosopher to commit a mistake in his subtile reasonings; and one mistake is the necessary parent of another, while he pushes on his consequences, and is not deterred from embracing any conclusion, by its unusual appearance, or its contradiction to popular opinion. But a philosopher, who purposes only to represent the common sense of mankind in more beautiful and more engaging colours, if by accident he falls into error, goes not farther; but renewing his appeal to common sense, and the natural sentiments of the mind, returns into the right path, and secures himself from any dangerous illusions. The fame of Cicero flourishes at present; but that of Aristotle is utterly decayed. La Bruyere passes the seas, and still maintains his reputation: But the glory of Malebranche is confined to his own nation, and to his own age. And Addison, perhaps, will be read with pleasure, when Locke shall be entirely forgotten.

The mere philosopher is a character, which is commonly but little acceptable in the world, as being supposed to contribute nothing either to the advantage or pleasure of society; while he lives remote from communication with mankind, and is wrapped up in principles and notions equally remote from their comprehension. On the other hand, the mere ignorant is still more despised; nor is any thing deemed a surer sign of an illiberal genius in an age and nation where the sciences flourish, than to be entirely destitute of all relish for those noble entertainments. The most perfect character is supposed to lie between those extremes; retaining an equal ability and taste for books, company, and business; preserving in conversation that discernment and delicacy which arise from polite letters; and in business, that probity and accuracy which are the natural result of a just philosophy. In order to diffuse and cultivate so accomplished a character, nothing can be more useful than compositions of the easy style and manner, which draw not too much from life, require no deep application or retreat to be comprehended, and send back the student among mankind full of noble sentiments and wise precepts, applicable to every exigence of human life. By means of such compositions, virtue becomes amiable, science agreeable, company instructive, and retirement entertaining.

Man is a reasonable being; and as such, receives from science his proper food and nourishment: But so narrow are the bounds of human understanding, that little satisfaction can be hoped for in this particular, either from the extent or security of his acquisitions. Man is a sociable, no less than a reasonable being: But neither can he always enjoy company agreeable and amusing, or preserve the proper relish for them. Man is also an active being; and from that disposition, as well as from the various necessities of human life, must submit to business and occupation: But the mind requires some relaxation, and cannot always support its bent to care and industry. It seems, then, that nature has pointed out a mixed kind of life as most suitable to the human race, and secretly admonished them to allow none of these biases to draw too much, so as to incapacitate them for other occupations and entertainments. Indulge your passion for science, says she, but let your science be human, and such as may have a direct reference to action and society. Abstruse thought and profound researches I prohibit, and will severely punish, by the pensive melancholy which they introduce, by the endless uncertainty in which they involve you, and by the cold reception which your pretended discoveries shall meet with, when communicated. Be a philosopher; but, amidst all your philosophy, be still a man.

Were the generality of mankind contented to prefer the easy philosophy to the abstract and profound, without throwing any blame or contempt on the latter, it might not be improper, perhaps, to comply with this general opinion, and allow every man to enjoy, without opposition, his own taste and sentiment. But as the matter is often carried farther, even to the absolute rejecting of all profound reasonings, or what is commonly called *metaphysics,* we shall now proceed to consider what can reasonably be pleaded in their behalf.

We may begin with observing, that one considerable advantage, which results from the accurate and abstract philosophy, is, its subserviency to the easy and humane, which, without the former, can never attain a sufficient degree of exactness in its sentiments, precepts, or reasonings. All polite letters are nothing but pictures of human life in various attitudes and situations; and inspire us with different sentiments, of praise or blame, admiration or ridicule, according to the qualities of the object, which they set before us. An artist must be better qualified to succeed in this undertaking, who, besides a delicate taste and a quick apprehension, possesses an accurate knowledge of the internal fabric, the operations of the understanding, the workings of the passions, and the various species of sentiment which discriminate vice and virtue. How painful soever this inward search or enquiry may appear, it becomes, in some measure, requisite to those, who would describe with success the obvious and outward appearances of life and manners. The anatomist presents to the eye the most hideous and disagreeable objects; but his science is useful to the painter in delineating even a Venus or an Helen. While the latter employs all the richest colours of his art, and gives his figures the most graceful and engaging airs; he must still carry his attention to the inward structure of the human body, the position of the muscles, the fabric of the bones, and the use and figure of every part or organ. Accuracy is, in every case, advantageous to beauty and just reasoning to delicate sentiment. In vain would we exalt the one by depreciating the other.

Besides, we may observe, in every art or profession, even those which most concern life or action, that a spirit of accuracy, however acquired, carries all of them nearer their perfection, and renders them more subservient to the interests of society. And though a philosopher may live remote from business, the genius of philosophy, if carefully cultivated by several, must gradually diffuse itself throughout the whole society, and bestow a similar correctness on every art and calling. The politician will acquire greater foresight and subtlety, in the subdividing and balancing of power; the lawyer more method and finer principles in his reasonings; and the general more regularity in his discipline, and more caution in his plans and operations. The stability of modern governments above the ancient, and the accuracy of modern philosophy, have improved, and probably will still improve, by similar gradations.

Were there no advantage to be reaped from these studies, beyond the gratification of an innocent curiosity, yet ought not even this to be despised; as being one accession to those few safe and harmless pleasures, which are bestowed on the human race. The sweetest and most inoffensive path of life leads through the avenues of science and

An Experiment on a Bird in the Air Pump, ca. 1767–1768, by Joseph Wright of Derby (1734–1797). The artist is showing the interplay between rational analysis and human emotion, between reason and feeling. The scientist in the center is demonstrating that a bird cannot fly in a vacuum. In doing so he is also killing the bird—a fact not lost on the little girls to the right. *(Tate Gallery, London)*

learning; and whoever can either remove any obstructions in this way, or open up any new prospect, ought so far to be esteemed a benefactor to mankind. And though these researches may appear painful and fatiguing, it is with some minds as with some bodies, which being endowed with vigorous and florid health, require severe exercise, and reap a pleasure from what, to the generality of mankind, may seem burdensome and laborious. Obscurity, indeed, is painful to the mind as well as to the eye; but to bring light from obscurity, by whatever labour, must needs be delightful and rejoicing.

But this obscurity in the profound and abstract philosophy, is objected to, not only as painful and fatiguing, but as the inevitable source of uncertainty and error. Here indeed lies the justest and most plausible objection against a considerable part of metaphysics, that they are not properly a science; but arise either from the fruitless efforts of human vanity, which would penetrate into subjects utterly inaccessible to the understanding, or from the craft of popular superstitions, which, being unable to defend themselves on fair ground, raise these entangling brambles to cover and protect their weakness. Chased from the open country, these robbers fly into the forest, and lie in wait to break in upon every unguarded avenue of the mind, and overwhelm it with religious fears and prejudices. The stoutest antagonist, if he remit his watch a moment, is oppressed. And many, through cowardice and folly, open the gates to the enemies, and willingly receive them with reverence and submission, as their legal sovereigns.

But is this a sufficient reason, why philosophers should desist from such researches, and leave superstition still in possession of her retreat? Is it not proper to draw an opposite conclusion, and perceive the necessity of carrying the war into the most secret recesses of the enemy? In vain do we hope, that men, from frequent disappointment, will at last abandon such airy sciences, and discover the proper province of human reason. For, besides, that many persons find too sensible an interest in perpetually recalling such topics; besides this, I say, the motive of blind despair can never reasonably have place in the sciences; since, however unsuccessful former attempts may have proved, there is still room to hope, that the industry, good fortune, or improved sagacity of succeeding generations may reach discoveries unknown to former ages. Each adventurous genius will leap at the arduous prize, and find himself stimulated, rather than discouraged, by the failures of his predecessors; while he hopes that the glory of achieving so hard an adventure is reserved for him alone. The only method of freeing learning, at once, from these abstruse questions, is to enquire seriously into the nature of human understanding, and show, from an exact analysis of its powers and capacity, that it is by no means fitted for such remote and abstruse subjects. We must submit to this fatigue, in order to live at ease ever after: And must cultivate true metaphysics with some care, in order to destroy the false and adulterate. Indolence, which, to some persons, affords a safeguard against this deceitful philosophy, is, with others, overbalanced by curiosity; and despair, which, at some moments, prevails, may give place afterwards to sanguine hopes and expectations. Accurate and just reasoning is the only catholic remedy, fitted for all persons and all dispositions; and is alone able to subvert that abstruse philosophy and metaphysical jargon, which, being mixed up with popular superstition, renders it in a manner impenetrable to careless reasoners, and gives it the air of science and wisdom.

Besides this advantage of rejecting, after deliberate enquiry, the most uncertain and disagreeable part of learning, there are many positive advantages, which result from an accurate scrutiny into the powers and faculties of human nature. It is remarkable concerning the operations of the mind, that, though most intimately present to us, yet, whenever they become the object of reflection, they seem involved in obscurity; nor can the eye readily find those lines and boundaries, which discriminate and distinguish them. The objects are too fine to remain long in the same aspect or situation; and must be apprehended in an instant, by a superior penetration, derived from nature, and improved by habit and reflection. It becomes, therefore, no inconsiderable part of science barely to know the different operations of the mind, to separate them from each other, to class them under their proper heads, and to correct all that seeming disorder, in which they lie involved, when made the object of reflection and enquiry. This talk of ordering and distinguishing, which has no merit, when performed with regard to external bodies, the objects of our senses, rises in its value, when directed towards the operations of the mind, in proportion to the difficulty and labour, which we meet with in performing it. And if we can go no farther than this mental geography, or delineation of the distinct parts and powers of the mind, it is at least a satisfaction to go so far; and the more obvious this science may appear (and it is by no means obvious) the more contemptible still must the ignorance of it be esteemed, in all pretenders to learning and philosophy.

Nor can there remain any suspicion, that this science is uncertain and chimerical; unless we should entertain such a scepticism as is entirely subversive of all speculation, and even action. It cannot be doubted, that the mind is endowed with several powers and faculties, that these powers are distinct from each other, that what is really distinct to the immediate perception may be distinguished by reflection; and consequently, that there is a truth and falsehood in all propositions on this subject, and a truth and falsehood, which lie not beyond the compass of human understanding. There are many obvious distinctions of this kind, such as those between the will and understanding, the imagination and passions, which fall within the comprehension of every human creature; and the finer and more philosophical distinctions are no less real and certain, though more difficult to be comprehended. Some instances, especially late ones, of success in these enquiries, may give us a juster notion of the certainty and solidity of this branch of learning. And shall we esteem it worthy the labour of a philosopher to give us a true system of the planets, and adjust the position and order of those remote bodies; while we affect to overlook those, who, with so much success, delineate the parts of the mind, in which we are so intimately concerned?

But may we not hope, that philosophy, if cultivated with care, and encouraged by the attention of the public, may carry its researches still farther, and discover, at least in some degree, the secret springs and principles, by which the human mind is actuated in its operations? Astronomers had long contented themselves with proving, from the phenomena, the true motions, order, and magnitude of the heavenly bodies: Till a philosopher, at last, arose, who seems, from the happiest reasoning, to have also determined the laws and forces, by which the revolutions of the planets are governed and directed. The like has been performed with regard to other parts of nature. And there is no reason to despair of equal success in our enquiries concerning the mental powers and economy, if prosecuted with equal capacity and caution. It is probable, that one operation and principle of the mind depends on another; which, again, may be resolved into one more general and universal: And how far these researches may possibly be carried, it will be difficult for us, before, or even after, a careful trial, exactly to determine. This is certain, that attempts of this kind are every day made even by those who philosophize the most negligently: And nothing can be more requisite than to enter upon the enterprize with thorough care and attention; that, if it lie within the compass of human understanding, it may at last be happily achieved; if not, it may, however, be rejected with some confidence and security. This last conclusion, surely, is not desirable; nor ought it to be embraced too rashly. For how much must we diminish from the beauty and value of this species of philosophy, upon such a supposition? Moralists have hitherto been accustomed, when they considered the vast multitude and diversity of those actions that excite our approbation or dislike, to search for some common principle, on which this variety of sentiments might depend. And though they have sometimes carried the matter too far, by their passion for some one general principle; it must, however, be confessed, that they are excusable in expecting to find some general principles, into which all the vices and virtues were justly to be resolved. The like has been the endeavour of critics, logicians, and even politicians: Nor have their attempts been wholly unsuccessful; though perhaps longer time, greater accuracy, and more ardent application may bring these sciences still nearer their perfection. To throw up at once all pretensions of this kind may justly be deemed more rash, precipitate, and dogmatical, than even the boldest and most affirmative philosophy, that has ever attempted to impose its crude dictates and principles on mankind.

What though these reasonings concerning human nature seem abstract, and of difficult comprehension? This affords no presumption of their falsehood. On the contrary, it seems impossible, that what has hitherto escaped so many wise and profound philosophers can be very obvious and easy. And whatever pains these researches may cost us, we may think ourselves sufficiently rewarded, not only in point of profit but of pleasure, if, by that means, we can make any addition to our stock of knowledge, in subjects of such unspeakable importance. But as, after all, the abstractedness of these speculations is no recommendation, but rather a disadvantage to them, and as this difficulty may perhaps be surmounted by care and art, and the avoiding of all unnecessary detail, we have, in the following enquiry, attempted to throw some light upon subjects, from which uncertainty has hitherto deterred the wise, and obscurity the ignorant. Happy, if we can unite the boundaries of the different species of philosophy, by reconciling profound enquiry with clearness, and truth with novelty! And still more happy, if reasoning in this easy manner, we can undermine the foundations of an abstruse philosophy, which seems to have hitherto served only as a shelter to superstition, and a cover to absurdity and error!

Section II. Of the Origin of Ideas

Every one will readily allow, that there is a considerable difference between the perceptions of the mind, when a man feels the pain of excessive heat, or the pleasure of moderate warmth, and when he afterwards recalls to his memory this sensation, or anticipates it by his imagination. These faculties may mimic or copy the perceptions of the senses; but they never can entirely reach the force and vivacity of the original sentiment. The utmost we say of them, even when they operate with greatest vigour, is, that they represent their object in so lively a manner, that we could almost say we feel or see it: But, except the mind be disordered by disease or madness, they never can arrive at such a pitch of vivacity, as to render these perceptions altogether undistinguishable. All the colours of poetry, however splendid, can never paint natural objects in such a manner as to make the description be taken for a real landscape. The most lively thought is still inferior to the dullest sensation.

We may observe a like distinction to run through all the other perceptions of the mind. A man in a fit of anger, is actuated in a very different manner from one who only thinks of that emotion. If you tell me, that any person is in love, I easily understand your meaning, and form a just conception of his situation; but never can mistake that conception for the real disorders and agitations of the passion. When we reflect on our past sentiments and affections, our thought is a faithful mirror, and copies its objects truly; but the colours which it employs are faint and dull, in comparison of those in which our original perceptions were clothed. It requires no nice discernment or metaphysical head to mark the distinction between them.

Here therefore we may divide all the perceptions of the mind into two classes or species, which are distinguished by their different degrees of force and vivacity. The less forcible and lively are commonly denominated *Thoughts* or *Ideas.* The other species want a name in our language, and in most others; I suppose, because it was not requisite for any, but philosophical purposes, to rank them under a general term or appellation. Let us, therefore, use a little freedom, and call them *Impressions;* employing that word in a sense somewhat different from the usual. By the term impression, then, I mean all our more lively perceptions, when we hear, or see, or feel, or love, or hate, or desire, or will. And *impressions* are distinguished from ideas which are the less lively perceptions, of which we are conscious, when we reflect on any of those sensations or movements above mentioned.

Nothing, at first view, may seem more unbounded than the thought of man, which not only escapes all human power and authority, but is not even restrained within the limits of nature and reality. To form monsters, and join incongruous shapes and appearances, costs the imagination no more trouble than to conceive the most natural and familiar objects. And while the body is confined to one planet, along which it creeps with pain and difficulty; the thought can in an instant transport us into the most distant regions of the universe; or even beyond the universe, into the unbounded chaos, where nature is supposed to lie in total confusion. What never was seen, or heard of, may yet be conceived; nor is any thing beyond the power of thought, except what implies an absolute contradiction.

But though our thought seems to possess this unbounded liberty, we shall find, upon a nearer examination, that it is really confined within very narrow limits, and that all this creative power of the mind amounts to no more than the faculty of compounding, transposing, augmenting, or diminishing the materials afforded us by the senses and experience. When we think of a golden mountain, we only join two consistent ideas, *gold* and *mountain,* with which we were formerly acquainted. A virtuous horse we can conceive; because, from our own feeling, we can conceive virtue; and this we may unite to the figure and shape of a horse, which is an animal familiar to us. In short, all the materials of thinking are derived either from our outward or inward sentiment: the mixture and composition of these belongs alone to the mind and will. Or, to express myself in philosophical language, all our ideas or more feeble perceptions are copies of our impressions or more lively ones.

To prove this, the two following arguments will, I hope, be sufficient. First, when we analyze our thoughts or ideas, however compounded or sublime, we always find that they resolve themselves into such simple ideas as were copied from a precedent feeling or sentiment. Even those ideas, which, at first view, seem the most wide of this origin, are found, upon a nearer scrutiny, to be derived from it. The idea of God, as meaning an infinitely intelligent, wise, and good Being, arises from reflecting on the operations of our own mind, and augmenting, without limit, those qualities of goodness and wisdom. We may prosecute this enquiry to what length we please; where we shall always find, that every idea which we examine is copied from a similar impression. Those who would assert that this position is not universally true nor without exception, have only one, and that an easy method of refuting it; by producing that idea, which, in their opinion, is not derived from this source. It will then be incumbent on us, if we would maintain our doctrine, to produce the impression, or lively perception, which corresponds to it.

Secondly. If it happens, from a defect of the organ, that a man is not susceptible of any species of sensation, we always find that he is as little susceptible of the correspondent ideas. A blind man can form no notion of colours; a deaf man of sounds. Restore either of them that sense in which he is deficient; by opening this new inlet for his sensations, you also open an inlet for the ideas; and he finds no difficulty in conceiving these objects. The case is the same, if the object, proper for exciting any sensation, has never been applied to the organ. A Laplander or Negro has no notion of the relish of wine. And though there are few or no instances of a like deficiency in the mind, where a person has never felt or is wholly incapable of a sentiment or passion that belongs to his species; yet we find the same observation to take place in a less degree. A man of mild manners can form no idea of inveterate revenge or cruelty; nor can a selfish heart easily conceive the heights of friendship and generosity. It is readily allowed, that other beings may possess many senses of which we can have no conception, because the ideas of them have never been introduced to us in the only manner by which an idea can have access to the mind, to wit, by the actual feeling and sensation.

There is, however, one contradictory phenomenon, which may prove that it is not absolutely impossible for ideas to arise, independent of their correspondent impressions. I believe it will readily be allowed, that the several distinct ideas of colour, which enter by the eye, or those of sound, which are conveyed by the ear, are really different from each other; though, at the same time, resembling. Now if this be true of different colours, it must be no less so of the different shades of the same colour; and each shade produces a distinct idea, independent of the rest. For if this should be denied, it is possible, by the continual gradation of shades, to run a colour insensibly into what is most remote from it; and if you will not allow any of the means to be different, you cannot, without absurdity, deny the extremes to be the same. Suppose, therefore, a person to have enjoyed his sight for thirty years, and to have become perfectly acquainted with colours of all kinds except one particular shade of blue, for instance, which it never has been his fortune to meet with. Let all the different shades of that colour, except that single one, be placed before him, descending gradually from the deepest to lightest; it is plain that he will perceive a blank, where that shade is wanting, and will be sensible that there is a greater distance in that place between the contiguous colours than in any other. Now I ask, whether it be possible for him, from his own imagination, to supply this deficiency, and raise up to himself the idea of that particular shade, though it had never been conveyed to him by his senses? I believe there are few but will be of opinion that he can: and this may serve as a proof that the simple ideas are not always, in every instance, derived from the correspondent impressions; though this instance is so singular, that it is scarcely worth our observing, and does not merit that for it alone we should alter our general maxim.

Here, therefore, is a proposition, which not only seems, in itself, simple and intelligible; but, if a proper use were made of it, might render every dispute equally intelligible, and banish all that jargon, which has so long taken possession of metaphysical reasonings, and drawn disgrace upon them. All ideas, especially abstract ones, are naturally faint and obscure: the mind has but a slender hold of them: they are apt to be confounded with other resembling ideas; and when we have often employed any term, though without a distinct meaning, we are apt to imagine it has a determinate idea annexed to it. On the contrary, all impressions, that is, all sensations, either outward or inward, are strong and vivid: the limits between them are more exactly determined: nor is it easy to fall into any error or mistake with regard to them. When we entertain, therefore, any suspicion that a philosophical term is employed without any meaning or idea (as is but too frequent), we need but enquire, *from what impressions is that supposed idea derived?* And if it be impossible to assign any, this will serve to confirm our suspicion.*

---

*It is probable that no more was meant by those, who denied innate ideas, than that all ideas were copies of our impressions; though it must be confessed, that the terms, which they employed, were not chosen with such caution, nor so exactly defined, as to prevent all mistakes about their doctrine. For what is meant by *innate?* If innate be equivalent to natural, then all the perceptions and ideas of the mind must be allowed to be innate or natural, in whatever sense we take the latter word, whether in opposition to what is uncommon, artificial, or miraculous. If by innate be meant, contemporary to our birth, the dispute seems to be frivolous; nor is it worth while to enquire at what time thinking begins, whether before, at, or after our birth. Again, the word idea, seems to be commonly taken in a very loose sense, by LOCKE and others; as standing for any of our perceptions, our sensations and passions, as well as thoughts. Now in this sense, I should desire to know, what can be meant by asserting, that self-love, or resentment of injuries, or the passion between the sexes is not innate?

But admitting these terms, *impressions* and *ideas,* in the sense above explained, and understanding by *innate,* what is original or copied from no precedent perception, then may we assert that all our impressions are innate and our ideas not innate.

To be ingenuous, I must own it to be my opinion, that LOCKE was betrayed into this question by the schoolmen, who, making use of undefined terms, draw out their disputes to a tedious length, without ever touching the point in question. A like ambiguity and circumlocution seem to run through that philosopher's reasonings on this as well as most other subjects.

By bringing ideas into so clear a light we may reasonably hope to remove all dispute, which may arise, concerning their nature and reality.

SECTION III. OF THE ASSOCIATION OF IDEAS

It is evident that there is a principle of connexion between the different thoughts or ideas of the mind, and that, in their appearance to the memory or imagination, they introduce each other with a certain degree of method and regularity. In our more serious thinking or discourse this is so observable that any particular thought, which breaks in upon the regular tract or chain of ideas, is immediately remarked and rejected. And even in our wildest and most wandering reveries, nay in our very dreams, we shall find, if we reflect, that the imagination ran not altogether at adventures, but that there was still a connexion upheld among the different ideas, which succeeded each other. Were the loosest and freest conversation to be transcribed, there would immediately be observed something which connected it in all its transitions. Or where this is wanting, the person who broke the thread of discourse might still inform you, that there had secretly revolved in his mind a succession of thought, which had gradually led him from the subject of conversation. Among different languages, even where we cannot suspect the least connexion or communication, it is found, that the words, expressive of ideas, the most compounded, do yet nearly correspond to each other: a certain proof that the simple ideas, comprehended in the compound ones, were bound together by some universal principle, which had an equal influence on all mankind.

Though it be too obvious to escape observation, that different ideas are connected together; I do not find that any philosopher has attempted to enumerate or class all the principles of association; a subject, however, that seems worthy of curiosity. To me, there appear to be only three principles of connexion among ideas, namely, *Resemblance, Contiguity* in time or place, and *Cause* or *Effect.*

That these principles serve to connect ideas will not, I believe, be much doubted. A picture naturally leads our thoughts to the original:* the mention of one apartment in a building naturally introduces an enquiry or discourse concerning the others:** and if we think of a wound, we can scarcely forbear reflecting on the pain which follows it. ***But that this enumeration is complete, and that there are no other principles of association except these, may be difficult to prove to the satisfaction of the reader, or even to a man's own satisfaction. All we can do, in such cases, is to run over several instances, and examine carefully the principle which binds the different thoughts to each other, never stopping till we render the principle as general as possible.† The more instances we examine, and the more care we employ, the more assurance shall we acquire, that the enumeration, which we form from the whole, is complete and entire.

---

*Resemblance.

**Contiguity.

***Cause and effect.

†For instance, Contrast or Contrariety is also a connexion among Ideas but it may, perhaps, be considered as a mixture of *Causation* and *Resemblance.* Where two objects are contrary, the one destroys the other; that is, the cause of its annihilation, and the idea of the annihilation of an object implies the idea of its former existence.

Section IV. Sceptical Doubts Concerning the Operations of the Understanding

Part I

All the objects of human reason or enquiry may naturally be divided into two kinds, to wit, *Relations of Ideas,* and *Matters of Fact.* Of the first kind are the sciences of Geometry, Algebra, and Arithmetic; and in short, every affirmation which is either intuitively or demonstratively certain. *That the square of the hypothenuse is equal to the squares of the two sides,* is a proposition which expresses a relation between these figures. *That three times five is equal to the half of thirty,* expresses a relation between these numbers. Propositions of this kind are discoverable by the mere operation of thought, without dependence on what is anywhere existent in the universe. Though there never were a circle or triangle in nature, the truths demonstrated by Euclid would for ever retain their certainty and evidence.

Matters of fact, which are the second objects of human reason, are not ascertained in the same manner; nor is our evidence of their truth however great, of a like nature with the foregoing. The contrary of every matter of fact is still possible; because it can never imply a contradiction, and is conceived by the mind with the same facility and distinctness, as if ever so conformable to reality. *That the sun will not rise to-morrow* is no less intelligible a proposition, and implies no more contradiction than the affirmation, *that it will rise.* We should in vain, therefore, attempt to demonstrate its falsehood. Were it demonstratively false, it would imply a contradiction, and could never be distinctly conceived by the mind.

It may, therefore, be a subject worthy of curiosity, to enquire what is the nature of that evidence which assures us of any real existence and matter of fact, beyond the present testimony of our senses, or the records of our memory. This part of philosophy, it is observable, has been little cultivated, either by the ancients or moderns; and therefore our doubts and errors, in the prosecution of so important an enquiry, may be the more excusable; while we march through such difficult paths without any guide or direction. They may even prove useful, by exciting curiosity, and destroying that implicit faith and security, which is the bane of all reasoning and free enquiry. The discovery of defects in the common philosophy, if any such there be, will not, I presume, be a discouragement, but rather an incitement, as is usual, to attempt something more full and satisfactory than has yet been proposed to the public.

All reasonings concerning matter of fact seem to be founded on the relation of *Cause and Effect.* By means of that relation alone we can go beyond the evidence of our memory and senses. If you were to ask a man, why he believes any matter of fact, which is absent; for instance, that his friend is in the country, or in France; he would give you a reason; and this reason would be some other fact; as a letter received from him, or the knowledge of his former resolutions and promises. A man finding a watch or any other machine in a desert island, would conclude that there had once been men in that island. All our reasonings concerning fact are of the same nature. And here it is constantly supposed that there is a connexion between the present fact and that which is inferred from it. Were there nothing to bind them together, the inference would be entirely precarious. The hearing of an articulate voice and rational discourse in the dark assures us of the presence of some person: Why? because these are the effects of the human make and fabric, and closely connected with it. If we anatomize all the other reasonings of this nature, we shall find that they are founded on the relation of cause and effect, and that this relation is either near or remote, direct or collateral. Heat and light are collateral effects of fire, and the one effect may justly be inferred from the other.

If we would satisfy ourselves, therefore, concerning the nature of that evidence, which assures us of matters of fact, we must enquire how we arrive at the knowledge of cause and effect.

I shall venture to affirm, as a general proposition, which admits of no exception, that the knowledge of this relation is not, in any instance, attained by reasonings *a priori*; but arises entirely from experience, when we find that any particular objects are constantly conjoined with each other. Let an object be presented to a man of ever so strong natural reason and abilities; if that object be entirely new to him, he will not be able, by the most accurate examination of its sensible qualities, to discover any of its causes or effects. Adam, though his rational faculties be supposed, at the very first, entirely perfect, could not have inferred from the fluidity and transparency of water that it would suffocate him, or from the light and warmth of fire that it would consume him. No object ever discovers, by the qualities which appear to the senses, either the causes which produced it, or the effects which will arise from it; nor can our reason, unassisted by experience, ever draw any inference concerning real existence and matter of fact.

This proposition, *that causes and effects are discoverable, not by reason but by experience,* will readily be admitted with regard to such objects, as we remember to have once been altogether unknown to us; since we must be conscious of the utter inability, which we then lay under, of foretelling what would arise from them. Present two smooth pieces of marble to a man who has no tincture of natural philosophy; he will never discover that they will adhere together in such a manner as to require great force to separate them in a direct line, while they make so small a resistance to a lateral pressure. Such events, as bear little analogy to the common course of nature, are also readily confessed to be known only by experience; nor does any man imagine that the explosion of gunpowder, or the attraction of a loadstone, could ever be discovered by arguments *a priori*. In like manner, when an effect is supposed to depend upon an intricate machinery or secret structure of parts, we make no difficulty in attributing all our knowledge of it to experience. Who will assert that he can give the ultimate reason, why milk or bread is proper nourishment for a man, not for a lion or a tiger?

But the same truth may not appear, at first sight, to have the same evidence with regard to events, which have become familiar to us from our first appearance in the world, which bear a close analogy to the whole course of nature, and which are supposed to depend on the simple qualities of objects, without any secret structure of parts. We are apt to imagine that we could discover these effects by the mere operation of our reason, without experience. We fancy, that were we brought on a sudden into this world, we could at first have inferred that one Billiard-ball would communicate motion to another upon impulse; and that we needed not to have waited for the event, in order to pronounce with certainty concerning it. Such is the influence of custom, that, where it is strongest, it not only covers our natural ignorance, but even conceals itself, and seems not to take place, merely because it is found in the highest degree.

But to convince us that all the laws of nature, and all the operations of bodies without exception, are known only by experience, the following reflections may, perhaps, suffice. Were any object presented to us, and were we required to pronounce concerning the effect, which will result from it, without consulting past observation; after what manner, I beseech you, must the mind proceed in this operation? It must invent or imagine some event, which it ascribes to the object as its effect; and it is plain that this invention must be entirely arbitrary. The mind can never possibly find the effect in the supposed cause, by the most accurate scrutiny and examination. For the effect is totally different from the cause, and consequently can never be discovered in it. Motion in the second Billiard-ball is a quite distinct event from motion in the first: nor is there anything in the one to suggest the smallest hint of the other. A stone or piece of metal raised into the air, and left without any support, immediately falls: but to consider the matter *a priori,* is there anything we discover in this situation which can beget the idea of a downward, rather than an upward, or any other motion, in the stone or metal?

And as the first imagination or invention of a particular effect, in all natural operations, is arbitrary, where we consult not experience; so must we also esteem the supposed tie or connexion between the cause and effect, which binds them together, and renders it impossible that any other effect could result from the operation of that cause. When I see, for instance, a Billiard-ball moving in a straight line towards another; even suppose motion in the second ball should by accident be suggested to me, as the result of their contact or impulse; may I not conceive, that a hundred different events might as well follow from that cause? May not both these balls remain at absolute rest? May not the first ball return in a straight line, or leap off from the second in any line or direction? All these suppositions are consistent and conceivable. Why then should we give the preference to one, which is no more consistent or conceivable than the rest? All our reasonings *a priori* will never be able to show us any foundation for this preference.

In a word, then, every effect is a distinct event from its cause. It could not, therefore, be discovered in the cause, and the first invention or conception of it, *a priori,* must be entirely arbitrary. And even after it is suggested, the conjunction of it with the cause must appear equally arbitrary; since there are always many other effects, which, to reason, must seem fully as consistent and natural. In vain, therefore, should we pretend to determine any single event, or infer any cause or effect, without the assistance of observation and experience.

Hence we may discover the reason why no philosopher, who is rational and modest, has ever pretended to assign the ultimate cause of any natural operation, or to show distinctly the action of that power, which produces any single effect in the universe. It is confessed, that the utmost effort of human reason is to reduce the principles, productive of natural phenomena, to a greater simplicity, and to resolve the many particular effects into a few general causes, by means of reasonings from analogy, experience, and observation. But as to the causes of these general causes, we should in vain attempt their discovery; nor shall we ever be able to satisfy ourselves, by any particular explication of them. These ultimate springs and principles are totally shut up from human curiosity and enquiry. Elasticity, gravity, cohesion of parts, communication of motion by impulse; these are probably the ultimate causes and principles which we ever discover in nature; and we may esteem ourselves sufficiently happy, if, by accurate inquiry and reasoning, we can trace up the particular phenomena to, or near to, these general principles. The most perfect philosophy of the natural kind only staves off our ignorance a little longer: as perhaps the most perfect philosophy of the moral or metaphysical kind serves only to discover larger portions of it. Thus the observation of human blindness and weakness is the result of all philosophy, and meets us at every turn, in spite of our endeavours to elude or avoid it.

Nor is geometry, when taken into the assistance of natural philosophy, ever able to remedy this defect, or lead us into the knowledge of ultimate causes, by all that accuracy of reasoning for which it is so justly celebrated. Every part of mixed mathematics proceeds upon the supposition that certain laws are established by nature in her operations; and abstract reasonings are employed, either to assist experience in the discovery of these laws, or to determine their influence in particular instances, where it depends upon any precise degree of distance and quantity. Thus, it is a law of motion, discovered by experience, that the moment or force of any body in motion is in the compound ratio or proportion of its solid contents and its velocity; and consequently, that a small force may remove the greatest obstacle or raise the greatest weight, if, by any contrivance or machinery, we can increase the velocity of that force, so as to make it an overmatch for its antagonist. Geometry assists us in the application of this law, by giving us the just dimensions of all the parts and figures which can enter into any species of machines; but still the discovery of the law itself is owing merely to experience, and all the abstract reasonings in the world could never lead us one step towards the knowledge of it. When we reason *a priori,* and consider merely any object or cause, as it appears to the mind, independent of all observation, it never could suggest to us the notion of any distinct object, such as its effect; much less, show us the inseparable and inviolable connexion between them. A man must be very sagacious who could discover by reasoning that crystal is the effect of heat, and ice of cold, without being previously acquainted with the operation of these qualities.

PART II

But we have not yet attained any tolerable satisfaction with regard to the question first proposed. Each solution still gives rise to a new question as difficult as the foregoing, and leads us on to farther enquiries. When it is asked, *What is the nature of all our reasonings concerning matter of fact?* the proper answer seems to be, that they are founded on the relation of cause and effect. When again it is asked, *What is the foundation of all our reasonings and conclusions concerning that relation?* it may be replied in one word, Experience. But if we still carry on our sifting humour, and ask, *What is the foundation of all conclusions from experience?* this implies a new question, which may be of more difficult solution and explication. Philosophers, that give themselves airs of superior wisdom and sufficiency, have a hard task when they encounter persons of inquisitive dispositions, who push them from every corner to which they retreat, and who are sure at last to bring them to some dangerous dilemma. The best expedient to prevent this confusion, is to be modest in our pretensions; and even to discover the difficulty ourselves before it is objected to us. By this means, we may make a kind of merit of our very ignorance.

I shall content myself, in this section, with an easy task, and shall pretend only to give a negative answer to the question here proposed. I say then, that, even after we have experience of the operations of cause and effect, our conclusions from that experience are not founded on reasoning, or any process of the understanding. This answer we must endeavour both to explain and to defend.

It must certainly be allowed, that nature has kept us at a great distance from all her secrets, and has afforded us only the knowledge of a few superficial qualities of objects; while she conceals from us those powers and principles on which the influence of those objects entirely depends. Our senses inform us of the colour, weight, and consistence of bread; but neither sense nor reason can ever inform us of those qualities which fit it for the nourishment and support of a human body. Sight or feeling conveys an idea of the actual motion of bodies; but as to that wonderful force or power, which would carry on a moving body for ever in a continued change of place, and which bodies never lose but by communicating it to others; of this we cannot form the most distant conception. But notwithstanding this ignorance of natural powers* and principles, we always presume, when we see like sensible qualities, that they have like secret powers, and expect that effects, similar to those which we have experienced, will follow from them. If a body of like colour and consistence with that bread, which we have formerly eat, be presented to us, we make no scruple of repeating the experiment, and foresee, with certainty, like nourishment and support. Now this is a process of the mind or thought, of which I would willingly know the foundation. It is allowed on all hands that there is no known connexion between the sensible qualities and the secret powers; and consequently, that the mind is not led to form such a conclusion concerning their constant and regular conjunction, by anything which it knows of their nature. As to past *Experience,* it can be allowed to give *direct* and *certain* information of those precise objects only, and that precise period of time, which fell under its cognizance: but why this experience should be extended to future times, and to other objects, which, for aught we know, may be only in appearance similar; this is the main question on which I would insist. The bread, which I formerly eat, nourished me; that is, a body of such sensible qualities was, at that time, endued with such secret powers: but does it follow, that other bread must also nourish me at another time, and that like sensible qualities must always be attended with like secret powers? The consequence seems nowise necessary. At least, it must be acknowledged that there is here a consequence drawn by the mind; that there is a certain step taken; a process of thought, and an inference, which wants to be explained. These two propositions are far from being the same, *I have found that such an object has always been attended with such an effect, and I foresee, that other objects, which are, in appearance, similar, will be attended with similar effects.* I shall allow, if you please, that the one proposition may justly be inferred from the other; I know, in fact, that it always is inferred. But if you insist that the inference is made by a chain of reasoning, I desire you to produce that reasoning. The connexion between these propositions is not intuitive. There is required a medium, which may enable the mind to draw such an inference, if indeed it be drawn by reasoning and argument. What that medium is, I must confess, passes my comprehension; and it is incumbent on those to produce it, who assert that it really exists, and is the origin of all our conclusions concerning matter of fact.

This negative argument must certainly, in process of time, become altogether convincing, if many penetrating and able philosophers shall turn their enquiries this way and no one be ever able to discover any connecting proposition or intermediate step, which supports the understanding in this conclusion. But as the question is yet new, every reader may not trust so far to his own penetration, as to conclude, because an argument escapes his enquiry, that therefore it does not really exist. For this reason it may be requisite to venture upon a more difficult task; and enumerating all the branches of human knowledge, endeavour to show that none of them can afford such an argument.

All reasonings may be divided into two kinds, namely, demonstrative reasoning, or that concerning relations of ideas, and moral reasoning, or that concerning matter of fact and existence. That there are no demonstrative arguments in the case seems evident; since it implies no contradiction that the course of nature may change, and that an object, seemingly like those which we have experienced, may be attended with different or contrary effects. May I not clearly and distinctly conceive that a body, falling from the clouds, and which, in all other respects, resembles snow, has yet the taste of

---

*The word, Power, is here used in a loose and popular sense. The most accurate explication of it would give additional evidence to this argument. See Sec. 7.

salt or feeling of fire? Is there any more intelligible proposition than to affirm, that all the trees will flourish in December and January, and decay in May and June? Now whatever is intelligible, and can be distinctly conceived, implies no contradiction, and can never be proved false by any demonstrative argument or abstract reasoning *a priori*.

If we be, therefore, engaged by arguments to put trust in past experience, and make it the standard of our future judgement, these arguments must be probable only, or such as regard matter of fact and real existence, according to the division above mentioned. But that there is no argument of this kind, must appear, if our explication of that species of reasoning be admitted as solid and satisfactory. We have said that all arguments concerning existence are founded on the relation of cause and effect; that our knowledge of that relation is derived entirely from experience; and that all our experimental conclusions proceed upon the supposition that the future will be conformable to the past. To endeavour, therefore, the proof of this last supposition by probable arguments, or arguments regarding existence, must be evidently going in a circle, and taking that for granted, which is the very point in question.

In reality, all arguments from experience are founded on the similarity which we discover among natural objects, and by which we are induced to expect effects similar to those which we have found to follow from such objects. And though none but a fool or madman will ever pretend to dispute the authority of experience, or to reject that great guide of human life, it may surely be allowed a philosopher to have so much curiosity at least as to examine the principle of human nature, which gives this mighty authority to experience, and makes us draw advantage from that similarity which nature has placed among different objects. From causes which appear similar we expect similar effects. This is the sum of all our experimental conclusions. Now it seems evident that, if this conclusion were formed by reason, it would be as perfect at first, and upon one instance, as after ever so long a course of experience. But the case is far otherwise. Nothing so like as eggs; yet no one, on account of this appearing similarity, expects the same taste and relish in all of them. It is only after a long course of uniform experiments in any kind, that we attain a firm reliance and security with regard to a particular event. Now where is that process of reasoning which, from one instance, draws a conclusion, so different from that which it infers from a hundred instances that are nowise different from that single one? This question I propose as much for the sake of information, as with an intention of raising difficulties. I cannot find, I cannot imagine any such reasoning. But I keep my mind still open to instruction, if any one will vouchsafe to bestow it on me.

Should it be said that, from a number of uniform experiments, we *infer* a connexion between the sensible qualities and the secret powers; this, I must confess, seems the same difficulty, couched in different terms. The question still recurs, on what process of argument this *inference* is founded? Where is the medium, the interposing ideas, which join propositions so very wide of each other? It is confessed that the colour, consistence, and other sensible qualities of bread appear not, of themselves, to have any connexion with the secret powers of nourishment and support. For otherwise we could infer these secret powers from the first appearance of these sensible qualities, without the aid of experience; contrary to the sentiment of all philosophers, and contrary to plain matter of fact. Here, then, is our natural state of ignorance with regard to the powers and influence of all objects. How is this remedied by experience? It only shows us a number of uniform effects, resulting from certain objects, and teaches us that those particular objects, at that particular time, were endowed with such powers and forces. When a new object, endowed with similar sensible qualities, is produced, we expect similar powers and forces, and look for a like effect. From a body of like colour and consistence with bread we expect like nourishment and support. But this surely is a step or progress of the mind, which wants to be explained. When a man says, *I have found, in all past instances, such sensible qualities conjoined with such secret powers:* And when he says, *Similar sensible qualities will always be conjoined with similar secret powers,* he is not guilty of a tautology, nor are these propositions in any respect the same. You say that the one proposition is an inference from the other. But you must confess that the inference is not intuitive; neither is it demonstrative: Of what nature is it, then? To say it is experimental, is begging the question. For all inferences from experience suppose, as their foundation, that the future will resemble the past, and that similar powers will be conjoined with similar sensible qualities. If there be any suspicion that the course of nature may change, and that the past may be no rule for the future, all experience becomes useless, and can give rise to no inference or conclusion. It is impossible, therefore, that any arguments from experience can prove this resemblance of the past to the future: since all these arguments are founded on the supposition of that resemblance. Let the course of things be allowed hitherto ever so regular; that alone, without some new argument or inference, proves not that, for the future, it will continue so. In vain do you pretend to have learned the nature of bodies from your past experience. Their secret nature, and consequently all their effects and influence, may change, without any change in their sensible qualities. This happens sometimes, and with regard to some objects: Why may it not happen always, and with regard to all objects? What logic, what process of argument secures you against this supposition? My practice, you say, refutes my doubts. But you mistake the purport of my question. As an agent, I am quite satisfied in the point; but as a philosopher, who has some share of curiosity, I will not say scepticism, I want to learn the foundation of this inference. No reading, no enquiry has yet been able to remove my difficulty, or give me satisfaction in a matter of such importance. Can I do better than propose the difficulty to the public, even though, perhaps, I have small hopes of obtaining a solution? We shall, at least, by this means, be sensible of our ignorance, if we do not augment our knowledge.

I must confess that a man is guilty of unpardonable arrogance who concludes, because an argument has escaped his own investigation, that therefore it does not really exist. I must also confess that, though all the learned, for several ages, should have employed themselves in fruitless search upon any subject, it may still, perhaps, be rash to conclude positively that the subject must, therefore, pass all human comprehension. Even though we examine all the sources of our knowledge, and conclude them unfit for such a subject, there may still remain a suspicion, that the enumeration is not complete, or the examination not accurate. But with regard to the present subject, there are some considerations which seem to remove all this accusation of arrogance or suspicion of mistake.

It is certain that the most ignorant and stupid peasants—nay infants, nay even brute beasts—improve by experience, and learn the qualities of natural objects, by observing the effects which result from them. When a child has felt the sensation of pain from touching the flame of a candle, he will be careful not to put his hand near any candle; but will expect a similar effect from a cause which is similar in its sensible qualities and appearance. If you assert, therefore, that the understanding of the child is led into this conclusion by any process of argument or ratiocination, I may justly require you to produce that argument; nor have you any pretense to refuse so equitable a demand. You cannot say that the argument is abstruse, and may possibly escape your enquiry; since you confess that it is obvious to the capacity of a mere infant. If you hesitate, therefore, a moment, or if, after reflection, you produce any intricate or profound argument, you, in a manner, give up the question, and confess that it is not reasoning which engages us to suppose the past resembling the future, and to expect similar effects from causes which are, to appearance, similar. This is the proposition which I intended to enforce in the present section. If I be right, I pretend not to have made any mighty discovery. And if I be wrong, I must acknowledge myself to be indeed a very backward scholar; since I cannot now discover an argument which, it seems, was perfectly familiar to me long before I was out of my cradle.

SECTION V. SCEPTICAL SOLUTION OF THESE DOUBTS

PART I

The passion for philosophy, like that for religion, seems liable to this inconvenience, that, though it aims at the correction of our manners, and extirpation of our vices, it may only serve, by imprudent management, to foster a predominant inclination, and push the mind, with more determined resolution, towards that side which already *draws* too much, by the bias and propensity of the natural temper. It is certain that, while we aspire to the magnanimous firmness of the philosophic sage, and endeavour to confine our pleasures altogether within our own minds, we may, at last, render our philosophy like that of Epictetus, and other *Stoics,* only a more refined system of selfishness, and reason ourselves out of all virtue as well as social enjoyment. While we study with attention the vanity of human life, and turn all our thoughts towards the empty and transitory nature of riches and honours, we are, perhaps, all the while flattering our natural indolence, which, hating the bustle of the world, and drudgery of business, seeks a pretence of reason to give itself a full and uncontrolled indulgence. There is, however, one species of philosophy which seems little liable to this inconvenience, and that because it strikes in with no disorderly passion of the human mind, nor can mingle itself with any natural affection or propensity; and that is the Academic or Sceptical philosophy. The academics always talk of doubt and suspense of judgement, of danger in hasty determinations, of confining to very narrow bounds the enquiries of the understanding, and of renouncing all speculations which lie not within the limits of common life and practice. Nothing, therefore, can be more contrary than such a philosophy to the supine indolence of the mind, its rash arrogance, its lofty pretensions, and its superstitious credulity. Every passion is mortified by it, except the love of truth; and that passion never is, nor can be, carried to too high a degree. It is surprising, therefore, that this philosophy, which, in almost every instance, must be harmless and innocent, should be the subject of so much groundless reproach and obloquy. But, perhaps, the very circumstance which renders it so innocent is what chiefly exposes it to the public hatred and resentment. By flattering no irregular passion, it gains few partizans: By opposing so many vices and follies, it raises to itself abundance of enemies, who stigmatize it as libertine, profane, and irreligious.

    Nor need we fear that this philosophy, while it endeavours to limit our enquiries to common life, should ever undermine the reasonings of common life, and carry its doubts so far as to destroy all action, as well as speculation. Nature will always maintain her rights, and prevail in the end over any abstract reasoning whatsoever. Though we should conclude, for instance, as in the foregoing section, that, in all reasonings from experience, there is a step taken by the mind which is not supported by any argument or process of the understanding; there is no danger that these reasonings, on which almost all knowledge depends, will ever be affected by such a discovery. If the mind be not engaged by argument to make this step, it must be induced by some other principle of equal weight and authority; and that principle will preserve its influence as long as human nature remains the same. What that principle is may well be worth the pains of enquiry.

Suppose a person, though endowed with the strongest faculties of reason and reflection, to be brought on a sudden into this world; he would, indeed, immediately observe a continual succession of objects, and one event following another; but he would not be able to discover anything farther. He would not, at first, by any reasoning, be able to reach the idea of cause and effect; since the particular powers, by which all natural operations are performed, never appear to the senses; nor is it reasonable to conclude, merely because one event, in one instance, precedes another, that therefore the one is the cause, the other the effect. Their conjunction may be arbitrary and casual. There may be no reason to infer the existence of one from the appearance of the other. And in a word, such a person, without more experience, could never employ his conjecture or reasoning concerning any matter of fact, or be assured of anything beyond what was immediately present to his memory and senses.

Suppose, again, that he has acquired more experience, and has lived so long in the world as to have observed familiar objects or events to be constantly conjoined together; what is the consequence of this experience? He immediately infers the existence of one object from the appearance of the other. Yet he has not, by all his experience, acquired any idea or knowledge of the secret power by which the one object produces the other; nor is it, by any process of reasoning, he is engaged to draw this inference. But still he finds himself determined to draw it: And though he should be convinced that his understanding has no part in the operation, he would nevertheless continue in the same course of thinking. There is some other principle which determines him to form such a conclusion.

This principle is Custom or Habit. For wherever the repetition of any particular act or operation produces a propensity to renew the same act or operation, without being impelled by any reasoning or process of the understanding, we always say, that this propensity is the effect of *Custom.* By employing that word, we pretend not to have given the ultimate reason of such a propensity. We only point out a principle of human nature, which is universally acknowledged, and which is well known by its effects. Perhaps we can push our enquiries no farther, or pretend to give the cause of this cause; but must rest contented with it as the ultimate principle, which we can assign, of all our conclusions from experience. It is sufficient satisfaction, that we can go so far, without repining at the narrowness of our faculties because they will carry us no farther. And it is certain we here advance a very intelligible proposition at least, if not a true one, when we assert that, after the constant conjunction of two objects—heat and flame, for instance, weight and solidity—we are determined by custom alone to expect the one from the appearance of the other. This hypothesis seems even the only one which explains the difficulty, why we draw, from a thousand instances, an inference which we are not able to draw from one instance, that is, in no respect, different from them. Reason is incapable of any such variation. The conclusions which it draws from considering one circle are the same which it would form upon surveying all the circles in the universe. But no man, having seen only one body move after being impelled by another, could infer that every other body will move after a like impulse. All inferences from experience, therefore, are effects of custom, not of reasoning.*

Custom, then, is the great guide of human life. It is that principle alone which renders our experience useful to us, and makes us expect, for the future, a similar train of events with those which have appeared in the past. Without the influence of custom, we should be entirely ignorant of every matter of fact beyond what is immediately present to the memory and senses. We should never know to adjust means to ends, or to employ our natural powers in the production of any effect. There would be an end at once of all action, as well as of the chief part of speculation.

But here it may be proper to remark, that though our conclusions from experience carry us beyond our memory and senses, and assure us of matters of fact which happened in the most distant places and most remote ages, yet some fact must always be present to the senses or memory, from which we may first proceed in drawing these conclusions. A man, who should find in a desert country the remains of pompous build-

---

*Nothing is more useful than for writers, even, on *moral, political,* or *physical* subjects to distinguish between *reason* and *experience,* and to suppose, that these species of argumentation are entirely different from each other. The former are taken for the mere result of our intellectual faculties, which, by considering *a priori* the nature of things, and examining the effects that must follow from their operation, establish particular principles of science and philosophy. The latter are supposed to be derived entirely from sense and observation, by which we learn what has actually resulted from the operation of particular objects, and are thence able to infer, what will, for the future, result from them. Thus, for instance, the limitations and restraints of civil government, and a legal constitution, may be defended, either from *reason,* which reflecting on the great frailty and corruption of human nature, teaches, that no man can safely be trusted with unlimited authority; or from *experience* and history which inform us of the enormous abuses, that ambition, in every age and country, has been found to make of so imprudent a confidence.

The same distribution between reason and experience is maintained in all our deliberations concerning the conduct of life; while the experienced statesman, general, physician, or merchant is trusted and followed; and the unpractised novice, with whatever natural talents endowed, neglected and despised. Though it be allowed, that reason may form very plausible conjectures with regard to the consequences of such a particular conduct in such the assistance of experience, which is alone able to give stability and certainty to the maxims, derived from study and reflection.

But notwithstanding that this distinction be thus universally received, both in the active speculative scenes of life, I shall not scruple to pronounce, that it is, at bottom, erroneous, at least, superficial.

If we examine those arguments, which, in any of the sciences above mentioned, are supposed to be the mere effects of reasoning and reflection, they will be found to terminate at last, in some general principle or conclusion, for which we can assign no reason but observation and experience. The only difference between them and those maxims, which are vulgarly esteemed the result of pure experience, is, that the former cannot be established without some process of thought, and some reflection on what we have observed, in order to distinguish its circumstances, and trace its consequences: Whereas in the latter, the experienced event is exactly and fully familiar to that which we infer as the result of any particular situation. The history of a Tiberius or a Nero makes us dread a like tyranny, were our monarchs freed from the restraints of laws and senates. But the observation of any fraud or cruelty in private life is sufficient, with the aid of a little thought, to give us the same apprehension; while it serves as an instance of the general corruption of human nature, and shows us the danger which we must incur by reposing an entire confidence in mankind. In both cases, it is experience which is ultimately the foundation of our inference and conclusion.

There is no man so young and experienced, as not to have formed, from observation, many general and just maxims concerning human affairs and the conduct of life; but it must be confessed, that, when a man comes to put these in practice, he will be extremely liable to error, till time and farther experience both enlarge these maxims, and teach him their proper use and application. In every situation or incident, there are many particular and seemingly minute circumstances, which the man of greatest talent is, at first, apt to overlook, though on them the justness of his conclusions, and consequently the prudence of his conduct, entirely depend. Not to mention, that, to a young beginner, the general observations and maxims occur not always on the proper occasions, nor can be immediately applied with due calmness and distinction. The truth is, an unexperienced reasoner could be no reasoner at all, were he absolutely unexperienced; and when we assign that character to any one, we mean it only in a comparative sense, and suppose him possessed of experience, in a smaller and more imperfect degree.

ings, would conclude that the country had, in ancient times, been cultivated by civilized inhabitants; but did nothing of this nature occur to him, he could never form such an inference. We learn the events of former ages from history; but then we must peruse the volumes in which this instruction is contained, and thence carry up our inferences from one testimony to another, till we arrive at the eyewitnesses and spectators of these distant events. In a word, if we proceed not upon some fact, present to the memory or senses, our reasonings would be merely hypothetical; and however the particular links might be connected with each other, the whole chain of inferences would have nothing to support it, nor could we ever, by its means, arrive at the knowledge of any real existence. If I ask why you believe any particular matter of fact, which you relate, you must tell me some reason; and this reason will be some other fact, connected with it. But as you cannot proceed after this manner, *in infinitum,* you must at last terminate in some fact, which is present to your memory or senses; or must allow that your belief is entirely without foundation.

What, then, is the conclusion of the whole matter? A simple one; though, it must be confessed, pretty remote from the common theories of philosophy. All belief of matter of fact or real existence is derived merely from some object, present to the memory or senses, and a customary conjunction between that and some other object. Or in other words; having found in many instances, that any two kinds of objects—flame and heat, snow and cold—have always been conjoined together; if flame or snow be presented anew to the senses, the mind is carried by custom to expect heat or cold, and to *believe* that such a quality does exist, and will discover itself upon a nearer approach. This belief is the necessary result of placing the mind in such circumstances. It is an operation of the soul, when we are so situated, as unavoidable as to feel the passion of love, when we receive benefits; or hatred, when we meet with injuries. All these operations are a species of natural instincts, which no reasoning or process of the thought and understanding is able either to produce or to prevent.

At this point, it would be very allowable for us to stop our philosophical researches. In most questions we can never make a single step farther; and in all questions we must terminate here at last, after our most restless and curious enquiries. But still our curiosity will be pardonable, perhaps commendable, if it carry us on to still farther researches, and make us examine more accurately the nature of this belief, and of the *customary conjunction,* whence it is derived. By this means we may meet with some explications and analogies that will give satisfaction; at least to such as love the abstract sciences, and can be entertained with speculations, which, however accurate, may still retain a degree of doubt and uncertainty. As to readers of a different taste; the remaining part of this section is not calculated for them, and the following enquiries may well be understood, though it be neglected.

PART II

Nothing is more free than the imagination of man; and though it cannot exceed that original stock of ideas furnished by the internal and external senses, it has unlimited power of mixing, compounding, separating, and dividing these ideas, in all the varieties of fiction and vision. It can feign a train of events, with all the appearance of reality, ascribe to them a particular time and place, conceive them as existent, and paint them out to itself with every circumstance, that belongs to any historical fact, which it believes with the greatest certainty. Wherein, therefore, consists the difference between such a fiction and belief? It lies not merely in any peculiar idea, which is annexed to such a conception as commands our assent, and which is wanting to every known fiction. For as the mind has authority over all its ideas, it could voluntarily annex this particular idea to any fiction, and consequently be able to believe whatever it pleases; contrary to what we find by daily experience. We can, in our conception, join the head of a man to the body of a horse; but it is not in our power to believe that such an animal has ever really existed.

It follows, therefore, that the difference between *fiction* and *belief* lies in some sentiment or feeling, which is annexed to the latter, not to the former, and which depends not on the will, nor can be commanded at pleasure. It must be excited by nature, like all other sentiments; and must arise from the particular situation, in which the mind is placed at any particular juncture. Whenever any object is presented to the memory or senses, it immediately, by the force of custom, carries the imagination to conceive that object, which is usually conjoined to it; and this conception is attended with a feeling or sentiment, different from the loose reveries of the fancy. In this consists the whole nature of belief. For as there is no matter of fact which we believe so firmly that we cannot conceive the contrary, there would be no difference between the conception assented to and that which is rejected, were it not for some sentiment which distinguishes the one from the other. If I see a billiard-ball moving towards another, on a smooth table, I can easily conceive it to stop upon contact. This conception implies no contradiction; but still it feels very differently from that conception by which I represent to myself the impulse and the communication of motion from one ball to another.

Were we to attempt a *definition* of this sentiment, we should, perhaps, find it a very difficult, if not an impossible task; in the same manner as if we should endeavour to define the feeling of cold or passion or anger, to a creature who never had any experience of these sentiments. Belief is the true and proper name of this feeling; and no one is ever at a loss to know the meaning of that term; because every man is every moment conscious of the sentiment represented by it. It may not, however, be improper to attempt a *description* of this sentiment; in hopes we may, by that means, arrive at some analogies, which may afford a more perfect explication of it. I say, then, that belief is nothing but a more vivid, lively, forcible, firm, steady conception of an object, than what the imagination alone is ever able to attain. This variety of terms, which may seem so unphilosophical, is intended only to express that act of the mind, which renders realities, or what is taken for such, more present to us than fictions, causes them to weigh more in the thought, and gives them a superior influence on the passions and imagination. Provided we agree about the thing, it is needless to dispute about the terms. The imagination has the command over all its ideas, and can join and mix and vary them, in all the ways possible. It may conceive fictitious objects with all the circumstances of place and time. It may set them, in a manner, before our eyes, in their true colours, just as they might have existed. But as it is impossible that this faculty of imagination can ever, of itself, reach belief, it is evident that belief consists not in the peculiar nature or order of ideas, but in the *manner* of their conception, and in their *feeling* to the mind. I confess, that it is impossible perfectly to explain this feeling or manner of conception. We may make use of words which express something near it. But its true and proper name, as we observed before, is *belief;* which is a term that every one sufficiently understands in common life. And in philosophy, we can go no farther than assert, that *belief* is something felt by the mind, which distinguishes the ideas of the judgement from the fictions of the imagination. It gives them more weight and influence; makes them appear of greater importance; enforces them in the mind; and renders them the governing principle of our actions. I hear at present, for instance, a person's voice, with whom I am acquainted; and the sound comes as from the next room. This impression of my senses immediately conveys my thought to the person, together with all the surrounding objects. I paint them out to myself as existing at present, with the same qualities and relations, of which I formerly knew them possessed. These ideas take faster hold of my mind than ideas of an enchanted castle. They are very different to the feeling, and have a much greater influence of every kind, either to give pleasure or pain, joy or sorrow.

Let us, then, take in the whole compass of this doctrine, and allow, that the sentiment of belief is nothing but a conception more intense and steady than what attends the mere fictions of the imagination, and that this manner of conception arises from a customary conjunction of the object with something present to the memory or senses: I believe that it will not be difficult, upon these suppositions, to find other operations of the mind analogous to it, and to trace up these phenomena to principles still more general.

We have already observed that nature has established connexions among particular ideas, and that no sooner one idea occurs to our thoughts than it introduces its correlative, and carries our attention towards it, by a gentle and insensible movement. These principles of connexion or association we have reduced to three, namely, *Resemblance, Contiguity* and *Causation;* which are the only bonds that unite our thoughts together, and beget that regular train of reflection or discourse, which, in a greater or less degree, takes place among mankind. Now here arises a question, on which the solution of the present difficulty will depend. Does it happen, in all these relations, that, when one of the objects is presented to the senses or memory the mind is not only carried to the conception of the correlative, but reaches a steadier and stronger conception of it than what otherwise it would have been able to attain? This seems to be the case with that belief which arises from the relation of cause and effect. And if the case be the same with the other relations or principles of associations, this may be established as a general law, which takes place in all the operations of the mind.

We may, therefore, observe, as the first experiment to our present purpose, that, upon the appearance of the picture of an absent friend, our idea of him is evidently enlivened by the *resemblance,* and that every passion, which that idea occasions, whether of joy or sorrow, acquires new force and vigour. In producing this effect, there concur both a relation and a present impression. Where the picture bears him no resemblance, at least was not intended for him, it never so much as conveys our thought to him: And where it is absent, as well as the person, though the mind may pass from the thought of the one to that of the other, it feels its idea to be rather weakened than enlivened by that transition. We take a pleasure in viewing the picture of a friend, when it is set before us; but when it is removed, rather choose to consider him directly than by reflection in an image, which is equally distant and obscure.

The ceremonies of the Roman Catholic religion may be considered as instances of the same nature. The devotees of that superstition usually plead in excuse for the mummeries, with which they were upbraided, that they feel the good effect of those external motions, and postures, and actions, in enlivening their devotion and quickening their fervour, which otherwise would decay, if directed entirely to distant and immaterial objects. We shadow out the objects of our faith, say they, in sensible types and images, and render them more present to us by the immediate presence of these types, than it is possible for us to do merely by an intellectual view and contemplation. Sensible objects have always a greater influence on the fancy than any other; and this influence they readily convey to those ideas to which they are related, and which they resemble. I shall only infer from these practices, and reasoning, that the effect of resemblance in enlivening the ideas is very common; and as in every case a resemblance and a present impression must concur, we are abundantly supplied with experiments to prove the reality of the foregoing principle.

We may add force to these experiments by others of a different kind, in considering the effects of *contiguity* as well as of *resemblance.* It is certain that distance diminishes the force of every idea, and that, upon our approach to any object; though it does not discover itself to our senses; it operates upon the mind with an influence, which imitates an immediate impression. The thinking on any object readily transports the mind to what is contiguous; but it is only the actual presence of an object, that transports it with a superior vivacity. When I am a few miles from home, whatever relates to it touches me more nearly than when I am two hundred leagues distant; though even at that distance the reflecting on any thing in the neighbourhood of my friends or family naturally produces an idea of them. But as in this latter case, both the objects of the mind are ideas; notwithstanding there is an easy transition between them; that transition alone is not able to give a superior vivacity to any of the ideas, for want of some immediate impression.* No one can doubt but causation has the same influence as the other two relations of resemblance and contiguity. Superstitious people are fond of the relics of saints and holy men, for the same reason, that they seek after types or images, in order to enliven their devotion, and give them a more intimate and strong conception of those exemplary lives, which they desire to imitate. Now it is evident, that one of the best relics, which a devotee could procure, would be the handywork of a saint; and if his clothes and furniture are ever to be considered in this light, it is because they were once at his disposal, and were moved and affected by him; in which respect they are to be considered as imperfect effects, and as connected with him by a shorter chain of consequences than any of those, by which we learn the reality of his existence.

Suppose, that the son of a friend, who had been long dead or absent, were presented to us; it is evident, that this object would instantly revive its correlative idea, and recall to our thoughts all past intimacies and familiarities, in more lively colours than they would otherwise have appeared to us. This is another phenomenon, which seems to prove the principle above mentioned.

We may observe, that, in these phenomena, the belief of the correlative object is always presupposed; without which the relation could have no effect. The influence of the picture supposes, that we *believe* our friend to have once existed. Contiguity to home can never excite our ideas of home, unless we *believe* that it really exists. Now I assert, that this belief, where it reaches beyond the memory or senses, is of a similar nature, and arises from similar causes, with the transition of thought and vivacity of conception here explained. When I throw a piece of dry wood into a fire, my mind is immediately carried to conceive, that it augments, not extinguishes the flame. This transition of thought from the cause to the effect proceeds not from reason. It derives its origin altogether from custom and experience. And as it first begins from an object, present to the senses, it renders the idea or conception of flame more strong and lively than any loose, floating reverie of the imagination. That idea arises immediately. The thought moves instantly towards it, and conveys to it all that force of conception, which is derived from the impression

---

*"Should I call it our nature or some error that leads us to feel more deeply moved upon seeing places where memorable men are said to have spent much time than we feel when hearing of their deeds or reading their writings? Thus I feel deeply moved now. For Plato comes to my mind, who is said to have been the first philosopher to have made a practice of holding discussions here; and his little garden nearby not only stirs memories but makes me all but see him in the flesh. Here is Speusippus, here Xenocrates, here his student Polemo; it was his seat that we see before us. Even looking at our senate building—that of Hostilius, not the new building which looks smaller to me since it was made larger—made me think of Scipio, Cato, Laelius, and above all my grandfather. Such power of stirring recollection resides in places: no wonder that the training of the memory is based on them." Cicero, *De Finibus,* Book V. [Hume's footnote is in Latin, translation by W.K.]

present to the senses. When a sword is levelled at my breast, does not the idea of wound and pain strike me more strongly, than when a glass of wine is presented to me, even though by accident this idea should occur after the appearance of the latter object? But what is there in this whole matter to cause such a strong conception, except only a present object and a customary transition to the idea of another object, which we have been accustomed to conjoin with the former? This is the whole operation of the mind, in all our conclusions concerning matter of fact and existence; and it is a satisfaction to find some analogies, by which it may be explained. The transition from a present object does in all cases give strength and solidity to the related idea.

Here, then, is a kind of pre-established harmony between the course of nature and the succession of our ideas; and though the powers and forces, by which the former is governed, be wholly unknown to us; yet our thoughts and conceptions have still, we find, gone on in the same train with the other work of nature. Custom is that principle, by which this correspondence has been effected; so necessary to the subsistence of our species, and the regulation of our conduct, in every circumstance and occurrence of human life. Had not the presence of an object, instantly excited the idea of those objects, commonly conjoined with it, all our knowledge must have been limited to the narrow sphere of our memory and senses; and we should never have been able to adjust means to ends, or employ our natural powers, either to the producing of good, or avoiding of evil. Those, who delight in the discovery and contemplation of *final causes,* have here ample subject to employ their wonder and admiration.

I shall add, for a further confirmation of the foregoing theory, that, as this operation of the mind, by which we infer like effects from like causes, and *vice versa,* is so essential to the subsistence of all human creatures, it is not probable, that it could be trusted to the fallacious deductions of our reason, which is slow in its operations; appears not, in any degree, during the first years of infancy; and at best is, in every age and period of human life, extremely liable to error and mistake. It is more conformable to the ordinary wisdom of nature to secure so necessary an act of the mind, by some instinct or mechanical tendency, which may be infallible in its operations, may discover itself at the first appearance of life and thought, and may be independent of all the laboured deductions of the understanding. As nature has taught us the use of our limbs, without giving us the knowledge of the muscles and nerves, by which they are actuated; so has she implanted in us an instinct, which carries forward the thought in a correspondent course to that which she has established among external objects; though we are ignorant of those powers and forces, on which this regular course and succession of objects totally depends.

Section VI. Of Probability*

Though there be no such thing as *Chance* in the world; our ignorance of the real cause of any event has the same influence on the understanding, and begets a like species of belief or opinion.

---

*Mr. Locke divides all arguments into demonstrative and probable. In this view, we must say, that it is only probable all men must die, or that the sun will rise to-morrow. But to conform our language more to common use, we ought to divide arguments into *demonstrations, proofs,* and *probabilities.* By proofs meaning such arguments from experience as leave no room for doubt or opposition.

There is certainly a probability, which arises from a superiority of chances on any side; and according as this superiority increases, and surpasses the opposite chances, the probability receives a proportionable increase, and begets still a higher degree of belief or assent to that side, in which we discover the superiority. If a dye were marked with one figure or number of spots on four sides, and with another figure or number of spots on the two remaining sides, it would be more probable, that the former would turn up than the latter; though, if it had a thousand sides marked in the same manner, and only one side different, the probability would be much higher, and our belief or expectation of the event more steady and secure. This process of the thought or reasoning may seem trivial and obvious; but to those who consider it more narrowly, it may, perhaps, afford matter for curious speculation.

It seems evident, that, when the mind looks forward to discover the event, which may result from the throw of such a dye, it considers the turning up of each particular side as alike probable; and this is the very nature of chance, to render all the particular events, comprehended in it, entirely equal. But finding a greater number of sides concur in the one event than in the other, the mind is carried more frequently to that event, and meets it oftener, in revolving the various possibilities or chances, on which the ultimate result depends. This concurrence of several views in one particular event begets immediately, by an inexplicable contrivance of nature, the sentiment of belief, and gives that event the advantage over its antagonist, which is supported by a smaller number of views, and recurs less frequently to the mind. If we allow, that belief is nothing but a firmer and stronger conception of an object than what attends the mere fictions of the imagination, this operation may, perhaps, in some measure, be accounted for. The concurrence of these several views or glimpses imprints the idea more strongly on the imagination; gives it superior force and vigour; renders its influence on the passions and affections more sensible; and in a word, begets that reliance or security, which constitutes the nature of belief and opinion.

The case is the same with the probability of causes, as with that of chance. There are some causes, which are entirely uniform and constant in producing a particular effect; and no instance has ever yet been found of any failure or irregularity in their operation. Fire has always burned, and water suffocated every human creature: The production of motion by impulse and gravity is an universal law, which has hitherto admitted of no exception. But there are other causes which have been found more irregular and uncertain; nor has rhubarb always proved a purge, or opium a soporific to every one, who has taken these medicines. It is true, when any cause fails of producing its usual effect, philosophers ascribe not this to any irregularity in nature; but suppose, that some secret causes, in the particular structure of parts, have prevented the operation. Our reasonings, however, and conclusions concerning the event are the same as if this principle had no place. Being determined by custom to transfer the past to the future, in all our inferences; where the past has been entirely regular and uniform, we expect the event with the greatest assurance, and leave no room for any contrary supposition. But where different effects have been found to follow from causes, which are to *appearance* exactly similar, all these various effects must occur to the mind in transferring the past to the future, and enter into our consideration, when we determine the probability of the event. Though we give the preference to that which has been found most usual, and believe that this effect will exist, we must not overlook the other effects, but must assign to each of them a particular weight and authority, in proportion as we have found it to be more or less frequent. It is more probable, in almost every country of Europe, that there will be frost sometime in January, than that the weather will continue open throughout the whole month; though this probability varies according to the different climates, and approaches to a certainty in the more northern kingdoms. Here then it seems evident, that, when we transfer the past to the future, in order to determine the effect, which will result from any cause, we transfer all the different events, in the same proportion as they have appeared in the past, and conceive one to have existed a hundred times, for instance, another ten times, and another once. As a great number of views do here concur in one event, they fortify and confirm it to the imagination, beget that sentiment which we call *belief,* and give its object the preference above the contrary event, which is not supported by an equal number of experiments, and recurs not so frequently to the thought in transferring the past to the future. Let any one try to account for this operation of the mind upon any of the received systems of philosophy, and he will be sensible of the difficulty. For my part, I shall think it sufficient, if the present hints excite the curiosity of philosophers, and make them sensible how defective all common theories are in treating of such curious and such sublime subjects.

Section VII. Of the Idea of Necessary Connexion

Part I

The great advantage of the mathematical sciences above the moral consists in this, that the ideas of the former, being sensible, are always clear and determinate, the smallest distinction between them is immediately perceptible, and the same terms are still expressive of the same ideas, without ambiguity or variation. An oval is never mistaken for a circle, nor an hyperbola for an ellipsis. The isosceles and scalenum are distinguished by boundaries more exact than vice and virtue, right and wrong. If any term be defined in geometry, the mind readily, of itself, substitutes, on all occasions, the definition for the term defined: Or even when no definition is employed, the object itself may be presented to the senses, and by that means be steadily and clearly apprehended. But the finer sentiments of the mind, the operations of the understanding, the various agitations of the passions, though really in themselves distinct, easily escape us, when surveyed by reflection; nor is it in our power to recall the original object, as often as we have occasion to contemplate it. Ambiguity, by this means, is gradually introduced into our reasonings: Similar objects are readily taken to be the same: And the conclusion becomes at last very wide of the premises.

One may safely, however, affirm, that, if we consider these sciences in a proper light, their advantages and disadvantages nearly compensate each other, and reduce both of them to a state of equality. If the mind, with greater facility, retains the ideas of geometry clear and determinate, it must carry on a much longer and more intricate chain of reasoning, and compare ideas much wider of each other, in order to reach the abstruser truths of that science. And if moral ideas are apt, without extreme care, to fall into obscurity and confusion, the inferences are always much shorter in these disquisitions, and the intermediate steps, which lead to the conclusion, much fewer than in the sciences which treat of quantity and number. In reality, there is scarcely a proposition in Euclid so simple, as not to consist of more parts, than are to be found in any moral reasoning which runs not into chimera and conceit. Where we trace the principles of the human mind through a few steps, we may be very well satisfied with our progress; considering how soon nature

A chemist's laboratory from Denis Diderot's *Encyclopedia* (1751–1772) illustrates the state of empirical science during Hume's lifetime. The symbols below are an early periodic table of elements. (*The Bettmann Archive*)

throws a bar to all our enquiries concerning causes, and reduces us to an acknowledgment of our ignorance. The chief obstacle, therefore, to our improvement in the moral or metaphysical sciences is the obscurity of the ideas, and ambiguity of the terms. The principal difficulty in the mathematics is the length of inferences and compass of thought, requisite to the forming of any conclusion. And, perhaps, our progress in natural philosophy is chiefly retarded by the want of proper experiments and phenomena, which are often discovered by chance, and cannot always be found, when requisite, even by the most diligent and prudent enquiry. As moral philosophy seems hitherto to have received less improvement than either geometry or physics, we may conclude, that, if there be any difference in this respect among these sciences, the difficulties, which obstruct the progress of the former, require superior care and capacity to be surmounted.

There are no ideas, which occur in metaphysics, more obscure and uncertain, than those of *power, force, energy* or *necessary connexion,* of which it is every moment necessary for us to treat in all our disquisitions. We shall, therefore, endeavour, in this section, to fix, if possible, the precise meaning of these terms, and thereby remove some part of that obscurity, which is so much complained of in this species of philosophy.

It seems a proposition, which will not admit of much dispute, that all our ideas are nothing but copies of our impressions, or, in other words, that it is impossible for us to *think* of any thing, which we have not antecedently *felt,* either by our external or internal senses. I have endeavoured* to explain and prove this proposition, and have ex-

*Section II.

pressed my hopes, that, by a proper application of it, men may reach a greater clearness and precision in philosophical reasonings, than what they have hitherto been able to attain. Complex ideas may, perhaps, be well known by definition, which is nothing but an enumeration of those parts or simple ideas, that compose them. But when we have pushed up definitions to the most simple ideas, and find still some ambiguity and obscurity; what resource are we then possessed of? By what invention can we throw light upon these ideas, and render them altogether precise and determinate to our intellectual view? Produce the impressions or original sentiments, from which the ideas are copied. These impressions are all strong and sensible. They admit not of ambiguity. They are not only placed in a full light themselves, but may throw light on their correspondent ideas, which lie in obscurity. And by this means, we may, perhaps, attain a new microscope or species of optics, by which, in the moral sciences, the most minute, and most simple ideas may be so enlarged as to fall readily under our apprehension, and be equally known with the grossest and most sensible ideas, that can be the object of our enquiry.

To be fully acquainted, therefore, with the idea of power or necessary connexion, let us examine its impression; and in order to find the impression with greater certainty, let us search for it in all the sources, from which it may possibly be derived.

When we look about us towards external objects, and consider the operation of causes, we are never able, in a single instance, to discover any power or necessary connexion; and quality, which binds the effect to the cause, and renders the one an infallible consequence of the other. We only find, that the one does actually, in fact, follow the other. The impulse of one billiard-ball is attended with motion in the second. This is the whole that appears to the *outward senses*. The mind feels no sentiment or *inward* impression from this succession of objects: Consequently there is not, in any single, particular instance of cause and effect, any thing which can suggest the idea of power or necessary connexion.

From the first appearance of an object, we never can conjecture what effect will result from it. But were the power or energy of any cause discoverable by the mind, we could foresee the effect, even without experience; and might, at first, pronounce with certainty concerning it, by mere dint of thought and reasoning.

In reality, there is no part of matter, that does ever, by its sensible qualities, discover any power or energy, or give us ground to imagine, that it could produce any thing, or be followed by any other object, which we could denominate its effect. Solidity, extension, motion; these qualities are all complete in themselves, and never point out any other event which may result from them. The scenes of the universe are continually shifting, and one object follows another in an uninterrupted succession; but the power of force, which actuates the whole machine, is entirely concealed from us, and never discovers itself in any of the sensible qualities of body. We know, that, in fact, heat is a constant attendant of flame; but what is the connexion between them, we have no room so much as to conjecture or imagine. It is impossible, therefore, that the idea of power can be derived from the contemplation of bodies, in single instances of their operation; because no bodies ever discover any power, which can be the original of this idea.*

Since, therefore, external objects as they appear to the senses, give us no idea of power or necessary connexion, by their operation in particular instances, let us see,

---

*Mr. Locke, in his chapter of power, says, that, finding from experience, that there are several new productions in matter, and concluding that there must somewhere be a power capable of producing them, we arrive at last by this reasoning at the idea of power. But no reasoning can ever give us a new, original, simple idea; as this philosopher himself confesses. This, therefore, can never be the origin of that idea.

whether this idea be derived from reflection on the operations of our own minds, and be copied from any internal impression. It may be said, that we are every moment conscious of internal power; while we feel, that, by the simple command of our will, we can move the organs of our body, or direct the faculties of our mind. An act of volition produces motion in our limbs, or raises a new idea in our imagination. This influence of the will we know by consciousness. Hence we acquire the idea of power or energy; and are certain, that we ourselves and all other intelligent beings are possessed of power. This idea, then, is an idea of reflection, since it arises from reflecting on the operations of our own mind, and on the command which is exercised by will, both over the organs of the body and faculties of the soul.

We shall proceed to examine this pretension; and first with regard to the influence of volition over the organs of the body. This influence, we may observe, is a fact, which, like all other natural events, can be known only by experience, and can never be foreseen from any apparent energy or power in the cause, which connects it with the effect, and renders the one an infallible consequence of the other. The motion of our body follows upon the command of our will. Of this we are every moment conscious. But the means, by which this is effected; the energy, by which the will performs so extraordinary an operation; of this we are so far from being immediately conscious, that it must for ever escape our most diligent enquiry.

For *first;* is there any principle in all nature more mysterious than the union of soul with body; by which a supposed spiritual substance acquires such an influence over a material one, that the most refined thought is able to actuate the grossest matter? Were we empowered, by a secret wish, to remove mountains, or control the planets in their orbit; this extensive authority would not be more extraordinary, nor more beyond our comprehension. But if by consciousness we perceived any power or energy in the will, we must know this power; we must know its connexion with the effect; we must know the secret union of soul and body, and the nature of both these substances; by which the one is able to operate, in so many instances, upon the other.

Secondly, We are not able to move all the organs of the body with a like authority; though we cannot assign any reason besides experience, for so remarkable a difference between one and the other. Why has the will an influence over the tongue and fingers, not over the heart and liver? This question would never embarrass us, were we conscious of a power in the former case, not in the latter. We should then perceive, independent of experience, why the authority of will over the organs of the body is circumscribed within such particular limits. Being in that case fully acquainted with the power or force, by which it operates, we should also know, why its influence reaches precisely to such boundaries, and no farther.

A man, suddenly struck with palsy in the leg or arm, or who had newly lost those members, frequently endeavours, at first to move them, and employ them in their usual offices. Here he is as much conscious of power to command such limbs, as a man in perfect health is conscious of power to actuate any member which remains in its natural state and condition. But consciousness never deceives. Consequently, neither in the one case nor in the other, are we ever conscious of any power. We learn the influence of our will from experience alone. And experience only teaches us, how one event constantly follows another; without instructing us in the secret connexion, which binds them together, and renders them inseparable.

Thirdly, We learn from anatomy, that the immediate object of power in voluntary motion, is not the member itself which is moved, but certain muscles, and nerves, and animal spirits, and, perhaps, something still more minute and more unknown, through which the motion is successfully propagated, ere it reach the member itself whose motion is the immediate object of volition. Can there be a more certain proof that the power, by which this whole operation is performed, so far from being directly and fully known by an inward sentiment or consciousness, is, to the last degree, mysterious and unintelligible? Here the mind wills a certain event: Immediately another event, unknown to ourselves, and totally different from the one intended, is produced: This event produces another, equally unknown: Till at last, through a long succession, the desired event is produced. But if the original power were felt, it must be known: Were it known, its effect also must be known; since all power is relative to its effect. And *vice versa,* if the effect be not known, the power cannot be known nor felt. How indeed can we be conscious of a power to move our limbs, when we have no such power; but only that to move certain animal spirits, which, though they produce at last the motion of our limbs, yet operate in such a manner as is wholly beyond our comprehension?

We may, therefore, conclude from the whole, I hope, without any temerity, though with assurance; that our idea of power is not copied from any sentiment or consciousness of power within ourselves, when we give rise to animal motion, or apply our limbs, to their proper use and office. That their motion follows the command of the will is a matter of common experience, like other natural events: But the power or energy by which this is effected, like that in other natural events, is unknown and inconceivable.*

Shall we then assert, that we are conscious of a power or energy in our own minds, when, by an act or command of our will, we raise up a new idea, fix the mind to the contemplation of it, turn it on all sides, and at last dismiss it for some other idea, when we think that we have surveyed it with sufficient accuracy? I believe the same arguments will prove, that even this command of the will gives us no real idea of force or energy.

First, It must be allowed, that, when we know a power, we know that very circumstance in the cause, by which it is enabled to produce the effect: For these are supposed to be synonymous. We must, therefore, know both the cause and effect, and the relation between them. But do we pretend to be acquainted with the nature of the human soul and the nature of an idea, or the aptitude of the one to produce the other? This is a real creation; a production of something out of nothing: Which implies a power so great, that it may seem, at first sight, beyond the reach of any being, less than infinite. At least it must be owned, that such a power is not felt, nor known, nor even conceivable by the mind. We only feel the event, namely, the existence of an idea, consequent to a command of the will: But the manner, in which this operation is performed, the power by which it is produced, is entirely beyond our comprehension.

Secondly, The command of the mind over itself is limited, as well as its command over the body; and these limits are not known by reason, or any acquaintance with the nature of cause and effect, but only by experience and observation, as in all other natural events and in the operation of external objects. Our authority over our sentiments

---

*It may be pretended, that the resistance which we meet with in bodies, obliging us frequently to exert our force, and call up all our power, this gives us the idea of force and power. It is this nisus, or strong endeavour, of which we are conscious, that is the original impression from which this idea is copied. But, *first,* we attribute power to a vast number of objects, where we never can suppose this resistance or exertion of force to take place, to the supreme Being, who never meets with any resistance; to the mind in its command over its ideas and limbs, in common thinking and motion, where the effect follows immediately upon the will, without any exertion or summoning up of force, to inanimate matter, which is not capable of this sentiment. *Secondly,* This sentiment of an endeavour to overcome resistance has no known connexion with any event: What follows it we know by experience; but could not know it *a priori.* It must, however, be confessed that the animal nisus, which we experience though it can afford no accurate precise idea of power, enters very much into that vulgar, inaccurate idea, which is formed of it.

and passions is much weaker than that over our ideas; and even the latter authority is circumscribed within very narrow boundaries, or show why the power is deficient in one case, not in another.

Thirdly, This self-command is very different at different times. A man in health possesses more of it than one languishing with sickness. We are more master of our thoughts in the morning than in the evening: Fasting, than after a full meal. Can we give any reason for these variations, except experience? Where then is the power, of which we pretend to be conscious? Is there not here, either in a spiritual or material substance, or both, some secret mechanism or structure of parts, upon which the effect depends, and which, being entirely unknown to us, renders the power or energy of the will equally unknown and incomprehensible?

Volition is surely an act of the mind, with which we are sufficiently acquainted. Reflect upon it. Consider it on all sides. Do you find anything in it like this creative power, by which it raises from nothing a new idea, and with a kind of *Fiat,* imitates the omnipotence of its Maker, if I may be allowed so to speak, who called forth into existence all the various scenes of nature? So far from being conscious of this energy in the will, it requires as certain experience as that of which we are possessed, to convince us that such extraordinary effects do ever result from a simple act of volition.

The generality of mankind never find any difficulty in accounting for the more common and familiar operations of nature—such as the descent of heavy bodies, the growth of plants, the generation of animals, or the nourishment of bodies by food: But suppose that, in all these cases, they perceive the very force or energy of the cause, by which it is connected with its effect, and is for ever infallible in its operation. They acquire, by long habit, such a turn of mind, that, upon the appearance of the cause, they immediately expect with assurance its usual attendant, and hardly conceive it possible that any other event could result from it. It is only on the discovery of extraordinary phenomena, such as earthquakes, pestilence, and prodigies of any kind, that they find themselves at a loss to assign a proper cause, and to explain the manner in which the effect is produced by it. It is usual for men, in such difficulties, to have recourse to some invisible intelligent principle as the Immediate cause of that event which surprises them, and which, they think, cannot be accounted for from the common powers of nature. But philosophers, who carry their scrutiny a little farther, immediately perceive that, even in the most familiar events, the energy of the cause is as unintelligible as in the most unusual, and that we only learn by experience the frequent *Conjunction* of objects, without being ever able to comprehend anything like *Connexion* between them. Here, then, many philosophers think themselves obliged by reason to have recourse, on all occasions, to the same principle, which the vulgar never appeal to but in cases that appear miraculous and supernatural. They acknowledge mind and intelligence to be, not only the ultimate and original cause of all things, but the immediate and sole cause of every event which appears in nature. They pretend that those objects which are commonly denominated *causes,* are in reality nothing but *occasions;* and that the true and direct principle of every effect is not any power or force in nature, but a volition of the Supreme Being, who wills that such particular objects should for ever be conjoined with each other. Instead of saying that one billiard-ball moves another by a force which it has derived from the author of nature, it is the Deity himself, they say, who, by a particular volition, moves the second ball, being determined to this operation by the impulse of the first ball, in consequence of those general laws which he has laid down to himself in the government of the universe. But philosophers advancing still in their inquiries, discover that, as we are totally ignorant of the power on which depends the mutual operation of bodies, we are no less ignorant of that power on which depends the operation of mind on body, or of body on mind; nor are we able, either from our sense or consciousness, to assign the ultimate principle in one case more than in the other. The same ignorance, therefore, reduces them to the same conclusion. They assert that the Deity is the immediate cause of the union between soul and body; and that they are not the organs of sense, which, being agitated by external objects, produce sensations in the mind; but that it is a particular volition of our omnipotent Maker, which excites such a sensation, in consequence of such a motion in the organ. In like manner, it is not any energy in the will that produces local motion in our members: It is God himself, who is pleased to second our will, in itself important, and to command that motion which we erroneously attribute to our own power and efficacy. Nor do philosophers stop at this conclusion. They sometimes extend the same inference to the mind itself, in its internal operations. Our mental vision or conception of ideas is nothing but a revelation made to us by our Maker. When we voluntarily turn our thoughts to any object, and raise up its image in the fancy, it is not the will which creates that idea: It is the universal Creator, who discovers it to the mind, and renders it present to us.

Thus, according to these philosophers, every thing is full of God. Not content with the principle, that nothing exists but by his will, that nothing possesses any power but by his concession: They rob nature, and all created beings, of every power, in order to render their dependence on the Deity still more sensible and immediate. They consider not that, by this theory, they diminish, instead of magnifying, the grandeur of those attributes, which they affect so much to celebrate. It argues surely more power in the Deity to delegate a certain degree of power to inferior creatures, than to produce every thing by his own immediate volition. It argues more wisdom to contrive at first the fabric of the world with such perfect foresight that, of itself, and by its proper operation, it may serve all the purposes of providence, than if the great Creator were obliged every moment to adjust its parts, and animate by his breath all the wheels of that stupendous machine.

But if we would have a more philosophical confutation of this theory, perhaps the two following reflections may suffice.

First, it seems to me that this theory of the universal energy and operation of the Supreme Being is too bold ever to carry conviction with it to a man, sufficiently apprized of the weakness of human reason, and the narrow limits to which it is confined in all its operations. Though the chain of arguments which conduct to it were ever so logical, there must arise a strong suspicion, if not an absolute assurance, that it has carried us quite beyond the reach of our faculties, when it leads to conclusions so extraordinary, and so remote from common life and experience. We are got into fairy land, long ere we have reached the last steps of our theory; and *there* we have no reason to trust our common methods of argument, or to think that our usual analogies and probabilities have any authority. Our line is too short to fathom such immense abysses. And however we may flatter ourselves that we are guided, in every step which we take, by a kind of verisimilitude and experience, we may be assured that this fancied experience has no authority when we thus apply it to subjects that lie entirely out of the sphere of experience. But on this we shall have occasion to touch afterwards.*

Secondly, I cannot perceive any force in the arguments on which this theory is founded. We are ignorant, it is true, of the manner in which bodies operate on each other: Their force or energy is entirely incomprehensible: But are we not equally ignorant of the manner of force by which a mind, even the supreme mind, operates either on

*Section XII.

itself or on body? Whence, I beseech you, do we acquire any idea of it? We have no sentiment or consciousness of this power in ourselves. We have no idea of the Supreme Being but what we learn from reflection on our own faculties. Were our ignorance, therefore, a good reason for rejecting any thing, we should be led into that principle of denying all energy in the Supreme Being as much as in the grossest matter. We surely comprehend as little the operations of one as of the other. Is it more difficult to conceive that motion may arise from impulse than that it may arise from volition? All we know is our profound ignorance in both cases.*

PART II

But to hasten to a conclusion of this argument, which is already drawn out to too great a length: We have sought in vain for an idea of power or necessary connexion in all the sources from which we could suppose it to be derived. It appears that, in single instances of the operation of bodies, we never can, by our utmost scrutiny, discover any thing but one event following another, without being able to comprehend any force or power by which the cause operates, or any connexion between it and its supposed effect. The same difficulty occurs in contemplating the operations of mind on body—where we observe the motion of the latter to follow upon the volition of the former, but are not able to observe or conceive the tie which binds together the motion and volition, or the energy by which the mind produces this effect. The authority of the will over its own faculties and ideas is not a whit more comprehensible: So that, upon the whole, there appears not, throughout all nature, any one instance of connexion which is conceivable by us. All events seem entirely loose and separate. One event follows another; but we never can observe any tie between them. They seem *conjoined,* but never *connected.* And as we can have no idea of any thing which never appeared to our outward sense or inward sentiment, the necessary conclusion *seems* to be that we have no idea of connexion or power at all, and that these words are absolutely without any meaning, when employed either in philosophical reasonings or common life.

But there still remains one method of avoiding this conclusion, and one source which we have not yet examined. When any natural object or event is presented, it is impossible for us, by any sagacity or penetration, to discover, or even conjecture, without experience, what event will result from it, or to carry our foresight beyond that object which is immediately present to the memory and senses. Even after one instance or experiment where we have observed a particular event to follow upon another, we are

---

*I need not examine at length the *vis inertiae* [force of inertia] which is so much talked of in the new philosophy, and which is ascribed to matter. We find by experience, that a body at rest or in motion continues for ever in its present state, till put from it by some new cause; and that a body impelled takes as much motion from the impelling body as it acquires itself. These are facts. When we call this a *vis inertiae,* we only mark these facts, without pretending to have any idea of the inert power; in the same manner as, when we talk of gravity, we mean certain effects without comprehending that active power. It was never the meaning of SIR ISAAC NEWTON to rob second causes of all forces of energy though some of his followers have endeavoured to establish that theory upon his authority. On the contrary, that great philosopher had recourse to an etherial active fluid to explain his universal attraction; though he was so cautious and modest as to allow that it was a mere hypothesis, not to be insisted on, without more experiments. I must confess, that there is something in the fate of opinions a little extraordinary. DESCARTES insinuated that doctrine of the universal and sole efficacy of the Diety, without insisting on it. MALEBRANCHE and other CARTESIANS made it the foundation of all their philosophy. It had, however, no authority in England. LOCKE, CLARKE, and CUDWORTH, never so much as take notice of it, but suppose all along, that matter has a real, though subordinate and derived power. By what means has it become so prevalent among our modern metaphysicians?

not entitled to form a general rule, or foretell what will happen in like cases; it being justly esteemed an unpardonable temerity to judge of the whole course of nature from one single experiment, however accurate or certain. But when one particular species of event has always, in all instances, been conjoined with another, we make no longer any scruple of foretelling one upon the appearance of the other, and of employing that reasoning which can alone assure us of any matter of fact or existence. We then call the one object, *Cause;* the other, *Effect.* We suppose that there is some connexion between them; some power in the one, by which it infallibly produces the other, and operates with the greatest certainty and strongest necessity.

It appears, then, that this idea of a necessary connexion among events arises from a number of similar instances which occur of the constant conjunction of these events; nor can that idea ever be suggested by any one of these instances, surveyed in all possible lights and positions. But there is nothing in a number of instances, different from every single instance, which is supposed to be exactly similar; except only, that after a repetition of similar instances, the mind is carried by habit, upon the appearance of one event, to expect its usual attendant, and to believe that it will exist. This connexion, therefore, which we *feel* in the mind, this customary transition of the imagination from one object to its usual attendant, is the sentiment or impression from which we form the idea of power or necessary connexion. Nothing farther is in the case. Contemplate the subject on all sides; you will never find any other origin of that idea. This is the sole difference between one instance, from which we can never receive the idea of connexion, and a number of similar instances, by which it is suggested. The first time a man saw the communication of motion by impulse, as by the shock of two billiard-balls, he could not pronounce that the one event was *connected:* but only that it was *conjoined* with the other. After he has observed several instances of this nature, he then pronounces them to be *connected.* What alteration has happened to give rise to this new idea of *connexion?* Nothing but that he now *feels* these events to be *connected* in his imagination, and can readily foretell the existence of one from the appearance of the other. When we say, therefore, that one object is connected with another, we mean only that they have acquired a connexion in our thought, and give rise to this inference, by which they become proofs of each other's existence: A conclusion which is somewhat extraordinary, but which seems founded on sufficient evidence. Nor will its evidence be weakened by any general diffidence of the understanding, or sceptical suspicion concerning every conclusion which is new and extraordinary. No conclusions can be more agreeable to scepticism than such as make discoveries concerning the weakness and narrow limits of human reason and capacity.

And what stronger instance can be produced of the surprising ignorance and weakness of the understanding than the present? For surely, if there be any relation among objects which it imports to us to know perfectly, it is that of cause and effect. On this are founded all our reasonings concerning matter of fact or existence. By means of it alone we attain any assurance concerning objects which are removed from the present testimony of our memory and senses. The only immediate utility of all sciences, is to teach us, how to control and regulate future events by their causes. Our thoughts and enquiries are, therefore, every moment, employed about this relation: Yet so imperfect are the ideas which we form concerning it, that it is impossible to give any just definition of cause, except what is drawn from something extraneous and foreign to it. Similar objects are always conjoined with similar. Of this we have experience. Suitably to this experience, therefore, we may define a cause to be *an object, followed by another, and where all the objects similar to the first are followed by objects similar to the second.* Or in other words *where, if the first object had not been, the second never had existed.* The appearance of a cause always conveys the mind, by a customary transition, to the idea of the effect. Of this also we have experience. We may, therefore, suitably to this experience, form another definition of cause, and call it, *an object followed by another and whose appearance always conveys the thought to that other.* But though both these definitions be drawn from circumstances foreign to the cause, we cannot remedy this inconvenience, or attain any more perfect definition, which may point out that circumstance in the cause, which gives it a connexion with its effect. We have no idea of this connexion, nor even any distinct notion what it is we desire to know, when we endeavour at a conception of it. We say, for instance, that the vibration of this string is the cause of this particular sound. But what do we mean by that affirmation? We either mean *that this vibration is followed by this sound, and that all similar vibrations have been followed by similar sounds: Or,* that this vibration is followed by this sound, and that upon the appearance of one the mind anticipates the senses, and forms immediately an idea of the other. We may consider the relation of cause and effect in either of these two lights; but beyond these, we have no idea of it.*

To recapitulate, therefore, the reasonings of this section: Every idea is copied from some preceding impression or sentiment; and where we cannot find any impression, we may be certain that there is no idea. In all single instances of the operation of bodies or minds, there is nothing that produces any impression, nor consequently can suggest any idea of power or necessary connexion. But when many uniform instances appear, and the same object is always followed by the same event; we then begin to entertain the notion of cause and connexion. We then *feel* a new sentiment or impression, to wit, a customary connexion in the thought or imagination between one object and its usual attendant; and this sentiment is the original of that idea which we seek for. For as this idea arises from a number of similar instances, and not from any single instance, it must arise from that circumstance, in which the number of instances differ from every individual instance. But this customary connexion or transition of the imagination is the only circumstance in which they differ. In every other particular they are alike. The first instance which we saw of motion communicated by the shock of two billiard-balls (to return to this obvious illustration) is exactly similar to any instance that may, at present, occur to us; except only, that we could not, at first, *infer* one event from the other; which we are enabled to do at present, after so long a course of uniform experience. I know not whether the reader will readily apprehend this reasoning. I am afraid that, should I mul-

---

*According to these explanations and definitions, the idea of *power* is relative as much as that of *cause;* and both have a reference to an effect, or some other event constantly conjoined with the former. When we consider the *unknown* circumstance of an object, by which the degree of quantity of its effect is fixed and determined, we call that its power: And accordingly, it is allowed by all philosophers, that the effect is the measure of the power. But if they had any idea of power, as it is in itself, why could not they measure it in itself? The dispute whether the force of a body in motion be as its velocity, or the square of its velocity; this dispute, I say, need not be decided by comparing its effects in equal or unequal times; but by a direct mensuration and comparison.

As to the frequent use of the words, Force, Power, Energy, &c., which every where occur in common conversation, as well as in philosophy; that is no proof, that we are acquainted, in any instance, with the connecting principle between cause and effect or can account ultimately for the production of one thing to another. These words, as commonly used, have very loose meanings annexed to them; and their ideas in motion without the sentiment of a *nisus* or endeavour; and every animal has a sentiment or feeling from the stroke or blow of an external object, that is in motion. These sensations, which are merely animal, and from which we can *a priori* draw no inference, we are apt to transfer to inanimate objects, and to suppose, that they have some such feelings, whenever they transfer or receive motion. With regard to energies, which are exerted, without our annexing to them any idea of communicated motion, we consider only the constant experienced conjunction of the events; and as we *feel* a customary connexion between the ideas, we transfer that feeling to the objects; as nothing is more usual than to apply to external bodies every internal sensation with they occasion.

tiply words about it, or throw it into a greater variety of lights, it would only become more obscure and intricate. In all abstract reasonings there is one point of view which, if we can happily hit, we shall go farther towards illustrating the subject than by all the eloquence in the world. This point of view we should endeavour to reach, and reserve the flowers of rhetoric for subjects which are more adapted to them.

Section VIII. Of Liberty and Necessity

Part I

It might reasonably be expected in questions which have been canvassed and disputed with great eagerness, since the first origin of science and philosophy, that the meaning of all the terms, at least, should have been agreed upon among the disputants; and our enquiries, in the course of two thousand years, been able to pass from words to the true and real subject of the controversy. For how easy may it seem to give exact definitions of the terms employed in reasoning, and make these definitions, not the mere sound of words, the object of future scrutiny and examination? But if we consider the matter more narrowly, we shall be apt to draw a quite opposite conclusion. From this circumstance alone, that a controversy has been long kept on foot, and remains still undecided, we may presume that there is some ambiguity in the expression, and that the disputants affix different ideas to the terms employed in the controversy. For as the faculties of the mind are supposed to be naturally alike in every individual; otherwise nothing could be more fruitless than to reason or dispute together; it were impossible, if men affix the same ideas to their terms, that they could so long form different opinions of the same subject; especially when they communicate their views, and each party turn themselves on all sides, in search of arguments which may give them the victory over their antagonists. It is true, if men attempt the discussion of questions which lie entirely beyond the reach of human capacity, such as those concerning the origin of worlds, or the economy of the intellectual system or region of spirits, they may long beat the air in their fruitless contests, and never arrive at any determinate conclusion. But if the question regard any subject of common life and experience, nothing, one would think, could preserve the dispute so long undecided but some ambiguous expressions, which keep the antagonists still at a distance, and hinder them from grappling with each other.

This has been the case in the long disputed question concerning liberty and necessity; and to so remarkable a degree that, if I be not much mistaken, we shall find, that all mankind, both learned and ignorant, have always been of the same opinion with regard to this subject, and that a few intelligible definitions would immediately have put an end to the whole controversy. I own that this dispute has been so much canvassed on all hands, and has led philosophers into such a labyrinth of obscure sophistry, that it is no wonder, if a sensible reader indulge his ease so far as to turn a deaf ear to the proposal of such a question, from which he can expect neither instruction nor entertainment. But the state of the argument here proposed may, perhaps, serve to renew his attention; as it has more novelty, promises at least some decision of the controversy, and will not much disturb his ease by any intricate or obscure reasoning.

I hope, therefore, to make it appear that all men have ever agreed in the doctrine both of necessity and of liberty, according to any reasonable sense, which can be put on these terms; and that the whole controversy has hitherto turned merely upon words. We shall begin with examining the doctrine of necessity.

It is universally allowed that matter, in all its operations, is actuated by a necessary force, and that every natural effect is so precisely determined by the energy of its cause that no other effect, in such particular circumstances, could possibly have resulted from it. The degree and direction of every motion is, by the laws of nature, prescribed with such exactness that a living creature may as soon arise from the shock of two bodies as motion in any other degree or direction than what is actually produced by it. Would we, therefore, form a just and precise idea of *necessity* we must consider whence that idea arises when we apply it to the operation of bodies.

It seems evident that, if all the scenes of nature were continually shifted in such a manner that no two events bore any resemblance to each other, but every object was entirely new, without any similitude to whatever had been seen before, we should never, in that case, have attained the least idea of necessity, or of a connexion among these objects. We might say, upon such a supposition, that one object or event has followed another; not that one was produced by the other. The relation of cause and effect must be utterly unknown to mankind. Inference and reasoning concerning the operations of nature would, from that moment, be at an end; and the memory and senses remain the only canals, by which the knowledge of any real existence could possibly have access to the mind. Our idea, therefore, of necessity and causation arises entirely from the uniformity observable in the operations of nature, where similar objects are constantly conjoined together, and the mind is determined by custom to infer the one from the appearance of the other. These two circumstances form the whole of that necessity, which we ascribe to matter. Beyond the constant conjunction of similar objects, and the consequent *inference* from one to the other, we have no notion of any necessity or connexion.

If it appear, therefore, that all mankind have ever allowed, without any doubt or hesitation, that these two circumstances take place in the voluntary actions of men, and in the operations of mind; it must follow, that all mankind have ever agreed in the doctrine of necessity, and that they have hitherto disputed, merely for not understanding each other.

As to the first circumstance, the constant and regular conjunction of similar events, we may possibly satisfy ourselves by the following considerations. It is universally acknowledged that there is a great uniformity among the actions of men, in all nations and ages, and that human nature remains still the same, in its principles and operations. The same motives always produce the same actions: The same events follow from the same causes. Ambition, avarice, self-love, vanity, friendship, generosity, public spirit: these passions, mixed in various degrees, and distributed through society, have been, from the beginning of the world, and still are, the source of all the actions and enterprises, which have ever been observed among mankind. Would you know the sentiments, inclinations, and course of life of the Greeks and Romans? Study well the temper and actions of the French and English: You cannot be much mistaken in transferring to the former *most* of the observations which you have made with regard to the latter. Mankind are so much the same, in all times and places, that history informs us of nothing new or strange in this particular. Its chief use is only to discover the constant and universal principles of human nature, by showing men in all varieties of circumstances and situations, and furnishing us with materials from which we may form our observations and become acquainted with the regular springs of human action and behaviour. These records of wars, intrigues, factions, and revolutions, are so many collections of experiments, by which the politician or moral philosopher fixes the principles of his science, in the same manner as the physician or natural philosopher becomes acquainted with the nature of plants, minerals, and other external objects, by the experiments which he forms concerning them. Nor are the earth, water, and other elements, examined by Aristotle, and Hippocrates, more like to those which at present lie under our observation than the men described by Polybius and Tacitus are to those who now govern the world.

Should a traveller, returning from a far country, bring us an account of men, wholly different from any with whom we were ever acquainted; men, who were entirely divested of avarice, ambition, or revenge; who knew no pleasure but friendship, generosity, and public spirit; we should immediately, from these circumstances, detect the falsehood, and prove him a liar, with the same certainty as if he had stuffed his narration with stories of centaurs and dragons, miracles and prodigies. And if we would explode any forgery in history, we cannot make use of a more convincing argument, than to prove, that the actions ascribed to any person are directly contrary to the course of nature, and that no human motives, in such circumstances, could ever induce him to such a conduct. The veracity of Quintus Curtius is as much to be suspected, when he describes the supernatural courage of Alexander, by which he was hurried on singly to attack multitudes, as when he describes his supernatural force and activity, by which he was able to resist them. So readily and universally do we acknowledge a uniformity in human motives and actions as well as in the operations of body.

Hence likewise the benefit of that experience, acquired by long life and a variety of business and company, in order to instruct us in the principles of human nature, and regulate our future conduct, as well as speculation. By means of this guide, we mount up to the knowledge of men's inclinations and motives, from their actions, expressions, and even gestures; and again descend to the interpretation of their actions from our knowledge of their motives and inclinations. The general observations treasured up by a course of experience, give us the clue of human nature, and teach us to unravel all its intricacies. Pretexts and appearances no longer deceive us. Public declarations pass for the specious colouring of a cause. And though virtue and honour be allowed their proper weight and authority, that perfect disinterestedness, so often pretended to, is never expected in multitudes and parties; seldom in their leaders; and scarcely even in individuals of any rank or station. But were there no uniformity in human actions, and were every experiment which we could form of this kind irregular and anomalous, it were impossible to collect any general observations concerning mankind; and no experience, however accurately digested by reflection, would ever serve to any purpose. Why is the aged husbandman more skillful in his calling than the young beginner but because there is a certain uniformity in the operation of the sun, rain, and earth towards the production of vegetables; and experience teaches the old practitioner the rules by which this operation is governed and directed.

We must not, however, expect that this uniformity of human actions should be carried to such a length as that all men, in the same circumstances, will always act precisely in the same manner, without making any allowance for the diversity of characters, prejudices, and opinions. Such a uniformity in every particular, is found in no part of nature. On the contrary, from observing the variety of conduct in different men, we are enabled to form a greater variety of maxims, which still suppose a degree of uniformity and regularity.

Are the manners of men different in different ages and countries? We learn thence the great force of custom and education, which mould the human mind from its infancy and form it into a fixed and established character. Is the behaviour and conduct of the one sex very unlike that of the other? Is it thence we become acquainted with the different characters which nature has impressed upon the sexes, and which she preserves with constancy and regularity? Are the actions of the same person much diversified in the different periods of his life, from infancy to old age? This affords room for many general observations concerning the gradual change of our sentiments and inclinations, and the different maxims which prevail in the different ages of human creatures. Even the characters, which are peculiar to each individual, have a uniformity in their influence; otherwise our acquaintance with the persons and our observation of their conduct could never teach us their dispositions, or serve to direct our behaviour with regard to them.

I grant it possible to find some actions, which seem to have no regular connexion with any known motives, and are exceptions to all the measures of conduct which have ever been established for the government of men. But if we would willingly know what judgement should be formed of such irregular and extraordinary actions, we may consider the sentiments commonly entertained with regard to those irregular events which appear in the course of nature, and the operations of external objects. All causes are not conjoined to their usual effects with like uniformity. An artificer, who handles only dead matter, may be disappointed of his aim, as well as the politician, who directs the conduct of sensible and intelligent agents.

The vulgar, who take things according to their first appearance, attribute the uncertainty of events to such an uncertainty in the causes as makes the latter often fail of their usual influence; though they meet with no impediment in their operation. But philosophers, observing that, almost in every part of nature, there is contained a vast variety of springs and principles, which are hid, by reason of their minuteness or remoteness, find, that it is at least possible the contrariety of events may not proceed from any contingency in the cause, but from the secret operation of contrary causes. This possibility is converted into certainty by farther observation, when they remark that, upon an exact scrutiny, a contrariety of effects always betrays a contrariety of causes, and proceeds from their mutual opposition. A peasant can give no better reason for the stopping of any clock or watch than to say that it does not commonly go right: But an artist easily perceives that the same force in the spring or pendulum has always the same influence on the wheels; but fails of its usual effect, perhaps by reason of a grain of dust, which puts a stop to the whole movement. From the observation of several parallel instances, philosophers form a maxim that the connexion between all causes and effects is equally necessary, and that its seeming uncertainty in some instances proceeds from the secret opposition of contrary causes.

Thus, for instance, in the human body, when the usual symptoms of health or sickness disappoint our expectation; when medicines operate not with their wonted powers; when irregular events follow from any particular cause; the philosopher and physician are not surprised at the matter, nor are ever tempted to deny, in general, the necessity and uniformity of those principles by which the animal economy is conducted. They know that a human body is a mighty complicated machine: That many secret powers lurk in it, which are altogether beyond our comprehension: That to us it must often appear very uncertain in its operations: And that therefore the irregular events, which outwardly discover themselves, can be no proof that the laws of nature are not observed with the greatest regularity in its internal operations and government.

The philosopher, if he be consistent, must apply the same reasoning to the actions and volitions of intelligent agents. The most irregular and unexpected resolutions of men may frequently be accounted for by those who know every particular circumstance of their character and situation. A person of an obliging disposition gives a peevish answer: But he has the toothache, or has not dined. A stupid fellow discovers an uncommon alacrity in his carriage: But he has met with a sudden piece of good fortune. Or even when an action, as sometimes happens, cannot be particularly accounted for, either by the person himself or by others; we know, in general, that the characters of men are, to a certain degree, inconstant and irregular. This is, in a manner, the constant character of human nature; though it be applicable, in a more particular manner, to some persons who have no fixed rule for their conduct, but proceed in a continued course of caprice and inconstancy. The internal principles and motives may operate in a uniform manner, notwithstanding these seeming irregularities; in the same manner as the winds, rain, clouds, and other variations of the weather are supposed to be governed by steady principles; though not easily discoverable by human sagacity and enquiry.

Thus it appears, not only that the conjunction between motives and voluntary actions is as regular and uniform as that between the cause and effect in any part of nature; but also that this regular conjunction has been universally acknowledged among mankind, and has never been the subject of dispute, either in philosophy or common life. Now, as it is from past experience that we draw all inferences concerning the future, and as we conclude that objects will always be conjoined together which we find to have always been conjoined; it may seem superfluous to prove that this experienced uniformity in human actions is a source whence we draw *inferences* concerning them. But in order to throw the argument into a greater variety of lights we shall also insist, though briefly, on this latter topic.

The mutual dependence of men is so great in all societies that scarce any human action is entirely complete in itself, or is performed without some reference to the actions of others, which are requisite to make it answer fully the intention of the agent. The poorest artificer, who labours alone, expects at least the protection of the magistrate, to ensure him the enjoyment of the fruits of his labour. He also expects that, when he carries his goods to market, and offers them at a reasonable price, he shall find purchasers, and shall be able, by the money he acquires, to engage others to supply him with those commodities which are requisite for his subsistence. In proportion as men extend their dealings, and render their intercourse with others more complicated, they always comprehend, in their schemes of life, a greater variety of voluntary actions, which they expect, from the proper motives, to co-operate with their own. In all these conclusions they take their measures from past experience, in the same manner as in their reasonings concerning external objects; and firmly believe that men, as well as all the elements, are to continue, in their operations, the same that they have ever found them. A manufacturer reckons upon the labour of his servants for the execution of any work as much as upon the tools which he employs, and would be equally surprised were his expectations disappointed. In short, this experimental inference and reasoning concerning the actions of others enters so much into human life, that no man, while awake, is ever a moment without employing it. Have we not reason, therefore, to affirm that all mankind have always agreed in the doctrine of necessity according to the foregoing definition and explication of it?

Nor have philosophers ever entertained a different opinion from the people in this particular. For, not to mention that almost every action of their life supposes that opinion, there are even few of the speculative parts of learning to which it is not essential. What would become of *history,* had we not a dependence on the veracity of the historian according to the experience which we have had of mankind? How could *politics* be a science, if laws and forms of government had not a uniform influence upon society? Where would be the foundation of *morals,* if particular characters had no certain or determinate power to produce particular sentiments, and if these sentiments had no constant operation on actions? And with what pretence could we employ our *criticism* upon any poet or polite author, if we could not pronounce the conduct and sentiments of his actors either natural or unnatural to such characters, and in such circumstances? It seems almost impossible, therefore, to engage either in science or action of any kind without acknowledging the doctrine of necessity, and this *inference* from motive to voluntary actions, from characters to conduct.

And indeed, when we consider how aptly *natural* and *moral* evidence link together, and form only one chain of argument, we shall make no scruple to allow that they are of the same nature, and derived from the same principles. A prisoner who has neither money nor interest, discovers the impossibility of his escape, as well when he considers the obstinacy of the gaoler, as the walls and bars with which he is surrounded; and, in all attempts for his freedom, chooses rather to work upon the stone and iron of the one, than upon the inflexible nature of the other. The same prisoner, when conducted to the scaffold, foresees his death as certainly from the constancy and fidelity of his guards, as from the operation of the axe or wheel. His mind runs along a certain train of ideas: The refusal of the soldiers to consent to his escape; the action of the executioner; the separation of the head and body; bleeding, convulsive motions, and death. Here is a connected chain of natural causes and voluntary actions; but the mind feels no difference between them in passing from one link to another: Nor is less certain of the future event than if it were connected with the objects present to the memory or senses, by a train of causes, cemented together by what we are pleased to call a *physical* necessity. The same experienced union has the same effect on the mind, whether the united objects be motives, volition, and actions; or figure and motion. We may change the name of things; but their nature and their operation on the understanding never change.

Were a man, whom I know to be honest and opulent, and with whom I live in intimate friendship, to come into my house, where I am surrounded with my servants, I rest assured that he is not to stab me before he leaves it in order to rob me of my silver standish; and I no more suspect this event than the falling of the house itself, which is new, and solidly built and founded.—*But he may have been seized with a sudden and unknown frenzy.*—So may a sudden earthquake arise, and shake and tumble my house about my ears. I shall therefore change the suppositions. I shall say that I know with certainty that he is not to put his hand into the fire and hold it there till it be consumed: And this event I think I can foretell with the same assurance, as that, if he throw himself out at the window, and meet with no obstruction, he will not remain a moment suspended in the air. No suspicion of an unknown frenzy can give the least possibility to the former event, which is so contrary to all the known principles of human nature. A man who at noon leaves his purse full of gold on the pavement at Charing-Cross, may as well expect that it will fly away like a feather, as that he will find it untouched an hour after. Above one half of human reasonings contain inferences of a similar nature, attended with more or less degrees of certainty proportioned to our experience of the usual conduct of mankind in such particular situations.

I have frequently considered, what could possibly be the reason why all mankind, though they have ever, without hesitation, acknowledged the doctrine of necessity in their whole practice and reasoning, have yet not discovered such a reluctance to acknowledge it in words, and have rather shown a propensity, in all ages, to profess the contrary opinion. The matter, I think, may be accounted for after the following manner. If we examine the operations of body, and the production of effects from their causes, we shall find that all our faculties can never carry us farther in our knowledge of this relation than barely to observe that particular objects are *constantly conjoined* together, and that the mind is carried, by a *customary transition,* from the appearance of one to the belief of the other. But though this conclusion concerning human ignorance be the result of the strictest scrutiny of this subject, men still entertain a strong propensity to believe that they penetrate farther into the powers of nature, and perceive something like a necessary connexion between the cause and the effect. When again they turn their reflections towards the operations of their own minds, and *feel* no such connexion of the motive and the action; they are thence apt to suppose, that there is a difference between the effects which result from material force, and those which arise from thought and intelligence. But being once convinced that we know nothing farther of causation of any kind than merely the *constant conjunction* of objects, and the consequent *inference* of the mind from one to another, and finding that these two circumstances are universally allowed to have place in voluntary actions; we may be more easily led to own the same necessity common to all causes. And though this reasoning may contradict the systems of many philosophers, in ascribing necessity to the determinations of the will, we shall find, upon reflection, that they dissent from it in words only, not in their real sentiment. Necessity, according to the sense in which it is here taken, has never yet been rejected, nor can ever, I think, be rejected by any philosopher. It may only, perhaps, be pretended that the mind can perceive, in the operations of matter, some farther connexion between the cause and effect; and connexion that has not place in voluntary actions of intelligent beings. Now whether it be so or not, can only appear upon examination; and it is incumbent on these philosophers to make good their assertion, by defining or describing that necessity, and pointing it out to us in the operations of material causes.

It would seem, indeed, that men begin at the wrong end of this question concerning liberty and necessity, when they enter upon it by examining the faculties of the soul, the influence of the understanding, and the operations of the will. Let them first discuss a more simple question, namely, the operations of body and of brute unintelligent matter; and try whether they can there form any idea of causation and necessity, except that of a constant conjunction of objects, and subsequent inference of the mind from one to another. If these circumstances form, in reality, the whole of that necessity, which we conceive in matter, and if these circumstances be also universally acknowledged to take place in the operations of the mind, the dispute is at an end; at least, must be owned to be thenceforth merely verbal. But as long as we will rashly suppose, that we have some farther idea of necessity and causation in the operations of external objects; at the same time, that we can find nothing farther in the voluntary actions of the mind; there is no possibility of bringing the question to any determinate issue, while we proceed upon so erroneous a supposition. The only method of undeceiving us is to mount up higher; to examine the narrow extent of science when applied to material causes; and to convince ourselves that all we know of them is the constant conjunction and inference above mentioned. We may, perhaps, find that it is with difficulty we are induced to fix such narrow limits to human understanding: But we can afterwards find no difficulty when we come to apply this doctrine to the actions of the will. For as it is evident that these have a regular conjunction with motives and circumstances and characters, and as we always draw inferences from one to the other, we must be obliged to acknowledge in words that necessity, which we have already avowed, in every deliberation of our lives, and in every step of our conduct and behaviour.*

But to proceed in this reconciling project with regard to the question of liberty and necessity; the most contentious question of metaphysics, the most contentious science; it will not require many words to prove, that all mankind have ever agreed in the doctrine of liberty as well as in that of necessity, and that the whole dispute, in this respect also, has been hitherto merely verbal. For what is meant by liberty, when applied to voluntary actions? We cannot surely mean that actions have so little connexion with motives, inclinations, and circumstances, that one does not follow with a certain degree of uniformity from the other, and that one affords no inference by which we can conclude the existence of the other. For these are plain and acknowledged matters of fact. By liberty, then, we can only mean *a power of acting or not acting, according to the determinations of the will;* that is, if we choose to remain at rest, we may; if we choose to move, we also may. Now this hypothetical liberty is universally allowed to belong to every one who is not a prisoner and in chains. Here, then, is no subject of dispute.

Whatever definition we may give of liberty, we should be careful to observe two requisite circumstances; *first,* that it be consistent with plain matter of fact; *secondly,* that it be consistent with itself. If we observe these circumstances, and render our definition intelligible, I am persuaded that all mankind will be found of one opinion with regard to it.

It is universally allowed that nothing exists without a cause of its existence, and that chance, when strictly examined, is a mere negative word, and means not any real power which has anywhere a being in nature. But it is pretended that some causes are necessary, some not necessary. Here then is the advantage of definitions. Let any one *define* a cause, without comprehending, as a part of the definition, a *necessary connexion* with its effect; and let him show distinctly the origin of the idea, expressed by the definition; and I shall readily give up the whole controversy. But if the foregoing explication of the matter be received, this must be absolutely impracticable. Had not objects a regular conjunction with each other, we should never have entertained any notion of

---

*The prevalence of the doctrine of liberty may be accounted for, from another cause viz. a false sensation or seeming experience which we have, or may have, of liberty or indifference, in many of our actions. The necessity of any action, whether of matter or of mind, is not, properly speaking, a quality in the agent, but in any thinking or intelligent being, who may consider the action; and it consists chiefly in the determination of his thoughts to infer the existence of that action from some preceding objects; as liberty, when opposed to necessity, is nothing but the want of that determination, and a certain looseness or indifference, which we feel, in passing or not passing, from the idea of one object to that of any succeeding one. Now we may observe, that, though, in *reflecting* on human actions, we seldom feel such a looseness, or indifference, but are commonly able to infer them with considerable certainty from their motives, and from the dispositions of the agent; yet it frequently happens, that, in *performing* the actions themselves, we are sensible of something like it: And as all resembling objects are readily taken for each other, this has been employed as a demonstrative and even intuitive proof of human liberty. We feel, that our actions are subject to our will, on most occasions; and imagine we feel, that the will itself is subject to nothing, because, when by a denial of it we are provoked to try, we feel, that it moves easily every way, and produces an image of itself (or a *Velleïty,* as it is called in the schools) even on that side, on which it did not settle. This image, or faint motion, we persuade ourselves, could, at that time, have been completed into the thing itself; because, should that be denied, we find, upon a second trial, that, at present it can. We consider not that the fantastical desire of showing liberty, is here the motive of our actions. And it seems certain, that, however, we may imagine we feel a liberty within ourselves, a spectator can commonly infer our actions from our motives and character, and even where he cannot, he concludes in general, that he might, were he perfectly acquainted with every circumstance of our situation and temper, and the most secret springs of our complexion and disposition. Now this is the very essence of necessity, according to the foregoing doctrine.

cause and effect; and this regular conjunction produces that inference of the understanding, which is the only connexion, that we can have any comprehension of. Whoever attempts a definition of cause, exclusive of these circumstances, will be obliged either to employ unintelligible terms or such as are synonymous to the term which he endeavours to define.* And if the definition above mentioned be admitted; liberty, when opposed to necessity, not to constraint, is the same thing with chance; which is universally allowed to have no existence.

PART II

There is no method of reasoning more common, and yet none more blameable, than, in philosophical disputes, to endeavour the refutation of any hypothesis, by a pretence of its dangerous consequences to religion and morality. When any opinion leads to absurdities, it is certainly false; but it is not certain that an opinion is false, because it is of dangerous consequence. Such topics, therefore, ought entirely to be forborne; as serving nothing to the discovery of truth, but only to make the person of an antagonist odious. This I observe in general, without pretending to draw any advantage from it. I frankly submit to an examination of this kind, and shall venture to affirm that the doctrines, both of necessity and of liberty, as above explained, are not only consistent with morality, but are absolutely essential to its support.

Necessity may be defined two ways, conformably to the two definitions of *cause,* of which it makes an essential part. It consists either in the constant conjunction of like objects, or in the inference of the understanding from one object to another. Now necessity, in both these senses, (which, indeed, are at bottom the same) has universally, though tacitly, in the schools, in the pulpit, and in common life, been allowed to belong to the will of man; and no one has ever pretended to deny that we can draw inferences concerning human actions, and that those inferences are founded on the experienced union of like actions, with like motives, inclinations, and circumstances. The only particular in which any one can differ, is, that either, perhaps, he will refuse to give the name of necessity to this property of human actions: But as long as the meaning is understood, I hope the word can do no harm: Or that he will maintain it possible to discover something farther in the operations of matter. But this, it must be acknowledged, can be of no consequence to morality or religion, whatever it may be to natural philosophy or metaphysics. We may here be mistaken in asserting that there is no idea of any other necessity or connexion in the actions of body: But surely we ascribe nothing to the actions of the mind, but what everyone does, and must readily allow of. We change no circumstance in the received orthodox system with regard to the will, but only in that with regard to material objects and causes. Nothing, therefore, can be more innocent, at least, than this doctrine.

All laws being founded on rewards and punishments, it is supposed as a fundamental principle, that these motives have a regular and uniform influence on the mind, and both produce the good and prevent the evil actions. We may give to this influence what name we please; but, as it is usually conjoined with the action, it must be esteemed

---

*Thus, if a cause be defined, *that which produces any thing;* it is easy to observe, that *producing* is synonymous to *causing.* In like manner, if a cause be defined, *that by which any thing exists;* this is liable to the same objection. For what is meant by these words, *by which?* Had it been said, that a cause is *that* after which *any thing constantly exists;* we should have understood the terms. For this is, indeed, all we know of the matter. And this constancy forms the very essence of necessity, nor have we any other idea of it.

a *cause,* and be looked upon as an instance of that necessity, which we would here establish.

The only proper object of hatred or vengeance is a person or creature, endowed with thought and consciousness; and when any criminal or injurious actions excite that passion, it is only by their relation to the person, or connexion with him. Actions are, by their very nature, temporary and perishing; and where they proceed not from some *cause* in the character and disposition of the person who performed them, they can neither redound to his honour, if good; not infamy, if evil. The actions themselves may be blameable; they may be contrary to all the rules of morality and religion: But the person is not answerable for them; and as they proceeded from nothing in him that is durable and constant, and leave nothing of that nature behind them, it is impossible he can, upon their account, become the object of punishment or vengeance. According to the principle, therefore, which denies necessity, and consequently causes, a man is as pure and untainted, after having committed the most horrid crime, as at the first moment of his birth, nor is his character anywise concerned in his actions, since they are not derived from it, and the wickedness of the one can never be used as a proof of the depravity of the other.

Men are not blamed for such actions as they perform ignorantly and casually, whatever may be the consequences. Why? but because the principles of these actions are only momentary, and terminate in them alone. Men are less blamed for such actions as they perform hastily and unpremeditately than for such as proceed from deliberation. For what reason? but because a hasty temper, though a constant cause or principle in the mind, operates only by intervals, and infects not the whole character. Again, repentance wipes off every crime, if attended with a reformation of life and manners. How is this to be accounted for? but by asserting that actions render a person criminal merely as they are proofs of criminal principles in the mind; and when, by an alteration of these principles, they cease to be just proofs, they likewise cease to be criminal. But, except upon the doctrine of necessity, they never were just proofs, and consequently never were criminal.

It will be equally easy to prove, and from the same arguments, that *liberty,* according to that definition above mentioned, in which all men agree, is also essential to morality, and that no human actions, where it is wanting, are susceptible of any moral qualities, or can be the objects either of approbation or dislike. For as actions are objects of our moral sentiment, so far only as they are indications of the internal character, passions, and affections; it is impossible that they can give rise either to praise or blame, where they proceed not from these principles, but are derived altogether from external violence.

I pretend not to have obviated or removed all objections to this theory, with regard to necessity and liberty. I can foresee other objections, derived from topics which have not here been treated of. It may be said, for instance, that, if voluntary actions be subjected to the same laws of necessity with the operations of matter, there is a continued chain of necessary causes, pre-ordained and pre-determined, reaching from the original cause of all to every single volition of every human creature. No contingency anywhere in the universe; no indifference; no liberty. While we act, we are, at the same time, acted upon. The ultimate Author of all our volitions is the Creator of the world, who first bestowed motion on this immense machine, and placed all beings in that particular position, whence every subsequent event, by an inevitable necessity, must result. Human actions, therefore, either can have no moral turpitude at all, as proceeding from so good a cause; or if they have any turpitude, they must involve our Creator in the same guilt, while he is acknowledged to be their ultimate cause and author. For as a man, who fired a mine, is answerable for all the consequences whether the train he employed be long or short; so wherever a continued chain of necessary causes is fixed, that Being, either finite or infinite, who produces the first, is likewise the author of all the rest, and must both bear the blame and acquire the praise which belong to them. Our clear and unalterable ideas of morality establish this rule, upon unquestionable reasons, when we examine the consequences of any human action; and these reasons must still have greater force when applied to the volitions and intentions of a Being infinitely wise and powerful. Ignorance or impotence may be pleaded for so limited a creature as man; but those imperfections have no place in our Creator. He foresaw, he ordained, he intended all those actions of men, which we so rashly pronounce criminal. And we must therefore conclude, either that they are not criminal, or that the Deity, not man, is accountable for them. But as either of these positions is absurd and impious, it follows, that the doctrine from which they are deduced cannot possibly be true, as being liable to all the same objections. An absurd consequence, if necessary, proves the original doctrine to be absurd in the same manner as criminal actions render criminal the original cause, if the connexion between them be necessary and inevitable.

This objection consists of two parts, which we shall examine separately; *First,* that, if human actions can be traced up, by a necessary chain, to the Deity, they can never be criminal; on account of the infinite perfection of that Being from whom they are derived, and who can intend nothing but what is altogether good and laudable. Or, *Secondly,* if they be criminal, we must retract the attribute of perfection, which we ascribe to the Deity, and must acknowledge him to be the ultimate author of guilt and moral turpitude in all his creatures.

The answer to the first objection seems obvious and convincing. There are many philosophers who, after an exact scrutiny of all the phenomena of nature, conclude, that the WHOLE, considered as one system is, in every period of its existence, ordered with perfect benevolence; and that the utmost possible happiness will, in the end, result to all created beings, without any mixture of positive or absolute ill or misery. Every physical ill, say they, makes an essential part of this benevolent system, and could not possibly be removed, even by the Deity himself, considered as a wise agent, without giving entrance to greater ill, or excluding greater good, which will result from it. From this theory, some philosophers, and the ancient *Stoics* among the rest, derived a topic of consolation under all afflictions, while they taught their pupils that those ills under which they laboured were, in reality, goods to the universe; and that to an enlarged view, which could comprehend the whole system of nature, every event became an object of joy and exultation. But though this topic be specious and sublime, it was soon found in practice weak and ineffectual. You would surely more irritate than appease a man lying under the racking pains of the gout by preaching up to him the rectitude of those general laws, which produced the malignant humours in his body, and led them through the proper canals, to the sinews and nerves, where they now excite such acute torments. These enlarged views may, for a moment, please the imagination of a speculative man, who is placed in ease and security; but neither can they dwell with constancy on his mind, even though undisturbed by the emotions of pain or passion; much less can they maintain their ground when attacked by such powerful antagonists. The affections take a narrower and more natural survey of their object; and by an economy, more suitable to the infirmity of human minds, regard alone the beings around us, and are actuated by such events as appear good or ill to the private system.

The case is the same with *moral* as with *physical* ill. It cannot reasonably be supposed, that those remote considerations, which are found of so little efficacy with regard to one, will have a more powerful influence with regard to the other. The mind of man is so formed by nature that, upon the appearance of certain characters, dispositions, and actions, it immediately feels the sentiment of approbation or blame; nor are there any emotions more essential to its frame and constitution. The characters which engage our approbation are chiefly such as contribute to the peace and security of human society; as the characters which excite blame are chiefly such as tend to public detriment and disturbance: Whence it may reasonably be presumed, that the moral sentiments arise, either mediately or immediately, from a reflection of these opposite interests. What though philosophical meditations establish a different opinion or conjecture; that everything is right with regard to the WHOLE, and that the qualities, which disturb society, are, in the main, as beneficial, and are as suitable to the primary intention of nature as those which more directly promote its happiness and welfare? Are such remote and uncertain speculations able to counterbalance the sentiments which arise from the natural and immediate view of the objects? A man who is robbed of a considerable sum; does he find his vexation for the loss anywise diminished by these sublime reflections? Why then should his moral resentment against the crime be supposed incompatible with them? Or why should not the acknowledgment of a real distinction between vice and virtue be reconcileable to all speculative systems of philosophy, as well as that of a real distinction between personal beauty and deformity? Both these distinctions are founded in the natural sentiments of the human mind: And these sentiments are not to be controlled or altered by any philosophical theory or speculation whatsoever.

The *second* objection admits not of so easy and satisfactory an answer; nor is it possible to explain distinctly, how the Deity can be the mediate cause of all the actions of men, without being the author of sin and moral turpitude. These are mysteries, which mere natural and unassisted reason is very unfit to handle; and whatever system she embraces, she must find herself involved in inextricable difficulties, and even contradictions, at every step which she takes with regard to such subjects. To reconcile the indifference and contingency of human actions with prescience; or to defend absolute decrees, and yet free the Deity from being the author of sin, has been found hitherto to exceed all the power of philosophy. Happy, if she be thence sensible of her temerity, when she pries into these sublime mysteries; and leaving a scene so full of obscurities and perplexities, return, with suitable modesty, to her true and proper province, the examination of common life; where she will find difficulties enough to employ her enquiries, without launching into so boundless an ocean of doubt, uncertainty, and contradiction!

SECTION IX. OF THE REASON OF ANIMALS

All our reasonings concerning matter of fact are founded on a species of Analogy, which leads us to expect from any cause the same events, which we have observed to result from similar causes. Where the causes are entirely similar, the analogy is perfect, and the inference, drawn from it, is regarded as certain and conclusive: nor does any man ever entertain a doubt, when he sees a piece of iron, that it will have weight and cohesion of parts; as in all other instances, which have ever fallen under his observation. But where the objects have not so exact a similarity, the analogy is less perfect, and the inference is less conclusive; though still it has some force, in proportion to the degree of similarity and resemblance. The anatomical observations, formed upon one animal, are, by this species of reasoning, extended to all animals; and it is certain, that when the circulation of the blood for instance, is clearly proved to have place in one creature, as a frog, or fish, it forms a strong presumption, that the same principle has place in all. These analogical observations may be carried farther, even to this science, of which we are now treating; and any theory, by which we explain the operations of the understanding, or the origin and connexion of the passions in man, will acquire additional authority, if we find, that the same theory is requisite to explain the same phenomena in all other animals. We shall make trial of this, with regard to the hypothesis, by which we have, in the foregoing discourse, endeavoured to account for all experimental reasonings; and it is hoped, that this new point of view will serve to confirm all our former observations.

First, It seems evident, that animals as well as men learn many things from experience, and infer, that the same events will always follow from the same causes. By this principle they become acquainted with the more obvious properties of external objects, and gradually, from their birth, treasure up a knowledge of the nature of fire, water, earth, stones, heights, depths, &c., and of the effects which result from their operation. The ignorance and inexperience of the young are here plainly distinguishable from the cunning and sagacity of the old, who have learned, by long observation, to avoid what hurt them, and to pursue what gave ease or pleasure. A horse, that has been accustomed to the field, becomes acquainted with the proper height which he can leap, and will never attempt what exceeds his force and ability. An old greyhound will trust the more fatiguing part of the chase to the younger, and will place himself so as to meet the hare in her doubles; nor are the conjectures, which he forms on this occasion, founded in any thing but his observation and experience.

This is still more evident from the effects of discipline and education on animals, who, by the proper application of rewards and punishments, may be taught any course of action, and most contrary to their natural instincts and propensities. Is it not experience, which renders a dog apprehensive of pain, when you menace him, or lift up the whip to beat him? Is it not even experience, which makes him answer to his name, and infer, from such an arbitrary sound, that you mean him rather than any of his fellows, and intend to call him, when you pronounce it in a certain manner, and with a certain tone and accent?

In all these cases, we may observe, that the animal infers some fact beyond what immediately strikes his senses; and that this inference is altogether founded on past experience, while the creature expects from the present object the same consequences, which it has always found in its observation to result from similar objects.

Secondly, It is impossible, that this inference of the animal can be founded on any process of argument or reasoning, by which he concludes, that like events must follow like objects, and that the course of nature will always be regular in its operations. For if there be in reality any arguments of this nature, they surely lie too abstruse for the observation of such imperfect understandings; since it may well employ the utmost care and attention of a philosophic genius to discover and observe them. Animals, therefore, are not guided in these inferences by reasoning: Neither are children: Neither are the generality of mankind, in their ordinary actions and conclusions: Neither are philosophers themselves, who, in all the active parts of life, are, in the main, the same with the vulgar, and are governed by the same maxims. Nature must have provided some other principle, of more ready, and more general use and application; nor can an operation of such immense consequence in life, as that of inferring effects from causes, be trusted to the uncertain process of reasoning and argumentation. Were this doubtful with regard to men, it seems to admit of no question with regard to the brute creation; and the conclusion being once firmly established in the one, we have a strong presumption, from all the rules of analogy, that it ought to be universally admitted, without any exception or reserve. It is custom alone, which engages animals, from every object, that strikes their senses, to infer its usual attendant, and carries their imagination, from the appearance of the one, to conceive the other, in that particular manner, which we denominate *belief.* No other explication can be given of this operation, in all the higher, as well as lower classes of sensitive beings, which fall under our notice and observation.*

But though animals learn many parts of their knowledge from observation, there are also many parts of it, which they derive from the original hand of nature; which much exceed the share of capacity they possess on ordinary occasions; and in which they improve, little or nothing, by the longest practice and experience. These we denominate Instincts, and are so apt to admire as something very extraordinary, and inexplicable by all the disquisitions of human understanding. But our wonder will, perhaps, cease or diminish, when we consider, that the experimental reasoning itself, which we possess in common with beasts, and on which the whole conduct of life depends, is nothing but a species of instinct or mechanical power, that acts in us unknown to ourselves; and in its chief operations, is not directed by any such relations or comparisons of ideas, as are the proper objects of our intellectual faculties. Though the instinct be different, yet still it is an instinct, which teaches a man to avoid the fire; as much as that, which teaches a bird, with such exactness, the art of incubation, and the whole economy and order of its nursery.

---

*Since all reasonings concerning facts or causes is derived merely from custom, it may be asked how it happens, that men so much surpass animals in reasoning, and one man so much surpasses another? Has not the same custom the same influence on all?

We shall here endeavour briefly to explain the great difference in human understandings: After which the reason of the difference between men and animals will easily be comprehended.

1. When we have lived any time, and have been accustomed to the uniformity of nature we acquire a general habit, by which we always transfer the known to the unknown, and conceive the latter to resemble the former. By means of this general habitual principle, we regard even one experiment as the foundation of reasoning, and expect a similar event with some degree of certainty, where the experiment has been made accurately, and free from all foreign circumstances. It is therefore considered as a matter of great importance to observe the consequences of things; and as one man may very much surpass another in attention and memory and observation, this will make a very great difference in their reasoning.

2. Where there is a complication of causes to produce any effect, one mind may be much larger than another, and better able to comprehend the whole system of objects, and to infer justly their consequences.

3. One man is able to carry on a chain of consequences to a greater length than another.

4. Few men can think long without running into a confusion of ideas, and mistaking one for another; and there are various degrees of this infirmity.

5. The circumstance, on which the effect depends, is frequently involved in other circumstances, which are foreign and extrinsic. The separation of it often requires great attention, accuracy, and subtilty.

6. The forming of general maxims from particular observation is a very nice operation; and nothing is more usual, from haste or narrowness of mind which sees not on all sides than to commit mistakes in this particular.

7. When we reason from analogies, the man, who has the greater experience of the greater promptitude of suggesting analogies, will be the better reasoner.

8. Biases from prejudice, education, passion, party, &c., hang more upon one mind than another.

9. After we have acquired a confidence in human testimony, books and conversation enlarge much more the sphere of one man's experience and thought than those of another.

It would be easy to discover many other circumstances that make a difference in the understandings of men.

Section X. Of Miracles

Part I

There is, in Dr. Tillotson's writings, an argument against the *real presence,* which is as concise, and elegant, and strong as any argument can possibly be supposed against a doctrine, so little worthy of a serious refutation. It is acknowledged on all hands, says that learned prelate, that the authority, either of the scripture or of tradition, is founded merely in the testimony of the apostles, who were eye-witnesses to those miracles of our Saviour, by which he proved his divine mission. Our evidence, then, for the truth of the *Christian* religion is less than the evidence for the truth of our senses; because, even in the first authors of our religion, it was no greater; and it is evident it must diminish in passing from them to their disciples; nor can any one rest such confidence in their testimony, as in the immediate object of his senses. But a weaker evidence can never destroy a stronger; and therefore, were the doctrine of the real presence ever so clearly revealed in scripture, it were directly contrary to the rules of just reasoning to give our assent to it. It contradicts sense, though both the scripture and tradition, on which it is supposed to be built, carry not such evidence with them as sense, when they are considered merely as external evidences, and are not brought home to every one's breast, by the immediate operation of the Holy Spirit.

Nothing is so convenient as a decisive argument of this kind, which must at least *silence* the most arrogant bigotry and superstition, and free us from their impertinent solicitations. I flatter myself, that I have discovered an argument of a like nature, which, if just, will, with the wise and learned, be an everlasting check to all kinds of superstitious delusion, and consequently, will be useful as long as the world endures; for so long, I presume, will the accounts of miracles and prodigies be found in all history, sacred and profane.

Though experience be our only guide in reasoning concerning matters of fact; it must be acknowledged, that this guide is not altogether infallible, but in some cases is apt to lead us into errors. One, who in our climate, should expect better weather in any week of June than in one of December, would reason justly, and conformably to experience; but it is certain, that he may happen, in the event, to find himself mistaken. However, we may observe, that, in such a case, he would have no cause to complain of experience; because it commonly informs us beforehand of the uncertainty, by that contrariety of events, which we may learn from a diligent observation. All effects follow not with like certainty from their supposed causes. Some events are found, in all countries and all ages, to have been constantly conjoined together: Others are found to have been more variable, and sometimes to disappoint our expectations; so that, in our reasonings concerning matter of fact, there are all imaginable degrees of assurance, from the highest certainty to the lowest species of moral evidence.

A wise man, therefore, proportions his belief to the evidence. In such conclusions as are founded on an infallible experience, he expects the event with the last degree of assurance, and regards his past experience as a full *proof* of the future existence of that event. In other cases, he proceeds with more caution: He weighs the opposite experiments: He considers which side is supported by the greater number of experiments: to that side he inclines, with doubt and hesitation; and when at last he fixes his judgement, the evidence exceeds not what we properly call *probability.* All probability, then, supposes an opposition of experiments and observations, where the one side is found to overbalance the other, and to produce a degree of evidence, proportioned to the superiority. A hundred instances or experiments on one side, and fifty on another, afford a doubtful expectation of any event; though a hundred uniform experiments, with only one that is contradictory, reasonably begets a pretty strong degree of assurance. In all cases, we must balance the opposite experiments, where they are opposite, and deduct the smaller number from the greater, in order to know the exact force of the superior evidence.

To apply these principles to a particular instance; we may observe, that there is no species of reasoning more common, more useful, and even necessary to human life, than that which is derived from the testimony of men, and the reports of eye-witnesses and spectators. This species of reasoning, perhaps, one may deny to be founded on the relation of cause and effect. I shall not dispute about a word. It will be sufficient to observe that our assurance in any argument of this kind is derived from no other principle than our observation of the veracity of human testimony, and of the usual conformity of facts to the reports of witnesses. It being a general maxim, that no objects have any discoverable connexion together, and that all the inferences, which we can draw from one to another, are founded merely on our experience of their constant and regular conjunction; it is evident, that we ought not to make an exception to this maxim in favour of human testimony, whose connexion with any event seems, in itself, as little necessary as any other. Were not the memory tenacious to a certain degree; had not men commonly an inclination to truth and a principle of probity, were they not sensible to shame, when detected in a falsehood: Were not these, I say, discovered by *experience* to be qualities, inherent in human nature, we should never repose the least confidence in human testimony. A man delirious, or noted for falsehood and villainy, has no manner of authority with us.

And as the evidence, derived from witnesses and human testimony, is founded on past experience, so it varies with the experience, and is regarded either as *proof* or a *probability,* according as the conjunction between any particular kind of report and any kind of object has been found to be constant or variable. There are a number of circumstances to be taken into consideration in all judgements of this kind; and the ultimate standard, by which we determine all disputes, that may arise concerning them, is always derived from experience and observation. Where this experience is not entirely uniform on any side, it is attended with an unavoidable contrariety in our judgements, and with the same opposition and mutual destruction of argument as in every other kind of evidence. We frequently hesitate concerning the reports of others. We balance the opposite circumstances, which cause any doubt or uncertainty; and when we discover a superiority on one side, we incline to it; but still with a diminution of assurance, in proportion to the force of its antagonist.

This contrariety of evidence, in the present case, may be derived from several different causes; from the opposition of contrary testimony; from the character or number of the witnesses; from the manner of their delivering their testimony; or from the union of all these circumstances. We entertain a suspicion concerning any matter of fact, when the witnesses contradict each other; when they are but few, or of a doubtful character; when they have an interest in what they affirm; when they deliver their testimony with hesitation, or on the contrary, with too violent asseverations. There are many other particulars of the same kind, which may diminish or destroy the force of any argument, derived from human testimony.

Suppose, for instance, that the fact, which the testimony endeavours to establish, partakes of the extraordinary and the marvellous; in that case, the evidence, resulting from the testimony, admits of a diminution, greater or less, in proportion as the fact is more or less unusual. The reason why we place any credit in witnesses and historians, is not derived from any *connexion,* which we perceive *a priori,* between testimony and reality, but because we are accustomed to find a conformity between them. But when the fact attested is such a one as has seldom fallen under our observation, here is a contest of two opposite experiences; of which the one destroys the other, as far as its force goes, and the superior can only operate on the mind by the force, which remains. The very same principle of experience, which gives us a certain degree of assurance in the testimony of witnesses, gives us also, in this case, another degree of assurance against the fact, which they endeavour to establish; from which contradiction there necessarily arises a counterpoise, and mutual destruction of belief and authority.

I should not believe such a story were it told me by Cato, was a proverbial saying in Rome, even during the lifetime of that philosophical patriot.* The incredibility of a fact, it was allowed, might invalidate so great an authority.

The Indian prince, who refused to believe the first relations concerning the effects of frost, reasoned justly; and it naturally required very strong testimony to engage his assent to facts, that arose from a state of nature, with which he was unacquainted, and which bore so little analogy to those events, of which he had had constant and uniform experience. Though they were not contrary to his experience, they were not conformable to it.**

But in order to increase the probability against the testimony of witnesses, let us suppose, that the fact, which they affirm, instead of being only marvellous, is really miraculous; and suppose also, that the testimony considered apart and in itself, amounts to an entire proof; in that case, there is proof against proof, of which the strongest must prevail, but still with a diminution of its force, in proportion to that of its antagonist.

A miracle is a violation of the laws of nature; and as a firm and unalterable experience has established these laws, the proof against a miracle, from the very nature of the fact, is as entire as any argument from experience can possibly be imagined. Why is it more than probable, that all men must die; that lead cannot, of itself, remain suspended in the air; that fire consumes wood, and is extinguished by water; unless it be, that these events are found agreeable to the laws of nature, and there is required a violation of these laws, or in other words, a miracle to prevent them? Nothing is esteemed a miracle, if it ever happen in the common course of nature. It is no miracle that a man, seemingly in good health, should die on a sudden: because such a kind of death, though more unusual than any other, has yet been frequently observed to happen. But it is a miracle, that a dead man should come to life; because that has never been observed in any age or country. There must, therefore, be a uniform experience against every miraculous event, otherwise the event would not merit that appellation. And as a uniform experience amounts to a proof, there is here a direct and full *proof,* from the nature of the

---

*Plutarch, *Marcus Cato [The Life of Cato].*

**No Indian, it is evident, could have experience that water did not freeze in cold climates. This is placing nature in a situation quite unknown to him; and it is impossible for him to tell *a priori* what will result from it. It is making a new experiment, the consequence of which is always uncertain. One may sometimes conjecture from analogy what will follow; but still this is but conjecture. And it must be confessed, that, in the present case of freezing, the event follows contrary to the rules of analogy, and is such as a rational Indian would not look for. The operations of cold upon water are not gradual according to the degrees of cold; but whenever it comes to the freezing point, the water passes in a moment, from the utmost liquidity to perfect hardness. Such an event, therefore, may be denominated *extraordinary,* and requires a pretty strong testimony, to render it credible to people in a warm climate: But still it is not *miraculous,* nor contrary to uniform experience of the course of nature in cases where all the circumstances are the same. The inhabitants of Sumatra have always seen water fluid in their own climate, and the freezing of their rivers ought to be deemed a prodigy: But they never saw water in Muscovy during the winter, and therefore they cannot reasonably be positive what would there be the consequence.

fact, against the existence of any miracle; nor can such a proof be destroyed, or the miracle rendered credible, but by an opposite proof, which is superior.*

The plain consequence is (and it is a general maxim worthy of our attention), "That no testimony is sufficient to establish a miracle, unless the testimony be of such a kind, that its falsehood would be more miraculous, than the fact, which it endeavours to establish; and even in that case there is a mutual destruction of arguments, and the superior only gives us an assurance suitable to that degree of force, which remains, after deducting the inferior." When anyone tells me, that he saw a dead man restored to life, I immediately consider with myself, whether it be more probable, that this person should either deceive or be deceived, or that the fact, which he relates, should really have happened. I weigh the one miracle against the other; and according to the superiority, which I discover, I pronounce my decision, and always reject the greater miracle. If the falsehood of his testimony would be more miraculous, than the event which he relates; then, and not till then, can he pretend to command my belief or opinion.

PART II

In the foregoing reasoning we have supposed, that the testimony, upon which a miracle is founded, may possibly amount to an entire proof, and that the falsehood of that testimony would be a real prodigy: But it is easy to shew, that we have been a great deal too liberal in our concession, and that there never was a miraculous event established on so full an evidence.

For *first,* there is not to be found, in all history, any miracle attested by a sufficient number of men, of such unquestioned good-sense, education, and learning, as to secure us against all delusion in themselves; of such undoubted integrity, as to place them beyond all suspicion of any design to deceive others; of such credit and reputation in the eyes of mankind, as to have a great deal to lose in case of their being detected in any falsehood; and at the same time, attesting facts performed in such a public manner and in so celebrated a part of the world, as to render the detection unavoidable: All which circumstances are requisite to give us a full assurance in the testimony of men.

Secondly. We may observe in human nature a principle which, if strictly examined, will be found to diminish extremely the assurance, which we might, from human testimony, have, in any kind of prodigy. The maxim, by which we commonly conduct ourselves in our reasonings, is, that the objects, of which we have no experience, resemble those, of which we have; that what we have found to be most usual is always most probable; and that where there is an opposition of arguments, we ought to give the preference to such as are founded on the greatest number of past observations. But

---

*Sometimes an event may not, *in itself,* seem to be contrary to the laws of nature, and yet, if it were real, it might, by reason of some circumstances, be denominated a miracle, because, *in fact,* it is contrary to these laws. Thus if a person, claiming a divine authority, should command a sick person to be well, a healthful man to fall down dead, the clouds to pour rain, the winds to blow, in short, should order many natural events, which immediately follow upon his command; these might justly be esteemed miracles, because they are really, in this case, contrary to the laws of nature. For if any suspicion remain, that the event and command concurred by accident, there is no miracle and no transgression of the laws of nature. If this suspicion be removed, there is evidently a miracle, and a transgression of these laws; because nothing can be more contrary to nature than that the voice or command of a man should have such an influence. A miracle may be accurately defined, *a transgression of a law of nature by a particular volition of the Deity, or by the interposition of some invisible agent.* A miracle may either be discovered by men or not. This alters not its nature and essence. The raising of a house or ship into the air is a visible miracle. The raising of a feather, when the wind wants ever so little of a force requisite for that purpose, is as real a miracle, though not so sensible with regard to us.

though, in proceeding by this rule, we readily reject any fact which is unusual and in-credible in an ordinary degree; yet in advancing farther, the mind observes not always the same rule; but when anything is affirmed utterly absurd and miraculous, it rather the more readily admits of such a fact, upon account of that very circumstance, which ought to destroy all its authority. The passion of *surprise* and *wonder,* arising from miracles, being an agreeable emotion, gives a sensible tendency towards the belief of those events, from which it is derived. And this goes so far, that even those who cannot enjoy this pleasure immediately, nor can believe those miraculous events, of which they are informed, yet love to partake of the satisfaction at second-hand or by rebound, and place a pride and delight in exciting the admiration of others.

With what greediness are the miraculous accounts of travellers received, their de-scriptions of sea and land monsters, their relations of wonderful adventures, strange men, and uncouth manners? But if the spirit of religion join itself to the love of wonder, there is an end of common sense; and human testimony, in these circumstances, loses all pretensions to authority. A religionist may be an enthusiast, and imagine he sees what has no reality: he may know his narrative to be false, and yet persevere in it, with the best intentions in the world, for the sake of promoting so holy a cause: or even where this delusion has not place, vanity, excited by so strong a temptation, operates on him more powerfully than on the rest of mankind in any other circumstances; and self-interest with equal force. His auditors may not have, and commonly have not, sufficient judgement to canvass his evidence: what judgement they have, they renounce by prin-

Ninewells, the Hume family estate, near Berwick in southern Scotland. David Hume lived here until age twelve when he went to the University of Edinburgh. (Culver Pictures, Inco)

ciple, in these sublime and mysterious subjects: or if they were ever so willing to employ it, passion and a heated imagination disturb the regularity of its operations. Their credulity increases his impudence: and his impudence overpowers their credulity.

Eloquence, when at its highest pitch, leaves little room for reason or reflection; but addressing itself entirely to the fancy or the affections, captivates the willing hearers, and subdues their understanding. Happily, this pitch it seldom attains. But what a Tully or a Demosthenes could scarcely effect over a Roman or Athenian audience, every *Capuchin,* every itinerant or stationary teacher can perform over the generality of mankind, and in a higher degree, by touching such gross and vulgar passions.

The many instances of forged miracles, and prophecies, and supernatural events, which, in all ages, have either been detected by contrary evidence, or which detect themselves by their absurdity, prove sufficiently the strong propensity of mankind to the extraordinary and the marvellous, and ought reasonably to beget a suspicion against all relations of this kind. This is our natural way of thinking, even with regard to the most common and most credible events. For instance: There is no kind of report which rises so easily, and spreads so quickly, especially in country places and provincial towns, as those concerning marriages; insomuch that two young persons of equal condition never see each other twice, but the whole neighbourhood immediately join them together. The pleasure of telling a piece of news so interesting, of propagating it, and of being the first reporters of it, spreads the intelligence. And this is so well known, that no man of sense gives attention to these reports, till he find them confirmed by some greater evidence. Do not the same passions, and others still stronger, incline the generality of mankind to believe and report, with the greatest vehemence and assurance, all religious miracles?

Thirdly. It forms a strong presumption against all supernatural and miraculous relations, that they are observed chiefly to abound among ignorant and barbarous nations; or if a civilized people has ever given admission to any of them, that people will be found to have received them from ignorant and barbarous ancestors, who transmitted them with that inviolable sanction and authority, which always attend received opinions. When we peruse the first histories of all nations, we are apt to imagine ourselves transported into some new world; where the whole frame of nature is disjointed, and every element performs its operations in a different manner, from what it does at present. Battles, revolutions, pestilence, famine and death, are never the effect of those natural causes, which we experience. Prodigies, omens, oracles, judgements, quite obscure the few natural events, that are intermingled with them. But as the former grow thinner every page, in proportion as we advance nearer the enlightened ages, we soon learn, that there is nothing mysterious or super-natural in the case, but that all proceeds from the usual propensity of mankind towards the marvellous, and that, though this inclination may at intervals receive a check from sense and learning, it can never be thoroughly extirpated from human nature.

It is strange, a judicious reader is apt to say, upon the perusal of these wonderful historians, *that such prodigious events never happen in our days.* But it is nothing strange, I hope, that men should lie in all ages. You must surely have seen instances enough of that frailty. You have yourself heard many such marvellous relations started, which, being treated with scorn by all the wise and judicious, have at last been abandoned even by the vulgar. Be assured, that those renowned lies, which have spread and flourished to such a monstrous height, arose from like beginnings; but being sown in a more proper soil, shot up at last into prodigies almost equal to those which they relate.

It was a wise policy in that false prophet, Alexander, who though now forgotten, was once so famous, to lay the first scene of his impostures in Paphlagonia, where, as Lucian tells us, the people were extremely ignorant and stupid, and ready to swallow even the grossest delusion. People at a distance, who are weak enough to think the matter at all worth enquiry, have no opportunity of receiving better information. The stories come magnified to them by a hundred circumstances. Fools are industrious in propagating the imposture; while the wise and learned are contented, in general, to deride its absurdity, without informing themselves of the particular facts, by which it may be distinctly refuted. And thus the impostor above mentioned was enabled to proceed, from his ignorant Paphlagonians, to the enlisting of votaries, even among the Grecian philosophers, and men of the most eminent rank and distinction in Rome: nay, could engage the attention of that sage emperor Marcus Aurelius; so far as to make him trust the success of a military expedition to his delusive prophecies.

The advantages are so great, of starting an imposture among an ignorant people, that, even though the delusion should be too gross to impose on the generality of them *(which, though seldom, is sometimes the case)* it has a much better chance for succeeding in remote countries, than if the first scene had been laid in a city renowned for arts and knowledge. The most ignorant and barbarous of these barbarians carry the report abroad. None of their countrymen have a large correspondence, or sufficient credit and authority to contradict and beat down the delusion. Men's inclination to the marvellous has full opportunity to display itself. And thus a story, which is universally exploded in the place where it was first started, shall pass for certain at a thousand miles distance. But had Alexander fixed his residence at Athens, the philosophers of that renowned mart of learning had immediately spread, throughout the whole Roman empire, their sense of the matter; which, being supported by so great authority, and displayed by all the force of reason and eloquence, had entirely opened the eyes of mankind. It is true; Lucian, passing by chance through Paphlagonia, had an opportunity of performing this good office. But, though much to be wished, it does not always happen, that every Alexander meets with a Lucian, ready to expose and detect his impostures.

I may add as a *fourth* reason, which diminishes the authority of prodigies, that there is no testimony for any, even those which have not been expressly detected, that is not opposed by an infinite number of witnesses; so that not only the miracle destroys the credit of testimony, but the testimony destroys itself. To make this the better understood, let us consider, that, in matters of religion, whatever is different is contrary; and that it is impossible the religions of ancient Rome, of Turkey, of Siam, and of China should, all of them, be established on any solid foundation. Every miracle, therefore, pretended to have been wrought in any of these religions (and all of them abound in miracles), as its direct scope is to establish the particular system to which it is attributed; so has it the same force, though more indirectly, to overthrow every other system. In destroying a rival system, it likewise destroys the credit of those miracles, on which that system was established; so that all the prodigies of different religions are to be regarded as contrary facts, and the evidences of these prodigies, whether weak or strong, as opposite to each other. According to this method of reasoning, when we believe any miracle of Mahomet or his successors, we have for our warrant the testimony of a few barbarous Arabians: And on the other hand, we are to regard the authority of Titus Livius, Plutarch, Tacitus, and, in short, of all the authors and witnesses, Grecian, Chinese, and Roman Catholic, who have related any miracle in their particular religion; I say, we are to regard their testimony in the same light as if they had mentioned that Mahometan miracle, and had in express terms contradicted it, with the same certainty as they have for the miracle they relate. This argument may appear over subtile and refined; but is not in reality different from the reasoning of a judge, who supposes, that the credit of two witnesses, maintaining a crime against any one, is destroyed by the testimony of two others, who affirm him to have been two hundred leagues distant, at the same instant when the crime is said to have been committed.

One of the best attested miracles in all profane history, is that which Tacitus reports of Vespasian, who cured a blind man in Alexandria, by means of his spittle, and a lame man by the mere touch of his foot; in obedience to a vision of the god Serapis, who had enjoined them to have recourse to the Emperor, for these miraculous cures. The story may be seen in that fine historian;* where every circumstance seems to add weight to the testimony, and might be displayed at large with all the force of argument and eloquence, if any one were now concerned to enforce the evidence of that exploded and idolatrous superstition. The gravity, solidity, age, and probity of so great an emperor, who, through the whole course of his life, conversed in a familiar manner with his friends and courtiers, and never affected those extraordinary airs of divinity assumed by Alexander and Demetrius. The historian, a contemporary writer, noted for candour and veracity, and withal, the greatest and most penetrating genius, perhaps, of all antiquity; and so free from any tendency to credulity, that he even lies under the contrary imputation, of atheism and profaneness: The persons, from whose authority he related the miracle, of established character for judgement and veracity, as we may well presume; eyewitnesses of the fact, and confirming their testimony, after the Flavian family was despoiled of the empire, and could no longer give any reward, as the price of a lie. *Utrumque, qui interfuere, nunc quoque memorant, postquam nullum mendacio pretium.*** To which if we add the public nature of the facts, as related, it will appear, that no evidence can well be supposed stronger for so gross and so palpable a falsehood.

There is also a memorable story related by Cardinal de Retz, which may well deserve our consideration. When that intriguing politician fled into Spain, to avoid the persecution of his enemies, he passed through Saragossa, the capital of Arragon, where he was shown, in the cathedral, a man, who had served seven years as a doorkeeper, and was well known to every body in town, that had ever paid his devotions at that church. He had been seen, for so long a time, wanting a leg; but recovered that limb by the rubbing of holy oil upon the stump; and the cardinal assures us that he saw him with two legs. This miracle was vouched by all the canons of the church; and the whole company in town were appealed to for a confirmation of the fact; whom the cardinal found, by their zealous devotion, to be thorough believers of the miracle. Here the relater was also contemporary to the supposed prodigy, of an incredulous and libertine character, as well as of great genius; the miracle of so *singular* a nature as could scarcely admit of a counterfeit, and the witnesses very numerous, and all of them, in a manner, spectators of the fact, to which they gave their testimony. And what adds mightily to the force of the evidence, and may double our surprise on this occasion, is, that the cardinal himself, who relates the story, seems not to give any credit to it, and consequently cannot be suspected of any concurrence in the holy fraud. He considered justly, that it was not requisite, in order to reject a fact of this nature, to be able accurately to disprove the testimony, and to trace its falsehood, through all the circumstances of knavery and credulity which produced it. He knew, that, as this was commonly altogether impossible at any small distance of time and place; so was it extremely difficult, even where one was immediately present, by reason of the bigotry, ignorance, cunning, and roguery of a great part of mankind. He therefore concluded, like a just reasoner, that such an evidence carried falsehood upon the very face of it, and that a miracle, supported by any human testimony, was more properly a subject of derision than of argument.

*Histories, iv. 81. Suetonius gives nearly the same account, *Lives of the Caesars* (Vespasian).
**[Those who were present recount both even now that a lie is no longer rewarded.]

There surely never was a greater number of miracles ascribed to one person, than those, which were lately said to have been wrought in France upon the tomb of Abbe Paris, the famous Jansenist, with whose sanctity the people were so long deluded.

The curing of the sick, giving hearing to the deaf, and sight to the blind, were every where talked of as the usual effects of that holy sepulchre. But what is more extraordinary; many of the miracles were immediately proved upon the spot, before judges of unquestioned integrity, attested by witnesses of credit and distinction, in a learned age, and on the most eminent theatre that is now in the world. Nor is this all: a relation of them was published and dispersed everywhere; nor were the *Jesuits,* though a learned body, supported by the civil magistrate, and determined enemies to those opinions, in whose favour the miracles were said to have been wrought, ever able distinctly to refute or detect them. Where shall we find such a number of circumstances, agreeing to the corroboration of one fact? And what have we to oppose to such a cloud of witnesses, but the absolute impossibility or miraculous nature of the events, which they relate? And this surely, in the eyes of all reasonable people, will alone be regarded as a sufficient refutation.

Is the consequence just, because some human testimony has the utmost force and authority in some cases, when it relates the battle of Philippi or Pharsalia for instance; that therefore all kinds of testimony must, in all cases, have equal force and authority? Suppose that the Caesarean and Pompeian factions had, each of them, claimed the victory in these battles, and that the historians of each party had uniformly ascribed the advantage to their own side; how could mankind, at this distance, have been able to determine between them? The contrariety is equally strong between the miracles related by Herodotus or Plutarch, and those delivered by Mariana, Bede, or any monkish historian.

The wise lend a very academic faith to every report which favours the passion of the reporter; whether it magnifies his country, his family, or himself, or in any other way strikes in with his natural inclinations and propensities. But what greater temptation than to appear a missionary, a prophet, an ambassador from heaven? Who would not encounter many dangers and difficulties, in order to attain so sublime a character? Or if, by the help of vanity and a heated imagination, a man has first made a convert of himself, and entered seriously into the delusion; who ever scruples to make use of pious frauds, in support of so holy and meritorious a cause?

The smallest spark may here kindle into the greatest flame; because the materials are always prepared for it. The *avidum genus auricularum,** the gazing populace, receive greedily, without examination, whatever soothes superstition, and promotes wonder.

How many stories of this nature have, in all ages, been detected and exploded in their infancy? How many more have been celebrated for a time, and have afterwards sunk into neglect and oblivion? Where such reports, therefore, fly about, the solution of the phenomenon is obvious; and we judge in conformity to regular experience and observation, when we account for it by the known and natural principles of credulity and delusion. And shall we, rather than have a recourse to so natural a solution, allow of a miraculous violation of the most established laws of nature?

I need not mention the difficulty of detecting, a falsehood in any private or even public history, at the place, where it is said to happen; much more when the scene is removed to ever so small a distance. Even a court of judicature, with all the authority, accuracy, and judgement, which they can employ, find themselves often at a loss to distin-

---

*[a genus hungry for gossip] Lucretius, *De Rerum Natura,* iv.

guish between truth and falsehood in the most recent actions. But the matter never comes to any issue, if trusted to the common method of altercations and debate and flying rumours; especially when men's passions have taken part on either side.

In the infancy of new religions, the wise and learned commonly esteem the matter too inconsiderable to deserve their attention or regard. And when afterwards they would willingly detect the cheat, in order to undeceive the deluded multitude, the season is now past, and the records and witnesses, which might clear up the matter, have perished beyond recovery.

No means of detection remain, but those which must be drawn from the very testimony itself of the reporters: and these, though always sufficient with the judicious and knowing, are commonly too fine to fall under the comprehension of the vulgar.

Upon the whole, then, it appears, that no testimony for any kind of miracle has ever amounted to a probability, much less to a proof; and that, even supposing it amounted to a proof, it would be opposed by another proof; derived from the very nature of the fact, which it would endeavour to establish. It is experience only, which gives authority to human testimony; and it is the same experience, which assures us of the laws of nature. When, therefore, these two kinds of experience are contrary, we have nothing to do but subtract the one from the other, and embrace an opinion, either on one side or the other, with that assurance which arises from the remainder. But according to the principle here explained, this substraction, with regard to all popular religions, amounts to an entire annihilation; and therefore we may establish it as a maxim, that no human testimony can have such force as to prove a miracle, and make it a just foundation for any such system of religion.

I beg the limitations here made may be remarked, when I say, that a miracle can never be proved, so as to be the foundation of a system of religion. For I own, that otherwise, there may possibly be miracles, or violations of the usual course of nature, of such a kind as to admit of proof from human testimony; though, perhaps, it will be impossible to find any such in all the records of history. Thus, suppose, all authors, in all languages, agree, that, from the first of January 1600, there was a total darkness over the whole earth for eight days: suppose that the tradition of this extraordinary event is still strong and lively among the people: that all travellers, who return from foreign countries, bring us accounts of the same tradition, without the least variation or contradiction: it is evident, that our present philosophers, instead of doubting the fact, ought to receive it as certain, and ought to search for the causes whence it might be derived. The decay, corruption, and dissolution of nature, is an event rendered probable by so many analogies, that any phenomenon, which seems to have a tendency towards that catastrophe, comes within the reach of human testimony, if that testimony be very extensive and uniform.

But suppose, that all the historians who treat of England, should agree, that, on the first of January 1600, Queen Elizabeth died; that both before and after her death she was seen by her physicians and the whole court, as is usual with persons of her rank; that her successor was acknowledged and proclaimed by the parliament; and that, after being interred a month, she again appeared, resumed the throne, and governed England for three years: I must confess that I should be surprised at the concurrence of so many odd circumstances, but should not have the least inclination to believe so miraculous an event. I should not doubt of her pretended death, and of those other public circumstances that followed it: I should only assert it to have been pretended, and that it neither was, nor possibly could be real. You would in vain object to me the difficulty, and almost impossibility of deceiving the world in an affair of such consequence; the wisdom and solid judgement of that renowned queen; with the little or no advantage which she could reap from so poor an artifice: All this might astonish me; but I would still reply, that the knavery and folly of men are such common phenomena, that I should rather believe the most extraordinary events to arise from their concurrence, then admit of so signal a violation of the laws of nature.

But should this miracle be ascribed to any new system of religion; men, in all ages, have been so much imposed on by ridiculous stories of that kind, that this very circumstance would be a full proof of a cheat, and sufficient, with all men of sense, not only to make them reject the fact, but even reject it without farther examination. Though the Being to whom the miracle is ascribed, be, in this case, Almighty, it does not, upon that account, become a whit more probable; since it is impossible for us to know the attributes or actions of such a Being, otherwise than from the experience which we have of his productions, in the usual course of nature. This still reduces us to past observation, and obliges us to compare the instances of the violation of truth in the testimony of men, with those of the violation of the laws of nature by miracles, in order to judge which of them is most likely and probable. As the violations of truth are more common in the testimony concerning religious miracles, than in that concerning any other matter of fact; this must diminish very much the authority of the former testimony, and make us form a general resolution, never to lend any attention to it, with whatever specious pretence it may be covered.

Lord Bacon seems to have embraced the same principles of reasoning. "We ought," says he, "to make a collection or particular history of all monsters and prodigious births or productions, and in a word of every thing new, rare, and extraordinary in nature. But this must be done with the most severe scrutiny, lest we depart from truth. Above all, every relation must be considered as suspicious, which depends in any degree upon religion, as the prodigies of Livy: And no less so, every thing that is to be found in the writers of natural magic or alchemy, or such authors, who seem, all of them, to have an unconquerable appetite for falsehood and fable.*

I am the better pleased with the method of reasoning here delivered, as I think it may serve to confound those dangerous friends or disguised enemies to the *Christian Religion*, who have undertaken to defend it by the principles of human reason. Our most holy religion is founded on *Faith*, not on reason; and it is a sure method of exposing it to put it to such a trial as it is, by no means, fitted to endure. To make this more evident, let us examine those miracles, related in scripture; and not to lose ourselves in too wide a field, let us confine ourselves to such as we find in the *Pentateuch*, which we shall examine, according to the principles of these pretended Christians, not as the word or testimony of God himself, but as the production of a mere human writer and historian. Here then we are first to consider a book, presented to us by a barbarous and ignorant people, written in an age when they were still more barbarous, and in all probability long after the facts which it relates, corroborated by no concurring testimony, and resembling those fabulous accounts, which every nation gives of its origin. Upon reading this book, we find it full of prodigies and miracles. It gives an account of a state of the world and of human nature entirely different from the present: Of our fall from that state: Of the age of man, extended to near a thousand years: Of the destruction of the world by a deluge: Of the arbitrary choice of one people, as the favourites of heaven; and that people the countrymen of the author: Of their deliverance from bondage by prodigies the most astonishing imaginable: I desire any one to lay his hand upon his heart, and after a serious consideration declare, whether he thinks that the falsehood of

Novum Organum, II, aphorism 29.

such a book, supported by such a testimony, would be more extraordinary and miraculous than all the miracles it relates; which is, however, necessary to make it be received, according to the measures of probability above established.

What we have said of miracles may be applied, without any variation, to prophecies; and indeed, all prophecies are real miracles, and as such only, can be admitted as proofs of any revelation. If it did not exceed the capacity of human nature to foretell future events, it would be absurd to employ any prophecy as an argument for a divine mission or authority from heaven. So that, upon the whole, we may conclude, that the *Christian Religion* not only was at first attended with miracles, but even at this day cannot be believed by any reasonable person without one. Mere reason is insufficient to convince us of its veracity: And whoever is moved by *Faith* to assent to it, is conscious of a continued miracle in his own person, which subverts all the principles of his understanding, and gives him a determination to believe what is most contrary to custom and experience.

SECTION XI. OF A PARTICULAR PROVIDENCE AND OF A FUTURE STATE

I was lately engaged in conversation with a friend who loves sceptical paradoxes; where, though he advanced many principles, of which I can by no means approve, yet as they seem to be curious, and to bear some relation to the chain of reasoning carried on throughout this enquiry, I shall here copy them from my memory as accurately as I can, in order to submit them to the judgement of the reader.

Our conversation began with my admiring the singular good fortune of philosophy, which, as it requires entire liberty above all other privileges, and chiefly flourishes from the free opposition of sentiments and argumentation, received its first birth in an age and country of freedom and toleration, and was never cramped, even in its most extravagant principles, by any creeds, concessions, or penal statutes. For, except the banishment of Protagoras, and the death of Socrates, which last event proceeded partly from other motives, there are scarcely any instances to be met with, in ancient history, of this bigoted jealousy, with which the present age is so much infested. Epicurus lived at Athens to an advanced age, in peace and tranquillity: Epicureans were even admitted to receive the sacerdotal character, and to officiate at the altar, in the most sacred rites of the established religion: And the public encouragement of pensions and salaries was afforded equally, by the wisest of all the Roman emperors, to the professors of every sect of philosophy. How requisite such kind of treatment was to philosophy, in her early youth, will easily be conceived, if we reflect, that, even at present, when she may be supposed more hardy and robust, she bears with much difficulty the inclemency of the seasons, and those harsh winds of calumny and persecution, which blow upon her.

You admire, says my friend, as the singular good fortune of philosophy, what seems to result from the natural course of things, and to be unavoidable in every age and nation. This pertinacious bigotry, of which you complain, as so fatal to philosophy, is really her offspring, who, after allying with superstition, separates himself entirely from the interest of his parent, and becomes her most inveterate enemy and persecutor. Speculative dogmas of religion, the present occasions of such furious dispute, could not possibly be conceived or admitted in the early ages of the world; when mankind, being wholly illiterate, formed an idea of religion more suitable to their weak apprehension, and composed their sacred tenets of such tales chiefly as were the objects of traditional belief, more than of argument or disputation. After the first alarm, therefore, was over, which arose from the new paradoxes and principles of the philosophers; these teachers seem ever after, during the ages of antiquity, to have lived in great harmony with the established superstition, and to have made a fair partition of mankind between them; the former claiming all the learned and wise, the latter possessing all the vulgar and illiterate.

It seems then, say I, that you leave politics entirely out of the question, and never suppose, that a wise magistrate can justly be jealous of certain tenets of philosophy, such as those of Epicurus, which, denying a divine existence, and consequently a providence and a future state, seem to loosen, in a great measure, the ties of morality, and may be supposed, for that reason, pernicious to the peace of civil society.

I know, replied he, that in fact these persecutions never, in any age, proceeded from calm reason, or from experience of the pernicious consequences of philosophy; but arose entirely from passion and prejudice. But what if I should advance farther, and assert, that if Epicurus had been accused before the people, by any of the *sycophants* or informers of those days, he could easily have defended his cause, and proved his principles of philosophy to be as salutary as those of his adversaries, who endeavoured, with such zeal, to expose him to the public hatred and jealousy?

I wish, said I, you would try your eloquence upon so extraordinary a topic, and make a speech for Epicurus, which might satisfy, not the mob of Athens, if you will allow that ancient and polite city to have contained any mob, but the more philosophical part of his audience, such as might be supposed capable of comprehending his arguments.

The matter would not be difficult, upon such conditions, replied he: And if you please, I shall suppose myself Epicurus for a moment, and make you stand for the Athenian people, and shall deliver you such an harangue as will fill all the urn with white beans, and leave not a black one to gratify the malice of my adversaries.

Very well: Pray proceed upon these suppositions.

I come hither, O ye Athenians, to justify in your assembly what I maintained in my school, and I find myself impeached by furious antagonists, instead of reasoning with calm and dispassionate enquirers. Your deliberations, which of right should be directed to questions of public good, and the interest of the commonwealth, are diverted to the disquisitions of speculative philosophy; and these magnificent, but perhaps fruitless enquiries, take place of your more familiar but more useful occupations. But so far as in me lies, I will prevent this abuse. We shall not here dispute concerning the origin and government of worlds. We shall only enquire how far such questions concern the public interest. And if I can persuade you, that they are entirely indifferent to the peace of society and security of government, I hope that you will presently send us back to our schools, there to examine, at leisure, the question the most sublime, but at the same time, the most speculative of all philosophy.

The religious philosophers, not satisfied with the tradition of your forefathers, and doctrine of your priests (in which I willingly acquiesce), indulge a rash curiosity, in trying how far they can establish religion upon the principles of reason; and they thereby excite, instead of satisfying, the doubts, which naturally arise from a diligent and scrutinous enquiry. They paint, in the most magnificent colours, the order, beauty, and wise arrangement of the universe; and then ask, if such a glorious display of intelligence could proceed from the fortuitous concourse of atoms, or if chance could produce what the greatest genius can never sufficiently admire. I shall not examine the justness of this argument. I shall allow it to be as solid as my antagonists and accusers can desire. It is sufficient, if I can prove, from this very reasoning, that the question is entirely speculative, and that, when, in my philosophical disquisitions, I deny a providence and a future state, I undermine not the foundations of society, but advance principles, which they themselves, upon their own topics, if they argue consistently, must allow to be solid and satisfactory.

You then, who are my accusers, have acknowledged, that the chief or sole argument for a divine existence (which I never questioned) is derived from the order of nature; where there appear such marks of intelligence and design, that you think it extravagant to assign for its cause, either chance, or the blind and unguided force of matter. You allow, that this is an argument drawn from effects to causes. From the order of the work, you infer, that there must have been project and forethought in the workman. If you cannot make out this point, you allow, that your conclusion fails; and you pretend not to establish the conclusion in a greater latitude than the phenomena of nature will justify. These are your concessions. I desire you to mark the consequences.

When we infer any particular cause from an effect, we must proportion the one to the other, and can never be allowed to ascribe to the cause any qualities, but what are exactly sufficient to produce the effect. A body of ten ounces raised in any scale may serve as a proof, that the counterbalancing weight exceeds ten ounces; but can never afford a reason that it exceeds a hundred. If the cause, assigned for any effect, be not sufficient to produce it, we must either reject that cause, or add to it such qualities as will give it a just proportion to the effect. But if we ascribe to it further qualities, or affirm it capable of producing other effects, we can only indulge the licence of conjecture, and arbitrarily suppose the existence of qualities and energies, without reason or authority.

The same rule holds, whether the cause assigned be brute unconscious matter, or a rational intelligent being. If the cause be known only by the effect, we never ought to ascribe to it any qualities, beyond what are precisely requisite to produce the effect: Nor can we, by any rules of just reasoning, return back from the cause, and infer other effects from it, beyond those by which alone it is known to us. No one, merely from the sight of one of Zeuxis's pictures, could know, that he was also a statuary or architect, and was an artist no less skillful in stone and marble than in colours. The talents and taste, displayed in the particular work before us; these we may safely conclude the workmen to be possessed of. The cause must be proportioned to the effect; and if we exactly and precisely proportion it, we shall never find in it any qualities, that point farther, or afford an inference concerning any other design or performance. Such qualities must be somewhat beyond what is merely requisite for producing the effect, which we examine.

Allowing, therefore, the gods to be the authors of the existence or order of the universe; it follows, that they possess that precise degree of power, intelligence, and benevolence, which appears in their workmanship; but nothing farther can ever be proved, except we call in the assistance of exaggeration and flattery to supply the defects of argument and reasoning. So far as the traces of any attributes, at present, appear, so far may we conclude these attributes to exist. The supposition of farther attributes is mere hypothesis; much more the supposition, that, in distant regions of space or periods of time, there has been, or will be, a more magnificent display of these attributes, and a scheme of administration more suitable to such imaginary virtues. We can never be allowed to mount up from the universe, the effect, to Jupiter, the cause; and then descend downwards, to infer any new effect from that cause; as if the present effects alone were not entirely worthy of the glorious attributes, which we ascribe to that deity. The knowledge of the cause being derived solely from the effect, they must be exactly adjusted to each other; and the one can never refer to anything farther, or be the foundation of any new inference and conclusion.

You find certain phenomena in nature. You seek a cause or author. You imagine that you have found him. You afterwards become so enamoured of this offspring of your brain, that you imagine it impossible, but he must produce something greater and more perfect than the present scene of things, which is so full of ill and disorder. You forget, that this superlative intelligence and benevolence are entirely imaginary, or, at least, without any foundation in reason; and that you have no ground to ascribe to him any qualities, but what you see he has actually exerted and displayed in his productions. Let your gods, therefore, O philosophers, be suited to the present appearances of nature: and presume not to alter these appearances by arbitrary suppositions, in order to suit them to the attributes, which you so fondly ascribe to your deities.

When priests and poets, supported by your authority, O Athenians, talk of a golden or silver age, which preceded the present state of vice and misery, I hear them with attention and with reverence. But when philosophers, who pretend to neglect authority, and to cultivate reason, hold the same discourse, I pay them not, I own, the same obsequious submission and pious deference. I ask, who carried them into the celestial regions, who admitted them into the councils of the gods, who opened to them the book of fate, that they thus rashly affirm, that their deities have executed, or will execute, any purpose beyond what has actually appeared? If they tell me, that they have mounted on the steps or by the gradual ascent of reason, and by drawing inferences from effects to causes, I still insist, that they have aided the ascent of reason by the wings of imagination; otherwise they could not thus change their manner of inference, and argue from causes to effects; presuming, that a more perfect production than the present world would be more suitable to such perfect beings as the gods, and forgetting that they have no reason to ascribe to these celestial beings any perfection or any attribute, but what can be found in the present world.

Hence all the fruitless industry to account for the ill appearance of nature, and save the honour of the gods; while we must acknowledge the reality of that evil and disorder, with which the world so much abounds. The obstinate and intractable qualities of matter, we are told, or the observance of general laws, or some such reason, is the sole cause, which controlled the power and benevolence of Jupiter, and obliged him to create mankind and every sensible creature so imperfect and so unhappy. These attributes then, are, it seems, beforehand, taken for granted, in their greatest latitude. And upon that supposition, I own that such conjectures may, perhaps, be admitted as plausible solutions of the ill phenomena. But still I ask, Why take these attributes for granted, or why ascribe to the cause any qualities but what actually appear in the effect? Why torture your brain to justify the course of nature upon suppositions, which, for aught you know, may be entirely imaginary, and of which there are to be found no traces in the course of nature?

The religious hypothesis, therefore, must be considered only as a particular method of accounting for the visible phenomena of the universe: but no just reasoner will ever presume to infer from it any single fact, and alter or add to the phenomena, in any single particular. If you think, that the appearances of things prove such causes, it is allowable for you to draw an inference concerning the existence of these causes. In such complicated and sublime subjects, every one should be indulged in the liberty of conjecture and argument. But here you ought to rest. If you come backward, and arguing from your inferred causes, conclude, that any other fact has existed, or will exist, in the course of nature, which may serve as a fuller display of particular attributes; I must admonish you, that you have departed from the method of reasoning, attached to the present subject, and have certainly added something to the attributes of the cause, beyond what appears in the effect; otherwise you could never, with tolerable sense or propriety, add anything to the effect, in order to render it more worthy of the cause.

Where, then, is the odiousness of that doctrine, which I teach in my school, or rather, which I examine in my gardens? Or what do you find in this whole question, wherein the security of good morals, or the peace and order of society, is in the least concerned?

I deny a providence, you say, and supreme governor of the world, who guides the course of events, and punishes the vicious with infamy and disappointment, and rewards the virtuous with honour and success, in all their undertakings. But surely, I deny not the course itself of events, which lies open to every one's inquiry and examination. I acknowledge, that, in the present order of things, virtue is attended with more peace of mind than vice, and meets with a more favourable reception from the world. I am sensible, that, according to the past experience of mankind, friendship is the chief joy of human life, and moderation the only source of tranquillity and happiness. I never balance between the virtuous and the vicious course of life; but am sensible, that, to a well-disposed mind, every advantage is on the side of the former. And what can you say more, allowing all your suppositions and reasonings? You tell me, indeed, that this disposition of things proceeds from intelligence and design. But whatever it proceeds from, the disposition itself, on which depends our happiness or misery, and consequently our conduct and deportment in life is still the same. It is still open for me, as well as you, to regulate my behaviour, by my experience of past events. And if you affirm, that, while a divine providence is allowed, and a supreme distributive justice in the universe, I ought to expect some more particular reward of the good, and punishment of the bad, beyond the ordinary course of events; I here find the same fallacy, which I have before endeavoured to detect. You persist in imagining, that, if we grant that divine existence, for which you so earnestly contend, you may safely infer consequences from it, and add something to the experienced order of nature, by arguing from the attributes which you ascribe to your gods. You seem not to remember, that all your reasonings on this subject can only be drawn from effects to causes; and that every argument, deducted from causes to effects, must of necessity be a gross sophism; since it is impossible for you to know anything of the cause, but what you have antecedently, not inferred, but discovered to the full, in the effect.

But what must a philosopher think of those vain reasoners, who, instead of regarding the present scene of things as the sole object of their contemplation, so far reverse the whole course of nature, as to render this life merely a passage to something farther; a porch, which leads to a greater, and vastly different building; a prologue, which serves only to introduce the piece, and give it more grace and propriety? Whence, do you think, can such philosophers derive their idea of the gods? From their own conceit and imagination surely. For if they derived it from the present phenomena, it would never point to anything farther, but must be exactly adjusted to them. That the divinity may *possibly* be endowed with attributes, which we have never seen exerted, may be governed by principles of action, which we cannot discover to be satisfied: all this will freely be allowed. But still this is mere *possibility* and hypothesis. We never can have reason to *infer* any attributes, or any principles of action in him, but so far as we know them to have been exerted and satisfied.

Are there *any marks of a distributive justice in the world?* If you answer in the affirmative, I conclude, that, since justice here exerts itself, it is satisfied. If you reply in the negative, I conclude, that you have then no reason to ascribe justice, in our sense of it, to the gods. If you hold a medium between affirmation and negation, by saying, that the justice of the gods, at present, exerts itself in part, but not in its full extent; I answer, that you have no reason to give it any particular extent, but only so far as you see it, *at present,* exert itself.

Thus I bring the dispute, O Athenians, to a short issue with my antagonists. The course of nature lies open to my contemplation as well as to theirs. The experienced train of events is the great standard, by which we all regulate our conduct. Nothing else can be appealed to in the field, or in the senate. Nothing else ought ever to be heard of in the schools, or in the closet. In vain would our limited understanding break through those boundaries, which are too narrow for our fond imagination. While we argue from the course of nature, and infer a particular intelligent cause, which first bestowed, and still preserves order in the universe, we embrace a principle, which is both uncertain and useless. It is uncertain; because the subject lies entirely beyond the reach of human experience. It is useless; because our knowledge of this cause being derived entirely from the course of nature, we can never, according to the rules of just reasoning, return back from the cause with any new inference, or making additions to the common and experienced course of nature, establish any new principles of conduct and behaviour.

I observe (said I, finding he had finished his harangue) that you neglect not the artifice of the demagogues of old; and as you were pleased to make me stand for the people, you insinuate yourself into my favour by embracing those principles, to which, you know, I have always expressed a particular attachment. But allowing you to make experience (as indeed I think you ought) the only standard of our judgement concerning this, and all other questions of fact; I doubt not but, from the very same experience, to which you appeal, it may be possible to refute this reasoning, which you have put into the mouth of Epicurus. If you saw, for instance, a half-finished building, surrounded with heaps of brick and stone and mortar, and all the instruments of masonry; could you not *infer* from the effect, that it was a work of design and contrivance? And could you not return again, from this inferred cause, to infer new additions to the effect, and conclude, that the building would soon be finished, and receive all the further improvements, which art could bestow upon it? If you saw upon the sea-shore the print of one human foot, you would conclude, that a man had passed that way, and that he had also left the traces of the other foot, though effaced by the rolling of the sands or inundation of the waters. Why then do you refuse to admit the same method of reasoning with regard to the order of nature? Consider the world and the present life only as an imperfect building, from which you can infer a superior intelligence; and arguing from that superior intelligence, which can leave nothing imperfect; why may you not infer a more finished scheme or plan, which will receive its completion in some distant point of space or time? Are not these methods of reasoning exactly similar? And under what pretence can you embrace the one, while you reject the other?

The infinite difference of the subjects, replied he, is a sufficient foundation for this difference in my conclusions. In works of *human* art and contrivance, it is allowable to advance from the effect to the cause, and returning back from the cause, to form new inferences concerning the effect, and examine the alterations, which it has probably undergone, or may still undergo. But what is the foundation of this method of reasoning? Plainly this: that man is a being, whom we know by experience, whose motives and designs we are acquainted with, and whose projects and inclinations have a certain connexion and coherence, according to the laws which nature has established for the government of such a creature. When, therefore, we find, that any work has proceeded from the skill and industry of man; as we are otherwise acquainted with the nature of the animal, we can draw a hundred inferences concerning what may be expected from him; and these inferences will all be founded in experience and observation. But did we know man only from the single work or production which we examine, it were impossible for us to argue in this manner; because our knowledge of all the qualities, which we ascribe to him, being in that case derived from the production, it is impossible they could point to anything further, or be the foundation of any new inference. The print of a foot in the sand can only prove, when considered alone, that there was some figure adapted to it, by which it was produced: but the print of a human foot proves likewise, from our other experience, that there was probably another foot, which also left its impression, though effaced by time or other accidents. Here we mount from the effect to the cause; and descending again from the cause, infer alterations in the effect; but this is not a continuation of the same simple chain of reasoning. We comprehend in this case a hundred other experiences and observations, concerning the *usual* figure and members of that species of animal, without which this method of argument must be considered as fallacious and sophistical.

The case is not the same with our reasonings from the works of nature. The Deity is known to us only by his productions, and is a single being in the universe, not comprehended under any species or genus, from whose experienced attributes or qualities, we can, by analogy, infer any attribute or quality in him. As the universe shows wisdom and goodness, we infer wisdom and goodness. As it shows a particular degree of these perfections, we infer a particular degree of them, precisely adapted to the effect which we examine. But further attributes or further degrees of the same attributes, we can never be authorized to infer or suppose, by any rules of just reasoning. Now, without some such license of supposition, it is impossible for us to argue from the cause, or infer any alteration in the effect, beyond what has immediately fallen under our observation. Greater good produced by this Being must still prove a greater degree of goodness: a more impartial distribution of rewards and punishments must proceed from a greater regard to justice and equity. Every supposed addition to the works of nature makes an addition to the attributes of the Author of nature; and consequently, being entirely unsupported by any reason or argument, can never be admitted but as mere conjecture and hypothesis.*

The great source of our mistake in this subject, and of the unbounded license of conjecture, which we indulge, is, that we tacitly consider ourselves, as in the place of the Supreme Being, and conclude, that he will, on every occasion, observe the same conduct, which we ourselves, in his situation, would have embraced as reasonable and eligible. But, besides that the ordinary course of nature may convince us, that almost everything is regulated by principles and maxims very different from ours; besides, this, I say, it must evidently appear contrary to all rules of analogy to reason, from the intentions and projects of men, to those of a Being so different, and so much superior. In human nature, there is a certain experienced coherence of designs and inclinations; so that when, from any fact, we have discovered one intention of any man, it may often be rea-

---

*In general, it may, I think, be established as a maxim, that where any cause is known only by its particular effects, it must be impossible to infer any new effects from that cause; since the qualities, which are requisite to produce these new effects along with the former, must either be different, or superior, or of more extensive operation, than those which simply produced the effect, whence alone the cause is supposed to be known to us. We can never, therefore, have any reason to suppose the existence of these qualities. To say, that the new effects proceed only from a continuation of the same energy, which is already known from the first effects, will not remove the difficulty. For even granting this to be the case (which can seldom be supposed), the very continuation and exertion of a like energy (for it is impossible it can be absolutely the same), I say, this exertion of a like energy, in a different period of space and time, is a very arbitrary supposition, and what there cannot possibly be any traces of in the effects, from which all our knowledge of the cause is originally derived. Let the *inferred* cause be exactly proportioned (as it should be) to the known effect; and it is impossible that it can possess any qualities, from which new or different effects can be *inferred*.

sonable, from experience, to infer another, and draw a long chain of conclusions concerning his past or future conduct. But this method of reasoning can never have place with regard to a Being, so remote and incomprehensible, who bears much less analogy to any other being in the universe than the sun to a waxen taper, and who discovers himself only by some faint traces or outlines, beyond which we have no authority to ascribe to him any attribute or perfection. What we imagine to be a superior perfection, may really be a defect. Or were it ever so much a perfection, the ascribing of it to the Supreme Being, where it appears not to have been really exerted, to the full, in his works, savours more of flattery and panegyric, than of just reasoning and sound philosophy. All the philosophy, therefore, in the world, and all the religion, which is nothing but a species of philosophy, will never be able to carry us beyond the usual course of experience, or give us measures of conduct and behaviour different from those which are furnished by reflections on common life. No new fact can ever be inferred from the religious hypothesis; no event foreseen or foretold: no reward or punishment expected or dreaded, beyond what is already known by practice and observation. So that my apology for Epicurus will still appear solid and satisfactory; nor have the political interests of society any connexion with the philosophical disputes concerning metaphysics and religion.

There is still one circumstance, replied I, which you seem to have overlooked. Though I should allow your premises, I must deny your conclusion. You conclude, that religious doctrines and reasonings *can* have no influence on life, because they *ought* to have no influence; never considering, that men reason not in the same manner you do, but draw many consequences from the belief of a divine Existence, and suppose that the Deity will inflict punishments on vice, and bestow rewards on virtue, beyond what appear in the ordinary course of nature. Whether this reasoning of theirs be just or not, is no matter. Its influence on their life and conduct must still be the same. And, those, who attempt to disabuse them of such prejudices, may, for aught I know, be good reasoners, but I cannot allow them to be good citizens and politicians; since they free men from one restraint upon their passions, and make the infringement of the laws of society, in one respect, more easy and secure.

After all, I may, perhaps, agree to your general conclusion in favour of liberty, though upon different premises from those, on which you endeavour to found it. I think, that the state ought to tolerate every principle of philosophy; nor is there an instance, that any government has suffered in its political interests by such indulgence. There is no enthusiasm among philosophers; their doctrines are not very alluring to the people; and no restraint can be put upon their reasonings, but what must be of dangerous consequences to the sciences, and even to the state, by paving the way for persecution and oppression in points, where the generality of mankind are more deeply interested and concerned.

But there occurs to me (continued I) with regard to your main topic, a difficulty, which I shall just propose to you without insisting on it; lest it lead into reasonings of too nice and delicate a nature. In a word, I much doubt whether it be possible for a cause to be known only by its effect (as you have all along supposed) or to be of so singular and particular a nature as to have no parallel and no similarity with any other cause or object, that has ever fallen under our observation. It is only when two *species* of objects are found to be constantly conjoined, that we can infer the one from the other; and were an effect presented, which was entirely singular, and could not be comprehended under any known *species,* I do not see, that we could form any conjecture or inference at all concerning its cause. If experience and observation and analogy be, indeed, the only guides which we can reasonably follow in inferences of this nature; both the effect and cause must bear a similarity and resemblance to other effects and causes, which we know, and which we have found, in many instances, to be conjoined with each other. I leave it to your own reflection to pursue the consequences of this principle. I shall just observe, that, as the antagonists of Epicurus always suppose the universe, an effect quite singular and unparalleled, to be the proof of a Deity, a cause no less singular and unparalleled; your reasonings, upon that supposition, seem, at least, to merit our attention. There is, I own, some difficulty, how we can ever return from the cause to the effect, and, reasoning from our ideas of the former, infer any alteration on the latter, or any addition to it.

Section XII. Of the Academical or Sceptical Philosophy

Part I

There is not a greater number of philosophical reasonings, displayed upon any subject, than those, which prove the existence of a Deity, and refute the fallacies of *Atheists;* and yet the most religious philosophers still dispute whether any man can be so blinded as to be a speculative atheist. How shall we reconcile these contradictions? The knights-errant, who wandered about to clear the world of dragons and giants, never entertained the least doubt with regard to the existence of these monsters.

The *Sceptic* is another enemy of religion, who naturally provokes the indignation of all divines and graver philosophers; though it is certain, that no man ever met with any such absurd creature, or conversed with a man, who had no opinion or principle concerning any subject, either of action or speculation. This begets a very natural question; What is meant by a sceptic? And how far is it possible to push these philosophical principles of doubt and uncertainty?

There is a species of scepticism, *antecedent* to all study and philosophy, which is much inculcated by Des Cartes and others, as a sovereign preservative against error and precipitate judgement. It recommends an universal doubt, not only of all our former opinions and principles, but also of our very faculties; of whose veracity, say they, we must assure ourselves, by a chain of reasoning, deduced from some original principle, which cannot possibly be fallacious or deceitful. But neither is there any such original principle, which has a prerogative above others, that are self-evident and convincing: or if there were, could we advance a step beyond it, but by the use of those very faculties, of which we are supposed to be already diffident. The Cartesian doubt, therefore, were it ever possible to be attained by any human creature (as it plainly is not) would be entirely incurable; and no reasoning could ever bring us to a state of assurance and conviction upon any subject.

It must, however, be confessed, that this species of scepticism, when more moderate, may be understood in a very reasonable sense, and is a necessary preparative to the study of philosophy, by preserving a proper impartiality in our judgements, and weaning our mind from all those prejudices, which we may have imbibed from education or rash opinion. To begin with clear and self-evident principles, to advance by timorous and sure steps, to review frequently our conclusions, and examine accurately all their consequences; though by these means we shall make both a slow and a short progress in our systems; are the only methods, by which we can ever hope to reach truth, and attain a proper stability and certainty in our determinations.

There is another species of scepticism, *consequent* to science and enquiry, when men are supposed to have discovered either the absolute fallaciousness of their mental faculties, or their unfitness to reach any fixed determination in all those curious subjects of speculation, about which they are commonly employed. Even our very senses are brought into dispute, by a certain species of philosophers; and the maxims of common life are subjected to the same doubt as the most profound principles or conclusions of metaphysics and theology. As these paradoxical tenets (if they may be called tenets) are to be met with in some philosophers, and the refutation of them in several, they naturally excite our curiosity, and make us enquire into the arguments, on which they may be founded.

I need not insist upon the more trite topics, employed by the sceptics in all ages, against the evidence of *sense;* such as those which are derived from the imperfection and fallaciousness of our organs, on numberless occasions; the crooked appearance of an oar in water; the various aspects of objects, according to their different distances; the double images which arise from the pressing one eye; with many other appearances of a like nature. These sceptical topics, indeed, are only sufficient to prove, that the senses alone are not implicitly to be depended on; but that we must correct their evidence by reason, and by considerations, derived from the nature of the medium, the distance of the object, and the disposition of the organ, in order to render them, without their sphere, the proper *criteria* of truth and falsehood. There are other more profound arguments against the senses, which admit not of so easy a solution.

It seems evident, that men are carried, by a natural instinct or prepossession, to repose faith in their senses; and that, without any reasoning, or even almost before the use of reason, we always suppose an external universe, which depends not on our perception, but would exist, though we and every sensible creature were absent or annihilated. Even the animal creation are governed by a like opinion, and preserve this belief of external objects, in all their thoughts, designs, and actions.

It seems also evident, that, when men follow this blind and powerful instinct of nature, they always suppose the very images, presented by the senses, to be the external objects, and never entertain any suspicion, that the one are nothing but representations of the other. This very table, which we see white, and which we feel hard, is believed to exist, independent of our perception, and to be something external to our mind, which perceives it. Our presence bestows not being on it: our absence does not annihilate it. It preserves its existence uniform and entire, independent of the situation of intelligent beings, who perceive or contemplate it.

But this universal and primary opinion of all men is soon destroyed by the slightest philosophy, which teaches us, that nothing can ever be present to the mind but an image or perception, and that the senses are only the inlets, through which these images are conveyed, without being able to produce any immediate intercourse between the mind and the object. The table, which we see, seems to diminish, as we remove farther from it: but the real table, which exists independent of us, suffers no alteration: it was, therefore, nothing but its image, which was present to the mind. These are the obvious dictates of reason; and no man, who reflects, ever doubted, that the existences, which we consider, when we say, *this house* and *that tree,* are nothing but perceptions in the mind, and fleeting copies or representations of other existences, which remain uniform and independent.

So far, then, are we necessitated by reasoning to contradict or depart from the primary instincts of nature, and to embrace a new system with regard to the evidence of our senses. But here philosophy finds herself extremely embarrassed, when she would justify this new system, and obviate the cavils and objections of the sceptics. She can no longer plead the infallible and irresistible instinct of nature: for that led us to a quite different system, which is acknowledged fallible and even erroneous. And to justify this pretended philosophical system, by a chain of clear and convincing argument, or even any appearance of argument, exceeds the power of all human capacity.

By what argument can it be proved, that the perceptions of the mind must be caused by external objects, entirely different from them, though resembling them (if that be possible) and could not arise either from the energy of the mind itself, or from the suggestion of some invisible and unknown spirit, or from some other cause still more unknown to us? It is acknowledged, that, in fact, many of these perceptions arise not from anything external, as in dreams, madness, and other diseases. And nothing can be more inexplicable than the manner, in which body should so operate upon mind as ever to convey an image of itself to a substance, supposed of so different, and even contrary a nature.

It is a question of fact, whether the perceptions of the senses be produced by external objects, resembling them: how shall this question be determined? By experience surely; as all other questions of a like nature. But here experience is, and must be entirely silent. The mind has never anything present to it but the perceptions, and cannot possibly reach any experience of their connexion with objects. The supposition of such a connexion is, therefore, without any foundation in reasoning.

To have recourse to the veracity of the supreme Being, in order to prove the veracity of our senses, is surely making a very unexpected circuit. If his veracity were at all concerned in this matter, our senses would be entirely infallible; because it is not possible that he can ever deceive. Not to mention, that, if the external world be once called in question, we shall be at a loss to find arguments, by which we may prove the existence of that Being or any of his attributes.

This is a topic, therefore, in which the profounder and more philosophical sceptics will always triumph, when they endeavour to introduce an universal doubt into all subjects of human knowledge and enquiry. Do you follow the instincts and propensities of nature, may they say, in assenting to the veracity of sense? But these lead you to believe that the very perception or sensible image is the external object. Do you disclaim this principle, in order to embrace a more rational opinion, that the perceptions are only representations of something external? You here depart from your natural propensities and more obvious sentiments; and yet are not able to satisfy your reason, which can never find any convincing argument from experience to prove, that the perceptions are connected with any external objects.

There is another sceptical topic of a like nature, derived from the most profound philosophy, which might merit our attention, were it requisite to dive so deep, in order to discover arguments and reasonings, which can so little serve to any serious purpose. It is universally allowed by modern enquirers, that all the sensible qualities of objects, such as hard, soft, hot, cold, white, black, &c. are merely secondary, and exist not in the objects themselves, but are perceptions of the mind, without any external archetype or model, which they represent. If this be allowed, with regard to secondary qualities, it must also follow, with regard to the supposed primary qualities of extension and solidity; nor can the latter be any more entitled to that denomination than the former. The idea of extension is entirely acquired from the senses of sight and feeling; and if all the qualities, perceived by the senses, be in the mind, not in the object, the same conclusion must reach the idea of extension, which is wholly dependent on the sensible ideas or the ideas of secondary qualities. Nothing can save us from this conclusion, but the asserting, that the ideas of those primary qualities are attained by *Abstraction,* an opinion, which, if we examine it accurately, we shall find to be unintelligible, and even absurd. An extension, that is neither tangible nor visible, cannot possibly be conceived: and a tangible or visible extension, which is neither hard nor soft, black or white, is equally beyond the reach of human conception. Let any man try to conceive a triangle in general, which is neither *Isosceles* nor *Scalenum,* nor has any particular length or proportion of sides; and he will soon perceive the absurdity of all the scholastic notions with regard to abstraction and general ideas.*

Thus the first philosophical objection to the evidence of sense or to the opinion of external existence consists in this, that such an opinion, if rested on natural instinct, is contrary to reason, and if referred to reason, is contrary to natural instinct, and at the same time carries no rational evidence with it, to convince an impartial enquirer. The second objection goes farther, and represents this opinion as contrary to reason: at least, if it be a principle of reason, that all sensible qualities are in the mind, not in the object. Bereave matter of all its intelligible qualities, both primary and secondary, you in a manner annihilate it, and leave only a certain unknown, inexplicable *something,* as the cause of our perceptions; a notion so imperfect, that no sceptic will think it worth while to contend against it.

Part II

It may seem a very extravagant attempt of the sceptics to *destroy* reason by argument and ratiocination; yet is this the grand scope of all their enquiries and disputes. They endeavour to find objections, both to our abstract reasonings, and to those which regard matter of fact and existence.

The chief objection against all *abstract* reasonings is derived from the ideas of space and time; ideas, which, in common life and to a careless view, are very clear and intelligible, but when they pass through the scrutiny of the profound sciences (and they are the chief object of these sciences) afford principles, which seem full of absurdity and contradiction. No priestly *dogmas,* invented on purpose to tame and subdue the rebellious reason of mankind, ever shocked common sense more than the doctrine of the infinite divisibility of extension, with its consequences; as they are pompously displayed by all geometricians and metaphysicians, with a kind of triumph and exultation. A real quantity, infinitely less than any finite quantity, containing quantities infinitely less than itself, and so on *in infinitum;* this is an edifice so bold and prodigious, that it is too weighty for any pretended demonstration to support, because it shocks the clearest and most natural principles of human reason.** But what renders the matter more ex-

---

*This argument is drawn from Dr. Berkeley; and indeed most of the writings of that very ingenious author form the best lessons of scepticism, which are to be found either among the ancient or modern philosophers. Bayle not excepted. He professes, however, in his title-page (and undoubtedly with great truth) to have composed his book against the sceptics as well as against the atheists and freethinkers. But that all his arguments, though otherwise intended, are, in reality, merely sceptical, appears from this, *that they admit of no answer and produce no conviction.* Their only effect is to cause that momentary amazement and irresolution and confusion, which is the result of scepticism.

**Whatever disputes there may be about mathematical points, we must allow that there are physical points; that is, parts of extension which cannot be divided or lessened, either by the eye or imagination. These images, then, which are present to the fancy or senses, are absolutely indivisible, and consequently must be allowed by mathematicians to be infinitely less than any real part of extension; and yet nothing appears more certain to reason, than that an infinite number of them composes an infinite extension. How much more an infinite number of those infinitely small parts of extension, which are still supposed infinitely divisible.

traordinary, is, that these seemingly absurd opinions are supported by a chain of reasoning, the clearest and most natural; nor is it possible for us to allow the premises without admitting the consequences. Nothing can be more convincing and satisfactory than all the conclusions concerning the properties of circles and triangles; and yet, when these are once received, how can we deny, that the angle of contact between a circle and its tangent is infinitely less than any rectilineal angle, that as you may increase the diameter of the circle *in infinitum,* this angle of contact becomes still less, even *in infinitum,* and that the angle of contact between other curves and their tangents may be infinitely less than those between any circle and its tangent, and so on, *in infinitum?* The demonstration of these principles seems as unexceptionable as that which proves the three angles of a triangle to be equal to two right ones, though the latter opinion be natural and easy, and the former big with contradiction and absurdity. Reason here seems to be thrown into a kind of amazement and suspense, which, without the suggestions of any sceptic, gives her a diffidence of herself, and of the ground on which she treads. She sees a full light, which illuminates certain places; but that light borders upon the most profound darkness. And between these she is so dazzled and confounded, that she scarcely can pronounce with certainty and assurance concerning any one object.

The absurdity of these bold determinations of the abstract sciences seems to become, if possible, still more palpable with regard to time than extension. An infinite number of real parts of time, passing in succession, and exhausted one after another, appears so evident a contradiction, that no man, one should think, whose judgment is not corrupted, instead of being improved, by the sciences, would ever be able to admit of it.

Yet still reason must remain restless, and unquiet, even with regard to that scepticism, to which she is driven by these seeming absurdities and contradictions. How any clear, distinct idea can contain circumstances, contradictory to itself, or to any other clear, distinct idea, is absolutely incomprehensible; and is, perhaps, as absurd as any proposition, which can be formed. So that nothing can be more sceptical, or more full of doubt and hesitation, than this scepticism itself, which arises from some of the paradoxical conclusions of geometry or the science of quantity.*

The sceptical objections to *moral* evidence, or to the reasonings concerning matter of fact, are either *popular* or *philosophical.* The popular objections are derived from the natural weakness of human understanding; the contradictory opinions, which have been entertained in different ages and nations; the variations of our judgement in sickness and health, youth and old age, prosperity and adversity; the perpetual contradiction of each particular man's opinions and sentiments; with many other topics of that kind. It is needless to insist farther on this head. These objections are but weak. For as, in common life, we reason every moment concerning fact and existence, and cannot possibly

---

*It seems to me not impossible to avoid these absurdities and contradictions, if it be admitted, that there is no such thing as abstract or general ideas, properly speaking; but that all general ideas are, in reality, particular ones, attached to a general term, which recalls, upon occasion, other particular ones that resemble, in certain circumstances, the idea, present to the mind. Thus when the term Horse is pronounced, we immediately figure to ourselves the idea of a black or a white animal, of a particular size or figure: But as that term is also usually applied to animals of other colours, figures and sizes these ideas, though not actually present to the imagination, are easily recalled, and our reasoning and conclusion proceed in the same way, as if they were actually present. If this be admitted (as seems reasonable) it follows that all the ideas of quantity, upon which mathematicians reason, are nothing but particular, and such as are suggested by the senses and imagination, and consequently, cannot be infinitely divisible. It is sufficient to have dropped this hint at present, without prosecuting it any farther. It certainly concerns all lovers of science not to expose themselves to the ridicule and contempt of the ignorant by their conclusions; and this seems the readiest solution of these difficulties.

subsist, without continually employing this species of argument, any popular objections, derived from thence, must be insufficient to destroy that evidence. The great subverter of *Pyrrhonism* or the excessive principles of scepticism is action, and employment, and the occupations of common life. These principles may flourish and triumph in the schools; where it is, indeed, difficult, if not impossible, to refute them. But as soon as they leave the shade, and by the presence of the real objects, which actuate our passions and sentiments, are put in opposition to the more powerful principles of our nature, they vanish like smoke, and leave the most determined sceptic in the same condition as other mortals.

The sceptic, therefore, had better keep within his proper sphere, and display those *philosophical* objections, which arise from more profound researches. Here he seems to have ample matter of triumph; while he justly insists, that all our evidence for any matter of fact, which lies beyond the testimony of sense or memory, is derived entirely from the relation of cause and effect; that we have no other idea of this relation than that of two objects, which have been frequently *conjoined* together; that we have no argument to convince us, that objects, which have, in our experience, been frequently conjoined, will likewise, in other instances, be conjoined in the same manner; and that nothing leads us to this inference but custom or a certain instinct of our nature; which it is indeed difficult to resist, but which, like other instincts, may be fallacious and deceitful. While the sceptic insists upon these topics, he shows his force, or rather, indeed, his own and our weakness; and seems, for the time at least, to destroy all assurance and conviction. These arguments might be displayed at greater length, if any durable good or benefit to society could ever be expected to result from them.

For here is the chief and most confounding objection to *excessive* scepticism, that no durable good can ever result from it; while it remains in its full force and vigour. We need only ask a sceptic, *What his meaning is? And what he proposes by all these curious researches?* He is immediately at a loss, and knows not what to answer. A Copernican or Ptolemaic, who supports each his different system of astronomy, may hope to produce a conviction, which will remain constant and durable, with his audience. A Stoic or Epicurean displays principles, which may not be durable, but which have an effect on conduct and behaviour. But a Pyrrhonian cannot expect, that his philosophy will have any constant influence on the mind: or if it had, that its influence would be beneficial to society. On the contrary, he must acknowledge, if he will acknowledge anything, that all human life must perish, were his principles universally and steadily to prevail. All discourse, all action would immediately cease; and men remain in a total lethargy, till the necessities of nature, unsatisfied, put an end to their miserable existence. It is true; so fatal an event is very little to be dreaded. Nature is always too strong for principle. And though a Pyrrhonian may throw himself or others into a momentary amazement and confusion by his profound reasonings; the first and most trivial event in life will put to flight all his doubts and scruples, and leave him the same, in every point of action and speculation, with the philosophers of every other sect, or with those who never concerned themselves in any philosophical researches. When he awakes from his dream, he will be the first to join in the laugh against himself, and to confess, that all his objections are mere amusement, and can have no other tendency than to show the whimsical condition of mankind, who must act and reason and believe; though they are not able, by their most diligent enquiry, to satisfy themselves concerning the foundation of these operations, or to remove the objections, which may be raised against them.

Part III

There is, indeed, a more *mitigated* scepticism or *academical* philosophy, which may be both durable and useful, and which may, in part, be the result of this Pyrrhonism, or excessive scepticism, when its undistinguished doubts are, in some measure, corrected by common sense and reflection. The greater part of mankind are naturally apt to be affirmative and dogmatical in their opinions; and while they see objects only on one side, and have no idea of any counterpoising argument, they throw themselves precipitately into the principles, to which they are inclined; nor have they any indulgence for those who entertain opposite sentiments. To hesitate or balance perplexes their understanding, checks their passion, and suspends their action. They are, therefore, impatient till they escape from a state, which to them is so uneasy: and they think, that they could never remove themselves far enough from it, by the violence of their affirmations and obstinacy of their belief. But could such dogmatical reasoners become sensible of the strange infirmities of human understanding, even in its most perfect state, and when most accurate and cautious in its determination; such a reflection would naturally inspire them with more modesty and reserve, and diminish their fond opinion of themselves, and their prejudice against antagonists. The illiterate may reflect on the disposition of the learned, who, amidst all the advantages of study and reflection, are commonly still diffident in their determinations: and if any of the learned be inclined, from their natural temper, to haughtiness and obstinacy, a small tincture of Pyrrhonism might abate their pride, by showing them, that the few advantages, which they may have attained over their fellows, are but inconsiderable, if compared with the universal perplexity and confusion, which is inherent in human nature. In general, there is a degree of doubt, and caution, and modesty, which, in all kinds of scrutiny and decision, ought for ever to accompany a just reasoner.

Another species of *mitigated* scepticism which may be of advantage to mankind, and which may be the natural result of the Pyrrhonian doubts and scruples, is the limitation of our enquiries to such subjects as are best adapted to the narrow capacity of human understanding. The *imagination* of man is naturally sublime, delighted with whatever is remote and extraordinary, and running, without control, into the most distant parts of space and time in order to avoid the objects, which custom has rendered too familiar to it. A correct *judgement* observes a contrary method, and avoiding all distant and high enquiries, confines itself to common life, and to such subjects as fall under daily practice and experience; leaving the more sublime topics to the embellishment of poets and orators, or to the arts of priests and politicians. To bring us to so salutary a determination, nothing can be more serviceable, than to be once thoroughly convinced of the force of the Pyrrhonian doubt, and of the impossibility, that anything, but the strong power of natural instinct, could free us from it. Those who have a propensity to philosophy, will still continue their researches; because they reflect, that, besides the immediate pleasure, attending such an occupation, philosophical decisions are nothing but the reflections of common life, methodized and corrected. But they will never be tempted to go beyond common life, so long as they consider the imperfection of those faculties which they employ, their narrow reach, and their inaccurate operations. While we cannot give a satisfactory reason, why we believe, after a thousand experiments, that a stone will fall, or fire burn; can we ever satisfy ourselves concerning any determination, which we may form, with regard to the origin of worlds, and the situation of nature, from, and to eternity?

This narrow limitation, indeed, of our enquiries, is, in every respect, so reasonable, that it suffices to make the slightest examination into the natural powers of the human mind and to compare them with their objects, in order to recommend it to us. We shall then find what are the proper subjects of science and enquiry.

It seems to me, that the only objects of the abstract science or of demonstration are quantity and number, and that all attempts to extend this more perfect species of knowledge beyond these bounds are mere sophistry and illusion. As the component parts of quantity and number are entirely similar, their relations become intricate and involved; and nothing can be more curious, as well as useful, than to trace, by a variety of mediums their equality or inequality, through their different appearances. But as all other ideas are clearly distinct and different from each other, we can never advance farther, by our utmost scrutiny, than to observe this diversity, and, by an obvious reflection, pronounce one thing not to be another. Or if there be any difficulty in these decisions, it proceeds entirely from the undeterminate meaning of words, which is corrected by juster definitions. That *the square of the hypothenuse is equal to the square of the other two sides,* cannot be known, let the terms be ever so exactly defined, without a train of reasoning and enquiry. But to convince us of this proposition, *that where there is no property, there can be no injustice,* it is only necessary to define the terms, and explain injustice to be a violation of property. This proposition is, indeed, nothing but a more imperfect definition. It is the same case with all those pretended syllogistical reasonings, which may be found in every other branch of learning, except the sciences of quantity and number and these may safely, I think, be pronounced the only proper objects of knowledge and demonstration.

All other enquiries of men regard only matter of fact and existence; and these are evidently incapable of demonstration. Whatever *is* may *not be.* No negation of a fact can involve a contradiction. The non-existence of any being, without exception, is as clear and distinct an idea as its existence. The proposition, which affirms it not to be, however false, is no less conceivable and intelligible, than that which affirms it to be. The case is different with the sciences, properly so called. Every proposition, which is not true, is there confused and unintelligible. That the cube root of 64 is equal to the half of 10, is a false proposition, and can never be distinctly conceived. But that Caesar, or the angel Gabriel, or any being never existed, may be a false proposition, but still is perfectly conceivable, and implies no contradiction.

The existence, therefore, of any being can only be proved by arguments from its cause or its effect; and these arguments are founded entirely on experience. If we reason *a priori,* anything may appear able to produce anything. The falling of a pebble may, for aught we know, extinguish the sun; or the wish of a man control the planets in their orbits. It is only experience, which teaches us the nature and bounds of cause and effect, and enables us to infer the existence of one object from that of another.* Such is the foundation of moral reasoning, which forms the greater part of human knowledge, and is the source of all human action and behaviour.

Moral reasonings are either concerning particular or general facts. All deliberations in life regard the former; as also all disquisitions in history, chronology, geography, and astronomy.

The sciences, which treat of general facts, are politics, natural philosophy, physic, chemistry, &c. where the qualities, causes and effects of a whole species of objects are enquired into.

---

*That impious maxim of the ancient philosophy, *Ex nihilo, nihil fit* [From nothing, nothing issues], by which the creation of matter was excluded, ceases to be a maxim according to this philosophy. Not only the will of the supreme Being may create matter; but, for aught we know *a priori,* the will of any other being might create it, or any other cause, that the most whimsical imagination can assign.

Divinity or Theology, as it proves the existence of a Deity, and the immortality of souls, is composed partly of reasonings concerning particular, partly concerning general facts. It has a foundation in *reason,* so far as it is supported by experience. But its best and most solid foundation is *faith* and divine revelation.

Morals and criticism are not so properly objects of the understanding as of taste and sentiment. Beauty, whether moral or natural, is felt, more properly than perceived. Or if we reason concerning it, and endeavour to fix its standard, we regard a new fact, to wit, the general tastes of mankind, or some such fact, which may be the object of reasoning and enquiry.

When we run over libraries, persuaded of these principles, what havoc must we make? If we take in our hand any volume; of divinity or school metaphysics, for instance; let us ask, *Does it contain any abstract reasoning concerning quantity or number?* No. *Does it contain any experimental reasoning concerning matter of fact and existence?* No. Commit it then to the flames: for it can contain nothing but sophistry and illusion.

IMMANUEL KANT
1724–1804

Whereas most modern philosophers (such as Descartes, Berkeley, and Hume) arrived at their basic philosophical positions early in life, Immanuel Kant did not work out his views until well into middle age. Whereas the earlier thinkers wrote major works when still young, Kant's important pieces were written between the ages of fifty-seven and sixty-seven. Whereas the others' works were written for a broad general audience and are relatively accessible to educated readers, Kant wrote in an academic style that is notoriously difficult to follow. Whereas most of the earlier philosophers traveled widely, Kant never left the provincial city in which he was born. Unlike his predecessors, who held many different positions and did philosophy on the side, Kant made his living as a professor of philosophy. Yet Kant is the most important and influential of all modern philosophers.

Kant was born, raised, lived, and died in the town of Königsberg in East Prussia. His parents were lower middle-class, hard-working, simple folk. They belonged to the Lutheran Pietist movement, which cultivated high moral standards and personal devotion to God in Christ. Like Hume, who had a similar religious upbringing (Calvinist Presbyterian), Kant was later critical of his background. But unlike Hume, he remained a deeply religious man.

Through the intervention of his mother's favorite preacher, who was also a professor at the University of Königsberg, young Immanuel gained admittance to a local high school. There he received a solid Pietist education and a firm grounding in the classics. At sixteen, Kant was admitted to the university, where he planned to study the classics. But under the influence of a strong teacher, Martin Knutzen, Kant moved into philosophy and was attracted to the comprehensive scholasticism of Christian Wolff (1679–1754), who had developed Leibniz's philosophy into a rationalistic system.

Following his university studies, Kant worked as a private tutor to wealthy families. By 1755, he was back in the university, where he was employed as an unsalaried lecturer for the next fifteen years. (Given the difficulty of his writing, it is worth noting that his lectures were very popular.) His early lectures focused on the external world, dealing with issues in physics and physical geography. He published an important early work, *Universal History of Nature and Theory of the Heavens* (1755), which explained the structure of the universe in terms of Newtonian physics, without reference to God. During this period, Kant's focus began to shift to the inner world of the mind and the nature of morality. At this time, he also encountered the writings of Hume, which challenged the rationalism he had imbibed from Wolff. He later said that Hume "interrupted my dogmatic slumber, and gave my investigations in the field of speculative philosophy quite a new direction."

In 1770, Kant was given what he had long desired—the chair of logic and metaphysics at the University of Königsberg. In his inaugural address, *Dissertation on the Form and Principles of Sensible and Intelligible Worlds,* Kant declared his intention to reconstruct philosophy. Over the next ten years, he carefully and quietly thought through all his ideas. Finally he wrote his major work, *Critique of Pure Reason.* He wrote it, as he later told a friend, "within four or five months, with the utmost attention to the contents, but with less concern for the presentation or for making things easy for the reader." Unfortunately, when the book appeared, his indifference to readers left most people lost. In 1783, he restated his main points in a work "for the benefit of teachers," the *Prolegomena to Any Future Metaphysics,* and in 1787 he rewrote the *Critique* itself.

Kant's first major work on ethics, *Foundation for the Metaphysics of Morals,* was published in 1785. A further development of his moral views, *Critique of Practical Reason,* appeared in 1788. In 1790, Kant published his third and last critique, the *Critique of Judgment,* which deals with aesthetic judgments and the question of purpose in nature. Kant's other important works include *Metaphysical Foundations of Natural Science* (1786), *Religion Within the Limits of Reason Alone* (1793), *Toward Eternal Peace* (1795), and *Metaphysics of Morals* (1797).

Whereas Kant's writings revolutionized the philosophical world, his personal life was quiet, almost boring. With one minor exception late in life, he was never involved in any scandals or controversies. He never traveled more than a few miles outside Königsberg. A lifelong bachelor, he is said to have awakened and gone to bed at exactly the same time each day. His daily walks were reportedly so regular that people could set their clocks by his approach. A rather frail man, he so carefully guarded his health that he lived a long, productive life. Yet he was also a delightful conversationalist and host, and he had many friends and admirers. At his death in 1804, he was the best-known philosopher in Germany, read, if not understood, throughout Europe.

*   *   *

Responding to the skeptical empiricism of Hume, Kant argued that the mind is not simply a repository of impressions and ideas but it is actively involved in knowing the objects it experiences. Prior to Kant, most thinkers believed that the mind, in knowing, conformed to objects: that the ideas of the mind took on the "shape" of the world outside the mind. Kant argued instead that objects conform to the mind:

that how one experiences the world is a result of the way the mind operates. Knowledge is a result of human understanding applied to sense experience.

Space and time are two ways the mind operates. They are not "objects" in the world, derived from sense experience; rather, they are the precondition for our having sense-experience at all: They are the *a priori* (meaning "known independently of sense perceptions," "indubitable") foundations of sensibility. Space and time must be presupposed in order to have experience at all.

Kant goes on to consider the *a priori* foundations of human understanding. He argues that there must be categories of the mind, such as causality and substance, that unify our perceptions. These categories are not found in sense experience; they are innate structures of the mind and the necessary conditions for having any knowledge at all. Without these categories, the world of experience would be utterly chaotic and unknowable.

Of course this knowledge is only a knowledge of things as we experience them in the "phenomenal world." The way things *really* are, apart from our experience of them, the "noumenal world" of the "things-in-themselves," is not available to us by pure reason. This, according to Kant, means that we cannot have knowledge of God, the world, or even the substantial self. But rather than letting this end in Humean skepticism, Kant suggests that these three "ideas of reason" (God, world, self) stimulate and unify knowledge. They point beyond themselves to possibilities in the noumenal world that pure reason cannot reach. As long as we do not think that we have real knowledge of their objects, these three ideas of reason serve a useful purpose.

Turning to moral theory, Kant develops a "deontological," or "duty-based," theory of morality. An action is good not because it produces consequences such as pleasure or happiness, but because it is done out of duty by a good will. To establish what a person's duty is, Kant develops the "categorical imperative." In the *Foundation for the Metaphysics of Morals,* Kant discusses several versions of this imperative, the most important of which is this: "Act only on that maxim whereby you can at the same time will that it should become a universal law."

Although Kant is best known for his work in epistemology and ethics, he wrote on many topics. His earlier essay "Idea for a Universal History with Cosmopolitan Intent" (1784) is an example of Kant at his nontechnical best. Here the Königsberg recluse shows himself as a brilliant citizen of the world when he introduces the idea of a League of Nations:

> By means of wars and the high tension of never relaxed armaments for these wars, and by means of the distress which every nation must thus suffer, even during times of peace, [Nature] drives man at first to imperfect attempts, but finally, after many devastations and disturbances and even exhaustion of all powers, she drives toward a situation which reason might have anticipated without so many sad experiences: Men leave the lawless state of savages and enter a League of Nations. Thus every state, including the smallest, can find a guarantee for its security and its rights, not in its own power or in its own views of what is just, but in this great League of Nations. . . .

*   *   *

Kant's condensation of the *Critique,* the *Prolegomena to Any Future Metaphysics,* and his *Foundation for the Metaphysics of Morals* are both given here (complete) in the Lewis White Beck translations.

Among the many available books on Kant, Stephen Körner, *Kant* (Baltimore, MD: Penguin Books, 1955) is almost universally accepted as the best introduction. John Kemp, *The Philosophy of Kant* (Oxford: Oxford University Press, 1968); Ralph C.S. Walker, *Kant: The Arguments of the Philosophers* (London: Routledge & Kegan Paul, 1978); C.D. Broad, *Kant: An Introduction* (Cambridge: Cambridge University Press, 1978); Ernst Cassirer, *Kant's Life and Thought,* translated by James Haden (New Haven, CT: Yale University Press, 1982); Ermanno Bencivenga, *Kant's Copernican Revolution* (Oxford: Oxford University Press, 1987); and Otfried Höffe, *Immanuel Kant,* translated by Marshall Farrier (Albany, NY: SUNY Press, 1994) are also helpful. A.C. Ewing, *A Short Commentary on Kant's Critique of Pure Reason* (London: Methuen, 1950) provides an accessible commentary to Kant's difficult *Critique of Pure Reason,* while Norman Kemp Smith, *A Commentary to Kant's Critique of Pure Reason* (London: Macmillan, 1930) is standard. H.J. Paton, *Kant's Metaphysic of Experience,* two vols. (New York: Humanities Press, 1936) is an alternative interpretation to the N.K. Smith study. T.D. Weldon, *Kant's Critique of Pure Reason* (Oxford: Oxford University Press, 1945, 2nd edition, 1958); and Henry E. Allison, *Kant's Transcendental Idealism: An Interpretation and Defense* (New Haven, CT: Yale University Press, 1983) are also useful. For works on Kant's moral theory, see W.D. Ross, *Kant's Ethical Theory: A Commentary on the Grundlegung zur Metaphysik der Sitten* [*Groundwork of the Metaphysic of Morals*] (Oxford: Clarendon Press, 1954); Lewis White Beck, *A Commentary on Kant's Critique of Practical Reason* (Chicago: University of Chicago Press, 1960); H.J. Paton, *The Categorical Imperative* (London: 1947; reprinted, New York: Harper & Row, 1967); and Roger Sullivan, *An Introduction to Kant's Ethics* (Cambridge: Cambridge University Press, 1994). Howard Caygill, *A Kant Dictionary* (Oxford: Basil Blackwell, 1995) provides a useful reference work. For collections of essays, see Lewis White Beck, ed., *Studies in the Philosophy of Kant* (Indianapolis, IN: Bobbs-Merrill, 1965); R.P. Wolff, *Kant* (Garden City, NY: Doubleday, 1967); and Ralph C.S. Walker, ed., *Kant on Pure Reason* (Oxford: Oxford University Press, 1982).

PROLEGOMENA TO ANY FUTURE METAPHYSICS

INTRODUCTION

These *Prolegomena* are for the use, not of mere learners, but of future teachers, and even the latter should not expect that they will be serviceable for the systematic exposition of a ready-made science, but merely for the discovery of the science itself.

There are scholarly men to whom the history of philosophy (both ancient and modern) is philosophy itself; for these the present *Prolegomena* are not written. They must wait till those who endeavor to draw from the fountain of reason itself have com-

Immanuel Kant, *Prolegomena to Any Future Metaphysics,* a revision of the Paul Carus translation with an introduction by Lewis White Beck (New York: Macmillan/Library of the Liberal Arts, 1950).

pleted their work; it will then be the turn of these scholars to inform the world of what has been done. Unfortunately, nothing can be said which, in their opinion, has not been said before, and truly the same prophecy applies to all future time; for since the human reason has for many centuries speculated upon innumerable objects in various ways, it is hardly to be expected that we should not be able to discover analogies for every new idea among the old sayings of past ages.

My purpose is to persuade all those who think metaphysics worth studying that it is absolutely necessary to pause a moment and, regarding all that has been done as though undone, to propose first the preliminary question, "Whether such a thing as metaphysics be even possible at all?"

If it be science, how is it that it cannot, like other sciences, obtain universal and lasting recognition? If not, how can it maintain its pretensions and keep the human mind in suspense with hopes never ceasing, yet never fulfilled? Whether then we demonstrate our knowledge or our ignorance in this field, we must come once for all to a definite conclusion respecting the nature of this so-called science, which cannot possibly remain on its present footing. It seems almost ridiculous, while every other science is continually advancing, that in this, which pretends to be wisdom incarnate, for whose oracle everyone inquires, we should constantly move round the same spot, without gaining a single step. And so its votaries having melted away, we do not find men confident of their ability to shine in other sciences venturing their reputation here, where everybody, however ignorant in other matters, presumes to deliver a final verdict, because in this domain there is actually as yet no standard weight and measure to distinguish sound knowledge from shallow talk.

After all it is nothing extraordinary in the elaboration of a science that, when men begin to wonder how far it has advanced, the question should at last occur whether and how such a science is possible at all. Human reason so delights building that it has several times built up a tower and then razed it to see how the foundation was laid. It is never too late to become reasonable and wise; but if the knowledge comes late, there is always more difficulty in starting a reform.

The question whether a science be possible presupposes a doubt as to its actuality. But such a doubt offends the men whose whole fortune consists of this supposed jewel; hence he who raises the doubt must expect opposition from all sides. Some, in the proud consciousness of their possessions, which are ancient and therefore considered legitimate, will take their metaphysical compendia in their hands and look down on him with contempt; others, who never see anything except it be identical with what they have elsewhere seen before, will not understand him, and everything will remain for a time as if nothing had happened to excite the concern or the hope for an impending change.

Nevertheless, I venture to predict that the independent reader of these *Prolegomena* will not only doubt his previous science, but ultimately be fully persuaded that it cannot exist unless the demands here stated on which its possibility depends be satisfied; and, as this has never been done, that there is, as yet, no such thing as metaphysics. But as it can never cease to be in demand*—since the interest of common sense are so

---

*Says Horace:
Rusticus expectat, dum defluat amnis, at ille
Labitur et labetur in omne volubilis aevum.
     ["A rustic fellow waiteth on the shore
     For the river to flow away,
     But the river flows, and flows on as before,
     And it flows forever and aye".]
                         Epistle I, 2, 42f.

intimately interwoven with it—he must confess that a radical reform, or rather a new birth of the science, after a new plan, is unavoidable, however men may struggle against it for a while.

Since the *Essays* of Locke and Leibniz, or rather since the origin of metaphysics so far as we know its history, nothing has ever happened which could have been more decisive to its fate than the attack made upon it by David Hume. He threw no light on this species of knowledge, but he certainly struck a spark by which light might have been kindled had it caught some inflammable substance and had its smouldering fire been carefully nursed and developed.

Hume started chiefly from a single but important concept in metaphysics, namely, that of the connection of cause and effect (including its derivatives force and action, and so on). He challenged reason, which pretends to have given birth to this concept of herself, to answer him by what right she thinks anything could be so constituted that if that thing be posited, something else also must necessarily be posited; for this is the meaning of the concept of cause. He demonstrated irrefutably that it was perfectly impossible for reason to think *a priori* and by means of concepts such a combination, for it implies necessity. We cannot at all see why, in consequence of the existence of one thing, another must necessarily exist or how the concept of such a combination can arise *a priori*. Hence he inferred that reason was altogether deluded with reference to this concept, which she erroneously considered as one of her own children, whereas in reality it was nothing but a bastard of imagination, impregnated by experience, which subsumed certain representations under the law of association and mistook a subjective necessity (habit) for an objective necessity arising from insight. Hence he inferred that reason had no power to think such combinations, even in general, because her concepts would then be purely fictitious and all her pretended *a priori* cognitions nothing but common experiences marked with a false stamp. In plain language, this means that there is not and cannot be any such thing as metaphysics at all.*

However hasty and mistaken Hume's inference may appear, it was at least founded upon investigation, and this investigation deserved the concentrated attention of the brighter spirits of his day as well as determined efforts on their part to discover, if possible, a happier solution of the problem in the sense proposed by him, all of which would have speedily resulted in a complete reform of the science.

But Hume suffered the usual misfortune of metaphysicians, of not being understood. It is positively painful to see how utterly his opponents, Reid, Oswald, Beattie, and lastly Priestley, missed the point of the problem; for while they were ever taking for granted that which he doubted, and demonstrating with zeal and often with impudence that which he never thought of doubting, they so misconstrued his valuable suggestion that everything remained in its old condition, as if nothing had happened. The question was not whether the concept of cause was right, useful, and even indispensable for our knowledge of nature, for this Hume had never doubted; but whether that concept could

---

*Nevertheless Hume called this destructive science metaphysics and attached to it great value. "Metaphysics and morals," he declares, "are the most considerable branches of science. Mathematics and natural philosophy are not half so valuable." ["Of the Rise and Progress of the Arts and Sciences," *Essays Moral, Political, and Literary,* XIV, edited by Green and Grose, I, 187]. But the acute man merely regarded the negative use arising from the moderation of extravagant claims of speculative reason, and the complete settlement of the many endless and troublesome controversies that mislead mankind. He overlooked the positive injury which results if reason be deprived of its most important prospects, which can alone supply to the will the highest aim for all its endeavors.

be thought by reason *a priori,* and consequently whether it possessed an inner truth, independent of all experience, implying a perhaps more extended use not restricted merely to objects of experience. This was Hume's problem. It was solely a question concerning the *origin,* not concerning the *indispensable* need of using the concept. Were the former decided, the conditions of the use and the sphere of its valid application would have been determined as a matter of course.

But to satisfy the conditions of the problem, the opponents of the great thinker should have penetrated very deeply into the nature of reason, so far as it is concerned with pure thinking—a task which did not suit them. They found a more convenient method of being defiant without any insight, namely, the appeal to *common sense.* It is indeed a great gift of God to possess right or (as they now call it) plain common sense. But this common sense must be shown in action by well-considered and reasonable thoughts and words, not by appealing to it as an oracle when no rational justification for one's position can be advanced. To appeal to common sense when insight and science fail, and no sooner—this is one of the subtle discoveries of modern times, by means of which the most superficial ranter can safely enter the lists with the most thorough thinker and hold his own. But as long as a particle of insight remains, no one would think of having recourse to this subterfuge. Seen clearly, it is but an appeal to the opinion of the multitude, of whose applause the philosopher is ashamed, while the popular charlatan glories and boasts in it. I should think that Hume might fairly have laid as much claim to common sense as Beattie and, in addition, to a critical reason (such as the latter did not possess), which keeps common sense in check and prevents it from speculating, or, if speculations are under discussion, restrains the desire to decide because it cannot satisfy itself concerning its own premises. By this means alone can common sense remain sound. Chisels and hammers may suffice to work a piece of wood, but for etching we require an etcher's needle. Thus common sense and speculative understanding are each serviceable, but each in its own way: the former in judgments which apply immediately to experience; the latter when we judge universally from mere concepts, as in metaphysics, where that which calls itself, in spite of the inappropriateness of the name, sound common sense, has no right to judge at all.

I openly confess my recollection* of David Hume was the very thing which many years ago first interrupted my dogmatic slumber and gave my investigations in the field of speculative philosophy a quite new direction. I was far from following him in the conclusions at which he arrived by regarding, not the whole of his problem, but a part, which by itself can give us no information. If we start from a well-founded, but undeveloped, thought which another has bequeathed to us, we may well hope by continued reflection to advance farther than the acute man to whom we owe the first spark of light.

I therefore first tried whether Hume's objection could not be put into a general form, and soon found that the concept of the connection of cause and effect was by no means the only concept by which the understanding thinks the connection of things *a priori,* but rather that metaphysics consists altogether of such concepts. I sought to ascertain their number; and when I had satisfactorily succeeded in this by starting from a single principle, I proceeded to the deduction of these concepts, which I was now certain were not derived from experience, as Hume had attempted to derive them, but sprang from the pure understanding. This deduction (which seemed impossible to my acute predecessor, which had never even occurred to anyone else, though no one had

*[*Erinnerung.* Kant had probably read Hume before 1760, but only much later (1772?) did he begin to follow "a new direction" under Hume's influence.—L.W.B.]

View of Königsberg Castle,
house of Kant in foreground, left.
(*British Museum*)

hesitated to use the concepts without investigating the basis of their objective validity)
was the most difficult task which ever could have been undertaken in the service of
metaphysics; and the worst was that metaphysics, such as it is, could not assist me in the
least because this deduction alone can render metaphysics possible. But as soon as I had
succeeded in solving Hume's problem, not merely in a particular case, but with respect
to the whole faculty of pure reason, I could proceed safely, though slowly, to determine
the whole sphere of pure reason completely and from universal principles, in its boundaries as well as in its contents. This was required for metaphysics in order to construct
its system according to a safe plan.

But I fear that the execution of Hume's problem in its widest extent (namely, my
Critique of Pure Reason) will fare as the problem itself fared when first proposed. It will
be misjudged because it is misunderstood, and misunderstood because men choose to
skim through the book and not to think through it—a disagreeable task, because the
work is dry, obscure, opposed to all ordinary notions, and moreover long-winded. I confess, however, I did not expect to hear from philosophers complaints of want of popularity, entertainment, and facility when the existence of highly prized and indispensable
knowledge is at stake, which cannot be established otherwise than by the strictest rules
of a scholastic precision. Popularity may follow, but is inadmissible at the beginning.
Yet as regards a certain obscurity, arising partly from the diffuseness of the plan, owing
to which the principal points of the investigation are easily lost sight of, the complaint
is just, and I intend to remove it by the present *Prolegomena*.

The first-mentioned work, which discusses the pure faculty of reason in its whole
compass and bounds, will remain the foundation, to which the *Prolegomena*, as a preliminary exercise, refer; for critique as a science must first be established as complete
and perfect before we can think of letting metaphysics appear on the scene or even have
the most distant hope of attaining it.

We have been long accustomed to seeing antiquated knowledge produced as new
by taking it out of its former context and fitting it into a systematic garment of any fancy
pattern with new titles. Most readers will set out by expecting nothing else from the *Critique;* but these *Prolegomena* may persuade him that it is a perfectly new science, of
which no one has ever even thought, the very idea of which was unknown, and for
which nothing hitherto accomplished can be of the smallest use, except it be the suggestion of Hume's doubts. Yet even he did not suspect such a formal science, but ran his

ship ashore, for safety's sake, landing on scepticism, there to let it lie and rot; whereas my object is rather to give it a pilot, who, by means of safe principles of navigation drawn from a knowledge of the globe, and provided with a complete chart and compass, may steer the ship safely whither he listeth.

If in a new science which is wholly isolated and unique in its kind, we started with the prejudice that we can judge of things by means of alleged knowledge previously acquired—though this is precisely what has first to be called in question—we should only fancy we saw everywhere what we had already known, because the expressions have a similar sound. But everything would appear utterly metamorphosed, senseless, and unintelligible, because we should have as a foundation our own thoughts, made by long habit a second nature, instead of the author's. But the long-windedness of the work, so far as it depends on the subject and not on the exposition, its consequent unavoidable dryness and its scholastic precision, are qualities which can only benefit the science, though they may discredit the book.

Few writers are gifted with the subtlety and, at the same time, with the grace of David Hume, or with the depth, as well as the elegance, of Moses Mendelssohn. Yet I flatter myself I might have made my own exposition popular had my object been merely to sketch out a plan and leave its completion to others, instead of having my heart in the welfare of the science to which I had devoted myself so long; in truth, it required no little constancy, and even self-denial, to postpone the sweets of an immediate success to the prospect of a slower, but more lasting, reputation.

Making plans is often the occupation of an opulent and boastful mind, which thus obtains the reputation of a creative genius by demanding what it cannot itself supply, by censuring what it cannot improve, and by proposing what it knows not where to find. And yet something more should belong to a sound plan of a general critique of pure reason than mere conjectures if this plan is to be other than the usual declamations of pious aspirations. But pure reason is a sphere so separate and self-contained that we cannot touch a part without affecting all the rest. We can do nothing without first determining the position of each part and its relation to the rest; for, as our judgment within this sphere cannot be corrected by anything without, the validity and use of every part depends upon the relation in which it stands to all the rest within the domain of reason. As in the structure of an organized body, the end of each member can only be deduced from the full conception of the whole. It may, then, be said of such a critique that it is never trustworthy except it be perfectly complete, down to the most minute elements of pure reason. In the sphere of this faculty you can determine and define either everything or nothing.

But although a mere sketch preceding the *Critique of Pure Reason* would be unintelligible, unreliable, and useless, it is all the more useful as a sequel. It enables us to grasp the whole, to examine in detail the chief points of importance in the science, and to improve in many respects our exposition, as compared with the first execution of the work.

With that work complete, I offer here a sketch based on an *analytical* method, while the *Critique* itself had to be executed in the *synthetical* style, in order that the science may present all its articulations, as the structure of a peculiar cognitive faculty, in their natural combination. But should any reader find this sketch, which I publish as the *Prolegomena to Any Future Metaphysics,* still obscure, let him consider that not everyone is bound to study metaphysics; that many minds will succeed very well in the exact and even in deep sciences more closely allied to the empirical, while they cannot succeed in investigations dealing exclusively with abstract concepts. In such cases men should apply their talents to other subjects. But he who undertakes to judge or, still more, to construct a system of metaphysics must satisfy the demands here made, either by adopting my solution or by thoroughly refuting it and substituting another. To evade it is impossible.

In conclusion, let it be remembered that this much abused obscurity (frequently serving as a mere pretext under which people hide their own indolence or dullness) has its uses, since all who in other sciences observe a judicious silence speak authoritatively in metaphysics and make bold decisions, because their ignorance is not here contrasted with the knowledge of others. Yet it does contrast with sound critical principles, which we may therefore commend in the words of Virgil:

*Ignavum, fucos, pecus a praesepibus arcent.**

PROLEGOMENA

PREAMBLE ON THE PECULIARITIES OF ALL METAPHYSICAL KNOWLEDGE

§ 1. Of the Sources of Metaphysics

If it becomes desirable to organize any knowledge as science, it will be necessary first to determine accurately those peculiar features which no other science has in common with it, constituting its peculiarity; otherwise the boundaries of all sciences become confused, and none of them can be treated thoroughly according to its nature.

The peculiar characteristic of a science may consist of a simple difference of object, or of the sources of knowledge, or of the kind of knowledge, or perhaps of all three conjointly. On these, therefore, depends the idea of a possible science and its territory.

First, as concerns the sources of metaphysical knowledge, its very concept implies that they cannot be empirical. Its principles (including not only its maxims but its basic notions) must never be derived from experience. It must not be physical but metaphysical knowledge, namely, knowledge lying beyond experience. It can therefore have for its basis neither external experience, which is the source of physics proper, nor internal, which is the basis of empirical psychology. It is therefore *a priori* knowledge, coming from pure understanding and pure reason.

But so far metaphysics would not be distinguishable from pure mathematics; it must therefore be called *pure philosophical* knowledge; and for the meaning of this term I refer to the *Critique of the Pure Reason,*** where the distinction between these two employments of reason is sufficiently explained. So far concerning the sources of metaphysical knowledge.

§ 2. Concerning the Kind of Knowledge Which Can Alone Be Called Metaphysical

---

*["They defend the hives against drones, those indolent creatures"—Georgics IV 168.]
***Critique of Pure Reason,* "Methodology," Ch. I, Sec. 2.

a. On the Distinction between Analytical and Synthetical Judgments in General.—The peculiarity of its sources demands that metaphysical knowledge must consist of nothing but *a priori* judgments. But whatever be their origin or their logical form, there is a distinction in judgments, as to their content, according to which they are either merely *explicative,* adding nothing to the content of knowledge, or *expansive,* increasing the given knowledge. The former may be called *analytical,* the latter *synthetical,* judgments.

Analytical judgments express nothing in the predicate but what has been already actually thought in the concept of the subject, though not so distinctly or with the same (full) consciousness. When I say: "All bodies are extended," I have not amplified in the least my concept of body, but have only analyzed it, as extension was really thought to belong to that concept before the judgment was made, though it was not expressed. This judgment is therefore analytical. On the contrary, this judgment, "All bodies have weight," contains in its predicate something not actually thought in the universal concept of body; it amplifies my knowledge by adding something to my concept, and must therefore be called synthetical.

b. The Common Principle of All Analytical Judgments Is the Law of Contradiction.—All analytical judgments depend wholly on the law of contradiction, and are in their nature *a priori* cognitions, whether the concepts that supply them with matter be empirical or not. For the predicate of an affirmative analytical judgment is already contained in the concept of the subject, of which it cannot be denied without contradiction. In the same way its opposite is necessarily denied of the subject in an analytical, but negative, judgment, by the same law of contradiction. Such is the nature of the judgments: "All bodies are extended," and "No bodies are unextended (that is, simple)."

For this very reason all analytical judgments are *a priori* even when the concepts are empirical, as, for example, "Gold is a yellow metal"; for to know this I require no experience beyond my concept of gold as a yellow metal. It is, in fact, the very concept, and I need only analyze it without looking beyond it.

c. Synthetical Judgments Require a Different Principle from the Law of Contradiction.—There are synthetical *a posteriori* judgments of empirical origin; but there are also others which are certain *a priori,* and which spring from pure understanding and reason. Yet they both agree in this, that they cannot possibly spring from the principle of analysis, namely, the law of contradiction, alone. They require a quite different principle from which they may be deduced, subject, of course, always to the law of contradiction, which must never be violated, even though everything cannot be deduced from it. I shall first classify synthetical judgments.

1. *Judgments of Experience* are always synthetical. For it would be absurd to base an analytical judgment on experience, as our concept suffices for the purpose without requiring any testimony from experience. That body is extended is a judgment established *a priori,* and not an empirical judgment. For before appealing to experience, we already have all the conditions of the judgment in the concept, from which we have but to elicit the predicate according to the law of contradiction, and thereby to become conscious of the necessity of the judgment, which experience could not in the least teach us.

2. *Mathematical Judgments* are all synthetical. This fact seems hitherto to have altogether escaped the observation of those who have analyzed human reason: it even seems directly opposed to all their conjectures, though it is incontestably certain and most important in its consequences. For as it was found that the conclusions of mathematicians all proceed according to the law of contradiction (as is demanded by all apodictic certainty), men persuaded themselves that the fundamental principles were

known from the same law. This was a great mistake, for a synthetical proposition can indeed be established by the law of contradiction, but only by presupposing another synthetical proposition from which it follows, but never by that law alone.

First of all, we must observe that all strictly mathematical judgments are *a priori,* and not empirical, because they carry with them necessity, which cannot be obtained from experience. But if this be not conceded to me, very good; I shall confine my assertion to *pure mathematics,* the very notion of which implies that it contains pure *a priori* and not empirical knowledge.

It must at first be thought that the proposition $7 + 5 = 12$ is a mere analytical judgment, following from the concept of the sum of seven and five, according to the law of contradiction. But on closer examination it appears that the concept of the sum of $7 + 5$ contains merely their union in a single number, without its being at all thought what the particular number is that unites them. The concept of twelve is by no means thought by merely thinking of the combination of seven and five; and, analyze this possible sum as we may, we shall not discover twelve in the concept. We must go beyond these concepts, by calling to our aid some intuition which corresponds to one of the concepts—that is, either our five fingers or five points (as Segner has it in his *Arithmetic*)—and we must add successively the units of the five given in the intuition to the concept of seven. Hence our concept is really amplified by the proposition $7 + 5 = 12$, and we add to the first concept a second concept not thought in it. Arithmetical judgments are therefore synthetical, and the more plainly according as we take larger numbers; for in such cases it is clear that, however closely we analyze our concepts without calling intuition to our aid, we can never find the sum by such mere dissection.

Just as little is any principle of geometry analytical. That a straight line is the shortest path between two points is a synthetical proposition. For my concept of straight contains nothing of quantity, but only a quality. The concept "shortest" is therefore altogether additional and cannot be obtained by any analysis of the concept "straight line." Here, too, intuition must come to aid us. It alone makes the synthesis possible. What usually makes us believe that the predicate of such apodictic judgments is already contained in our concept, and that the judgment is therefore analytical, is the duplicity of the expression. We must think a certain predicate as attached to a given concept, and necessity indeed belongs to the concepts. But the question is not what we must join in thought *to* the given concept, but what we actually think together with and in it, though obscurely; and so it appears that the predicate belongs to this concept necessarily indeed, yet not directly but indirectly by means of an intuition which must be present.

Some other principles, assumed by geometers, are indeed actually analytical, and depend on the law of contradiction; but they only serve, as identical propositions, as a method of concatenation, and not as principles—for example, $a = a$, the whole is equal to itself, or $a + b > a$, the whole is greater than its part. And yet even these, though they are recognized as valid from mere concepts, are admitted in mathematics only because they can be represented in some intuition.

The essential and distinguishing feature of pure mathematical knowledge among all other *a priori* knowledge is that it cannot at all proceed from concepts, but only by means of the construction of concepts.* As therefore in its propositions it must proceed beyond the concept to that which its corresponding intuition contains, these propositions neither can, nor ought to, arise analytically, by dissection of the concept, but are all synthetical.

Critique of Pure Reason, "Methodology," Ch. I, Sec. 1.

I cannot refrain from pointing out the disadvantage resulting to philosophy from the neglect of this easy and apparently insignificant observation. Hume being prompted to cast his eye over the whole field of *a priori* cognitions in which human understanding claims such mighty possessions (a calling he felt worthy of a philosopher) heedlessly severed from it a whole, and indeed its most valuable, province, namely, pure mathematics; for he imagined its nature or, so to speak, the state constitution of this empire depended on totally different principles, namely, on the law of contradiction alone; and although he did not divide judgments in this manner formally and universally as I have done here, what he said was equivalent to this: that mathematics contains only analytical, but metaphysics synthetical, *a priori* propositions. In this, however, he was greatly mistaken, and the mistake had a decidedly injurious effect upon his whole conception. But for this, he would have extended his question concerning the origin of our synthetical judgments far beyond the metaphysical concept of causality and included in it the possibility of mathematics *a priori* also, for this latter he must have assumed to be equally synthetical. And then he could not have based his metaphysical propositions on mere experience without subjecting the axioms of mathematics equally to experience, a thing which he was far too acute to do. The good company into which metaphysics would thus have been brought would have saved it from the danger of a contemptuous ill-treatment, for the thrust intended for it must have reached mathematics, which was not and could not have been Hume's intention. Thus that acute man would have been led into considerations which must needs be similar to those that now occupy us, but which would have gained inestimably by his inimitably elegant style.

[3.] *Metaphysical Judgments,* properly so called, are all synthetical. We must distinguish judgments pertaining to metaphysics from metaphysical judgments properly so called. Many of the former are analytical, but they only afford the means for metaphysical judgments, which are the whole end of the science and which are always synthetical. For if there be concepts pertaining to metaphysics (as, for example, that of substance), the judgments springing from simple analysis of them also pertain to metaphysics, as, for example, substance is that which only exists as subject, etc.; and by means of several such analytical judgments we seek to approach the definition of the concepts. But as the analysis of a pure concept of the understanding (the kind of concept pertaining to metaphysics) does not proceed in any different manner from the dissection of any other, even empirical, concepts, not belonging to metaphysics (such as, air is an elastic fluid, the elasticity of which is not destroyed by any known degree of cold), it follows that the concept indeed, but not the analytical judgment, is properly metaphysical. This science has something peculiar in the production of its *a priori* cognitions, which must therefore be distinguished from the features it has in common with other rational knowledge. Thus the judgment that all the substance in things is permanent is a synthetical and properly metaphysical judgment.

If the *a priori* concepts which constitute the materials and tools of metaphysics have first been collected according to fixed principles, then their analysis will be of great value; it might be taught as a particular part (as a *philosophia definitiva*), containing nothing but analytical judgments pertaining to metaphysics, and could be treated separately from the synthetical which constitute metaphysics proper. For indeed these analyses are not of much value except in metaphysics, that is, as regards the synthetical judgments which are to be generated by these previously analyzed concepts.

The conclusion drawn in this section then is that metaphysics is properly concerned with synthetical propositions *a priori,* and these alone constitute its end, for which it indeed requires various dissections of its concepts, namely, analytical judgments, but wherein the procedure is not different from that in every other kind of knowledge, in which we merely seek to render our concepts distinct by analysis. But the generation of *a priori* knowledge by intuition as well as by concepts, in fine, of synthetical propositions *a priori,* especially in philosophical knowledge, constitutes the essential subject of metaphysics.

§ 3. A Remark on the General Division of Judgment into Analytical and Synthetical

This division is indispensable, as concerns the critique of human understanding, and therefore deserves to be called classical in such critical investigation, though otherwise it is of little use. But this is the reason why dogmatic philosophers, who always seek the sources of metaphysical judgments in metaphysics itself, and not apart from it in the pure laws of reason generally, altogether neglected this apparently obvious distinction. Thus the celebrated Wolff and his acute follower Baumgarten came to seek the proof of the principle of sufficient reason, which is clearly synthetical, in the principle of contradiction. In Locke's *Essay,* however, I find an indication of my division. For in the fourth book (Chapter III, § 9, seq.), having discussed the various connections of representations in judgments, and their sources, one of which he makes "identity or contradiction" (analytical judgments) and another the coexistence of ideas in a subject (synthetical judgments), he confesses (§ 10) that our *(a priori)* knowledge of the latter is very narrow and almost nothing. But in his remarks on this species of knowledge, there is so little of what is definite and reduced to rules that we cannot wonder if no one, not even Hume, was led to make investigations concerning this sort of proposition. For such general and yet definite principles are not easily learned from other men, who have had them only obscurely in their minds. One must hit on them first by one's own reflection; then one finds them elsewhere, where one could not possibly have found them at first because the authors themselves did not know that such an idea lay at the basis of their observations. Men who never think independently have nevertheless the acuteness to discover everything, after it has been once shown them, in what was said long since, though no one was ever able to see it there before.

§ 4. The General Question of the Prolegomena: Is Metaphysics at All Possible?

Were a metaphysics which could maintain its place as a science really in existence, could we say: "Here is metaphysics; learn it and it will convince you irresistibly and irrevocably of its truth"? This question would then be useless, and there would only remain that other question (which would rather be a test of our acuteness than a proof of the existence of the thing itself): "How is the science possible, and how does reason come to attain it?" But human reason has not been so fortunate in this case. There is no single book to which you can point as you do to Euclid, and say: "This is metaphysics; here you may find the noblest objects of this science, the knowledge of a highest being and of a future existence, proved from principles of pure reason." We can be shown indeed many propositions, demonstrably certain and never questioned; but these are all analytical, and rather concern the materials and the scaffolding for metaphysics than the extension of knowledge, which is our proper object in studying it (§ 2). Even supposing you produce synthetical judgments (such as the law of sufficient reason, which you have never proved, as you ought to, from pure reason *a priori,* though we gladly concede its truth), you lapse, when you try to employ them for your principal purpose, into such doubtful assertions that in all ages one metaphysics has contradicted another, either in its assertions or their proofs, and thus has itself destroyed its own claim to lasting assent. Nay, the very attempts to set up such a science are the main cause of the early appearance of skepticism, a mental attitude in which reason treats itself with such violence that it could never have arisen save from complete despair of ever satisfying its most important aspirations. For long before men began to inquire into nature methodically, they consulted abstract reason, which had to some extent been exercised by means of ordinary experience; for reason is ever present, while laws of nature must usually be discovered with labor. So metaphysics floated to the surface, like foam, which dissolved the moment it was scooped off. But immediately there appeared a new supply on the surface, to be ever eagerly gathered up by some; while others, instead of seeking in the depths the cause of the phenomenon, thought they showed their wisdom by ridiculing the idle labor of their neighbors.

Weary therefore of dogmatism, which teaches us nothing, and of skepticism, which does not even promise us anything—even the quiet state of a contented ignorance—disquieted by the importance of knowledge so much needed, and rendered suspicious by long experience of all knowledge which we believe we possess or which offers itself in the name of pure reason, there remains but one critical question on the answer to which our future procedure depends, namely, "Is metaphysics at all possible?" But this question must be answered, not by skeptical objections to the asseverations of some actual system of metaphysics (for we do not as yet admit such a thing to exist), but from the conception, as yet only problematical, of a science of this sort.

In the *Critique of Pure Reason* I have treated this question synthetically, by making inquiries into pure reason itself and endeavoring in this source to determine the elements as well as the laws of its pure use according to principles. The task is difficult and requires a resolute reader to penetrate by degrees into a system based on no data except reason itself, and which therefore seeks, without resting upon any fact, to unfold knowledge from its original germs. The *Prolegomena,* however, are designed for preparatory exercises; they are intended to point out what we have to do in order to make a science actual if it is possible, rather than to propound it. The *Prolegomena* must therefore rest upon something already known as trustworthy, from which we can set out with confidence and ascend to sources as yet unknown, the discovery of which will not only explain to us what we knew but exhibit a sphere of many cognitions which all spring from the same sources. The method of prolegomena, especially of those designed as a preparation for future metaphysics, is consequently analytical.

But it happens, fortunately, that though we cannot assume metaphysics to be an actual science, we can say with confidence that there is actually given certain pure *a priori* synthetical cognitions, pure mathematics and pure physics; for both contain propositions which are unanimously recognized, partly apodictically certain by mere reason, partly by general consent arising from experience and yet as independent of experience. We have therefore at least some uncontested synthetical knowledge *a priori* and need not ask *whether* it be possible, for it is actual, but *how* it is possible, in order that we may deduce from the principle which makes the given knowledge possible the possibility of all the rest.

§ 5. The General Problem: How Is
Knowledge from Pure Reason Possible?

We have already learned the significant distinction between analytical and synthetical judgments. The possibility of analytical propositions was easily comprehended, being entirely founded on the law of contradiction. The possibility of synthetical *a pos-*

teriori judgments, of those which are gathered from experience, also requires no particular explanations, for experience is nothing but a continued synthesis of perceptions. There remain therefore only synthetical propositions *a priori,* of which the possibility must be sought or investigated, because they must depend upon other principles than the law of contradiction.

But here we need not first establish the possibility of such propositions so as to ask whether they are possible. For there are enough of them which indeed are of undoubted certainty; and, as our present method is analytical, we shall start from the fact that such synthetical but purely rational knowledge actually exists; but we must now inquire into the ground of this possibility and ask *how* such knowledge is possible, in order that we may, from the principles of its possibility, be enabled to determine the conditions of its use, its sphere and its limits. The real problem upon which all depends, when expressed with scholastic precision, is therefore: "How are synthetic propositions *a priori* possible?"

For the sake of popular understanding I have above expressed this problem somewhat differently, as an inquiry into purely rational knowledge, which I could do for once without detriment to the desired insight, because, as we have only to do here with metaphysics and its sources, the reader will, I hope, after the foregoing reminders, keep in mind that when we speak of knowing by pure reason we do not mean analytical but synthetical knowledge.*

Metaphysics stands or falls with the solution of this problem; its very existence depends upon it. Let anyone make metaphysical assertions with ever so much plausibility, let him overwhelm us with conclusions; but if he has not previously proved able to answer this question satisfactorily, I have a right to say: This is all vain, baseless philosophy and false wisdom. You speak through pure reason and claim, as it were, to create cognitions *a priori* not only by dissecting given concepts, but also by asserting connections which do not rest upon the law of contradiction, and which you claim to conceive quite independently of all experience; how do you arrive at this, and how will you justify such pretensions? An appeal to the consent of the common sense of mankind cannot be allowed, for that is a witness whose authority depends merely upon rumor. Says Horace:

*Quodcunque ostendis mihi sic, incredulus odi.***

The answer to this question is as indispensable as it is difficult; and although the principal reason that it was not sought long ago is that the possibility of the question never occurred to anybody, there is yet another reason, namely, that a satisfactory answer to this one question requires a much more persistent, profound, and painstaking reflection than the most diffuse work on metaphysics, which on its first appearance

---

*It is unavoidable that, as knowledge advances, certain expressions which have become classical after having been used since the infancy of science will be found inadequate and unsuitable, and a newer and more appropriate application of the terms will give rise to confusion. [This is the case with the term "analytical."] The analytical method, so far as it is opposed to the synthetical, is very different from one that consists of analytical propositions; it signifies only that we start from what is sought, as if it were given, and ascend to the only conditions under which it is possible. In this method we often use nothing but synthetical propositions, as in mathematical analysis, and it were better to term it the *regressive* method, in contradistinction to the *synthetic* or *progressive.* A principal part of logic too is distinguished by the name of analytic, which here signifies the logic of truth in contrast to dialectic, without considering whether the cognitions belonging to it are analytical or synthetical.

**["To all that which thou provest me thus, I refuse to give credence, and hate"—*Epistle* II, 3, 188.]

promised immortal fame to its author. And every intelligent reader, when he carefully reflects what this problem requires, must at first be struck with its difficulty, and would regard it as insoluble and even impossible did there not actually exist pure synthetical cognitions *a priori*. This actually happened to David Hume, though he did not conceive the question in its entire universality as is done here and as must be done if the answer is to be decisive for all metaphysics. For how is it possible, says that acute man, that when a concept is given me I can go beyond it and connect with it another which is not contained in it, in such a manner as if the latter *necessarily* belonged to the former? Nothing but experience can furnish us with such connections (thus he concluded from the difficulty which he took to be impossibility), and all that vaunted necessity or, what is the same thing, knowledge assumed to be *a priori* is nothing but a long habit of accepting something as true, and hence of mistaking subjective necessity for objective.

Should my reader complain of the difficulty and the trouble which I shall occasion him in the solution of this problem, he is at liberty to solve it himself in an easier way. Perhaps he will then feel under obligation to the person who has undertaken for him a labor of so profound research and will rather feel some surprise at the facility with which, considering the nature of the subject, the solution has been attained. Yet it has cost years of work to solve the problem in its whole universality (using the term in the mathematical sense, namely, for that which is sufficient for all cases), and finally to exhibit it in the analytical form, as the reader will find it here.

All metaphysicians are therefore solemnly and legally suspended from their occupations till they shall have adequately answered the question, "How are synthetic cognitions *a priori* possible?" For the answer contains the only credentials which they must show when they have anything to offer us in the name of pure reason. But if they do not possess these credentials, they can expect nothing else of reasonable people, who have been deceived so often, than to be dismissed without further inquiry.

If they, on the other hand, desire to carry on their business, not as a science, but as an art of wholesome persuasion suitable to the common sense of man, this calling cannot in justice be denied them. They will then speak the modest language of a rational belief; they will grant that they are not allowed even to conjecture, far less to know, anything which lies beyond the bounds of all possible experience, but only to assume (not for speculative use, which they must abandon, but for practical use only) the existence of something possible and even indispensable for the guidance of the understanding and of the will in life. In this manner alone can they be called useful and wise men, and the more so as they renounce the title of metaphysicians. For the latter profess to be speculative philosophers; and since, when judgments *a priori* are under discussion, poor probabilities cannot be admitted (for what is declared to be known *a priori* is thereby announced as necessary), such men cannot be permitted to play with conjectures, but their assertion must be either science or nothing at all.

It may be said that the entire transcendental philosophy, which necessarily precedes all metaphysics, is nothing but the complete solution of the problem here propounded, in systematic order and completeness, and hence we have hitherto never had any transcendental philosophy. For what goes by its name is properly a part of metaphysics, whereas the former science is intended only to constitute the possibility of the latter and must therefore precede all metaphysics. And it is not surprising that when a whole science, deprived of all help from other sciences and consequently in itself quite new, is required to answer a single question satisfactorily, we should find the answer troublesome and difficult, nay, even shrouded in obscurity.

As we now proceed to this solution according to the analytical method, in which we assume that such cognitions from pure reason actually exist, we can only appeal to two sciences of theoretical knowledge (which alone is under consideration here), namely, pure mathematics and pure natural science. For these alone can exhibit to us objects in intuition, and consequently (if there should occur in them a cognition *a priori*) can show the truth or conformity of the cognition to the object *in concreto,* that is, its actuality, from which we could proceed to the ground of its possibility by the analytical method. This facilitates our work greatly for here universal considerations are not only applied to facts, but even start from them, while in a synthetic procedure they must strictly be derived *in abstracto* from concepts.

But in order to rise from these actual and, at the same time, well-grounded pure cognitions *a priori* to a possible knowledge of the kind as we are seeking, namely, to metaphysics as a science, we must comprehend that which occasions it—I mean the mere natural, though in spite of its truth still suspect, cognition *a priori* which lies at the basis of that science, the elaboration of which without any critical investigation of its possibility is commonly called metaphysics. In a word, we must comprehend the natural conditions of such a science as a part of our inquiry, and thus the transcendental problem will be gradually answered by a division into four questions:

1. How is pure mathematics possible?
2. How is pure natural science possible?
3. How is metaphysics in general possible?
4. How is metaphysics as a science possible?

It may be seen that the solution of these problems, though chiefly designed to exhibit the essential matter of the *Critique,* has yet something peculiar, which for itself alone deserves attention. This is the search for the sources of given sciences in reason itself, so that its faculty of knowing something *a priori* may by its own deeds be investigated and measured. By this procedure these sciences gain, if not with regard to their contents, yet as to their proper use; and while they throw light on the higher question concerning their common origin, they give, at the same time, an occasion better to explain their own nature.

FIRST PART OF THE MAIN TRANSCENDENTAL PROBLEM

How Is Pure Mathematics Possible?

§ 6. Here is a great and established branch of knowledge, encompassing even now a wonderfully large domain and promising an unlimited extension in the future, yet carrying with it thoroughly apodictic certainty, that is, absolute necessity, and therefore resting upon no empirical grounds. Consequently it is a pure product of reason; and, moreover, it is thoroughly synthetical. [Hence the question arises:] "How then is it possible for human reason to produce such knowledge entirely *a priori?*"

Does not this faculty [which produces mathematics], as it neither is nor can be based upon experience, presuppose some ground of knowledge *a priori,* which lies deeply hidden but which might reveal itself by these its effects if their first beginnings were but diligently ferreted out?

§ 7. But we find that all mathematical cognition has this peculiarity: it must first exhibit its concept in intuition and indeed *a priori;* therefore in an intuition which is not empirical but pure. Without this mathematics cannot take a single step; hence its judgments are always *intuitive;* whereas philosophy must be satisfied with *discursive* judgments from mere concepts, and though it may illustrate its doctrines through an intuition, can never derive them from it. This observation on the nature of mathematics gives us a clue to the first and highest condition of its possibility, which is that some pure intuition must form its basis, in which all its concepts can be exhibited or constructed, *in concreto* and yet *a priori.* If we can uncover this pure intuition and its possibility, we may thence easily explain how synthetical propositions *a priori* are possible in pure mathematics, and consequently how this science itself is possible. For just as empirical intuition [namely, sense-perception] enables us without difficulty to enlarge the concept which we frame of an object of intuition by new predicates which intuition itself presents synthetically in experience, so also pure intuition does likewise, only with this difference, that in the latter case the synthetical judgment is *a priori* certain and apodictic, in the former only *a posteriori* and empirically certain; because this latter contains only that which occurs in contingent empirical intuition, but the former that which must necessarily be discovered in pure intuition. Here intuition, being an intuition *a priori,* is inseparably joined with the concept *prior to all experience* or particular perception.

§ 8. But with this step our perplexity seems rather to increase than to lessen. For the question now is, "How is it possible to intuit anything *a priori?*" An intuition is such a representation as would immediately depend upon the presence of the object. Hence it seems impossible to intuit spontaneously *a priori,* because intuition would in that event have to take place without either a former or a present object to refer to, and in consequence could not be intuition. Concepts indeed are such that we can easily form some of them *a priori,* namely, such as contain nothing but the thought of an object in general; and we need not find ourselves in an immediate relation to the object. Take, for instance, the concepts of quantity, of cause, etc. But even these require, in order to be meaningful and significant, a certain concrete use—that is, an application to some intuition by which an object of them is given us. But how can the intuition of the object precede the object itself?

§ 9. If our intuition were of such a nature as to represent things as they are in themselves, there would not be any intuition *a priori,* but intuition would be always empirical. For I can only know what is contained in the object in itself if it is present and given to me. It is indeed even then incomprehensible how the intuition of a present thing should make me know this thing as it is in itself, as its properties cannot migrate into my faculty of representation. But even granting this possibility, an intuition of that sort would not take place *a priori,* that is, before the object were presented to me; for without this latter fact no ground of a relation between my representation and the object can be imagined, unless it depend upon a direct implantation.

Therefore in one way only can my intuition anticipate the actuality of the object, and be a cognition *a priori,* namely: *if my intuition contains nothing but the form of sensibility, antedating in my mind all the actual impressions through which I am affected by objects.*

For that objects of sense can only be intuited according to this form of sensibility I can know *a priori.* Hence it follows that propositions which concern this form of sensuous intuition only are possible and valid for objects of the senses; as also, conversely, that intuitions which are possible *a priori* can never concern any other things than objects of our senses.

§ 10. Accordingly, it is only the form of sensuous intuition by which we can intuit things *a priori,* but by which we can know objects only as they *appear* to us (to our senses), not as they are in themselves; and this assumption is absolutely necessary if synthetical propositions *a priori* be granted as possible or if, in case they actually occur, their possibility is to be comprehended and determined beforehand.

Now, the intuitions which pure mathematics lays at the foundation of all its cognitions and judgments which appear at once apodictic and necessary are space and time. For mathematics must first present all its concepts in intuition, and pure mathematics in pure intuition; that is, it must construct them. If it proceeded in any other way, it would be impossible to take a single step; for mathematics proceeds, not analytically by dissection of concepts, but synthetically, and if pure intuition be wanting there is nothing in which the matter for synthetical judgments *a priori* can be given. Geometry is based upon the pure intuition of space. Arithmetic achieves its concept of number by the successive addition of units in time, and pure mechanics cannot attain its concepts of motion without employing the representation of time. Both representations, however, are only intuitions; for if we omit from the empirical intuitions of bodies and their alterations (motion) everything empirical, that is, belonging to sensation, space and time still remain, which are therefore pure intuitions that lie *a priori* at the basis of the empirical. Hence they can never be omitted; but at the same time, by their being pure intuitions *a priori,* they prove that they are mere forms of our sensibility, which must precede all empirical intuition, that is, perception of actual objects, and conformably to which objects can be known *a priori,* but only as they appear to us.

§ 11. The problem of the present section is therefore solved. Pure mathematics, as synthetical cognition *a priori,* is possible only by referring to no other objects than those of the senses. At the basis of their empirical intuition lies a pure intuition (of space and of time) which is *a priori,* because the latter intuition is nothing but the mere form of sensibility, which precedes the actual appearance of the objects, since in fact it makes them possible. Yet this faculty of intuiting *a priori* affects not the matter of the phenomenon (that is, the sensation in it, for this constitutes that which is empirical), but its form, namely, space and time. Should any man venture to doubt that these are determinations adhering not to things in themselves, but to their relation to our sensibility, I should be glad to know how he can find it possible to know *a priori* how their intuition will be characterized before we have any acquaintance with them and before they are presented to us. Such, however, is the case with space and time. But this is quite comprehensible as soon as both count for nothing more than formal conditions of our sensibility, while the objects count merely as phenomena; for then the form of the phenomenon, that is, pure intuition, can by all means be represented as proceeding from ourselves, that is, *a priori.*

§ 12. In order to add something by way of illustration and confirmation, we need only watch the ordinary and unavoidable procedure of geometers. All proofs of the complete congruence of two given figures (where the one can in every respect be substituted for the other) come ultimately to this, that they may be made to coincide, which is evidently nothing else than a synthetical proposition resting upon immediate intuition; and this intuition must be pure or given *a priori,* otherwise the proposition could not rank as apodictically certain, but would have empirical certainty only. In that case, it could only be said that it is always found to be so and holds good only as far as our perception reaches. That everywhere space (which [in its entirety] is itself no longer the boundary of another space) has three dimensions and that space cannot in any way have more is based on the proposition that not more than three lines can intersect at right angles in one point; but this proposition cannot by any means be shown from concepts, but rests immediately on intuition, and indeed on pure and *a priori* intuition because it is apodictically certain. That we can require a line to be drawn to infinity *(in indefinitum)* or that a series of changes (for example, spaces traversed by motion) shall be infinitely continued presupposes a representation of space and time, which can only attach to intuition—namely, so far as it in itself is bounded by nothing—for from concepts it could never be inferred. Consequently, the basis of mathematics actually is pure intuitions, which make its synthetical and apodictically valid propositions possible. Hence our transcendental deduction of the notions of space and of time explains at the same time the possibility of pure mathematics. Without such a deduction and the assumption "that everything which can be given to our senses (to the external senses in space, to the internal one in time) is intuited by us as it appears to us, not as it is in itself," the truth of pure mathematics may be granted, but its existence could by no means be understood.

§ 13. Those who cannot yet rid themselves of the notion that space and time are actual qualities inherent in things in themselves may exercise their acumen on the following paradox. When they have in vain attempted its solution and are free from prejudices at least for a few moments, they will suspect that the degradation of space and time to mere forms of our sensuous intuition may perhaps be well founded.

If two things are quite equal in all respects as much as can be ascertained by all means possible, quantitatively and qualitatively, it must follow that the one can in all cases and under all circumstances replace the other, and this substitution would not occasion the least perceptible difference. This in fact is true of plane figures in geometry; but some spherical figures exhibit, notwithstanding a complete internal agreement, such a difference in their external relation that the one figure cannot possibly be put in the place of the other. For instance, two spherical triangles on opposite hemispheres, which have an arc of the equator as their common base, may be quite equal, both as regards sides and angles, so that nothing is to be found in either, if it be described for itself alone and completed, that would not equally be applicable to both; and yet the one cannot be put in the place of the other (that is, upon the opposite hemisphere). Here, then, is an internal difference between the two triangles, which difference our understanding cannot describe as internal and which only manifests itself by external relations in space. But I shall adduce examples, taken from common life, that are more obvious still.

What can be more similar in every respect and in every part more alike to my hand and to my ear than their images in a mirror? And yet I cannot put such a hand as is seen in the glass in the place of its original; for if this is a right hand, that in the glass is a left one, and the image or reflection of the right ear is a left one, which never can take the place of the other. There are in this case no internal differences which our understanding could determine by thinking alone. Yet the differences are internal as the senses teach, for, notwithstanding their complete equality and similarity, the left hand cannot be enclosed in the same bounds as the right one (they are not congruent); the glove of one hand cannot be used for the other. What is the solution? These objects are not representations of things as they are in themselves and as some mere* understanding would know them, but sensuous intuitions, that is, appearances whose possibility rests upon the relation of certain things unknown in themselves to something else, namely, to our sensibility. Space is the form of the external intuition of this sensibility, and the internal determination of every space is possible only by the determination of its external relation to the whole of space, of which it is a part (in other words, by its relation to the outer sense). That is to say, the part is possible only through the whole, which is never the case with things in themselves, as objects of the mere understanding, but which may well be the case with mere appearances. Hence the difference between sim-

---

*[In German, *pure*. The clause is meant ironically.—L.W.B.]

ilar and equal things which are not congruent (for instance, two symmetric helices) cannot be made intelligible by any concept, but only by the relation to the right and the left hands which immediately refers to intuition.

Remark I

Pure mathematics, and especially pure geometry, can have objective reality only on condition that they refer merely to objects of sense. But in regard to the latter the principle holds good that our sense representation is not a representation of things in themselves, but of the way in which they appear to us. Hence it follows that the propositions of geometry are not the results of a mere creation of our poetic imagination, and that therefore they cannot be referred with assurance to actual objects; but rather that they are necessarily valid of space, and consequently of all that may be found in space, because space is nothing else than the form of all external appearances, and it is this form alone in which objects of sense can be given to us. Sensibility, the form of which is the basis of geometry, is that upon which the possibility of external appearance depends. Therefore these appearances can never contain anything but what geometry prescribes to them.

It would be quite otherwise if the senses were so constituted as to represent objects as they are in themselves. For then it would not by any means follow from the representation of space, which, with all its properties, serves to the geometer as an *a priori* foundation, that this foundation and everything which is thence inferred must be so in nature. The space of the geometer would be considered a mere fiction, and it would not be credited with objective validity because we cannot see how things must of necessity agree with an image of them which we make spontaneously and previous to our acquaintance with them. But if this image, or rather this formal intuition, is the essential property of our sensibility by means of which alone objects are given to us, and if this sensibility represents not things in themselves but their appearances, then we shall easily comprehend, and at the same time indisputably prove, that all external objects of our world of sense must necessarily coincide in the most rigorous way with the propositions of geometry; because sensibility, by means of its form of external intuition, namely, by space, with which the geometer is occupied, makes those objects possible as mere appearances.

It will always remain a remarkable phenomenon in the history of philosophy that there was a time when even mathematicians who at the same time were philosophers began to doubt, not of the accuracy of their geometrical propositions so far as they concerned space, but of their objective validity and the applicability of this concept itself, and of all its corollaries, to nature. They showed much concern whether a line in nature might not consist of physical points, and consequently that true space in the object might consist of simple parts, while the space which the geometer has in his mind cannot be such. They did not recognize that this thought space renders possible the physical space, that is, the extension of matter itself; that this pure space is not at all a quality of things in themselves, but a form of our sensuous faculty of representation; and that all objects in space are mere appearances, that is, not things in themselves but representations of our sensuous intuition. But such is the case, for the space of the geometer is exactly the form of sensuous intuition which we find *a priori* in us, and contains the ground of the possibility of all external appearances (according to their form); and the latter must necessarily and most rigorously agree with the propositions of the geometer, which he draws, not from any fictitious concept, but from the subjective basis of all external appearances which is sensibility itself. In this and no other way can geometry be made secure as to the undoubted objective reality of its propositions against all the intrigues of a shallow metaphysics, which is surprised at them [the geometrical propositions] because it has not traced them to the sources of their concepts.

Remark II

Whatever is given us as object must be given us in intuition. All our intuition, however, takes place by means of the senses only; the understanding intuits nothing but only reflects. And as we have just shown that the senses never and in no manner enable us to know things in themselves, but only their appearances, which are mere representations of the sensibility, we conclude that "all bodies, together with the space in which they are, must be considered nothing but mere representations in us, and exist nowhere but in our thoughts." Is not this manifest idealism?

Idealism consists in the assertion that there are none but thinking beings, all other things which we think are perceived in intuition, being nothing but representations in the thinking beings, to which no object external to them in fact corresponds. I, on the contrary, say that things as objects of our senses existing outside us are given, but we know nothing of what they may be in themselves, knowing only their appearances, that is, the representations which they cause in us by affecting our senses. Consequently I grant by all means that there are bodies without us, that is, things which, though quite unknown to us as to what they are in themselves, we yet know by the representations which their influence on our sensibility procures us. These representations we call "bodies," a term signifying merely the appearance of the thing which is unknown to us, but not therefore less actual. Can this be termed idealism? It is the very contrary.

Long before Locke's time, but assuredly since him, it has been generally assumed and granted without detriment to the actual existence of external things that many of their predicates may be said to belong, not to the things in themselves, but to their appearances, and to have no proper existence outside our representation. Heat, color, and taste, for instance, are of this kind. Now, if I go farther and, for weighty reasons, rank as mere appearances the remaining qualities of bodies also, which are called primary—such as extension, place, and, in general, space, with all that which belongs to it (impenetrability or materiality, shape, etc.)—no one in the least can adduce the reason of its being inadmissible. As little as the man who admits colors not to be properties of the object in itself, but only as modifications of the sense of sight, should on that account be called an idealist, so little can my thesis be named idealistic merely because I find that more, nay, *all the properties which constitute the intuition of a body belong merely to its appearance.*

The existence of the thing that appears is thereby not destroyed, as in genuine idealism, but it is only shown that we cannot possibly know it by the senses as it is in itself.

I should be glad to know what my assertions must be in order to avoid all idealism. Undoubtedly, I should say that the representation of space is not only perfectly conformable to the relation which our sensibility has to objects—that I have said—but that it is quite similar to the object—an assertion in which I can find as little meaning as if I said that the sensation of red has a similarity to the property of cinnabar which excites this sensation in me.

Remark III

Hence we may at once dismiss an easily foreseen but futile objection, "that by admitting the ideality of space and of time the whole sensible world would be turned into mere sham." After all philosophical insight into the nature of sensuous cognition was spoiled by making the sensibility merely a confused mode of representation, according to which we still know things as they are, but without being able to reduce everything in this our representation to a clear consciousness, I proved that sensibility consists, not in this logical distinction of clearness and obscurity, but in the genetic one of the origin of knowledge itself. For sensuous perception represents things not at all as they are, but only the mode in which they affect our senses; and consequently by sensuous perception appearances only, and not things themselves, are given to the understanding for reflection. After this necessary correction an objection rises from an unpardonable and almost intentional misconception, as if my doctrine turned all the things of the world of sense into mere illusion.

When an appearance is given us, we are still quite free as to how we should judge the matter. The appearance depends upon the senses, but the judgment upon the understanding; and the only question is whether in the determination of the object there is truth or not. But the difference between truth and dreaming is not ascertained by the nature of the representations which are referred to objects (for they are the same in both cases), but by their connection according to those rules which determine the coherence of the representations in the concept of an object, and by ascertaining whether they can subsist together in experience or not. And it is not the fault of the appearances if our cognition takes illusion for truth, that is, if the intuition, by which an object is given us, is considered a concept of the thing or even of its existence which the understanding can only think. The senses represent to us the course of the planets as now progressive, now retrogressive; and herein is neither falsehood nor truth, because as long as we hold this to be nothing but appearance we do not judge of the objective character of their motion. But as a false judgment may easily arise when the understanding is not on its guard against this subjective mode of representation being considered objective, we say they appear to move backward; it is not the senses however which must be charged with the illusion, but the understanding, whose province alone it is to make an objective judgment from appearances.

Thus, even if we did not at all reflect on the origin of our representations, whenever we connect our intuitions of sense (whatever they may contain) in space and in time, according to the rules of the coherence of all knowledge in experience, illusion or truth will arise according as we are negligent or careful. It is merely a question of the use of sensuous representations in the understanding, and not of their origin. In the same way, if I consider all the representations of the senses, together with their form, space and time, to be nothing but appearances, and space and time to be a mere form of the sensibility, which is not to be met with in objects out of it, and if I make use of these representations in reference to possible experience only, there is nothing in my regarding them as appearances that can lead astray or cause illusion. For all that they can correctly cohere according to rules of truth in experience. Thus all the propositions of geometry hold good of space as well as of all the objects of the senses, consequently, of all possible experience, whether I consider space as a mere form of the sensibility or as something cleaving to the things themselves. In the former case, however, I comprehend how I can know *a priori* these propositions concerning all the objects of external intuition. Otherwise, everything else as regards all possible experience remains just as if I had not departed from the common view.

But if I venture to go beyond all possible experience with my concepts of space and time, which I cannot refrain from doing if I proclaim them characters inherent in things in themselves (for what should prevent me from letting them hold good of the same things, even though my senses might be different, and unsuited to them?), then a grave error may arise owing to an illusion, in which I proclaim to be universally valid what is merely a subjective condition of the intuition of things and certain only for all objects of senses—namely, for all possible experience; I would refer this condition to things in themselves, and not limit it to conditions of experience.

My doctrine of the ideality of space and of time, therefore, far from reducing the whole sensible world to mere illusion, is the only means of securing the application of one of the most important kinds of knowledge (that which mathematics propounds *a priori*) to actual objects and of preventing its being regarded as mere illusion. For without this observation it would be quite impossible to make out whether the intuitions of space and time, which we borrow from no experience and which yet lie in our representation *a priori,* are not mere phantasms of our brain to which objects do not correspond, at least not adequately; and, consequently, whether we have been able to show its unquestionable validity with regard to all the objects of the sensible world just because they are mere appearances.

Secondly, though these my principles make appearances of the representations of the senses, they are so far from turning the truth of experience into mere illusion that they are rather the only means of preventing the transcendental illusion, by which metaphysics has hitherto been deceived and led to the childish endeavor of catching at bubbles, because appearances, which are mere representations, were taken for things in themselves. Here originated the remarkable occurrence of the antinomy of reason which I shall mention later and which is solved by the single observation that appearance, as long as it is employed in experience, produces truth; but the moment it transgresses the bounds of experience, and consequently becomes transcendent, produces nothing but illusion.

Inasmuch, therefore, as I leave to things as we obtain them by the senses their actuality and only limit our sensuous intuition of these things to this: that it represents in no respect, not even in the pure intuitions of space and of time, anything more than mere appearance of those things, but never their constitution in themselves, this is not a sweeping illusion invented for nature by me. My protestation, too, against all charges of idealism is so valid and clear as even to seem superfluous, were there not incompetent judges who, while they would have an old name for every deviation from their perverse though common opinion and never judge of the spirit of philosophic nomenclature, but cling to the letter only, are ready to put their own conceits in the place of well-defined notions, and thereby deform and distort them. I have myself given this my theory the name of transcendental idealism, but that cannot authorize anyone to confound it either with the empirical idealism of Descartes (indeed, his was only an insoluble problem, owing to which he thought everyone at liberty to deny the existence of the corporeal world because it could never be proved satisfactorily), or with the mystical and visionary idealism of Berkeley, against which and other similar phantasms our *Critique* contains the proper antidote. My idealism concerns not the existence of things (the doubting of which, however, constitutes idealism in the ordinary sense), since it never came into my head to doubt it, but it concerns the sensuous representation of things to which space and time especially belong. Of these [namely, space and time], consequently of all appearances in general, I have only shown that they are neither things (but mere modes of representation) nor determinations belonging to things in themselves. But the word "transcendental," which with me never means a reference of our knowledge to things, but only to the cognitive faculty, was meant to obviate this misconception. Yet rather than give further occasion to it by this word, I now retract it and desire this idealism of mine to be called "critical." But if it be really an objectionable idealism to convert actual things (not appearances) into mere representations, by what name shall we call him who conversely changes mere representations to things? It may, I think, be called "dreaming idealism," in contradistinction to the former, which may be called "visionary," both of which are to be refuted by my transcendental or, better, *critical* idealism.

SECOND PART OF THE MAIN TRANSCENDENTAL PROBLEM
How Is Pure Science of Nature Possible?

§ 14. Nature is the existence of things, so far as it is determined according to universal laws. Should nature signify the existence of things in themselves, we could never know it either *a priori* or *a posteriori*. Not *a priori,* for how can we know what belongs to things in themselves, since this never can be done by the dissection of our concepts (in analytical propositions)? For I do not want to know what is contained in my concept of a thing (for that belongs to its logical essence), but what in the actuality of the thing is superadded to my concept and by which the thing itself is determined in its existence apart from the concept. My understanding and the conditions on which alone it can connect the determination of things in their existence do not prescribe any rule to things [in] themselves; these do not conform to my understanding, but it would have to conform itself to them; they would therefore have to be first given me in order to gather these determinations from them, wherefore they would not be known *a priori.*

But knowledge of the nature of things in themselves *a posteriori* would be equally impossible. For, if experience is to teach us laws to which the existence of things is subject, these laws, if they have reference to things in themselves, would have to hold them of necessity even outside our experience. But experience teaches us what exists and how it exists, but never that it must necessarily exist so and not otherwise. Experience therefore can never teach us the nature of things in themselves.

§ 15. We nevertheless actually possess a pure science of nature in which are propounded, *a priori* and with all the necessity requisite to apodictical propositions, laws to which nature is subject. I need only call to witness that propaedeutic of natural science which, under the title of the universal science of nature, precedes all physics (which is founded upon empirical principles). In it we have mathematics applied to appearances, and also merely discursive principles (or those derived from concepts), which constitute the philosophical part of the pure knowledge of nature. But there are several things in it which are not quite pure and independent of empirical sources, such as the concept of *motion,* that of *impenetrability* (upon which the empirical concept of matter rests), that of *inertia,* and many others, which prevent its being called a perfectly pure science of nature. Besides, it only refers to objects of the outer sense, and therefore does not give an example of a universal science of nature, in the strict sense, for such a science must bring nature in general, whether it regards the object of the outer or that of the inner sense (the object of physics as well as psychology), under universal laws. But among the principles of this universal physics there are a few which actually have the required universality; for instance, the propositions that "substance is permanent," that "every event is determined by a cause according to constant laws," etc. These are actually universal laws of nature, which hold completely *a priori*. There is then in fact a pure science of nature, and the question arises, *How is it possible?*

§ 16. The word *nature* assumes yet another meaning which defines the object, whereas in the former sense it only denotes the conformity to law of the determinations of the existence of things generally. If we consider it *materialiter,* "nature is the complex of all the objects of experience." And with this only are we now concerned, for anyhow things which can never be objects of experience, if they had to be known as to their nature, would oblige us to have recourse to concepts whose meaning could never be given *in concreto* (by any example of possible experience). Consequently we would have to form for ourselves a list of concepts of their nature, the reality whereof could never be determined. That is, we could never learn whether they actually referred to objects or were mere creations of thought. The knowledge of what cannot be an object of experience would be hyperphysical, and with things hyperphysical we are here not concerned, but only with the knowledge of nature, the actuality of which can be confirmed by experience, though this knowledge is possible *a priori* and precedes all experience.

§ 17. The formal aspect of nature in this narrower sense is therefore the conformity to law of all the objects of experience and, so far as it is known *a priori,* their *necessary* conformity. But it has just been shown that the laws of nature can never be known *a priori* in objects so far as they are considered, not in reference to possible experience, but as things in themselves. And our inquiry here extends, not to things in themselves (the properties of which we pass by), but to things as objects of possible experience, and the complex of these is what we here properly designate as nature. And now I ask, when the possibility of knowledge of nature *a priori* is in question, whether it is better to arrange the problem thus: "How can we know *a priori* that things as objects of experience necessarily conform to law?" or thus: "How is it possible to know *a priori* the necessary conformity to law of experience itself as regards all its objects generally?"

Closely considered, the solution of the problem represented in either way amounts, with regard to the pure knowledge of nature (which is the point of the question at issue), entirely to the same thing. For the subjective laws, under which alone an empirical knowledge of things is possible, hold good of these things as objects of possible experience (not as things in themselves, which are not considered here). It is all the same whether I say: "A judgment of perception can never rank as experience without the law that, whenever an event is observed, it is always referred to some antecedent, which it follows according to a universal rule," or: "Everything of which experience teaches that it happens must have a cause."

It is, however, more suitable to choose the first formula. For we can *a priori* and prior to all given objects have a knowledge of those conditions on which alone experience of them is possible, but never of the laws to which things may in themselves be subject, without reference to possible experience. We cannot, therefore, study the nature of things *a priori* otherwise than by investigating the conditions and the universal (though subjective) laws, under which alone such a cognition as experience (as to mere form) is possible, and we determine accordingly the possibility of things as objects of experience. For if I should choose the second formula and seek the *a priori* conditions under which nature as an object of experience is possible, I might easily fall into error and fancy that I was speaking of nature as a thing in itself, and then move round in endless circles, in a vain search for laws concerning things of which nothing is given me.

Accordingly, we shall here be concerned with experience only and the universal conditions of its possibility, which are given *a priori*. Thence we shall define nature as the whole object of all possible experience. I think it will be understood that I here do not mean the rules of the observation of a nature that is already given, for these already presuppose experience. Thus I do not mean how (through experience) we can study the laws of nature, for these would not then be laws *a priori* and would yield us no pure science of nature; but [I mean to ask] how the conditions *a priori* of the possibility of experience are at the same time the sources from which all universal laws of nature must be derived.

§ 18. In the first place we must state that, while all judgments of experience are empirical (that is, have their ground in immediate sense-perception), all empirical judgments are not judgments of experience; but, besides the empirical, and in general besides what is given to the sensuous intuition, special concepts must yet be superadded— concepts which have their origin wholly *a priori* in the pure understanding, and under which every perception must be first of all subsumed and then by their means changed into experience.

Empirical judgments, so far as they have objective validity, are *judgments of experience,* but those which are only subjectively valid I name mere *judgments of perception.* The latter require no pure concept of the understanding, but only the logical connection of perception in a thinking subject. But the former always require, besides the representation of the sensuous intuition, special *concepts originally begotten in the understanding,* which make possible the objective validity of the judgment of experience.

All our judgments are at first merely judgments of perception; they hold good only for us (that is, for our subject), and we do not till afterward give them a new reference (to an object) and desire that they shall always hold good for us and in the same way for everybody else; for when a judgment agrees with an object, all judgments concerning the same object must likewise agree among themselves, and thus the objective validity of the judgment of experience signifies nothing else than its necessary universal validity. And conversely when we have ground for considering a judgment as necessarily having universal validity (which never depends upon perception, but upon the pure concept of the understanding under which the perception is subsumed), we must consider that it is objective also—that is, that it expresses not merely a reference of our perception to a subject, but a characteristic of the object. For there would be no reason for the judgments of other men necessarily agreeing with mine if it were not the unity of the object to which they all refer and with which they accord; hence they must all agree with one another.

§ 19. Therefore objective validity and necessary universality (for everybody) are equivalent terms, and though we do not know the object in itself, yet when we consider a judgment as universal, and hence necessary, we thereby understand it to have objective validity. By this judgment we know the object (though it remains unknown as it is in itself) by the universal and necessary connection of the given perceptions. As this is the case with all objects of sense, judgments of experience take their objective validity, not from the immediate knowledge of the object (which is impossible), but from the condition of universal validity of empirical judgments, which, as already said, never rests upon empirical or, in short, sensuous conditions, but upon a pure concept of the understanding. The object in itself always remains unknown; but when by the concept of the understanding the connection of the representations of the object, which it gives to our sensibility, is determined as universally valid, the object is determined by this relation, and the judgment is objective.

To illustrate the matter: when we say, "The room is warm, sugar sweet, and wormwood bitter,"* we have only subjectively valid judgments. I do not at all expect

---

*I freely grant that these examples do not represent such judgments of perception as ever could become judgments of experience, even though a concept of the understanding were superadded, because they refer merely to feeling, which everybody knows to be merely subjective and which of course can never be attributed to the object, and consequently never become objective. I only wished to give here an example of a judgment that is merely subjectively valid, containing no ground for necessary universal validity and thereby for a relation to the object. An example of the judgments of perception which become judgments of experience by superadded concepts of the understanding will be given in the next note.

that I or any other person shall always find it as I now do; each of these sentences only expresses a relation of two sensations to the same subject, that is, myself, and that only in my present state of perception; consequently they are not valid of the object. Such are judgments of perception. Judgments of experience are of quite a different nature. What experience teaches me under certain circumstances, it must always teach me and everybody; and its validity is not limited to the subject nor to its state at a particular time. Hence I pronounce all such judgments objectively valid. For instance, when I say the air is elastic, this judgment is as yet a judgment of perception only; I do nothing but refer two of my sensations to each other. But if I would have it called a judgment of experience, I require this connection to stand under a condition which makes it universally valid. I desire therefore that I and everybody else should always connect necessarily the same perceptions under the same circumstances.

§ 20. We must consequently analyze experience in general in order to see what is contained in this product of the senses and of the understanding, and how the judgment of experience itself is possible. The foundation is the intuition of which I become conscious, that is, perception *(perceptio)*, which pertains merely to the senses. But in the next place, there is judging (which belongs only to the understanding). But this judging may be twofold: first, I may merely compare perceptions and connect them in a consciousness of my particular state; or, secondly, I may connect them in consciousness in general. The former judgment is merely a judgment of perception, and hence is of subjective validity only; it is merely a connection of perceptions in my mental state, without reference to the object. Hence it does not, as is commonly imagined, suffice for experience that perceptions are compared and connected in consciousness through judgment; thence arises no universal validity and necessity by virtue of which alone consciousness can be objectively valid, that is, can be called experience.

Quite another judgment therefore is required before perception can become experience. The given intuition must be subsumed under a concept which determines the form of judging in general relatively to the intuition, connects empirical consciousness of intuition in consciousness in general, and thereby procures universal validity for empirical judgments. A concept of this nature is a pure *a priori* concept of the understanding, which does nothing but determine for an intuition the general way in which it can be used for judgments. Let the concept be that of cause; then it determines the intuition which is subsumed under it, for example, that of air, relative to judging in general— namely, the concept of air in respect to its expansion serves in the relation of antecedent to consequent in a hypothetical judgment. The concept of cause accordingly is a pure concept of the understanding, which is totally disparate from all possible perception and only serves to determine the representation subsumed under it, with respect to judging in general, and so to make a universally valid judgment possible.

Before, therefore, a judgment of perception can become a judgment of experience, it is requisite that the perception should be subsumed under some such concept of the understanding; for instance, air belongs under the concept of cause, which determines our judgment about it in respect to its expansion as hypothetical.* Thereby the expansion of the air is represented, not as merely belonging to the perception of the air

---

*As an easier example, we may take the following: "When the sun shines on the stone, it grows warm." This judgment, however often I and others may have perceived it, is a mere judgment of perception and contains no necessity; perceptions are only usually conjoined in this manner. But if I say, "The sun warms the stone," I add to the perception a concept of the understanding, namely, that of cause, which necessarily connects with the concept of sunshine that of heat, and the synthetical judgment becomes of necessity universally valid, namely, objective, and is converted from a perception into experience.

in my present state or in several states of mine, or in the perceptual state of others, but as belonging to it necessarily. The judgment, "Air is elastic," becomes universally valid and a judgment of experience only because certain judgments precede it which subsume the intuition of air under the concept of cause and effect; and they thereby determine the perceptions, not merely with respect to one another in me, but with respect to the form of judging in general (which is here hypothetical), and in this way they render the empirical judgment universally valid.

If all our synthetical judgments are analyzed so far as they are objectively valid, it will be found that they never consist of mere intuitions connected only (as is commonly believed) by comparison into a judgment; but that they would be impossible were not a pure concept of the understanding superadded to the concepts abstracted from intuition, under which concept these latter are subsumed and in this manner only combined into an objectively valid judgment. Even the judgments of pure mathematics in their simplest axioms are not exempt from this condition. The principle, "A straight line is the shortest distance between two points," presupposes that the line is subsumed under the concept of magnitude, which certainly is no mere intuition, but has its seat in the understanding alone and serves to determine the intuition (of the line) with regard to the judgments which may be made about it, in respect to their quantity, that is, to plurality (as *judicia plurativa*).* For under them it is understood that in a given intuition there is contained a plurality of homogeneous parts.

§ 21. To prove, then, the possibility of experience so far as it rests upon pure concepts of the understanding *a priori,* we must first represent what belongs to judging in general and the various functions of the understanding in a complete table. For the pure concepts of the understanding must run parallel to these functions, as such concepts are nothing more than concepts of intuitions in general, so far as these are determined by one or other of these functions of judging, in themselves, that is, necessarily and universally. Hereby also the *a priori* principles of the possibility of all experience, as objectively valid empirical knowledge, will be precisely determined. For they are nothing but propositions which subsume all perception (under certain universal conditions of intuition) under those pure concepts of the understanding.

LOGICAL TABLE OF JUDGMENTS

1 *As to Quantity*	2 *As to Quality*
Universal	Affirmative
Particular	Negative
Singular	Infinite

3 *As to Relation*	4 *As to Modality*
Categorical	Problematic
Hypothetical	Assertoric
Disjunctive	Apodeicticer

*This name seems preferable to the term *particularia,* which is used for these judgments in logic. For the latter implies the idea that they are not universal. But when I start from unity (in singular judgments) and so proceed to totality, I must not [even indirectly and negatively] imply any reference to totality. I think plurality merely without totality, and not the exception from totality. This is necessary if logical distinctions are to form the basis of the pure concepts of the understanding. However, logical usage need not be changed.

TRANSCENDENTAL TABLE OF THE CONCEPTS
OF THE UNDERSTANDING

1 *As to Quantity* Unity (Measure) Plurality (Magnitude) Totality (Whole)	2 *As to Quality* Reality Negation Limitation
3 *As to Relation* Substance Cause Community	4 *As to Modality* Possibility Existence Necessity

PURE PHYSICAL TABLE OF THE UNIVERSAL PRINCIPLES
OF THE SCIENCE OF NATURE

1 Axioms of Intuition	2 Anticipations of Perception
3 Analogies of Experience	4 Postulates of Empirical Thinking Generally

§ 21a. In order to comprise the whole matter in one idea, it is first necessary to remind the reader that we are discussing, not the origin of experience, but that which lies in experience. The former pertains to empirical psychology and would even then never be adequately explained without the latter, which belongs to the critique of knowledge, and particularly of the understanding.

Experience consists of intuitions, which belong to the sensibility, and of judgments, which are entirely a work of the understanding. But the judgments which the understanding forms solely from sensuous intuitions are far from being judgments of experience. For in the one case the judgment connects only the perceptions as they are given in sensuous intuition, while in the other the judgments must express what experience in general and not what the mere perception (which possesses only subjective validity) contains. The judgment of experience must therefore add to the sensuous intuition and its logical connection in a judgment (after it has been rendered universal by comparison) something that determines the synthetical judgment as necessary and therefore as universally valid. This can be nothing else than that concept which represents the intuition as determined in itself with regard to one form of judgment rather than another, namely, a concept of that synthetical unity of intuitions which can only be represented by a given logical function of judgments.

§ 22. The sum of the matter is this: the business of the senses is to intuit, that of the understanding is to think. But thinking is uniting representations in one consciousness. This union originates either merely relative to the subject and is accidental and subjective, or takes place absolutely and is necessary or objective. The union of representations in one consciousness is judgment. Thinking, therefore, is the same as judging or referring representations to judgments in general. Hence judgments are either merely subjective, when representations are referred to a consciousness in one subject only and united in it, or objective, when they are united in consciousness in general, that is, necessarily. The logical functions of all judgments are but various modes of uniting representations in consciousness. But if they serve for concepts, they are concepts of the necessary union of representations in [any] consciousness, and so are principles of objectively valid judgments. This union in consciousness is either analytical, by identity, or synthetical, by the combination and addition of various representations one to another. Experience consists in the synthetical connection of phenomena (perceptions) in consciousness, so far as this connection is necessary. Hence the pure concepts of the understanding are those under which all perceptions must be subsumed ere they can serve for judgments of experience, in which the synthetical unity of the perceptions is represented as necessary and universally valid.*

§ 23. Judgments, when considered merely as the condition of the union of given representations in a consciousness, are rules. These rules, so far as they represent the union as necessary, are rules *a priori,* and, insofar as they cannot be deduced from higher rules, are principles. But in regard to the possibility of all experience, merely in relation to the form of thinking in it, no conditions of judgments of experience are higher than those which bring the appearances, according to the various form of their intuition, under pure concepts of the understanding, which render the empirical judgment objectively valid. These are therefore the *a priori* principles of possible experience.

The principles of possible experience are then at the same time universal laws of nature, which can be known *a priori.* And thus the problem of our second question, "How is the pure science of nature possible?" is solved. For the system which is required for the form of a science is to be met with in perfection here, because, beyond the above-mentioned formal conditions of all judgments in general (and hence of all rules in general) offered in logic, no others are possible, and these constitute a logical system. The concepts grounded thereupon, which contain the *a priori* conditions of all synthetical and necessary judgments, accordingly constitute a transcendental system. Finally the principles, by means of which all phenomena are subsumed under these concepts, constitute a physical system, that is, a system of nature, which precedes all empirical knowledge of nature, and makes it possible. It may in strictness be denominated the universal and pure science of nature.

§ 24. The first of the physical principles subsumes all phenomena, as intuitions in space and time, under the concept of quantity, and is thus a principle of the application of mathematics to experience. The second one subsumes the strictly empirical element, namely, sensation, which denotes the real in intuitions, not indeed directly under the concept of quantity, because sensation is not an intuition that *contains* either space or time, though it places the respective object corresponding to it in both. But still there is between reality (sense-representation) and the zero, or total void of intuition in time, a difference which has a quantity. For between every given degree of light and of darkness, between every degree of heat and of absolute cold, between every degree of weight and of absolute lightness, between every degree of occupancy space and of to-

---

*But how does the proposition that judgments of experience contain necessity in the synthesis of perceptions agree with my statement so often before inculcated that experience as cognition *a posteriori* can afford contingent judgments only? When I say that experience teaches me something, I mean only the perception that lies in experience—for example, that heat always follows the shining of the sun on a stone; consequently the proposition of experience is always so far accidental. That this heat necessarily follows the shining of the sun is contained indeed in the judgment of experience (by means of the concept of cause), yet is a fact not learned by experience; for conversely, experience is first of all generated by this addition of the concept of the understanding (of cause) to perception. How perception attains this addition may be seen by referring in the *Critique* itself to the [first] section of the "Transcendental Faculty of Judgment."

tally void space, diminishing degrees can be conceived, in the same manner as between consciousness and total unconsciousness (psychological darkness) ever-diminishing degrees obtain. Hence there is no perception that can prove an absolute absence; for instance, no psychological darkness that cannot be considered as consciousness which is only outbalanced by a stronger consciousness. This occurs in all cases of sensation, and so the understanding can anticipate even sensations, which constitute the peculiar quality of empirical representations (appearances), by means of the principle that they all have degree (and consequently that what is real in all appearance has degree). Here is the second application of mathematics *(mathesis intensorum)* to the science of nature.

§ 25. Anent the relation of appearances merely with a view to their existence, the determination of the relation is not mathematical but dynamical, and can never be objectively valid, consequently never fit for experience, if it does not come under *a priori* principles by which the empirical knowledge relative to appearances first becomes possible. Hence appearances must be subsumed under the concept of substance, which as a concept of a thing is the foundation of all determination of existence; or, secondly—so far as a succession is found among appearances, that is, an event—under the concept of an effect with reference to cause; or lastly—so far as coexistence is to be known objectively, that is, by a judgment of experience—under the concept of community (action and reaction). Thus *a priori* principles form the basis of objectively valid, though empirical, judgments—that is, of the possibility of experience so far as it must connect objects as existing in nature. These principles are the real laws of nature, which may be termed "dynamical."

Finally knowledge of the agreement and connection, not only of appearances among themselves in experience, but of their relation to experience in general, belongs to the judgments of experience. This relation contains either their agreement with the formal conditions, which the understanding recognizes, or their coherence with the materials of the senses and of perception, or combines both into one concept. Consequently, their relation to experience in general entails possibility, actuality, and necessity, according to universal laws of nature. This would constitute the physical doctrine of method for distinguishing truth from hypotheses and for determining the limits of certainty of the latter.

§ 26. The third table of principles drawn by the critical method from the nature of the understanding itself shows an inherent perfection, which raises it far above every other table which has hitherto, though in vain, been tried or may yet be tried by analyzing the objects themselves dogmatically. It exhibits all synthetical *a priori* principles completely and according to one principle, namely, the faculty of judging in general, constituting the essence of experience as regards the understanding; so that we can be certain that there are no more such principles. This affords a satisfaction which can never be attained by the dogmatic method. Yet this is not all; there is a still greater merit in it.

We must carefully bear in mind the premise which shows the possibility of this cognition *a priori* and, at the same time, limits all such principles to a condition which must never be lost sight of if we desire it not to be misunderstood and extended in use beyond the original sense which the understanding attaches to it. This limit is that they contain nothing but the conditions of possible experience in general so far as it is subjected to laws *a priori*. Consequently, I do not say that things *in themselves* possess a magnitude; that their reality possesses a degree, their existence a connection of accidents in a substance, etc. This nobody can prove, because such a synthetical connection from mere concepts, without any reference to sensuous intuition on the one side or connection of it in a possible experience on the other, is absolutely impossible. The essential limitation of the concepts in these principles then is that all things *as objects of experience only* stand necessarily *a priori* under the aforementioned conditions.

Hence there follows, secondly, a specifically peculiar mode of proof of these principles; they are not directly referred to appearances and to their relation, but to the possibility of experience, of which appearances constitute the matter only, not the form. Thus they are referred to objectively and universally valid synthetical propositions, in which we distinguish judgments of experience from those of perception. This takes place because appearances, as mere intuitions *occupying a part of space and time,* come under the concept of quantity, which synthetically unites their multiplicity *a priori* according to rules. Again, insofar as the perception contains, besides intuition, sensation, and between the latter and nothing (that is, the total disappearance of sensation), there is an ever-decreasing transition, it is apparent that the real within appearances must have a degree, so far as it (namely, the sensation) *does not itself occupy any part of space or of time.** Still the transition to this real from empty time or empty space is possible only in time. Consequently, although sensation, as the quality of empirical intuition specifically differentiating it from other sensations, can never be known *a priori,* yet it can, in a possible experience in general, as quantity of perception be intensively distinguished from every other similar perception. Hence the application of mathematics to nature, as regards the sensuous intuition by which nature is given to us, thus becomes possible and definite.

Above all, the reader must pay attention to the mode of proof of the principles which occur under the title of "analogies of experience." For these do not refer to the genesis of intuitions, as do the principles of applying mathematics to natural science in general, but to the connection of their existence in an experience; and this can be nothing but the determination of their existence in time according to necessary laws, under which alone the connection is objectively valid and thus becomes experience. The proof, therefore, does not turn on the synthetical unity in the connection of things in themselves, but merely of perceptions; and of these, not in regard to their matter, but to the determination of time and of the relation of their existence in it according to universal laws. If the empirical determination in relative time is indeed to be objectively valid (that is, to be experience), these universal laws must contain the necessary determination of existence in time generally (namely, according to a rule of the understanding *a priori*).

As these are prolegomena I cannot here further descant on the subject, but my reader (who has probably been long accustomed to consider experience a mere empirical synthesis of perceptions, and hence has not considered that it goes much beyond them since it imparts to empirical judgments universal validity, and for that purpose requires a pure and *a priori* unity of the understanding) is recommended to pay special attention to this distinction of experience from a mere aggregate of perceptions and to judge the mode of proof from this point of view.

§ 27. Now we are prepared to remove Hume's doubt. He justly maintains that we cannot comprehend by reason the possibility of causality, that is, of the reference of

---

*Heat and light are in a small space just as large, as to degree, as in a large one; in like manner the internal representations, pain, consciousness generally, whether they last a short or a long time, need not vary as to the degree. Hence the quantity is here in a point and in a moment just as great as in any space or time, however great. Degrees are quantities not in intuition, but in mere sensation (or the quantity of the content *[Grundes]* of an intuition). Hence they can only be estimated quantitatively by the relation of 1 to 0, namely, by their capability of decreasing by infinite intermediate degrees to disappearance, or of increasing from naught through infinite gradations to a determinate sensation in a certain time. *Quantitas qualitatis est gradus.* [meaning,] "The quantity of quality is degree."

the existence of one thing to the existence of another which is necessitated by the former. I add that we comprehend just as little the concept of subsistence, that is, the necessity that at the foundation of the existence of things there lies a subject which cannot itself be a predicate of any other thing; nay, we cannot even form a notion of the possibility of such a thing (though we can point out examples of its use in experience). The very same incomprehensibility affects the community of things, as we cannot comprehend how from the state of one thing an inference to the state of quite another thing beyond it, and *vice versa,* can be drawn, and how substances which have each their own separate existence should depend upon one another necessarily. But I am very far from holding these concepts to be derived merely from experience, and the necessity represented in them to be imaginary and a mere illusion produced in us by long habit. On the contrary, I have amply shown that they and the principles derived from them are firmly established *a priori* before all experience and have their undoubted objective value, though only with regard to experience.

§ 28. Although I have no notion of such a connection of things in themselves, how they can either exist as substances, or act as causes, or stand in community with others (as parts of a real whole), and I can just as little conceive such properties in appearances as such (because those concepts contain nothing that lies in the appearances, but only what the understanding alone must think), we have yet a concept of such a connection of representations in our understanding and in judgments generally. This concept is: that representations appear, in one sort of judgments, as subject in relation to predicates; in another, as ground in relation to consequent; and, in a third, as parts which constitute together a total possible cognition. Furthermore, we know *a priori* that without considering the representation of an object as determined in one or the other of these respects, we can have no valid knowledge of the object; and, if we should occupy ourselves about the object in itself, there is not a single possible attribute by which I could know that it is determined under any of these aspects, that is, under the concept either of substance, or of cause, or (in relation to other substances) of community, for I have no concept of the possibility of such a connection of existence. But the question is not how things in themselves but how the empirical knowledge of things is determined, as regards the above aspects of judgments in general; that is, how things, as objects of experience, can and must be subsumed under these concepts of the understanding. And then it is clear that I completely comprehend, not only the possibility, but also the necessity, of subsuming all appearances under these concepts—that is, of using them for principles of the possibility of experience.

§ 29. In order to test Hume's problematical concept (his *crux metaphysicorum*), the concept of cause, we are first given *a priori,* by means of logic, the form of a conditional judgment in general; that is, we have one cognition given as antecedent and another as consequent. But it is possible that in perception we may meet with a rule of relation which runs thus: that a certain appearance is constantly followed by another (though not conversely); and this is a case for me to use the hypothetical judgment and, for instance, to say if the sun shines long enough upon a body it grows warm. Here there is indeed as yet no necessity of connection or concept of cause. But I proceed and say that, if this proposition, which is merely a subjective connection of perceptions, is to be a proposition of experience, it must be seen as necessary and universally valid. Such a proposition would be that the sun is by its light the cause of heat. The empirical rule is now considered as a law, and as valid, not merely of appearances but valid of them for the purposes of a possible experience which requires universal and therefore necessarily valid rules. I therefore easily comprehend the concept of cause, as a concept necessarily belonging to the mere form of experience, and its possibility as a synthetical union of perceptions in consciousness in general; but I do not at all comprehend the possibility of a thing in general as a cause, because the concept of cause denotes a condition not at all belonging to things, but to experience. For experience can be nothing but objectively valid knowledge of appearances and of their succession, only so far as the earlier can be conjoined with the later according to the rule of hypothetical judgments.

§ 30. Hence if even the pure concepts of the understanding are thought to go beyond objects of experience to things in themselves *(noumena)*, they have no meaning whatever. They serve, as it were, only to decipher appearances, that we may be able to read them as experience. The principles which arise from their reference to the sensible world only serve our understanding for empirical use. Beyond this they are arbitrary combinations without objective reality, and we can neither know their possibility *a priori* nor verify—or even render intelligible by any example—their reference to objects; because examples can only be borrowed from some possible experience, and consequently the objects of these concepts can be found nowhere but in a possible experience.

This complete (though to its originator unexpected) solution of Hume's problem rescues for the pure concepts of the understanding their *a priori* origin and for the universal laws of nature their validity as laws of the understanding, yet in such a way as to limit their use to experience, because their possibility depends solely on the reference of the understanding to experience, but with a completely reversed mode of connection which never occurred to Hume—they do not derive from experience, but experience derives from them.

This is, therefore, the result of all our foregoing inquiries: "All synthetical principles *a priori* are nothing more than principles of possible experience" and can never be referred to things in themselves, but to appearances as objects of experience. And hence pure mathematics as well as a pure science of nature can never be referred to anything more than mere appearances, and can only represent either that which makes experience in general possible, or else that which, as it is derived from these principles, must always be capable of being represented in some possible experience.

§ 31. And thus we have at last something definite upon which to depend in all metaphysical enterprises, which have hitherto, boldly enough but always blindly, attempted everything without discrimination. That the aim of their exertions should be so near struck neither the dogmatic thinkers nor those who, confident in their supposed sound common sense, started with concepts and principles of pure reason (which were legitimate and natural, but destined for mere empirical use) in quest of insights to which they neither knew nor could know any definite bounds, because they had never reflected nor were able to reflect on the nature or even on the possibility of such a pure understanding.

Many a naturalist of pure reason (by which I mean the man who believes he can decide in matters of metaphysics without any science) may pretend that he, long ago, by the prophetic spirit of his sound sense, not only suspected but knew and comprehended what is here propounded with so much ado, or, if he likes, with prolix and pedantic pomp: "that with all our reason we can never reach beyond the field of experience." But when he is questioned about his rational principles individually, he must grant that there are many of them which he has not taken from experience and which are therefore independent of it and valid *a priori.* How then and on what grounds will he restrain both himself and the dogmatist, who makes use of these concepts and principles beyond all possible experience because they are recognized to be independent of it? And even he, this adept in sound sense, in spite of all his assumed and cheaply acquired wisdom, is not exempt from wandering inadvertently beyond objects of experience into the field of chimeras. He is often deeply enough involved in them; though, in announcing everything as mere probability, rational conjecture, or analogy, he gives by his popular language a color to his groundless pretensions.

§ 32. Since the oldest days of philosophy, inquirers into pure reason have conceived, besides the things of sense, or appearances *(phenomena)*, which make up the sensible world, certain beings of the understanding *(noumena)*, which should constitute an intelligible world. And as appearance and illusion were by those men identified (a thing which we may well excuse in an undeveloped epoch), actuality was only conceded to the beings of the understanding.

And we indeed, rightly considering objects of sense as mere appearances, confess thereby that they are based upon a thing in itself, though we know not this thing as it is in itself but only know its appearances, namely, the way in which our senses are affected by this unknown something. The understanding, therefore, by assuming appearances, grants the existence of things in themselves also; and to this extent we may say that the representation of such things as are the basis of appearances, consequently of mere beings of the understanding, is not only admissible but unavoidable.

Our critical deduction by no means excludes things of that sort *(noumena)*, but rather limits the principles of the Aesthetic* to this, that they shall not extend to all things—as everything would then be turned into mere appearance—but that they shall hold good only of objects of possible experience. Hereby, then, beings of the understanding are granted, but with the inculcation of this rule which admits of no exception: that we neither know nor can know anything at all definite of these pure beings of the understanding, because our pure concepts of the understanding as well as our pure intuitions extend to nothing but objects of possible experience, consequently to mere things of sense; and as soon as we leave this sphere, these concepts retain no meaning whatever.

§ 33. There is indeed something seductive in our pure concepts of the understanding which tempts us to a transcendent use—a use which transcends all possible experience. Not only are our concepts of substance, of power, of action, of reality, and others, quite independent of experience, containing nothing of sense appearance, and so apparently applicable to things in themselves *(noumena)*, but, what strengthens this conjecture, they contain a necessity of determination in themselves, which experience never attains. The concept of cause implies a rule according to which one state follows another necessarily; but experience can only show us that one state of things often or, at most, commonly follows another, and therefore affords neither strict universality nor necessity.

Hence the concepts of the understanding seem to have a deeper meaning and import than can be exhausted by their merely empirical use, and so the understanding inadvertently adds for itself to the house of experience a much more extensive wing, which it fills with nothing but beings of thought, without ever observing that it has transgressed with its otherwise legitimate concepts the bounds of their use.

§ 34. Two important and even indispensable, though very dry, investigations therefore became indispensable in the *Critique of Pure Reason* [namely, the chapters "The Schematism of the Pure Concepts of the Understanding" and "On the Ground of the Distinction of All Objects as Phenomena and Noumena."] In the former it is shown that the senses furnish, not the pure concepts of the understanding *in concreto,* but only the schema for their use, and that the object conformable to it occurs only in experience (as the product of the understanding from materials of the sensibility). In the latter it is shown that, although our pure concepts of the understanding and our principles are independent of experience, and despite the apparently greater sphere of their use, still nothing whatever can be thought by them beyond the field of experience, because they

---

*[That is, the first part of the *Critique of Pure Reason*, establishing space and time as pure intuitions.—L.W.B.]

can do nothing but merely determine the logical form of the judgment relatively to given intuitions. But as there is no intuition at all beyond the field of the sensibility, these pure concepts, as they cannot possibly be exhibited *in concreto,* are void of all meaning; consequently all these *noumena,* together with their complex, the intelligible world,* are nothing but representation of a problem, of which the object in itself is possible but the solution, from the nature of our understanding, totally impossible. For our understanding is not a faculty of intuition, but of the connection of given intuitions in one experience. Experience must therefore contain all the objects for our concepts; but beyond it no concepts have any significance, as there is no intuition that might offer them a foundation.

§ 35. The imagination may perhaps be forgiven for occasional vagaries and for not keeping carefully within the limits of experience, since it gains life and vigor by such flights and since it is always easier to moderate its boldness than to stimulate its languor. But the understanding which ought to *think* can never be forgiven for indulging in vagaries; for we depend upon it alone for assistance to set bounds, when necessary, to the vagaries of the imagination.

But the understanding begins its aberrations very innocently and modestly. It first brings to light the elementary cognitions which inhere in it prior to all experience, but which yet must always have their application in experience. It gradually drops these limits—and what is there to prevent it, as it has quite freely derived its principles from itself? It then proceeds first to newly imagined powers in nature, then to beings outside nature—in short, to a world for whose construction the materials cannot be wanting, because fertile fiction furnishes them abundantly, and though not confirmed it is never refuted by experience. This is the reason that young thinkers are so partial to metaphysics constructed in a truly dogmatic manner, and often sacrifice to it their time and their talents, which might be otherwise better employed.

But there is no use in trying to moderate these fruitless endeavors of pure reason by all manner of cautions as to the difficulties of solving questions so occult, by complaints of the limits of our reason, and by degrading our assertions into mere conjectures. For if their impossibility is not distinctly shown, and reason's knowledge of itself does not become a true science, in which the field of its right use is distinguished, so to say, with geometrical certainty from that of its worthless and idle use, these fruitless efforts will never be wholly abandoned.

§ 36. How is nature itself possible? This question—the highest point that transcendental philosophy can ever reach, and to which, as its boundary and completion, it must proceed—really contains two questions.

First: How is nature in the material sense, that is, as to intuition, or considered as the totality of appearances, possible; how are space, time, and that which fills both—the object of sensation—possible generally? The answer is: By means of the constitution of our sensibility, according to which it is in its own way affected by objects which are in themselves unknown to it and totally distinct from those appearances. This answer is given in the *Critique* itself in the "Transcendental Aesthetic," and in these *Prolegomena* by the solution of the first general problem.

---

*We speak of the "intelligible world," not (as the usual expression is) "intellectual world." For cognitions are intellectual through the understanding and refer to our world of sense also; but objects, in so far as they can be represented merely by the understanding, and to which none of our sensible intuitions can refer, are termed "intelligible." But as some possible intuition must correspond to every object, we would have to assume an understanding that intuits things immediately; but of such we have not the least notion, nor have we any notion of the *beings of the understanding* to which it should be applied.

Secondly: How is nature possible in the formal sense, as the totality of the rules under which all appearances must come in order to be thought as connected in experience? The answer must be this: It is only possible by means of the constitution of our understanding, according to which all the above representations of the sensibility are necessarily referred to a consciousness, and by which the peculiar way in which we think (namely, by rules) and hence experience also are possible, but must be clearly distinguished from an insight into the objects in themselves. This answer is given in the *Critique* itself in the "Transcendental Logic" and in these *Prolegomena,* in the course of the solution of the second main problem.

But how this peculiar property of our sensibility itself is possible, or that of our understanding and of the apperception which is necessarily its basis and that of all thinking, cannot be further analyzed or answered, because it is of them that we are in need for all our answers and for all our thinking about objects.

There are many laws of nature which we can know only by means of experience; but conformity to law in the connection of appearances, that is, in nature in general, we cannot discover by any experience, because experience itself requires laws which are *a priori* at the basis of its possibility.

The possibility of experience in general is therefore at the same time the universal law of nature, and the principles of experience are the very laws of nature. For we know nature only as the totality of appearances, that is, of representations in us; and hence we can only derive the laws of their connection from the principles of their connection in us, that is, from the conditions of their necessary union in one consciousness which constitutes the possibility of experience.

Even the main proposition expounded throughout this section—that universal laws of nature can be known *a priori*—leads naturally to the proposition that the highest legislation of nature must lie in ourselves, that is, in our understanding; and that we must not seek the universal laws of nature in nature by means of experience, but conversely must seek nature, as to its universal conformity to law, in the conditions of the possibility of experience which lie in our sensibility and in our understanding. For how were it otherwise possible to know *a priori* these laws, as they are not rules of analytical knowledge but truly synthetical extensions of it?

Such a necessary agreement of the principles of possible experience with the laws of the possibility of nature can only proceed from one of two causes: either these laws are drawn from nature by means of experience, or conversely nature is derived from the laws of the possibility of experience in general and is quite the same as the mere universal conformity to law of the latter. The former is self-contradictory, for the universal laws of nature can and must be known *a priori* (that is, independently of all experience) and be the foundation of all empirical use of the understanding; the latter alternative therefore alone remains.*

But we must distinguish the empirical laws of nature, which always presuppose particular perceptions, from the pure or universal laws of nature, which, without being based on particular perceptions, contain merely the conditions of their necessary union in experience. In relation to the latter, nature and possible experience are quite the same; and as the conformity to law in the latter depends upon the necessary connection of ap-

---

*Crusius alone thought of a compromise: that a spirit, who can neither err nor deceive, implanted these laws in us originally. But since false principles often intrude themselves, as indeed the very system of this man shows in not a few instances, we are involved in difficulties as to the use of such a principle in the absence of sure criteria to distinguish the genuine origin from the spurious, since we never can know certainly what the spirit of truth or the father of lies may have instilled into us.

pearances in experience (without which we cannot know any object whatever in the sensible world), consequently upon the original laws of the understanding, it seems at first strange, but is not the less certain, to say: *The understanding does not derive its laws* (a priori) *from, but prescribes them to, nature.*

§ 37. We shall illustrate this seemingly bold proposition by an example, which will show that laws which we discover in objects of sensuous intuition (especially when these laws are known as necessary) are commonly held by us to be such as have been placed there by the understanding, in spite of their being similar in all points to the laws of nature which we ascribe to experience.

§ 38. If we consider the properties of the circle, by which this figure combines in itself so many arbitrary determinations of space in a universal rule, we cannot avoid attributing a constitution to this geometrical thing. Two straight lines, for example, which intersect each other and the circle, howsoever they may be drawn, are always divided so that the rectangle constructed with the segments of the one is equal to that constructed with the segments of the other. The question now is: Does this law lie in the circle or in the understanding? That is, does this figure, independently of the understanding, contain in itself the ground of the law; or does the understanding, having constructed according to its concepts (of the equality of the radii) the figure itself, introduce into it this law of the chords intersecting in geometrical proportion? When we follow the proofs of this law, we soon perceive that it can only be derived from the condition on which the understanding founds the construction of this figure, namely, the concept of the equality of the radii. But if we enlarge this concept to pursue further the unity of various properties of geometrical figures under common laws and consider the circle as a conic section, which of course is subject to the same fundamental conditions of construction as other conic sections, we shall find that all the chords which intersect within the ellipse, parabola, and hyperbola always intersect so that the rectangles of their segments are not indeed equal but always bear a constant ratio to one another. If we proceed still farther to the fundamental teachings of physical astronomy, we find a physical law of reciprocal attraction applicable to all material nature, the rule of which is that it decreases inversely as the square of the distance from each attracting point, that is, as the spherical surfaces increase over which this force spreads, which law seems to be necessarily inherent in the very nature of things, and hence is usually propounded as knowable *a priori*. Simple as the sources of this law are, merely resting upon the relation of spherical surfaces of different radii, its consequences are so valuable with regard to the variety and simplicity of their agreement that not only are all possible orbits of the celestial bodies conic sections, but such a relation of these orbits to one another results that no other law of attraction than that of the inverse square of the distance can be imagined as fit for a cosmical system.

Here accordingly is nature, which rests upon laws that the understanding knows *a priori,* and chiefly from the universal principles of the determination of space. Now I ask: Do the laws of nature lie in space, and does the understanding learn them by merely endeavoring to find out the enormous wealth of meaning that lies in space; or do they inhere in the understanding and in the way in which it determines space according to the conditions of the synthetical unity in which its concepts are all centered?

Space is something so uniform and as to all particular properties so indeterminate that we should certainly not seek a store of laws of nature in it. Whereas that which determines space to assume the form of a circle, or the figures of a cone and a sphere, is the understanding, so far as it contains the ground of the unity of their constructions.

The mere universal form of intuition, called space, must therefore be the substratum of all intuitions determinable to particular objects; and in it, of course, the condition of the possibility and of the variety of these intuitions lies. But the unity of the objects is entirely determined by the understanding and on conditions which lie in its own na-

A drawing from Andreas Cellarius' *Harmonica Macrocosmica* (1661) with some of the greatst names of astronomy and cosmology, including (from left to right): Tycho Brahe (1546–1601), Ptolemy (fl. A.D. 130), St. Augustine (A.D. 354–430), Nicholas Copernicus (1473–1543), Galileo Galilei (with pointer) (1564–1642), and Andreas Cellarius (seated at right). (*Library of Congress*)

ture; and thus the understanding is the origin of the universal order of nature, in that it comprehends all appearances under its own laws and thereby produces, in an *a priori* manner, experience (as to its form), by means of which whatever is to be known only by experience is necessarily subjected to its laws. For we are not concerned with the nature of things in themselves, which is independent of the conditions both of our sensibility and our understanding, but with nature as an object of possible experience; and in this case the understanding, since it makes experience possible, thereby insists that the sensuous world is either not an object of experience at all or that it is nature [namely, the existence of things determined according to universal laws].

Appendix to the Pure Science of Nature

OF THE SYSTEM OF THE CATEGORIES

§ 39. There can be nothing more desirable to a philosopher than to be able to derive the scattered multiplicity of the concepts or principles which had occurred to him in concrete use from a principle *a priori,* and to unite everything in this way in one cognition. He formerly only believed that those things which remained after a certain abstraction, and seemed by comparison among one another to constitute a particular kind of cognitions, were completely collected; but this was only an *aggregate.* Now he knows that just so many, neither more nor less, can constitute the kind of cognition, and perceives the necessity of his division. This constitutes comprehension; and only then has he attained a *system.*

To search in our common knowledge for the concepts which do not rest upon particular experience and yet occur in all knowledge from experience, of which they as it were constitute the mere form of connection, presupposes neither greater reflection nor deeper insight than to detect in a language the rules of the actual use of words generally and thus to collect elements for a grammar (in fact both researches are very nearly related), even though we are not able to give a reason why each language has just this and no other formal constitution, and still less why any precise number of such formal determinations in general, neither more nor less, can be found in it.

Aristotle collected ten pure elementary concepts under the name of *categories.** To these, which are also called "predicaments," he found himself obliged afterward to add five post-predicaments,** some of which however *(prius, simul,* and *motus)* are contained in the former; but this rhapsody must be considered (and commended) as a mere hint for future inquirers, not as an idea developed according to rule; and hence it has, in the present more advanced state of philosophy, been rejected as quite useless.

After long reflection on the pure elements of human knowledge (those which contain nothing empirical), I at last succeeded in distinguishing with certainty and in separating the pure elementary notions of the sensibility (space and time) from those of the understanding. Thus the seventh, eighth, and ninth categories had to be excluded from the old list. And the others were of no service to me because there was no principle on which the understanding could be exhaustively investigated, and all the functions, whence its pure concepts arise, determined exhaustively and precisely.

But in order to discover such a principle, I looked about for an act of the understanding which comprises all the rest and is distinguished only by various modifications or phases, in reducing the multiplicity of representation to the unity of thinking in general. I found this act of the understanding to consist in judging. Here, then, the labors of the logicians were ready at hand, though not yet quite free from defects; and with this help I was enabled to exhibit a complete table of the pure functions of the understanding, which are however undetermined with respect to any object. I finally referred these functions of judging to objects in general, or rather to the condition of determining judgments as objectively valid; and so there arose the pure concepts of the understanding, concerning which I could make certain that these, and this exact number only, constitute our whole knowledge of things by pure understanding. I was justified in calling them by their old name "categories," while I reserved for myself the liberty of adding, under the title of "predicables," a complete list of all the concepts deducible from them by combinations, whether among themselves, or with the pure form of the appearance, that is, space or time, or with its matter, so far as it is not yet empirically determined (namely, the object of sensation in general), as soon as a system of transcendental philosophy should be completed, with the construction of which I was engaged in the *Critique of Pure Reason* itself.

---

*1. *Substantia.* 2. *Qualitas.* 3. *Quantitas.* 4. *Relatio.* 5. *Actio.* 6. *Passio.* 7. *Quando.* 8. *Ubi.* 9. *Situs.* 10. *Habitus.*
**Oppositum. Prius. Simul. Motus. Habere.*

Now the essential point in this system of categories, which distinguishes it from the old rhapsody which proceeded without any principle and for which alone it deserves to be considered as philosophy, consists in this: that, by means of it, the true significance of the pure concepts of the understanding and the condition of their use could be precisely determined. For here it became obvious that they are themselves nothing but logical functions, and as such do not produce the least concept of an object, but require sensuous intuition as a basis. These concepts, therefore, only serve to determine empirical judgments (which are otherwise undetermined and indifferent as regards all functions of judging) with respect to the functions of judging, thereby procuring them universal validity and, by means of them, making judgments of experience in general possible.

Such an insight into the nature of the categories, which limits them at the same time to use merely in experience, never occurred either to their first author or to any of his successors; but without this insight (which immediately depends upon their derivation or deduction), they are quite useless and only a miserable list of names, without explanation or rule for their use. Had the ancients ever conceived such a notion, doubtless the whole study of pure rational knowledge, which under the name of metaphysics has for centuries spoiled many a sound mind, would have reached us in quite another shape and would have enlightened the human understanding, instead of actually exhausting it in obscure and vain speculations and rendering it unfit for true science.

This system of categories makes all treatment of every object of pure reason itself systematic, and affords a direction or clue how and through what points of inquiry every metaphysical consideration must proceed in order to be complete; for it exhausts all the possible functions of the understanding, among which every concept must be classed. In like manner the table of principles has been formulated, the completeness of which we can only vouch for by the system of the categories. Even in the division of the concepts,* which must go beyond the physical application of the understanding, it is always the very same clue, which, as it must always be determined *a priori* by the same fixed points of the human understanding, always forms a closed circle. There is no doubt that the object of a pure concept, either of the understanding or of reason, so far as it is to be estimated philosophically and on *a priori* principles, can in this way be completely known. I could not therefore omit to make use of this clue with regard to one of the most abstract ontological divisions, namely, the various distinctions of the concepts of something and of nothing, and to construct accordingly** a systematic and necessary table of their divisions.***

And this system, like every other true one founded on a universal principle, shows its inestimable value in that it excludes all foreign concepts which might otherwise in-

---

*Cf. the tables in the *Critique of Pure Reason* in the chapters on "The Paralogisms of Pure Reason" and the "System of Cosmological Ideas."

**In the chapter on "The Amphiboly of the Concepts of Reflection," in the *Critique of Pure Reason.*

***On the table of the categories many neat observations may be made, for instance: (1) that the third arises from the first and the second, joined in one concept; (2) that in those of quantity and of quality there is merely a progress from unity to totality or from something to nothing (for this purpose the categories of quality must stand thus: reality, limitation, total negation), without *correlata* or *opposita*, whereas those of relation and of modality have them; (3) that, as in logic categorical judgments are the basis of all others, so the category of substance is the basis of all concepts of actual things; (4) that, as modality in the judgment is not a particular predicate, so by the modal concepts a determination is not superadded to things, etc. Such observations are of great use. If we enumerate all the predicables, which we can find pretty completely in any good ontology (for example, Baumgarten's), and arrange them in classes under the categories, in which operation we must not neglect to add as complete a dissection of all these concepts as possible, there will then arise a merely analytical part of metaphysics which does not contain a single synthetical proposition, which might precede the second (the synthetical) and would, by its precision and completeness, be not only useful but, in virtue of its system, be even to some extent elegant.

trude among the pure concepts of the understanding, and determines the place of every cognition. Those concepts, which under the name of "concepts of reflection" have been likewise arranged in a table according to the clue of the categories, intrude into ontology without any privilege or just claim to be among the pure concepts of the understanding. The latter are concepts of connection, and thereby of the objects themselves, whereas the former are only concepts of mere comparison of concepts already given, and hence are of quite another nature and use. By my systematic division* they are saved from this confusion. But the value of the special table of the categories will be still more obvious when we separate—as we are about to do—the table of the transcendental concepts of reason from the concepts of the understanding. As the transcendental concepts of reason are of an entirely different nature and origin, the table of them must have quite another form than the table of categories. This so necessary separation has never yet been made in any system of metaphysics, where, as a rule, these Ideas of reason are all mixed up with the concepts of the understanding, as if they were children of the same family—a confusion which was unavoidable in the absence of a definite system of categories.

THIRD PART OF THE MAIN
TRANSCENDENTAL PROBLEM

How Is Metaphysics in General Possible?

§ 40. Pure mathematics and pure science of nature had, for their own safety and certainty, no need for such a deduction as we have made of both. For the former rests upon its own evidence, and the latter (though sprung from pure sources of the understanding) upon experience and its thorough confirmation. The pure science of nature cannot altogether refuse and dispense with the testimony of experience; because with all its certainty it can never, as philosophy, rival mathematics. Both sciences, therefore, stood in need of this inquiry, not for themselves, but for the sake of another science: metaphysics.

Metaphysics has to do not only with concepts of nature, which always find their application in experience, but also with pure rational concepts, which never can be given in any possible experience whatever. Consequently it deals with concepts whose objective reality (namely, that they are not mere chimeras) and with assertions whose truth or falsity cannot be discovered or confirmed by any experience. This part of metaphysics, however, is precisely what constitutes its essential end, to which the rest is only a means, and thus this science is in need of such a deduction for its own sake. The third question now proposed relates therefore as it were to the root and peculiarity of metaphysics, that is, the occupation of reason merely with itself and the supposed knowledge of objects arising immediately from this brooding over its own concepts, without requiring, or indeed being able to reach that knowledge through, experience.**

Without solving this problem, reason can never satisfy itself. The empirical use to which reason limits the pure understanding does not fully satisfy the proper calling of reason. Every single experience is only a part of the whole sphere of its domain, but the

---

*See *Critique of Pure Reason,* "The Amphiboly of the Concepts of Reflection."

**If we can say that a science is actual, at least in the idea of all men, as soon as it appears that the problems which lead to it are proposed to everybody by the nature of human reason, and that therefore many (though faulty) endeavors are unavoidably made in its behalf, then we are bound to say that metaphysics is subjectively (and indeed necessarily) actual, and therefore, we justly ask, how is it (objectively) possible.

absolute totality of all possible experience is itself not experience. Yet it is a necessary problem for reason, the mere representation of which requires concepts quite different from the pure concepts of the understanding, whose use is only *immanent,* or refers to experience, so far as it can be given. Whereas the concepts of reason aim at the completeness, that is, the collective unity of all possible experience, and thereby transcend every given experience. Thus they become *transcendent.*

As the understanding stands in need of categories for experience, reason contains in itself the source of Ideas, by which I mean necessary concepts whose object *cannot* be given in any experience. The latter are inherent in the nature of reason, as the former are in that of the understanding. While the former carry with them an illusion likely to mislead, the illusion of the latter is inevitable, though it certainly can be kept from misleading us.

Since all illusion consists in holding the subjective ground of our judgments to be objective, a self-knowledge of pure reason in its transcendent (presumptuous) use is the sole preservative from the aberrations into which reason falls when it mistakes its calling and transcendently refers to the object that which concerns only its own subject and its guidance in all immanent use.

§ 41. The distinction of Ideas—that is, of pure concepts of reason—from categories, or pure concepts of the understanding, as cognitions of a quite distinct species, origin, and use, is so important a point in founding a science which is to contain the system of all these *a priori* cognitions that, without this distinction, metaphysics is absolutely impossible or is at best a random, bungling attempt to build a castle in the air without a knowledge of the materials or of their fitness for this or any purpose. Had the *Critique of Pure Reason* done nothing but first point out this distinction, it would thereby have contributed more to clear up our conception of, and to guide our inquiry in, the field of metaphysics than all the vain efforts which had hitherto been made to satisfy the transcendent problems of pure reason, but which had never surmised that we were in quite another field than that of the understanding, and hence classed concepts of the understanding and those of reason together as if they were of the same kind.

§ 42. All pure cognitions of the understanding have this feature that their concepts present themselves in experience, and their principles can be confirmed by it; whereas the transcendent cognitions of reason cannot either, as Ideas, appear in experience or, as propositions, ever be confirmed or refuted by it. Hence whatever errors may slip in unawares can only be discovered by pure reason itself—a discovery of much difficulty, because this very reason naturally becomes dialectical by means of its Ideas; and this unavoidable illusion cannot be limited by any objective and dogmatic researches into things, but only by a subjective investigation of reason itself as a source of ideas.

§ 43. In the *Critique of Pure Reason* it was always my greatest care to endeavor, not only carefully to distinguish the several species of knowledge, but to derive concepts belonging to each one of them from their common source. I did this in order that, by knowing whence they originated, I might determine their use with safety and also have the unanticipated but invaluable advantage of knowing, according to principles, the completeness of my enumeration, classification, and specification of concepts *a priori.* Without this, metaphysics is mere rhapsody, in which no one knows whether he has enough or whether and where something is still wanting. We can indeed have this advantage only in pure philosophy, but of this philosophy it constitutes the very essence.

As I had found the origin of the categories in the four logical forms of all the judgments of the understanding, it was quite natural to seek the origin of the Ideas in the three forms of syllogisms. For as soon as these pure concepts of reason (the transcendental Ideas) are given, they could hardly, except they be held innate, be found anywhere else than in the same activity of reason, which, so far as it regards mere form, constitutes the logical element of syllogisms; but, so far as it represents judgments of the understanding as determined *a priori* with respect to one or another form, constitutes transcendental concepts of pure reason.

The formal distinction of syllogisms renders necessary their division into categorical, hypothetical, and disjunctive. The concepts of reason founded on them contain therefore, first, the Idea of the complete subject (the substantial); secondly, the Idea of the complete series of conditions; thirdly, the determination of all concepts in the Idea of a complete complex of that which is possible.* The first idea is psychological, the second cosmological, the third theological; and, as all three give occasion to dialectic, yet each in its own way, the division of the whole dialectic of pure reason into its paralogism, its antinomy, and its Ideal was arranged accordingly. Through this deduction we may feel assured that all the claims of pure reason are completely represented and that none can be wanting, because the faculty of reason itself, whence they all take their origin, is thereby completely surveyed.

§ 44. In these general considerations it is also remarkable that the Ideas of reason, unlike the categories, are of no service to the use of our understanding in experience, but quite dispensable, and become even an impediment to the maxims of a rational knowledge of nature. Yet in another aspect still to be determined they are necessary. Whether the soul is or is not a simple substance is of no consequence to us in the explanation of its phenomena. For we cannot render the concept of a simple being sensuous and thus concretely intelligible by any possible experience. The concept is therefore quite void as regards all hoped-for insight into the cause of appearances and cannot at all serve as a principle of the explanation of that which inner or outer experience supplies. Similarly, the cosmological Ideas of the beginning of the world or of its eternity *(a parte ante)* cannot be of any service to us for the explanation of any event in the world itself. And finally we must, according to a right maxim of the philosophy of nature, refrain from explaining the design of nature as drawn from the will of a Supreme Being, because this would not be natural philosophy but a confession that we have come to the end of it. The use of these Ideas, therefore, is quite different from that of those categories by which (and by the principles built upon which) experience itself first becomes possible. But our laborious Analytic of the understanding would be superfluous if we had nothing else in view than the mere knowledge of nature as it can be given in experience; for reason does its work, both in mathematics and in the science of nature, quite safely and well without any of this subtle deduction. Therefore our critical examination of the understanding combines with the Ideas of pure reason for a purpose which lies beyond the empirical use of the understanding; but such an extended use of the understanding we have above declared to be totally inadmissible and without any object or meaning. Yet there must be a harmony between the nature of reason and that of the understanding, and the former must contribute to the perfection of the latter and cannot possibly upset it.

---

*In disjunctive judgments, we consider all possibility as divided in respect to a particular concept. By the ontological principle of the universal determination of a thing in general, I understand the principle that either the one or the other of all possible contradictory predicates must be assigned to any object. This is, at the same time, the principle of all disjunctive judgments, constituting the foundation of a complete whole of possibility, and in it the possibility of every object in general is considered as determined. This may serve as a slight explanation of the above propositions: that the activity of reason in disjunctive syllogisms is formally the same as that by which it fashions the idea of a complete whole of all reality, containing in itself that which is positive in all pairs of contradictory predicates.

The solution of this question is as follows: Pure reason does not in its Ideas point to particular objects which lie beyond the field of experience, but only requires completeness of the use of the understanding in the system of experience. But this completeness can be a completeness of principles only, not of intuitions and of objects. In order, however, to represent the Ideas definitely, reason conceives them after the fashion of the knowledge of an object. This knowledge is, as far as these rules are concerned, completely determined; but the object is only an Idea [invented for the purpose of] bringing the knowledge of the understanding as near as possible to the completeness indicated by that Idea.

Prefatory Remark to the Dialectic
of Pure Reason

§ 45. We have shown in §§ 33 and 34 that the purity of the categories from all admixture of sensuous restrictions may mislead reason into extending their use beyond all experience to things in themselves; for though these categories themselves find no intuition which can give them meaning or sense *in concreto,* they, as mere logical functions, can represent a thing in general, but not give by themselves alone a determinate concept of anything. Such hyperbolical objects are distinguished by the appellation of *noumena,* or pure beings of the understanding (or better, beings of thought)—such as, for example, "substance"—but conceived without permanence in time, or "cause," but not acting in time, etc. Here predicates that only serve to make the conformity-to-law of experience possible are applied to these concepts, and yet they are deprived of all the conditions of intuition on which alone experience is possible, and so these concepts lose all significance.

There is no danger, however, of the understanding spontaneously making an excursion so very wantonly beyond its own bounds into the field of the mere beings of thought unless it is impelled by foreign laws. But when reason, which cannot be fully satisfied with any empirical use of the rules of the understanding, as being always conditioned, requires a completion of this chain of conditions, then the understanding is forced out of its sphere. And then it partly represents objects of experience in a series so extended that no experience can grasp it; partly even (with a view to complete the series) it seeks entirely beyond it *noumena,* to which it can attach that chain; and so, having at last escaped from the conditions of experience, it makes its stand as it were final. These are then the transcendental Ideas, which, in accord with the true but hidden ends of the natural destiny of our reason, aim, not at extravagant concepts, but at an unbounded extension of their empirical use, yet seduce the understanding by an unavoidable illusion to a transcendent use, which, though deceitful, cannot be restrained within the bounds of experience by any resolution, but only by scientific instruction and with much difficulty.

I. The Psychological Ideas*

§ 46. People have long since observed that in all substances the subject proper, that which remains after all the accidents (as predicates) are abstracted, consequently the *substantial,* remains unknown, and various complaints have been made concerning these limits to our knowledge. But it will be well to consider that the human under-

---

*See *Critique of Pure Reason,* "The Paralogisms of Pure Reason."

standing is not to be blamed for its inability to know the substance of things—that is, to determine it by itself—but rather for demanding definitely to know substance, which is a mere Idea, as though it were a given object. Pure reason requires us to seek for every predicate of a thing its own subject, and for this subject, which is itself necessarily nothing but a predicate, its subject, and so on indefinitely (or as far as we can reach). But hence it follows that we must not hold anything at which we can arrive to be an ultimate subject, and that substance itself never can be thought by our understanding, however deep we may penetrate, even if all nature were unveiled to us. For the specific nature of our understanding consists in thinking everything discursively, that is, by concepts, and so by mere predicates, to which, therefore, the absolute subject must always be wanting. Hence all the real properties by which we know bodies are mere accidents—not excepting even impenetrability, which we can only represent to ourselves as the effect of a power of which the subject is unknown to us.

Now we appear to have this substance in the consciousness of ourselves (in the thinking subject), and indeed in an immediate intuition; for all the predicates of an internal sense refer to the *ego,* as a subject, and I cannot conceive myself as the predicate of any other subject. Hence completeness in the reference of the given concepts as predicates to a subject—not merely an Idea, but an object—that is, the absolute subject itself, seems to be given in experience. But this expectation is disappointed. For the ego is not a concept,* but only the indication of the object of the inner sense, so far as we know it by no further predicate. Consequently it cannot indeed be itself a predicate of any other thing; but just as little can it be a definite concept of an absolute subject, but is, as in all other cases, only the reference of the inner phenomena to their unknown subject. Yet this idea (which serves very well as a regulative principle totally to destroy all materialistic explanations of the internal phenomena of the soul) occasions by a very natural misunderstanding a very specious argument, which infers its nature from this supposed knowledge of the substance of our thinking being. This is specious so far as the knowledge of it falls quite without the complex of experience.

§ 47. But though we may call this thinking self (the soul) "substance," as being the ultimate subject of thinking which cannot be further represented as the predicate of another thing, it remains quite empty and without significance if permanence—the quality which renders the concept of substances in experience fruitful—cannot be proved of it.

But permanence can never be proved of the concept of a substance as a thing in itself, but for the purposes of experience only. This is sufficiently shown by the first Analogy of Experience,** and whoever will not yield to this proof may try for himself whether he can succeed in proving, from the concept of a subject which does not exist itself as the predicate of another thing, that its existence is absolutely permanent and that it cannot either in itself or by any natural cause originate or be annihilated. These synthetical *a priori* propositions can never be proved in themselves, but only in reference to things as objects of possible experience.

§ 48. If, therefore, from the concept of the soul as a substance we would infer its permanence, this can hold good as regards possible experience only, not of the soul as a thing in itself and beyond all possible experience. Life is the subjective condition of all

---

*Were the representation of the apperception (the Ego) a concept, by which anything whatever could be thought, it could be used as a predicate of other things or contain predicates in itself. But it is nothing more than the feeling of an existence without the least concept and is only the representation of that to which all thinking stands in relation *(relatione accidentis).*
**In the *Critique of Pure Reason.*

our possible experience; consequently we can only infer the permanence of the soul in life, for the death of a man is the end of all experience which concerns the soul as an object of experience, except the contrary be proved—which is the very question in hand. The permanence of the soul can therefore only be proved (and no one cares to do that) during the life of man, but not, as we desire to do, after death. The reason for this is that the concept of substance, so far as it is to be considered necessarily combined with the concept of permanence, can be so combined only according to the principles of possible experience, and therefore for the purposes of experience only.*

§ 49. That there is something real outside us which not only corresponds but must correspond to our outer perceptions can likewise be proved to be, not a connection of things in themselves, but for the sake of experience. This means that there is something empirical, that is, some appearance in space without us, that admits of a satisfactory proof; for we have nothing to do with other objects than those which belong to possible experience, because objects which cannot be given us in any experience are nothing for us. Empirically outside me is that which is intuited in space; and space, together with all the appearances it contains, belongs to the representations whose connection, according to laws of experience, proves their objective truth, just as the connection of the appearances of the inner sense proves the actuality of my soul (as an object of the inner sense). By means of outer experience I am conscious of the actuality of bodies as external appearances in space, in the same manner as by means of the inner experience I am conscious of the existence of my soul in time; but this soul is known only as an object of the inner sense by appearances that constitute an inner state and of which the being in itself, which forms the basis of these appearances, is unknown. Cartesian idealism therefore does nothing but distinguish outer experience from a dream and the conformity to law (as a criterion of its truth) of the former from the irregularity and false illusion of the latter. In both it presupposes space and time as conditions of the existence of objects, and it only inquires whether the objects of the outer senses which we, when awake, put in space, are as actually to be found in it as the object of the internal sense, the soul, is in time; that is, whether experience carries with it sure criteria to distinguish it from imagination. This doubt, however, may easily be disposed of, and we always do so in common life by investigating the connection of appearances in both space and time according to universal laws of experience, and we cannot doubt, when the representation of external things throughout agrees therewith that they constitute truthful experience. Material idealism, in which appearances are considered as such only according to their connection in experience may accordingly be very easily refuted; and it is just as sure an experience that bodies exist outside us (in

---

*It is indeed very remarkable how carelessly metaphysicians have always passed over the principle of the permanence of substances without ever attempting a proof of it; doubtless because they found themselves abandoned by all proofs as soon as they began to deal with the concept of substance. Common sense, which felt distinctly that without this presupposition no union of perceptions in experience is possible, supplied the want by a postulate. From experience itself it never could derive such a principle, partly because material things (substances) cannot be so traced in all their alterations and dissolutions that the matter can always be found undiminished, partly because the principle contains *necessity*, which is always the sign of an *a priori* principle. People then boldly applied this postulate to the concept of soul as a *substance*, and concluded a necessary continuance of the soul after the death of man (especially as the simplicity of this substance, which is inferred from the indivisibility of consciousness, secured it from destruction by dissolution). Had they found the genuine source of this principle—a discovery which requires deeper researches than they were ever inclined to make—they would have seen that the law of the permanence of substances arises for the purposes of experience only, and hence can hold good of things so far as they are to be known and conjoined with others in experience, but never independently of all possible experience, and consequently cannot hold good of the soul after death.

space) as that I myself exist according to the representation of the inner sense (in time), for the concept "outside us" only signifies existence in space. However, as the Ego in the proposition "I am" means not only the object of inner intuition (in time) but the subject of consciousness, just as body means not only outer intuition (in space) but the thing in itself which is the basis of this appearance, then the question whether bodies (as appearances of the outer sense) exist as bodies in nature apart from my thoughts may without any hesitation be denied. But the question whether I myself as an appearance of the inner sense (the soul according to empirical psychology) exist apart from my faculty of representation in time is an exactly similar one and must likewise be answered in the negative. And in this manner everything, when it is reduced to its true meaning, is decided and certain. The formal (which I have also called "transcendental") actually abolishes the material, or Cartesian, idealism. For if space be nothing but a form of my sensibility, it is as a representation in me just as actual as I myself am, and nothing but the empirical truth of the appearances in it remains for consideration. But if this is not the case, if space and the appearances in it are something existing outside us, then all the criteria of experience besides our perception can never prove the actuality of these objects outside us.

II. The Cosmological Ideas*

§ 50. This product of pure reason in its transcendent use is its most remarkable phenomenon. It serves as a very powerful agent to rouse philosophy from its dogmatic slumber and to stimulate it to the arduous task of undertaking a critical examination of reason itself.

I term this Idea cosmological because it always takes its object only in the sensible world and does not need any other world than one whose object is given to sense; consequently it remains in this respect in its native home, does not become transcendent, and is therefore so far not an Idea; whereas to conceive the soul as a simple substance, on the contrary, means to conceive such an object (the simple) as cannot be presented to the senses. Yet, in spite of this, the cosmological idea extends the connection of the conditioned with its condition (whether this is mathematical or dynamical) so far that experience never can keep up with it. It is therefore with regard to this point always an Idea, whose object never can be adequately given in any experience.

§ 51. In the first place, the use of a system of categories becomes here so obvious and unmistakable that, even if there were not several other proofs of it, this alone would sufficiently prove it indispensable in the system of pure reason. There are only four such transcendent Ideas, as many as there are classes of categories; in each of which, however, they refer only to the absolute completeness of the series of the conditions for a given condition. In accordance with these cosmological Ideas, there are only four kinds of dialectical assertions of pure reason, which, being dialectical, prove that to each of them, on equally specious principles of pure reason, a contradictory assertion stands opposed. As all the metaphysical art of the most subtle distinction cannot prevent this opposition, it compels the philosopher to recur to the first sources of pure reason itself. This antinomy, not arbitrarily invented but founded in the nature of human reason, and hence unavoidable and never ceasing, contains the following four theses together with their antitheses:

---

*Cf. *Critique of Pure Reason,* "The Antinomy of Pure Reason."

1

Thesis

The world has, as to time and space, a beginning (limit).

Antithesis

The world is, as to time and space, infinite.

2

Thesis

Everything in the world consists of [elements that are] simple.

Antithesis

There is nothing simple, but everything is composite.

3

Thesis

There are in the world causes through freedom.

Antithesis

There is no freedom, but all is nature.

4

Thesis

In the series of the world-causes there is some necessary being.

Antithesis

There is nothing necessary in the world, but in this series all is contingent.

§ 52a. Here is the most singular phenomenon of human reason, no other instance of which can be shown in any other use of reason. If we, as is commonly done, represent to ourselves the appearances of the sensible world as things in themselves, if we assume the principles of their combination as principles universally valid of things in themselves and not merely of experience, as is usually, nay, without our *Critique* unavoidably, done, there arises an unexpected conflict which never can be removed in the common dogmatic way; because the thesis, as well as the antithesis, can be shown by equally clear, evident, and irresistible proofs—for I pledge myself as to the correctness of all these proofs—and reason therefore perceives that it is divided against itself, a state at which the skeptic rejoices, but which must make the critical philosopher pause and feel ill at ease.

§ 52b. We may blunder in various ways in metaphysics without any fear of being detected in falsehood. If we but avoid self-contradiction, which in synthetical though purely fictitious propositions is quite possible, then whenever the concepts which we connect are mere Ideas that cannot be given (with respect to their whole content) in experience, we cannot be refuted by experience. For how can we make out by experience whether the world is from eternity or had a beginning, whether matter is infinitely divisible or consists of simple parts? Such concepts cannot be given in any experience, however extensive, and consequently the falsehood either of the affirmative or the negative proposition cannot be discovered by this touchstone.

The only possible way in which reason could have revealed unintentionally its secret dialectic, falsely announced as its dogmatics, would be when it were made to ground an assertion upon a universally admitted principle and to deduce the exact contrary with the greatest accuracy of inference from another which is equally granted. This is actually here the case with regard to four natural Ideas of reason, whence four assertions on the one side and as many counterassertions on the other arise, each consistently following from universally acknowledged principles. Thus they reveal, by the use of these principles, the dialectical illusion of pure reason, which would otherwise forever remain concealed.

This is therefore a decisive experiment, which must necessarily expose any error lying hidden in the assumptions of reason.* Contradictory propositions cannot both be false, except the concept on which each is founded is self-contradictory; for example, the propositions, "A square circle is round," and "A square circle is not round," are both false. For, as to the former, it is false that the circle is round because it is quadrangular; and it is likewise false that it is not round, that is, angular, because it is a circle. For the logical criterion of the impossibility of a concept consists in this that, if we presuppose it, two contradictory propositions both become false; consequently, as no middle between them is conceivable, nothing at all is thought by that concept.

§ 52c. The first two antinomies, which I call mathematical because they are concerned with the addition or division of the homogeneous, are founded on such a contradictory concept; and hence I explain how it happens that both the thesis and antithesis of the two are false.

When I speak of objects in time and in space, it is not of things in themselves, of which I know nothing, but of things in appearance, that is, of experience, as the particular way of knowing objects which is afforded to man. I must not say of what I think in time or in space, that in itself, and independent of these my thoughts, it exists in space and in time, for in that case I should contradict myself; because space and time, together with the appearances in them, are nothing existing in themselves and outside of my representations, but are themselves only modes of representation, and it is palpably contradictory to say that a mere mode of representation exists without our representation. Objects of the senses therefore exist only in experience, whereas to give them a self-subsisting existence apart from experience or before it is merely to represent to ourselves that experience actually exists apart from experience or before it.

Now if I inquire into the magnitude of the world, as to space and time, it is equally impossible, as regards all my concepts, to declare it infinite or to declare it finite. For neither assertion can be contained in experience, because experience either of an infi-

---

*I therefore would be pleased to have the critical reader to devote to this antinomy of pure reason his chief attention, because nature itself seems to have established it with a view to stagger reason in its daring pretensions and to force it to self-examination. For every proof which I have given of both thesis and antithesis I undertake to be responsible, and thereby to show the certainty of the inevitable antinomy of reason. When the reader is brought by this curious phenomenon to fall back upon the proof of the presumption upon which it rests, he will feel himself obliged to investigate the ultimate foundation of all knowledge by pure reason with me more thoroughly.

nite space or of an infinite elapsed time, or again, of the boundary of the world by a void space or by an antecedent void time, is impossible; these are mere Ideas. The magnitude of the world, decided either way, would therefore have to exist in the world itself apart from all experience. But this contradicts the concept of a world of sense, which is merely a complex of the appearances whose existence and connection occur only in our representations, that is, in experience; since this latter is not an object in itself but a mere mode of representation. Hence it follows that, as the concept of an absolutely existing world of sense is self-contradictory, the solution of the problem concerning its magnitude, whether attempted affirmatively or negatively, is always false.

The same holds of the second antinomy, which relates to the division of appearances. For these are mere representations; and the parts exist merely in their representation, consequently in the division—that is, in a possible experience in which they are given—and the division reaches only as far as the possible experience reaches. To assume that an appearance, for example, that of body, contains in itself before all experience all the parts which any possible experience can ever reach is to impute to a mere appearance, which can exist only in experience, an existence previous to experience. In other words, it would mean that mere representations exist before they can be found in our faculty of representation. Such an assertion is self-contradictory, as also every solution of our misunderstood problem, whether we maintain that bodies in themselves consist of an infinite number of parts or of a finite number of simple parts.

§ 53. In the first (the mathematical) class of antinomies the falsehood of the presupposition consists in representing in one concept something self-contradictory as if it were compatible (that is, an appearance as a thing in itself). But, as to the second (the dynamical) class of antinomies, the falsehood of the presupposition consists in representing as contradictory what is compatible; so that while in the former case the opposed assertions were both false, in this case, on the other hand, where they are opposed to one another by mere misunderstanding, they may both be true.

Any mathematical connection necessarily presupposes homogeneity of what is connected (in the concept of magnitude), while the dynamical one by no means requires this. When we have to deal with extended magnitudes all the parts must be homogeneous with one another and with the whole, whereas in the connection of cause and effect homogeneity may indeed likewise be found but is not necessary; for the concept of causality (by means of which something is posited through something else quite different from it) does not in the least require it.

If the objects of the world of sense are taken for things in themselves and the above laws of nature for laws of things in themselves, the contradiction would be unavoidable. So also, if the subject of freedom were, like other objects, represented as mere appearance, the contradiction would be just as unavoidable; for the same predicate would at once be affirmed and denied of the same kind of object in the same sense. But if natural necessity is referred merely to appearances and freedom merely to things in themselves, no contradiction arises if we at the same time assume or admit both kinds of causality, however difficult or impossible it may be to make the latter kind conceivable.

In appearance every effect is an event, or something that happens in time; it must, according to the universal law of nature, be preceded by a determination of the causal act of its cause—this determination being a state of the cause—which it follows according to a constant law. But this determination of the cause to a causal act must likewise be something that takes place or happens; the cause must have begun to act, otherwise no succession between it and the effect could be conceived. Otherwise the effect, as well as the causal act of the cause, would have always existed. Therefore the determination of the cause to act must also have originated among appearances and must consequently, like its effect, be an event, which must again have its cause, and so on; hence natural necessity must be the condition on which efficient causes are determined. Whereas if freedom is to be a property of certain causes of appearances, it must, as regards these, which are events, be a faculty of starting them spontaneously. That is, it would not require that the causal act of the cause should itself begin [in time], and hence it would not require any other ground to determine its start. But then the cause, as to its causal act, could not rank under time-determinations of its state; that is, it could not be an appearance, but would have to be considered a thing in itself, while only its effects would be appearances.* If without contradiction we can think of the beings of understanding as exercising such an influence on appearances, then natural necessity will attach to all connections of cause and effect in the sensuous world; though, on the other hand, freedom can be granted to the cause which is itself not an appearance (but the foundation of appearance). Nature and freedom therefore can without contradiction be attributed to the very same thing, but in different relations—on one side as an appearance, on the other as a thing in itself.

We have in us a faculty which not only stands in connection with its subjective determining grounds [motives] which are the natural causes of its actions and is so far the faculty of a being that itself belongs to appearances, but is also related to objective grounds which are only Ideas so far as they can determine this faculty. This connection is expressed by the word *ought*. This faculty is called "reason," and, so far as we consider a being (man) entirely according to this objectively determinable reason, he cannot be considered as a being of sense; this property is a property of a thing in itself, a property whose possibility we cannot comprehend. I mean we cannot comprehend how the *ought* should determine (even if it never has actually determined) its activity and could become the cause of actions whose effect is an appearance in the sensible world. Yet the causality of reason would be freedom with regard to the effects in the sensuous world, so far as we can consider *objective grounds,* which are themselves Ideas, as their determinants. For its action in that case would not depend upon subjective conditions, consequently not upon those of time, and of course not upon the law of nature which serves to determine them, because grounds of reason give the rule universally to actions, according to principles, without influence of the circumstances of either time or place.

What I adduce here is merely meant as an example to make the thing intelligible and does not necessarily belong to our problem, which must be decided from mere concepts independently of the properties which we meet in the actual world.

Now I may say without contradiction that all the actions of rational beings, so far as they are appearances (met with in any experience), are subject to the necessity of nature, but the very same actions, as regards merely the rational subject and its faculty of

---

*The Idea of freedom occurs only in the relation of the intellectual, as cause, to the appearance, as effect. Hence we cannot attribute freedom to matter in regard to the incessant action by which it fills its space, though this action takes place from an internal principle. We can likewise find no notion of freedom suitable to purely rational beings, for instance, to God, so far as his action is immanent. For his action, though independent of external determining causes, is determined in his eternal reason, that is, in the divine *nature.* It is only if *something is to start* by an action, and so the effect occurs in the sequence of time, or in the world of sense (for example, the beginning of the world), that we can put the question whether the causal act of the cause must in its turn have been started or whether the cause can originate an effect without its causal act itself beginning. In the former case, the concept of this activity is a concept of natural necessity; in the latter, that of freedom. From this the reader will see that as I explained freedom to be the faculty of starting an event spontaneously, I have exactly hit the concept which is the problem of metaphysics.

acting according to mere reason, are free. For what is required for the necessity of nature? Nothing more than the determinability of every event in the world of sense according to constant laws, that is, a reference to cause in the [world of] appearance; in this process the thing in itself at its foundation and its causality remain unknown. But, I say, the law of nature remains, whether the rational being is the cause of the effects in the sensuous world from reason—that is, through freedom—or whether it does not determine them on grounds of reason. For if the former is the case, the action is performed according to maxims, the effect of which as appearance is always conformable to constant laws; if the latter is the case, and the action not performed on principles of reason, it is subjected to the empirical laws of the sensibility, and in both cases the effects are connected according to constant laws; more than this we do not require or know concerning natural necessity. But in the former case reason is the cause of these laws of nature, and therefore free; in the latter, the effects follow according to mere natural laws of sensibility, because reason does not influence it. But reason itself is not determined on that account by the sensibility (which is impossible) and is therefore free in this case too. Freedom is therefore no hindrance to natural law in appearances; neither does this law abrogate the freedom of the practical use of reason, which is connected with things in themselves, as determining grounds.

Thus practical freedom, namely, the freedom in which reason possesses causality according to objectively determining grounds, is rescued; and yet natural necessity is not in the least curtailed with regard to the very same effects, as appearances. The same remarks will serve to explain what we had to say concerning transcendental freedom and its compatibility with natural necessity in the same subject, but not taken in the same context. For, as to this, every beginning of the action of a being from objective causes regarded as determining grounds is always a *first beginning,* though the same action is in the series of appearances only a *subordinate beginning,* which must be preceded by a state of the cause which determines it and is itself determined in the same manner by another immediately preceding. Thus we are able, in rational beings, or in beings generally so far as their causality is determined in them as things in themselves, to think of a faculty of beginning from themselves a series of states without falling into contradiction with the laws of nature. For the relation of the action to objective grounds of reason is not a time relation; in this case that which determines the causality does not precede in time the action, because such determining grounds represent, not a reference to objects of sense, for example, to causes in the appearances, but to determining causes as things in themselves, which do not fall under conditions of time. And in this way the action, with regard to the causality of reason, can be considered as a first beginning, while in respect to the series of appearances as merely a subordinate beginning. We may therefore without contradiction consider it in the former aspect as free, but in the latter (as it is merely appearance) as subject to natural necessity.

As to the fourth antinomy, it is solved in the same way as the conflict of reason with itself in the third. For, provided the cause *in* the appearance is distinguished from the cause *of* the appearances (so far as it can be thought as a thing in itself), both propositions are perfectly reconcilable: the one, that there is nowhere in the sensuous world a cause (according to similar laws of causality) whose existence is absolutely necessary; the other, that this world is nevertheless connected with a necessary being as its cause (but of another kind and according to another law). The incompatibility of these propositions rests entirely upon the mistake of extending what is valid merely of appearances to things in themselves and in confusing both in one concept.

§ 54. This, then, is the exposition, and this the solution of the whole antinomy in which reason finds itself involved in the application of its principles to the sensible world. The former alone (the mere exposition) would be a considerable service in the cause of our knowledge of human reason, even though the solution might fail fully to satisfy the reader, who has here to combat a natural illusion which has been but recently exposed to him and which he had hitherto always regarded as genuine. For one result at least is unavoidable. As it is quite impossible to prevent this conflict of reason with itself—so long as the objects of the sensible world are taken for things in themselves and not for mere appearances, which they are in fact—the reader is thereby compelled to examine over again the deduction of all our *a priori* knowledge and the proof which I have given of my deduction in order to come to a decision on the question. This is all I require at present; for when in this occupation he shall have thought himself deep enough into the nature of pure reason, those concepts by which alone the solution of the conflict of reason is possible will become sufficiently familiar to him. Without this preparation, I cannot expect an unreserved assent even from the most attentive reader.

III. The Theological Idea*

§ 55. The third transcendental Idea, which affords matter for the most important but (if pursued only speculatively) transcendent and thereby dialectical use of reason, is the Ideal of pure reason. Reason in this case does not, as with the psychological and the cosmological Ideas, begin from experience and err by exaggerating its grounds in striving to attain, if possible, the absolute completeness of their series. Rather, it totally breaks with experience and from mere concepts of what constitutes the absolute completeness of a thing in general; and thus, by means of the Idea of a most perfect primal Being, it proceeds to determine the possibility and therefore the actuality of all other things. And so the mere presupposition of a Being conceived, not in the series of experience yet for the purposes of experience, for the sake of comprehending its connection, order, and unity—in a word, the Idea—is more easily distinguished from the concept of the understanding here than in the former cases. Hence we can easily expose the dialectical illusion which arises from our making the subjective conditions of our thinking objective conditions of objects themselves, and from making an hypothesis necessary for the satisfaction of our reason into a dogma. As the observations of the *Critique* on the pretensions of transcendental theology are intelligible, clear, and decisive, I have nothing more to add on the subject.

General Remark
on the Transcendental Ideas

§ 56. The objects which are given us by experience are in many respects incomprehensible, and many questions to which the law of nature leads us when carried beyond a certain point (though still quite conformably to the laws of nature) admit of no answer. An example is the question: Why do material things attract one another? But if we entirely quit nature or, in pursuing its combinations, exceed all possible experience, and so enter the realm of mere Ideas, we cannot then say that the object is incomprehensible and that the nature of things proposes to us insoluble problems. For we are not then concerned with nature or even with given objects, but with mere concepts which have their origin solely in our reason, and with mere beings of thought; and all the problems that arise from our concepts of them must be solved, because of course reason can

---

*Cf. *Critique of Pure Reason*, "The Transcendental Ideal."

and must give a full account of its own procedure.* As the psychological, cosmological, and theological Ideas are nothing but pure concepts of reason which cannot be given in any experience, the questions which reason asks us about them are put to us, not by the objects, but by mere maxims of our reason for the sake of its own satisfaction. They must all be capable of satisfactory answers, which are given by showing that they are principles which bring our use of the understanding into thorough agreement, completeness, and synthetical unity, and that they thus hold good of experience only, but of experience as a whole.

Although an absolute whole of experience is impossible, the Idea of a whole of knowledge according to principles must impart to our knowledge a peculiar kind of unity, that of a system, without which it is nothing but piecework and cannot be used for proving the existence of a highest purpose (which can only be the general system of all purposes). I do not here refer only to the practical, but also to the highest purpose of the speculative use of reason.

The transcendental Ideas therefore express the peculiar vocation of reason as a principle of systematic unity in the use of the understanding. Yet if we assume this unity of the mode of knowledge to pertain to the object of knowledge, if we regard that which is merely *regulative* to be *constitutive,* and if we persuade ourselves that we can by means of these Ideas widen our knowledge transcendently or far beyond all possible experience, while it only serves to render experience within itself as nearly complete as possible, that is, to limit its progress by nothing that cannot belong to experience—if we do this, I say—we suffer from a mere misunderstanding in our estimate of the proper role of our reason and of its principles, and a dialectic arises which both confuses the empirical use of reason and sets reason at variance with itself.

CONCLUSION

On the Determination of the Bounds of Pure Reason

§ 57. Having adduced the clearest arguments, it would be absurd for us to hope that we can know more of any object than belongs to the possible experience of it or lay claim to the least knowledge of anything not assumed to be an object of possible experience which would determine it according to the constitution it has in itself. For how could we determine anything in this way, since time, space, and all the concepts of the understanding, and still more all the concepts formed by empirical intuition (perception) in the sensible world, have and can have no other use than to make experience possible? And if this condition is omitted from the pure concepts of the understanding, they do not determine any object and have no meaning whatever.

But it would be, on the other hand, a still greater absurdity if we conceded no things in themselves or set up our experience as the only possible mode of knowing things, our intuition of them in space and in time for the only possible intuition and our discursive understanding for the archetype of every possible understanding; for this

---

*Herr Platner, in his *Aphorismen,* acutely says (§§ 728, 729), "If reason be a criterion, no concept which is incomprehensible to human reason can be possible. Incomprehensibility has place in what is actual only. Here incomprehensibility arises from the insufficiency of the acquired ideas." It sounds paradoxical, but is otherwise not strange to say that in nature there is much that is incomprehensible (for example, the faculty of reproduction); but if we mount still higher and go even beyond nature, everything again becomes comprehensible. For we then quit entirely the objects which can be given us and occupy ourselves merely about Ideas, in which occupation we can easily comprehend the law that reason prescribes by them to the understanding for its use in experience, because the law is the reason's own production.

would be to wish to have the principles of the possibility of experience considered universal conditions of things in themselves.

Our principles, which limit the use of reason to possible experience, might in this way become transcendent and the limits of our reason be set up as limits of the possibility of things in themselves (as Hume's *Dialogues* may illustrate) if a careful critique did not guard the bounds of our reason with respect to its empirical use and set a limit to its pretensions. Skepticism originally arose from metaphysics and its anarchic dialectic. At first it might, merely to favor the empirical use of reason, announce everything that transcends this use as worthless and deceitful; but by and by, when it was perceived that the very same principles that are used in experience insensibly and apparently with the same right led still further than experience extends, then men began to doubt even the principles of experience. But here there is no danger, for common sense will doubtless always assert its rights. A certain confusion, however, arose in science, which cannot determine how far reason is to be trusted, and why only so far and no farther; and this confusion can only be cleared up and all future relapses obviated by a formal determination, on principle, of the boundary of the use of our reason.

We cannot indeed, beyond all possible experience, form a definite concept of what things in themselves may be. Yet we are not at liberty to abstain entirely from inquiring into them; for experience never satisfies reason fully but, in answering questions, refers us further and further back and leaves us dissatisfied with regard to their complete solution. This anyone may gather from the dialectic of pure reason, which therefore has its good subjective grounds. Having acquired, as regards the nature of our soul, a clear conception of the subject, and having come to the conviction that its manifestations cannot be explained materialistically, who can refrain from asking what the soul really is and, if no concept of experience suffices for the purpose, from accounting for it by a concept of reason (that of a simple immaterial being), though we cannot by any means prove its objective reality? Who can satisfy himself with mere empirical knowledge in all the cosmological questions of the duration and of the magnitude of the world, of freedom or of natural necessity, since every answer given on principles of experience begets a fresh question, which likewise requires its answer and thereby clearly shows the insufficiency of all physical modes of explanation to satisfy reason? Finally, who does not see in the thoroughgoing contingency and dependence of all his thoughts and assumptions on mere principles of experience the impossibility of stopping there? And who does not feel himself compelled, notwithstanding all interdictions against losing himself in transcendent Ideas, to seek rest and contentment, beyond all the concepts which he can vindicate by experience, in the concept of a Being the possibility of the Idea of which cannot be conceived but at the same time cannot be refuted, because it relates to a mere being of the understanding and without it reason must needs remain forever dissatisfied?

Bounds (in extended beings) always presuppose a space existing outside a certain definite place and inclosing it; limits do not require this, but are mere negations which affect a quantity so far as it is not absolutely complete. But our reason, as it were, sees in its surroundings a space for knowledge of things in themselves, though we can never have definite concepts of them and are limited to appearances only.

As long as the knowledge of reason is homogeneous, definite bounds to it are inconceivable. In mathematics and in natural philosophy, human reason admits of limits but not of bounds, namely, it admits that something indeed lies without it, at which it can never arrive, but not that it will at any point find completion in its internal progress. The enlarging of our views in mathematics and the possibility of new discoveries are infinite; and the same is the case with the discovery of new properties of nature, of new powers and laws, by continued experience and its rational combination. But limits cannot be mistaken here, for mathematics refers to appearances only, and what cannot be an object of sensuous intuition, such as the concepts of metaphysics and of morals, lies entirely without its sphere; it can never lead to them, but neither does it require them. There is, therefore, not a continual progress and approximation towards these sciences, and there is not, as it were, any point or line of contact. Natural science will never reveal to us the internal constitution of things, which, though not appearance, yet can serve as the ultimate ground for explaining appearances. Nor does that science require this for its physical explanations. Nay, even if such grounds should be offered from other sources (for instance, the influence of immaterial beings), they must be rejected and not used in the progress of its explanations. For these explanations must only be grounded upon that which as an object of sense can belong to experience, and be brought into connection with our actual perceptions and empirical laws.

But metaphysics leads us towards bounds in the dialectical attempts of pure reason (not undertaken arbitrarily or wantonly, but stimulated thereto by the nature of reason itself). And the transcendental Ideas, as they do not admit of evasion but are never capable of realization, serve to point out to us actually not only the bounds of the pure use of reason, but also the way to determine them. Such is the end and the use of this natural predisposition of our reason, which has brought forth metaphysics as its favorite child, whose generation, like every other in the world, is not to be ascribed to blind chance but to an original germ, wisely organized for great ends. For metaphysics, in its fundamental features, perhaps more than any other science, is placed in us by nature itself and cannot be considered the production of an arbitrary choice or a casual enlargement in the progress of experience from which it is quite disparate.

Reason through all its concepts and laws of the understanding which are sufficient to it for empirical use, that is, within the sensible world, finds in it no satisfaction, because ever-recurring questions deprive us of all hope of their complete solution. The transcendental Ideas which have that completion in view are such problems of reason. But it sees clearly that the sensuous world cannot contain this completion; neither, consequently, can all the concepts which serve merely for understanding the world of sense, for example, space and time, and what we have adduced under the name of pure concepts of the understanding. The sensuous world is nothing but a chain of appearances connected according to universal laws; it has therefore no subsistence by itself; it is not the thing in itself, and consequently must point to that which contains the basis of this appearance, to beings which cannot be known merely as appearances, but as things in themselves. In the knowledge of them alone can reason hope to satisfy its desire for completeness in proceeding from the conditioned to its conditions.

We have above (§§ 33 and 34) indicated the limits of reason with regard to all knowledge of mere beings of thought. Now, since the transcendental Ideas have made it necessary to approach them and thus have led us, as it were, to the spot where the occupied space (namely, experience) touches the void (that of which we can know nothing, namely, *noumena*), we can determine the bounds of pure reason. For in all bounds there is something positive (for example, a surface is the boundary of corporeal space, and is therefore itself a space; a line is a space, which is the boundary of the surface, a point the boundary of the line, but yet always a place in space), but limits contain mere negations. The limits pointed out in those paragraphs are not enough after we have discovered that beyond them there still lies something (though we can never know what it is in itself). For the question now is, What is the attitude of our reason in this connection of what we know with what we do not, and never shall, know? This is an actual connection of a known thing with one quite unknown (and which will always remain so), and though what is unknown should not become in the least more known—which we cannot even hope—yet the concept of this connection must be definite and capable of being rendered distinct.

We must therefore think an immaterial being, a world of understanding, and a Supreme Being (all mere *noumena*), because in them only, as things in themselves, reason finds that completion and satisfaction which it can never hope for in the derivation of appearances from their homogeneous grounds, and because these actually have reference to something distinct from them (and totally heterogeneous), as appearances always presuppose an object in itself and therefore suggest its existence whether we can know more of it or not.

But as we can never know these beings of understanding as they are in themselves, that is, as definite, yet must assume them as regards the sensible world and connect them with it by reason, we are at least able to think this connection by means of such concepts as express their relation to the world of sense. If we represent to ourselves a being of the understanding by nothing but pure concepts of the understanding, we then indeed represent nothing definite to ourselves, and consequently our concept has no significance; but if we think of it by properties borrowed from the sensuous world, it is no longer a being of understanding, but is conceived phenomenally and belongs to the sensible world. Let us take an instance from the notion of the Supreme Being.

The deistic conception is a quite pure concept of reason, but represents only a thing containing all reality, without being able to determine any one reality [in it]; because for that purpose an example must be taken from the world of sense, in which case I should have an object of sense only, not something quite heterogeneous which can never be an object of sense. Suppose I attribute to the Supreme Being understanding, for instance; I have no concept of an understanding other than my own, one that must receive its intuitions by the senses and which is occupied in bringing them under rules of the unity of consciousness. Then the elements of my concept would always lie in the appearance; I should, however, by the insufficiency of the appearance have to go beyond them to the concept of a being which neither depends upon appearances nor is bound up with them as conditions of its determination. But if I separate understanding from sensibility to obtain a pure understanding, then nothing remains but the mere form of thinking without intuition, by which form alone I can know nothing definite and consequently no object. For that purpose I should finally have to conceive another understanding, such as would intuit its objects but of which I have not the least concept, because the human understanding is discursive and can know only by means of general concepts. And the very same difficulties arise if we attribute a will to the Supreme Being, for I have this concept only by drawing it from my inner experience, and therefore from my dependence for satisfaction upon objects whose existence I require; and so the concept rests upon sensibility, which is absolutely incompatible with the pure concept of the Supreme Being.

Hume's objections to deism are weak, and affect only the proofs and not the deistic assertion itself. But as regards theism, which depends on a stricter determination of the concept of the Supreme Being, which in deism is merely transcendent, they are very strong and, as this concept is formed, in certain (in fact in all common) cases irrefutable. Hume always insists that by the mere concept of an original being to which we apply only ontological predicates (eternity, omnipresence, omnipotence) we think nothing definite, and that properties which could yield a concept *in concreto* would have to be superadded. He further insists that it is not enough to say it is cause, but we must explain the nature of its causality, for example, that it is that of an understanding and of a will. He then begins his attacks on the essential point itself, that is, theism, as he had previously directed his battery only against the proofs of deism, an attack which is not very dangerous to it in its consequences. All his dangerous arguments refer to anthropomorphism, which he holds to be inseparable from theism and to make it contradictory in itself; but if the former be abandoned, the latter must vanish with it and nothing remain but deism, of which nothing can come, which is of no value and which cannot serve as any foundation to religion or morals. If this anthropomorphism were really unavoidable, no proofs whatever of the existence of a Supreme Being, even were they all granted, could determine for us the concept of this Being without involving us in contradictions.

If we connect with the command to avoid all transcendent judgments of pure reason the command (which apparently conflicts with it) to proceed to concepts that lie beyond the field of its immanent (empirical) use, we discover that both can subsist together, but only at the boundary of all permitted use of reason. For this boundary belongs to the field of experience as well as to that of the beings of thought, and we are thereby taught how these so remarkable Ideas serve merely for marking the bounds of human reason. On the one hand, they give warning not boundlessly to extend knowledge of experience, as if nothing but world remained for us to know, and yet, on the other hand, not to transgress the bounds of experience and to think of judging about things beyond them as things in themselves.

But we stop at this boundary if we limit our judgment merely to the relation which the world may have to a Being whose very concept lies beyond all the knowledge which we can attain within the world. For we then do not attribute to the Supreme Being any of the properties in themselves by which we represent objects of experience, and thereby avoid *dogmatic* anthropomorphism; but we attribute them to the relation of this Being to the world and allow ourselves a *symbolical* anthropomorphism, which in fact concerns language only and not the object itself.

If I say that we are compelled to consider the world *as if* it were the work of a Supreme Understanding and Will, I really say nothing more than that a watch, a ship, a regiment, bears the same relation to the watchmaker, the shipbuilder, the commanding officer as the world of sense (or whatever constitutes the substratum of this complex of appearances) does to the unknown, which I do not hereby know as it is in itself but as it is for me, that is, in relation to the world of which I am a part.

§ 58. Such a cognition is one of analogy and does not signify (as is commonly understood) an imperfect similarity of two things, but a perfect similarity of relations between two quite dissimilar things.* By means of this analogy, however, there remains a concept of the Supreme Being sufficiently determined *for us,* though we have left out everything that could determine it absolutely or *in itself;* for we determine it as regards the world and hence as regards ourselves, and more do we not require. The attacks which Hume makes upon those who would determine this concept absolutely, by taking the materials for so doing from themselves and the world, do not affect us; and he can-

---

*There is, for example, an analogy between the juridical relation of human actions and the mechanical relation of moving forces. I never can do anything to another man without giving him a right to do the same to me on the same conditions; just as no mass can act with its moving forces on another mass without thereby occasioning the other to react equally against it. Here right and moving force are quite dissimilar things, but in their relation there is complete similarity. By means of such an analogy, I can obtain a notion of the relation of things which absolutely are unknown to me. For instance, as the promotion of the welfare of children ($= a$) is to the love of parents ($= b$), so the welfare of the human species ($= c$) is to that unknown character in God ($= x$), which we call love; not as if it had the least similarity to any human inclination, but because we can suppose its relation to the world to be similar to that which things of the world bear one another. But the concept of relation in this case is a mere category, namely, the concept of cause, which has nothing to do with sensibility.

not object to us that we have nothing left if we give up the objective anthropomorphism of the concept of the Supreme Being.

For let us assume at the outset (as Hume in his *Dialogues* makes Philo grant Cleanthes), as a necessary hypothesis, the deistic concept of the First Being, in which this Being is thought by the mere ontological predicates of substance, of cause, and so on. This must be done because reason, actuated in the sensible world by mere conditions which are themselves always conditional, cannot otherwise have any satisfaction; and it therefore can be done without falling into anthropomorphism (which transfers predicates from the world of sense to a Being quite distinct from the world) because those predicates are mere categories which, though they do not give a determinate concept of that Being, yet give a concept not limited to any conditions of sensibility. Thus nothing can prevent our predicating of this Being a causality through reason with regard to the world, and thus passing to theism, without being obliged to attribute to this Being itself this kind of reason, as a property inherent in it. For as to the former, the only possible way of prosecuting the use of reason (as regards all possible experience in complete harmony with itself) in the world of sense to the highest point is to assume a supreme reason as a cause of all the connections in the world. Such a principle must be quite advantageous to reason and can hurt it nowhere in its application to nature. As to the latter, reason is thereby not transferred as a property to the First Being in itself, but only to its relation to the world of sense, and so anthropomorphism is entirely avoided. For nothing is considered here but the cause of the form of reason which is perceived everywhere in the world, and reason is indeed attributed to the Supreme Being so far as it contains the ground of this form of reason in the world, but according to analogy only—that is, so far as this expression shows merely the relation which the Supreme Cause, unknown to us, has to the world in order to determine everything in it conformably to reason in the highest degree. We are thereby kept from using reason as an attribute for the purpose of conceiving God, but not from conceiving the world in such a manner as is necessary to have the greatest possible use of reason within it according to principle. We thereby acknowledge that the Supreme Being is quite inscrutable and even unthinkable in any definite way as to what it is in itself. We are thereby kept, on the one hand, from making a transcendent use of the concepts which we have of reason as an efficient cause (by means of the will), in order to determine the Divine Nature by properties which are only borrowed from human nature, and from losing ourselves in gross and extravagant notions; and, on the other hand, from deluging the contemplation of the world with hyperphysical modes of explanation according to our notions of human reason which we transfer to God, and so from losing for this contemplation its proper rôle, according to which it should be a rational study of mere nature and not a presumptuous derivation of its appearances from a Supreme Reason. The expression suited to our feeble notions is: we conceive the world *as if* it came, in its existence and internal plan, from a Supreme Reason. By this, on the one hand, we know the constitution which belongs to the world itself without pretending to determine the nature of its cause in itself; and, on the other hand, we transfer the ground of this constitution (of the form of reason in the world) upon the *relation* of the Supreme Cause to the world, without finding the world sufficient by itself for that purpose.*

---

*I may say that the causality of the Supreme Cause holds the same place with regard to the world that human reason does with regard to its works of art. Here the nature of the Supreme Cause itself remains unknown to me; I only compare its effects (the order of the world), which I know, and their conformity to reason to the effects of human reason, which I also know; and hence I term the former "reason," without attributing to it on that account what I understand in man by this term, or attaching to it anything else known to me as its property.

Thus the difficulties which seem to oppose theism disappear by combining with Hume's principle, "not to carry the use of reason dogmatically beyond the field of all possible experience," this other principle, which he quite overlooked, "not to consider the field of experience as one which bounds itself in the eyes of our reason." The *Critique of Pure Reason* here points out the true mean between dogmatism, which Hume combats, and skepticism, which he would substitute for it—a mean which is not like others that we find advisable to determine for ourselves, as it were mechanically (by adopting something from one side and something from the other), and by which nobody is taught a better way, but such a one as can be precisely determined on principles.

§ 59. At the beginning of this note I made use of the metaphor of a boundary, in order to establish the limits of reason in regard to its suitable use. The world of sense contains merely appearances, which are not things in themselves; but the understanding, because it recognizes that the objects of experience are mere appearances, must assume that there are things in themselves, namely, *noumena.* In our reason both are comprehended, and the question is, How does reason proceed to set boundaries to the understanding as regards both these fields? Experience, which contains all that belongs to the sensible world, does not bound itself; it only proceeds in every case from the conditioned to some other equally conditioned object. That which bounds it must lie quite without it, and this is the field of the pure beings of the understanding. But this field, so far as the *determination* of the nature of these beings is concerned, is an empty space for us; and apart from dogmatically defined concepts, we cannot pass beyond the field of possible experience. But as a boundary itself is something positive, which belongs to that which lies within as well as to the space that lies without the given content, it is still an actual positive cognition which reason only acquires by enlarging itself to this boundary, yet without attempting to pass it because it there finds itself in the presence of an empty space in which it can conceive forms of things, but not things themselves. But the setting of a boundary to the field of the understanding by something which is otherwise unknown to it is still a cognition which belongs to reason even at this point, and by which it is neither confined within the sensible nor strays beyond it, but only limits itself, as befits the knowledge of a boundary, to the relation between that which lies beyond it and that which is contained within it.

Natural theology is such a concept at the boundary of human reason, being constrained to look beyond this boundary to the Idea of a Supreme Being (and, for practical purposes, to that of an intelligible world also), not in order to determine anything relatively to this pure being of the understanding, and thus to determine something that lies beyond the world of sense, but in order to guide the use of reason within it according to principles of the greatest possible (theoretical as well as practical) unity. For this purpose, it makes use of the reference of the world of sense to an independent reason as the cause of all its connections. Thereby it does not just *invent* a being, but, as beyond the sensible world there must be something that can be thought only by the pure understanding, it determines that something in this particular way, though only of course by analogy.

And thus there remains our original proposition, which is the *résumé* of the whole *Critique:* "Reason by all its *a priori* principles never teaches us anything more than objects of possible experience, and even of these nothing more than can be known in experience." But this limitation does not prevent reason from leading us to the objective boundary of experience, namely, to the relation to something which is not itself an object of experience but is the ground of all experience. Reason does not, however, teach us anything concerning the thing in itself; it only instructs us as regards its own complete and highest use in the field of possible experience. But this is all that can be reasonably desired in the present case, and with it we have cause to be satisfied.

§ 60. Thus we have fully exhibited metaphysics, in its subjective possibility, as it is actually given in the natural predisposition of human reason and in that which constitutes the essential end of its pursuit. Though we have found that this merely natural use of such a predisposition of our reason, if no discipline arising only from a scientific critique bridles and sets limits to it, involves it in transcendent and specious inferences and really conflicting dialectical inferences, and this fallacious metaphysics is not only unnecessary as regards the promotion of our knowledge of nature but even disadvantageous to it, there yet remains a problem worthy of investigation, which is to find out the natural ends intended by this disposition to transcendent concepts in our nature, because everything that lies in nature must be originally intended for some useful purpose.

Such an inquiry is of a doubtful nature, and I acknowledge that what I can say about it is conjecture only, like every speculation about the ultimate ends of nature. Such conjecture may be allowed me here, for the question does not concern the objective validity of metaphysical judgments but our natural predisposition to them, and therefore does not belong to the system of metaphysics but to anthropology.

When I compare all the transcendental Ideas, the totality of which constitutes the proper problem of natural pure reason, compelling it to quit the mere contemplation of nature, to transcend all possible experience, and in this endeavor to produce the thing (be it knowledge or fiction) called metaphysics, I think I perceive that the aim of this natural tendency is to free our concepts from the fetters of experience and from the limits of the mere contemplation of nature so far as at least to open to us a field containing mere objects for the pure understanding which no sensibility can reach, not indeed for the purpose of speculatively occupying ourselves with them (for there we can find no ground to stand on), but in order that practical principles [may be assumed as at least possible]; for practical principles, unless they find scope for their necessary expectation and hope, could not expand to the universality which reason unavoidably requires from a moral point of view.

So I find that the psychological Idea (however little it may reveal to me the nature of the human soul, which is elevated above all concepts of experience), shows the insufficiency of these concepts plainly enough and thereby deters me from materialism, a psychological concept which is unfit for any explanation of nature and which moreover confines reason in practical respects. The cosmological Ideas, by the obvious insufficiency of all possible knowledge of nature to satisfy reason in its legitimate inquiry, serve in the same manner to keep us from naturalism, which asserts nature to be sufficient for itself. Finally, all natural necessity in the sensible world is conditional, as it always presupposes the dependence of things upon others, and unconditional necessity must be sought only in the unity of a cause different from the world of sense. But as the causality of this cause, in its turn, were it merely nature, could never render the existence of the contingent (as its consequent) comprehensible, reason frees itself by means of the theological Idea from fatalism (both as a blind natural necessity in the coherence of nature itself, without a first principle, and as a blind causality of this principle itself) and leads to the concept of a cause possessing freedom or of a Supreme Intelligence. Thus the transcendental Ideas serve, if not to instruct us positively, at least to destroy the narrowing assertions of materialism, of naturalism, and of fatalism, and thus to afford scope for the moral Ideas beyond the field of speculation. These considerations, I should think, explain in some measure the natural predisposition of which I spoke.

The practical value, which a merely speculative science may have, lies without the bounds of this science, and can therefore be considered as a scholium merely, and like all scholia does not form part of the science itself. This application, however, surely lies within the bounds of philosophy, especially of philosophy drawn from the pure sources of reason, where its speculative use in metaphysics must necessarily be at one with its practical use in morals. Hence the unavoidable dialectic of pure reason, considered in metaphysics as a natural tendency, deserves to be explained not as a mere illusion, which is to be removed, but also, if possible, as a natural provision as regards its end, though this task, a work of supererogation, cannot justly be assigned to metaphysics proper.

The solutions of these questions which are treated in the *Critique** should be considered a second scholium, which, however, has a greater affinity with the subject of metaphysics. For there certain rational principles are expounded which determine *a priori* the order of nature or rather of the understanding, which seeks nature's laws through experience. They seem to be constitutive and legislative with regard to experience, though they spring from pure reason, which cannot be considered, like the understanding, as a principle of possible experience. Now whether or not this harmony rests upon the fact that, just as nature does not inhere in appearances or in their source (the sensibility) itself, but only in the relation of the latter to the understanding, a thorough unity in applying the understanding to bring about an entirety of all possible experience (in a system) can only belong to the understanding when in relation to reason, with the consequence that experience is in this way mediately subordinate to the legislation of reason—this question may be discussed by those who desire to trace the nature of reason even beyond its use in metaphysics, into the general principles, which will make a history of nature in general systematic. I have presented this task as important, but not attempted its solution in the book itself.**

And thus I conclude the analytical solution of the main question which I had proposed: "How is metaphysics in general possible?" by ascending from the data of its actual use, as shown in its consequences, to the grounds of its possibility.

SOLUTION OF THE GENERAL QUESTION OF THE *PROLEGOMENA*

How Is Metaphysics Possible as Science?

Metaphysics, as a natural disposition of reason, is actual; but if considered by itself alone (as the analytical solution of the third principal question showed), dialectical and illusory. If we think of taking principles from it, and in using them follow the natural, but on that account not less false, illusion, we can never produce science, but only a vain dialectical art, in which one school may outdo another but none can ever acquire a just and lasting approbation.

In order that as a science metaphysics may be entitled to claim, not mere fallacious plausibility, but insight and conviction, a critique of reason itself must exhibit the whole stock of *a priori* concepts, their division according to their various sources (sensibility, understanding, and reason), together with a complete table of them, the analysis of all these concepts, with all their consequences, and especially the possibility of syn-

---

*Critique of Pure Reason, "Regulative Use of the Ideas of Pure Reason."

**Throughout in the *Critique,* I never lost sight of the plan not to neglect anything, were it ever so recondite, that could render the inquiry into the nature of pure reason complete. Everybody may afterward carry his research as far as he pleases, when he has been merely shown what yet remains to be done. This can reasonably be expected of him who has made it his business to survey the whole field, in order to consign it to others for future cultivation and allotment. And to this branch both the scholia belong, which will hardly recommend themselves because of their dryness to amateurs, and hence are added here for connoisseurs only.

thetical knowledge *a priori* by means of a deduction of these concepts, the principles and the bounds of their application, all in a complete system. Critique, therefore, and critique alone contains in itself the whole well-proved and well-tested plan, and even all the means, required to establish metaphysics as a science; by other ways and means it is impossible. The question here, therefore, is not so much how this performance is possible as how to set it going and to induce men of clear heads to quit their hitherto perverted and fruitless cultivation for one that will not deceive, and how such a union for the common end may best be directed.

This much is certain, that whoever has once tasted critique will be ever after disgusted with all dogmatic twaddle which he formerly had to put up with because his reason had to have something and could find nothing better for its support.

Critique stands in the same relation to the common metaphysics of the schools as chemistry does to alchemy, or as astronomy to the astrology of the fortune teller. I pledge myself that nobody who has thought through and grasped the principles of critique, even in these *Prolegomena* only, will ever return to that old and sophistical pseudo-science; but will rather with a certain delight look forward to metaphysics, which is now indeed in his power, requiring no more preparatory discoveries and affording permanent satisfaction to reason at last. For here is an advantage upon which, of all possible sciences, metaphysics alone can with certainty reckon: that it can be brought to such completion and fixity as to be in need of no further change or be subject to any augmentation by new discoveries; because here reason has the sources of its knowledge in itself, not in objects and their observation, by which its stock of knowledge could be further increased. When, therefore, it has exhibited the fundamental laws of its faculty completely and so definitely as to avoid all misunderstanding, there remains nothing further which pure reason could know *a priori;* nay, there is no ground even to raise further questions. The sure prospect of knowledge so definite and so compact has a peculiar charm, even though we should set aside all its advantages, of which I shall hereafter speak.

All false art, all vain wisdom, lasts its time but finally destroys itself, and its highest culture is also the epoch of its decay. That this time is come for metaphysics appears from the state into which it has fallen among all learned nations, despite all the zeal with which other sciences of every kind are prosecuted. The old arrangement of our university studies still preserves its shadow. Now and then an academy of science tempts men by offering prizes to write some essay on it, but it is no longer numbered among the rigorous sciences; and let anyone judge for himself how a sophisticated man, if he were called a great metaphysician, would receive the compliment, which may be well meant but is scarcely envied by anybody.

Yet, though the period of the downfall of all dogmatic metaphysics has undoubtedly arrived, we are yet far from being able to say that the period of its regeneration is come by means of a thorough and complete critique of reason. All transitions from a tendency to its contrary pass through the stage of indifference, and this moment is the most dangerous for an author but, in my opinion, the most favorable for the science. For when party spirit has died out by a total dissolution of former connections, minds are in the best state to listen to several proposals for an organization according to a new plan.

When I say that I hope these *Prolegomena* will excite investigation in the field of critique and afford a new and promising object to sustain the general spirit of philosophy, which seems on its speculative side to want sustenance, I can imagine beforehand that everyone whom the thorny paths of my *Critique* have tired and put out of humor will ask me upon what I found this hope. My answer is: upon the irresistible law of necessity.

That the human mind will ever give up metaphysical researches is as little to be expected as that we, to avoid inhaling impure air, should prefer to give up breathing altogether. There will, therefore, always be metaphysics in the world; nay, everyone, especially every reflective man, will have it and, for want of a recognized standard, will shape it for himself after his own pattern. What has hitherto been called metaphysics cannot satisfy any critical mind, but to forego it entirely is impossible; therefore a *Critique of Pure Reason* itself must now be attempted or, if one exists, investigated and brought to the full test, because there is no other means of supplying this pressing want which is something more than mere thirst for knowledge.

Ever since I have come to know critique, whenever I finish reading a book of metaphysical contents which, by the preciseness of its notions, by variety, order, and an easy style, was not only entertaining but also helpful, I cannot help asking, "Has this author indeed advanced metaphysics a single step?" The learned men whose works have been useful to me in other respects and always contributed to the culture of my mental powers will, I hope, forgive me for saying that I have never been able to find either their essays or my own less important ones (though self-love may recommend them to me) to have advanced the science of metaphysics in the least.

There is a very obvious reason for this: metaphysics did not then exist as a science, nor can it be gathered piecemeal; but its germ must be fully preformed in critique. But, in order to prevent all misconception, we must remember what has been already said—that, by the analytical treatment of our concepts, the understanding gains indeed a great deal; but the science of metaphysics is thereby not in the least advanced, because these dissections of concepts are nothing but the materials from which the intention is to carpenter our science. Let the concepts of substance and of accident be ever so well dissected and determined; all this is very well as a preparation for some future use. But if we cannot prove that in all which exists the substance endures and only the accidents vary, our science is not the least advanced by all our analyses.

Metaphysics has hitherto never been able to prove *a priori* either this proposition or that of sufficient reason, still less any more complex theorem such as belongs to psychology or cosmology, or indeed any synthetical proposition. By all its analyzing, therefore, nothing is affected, nothing obtained or forwarded; and the science, after all this bustle and noise, still remains as it was in the days of Aristotle, though there were far better preparations for it than of old if only the clue to synthetical cognitions had been discovered.

If anyone thinks himself offended, he is at liberty to refute my charge by producing a single synthetical proposition belonging to metaphysics which he would prove dogmatically *a priori;* for until he has actually performed this feat I shall not grant that he has truly advanced the science, even if this proposition should be sufficiently confirmed by common experience. No demand can be more moderate or more equitable and, in the (inevitably certain) event of its nonperformance, no assertion more just than that hitherto metaphysics has never existed as a science.

But there are two things which, in case the challenge be accepted, I must deprecate: first, trifling about probability and conjecture, which are suited as little to metaphysics as to geometry; and secondly, a decision by means of the magic wand of so-called common sense, which does not convince everyone but accommodates itself to personal peculiarities.

For as to the former, nothing can be more absurd than in metaphysics, a philosophy from pure reason, to think of grounding our judgments upon probability and conjecture. Everything that is to be known *a priori* is thereby announced as apodictically certain, and must therefore be proved in this way. We might as well think of grounding geometry or arithmetic upon conjectures. As to the calculus of probabilities in the latter, it does not contain probable but perfectly certain judgments concerning the degree of the possibility of certain cases under given uniform conditions, which, in the sum of all possible cases, must infallibly happen according to the rule, though the rule is not sufficiently definite with respect to every single instance. Conjectures (by means of induction and of analogy) can be suffered in an empirical science of nature only, yet even there at least the possibility of what we assume must be quite certain.

The appeal to common sense is even more absurd—if anything more absurd can be imagined—when it is a question of concept and principles claimed as valid, not in so far as they hold with regard to experience, but beyond the conditions of experience. For what is common sense? It is normal good sense, so far it judges right. But what is normal good sense? It is the faculty of the knowledge and use of rules *in concreto,* as distinguished from the speculative understanding, which is a faculty of knowing rules *in abstracto.* Common sense can hardly understand the rule that every event is determined by means of its cause and can never comprehend it in its generality. It therefore demands an example from experience; and when it hears that this rule means nothing but what it always thought when a pane was broken or a kitchen utensil missing, it then understands the principle and grants it. Common sense, therefore, is only of use so far as it can see its rules (though they actually are *a priori*) confirmed by experience; consequently to comprehend them *a priori,* or independently of experience, belongs to the speculative understanding and lies quite beyond the horizon of common sense. But the province of metaphysics is entirely confined to the latter kind of knowledge, and it is certainly a bad sign of common sense to appeal to it as a witness, for it cannot here form any opinion whatever, and men look down upon it with contempt until they are in straits and can find in their speculation neither advice nor help.

It is a common subterfuge of those false friends of common sense (who occasionally prize it highly, but usually despise it) to say that there must surely be at all events some propositions which are immediately certain and of which there is no occasion to give any proof, or even any account at all, because we otherwise could never stop inquiring into the grounds of our judgments. But if we except the principle of contradiction, which is not sufficient to show the truth of synthetical judgments, they can never adduce, in proof of this privilege, anything else indubitable which they can immediately ascribe to common sense, except mathematical propositions, such as twice two make four, between two points there is but one straight line, etc. But these judgments are radically different from those of metaphysics. For in mathematics I can by thinking itself construct whatever I represent to myself as possible by a concept: I add to the first two the other two, one by one, and myself make the number four, or I draw in thought from one point to another all manner of lines, equal as well as unequal; yet I can draw one only which is like itself in all its parts. But I cannot, by all my power of thinking, extract from the concept of a thing the concept of something else whose existence is necessarily connected with the former; for this I must call in experience. And though my understanding furnishes me *a priori* (yet only in reference to possible experience) with the concept of such a connection (that is causation), I cannot exhibit it, like the concepts of mathematics, by intuiting it *a priori,* and so show its possibility *a priori.* This concept, together with the principles of its application, always requires, if it shall hold *a priori*— as is requisite in metaphysics—a justification and deduction of its possibility, because we cannot otherwise know how far it holds good and whether it can be used in experience only or beyond it also.

Therefore in metaphysics, as a speculative science of pure reason, we can never appeal to common sense, but may do so only when we are forced to surrender it and to renounce all pure speculative knowledge which must always be theoretical cognition, and thereby under some circumstances to forego metaphysics itself and its instruction for the sake of adopting a rational faith which alone may be possible for us, sufficient to our wants, and perhaps even more salutary than knowledge itself. For in this case the state of affairs is quite altered. Metaphysics must be science, not only as a whole, but in all its parts; otherwise it is nothing at all; because, as speculation of pure reason, it finds a hold only on common convictions. Beyond its field, however, probability and common sense may be used justly and with advantage, but on quite special principles, the importance of which always depends on their reference to practical life.

This is what I hold myself justified in requiring for the possibility of metaphysics as a science.

APPENDIX

ON WHAT CAN BE DONE TO MAKE METAPHYSICS AS A SCIENCE ACTUAL

Since all the ways heretofore taken have failed to attain the goal, and since without a preceding critique of pure reason it is not likely ever to be attained, the present attempt has a right to an accurate and careful examination, unless it be thought more advisable to give up all pretensions to metaphysics, to which, if men but would consistently adhere to their purpose, no objection can be made.

If we take the course of things as it is, not as it ought to be, there are two sorts of judgments: (1) one a judgment which precedes investigation (in our case one in which the reader from his own metaphysics pronounces judgment on the *Critique of Pure Reason,* which was intended to discuss the very possibility of metaphysics); (2) the other a judgment subsequent to investigation. In the latter, the reader is enabled to ignore for a while the consequences of the critical researches that may be repugnant to his formerly adopted metaphysics, and first examines the grounds whence those consequences are derived. If what common metaphysics propounds were demonstrably certain, as is the case with the theorems of geometry, the former way of judging would hold good. For if the consequences of certain principles are repugnant to established truths, these principles are false and without further inquiry to be repudiated. But if metaphysics does not possess a stock of indisputably certain (synthetical) propositions, and should it even be the case that there are a number of them, which, though among the most plausible, are by their consequences in mutual conflict, and if no sure criterion of the truth of peculiarly metaphysical (synthetical) propositions is to be met with in it, then the former way of judging is not admissible, but the investigation of the principles of the *Critique* must precede all judgments as to its value.

A SPECIMEN OF A JUDGMENT OF THE CRITIQUE PRIOR TO ITS EXAMINATION

Such a judgment is to be found in the *Göttingische gelehrte Anzeigen,* in the supplement to the third part, of January 19, 1782, pages 40 *et seq.*

When an author who is familiar with the subject of his work and endeavors to present his independent reflections in its elaboration falls into the hands of a reviewer who, in his turn, is keen enough to discern the points on which the worth or worthlessness of the book rests, who does not cling to words but goes to the heart of the subject, sifting and testing the principles which the author takes as his point of departure, the severity of the judgment may indeed displease the author, but the public does not care, as it gains thereby. And the author himself may be contented, as an opportunity of correcting or explaining his positions is afforded to him at an early date by the examination of a competent judge, in such a manner that if he believes himself fundamentally right, he can remove in time any stumbling block that might hurt the success of his work.

I find myself, with my reviewer, in quite another position. He seems not to see at all the real matter of the investigation with which (successfully or unsuccessfully) I have been occupied. It is either impatience at thinking out a lengthy work, or vexation at a threatened reform of a science in which he believed he had brought everything to perfection long ago, or, what I am reluctant to suspect, real narrow-mindedness that prevents him from ever carrying his thoughts beyond his school metaphysics. In short, he passes impatiently in review a long series of propositions, of which, without knowing their premises, one can understand nothing, intersperses here and there his censure, the reason of which the reader understands just as little as the propositions against which it is directed; and hence [his report] can neither serve the public nor damage me in the judgment of experts. I should, for these reasons, have passed over this judgment altogether, were it not that it may afford me occasion for some explanations which may in some cases save the readers of these *Prolegomena* from a misconception.

In order to take a position from which my reviewer could most easily set the whole work in a most unfavorable light, without venturing to trouble himself with any special investigation, he begins and ends by saying: "This work is a system of transcendental (or, as he translates it, of higher*) idealism."

A glance at this line soon showed me the sort of criticism that I had to expect, much as though the reviewer were one who had never seen or heard of geometry, having found a Euclid and coming upon various figures in turning over its leaves, were to say, on being asked his opinion of it: "The work is a textbook of drawing; the author introduces a peculiar terminology, in order to give dark, incomprehensible directions, which in the end teach nothing more than what everyone can effect by a fair natural accuracy of eye, etc."

Let us see, in the meantime, what sort of an idealism it is that goes through my whole work, although it does not by a long way constitute the soul of the system.

The dictum of all genuine idealists, from the Eleatic school to Bishop Berkeley, is contained in this formula: "All knowledge through the senses and experience is nothing but sheer illusion, and only in the ideas of the pure understanding and reason is there truth."

The principle that throughout dominates and determines my idealism, is on the contrary: "All knowledge of things merely from pure understanding or pure reason is nothing but sheer illusion, and only in experience is there truth."

---

*By no means "higher." High towers and metaphysically great men resembling them, round both of which there is commonly much wind, are not for me. My place is the fruitful bathos of experience; and the word "transcendental," the meaning of which is so often explained by me but not once grasped by my reviewer (so carelessly has he regarded everything), does not signify something passing beyond all experience but something that indeed precedes it *a priori,* but that is intended simply to make knowledge of experience possible. If these conceptions overstep experience, their employment is termed "transcendent," which must be distinguished from the immanent use, that is, use restricted to experience. All misunderstandings of this kind have been sufficiently guarded against in the work itself, but my reviewer found his advantage in misunderstanding me.

But this is directly contrary to idealism proper. How came I then to use this expression for quite an opposite purpose, and how came my reviewer to see it everywhere?

The solution of this difficulty rests on something that could have been very easily understood from the general bearing of the work if the reader had only desired to understand it. Space and time, together with all that they contain, are not things in themselves or their qualities, but belong merely to the appearances of the things in themselves. Up to this point I am one in confession with the above idealists. But these, and among them more particularly Berkeley, regarded space as a mere empirical representation that, like the appearances it contains, is, together with its determinations, known to us only by means of experience or perception. I, on the contrary, prove in the first place that space (and also time, which Berkeley did not consider) and all its *a priori* determinations can be known by us, because, no less than time, it inheres in us as a pure form of our sensibility before all perception or experience and makes all intuition of the form, and therefore all appearances, possible. It follows from this that, as truth rests on universal and necessary laws as its criteria, experience, according to Berkeley, can have no criteria of truth because its phenomena* (according to him) have nothing *a priori* at their foundation, whence it follows that experience is nothing but sheer illusion; whereas with us, space and time (in conjunction with the pure concept of the understanding) prescribe their law to all possible experience *a priori* and, at the same time, afford the certain criterion for distinguishing truth from illusion therein.

My so-called (properly critical) idealism is of quite a special character, in that it subverts the ordinary idealism and in that only through it all *a priori* knowledge, even that of geometry, receives objective reality, which, without my demonstrated ideality of space and time, could not be maintained by the most zealous realists. This being the state of the case, I could wish, in order to avoid all misunderstanding, to have named this conception of mine otherwise, but to alter it altogether is probably impossible. It may be permitted me however, in future, as has been above intimated, to term it "formal" or, better still, "critical" idealism, to distinguish it from the dogmatic idealism of Berkeley and from the skeptical idealism of Descartes.

Beyond this, I find nothing remarkable in the judgment of my book. The reviewer makes sweeping criticisms, a mode prudently chosen, since it does not betray one's own knowledge or ignorance; a single thorough criticism in detail, had it touched the main question, as is only fair, would have exposed either my error or my reviewer's measure of insight into this species of research. It was, moreover, not a badly conceived plan, in order at once to take from readers (who are accustomed to form their conceptions of books from newspaper reports) the desire to read the book itself, to pour out in one breath a number of passages in succession which, torn from their connection with their premises and explanations, must necessarily sound senseless, especially considering how antipathetic they are to all school-metaphysics; to exhaust the reader's patience *ad nauseam,* and then, having made me acquainted with the lucid proposition that persistent illusion is truth, to conclude with the crude paternal moralization: to what end, then, the quarrel with accepted language; to what end, and whence, the idealistic distinction?

---

*Idealism proper always has a mystical tendency, and can have no other, but mine is solely designed for the purpose of comprehending the possibility of our *a priori* knowledge of objects of experience, which is a problem never hitherto solved or even suggested. In this way all mystical idealism falls to the ground, for (as may be seen in Plato) it inferred from our cognitions *a priori* (even from those of geometry) another intuition different from that of the senses (namely, an intellectual intuition), because it never occurred to anyone that the senses themselves might intuit *a priori.*

A judgment which seeks all that is characteristic of my book, first supposed to be meta-physically heterodox, in a mere innovation of the nomenclature proves clearly that my would-be judge has understood nothing of the subject and, in addition, has not under-stood himself.*

My reviewer speaks like a man who is conscious of important and superior in-sight which he keeps hidden, for I am aware of nothing recent with respect to meta-physics that could justify his tone. But he should not withhold his discoveries from the world, for there are doubtless many who, like myself, have not been able to find in all the fine things that have for long past been written in this department anything that has advanced the science by so much as a finger's breadth; we find indeed the giving a new point to definitions, the supplying of lame proofs with new crutches, the adding to the crazy-quilt of metaphysics fresh patches or changing its pattern. But all this is not what the world requires. The world is tired of metaphysical assertions; it wants [to know] the possibility of this science, the sources from which certainty therein can be derived, and certain criteria by which it may distinguish the dialectical illusion of pure reason from truth. To this the critic seems to possess a key, otherwise he would never have spoken out in such a high tone.

But I am inclined to suspect that no such requirement of the science has ever en-tered his thoughts, for in that case he would have directed his judgment to this point, and even a mistaken attempt in such an important matter would have won his respect. If that be the case, we are once more good friends. He may penetrate as deeply as he likes into his metaphysics, without any one hindering him; only as concerns that which lies outside metaphysics, its sources, which are to be found in reason, he cannot form a judgment. That my suspicion is not without foundation is proved by the fact that he does not mention a word about the possibility of synthetic knowledge *a priori,* the spe-cial problem upon the solution of which the fate of metaphysics wholly rests and upon which my *Critique* (as well as the present *Prolegomena*) entirely hinges. The idealism he encountered and which he hung upon was only taken up in the doctrine as the sole means of solving the above problem (although it received its confirmation on other grounds), and hence he must have shown either that the above problem does not possess the importance I attribute to it (even in these *Prolegomena*) or that, by my conception of appearances, it is either not solved at all or can be better solved in another way; but I do not find a word of this in the criticism. The reviewer, then, understands nothing of my work and possibly also nothing of the spirit and essential nature of metaphysics itself; and it is not, what I would rather assume, the hurry of a reviewer to finish his review, in-censed at the labor of plodding through so many obstacles, that threw an unfavorable shadow over the work lying before him and made its fundamental features unrecog-nizable.

There is a good deal to be done before a learned journal, it matters not with what care its writers may be selected, can maintain its otherwise well-merited reputation in the field of metaphysics as elsewhere. Other sciences and branches of knowledge have

---

*The reviewer often fights with his own shadow. When I oppose the truth of experience to dream, he never thinks that I am here speaking simply of the well-known *somnio objective sumto* of the Wolffian phi-losophy, which is merely formal, and with which the distinction between sleeping and waking is in no way concerned—a distinction which can indeed have no place in a transcendental philosophy. For the rest, he calls my deduction of the categories and table of the principles of the understanding "common well-known axioms of logic and ontology, expressed in an idealistic manner." The reader need only consult these *Prolegomena* upon this point to convince himself that a more miserable and historically incorrect judgment could hardly be made.

their standard. Mathematics has it in itself, history and theology in profane or sacred books, natural science and the art of medicine in mathematics and experience, jurisprudence in law books, and even matters of taste in the examples of the ancients. But for the judgment of the thing called metaphysics, the standard has yet to be found. I have made an attempt to determine it, as well as its use. What is to be done, then, until it be found when works of this kind have to be judged of? If they are of a dogmatic character, one may do what one likes; no one will play the master over others here for long before someone else appears to deal with him in the same manner. If, however, they are critical in character, not indeed with reference to other works but to reason itself, so that the standard of judgment cannot be assumed but has first of all to be sought for, then, though objection and blame may indeed be permitted, yet a certain degree of leniency is indispensable, since the need is common to us all and the lack of the necessary insight makes the high-handed attitude of judge unwarranted.

In order, however, to connect my defense with the interest of the philosophical commonwealth, I propose a test, which must be decisive as to the mode whereby all metaphysical investigations may be directed to their common purpose. This is nothing more than what mathematicians have done in establishing the advantage of their methods by competition. I challenge my critic to demonstrate, as is only just, on *a priori* grounds, in his own way, any single really metaphysical proposition asserted by him. Being metaphysical, it must be synthetical and known *a priori* from concepts, but it may also be any one of the most indispensable propositions, as, for instance, the principle of the persistence of substance or of the necessary determination of events in the world by their causes. If he cannot do this (silence however is confession), he must admit that, since metaphysics without apodictic certainty of propositions of this kind is nothing at all, its possibility or impossibility must before all things be established in a critique of pure reason. Thus he is bound either to confess that my principles in the *Critique* are correct, or he must prove their invalidity. But as I can already foresee that, confidently as he has hitherto relied on the certainty of his principles, when it comes to a strict test he will not find a single one in the whole range of metaphysics he can boldly bring forward, I will concede to him an advantageous condition, which can only be expected in such a competition, and will relieve him of the *onus probandi* by laying it on myself.

He finds in these *Prolegomena* and in my *Critique** eight propositions, of which one in each pair contradicts the other, but each of which necessarily belongs to metaphysics, by which it must either be accepted or rejected (although there is not one that has not in its time been assumed by some philosopher). Now he has the liberty of selecting any one of these eight propositions at his pleasure and accepting it without any proof, of which I shall make him a present, but only one (for waste of time will be just as little serviceable to him as to me), and then of attacking my proof of the opposite proposition. If I can save this one and at the same time show that, according to principles which every dogmatic metaphysics must necessarily recognize, the opposite of the proposition adopted by him can be just as clearly proved, it is thereby established that metaphysics has an hereditary failing not to be explained, much less set aside, until we ascend to its birthplace, pure reason itself. And thus my *Critique* must either be accepted or a better one take its place; at least it must be studied, which is the only thing I now require. If, on the other hand, I cannot save my demonstration, then a synthetic proposition *a priori* from dogmatic principles is to be reckoned to the score of my op-

---

*[The reference is to the theses and antitheses of the antinomies.—L.W.B.]

ponent, and I shall deem my impeachment of ordinary metaphysics unjust and pledge myself to recognize his stricture on my *Critique* as justified (although this would not be the consequence by a long way). To this end it would be necessary, it seems to me, that he should step out of his incognito. Otherwise I do not see how it could be avoided that, instead of dealing with one, I should be honored or besieged by several challenges coming from anonymous and unqualified opponents.

PROPOSALS AS TO AN INVESTIGATION OF THE "CRITIQUE" UPON WHICH A JUDGMENT MAY FOLLOW

I feel obliged to the learned public even for the silence with which it for a long time honored my *Critique,* for this proves at least a postponement of judgment and some supposition that, in a work leaving all beaten tracks and striking out on a new path, in which one cannot at once perhaps so easily find one's way, something may perchance lie from which an important but at present dead branch of human knowledge may derive new life and productiveness. Hence may have originated a solicitude for the as yet tender shoot, lest it be destroyed by a hasty judgment. A specimen of a judgment, delayed for the above reasons, is now before my eye in the *Gothaische gelehrte Zeitung,* the thoroughness of which—disregarding my praise, which might be suspicious—every reader will himself perceive from the clear and unperverted presentation of a fragment of one of the first principles of my work.

Since an extensive structure cannot be judged of as a whole from a hurried glance, I suggest that it be tested piece by piece from the ground up, and in this, the present *Prolegomena* may fitly be used as a general outline with which the work itself may occasionally be compared. This notion, if it were founded on nothing more than my conceit of importance, such as vanity commonly attributes to all of one's own productions, would be immodest and would deserve to be repudiated with indignation. But now the interests of speculative philosophy have arrived at the point of total extinction, while human reason hangs upon them with inextinguishable affection; and only after having been ceaselessly deceived, does it vainly attempt to change this into indifference.

In our thinking age, it is not to be supposed but that many deserving men would use any good opportunity of working for the common interest of the more and more enlightened reason, if there were only some hope of attaining the goal. Mathematics, natural science, laws, arts, even morality, etc., do not completely fill the soul; there is always a space left over reserved for pure and speculative reason, the emptiness of which prompts us to seek in vagaries, buffooneries, and mysticism for what seems to be employment and entertainment, but what actually is mere pastime undertaken in order to deaden the troublesome voice of reason, which, in accordance with its nature, requires something that can satisfy it and does not merely subserve other ends or the interests of our inclinations. A consideration, therefore, which is concerned only with reason as it exists for it itself has, as I may reasonably suppose, a great fascination for everyone who has attempted thus to extend his conceptions, and I may even say a greater fascination than any other theoretical branch of knowledge, for which he would not willingly exchange it because here all other branches of knowledge and even purposes must meet and unite themselves in a whole.

I offer, therefore, these *Prolegomena* as a sketch and textbook for this investigation, and not the work itself. Although I am even now perfectly satisfied with the latter as far as contents, order, and mode of presentation, and the care that I have expended in weighing and testing every sentence before writing it down are concerned (for it has taken me years to satisfy myself fully, not only as regards the whole, but in some cases even as to the sources of one particular proposition); yet I am not quite satisfied with my exposition in some sections of the Doctrine of Elements,* as for instance in the deduction of the concepts of the understanding or in the chapter on the paralogisms of pure reason, because a certain diffuseness takes away from their clearness, and in place of them what is here said in the *Prolegomena* respecting these sections may be made the basis of the test.**

It is the boast of the Germans that, where steady and continuous industry are requisite, they can carry things farther than other nations. If this opinion be well founded, an opportunity, a task, presents itself the successful issue of which we can scarcely doubt and in which all thinking men can equally take part, though they have hitherto been unsuccessful in accomplishing it and in thus confirming the above good opinion. This is chiefly because the science in question is of so peculiar a kind that it can all at once be brought to completion and to that enduring state beyond which it can never be developed, in the least degree enlarged by later discoveries, or changed if we leave out of account adornment by greater clearness in some places or additional uses. This is an advantage no other science has or can have, because there is none so fully isolated and independent of others and so exclusively concerned with the faculty of cognition pure and simple. And the present moment seems not to be unfavorable to my expectation, for just now, in Germany, no one seems to know wherewith to occupy himself, apart from the so-called useful sciences, so as to pursue not mere play but a business possessing an enduring purpose.

To discover how the endeavors of the learned may be united in such a purpose I must leave to others. In the meantime, it is not my intention to persuade anyone merely to follow my propositions or even to flatter me with the hope that he will do so; but attacks, repetitions, limitations, or confirmation, completion, and extension, as the case may be, should be appended. If the matter be but investigated from its foundation, it cannot fail that a system, albeit not my own, shall be erected that shall be a possession for future generations for which they may have reason to be grateful.

It would lead us too far here to show what kind of metaphysics may be expected when the principles of criticism have been perfected and how, though the old false feathers have been pulled out, it need by no means appear poor and reduced to an insignificant figure but may be in other respects richly and respectably adorned. But other and great uses which would result from such a reform strike one immediately. The ordinary metaphysics had its uses, in that it sought out the elementary concepts of the pure understanding in order to make them clear through analysis and definite through definitions. In this way it was a training for reason, in whatever direction it might be turned. But this was all the good it did. The service was subsequently effaced when it favored conceit by venturesome assertions, sophistry by subtle distinctions and adornment, and shallowness by the ease with which it decided the most difficult problems by means of a little school wisdom, which is only the more seductive the more it has the choice, on the one hand, of taking something from the language of science and, on the other, from that of popular discourse—thus being everything to everybody but in reality nothing at all. By criticism, however, a standard is given to our judgment whereby knowledge may be with certainty distinguished from pseudo-science and firmly founded, being brought into full operation in metaphysics—a mode of thought extending by degrees its benefi-

---

*[The first part of the *Critique of Pure Reason,* the other being the Methodology.—L.W.B.]

**[These sections were almost completely rewritten in the second edition of the *Critique* (1787), though the new deduction of the categories does not follow the argument of the *Prolegomena.*—L.W.B.]

cial influence over every other use of reason, at once infusing into it the true philosophical spirit. But the service that metaphysics performs also for theology, by making it independent of the judgment of dogmatic speculation and thereby assuring it completely against the attacks of all such opponents, is certainly not to be valued lightly. For ordinary metaphysics, although it promised theology much advantage, could not keep this promise, and by summoning speculative dogmatics to its assistance did nothing but arm enemies against itself. Mysticism, which can prosper in a rationalistic age only when it hides itself behind a system of school metaphysics, under the protection of which it may venture to rave with a semblance of rationality, is driven from theology, its last hiding place, by critical philosophy. Last, but not least, it cannot be otherwise than important to a teacher of metaphysics to be able to say with universal assent that what he expounds is *science,* and that by it genuine services will be rendered to the commonweal.

FOUNDATION FOR THE METAPHYSICS OF MORALS

PREFACE

Ancient Greek philosophy was divided into three sciences: physics, ethics, and logic. This division conforms perfectly to the nature of the subject, and one need improve on it perhaps only by supplying its principle in order both to insure its exhaustiveness and to define correctly the necessary subdivisions.

All rational knowledge is either material, and concerns some object, or formal, and is occupied only with the form of understanding and reason itself and with the universal rules of thinking, without regard to distinctions among objects. Formal philosophy is called logic. Material philosophy, however, which has to do with definite objects and the laws to which they are subject, is divided into two parts. This is because these laws are either laws of nature or laws of freedom. The science of the former is called physics, and that of the latter ethics. The former is also called theory of nature and the latter theory of morals.

Logic can have no empirical part—a part in which universal and necessary laws of thinking would rest upon grounds taken from experience. For in that case it would not be logic (i.e., a canon for understanding or reason which is valid for all thinking and which must be demonstrated). Natural and moral philosophy, on the other hand, can each have its empirical part. The former must do so, for it must determine the laws of nature as an object of experience, and the latter must do so because it must determine the human will so far as it is affected by nature. The laws of the former are laws according to which everything happens; those of the latter are laws according to which everything ought to happen, but allow for conditions under which what ought to happen often does not.

All philosophy, so far as it is based on experience, may be called empirical; but, so far as it presents its doctrines solely on the basis of a priori principles, it may be

Immanuel Kant, *Foundation for the Metaphysics of Morals,* 2nd edition, translated by Lewis White Beck (New York: Macmillan/Library of the Liberal Arts, 1990).

called pure philosophy. Pure philosophy, when formal only, is logic; when limited to definite objects of the understanding, it is metaphysics.

In this way there arises the idea of a two-fold metaphysics—a metaphysics of nature and a metaphysics of morals. Physics, therefore, will have an empirical part and also a rational part, and ethics likewise. In ethics, however, the empirical part may be called more specifically practical anthropology; the rational part, morals proper.

All crafts, handiworks, and arts have gained by the division of labor, for when one person does not do everything but each limits himself to a particular job which is distinguished from all the others by the treatment it requires, he can do it with greater perfection and more facility. Where work is not thus differentiated and divided, where everyone is a jack-of-all-trades, the crafts remain at a primitive level. It might be worth considering whether pure philosophy in each of its parts does not require a man particularly devoted to it, and whether it would not be better for the learned profession as a whole to warn those who are in the habit of catering to the taste of the public by mixing up the empirical with the rational in all sorts of proportions which they themselves do not know—a warning to those who call themselves independent thinkers and who give the name of speculator to those who apply themselves exclusively to the rational part of philosophy. This warning would be that they should not, at one and the same time, carry on two employments which differ widely in the treatment they require, and for each of which perhaps a special talent is required, since the combination of these talents in one person produces only bunglers. I only ask whether the nature of the science does not require that a careful separation of the empirical from the rational part be made, with a metaphysics of nature put before real (empirical) physics and a metaphysics of morals before practical anthropology. Each branch of metaphysics must be carefully purified of everything empirical so that we can know how much pure reason can accomplish in each case and from what sources it creates its a priori teaching, whether the latter inquiry be conducted by all moralists (whose name is legion) or only by some who feel a calling to it.

Since my purpose here is directed to moral philosophy, I narrow my proposed question to this: Is it not of the utmost necessity to construct a pure moral philosophy which is completely freed from everything which may be only empirical and thus belong to anthropology? That there must be such a philosophy is self-evident from the common idea of duty and moral laws. Everyone must admit that a law, if it is to hold morally (i.e., as a ground of obligation), must imply absolute necessity; he must admit that the command: Thou shalt not lie, does not apply to men only as if other rational beings had no need to observe it. The same is true for all other moral laws properly so called. He must concede that the ground of obligation here must not be sought in the nature of man or in the circumstances in which he is placed but a priori solely in the concepts of pure reason, and that every precept which rests on principles of mere experience, even a precept which is in certain respects universal, so far as it leans in the least on empirical grounds (perhaps only in regard to the motive involved) may be called a practical rule but never a moral law.

Thus not only are moral laws together with their principles essentially different from all practical knowledge in which there is anything empirical, but all moral philosophy rests solely on its pure part. Applied to man, it borrows nothing from knowledge of him (anthropology) but gives man, as a rational being, a priori laws. No doubt these laws require a power of judgment sharpened by experience partly in order to decide in which cases they apply and partly to procure for them access to man's will and to provide an impetus to their practice. For man is affected by so many inclinations that, though he is capable of the Idea of a practical pure reason, he is not so easily able to make it concretely effective in the conduct of his life.

A metaphysics of morals is therefore indispensable, not merely because of motives to speculation on the source of the a priori practical principles which lie in our reason, but also because morals themselves remain subject to all kinds of corruption so long as the guide and supreme norm for their correct estimation is lacking. For it is not sufficient to that which should be morally good that it conform to the law; it must be done for the sake of the law. Otherwise its conformity is merely contingent and spurious because, though the unmoral ground may indeed now and then produce lawful actions, more often it brings forth unlawful ones. But the moral law can be found in its purity and genuineness (which is the central concern in the practical) nowhere else than in a pure philosophy; therefore metaphysics must lead the way, and without it there can be no moral philosophy. Philosophy which mixes pure principles with empirical ones does not deserve the name, for what distinguishes philosophy from common sense knowledge is its treatment in separate sciences of what is confusedly apprehended in such knowledge. Much less does it deserve the name of moral philosophy, since by this confusion it spoils the purity of morals themselves, and works contrary to its own end.

It should not be thought that what is here required is already present in the celebrated Wolff's propaedeutic to his moral philosophy (i.e., in what he calls *Universal Practical Philosophy*) and that it is not an entirely new field which is to be opened. Precisely because his work was to be universal practical philosophy, it contained no will of any particular kind, such as one determined without any empirical motives by a priori principles; in a word, it had nothing which could be called a pure will, since it considered only volition in general with all the actions and conditions which pertain to it in this general sense. Thus his propaedeutic differs from a metaphysic of morals in the same way that general logic is distinguished from transcendental philosophy, the former expounding the actions and rules of thinking in general, and the latter presenting the actions and rules of pure thinking (thinking by which objects are known completely a priori). For the metaphysics of morals is meant to investigate the Idea and principles of a possible pure will and not the actions and conditions of human volition as such, which for the most part are drawn from psychology.

That universal practical philosophy discussed (though improperly) laws and duty is no objection to my assertion. For the authors of this science remain even here true to their idea of it. They do not distinguish the motives which are presented completely a priori by reason alone and which are thus moral in the proper sense of the world, from empirical motives which the understanding raises to universal concepts by comparing experiences. Rather, they consider motives without regard to the difference in their source but only with reference to their larger or smaller number (as they are considered to be all of the same kind); they thus formulate their concept of obligation, which is anything but moral, but which is all that can be desired in a philosophy which does not decide whether the origin of all possible practical concepts is a priori or a posteriori.

As a preliminary to a *Metaphysics of Morals* which I intend to publish someday, I issue these *Foundations*. There is, to be sure, no other foundation for such a metaphysics than a critical examination of pure practical reason, just as there is no other foundation for metaphysics than the already published critical examination of pure speculative reason. But, in the first place, a critical examination of pure practical reason is not of such extreme importance as that of the speculative reason, because human reason, even in the commonest mind, can easily be brought to a high degree of correctness and completeness in moral matters while, on the other hand, in its theoretical but pure use it is wholly dialectical. In the second place, I require of a critical examination of pure practical reason, if it is to be complete, that its unity with the speculative be subject to presentation under a common principle, because in the final analysis there can be but one and the same reason which must be different only in application. But I could not bring this to such a completeness without bringing in observations of an altogether different kind and without thereby confusing the reader. For these reasons I have employed the title, *Foundations of the Metaphysics of Morals,* instead of *Critique of Pure Practical Reason.*

Because, in the third place, a *Metaphysics of Morals,* in spite of its forbidding title, is capable of a high degree of popular adaptation to common understanding, I find it useful to separate this preliminary work of laying the foundation, in order not to have to introduce unavoidable subtleties into the latter, more comprehensible work.

The present foundations, however, are nothing more than the search for and establishment of the supreme principle of morality. This constitutes a task altogether complete in design and one which should be kept separate from all other moral inquiry. My conclusions concerning this important question, which has not yet been discussed nearly enough, would, of course, be clarified by application of the principle to the whole system of morality, and it would receive much confirmation by the adequacy which it would everywhere show. But I must forego this advantage which would be, in the final analysis, more personally gratifying than commonly useful, because ease of use and apparent adequacy of a principle are not any sure proof of correctness, but rather awaken a certain partiality which prevents a rigorous investigation and evaluation of it for itself without regard to consequences.

I have adopted in this writing the method which is, I think, most suitable if one wishes to proceed analytically from common knowledge to the determination of its supreme principle, and then synthetically from the examination of this principle and its sources back to common knowledge where it finds its application. The division is therefore as follows:

1. First Section. Transition from Common Sense Knowledge of Morals to the Philosophical
2. Second Section. Transition from Popular Moral Philosophy to the Metaphysics of Morals
3. Third Section. Final Step from the Metaphysics of Morals to the Critical Examination of Pure Practical Reason

FIRST SECTION

TRANSITION FROM COMMON SENSE* KNOWLEDGE OF MORALS TO THE PHILOSOPHICAL

Nothing in the world—indeed nothing even beyond the world—can possibly be conceived which could be called good without qualification except a *GOOD WILL.* Intelligence, wit, judgment, and other talents of the mind however they may be named, or courage, resoluteness, and perseverence as qualities of temperament, are doubtless in

---

*[*gemeine Vernunfterkenntnis* ("common rational knowledge") is one of several expressions Kant uses which may sometimes best be translated as "common sense." Kant is very strict in his censure of those who appeal to common sense as an arbiter in philosophical disputes, yet he accepts it as a starting point, especially in ethics, where he says that the man of common sense has at least as much chance to be right as the philosopher. In this title "common sense" is not being used as a technical term; it just means "what everyone knows" about morality.]

many respects good and desirable; but they can become extremely bad and harmful if the will, which is to make use of these gifts of nature and which in its special constitution is called character, is not good. It is the same with gifts of fortune. Power, riches, honor, even health, general well-being and the contentment with one's condition which is called happiness make for pride and even arrogance if there is not a good will to correct their influence on the mind and on its principle of action, so as to make it generally fitting to its entire end. It need hardly be mentioned that the sight of a being adorned with no feature of a pure and good will yet enjoying lasting good fortune can never give pleasure to an impartial rational observer. Thus the good will seems to constitute the indispensable condition even of worthiness to be happy.

Some qualities seem to be conducive to this good will and can facilitate its action, but in spite of that they have no intrinsic unconditional worth. They rather presuppose a good will, which limits the high esteem which one otherwise rightly has for them and prevents their being held to be absolutely good. Moderation in emotions and passions, self-control, and calm deliberation not only are good in many respects but seem even to constitute part of the inner worth of the person. But however unconditionally they were esteemed by the ancients, they are far from being good without qualification, for without the principles of a good will they can become extremely bad, and the coolness of a villain makes him not only far more dangerous but also more directly abominable in our eyes than he would have seemed without it.

The good will is not good because of what it effects or accomplishes or because of its competence to achieve some intended end; it is good only because of its willing (i.e., it is good in itself). And, regarded for itself, it is to be esteemed as incomparably higher than anything which could be brought about by it in favor of any inclination or even of the sum total of all inclinations. Even if it should happen that, by a particularly unfortunate fate or by the niggardly provision of a step-motherly nature, this will should be wholly lacking in power to accomplish its purpose, and if even the greatest effort should not avail it to achieve anything of its end, and if there remained only the good will—not as a mere wish, but as the summoning of all the means in our power—it would sparkle like a jewel all by itself, as something that had its full worth in itself. Usefulness or fruitlessness can neither diminish nor augment this worth. Its usefulness would be only its setting, as it were, so as to enable us to handle it more conveniently in commerce or to attract the attention of those who are not yet connoisseurs, but not to recommend it to those who are experts or to determine its worth.

But there is something so strange in this idea of the absolute worth of the will alone, in which no account is taken of any use, that, notwithstanding the agreement even of common sense, the suspicion must arise that perhaps only high-flown fancy is its hidden basis, and that we may have misunderstood the purpose of nature in appointing reason as the ruler of our will. We shall therefore examine this idea from this point of view.

In the natural constitution of an organized being (i.e., one suitably adapted to life), we assume as an axiom that no organ will be found for any purpose which is not the fittest and best adapted to that purpose. Now if its preservation, its welfare, in a word its happiness, were the real end of nature in a being having reason and will, then nature would have hit upon a very poor arrangement in appointing the reason of the creature to be the executor of this purpose. For all the actions which the creature has to perform with this intention of nature, and the entire rule of his conduct, would be dictated much more exactly by instinct, and the end would be far more certainly attained by instinct than it ever could be by reason. And if, over and above this, reason should have been granted to the favored creature, it would have served only to let him contemplate the happy constitution of his nature, to admire it, to rejoice in it, and to be grateful for it to its beneficent cause. But reason would not have been given in order that the being should subject his faculty of desire to that weak and delusive guidance and to meddle with the purpose of nature. In a word, nature would have taken care that reason did not break forth into practical use nor have the presumption, with its weak insight, to think out for itself the plan of happiness and the means of attaining it. Nature would have taken over the choice not only of ends but also of the means, and with wise foresight she would have entrusted both to instinct alone.

And, in fact, we find that the more a cultivated reason deliberately devotes itself to the enjoyment of life and happiness, the more the man falls short of true contentment. From this fact there arises in many persons, if only they are candid enough to admit it, a certain degree of misology, hatred of reason. This is particularly the case with those who are most experienced in its use. After counting all the advantages which they draw—I will not say from the invention of the arts of common luxury—from the sciences (which in the end seem to them to be also a luxury of the understanding), they nevertheless find that they have actually brought more trouble on their shoulders instead of gaining in happiness; they finally envy, rather than despise, the common run of men who are better guided by merely natural instinct and who do not permit their reason much influence on their conduct. And we must at least admit that a morose attitude or ingratitude to the goodness with which the world is governed is by no means found always among those who temper or refute the boasting eulogies which are given of the advantages of happiness and contentment with which reason is supposed to supply us. Rather, their judgment is based on the Idea of another and far more worthy purpose of their existence for which, instead of happiness, their reason is properly intended; this purpose, therefore, being the supreme condition to which the private purposes of men must, for the most part, defer.

Since reason is not competent to guide the will safely with regard to its objects and the satisfaction of all our needs (which it in part multiplies), to this end an innate instinct would have led with far more certainty. But reason is given to us as a practical faculty (i.e., one which is meant to have an influence on the will). As nature has elsewhere distributed capacities suitable to the functions they are to perform, reason's proper function must be to produce a will good in itself and not one good merely as a means, since for the former, reason is absolutely essential. This will need not be the sole and complete good, yet it must be the condition of all others, even of the desire for happiness. In this case it is entirely compatible with the wisdom of nature that the cultivation of reason, which is required for the former unconditional purpose, at least in this life restricts in many ways—indeed, can reduce to nothing—the achievement of the latter unconditional purpose, happiness. For one perceives that nature here does not proceed unsuitably to its purpose, because reason, which recognizes its highest practical vocation in the establishment of a good will, is capable of a contentment of its own kind (i.e., one that springs from the attainment of a purpose determined by reason), even though this injures the ends of inclination.

We have, then, to develop the concept of a will which is to be esteemed as good in itself without regard to anything else. It dwells already in the natural and sound understanding and does not need so much to be taught as only to be brought to light. In the estimation of the total worth of our actions it always takes first place and is the condition of everything else. In order to show this, we shall take the concept of duty. It contains the concept of a good will, though with certain subjective restrictions and hindrances, but these are far from concealing it and making it unrecognizable, for they rather bring it out by contrast and make it shine forth all the more brightly.

I here omit all actions which are recognized as opposed to duty, even though they may be useful in one respect or another, for with these the question does not arise as to whether they may be done *from* duty, since they conflict with it. I also pass over actions which are really in accord with duty and to which one has no direct inclination, rather doing them because impelled to do so by another inclination. For it is easily decided whether an action in accord with duty is done from duty or for some selfish purpose. It is far more difficult to note this difference when the action is in accord with duty and, in addition, the subject has a direct inclination to do it. For example, it is in accord with duty that a dealer should not overcharge an inexperienced customer, and wherever there is much trade the prudent merchant does not do so, but has a fixed price for everyone so that a child may buy from him as cheaply as any other. Thus the customer is honestly served, but this is far from sufficient to warrant the belief that the merchant has behaved in this way from duty and principles of honesty. His own advantage required this behavior, but it cannot be assumed that over and above that he had a direct inclination to his customers and that, out of love, as it were, he gave none an advantage in price over another. The action was done neither from duty nor from direct inclination but only for a selfish purpose.

On the other hand, it is a duty to preserve one's life, and moreover everyone has a direct inclination to do so. But for that reason, the often anxious care which most men take of it has no intrinsic worth, and the maxim of doing so has no moral import. They preserve their lives according to duty, but not from duty. But if adversities and hopeless sorrow completely take away the relish for life; if an unfortunate man, strong in soul, is indignant rather than despondent or dejected over his fate and wishes for death, and yet preserves his life without loving it and from neither inclination nor fear but from duty—then his maxim has moral merit.

To be kind where one can is a duty, and there are, moreover, many persons so sympathetically constituted that without any motive of vanity or selfishness they find an inner satisfaction in spreading joy and rejoice in the contentment of others which they have made possible. But I say that, however dutiful and however amiable it may be, that kind of action has no true moral worth. It is on a level with [actions done from] other inclinations, such as the inclination to honor, which, if fortunately directed to what in fact accords with duty and is generally useful and thus honorable, deserve praise and encouragement, but no esteem. For the maxim lacks the moral import of an action done not from inclination but from duty. But assume that the mind of that friend to mankind was clouded by a sorrow of his own which extinguished all sympathy with the lot of others, and though he still had the power to benefit others in distress their need left him untouched because he was preoccupied with his own. Now suppose him to tear himself, unsolicited by inclination, out of his dead insensibility and to do this action only from duty and without any inclination—then for the first time his action has genuine moral worth. Furthermore, if nature has put little sympathy into the heart of a man, and if he, though an honest man, is by temperament cold and indifferent to the sufferings of others perhaps because he is provided with special gifts of patience and fortitude and expects and even requires that others should have them too—and such a man would certainly not be the meanest product of nature—would not he find in himself a source from which to give himself a far higher worth than he could have got by having a good-natured temperament? This is unquestionably true even though nature did not make him philanthropic, for it is just here that the worth of character is brought out, which is morally the incomparably highest of all: he is beneficent not from inclination, but from duty.

To secure one's own happiness is at least indirectly a duty, for discontent with one's condition under pressure from many cares and amid unsatisfied wants could easily become a great temptation to transgress against duties. But, without any view to duty, all men have the strongest and deepest inclination to happiness, because in this Idea all inclinations are summed up. But the precept of happiness is often so formulated that it definitely thwarts some inclinations, and men can make no definite and certain concept of the sum of satisfaction of all inclinations, which goes under the name of happiness. It is not to be wondered at, therefore, that a single inclination, definite as to what it promises and as to the time at which it can be satisfied, can outweigh a fluctuating idea and that, for example, a man with the gout can choose to enjoy what he likes and to suffer what he may, because according to his calculations at least on this occasion he has not sacrificed the enjoyment of the present moment to a perhaps groundless expectation of a happiness supposed to lie in health. But even in this case if the universal inclination to happiness did not determine his will, and if health were not at least for him a necessary factor in these calculations, there would still remain, as in all other cases, a law that he ought to promote his happiness not from inclination but from duty. Only from this law could his conduct have true moral worth.

It is in this way, undoubtedly, that we should understand those passages of Scripture which command us to love our neighbor and even our enemy, for love as an inclination cannot be commanded. But beneficence from duty, even when no inclination impels it and even when it is opposed by a natural and unconquerable aversion, is practical love, not pathological* love; it resides in the will and not in the propensities of feeling, in principles of action and not in tender sympathy; and it alone can be commanded.

[Thus the first proposition of morality is that to have genuine moral worth, an action must be done from duty.] The second proposition is: An action done from duty does not have its moral worth in the purpose which is to be achieved through it but in the maxim whereby it is determined. Its moral value, therefore, does not depend upon the realization of the object of the action but merely on the principle of the volition by which the action is done irrespective of the objects of the faculty of desire. From the preceding discussion it is clear that the purposes we may have for our actions and their effects as ends and incentives of the will cannot give the actions any unconditional and moral worth. Wherein, then, can this worth lie, if it is not in the will in its relation to its hoped-for effect? It can lie nowhere else than in the principle of the will irrespective of the ends which can be realized by such action. For the will stands, as it were, at the crossroads halfway between its a priori principle which is formal and its posteriori incentive which is material. Since it must be determined by something, if it is done from duty it must be determined by the formal principle of volition as such, since every material principle has been withdrawn from it.

The third principle, as a consequence of the two preceding, I would express as follows: Duty is the necessity to do an action from respect for law. I can certainly have an inclination to an object as an effect of the proposed action, but I can never have respect for it precisely because it is a mere effect and not an activity of a will. Similarly, I can have no respect for any inclination whatsoever, whether my own or that of another; in the former case I can at most approve of it and in the latter I can even love it (i.e., see it as favorable to my own advantage). But that which is connected with my will merely as ground and not as consequence, that which does not serve my inclination but overpowers it or at least excludes it from being considered in making a choice—in a word, law itself—can be an object of respect and thus a command. Now as an act from duty

---

*[Here as elsewhere Kant uses the word *pathological* to describe motives and actions arising from feeling or bodily impulses, with no suggestion of abnormality or disease.]

wholly excludes the influence of inclination and therewith every object of the will, nothing remains which can determine the will objectively except law and subjectively except pure respect for this practical law. This subjective element is the maxim* that I should follow such a law even if it thwarts all my inclinations.

Thus the moral worth of an action does not lie in the effect which is expected from it or in any principle of action which has to borrow its motive from this expected effect. For all these effects (agreeableness of my own condition, indeed even the promotion of the happiness of others) could be brought about through other causes and would not require the will of a rational being, while the highest and unconditional good can be found only in such a will. Therefore the preeminent good can consist only in the conception of law in itself (which can be present only in a rational being) so far as this conception and not the hoped-for effect is the determining ground of the will. This preeminent good, which we call moral, is already present in the person who acts according to this conception, and we do not have to look for it first in the result.**

But what kind of law can that be, the conception of which must determine the will without reference to the expected result? Under this condition alone can the will be called absolutely good without qualification. Since I have robbed the will of all impulses which could come to it from obedience to any law, nothing remains to serve as a principle of the will except universal conformity to law as such. That is, I ought never to act in such a way that I could not also will that my maxim should be a universal law. Strict conformity to law as such (without assuming any particular law applicable to certain actions) serves as the principle of the will, and it must serve as such a principle if duty is not to be a vain delusion and chimerical concept. The common sense of mankind *(gemeine Menschenvernunft)* in its practical judgments is in perfect agreement with this and has this principle constantly in view.

Let the question, for example, be: May I, when in distress, make a promise with the intention not to keep it? I easily distinguish the two meanings which the question can have, viz., whether it is prudent to make a false promise, or whether it conforms to duty. The former can undoubtedly be often the case, though I do see clearly that it is not sufficient merely to escape from the present difficulty by this expedient, but that I must consider whether inconveniences much greater than the present one may not later spring from this lie. Even with all my supposed cunning, the consequences cannot be so easily foreseen. Loss of credit might be far more disadvantageous than the misfortune I am now seeking to avoid, and it is hard to tell whether it might not be more prudent to

---

*A maxim is the subjective principle of volition. The objective principle (i.e., that which would serve all rational beings also subjectively as a practical principle if reason had full power over the faculty of desire) is the practical law.

**It might be objected that I seek to take refuge in an obscure feeling behind the word "respect," instead of clearly resolving the question with a concept of reason. But though respect is a feeling, it is not one received through any [outer] influence but is self-wrought by a rational concept; thus it differs specifically from all feelings of the former kind which may be referred to inclination or fear. What I recognize directly as a law for myself I recognize with respect, which means merely the consciousness of the submission of my will to a law without the intervention of other influences on my mind. The direct determination of the will by law and the consciousness of this determination is respect; thus respect can be regarded as the effect of the law on the subject and not as the cause of the law. Respect is properly the conception of a worth which thwarts my self-love. Thus it is regarded as an object neither of inclination nor of fear, though it has something analogous to both. The only object of respect is law, and indeed only the law which we impose on ourselves and yet recognize as necessary in itself. As a law we are subject to it without consulting self-love; as imposed on us by ourselves, it is a consequence of our will. In the former respect it is analogous to fear and in the latter to inclination. All respect for a person is only respect for the law (of righteousness, etc.) of which the person provides an example. Because we see the improvement of our talents as a duty, we think of a person of talent as the example of a law, as it were (the law that we should by practice become like him in his talents), and that constitutes our respect. All so-called moral interest consists solely in respect for the law.

act according to a universal maxim and to make it a habit not to promise anything without intending to fulfill it. But it is soon clear to me that such a maxim is based only on an apprehensive concern with consequences.

To be truthful from duty, however, is an entirely different thing from being truthful out of fear of untoward consequences, for in the former case the concept of the action itself contains a law for me, while in the latter I must first look about to see what results for me may be connected with it. To deviate from the principle of duty is certainly bad, but to be unfaithful to my maxim of prudence can sometimes be very advantageous to me, though it is certainly safer to abide by it. The shortest but most infallible way to find the answer to the question as to whether a deceitful promise is consistent with duty is to ask myself: Would I be content that my maxim of extricating myself from difficulty by a false promise should hold as a universal law for myself as well as for others? And could I say to myself that everyone may make a false promise when he is in a difficulty from which he otherwise cannot escape? Immediately I see that I could will the lie but not a universal law to lie. For with such a law there would be no promises at all, inasmuch as it would be futile to make a pretense of my intention in regard to future actions to those who would not believe this pretense or—if they overhastily did so—would pay me back in my own coin. Thus my maxim would necessarily destroy itself as soon as it was made a universal law.

I do not, therefore, need any penetrating acuteness to discern what I have to do in order that my volition may be morally good. Inexperienced in the course of the world, incapable of being prepared for all its contingencies, I only ask myself: Can I will that my maxim become a universal law? If not, it must be rejected, not because of any disadvantage accruing to myself or even to others, but because it cannot enter as a principle into a possible enactment of universal law, and reason extorts from me an immediate respect for such legislation. I do not as yet discern on what it is grounded (this is a question the philosopher may investigate), but I at least understand that it is an estimation of a worth which far outweighs all the worth of whatever is recommended by the inclinations, and that the necessity that I act from pure respect for the practical law constitutes my duty. To duty every other motive must give place, because duty is the condition of a will good in itself, whose worth transcends everything.

Thus within the moral knowledge of ordinary human reason *(gemeine Menschen-vernunft)* we have attained its principle. To be sure, ordinary human reason does not think this principle abstractly in such a universal form, but it always has the principle in view and uses it as the standard for its judgments. It would be easy to show how ordinary human reason, with this compass, knows well how to distinguish what is good, what is bad, and what is consistent or inconsistent with duty. Without in the least teaching common reason anything new, we need only to draw its attention to its own principle (in the manner of Socrates), thus showing that neither science nor philosophy is needed in order to know what one has to do in order to be honest and good, and even wise and virtuous. We might have conjectured beforehand that the knowledge of what everyone is obliged to do and thus also to know would be within the reach of everyone, even of the most ordinary man. Here we cannot but admire the great advantages which the practical faculty of judgment has over the theoretical in ordinary human understanding. In the theoretical, if ordinary reason ventures to go beyond the laws of experience and perceptions of the senses, it falls into sheer inconceivabilities and self-contradictions, or at least into a chaos of uncertainty, obscurity, and instability. In the practical, on the other hand, the power of judgment first shows itself to advantage when common understanding excludes all sensuous incentives from practical laws. It then even becomes subtle, quibbling with its own conscience or with other claims to what should be called right, or wishing to determine accurately, for its own instruction, the worth of certain actions. But the most remarkable thing about ordinary human under-standing in its practical concern is that it may have as much hope as any philosopher of hitting the mark. In fact, it is almost more certain to do so than the philosopher, for while he has no principle which common understanding lacks, his judgment is easily con-fused by a mass of irrelevant considerations so that it easily turns aside from the correct way. Would it not, therefore, be wiser in moral matters to acquiesce in ordinary reason-able judgment and at most to call in philosophy in order to make the system of morals more complete and comprehensible and its rules more convenient for use (especially in disputation), than to steer the ordinary understanding from its happy simplicity in practical matters and to lead it through philosophy into a new path of inquiry and in-struction?

Innocence is indeed a glorious thing, but it is very sad that it cannot well maintain itself, being easily led astray. For this reason, even wisdom—which consists more in acting than in knowing—needs science, not so as to learn from it but to secure admis-sion and permanence to its precepts. Man feels in himself a powerful counterpoise against all commands of duty which reason presents to him as so deserving of respect. This counterpoise is his needs and inclinations, the complete satisfaction of which he sums up under the name of happiness. Now reason issues inexorable commands with-out promising anything to the inclinations. It disregards, as it were, and holds in con-tempt those claims which are so impetuous and yet so plausible, and which refuse to be suppressed by any command. From this a natural dialectic arises, i.e., a propensity to ar-gue against the stern laws of duty and their validity, or at least to place their purity and strictness in doubt and, where possible, to make them more accordant with our wishes and inclinations. This is equivalent to corrupting them in their very foundations and destroying their dignity—a thing which even ordinary practical reason cannot finally call good.

In this way ordinary human reason is impelled to go outside its sphere and to take a step into the field of practical philosophy. But it is forced to do so not by any specula-tive need, which never occurs to it so long as it is satisfied to remain merely healthy rea-son; rather, it is impelled on practical grounds to obtain information and clear instruc-tion respecting the source of its principle and the correct definition of this principle in its opposition to the maxims based on need and inclination. It seeks this information in order to escape from the perplexity of opposing claims and to avoid the danger of los-ing all genuine moral principles through the equivocation in which it is easily involved. Thus when ordinary practical reason cultivates itself, a dialectic surreptitiously ensues which forces it to seek aid in philosophy, just as the same thing happens in the theoreti-cal use of reason. Ordinary practical reason, like theoretical reason, will find rest only in a complete critical examination of our reason.

SECOND SECTION

TRANSITION FROM POPULAR MORAL PHILOSOPHY TO THE METAPHYSICS OF MORALS

Although we have derived our earlier concept of duty from the ordinary use of our prac-tical reason, it is by no means to be inferred that we have treated it as an empirical con-cept. On the contrary, if we attend to our experience of the way men act, we meet frequent and, as we must confess, justified complaints that we cannot cite a single sure example of the disposition to act from pure duty. There are also justified complaints that, though much may be done that accords with what duty commands, it is nevertheless always doubtful whether it is done from duty and thus whether it has moral worth. There have always been philosophers who for this reason have absolutely denied the reality of this disposition in human actions, attributing everything to more or less refined self-love. They have done so without questioning the correctness of the concept of morality. Rather they spoke with sincere regret of the frailty and corruption of human nature, which is noble enough to take as its precept an Idea so worthy of respect but which at the same time is too weak to follow it, employing reason, which should give laws for human nature, only to provide for the interest of the inclinations either singly or, at best, in their greatest possible harmony with one another.

It is, in fact, absolutely impossible by experience to discern with complete certainty a single case in which the maxim of an action, however much it might conform to duty, rested solely on moral grounds and on the conception of one's duty. It sometimes happens that in the most searching self-examination we can find nothing except the moral ground of duty which could have been powerful enough to move us to this or that good action and to such great sacrifice. But from this we cannot by any means conclude with certainty that a secret impulse of self-love, falsely appearing as the Idea of duty, was not actually the true determining cause of the will. For we like to flatter ourselves with a pretended nobler motive, while in fact even the strictest examination can never lead us entirely behind the secret incentives, for when moral worth is in question it is not a matter of actions which one sees but of their inner principles which one does not see.

Moreover, one cannot better serve the wishes of those who ridicule all morality as a mere phantom of human imagination overreaching itself through self-conceit than by conceding that the concepts of duty must be derived only from experience (for they are ready, from indolence, to believe that this is true of all other concepts too). For, by this concession, a sure triumph is prepared for them. Out of love for humanity I am willing to admit that most of our actions are in accord with duty; but if we look more closely at our thoughts and aspirations, we come everywhere upon the dear self, which is always turning up, and it is this instead of the stern command of duty (which would often require self-denial) which supports our plans. One need not be an enemy of virtue, but only a cool observer who does not confuse even the liveliest aspiration for the good with its actuality, to be sometimes doubtful whether true virtue can really be found anywhere in the world. This is especially true as one's years increase and the power of judgment is made wiser by experience and more acute in observation. This being so, nothing can secure us against the complete abandonment of our ideas of duty and preserve in us a well-founded respect for its law except the conviction that, even if there never were actions springing from such pure sources, our concern is not whether this or that was done, but that reason of itself and independently of all appearances commanded what ought to be done. Our concern is with actions of which perhaps the world has never had an example, with actions whose feasibility might be seriously doubted by those who base everything on experience, and yet with actions inexorably commanded by reason. For example, pure sincerity in friendship can be demanded of every man, and this demand is not in the least diminished if a sincere friend has never existed, because this duty, as duty in general, prior to all experience lies in the Idea of reason which determines the will on a priori grounds.

No experience, it is clear, can give occasion for inferring the possibility of such apodictic laws. This is especially clear when we add that, unless we wish to deny all truth to the concept of morality and renounce its application to any possible object, we

Immanuel Kant and Luncheon Guests, 1893, by E. Doestling. While Kant led a simple, routine-filled life, he was known as a delightful conversationalist and host who had many friends and admirers. (*The Bettmann Archive*)

cannot refuse to admit that the law is of such broad significance that it holds not merely for men but for all rational beings as such; we must grant that it must be valid with absolute necessity, and not merely under contingent conditions and with exceptions. For with what right could we bring into unlimited respect something that might be valid only under contingent human conditions? And how could laws of the determination of our will be held to be laws of the determination of the will of any rational being whatever and of ourselves in so far as we are rational beings, if they were merely empirical and did not have their origin completely a priori in pure, but practical, reason?

Nor could one given poorer counsel to morality than to attempt to derive it from examples. For each example of morality which is exhibited must itself have been previously judged according to principles of morality to see whether it was worthy to serve as an original example or model. By no means could it authoritatively furnish the concept of morality. Even the Holy One of the Gospel must be compared with our ideal of moral perfection before He is recognized as such; even He says of Himself, "Why call ye Me (Whom you see) good? None is good (the archetype of the good) except God only (Whom you do not see)." But whence do we have the concept of God as the highest good? Solely from the Idea of moral perfection which reason formulates a priori and which it inseparably connects with the concept of a free will. Imitation has no place in moral matters, and examples serve only for encouragement. That is, they put beyond question the possibility of performing what the law commands, and they make visible that which the practical rule expresses more generally. But they can never justify our guiding ourselves by examples and our setting aside their true original, which lies in reason.

If there is thus no genuine supreme principle of morality which does not rest on pure reason alone independent of all possible experience, I do not believe it is necessary even to ask whether it is well to exhibit these concepts generally *(in abstracto)*, which, together with the principles belonging to them, are established a priori. At any rate, the question need not be asked if knowledge of them is to be distinguished from ordinary knowledge and called philosophical. But in our times this question may be necessary. For if we collected votes as to whether pure rational knowledge separated from all experience (i.e., a metaphysics of morals) or popular practical philosophy is to be preferred, it is easily guessed on which side the majority would stand.

This condescension to popular notions is certainly very commendable once the ascent to the principles of pure reason has been satisfactorily accomplished. That would mean the prior establishment of the doctrine of morals on metaphysics and then, when it is established, procuring a hearing for it through popularization. But it is extremely absurd to want to achieve popular appeal in the first investigation, where everything depends on the correctness of the fundamental principles. Not only can this procedure never make claim to that rarest merit of true philosophical popularity, since there is really no art in being generally comprehensible if one thereby renounces all basic insight; but it produces a disgusting jumble of patched-up observations and half-reasoned principles. Shallow pates enjoy this, for it is very useful in everyday chitchat, while the more sensible feel confused and dissatisfied and avert their eyes without being able to help themselves. But philosophers, who see through this delusion, get little hearing when they call people away from this would-be popularity so that they may have genuine popular appeal once they have gained a definite understanding.

One need only look at the essays on morality favored by popular taste. One will sometimes meet with the particular vocation of human nature (but occasionally with the Idea of a rational nature in general), sometimes perfection and sometimes happiness, here moral feeling, there fear of God, a little of this and a little of that in a marvelous mixture. It never occurs to the authors, however, to ask whether the principles of morality are, after all, to be sought anywhere in knowledge of human nature (which we can derive only from experience). And if this is not the case, if the principles are a priori, free from everything empirical, and found exclusively in pure rational concepts and not at all in any other place, they never ask whether they should undertake this investigation as a separate inquiry (i.e., as pure practical philosophy) or (if one may use a name so decried) a metaphysics* of morals. They never think of dealing with it alone and bringing

---

*If one wishes, the pure philosophy (metaphysics) of morals can be distinguished from the applied (i.e., applied to human nature), just as pure mathematics and pure logic are distinguished from applied mathematics and applied logic. By this designation one is immediately reminded that moral principles are not founded on the peculiarities of human nature but must stand of themselves a priori, and that from such principles practical rules for every rational nature, and accordingly for man, must be derivable.

it by itself to completeness and of requiring the public, which desires popularization, to await the outcome of this undertaking.

But a completely isolated metaphysics of morals, mixed with no anthropology, no theology, no physics or hyperphysics, and even less with occult qualities (which might be called hypophysical), is not only an indispensable substrate of all theoretically sound and definite knowledge of duties; it is also a desideratum of the highest importance to the actual fulfillment of its precepts. For the thought of duty and of the moral law generally, with no admixture of empirical inducements, has an influence on the human heart so much more powerful than all other incentives* which may be derived from the empirical field that reason, in the consciousness of its dignity, despises them and gradually becomes master over them. It has this influence only through reason alone, which thereby first realizes that it can of itself be practical. A mixed theory of morals which is put together from incentives of feelings and inclinations and from rational concepts must, on the other hand, make the mind vacillate between motives which cannot be brought together under any principle and which can lead only accidentally to the good, and frequently lead to the bad.

From what has been said it is clear that all moral concepts have their seat and origin entirely a priori in reason. This is just as much the case in the most ordinary reason as in the reason which is speculative to the highest degree. It is obvious that they can be abstracted from no empirical and hence merely contingent cognitions. In the purity of origin lies their worthiness to serve us as supreme practical principles, and to the extent that something empirical is added to them, just this much is subtracted from their genuine influence and from the unqualified worth of actions. Furthermore, it is evident that it is not only of the greatest necessity from a theoretical point of view when it is a question of speculation but also of the utmost practical importance to derive the concepts and laws of morals from pure reason and to present them pure and unmixed, and to determine the scope of this entire practical but pure rational knowledge (the entire faculty of pure practical reason) without making the principles depend upon the particular nature of human reason, as speculative philosophy may permit and even find necessary. But since moral laws should hold for every rational being as such, the principles must be derived from the universal concept of a rational being in general. In this manner all morals, which need anthropology for their application to men, must be completely developed first as pure philosophy (i.e., metaphysics), independently of anthropology (a thing feasibly done in such distinct fields of knowledge). For we know well that if we are not in possession of such a metaphysics, it is not merely futile [to try to] define accurately for the purposes of speculative judgment the moral element of duty in all actions which accord with duty, but impossible to base morals on legitimate principles for even ordinary practical use, especially in moral instruction; and it is only in this manner that pure moral dispositions can be produced and engrafted on men's minds for the purpose of the highest good in the world.

*I have a letter from the late excellent Sulzer in which he asks me why the theories of virtue accomplish so little even though they contain so much that is convincing to reason. My answer was delayed in order that I might make it complete. The answer is only that the teachers themselves have not completely clarified their concepts, and when they wish to make up for this by hunting in every quarter for motives to the morally good so as to make their physic right strong, they spoil it. For the commonest observation shows that if we imagine an act of honesty performed with a steadfast soul and sundered from all view to any advantage in this or another world and even under the greatest temptations of need or allurement, it far surpasses and eclipses any similar action which was affected in the least by any foreign incentive; it elevates the soul and arouses the wish to be able to act in this way. Even moderately young children feel this impression, and one should never represent duties to them in any other way.

In this study we do not advance merely from the common moral judgment (which here is very worthy of respect) to the philosophical, as this has already been done; but we advance by natural stages from popular philosophy (which goes no farther than it can grope by means of examples) to metaphysics (which is not held back by anything empirical and which, as it must measure out the entire scope of rational knowledge of this kind, reaches even Ideas, where examples fail us). In order to make this advance, we must follow and clearly present the practical faculty of reason from its universal rules of determination to the point where the concept of duty arises from it.

Everything in nature works according to laws. Only a rational being has the capacity of acting according to the *conception* of laws (i.e., according to principles). This capacity is the will. Since reason is required for the derivation of actions from laws, will is nothing less than practical reason. If reason infallibly determines the will, the actions which such a being recognizes as objectively necessary are also subjectively necessary. That is, the will is a faculty of choosing only that which reason, independently of inclination, recognizes as practically necessary (i.e., as good). But if reason of itself does not sufficiently determine the will, and if the will is subjugated to subjective conditions (certain incentives) which do not always agree with the objective conditions—in a word, if the will is not of itself in complete accord with reason (which is the actual case with men), then the actions which are recognized as objectively necessary are subjectively contingent, and the determination of such a will according to objective laws is a constraint. That is, the relation of objective laws to a will which is not completely good is conceived as the determination of the will of a rational being by principles of reason to which this will is not by its nature necessarily obedient.

The conception of an objective principle, so far as it constrains a will, is a command (of reason), and the formula of this command is called an *imperative*.

All imperatives are expressed by an "ought" and thereby indicate the relation of an objective law of reason to a will which is not in its subjective constitution necessarily determined by this law. This relation is that of constraint. Imperatives say that it would be good to do or to refrain from doing something, but they say it to a will which does not always do something simply because the thing is presented to it as good to do. Practical good is what determines the will by means of the conception of reason and hence not by subjective causes but objectively, on grounds which are valid for every rational being as such. It is distinguished from the pleasant, as that which has an influence on the will only by means of a sensation from purely subjective causes, which hold for the senses only of this or that person and not as a principle of reason which holds for everyone.*

A perfectly good will, therefore, would be equally subject to objective laws of the good, but it could not be conceived as constrained by them to accord with them, be-

---

*The dependence of the faculty of desire on sensations is called inclination, and inclination always indicates a need. The dependence of a contingently determinable will on principles of reason, however, is called interest. An interest is present only in a dependent will which is not of itself always in accord with reason; in the divine will we cannot conceive of an interest. But even the human will can take an interest in something without thereby acting from interest. The former means the practical interest in the action; the latter, the pathological interest in the object of the action. The former indicates only the dependence of the will on principles of reason in themselves, while the latter indicates dependence on the principles of reason for the purpose of inclination, since reason gives only the practical rule by which the needs of inclination are to be aided. In the former case the action interests me, and in the latter the object of the action (so far as it is pleasant for me) interests me. In the First Section we have seen that, in the case of an action done from duty, no regard must be given to the interest in the object, but merely to the action itself and its principle in reason (i.e., the law).

cause it can be determined to act by its own subjective constitution only through the conception of the good. Thus no imperatives hold for the divine will or, more generally, for a holy will. The "ought" here is out of place, for the volition of itself is necessarily in unison with the law. Therefore imperatives are only formulas expressing the relation of objective laws of volition in general to the subjective imperfection of the will of this or that rational being, for example, the human will.

All imperatives command either *hypothetically* or *categorically*. The former present the practical necessity of a possible action as a means to achieving something else which one desires (or which one may possibly desire). The categorical imperative would be one which presented an action as of itself objectively necessary, without regard to any other end.

Since every practical law presents a possible action as good and thus as necessary for a subject practically determinable by reason, all imperatives are formulas of the determination of action which is necessary by the principle of a will which is in any way good. If the action is good only as a means to something else, the imperative is hypothetical; but if it is thought of as good in itself, and hence as necessary in a will which of itself conforms to reason as the principle of this will, the imperative is categorical.

The imperative thus says what action possible for me would be good, and it presents the practical rule in relation to a will which does not forthwith perform an action simply because it is good, in part because the subject does not always know that the action is good, and in part (when he does know it) because his maxims can still be opposed to the objective principles of a practical reason.

The hypothetical imperative, therefore, says only that the action is good to some purpose, possible or actual. In the former case, it is a problematical, in the latter an assertorical, practical principle. The categorical imperative, which declares the action to be of itself objectively necessary without making any reference to any end in view (i.e., without having any other purpose), holds as an apodictical practical principle.

We can think of what is possible only through the powers of some rational being as a possible end in view of any will. As a consequence, the principles of action thought of as necessary to attain a possible end in view which can be achieved by them, are in reality infinitely numerous. All sciences have some practical part consisting of problems which presuppose some purpose as well as imperatives directing how it can be reached. These imperatives can therefore be called, generally, imperatives of skill. Whether the purpose is reasonable and good is not in question at all, for the questions concerns only what must be done in order to attain it. The precepts to be followed by a physician in order to cure his patient and by a poisoner to bring about certain death are of equal value in so far as each does that which will perfectly accomplish his purpose. Since in early youth we do not know what purposes we may have in the course of our life, parents seek to let their children learn a great many things and provide for skill in the use of means to all sorts of ends which they might choose, among which they cannot determine whether any one of them will become their child's actual purpose, though it may be that someday he may have it as his actual purpose. And this anxiety is so great that they commonly neglect to form and correct their children's judgment on the worth of the things which they may make their ends.

There is one end, however, which we may presuppose as actual in all rational beings so far as imperatives apply to them, that is, so far as they are dependent beings. There is one purpose which they not only *can* have but which we can presuppose that they all *do* have by a necessity of nature. This purpose is happiness. The hypothetical imperative which represents the practical necessity of an action as means to the promotion of happiness is an assertorical imperative. We may not expound it as necessary to a merely uncertain and merely possible purpose, but as necessary to a purpose which we can a priori and with assurance assume for everyone because it belongs to his essence. Skill in the choice of means to one's own highest well-being can be called prudence* in the narrowest sense. Thus the imperative which refers to the choice of means to one's own happiness (i.e., the precept of prudence) is still only hypothetical, and the action is not commanded absolutely but commanded only as a means to another end in view.

Finally, there is one imperative which directly commands certain conduct without making its condition some purpose to be reached by it. This imperative is categorical. It concerns not the material of the action and its intended result, but the form and principle from which it originates. What is essentially good in it consists in the mental disposition, the result being what it may. This imperative may be called the imperative of morality.

Volition according to these three principles is plainly distinguished by the dissimilarity in the constraints by which they subject the will. In order to clarify this dissimilarity, I believe that they are most suitably named if one says that they are either rules of skill, counsels of prudence, or commands (laws) of morality, respectively. For law alone implies the concept of an unconditional and objective and hence universally valid necessity, and commands are laws which must be obeyed even against inclination. Counsels do indeed involve necessity, but a necessity that can hold only under a subjectively contingent condition (i.e., whether this or that man counts this or that as part of his happiness). The categorical imperative, on the other hand, is restricted by no condition. As absolutely, though practically, necessary it can be called a command in the strict sense. We could also call the first imperatives *technical* (belonging to art), the second *pragmatic***** (belonging to well-being), and the third *moral* (belonging to free conduct as such, i.e., to morals).

The question now arises: How are all these imperatives possible? This question does not require an answer as to how the action which the imperative commands can be performed, but only an answer as to how the constraint of the will, which the imperative expresses in setting the problem, can be conceived. How an imperative of skill is possible requires no particular discussion. Whoever wills the end, so far as reason has decisive influence on his action, wills also the indispensably necessary steps to it that he can take. This proposition, in what concerns the will, is analytical; for, in the willing of an object as an effect, my causality, as an acting cause of this effect shown in my use of the means to it, is already thought, and the imperative derives the concept of actions necessary to this purpose from the concept of willing this purpose. Synthetical propositions undoubtedly are necessary for determining the means to a proposed end, but they do not concern the ground, the act of the will, but only the way to achieve the object. Mathematics teaches, by synthetical propositions only, that in order to bisect a line according to an infallible principle, I must make two intersecting arcs from each of its extremities;

*The word "prudence" may be taken in two senses, and it may bear the names of prudence with reference to things of the world and private prudence. The former sense means the skill of a man in having an influence on others so as to use them for his own purposes. The latter is the ability to unite all these purposes to his own lasting advantage. The worth of the first is finally reduced to the latter, and of one who is prudent in the former sense but not in the latter we might better say that he is clever and cunning yet, on the whole, imprudent.

**It seems to me that the proper meaning of the word "pragmatic" could be most accurately defined in this way. For sanctions which properly flow not from the law of states as necessary statutes but from provision for the general welfare are called pragmatic. A history is pragmatically composed when it teaches prudence (i.e., instructs the world how it could provide for its interest better than, or at least as well as, has been done in the past).

but if I know the proposed result can be obtained only by such an action, then it is an analytical proposition that, if I fully will the effect, I must also will the action necessary to produce it. For it is one and the same thing to conceive of something as an effect which is in a certain way possible through me, and to conceive of myself as acting in this way.

If it were only easy to give a definite concept of happiness, the imperatives of prudence would perfectly correspond to those of skill and would likewise be analytical. For it could then be said in this case as well as in the former that whoever wills the end wills also (necessarily according to reason) the only means to it which are in his power. But it is a misfortune that the concept of happiness is so indefinite that, although each person wishes to attain it, he can never definitely and self-consistently state what it is that he really wishes and wills. The reason for this is that all elements which belong to the concept of happiness are empirical (i.e., they must be taken from experience), while for the Idea of happiness an absolute whole, a maximum, of well-being is needed in my present and in every future condition. Now it is impossible for even a most clear-sighted and most capable but finite being to form here a definite concept of that which he really wills. If he wills riches, how much anxiety, envy, and intrigues might he not thereby draw upon his shoulders! If he wills much knowledge and vision, perhaps it might become only an eye that much sharper to show him as more dreadful the evils which are now hidden from him and which are yet unavoidable; or it might be to burden his desires—which already sufficiently engage him—with even more needs! If he wills long life, who guarantees that it will not be long misery! If he wills at least health, how often has not the discomfort of his body restrained him from excesses into which perfect health would have led him? In short, he is not capable, on any principle and with complete certainty, of ascertaining what would make him truly happy; omniscience would be needed for this. He cannot, therefore, act according to definite principles so as to be happy, but only according to empirical counsels (e.g., those of diet, economy, courtesy, restraint, etc.) which are shown by experience best to promote well-being on the average. Hence the imperatives of prudence cannot, in the strict sense, command (i.e., present actions objectively as practically necessary); thus they are to be taken as counsels (*consilia*) rather than as commands (*praecepta*) of reason, and the task of determining infallibly and universally what action will promote the happiness of a rational being is completely unsolvable. There can be no imperative which would, in the strict sense, command us to do what makes for happiness, because happiness is an ideal not of reason but of imagination, depending only on empirical grounds which one would expect in vain to determine an action through which the totality of consequences—which in fact is infinite—could be achieved. Assuming that the means to happiness could be infallibly stated, this imperative of prudence would be an analytically practical proposition for it differs from the imperative of skill only in that its purpose is given, while in the imperative of skill it is merely a possible purpose. Since both, however, command the means to that which one presupposes as a willed purpose, the imperative which commands the willing of the means to him who wills the end is in both cases analytical. There is, consequently, no difficulty in seeing the possibility of such an imperative.

To see how the imperative of morality is possible, then, is without doubt the only question needing an answer. It is not hypothetical, and thus the objectively conceived necessity cannot be supported by any presupposed purpose, as was the case with the hypothetical imperatives. But it must not be overlooked that it cannot be shown by any example (i.e., it cannot be empirically shown) that there is such an imperative. Rather, it is to be suspected that all imperatives which appear to be categorical are tacitly hypothetical. For instance, when it is said, "Thou shalt not make a false promise," we assume that the necessity of this prohibition is not a mere counsel for the sake of escaping some other evil, so that it would read: "Thou shalt not make a false promise, lest, if it comes to light, thou ruinest thy credit." [In so doing] we assume that an action of this kind must be regarded as in itself bad and that the imperative prohibiting it is categorical, but we cannot show with certainty by any example that the will is here determined by the law alone without any other incentives, although it appears to be so. For it is always possible that secretly fear of disgrace, and perhaps also obscure apprehension of other dangers, may have had an influence on the will. Who can prove by experience the nonexistence of a cause when experience shows us only that we do not perceive the cause? In such a case the so-called moral imperative, which as such appears to be categorical and unconditional, would be actually only a pragmatic precept which makes us attentive to our own advantage and teaches us to consider it.

Thus we shall have to investigate purely a priori the possibility of a categorical imperative, for we do not have the advantage that experience would show us the reality of this imperative so that the [demonstration of its] possibility would be necessary only for its explanation, and not for its establishment. In the meantime, this much at least may be seen: the categorical imperative alone can be taken as a practical *law,* while all other imperatives may be called principles of the will but not laws. This is because what is necessary merely for the attainment of some chosen end can be regarded as itself contingent and we get rid of the precept once we give up the end in view, whereas the unconditional command leaves the will no freedom to choose the opposite. Thus it alone implies the necessity which we require of a law.

Secondly, in the case of the categorical imperative or law of morality, the cause of the difficulty in discerning its possibility is very weighty. This imperative is an a priori synthetical practical proposition* and since to discern the possibility of propositions of this sort is so difficult in theoretical knowledge it may well be gathered that it will be no less difficult in practical knowledge.

In attacking this problem, we will first inquire whether the mere concept of a categorical imperative does not also furnish the formula containing the proposition which alone can be a categorical imperative. For even when we know the formula of the imperative, to learn how such an absolute command is possible will require difficult and special labors which we shall postpone to the last Section.

If I think of a hypothetical imperative as such, I do not know what it will contain until the condition is stated [under which it is an imperative]. But if I think of a categorical imperative, I know immediately what it will contain. For since the imperative contains, besides the law, only the necessity of the maxim** of acting in accordance with the law, while the law contains no condition to which it is restricted, nothing remains except the universality of law as such to which the maxim of the action should conform; and this conformity alone is what is represented as necessary by the imperative.

---

*I connect a priori, and hence necessarily, the action with the will without supposing as a condition that there is any inclination [to the action] (though I do so only objectively, i.e., under the Idea of a reason which would have complete power over all subjective motives). This is, therefore, a practical proposition which does not analytically derive the willing of an action from some other volition already presupposed (for we do not have such a perfect will); it rather connects it directly with the concept of the will of a rational being as something which is not contained within it.

**A maxim is the subjective principle of acting and must be distinguished from the objective principle (i.e., the practical law). The former contains the practical rule which reason determines according to the conditions of the subject (often his ignorance or inclinations) and is thus the principle according to which the subject acts. The law, on the other hand, is the objective principle valid for every rational being, and the principle by which it ought to act, i.e., an imperative.

There is, therefore, only one categorical imperative. It is: Act only according to that maxim by which you can at the same time will that it should become a universal law.

Now if all imperatives of duty can be derived from this one imperative as a principle, we can at least show what we understand by the concept of duty and what it means, even though it remain undecided whether that which is called duty is an empty concept or not.

The universality of law according to which effects are produced constitutes what is properly called nature in the most general sense (as to form) (i.e., the existence of things so far as it is determined by universal laws). [By analogy], then, the universal imperative of duty can be expressed as follows: Act as though the maxim of your action were by your will to become a universal law of nature.

We shall now enumerate some duties, adopting the usual division of them into duties to ourselves and to others and into perfect and imperfect duties.*

1. A man who is reduced to despair by a series of evils feels a weariness with life but is still in possession of his reason sufficiently to ask whether it would not be contrary to his duty to himself to take his own life. Now he asks whether the maxim of his action could become a universal law of nature. His maxim, however is: For love of myself, I make it my principle to shorten my life when by a longer duration it threatens more evil than satisfaction. But it is questionable whether this principle of self-love could become a universal law of nature. One immediately sees a contradiction in a system of nature whose law would be to destroy life by the feeling whose special office is to impel the improvement of life. In this case it would not exist as nature; hence that maxim cannot obtain as a law of nature, and thus it wholly contradicts the supreme principle of all duty.

2. Another man finds himself forced by need to borrow money. He well knows that he will not be able to repay it, but he also sees that nothing will be lent him if he does not firmly promise to repay it at a certain time. He desires to make such a promise, but he has enough conscience to ask himself whether it is not improper and opposed to duty to relieve his distress in such a way. Now, assuming he does decide to do so, the maxim of his action would be as follows: When I believe myself to be in need of money, I will borrow money and promise to repay it, although I know I shall never be able to do so. Now this principle of self-love or of his own benefit may very well be compatible with his whole future welfare, but the question is whether it is right. He changes the pretension of self-love into a universal law and then puts the question: How would it be if my maxim became a universal law? He immediately sees that it could never hold as a universal law of nature and be consistent with itself; rather it must necessarily contradict itself. For the universality of a law which says that anyone who believes himself to be in need could promise what he pleased with the intention of not fulfilling it would make the promise itself and the end to be accomplished by it impossible; no one would believe what was promised to him but would only laugh at any such assertion as vain pretense.

3. A third finds in himself a talent which could, by means of some cultivation, make him in many respects a useful man. But he finds himself in comfortable circum-

*It must be noted here that I reserve the division of duties for a future *Metaphysics of Morals* and that the division here stands as only an arbitrary one (chosen in order to arrange my examples). For the rest, by a perfect duty I here understand a duty which permits no exception in the interest of inclination; thus I have not merely outer but also inner perfect duties. This runs contrary to the usage adopted in the schools, but I am not disposed to defend it here because it is all one to my purpose whether this is conceded or not.

stances and prefers indulgence in pleasure to troubling himself with broadening and improving his fortunate natural gifts. Now, however, let him ask whether his maxim of neglecting his gifts, besides agreeing with his propensity to idle amusement, agrees also with what is called duty. He sees that a system of nature could indeed exist in accordance with such a law, even though man (like the inhabitants of the South Sea Islands) should let his talents rust and resolve to devote his life merely to idleness, indulgence, and propagation—in a word, to pleasure. But he cannot possibly will that this should become a universal law of nature or that it should be implanted in us by a natural instinct. For, as a rational being, he necessarily wills that all his faculties should be developed, inasmuch as they are given him and serve him for all sorts of purposes.

4. A fourth man, for whom things are going well, sees that others (whom he could help) have to struggle with great hardships, and he asks, "What concern of mine is it? Let each one be as happy as heaven wills, or as he can make himself; I will not take anything from him or even envy him; but to his welfare or to his assistance in time of need I have no desire to contribute." If such a way of thinking were a universal law of nature, certainly the human race could exist, and without doubt even better than in a state where everyone talks of sympathy and good will or even exerts himself occasionally to practice them while, on the other hand, he cheats when he can and betrays or otherwise violates the right of man. Now although it is possible that a universal law of nature according to that maxim could exist, it is nevertheless impossible to will that such a principle should hold everywhere as a law of nature. For a will which resolved this would conflict with itself, since instances can often arise in which he would need the love and sympathy of others, and in which he would have robbed himself, by such a law of nature springing from his own will, of all hope of the aid he desires.

The foregoing are a few of the many actual duties, or at least of duties we hold to be actual, whose derivation from the one stated principle is clear. We must be able to will that a maxim of our action become a universal law; this is the canon of the moral estimation of our action generally. Some actions are of such a nature that their maxim cannot even be *thought* as a universal law of nature without contradiction, far from it being possible that one could will that it should be such. In others this internal impossibility is not found, though it is still impossible to *will* that that maxim should be raised to the universality of a law of nature, because such a will would contradict itself. We easily see that a maxim of the first kind conflicts with stricter or narrower (imprescriptable) duty, that of the latter with broader (meritorious) duty. Thus all duties, so far as the kind of obligation (not the object of their action) is concerned, have been completely exhibited by these examples in their dependence upon the same principle.

When we observe ourselves in any transgression of a duty, we find that we do not actually will that our maxim should become a universal law. That is impossible for us; rather, the contrary of this maxim should remain as a law generally, and we only take the liberty of making an exception to it for ourselves or for the sake of our inclination, and for this one occasion. Consequently, if we weighed everything from one and the same standpoint, namely, reason, we would come upon a contradiction in our own will, viz., that a certain principle is objectively necessary as a universal law and yet subjectively does not hold universally but rather admits exceptions. However, since we regard our action at one time from the point of view of a will wholly conformable to reason and then from that of a will affected by inclinations, there is actually no contradiction, but rather an opposition of inclination to the precept of reason *(antagonismus)*. In this the universality of the principle *(universalitas)* is changed into mere generality *(generalitas)*, whereby the practical principle of reason meets the maxim halfway. Although this cannot be justified in our own impartial judgment, it does show that we actually acknowledge the validity of the categorical imperative and allow ourselves (with all respect to it) only a few exceptions which seem to us to be unimportant and forced upon us.

We have thus at least established that if duty is a concept which is to have significance and actual law-giving authority for our actions, it can be expressed only in categorical imperatives and not at all in hypothetical ones. For every application of it we have also clearly exhibited the content of the categorical imperative which must contain the principle of all duty (if there is such). This is itself very much. But we are not yet advanced far enough to prove a priori that that kind of imperative really exists, that there is a practical law which of itself commands absolutely and without any incentives, and that obedience to this law is duty.

With a view to attaining this, it is extremely important to remember that we must not let ourselves think that the reality of this principle can be derived from the particular constitution of human nature. For duty is practical unconditional necessity of action; it must, therefore, hold for all rational beings (to which alone an imperative can apply), and only for that reason can it be a law for all human wills. Whatever is derived from the particular natural situation of man as such, or from certain feelings and propensities, or even from a particular tendency of the human reason which might not hold necessarily for the will of every rational being (if such a tendency is possible), can give a maxim valid for us but not a law; that is, it can give a subjective principle by which we might act if only we have the propensity and inclination, but not an objective principle by which we would be directed to act even if all our propensity, inclination, and natural tendency were opposed to it. This is so far the case that the sublimity and intrinsic worth of the command is the better shown in a duty the fewer subjective causes there are for it and the more they are against it; the latter do not weaken the constraint of the law or diminish its validity.

Here we see philosophy brought to what is, in fact, a precarious position, which should be made fast even though it is supported by nothing in either heaven or earth. Here philosophy must show its purity, as the absolute sustainer of its laws, and not as the herald of laws which an implanted sense or who knows what tutelary nature whispers to it. Those may be better than nothing at all, but they can never afford fundamental principles, which reason alone dictates. These fundamental principles must originate entirely a priori and thereby obtain their commanding authority; they can expect nothing from the inclination of men but everything from the supremacy of the law and due respect for it. Otherwise they condemn man to self-contempt and inner abhorrence.

Thus everything empirical is not only wholly unworthy to be an ingredient in the principle of morality but is even highly prejudicial to the purity of moral practices themselves. For, in morals, the proper and inestimable worth of an absolutely good will consists precisely in the freedom of the principle of action from all influences from contingent grounds which only experience can furnish. We cannot too much or too often warn against the lax or even base manner of thought which seeks its principles among empirical motives and laws, for human reason in its weariness is glad to rest on this pillow. In a dream of sweet illusions (in which it embraces not Juno but a cloud), it substitutes for morality a bastard patched up from limbs of very different parentage, which looks like anything one wishes to see in it, but not like virtue to anyone who has ever beheld her in her true form.*

---

*To behold virtue in her proper form is nothing else than to exhibit morality stripped of all admixture of sensuous things and of every spurious adornment of reward or self-love. How much she then eclipses everything which appears charming to the senses can easily be seen by everyone with the least effort of his reason, if it be not spoiled for all abstraction.

The question then is: Is it a necessary law for all rational beings that they should always judge their actions by such maxims as they themselves could will to serve as universal laws? If there is such a law, it must be connected wholly a priori with the concept of the will of a rational being as such. But in order to discover this connection, we must, however reluctantly, take a step into metaphysics, although in a region of it different from speculative philosophy, namely into the metaphysics of morals. In a practical philosophy it is not a question of assuming grounds for what happens but of assuming laws of what ought to happen even though it may never happen (that is to say, we assume objective practical laws). Hence in practical philosophy we need not inquire into the reasons why something pleases or displeases, how the pleasure of mere feeling differs from taste, and whether this is distinct from a general satisfaction of reason. Nor need we ask on what the feeling of pleasure or displeasure rests, how desires and inclinations arise, and how, finally, maxims arise from desires and inclination under the co-operation of reason. For all these matters belong to empirical psychology, which would be the second part of physics if we consider it as philosophy of nature so far as it rests on empirical laws. But here it is a question of objectively practical laws and thus of the relation of a will to itself so far as it determines itself only by reason, for everything which has a relation to the empirical automatically falls away, because if reason of itself alone determines conduct, it must necessarily do so a priori. The possibility of reason's thus determining conduct must now be investigated.

The will is thought of as a faculty of determining itself to action in accordance with the conception of certain laws. Such a faculty can be found only in rational beings. That which serves the will as the objective ground of its self-determination is a purpose, and if it is given by reason alone it must hold alike for all rational beings. On the other hand, that which contains the ground of the possibility of the action, whose result is an end, is called the means. The subjective ground of desire is the incentive *(Triebfeder)* while the objective ground of volition is the motive *(Bewegungsgrund)*. Thus arises the distinction between subjective purposes, which rest on incentives, and objective purposes, which depend on motives valid for every rational being. Practical principles are formal when they disregard all subjective purposes; they are material when they have subjective purposes and thus certain incentives as their basis. The purposes that a rational being holds before himself by choice as consequences of his action are material purposes and are without exception only relative, for only their relation to a particularly constituted faculty of desire in the subject gives them their worth. And this worth cannot afford any universal principles for all rational beings or any principles valid and necessary for every volition. That is, they cannot give rise to any practical laws. All these relative purposes, therefore, are grounds for hypothetical imperatives only.

But suppose that there were something the existence of which in itself had absolute worth, something which, as an end in itself, could be a ground of definite laws. In it and only in it could lie the ground of a possible categorical imperative (i.e., of a practical law).

Now, I say, man and, in general, every rational being exists as an end in himself and not merely as a means to be arbitrarily used by this or that will. In all his actions, whether they are directed toward himself or toward other rational beings, he must always be regarded at the same time as an end. All objects of inclination have only conditional worth, for if the inclinations and needs founded on them did not exist, their object would be worthless. The inclinations themselves as the sources of needs, however, are so lacking in absolute worth that the universal wish of every rational being must be indeed to free himself completely from them. Therefore, the worth of any objects to be obtained by our actions is at times conditional. Beings whose existence does not depend on our will but on nature, if they are not rational beings, have only relative worth as means, and are therefore called "things"; rational beings, on the other hand, are designated "persons" because their nature indicates that they are ends in themselves (i.e., things which may not be used merely as means). Such a being is thus an object of respect, and as such restricts all [arbitrary] choice. Such beings are not merely subjective ends whose existence as a result of our action has a worth for us, but are objective ends (i.e., beings whose existence is an end in itself). Such an end is one in the place of which no other end, to which these beings should serve merely as means, can be put. Without them, nothing of absolute worth could be found, and if all worth is conditional and thus contingent, no supreme practical principle for reason could be found anywhere.

Thus if there is to be a supreme practical principle and a categorical imperative for the human will, it must be one that forms an objective principle of the will from the conception of that which is necessarily an end for everyone because it is an end in itself. Hence this objective principle can serve as a universal law. The ground of this principle is: rational nature exists as an end in itself. Man necessarily thinks of his own existence in this way, and thus far it is a subjective principle of human actions. Also every other rational being thinks of his existence on the same rational ground which holds also for myself;* thus it is at the same time an objective principle from which, as a supreme practical ground, it must be possible to derive all laws of the will. The practical imperative, therefore, is the following: Act so that you treat humanity, whether in your own person or in that of another, always as an end and never as a means only. Let us now see whether this can be achieved. To return to our previous examples:

First, according to the concept of necessary duty to oneself, he who contemplates suicide will ask himself whether his action can be consistent with the idea of humanity as an end in itself. If in order to escape from burdensome circumstances he destroys himself, he uses a person merely as a means to maintain a tolerable condition up to the end of life. Man, however, is not a thing, and thus not something to be used merely as a means; he must always be regarded in all his actions as an end in himself. Therefore I cannot dispose of man in my own person so as to mutilate, corrupt, or kill him. (It belongs to ethics proper to define more accurately this basic principle so as to avoid all misunderstanding, e.g., as to amputating limbs in order to preserve myself, or to exposing my life to danger in order to save it; I must therefore omit them here.)

Second, as concerns necessary or obligatory duties to others, he who intends a deceitful promise to others sees immediately that he intends to use another man merely as a means, without the latter at the same time containing the end in himself. For he whom I want to use for my own purposes by means of such a promise cannot possibly assent to my mode of acting against him and thus share in the purpose of this action. This conflict with the principle of other men is even clearer if we cite examples of attacks on their freedom and property, for then it is clear that he who violates the rights of men intends to make use of the person of others merely as means, without considering that, as rational beings, they must always be esteemed at the same time as ends (i.e., only as beings who must be able to embody in themselves the purpose of the very same action).**

Third, with regard to contingent (meritorious) duty to oneself, it is not sufficient that the action not conflict with humanity in our person as an end in itself; it must also harmonize with it. In humanity there are capacities for greater perfection which belong

---

*Here I present this proposition as a postulate, but in the last Section grounds for it will be found.

**Let it not be thought that the banal "what you do not wish to be done to you . . ." could here serve as guide or principle, for it is only derived from the principle and is restricted by various limitations. It cannot be a universal law, because it contains the ground neither of duties to one's self nor of the benevolent duties to others (for many a man would gladly consent that others should not benefit him, provided only that he might be excused from showing benevolence to them). Nor does it contain the ground of obligatory duties to another, for the criminal would argue on this ground against the judge who sentences him. And so on.

to the purpose of nature with respect to humanity in our own person, and to neglect these might perhaps be consistent with the preservation of humanity as an end in itself, but not with the furtherance of that end.

Fourth, with regard to meritorious duty to others, the natural purpose that all men have is their own happiness. Humanity might indeed exist if no one contributed to the happiness of others, provided he did not intentionally detract from it, but this harmony with humanity as an end in itself is only negative, not positive, if everyone does not also endeavor, as far as he can, to further the purposes of others. For the ends of any person, who is an end in himself, must as far as possible be also my ends, if that conception of an end in itself is to have its full effect on me.

This principle of humanity, and in general of every rational creature an end in itself, is the supreme limiting condition on the freedom of action of each man. It is not borrowed from experience, first, because of its universality, since it applies to all rational beings generally, and experience does not suffice to determine anything about them; and secondly, because in experience humanity is not thought of (subjectively) as the purpose of men (i.e., as an object which we of ourselves really make our purpose). Rather it is thought of as the objective end which ought to constitute the supreme limiting condition of all subjective ends whatever they may be. Thus this principle must arise from pure reason. Objectively the ground of all practical legislation lies (according to the first principle) in the rule and form of universality, which makes it capable of being a law (at least a natural law); subjectively it lies in the end. But the subject of all ends is every rational being as an end in itself (by the second principle); from this there follows the third practical principle of the will as the supreme condition of its harmony with universal practical reason, viz., the Idea of the will of every rational being as making universal law.

By this principle all maxims are rejected which are not consistent with the will's giving universal law. The will is not only subject to the law, but subject in such a way that it must be conceived also as itself prescribing the law, of which reason can hold itself to be the author; it is on this ground alone that the will is regarded as subject to the law.

By the very fact that the imperatives are thought of as categorical, either way of conceiving them—as imperatives demanding the lawfulness of actions, resembling the lawfulness of the natural order; or as imperatives of the universal prerogative of the purposes of rational beings as such—excludes from their sovereign authority all admixture of any interest as an incentive to obedience. But we have been *assuming* the imperatives to be categorical, for that was necessary if we wished to explain the concept of duty; that there are practical propositions which command categorically could not of itself be proved independently, just as little as it can be proved anywhere in this section. One thing, however could have been done: to indicate in the imperative itself, by some determination inherent in it, that in willing from duty the renunciation of all interest is the specific mark of the categorical imperative, distinguishing it from the hypothetical. And this is now done in the third formulation of the principle, viz., in the Idea of the will of every rational being as a will giving universal law. A will which is subject to laws can be bound to them by an interest, but a will giving the supreme law cannot possibly depend upon any interest, for such a dependent will would itself need still another law which would restrict the interest of its self-love to the condition that its [maxim] should be valid as a universal law.

Thus the principle of every human will as a will giving universal law in all its maxims* is very well adapted to being a categorical imperative, provided it is otherwise

---

*I may be excused from citing examples to elucidate this principle, for those that have already illustrated the categorical imperative and its formula can here serve the same purpose.

correct. Because of the Idea of giving universal law, it is based on no interest; and thus of all possible imperatives, it alone can be unconditional. Or, better, converting the proposition: if there is a categorical imperative (a law for the will of every rational being), it can command only that everything be done from the maxim of its will as one which could have as its object only itself considered as giving universal law. For only in this case are the practical principle and the imperative which the will obeys unconditional, because the will can have no interest as its foundation.

If now we look back upon all previous attempts which have ever been undertaken to discover the principle of morality, it is not to be wondered at that they all had to fail. Man was seen to be bound to laws by his duty, but it was not seen that he is subject to his own, but still universal, legislation, and that he is bound to act only in accordance with his own will, which is, however, designed by nature to be a will giving universal law. For if one thought of him as only subject to a law (whatever it may be), this necessarily implied some interest as a stimulus or compulsion to obedience because the law did not arise from his will. Rather, his will had to be constrained by something else to act in a certain way. By this strictly necessary consequence, however, all the labor of finding a supreme ground for duty was irrevocably lost, and one never arrived at duty but only at the necessity of acting from a certain interest. This might be his own interest or that of another, but in either case the imperative always had to be conditional, and could not at all serve as a moral command. The moral principle I will call the principle of *autonomy* of the will in contrast to all other principles which I accordingly count under *heteronomy*.

The concept of any rational being as a being that must regard itself as giving universal law through all the maxims of its will, so that it may judge itself and its actions from this standpoint, leads to a very fruitful concept, namely that of a *realm of ends*.

By *realm* I understand the systematic union of different rational beings through common laws. Because laws determine which ends have universal validity, if we abstract from personal differences of rational beings, and thus from all content of their private purposes, we can think of a whole of all ends in systematic connection, a whole of rational beings as ends in themselves as well as a whole of particular purposes which each may set for himself. This is a realm of ends, which is possible on the principles stated above. For all rational beings stand under the law that each of them should treat himself and all others never merely as means, but in every case at the same time as an end in himself. Thus there arises a systematic union of rational beings through common objective laws. This is a realm which may be called a realm of ends (certainly only an ideal) because what these laws have in view is just the relation of these beings to each other as ends and means.

A rational being belongs to the realm of ends as a member when he gives universal laws in it while also himself subject to these laws. He belongs to it as sovereign when, as legislating, he is subject to the will of no other. The rational being must regard himself always as legislative in a realm of ends possible through the freedom of the will whether he belongs to it as member or as sovereign. He cannot maintain his position as sovereign merely through the maxims of his will, but only when he is a completely independent being without need and with unlimited power adequate to his will.

Morality, therefore, consists in the relation of every action to the legislation through which alone a realm of ends is possible. This legislation must be found in every rational being. It must be able to arise from his will, whose principle then is to do no action according to any maxim which would be inconsistent with its being a universal law, and thus to act only so that the will through its maxims could regard itself at the same time as giving universal law. If the maxims do not by their nature already necessarily conform to this objective principle of rational beings as giving universal law, the necessity of acting according to that principle is called practical constraint, which is to say: duty. Duty pertains not to the sovereign of the realm of ends, but rather to each member and to each in the same degree.

The practical necessity of acting according to this principle (duty) does not rest at all on feelings, impulses, and inclinations; it rests solely on the relation of rational beings to one another, in which the will of a rational being must always be regarded as legislative, for otherwise it could not be thought of as an end in itself. Reason, therefore, relates every maxim of the will as giving universal laws to every other will and also to every action towards itself; it does not do so for the sake of any other practical motive or future advantage but rather from the Idea of the dignity of a rational being who obeys no law except one which he himself also gives.

In the realm of ends everything has either a *price* or a *dignity*. Whatever has a price can be replaced by something else as its equivalent; on the other hand, whatever is above all price and therefore admits of no equivalent, has dignity.

That which is related to general human inclinations and needs has a *market price*. That which, without presupposing any need, accords with a certain taste (i.e., with pleasure in the purposeless play of our faculties) has a *fancy price*. But that which constitutes the condition under which alone something can be an end in itself does not have mere relative worth *(price)* but an intrinsic worth *(dignity)*.

Morality is the condition under which alone a rational being can be an end in himself, because only through it is it possible to be a lawgiving member in the realm of ends. Thus morality, and humanity so far as it is capable of morality, alone have dignity. Skill and diligence in work have a market value; wit, lively imagination, and humor have a fancy price; but fidelity in promises and benevolence on principle (not benevolence from instinct) have intrinsic worth. Nature and likewise art contain nothing which could make up for their lack, for their worth consists not in the effects which flow from them nor in any advantage and utility which they procure; it consists only in mental dispositions, maxims of the will, which are ready to reveal themselves in this manner through actions even though success does not favor them. These actions need no recommendation from my subjective disposition or taste in order that they may be looked upon with immediate favor and satisfaction, nor do they have need of any direct propensity or feeling directed to them. They exhibit the will which performs them as the object of an immediate respect, since nothing but reason is required in order to impose them upon the will. The will is not to be cajoled into them, for this, in the case of duties, would be a contradiction. This esteem lets the worth of such a turn of mind be recognized as dignity and puts it infinitely beyond any price; with things of price it cannot in the least be brought into any competition or comparison without, as it were, violating its holiness.

And what is it that justifies the morally good disposition or virtue in making such lofty claims? It is nothing less than the participation it affords the rational being in giving universal laws. He is thus fitted to be a member in a possible realm of ends, to which his own nature already destined him. For, as an end in himself, he is destined to be a lawgiver in the realm of ends, free from all laws of nature and obedient only to those laws which he himself gives. Accordingly, his maxims can belong to a universal legislation to which he is at the same time subject. A thing has no worth other than that determined for it by the law. The lawgiving which determines all worth must therefore have a dignity (i.e., an unconditional and incomparable worth). For the esteem which a rational being must have for it, only the word "respect" is suitable. Autonomy is thus the basis of the dignity of both human nature and every rational nature.

The three aforementioned ways of presenting the principle of morality are fundamentally only so many formulas of the very same law, and each of them unites the others in itself. There is, nevertheless, a difference between them, but the difference is more subjectively than objectively practical, for the difference is intended to bring an Idea of reason closer to intuition (by means of a certain analogy) and thus nearer to feeling. All maxims have:

1. A form, which consists in universality, and in this respect the formula of the moral imperative requires that maxims be chosen as though they should hold as universal laws of nature.
2. A material (i.e., an end), and in this respect the formula says that the rational being, as by its nature an end and thus as an end in itself, must serve in every maxim as the condition restricting all merely relative and arbitrary ends.
3. A complete determination of all maxims by the formula that all maxims which stem from autonomous legislation ought to harmonize with a possible realm of ends as with a realm of nature.*

There is a progression here like that through the categories of the unity of the form of the will (its universality), the plurality of material (the objects, ends), to the all-comprehensiveness or totality of the system of ends. But it is better in moral valuation to follow the rigorous method and to make the universal formula of the categorical imperative the basis: Act according to the maxim which can at the same time make itself a universal law. But if one wishes to gain a hearing for the moral law, it is very useful to bring one and the same action under the three stated principles and thus, so far as possible, bring it nearer to intuition.

We can now end where we started, with the concept of an unconditionally good will. That will is absolutely good which cannot be bad, and thus it is a will whose maxim, when made universal law, can never conflict with itself. Thus this principle is also its supreme law: Always act according to that maxim whose universality as law you can at the same time will. This is the only condition under which a will can never come into conflict with itself, and such an imperative is categorical. Because the validity of the will as a universal law for possible actions has an analogy with the universal connection of the existence of things under universal laws, which is the formal element of nature in general, the categorical imperative can be expressed also as follows: Act on those maxims which can at the same time have themselves as universal laws of nature as their object. Such, then, is the formula of an absolutely good will.

Rational nature is distinguished from others in that it proposes an end to itself. This end would be the material of every good will. Since, however, in the Idea of an absolutely good will without the limiting condition that this or that end be achieved, we must abstract from every end to be actually effected (as any particular end would make each will only relatively good), we must conceive the end here not as one to be brought about, but as a self-existent end, and thus merely negatively, as that which must never be acted against and which consequently must never be valued merely as a means but in every volition also as an end. Now this end can never be other than the subject of all possible ends themselves, because this is at the same time the subject of a possible will which is absolutely good, for the latter cannot without contradiction be made secondary

---

*Teleology considers nature as a realm of ends; morals regards a possible realm of ends as a realm of nature. In the former the realm of ends is a theoretical Idea for the explanation of what actually is. In the latter it is a practical Idea for bringing about that which does not exist but which can become actual through our conduct and for making it conform with this Idea.

to any other object. The principle: Act with reference to every rational being (whether yourself or another) so that in your maxim it is an end in itself, is thus basically identical with the principle: Act by a maxim which involves its own universal validity for every rational being.

That in the use of means to any end I should restrict my maxim to the condition of its universal validity as a law for every subject is tantamount to saying that the subject of ends (i.e., the rational being itself) must be made the basis of all maxims of actions and thus be treated never as a mere means but as the supreme limiting condition in the use of all means (i.e., as at the same time an end).

It follows incontestably that every rational being must be able to regard himself as an end in himself with reference to all laws to which he may be subject whatever they may be, and thus see himself as giving universal laws. For it is just the fitness of his maxims to universal legislation that indicates that he is an end in himself. It also follows that his dignity (his prerogative) over all merely natural beings entails that he must take his maxims from the point of view that regards himself, and hence also every other rational being, as legislative. Rational beings are, on this account, called persons. In this way, a world of rational beings (*mundus intelligibilis*) is possible as a realm of ends, because of the legislation belonging to all persons as members. Consequently every rational being must act as if by his maxims he were at all times a legislative member of the universal realm of ends. The formal principle of these maxims is: So act as if your maxims should serve at the same time as universal law (for all rational beings).

A realm of ends is thus possible only by analogy with a realm of nature. The former is possible only by maxims (i.e., self-imposed rules), while the latter is possible by laws of efficient causes of things externally necessitated. Regardless of this difference, by analogy we call the natural whole a realm of nature so far as it is related to rational beings as its end; we do so even though the natural whole is looked upon as a machine. Such a realm of ends would actually be realized through maxims whose rule is prescribed to all rational beings by the categorical imperative, if they were universally obeyed. But a rational being, though he scrupulously follow this maxim, cannot for that reason expect every other rational being to be true to it, nor can he expect the realm of nature and its orderly design to harmonize with him as a fitting member of a realm of ends which is possible through himself. That is, he cannot count on its favoring his expectation of happiness. Still the law: Act according to the maxim of a member of a merely potential realm of ends who gives universal law, remains in full force because it commands categorically. And just in this lies the paradox that simply the dignity of humanity as rational nature without any end or advantage to be gained by it, and thus respect for a mere Idea, should serve as the inflexible precept of the will. [There is the further paradox that] the sublimity of the maxims and the worthiness of every rational subject to be a law-giving member in the realm of ends consist precisely in the independence of his maxims from all such incentives. Otherwise he would have to be viewed as subject to only the natural law of his needs. Although the realm of nature as well as that of ends would be thought of as united under a sovereign, so that the latter would no longer remain a mere Idea but would receive true reality, the realm of ends would undoubtedly gain a strong urge in its favor though its intrinsic worth would not be augmented. Regardless of this, even the one and only absolute legislator would still have to be conceived as judging the worth of rational beings only by the disinterested conduct which they prescribe to themselves merely from the Idea. The essence of things is not changed by their external relations, and without reference to these relations a man must be judged only by what constitutes his absolute worth, and this is true whoever his judge may be, even if it be the Supreme Being. Morality is thus the relation of actions to the autonomy of the will (i.e., to the possible giving of universal law by the maxims of the will). The action which can be compatible with the autonomy of the will is permitted; that which does not agree with it is prohibited. The will whose maxims are necessarily in harmony with the laws of autonomy is a holy will or an absolutely good will. The dependence of a will not absolutely good on the principle of autonomy (moral constraint) is *obligation*. Hence obligation cannot be predicated of a holy will. The objective necessity of an action from obligation is called *duty*.

From what has just been said, it can easily be explained how it happens that, although in the concept of duty we think of subjection to law, we do nevertheless at the same time ascribe a certain sublimity and dignity to the person who fulfills all his duties. For though there is no sublimity in him in so far as he is subject to the moral law, yet he is sublime in so far as he is the giver of the law and subject to it for this reason only. We have also shown above how neither fear of nor inclination to the law is the incentive which can give moral worth to action; only respect for it can do so. Our own will, so far as it would act only under the condition of a universal legislation rendered possible by its maxims—this will ideally possible for us—is the proper object of respect, and the dignity of humanity consists just in its capacity to give universal laws under the condition that it is itself subject to this same legislation.

The Autonomy of the Will as the Supreme Principle of Morality

Autonomy of the will is that property of it by which it is a law to itself independent of any property of the objects of its volition. Hence the principle of autonomy is: Never choose except in such a way that the maxims of the choice are comprehended as universal law in the same volition. That this practical rule is an imperative, that is, that the will of every rational being is necessarily bound to it as a condition, cannot be proved by a mere analysis of the concepts occurring in it, because it is a synthetical proposition. To prove it, we would have to go beyond the knowledge of objects to a critical examination of the subject (i.e., to a critique of pure practical reason), for this synthetical proposition which commands apodictically must be susceptible of being known a priori. This matter, however, does not belong in the present section. But that the principle of autonomy, which is now in question, is the sole principle of morals can be readily shown by mere analysis of the concepts of morality; for by this analysis we find that its principle must be a categorical imperative and that the imperative commands neither more nor less than this very autonomy.

The Heteronomy of the Will as the Source of All Spurious Principles of Morality

If the will seeks the law which is to determine it elsewhere than in the fitness of its maxims to be given as universal law, and if thus it goes outside and seeks the law in the property of any of its objects, heteronomy always results. For then the will does not give itself the law, but the object through its relation to the will gives the law to it. This relation, whether it rests on inclination or on conceptions of reason, admits of only hypothetical imperatives: I should do something for the reason that I will something else. The moral (categorical) imperative, on the other hand, says that I should act in this or that way even though I have not willed anything else. For example, the former says that I should not lie if I wish to keep my good name. The latter says that I should not lie even though it would not cause me the least injury. The latter, therefore, must disregard every object to such an extent that it has absolutely no influence on the will; it must so disregard it that practical reason (will) may not just minister to any interest not its own but rather show its commanding authority as the supreme legislation. Thus, for instance, I should seek to further the happiness of others, not as though its realization were of consequence to me (because of a direct inclination or some satisfaction related to it indirectly through reason); I should do so solely because the maxim which excludes it from my duty cannot be comprehended as a universal law in one and the same volition.

Classification of All Possible Principles
of Morality Following from the Assumed
Principle of Heteronomy

Here as everywhere in the pure use of reason so long as a critical examination of it is lacking, human reason tries all possible wrong ways before it succeeds in finding the one true way.

All principles which can be taken from this point of view are either empirical or rational. The former, drawn from the principles of happiness, are based on physical or moral feeling; the latter, drawn from the principle of perfection, are based either on the rational concept of perfection as a possible result or on the concept of an independent perfection (the will of God) as the determining ground of the will.

Empirical principles are not at all suited to serve as the basis of moral laws. For if the basis of the universality by which they should be valid for all rational beings without distinction (the unconditional practical necessity which is thereby imposed upon them) is derived from a particular tendency of human nature or the accidental circumstance in which it is found, that universality is lost. But the principle of one's own happiness is the most objectionable of the empirical principles. This is not merely because it is false and because experience contradicts the supposition that well-being is always proportional to good conduct, nor yet because this principle contributes nothing to the establishment of morality inasmuch as it is a very different thing to make a man happy from making him good, and to make him prudent and farsighted for his own advantage is far from making him virtuous. Rather, it is because this principle supports morality with incentives which undermine it and destroy all its sublimity, for it puts the motives to virtue and those to vice in the same class, teaching us only to make a better calculation while obliterating the specific difference between them. On the other hand, there is the alleged special sense,* the moral feeling. The appeal to it is superficial, since those who cannot think expect help from feeling, even with respect to that which concerns universal laws; they do so even though feelings naturally differ so infinitely in degree that they are incapable of furnishing a uniform standard of the good and bad, and also in spite of the fact that one cannot validly judge for others by means of one's own feeling. Nevertheless, the moral feeling is nearer to morality and its dignity, inasmuch as it pays virtue the honor of ascribing the satisfaction and esteem for her directly to morality, and does not, as it were, say to her face that it is not her beauty but only our advantage which attaches us to her.

Among the rational principles of morality, there is the ontological concept of perfection. It is empty, indefinite, and consequently useless for finding in the immeasurable

---

*I count the principle of moral feeling under that of happiness, because every empirical interest promises to contribute to our well-being by the agreeableness that a thing affords, either directly and without a view to future advantage or with a view to it. We must likewise, with Hutcheson, count the principle of sympathy with the happiness of others under the moral sense which he assumed.

field of possible reality the greatest possible sum which is suitable to us; and, in specifically distinguishing the reality which is here in question from all other reality, it inevitably tends to move in a circle and cannot avoid tacitly presupposing the morality which it ought to explain. Nevertheless, it is better than the theological concept, which derives morality from a most perfect divine will. It is better not merely because we cannot intuit the perfection of the divine will, having rather to derive it only from our own concepts of which morality itself is foremost, but also because if we do not so derive it (and to do so would involve a most flagrant circle in explanation), the only remaining concept of the divine will is made up of the attributes of desire for glory and dominion combined with the awful conceptions of might and vengeance, and any system of ethics based on them would be directly opposed to morality.

But if I had to choose between the concept of the moral sense and that of perfection in general (neither of which at any rate weakens morality, though neither is capable of serving as its foundation), I would decide for the latter, because it preserves the indefinite Idea of a will good in itself free from corruption until it can be more narrowly defined. It at least withdraws the decision on the question from the realm of sensibility and brings it to the court of pure reason, although it does not even there decide the question.

For the rest, I think I may be excused from a lengthy refutation of all these doctrines. It is so easy, and presumably so well understood even by those whose office requires them to decide for one of these theories (since their students would not tolerate suspension of judgment), that such a refutation would be superfluous. What interests us more, however, is to know that all these principles set up nothing other than heteronomy of the will as the first ground of morality, and thus they necessarily miss their goal.

In every case in which the object of the will must be assumed as prescribing the rule which is to determine the will, the rule is nothing else than heteronomy. The imperative in this case is conditional, stating that if or because one wills such and such an object, one ought to act thus or so. Therefore the imperative can never command morally, that is, categorically. The object may determine the will by means of inclination, as in the principle of one's own happiness, or by means of reason directed to objects of our possible volition in general, as in the principle of perfection; but the will in these cases never determines itself directly by the conception of the action itself but only by the incentive which the foreseen result of the action incites in the will—that is: I ought to do something because I will something else. And here still another law must be assumed in me as the basis for this imperative; it would be a law by which I would necessarily will that other thing; but this law would in its turn require an imperative to restrict this maxim. Since the conception of a result to be obtained by one's own powers incites in the will an impulse which depends upon the natural characteristic of the subject, either of his sensibility (inclination and taste) or understanding and reason; and since these faculties according to the particular constitution of their nature find satisfaction in exercising themselves on the result of the voluntary action, it follows that it would really be nature which would give the law [to the action]. This law, as a law of nature, would have to be known and proved by experience, and as in itself contingent it would be unfit to be an apodictical practical rule such as the moral rule must be. Such a law always represents heteronomy of the will: the will does not give itself the law, but an external impulse gives the law to the will according to nature of the subject which is susceptible to receive it.

The absolutely good will, the principle of which must be a categorical imperative, is thus undetermined with reference to any object. It contains only the form of volition in general, and this form is autonomy. That is, the capability of the maxims of every good will to make themselves universal laws is itself the sole law which the will of every rational being imposes on himself, and it does not need to support this by any incentive or interest.

How such a synthetical practical a priori proposition is possible and why it is necessary is a problem whose solution does not lie within the boundaries of the metaphysics of morals. Moreover, we have not here affirmed its truth, and even less professed to command a proof of it. We showed only through the development of the generally received concept of morals that autonomy of the will is unavoidably connected with it, or rather that it is its foundation. Whoever, therefore, holds morality to be something real and not a chimerical idea without truth must also concede its principle which has been derived here. Consequently, this section, like the first, was merely analytical. To prove that morality is not a mere phantom of the mind—and if the categorical imperative, and with it the autonomy of the will, is true and absolutely necessary as an a priori proposition, it follows that it is no phantom—requires that a synthetical use of pure practical reason be possible. But we must not venture on this use without first making a critical examination of this faculty of reason. In the last section we shall give the principal features of such an examination that will be sufficient for our purpose.

THIRD SECTION

TRANSITION FROM THE METAPHYSICS OF MORALS
TO THE CRITICAL EXAMINATION OF PURE PRACTICAL REASON

*The Concept of Freedom Is the Key
to the Explanation of the Autonomy
of the Will*

As will is a kind of causality of living beings so far as they are rational, freedom would be that property of this causality by which it can be effective independent of foreign causes determining it, just as natural necessity is the property of the causality of all irrational beings by which they are determined to activity by the influence of foreign causes.

The preceding definition of freedom is negative and therefore affords no insight into its essence. But a positive concept of freedom flows from it which is so much the richer and more fruitful. Since the concept of a causality entails that of laws according to which something (i.e., the effect) must be established through something else which we call cause, it follows that freedom is by no means lawless even though it is not a property of the will according to laws of nature. Rather, it must be a causality of a peculiar kind according to immutable laws. Otherwise a free will would be an absurdity. Natural necessity is, as we have seen, a heteronomy of efficient causes, for every effect is possible only according to the law that something else determines the efficient cause to its causality. What else, then, can the freedom of the will be but autonomy (i.e., the property of the will to be law to itself)? The proposition that the will is a law to itself in all its actions, however, only expresses the principle that we should act according to no other maxim than that which can also have itself as a universal law for its object. And this is just the formula of the categorical imperative and the principle of morality. Therefore a free will and a will under moral laws are identical.

Thus if freedom of the will is presupposed, morality together with its principle follows from it by the mere analysis of its concepts. But the principle: An absolutely good will is one whose maxim can always include itself as a universal law, is nevertheless a synthetical proposition. It is synthetical because by analysis of the concept of an absolutely good will that property of the maxim cannot be found in it. Such synthetical propositions, however, are made possible only by the fact that the two cognitions are connected with each other through their union with a third in which both are to be found. The positive concept of freedom furnishes this third cognition, which cannot be, as in the case of physical causes, the sensible world of nature, in the concept of which we find conjoined the concepts of something as cause in relation to something else as effect. We cannot yet show directly what this third cognition is to which freedom directs us and of which we have an a priori Idea, nor can we yet explain the deduction of the concept of freedom from pure practical reason, and therewith the possibility of a categorical imperative. For this, some further preparation is needed.

Freedom Must be Presupposed as the Property of the Will of All Rational Beings

It is not enough to ascribe freedom to our will, on whatever grounds, if we do not also have sufficient grounds for attributing it to all rational beings. For since morality serves as a law for us only as rational beings, it must hold for all rational beings, and since it must be derived exclusively from the property of freedom, freedom as a property of the will of all rational beings must be demonstrated. And it does not suffice to prove it from certain alleged experiences of human nature (which is indeed impossible, as it can be proved only a priori), but we must prove it as belonging universally to the activity of rational beings endowed with a will. Now I say that every being which cannot act otherwise than under the Idea of freedom is thereby really free in a practical respect. That is to say, all laws which are inseparably bound with freedom hold for it just as if its wills were proved free in itself by theoretical philosophy.* Now I affirm that we must necessarily grant that every rational being who has a will also has the Idea of freedom and that it acts only under this Idea. For in such a being we think of a reason which is practical (i.e., a reason which has causality with respect to its object). Now we cannot conceive of a reason which, in making its judgments, consciously responds to a bidding from the outside, for then the subject would attribute the determination of its power of judgment not to reason but to an impulse. Reason must regard itself as the author of its principles, independently of alien influences; consequently as practical reason or as the will of a rational being it must regard itself as free. That is to say, the will of a rational being can be a will of its own only under the Idea of freedom, and therefore from a practical point of view such a will must be ascribed to all rational beings.

Of the Interest Attaching to the Ideas of Morality

We have finally reduced the definite concept of morality to the Idea of freedom, but we could not prove freedom to be actual in ourselves and in human nature. We saw only that we must presuppose it if we would think of a being as rational and conscious

---

*I propose this argument as sufficient to our purpose: Freedom as an Idea is posited by all rational beings as the basis for their actions. I do so in order to avoid having to prove freedom also in its theoretical aspect. For even if the latter is left unproved, the laws which would obligate a being who was really free would hold for a being who cannot act except under the Idea of his own freedom. Thus we escape the onus which has been pressed on theory.

of its causality with respect to actions, that is, as endowed with a will; and so we find that on the very same grounds we must ascribe to each being endowed with reason and will the property of determining itself to action under the Idea of its freedom.

From presupposing this Idea [of freedom] there followed also the consciousness of a law of action: that the subjective principles of actions (i.e., maxims) must in every instance be so chosen that they can hold also as objective (i.e., universal) principles, and can thus serve as principles for our giving universal laws. But why should I, as a rational being, and why should all other beings endowed with reason, subject ourselves to this law? I will admit that no interest impels me to do so, for that would then give no categorical imperative. But I must nevertheless take an interest in it and see how it comes about, for this *ought* is properly a *would* that is valid for every rational being provided reason were practical for it without hindrance [i.e., exclusively determined its action]. For beings who, like ourselves, are affected by the senses as incentives different from reason, and who do not always do that which reason by itself alone would have done, that necessity of action is expressed as only an *ought*. The subjective necessity is thus distinguished from the objective.

It therefore seems that we have only presupposed the moral law, the principle of the autonomy of the will in the Idea of freedom, as if we could not prove its reality and objective necessity by itself. Even if that were so, we would still have gained something because we would at least have defined the genuine principle more accurately than had been done before; but with regard to its validity and the practical necessity of subjection to it, we would not have advanced a single step, for we could give no satisfactory answer to anyone who asked us why the universal validity of our maxim as a law had to be the restricting condition of our action. We could not tell on what is based the worth which we ascribe to actions of this kind—a worth so great that there can be no higher interest—nor could we tell how it happens that man believes that it is only through this that he feels his own personal worth, in contrast to which the worth of a pleasant or unpleasant state is to be regarded as nothing.

We do find sometimes that we can take an interest in a personal quality which involves no [personal] interest in any [external] condition, provided only that the [possession of] this quality makes us fit to participate in the [desired] condition in case reason were to effect the allotment of this condition. That is, being worthy of happiness, even without the motive of partaking in happiness, can interest of itself. But this judgment is in fact only the effect of the importance already ascribed to moral laws (if by the Idea of freedom we detach ourselves from every empirical interest). But that we ought so to detach ourselves from every empirical interest, to regard ourselves as free in acting and yet as subject to certain laws, in order to find a worth wholly in our person which would compensate for the loss of everything which could make our situation desirable—how this is possible and hence on what grounds the moral law obligates us still cannot be seen in this way.

We must openly confess that there is a kind of circle here from which it seems that there is no escape. We assume that we are free in the order of efficient causes so that we can conceive of ourselves as subject to moral laws in the order of ends. And then we think of ourselves subject to these laws because we have ascribed freedom of the will to ourselves. This is circular because freedom and self-legislation of the will are both autonomy and thus are reciprocal concepts, and for that reason one of them cannot be used to explain the other and to furnish a ground for it. At most they can be used for the logical purpose of bringing apparently different conceptions of the same object under a single concept (as we reduce different fractions of the same value to the lowest common terms).

One recourse, however, remains open to us, namely, to inquire whether we do not assume a different standpoint when we think of ourselves as causes a priori efficient through freedom from that which we occupy when we conceive of ourselves in the light of our actions as effects which we see before our eyes.

The following remark requires no subtle reflection, and we may suppose that even the commonest understanding can make it, though it does so, after its fashion, by an obscure discernment of judgment which it calls feeling: all conceptions, like those of the senses, which come to us without our choice enable us to know objects only as they affect us, while what they are in themselves remains unknown to us; therefore, as regards this kind of conception, even with the closest attention and clearness which understanding may ever bring to them we can attain only a knowledge of appearances and never a knowledge of things as they are in themselves. When this distinction is once made (perhaps merely because of a difference noticed between conceptions which are given to us from somewhere else and to which we are passive, and those which we produce from ourselves only and in which we show our own activity), it follows of itself that we must admit and assume behind the appearances something else which is not appearance, i.e., things as they are in themselves, although we must admit that we cannot approach them more closely and can never know what they are in themselves, since they can never be known by us except as they affect us. This must furnish a distinction, though a crude one, between a world of sense and a world of understanding. The former, by differences in our sensible faculties, can be very different to various observers, while the latter, which is its foundation, remains always the same. A man may not presume to know even himself as he really is by knowing himself through inner sensation. For since he does not, as it were, produce himself or derive his concept of himself a priori but only empirically, it is natural that he obtain his knowledge of himself through inner sense and consequently only through the appearance of his nature and the way in which his consciousness is affected. But beyond the characteristic of his own subject which is compounded of these mere appearances, he necessarily assumes something else as its basis, namely, his ego as it is in itself. Thus in respect to mere perception and receptivity to sensations he must count himself as belonging to the world of sense; but in respect to that which may be pure activity in himself (i.e., in respect to that which reaches consciousness directly and not by affecting the senses) he must reckon himself as belonging to the intellectual world. But he has no further knowledge of that world.

To such a conclusion the thinking man must come with respect to all things which may present themselves to him. Presumably it is to be met with in the commonest understanding which, as is well known, is very much inclined to expect behind the objects of the senses something else invisible and acting of itself. But common understanding soon spoils it by trying to make the invisible again sensible (i.e., to make it an object of intuition). Thus the common understanding becomes not in the least wiser.

Now man really finds in himself a faculty by which he distinguishes himself from all other things, even from himself so far as he is affected by objects. This faculty is reason. As a pure, spontaneous activity it is elevated even above understanding. For though the latter is also a spontaneous activity and does not, like sense, which is passive, merely contain representations which arise only when one is affected by things, it cannot produce by its activity any other concepts than those which serve to bring the sensible representations under rules and thereby to unite them in one consciousness. Without this use of sensibility it would think nothing at all; on the other hand, reason shows such a pure spontaneity in the case of Ideas that it far transcends anything that sensibility can give to consciousness, and shows its chief occupation in distinguishing the world of sense from the world of understanding, thereby prescribing limits to the understanding itself.

For this reason a rational being must regard itself *qua* intelligence (and not from the side of his lower faculties) as belonging to the world of understanding and not to that of the senses. Thus it has two standpoints from which it can consider itself and recognize the laws [governing] the employment of its powers and all its actions: first, as belonging to the world of sense, under the laws of nature (heteronomy), and, second, as belonging to the intelligible world under laws which, independent of nature, are not empirical but founded on reason alone.

As a rational being and thus as belonging to the intelligible world, man cannot think of the causality of his own will except under the Idea of freedom, for independence from the determining causes of the world of sense (an independence which reason must always ascribe to itself) is freedom. The concept of autonomy is inseparably connected with the Idea of freedom, and with the former there is inseparably bound the universal principle of morality, which is the ground in Idea of all actions of rational beings, just as natural law is the ground of all appearances.

We have now removed the suspicion which we raised that there might be a hidden circle in our reasoning from freedom to autonomy and from the latter to the moral law. This suspicion was that we laid down the Idea of freedom for the sake of the moral law in order later to derive the law from freedom, and that we were thus unable to give any basis for the law, presenting it only as a *petitio principii* [begging the question] which well-disposed minds might gladly allow us, but which we could never advance as a demonstrable proposition. But we now see that, if we think of ourselves as free, we transport ourselves into the intelligible world as members of it and know the autonomy of the will together with its consequence, morality; whereas if we think of ourselves as obligated, we consider ourselves as belonging both to the world of sense and at the same time to the intelligible world.

How Is a Categorical Imperative Possible?

The rational being counts himself, *qua* intelligence, as belonging to the intelligible world, and only as an efficient cause belonging to it does he call his causality will. On the other side, however, he is conscious of himself as a part of the world of sense in which his actions are found as mere appearances of that causality. But we do not discern how they are possible on the basis of that causality which we do not know; rather, those actions must be regarded as determined by other appearances, namely, desires and inclinations belonging to the world of sense. As a member of the intelligible world only, all my actions would completely accord with the principle of the autonomy of the pure will, and as a part only of the world of sense would they have to be assumed to conform wholly to the natural law of desires and inclinations and thus to the heteronomy of nature. (The former actions would rest on the supreme principle of morality, and the latter on that of happiness.) But since the intelligible world contains the ground of the world of sense and hence of its laws, the intelligible world is (and must be conceived as) directly legislative for my will, which belongs wholly to the intelligible world. Therefore I recognize myself *qua* intelligence as subject to the law of the world of understanding and to the autonomy of the will. That is, I recognize myself as subject to the law of reason which contains in the Idea of freedom the law of the intelligible world, while at the same time I must acknowledge that I am a being which belongs to the world of sense. Therefore I must regard the laws of the intelligible world as imperatives for me, and actions in accord with this principle as duties.

Thus categorical imperatives are possible because the Idea of freedom makes me a member of an intelligible world. Consequently, if I were a member of that world only, all my actions *would* always be in accordance with the autonomy of the will. But since I intuit myself at the same time as a member of the world of sense, my actions *ought* to conform to it, and this categorical "ought" presents a synthetic a priori proposition, since besides my will affected by my sensuous desires there is added the Idea of exactly the same will as pure, practical of itself, and belonging to the intelligible world, which according to reason contains the supreme condition of the sensuously affected will. It is similar to the manner in which concepts of the understanding, which of themselves mean nothing but lawful form in general, are added to the intuitions of the sensible world, thus rendering possible a priori synthetic propositions on which all knowledge of a system of nature rests.

The practical use of ordinary human reason confirms the correctness of this deduction. When we present examples of honesty of purpose, of steadfastness in following good maxims, and of sympathy and general benevolence even with great sacrifices of advantage and comfort, there is no man, not even the most malicious villain (provided he is otherwise accustomed to using his reason), who does not wish that he also might have these qualities, but because of his inclinations and impulses cannot bring this about, yet at the same time wishes to be free from such inclinations which are burdensome even to him. He thus proves that with a will free from all impulses of sensibility, he in thought transfers himself into an order of things altogether different from that of his desires in the field of sensibility. He cannot expect to obtain by that wish any gratification of desires or any state which would satisfy his actual or even imagined inclinations, for the Idea itself, which elicits this wish from him, would lose its preeminence if he had any such expectation. He imagines himself to be this better person when he transfers himself to the standpoint of a member of the intelligible world to which he is involuntarily impelled by the Idea of freedom (i.e., of independence from the determining causes in the world of sense); and from this standpoint he is conscious of a good will, which on his own confession constitutes the law for his bad will as a member of the world of sense. He acknowledges the authority of the law even while he transgresses it. The moral "ought" is therefore his own volition as a member of the intelligible world, and it is conceived by him as an "ought" only insofar as he regards himself at the same time as a member of the world of sense.

On the Extreme Boundary of All Practical Philosophy

In respect to their will, all men think of themselves as free. Hence arise all judgments of acts as being such as ought to have been done, although they were not done. But this freedom is not an empirical concept and cannot be such, for it continues to hold even though experience shows the contrary of the demands which are necessarily conceived to be consequences of the supposition of freedom. On the other hand it is equally necessary that everything that happens should be inexorably determined by natural laws, and this natural necessity is likewise no empirical concept because it implies the concept of necessity and thus of a priori knowledge. But this concept of a system of nature is confirmed by experience, and it is inevitably presupposed if experience, which is knowledge of the objects of the sense interconnected by universal laws, is to be possible. Therefore freedom is only an Idea of reason whose objective reality in itself is doubtful, while nature is a concept of the understanding which shows and must necessarily show its reality by examples of experience.

There now arises a dialectic of reason, since the freedom ascribed to the will seems to stand in contradiction to natural necessity. At this parting of the ways reason in its speculative aspect finds the path of natural necessity more well-beaten and usable than that of freedom, but in its practical aspect the path of freedom is the only one on which it is possible to make use of reason in our conduct. Hence it is as impossible for the subtlest philosophy as for the commonest reasoning to argue freedom away. Philosophy must therefore assume that no true contradiction will be found between freedom and natural necessity in the same human actions, for it cannot give up the concept of nature any more than that of freedom.

Hence if we should never be able to conceive how freedom is possible, at least this apparent contradiction must be convincingly eradicated. For if even the thought of freedom contradicted itself or nature, it would have to be surrendered in competition with natural necessity.

But it would be impossible to escape this contradiction if the subject, who seems to himself to be free, thought of himself in the same sense or in the same relationship when he calls himself free as when he assumes that in the same action he is subject to natural law. Therefore it is an inescapable task of speculative philosophy to show at least that its illusion of contradiction rests on the fact that we [do not] think of man in a different sense and relationship when we call him free from that in which we consider him as part of nature and subject to its laws. It must show not only that they can very well coexist but also that they must be thought of as necessarily united in one and the same subject; for otherwise no ground could be given as to why we should burden reason with an Idea which, though it may without contradiction be united with another that is sufficiently established, nevertheless involves us in a perplexity which sorely embarrasses reason in its theoretical use. This duty is imposed only on theoretical philosophy, so that it may clear the way for practical philosophy. Thus the philosopher has no choice as to whether he will remove the apparent contradiction or leave it untouched, for in the latter case the theory of it would be unoccupied land, into the possession of which the fatalist could rightly enter and drive all morality from its alleged property as occupying it without title.

Yet we cannot say here that we have reached the boundary of practical philosophy. For the settlement of the controversy does not belong to practical philosophy, as the latter only demands from theoretical reason that it put an end to the discord in which it entangles itself in theoretical questions, so that practical reason may have rest and security from outward attacks which could dispute it the ground on which it desires to erect its edifice.

The title to freedom of the will claimed by ordinary reason is based on the consciousness and the conceded presupposition of the independence of reason from merely subjectively determining causes which together constitute what belongs only to sensation and is included under the general name of sensibility. Man, who in this way regards himself as intelligence, puts himself in a different order of things and in a relationship to determining grounds of an altogether different kind when he thinks of himself as intelligence with a will and thus as endowed with causality, compared with that other order of things and that other set of determining grounds which become relevant when he perceives himself as a phenomenon in the world of sense (as he really is also) and submits his causality to external determination according to natural laws. Now he soon realizes that both can subsist together—indeed, that they must. For there is not the least contradiction between a thing in appearance (as belonging to the world of sense) being subject to certain laws from which, as a thing or being regarded as it is in itself, it is independent. That he must think of himself in this twofold manner rests, with regard to the first, on the consciousness of himself as an object affected through the senses, and, with regard to what is required by the second, on the consciousness of himself as intelligence (i.e., as independent of sensible impressions in the use of reason), and thus as belonging to the intelligible world.

This is why man claims to possess a will which does not make him accountable for what belongs only to his desires and inclinations, but thinks of actions which can be done only by disregarding all his desires and sensuous attractions as possible and indeed as necessary for him. The causality of these actions lies in him as an intelligence and in effects and actions in accordance with principles of an intelligible world, of which he knows only that reason alone, and indeed pure reason independent of sensibility, gives the law in it. Moreover, since it is only as intelligence that he is his proper self (as man he is only appearance of himself), he knows that those laws apply to him directly and categorically, so that that to which inclinations and impulses and hence the entire nature of the world of sense incite him cannot in the least impair the laws of his volition as an intelligence. He does not even hold himself responsible for these inclinations and impulses or attribute them to his proper self (i.e., his will), though he does impute to his will the indulgence which he may grant to them when he permits them to influence his maxims to the detriment of the rational laws of his will.

When practical reason thinks itself into an intelligible world, it does in no way transcend its boundaries. It would do so, however, if it tried to intuit or feel itself into it. The intelligible world is only a negative thought with respect to the world of sense, which does not give reason any laws for determining the will. It is positive only in the single point that freedom as negative determination is at the same time connected with a positive power and even a causality of reason. This causality we call a will to act so that the principle of actions will accord with the essential characteristic of a rational cause (i.e., with the condition of universal validity of a maxim as law). But if it were to borrow an object of the will (i.e., a motive) from the intelligible world, it would overstep its boundaries and pretend to be acquainted with something of which it knows nothing. The concept of a world of understanding is therefore only a standpoint from which reason sees itself forced to take outside appearances, in order to think of itself as practical. If the influences of sensibility were determining for man, this would not be possible; but it is necessary unless he is to be denied the consciousness of himself as an intelligence, and thus as a rational and rationally active cause (i.e., a cause acting in freedom). This thought certainly implies the Idea of an order and legislation different from that of natural mechanism, which applies to the world of sense; and it makes necessary the concept of an intelligible world, the whole of rational beings as things regarded as they are in themselves. But it does not give us the least occasion to think of it otherwise than according to its formal condition only (i.e., the universality of the maxim of the will as law and thus the autonomy of the will), which alone is consistent with freedom. All laws, on the other hand, which are directed to an object make for heteronomy, which belongs only to natural laws and which can apply only to the world of sense.

But reason would overstep its bounds if it undertook to explain how pure reason can be practical, which is the same problem as explaining how freedom is possible.

We can explain nothing but what we can reduce to laws whose object can be given in some possible experience. But freedom is only an Idea, the objective reality which can in no way be shown to accord with natural laws or to be in any possible experience. Since no example in accordance with any analogy can support it, it can never be comprehended or even imagined. It holds only as the necessary presupposition of reason in a being who believes himself conscious of a will (i.e., of a faculty different from the mere faculty of desire, or a faculty of determining himself to act as an intelligence and thus according to laws of reason independently of natural instincts. But where determination according to natural laws comes to an end, there too all explanation ceases, and nothing remains but defense (i.e., refutation of the objections from those who pretend to have seen more deeply into the essence of things and who boldly declare freedom to be impossible). We can show them only that the supposed contradiction they have discovered lies nowhere else than in their necessarily regarding man [only] as appearance in order to make natural law valid with respect to human actions, and now when we require them to think of man *qua* intelligence as a thing regarded as it is in itself, they still persist in considering him as appearance [only]. Obviously, then, the detachment of his causality (his will) from all natural laws of the world of sense in one and the same subject is a contradiction, but this disappears when they reconsider and confess, as is reasonable, that behind the appearances things regarded as they are in themselves must stand as their hidden ground, and that we cannot expect the laws of the activity of these grounds to be the same as those under which their appearances stand.

The subjective impossibility of explaining the freedom of the will is the same as the impossibility of discovering and explaining an interest* which man can take in moral laws. Nevertheless, he does actually take an interest in them, and the foundation of this interest in us we will call the moral feeling. This moral feeling has been erroneously construed by some as the standard for our moral judgment, whereas it must be regarded rather as the subjective effect which the law has upon the will to which reason alone gives objective grounds.

In order to will an action which reason alone prescribes to the sensuously affected rational being as the action which he ought to will, there is certainly required a power of will to instill a feeling of pleasure of satisfaction in the fulfilment of duty, and hence there must be a causality of reason to determine sensibility in accordance with its own principles. But it is wholly impossible to discern, i.e., to make a priori conceivable, how a mere thought containing nothing sensuous is able to produce a sensation of pleasure or displeasure. For that is a particular kind of causality of which, as of all causality, we cannot determine anything a priori but must consult experience only. But since experience can exemplify the relation of cause to effect only as subsisting between two objects of experience, while here pure reason by mere Ideas (which furnish no object for experience) is to be the cause of an effect which does lie within experience, an explanation of how and why the universality of the maxim as law (and hence morality) interests us is completely impossible for us men. Only this much is certain: that it is valid for us not because it interests us (for that is heteronomy and dependence of practical reason on sensibility, i.e., on a basic feeling; and thus it could never be morally legislating); but that it interests us because it is valid for us as men, inasmuch as it has arisen from our will as intelligence and hence from our proper self; but what belongs to mere appearance is necessarily subordinated to the character of the thing regarded as it is in itself.

Thus the question *How is a categorical imperative possible?* can be answered to this extent: We can cite the only presupposition under which it is possible. This is the Idea of freedom, and we can have insight into the necessity of this presupposition which is sufficient to the practical use of reason (i.e., to the conviction of the validity of this imperative and hence also of the moral law). But how this presupposition itself is possible can never be discerned by any human reason. However, on the presupposition of freedom of the will as an intelligence, its autonomy as the formal condition under which

---

*Interest is that by which reason becomes practical (i.e., a cause determining the will). We therefore say only of a rational being that he takes an interest in something; irrational creatures feel only sensuous impulses. A direct interest in the action is taken by reason only if the universal validity of its maxim is a sufficient determining ground of the will. Only such an interest is pure. But if reason can determine the will only by means of another object of desire or under the presupposition of a particular feeling of the subject, reason takes merely an indirect interest in the action, and since reason for itself alone without experience can discover neither objects of the will nor a particular feeling which lies at its root, that indirect interest would be only empirical and not a pure interest of reason. The logical interest of reason in advancing its insights is never direct but rather presupposes purposes for which they are to be used.

alone it can be determined is a necessary consequence. To presuppose the freedom of the will is not only quite possible, as speculative philosophy itself can prove, for it does not involve itself in a contradiction with the principle of natural necessity in the inter-connection of appearances in the world of sense. But it is also unconditionally neces-sary that a rational being conscious of its causality through reason, and thus conscious of a will different from desires, should practically presuppose freedom (i.e., presuppose it in the Idea as the fundamental condition of all his voluntary acts). Yet how pure rea-son, without any other incentives whencesoever derived, can by itself be practical (i.e., how the simple principle of the universal validity of its maxims as laws—which would certainly be the form of a pure practical reason—without any material (object) of the will in which we might in advance take some interest), and can itself furnish an incen-tive and produce an interest which would be called purely moral; or, in other words, *how pure reason can be practical*—to explain this, all human reason is wholly incom-petent, and all the pain and work of seeking an explanation of it are wasted.

It is just the same as if I sought to find out how freedom itself as the causality of a will is possible, for in so doing I would leave the philosophical basis of explanation be-hind, and I have no other. Certainly I could revel in the intelligible world, the world of intelligences, which still remains to me; but although I have a well-founded Idea of it, still I do not have the least knowledge of it, nor can I ever attain knowledge of it by all the exertions of my natural faculty of reason. This intelligible world signifies only a something which remains when I have excluded from the determining grounds of my will everything belonging to the world of sense, in order to isolate the principle of mo-tives from the field of sensibility. I do so by limiting it and showing that it does not con-tain absolutely everything in itself but that outside it there is still more; but this more I do not know. After banishing all material (i.e., knowledge of objects) from pure reason which formulates this ideal, there remain to me only the form, the practical law of the universal validity of maxims, and, in accordance with this, reason in relation to a pure intelligible world as a possible efficient cause determining the will. Any incentive must here be totally absent unless this Idea of an intelligible world or that in which reason di-rectly takes an interest be the incentive. But to make this conceivable is precisely the problem we cannot solve.

Here, then, is the outermost boundary of all moral inquiry. To define it is very im-portant, both in order that reason may not seek around, on the one hand, in the world of sense, in a way harmful to morals, for the supreme motive and for a comprehensible but empirical interest; and so that it will not, on the other hand, impotently flap its wings in the space (for it, an empty space) of transcendent concepts which we call the intelligible world, without being able to move from its starting point and so losing itself amid phan-toms. Furthermore, the Idea of a pure intelligible world as a whole of all intelligences to which we ourselves belong as rational beings (though on the other side we are at the same time members of the world of sense) is always a useful and permissible Idea for the purpose of a rational faith. This is so even though all knowledge terminates at its boundary, for the glorious ideal of a universal realm of ends regarded as they are in themselves (rational beings) can awaken in us a lively interest in the moral law. To that realm we can belong as members only when we scrupulously conduct ourselves by maxims of freedom as if they were laws of nature.

Concluding Remark

The speculative use of reason with respect to nature leads to the absolute neces-sity of some supreme cause of the world. The practical use of reason with respect to freedom leads also to an absolute necessity, but to the necessity only of laws of actions of a rational being as such. Now it is an essential principle of all use of reason to push its knowledge to an awareness of its necessity, for otherwise it would not be rational knowledge. But it is also an equally essential restriction of this very same reason that it cannot discern the necessity of what is or of what occurs or of what ought to be done unless a condition under which it is or occurs or ought to be done is presupposed. In this way, however, the satisfaction of reason is only postponed further and further by the unceasing search for the condition. Reason, therefore, restlessly seeking the unconditionally necessary, sees itself compelled to assume it though it has no means by which to make it comprehensible; it is happy enough if it can discover only the concept which is compatible with this presupposition. It is, therefore, no objection to our deduction of the supreme principle of morality, but a reproach that we must make to human reason generally, that it cannot render comprehensible the absolute necessity of an unconditional practical law (such as the categorical imperative must be). Reason cannot be blamed for being unwilling to explain it by a condition (i.e., by making some interest its basis), for then the law would cease to be moral and would no longer be the supreme law of freedom. And so we do not indeed comprehend the unconditional practical necessity of the moral imperative; yet we do comprehend its incomprehensibility, which is all that can fairly be demanded of a philosophy which in its principles strives to reach the boundary of human reason.

NINETEENTH-CENTURY PHILOSOPHY

The nineteenth century has often been been described as the Age of Progress. The scientific discoveries of the seventeenth and eighteenth centuries led to numerous technological advances in Europe and America. These advances, in turn, made possible the Industrial Revolution and the incredible outpouring of goods it produced. Millions left the hard life of the farm, moving to cities and working in factories. In England, for example, in 1800 only twenty-one percent of the population lived in cities with a population more than ten thousand. By 1890, city-dwellers had become sixty-two percent of the population. Life in the city seemed full of promise, and the good life seemed within reach of all.

The early nineteenth-century philosophies of Hegel and Mill epitomized this optimism about the future. Hegel claimed that "Idea" (or "Spirit" or "Mind") was guiding all of history. Contradictions in thought and practice would be overcome as history progressed. For his part, Mill wrote in his major work, *Utilitarianism,* of the "progress of science [which] holds out a promise for the future." Mill argued that free individuals representing the "wisdom of society" could overcome the social problems of the nineteenth century.

Yet by the middle of the century doubts were beginning to emerge among some thinkers. Kierkegaard questioned the optimistic assumptions of Hegel and expressed skepticism about the inevitability of progress. More fundamentally, Kierkegaard claimed that Hegel's entire system was flawed, because it assumed an objectivity that is unavailable and a finality that does not exist within history. For his part, Marx noted the effect of the Industrial Revolution on the factory worker and called for a change in the social and economic order. Marx also raised questions about Hegel, focusing his attack on Hegel's concept of "Idea."

Towards the end of the century, Nietzsche added his voice to those of the skeptics about nineteenth-century progress. Nietzsche decried the lack of passion brought on by the comforts of the Industrial Revolution. He called on thinking persons to recognize that there are no standards, that "God is dead," and he wished them to assert their "will to power" in overcoming the comfortable mediocrity of his age.

Though Nietzsche died in 1900, the nineteenth century really did not come to an end, in terms of ideas, until 1914. In that year, all the impressive technology that had been developed over the previous century was brought to bear in the first world war with the goal of killing people. A system of alliances that had been established in the mid-nineteenth century on the basis of rational, pragmatic considerations ensured that virtually the entire world was involved in the struggle. By the time the war ended, the nineteenth-century optimistic assumption of progress had died.

*   *   *

There are a number of general introductions to nineteenth-century philosophy. Among the classics in this area are Étienne Gilson, *Recent Philosophy: Hegel to the Present* (New York: Random House, 1966); the appropriate works from Frederick Copleston's series, *A History of Philosophy: Volume VII, Fichte to Nietzsche; Volume VIII, Bentham to Russell;* and *Volume IX, Maine de Biran to Sartre* (New York: Image Doubleday, 1963, 1966, 1974); and from Emile Brehier's series, *The History of Philosophy: Volume 6, The Nineteenth Century: Period of Systems, 1800–1850; Volume 7, Contemporary Philosophy, Since 1850,* translated by Joseph Thomas (Chicago: University of Chicago Press, 1969); Karl Löwith, *From Hegel to Nietzsche: The Revolution in Nineteenth-Century Thought,* translated by David E. Green (1964; reprinted New York: Columbia University Press, 1991); and W.T. Jones, *Kant and the Nineteenth Century* 2nd edition, revised (New York: Harcourt, Brace & World, 1975). More recent general surveys include Roger Scruton, *A Short History of Modern Philosophy: From Descartes to Wittgenstein* (London: Routledge, 1984); and Wallace I. Matson, *A New History of Philosophy: Volume II, Modern* (San Diego, CA: Harcourt Brace Jovanovich, 1987). The following is a sampling of the many books on specific topics from this era: William Barrett, *Irrational Man* (New York: Doubleday. 1958); David Knight, *The Age of Science: The Scientific World-View in the Nineteenth Century* (Oxford: Blackwell, 1986); Robert C. Solomon, *Hegel to Existentialism* (Oxford: Oxford University Press, 1987); David Jasper and T.R. Wright, eds., *The Critical Spirit and the Will to Believe: Essays in Nineteenth-Century Literature and Religion* (London: Macmillan, 1989); Mary Ellen Waithe, *A History of Women Philosophers: Volume III, Modern Women Philosophers, 1600–1900* (Dordrecht, Netherlands: Kluwer Academic, 1991); and Mark Francis and John Morrow, *A History of English Political Thought in the Nineteenth Century* (London: Duckworth, 1994).

G.W.F. HEGEL
1770–1831

Georg Wilhelm Friedrich Hegel was born in Stuttgart, in southern Germany. Hegel and his father, a minor government official, his mother, a loving *Haus Frau* (housewife), and his sister and brother were all close, affectionate, and loving. It is easy to see why Hegel would later describe the family as the "immediate Ethical Substance." Following grade school in Stuttgart, at age eighteen, Hegel won a scholarship to Tübingen University, where he studied theology. While there, he met and befriended the poet Hölderlin and the philosopher Schelling. The work Hegel submitted to his professors at the university gave no indication of the brilliant philosophical career that was to follow. In fact, his diploma from the university recorded that his knowledge of theology was fair, but his knowledge of philosophy was inadequate. Nevertheless Hegel was already beginning to write insightful essays, not for classroom assignments, but to clarify his own thoughts.

After graduating from the university in 1793, Hegel spent seven years as a tutor for wealthy families in Bern and Frankfurt. During this time he continued to write essays—mostly on religious topics—that indicated he had moved far away from orthodox Christianity. For example, one early essay compared Jesus and Socrates, and Socrates' ethical teaching was seen as superior.

Following his father's death in 1799, Hegel inherited a modest sum of money, quit tutoring, and joined his friend Schelling at the University of Jena. There Hegel became a *Privatdozent* (an unsalaried lecturer) and coedited a philosophic journal with Schelling. While at Jena, Hegel wrote his first great work, *The Phenomenology of Spirit* (1807), which laid out the major themes of his philosophy. This work included a critique of Schelling's ideas, ending the friendship. Before this important work could be published, Napoleon's war with Prussia closed the

University of Jena, and so Hegel, whose inheritance had now been exhausted, was forced to find other employment.

After a stint as a newspaper editor, Hegel served eight years in Nürnberg as the rector of a *Gymnasium* (high school). There he published his second major work, *Science of Logic* (1812–1816). He also met and married a young woman from a distinguished family who was half his age, and they had two sons. In 1816, Hegel accepted a chair of philosophy at the University of Heidelberg. He continued his practice of producing a major book at each place he worked by publishing the *Encyclopedia of the Philosophical Sciences in Outline* in 1817. In 1818, Hegel moved to his final institution, the University of Berlin. There he published his *Philosophy of Right* (1821)—and became famous throughout Europe. He remained in Berlin until his death from cholera in 1831.

Following his death, a group of his friends published an eighteen-volume collection of his works, including his early essays and his lectures on aesthetics, the history of philosophy, the philosophy of history (portions of which are reprinted here), and the philosophy of religion.

*   *   *

Like all philosophers of his age, Hegel was greatly influenced by Kant. Kant had managed to synthesize two previously disparate realities—the rational world of ideas (emphasized by rationalists) with the phenomenal world of perception (emphasized by empiricists). But in so doing, Kant separated the noumenal world of "things-in-themselves" from the phenomenal world of experience and declared the noumenal world unknowable. In a sense he had reconciled two competing epistemologies—Continental Rationalism and British Empiricism—at the expense of abandoning metaphysics. Hegel sought to go one step further than Kant and effect a complete synthesis that would not only draw together competing epistemologies, but would also show the connection between epistemology and metaphysics. The key to this synthesis is the recognition that consciousness is the ultimate reality, or, to use his famous phrase, "What is real is rational—what is rational is real." That is, metaphysical reality (the real) *is* Idea or Spirit or Mind (that which knows). The resulting philosophy is called "Absolute Idealism" because all things that exist are essentially related to absolute Idea or Spirit or Mind.

According to Hegel, traditional rationalism (what he calls *raisonnement*) tends to classify all experience formally into abstract, lifeless universals. Taken to its logical extreme, rationalists end up with the abstraction "Being": "But this mere Being, as it is mere abstraction, is therefore the absolutely negative: which, in a similarly immediate aspect, is just NOTHING." By abstracting away the concreteness or particularity of actual experience, one is left with Being which is Nothing. The short article "Who Thinks Abstractly?" (1807–1808?), reprinted here in Walter Kaufmann's translation, clearly conveys Hegel's contempt for the process of abstraction.

Whereas Being and Nothing are both identical and yet contradictory, according to Hegel, "the truth of Being and Nothing is . . . the unity of the two: and this unity is BECOMING." The unity of Becoming does not obliterate Being and Nothing but holds both in tension in a higher truth. The two parts of the contradiction, together with that which unites or overcomes them, make up a triad. This method of overcoming contradictions by moving to a higher level of truth is known as the "dialectic." Hegel proposed to develop a complete dialectical System of reality based on the three foundational triads of "Being–Nothing–

Becoming," "Being–Essence–Notion," and "Idea–Nature–Spirit." Though he developed several proposals for this System, he never completed any of them. But he did use the dialectical method to explain consciousness.

In the section entitled "Relations of Master and Servant" from *The Phenomenology of Spirit* (1807), reprinted here in the J.L.H. Thomas translation, Hegel explains one stage in the dialectical development of consciousness. He begins by pointing out that only by acknowledging an "other" is self-consciousness possible. But if there is an other, then the original self-consciousness feels threatened and asserts its freedom by trying to dominate that other and force acknowledgment of its dominance. The ensuing struggle results in a master who dominates and a servant who is dominated. The master then forces the servant to produce material goods for the enjoyment of the master.

But at this point the master is now dependent upon the servant he has dominated. In the first place, his self-consciousness as master is subject to his recognition as master by the servant. But more important, while the master has been consuming or destroying what the servant makes, the servant has been learning to create—to bend nature to his will—and so has established his own self-consciousness in relation to what he has created. Furthermore, the labor of the servant has a permanent quality while the master's consumption is again dependent on the servant's production. So by dominating the servant, the master is dominated.

The solution to this contradiction is to acknowledge that neither master nor servant is free and that freedom is not possible in relationships of domination. The next stage in the dialectic is for the mind to seek freedom within itself.

This dialectical development of the consciousness of freedom can also be understood in relation to world history. As Hegel says in his "General Introduction" to the *Philosophy of History* (1832), presented here in the Robert S. Hartman translation, "the study of world history . . . represents the rationally necessary course of the World Spirit, the Spirit whose nature is indeed always one and the same, but whose one nature unfolds in the course of the world." In other words, the Absolute Spirit as manifested in history through human consciousness is the World Spirit *(Weltgeist),* and all of human history is a process whereby this World Spirit comes to self-consciousness of itself as free. To understand this development of Spirit, Hegel examines the three elements that structure historical movement: (1) the nature of Spirit, (2) its means of actualization, and (3) the shape of its perfect embodiment. This final embodiment of Spirit as freedom is found in the State. As Hegel explains each of these three elements, he makes it clear that the individual is unimportant: "In world history the 'individuals' that we have to deal with are peoples." In fact, the individual as an individual is outside of history entirely and only finds freedom and meaning within the unified self-consciousness of a people known as the State.

Hegel's ideas have been both lauded and attacked. His insights on the master-servant relationship made a powerful impression on Marx and Nietzsche. Indeed, Hegel's understanding of dialectical development became a central feature of Marx's thought—though Marx rejected the notion of Absolute Spirit. Phenomenology developed Hegel's insights about the different types of consciousness. The sociology of knowledge developed his notions about the connection between consciousness and the culture of a particular epoch. Chief among Hegel's critics was Kierkegaard, who objected strenuously to the devaluing of the individual, questioned the implicit optimism of the dialectic, and mocked the incompleteness of Hegel's "System." Perhaps Hegel's greatest legacy was not any specific idea, but the vision of a complete historical development of thought.

*   *   *

For a selection of primary source readings for Hegel, see *Hegel, The Essential Writings,* edited by Frederick G. Weiss (New York: Harper & Row, 1974). Many secondary books about Hegel are difficult for beginning students. Two accessible classics are W.T. Stace, *The Philosophy of Hegel* (1924; reprinted New York: Dover, 1955), and G.R.G. Mure, *An Introduction to Hegel* (Oxford: Clarendon Press, 1940). Recent helpful studies include J.N. Findlay, *Hegel: A Re-examination* (New York: Macmillan, 1958); Walter Kaufmann, *Hegel: Reinterpretation, Texts and Commentary* (Garden City, NY: Doubleday, 1965); and, especially, Peter Singer, *Hegel* (Oxford: Oxford University Press, 1983). Charles Taylor's massive *Hegel* (Cambridge: Cambridge University Press, 1975) can be consulted for particular topics. For specialized topics, see H.A. Reyburn, *Ethical Theory of Hegel* (Oxford: Oxford University Press, 1965); Ivan Soll, *An Introduction to Hegel's Metaphysics* (Chicago: University of Chicago Press, 1969); Walter Kaufmann, ed., *Hegel's Political Philosophy* (New York: Atherton Press, 1970); Quentin Lauer, *Hegel's Idea of Philosophy* (New York: Fordham University Press, 1971); Quentin Lauer, *A Reading of Hegel's "Phenomenology of Spirit"* (New York: Fordham University Press, 1976); Robert C. Solomon, *From Hegel to Existentialism* (New York: Oxford University Press, 1987); Michael N. Forster, *Hegel and Skepticism* (Cambridge, MA: Harvard University Press, 1989); and Merold Westphal, *History and Truth in Hegel's "Phenomenology"* (Atlantic Highlands, NJ: Humanities Press, 1990). Karl Marx, *Critique of Hegel's "Philosophy of Right,"* edited by Joseph O'Malley (Cambridge: Cambridge University Press, 1970), is both a critical review of Hegel's work and a major work in its own right. Michael Inwood, *A Hegel Dictionary* (Oxford: Basil Blackwell, 1992) provides a useful reference work. General collections of critical essays include W.E. Steinkraus, ed., *New Studies in Hegel's Philosophy* (New York: Holt, Rinehart and Winston, 1971); Alasdair MacIntyre, ed., *Hegel: A Collection of Critical Essays* (Notre Dame, IN: University of Notre Dame Press, 1972); Michael Inwood, ed., *Hegel* (Oxford: Oxford University Press, 1985); and Frederick C. Beiser, ed., *The Cambridge Companion to Hegel* (Cambridge: Cambridge University Press, 1993).

PHENOMENOLOGY OF SPIRIT (in part)

INDEPENDENCE AND DEPENDENCE OF SELF-CONSCIOUSNESS: RELATIONS OF MASTER AND SERVANT

Self-consciousness is *in* and *for itself* in and through being in and for itself for another self-consciousness; that is, it is only as something acknowledged, or recognized. The concept of this unity of self-consciousness in its duplication, of the infinitude realising

G.W.F. Hegel, *Phenomenology of Spirit,* B, IV, A: "Independence and Dependence of Self-Consciousness: Relations of Master and Servant," translated by J.L.H. Thomas. Reprinted from *Hegel: Selections,* edited by M.J. Inwood, *The Great Philosophers,* series, Paul Edwards, general editor (New York: Macmillan, 1989).

itself in self-consciousness, is a many-sided and many-sensed complex, so that the moments of this complex must both be held carefully apart, and at the same time taken and understood in this differentiation as not distinct, or always also in their opposed sense. The double-sensedness of what is distinguished lies in the essence of self-consciousness, of being infinite, or boundless, that is, immediately the contrary of the determination in which it is established. The laying-apart of the concept of this spiritual unity in its duplication presents to us the movement of *acknowledging*.

There is for self-consciousness another self-consciousness; it has come *outside itself*. This has a twofold significance: *first*, self-consciousness has lost itself, for it finds itself as *another* being; *second*, it has thereby done away with the other, for it does not see the other either as the essential being, but *it itself* in the *other.*

Self-consciousness must do away with this *otherness it* has; this is the doing away with of the first double-sense, and hence itself a second double-sense: *first*, it must set out to do away with *the other* independent being in order thereby to become certain of *itself* as the essential being; *second*, in so doing it sets out to do away with *itself*, for this other being is itself.

This double-sensed doing away with its double-sensed otherness is equally a double-sensed return *into itself;* for, *first*, through doing away it gets itself back, for it becomes once more equal to itself through doing away with *its* otherness; *second*, however, it no less gives back the other self-consciousness to the latter again, for it had itself in the other, it does away with this being *it* has in the other, thus letting the other go free again.

This movement of self-consciousness in its relation to another self-consciousness has been presented in this way now, as *the doing of the one;* but this doing of the one has itself the two-fold significance of being as much *its doing* as *the doing of the other;* for the other is no less independent, shut up within itself, and there is nothing in it that is not owing to itself. The first self-consciousness does not have the object before it as the latter to begin with is merely for desire, but an independent object existing for itself, over which therefore it has of itself no power, unless the object does with itself what self-consciousness does with it. The movement is thus in all respects the double movement of both self-consciousnesses. Each sees the *other one* do the same as it does; each does itself what it demands of the other, and so does what it does only inasmuch as the other does the same; a one-sided doing would be unavailing, because what it is intended should occur can come about only through both.

The doing is therefore double-sensed not only inasmuch as it is a doing as much *to itself* as *to the other,* but also inasmuch as it is undividedly as much the *doing of the one* as *of the other.*

In this movement we see the process repeat itself which presented itself as the play of forces, but in consciousness. What in the earlier process was for us, is here for the extremes themselves. The centre is self-consciousness, which puts itself apart into the extremes; and each extreme is this exchanging of its determination and absolute going over into the opposed extreme. But though, as consciousness, it does indeed come *out of itself,* yet it is in its being-out-of-itself at the same time held back within itself, is *for itself,* and its "outside-itself" is *for it.* It is for consciousness that it immediately *is* and *is not* another consciousness; and, equally, that this other is only for itself in doing away with itself as something being for itself, and only in the being-for-itself of the other is for itself. Each is to the other the centre through which each brings into relation and connects itself with itself, and each is to itself and to the other an immediate entity existing for itself, which at the same time is thus for itself only through this relating, or mediation. They *acknowledge* one another as *mutually acknowledging one other.*

This pure concept of acknowledgement, the duplication of self-consciousness in its unity, will now be studied in the way in which its process appears for self-consciousness. This process will first present the facet of the *inequality* of the two, or the coming out of the centre into the extremes, which, being extremes, are opposed to one another, the one acknowledged only, the other acknowledging only.

Self-consciousness is to begin with simple being-for-itself, equal-with-itself through the exclusion of everything *other from itself;* its essence and absolute object is to it "*I*"; and it is in this *immediacy,* or in this *being* of its being-for-itself, an *individual.* Whatever else there is for it, is as an inessential object, one marked with the character of the negative. But the other is also a self-consciousness: an individual comes on opposite an individual. Thus *immediately* coming on, they are for each other in the way of common objects: *independent* forms, consciousnesses immersed in the *existence* of *life*—for it is as life that the existent object has here determined itself—which have not yet carried out *for each other* the movement of absolute abstraction, of expunging all immediate existence and of being merely the purely negative existence of consciousness equal-with-itself, or which have not yet presented themselves to each other as pure *being-for-self,* that is, as *self*-consciousness. Each is indeed certain of itself, but not of the other, and consequently each's own certainty of itself has as yet no truth; for its truth could only be that its own being-for-itself had presented itself to it as an independent object or, what amounts to the same thing, that the object had presented itself as this pure certainty of itself. This, however, on the concept of acknowledgement is not possible, save that as the other does for the one, so the one does for the other, each with itself through its own activity, and again through the activity of the other, carrying out this pure abstraction of being-for-itself.

The *presentation* of oneself as the pure abstraction of self-consciousness, however, consists in showing oneself to be the pure negation of one's objective way of being, that is, in showing oneself not to be attached to a particular *concrete existence,* nor to the universal individuality of concrete existence in general, nor even to life. This presentation is a *double* doing: doing of the other, and doing through oneself. Inasmuch as it is the doing *of the other,* each then is set upon the death of the other. But in this there is present also the second doing, *the doing through oneself;* for the former contains within itself the staking of one's own life. The relation of the two self-consciousnesses is hence determined in such a way that through the combat for life and death they *prove* themselves and each other.—They must enter this combat, for they must raise the certainty of themselves, *of being for themselves,* to truth in the other and in themselves. And it is solely through the staking of life that freedom arises, that it is confirmed to self-consciousness that it is not *being,* not the *immediate* way in which it comes on, not its being immersed in the expanse of life which is its essence—but that there is nothing present in it which is not for it a vanishing moment, that it is just pure *being-for-itself.* The individual that has not risked life can indeed be acknowledged as a *person;* but it has not attained the truth of this state of acknowledgement as that of an independent self-consciousness. Likewise, each must as much aim at the death of the other as it stakes its own life; for the other means no more to it than it itself does; the individual's essence presents itself to it as another, it is outside itself, it must do away with its being-outside-itself; the other is a consciousness engaged and existing in manifold ways; it must view its otherness as pure being-for-self, or as absolute negation.

This proving through death does away, however, with the truth that was to result from it, just as much as it thereby also does away with the certainty of oneself altogether; for just as life was the *natural* position of consciousness, independence without absolute negativity, so death is the *natural* negation of consciousness, negation without

independence, which therefore remains without the required sense of acknowledgement. Through death the certainty has indeed arisen that both risked their life and despised it in themselves and in the other; though not for those who underwent this combat. They do away with their consciousness set in this alien essentiality that is natural
concrete existence, or they do away with themselves, and are done away with as the *extremes* which would be for themselves. There thereby vanishes, however, from the play
of exchange the essential moment of setting oneself apart into extremes of opposed determinations; and the centre collapses into a dead unity, which is set apart into dead,
merely existent, not opposed, extremes; and the two do not mutually give back and receive back themselves from each other through consciousness, but let each other free
merely indifferently, as things. Their deed is abstract negation, not the negation of consciousness, which *does away* in such a manner that it *puts by* and *preserves* what is done
away, and consequently survives its being-done-away.

In this experience self-consciousness comes to realise that life is as essential to it
as pure self-consciousness is. In immediate self-consciousness the simple "I" is the absolute object, which however, for us or in itself, is absolute mediation and has existent
independence as an essential moment. The dissolution of that simple unity is the result
of the first experience; through it there is established a pure self-consciousness, and a
consciousness which is not purely for itself, but is for another consciousness, that is, is
as *existent,* or is consciousness in the form of *thinghood.* Both moments are essential;—
but as they are to begin with unequal and opposed, and their reflexion into unity is not
yet a reality, they are as two opposed forms of consciousness: one, the independent consciousness, to which being-for-self is the essence; the other, the dependent consciousness, to which life or being for another is the essence: the former is the *master,* the latter the *servant.*

The master is the consciousness existing *for itself,* though no longer merely the
concept of the latter, but a consciousness existing for itself which is in mediate relation
with itself through *another* consciousness, namely through one to whose essence it pertains to be synthesised with independent *being* or thinghood in general. The master relates himself to both these moments, to a *thing* as such, the object of desire, and to the
consciousness to whom thinghood is what is essential; and since he (a), *qua* concept of
self-consciousness, is immediate relation of *being-for-himself,* but (b) now is also as
mediation, or as a being-for-self which is for itself only through another, so he relates
himself (a) immediately to both and (b) mediately to each through the other. The master
relates himself *to the servant mediately through independent being;* for it is precisely to
this that the servant is kept; it is his chain, from which in the combat he could not abstract, and consequently showed himself to be dependent, to have his independence in
thinghood. The master, however, is the power over the being in question, for he showed
in the combat that it meant merely something negative to him; since he is the power
over this being, while this being is the power over the other, the master thus has in this
conjunction the other under himself. Likewise the master relates himself *mediately
through the servant to the thing,* the servant relates himself, qua self-consciousness as
such, to the thing negatively also, and does away with it; but the thing is at the same
time independent for him, and hence he cannot through his negating dispose of it so far
as to destroy it, or he *works* it merely. The master on the other hand *gains* through this
mediation the *immediate* relation as the pure negation of the thing, or the *enjoyment;*
where desire did not succeed, he succeeds, namely in disposing of the thing and in satisfying himself in the enjoyment of it. Desire did not succeed in this on account of the
independence of the thing; the master, however, who has interposed the servant between the thing and himself, thereby connects himself only with the non-independence

of the thing, and enjoys it in its purity; the facet of independence, on the other hand, he leaves to the servant, who works it.

In these two moments the master has his acknowledgement, or recognition, by another consciousness granted him; for the other consciousness establishes itself in these moments as something inessential, first, in the working of the thing, second, in the dependence upon a particular existence; in both it cannot achieve mastery over being and attain absolute negation. There is therefore present here the following moment of recognition, that the other consciousness does away with itself as being-for-itself, and so itself does what the other does to it. Likewise the other moment is present, that this doing of the second consciousness is the first's own doing for what the servant does is really the doing of the master; to the latter, solely being-for-himself is the essence; he is the pure negative power to which the thing is nothing, and hence the pure essential doing in this situation; while the servant is not a pure doing, but an inessential one. But for true recognition there is lacking the moment that what the master does to the other he also does to himself, and what the servant does to himself he also does to the other. Thus there has arisen a one-sided and unequal recognizing.

The inessential consciousness is here for the master the object which constitutes the *truth* of the certainty of oneself. But it is evident that this object does not match its concept, and that there where the master has fulfilled himself, he has instead had something quite other than an independent consciousness come to be. It is not such a consciousness that is for him, but a dependent one rather; he is consequently not certain of *being-for-himself* as the truth, and his truth is rather the inessential consciousness, and the inessential doing of the latter.

The *truth* of independent consciousness is accordingly the servile or *subject consciousness*. The latter admittedly appears at first *outside* itself, and not as the truth of self-consciousness. But just as masterhood or dominion, showed that its essence is the converse of what it itself would be, so too, as we shall see, subjection will in its fulfillment turn rather into the contrary of what it is immediately; it will, *qua* consciousness *driven back* into itself, go into itself and turn about to true independence.

We have seen only what subjection is in the context of dominion. But the former is self-consciousness, and accordingly we shall now see what it is in and for itself. First of all, for subjection the master is the essence; hence the *independent consciousness existing for itself* is to subjection *the truth,* which however *for subjection* is not yet *in subjection.* But it has this truth of pure negativity and of *being-for-itself in the event in itself;* for subjection has *experienced* this essence within itself. This consciousness was, namely, not afraid for this or that, or for this instant or that, but for its whole being; for it has felt the fear of death, the absolute lord, or master. In this fear it has been internally broken up, it has been thoroughly shaken in itself, and everything fixed has trembled within it. This pure universal movement, the absolute becoming fluid of all that is permanent, is however the simple essence of self-consciousness, absolute negativity, *pure being-for-itself,* which is consequently *in* this consciousness. This moment of pure being-for-itself is also *for it,* for in the master it has it as its *object.* It is further not merely this universal dissolution *in general,* but in serving it *actually* brings it about; in serving it does away in all *particular* moments with its dependency on natural existence, and works that existence off.

But the feeling of absolute power, in general and in the particulars of service, is only the dissolution *in itself,* and although "the fear of the Lord is the beginning of wisdom," consciousness in this fear is *for its self,* not *being-for-itself.* Through work, however, it comes to itself. In the moment which corresponds to desire in the consciousness of the master, the facet of the inessential relation to the thing seemed to have fallen to the consciousness that serves, inasmuch as in this relation the thing retains its independence. Desire has reserved to itself the pure negating of the object and thereby the unmixed feeling-of-self. This satisfaction is on that account, however, itself just a vanishing, for it lacks the facet of the *object*, or *permanency*. Work by contrast is *contained* desire, *arrested* vanishing, or work *improves*. The negative relation to the object turns into the *form* of the object and into something *enduring*, precisely because to the worker the object has independence. This *negative* centre, or the *activity* that forms, or fashions, is at the same time *the particularity*, or the pure being-for-self of consciousness, which now in work steps out of consciousness into the element of permanency; the consciousness that works therefore attains as a consequence a view of independent being *as itself*.

The fashioning has not only this positive significance, however, that in it the consciousness that serves has itself as pure *being-for-itself* become something *existent;* but also a negative significance as against its first moment, the fear. For, in the improving of the thing, the consciousness which serves has its own negativity, its being-for-itself, become object only by doing away with the opposed existent *form*. But this objective, *negative* thing is precisely the alien being before which it trembled. Now, however, it destroys this alien negative thing, sets *itself* as something negative into the element of permanency, and thereby comes to be *for itself,* something *existing-for-itself.* In the master it has being-for-self as *an other,* or as merely *for it;* in the fear being-for-self is *in the consciousness itself that serves;* in the improving being-for-self comes to be for the consciousness that serves as *its own,* and the latter becomes conscious that it itself is in and for itself. Through being *set outside,* the form does not become to the consciousness that serves something other than the consciousness itself; for it is precisely the form that is its pure being-for-itself, which thereby to consciousness becomes the truth. Through this refinding of itself by itself, then, the consciousness that serves becomes a mind or *sense of its own,* and in the very work in which it seemed to be only *another's sense.*—For this reflexion both moments, that of fear and service in general, as well as that of improving, are necessary, and at the same time both in a general way. Without the discipline of service and obedience, fear remains at the formal stage, and does not spread itself upon the known reality of concrete existence. Without the improving, fear remains inward and silent, and consciousness does not become for itself. If consciousness fashions, or forms, without the initial absolute fear, it is merely a vain sense of self; for its form or negativity is not negativity *in itself,* and its fashioning cannot therefore give it the consciousness of itself as the essence. If it has not endured absolute fear, but only some anxiety, then it has the negative essence remain something external, its substance has not been infected through and through by the negative essence. Inasmuch as not all aspects of its natural consciousness have become insecure, it still *in itself* belongs to some particular existence; its self-sense is *self-will,* a freedom which as yet remains within subjection. No more than it can have the pure form become essence, no more is the form, regarded as something spread over individual things, a universal cultivating, an absolute concept, but is instead a dexterity which has power over merely some things, not over universal power and the whole objective realm of being.

WHO THINKS ABSTRACTLY?

Think? Abstractly?—*Sauve qui peut!* Let those who can save themselves! Even now I can hear a traitor, bought by the enemy, exclaim these words, denouncing this essay because it will plainly deal with metaphysics. For *metaphysics* is a word, no less than *abstract,* and almost *thinking* as well, from which everybody more or less runs away as from a man who has caught the plague.

But the intention here really is not so wicked, as if the meaning of thinking and of abstract were to be explained here. There is nothing the beautiful world finds as intolerable as explanations. I, too, find it terrible when somebody begins to explain, for when worst comes to worst I understand everything myself. Here the explanation of thinking and abstract would in any case be entirely superfluous; for it is only because the beautiful world knows what it means to be abstract that it runs away. Just as one does not desire what one does not know, one also cannot hate it. Nor is it my intent to try craftily to reconcile the beautiful world with thinking or with the abstract as if, under the semblance of small talk, thinking and the abstract were to be put over till in the end they had found their way into society incognito, without having aroused any disgust; even as if they were to be adopted imperceptibly by society, or, as the Swabians say, *hereingezäunselt,* before the author of this complication suddenly exposed this strange guest, namely the abstract, whom the whole party had long treated and recognized under a different title as if he were a good old acquaintance. Such scenes of recognition which are meant to instruct the world against its will have the inexcusable fault that they simultaneously humiliate, and the wirepuller tries with his artifice to gain a little fame; but this humiliation and this vanity destroy the effect, for they push away again an instruction gained at such a price.

In any case, such a plan would be ruined from the start, for it would require that the crucial word of the riddle is not spoken at the outset. But this has already happened in the title. If this essay toyed with such craftiness, these words should not have been allowed to enter right in the beginning; but like the cabinet member in a comedy, they should have been required to walk around during the entire play in their overcoat, unbuttoning it only in the last scene, disclosing the flashing star of wisdom. The unbuttoning of the metaphysical overcoat would be less effective, to be sure, than the unbuttoning of the minister's: it would bring to light no more than a couple of words, and the best part of the joke ought to be that it is shown that society has long been in possession of the matter itself, so what they would gain in the end would be the mere name, while the minister's star signifies something real—a bag of money.

That everybody present should know what thinking is and what is abstract is presupposed in good society, and we certainly are in good society. The question is merely *who* thinks abstractly. The intent, as already mentioned, is not to reconcile society with these things, to expect it to deal with something difficult, to appeal to its conscience not frivolously to neglect such a matter that befits the rank and status of beings gifted with reason. Rather it is my intent to reconcile the beautiful world with itself, although it does not seem to have a bad conscience about this neglect, still, at least deep down, it has a certain respect for abstract thinking as something exalted, and it looks the other way not because it seems too lowly but because it appears too exalted, not because it

Translated by Walter Kaufmann.

seems too mean but rather too noble, or conversely because it seems an *Espèce,* something special; it seems something that does not lend one distinction in general society, like new clothes, but rather something that—like wretched clothes, or rich ones if they are decorated with precious stones in ancient mounts or embroidery that, be it ever so rich, has long become quasi–Chinese—excludes one from society or makes one ridiculous in it.

Who thinks abstractly? The uneducated, not the educated. Good society does not think abstractly because it is too easy, because it is too lowly (not referring to the external status)—not from an empty affectation of nobility that would place itself above that of which it is not capable, but on account of the inward inferiority of the matter.

The prejudice and respect for abstract thinking are so great that sensitive nostrils will begin to smell some satire or irony at this point; but since they read the morning paper they know that there is a prize to be had for satires and that I should therefore sooner earn it by competing for it than give up here without further ado.

I have only to adduce examples for my proposition: everybody will grant that they confirm it. A murderer is led to the place of execution. For the common populace he is nothing but a murderer. Ladies perhaps remark that he is a strong, handsome, interesting man. The populace finds this remark terrible: What? A murderer handsome? How can one think so wickedly and call a murderer handsome; no doubt, you yourselves are something not much better! This is the corruption of morals that is prevalent in the upper classes, a priest may add, knowing the bottom of things and human hearts.

One who knows men traces the development of the criminal's mind: he finds in his history, in his education, a bad family relationship between his father and mother, some tremendous harshness after this human being had done some minor wrong, so he became embittered against the social order—a first reaction to this that in effect expelled him and henceforth did not make it possible for him to preserve himself except through crime.—There may be people who will say when they hear such things: he wants to excuse this murderer! After all I remember how in my youth I heard a mayor lament that writers of books were going too far and sought to extirpate Christianity and righteousness altogether; somebody had written a defense of suicide; terrible, really too terrible!—Further questions revealed that *The Sufferings of Werther* [by Goethe, 1774] were meant.

This is abstract thinking: to see nothing in the murderer except the abstract fact that he is a murderer, and to annul all other human essence in him with this simple quality.

It is quite different in refined, sentimental circles—in Leipzig. There they strewed and bound flowers on the wheel and on the criminal who was tied to it.—But this again is the opposite abstraction. The Christians may indeed trifle with Rosicrucianism, or rather cross-rosism, and wreathe roses around the cross. The cross is the gallows and wheel that have long been hallowed. It has lost its one-sided significance of being the instrument of dishonorable punishment and, on the contrary, suggests the notion of the highest pain and the deepest rejection together with the most joyous rapture and divine honor. The wheel in Leipzig, on the other hand, wreathed with violets and poppies, is a reconciliation à la Kotzebue, a kind of slovenly sociability between sentimentality and badness.

In quite a different manner I once heard a common old woman who worked in a hospital kill the abstraction of the murderer and bring him to life for honor. The severed head had been placed on the scaffold, and the sun was shining. How beautifully, she said, the sun of God's grace shines on Binder's head!—You are not worthy of having the sun shine on you, one says to a rascal with whom one is angry. This woman saw that the murderer's head was struck by the sunshine and thus was still worthy of it. She raised it from the punishment of the scaffold into the sunny grace of God, and instead of accomplishing the reconciliation with violets and sentimental vanity, saw him accepted in grace in the higher sun.

Old woman, your eggs are rotten! the maid says to the market woman. What? she replies, my eggs rotten? You may be rotten! You say that about my eggs? You? Did not lice eat your father on the highways? Didn't your mother run away with the French, and didn't your grandmother die in a public hospital? Let her get a whole shirt instead of that flimsy scarf; we know well where she got that scarf and her hats: if it were not for those officers, many wouldn't be decked out like that these days, and if their ladyships paid more attention to their households, many would be in jail right now. Let her mend the holes in her stockings!—In brief, she does not leave one whole thread on her. She thinks abstractly and subsumes the other woman—scarf, hat, shirt, etc., as well as her fingers and other parts of her, and her father and whole family, too—solely under the crime that she has found the eggs rotten. Everything about her is colored through and through by these rotten eggs, while those officers of which the market woman spoke— if, as one may seriously doubt, there is anything to that—may have got to see very different things.

To move from the maid to a servant, no servant is worse off than one who works for a man of low class and low income; and he is better off the nobler his master is. The common man again thinks more abstractly, he gives himself noble airs vis-à-vis the servant and relates himself to the other man merely as to a servant; he clings to this one predicate. The servant is best off among the French. The nobleman is familiar with his servant, the Frenchman is his friend. When they are alone, the servant does the talking: see Diderot's *Jacques et son maître;* the master does nothing but take snuff and see what time it is and lets the servant take care of everything else. The nobleman knows that the servant is not merely a servant, but also knows the latest city news, the girls, and harbors good suggestions; he asks him about these matters, and the servant may say what he knows about these questions. With a French master, the servant may not only do this; he may also broach a subject, have his own opinions and insist on them; and when the master wants something, it is not done with an order but he has to argue and convince the servant of his opinion and add a good word to make sure that this opinion retains the upper hand.

In the army we encounter the same difference. Among the Austrians a soldier may be beaten, he is canaille; for whatever has the passive right to be beaten is canaille. Thus the common soldier is for the officer this *abstractum* of a beatable subject with whom a gentleman who has a uniform and port *d'epée* must trouble himself—and that could drive one to make a pact with the devil.

REASON IN HISTORY (in part)

I. THE THREE METHODS OF WRITING HISTORY

*   *   *

3. The third method of history, the *philosophical*.* There was little in the two preceding methods that had to be clarified; their concept was self-explanatory. But it is different with this last one, which indeed seems to require some commentary or justification. The most universal definition would be that philosophy of history is nothing but the thoughtful contemplation of history. To think is one of those things we cannot help doing; in this we differ from the animals. In our sensation, cognition, and intellection, in our instincts and volitions, in as far as they are human, there is an element of thinking. But reference to thinking may here appear inadequate. In history, thinking is subordinate to the data of reality, which latter serve as guide and basis for historians. Philosophy, on the other hand, allegedly produces its own ideas out of speculation, without regard to given data. If philosophy approached history with such ideas, it may be held, it would treat history as its raw material and not leave it as it is, but shape it in accordance with these ideas, and hence construct it, so to speak, a priori. But since history is supposed to understand events and actions merely for what they are and have been, and is the truer, the more factual it is, it seems that the method of philosophy would be in contradiction to the function of history. This contradiction and the charge consequently brought against philosophy shall here be explained and refuted. But we shall not, for that matter, attempt to correct the innumerable specific misrepresentations which are current and continuously recur about the aims, interests, and methods of history, and its relations to philosophy.

II. REASON AS THE BASIS OF HISTORY

The sole thought which philosophy brings to the treatment of history is the simple concept of *Reason:* that Reason is the law of the world and that, therefore, in world history, things have come about rationally. This conviction and insight is a presupposition of history as such; in philosophy itself it is not presupposed. Through its speculative reflection philosophy has demonstrated that Reason—and this term may be accepted here without closer examination of its relation to God—is both *substance and infinite power,* in itself the infinite material of all natural and spiritual life as well as the *infinite form,* the actualization of itself as content. It is *substance,* that is to say, that by which and in which all reality has its being and subsistence. It is infinite *power,* for

*[The first two methods are "Original History" (descriptions of events which the historian has witnessed) and "Reflective History" (a general history which includes events and deeds the historian has not observed).]

Hegel, *Reason in History: A General Introduction to the Philosophy of History,* 1–3, translated by Robert S. Hartman (New York: Macmillan/Library of the Liberal Arts, 1953).

Reason is not so impotent as to bring about only the ideal, the ought, and to remain in an existence outside of reality—who knows where—as something peculiar in the heads of a few people. It is the infinite *content* of all essence and truth, for it does not require, as does finite activity, the condition of external materials, of given data from which to draw nourishment and objects of its activity; it supplies its own nourishment and is its own reference. And it is infinite *form,* for only in its image and by its fiat do phenomena arise and begin to live. It is its own exclusive presupposition and absolutely final purpose, and itself works out this purpose from potentiality into actuality, from inward source to outward appearance, not only in the natural but also in the spiritual universe, in world history. That this *Idea* or *Reason* is the True, the Eternal, the Absolute Power and that it and nothing but it, its glory and majesty, manifests itself in the world—this, as we said before, has been proved in philosophy and is being presupposed here as proved.

Those among you, gentlemen, who are not yet acquainted with philosophy could perhaps be asked to come to these lectures on world history with the belief in Reason, with a desire, a thirst for its insight. It is indeed this desire for rational insight, for cognition, and not merely for a collection of various facts, which ought to be presupposed as a subjective aspiration in the study of the sciences. For even though one were not approaching world history with the thought and knowledge of Reason, at least one ought to have the firm and invincible faith that there is Reason in history and to believe that the world of intelligence and of self-conscious willing is not abandoned to mere chance, but must manifest itself in the light of the rational Idea. Actually, however, I do not have to demand such belief in advance. What I have said here provisionally, and shall have to say later on, must, even in our branch of science, be taken as a summary view of the whole. It is not a presupposition of study; it is a *result* which happens to be known to myself because I already know the whole. Therefore, only the study of world history itself can show that it has proceeded rationally, that it represents the rationally necessary course of the World Spirit, the Spirit whose nature is indeed always one and the same, but whose one nature unfolds in the course of the world. This, as I said, must be the result of history. History itself must be taken as it is; we have to proceed historically, empirically. Among other things, we must not let ourselves be tempted by the professional historians, for these, particularly the Germans, who possess great authority, practice precisely what they accuse the philosophers of, namely, a priori historical fiction. For example, it is a widespread fabrication that there was an original, primeval people taught immediately by God, endowed with perfect insight and wisdom, possessing a thorough knowledge of all natural laws and spiritual truths; or that there were such or such sacerdotal peoples; or, to mention a more specific matter, that there was a Roman epos from which the Roman historians derived the earliest history—and so on. Apriorities of this kind we shall leave to these talented professional historians, among whom, at least in our country, their use is quite common. As our first condition we must therefore state that we apprehend the historical faithfully. In such general terms, however, as "faithfully" and "apprehend" lies an ambiguity. Even the average and mediocre historian, who perhaps believes and pretends that he is merely receptive, merely surrendering himself to the data, is not passive in his thinking. He brings his categories with him and sees the data through them. In everything that is supposed to be scientific, Reason must be awake and reflection applied. To him who looks at the world rationally the world looks rationally back. The relation is mutual. But we cannot treat here the various modes of reflection, of points of view, of judgment, not even those concerning the relative importance or unimportance of facts—the most elementary category.

Only two aspects of the general conviction that Reason has ruled in the world and in world history may be called to your attention. They will give us an immediate opportunity to examine our most difficult question and to point ahead to the main theme.

1. The first is the historical fact of the Greek, Anaxagoras, who was the first to point out that *nous,* understanding in general or Reason, rules the world—but not an intelligence in the sense of an individual consciousness, not a spirit as such. These two must be carefully distinguished. The motion of the solar system proceeds according to immutable laws; these laws are its reason. But neither the sun nor the planets, which according to these laws rotate around it, have any consciousness of it. Thus, the thought that there is Reason in nature, that nature is ruled by universal, unchangeable laws, does not surprise us; we are used to it and make very little of it. Also, this historical circumstance teaches us a lesson of history: things which may seem trivial to us have not always been in the world; a new thought like this one marks an epoch in the development of the human spirit. Aristotle says of Anaxagoras, as the originator of this thought, that he appeared like a sober man among the drunken. From Anaxagoras, Socrates adopted the doctrine, which became forthwith the ruling idea in philosophy, except in the school of Epicurus, who ascribed all events to chance. "I was delighted about this," Plato makes Socrates say, "and hoped to have found a teacher who would interpret Nature by Reason and would show me in the particular its particular purpose, and in the universal, the universal purpose. I should not have given up this hope for anything. But how greatly was I disappointed when, having zealously applied myself to the writings of Anaxagoras, I found that he mentions only external causes, such as Air, Ether, Water, and the like, instead of Reason."* It is evident that the insufficiency which Socrates found in the principle of Anaxagoras has nothing to do with the principle itself, but with Anaxagoras' failure to apply it to concrete nature. Nature was not understood or comprehended through this principle; the principle remained abstract—nature was not understood as a development of Reason, as an organization brought forth by it. I wish at the very outset to draw your attention to this difference between a concept, a principle, a truth, as confined to the abstract and as determining concrete application and development. This difference is fundamental; among other things we shall come back to precisely this point at the end of our world history, when we deal with the most recent political events.

2. The second point is the historical connection of the thought that Reason rules the world with another form of it, well known to us—that of religious truth: that the world is not abandoned to chance and external accident but controlled by *Providence.* I said before that I do not make any demand on your belief in the principle announced; but I think I may appeal to this belief in its religious form, unless the nature of scientific philosophy precludes, as a general rule, the acceptance of any presuppositions; or, seen from another angle, unless the science itself which we want to develop should first give the proof, if not of the truth, at least of the correctness of our principle. The truth that a Providence, that is to say, a divine Providence, presides over the events of the world corresponds to our principle; for divine Providence is wisdom endowed with infinite power which realizes its own aim, that is, the absolute, rational, final purpose of the world. Reason is Thought determining itself in absolute freedom.

On the other hand, a difference, indeed an opposition, now appears between this faith and our principle, very much like that between Socrates' expectation and the principle of Anaxagoras. For this faith is also indefinite, it is what is called faith in Providence in general; it is not followed up in definite application to the whole, the compre-

---

*[*Phaedo,* 97–98. Hegel paraphrases this passage.]

hensive course of world history. To explain history means to reveal the passions of men, their genius, their active powers. This definiteness of Providence is usually called its *plan*. Yet this very plan is supposed to be hidden from our view; indeed, the wish to recognize it is deemed presumption. The ignorance of Anaxagoras about the manifestation of Reason in reality was naïve; the knowledge of the principle had not yet developed, either in him or in Greece in general. He was not yet able to apply his general principle to the concrete, to deduce the latter from the former. Only Socrates took the first step in comprehending the union of the concrete and the universal. Anaxagoras, then, was not opposed to such application; but the faith in Providence *is*. It is opposed at least to the application at large of our principle, to the *cognition* of the plan of Providence. In particular cases, it is true, one allows it here and there, when pious minds see in particular events not only chance but God's will—when, for example, an individual in great perplexity and need gets unexpected help. But these instances are limited to the particular purposes of this individual. In world history the "individuals" that we have to deal with are peoples; they are totalities which are states. We cannot, therefore, be satisfied with what we may call this "retail" view of faith in Providence, nor with the merely abstract, undetermined faith in the universal statement that there is a Providence, without determining its definite acts. On the contrary, we must seriously try to recognize the ways of Providence, its means and manifestations in history, and their relation to our universal principle.

But in mentioning at all the recognition of the plan of divine Providence I have touched on a prominent question of the day, the question, namely, whether it is possible to recognize God—or, since it has ceased to be a question, the doctrine, which has now become a prejudice, that it is impossible to know God. Following this doctrine we now contradict what the Holy Scripture commands as our highest duty, namely, not only to love but also to know God. We now categorically deny what is written, namely, that it is the spirit which leads to truth, knows all things, and penetrates even the depths of divinity. Thus, in placing the Divine Being beyond our cognition and the pale of all human things, we gain the convenient license of indulging in our own fancies. We are freed from the necessity of referring our knowledge to the True and Divine. On the contrary, the vanity of knowledge and the subjectivity of sentiment now have ample justification. And pious humility, in keeping true recognition of God at arm's length, knows very well what it gains for its arbitrary and vain striving.

I wanted to discuss the connection of our thesis—that Reason governs and has governed the world—with the question of the possible knowledge of God, chiefly in order to mention the accusation that philosophy avoids, or must avoid, the discussion of religious truths because it has, so to speak, a bad conscience about them. On the contrary, the fact is that in recent times philosophy has had to take over the defense of religious truths against many a theological system. In the Christian religion God has revealed Himself, which means He has given man to understand what He is, and thus is no longer concealed and secret. With this *possibility* of knowing God the *obligation* to know Him is imposed upon us. God wishes no narrow souls and empty heads for his children; He wishes our spirit, of itself indeed poor, rich in the knowledge of Him and holding this knowledge to be of supreme value. The development of the thinking spirit only *began* with this revelation of divine essence. It must now advance to the intellectual comprehension of that which originally was present only to the feeling and imagining spirit.

[Feeling is the lowest form in which any mental content can exist. God is the Eternal Being in and for itself; and what is universal in and for itself is subject of thought, not of feeling. It is true that everything spiritual, every content of consciousness, any-

thing that is product and subject of thought—in particular religion and morality—must also, and originally does, exist in the mode of feeling. But feeling is not the fount from which this content flows to man, but only a primal mode in which it exists in him. It is indeed the worst mode, a mode which he has in common with the animal. What is substantial must also exist in feeling, but it does mainly exist in a higher, more dignified form. If one wants to relegate the moral, the true, the most spiritual mental content necessarily to feeling and emotion and keep it there on general principle, one would ascribe to it essentially the animalic form; but this is not at all capable of containing the spirit. In feeling, the mental content is the smallest possible; it is present in its lowest possible form. As long as it is still in feeling it is veiled and entirely indefinite. It is still entirely subjective, present exclusively in the subjective form. If one says: "I feel such and such and so and so," then one has secluded himself in himself. Everybody else has the same right to say: "I don't feel it that way." And hence one has retreated from the common soil of understanding. In wholly particular affairs feeling is entirely in its right. But to maintain that all men had this or that in their feeling is a contradiction in terms; it contradicts the concept of feeling, the point of view of the individual subjectivity of each which one has taken with this statement. As soon as mental content is placed into feeling, everybody is reduced to his subjective point of view. If someone called anyone else by this or that epithet, the other would be entitled to give it back; and both, from their respective points of view, would be entitled to offend each other. If someone says he has religion in his feeling and the other that he does not find any God in his feeling, then both are right. If in this manner the divine content—the revelation of God, the relationship of man to God, the being of God for man—is reduced to pure feeling, then it is reduced to pure subjectivity, to the arbitrary, to whim. In this way one actually gets rid of truth as it is in and for itself. The true is universal in and for itself, essential, substantial; as such it can be only in and for thought.] The time has finally come to understand also the rich product of creative Reason which is world history.

It was for a while the fashion to admire God's wisdom in animals, plants, and individual lives. If it is conceded that Providence manifests itself in such objects and materials, why not also in world history? Because its scope seems to be too large. But the divine wisdom, or Reason, is the same in the large as in the small. We must not deem God too weak to exercise his wisdom on a grand scale. Our intellectual striving aims at recognizing that what eternal wisdom *intended* it has actually *accomplished*, dynamically active in the world, both in the realm of nature and that of the spirit. In this respect our method is a theodicy, a justification of God, which Leibniz attempted metaphysically, in his way, by undetermined abstract categories. Thus the evil in the world was to be comprehended and the thinking mind reconciled with it. Nowhere, actually, exists a larger challenge to such reconciliation than in world history. This reconciliation can only be attained through the recognition of the positive elements in which that negative element disappears as something subordinate and vanquished. This is possible through the consciousness, on the one hand, of the true ultimate purpose of the world and, on the other hand, of the fact that this purpose has been actualized in the world and that the evil cannot ultimately prevail beside it. But for this end the mere belief in *nous* and providence is not sufficient. "Reason," which is said to govern the world, is as indefinite a term as "Providence."

One always speaks of Reason without being able to indicate its definition, its content, which alone would enable us to judge whether something is rational or irrational. What we need is an adequate definition of Reason. Without such definition we can get no further than mere words. With this let us proceed to the second point that we want to consider in this introduction.

Coalbrookdale by Night, 1801, by Phillip James De Loutherbourg. The coal furnaces in the background light the sky and illuminate the fragments from the past in the foreground, symbolizing the onward march of history. (*Science Museum, London*)

III. THE IDEA OF HISTORY AND ITS REALIZATION

The question of how Reason is determined in itself and what its relation is to the world coincides with the question, *What is the ultimate purpose of the world?* This question implies that the purpose is to be actualized and realized. Two things, then, must be considered: first, the content of this ultimate purpose, the determination as such, and, secondly, its realization.

To begin with, we must note that world history goes on within the realm of Spirit. The term "world" includes both physical and psychical nature. Physical nature does play a part in world history, and from the very beginning we shall draw attention to the fundamental natural relations thus involved. But Spirit, and the course of its development, is the substance of history. We must not contemplate nature as a rational system in itself, in its own particular domain, but only in its relation to Spirit.

[*After the creation of nature appears Man. He constitutes the antithesis to the natural world; he is the being that lifts itself up to the second world. We have in our universal consciousness two realms, the realm of Nature and the realm of Spirit. The realm of Spirit consists in what is produced by man. One may have all sorts of ideas about the Kingdom of God; but it is always a realm of Spirit to be realized and brought about in man.*

The realm of Spirit is all-comprehensive; it includes everything that ever has interested or ever will interest man. Man is active in it; whatever he does, he is the crea-

ture within which the Spirit works. Hence it is of interest, in the course of history, to learn to know spiritual nature in its existence, that is, the point where Spirit and Nature unite, namely, human nature. In speaking of human nature we mean something permanent. The concept of human nature must fit all men and all ages, past and present. This universal concept may suffer infinite modifications; but actually the universal is one and the same essence in its most various modifications. Thinking reflection disregards the variations and adheres to the universal, which under all circumstances is active in the same manner and shows itself in the same interest. The universal type appears even in what seems to deviate from it most strongly; in the most distorted figure we can still discern the human . . . .

This kind of reflection abstracts from the content, the purpose of human activity. . . . But the cultured human mind cannot help making distinctions between inclinations and desires as they manifest themselves in small circumstances and as they appear in the struggle of world-wide historical interests. Here appears an objective interest, which impresses us in two aspects, that of the universal aim and that of the individual who represents this aim. It is this which makes history so fascinating. These are the aims and individuals whose loss and decline we mourn. When we have before us the struggle of the Greeks against the Persians or Alexander's mighty dominion, we know very well what interests us. We want to see the Greeks saved from barbarism, we want the Athenian state preserved, and we are interested in the ruler under whose leadership the Greeks subjugated Asia. If it were only a matter of human passion, we would not feel any loss in imagining that Alexander would have failed in his enterprise. We could very well content ourselves in seeing here a mere play of passions, but we would not feel satisfied. We have here a substantial, an objective interest. . . .

In contemplating world history we must thus consider its ultimate purpose. This ultimate purpose is what is willed in the world itself. We know of God that He is the most perfect; He can will only Himself and what is like Him. God and the nature of His will are one and the same; these we call, philosophically, the Idea. Hence, it is the Idea in general, in its manifestation as human spirit, which we have to contemplate. More precisely, it is the idea of human freedom. The purest form in which the Idea manifests itself is Thought itself. In this aspect the Idea is treated in Logic. Another form is that of physical Nature.* The third form, finally, is that of Spirit in general.] Spirit, on the stage on which we observe it, that of world history, is in its most concrete reality. But nevertheless—or rather in order to understand also the general idea of this concrete existence of Spirit—we must set forth, first, some general definition of the *nature of Spirit*. But this can only be done here as a mere assertion; this is not the place to develop the idea of Spirit through philosophical speculation. As was mentioned above, what can be said in an introduction can be taken only historically—as an assumption to be explained and proved elsewhere or to be verified by the science of history itself.

We have therefore to indicate here:

(1) The abstract characteristics of the nature of Spirit.

(2) The means Spirit uses in order to realize its Idea.

(3) The form which the complete realization of Spirit assumes in existence—the State.

---

*[In this aspect the Idea is treated in the Philosophy of Nature.]

1. THE IDEA OF FREEDOM

The nature of Spirit may be understood by a glance at its direct opposite—Matter. The essence of matter is gravity, the essence of Spirit—its substance—is Freedom. It is immediately plausible to everyone that, among other properties, Spirit also possesses Freedom. But philosophy teaches us that *all* the properties of Spirit exist only through Freedom. All are but means of attaining Freedom; all seek and produce this and this alone. It is an insight of speculative philosophy that Freedom is the sole truth of Spirit. Matter possesses gravity by virtue of its tendency toward a central point; it is essentially composite, consisting of parts that exclude each other. It seeks its unity and thereby its own abolition; it seeks its opposite. If it would attain this it would be matter no longer, but would have perished. It strives toward ideality, for in unity it exists ideally. Spirit, on the contrary, is that which has its center in itself. It does not have unity outside of itself but has found it; it is in itself and with itself. Matter has its substance outside of itself; Spirit is Being-within-itself (self-contained existence). But this, precisely, is Freedom. For when I am dependent, I refer myself to something else which I am not; I cannot exist independently of something external. I am free when I am within myself. This self-contained existence of Spirit is self-consciousness, consciousness of self.

Two things must be distinguished in consciousness, first, *that* I know and, secondly, *what* I know. In self-consciousness the two coincide, for Spirit knows itself. It is the judgment of its own nature and, at the same time, the operation of coming to itself, to produce itself, to make itself (actually) into that which it is in itself (potentially). Following this abstract definition it may be said that world history is the exhibition of spirit striving to attain knowledge of its own nature. As the germ bears in itself the whole nature of the tree, the taste and shape of its fruit, so also the first traces of Spirit virtually contain the whole of history. Orientals do not yet know that Spirit—Man as such—is free. And because they do not know it, they are not free. They only know that *one* is free; but for this very reason such freedom is mere caprice, ferocity, dullness of passion, or, perhaps, softness and tameness of desire—which again is nothing but an accident of nature and thus, again, caprice. This *one* is therefore only a despot, not a free man. The consciousness of freedom first arose among the Greeks, and therefore they were free. But they, and the Romans likewise, only knew that some are free—not man as such. This not even Plato and Aristotle knew. For this reason the Greeks not only had slavery, upon which was based their whole life and the maintenance of their splendid liberty, but their freedom itself was partly an accidental, transient, and limited flowering and partly a severe thralldom of human nature. Only the Germanic peoples came, through Christianity, to realize that man as man is free and that freedom of Spirit is the very essence of man's nature. This realization first arose in religion, in the innermost region of spirit; but to introduce it in the secular world was a further task which could only be solved and fulfilled by a long and severe effort of civilization. Thus slavery did not cease immediately with the acceptance of the Christian religion. Liberty did not suddenly predominate in states nor reason in governments and constitutions. The application of the principle to secular conditions, the thorough molding and interpenetration of the secular world by it, is precisely the long process of history. I have already drawn attention to this distinction between a principle as such and its application, its introduction and execution in the actuality of life and spirit. This is a fundamental fact in our science and must be kept constantly in mind. Just as we noted it in the Christian principle of self-consciousness and freedom, so it shows itself in the principle of freedom in general. World history is the progress of the consciousness of freedom—a progress whose necessity we have to investigate.

The preliminary statement given above of the various grades in the consciousness of freedom—that the Orientals knew only that *one* is free, the Greeks and Romans that *some* are free, while we know that *all* men absolutely, that is, as men, are free—is at the same time the natural division of world history and the manner in which we shall treat it. But this is only mentioned in passing; first, we must explain some other concepts.

We have established Spirit's consciousness of its freedom, and thereby the actualization of this Freedom as the final purpose of the world. For the spiritual world is the substance of reality, and the physical world remains subordinate to it, or, in terms of speculative philosophy, has no truth compared with the former. But the term "freedom," without further qualification, is indefinite and infinitely ambiguous. Being the highest concept, it is liable to an infinity of misunderstandings, confusions, and errors and may give rise to all possible kinds of extravagances. All this has never been more clearly known and experienced than today. Yet for the time being we must content ourselves with this general, as yet undefined term. Attention was also drawn to the importance of the infinite difference between the principle, as that which so far is only in itself, and that which is real. At the same time, it is Freedom in itself that comprises within itself the infinite necessity of bringing itself to consciousness and thereby, since knowledge about itself is its very nature, to reality. Freedom is itself its own object of attainment and the sole purpose of Spirit. It is the ultimate purpose toward which all world history has continually aimed. To this end all the sacrifices have been offered on the vast altar of the earth throughout the long lapse of ages. Freedom alone is the purpose which realizes and fulfills itself, the only enduring pole in the change of events and conditions, the only truly efficient principle that pervades the whole. This final aim is God's purpose with the world. But God is the absolutely perfect Being and can, therefore, will nothing but Himself, His own will. The nature of His own will, His own nature, is what we here call the Idea of freedom. Thus we translate the language of religion into that of philosophy. Our next question then is: what are the means the Idea uses for its realization? This is the second point that we have to consider.

2. THE MEANS OF REALIZATION

(A) THE IDEA AND THE INDIVIDUAL

The question of the *means* whereby Freedom develops itself into a world leads us directly to the phenomenon of history. Although Freedom as such is primarily an internal idea, the means it uses are the external phenomena which in history present themselves directly before our eyes. The first glance at history convinces us that the actions of men spring from their needs, their passions, their interests, their characters, and their talents. Indeed, it appears as if in this drama of activities these needs, passions, and interests are the sole springs of action and the main efficient cause. It is true that this drama involves also universal purposes, benevolence, or noble patriotism But such virtues and aims are insignificant on the broad canvas of history. We may, perhaps, see the ideal of Reason actualized in those who adopt such aims and in the spheres of their influence; but their number is small in proportion to the mass of the human race and their influence accordingly limited. Passions, private aims, and the satisfaction of selfish desires are, on the contrary, tremendous springs of action. Their power lies in the fact that they respect none of the limitations which law and morality would impose on them; and that these natural impulses are closer to the core of human nature than the artificial and troublesome discipline that tends toward order, self-restraint, law, and morality.

When we contemplate this display of passions and the consequences of their violence, the unreason which is associated not only with them, but even—rather we might say *especially*—with *good* designs and righteous aims; when we see arising therefrom the evil, the vice, the ruin that has befallen the most flourishing kingdoms which the mind of man ever created, we can hardly avoid being filled with sorrow at this universal taint of corruption. And since this decay is not the work of mere nature, but of human will, our reflections may well lead us to a moral sadness, a revolt of the good will (spirit)—if indeed it has a place within us. Without rhetorical exaggeration, a simple, truthful account of the miseries that have overwhelmed the noblest of nations and politics and the finest exemplars of private virtue forms a most fearful picture and excites emotions of the profoundest and most hopeless sadness, counter-balanced by no consoling result. We can endure it and strengthen ourselves against it only by thinking that this is the way it had to be—it is fate; nothing can be done. And at last, out of the boredom with which this sorrowful reflection threatens us, we draw back into the vitality of the present, into our aims and interests of the moment; we retreat, in short, into the selfishness that stands on the quiet shore and thence enjoys in safety the distant spectacle of wreckage and confusion.

But in contemplating history as the slaughter-bench at which the happiness of peoples, the wisdom of states, and the virtue of individuals have been sacrificed, a question necessarily arises: To what principle, to what final purpose, have these monstrous sacrifices been offered?

From here one usually proceeds to the starting point of our investigation: the events which make up this picture of gloomy emotion and thoughtful reflection are only the means for realizing the essential destiny, the absolute and final purpose, or, what amounts to the same thing, the true result of world history. We have all along purposely eschewed that method of reflection which ascends from this scene of particulars to general principles. Besides, it is not in the interest of such sentimental reflections really to rise above these depressing emotions and to solve the mysteries of Providence presented in such contemplations. It is rather their nature to dwell melancholically on the empty and fruitless sublimities of their negative result. For this reason we return to our original point of view. What we shall have to say about it will also answer the questions put to us by this panorama of history.

The first thing we notice—something which has been stressed more than once before but which cannot be repeated too often, for it belongs to the central point of our inquiry—is the merely general and abstract nature of what we call principle, final purpose, destiny, or the nature and concept of Spirit. A principle, a law is something implicit, which as such, however true in itself, is not completely real (actual). Purposes, principles, and the like, are at first in our thoughts, our inner intention. They are not yet in reality. That which is in itself is a possibility, a faculty. It has not yet emerged out of its implicitness into existence. A second element must be added for it to become reality, namely, activity, actualization. The principle of this is the will, man's activity in general. It is only through this activity that the concept and its implicit ("being-in-themselves") determinations can be realized, actualized; for of themselves they have no immediate efficacy. The activity which puts them in operation and in existence is the need, the instinct, the inclination, and passion of man. When I have an idea I am greatly interested in transforming it into action, into actuality. In its realization through my participation I want to find my own satisfaction. A purpose for which I shall be active must in some way be my purpose; I must thereby satisfy my own desires, even though it may have ever so many aspects which do not concern me. This is the infinite right of the individual to find itself satisfied in its activity and labor. If men are to be interested in anything they must have "their heart" in it. Their feelings of self-importance must be satisfied. But here a misunderstanding must be avoided. To say that an individual "has an interest" in something is justly regarded as a reproach or blame; we imply that he seeks only his private advantage. Indeed, the blame implies not only his disregard of the common interest, but his taking advantage of it and even his sacrificing it to his own interest. Yet, he who is active for a cause is not simply "interested," but "interested *in it.*" Language faithfully expresses this distinction. Nothing therefore happens, nothing is accomplished, unless those concerned with an issue find their own satisfaction in it. They are particular individuals; they have their special needs, instincts, and interests. They have their own particular desires and volitions, their own insight and conviction, or at least their own attitude and opinion, once the aspirations to reflect, understand, and reason have been awakened. Therefore people demand that a cause for which they should be active accord with their ideas. And they expect their opinion—concerning its goodness, justice, advantage, profit—to be taken into account. This is of particular importance today when people are moved to support a cause not by faith in other people's authority, but rather on the basis of their own independent judgment and conviction.

We assert then that nothing has been accomplished without an interest on the part of those who brought it about. And if "interest" be called "passion"—because the whole individuality is concentrating all its desires and powers, with every fiber of volition, to the neglect of all other actual or possible interests and aims, on one object—we may then affirm without qualification that *nothing great in the world* has been accomplished without passion.

Two elements therefore enter into our investigation: first, the Idea, secondly, the complex of human passions; the one the warp, the other the woof of the vast tapestry of world history. Their contact and concrete union constitutes moral liberty in the state. We have already spoken of the Idea of freedom as the essence of Spirit and absolutely final purpose of history. Passion is regarded as something wrong, something more or less evil; man is not supposed to have passions. "Passion," it is true, is not quite the right word for what I wish to express. I mean here nothing more than human activity resulting from private interest, from special or, if you will, self-seeking designs—with this qualification: that the whole energy of will and character is devoted to the attainment of one aim and that other interests or possible aims, indeed everything else, is sacrificed to this aim. This particular objective is so bound up with the person's will that it alone and entirely determines its direction and is inseparable from it. It is that which makes the person what he is. For a person is a specific existence. He is not man in general—such a thing does not exist—but a particular human being. The term "character" also expresses this uniqueness of will and intelligence. But character comprises all individual features whatever—the way in which a person conducts himself in his private and other relations. It does not connote this individuality itself in its practical and active phase. I shall therefore use the term "passion" to mean the particularity of a character insofar as its individual volitions not only have a particular content but also supply the impelling and actuating force for deeds of universal scope. Passion is thus the subjective and therefore the formal aspect of energy, will, and activity, whose content and aim are at this point still undetermined. And a similar relation exists between individual conviction, insight, and conscience, on the one hand, and their content, on the other. If someone wants to decide whether my conviction and passion are true and substantial, he must consider the *content* of my conviction and the *aim* of my passion. Conversely, if they are true and substantial, they cannot help but attain actual existence.

From this comment on the second essential element in the historical embodiment of an aim, we infer—considering for a moment the institution of the state—that a state is then well constituted and internally vigorous when the private interest of its citizens is one with the common interest of the state, and the one finds gratification and realization in the other—a most important proposition. But in a state many institutions are necessary—inventions, appropriate arrangements, accompanied by long intellectual struggles in order to find out what is really appropriate, as well as struggles with private interests and passions, which must be harmonized in difficult and tedious discipline. When a state reaches this harmony, it has reached the period of its bloom, its excellence, its power and prosperity. But world history does not begin with any conscious aim, as do the *particular* circles of men. Already the simple instinct of living together contains the conscious purpose of securing life and property; once this primal society has been established, the purpose expands. But world history begins its *general* aim—to realize the idea of Spirit—only in an implicit form *(an sich)*, namely, as Nature—as an innermost, unconscious instinct. And the whole business of history, as already observed, is to bring it into consciousness. Thus, appearing in the form of nature, of natural will, what we have called the subjective side is immediate, actual existence *(für sich)*: need, instinct, passion, private interest, even opinion and subjective representation. These vast congeries of volitions, interests, and activities constitute the tools and means of the World Spirit for attaining its purpose, bringing it to consciousness, and realizing it. And this purpose is none other than finding itself—coming to itself—and contemplating itself in concrete actuality. But one may indeed question whether those manifestations of vitality on the part of individuals and peoples in which they seek and satisfy their own purposes are, at the same time, the means and tools of a higher and broader purpose of which they know nothing, which they realize unconsciously. This purpose has been questioned, and in every variety of form denied, decried, and denounced as mere dreaming and "philosophy." On this point, however, I announced my view at the very outset, and asserted our hypothesis—which eventually will appear as the result of our investigation—namely, that Reason governs the world and has consequently governed its history. In relation to this Reason, which is universal and substantial, in and for itself, all else is subordinate, subservient, and the means for its actualization. Moreover, this Reason is immanent in historical existence and reaches its own perfection in and through this existence. The union of the abstract universal, existing in and for itself, with the particular or subjective, and the fact that this union alone constitutes truth are a matter of speculative philosophy which, in this general form, is treated in logic. But in its historical development *[the subjective side, consciousness, is not yet able to know what is]* the abstract final aim of history, the idea of Spirit, for it is then itself in process and incomplete. The idea of Spirit is not yet its distinct object of desire and interest. Thus desire is still unconscious of its purpose; yet it already exists in the particular purposes and realizes itself through them. The problem concerning the union of the general and the subjective may also be raised under the form of the union of freedom and necessity. We consider the immanent development of the Spirit, existing in and for itself, as necessary, while we refer to freedom the interests contained in men's conscious volitions. Since, as was said, the speculative, that is, the conceptual aspect of this connection belongs to logic, it would be out of place to analyze it here. But the chief and cardinal points may be mentioned.

In philosophy we show that the Idea proceeds to its infinite antithesis. . . . *[The Idea has within itself the determination of its self-consciousness, of activity. Thus it is God's own eternal life, as it was, so to speak, before the creation of the world, (the) log-*

*ical connection (of all things). It still lacks at this point the form of being which is actu-
ality. It still is the universal, the immanent, the represented. The second stage begins
when the Idea satisfies the contrast which originally is only ideally in it and posits the
difference between itself in its free universal mode, in which it remains within itself, and
itself as purely abstract reflection in itself. In thus stepping over to one side (in order to
be object of reflection) the Idea sets the other side as formal actuality (Fürsichsein), as
formal freedom, as abstract unity of self-consciousness, as infinite reflection in itself,
and as infinite negativity (antithesis).*

> *Thus it becomes Ego, which, as an atom (indivisible), opposes itself to all content
and thus is the most complete antithesis—the antithesis, namely, of the whole plenitude
of the Idea. The absolute Idea is thus, on the one hand, substantial fullness of content
and, on the other hand, abstract free volition. God and universe have separated, and set
each other as opposites. Consciousness, the Ego, has a being such that the other (everything else) is for it (its object). In developing this train of thought one arrives at the creation of free spirits, the world, and so on. The absolute antithesis, the atom (i.e., the
Ego), which at the same time is a manifold (of contents of consciousness), is finiteness
itself. It is for itself (in actuality) merely exclusion of its antithesis (the absolute Idea). It
is its limit and barrier. Thus it is the Absolute itself become finite. Reflection in itself, individual self-consciousness, is the antithesis of the absolute Idea and hence the Idea in
absolute finiteness. This finitude, the acme of freedom, this formal knowledge—when referred to the glory of God as to the absolute Idea which recognizes what ought to be—
is the soil on which the spiritual element of knowledge as such is falling; thus it constitutes the absolute aspect of its actuality, though it remains merely formal.]*

To comprehend the absolute connection of this opposition is the profound task of
metaphysics. *[The Divine, and hence religion, exists for the Ego, and likewise also the
world in general, that is, the universal totality of finite existence, exists for the Ego. The
Ego, in this relation, is itself its own finiteness and comprehends itself as finite. Thus it
is the viewpoint of finite purposes, of mere appearance. (At the same time it is particularity of consciousness.) Consciousness in itself, freedom abstractly considered, is the
formal aspect of the activity of the absolute Idea. This self-consciousness, first of all,
wills itself in general and, secondly, wills itself in every particular. This self-knowing
subjectivity projects itself into all objectivity. This constitutes the Ego's certainty of its
own existence. Inasmuch as this subjectivity has no other content, it must be called the
rational desire—just as piety is nothing but the desire for the subject's salvation. The
Ego thus wills itself primarily not as conscious but as finite in its immediacy. This is
the sphere of its phenomenality. It wills itself in its particularity. At this point we find
the passions, where individuality realizes its particularity. If it succeeds in thus realizing its finiteness, it doubles itself (its potential finiteness becomes actual finiteness).
Through this reconciliation of the atom and its othernesses individuals are what we call
happy, for happy is he who is in harmony with himself. One may contemplate history
from the point of view of happiness.]* But actually history is not the soil of happiness.
The periods of happiness are blank pages in it. *[There is, it is true, satisfaction in world
history. But it is not the kind that is called happiness, for it is satisfaction of purposes
that are above particular interests. Purposes that are relevant for world history must
be grasped in abstract volition and with energy. The world-historical individuals who
have pursued such purposes have satisfied themselves, it is true, but they did not want
to be happy.**

---

*[They wanted to be great. Greatness is satisfaction in large situations, happiness satisfaction in small
situations.]

This element of abstract action is to be regarded as the bond, the middle term, between the universal Idea, which reposes in the inner recesses of Spirit, and the external world. *[It is that which carries the Idea from its immanence into its external state. Universality, in being externalized, is at the same time made particular. The immanent by itself would be dead, abstract. Through action it becomes existent. Conversely, activity elevates (the) empty objectivity (of nature) to be the appearance of the essence which is in and for itself.]*

(B) THE INDIVIDUAL AS SUBJECT OF HISTORY

[In world history we deal with the Idea as it manifests itself in the element of human will, of human freedom. . . . Objectively seen, the Idea and the particular individual stand in the great opposition of Necessity and Freedom—the struggle of man against fate. But we take necessity not as the external necessity of fate, but as that of the divine Idea. The question then is: How is this high Idea to be united with human freedom? The will of the individual is free when it can posit abstractly, absolutely, and in and for itself that which it wills. How then can the universal, the rational in general, be determinant in history? This contradiction cannot be clarified here in complete detail. But think of the following:

The flame consumes the air; it is nourished by wood. The air is the sole condition for the growing of trees. In the wood's endeavor to consume the air through fire, it fights against itself and against its own source. And yet oxygen continues in the air and the trees do not cease to grow green. So also when someone starts building a house, his decision to do so is freely made. But all the elements must help. And yet the house is being built to protect man against the elements. Hence the elements are here used against themselves. But the general law of nature is not disturbed thereby.] The building of a house is, in the first instance, a subjective aim and design. On the other hand we have, as means, the several substances required for the work—iron, wood, stones. The elements are used in preparing this material: fire to melt the iron, wind to blow the fire, water to set wheels in motion in order to cut the wood, etc. The result is that the wind, which has helped to build the house, is shut out by the house; so also are the violence of rains and floods and the destructive powers of fire, so far as the house is made fireproof. The stones and beams obey the law of gravity and press downwards so that the high walls are held up. Thus the elements are made use of in accordance with their nature and cooperate for a product by which they become constrained. In a similar way the passions of men satisfy themselves; they develop themselves and their purposes in accordance with their natural destination and produce the edifice of human society. Thus they fortify a structure for law and order *against* themselves. *[Thus the passions are by no means always opposed to morality but actualize the universal. As far as their own morality is concerned, it is true, they strive to realize their own interests. Thus they appear bad and self-seeking. But action is always individual; it is always I who act. It is my purpose which I want to fulfill. This purpose may be a good one, a universal aim; on the other hand, the interest may be a particular, a private one. This does not mean that it is necessarily opposed to the universal good. On the contrary, the universal must be actualized through the particular.]*

This connection implies that human actions in history produce additional results, beyond their immediate purpose and attainment, beyond their immediate knowledge and desire. They gratify their own interests; but something more is thereby accomplished, which is latent in the action though not present in their consciousness and not included in their design. An analogous example is offered in the case of a man who, thirsting for revenge perhaps justly to redress an unjust injury, sets fire to another man's house. The deed immediately establishes a train of circumstances not directly connected with it, taken in itself. In itself it consists in merely presenting a small flame to a small portion of a beam. Events not involved in that simple act follow of themselves. The part of the beam which was set afire is connected with its remote portions; the beam itself is united with the woodwork of the house and this with other houses, and a wide conflagration ensues. It destroys the goods and chattels of many other persons besides those of the original victim and may even cost their lives. This lay neither in the deed itself, nor in the design of the man who committed it. But the action has a further general bearing. In the design of the doer it was only revenge executed against an individual through the destruction of his property. But it is moreover a crime, and that involves punishment. All this may not have been present to the mind of the perpetrator, still less in his intention; but his deed itself, the general principles that it calls into play, its substantial content, entail it. By this example I wish only to impress on you the consideration that in a simple act something further may be implicated than lies in the intention and consciousness of the agent. The example before us involves, however, this additional consideration, that the substance of the act—consequently we may say the act itself—recoils upon the perpetrator, reacts upon him and destroys him.

This union of the two extremes—the embodiment of a general idea in immediate actuality and the elevation of a particularity into universal truth—comes about under the condition of the diversity and mutual indifference of the two extremes. The human agents have before them limited aims, special interests. But they are also intelligent, thinking beings. Their purposes are interwoven with general and essential considerations of law, the good, duty, etc. For mere desire, volition in its raw and savage form, falls outside the scene and sphere of world history. These general considerations, which at the same time form norms for directing purposes and actions, have a definite content. For such empty abstractions as "good for its own sake" have no place in living actuality. If men are to act, they must not only intend the good but must know whether this or that particular course is good. What special course of action is good or not, right or wrong, is determined, for the ordinary circumstances of private life, by the laws and customs of a state. It is not too difficult to know them. *[It is part of the freedom in the state . . . that no apportionment in castes determines to which business an individual should dedicate himself. The morality of the individual, then, consists in his fulfilling the duties of his social position. And it is an easy matter to know what these duties are; they are determined by this position. The substantial content of such a relationship, its rationale, is known. It is, precisely, what is called duty. To investigate the content of duty is unnecessary speculation; in the tendency to regard the moral as a difficult problem, we rather sense the desire to get rid of one's duties.]* Each individual has his position; he knows, on the whole, what a lawful and honorable course of conduct is. To assert in ordinary private relations that it is difficult to choose the right and good, and to regard it as mark of an exalted morality to find difficulties and raise scruples on that score indicates an evil and perverse will. It indicates a will that seeks to evade obvious duties or, at least, a petty will that gives its mind too little to do. The mind, then, in idle reflection, busies itself with itself and indulges in moral smugness.

[The essence of a moral relation lies in the substantial nature that duty indicates. Thus, the nature of the relation between children and parents simply lies in the duty to behave accordingly. Or, to mention a legal relationship, if I owe money to someone, I just have to act according to law and the nature of the relation and return the money. There is nothing problematic in all this. The basis of duty is the civil life: the individu-

als have their assigned business and hence their assigned duties. *Their morality consists in acting accordingly. . . .*

But each individual is also the child of a people at a definite stage of its development. One cannot skip over the spirit of his people any more than one can skip over the earth. The earth is the center of gravity; a body imagined as leaving this center can only be imagined as exploding into the air. So it is with an individual. But only through his own effort can he be in harmony with his substance; he must bring the will demanded by his people to his own consciousness, to articulation. The individual does not invent his own content; he is what he is by acting out the universal as his own content.

This universal content everyone must activate within himself. Through this activity he maintains the whole of ethical life. But there is another element active in history which does bring about just this difficulty of acting according to ethical norms. We saw earlier, in the discussion of the dialectic of the Idea, where this universal content originates. It cannot originate within the ethical community. There particular events may occur that violate its determinate universality, such as vice, fraud, and the like, which are suppressed. But a moral whole, as such, is limited. It must have above it a higher universality, which makes it disunited in itself. The transition from one spiritual pattern to the next is just this, that the former moral whole, in itself a universal, through being thought (in terms of the higher universal), is abolished as a particular.* The later universal, so to speak, the next higher genus of the preceding species, is potentially but not yet actually present in the preceding one. This makes all existing reality unstable and disunited.

In the course of history two factors are important. One is the preservation of a people, a state, of the well-ordered spheres of life. This is the activity of individuals participating in the common effort and helping to bring about its particular manifestations. It is the preservation of ethical life. The other important factor, however, is the decline of a state. The existence of a national spirit is broken when it has used up and exhausted itself. World history, the World Spirit, continues on its course. We cannot deal here with the position of the individuals within the moral whole and their moral conduct and duty. We are concerned with the Spirit's development, its progression and ascent to an ever higher concept of itself. But this development is connected with the degradation, destruction, annihilation of the preceding mode of actuality which the concept of the Spirit had evolved. This is the result, on the one hand, of the inner development of the Idea and, on the other, of the activity of individuals, who are its agents and bring about its actualization.] It is at this point that appear those momentous collisions between existing, acknowledged duties, laws, and rights and those possibilities which are adverse to this system, violate it, and even destroy its foundations and existence. Their tenor may nevertheless seem good, on the whole advantageous—yes, even indispensable and necessary. These possibilities now become historical fact; they involve a universal of an order different from that upon which depends the permanence of a people or a state. This universal is an essential phase in the development of the creating Idea, of truth striving and urging toward itself. The historical men, *world-historical individuals,* are those *[who grasp just such a higher universal, make it their own purpose, and realize this purpose in accordance with the higher law of the spirit].*

Caesar was such a man. Before reaching his position of superiority he was in danger of losing his place of equality with the other leaders of Rome. He was about to succumb to those who were just becoming his enemies. These enemies, who at the same

---

*[For it is elevated into the universal.]

time pursued their own personal interests, had on their side the formal constitution of Rome and the power of legal appearance. Caesar fought to keep his position, honor, and safety. But victory over his enemies, who held the power over all the Roman provinces, became at the same time conquest of the entire empire. Thus Caesar, without changing the form of the constitution, became the sole ruler of the state. In accomplishing his originally negative purpose—the autocracy over Rome—he at the same time fulfilled the necessary historical destiny of Rome and the world. Thus he was motivated not only by his own private interest, but acted instinctively to bring to pass that which the times required. It is the same with all great historical individuals: their own particular purposes contain the substantial will of the World Spirit. They must be called "heroes," insofar as they have derived their purpose and vocation not from the calm, regular course of things, sanctioned by the existing order, but from a secret source whose content is still hidden and has not yet broken through into existence. The source of their actions is the inner spirit, still hidden beneath the surface but already knocking against the outer world as against a shell, in order, finally, to burst forth and break it into pieces; for it is a kernel different from that which belongs to the shell. They are men, therefore, who appear to draw the impulses of their lives from themselves. Their deeds have produced a condition of things and a complex of historical relations that appear to be their own interest and their own work.

Such individuals have no consciousness of the Idea as such. They are practical and political men. But at the same time they are thinkers with insight into what is needed and timely. They see the very truth of their age and their world, the next genus, so to speak, which is already formed in the womb of time. It is theirs to know this new universal, the necessary next stage of their world, to make it their own aim and put all their energy into it. The world-historical persons, the heroes of their age, must therefore be recognized as its seers—their words and deeds are the best of the age. Great men have worked for their own satisfaction and not that of others. Whatever prudent designs and well-meant counsels they might have gotten from others would have been limited and inappropriate under the circumstances. For it is they who knew best and from whom the others eventually learned and with whom they agreed or, at least, complied. For Spirit, in taking this new historical step, is the innermost soul of all individuals— but in a state of unconsciousness, which the great men arouse to consciousness. For this reason their fellow men follow these soul-leaders, *[they stream to their banner]*. For they feel the irresistible power of their own spirit embodied in them.

Let us now cast a look at the fate of these world-historical individuals. *[They were fortunate in being the agents of a purpose which constitutes a step in the progress of the universal Spirit. But as individuals distinguished from their substantial aim, they were not what is commonly called happy, nor did they want to be. They wanted to achieve their aim, and they achieved it by their toil and labor. They succeeded in finding their satisfaction in bringing about their purpose, the universal purpose. With such a grand aim they had the boldness to challenge all the opinions of men.]* Thus they attained no calm enjoyment. Their whole life was labor and trouble, their whole being was in their passion. Once their objective is attained, they fall off like empty hulls from the kernel. They die early like Alexander, they are murdered like Caesar, transported to Saint Helena like Napoleon. This awful fact, that historical men were not what is called happy—for only private life in its manifold external circumstances can be "happy"— may serve as a consolation for those people who need it, the envious ones who cannot tolerate greatness and eminence. They strive to criticize the great and belittle greatness. Thus in modern times it has been demonstrated *ad nauseam* that princes are generally unhappy on their thrones. For this reason one does not begrudge them their position and finds it tolerable that *they* rather than oneself sit on the throne. The free man, however, is not envious, but gladly recognizes what is great and exalted and rejoices in its existence. . . . *[But to such great men attaches a whole train of envy, which tries to demonstrate that their passion is a vice. One can indeed apply the term "passion" to the phenomenon of the great men and can judge them morally by saying that passion had driven them. They were indeed men of passion: they had the passion of their conviction and put their whole character, genius, and energy into it. Here, then, what is necessary in and for itself appears in the form of passion. These great men seem only to follow their passion and their arbitrary wills. But what they pursue is the universal; that alone is their pathos. The passion precisely has been the energy of their ego; without it they would not have been able to achieve anything.*

In this way the purpose of passion and the purpose of the Idea are one and the same. Passion is the absolute unity of individual character and the universal. It is something almost animalic how the spirit in its subjective particularity here becomes identified with the Idea. . . .

By fulfilling their own great purpose in accordance with the necessity of the universal Spirit, these world-historical men also satisfy themselves. These two things belong inseparably together: the cause and its hero. They must both be satisfied. . . . It is psychological pedantry to make a separation and, by giving passion the name of addiction, to suspect the morality of these men. By saying they acted only from morbid craving, one presents the consequences of their actions as their purposes and degrades the actions themselves to means.] Alexander of Macedon partly conquered Greece and then Asia; it is said, therefore, that he craved conquest, and as proof it is offered that he did things which resulted in fame. What schoolmaster has not demonstrated that Alexander the Great and Julius Caesar were driven by such passions and were, consequently, immoral? From which it immediately follows that he, the schoolmaster, is a better man than they because he has no such passions, and proves it by the fact that he has not conquered Asia nor vanquished Darius and Porus, but enjoys life and allows others to enjoy it too. These psychologists are particularly fond of contemplating those peculiarities that belong to great historical figures as private persons. Man must eat and drink; he has relations with friends and acquaintances; he has emotions and fits of temper. "No man is a hero to his *valet de chambre,*" is a well-known proverb; I have added—and Goethe repeated it two years later—"but not because the former is no hero, but because the latter is a valet." He takes off the hero's boots, helps him into bed, knows that he prefers champagne, and the like. Historical personages fare badly in historical literature when served by such psychological valets. These attendants degrade them to their own level, or rather a few degrees below the level of their own morality, these exquisite discerners of spirits. Homer's Thersites, who abuses the kings, is a standing figure for all times. Not in every age, it is true, does he get blows—that is, beating with a solid cudgel—as in the Homeric one. But his envy, his egotism, is the thorn that he has to carry in his flesh; and the undying worm that gnaws him is the tormenting thought that his excellent intentions and criticisms get absolutely no result in the world. One may be allowed a certain glee over Thersites' fate.

A world-historical individual is not so sober as to adjust his ambition to circumstances; nor is he very considerate. He is devoted, come what may, to one purpose. Therefore such men may treat other great and even sacred interests inconsiderately—a conduct which indeed subjects them to moral reprehension. But so mighty a figure must trample down many an innocent flower, crush to pieces many things in its path.

(C) THE INDIVIDUAL AS OBJECT OF HISTORY

The special interest of passion is thus inseparable from the actualization of the universal; for the universal results from the particular and definite and its negation. *[The particular has its own role to play in world history; it is finite and must, as such, perish.]* It is the particular which exhausts itself in the struggle and part of which is destroyed. *[But the universal results precisely from this struggle, from the destruction of the particular.]* It is not the general Idea that involves itself in opposition and combat and exposes itself to danger; it remains in the background, untouched and uninjured. This may be called the *cunning of Reason*—that it sets the passions to work for itself, while that through which it develops itself pays the penalty and suffers the loss. For it is the phenomenal which in part is negative, in part positive. The particular in most cases is too trifling as compared with the universal; the individuals are sacrificed and abandoned. The Idea pays the tribute of existence and transience, not out of its own funds but with the passions of the individuals.

We might find it tolerable that individuals, their purposes and gratifications, are thus sacrificed, their happiness abandoned to the realm of *[natural forces and hence of]* chance to which it belongs; and that individuals in general are regarded under the category of means. Yet there is one aspect of human individuality that we must refuse to take exclusively in this light even in relation to the highest, an element which is absolutely not subordinate but exists in individuals as essentially eternal and divine. I mean morality, ethics, religion. Already in discussing the role of individuals in the realization of the rational aim we said that the subjective element in them, their interests, cravings, and impulses, their views and judgments had an infinite right to be satisfied, although we regarded these as only the formal aspect of the process. In speaking of means we imagine, first of all, something external to the end which has no share in it. But actually even merely natural things, the most common lifeless objects used as means, must somehow be adapted to their purpose; they must have something in common with it. This bare external relation of mere means is the least relation human beings have to the rational purpose. In the very act of realizing it they make it the occasion of satisfying their personal desires, whose import is different from that purpose. Moreover, they share in the rational purpose itself and for that very reason are ends in themselves—not merely formally, as is the world of other living beings, whose individual life is essentially subordinate to that of man and is properly used up as an instrument. Men, on the contrary, are ends in themselves in regard to the content of the end. This defines those elements which we demand to be exempt from the category of means: morality, ethics, religion.

Man is an end in himself only by virtue of the divine in him—that which we designated at the outset as *Reason,* or, insofar as it has activity and power of self-determination, as *Freedom.* And we say—without entering at present into further discussion—that religiosity, morality, etc., have their foundation and source in it and are thus essentially exempt from external necessity and chance. *[But we must not forget that here we speak of morality, religiosity, etc., only insofar as they exist in individuals, hence, subject to individual freedom. In this sense, that is,]* to the extent of their freedom, individuals are responsible for the depravation and enfeeblement of morality and religion. This is the seal of the absolute and sublime destiny of man, that he knows what is good and what is evil, and that his destiny is his very ability to will either good or evil. In one word, he can be guilty—guilty not only of evil but of good, and not only concerning this or that particular matter and all that happens in and around him *(Sitt-*

lichkeit), but also the good and evil attaching to his individual freedom *(Moralität)*. The animal alone is truly innocent. It would, however, require an extensive explanation—as extensive as that of freedom itself—to avoid or refute all the misunderstandings which usually arise from the statement that the word "innocence" means ignorance of evil.

In contemplating the fate which virtue, morality, even piety have in history, we must not fall into the litany of lamentations that the good and pious often, or for the most part, fare ill in the world, while the evil and wicked prosper. By prosperity one may understand a variety of things—riches, outward honor, and the like. But in speaking of purpose in and for itself, the so-called prosperity or misfortune of this or that isolated individual cannot be regarded as an essential element in the rational order of the universe. With more reason than merely the happiness or fortunate circumstances of individuals we demand of the purpose of the world that good, moral, righteous purposes should find in and under it their satisfaction and security. What makes men morally discontented—a discontent on which they pride themselves—is that they do not find the present appropriate for the realization of aims which in their opinion are right and good—especially the ideals of political institutions of our time. They contrast things as they are with their ideal of things as they ought to be. In this case it is neither private interest nor passion that desires gratification, but reason, justice, liberty. In their name people demand their due and often are not merely discontent but rebellious against the condition of the world. To estimate such views and feelings one would have to examine the stubborn demands and dogmatic opinions in question. At no time as much as in our own have such general principles and notions been advanced with so much pretentiousness. At other times history seems to present itself as a struggle of passions. In our time, however, though passions are not wanting, history exhibits partly and predominantly a struggle of justifiable ideas and partly a struggle of passions and subjective interests under the mask of such higher pretensions. These pretensions, regarded as legitimate in the name of the supposed destiny of Reason, are thereby validated as absolute ends—in the same way as religion, morality, ethics.

As was said earlier, nothing is now more common than the complaint that the *ideals* which imagination sets up are not actualized, that these glorious dreams are destroyed by cold actuality. These ideals, which in the voyage of life founder on the rocks of hard reality, may be merely subjective to begin with and belong to the peculiarity of an individual who regards himself as supremely wise. Such ideals do not belong here. For what an individual fancies for himself in his isolation cannot be the norm for universal reality. The universal law is not designed for individuals, as such, who indeed may find themselves very much the losers. But by the term "ideal" we also understand the ideal of Reason, of the good and true. Poets, like Schiller, have painted such ideals touchingly and with strong emotion, and with the deeply melancholy conviction that they could never be actualized. In affirming, on the contrary, that the universal Reason *does* actualize itself, we have nothing to do with the empirical detail. For this can be better or worse; here chance and particularity have received authority to exercise their tremendous power. Much fault, therefore, might be found in phenomenal details. This subjective fault-finding is easy, particularly since it keeps in view only the detail and its deficiency, without understanding the universal Reason in it. In asserting good intentions for the welfare of the whole and exhibiting a semblance of good-heartedness, it can swagger about with great airs. It is easier to discover the deficiency in individuals, in states, and in Providence, than to see their real meaning. For in negative fault-finding one stands nobly and with proud mien above the matter, without penetrating into it and without comprehending its positive aspects. Age generally makes people more tolerant; youth is always discontented. For older people have a more mature judgment, which accepts even the bad, not out of mere indifference but because it has been more deeply taught by the grave experience of life. It has thus been led to the essence, the intrinsic value of the matter in question.

The insight then to which—in opposition to these ideals—philosophy should lead us is that the actual world is as it ought to be, that the truly good, the universal divine Reason is the power capable of actualizing itself. This good, this Reason, in its most concrete representation, is God. God governs the world. The actual working of His government, the carrying out of His plan is the history of the world. Philosophy strives to comprehend this plan, for only that which has been carried out according to it has reality; whatever does not accord with it is but worthless existence. Before the pure light of this divine Idea, which is no mere ideal, the illusion disappears as though the world were a crazy, inane process. Philosophy wishes to recognize the content, the reality of the divine Idea, and to justify the spurned actuality; for Reason is the comprehension of the divine work.

But then what about the atrophy, corruption, and ruin of religious, ethical, and moral purposes and social conditions in general? It must be said that essentially these purposes are infinite and eternal. But the forms that they assume may be of a limited order and consequently belong to the realm of mere nature, subject to the sway of chance. They are therefore transitory and exposed to atrophy and corruption. Religion and morality, as the universal essences in themselves, have the peculiarity of being present, conformably to their concepts and therefore truthfully, in the individual soul, although they may not be represented there fully elaborated and applied to completely developed conditions. The religiousness, the morality of a limited life—of a shepherd, a peasant—in their concentrated inward limitation to a few and quite simple circumstances of life, has infinite value. It has the same value as the religiousness and morality of a trained intellect and of an existence rich in scope of relations and activities. This inner focus, this simple region of the claims of subjective freedom—the seat of volition, resolution, and action, the abstract content of conscience, that wherein responsibility and worth of the individual are enclosed—remains untouched. It is quite shut out from the noisy din of world history, not only from its external and temporal changes but also from all alterations entailed by the absolute necessity of the concept of freedom itself. In general, however, it must be noted that for whatever in the world is acclaimed as noble and glorious there is something even higher. The claim of the World Spirit rises above all special claims.

So much concerning the means which the World Spirit uses for actualizing its concept. Simply and abstractedly, it is the activity of the subjects in whom Reason is present as their substantial essence in itself, but still obscure and concealed from them. The matter becomes more complicated and difficult when we regard the individuals not merely as active but, more concretely, consider the definite content of their religion and morality—features which have part in Reason and thereby in its absolute claims. Here the relation of mere means to an end disappears. The main points of this seeming difficulty with regard to the absolute purpose of Spirit have been briefly considered.

3. THE STATE

(A) THE STATE AS REALIZATION OF THE IDEA

The third point, then, concerns the end to be attained by these means, that is, the form it assumes in the realm of the actual. We have spoken of means; but the carrying out of a subjective, limited aim also requires a *material* element, either already present or to be procured or to serve this actualization. Thus the question would arise: What is the material in which the final end of Reason is to be realized? It is first of all the subjective agent itself, human desires, subjectivity in general. In human knowledge and volition, as its material basis, the rational attains existence. We have considered subjective volition with its purpose, namely, the truth of reality, insofar as moved by a great world-historical passion. As a subjective will in limited passions it is dependent; it can gratify its particular desires only within this dependence. But the subjective will has also a substantial life, a reality where it moves in the region of essential being and has the essential itself as the object of its existence. This essential being is the union of the subjective with the rational will; it is the moral whole, the *State*. It is that actuality in which the individual has and enjoys his freedom, but only as knowing, believing, and willing the universal. This must not be understood as if the subjective will of the individual attained its gratification and enjoyment through the common will and the latter were a means for it—as if the individual limited his freedom among the other individuals, so that this common limitation, the mutual constraint of all, might secure a small space of liberty for each. (This would only be negative freedom.) Rather, law, morality, the State, and they alone, are the positive reality and satisfaction of freedom. The caprice of the individual is not freedom. It is this caprice which is being limited, the license of particular desires.

The subjective will, passion, is the force which actualizes and realizes. The Idea is the interior; the State is the externally existing, genuinely moral life. It is the union of the universal and essential with the subjective will, and as such it is *Morality*. The individual who lives in this unity has a moral life, a value which consists in this substantiality alone.* Sophocles' Antigone says: "The divine commands are not of yesterday nor of today; no, they have an infinite existence, and no one can say whence they came." The laws of ethics are not accidental, but are rationality itself. It is the end of the State to make the substantial prevail and maintain itself in the actual doings of men and in their convictions. It is the absolute interest of Reason that this moral whole exist; and herein lies the justification and merit of heroes who have founded states, no matter how crude.

[What counts in a state is the practice of acting according to a common will and adopting universal aims. Even in the crude state there is subjection of one will under another; but this does not mean that the individual does not have a will of his own. It means that his particular will has no validity. Whims, lusts are not valid. The particularity of the will is being renounced already in such crude political formations. What counts is the common will. In thus being suppressed the individual will retires into itself. And this is the first condition necessary for the existence of the universal, the condition, namely, of knowledge, of thought—for it is thought that man has in common with the divine. It thus makes its appearance in the state. Only on this soil, that is, in the state, can art and religion exist. The objects of our considerations are peoples that have organized themselves rationally.] In world history only those peoples that form states can come to our notice. *[One must not imagine that such organizations could appear on a desert island or in isolation. Although it is true that all great men have formed themselves in solitude, they have done so only by assimilating what the state had already created. The universal must be not only something which the individual merely intends, but which is*

---

*[Social institutions, originally extrinsic to the individual and his intrinsic morality, grow up to complete this morality in the course of their development. Their totality, the State, thus becomes itself intrinsic morality, both with respect to the individual, as completion of his intrinsic freedom, and to the World Spirit, as concretion of its universal Freedom.]

in existence. As such it is present in the state; it is that which is valid in it. Here inward-
ness is at the same time actuality. It is but actuality of an external manifold, yet com-
prehended here in universality.

The universal Idea manifests itself in the state. The term "manifestation" has here
a meaning different from the usual one. Usually we distinguish between power (poten-
tiality) and manifestation, as if the former were the essential, the latter the unessential
or external. But no concrete determination lies as yet in the category of power itself,
while where Spirit is, or the concrete concept, manifestation itself is the essential. The
criterion of Spirit is its action, its active essence. Man is his own action, the sequence of
his actions, that into which he has been making himself. Thus Spirit is essentially En-
ergy; and in regard to Spirit one cannot set aside its manifestation. The manifestation of
Spirit is its actual self-determination, and this is the element of its concrete nature.
Spirit which does not determine itself is an abstraction of the intellect. The manifesta-
tion of Spirit is its self-determination, and it is this manifestation that we have to inves-
tigate in the form of states and individuals.

The spiritual individual, the people, insofar as it is organized in itself, an organic
whole, is what we call the State. This designation is ambiguous in that by "state" and
"constitutional law" one usually means the simple political aspect as distinct from reli-
gion, science, and art. But when we speak of the manifestation of the spiritual we un-
derstand the term "state" in a more comprehensive sense, similar to the term Reich
(empire, realm). For us, then, a people is primarily a spiritual individual. We do not em-
phasize the external aspects but concentrate on what has been called the spirit of a peo-
ple. We mean its consciousness of itself, of its own truth, its own essence, the spiritual
powers which live and rule in it. The universal which manifests itself in the State and is
known in it—the form *under which everything that is, is subsumed—is that which con-*
stitutes the culture *of a nation. The definite* content *which receives this universal form*
and is contained in the concrete actuality of the state is the spirit of the people. *The ac-*
tual state is animated by this spirit in all its particular affairs, wars, institutions, etc.
This spiritual content is something definite, firm, solid, completely exempt from caprice,
the particularities, the whims of individuality, of chance. That which is subject to the
latter is not the nature of the people: it is like the dust playing over a city or a field,
which does not essentially transform it. This spiritual content then constitutes the
essence of the individual as well as that of the people. It is the holy bond that ties the
men, the spirits together. It is one life in all, a grand object, a great purpose and content
on which depend all individual happiness and all private decisions. [The state does not
exist for the citizens; on the contrary, one could say that the state is the end and they are
its means. But the means-end relation is not fitting here. For the state is not the abstract
confronting the citizens; they are parts of it, like members of an organic body, where no
member is end and none is means.] It is the realization of Freedom, of the absolute, final purpose, and exists for its own sake. All the value man has, all spiritual reality, he
has only through the state. For his spiritual reality is the knowing presence to him of his
own essence, of rationality, of its objective, immediate actuality present in and for him.
Only thus is he truly a consciousness, only thus does he partake in morality, in the legal
and moral life of the state. For the True is the unity of the universal and particular will.
And the universal in the state is in its laws, its universal and rational provisions. The
state is the divine Idea as it exists on earth.

Thus the State is the definite object of world history proper. In it freedom
achieves its objectivity and lives in the enjoyment of this objectivity. For law is the objectivity of Spirit; it is will in its true form. Only the will that obeys the law is free, for
it obeys itself and, being in itself, is free. In so far as the state, our country, constitutes a

community of existence, and as the subjective will of man subjects itself to the laws, the antithesis of freedom and necessity disappears. The rational, like the substantial, is necessary. We are free when we recognize it as law and follow it as the substance of our own being. The objective and the subjective will are then reconciled and form one and the same harmonious whole. For the ethos of the state is not of the moral, the reflective kind in which one's own conviction rules supreme. This latter is rather the peculiarity of the modern world. The true and antique morality is rooted in the principle that everybody stands in his place of duty. An Athenian citizen did what was required of him, as it were from instinct. But if I reflect on the object of my activity, I must have the consciousness that my will counts. Morality, however, is the duty, the substantial law, the second nature, as it has been rightly called; for the first nature of man is his immediate, animalic existence.

(B) LAW AS REALIZATION OF FREEDOM

The detailed development of the state is the subject of legal philosophy. But it must be observed that in present-day theories various errors are current respecting the state, which pass for established truths and have become prejudices. We will mention only a few of them, particularly those which refer to the subject of history.

The first error that we encounter is the direct contradiction of our principle that the State is the realization of freedom: the view, namely, that man is free by nature but that in society and in the state, to which he necessarily belongs, he must limit this natural freedom. That man is free "by nature" is quite correct in the sense that he is free according to the very concept of man, that is, in his *destination* only, as he is, in himself; the "nature" of a thing is indeed tantamount to its concept. But the view in question also introduces into the concept of man his immediate and natural way of *existence.* In this sense a state of nature is assumed in which man is imagined in the possession of his natural rights and the unlimited exercise and enjoyment of his freedom. This assumption is not presented as a historical fact; it would indeed be difficult, were the attempt seriously made, to detect any such condition anywhere, either in the present or the past. Primitive conditions can indeed be found, but they are marked by brute passions and acts of violence. Crude as they are, they are at the same time connected with social institutions which, to use the common expression, restrain freedom. The assumption (of the noble savage) is one of those nebulous images which theory produces, an idea which necessarily flows from that theory and to which it ascribes real existence without sufficient historical justification.

Such a state of nature is in theory exactly as we find it in practice. Freedom as the *ideal* of the original state of nature does not *exist* as original and natural. It must first be acquired and won; and that is possible only through an infinite process of the discipline of knowledge and will power. The state of nature, therefore, is rather the state of injustice, violence, untamed natural impulses, of inhuman deeds and emotions. There is, it is true, a limitation by society and the state, but it is a limitation of the brute emotions and rude instincts, as well as (in a more advanced stage of culture) of self-reflecting caprice and passion. This constraint is part of the process through which is first produced the consciousness of and the desire for freedom in its true, that is, rational and ideal form. The idea of freedom necessarily implies law and morality. These are in and for themselves universal essences, objects, and aims, to be discovered only by the activity of thought, emancipating itself from, and developing itself in opposition to, the merely sensuous; it must be assimilated to and incorporated with the originally sensuous will against its natural inclination. The perpetual misunderstanding of freedom is this: that one knows it only in its formal subjective sense, abstracted from its essential objects and aims. Thus the limitation of impulse, desire, passion—pertaining merely to the particular individual as such—of caprice and willfulness, is taken as a limitation of freedom. On the contrary, such limitation is the very condition leading to liberation; and society and the state are the very conditions in which freedom is realized.

Secondly, there is another theory that objects to the development of morality into legal form. The *patriarchal* state is viewed, either in relation to the whole or to some branches (of the human family), as that condition in which, together with the legal element, the moral and emotional find their fulfillment. Hence justice, it is believed, can be truly carried out only through the union of its content with the moral and emotional elements. The basis of the patriarchal condition is the family relation. It develops as the first phase of conscious morality, to be followed by that of the state as its second phase. The patriarchal condition is one of transition, in which the family has already advanced to a race or people. The union, therefore, has already ceased to be simply a bond of love and confidence and has become one of service. To understand this transition we must first examine the ethical principle of the family. The family is a single person; its members have either, as parents, mutually surrendered their individuality—and consequently their legal relations to one another, as well as their particular interests and desires—or have not yet attained individuality, as children, who are at first in the merely natural condition already mentioned. They live therefore in a unity of feeling, love, confidence, and faith in each other. In love, the one individual has the consciousness of himself in the consciousness of the other; he lives selflessly. In this mutual self-renunciation each gains the life of the other, as well as his own which is one with the other. All other interests of life, its necessities and external concerns, education of the children, form a common purpose for the members of the family. The spirit of the family—the Penates—are as much one substantial being as the spirit of a people in the State. Morality in both cases consists in a feeling, a consciousness, and a will not of the individual personality and its interests but of the common personality, the interest of all members as such. But this unity is in the case of the family essentially one of feeling, remaining within the limits of the natural. The sacredness of the family relation should be respected in the highest degree by the state. Through it the state has as members individuals who are already, as such and in themselves, moral—for as mere persons they are not; and who, in uniting to form a state, bring with them the sound basis of a political edifice, the capacity of feeling one with a whole. But the expansion of the family to a patriarchal whole extends beyond the ties of blood relationship, the simple, natural basis of the state. Beyond that the individuals must acquire the status of personality. A detailed review of the patriarchal condition would lead us to the discussion of theocracy. The head of the patriarchal clan is also its priest. When the family is not yet distinct from civil society and the state, the separation of religion from it has not yet taken place either; and so much the less since its piety is itself (like religion) an inwardness of feeling.

(C) THE LEGAL FOUNDATION OF THE STATE
(THE CONSTITUTION)

We have discussed two aspects of freedom, the objective and the subjective. If freedom implies the consent of each individual, then of course only the subjective aspect is meant. From this principle follows as a matter of course that no law is valid except by agreement of all. This implies that the majority decides; hence the minority must yield to the majority. But already Rousseau has remarked that this means the absence of freedom, for the will of the minority is disregarded. In the Polish diet all decisions had to be unanimous, and it was from this kind of freedom that the state perished. Moreover, it is a dangerous and false presupposition that the people *alone* has reason and insight and knows what is right; for each popular faction can set itself up as the People. What constitutes the state is a matter of trained intelligence, not a matter of "the people."

If the principle of individual will and consent of all is laid down as the only basis of constitutional freedom, then actually there is no *Constitution*. The only institution necessary would be a neutral, centrally located observer who would announce what in his opinion were the needs of the state, a mechanism of assembling the individuals, casting their vote, and the arithmetical counting and comparison of the votes on the various propositions—and this would already be the decision. The state is an abstract entity which has its—merely general—reality in the citizens. But it is real, and the merely general existence must be translated into individual will and activity. Thus arises the necessity of government and administration, the selection of individuals who have to take the helm of political administration, decide its execution, and command the citizens entrusted with it. Thus, even in a democracy the people's decision on a war requires a general as leader of the army. Only in the constitution does the abstract entity of the state assume life and reality; but this involves a distinction between those who command and those who obey. Yet, it does not seem to be in accordance with freedom to obey, and those who command seem to act in opposition to the concept of freedom, the very basis of the state.

Thus the distinction between commanding and obeying seems necessary for the very function of the state. Hence one recommends—as a matter of purely external necessity, which is in opposition to the nature of freedom in its abstract aspect—that the constitution should at least be so framed that the citizens have to obey as little as possible and the authorities are allowed to command as little as possible. The nature and degree of whatever authority is necessary should be determined and decided in large measure by the people, that is to say, by the will of the majority; yet, at the same time the state, as reality, as individual unit, should have power and strength.

The primary distinction to be made is, then, between the governing and the governed. Constitutions have rightly been classified as monarchic, aristocratic, and democratic; the monarchy proper, however, must be distinguished again from despotism. Also, it must be understood that such classifications are drawn from abstract concepts so as to emphasize the fundamental differences only. They are types or genera or species which cannot exhaustively account for the concrete realities. Particularly, they admit of a great number of special modifications, not only within the types but also among the types; even though such fusions or mixtures of type conduce to misshapen, unstable, and inconsistent forms. The problem, in such collisions, therefore, is to determine the *best constitution*, namely, that institution, organization, or mechanism of government which most securely guarantees the purpose of the state. This goal can of course be considered in various ways, for example, as the quiet enjoyment of life, as universal happiness. Such aims have brought about the so-called ideals of government and, particularly, the ideals of the education of princes, as in Fénelon,* or of the rulers

*[In his *Télémaque* (1699), written after Fénelon's tutorship of the Duke of Burgundy, who for a year (1711–1712) was heir-apparent to the throne of Louis XIV. Fénelon (1651–1715) also wrote a *Treatise on the Education of Girls,* which for a century became the standard handbook on the subject. In 1695 he became archbishop of Cambrai. His writings form the transition from absolutism to enlightenment.]

or the aristocracy in general, as in Plato. The emphasis is here put on the nature of the ruling individuals; the content of the organic institutions of the state is not at all considered. It is often thought that the question of the best or a better constitution is not only in theory a matter of free individual conviction, but that its actual introduction could also be only a matter of purely theoretical decisions; so that the constitution would be a matter of free choice, determined by nothing but reflection. In this quite naïve sense the Persian magnates—though not the Persian people—deliberated upon the constitution which they wanted to introduce in Persia, after their conspiracy against the pseudo-Smerdis and the Magi had succeeded and there was no royal heir. And the account that Herodotus gives of this deliberation is equally naïve.

Today the constitution of a country and people is not regarded as so entirely dependent upon free choice. The underlying, but abstractly entertained conception of freedom has resulted in the Republic's being quite universally regarded—in theory—as the only just and true constitution. Many of those who even have high official positions under monarchical constitutions do not resist but rather incline toward such views. They understand, however, that such a constitution, though ideal, cannot be realized under all circumstances. People being what they are, one has to be content with less freedom; so that the monarchical constitution, under the given circumstances and the moral condition of the people, is regarded the most useful. Even in this view the actual condition on which the constitution is thought to depend is regarded as a merely external accident. This opinion is based on the separation which reflection and understanding make between the concept and its reality. Holding to an abstract and hence untrue concept they do not grasp the idea; or—which comes to the same thing insofar as the content, though not the form, is concerned—they have no concrete view of a people and a state. We shall show later that the constitution of a people is of the same substance, the same spirit as its art and philosophy, or at least its imagination, its thoughts, and its general culture—not to mention the additional, external influences of climate, neighbors, and global position. A state is an individual totality from which no particular aspect, not even one as highly important as the constitution, can be separated and considered by itself alone. Nor can this constitution be considered, discussed, and selected in isolation. Not only is the constitution intimately connected with those other spiritual forces and dependent on them, but the determination of the whole spiritual individuality, including all its forces, is only a moment in the history of the whole and predetermined in its course. It is this that gives to the constitution its highest sanction and necessity. The origin of the state is domination on the one hand, instinctive obedience on the other. But obedience and force, fear of a ruler, is already a connection of wills. Already in primitive states we found that the will of the individual does not count, that particularity is renounced and the universal will is the essential. This unity of the universal and the particular is the Idea itself, present as the State and as such developing itself further. The abstract but necessary course of the development of truly independent states begins then with royal power, either patriarchal or military. After that, individuality and particularity must assert themselves in aristocracy and democracy. The end is the subjection of this particularity under one power which must be absolutely of such a nature that the two spheres have their independence outside of it: it must be monarchical. Thus we must distinguish a first (or original) and a second phase of royalty. This course is a necessary one; each concrete constitution must enter it. A constitution is therefore not a matter of choice but depends on the stage of the people's spiritual development.

What is important in a constitution is the internal development of the rational, that is, the political condition, the setting free of the successive moments of the concept. The particular powers must become distinct, each one completing itself, but at the same time they must freely cooperate for one purpose and be held together by it, thus forming an organic whole. Thus the State is rational and self-conscious freedom, objectively knowing itself. For its objectivity resides precisely in the fact that its moments are not merely ideally present but actualized in their particularity; that they pass over from their own self-related activity into that activity from which results the whole, the soul, the individual unity.

The State is the idea of Spirit in the externality of human will and its freedom. It therefore is essentially the medium of historical change, and the stages of the Idea represent in it various *principles.* The constitutions wherein world-historical peoples have reached their flowering are peculiar to them, hence give us no universally valid basis. Their differences consist not in the individual manners of elaboration and development, but rather in the differences of principles. Thus we can learn little for the political principle of our time, as the last constitutional principle, from a comparison with the constitutions of earlier world-historical peoples. It is different with science and art. The philosophy of the ancients, for example, is so much the basis of modern philosophy that it must be contained in the latter as its fundament. The relation is here one of uninterrupted development of an identical structure, whose foundations, walls, and roof are still the same. In art that of the Greeks is the highest model. But in respect to the constitution it is different; here the old and the new do not have the essential principle in common, although we do have in common abstract speculations and doctrines of just government, of insight and virtue of the ruler. Yet, nothing is so inappropriate as to use as models for our constitutional institutions examples from Greece, Rome, or the Orient. From the Orient we can take agreeable pictures of patriarchal conditions, fatherly government, popular devotion; from the Greeks and Romans descriptions of popular liberty. The Greeks and Romans understood the concept of a free constitution as granting all citizens a share in the council and decisions of communal affairs and laws. Also in our times this is the general opinion, but with one modification: our states are so big and their people so many, that they cannot directly, but only indirectly through representatives, contribute their will to political decisions. For purposes of legislation the people must be represented by deputies. A free constitution is for us dependent upon the idea of representative government, and this has become a firm prejudice. Thus people and government are separated. But there is something malicious in this opposition, a trick of bad will, as if the people were the whole. Also, at the bottom of this idea lies the principle of individuality, the absoluteness of the subjective will of which we spoke above. The main thing is that freedom, as it is determined by the concept, is *not* based on the subjective will and caprice but on the understanding of the general will, and that the system of freedom is the free development of its stages. The subjective will is a purely formal concept which does not say at all *what* it wills. Only the rational will is the universal which determines and develops itself in itself and unfolds its successive moments in an organic manner. Of such Gothic cathedral architecture the ancients knew nothing.

(D) THE RELIGIOUS FOUNDATION OF THE STATE

We have established as the two points of our discussion, first, the idea of Freedom as absolute final aim, and, secondly, the means of its realization, the subjective side of knowledge and volition with their vitality, mobility, and activity. We then discussed the State as the moral whole and the reality of freedom, and thus as the objective unity of the two preceding factors. Although for analysis we separated the two elements, it must be well remembered that they are closely connected and that this connection is within each of them when we examine them singly. On the one hand we recognized the Idea in its determination, as self-knowing and self-willing freedom which has only itself as its aim. As such, it is at the same time the simple idea of reason and likewise that which we have called subject, the consciousness of self, the Spirit existing in the world. On the other hand, in considering this subjectivity, we find that subjective knowing and willing are Thinking. But in thoughtful knowing and willing I will the universal object, the substance of actualized rationality (of what is in and for itself rational). We thus observe a union which is in itself, between the objective element, the concept, and the subjective element. The objective existence of this unity is the State. The State, thus, is the foundation and center of the other concrete aspects of national life, of art, law, morality, religion, science. All spiritual activity, then, has the aim of becoming conscious of this union, that is, of its freedom. Among the forms of these conscious unions *religion* is the highest. In it the spirit existing in the world becomes conscious of absolute Spirit. In this consciousness of actualized ("being-in-and-for-itself") essence the will of man renounces particular interest; it puts it aside in devotion in which he is not concerned any more with particulars. Through sacrifice man expresses his renunciation of property, his will, his private feelings. The religious concentration of the mind appears as emotion, but passes also into contemplation; ritual is an expression of contemplation. The second form of the spiritual union between the objective and the subjective is *Art:* it appears more in sensible reality than does religion; in its most noble attitude it has to represent, not indeed the spirit of God but the form of the God—and then the divine, the spiritual in general. It renders the divine visible to imagination and the senses. The True, however, not only achieves representation and feeling, as in religion, and for the senses, as in art, but also for the thinking spirit; this leads to the third form of the union, *Philosophy.* It is in this respect the highest, freest, and wisest product. We cannot here discuss these three forms in any detail. They had to be mentioned only because they occupy the same ground as the object of our study, the *State.*

The universal which appears and becomes known in the state, the form into which is cast all reality, constitutes what is generally called the *culture* of a nation. The definite content, however, which receives the form of universality and is contained in the concrete reality of the State, is the *spirit of the people.* The true State is animated by this spirit in all its affairs, wars, institutions, etc. But man must himself know of this—his own—spirit and essence and give himself the consciousness of his original union with it. For we said that all morality is the unity of subjective and general will. The spirit, then, must give itself an express consciousness of this unity, and the center of this knowledge is religion. Art and science are only different aspects of this very same content.

In discussing religion it is important to ask whether it recognizes truth, or the Idea, only in its separation or in its true unity. In its separation: when God is conceived as the abstract highest Being, Lord of Heaven and Earth, transcending the world, beyond, and excluded from, human reality—or in its unity: God as unity of the universal and particular, in Whom even the particular is positively regarded, in the idea of incarnation. Religion is the sphere where a people gives itself the definition of what it regards as the True. Such a definition contains everything which belongs to the essence of the object, reducing its nature to a simple fundamental characteristic as focus for all other characteristics—the universal soul of all particulars. The idea of God thus is the general fundament of a people.

In this respect religion stands in closest connection with the principle of the State. Freedom can only exist where individuality is known as positive in the divine Being. There is a further connection between religion and the state: secular existence is temporal and moves within private interest. Hence it is relative and unjustified. Its justification can only be derived from the absolute justification of its universal soul, its principle. And this is justified only as determination and existence of the essence of God. For this reason the State is based on religion. We hear this often repeated in our time. But mostly nothing more is meant than that individuals should be pious in order to be more willing and prepared to do their duty; for obedience to prince and law is so easily connected with reverence toward God. It is true that reverence toward God, in elevating the universal over the particular, can turn against the particular in fanaticism, and work against the State, burning and destroying its buildings and institutions. Hence reverence for God, it is believed, should be temperate and kept in a certain degree of coolness, lest it storm against and destroy that which ought to be protected and preserved by it. The possibility of such disaster is at least latent in it.

The correct conviction that the State rests on religion may give religion a position which presupposes the existence of the State. Then, in order to preserve the State, religion must be carried into it, in buckets and bushels, in order to impress it upon people's minds. It is quite correct that man must be educated to religion, but not as to something which does not yet exist. For, when we say that the State is based on religion and that it has its roots in it, we mean essentially that it has arisen from it and now and always continues to arise out of it. That is, the principles of the State must be regarded as valid in and for themselves, which they can only insofar as they are known to be determinations of divine nature itself. The nature of its religion, therefore, determines that of the State and its constitution. It actually has originated from it: the Athenian and the Roman states were possible only through the specific paganism of these peoples, just as a Catholic state has a spirit and constitution different from a Protestant one.

It would be bad if this appeal, this urge and drive to implant religion, were a call of anguish and distress, as it looks so often—as if it expressed the danger that religion were about to disappear or already had disappeared from the State. Indeed, it would be worse than this appeal assumes; for it assumes it can still implant and inculcate religion as a means against this evil. But religion is not such an artifact. Its self-production is a much more profound process. Another and opposite folly which we meet in our time is the tendency to invent and institute constitutions independently from religion. The Catholic religion, although, like the Protestant, part of Christianity, does not concede to the State the inner justice and morality which follows from the inwardness of the Protestant principle. This separation of constitutional law and of constitutions themselves from morality is necessary because of the peculiarity of that religion; it does not regard law and morality as independent and substantial. But thus torn away from inwardness, from the last sanctuary of conscience, from the quiet corner where religion has its abode, the constitutional principles and institutions lack a real center and remain abstract and indeterminate.

In summary, the vitality of the State in individuals is what we call Morality. The State, its laws, its institutions are the rights of the citizens; its nature, its soil, its mountains, air, and waters are their land, their country, their external property. The history of the State are their deeds, and what their ancestors have accomplished belongs to them and lives in their memory. Everything is their possession just as they are possessed by it, for it constitutes their substance and being.

Their minds are full of it and their wills are their willing of these laws and of their country. It is this temporal totality which is One Being, the spirit of One People. To it the individuals belong; each individual is the son of his people and, at the same time, insofar as his state is in development, the son of his age. No one remains behind it, no one can leap ahead of it. This spiritual being is his—he is one of its representatives—it is that from which he arises and wherein he stands. For the Athenians Athens had a double meaning, the totality of their institutions as well as the goddess which represented the spirit and the unity of the people.

This spirit of a people is a *definite* spirit and, as was just said, is also determined according to the historical state of its development. This spirit, then, is the basis and content of the other forms of consciousness which have been mentioned. For the spirit in its consciousness of itself must be concrete to itself. Its objectivity immediately contains the origin of differences, which in their totality are the various spheres of the objective spirit itself—just as the soul exists only as the organization of its members which constitute it by combining themselves into simple unity. Thus it is one individuality. Its essence is represented, revered, and enjoyed as God, in religion; presented as image and intuition, in art; apprehended cognitively and conceived as thought, in philosophy. Because of the original identity of their substance, their content, and their subject matter with that of the State these products are inseparably united with the spirit of the State. Only with such a religion can there be such a form of the State, and only with such a State such art and such philosophy.

Furthermore, the definite national spirit itself is only one individual in the course of world history. For world history is the manifestation of the Divine, the absolute process of Spirit in its highest forms. It is this development wherein it achieves its truth and the consciousness of itself. The products of its stages are the world-historical national spirits, the definiteness of their moral life, their constitution, art, religion, and science. To realize these stages is the infinite élan of the World Spirit, its irresistible urge; for this differentiation and its realization constitute its concept. World history only shows how the World Spirit gradually attains the consciousness and willing of truth. Dawn rises in the Spirit; it discovers focal points; and finally, it attains full consciousness.

JOHN STUART MILL
1806–1873

John Stuart Mill was born in London, the eldest of James and Harriet Burrow Mills' nine children. His father, a well-known philosopher and follower of Jeremy Bentham, educated young John at home. Beginning with Greek at age three and Latin at age eight, the younger Mill had read six of Plato's dialogues by the age of ten. John spent most of the day in the study with his father, who was writing a history of India. Each morning, they would go on a walk and James would quiz his son on what he had learned the previous day. During these walks, James would often discourse on various topics and then expect his son to prepare a summary of his points for the following day. Given the severity of this schooling—and the fact that his father showed no "signs of feeling"—it is not surprising that John later concluded, "I never was a boy."

The publication of the elder Mill's work on India in 1818 resulted in his receiving a government post as an Assistant Examiner at the East India House. Five years later, James managed to arrange a similar position for his seventeen-year-old son. John worked for the East India House for the next thirty-four years, eventually becoming chief of his department. In his early years as a clerk, John was, like his father, a disciple of Bentham's utilitarianism. John established the Utilitarian Society, contributed articles to the *Westminster Review,* and was active in the London Debating Society. He was developing a reputation as a polemicist for the "philosophic radicals"—those who sought social changes along the lines of Bentham's theories.

But in 1826, at age twenty, Mill suffered a breakdown and went through a period of severe depression. He discovered to his horror that even if all the social changes he was advocating were enacted and all the ideas he had been taught about happiness were proven correct, it would not make *him* happy. As he later wrote in his *Autobiography*, "All my happiness was to have been found in the continual pursuit of this end. The end had ceased to charm, and how could there ever again be any interest in the means? I seemed to have nothing left to live for." He eventually came to the conclusion that his rigorous intellectual training had weakened his ability to feel emotion. Reading such writers as Wordsworth and Coleridge, he began to teach himself to feel as his father had taught him to think. During this period, he encountered divergent philosophies, such as those of socialist philosopher Claude-Henry Saint-Simon and positivist thinker Auguste Comte, and he began to see some of the inadequacies of the strict quantificational method of Bentham.

In 1831, Mill was introduced to Harriet Taylor, the wife of a successful merchant. They quickly developed a strong friendship and collaborated on a number of works, including *Principles of Political Economy, On Liberty,* and *The Subjection of Women.* Mill attributed to Taylor a number of his most important ideas, including his liberal feminism, and claimed that next to his father, she was the chief intellectual influence on his life. He even claimed she was the inspiration for his major epistemological work, *A System of Logic* (1843). Following her husband's death in 1849, they were finally married in 1851.

John and Harriet Mill moved to Avignon, France, in 1858, with neither of them in good health. Shortly after arriving, Harriet Taylor Mill died, and her daughter came to take care of her stepfather. Over the next seven years, Mill published *On Liberty* (1859), *Utilitarianism* (1861), *Considerations on Representative Government* (1861), *Auguste Comte and Positivism* (1865), and *The Subjection of Women* (written 1861, published 1869). In 1865, Mill was surprised by an offer to run for Parliament. Without campaigning he was elected and spent two years working on behalf of women's suffrage, Irish land reform, and the rights of blacks in Jamaica. Returning once again to the south of France, he wrote his *Autobiography* just before dying in 1873.

* * *

Although Mill wrote on a variety of topics and his work in induction is still used today, he is best known for his modification of Bentham's utilitarianism and his defense of individual liberty. Bentham had taught that ethics should be grounded on maximizing pleasure and minimizing pain, rather than on such abstractions as Kant's "duty" or conscience. Accordingly, Bentham developed a "hedonistic calculus," a mathematical method of determining which actions would most likely provide a greater quantity of pleasure over pain and hence yield happiness. Whereas this system might seem egoistic and individualistic, Bentham claimed that it would be to each individual person's advantage to seek the "greatest happiness of the greatest number."

In his *Utilitarianism*, given here (complete), Mill accepts Bentham's quantitative hedonism and argues that happiness, or pleasure, is the one thing that all people seek. But whereas Bentham's system merely measured quantities of pleasure and pain, Mill maintains that the *quality* of a given pleasure or pain has to be considered as well. Even though a pig might gain a great *quantity* of pleasure from wallowing in the mud, it would be a very low *quality* pleasure; and "It is better to be a human being dissatisfied than a pig satisfied; better to be Socrates dissatisfied than a fool satisfied." According to Mill, the person best able to make a qualitative determination between rival pleasures is the one who has experienced both. Presumably anyone who has both wallowed in the mud *and* studied philosophy would prefer the difficult but fulfilling pleasures of the latter.

In *On Liberty,* Mill asserts that society should maximize individual liberty. In fact, he claims that "the only purpose for which power can be rightfully exercised over any member of a civilized community, against his will, is to prevent harm to others." What an individual does in private does not concern society—even if such actions are not to that individual's own best interests. "Over himself, over his own body and mind, the individual is sovereign," and society should make no paternalistic rules. In Chapter 3, reprinted here, Mill argues that the "free development of individuality is one of the leading essentials of well-being." Mill claims that contrary to the Calvinists, self-will is a fundamental good and "He who chooses his plan for himself, employs all his faculties."

Mill's contemporary critics pointed out that there seem to be discrepancies between the philosophy of *Utilitarianism* and that of *On Liberty.* For example, following the greatest happiness principle of *Utilitarianism,* wouldn't it make sense for society to increase general happiness by intruding on an individual's liberty? Mill countered this objection by arguing that on balance *laissez-faire* individualism will ultimately benefit society; that the diversity of individual choices is more conducive to general happiness than any socially imposed standard. More recent critics have questioned Mill's distinction between private and public—for example, what you choose to do to yourself in the privacy of your home may cost the public money if you end up in a tax-supported hospital. But there is no question that as a reforming impulse, Mill's beliefs—about the rights of the individual, the rights of women and minorities, freedom from societal intrusion into personal affairs, and utility rather than tradition—have had an enormous influence.

*   *   *

There are several good overviews of Mill's life and thought, including R.P. Anschutz, *The Philosophy of John Stuart Mill* (Oxford: Oxford University Press, 1953); Karl Britton, *John Stuart Mill* (1953; reprinted New York: Dover, 1969); Alan Ryan, *J.S. Mill* (London: Routledge & Kegan Paul, 1974); and William Thomas, *Mill* (Oxford: Oxford University Press, 1985). F.A. Hayek, *John Stuart Mill and Harriet Taylor* (Chicago: University of Chicago Press, 1951), presents a study of Mill's relationship with Harriet Taylor. For a critical evaluation of his work, see H.J. McCloskey, *John Stuart Mill: A Critical Study* (London: Macmillan, 1971). For more specialized studies, see Denise F. Thompson, *John Stuart Mill and Representative Government* (Princeton, NJ: Princeton University Press, 1976); Gertrude Himmelfarb, *On Liberty and Liberalism: The Case of John Stuart Mill* (New York: Knopf, 1974); and John Gray and G.W. Smith, eds., *J.S. Mill's "On Liberty" in Focus* (London: Routledge, 1991). For collections of essays, see J.B. Schneewind, ed., *Mill: A Collection of Critical Essays* (Garden City, NY: Anchor Doubleday, 1968), and J.M. Smith and E. Sosa, eds., *Mill's Utilitarianism* (Belmont, CA: Wadsworth, 1969).

UTILITARIANISM

CHAPTER 1: GENERAL REMARKS

There are few circumstances among those which make up the present condition of human knowledge, more unlike what might have been expected, or more significant of the backward state in which speculation on the most important subjects still lingers, than the little progress which has been made in the decision of the controversy respecting the criterion of right and wrong. From the dawn of philosophy, the question concerning the *summum bonum,* or, what is the same thing, concerning the foundation of morality, has been accounted the main problem in speculative thought, has occupied the most gifted intellects, and divided them into sects and schools, carrying on a vigorous warfare against one another. And after more than two thousand years the same discussions continue, philosophers are still ranged under the same contending banners, and neither thinkers nor mankind at large seem nearer to being unanimous on the subject, than when the youth Socrates listened to the old Protagoras, and asserted (if Plato's dialogue be grounded on a real conversation) the theory of utilitarianism against the popular morality of the so-called sophist.

It is true that similar confusion and uncertainty, and in some cases similar discordance, exist respecting the first principles of all the sciences, not excepting that which is deemed the most certain of them, mathematics; without much impairing, generally indeed without impairing at all, the trustworthiness of the conclusions of those sciences. An apparent anomaly, the explanation of which is, that the detailed doctrines of a science are not usually deduced from, nor depend for their evidence upon, what are called its first principles. Were it not so, there would be no science more precarious, or whose conclusions were more insufficiently made out, than algebra; which derives none of its certainty from what are commonly taught to learners as its elements, since these, as laid down by some of its most eminent teachers, are as full of fictions as English law, and of mysteries as theology. The truths which are ultimately accepted as the first principles of a science, are really the last results of metaphysical analysis, practised on the elementary notions with which the science is conversant; and their relation to the science is not that of foundations to an edifice, but of roots to a tree, which may perform their office equally well though they be never dug down to and exposed to light. But though in science the particular truths precede the general theory, the contrary might be expected to be the case with a practical art, such as morals or legislation. All action is for the sake of some end, and rules of action, it seems natural to suppose, must take their whole character and colour from the end to which they are subservient. When we engage in a pursuit, a clear and precise conception of what we are pursuing would seem to be the first thing we need, instead of the last we are to look forward to. A test of right and wrong must be the means, one would think, of ascertaining what is right or wrong, and not a consequence of having already ascertained it.

The difficulty is not avoided by having recourse to the popular theory of a natural faculty, a sense or instinct, informing us of right and wrong. For—besides that the existence of such a moral instinct is itself one of the matters in dispute—those believers in it who have any pretensions to philosophy, have been obliged to abandon the idea that it discerns what is right or wrong in the particular case in hand, as our other senses discern the sight or sound actually present. Our moral faculty, according to all those of its inter-

preters who are entitled to the name of thinkers, supplies us only with the general principles of moral judgments; it is a branch of our reason, not of our sensitive faculty; and
must be looked to for the abstract doctrines of morality, not for perception of it in the
concrete. The intuitive, no less than what may be termed the inductive, school of ethics,
insists on the necessity of general laws. They both agree that the morality of an individual action is not a question of direct perception, but of the application of a law to an individual case. They recognise also, to a great extent, the same moral laws; but differ as
to their evidence, and the source from which they derive their authority. According to
the one opinion, the principles of morals are evident *a priori,* requiring nothing to command assent, except that the meaning of the terms be understood. According to the other
doctrine, right and wrong, as well as truth and falsehood, are questions of observation
and experience. But both hold equally that morality must be deduced from principles;
and the intuitive school affirm as strongly as the inductive, that there is a science of
morals. Yet they seldom attempt to make out a list of the *a priori* principles which are to
serve as the premises of the science; still more rarely do they make any effort to reduce
those various principles to one first principle, or common ground of obligation. They either assume the ordinary precepts of morals as of *a priori* authority, or they lay down as
the common groundwork of those maxims, some generality much less obviously authoritative than the maxims themselves, and which has never succeeded in gaining popular acceptance. Yet to support their pretensions there ought either to be some one fundamental principle or law, at the root of all morality, or if there be several, there should
be a determinate order of precedence among them; and the one principle, or the rule for
deciding between the various principles when they conflict, ought to be self-evident.

To inquire how far the bad effects of this deficiency have been mitigated in practice, or to what extent the moral beliefs of mankind have been vitiated or made uncertain by the absence of any distinct recognition of an ultimate standard, would imply a
complete survey and criticism of past and present ethical doctrine. It would, however,
be easy to show that whatever steadiness or consistency these moral beliefs have attained, has been mainly due to the tacit influence of a standard not recognised. Although
the non-existence of an acknowledged first principle has made ethics not so much a
guide as a consecration of men's actual sentiments, still, as men's sentiments, both of
favour and of aversion, are greatly influenced by what they suppose to be the effects of
things upon their happiness, the principle of utility, or as Bentham latterly called it, the
Greatest Happiness Principle, has had a large share in forming the moral doctrines even
of those who most scornfully reject its authority. Nor is there any school of thought
which refuses to admit that the influence of actions on happiness is a most material and
even predominant consideration in many of the details of morals, however unwilling to
acknowledge it as the fundamental principle of morality, and the source of moral obligation. I might go much further, and say that to all those *a priori* moralists who deem it
necessary to argue at all, utilitarian arguments are indispensable. It is not my present
purpose to criticise these thinkers; but I cannot help referring, for illustration, to a systematic treatise by one of the most illustrious of them, the *Metaphysics of Ethics* by
Kant. This remarkable man, whose system of thought will long remain one of the landmarks in the history of philosophical speculation, does, in the treatise in question, lay
down a universal first principle as the origin and ground of moral obligation; it is this:—
"So act, that the rule on which thou actest would admit of being adopted as a law by all
rational beings." But when he begins to deduce from this precept any of the actual duties of morality, he fails, almost grotesquely, to show that there would be any contradiction, any logical (not to say physical) impossibility, in the adoption by all rational beings of the most outrageously immoral rules of conduct. All he shows is that the

consequences of their universal adoption would be such as no one would choose to incur.

On the present occasion, I shall, without further discussion of the other theories, attempt to contribute something towards the understanding and appreciation of the Utilitarian or Happiness theory, and towards such proof as it is susceptible of. It is evident that this cannot be proof in the ordinary and popular meaning of the term. Questions of ultimate ends are not amenable to direct proof. Whatever can be proved to be good, must be so by being shown to be a means to something admitted to be good without proof. The medical art is proved to be good by its conducing to health; but how is it possible to prove that health is good? The art of music is good, for the reason, among others, that it produces pleasure; but what proof is it possible to give that pleasure is good? If, then, it is asserted that there is a comprehensive formula, including all things which are in themselves good, and that whatever else is good, is not so as an end, but as a mean, the formula may be accepted or rejected, but is not a subject of what is commonly understood by proof. We are not, however, to infer that its acceptance or rejection must depend on blind impulse, or arbitrary choice. There is a larger meaning of the word proof, in which this question is as amenable to it as any other of the disputed questions of philosophy. The subject is within the cognisance of the rational faculty; and neither does that faculty deal with it solely in the way of intuition. Considerations may be presented capable of determining the intellect either to give or withhold its assent to the doctrine; and this is equivalent to proof.

We shall examine presently of what nature are these considerations; in what manner they apply to the case, and what rational grounds, therefore, can be given for accepting or rejecting the utilitarian formula. But it is a preliminary condition of rational acceptance or rejection, that the formula should be correctly understood. I believe that the very imperfect notion ordinarily formed of its meaning, is the chief obstacle which impedes its reception; and that could it be cleared, even from only the grosser misconceptions, the question would be greatly simplified, and a large proportion of its difficulties removed. Before, therefore, I attempt to enter into the philosophical grounds which can be given for assenting to the utilitarian standard, I shall offer some illustrations of the doctrine itself; with the view of showing more clearly what it is, distinguishing it from what it is not, and disposing of such of the practical objections to it as either originate in, or are closely connected with, mistaken interpretations of its meaning. Having thus prepared the ground, I shall afterwards endeavour to throw such light as I can upon the question, considered as one of philosophical theory.

CHAPTER 2: WHAT UTILITARIANISM IS

A passing remark is all that needs be given to the ignorant blunder of supposing that those who stand up for utility as the test of right and wrong, use the term in that restricted and merely colloquial sense in which utility is opposed to pleasure. An apology is due to the philosophical opponents of utilitarianism, for even the momentary appearance of confounding them with any one capable of so absurd a misconception; which is the more extraordinary, inasmuch as the contrary accusation, of referring everything to pleasure, and that too in its grossest form, is another of the common charges against utilitarianism: and, as has been pointedly remarked by an able writer, the same sort of persons, and often the very same persons, denounce the theory "as impracticably dry when the word 'utility' precedes the word 'pleasure,' and as too practicably voluptuous when the word 'plea-sure' precedes the word 'utility.'" Those who know anything about the matter are aware that every writer, from Epicurus to Bentham, who maintained the theory of utility, meant by it, not something to be contradistinguished from pleasure, but pleasure itself, together with exemption from pain; and instead of opposing the useful to the agreeable or the or-namental, have always declared that the useful means these, among other things. Yet the common herd, including the herd of writers, not only in newspapers and periodicals, but in books of weight and pretension, are perpetually falling into this shallow mistake. Hav-ing caught up the word Utilitarian, while knowing nothing whatever about it but its sound, they habitually express by it the rejection, or the neglect, of pleasure in some of its forms; of beauty, of ornament, or of amusement. Nor is the term thus ignorantly misap-plied solely in disparagement, but occasionally in compliment; as though it implied supe-riority to frivolity and the mere pleasures of the moment. And this perverted use is the only one in which the word is popularly known, and the one from which the new genera-tion are acquiring their sole notion of its meaning. Those who introduced the word, but who had for many years discontinued it as a distinctive appellation, may well feel them-selves called upon to resume it, if by doing so they can hope to contribute anything to-wards rescuing it from this utter degradation.*

The creed which accepts as the foundation of morals Utility or the Greatest Hap-piness Principle holds that actions are right in proportion as they tend to promote hap-piness, wrong as they tend to produce the reverse of happiness. By happiness is in-tended pleasure, and the absence of pain; by unhappiness, pain, and the privation of pleasure. To give a clear view of the moral standard set up by the theory, much more re-quires to be said; in particular, what things it includes in the ideas of pain and pleasure; and to what extent this is left an open question. But these supplementary explanations do not affect the theory of life on which this theory of morality is grounded—namely, that pleasure, and freedom from pain, are the only things desirable as ends; and that all desirable things (which are as numerous in the utilitarian as in any other scheme) are desirable either for the pleasure inherent in themselves, or as means to the promotion of pleasure and the prevention of pain.

Now, such a theory of life excites in many minds, and among them in some of the most estimable in feeling and purpose, inveterate dislike. To suppose that life has (as they express it) no higher end than pleasure—no better and nobler object of desire and pursuit—they designate as utterly mean and grovelling; as a doctrine worthy only of swine, to whom the followers of Epicurus were, at a very early period, contemptuously likened; and modern holders of the doctrine are occasionally made the subject of equally polite comparisons by its German, French, and English assailants.

When thus attacked, the Epicureans have always answered, that it is not they, but their accusers, who represent human nature in a degrading light; since the accusation supposes human beings to be capable of no pleasures except those of which swine are capable. If this supposition were true, the charge could not be gainsaid, but would then be no longer an imputation; for if the sources of pleasure were precisely the same to hu-

---

*The author of this essay has reason for believing himself to be the first person who brought the word "utilitarian" into use. He did not Invent it, but adopted It from a passing expression in Mr. Galt's *Annals of the Parish*. After using it as a designation for several years, he and others abandoned it from a growing dislike to anything resembling a badge or watchword of sectarian distinction. But as a name for one single opinion, not a set of opinions—to denote the recognition of utility as a standard not any particular way of applying it—the term supplies a want in the language, and offers, in many cases, a convenient mode of avoiding tiresome cir-cumlocution.

man beings and to swine, the rule of life which is good enough for the one would be good enough for the other. The comparison of the Epicurean life to that of beasts is felt as degrading, precisely because a beast's pleasures do not satisfy a human being's conceptions of happiness. Human beings have faculties more elevated than the animal appetites, and when once made conscious of them, do not regard anything as happiness which does not include their gratification. I do not, indeed, consider the Epicureans to have been by any means faultless in drawing out their scheme of consequences from the utilitarian principle. To do this in any sufficient manner, many Stoic, as well as Christian elements require to be included. But there is no known Epicurean theory of life which does not assign to the pleasures of the intellect, of the feelings and imagination, and of the moral sentiments, a much higher value as pleasures than to those of mere sensation. It must be admitted, however, that utilitarian writers in general have placed the superiority of mental over bodily pleasures chiefly in the greater permanency, safety, uncostliness, etc., of the former—that is, in their circumstantial advantages rather than in their intrinsic nature. And on all these points utilitarians have fully proved their case; but they might have taken the other, and, as it may be called, higher ground, with entire consistency. It is quite compatible with the principle of utility to recognise the fact, that some kinds of pleasure are more desirable and more valuable than others. It would be absurd that while, in estimating all other things, quality is considered as well as quantity, the estimation of pleasures should be supposed to depend on quantity alone.

If I am asked, what I mean by difference of quality in pleasures, or what makes one pleasure more valuable than another, merely as a pleasure, except its being greater in amount, there is but one possible answer. Of two pleasures, if there be one to which all or almost all who have experience of both give a decided preference, irrespective of any feeling of moral obligation to prefer it, that is the more desirable pleasure. If one of the two is, by those who are competently acquainted with both, placed so far above the other that they prefer it, even though knowing it to be attended with a greater amount of discontent, and would not resign it for any quantity of the other pleasure which their nature is capable of, we are justified in ascribing to the preferred enjoyment a superiority in quality, so far outweighing quantity as to render it, in comparison, of small account.

Now it is an unquestionable fact that those who are equally acquainted with, and equally capable of appreciating and enjoying, both, do give almost marked preference to the manner of existence which employs their higher faculties. Few human creatures would consent to be changed into any of the lower animals, for a promise of the fullest allowance of a beast's pleasures; no intelligent human being would consent to be a fool, no instructed person would be an ignoramus, no person of feeling and conscience would be selfish and base, even though they should be persuaded that the fool, the dunce, or the rascal is better satisfied with his lot than they are with theirs. They would not resign what they possess more than he for the most complete satisfaction of all the desires which they have in common with him. If they ever fancy they would, it is only in cases of unhappiness so extreme, that to escape from it they would exchange their lot for almost any other, however undesirable in their own eyes. A being of higher faculties requires more to make him happy, is capable probably of more acute suffering, and certainly accessible to it at more points, than one of an inferior type; but in spite of these liabilities, he can never really wish to sink into what he feels to be a lower grade of existence. We may give what explanation we please of this unwillingness; we may attribute it to pride, a name which is given indiscriminately to some of the most and to some of the least estimable feelings of which mankind are capable: we may refer it to the love of liberty and personal independence, an appeal to which was with the Stoics one of the most effective means for the inculcation of it; to the love of power, or to the love of excitement, both of which do really enter into and contribute to it: but its most appropriate appellation is a sense of dignity, which all human beings possess in one form or other, and in some, though by no means in exact, proportion to their higher faculties, and which is so essential a part of the happiness of those in whom it is strong, that nothing which conflicts with it could be, otherwise than momentarily, an object of desire to them. Whoever supposes that this preference takes place at a sacrifice of happiness— that the superior being, in anything like equal circumstances, is not happier than the inferior—confounds the two very different ideas, of happiness, and content. It is indisputable that the being whose capacities of enjoyment are low, has the greatest chance of having them fully satisfied; and a highly endowed being will always feel that any happiness which he can look for, as the world is constituted, is imperfect. But he can learn to bear its imperfections, if they are at all bearable; and they will not make him envy the being who is indeed unconscious of the imperfections, but only because he feels not at all the good which those imperfections qualify. It is better to be a human being dissatisfied than a pig satisfied; better to be Socrates dissatisfied than a fool satisfied. And if the fool, or the pig, are of a different opinion, it is because they only know their own side of the question. The other party to the comparison knows both sides.

It may be objected, that many who are capable of the higher pleasures, occasionally, under the influence of temptation, postpone them to the lower. But this is quite compatible with a full appreciation of the intrinsic superiority of the higher. Men often, from infirmity of character, make their election for the nearer good, though they know it to be the less valuable; and this no less when the choice is between two bodily pleasures, than when it is between bodily and mental. They pursue sensual indulgences to the injury of health, though perfectly aware that health is the greater good. It may be further objected, that many who begin with youthful enthusiasm for everything noble, as they advance in years sink into indolence and selfishness. But I do not believe that those who undergo this very common change, voluntarily choose the lower description of pleasures in preference to the higher. I believe that before they devote themselves exclusively to the one, they have already become incapable of the other. Capacity for the nobler feelings is in most natures a very tender plant, easily killed, not only by hostile influences, but by mere want of sustenance; and in the majority of young persons it speedily dies away if the occupations to which their position in life has devoted them, and the society into which it has thrown them, are not favourable to keeping that higher capacity in exercise. Men lose their high aspirations as they lose their intellectual tastes, because they have not time or opportunity for indulging them; and they addict themselves to inferior pleasures, not because they deliberately prefer them, but because they are either the only ones to which they have access, or the only ones which they are any longer capable of enjoying. It may be questioned whether any one who has remained equally susceptible to both classes of pleasures, ever knowingly and calmly preferred the lower; though many, in all ages, have broken down in an ineffectual attempt to combine both.

From this verdict of the only competent judges, I apprehend there can be no appeal. On a question which is the best worth having of two pleasures, or which of two modes of existence is the most grateful to the feelings, apart from its moral attributes and from its consequences, the judgment of those who are qualified by knowledge of both, or, if they differ, that of the majority among them, must be admitted as final. And there needs be the less hesitation to accept this judgment respecting the quality of pleasures, since there is no other tribunal to be referred to even on the question of quantity. What means are there of determining which is the acutest of two pains, or the intensest of two pleasurable sensations, except the general suffrage of those who are familiar with both? Neither pains nor pleasures are homogeneous, and pain is always heterogeneous with pleasure. What is there to decide whether a particular pleasure is worth purchasing at the cost of a particular pain, except the feelings and judgment of the experienced? When, therefore, those feelings and judgment declare the pleasures derived from the higher faculties to be preferable *in kind,* apart from the question of intensity, to those of which the animal nature, disjoined from the higher faculties, is suspectible, they are entitled on this subject to the same regard.

I have dwelt on this point, as being a necessary part of a perfectly just conception of Utility or Happiness, considered as the directive rule of human conduct. But it is by no means an indispensable condition to the acceptance of the utilitarian standard; for that standard is not the agent's own greatest happiness, but the greatest amount of happiness altogether; and if it may possibly be doubted whether a noble character is always the happier for its nobleness, there can be no doubt that it makes other people happier, and that the world in general is immensely a gainer by it. Utilitarianism, therefore, could only attain its end by the general cultivation of nobleness of character, even if each individual were only benefited by the nobleness of others, and his own, so far as happiness is concerned, were a sheer deduction from the benefit. But the bare enunciation of such an absurdity as this last, renders refutation superfluous.

According to the Greatest Happiness Principle, as above explained, the ultimate end, with reference to and for the sake of which all other things are desirable (whether we are considering our own good or that of other people), is an existence exempt as far as possible from pain, and as rich as possible in enjoyments, both in point of quantity and quality; the test of quality, and the rule for measuring it against quantity, being the preference felt by those who in their opportunities of experience, to which must be added their habits of self-consciousness and self-observation, are best furnished with the means of comparison. This, being, according to the utilitarian opinion, the end of human action, is necessarily also the standard of morality; which may accordingly be defined "the rules and precepts for human conduct" by the observance of which an existence such as has been described might be, to the greatest extent possible, secured to all mankind; and not to them only, but, so far as the nature of things admits, to the whole sentient creation.

Against this doctrine, however, arises another class of objectors, who say that happiness, in any form, cannot be the rational purpose of human life and action; because, in the first place, it is unattainable: and they contemptuously ask, what right hast thou to be happy? a question which Mr. Carlyle clenches by the addition, What right, a short time ago, hadst thou even *to be?* Next, they say, that men can do *without* happiness; that all noble human beings have felt this, and could not have become noble but by learning the lesson of *Entsagen,* or renunciation; which lesson, thoroughly learnt and submitted to, they affirm to be the beginning and necessary condition of all virtue.

The first of these objections would go to the root of the matter were it well founded; for if no happiness is to be had at all by human beings, the attainment of it cannot be the end of morality, or of any rational conduct. Though, even in that case, something might still be said for the utilitarian theory; since utility includes not solely the pursuit of happiness, but the prevention or mitigation of unhappiness; and if the former aim be chimerical, there will be all the greater scope and more imperative need for the latter, so long at least as mankind think fit to live, and do not take refuge in the simultaneous act of suicide recommended under certain conditions by Novalis.* When, how-

---

*[The German poet Friedrich Leopold Freiherr von Hardenberg (1772–1801).]

ever, it is thus positively asserted to be impossible that human life should be happy, the assertion, if not something like a verbal quibble, is at least an exaggeration. If by happiness be meant a continuity of highly pleasurable excitement, it is evident enough that this is impossible. A state of exalted pleasure lasts only moments, or in some cases, and with some intermissions, hours or days, and is the occasional brilliant flash of enjoyment, not its permanent and steady flame. Of this the philosophers who have taught that happiness is the end of life were as fully aware as those who taunt them. The happiness which they meant was not a life of rapture; but moments of such, in an existence made up of few and transitory pains, many and various pleasures, with a decided predominance of the active over the passive, and having as the foundation of the whole, not to expect more from life than it is capable of bestowing. A life thus composed, to those who have been fortunate enough to obtain it, has always appeared worthy of the name of happiness. And such an existence is even now the lot of many, during some considerable portion of their lives. The present wretched education, and wretched social arrangements, are the only real hindrance to its being attainable by almost all.

The objectors perhaps may doubt whether human beings, if taught to consider happiness as the end of life, would be satisfied with such a moderate share of it. But great numbers of mankind have been satisfied with much less. The main constituents of a satisfied life appear to be two, either of which by itself is often found sufficient for the purpose: tranquillity, and excitement. With much tranquillity, many find that they can be content with very little pleasure: with much excitement, many can reconcile themselves to a considerable quantity of pain. There is assuredly no inherent impossibility in enabling even the mass of mankind to unite both; since the two are so far from being incompatible that they are in natural alliance, the prolongation of either being a preparation for, and exciting a wish for, the other. It is only those in whom indolence amounts to a vice, that do not desire excitement after an interval of repose: it is only those in whom the need of excitement is a disease, that feel the tranquillity which follows excitement dull and insipid, instead of pleasurable in direct proportion to the excitement which preceded it. When people who are tolerably fortunate in their outward lot do not find in life sufficient enjoyment to make it valuable to them, the cause generally is, caring for nobody but themselves. To those who have neither public nor private affections, the excitements of life are much curtailed, and in any case dwindle in value as the time approaches when all selfish interests must be terminated by death: while those who leave after them objects of personal affection, and especially those who have also cultivated a fellow-feeling with the collective interests of mankind, retain as lively an interest in life on the eve of death as in the vigour of youth and health. Next to selfishness, the principal cause which makes life unsatisfactory is want of mental cultivation. A cultivated mind—I do not mean that of a philosopher, but any mind to which the fountains of knowledge have been opened, and which has been taught, in any tolerable degree, to exercise its faculties—finds sources of inexhaustible interest in all that surrounds it; in the objects of nature, the achievements of art, the imaginations of poetry, the incidents of history, the ways of mankind, past and present, and their prospects in the future. It is possible, indeed, to become indifferent to all this, and that too without having exhausted a thousandth part of it; but only when one has had from the beginning no moral or human interest in these things, and has sought in them only the gratification of curiosity.

Now there is absolutely no reason in the nature of things why an amount of mental culture sufficient to give an intelligent interest in these objects of contemplation, should not be the inheritance of every one born in a civilised country. As little is there an inherent necessity that any human being should be a selfish egotist, devoid of every feeling or care but those which centre in his own miserable individuality. Something far superior to this is sufficiently common even now, to give ample earnest of what the human species may be made. Genuine private affections, and a sincere interest in the public good, are possible, though in unequal degrees, to every rightly brought up human being. In a world in which there is so much to interest, so much to enjoy, and so much also to correct and improve, every one who has this moderate amount of moral and intellectual requisites is capable of an existence which may be called enviable; and unless such a person, through bad laws, or subjection to the will of others, is denied the liberty to use the sources of happiness within his reach, he will not fail to find this enviable existence, if he escape the positive evils of life, the great sources of physical and mental suffering—such as indigence, disease, and the unkindness, worthlessness, or premature loss of objects of affection. The main stress of the problem lies, therefore, in the contest with these calamities, from which it is a rare good fortune entirely to escape; which, as things now are, cannot be obviated, and often cannot be in any material degree mitigated. Yet no one whose opinion deserves a moment's consideration can doubt that most of the great positive evils of the world are in themselves removable, and will, if human affairs continue to improve, be in the end reduced within narrow limits. Poverty, in any sense implying suffering, may be completely extinguished by the wisdom of society, combined with the good sense and providence of individuals. Even that most intractable of enemies, disease, may be indefinitely reduced in dimensions by good physical and moral education, and proper control of noxious influences; while the progress of science holds out a promise for the future of still more direct conquests over this detestable foe. And every advance in that direction relieves us from some, not only of the chances which cut short our own lives, but, what concerns us still more, which deprive us of those in whom our happiness is wrapt up. As for vicissitudes of fortune, and other disappointments connected with worldly circumstances, these are principally the effect either of gross imprudence, of ill-regulated desires, or of bad or imperfect social institutions. All the grand sources, in short, of human suffering are in a great degree, many of them almost entirely, conquerable by human care and effort; and though their removal is grievously slow—though a long succession of generations will perish in the breach before the conquest is completed, and this world becomes all that, if will and knowledge were not wanting, it might easily be made—yet every mind sufficiently intelligent and generous to bear a part, however small and unconspicuous, in the endeavour, will draw a noble enjoyment from the contest itself, which he would not for any bribe in the form of selfish indulgence consent to be without.

And this leads to the true estimation of what is said by the objectors concerning the possibility, and the obligation, of learning to do without happiness. Unquestionably it is possible to do without happiness; it is done involuntarily by nineteen-twentieths of mankind, even in those parts of our present world which are least deep in barbarism; and it often has to be done voluntarily by the hero or the martyr, for the sake of something which he prizes more than his individual happiness. But this something, what is it, unless the happiness of others, or some of the requisites of happiness? It is noble to be capable of resigning entirely one's own portion of happiness, or chances of it: but, after all, this self-sacrifice must be for some end; it is not its own end; and if we are told that its end is not happiness, but virtue, which is better than happiness, I ask, would the sacrifice be made if the hero or martyr did not believe that it would earn for others immunity from similar sacrifices? Would it be made if he thought that his renunciation of happiness for himself would produce no fruit for any of his fellow creatures, but to make their lot like his, and place them also in the condition of persons who have renounced happiness? All honour to those who can abnegate for themselves the personal enjoyment of life, when by such renunciation they contribute worthily to increase the amount of happiness in the world; but

Crystal Palace, London, 1851, designed by Joseph Paxton (1801–1865). Built
for the Works of Industry of All Nations exhibit, the building covered ninteen
acres and enclosed over thirty million cubic feet. *(The Bettmann Archive)*

he who does it, or professes to do it, for any other purpose, is no more deserving of admiration than the ascetic mounted on his pillar. He may be an inspiriting proof of what men
can do, but assuredly not an example of what they *should*.

Though it is only in a very imperfect state of the world's arrangements that any
one can best serve the happiness of others by the absolute sacrifice of his own, yet so
long as the world is in that imperfect state, I fully acknowledge that the readiness to
make such a sacrifice is the highest virtue which can be found in man. I will add, that in
this condition of the world, paradoxical as the assertion may be, the conscious ability to
do without happiness gives the best prospect of realising such happiness as is attainable.
For nothing except that consciousness can raise a person above the chances of life, by
making him feel that, let fate and fortune do their worst, they have not power to subdue
him: which, once felt, frees him from excess of anxiety concerning the evils of life, and
enables him, like many a Stoic in the worst times of the Roman Empire, to cultivate in
tranquillity the sources of satisfaction accessible to him, without concerning himself
about the uncertainty of their duration, any more than about their inevitable end.

Meanwhile, let utilitarians never cease to claim the morality of self devotion as a
possession which belongs by as good a right to them, as either to the Stoic or to the
Transcendentalist. The utilitarian morality does recognise in human beings the power of
sacrificing their own greatest good for the good of others. It only refuses to admit that
the sacrifice is itself a good. A sacrifice which does not increase, or tend to increase, the
sum total of happiness, it considers as wasted. The only self-renunciation which it applauds, is devotion to the happiness, or to some of the means of happiness, of others; either of mankind collectively, or of individuals within the limits imposed by the collective interests of mankind.

Interior, Crystal Palace. The palace was a shrine to science, industrialization, and progress. This architectural marvel represented in concrete form Mill's optimism when he spoke of the "wisdom of society" and the "progress of science [which] holds out a promise for the future." (*Victoria and Albert Museum, London*)

I must again repeat, what the assailants of utilitarianism seldom have the justice to acknowledge, that the happiness which forms the utilitarian standard of what is right in conduct, is not the agent's own happiness, but that of all concerned. As between his own happiness and that of others, utilitarianism requires him to be as strictly impartial as a disinterested and benevolent spectator. In the golden rule of Jesus of Nazareth, we read the complete spirit of the ethics of utility. "To do as you would be done by," and "to love your neighbour as yourself," constitute the ideal perfection of utilitarian morality. As the means of making the nearest approach to this ideal, utility would enjoin, first, that laws and social arrangements should place the happiness, or (as speaking practically it may be called) the interest, of every individual, as nearly as possible in harmony with the interest of the whole; and secondly, that education and opinion, which have so vast a power over human character, should so use that power as to establish in the mind of every individual an indissoluble association between his own happiness and the good of the whole; especially between his own happiness and the practice of such modes of conduct, negative and positive, as regard for the universal happiness prescribes; so that not only he may be unable to conceive the possibility of happiness to himself, consistently with conduct opposed to the general good, but also that a direct impulse to promote the general good may be in every individual one of the habitual motives of action, and the sentiments connected therewith may fill a large and prominent place in every human being's sentient existence. If the impugners of the utilitarian morality represented it to their own minds in this its true character, I know not what recommendation possessed by any other morality they could possibly affirm to be wanting to it; what more beautiful or more exalted developments of human nature any other ethical system can be supposed to foster, or what springs of action, not accessible to the utilitarian, such systems rely on for giving effect to their mandates.

The objectors to utilitarianism cannot always be charged with representing it in a discreditable light. On the contrary, those among them who entertain anything like a just idea of its disinterested character, sometimes find fault with its standard as being too high for humanity. They say it is exacting too much to require that people shall always act from the inducement of promoting the general interests of society. But this is to mistake the very meaning of a standard of morals, and confound the rule of action with the motive of it. It is the business of ethics to tell us what are our duties, or by what test we may know them; but no system of ethics requires that the sole motive of all we do shall be a feeling of duty; on the contrary, ninety-nine hundredths of all our actions are done from other motives, and rightly so done, if the rule of duty does not condemn them. It is the more unjust to utilitarianism that this particular misapprehension should be made a ground of objection to it, inasmuch as utilitarian moralists have gone beyond almost all others in affirming that the motive has nothing to do with the morality of the action, though much with the worth of the agent. He who saves a fellow creature from drowning does what is morally right, whether his motive be duty, or the hope of being paid for his trouble; he who betrays the friend that trusts him, is guilty of a crime, even if his object be to serve another friend to whom he is under greater obligations. But to speak only of actions done from the motive of duty, and in direct obedience to principle: it is a misapprehension of the utilitarian mode of thought, to conceive it as implying that people should fix their minds upon so wide a generality as the world, or society at large. The great majority of good actions are intended not for the benefit of the world, but for that of individuals, of which the good of the world is made up; and the thoughts of the most virtuous man need not on these occasions travel beyond the particular persons concerned, except so far as is necessary to assure himself that in benefiting them he is not violating the rights, that is, the legitimate and authorised expectations, of any one else. The multiplication of happiness is, according to the utilitarian ethics, the object of virtue: the occasions on which any person (except one in a thousand) has it in his power to do this on an extended scale, in other words to be a public benefactor, are but exceptional; and on these occasions alone is he called on to consider public utility; in every other case, private utility, the interest or happiness of some few persons, is all he has to attend to. Those alone the influence of whose actions extends to society in general, need concern themselves habitually about so large an object. In the case of abstinences indeed—of things which people forbear to do from moral considerations, though the consequences in the particular case might be beneficial—it would be unworthy of an intelligent agent not to be consciously aware that the action is of a class which, if practised generally, would be generally injurious, and that this is the ground of the obligation to abstain from it. The amount of regard for the public interest implied in this recognition, is no greater than is demanded by every system of morals, for they all enjoin to abstain from whatever is manifestly pernicious to society.

The same considerations dispose of another reproach against the doctrine of utility, founded on a still grosser misconception of the purpose of a standard of morality, and of the very meaning of the words "right" and "wrong." It is often affirmed that utilitarianism renders men cold and unsympathising; that it chills their moral feelings towards individuals; that it makes them regard only the dry and hard consideration of the consequences of actions, not taking into their moral estimate the qualities from which those actions emanate. If the assertion means that they do not allow their judgment respecting the rightness or wrongness of an action to be influenced by their opinion of the qualities of the person who does it, this is a complaint not against utilitarianism, but against having any standard of morality at all; for certainly no known ethical standard decides an action to be good or bad because it is done by a good or a bad man, still less because done by an amiable, a brave, or a benevolent man, or the contrary. These considerations are relevant, not to the estimation of actions, but of persons; and there is nothing in the utilitarian theory inconsistent with the fact that there are other things which interest us in persons besides the rightness and wrongness of their actions. The Stoics, indeed, with the paradoxical misuse of language which was part of their system, and by which they strove to raise themselves above all concern about anything but virtue, were fond of saying that he who has that has everything; that he, and only he, is rich, is beautiful, is a king. But no claim of this description is made for the virtuous man by the utilitarian doctrine. Utilitarians are quite aware that there are other desirable possessions and qualities besides virtue, and are perfectly willing to allow to all of them their full worth. They are also aware that a right action does not necessarily indicate a virtuous character, and that actions which are blamable, often proceed from qualities entitled to praise. When this is apparent in any particular case, it modifies their estimation, not certainly of the act, but of the agent. I grant that they are, notwithstanding, of opinion, that in the long run the best proof of a good character is good actions; and resolutely refuse to consider any mental disposition as good, of which the predominant tendency is to produce bad conduct. This makes them unpopular with many people; but it is an unpopularity which they must share with every one who regards the distinction between right and wrong in a serious light; and the reproach is not one which a conscientious utilitarian need be anxious to repel.

If no more be meant by the objection than that many utilitarians look on the morality of actions, as measured by the utilitarian standard, with too exclusive a regard, and do not lay sufficient stress upon the other beauties of character which go towards making a human being lovable or admirable, this may be admitted. Utilitarians who have cultivated their moral feelings, but not their sympathies nor their artistic perceptions, do fall into this mistake; and so do all other moralists under the same conditions. What can be said in excuse for other moralists is equally available for them, namely, that, if there is to be any error, it is better that it should be on that side. As a matter of fact, we may affirm that among utilitarians as among adherents of other systems, there is every imaginable degree of rigidity and of laxity in the application of their standard: some are even puritanically rigorous, while others are as indulgent as can possibly be desired by sinner or by sentimentalist. But on the whole, a doctrine which brings prominently forward the interest that mankind have in the repression and prevention of conduct which violates the moral law, is likely to be inferior to no other in turning the sanctions of opinion against such violations. It is true, the question, "What does violate the moral law?" is one on which those who recognise different standards of morality are likely now and then to differ. But difference of opinion on moral questions was not first introduced into the world by utilitarianism, while that doctrine does supply, if not always an easy, at all events a tangible and intelligible mode of deciding such differences.

It may not be superfluous to notice a few more of the common misapprehensions of utilitarian ethics, even those which are so obvious and gross that it might appear impossible for any person of candour and intelligence to fall into them; since persons, even of considerable mental endowments, often give themselves so little trouble to understand the bearings of any opinion against which they entertain a prejudice, and men are in general so little conscious of this voluntary ignorance as a defect, that the vulgarest misunderstandings of ethical doctrines are continually met with in the deliberate writings of persons of the greatest pretensions both to high principle and to philosophy.

We not uncommonly hear the doctrine of utility inveighed against as a godless doctrine. If it be necessary to say anything at all against so mere an assumption, we may say that the question depends upon what idea we have formed of the moral character of the Deity. If it be a true belief that God desires, above all things, the happiness of his creatures, and that this was his purpose in their creation, utility is not only not a godless doctrine, but more profoundly religious than any other. If it be meant that utilitarianism does not recognise the revealed will of God as the supreme law of morals, I answer, that a utilitarian who believes in the perfect goodness and wisdom of *God,* necessarily believes that whatever God has thought fit to reveal on the subject of morals, must fulfil the requirements of utility in a supreme degree. But others besides utilitarians have been of opinion that the Christian revelation was intended, and is fitted, to inform the hearts and minds of mankind with a spirit which should enable them to find for themselves what is right, and incline them to do it when found, rather than to tell them, except in a very general way, what it is; and that we need a doctrine of ethics, carefully followed out, to *interpret* to us the will of God. Whether this opinion is correct or not, it is superfluous here to discuss; since whatever aid religion, either natural or revealed, can afford to ethical investigation, is as open to the utilitarian moralist as to any other. He can use it as the testimony of God to the usefulness or hurtfulness of any given course of action, by as good a right as others can use it for the indication of a transcendental law, having no connection with usefulness or with happiness.

Again, Utility is often summarily stigmatised as an immoral doctrine by giving it the name of "expediency," and taking advantage of the popular use of that term to contrast it with Principle. But the Expedient, in the sense in which it is opposed to the Right, generally means that which is expedient for the particular interest of the agent himself; as when a minister sacrifices the interests of his country to keep himself in place. When it means anything better than this, it means that which is expedient for some immediate object, some temporary purpose, but which violates a rule whose observance is expedient in a much higher degree. The Expedient, in this sense, instead of being the same thing with the useful, is a branch of the hurtful. Thus, it would often be expedient, for the purpose of getting over some momentary embarrassment, or attaining some object immediately useful to ourselves or others, to tell a lie. But inasmuch as the cultivation in ourselves of a sensitive feeling on the subject of veracity, is one of the most useful, and the enfeeblement of that feeling one of the most hurtful, things to which our conduct can be instrumental; and inasmuch as any, even unintentional, deviation from truth, does that much towards weakening the trustworthiness of human assertion, which is not only the principal support of all present social well-being, but the insufficiency of which does more than any one thing that can be named to keep back civilisation, virtue, everything on which human happiness on the largest scale depends; we feel that the violation, for a present advantage, of a rule of such transcendant expediency, is not expedient, and that he who, for the sake of a convenience to himself or to some other individual, does what depends on him to deprive mankind of the good, and inflict upon them the evil, involved in the greater or less reliance which they can place in each other's word, acts the part of one of their worst enemies. Yet that even this rule, sacred as it is, admits of possible exceptions, is acknowledged by all moralists; the chief of which is when the withholding of some fact (as of information from a malefactor, or of bad news from a person dangerously ill) would save an individual (especially an individual other than oneself) from great and unmerited evil, and when the withholding can only be effected by denial. But in order that the exception may not extend itself beyond the need, and may have the least possible effect in weakening reliance on veracity, it ought to be recognised, and, if possible, its limits defined; and if the principle of utility is good for anything, it must be good for weighing these conflicting utilities against one another, and marking out the region within which one or the other preponderates.

Again, defenders of utility often find themselves called upon to reply to such objections as this—that there is not time, previous to action, for calculating and weighing the effects of any line of conduct on the general happiness. This is exactly as if any one were to say that it is impossible to guide our conduct by Christianity, because there is not time, on every occasion on which anything has to be done, to read through the Old and New Testaments. The answer to the objection is, that there has been ample time, namely, the whole past duration of the human species. During all that time, mankind have been learning by experience the tendencies of actions; on which experience all the prudence, as well as all the morality of life, are dependent. People talk as if the commencement of this course of experience had hitherto been put off, and as if, at the moment when some man feels tempted to meddle with the property or life of another, he had to begin considering for the first time whether murder and theft are injurious to human happiness. Even then I do not think that he would find the question very puzzling; but, at all events, the matter is now done to his hand. It is truly a whimsical supposition that, if mankind were agreed in considering utility to be the test of morality, they would remain without any agreement as to what is useful, and would take no measures for having their notions on the subject taught to the young, and enforced by law and opinion. There is no difficulty in proving any ethical standard whatever to work ill, if we suppose universal idiocy to be conjoined with it; but on any hypothesis short of that, mankind must by this time have acquired positive beliefs as to the effects of some actions on their happiness; and the beliefs which have thus come down are the rules of morality for the multitude, and for the philosopher until he has succeeded in finding better. That philosophers might easily do this, even now, on many subjects; that the received code of ethics is by no means of divine right; and that mankind have still much to learn as to the effects of actions on the general happiness, I admit, or rather, earnestly maintain. The corollaries from the principle of utility, like the precepts of every practical art, admit of indefinite improvement, and, in a progressive state of the human mind, their improvement is perpetually going on. But to consider the rules of morality as improvable, is one thing; to pass over the intermediate generalisations entirely, and endeavour to test each individual action directly by the first principle, is another. It is a strange notion that the acknowledgment of a first principle is inconsistent with the admission of secondary ones. To inform a traveller respecting the place of his ultimate destination, is not to forbid the use of landmarks and direction-posts on the way. The proposition that happiness is the end and aim of morality, does not mean that no road ought to be laid down to that goal, or that persons going thither should not be advised to take one direction rather than another. Men really ought to leave off talking a kind of nonsense on this subject, which they would neither talk nor listen to on other matters of practical concernment, Nobody argues that the art of navigation is not founded on astronomy, because sailors cannot wait to calculate the Nautical Almanac. Being rational creatures, they go to sea with it ready calculated; and all rational creatures go out upon the sea of life with their minds made up on the common questions of right and wrong, as well as on many of the far more difficult questions of wise and foolish. And this, as long as foresight is a human quality, it is to be presumed they will continue to do. Whatever we adopt as the fundamental principle of morality, we require subordinate principles to apply it by; the impossibility of doing without them, being common to all systems, can afford no argument against any one in particular; but gravely to argue as if no such secondary principles could be had, and as if mankind had remained till no, and always must remain, without drawing any general conclusions from the experience of human life, is as high a pitch, I think, as absurdity has ever reached in philosophical controversy.

The remainder of the stock arguments against utilitarianism mostly consist in laying to its charge the common infirmities of human nature, and the general difficulties which embarrass conscientious persons in shaping their course through life. We are told that a utilitarian will be apt to make his own particular case an exception to moral rules, and, when under temptation, will see a utility in the breach of a rule, greater than he will see in its observance. But is utility the only creed which is able to furnish us with excuses for evil doing, and means of cheating our own conscience? They are afforded in abundance by all doctrines which recognise as a fact in morals the existence of conflicting considerations; which all doctrines do, that have been believed by sane persons. It is not the fault of any creed, but of the complicated nature of human affairs, that rules of conduct cannot be so framed as to require no exceptions, and that hardly any kind of action can safely be laid down as either always obligatory or always condemnable. There is no ethical creed which does not temper the rigidity of its laws, by giving a certain latitude, under the moral responsibility of the agent, for accommodation to peculiarities of circumstances; and under every creed, at the opening thus made, self-deception and dishonest casuistry get in. There exists no moral system under which there do not arise unequivocal cases of conflicting obligation. These are the real difficulties, the knotty points both in the theory of ethics, and in the conscientious guidance of personal conduct. They are overcome practically, with greater or with less success, according to the intellect and virtue of the individual; but it can hardly be pretended that any one will be the less qualified for dealing with them, from possessing an ultimate standard to which conflicting rights and duties can be referred. If utility is the ultimate source of moral obligations, utility may be invoked to decide between them when their demands are incompatible. Though the application of the standard may be difficult, it is better than none at all: while in other systems, the moral laws all claiming independent authority, there is no common umpire entitled to interfere between them; their claims to precedence one over another rest on little better than sophistry, and unless determined, as they generally are, by the unacknowledged influence of considerations of utility, afford a free scope for the action of personal desires and partialities. We must remember that only in these cases of conflict between secondary principles is it requisite that first principles should be appealed to. There is no case of moral obligation in which some secondary principle is not involved; and if only one, there can seldom be any real doubt which one it is, in the mind of any person by whom the principle itself is recognised.

CHAPTER 3: OF THE ULTIMATE SANCTION OF THE PRINCIPLE OF UTILITY

The question is often asked, and properly so, in regard to any supposed moral standard—What is its sanction? what are the motives to obey it? or more specifically, what is the source of its obligation? whence does it derive its binding force? It is a necessary part of moral philosophy to provide the answer to this question; which, though frequently assuming the shape of an objection to the utilitarian morality, as if it had some special applicability to that above others, really arises in regard to all standards. It arises, in fact, whenever a person is called on to *adopt* a standard, or refer morality to any basis on which he has not been accustomed to rest it. For the customary morality, that which education and opinion have consecrated, is the only one which presents itself to the mind with the feeling of being *in itself* obligatory; and when a person is asked to believe that this morality *derives* its obligation from some general principle round which custom has not thrown the same halo, the assertion is to him a paradox; the supposed corollaries seem to have a more binding force than the original theorem; the superstructure seems to stand better without, than with, what is represented as its foundation. He says to himself, I feel that I am bound not to rob or murder, betray or deceive; but why am I bound to promote the general happiness? If my own happiness lies in something else, why may I not give that the preference?

If the view adopted by the utilitarian philosophy of the nature of the moral sense be correct, this difficulty will always present itself, until the influences which form moral character have taken the same hold of the principle which they have taken of some of the consequences—until, by the improvement of education, the feeling of unity with our fellow-creatures shall be (what it cannot be denied that Christ intended it to be) as deeply rooted in our character, and to our own consciousness as completely a part of our nature, as the horror of crime is in an ordinarily well brought up young person. In the meantime, however, the difficulty has no peculiar application to the doctrine of utility, but is inherent in every attempt to analyse morality and reduce it to principles; which, unless the principle is already in men's minds invested with as much sacredness as any of its applications, always seems to divest them of a part of their sanctity.

The principle of utility either has, or there is no reason why it might not have, all the sanctions which belong to any other system of morals. Those sanctions are either external or internal. Of the external sanctions it is not necessary to speak at any length. They are, the hope of favour and the fear of displeasure, from our fellow-creatures or from the Ruler of the Universe, along with whatever we may have of sympathy or affection for them, or of love and awe of Him, inclining us to do his will independently of selfish consequences. There is evidently no reason why all these motives for observance should not attach themselves to the utilitarian morality, as completely and as powerfully as to any other. Indeed, those of them which refer to our fellow-creatures are sure to do so, in proportion to the amount of general intelligence; for whether there be any other ground of moral obligation than the general happiness or not, men do desire happiness; and however imperfect may be their own practice, they desire and commend all conduct in others towards themselves, by which they think their happiness is promoted. With regard to the religious motive, if men believe, as most profess to do, in the goodness of God, those who think that conduciveness to the general happiness is the essence, or even only the criterion of good, must necessarily believe that it is also that which God approves. The whole force therefore of external reward and punishment, whether physical or moral, and whether proceeding from God or from our fellow men, together with all that the capacities of human nature admit of disinterested devotion to either, become available to enforce the utilitarian morality, in proportion as that morality is recognised; and the more powerfully, the more the appliances of education and general cultivation are bent to the purpose.

So far as to external sanctions. The internal sanction of duty, whatever our standard of duty may be, is one and the same—a feeling in our own mind; a pain, more or less intense, attendant on violation of duty, which in properly cultivated moral natures rises, in the more serious cases, into shrinking from it as an impossibility. This feeling, when disinterested, and connecting itself with the pure idea of duty, and not with some particular form of it, or with any of the merely accessory circumstances, is the essence of Conscience; though in that complex phenomenon as it actually exists, the simple fact is in general all encrusted over with collateral associations, derived from sympathy, from love, and still more from fear; from all the forms of religious feeling; from the recollections of childhood and of all our past life; from self-esteem, desire of the esteem of others, and occasionally even self-abasement. This extreme complication is, I apprehend, the origin of the sort of mystical character which, by a tendency of the human mind of which there are many other examples, is apt to be attributed to the idea of moral obligation, and which leads people to believe that the idea cannot possibly attach itself to any other objects than those which, by a supposed mysterious law, are found in our present experience to excite it. Its binding force, however, consists in the existence of a mass of feeling which must be broken through in order to do what violates our standard of right, and which, if we do nevertheless violate that standard, will probably have to be encountered afterwards in the form of remorse. Whatever theory we have of the nature or origin of conscience, this is what essentially constitutes it.

The ultimate sanction, therefore, of all morality (external motives apart) being a subjective feeling in our own minds, I see nothing embarrassing to those whose standard is utility, in the question, "What is the sanction of that particular standard?" We may answer, the same as of all other moral standards—the conscientious feelings of mankind. Undoubtedly this sanction has no binding efficacy on those who do not possess the feelings it appeals to; but neither will these persons be more obedient to any other moral principle than to the utilitarian one. On them morality of any kind has no hold but through the external sanctions. Meanwhile the feelings exist, a fact in human nature, the reality of which, and the great power with which they are capable of acting on those in whom they have been duly cultivated, are proved by experience. No reason has ever been shown why they may not be cultivated to as great intensity in connection with the utilitarian, as with any other rule of morals.

There is, I am aware, a disposition to believe that a person who sees in moral obligation a transcendental fact, an objective reality belonging to the province of "things in themselves," is likely to be more obedient to it than one who believes it to be entirely subjective, having its seat in human consciousness only. But whatever a person's opinion may be on this point of Ontology, the force he is really urged by is his own subjective feeling, and is exactly measured by its strength. No one's belief that duty is an objective reality is stronger than the belief that God is so; yet the belief in God, apart from the expectation of actual reward and punishment, only operates on conduct through, and in proportion to, the subjective religious feeling. The sanction, so far as it is disinterested, is always in the mind itself; and the notion therefore of the transcendental moralists must be, that this sanction will not exist *in* the mind unless it is believed to have its root out of the mind; and that if a person is able to say to himself, "This which is restraining me, and which is called my conscience, is only a feeling in my own mind," he may possibly draw the conclusion that when the feeling ceases the obligation ceases, and that if he find the feeling inconvenient, he may disregard it, and endeavour to get rid of it. But is this danger confined to the utilitarian morality? Does the belief that moral obligation has its seat outside the mind make the feeling of it too strong to be got rid of? The fact is so far otherwise, that all moralists admit and lament the ease with which, in the generality of minds, conscience can be silenced or stifled. The question, "Need I obey my conscience?" is quite as often put to themselves by persons who never heard of the principle of utility, as by its adherents. Those whose conscientious feelings are so weak as to allow of their asking this question, if they answer it affirmatively, will not do so because they believe in the transcendental theory, but because of the external sanctions.

It is not necessary, for the present purpose, to decide whether the feeling of duty is innate or implanted. Assuming it to be innate, it is an open question to what objects it naturally attaches itself; for the philosophic supporters of that theory are now agreed that the intuitive perception is of principles of morality and not of the details. If there be anything innate in the matter, I see no reason why the feeling which is innate should not be that of regard to the pleasures and pains of others. If there is any principle of morals which is intuitively obligatory, I should say it must be that. If so, the intuitive ethics would coincide with the utilitarian, and there would be no further quarrel between them. Even as it is, the intuitive moralists, though they believe that there are other intuitive moral obligations, do already believe this to be one; for they unanimously hold that a large *portion* of morality turns upon the consideration due to the interests of our fellow-creatures. Therefore, if the belief in the transcendental origin of moral obligation gives any additional efficacy to the internal sanction, it appears to me that the utilitarian principle has already the benefit of it.

On the other hand, if, as is my own belief, the moral feelings are not innate, but acquired, they are not for that reason the less natural. It is natural to man to speak, to reason, to build cities, to cultivate the ground, though these are acquired faculties. The moral feelings are not indeed a part of our nature, in the sense of being in any perceptible degree present in all of us; but this, unhappily, is a fact admitted by those who believe the most strenuously in their transcendental origin. Like the other acquired capacities above referred to, the moral faculty, if not a part of our nature, is a natural outgrowth from it; capable, like them, in a certain small degree, of springing up spontaneously; and susceptible of being brought by cultivation to a high degree of development. Unhappily it is also susceptible, by a sufficient use of the external sanctions and of the force of early impressions, of being cultivated in almost any direction: so that there is hardly anything so absurd or so mischievous that it may not, by means of these influences, be made to act on the human mind with all the authority of conscience. To doubt that the same potency might be given by the same means to the principle of utility, even if it had no foundation in human nature, would be flying in the face of all experience.

But moral associations which are wholly of artificial creation, when intellectual culture goes on, yield by degrees to the dissolving force of analysis: and if the feeling of duty, when associated with utility, would appear equally arbitrary; if there were no leading department of our nature, no powerful class of sentiments, with which that association would harmonise, which would make us feel it congenial, and incline us not only to foster it in others (for which we have abundant interested motives), but also to cherish it in ourselves; if there were not, in short, a natural basis of sentiment for utilitarian morality, it might well happen that this association also, even after it had been implanted by education, might be analysed away.

But there *is* this basis of powerful natural sentiment; and this it is which, when once the general happiness is recognised as the ethical standard, will constitute the strength of the utilitarian morality. This firm foundation is that of the social feelings of mankind; the desire to be in unity with our fellow creatures, which is already a powerful principle in human nature, and happily one of those which tend to become stronger, even without express inculcation, from the influences of advancing civilisation. The social state is at once so natural, so necessary, and so habitual to man, that, except in some unusual circumstances or by an effort of voluntary abstraction, he never conceives himself otherwise than as a member of a body; and this association is riveted more and more, as mankind are further removed from the state of savage independence. Any condition, therefore, which is essential to a state of society, becomes more and more an inseparable part of every person's conception of the state of things which he is born into, and which is the destiny of a human being. Now, society between human beings, except in the relation of master and slave, is manifestly impossible on any other footing than that the interests of all are to be consulted. Society between equals can only exist on the understanding that the interests of all are to be regarded equally. And since in all states of civilisation, every person, except an absolute monarch, has equals, every one is obliged to live on these terms with somebody; and in every age some advance is made towards a state in which it will be impossible to live permanently on other terms with anybody. In this way people grow up unable to conceive as possible to them a state of total disregard of other people's interests. They are under a necessity of conceiving themselves as at least abstaining from all the grosser injuries, and (if only for their own protection) living in a state of constant protest against them. They are also familiar with the fact of cooperating with others and proposing to themselves a collective, not an individual interest as the aim (at least for the time being) of their actions. So long as they are cooperating, their ends are identified with those of others; there is at least a temporary feeling that the interests of others are their own interests. Not only does all strengthening of social ties, and all healthy growth of society, give to each individual a stronger personal interest in practically consulting the welfare of others; it also leads him to identify his *feelings* more and more with their good, or at least with an even greater degree of practical consideration for it. He comes, as though instinctively, to be conscious of himself as a being who *of course* pays regard to others. The good of others becomes to him a thing naturally and necessarily to be attended to, like any of the physical conditions of our existence. Now, whatever amount of this feeling a person has, he is urged by the strongest motives both of interest and of sympathy to demonstrate it, and to the utmost of his power encourage it in others; and even if he has none of it himself, he is as greatly interested as any one else that others should have it. Consequently the smallest germs of the feeling are laid hold of and nourished by the contagion of sympathy and the influences of education; and a complete web of corroborative association is woven round it, by the powerful agency of the external sanctions. This mode of conceiving ourselves and human life, as civilisation goes on, is felt to be more and more natural. Every step in political improvement renders it more so, by removing the sources of opposition of interest, and levelling those inequalities of legal privilege between individuals or classes, owing to which there are large portions of mankind whose happiness it is still practicable to disregard. In an improving state of the human mind, the influences are constantly on the increase, which tend to generate in each individual a feeling of unity with all the rest; which, if perfect, would make him never think of, or desire, any beneficial condition for himself, in the benefits of which they are not included. If we now suppose this feeling of unity to be taught as a religion, and the whole force of education, of institutions, and of opinion, directed, as it once was in the case of religion, to make every person grow up from infancy surrounded on all sides both by the profession and the practice of it, I think that no one, who can realise this conception, will feel any misgiving about the sufficiency of the ultimate sanction for the Happiness morality. To any ethical student who finds the realisation difficult, I recommend, as a means of facilitating it, the second of M. Comte's two principal works, the *Traité de Politique Positive*. I entertain the strongest objections to the system of politics and morals set forth in that treatise; but I think it has superabundantly shown the possibility of giving to the service of humanity, even without the aid of belief in a Providence, both the psychological power and the social efficacy of a religion; making it take hold of human life, and colour all thought, feeling, and action, in a manner of which the greatest ascendancy ever exercised by any religion may be but a type and foretaste; and of which the danger is, not that it should be insufficient, but that it should be so excessive as to interfere unduly with human freedom and individuality.

Neither is it necessary to the feeling which constitutes the binding force of the utilitarian morality on those who recognise it, to wait for those social influences which would make its obligation felt by mankind at large. In the comparatively early state of human advancement in which we now live, a person cannot indeed feel that entireness of sympathy with all others, which would make any real discordance in the general direction of their conduct in life impossible; but already a person in whom the social feeling is at all developed, cannot bring himself to think of the rest of his fellow-creatures as struggling rivals with him for the means of happiness, whom he must desire to see defeated in their object in order that he may succeed in his. The deeply rooted conception which every individual even now has of himself as a social being, tends to make him feel it one of his natural wants that there should be harmony between his feelings and aims and those of his fellow-creatures. If differences of opinion and of mental culture make it impossible for him to share many of their actual feelings—perhaps make him denounce and defy those feelings—he still needs to be conscious that his real aim and theirs do not conflict; that he is not opposing himself to what they really wish for, namely their own good, but is, on the contrary, promoting it. This feeling in most individuals is much inferior in strength to their selfish feelings, and is often wanting altogether. But to those who have it, it possesses all the characters of a natural feeling. It does not present itself to their minds as a superstition of education, or a law despotically imposed by the power of society, but as an attribute which it would not be well for them to be without. This conviction is the ultimate sanction of the greatest happiness morality. This it is which makes any mind, of well-developed feelings, work with, and not against, the outward motives to care for others, afforded by what I have called the external sanctions; and when those sanctions are wanting, or act in an opposite direction, constitutes in itself a powerful internal binding force, in proportion to the sensitiveness and thoughtfulness of the character; since few but those whose mind is a moral blank, could bear to lay out their course of life on the plan of paying no regard to others except so far as their own private interest compels.

Chapter 4: Of What Sort of Proof the Principle of Utility Is Susceptible

It has already been remarked, that questions of ultimate ends do not admit of proof, in the ordinary acceptation of the term. To be incapable of proof by reasoning is common to all first principles; to the first premises of our knowledge, as well as to those of our conduct. But the former, being matters of fact, may be the subject of a direct appeal to the faculties which judge of fact—namely, our senses, and our internal consciousness. Can an appeal be made to the same faculties on questions of practical ends? Or by what other faculty is cognisance taken of them?

Questions about ends are, in other words, questions what things are desirable. The utilitarian doctrine is, that happiness is desirable, and the only thing desirable, as an end; all other things being only desirable as means to that end. What ought to be required of this doctrine—what conditions is it requisite that the doctrine should fulfil—to make good its claim to be believed?

The only proof capable of being given that an object is visible, is that people actually see it. The only proof that a sound is audible, is that people hear it: and so of the other sources of our experience. In like manner, I apprehend, the sole evidence it is possible to produce that anything is desirable, is that people do actually desire it. If the end which the utilitarian doctrine proposes to itself were not, in theory and in practice, acknowledged to be an end, nothing could ever convince any person that it was so. No reason can be given why the general happiness is desirable, except that each person, so far as he believes it to be attainable, desires his own happiness. This, however, being a fact, we have not only all the proof which the case admits of, but all which it is possible to require, that happiness is a good: that each person's happiness is a good to that person, and the general happiness, therefore, a good to the aggregate of all persons. Happiness has made out its title as *one* of the ends of conduct, and consequently one of the criteria of morality.

But it has not, by this alone, proved itself to be the sole criterion. To do that, it would seem, by the same rule, necessary to show, not only that people desire happiness, but that they never desire anything else. Now it is palpable that they do desire things which, in common language, are decidedly distinguished from happiness. They desire, for example, virtue, and the absence of vice, no less really than pleasure and the absence of pain. The desire of virtue is not as universal, but it is as authentic a fact, as the desire of happiness. And hence the opponents of the utilitarian standard deem that they have a right to infer that there are other ends of human action besides happiness, and that happiness is not the standard of approbation and disapprobation.

But does the utilitarian doctrine deny that people desire virtue, or maintain that virtue is not a thing to be desired? The very reverse. It maintains not only that virtue is to be desired, but that it is to be desired disinterestedly, for itself. Whatever may be the opinion of utilitarian moralists as to the original conditions by which virtue is made virtue; however they may believe (as they do) that actions and dispositions are only virtuous because they promote another end than virtue; yet this being granted, and it having been decided, from considerations of this description, what is virtuous, they not only place virtue at the very head of the things which are good as means to the ultimate end, but they also recognise as a psychological fact the possibility of its being, to the individual, a good in itself, without looking to any end beyond it; and hold, that the mind is not in a right state, not in a state conformable to Utility, not in the state most conducive to the general happiness, unless it does love virtue in this manner—as a thing desirable in itself, even although, in the individual instance, it should not produce those other desirable consequences which it tends to produce, and on account of which it is held to be virtue. This opinion is not, in the smallest degree, a departure from the Happiness principle. The ingredients of happiness are very various, and each of them is desirable in itself, and not merely when considered as swelling an aggregate. The principle of utility does not mean that any given pleasure, as music, for instance, or any given exemption from pain, as for example health, is to be looked upon as means to a collective something termed happiness, and to be desired on that account. They are desired and desirable in and for themselves; besides being means, they are a part of the end. Virtue, according to the utilitarian doctrine, is not naturally and originally part of the end, but it is capable of becoming so; and in those who love it disinterestedly it has become so, and is desired and cherished, not as a means to happiness, but as a part of their happiness.

To illustrate this farther, we may remember that virtue is not the only thing, originally a means, and which if it were not a means to anything else, would be and remain indifferent, but which by association with what it is a means to, comes to be desired for itself, and that too with the utmost intensity. What, for example, shall we say of the love of money? There is nothing originally more desirable about money than about any heap of glittering pebbles. Its worth is solely that of the things which it will buy; the desires for other things than itself, which it is a means of gratifying. Yet the love of money is not only one of the strongest moving forces of human life, but money is, in many cases, desired in and for itself; the desire to possess it is often stronger than the desire to use it, and goes on increasing when all the desires which point to ends beyond it, to be compassed by it, are falling off. It may, then, be said truly, that money is desired not for the sake of an end, but as part of the end. From being a means to happiness, it has come to be itself a principal ingredient of the individual's conception of happiness. The same may be said of the majority of the great objects of human life—power, for example, or fame; except that to each of these there is a certain amount of immediate pleasure annexed, which has at least the semblance of being naturally inherent in them; a thing which cannot be said of money. Still, however, the strongest natural attraction, both of power and of fame, is the immense aid they give to the attainment of our other wishes; and it is the strong association thus generated between them and all our objects of desire, which gives to the direct desire of them the intensity it often assumes, so as in some characters to surpass in strength all other desires. In these cases the means have become a part of the end, and a more important part of it than any of the things which they are means to. What was once desired as an instrument for the attainment of happiness, has come to be desired for its own sake. In being desired for its own sake it is, however, desired as *part* of happiness. The person is made, or thinks he would be made, happy by its mere possession; and is made unhappy by failure to obtain it. The desire of it is not a different thing from the desire of happiness, any more than the love of music, or the desire of health. They are included in happiness. They are some of the elements of which the desire of happiness is made up. Happiness is not an abstract idea, but a concrete whole; and these are some of its parts. And the utilitarian standard sanctions and approves their being so. Life would be a poor thing, very ill provided with sources of happiness, if there were not this provision of nature, by which things originally indifferent, but conducive to, or otherwise associated with, the satisfaction of our primitive desires, become in themselves sources of pleasure more valuable than the primitive pleasures, both in permanency, in the space of human existence that they are capable of covering, and even in intensity.

Virtue, according to the utilitarian conception, is a good of this description. There was no original desire of it, or motive to it, save its conduciveness to pleasure, and especially to protection from pain. But through the association thus formed, it may be felt a good in itself, and desired as such with as great intensity as any other good; and with this difference between it and the love of money, of power, or of fame, that all of these may, and often do, render the individual noxious to the other members of the society to which he belongs, whereas there is nothing which makes him so much a blessing to them as the cultivation of the disinterested love of virtue. And consequently, the utilitarian standard, while it tolerates and approves those other acquired desires, up to the point beyond which they would be more injurious to the general happiness than promotive of it, enjoins and requires the cultivation of the love of virtue up to the greatest strength possible, as being above all things important to the general happiness.

It results from the preceding considerations, that there is in reality nothing desired except happiness. Whatever is desired otherwise than as a means to some end beyond itself, and ultimately to happiness, is desired as itself a part of happiness, and is not desired for itself until it has become so. Those who desire virtue for its own sake, desire it either because the consciousness of it is a pleasure, or because the consciousness of being without it is a pain, or for both reasons united; as in truth the pleasure and pain seldom exist separately, but almost always together, the same person feeling pleasure in the degree of virtue attained, and pain in not having attained more. If one of these gave him no pleasure, and the other no pain, he would not love or desire virtue, or would desire it only for the other benefits which it might produce to himself or to persons whom he cared for.

We have now, then, an answer to the question, of what sort of proof the principle of utility is susceptible. If the opinion which I have now stated is psychologically true— if human nature is so constituted as to desire nothing which is not either a part of happiness or a means of happiness—we can have no other proof, and we require no other, that these are the only things desirable. If so, happiness is the sole end of human action, and the promotion of it the test by which to judge of all human conduct; from whence it necessarily follows that it must be the criterion of morality, since a part is included in the whole.

And now to decide whether this is really so; whether mankind do desire nothing for itself but that which is a pleasure to them, or of which the absence is a pain; we have evidently arrived at a question of fact and experience, dependent, like all similar questions, upon evidence. It can only be determined by practised self-consciousness and self-observation, assisted by observation of others. I believe that these sources of evidence, impartially consulted, will declare that desiring a thing and finding it pleasant, aversion to it and thinking of it as painful, are phenomena entirely inseparable, or rather two parts of the same phenomenon—in strictness of language, two different modes of naming the same psychological fact: that to think of an object as desirable (unless for the sake of its consequences), and to think of it as pleasant, are one and the same thing; and that to desire anything, except in proportion as the idea of it is pleasant, is a physical and metaphysical impossibility.

So obvious does this appear to me, that I expect it will hardly be disputed: and the objection made will be, not that desire can possibly be directed to anything ultimately except pleasure and exemption from pain, but that the will is a different thing from desire; that a person of confirmed virtue, or any other person whose purposes are fixed, carries out his purposes without any thought of the pleasure he has in contemplating them, or expects to derive from their fulfilment; and persists in acting on them, even though these pleasures are much diminished, by changes in his character or decay of his passive sensibilities, or are out weighed by the pains which the pursuit of the purposes may bring upon him. All this I fully admit, and have stated it elsewhere, as positively and emphatically as any one. Will, the active phenomenon, is a different thing from desire, the state of passive sensibility, and though originally an offshoot from it, may in time take root and detach itself from the parent stock; so much so, that in the case of an habitual purpose, instead of willing the thing because we desire it, we often desire it only because we will it. This, however, is but an instance of that familiar fact, the power of habit, and is no wise confined to the case of virtuous actions. Many indifferent things, which men originally did from a motive of some sort, they continue to do from habit. Sometimes this is done unconsciously, the consciousness coming only after the action: at other times with conscious volition, but volition which has become habitual, and is put in operation by the force of habit, in opposition perhaps to the deliberate preference, as often happens with those who have contracted habits of vicious or hurtful indulgence. Third and last comes the case in which the habitual act of will in the individual instance is not in contradiction to the general intention prevailing at other times, but in fulfilment of it; as in the case of the person of confirmed virtue, and of all who pursue deliberately and consistently any determinate end. The distinction between will and desire thus understood is an authentic and highly important psychological fact; but the fact consists solely in this—that will, like all other parts of our constitution, is amenable to habit, and that we may will from habit what we no longer desire for itself, or desire only because we will it. It is not the less true that will, in the beginning, is entirely produced by desire; including in that term the repelling influence of pain as well as the attractive one of pleasure. Let us take into consideration, no longer the person who has a confirmed will to do right, but him in whom that virtuous will is still feeble, conquerable by temptation, and not to be fully relied on; by what means can it be strengthened? How can the will to be virtuous, where it does not exist in sufficient force, be implanted or awakened? Only by making the person *desire* virtue—by making him think of it in a pleasurable light, or of its absence in a painful one. It is by associating the doing right with pleasure, or the doing wrong with pain, or by eliciting and impressing and bringing home to the person's experience the pleasure naturally involved in the one or the pain in the other, that it is possible to call forth that will to be virtuous, which, when confirmed, acts without any thought of either pleasure or pain. Will is the child of desire, and passes out of the dominion of its parent only to come under that of habit. That which is the result of habit affords no presumption of being intrinsically good; and there would be no reason for wishing that the purpose of virtue should become independent of pleasure and pain, were it not that the influence of the pleasurable and painful associations which prompt to virtue is not sufficiently to be depended on for unerring constancy of action until it has acquired the support of habit. Both in feeling and in conduct, habit is the only thing which imparts certainty; and it is because of the importance to others of being able to rely absolutely on one's feelings and conduct, and to oneself of being able to rely on one's own, that the will to do right ought to be cultivated into this habitual independence. In other words, this state of the will is a means to good, not intrinsically a good; and does not contradict the doctrine that nothing is a good to human beings but in so far as it is either itself pleasurable, or a means of attaining pleasure or averting pain.

But if this doctrine be true, the principle of utility is proved. Whether it is so or not, must now be left to the consideration of the thoughtful reader.

CHAPTER 5: ON THE CONNECTION BETWEEN JUSTICE AND UTILITY

In all ages of speculation, one of the strongest obstacles to the reception of the doctrine that Utility or Happiness is the criterion of right and wrong, has been drawn from the idea of Justice. The powerful sentiment, and apparently clear perception, which that word recalls with a rapidity and certainty resembling an instinct, have seemed to the majority of thinkers to point to an inherent quality in things; to show that the Just must have an existence in Nature as something absolute, generically distinct from every variety of the Expedient, and, in idea, opposed to it, though (as is commonly acknowledged) never, in the long run, disjoined from it in fact.

In the case of this, as of our other moral sentiments, there is no necessary connection between the question of its origin, and that of its binding force. That a feeling is bestowed on us by Nature, does not necessarily legitimate all its promptings. The feeling of justice might be a peculiar instinct, and might yet require, like our other instincts, to be controlled and enlightened by a higher reason. If we have intellectual instincts, leading us to judge in a particular way, as well as animal instincts that prompt us to act in a particular way, there is no necessity that the former should be more infallible in their sphere than the latter in theirs: it may as well happen that wrong judgments are occasionally suggested by those, as wrong actions by these. But though it is one thing to believe that we have natural feelings of justice, and another to acknowledge them as an ultimate criterion of conduct, these two opinions are very closely connected in point of fact. Mankind are always predisposed to believe that any subjective feeling, not otherwise accounted for, is a revelation of some objective reality. Our present object is to determine whether the reality, to which the feeling of justice corresponds, is one which needs any such special revelation; whether the justice or injustice of an action is a thing intrinsically peculiar, and distinct from all its other qualities, or only a combination of certain of those qualities, presented under a peculiar aspect. For the purpose of this inquiry it is practically important to consider whether the feeling itself, of justice and injustice, is *sui generis* like our sensations of colour and taste, or a derivative feeling, formed by a combination of others. And this it is the more essential to examine, as people are in general willing enough to allow, that objectively the dictates of Justice coincide with a part of the field of General Expediency; but inasmuch as the subjective mental feeling of Justice is different from that which commonly attaches to simple expediency, and, except in the extreme cases of the latter, is far more imperative in its demands, people find it difficult to see, in Justice, only a particular kind or branch of general utility, and think that its superior binding force requires a totally different origin.

To throw light upon this question, it is necessary to attempt to ascertain what is the distinguishing character of justice, or of injustice: what is the quality, or whether there is any quality, attributed in common to all modes of conduct designated as unjust (for justice, like many other moral attributes, is best defined by its opposite), and distinguishing them from such modes of conduct as are disapproved, but without having that particular epithet of disapprobation applied to them. If in everything which men are accustomed to characterise as just or unjust, some one common attribute or collection of attributes is always present, we may judge whether this particular attribute or combination of attributes would be capable of gathering round it a sentiment of that peculiar character and intensity by virtue of the general laws of our emotional constitution, or whether the sentiment is inexplicable, and requires to be regarded as a special provision of Nature. If we find the former to be the case, we shall, in resolving this question, have resolved also the main problem: if the latter, we shall have to seek for some other mode of investigating it.

To find the common attributes of a variety of objects, it is necessary to begin by surveying the objects themselves in the concrete. Let us therefore advert successively to the various modes of action, and arrangements of human affairs, which are classed, by universal or widely spread opinion, as Just or as Unjust. The things well known to excite the sentiments associated with those names are of a very multifarious character. I shall pass them rapidly in review, without studying any particular arrangement.

In the first place, it is mostly considered unjust to deprive any one of his personal liberty, his property, or any other thing which belongs to him by law. Here, therefore, is one instance of the application of the terms "just" and "unjust" in a perfectly definite sense, namely, that it is just to respect, unjust to violate, the *legal rights* of any one. But this judgment admits of several exceptions, arising from the other forms in which the notions of justice and injustice present themselves. For example, the person who suffers the deprivation may (as the phrase is) have *forfeited* the rights which he is so deprived of: a case to which we shall return presently. But also,

Secondly; the legal rights of which he is deprived, may be rights which *ought* not to have belonged to him; in other words, the law which confers on him these rights, may be a bad law. When it is so, or when (which is the same thing for our purpose) it is supposed to be so, opinions will differ as to the justice or injustice of infringing it. Some maintain that no law, however bad, ought to be disobeyed by an individual citizen; that his opposition to it, if shown at all, should only be shown in endeavouring to get it altered by competent authority. This opinion (which condemns many of the most illustrious benefactors of mankind, and would often protect pernicious institutions against the only weapons which, in the state of things existing at the time, have any chance of succeeding against them) is defended, by those who hold it, on grounds of expediency; principally on that of the importance, to the common interest of mankind, of maintaining inviolate the sentiment of submission to law. Other persons, again, hold the directly contrary opinion, that any law, judged to be bad, may blamelessly be disobeyed, even though it be not judged to be unjust, but only inexpedient; while others would confine the licence of disobedience to the case of unjust laws: but again, some say, that all laws which are inexpedient are unjust; since every law imposes some restriction on the natural liberty of mankind, which restriction is an injustice, unless legitimated by tending to their good. Among these diversities of opinion, it seems to be universally admitted that there may be unjust laws, and that law, consequently, is not the ultimate criterion of justice, but may give to one person a benefit, or impose on another an evil, which justice condemns. When, however, a law is thought to be unjust, it seems always to be regarded as being so in the same way in which a breach of law is unjust, namely, by infringing somebody's right; which, as it cannot in this case be a legal right, receives a different appellation, and is called a moral right. We may say, therefore, that a second case of injustice consists in taking or withholding from any person that to which he has a *moral right*.

   Thirdly, it is universally considered just that each person should obtain that (whether good or evil) which he *deserves* and unjust that he should obtain a good, or be made to undergo an evil, which he does not deserve. This is, perhaps, the clearest and most emphatic form in which the idea of justice is conceived by the general mind. As it involves the notion of desert, the question arises, what constitutes desert? Speaking in a general way, a person is understood to deserve good if he does right, evil if he does wrong; and in a more particular sense, to deserve good from those to whom he does or has done good, and evil from those to whom he does or has done evil. The precept of returning good for evil has never been regarded as a case of the fulfilment of justice, but as one in which the claims of justice are waived, in obedience to other considerations.

   Fourthly, it is confessedly unjust to *break faith* with any one: to violate an engagement, either express or implied, or disappoint expectations raised by our own conduct, at least if we have raised those expectations knowingly and voluntarily. Like the other obligations of justice already spoken of, this one is not regarded as absolute, but as capable of being overruled by a stronger obligation of justice on the other side; or by such conduct on the part of the person concerned as is deemed to absolve us from our obligation to him, and to constitute a *forfeiture* of the benefit which he has been led to expect.

   Fifthly, it is, by universal admission, inconsistent with justice to be *partial*—to show favour or preference to one person over another, in matters to which favour and preference do not properly apply. Impartiality, however, does not seem to be regarded as a duty in itself, but rather as instrumental to some other duty; for it is admitted that favour and preference are not always censurable, and indeed the cases in which they are condemned are rather the exception than the rule. A person would be more likely to be blamed than applauded for giving his family or friends no superiority in good offices over strangers, when he could do so without violating any other duty; and no one thinks it unjust to seek one person in preference to another as a friend, connection, or companion. Impartiality where rights are concerned is of course obligatory, but this is involved in the more general obligation of giving to every one his right. A tribunal, for example, must be impartial, because it is bound to award, without regard to any other consideration, a disputed object to the one of two parties who has the right to it. There are other cases in which impartiality means, being solely influenced by desert; as with those who, in the capacity of judges, preceptors, or parents, administer reward and punishment as such. There are cases, again, in which it means, being solely influenced by consideration for the public interest; as in making a selection among candidates for a government employment. Impartiality, in short, as an obligation of justice, may be said to mean, being exclusively influenced by the considerations which it is supposed ought to influence the particular case in hand; and resisting the solicitation of any motives which prompt to conduct different from what those considerations would dictate.

Nearly allied to the idea of impartiality is that of *equality,* which often enters as a component part both into the conception of justice and into the practice of it, and, in the eyes of many persons, constitutes its essence. But in this, still more than in any other case, the notion of justice varies in different persons, and always conforms in its variations to their notion of utility. Each person maintains that equality is the dictate of justice, except where he thinks that expediency requires inequality. The justice of giving equal protection to the rights of all, is maintained by those who support the most outrageous inequality in the rights themselves. Even in slave countries it is theoretically admitted that the rights of the slave, such as they are, ought to be as sacred as those of the master; and that a tribunal which fails to enforce them with equal strictness is wanting in justice; while, at the same time, institutions which leave to the slave scarcely any rights to enforce, are not deemed unjust, because they are not deemed inexpedient. Those who think that utility requires distinctions of rank, do not consider it unjust that riches and social privileges should be unequally dispensed; but those who think this inequality inexpedient, think it unjust also. Whoever thinks that government is necessary, sees no injustice in as much inequality as is constituted by giving to the magistrate powers not granted to other people. Even among those who hold levelling doctrines, there are as many questions of justice as there are differences of opinion about expediency. Some Communists consider it unjust that the produce of the labour of the community should be shared on any other principle than that of exact equality; others think it just that those should receive most whose wants are greatest; while others hold that those who work harder, or who produce more, or whose services are more valuable to the community, may justly claim a larger quota in the division of the produce. And the sense of natural justice may be plausibly appealed to in behalf of every one of these opinion.

Among so many diverse applications of the term "justice," which yet is not regarded as ambiguous, it is a matter of some difficulty to seize the mental link which holds them together, and on which the moral sentiment adhering to the term essentially depends. Perhaps, in this embarrassment, some help may be derived from the history of the word, as indicated by its etymology.

In most, if not in all, languages, the etymology of the word which corresponds to "just" points distinctly to an origin connected with the ordinances of law. *Justum* is a form of *jussum,* that which has been ordered. ⟨*Dikaion*⟩ comes directly from ⟨*dike*⟩, a suit at law. *Recht,* from which came *right* and *righteous,* is synonymous with law. The courts of justice, the administration of justice, are the courts and the administration of law. *La justice,* in French, is the established term for judicature. I am not committing the fallacy imputed with some show of truth to Horne Tooke,* of assuming that a word must still continue to mean what it originally meant. Etymology is slight evidence of what the idea now signified is, but the very best evidence of how it sprang up. There can, I think, be no doubt that the *idée mère,* the primitive element, in the formation of the notion of justice, was conformity to law. It constituted the entire idea among the Hebrews, up to the birth of Christianity; as might be expected in the case of a people whose laws attempted to embrace all subjects on which precepts were required, and who believed those laws to be a direct emanation from the Supreme Being. But other nations, and in particular the Greeks and Romans, who knew that their laws had been made originally, and still continued to be made, by men, were not afraid to admit that those men might make bad laws; might do, by law, the same things, and from the same motives, which if done by individuals without the sanction of law, would be called unjust. And hence the sentiment of injustice came to be attached, not to all violations of law, but only to violations of such laws as *ought* to exist, including such as ought to exist, but do not; and to laws themselves, if supposed to be contrary to what ought to be law. In this manner the idea of law and of its injunctions was still predominant in the notion of justice, even when the laws actually in force ceased to be accepted as the standard of it.

It is true that mankind consider the idea of justice and its obligations as applicable to many things which neither are, nor is it desired that they should be, regulated by law. Nobody desires that laws should interfere with the whole detail of private life; yet every one allows that in all daily conduct a person may and does show himself to be either just or unjust. But even here, the idea of the breach of what ought to be law, still lingers in a modified shape. It would always give us pleasure, and chime in with our feelings of fitness, that acts which we deem unjust should be punished, though we do not always think it expedient that this should be done by the tribunals. We forego that gratification on account of incidental inconveniences. We should be glad to see just conduct enforced and injustice repressed, even in the minutest details, if we were not, with reason, afraid of trusting the magistrate with so unlimited an amount of power over individuals. When we think that a person is bound in justice to do a thing, it is an ordinary form of language to say, that he ought to be compelled to do it. We should be gratified to see the obligation enforced by anybody who had the power. If we see that its enforcement by law would be inexpedient, we lament the impossibility, we consider the impunity given to injustice as an evil, and strive to make amends for it by bringing a strong expression of our own and the public disapprobation to bear upon the offender. Thus the idea of legal constraint is still the generating idea of the notion of justice, though undergoing several transformations before that notion, as it exists in an advanced state of society, becomes complete.

The above is, I think, a true account, as far as it goes, of the origin and progressive growth of the idea of justice. But we must observe, that it contains, as yet, nothing to distinguish that obligation from moral obligation in general. For the truth is, that the idea of penal sanction, which is the essence of law, enters not only into the conception of injustice, but into that of any kind of wrong. We do not call anything wrong, unless we mean to imply that a person ought to be punished in some way or other for doing it; if not by law, by the opinion of his fellow-creatures; if not by opinion, by the reproaches of his own conscience. This seems the real turning point of the distinction between morality and simple expediency. It is a part of the notion of Duty in every one of its

---

*[John Tooke (1736–1812), a radical writer and close friend of Bentham.]

forms, that a person may rightfully be compelled to fulfil it. Duty is a thing which may be *exacted* from a person, as one exacts a debt. Unless we think that it may be exacted from him, we do not call it his duty. Reasons of prudence, or the interest of other people, may militate against actually exacting it; but the person himself, it is clearly understood, would not be entitled to complain. There are other things, on the contrary, which we wish that people should do, which we like or admire them for doing, perhaps dislike or despise them for not doing, but yet admit that they are not bound to do; it is not a case of moral obligation; we do not blame them, that is, we do not think that they are proper objects of punishment. How we come by these ideas of deserving and not deserving punishment, will appear, perhaps, in the sequel; but I think there is no doubt that this distinction lies at the bottom of the notions of right and wrong; that we call any conduct wrong, or employ, instead, some other term of dislike or disparagement, according as we think that the person ought, or ought not, to be punished for it; and we say, it would be right to do so and so, or merely that it would be desirable or laudable, according as we would wish to see the person whom it concerns, compelled, or only persuaded and exhorted, to act in that manner.*

This, therefore, being the characteristic difference which marks off, not justice, but morality in general, from the remaining provinces of Expediency and Worthiness; the character is still to be sought which distinguishes justice from other branches of morality. Now it is known that ethical writers divide moral duties into two classes, denoted by the ill-chosen expressions, duties of perfect and of imperfect obligation; the latter being those in which, though the act is obligatory, the particular occasions of performing it are left to our choice; as in the case of charity or beneficence, which we are indeed bound to practise, but not towards any definite person, nor at any prescribed time. In the more precise language of philosophic jurists, duties of perfect obligation are those duties in virtue of which a correlative *right* resides in some person or persons; duties of imperfect obligation are those moral obligations which do not give birth to any right. I think it will be found that this distinction exactly coincides with that which exists between justice and the other obligations of morality. In our survey of the various popular acceptations of justice, the term appeared generally to involve the idea of a personal right—a claim on the part of one or more individuals, like that which the law gives when it confers a proprietary or other legal right. Whether the injustice consists in depriving a person of a possession, or in breaking faith with him, or in treating him worse than he deserves, or worse than other people who have no greater claims, in each case the supposition implies two things—a wrong done, and some assignable person who is wronged. Injustice may also be done by treating a person better than others; but the wrong in this case is to his competitors, who are also assignable persons. It seems to me that this feature in the case—a right in some person, correlative to the moral obligation—constitutes the specific difference between justice, and generosity or beneficence. Justice implies something which it is not only right to do, and wrong not to do, but which some individual person can claim from us as his moral right. No one has a moral right to our generosity or beneficence, because we are not morally bound to practise those virtues towards any given individual. And it will be found with respect to this as to every correct definition, that the instances which seem to conflict with it are those which most confirm it. For if a moralist attempts, as some have done, to make out that mankind generally, though not any given individual, have a right to all the good we can

---

*I see this point enforced and illustrated by Professor Bain, in an admirable chapter (entitled "The Ethical Emotions, or the Moral Sense"), of the second of the two treatises composing his elaborate and profound work on the Mind.

do them, he at once, by that thesis, includes generosity and beneficence within the category of justice. He is obliged to say, that our utmost exertions are due to our fellow-creatures, thus assimilating them to a debt; or that nothing less can be a sufficient *return* for what society does for us, thus classing the case as one of gratitude; both of which are acknowledged cases of justice. Wherever there is a right, the case is one of justice, and not of the virtue of beneficence: and whoever does not place the distinction between justice and morality in general, where we have now placed it, will be found to make no distinction between them at all, but to merge all morality in justice.

Having thus endeavoured to determine the distinctive elements which enter into the composition of the idea of justice, we are ready to enter on the inquiry, whether the feeling, which accompanies the idea, is attached to it by a special dispensation of nature, or whether it could have grown up, by any known laws, out of the idea itself; and in particular, whether it can have originated in considerations of general expediency.

I conceive that the sentiment itself does not arise from anything which would commonly, or correctly, be termed an idea of expediency; but that though the sentiment does not, whatever is moral in it does.

We have seen that the two essential ingredients in the sentiment of justice are, the desire to punish a person who has done harm and the knowledge or belief that there is some definite individual or individuals to whom harm has been done.

Now it appears to me, that the desire to punish a person who has done harm to some individual is a spontaneous outgrowth from two sentiments, both in the highest degree natural, and which either are or resemble instincts; the impulse of self-defence, and the feeling of sympathy.

It is natural to resent, and to repel or retaliate, any harm done or attempted against ourselves, or against those with whom we sympathise. The origin of this sentiment it is not necessary here to discuss. Whether it be an instinct or a result of intelligence, it is, we know, common to all animal nature; for every animal tries to hurt those who have hurt, or who it thinks are about to hurt, itself or its young. Human beings, on this point, only differ from other animals in two particulars. First, in being capable of sympathising, not solely with their offspring, or, like some of the more noble animals, with some superior animal who is kind to them, but with all human, and even with all sentient, beings. Secondly, in having a more developed intelligence, which gives a wider range to the whole of their sentiments, whether self-regarding or sympathetic. By virtue of his superior intelligence, even apart from his superior range of sympathy, a human being is capable of apprehending a community of interest between himself and the human society of which he forms a part, such that any conduct which threatens the security of the society generally, is threatening to his own, and calls forth his instinct (if instinct it be) of self-defence. The same superiority of intelligence, joined to the power of sympathising with human beings generally, enables him to attach himself to the collective idea of his tribe, his country, or mankind, in such a manner that any act hurtful to them, raises his instinct of sympathy, and urges him to resistance.

The sentiment of justice, in that one of its elements which consists of the desire to punish, is thus, I conceive, the natural feeling of retaliation or vengeance, rendered by intellect and sympathy applicable to those injuries, that is, to those hurts, which wound us through, or in common with, society at large. This sentiment, in itself, has nothing moral in it; what is moral is, the exclusive subordination of it to the social sympathies, so as to wait on and obey their call. For the natural feeling would make us resent indiscriminately whatever any one does that is disagreeable to us; but when moralised by the social feeling, it only acts in the directions conformable to the general good: just persons resenting a hurt to society, though not otherwise a hurt to themselves, and not resenting a hurt to themselves, however painful, unless it be of the kind which society has a common interest with them in the repression of.

It is no objection against this doctrine to say, that when we feel our sentiment of justice outraged, we are not thinking of society at large, or of any collective interest, but only of the individual case. It is common enough certainly, though the reverse of commendable, to feel resentment merely because we have suffered pain; but a person whose resentment is really a moral feeling, that is, who considers whether an act is blamable before he allows himself to resent it—such a person, though he may not say expressly to himself that he is standing up for the interest of society, certainly does feel that he is asserting a rule which is for the benefit of others as well as for his own. If he is not feeling this—if he is regarding the act solely as it affects him individually—he is not consciously just; he is not concerning himself about the justice of his actions. This is admitted even by anti-utilitarian moralists. When Kant (as before remarked) propounds as the fundamental principle of morals, "So act, that thy rule of conduct might be adopted as a law by all rational beings," he virtually acknowledges that the interest of mankind collectively, or at least of mankind indiscriminately, must be in the mind of the agent when conscientiously deciding on the morality of the act. Otherwise he uses words without a meaning: for, that a rule even of utter selfishness could not *possibly* be adopted by all rational beings—that there is any insuperable obstacle in the nature of things to its adoption—cannot be even plausibly maintained. To give any meaning to Kant's principle, the sense put upon it must be, that we ought to shape our conduct by a rule which all rational beings might adopt *with benefit to their collective interest.*

To recapitulate: the idea of justice supposes two things—a rule of conduct, and a sentiment which sanctions the rule. The first must be supposed common to all mankind, and intended for their good. The other (the sentiment) is a desire that punishment may be suffered by those who infringe the rule. There is involved, in addition, the conception of some definite person who suffers by the infringement; whose rights (to use the expression appropriated to the case) are violated by it. And the sentiment of justice appears to me to be, the animal desire to repel or retaliate a hurt or damage to oneself, or to those with whom one sympathises, widened so as to include all persons, by the human capacity of enlarged sympathy, and the human conception of intelligent self-interest. From the latter elements, the feeling derives its morality; from the former, its peculiar impressiveness, and energy of self-assertion.

I have, throughout, treated the idea of a *right* residing in the injured person, and violated by the injury, not as a separate element in the composition of the idea and sentiment, but as one of the forms in which the other two elements clothe themselves. These elements are, a hurt to some assignable person or persons on the one hand, and a demand for punishment on the other. An examination of our own minds, I think, will show, that these two things include all that we mean when we speak of violation of a right. When we call anything a person's right, we mean that he has a valid claim on society to protect him in the possession of it, either by the force of law, or by that of education and opinion. If he has what we consider a sufficient claim, on whatever account, to have something guaranteed to him by society, we say that he has a right to it. If we desire to prove that anything does not belong to him by right, we think this done as soon as it is admitted that society ought not to take measures for securing it to him, but should leave him to chance, or to his own exertions. Thus, a person is said to have a right to what he can earn in fair professional competition; because society ought not to allow any other person to hinder him from endeavouring to earn in that manner as much as he can. But he has not a right to three hundred a year, though he may happen to be earning it; because society is not called on to provide that he shall earn that sum. On the contrary, if he owns ten thousand pounds three percent stock, he *has* a right to three hundred a year because society has come under an obligation to provide him with an income of that amount.

To have a right, then, is, I conceive, to have something which society ought to defend me in the possession of. If the objector goes on to ask, why it ought? I can give him no other reason than general utility. If that expression does not seem to convey a sufficient feeling of the strength of the obligation, nor to account for the peculiar energy of the feeling, it is because there goes to the composition of the sentiment, not a rational only, but also an animal element, the thirst for retaliation; and this thirst derives its intensity, as well as its moral justification, from the extraordinarily important and impressive kind of utility which is concerned. The interest involved is that of security, to every one's feelings the most vital of all interests. All other earthly benefits are needed by one person, not needed by another; and many of them can, if necessary, be cheerfully foregone, or replaced by something else; but security no human being can possibly do without; on it we depend for all our immunity from evil, and for the whole value of all and every good, beyond the passing moment; since nothing but the gratification of the instant could be of any worth to us, if we could be deprived of anything the next instant by whoever was momentarily stronger than ourselves. Now this most indispensable of all necessaries, after physical nutriment, cannot be had, unless the machinery for providing it is kept unintermittedly in active play. Our notion, therefore, of the claim we have on our fellow-creatures to join in making safe for us the very groundwork of our existence, gathers feelings around it so much more intense than those concerned in any of the more common cases of utility, that the difference in degree (as is often the case in psychology) becomes a real difference in kind. The claim assumes that character of absoluteness, that apparent infinity, and incommensurability with all other considerations, which constitute the distinction between the feeling of right and wrong and that of ordinary expediency and inexpediency. The feelings concerned are so powerful, and we count so positively on finding a responsive feeling in others (all being alike interested), that *ought* and *should* grow into *must*, and recognised indispensability becomes a moral necessity, analogous to physical, and often not inferior to it in binding force.

If the preceding analysis, or something resembling it, be not the correct account of the notion of justice; if justice be totally independent of utility, and be a standard *per se*, which the mind can recognise by simple introspection of itself; it is hard to understand why that internal oracle is so ambiguous, and why so many things appear either just or unjust, according to the light in which they are regarded.

We are continually informed that Utility is an uncertain standard, which every different person interprets differently, and that there is no safety but in the immutable, ineffaceable, and unmistakable dictates of Justice, which carry their evidence in themselves, and are independent of the fluctuations of opinion. One would suppose from this that on questions of justice there could be no controversy; that if we take that for our rule, its application to any given case could leave us in as little doubt as a mathematical demonstration. So far is this from being the fact, that there is as much difference of opinion, and as much discussion, about what is just, as about what is useful to society. Not only have different nations and individuals different notions of justice, but in the mind of one and the same individual, justice is not some one rule, principle, or maxim, but many, which do not always coincide in their dictates, and in choosing between which, he is guided either by some extraneous standard, or by his own personal predilections.

For instance, there are some who say, that it is unjust to punish any one for the sake of example to others; that punishment is just, only when intended for the good of the sufferer himself. Others maintain the extreme reverse, contending that to punish persons who have attained years of discretion, for their own benefit, is despotism and injustice, since if the matter at issue is solely their own good, no one has a right to control their own judgment of it; but that they may justly be punished to prevent evil to others, this being the exercise of the legitimate right of self-defence. Mr. Owen,* again, affirms that it is unjust to punish at all; for the criminal did not make his own character; his education, and the circumstances which surrounded him, have made him a criminal, and for these he is not responsible. All these opinions are extremely plausible; and so long as the question is argued as one of justice simply, without going down to the principles which lie under justice and are the source of its authority, I am unable to see how any of these reasoners can be refuted. For in truth every one of the three builds upon rules of justice confessedly true. The first appeals to the acknowledged injustice of singling out an individual, and making him a sacrifice, without his consent, for other people's benefit. The second relies on the acknowledged justice of self-defence, and the admitted injustice of forcing one person to conform to another's notions of what constitutes his good. The Owenite invokes the admitted principle, that it is unjust to punish any one for what he cannot help. Each is triumphant so long as he is not compelled to take into consideration any other maxims of justice than the one he has selected; but as soon as their several maxims are brought face to face, each disputant seems to have exactly as much to say for himself as the others. No one of them can carry out his own notion of justice without trampling upon another equally binding. These are difficulties; they have always been felt to be such; and many devices have been invented to turn rather than to overcome them. As a refuge from the last of the three, men imagined what they called the freedom of the will; fancying that they could not justify punishing a man whose will is in a thoroughly hateful state, unless it be supposed to have come into that state through no influence of anterior circumstances. To escape from the other difficulties, a favourite contrivance has been the fiction of a contract, whereby at some unknown period all the members of society engaged to obey the laws, and consented to be punished for any disobedience to them; thereby giving to their legislators the right, which it is assumed they would not otherwise have had, of punishing them, either for their own good or for that of society. This happy thought was considered to get rid of the whole difficulty, and to legitimate the infliction of punishment, in virtue of another received maxim of justice, *volenti non fit injuria;* that is not unjust which is done with the consent of the person who is supposed to be hurt by it. I need hardly remark, that even if the consent were not a mere fiction, this maxim is not superior in authority to the others which it is brought in to supersede. It is, on the contrary, an instructive specimen of the loose and irregular manner in which supposed principles of justice grow up. This particular one evidently came into use as a help to the coarse exigencies of courts of law, which are sometimes obliged to be content with very uncertain presumptions, on account of the greater evils which would often arise from any attempt on their part to cut finer. But even courts of law are not able to adhere consistently to the maxim, for they allow voluntary engagements to be set aside on the ground of fraud, and sometimes on that of mere mistake or misinformation.

Again, when the legitimacy of inflicting punishment is admitted, how many conflicting conceptions of justice come to light in discussing the proper apportionment of punishments to offences. No rule on the subject recommends itself so strongly to the primitive and spontaneous sentiment of justice, as the *lex talionis,* an eye for an eye and

---

*[Robert Owen (1771–1858), a British reformer who argued for environmental determinism.]

a tooth for a tooth. Though this principle of the Jewish and of the Mohammedan law has been generally abandoned in Europe as a practical maxim, there is, I suspect, in most minds, a secret hankering after it; and when retribution accidentally falls on an offender in that precise shape, the general feeling of satisfaction evinced bears witness how natural is the sentiment to which this repayment in kind is acceptable. With many, the test of justice in penal infliction is that the punishment should be proportioned to the offence; meaning that it should be exactly measured by the moral guilt of the culprit (whatever be their standard for measuring moral guilt): the consideration, what amount of punishment is necessary to deter from the offence, having nothing to do with the question of justice, in their estimation: while there are others to whom that consideration is all in all; who maintain that it is not just, at least for man, to inflict on a fellow-creature, whatever may be his offences, any amount of suffering beyond the least that will suffice to prevent him from repeating, and others from imitating, his misconduct.

To take another example from a subject already once referred to. In a co-operative industrial association, is it just or not that talent or skill should give a title to superior remuneration? On the negative side of the question it is argued, that whoever does the best he can, deserves equally well, and ought not in justice to be put in a position of inferiority for no fault of his own; that superior abilities have already advantages more than enough, in the admiration they excite, the personal influence they command, and the internal sources of satisfaction attending them, without adding to these a superior share of the world's goods; and that society is bound in justice rather to make compensation to the less favoured, for this unmerited inequality of advantages, than to aggravate it. On the contrary side it is contended, that society receives more from the more efficient labourer; that his services being more useful, society owes him a larger return for them; that a greater share of the joint result is actually his work, and not to allow his claim to it is a kind of robbery; that if he is only to receive as much as others, he can only be justly required to produce as much, and to give a smaller amount of time and exertion, proportioned to his superior efficiency. Who shall decide between these appeals to conflicting principles of justice? Justice has in this case two sides to it, which it is impossible to bring into harmony, and the two disputants have chosen opposite sides; the one looks to what it is just that the individual should receive, the other to what it is just that the community should give. Each, from his own point of view, is unanswerable; and any choice between them, on grounds of justice, must be perfectly arbitrary. Social utility alone can decide the preference.

How many, again, and how irreconcilable, are the standards of justice to which reference is made in discussing the repartition of taxation. One opinion is, that payment to the State should be in numerical proportion to pecuniary means. Others think that justice dictates what they term graduated taxation; taking a higher percentage from those who have more to spare. In point of natural justice a strong case might be made for disregarding means altogether, and taking the same absolute sum (whenever it could be got) from every one: as the subscribers to a mess, or to a club, all pay the same sum for the same privileges, whether they can all equally afford it or not. Since the protection (it might be said) of law and government is afforded to, and is equally required by all, there is no injustice in making all buy it at the same price. It is reckoned justice, not injustice, that a dealer should charge to all customers the same price for the same article, not a price varying according to their means of payment. This doctrine, as applied to taxation, finds no advocates, because it conflicts so strongly with man's feelings of humanity and of social expediency; but the principle of justice which it invokes is as true and as binding as those which can be appealed to against it. Accordingly it exerts a tacit influence on the line of defence employed for other modes of assessing taxation. People feel obliged to argue that the State does more for the rich than for the poor, as a justification for its taking more from them: though this is in reality not true, for the rich would be far better able to protect themselves, in the absence of law or government, than the poor, and indeed would probably be successful in converting the poor into their slaves. Others, again, so far defer to the same conception of justice, as to maintain that all should pay an equal capitation tax for the protection of their persons (these being of equal value to all), and an unequal tax for the protection of their property, which is unequal. To this others reply, that the all of one man is as valuable to him as the all of another. From these confusions there is no other mode of extrication than the utilitarian.

Is, then, the difference between the Just and the Expedient a merely imaginary distinction? Have mankind been under a delusion in thinking that justice is a more sacred thing than policy, and that the latter ought only to be listened to after the former has been satisfied? By no means. The exposition we have given of the nature and origin of the sentiment, recognises a real distinction; and no one of those who profess the most sublime contempt for the consequences of actions as an element in their morality, attaches more importance to the distinction than I do. While I dispute the pretensions of any theory which sets up an imaginary standard of justice not grounded on utility, I account the justice which is grounded on utility to be the chief part, and incomparably the most sacred and binding part, of all morality. Justice is a name for certain classes of moral rules, which concern the essentials of human well-being more nearly, and are therefore of more absolute obligation, than any other rules for the guidance of life; and the notion which we have found to be of the essence of the idea of justice, that of a right residing in an individual, implies and testifies to this more binding obligation.

The moral rules which forbid mankind to hurt one another (in which we must never forget to include wrongful interference with each other's freedom) are more vital to human well-being than any maxims, however important, which only point out the best mode of managing some department of human affairs. They have also the peculiarity, that they are the main element in determining the whole of the social feelings of mankind. It is their observance which alone preserves peace among human beings: if obedience to them were not the rule, and disobedience the exception, every one would see in every one else an enemy, against whom he must be perpetually guarding himself. What is hardly less important, these are the precepts which mankind have the strongest and the most direct inducements for impressing upon one another. By merely giving to each other prudential instruction or exhortation, they may gain, or think they gain, nothing: in inculcating on each other the duty of positive beneficence they have an unmistakable interest, but far less in degree: a person may possibly not need the benefits of others; but he always needs that they should not do him hurt. Thus the moralities which protect every individual from being harmed by others, either directly or by being hindered in his freedom of pursuing his own good, are at once those which he himself has most at heart, and those which he has the strongest interest in publishing and enforcing by word and deed. It is by a person's observance of these that his fitness to exist as one of the fellowship of human beings is tested and decided; for on that depends his being a nuisance or not to those with whom he is in contact. Now it is these moralities primarily which compose the obligations of justice. The most marked cases of injustice, and those which give the tone to the feeling of repugnance which characterises the sentiment, are acts of wrongful aggression, or wrongful exercise of power over some one; the next are those which consist in wrongfully withholding from him something which is his due; in both cases, inflicting on him a positive hurt, either in the form of direct suffering, or of the privation of some good which he had reasonable ground, either of a physical or of a social kind, for counting upon.

The same powerful motives which command the observance of these primary moralities, enjoin the punishment of those who violate them; and as the impulses of self-defence, of defence of others, and of vengeance, are all called forth against such persons, retribution, or evil for evil, becomes closely connected with the sentiment of justice, and is universally included in the idea. Good for good is also one of the dictates of justice; and this, though its social utility is evident, and though it carries with it a natural human feeling, has not at first sight that obvious connection with hurt or injury, which, existing in the most elementary cases of just and unjust, is the source of the characteristic intensity of the sentiment. But the connection, though less obvious, is not less real. He who accepts benefits, and denies a return of them when needed, inflicts a real hurt, by disappointing one of the most natural and reasonable of expectations, and one which he must at least tacitly have encouraged, otherwise the benefits would seldom have been conferred. The important rank, among human evils and wrongs, of the disappointment of expectation, is shown in the fact that it constitutes the principal criminality of two such highly immoral acts as a breach of friendship and a breach of promise. Few hurts which human beings can sustain are greater, and none wound more, than when that on which they habitually and with full assurance relied, fails them in the hour of need; and few wrongs are greater than this mere withholding of good; none excite more resentment, either in the person suffering, or in a sympathising spectator. The principle, therefore, of giving to each what they deserve, that is, good for good as well as evil for evil, is not only included within the idea of Justice as we have defined it, but is a proper object of that intensity of sentiment, which places the Just, in human estimation, above the simply Expedient.

Most of the maxims of justice current in the world, and commonly appealed to in its transactions, are simply instrumental to carrying into effect the principles of justice which we have now spoken of. That a person is only responsible for what he has done voluntarily, or could voluntarily have avoided; that it is unjust to condemn any person unheard; that the punishment ought to be proportioned to the offence, and the like, are maxims intended to prevent the just principle of evil for evil from being perverted to the infliction of evil without that justification. The greater part of these common maxims have come into use from the practice of courts of justice, which have been naturally led to a more complete recognition and elaboration than was likely to suggest itself to others, of the rules necessary to enable them to fulfil their double function, of inflicting punishment when due, and of awarding to each person his right.

That first of judicial virtues, impartiality, is an obligation of justice, partly for the reason last mentioned; as being a necessary condition of the fulfilment of the other obligations of justice. But this is not the only source of the exalted rank, among human obligations, of those maxims of equality and impartiality, which, both in popular estimation and in that of the most enlightened, are included among the precepts of justice. In one point of view, they may be considered as corollaries from the principles already laid down. If it is a duty to do to each according to his deserts, returning good for good as well as repressing evil by evil, it necessarily follows that we should treat all equally well (when no higher duty forbids) who have deserved equally well of *us*, and that society should treat all equally well who have deserved equally well of *it*, that is, who have deserved equally well absolutely. This is the highest abstract standard of social and distributive justice; towards which all institutions, and the efforts of all virtuous citizens, should be made in the utmost possible degree to converge. But this great moral duty rests upon a still deeper foundation, being a direct emanation from the first principle of morals, and not a mere logical corollary from secondary or derivative doctrines. It is involved in the very meaning of Utility, or the Greatest Happiness Principle. That principle is a mere form of words without rational signification, unless one person's happiness, supposed equal in degree (with the proper allowance made for kind), is counted for exactly as much as another's. Those conditions being supplied, Bentham's dictum, "everybody to count for one, nobody for more than one," might be written under the principle of utility as an explanatory commentary.* The equal claim of everybody to happiness in the estimation of the moralist and of the legislator, involves an equal claim to all the means of happiness, except in so far as the inevitable conditions of human life, and the general interest, in which that of every individual is included, set limits to the maxim; and those limits ought to be strictly construed. As every other maxim of justice, so this is by no means applied or held applicable universally; on the contrary, as I have already remarked, it bends to every person's ideas of social expediency. But in whatever case it is deemed applicable at all, it is held to be the dictate of justice. All persons are deemed to have a *right* to equality of treatment, except when some recognised social expediency requires the reverse. And hence all social inequalities which have ceased to be considered expedient, assume the character not of simple inexpediency, but of injustice, and appear so tyrannical, that people are apt to wonder how they ever could have been tolerated; forgetful that they themselves perhaps tolerate other inequalities under an equally mistaken notion of expediency, the correction of which would make that which they approve seem quite as monstrous as what they have at last learnt to condemn. The entire history of social improvement has been a series of transitions, by which one custom or institution after another, from being a supposed primary necessity of social existence, has passed into the rank of a universally stigmatised injustice and tyranny. So it has been with the distinctions of slaves and freemen, nobles and serfs, patricians and plebeians; and so it will be, and in part already is, with the aristocracies of colour, race, and sex.

It appears from what has been said, that justice is a name for certain moral requirements, which, regarded collectively, stand higher in the scale of social utility, and are therefore of more paramount obligation, than any others; though particular cases may occur in which some other social duty is so important, as to overrule any one of the general maxims of justice. Thus, to save a life, it may not only be allowable, but a duty,

---

*This implication, in the first principle of the utilitarian scheme, of perfect impartiality between persons, is regarded by Mr. Herbert Spencer (in his *Social Statics*) as a disproof of the pretensions of utility to be a sufficient guide to right, since (he says) the principle of utility presupposes the anterior principle that everybody has an equal right to happiness. It may be more correctly described as supposing that equal amounts of happiness are equally desirable whether felt by the same or by different persons. This, however, is not a *presupposition*; not a premise needful to support the principle of utility, but the very principle itself; for what is the principle of utility, if it be not that "happiness" and "desirable" are synonymous terms? If there Is any anterior principle Implied, it can be no other than this, that the truths of arithmetic are applicable to the valuation of happiness, as of all other measurable quantities.

(Mr. Herbert Spencer in a private communication on the subject of the preceding note, objects to being considered an opponent of utilitarianism, and states that he regards happiness as the ultimate end of morality; but deems that end only partially attainable by empirical generalisations from the observed results of conduct, and completely attainable only by deducing, from the laws of life and the conditions of existence, what kinds of action necessarily tend to produce happiness, and what kinds to produce unhappiness. With the exception of the word "necessarily," I have no dissent to express from this doctrine; and (omitting that word) I am not aware that any modern advocate of utilitarianism is of a different opinion. Bentham, certainly, to whom in the *Social Statics* Mr. Spencer particularly referred, is, least of all writers, chargeable with unwillingness to deduce the effect of actions on happiness from the laws of human nature and the universal conditions of human life. The common charge against him is of relying too exclusively upon such deductions, and declining altogether to be bound by the generalisations from specific experience which Mr. Spencer thinks that utilitarians generally confine themselves to. My own opinion (and, as I collect, Mr. Spencer's) is, that in ethics, as in all other branches of scientific study, the consilience of the results of both these processes, each corroborating and verifying the other, is requisite to give to any general proposition the kind and degree of evidence which constitutes scientific proof.)

to steal, or take by force, the necessary food or medicine, or to kidnap, and compel to officiate, the only qualified medical practitioner. In such cases, as we do not call anything justice which is not a virtue, we usually say, not that justice must give way to some other moral principle, but that what is just in ordinary cases is, by reason of that other principle, not just in the particular case. By this useful accommodation of language, the character of indefeasibility attributed to justice is kept up, and we are saved from the necessity of maintaining that there can be laudable injustice.

The considerations which have now been adduced resolve, I conceive, the only real difficulty in the utilitarian theory of morals. It has always been evident that all cases of justice are also cases of expediency: the difference is in the peculiar sentiment which attaches to the former, as contradistinguished from the latter. If this characteristic sentiment has been sufficiently accounted for; if there is no necessity to assume for it any peculiarity of origin; if it is simply the natural feeling of resentment, moralised by being made coextensive with the demands of social good; and if this feeling not only does but ought to exist in all the classes of cases to which the idea of justice corresponds; that idea no longer presents itself as a stumbling-block to the utilitarian ethics. Justice remains the appropriate name for certain social utilities which are vastly more important, and therefore more absolute and imperative, than any others are as a class (though not more so than others may be in particular cases); and which, therefore, ought to be, as well as naturally are, guarded by a sentiment not only different in degree, but also in kind; distinguished from the milder feeling which attaches to the mere idea of promoting human pleasure or convenience, at once by the more definite nature of its commands, and by the sterner character of its sanctions.

ON LIBERTY (in part)

CHAPTER 3: OF INDIVIDUALITY, AS ONE OF THE ELEMENTS OF WELL-BEING

Such being the reasons which make it imperative that human beings should be free to form opinions and to express their opinions without reserve; and such the baneful consequences to the intellectual, and through that to the moral nature of man, unless this liberty is either conceded, or asserted in spite of prohibition; let us next examine whether the same reasons do not require that men should be free to act upon their opinions—to carry these out in their lives, without hindrance, either physical or moral, from their fellow men, so long as it is at their own risk and peril. This last proviso is of course indispensable. No one pretends that actions should be as free as opinions. On the contrary, even opinions lose their immunity, when the circumstances in which they are expressed are such as to constitute their expression a positive instigation to some mischievous act. An opinion that corn dealers are starvers of the poor, or that private property is robbery, ought to be unmolested when simply circulated through the press, but may justly incur punishment when delivered orally to an excited mob assembled before the house of a corn dealer, or when handed about among the same mob in the form of a placard. Acts, of whatever kind, which, without justifiable cause, do harm to others, may be, and in the more important cases absolutely require to be, controlled by the unfavourable sentiments, and, when needful, by the active interference of mankind. The liberty of the individual must be thus far limited; he must not make himself a nuisance to other people. But if he refrains from molesting others in what concerns them, and merely acts according to his own inclination and judgement in things which concern himself, the same reasons which show that opinion should be free, prove also that he should be allowed without molestation, to carry his opinions into practice at his own cost. That mankind are not infallible that their truths, for the most part, are only half-truths; that unity of opinion, unless resulting from the fullest and freest comparison of opposite opinions is not desirable, and diversity not an evil, but a good, until mankind are much more capable than at present of recognizing all sides of the truth, are principles applicable to men's modes of action, not less than to their opinions. As it is useful that while mankind are imperfect there should be different opinions, so is it that there should be different experiments of living; that free scope should be given to varieties of character short of injury to others; and that the worth of different modes of life should be proved practically, when any one thinks fit to try them. It is desirable, in short, that in things which do not primarily concern others, individuality should assert itself. Where, not the person's own character, but the traditions or customs of other people are the rule of conduct, there is wanting one of the principal ingredients of human happiness, and quite the chief ingredient of individual and social progress.

In maintaining this principle, the greatest difficulty to be encountered does not lie in the appreciation of means towards an acknowledged end, but in the indifference of persons in general to the end itself. If it were felt that the free development of individuality is one of the leading essentials of well-being; that it is not only a co-ordinate element with all that is designated by the terms civilization, instruction, education culture, but is itself a necessary part and condition of all those things; there would be no danger that liberty should be undervalued, and the adjustment of the boundaries between it and social control would present no extraordinary difficulty. But the evil is, that individual spontaneity is hardly recognized by the common modes of thinking, as having any intrinsic worth, or deserving any regard on its own account. The majority being satisfied with the ways of mankind as they now are (for it is they who make them what they are), cannot comprehend why those ways should not be good enough for everybody; and what is more, spontaneity forms no part of the ideal of the majority of moral and social reformers, but is rather looked on with jealousy as a troublesome and perhaps rebellious obstruction to the general acceptance of what these reformers, in their own judgement, think would be best for mankind. Few persons, out of Germany, even comprehend the meaning of the doctrine which Wilhelm von Humboldt, so eminent both as a *savant* and as a politician, made the text of a treatise—that "the end of man, or that which is prescribed by the eternal or immutable dictates of reason, and not suggested by vague and transient desires, is the highest and most harmonious development of his powers to a complete and consistent whole"; that, therefore, the object "towards which every human being must ceaselessly direct his efforts, and on which especially those who design to influence their fellow men must ever keep their eyes, is the individuality of power and development"; that for this there are two requisites, "freedom, and variety of situations," and that from the union of these arise "individual vigour and manifold diversity," which combine themselves in "originality."*

*The Sphere and Duties of Government, from the German of Baron Wilhelm von Humboldt, pp. 11–13. [Wilhelm von Humboldt (1767–1835) wrote this work in 1792 to oppose Fichte's and Hegel's theories of the state. The work shows the influence of the French Revolution on von Humboldt's thinking following his visit to Paris in 1789.]

Little, however, as people are accustomed to a doctrine like that of von Humboldt, and surprising as it may be to them to find so high a value attached to individuality, the question, one must nevertheless think, can only be one of degree. No one's idea of excellence in conduct is that people should do absolutely nothing but copy one another. No one would assert that people ought not to put into their mode of life, and into the conduct of their concerns, any impress whatever of their own judgement, or of their own individual character. On the other hand it would be absurd to pretend that people ought to live as if nothing whatever had been known in the world before they came into it; as if experience had as yet done nothing towards showing that one mode of existence, or of conduct, is preferable to another. Nobody denies that people should be so taught and trained in youth, as to know and benefit by the ascertained results of human experience. But it is the privilege and proper condition of a human being, arrived at the maturity of his faculties, to use and interpret experience in his own way. It is for him to find out what part of recorded experience is properly applicable to his own circumstances and character. The traditions and customs of other people are, to a certain extent, evidence of what their experience has taught *them;* presumptive evidence, and as such, have a claim to his deference: but, in the first place, their experience may be too narrow; or they may not have interpreted it rightly. Secondly, their interpretation of experience may be correct, but unsuitable to him. Customs are made for customary circumstances, and customary characters; and his circumstances or his character may be uncustomary. Thirdly, though the customs be both good as customs, and suitable to him, yet to conform to custom, merely *as* custom, does not educate or develop in him any of the qualities which are the distinctive endowment of a human being. The human faculties of perception, judgement, discriminative feeling, mental activity, and even moral preference, are exercised only in making a choice. He who does anything because it is the custom, makes no choice. He gains no practice either in discerning or in desiring what is best. The mental and moral, like the muscular powers, are improved only by being used. The faculties are called into no exercise by doing a thing merely because others do it, no more than by believing a thing only because others believe it. If the grounds of an opinion are not conclusive to the person's own reason, his reason cannot be strengthened, but is likely to be weakened, by his adopting it: and if the inducements to an act are not such as are consentaneous to his own feelings and character (where affection, or the rights of others, are not concerned) it is so much done towards rendering his feelings and character inert and torpid, instead of active and energetic.

He who lets the world, or his own portion of it, choose his plan of life for him, has no need of any other faculty than the ape-like one of imitation. He who chooses his plan for himself, employs all his faculties. He must use observation to see, reasoning and judgement to foresee, activity to gather materials for decision, discrimination to decide, and when he has decided, firmness and self-control to hold to his deliberate decision. And these qualities he requires and exercises exactly in proportion as the part of his conduct which he determines according to his own judgement and feelings is a large one. It is possible that he might be guided in some good path, and kept out of harm's way, without any of these things. But what will be his comparative worth as a human being? It really is of importance, not only what men do, but also what manner of men they are that do it. Among the works of man, which human life is rightly employed in perfecting and beautifying, the first in importance surely is man himself. Supposing it were possible to get houses built, corn grown, battles fought, causes tried, and even churches erected and prayers said, by machinery—by automatons in human form—it would be a considerable loss to exchange for these automatons even the men and women who at present inhabit the more civilized parts of the world, and who assuredly are but starved specimens of what nature can and will produce. Human nature is not a machine to be built after a model, and set to do exactly the work prescribed for it, but a tree, which requires to grow and develop itself on all sides, according to the tendency of the inward forces which make it a living thing.

It will probably be conceded that it is desirable people should exercise their understandings, and that an intelligent following of custom, or even occasionally an intelligent deviation from custom, is better than a blind and simply mechanical adhesion to it. To a certain extent it is admitted, that our understanding should be our own: but there is not the same willingness to admit that our desires and impulses should be our own likewise; or that to possess impulses of our own, and of any strength, is anything but a peril and a snare. Yet desires and impulses are as much a part of a perfect human being, as beliefs and restraints: and strong impulses are only perilous when not properly balanced; when one set of aims and inclinations is developed into strength, while others, which ought to coexist with them, remain weak and inactive. It is not because men's desires are strong that they act ill; it is because their consciences are weak. There is no natural connexion between strong impulses and a weak conscience. The natural connexion is the other way. To say that one person's desires and feelings are stronger and more various than those of another, is merely to say that he has more of the raw material of human nature, and is therefore capable, perhaps of more evil, but certainly of more good. Strong impulses are but another name for energy. Energy may be turned to bad uses; but more good may always be made of an energetic nature, than of an indolent and impassive one. Those who have most natural feeling, are always those whose cultivated feelings may be made the strongest. The same strong susceptibilities which make the personal impulses vivid and powerful, are also the source from whence are generated the most passionate love of virtue, and the sternest self-control. It is through the cultivation of these, that society both does its duty and protects its interests: not by rejecting the stuff of which heroes are made, because it knows not how to make them. A person whose desires and impulses are his own—are the expression of his own nature, as it has been developed and modified by his own culture—is said to have a character. One whose desires and impulses are not his own, has no character, no more than a steam engine has a character. If, in addition to being his own, his impulses are strong, and are under the government of a strong will, he has an energetic character. Whoever thinks that individuality of desires and impulses should not be encouraged to unfold itself, must maintain that society has no need of strong natures—is not the better for containing many persons who have much character—and that a high general average of energy is not desirable.

In some early states of society, these forces might be, and were, too much ahead of the power which society then possessed of disciplining and controlling them. There has been a time when the element of spontaneity and individuality was in excess, and the social principle had a hard struggle with it. The difficulty then was to induce men of strong bodies or minds to pay obedience to any rules which required them to control their impulses. To overcome this difficulty, law and discipline, like the Popes struggling against the Emperors, asserted a power over the whole man, claiming to control all his life in order to control his character—which society had not found any other sufficient means of binding. But society has now fairly got the better of individuality; and the danger which threatens human nature is not the excess, but the deficiency, of personal impulses and preferences. Things are vastly changed, since the passions of those who were strong by station or by personal endowment were in a state of habitual rebellion against laws and ordinances, and required to be rigorously chained up to enable the persons within their reach to enjoy any particle of security. In our times, from the highest class of society down to the lowest, every one lives as under the eye of a hostile and dreaded censorship. Not only in what concerns others, but in what concerns only themselves, the individual or the family do not ask themselves—what do I prefer? or, what would suit my character and disposition? or, what would allow the best and highest in me to have fair play, and enable it to grow and thrive? They ask themselves, what is suitable to my position? what is usually done by persons of my station and pecuniary circumstances? or (worse still) what is usually done by persons of a station and circumstances superior to mine? I do not mean that they choose what is customary, in preference to what suits their own inclination. It does not occur to them to have any inclination, except for what is customary. Thus the mind itself is owed to the yoke: even in what people do for pleasure, conformity is the first thing thought of; they like in crowds, they exercise choice only among things commonly done: peculiarity of taste, eccentricity of conduct, are shunned equally with crimes: until by dint of not following their own nature, they have no nature to follow: their human capacities are withered and starved: they become incapable of any strong wishes or native pleasures, and are generally without either opinions or feelings of home growth, or properly their own. Now is this, or is it not, the desirable condition of human nature?

It is so, on the Calvinistic theory. According to that, the one great offence of man is self-will. All the good of which humanity is capable, is comprised in obedience. You have no choice; thus you must do, and no otherwise: "Whatever is not a duty, is a sin." Human nature being radically corrupt, there is no redemption for any one until human nature is killed within him. To one holding this theory of life, crushing out any of the human faculties, capacities, and susceptibilities, is no evil: man needs no capacity, but that of surrendering himself to the will of God: and if he uses any of his faculties for any other purpose but to do that supposed will more effectually, he is better without them. This is the theory of Calvinism; and it is held, in a mitigated form, by many who do not consider themselves Calvinists; the mitigation consisting in giving a less ascetic interpretation to the alleged will of God, asserting it to be his will that mankind should gratify some of their inclinations; of course not in the manner they themselves prefer, but in the way of obedience, that is, in a way prescribed to them by authority, and, therefore by the necessary conditions of the case, the same for all.

In some such insidious form there is at present a strong tendency to this narrow theory of life, and to the pinched and hidebound type of human character which it patronizes. Many persons, no doubt, sincerely think that human beings thus cramped and dwarfed, are as their Maker designed them to be, just as many have thought that trees are a much finer thing when clipped into pollards, or cut out into figures of animals, than as nature made them. But if it be any part of religion to believe that man was made by a good Being, it is more consistent with that faith to believe that this Being gave all human faculties that they might be cultivated and unfolded, not rooted out and consumed, and that he takes delight in every nearer approach made by his creatures to the ideal conception embodied in them, every increase in any of their capabilities of comprehension, of action, or of enjoyment. There is a different type of human excellence from the Calvinistic, a conception of humanity as having its nature bestowed on it for other purposes than merely to be abnegated. "Pagan self-assertion" is one of the elements of human worth, as well as "Christian self-denial."* There is a Greek ideal of self-development, which the Platonic and Christian ideal of self-government blends with, but does not supersede. It may be better to be a John Knox than an Alcibiades, but it is

---

*Sterling's *Essays*. [John Sterling (1806–1844) was a British writer.]

better to be a Pericles* than either, nor would a Pericles, if we had one in these days, be without anything good which belonged to John Knox.

It is not by wearing down into uniformity all that is individual in themselves but by cultivating it and calling it forth, within the limits imposed by the rights and interests of others, that human beings become a noble and beautiful object of contemplation; and as the works partake the character of those who do them, by the same process human life also becomes rich, diversified, and animating, furnishing more abundant aliment [sustenance] to high thoughts and elevating feelings, and strengthening the tie which binds every individual to the race, by making the race infinitely better worth belonging to. In proportion to the development of his individuality, each person becomes more valuable to himself, and is therefore capable of being more valuable to others. There is a greater fullness of life about his own existence, and when there is more life in the units there is more in the mass which is composed of them. As much compression as is necessary to prevent the stronger specimens of human nature from encroaching on the rights of others, cannot be dispensed with; but for this there is ample compensation even in the point of view of human development. The means of development which the individual loses by being prevented from gratifying his inclinations to the injury of others are chiefly obtained at the expense of the development of other people. And even to himself there is a full equivalent in the better development of the social part of his nature, rendered possible by the restraint put upon the selfish part. To be held to rigid rules of justice for the sake of others develops the feelings and capacities which have the good of others for their object. But to be restrained in things not affecting their good, by their mere displeasure, develops nothing valuable, except such force of character as may unfold itself in resisting the restraint. If acquiesced in, it dulls and blunts the whole nature. To give any fair play to the nature of each, it is essential that different persons should be allowed to lead different lives. In proportion as this latitude has been exercised in any age, has that age been noteworthy to posterity. Even despotism does not produce its worst effects, so long as individuality exists under it; and whatever crushes individuality is despotism, by whatever name it may be called, and whether it professes to be enforcing the will of God or the injunctions of men.

Having said that individuality is the same thing with development, and that it is only the cultivation of individuality which produces, or can produce, well-developed human beings, I might here close the argument: for what more or better can be said of any condition of human affairs, than that it brings human beings themselves nearer to the best thing they can be? Or what worse can be said of any obstruction to good, than that it prevents this? Doubtless, however, these considerations will not suffice to convince those who most need convincing; and it is necessary further to show that these developed human beings are of some use to the undeveloped—to point out to those who do not desire liberty, and would not avail themselves of it, that they may be in some intelligible manner rewarded for allowing other people to make use of it without hindrance.

In the first place, then, I would suggest that they might possibly learn something from them. It will not be denied by anybody, that originality is a valuable element in human affairs. There is always need of persons not only to discover new truths, and point out when what were once truths are true no longer, but also to commence new practices, and set the example of more enlightened conduct, and better taste and sense in human

*[John Knox (1505–1572) was a leader of the Reformation and the founder of the Scottish Presbyterian Church; Alcibiades (ca. 450–404 B.C.) was a disreputable Athenian general who symbolized for many the decline of Athens; Pericles (ca. 495–429 B.C.) was a famous and beloved Athenian statesman.]

life. This cannot well be gainsaid by anybody who does not believe that the world has already attained perfection in all its ways and practices. It is true that this benefit is not capable of being rendered by everybody alike: there are but few persons, in comparison with the whole of mankind, whose experiments, if adopted by others, would be likely to be any improvement on established practice. But these few are the salt of the earth, without them human life would become a stagnant pool. Not only is it they who introduce good things which did not before exist; it is they who keep the life in those which already existed. If there were nothing new to be done would human intellect cease to be necessary? Would it be a reason why those who do the old things should forget why they are done, and do them like cattle, not like human beings? There is only too great a tendency in the best beliefs and practices to degenerate into the mechanical; and unless there were a succession of persons whose ever-recurring originality prevents the grounds of those beliefs and practices from becoming merely traditional, such dead matter would not resist the smallest shock from anything really alive, and there would be no reason why civilization should not die out, as in the Byzantine Empire. Persons of genius, it is true, are, and are always likely to be, a small minority; but in order to have them, it is necessary to preserve the soil in which they grow. Genius can only breathe freely in an *atmosphere* of freedom. Persons of genius are, *ex vi termini* [by definition], more individual than any other people—less capable, consequently, of fitting themselves, without hurtful compression, into any of the small number of moulds which society provides in order to save its members the trouble of forming their own character. If from timidity they consent to be forced into one of these moulds, and to let all that part of themselves which cannot expand under the pressure remain unexpanded, society will be little the better for their genius. If they are of a strong character, and break their fetters, they become a mark for the society which has not succeeded in reducing them to commonplace, to point at with solemn warning as "wild," "erratic," and the like, much as if one should complain of the Niagara river for not flowing smoothly between its banks like a Dutch canal.

I insist thus emphatically on the importance of genius, and the necessity of allowing it to unfold itself freely both in thought and in practice, being well aware that no one will deny the position in theory, but knowing also that almost every one, in reality, is totally indifferent to it. People think genius a fine thing if it enables a man to write an exciting poem, or paint a picture. But in its true sense, that of originality in thought and action, though no one says that it is not a thing to be admired, nearly all, at heart, think that they can do very well without it. Unhappily this is too natural to be wondered at. Originality is the one thing which unoriginal minds cannot feel the use of. They cannot see what it is to do for them: how should they? If they could see what it would do for them, it would not be originality. The first service which originality has to render them, is that of opening their eyes: which being once fully done, they would have a chance of being themselves original. Meanwhile, recollecting that nothing was ever yet done which some one was not the first to do, and that all good things which exist are the fruits of originality let them be modest enough to believe that there is something still left for it to accomplish, and assure themselves that they are more in need of originality the less they are conscious of the want.

In sober truth, whatever homage may be professed, or even paid, to real or supposed mental superiority, the general tendency of things throughout the world is to render mediocrity the ascendant power among mankind. In ancient history, in the middle ages, and in a diminishing degree through the long transition from feudality to the present time, the individual was a power in himself; and if he had either great talents or a high social position, he was a considerable power. At present individuals are lost in the crowd. In politics it is almost a triviality to say that public opinion now rules the world. The only power deserving the name is that of masses, and of governments while they make themselves the organ of the tendencies and instincts of masses. This is as true in the moral and social relations of private life as in public transactions. Those whose opinions go by the name of public opinion, are not always the same sort of public: in America they are the whole white population; in England, chiefly the middle class. But they are always a mass, that is to say, collective mediocrity. And what is a still greater novelty, the mass do not now take their opinions from dignitaries in Church or State, from ostensible leaders, or from books. Their thinking is done for them by men much like themselves, addressing them or speaking in their name, on the spur of the moment, through the newspapers. I am not complaining of all this. I do not assert that anything better is compatible, as a general rule, with the present low state of the human mind. But that does not hinder the government of mediocrity from being mediocre government. No government by a democracy or a numerous aristocracy, either in its political acts or in the opinions, qualities, and tone of mind which it fosters, ever did or could rise above mediocrity, except in so far as the sovereign Many have let themselves be guided (which in their best times they always have done) by the counsels and influence of a more highly gifted and instructed *One* or *Few*. The initiation of all wise or noble things, comes and must come from individuals; generally at first from some one individual. The honour and glory of the average man is that he is capable of following that initiative; that he can respond internally to wise and noble things, and be led to them with his eyes open. I am not countenancing the sort of "hero-worship" which applauds the strong man of genius for forcibly seizing on the government of the world and making it do his bidding in spite of itself. All he can claim is freedom to point out the way. The power of compelling others into it is not only inconsistent with the freedom and development of all the rest, but corrupting to the strong man himself. It does seem, however, that when the opinions of masses of merely average men are everywhere become or becoming the dominant power, the counterpoise and corrective to that tendency would be the more and more pronounced individuality of those who stand on the higher eminences of thought. It is in these circumstances most especially, that exceptional individuals, instead of being deterred, should be encouraged in acting differently from the mass. In other times there was no advantage in their doing so unless they acted not only differently, but better. In this age, the mere example of nonconformity, the mere refusal to bend the knee to custom, is itself a service. Precisely because the tyranny of opinion is such as to make eccentricity a reproach, it is desirable, in order to break through that tyranny, that people should be eccentric. Eccentricity has always abounded when and where strength of character has abounded; and the amount of eccentricity in a society has generally been proportional to the amount of genius, mental vigour; and moral courage which it contained. That so few now dare to be eccentric marks the chief danger of the time.

I have said that it is important to give the freest scope possible to uncustomary things, in order that it may in time appear which of these are fit to be converted into customs. But independence of action, and disregard of custom, are not solely deserving of encouragement for the chance they afford that better modes of action, and customs more worthy of general adoption, may be struck out; nor is it only persons of decided mental superiority who have a just claim to carry on their lives in their own way. There is no reason that all human existence should be constructed on some one or some small number of patterns. If a person possesses any tolerable amount of common sense and experience, his own mode of laying out his existence is the best, not because it is the best in itself, but because it is his own mode. Human beings are not like sheep; and even sheep are not undistinguishably alike. A man cannot get a coat or a pair of boots to fit him, unless they are either made to his measure or he has a whole warehouseful to choose from: and is it easier to fit him with a life than with a coat, or are human beings more like one another in their whole physical and spiritual conformation than in the shape of their feet? If it were only that people have diversities of taste, that is reason enough for not attempting to shape them all after one model. But different persons also require different conditions for their spiritual development; and can no more exist healthily in the same moral, than all the variety of plants can in the same physical, atmosphere and climate. The same things which are helps to one person towards the cultivation of his higher nature are hindrances to another. The same mode of life is a healthy excitement to one, keeping all his faculties of action and enjoyment in their best order, while to another it is a distracting burden, which suspends or crushes all internal life. Such are the differences among human beings in their sources of pleasure, their susceptibilities of pain, and the operation on them of different physical and moral agencies, that unless there is a corresponding diversity in their modes of life, they neither obtain their fair share of happiness, nor grow up to the mental, moral, and aesthetic stature of which their nature is capable. Why then should tolerance, as far as the public sentiment is concerned, extend only to tastes and modes of life which extort acquiescence by the multitude of their adherents? Nowhere (except in some monastic institutions) is diversity of taste entirely unrecognized; a person may, without blame, either like or dislike rowing, or smoking, or music, or athletic exercises, or chess, or cards, or study, because both those who like each of these things, and those who dislike them, are too numerous to be put down. But the man, and still more the woman, who can be accused either of doing "what nobody does," or of not doing "what everybody does," is the subject of as much depreciatory remark as if he or she had committed some grave moral delinquency. Persons require to possess a title, or some other badge of rank, or of the consideration of people of rank, to be able to indulge somewhat in the luxury of doing as they like without detriment to their estimation. To indulge somewhat, I repeat: for whoever allow themselves much of that indulgence, incur the risk of something worse than disparaging speeches—they are in peril of a commission *de lunatico,* and of having their property taken from them and given to their relations.*

There is one characteristic of the present direction of public opinion, peculiarly calculated to make it intolerant of any marked demonstration of individuality. The general average of mankind are not only moderate in intellect, but also moderate in inclinations: they have no tastes or wishes strong enough to incline them to do anything un-

---

*There is something both contemptible and frightful in the sort of evidence on which, of late years, any person can be judicially declared unfit for the management of his affairs, and after his death, his disposal of his property can be set aside, if there is enough of it to pay the expenses of litigation—which are charged on the property itself. All the minute details of his daily life are pried into, and whatever is found which, seen through the medium of the perceiving and describing faculties of the lowest of the low, bears an appearance unlike absolute commonplace, is laid before the jury as evidence of insanity, and often with success; the jurors being little, if at all, less vulgar and ignorant that the witnesses; while the judges, with that extraordinary want of knowledge of human nature and life which continually astonishes us in English lawyers, often help to mislead them. These trials speak volumes as to the state of feeling and opinion among the vulgar with regard to human liberty. So far from setting any value on individuality—so far from respecting the right of each individual to act, in things indifferent, as seems good to his own judgement and inclinations, judges and juries cannot even conceive that a person in a state of sanity can desire such freedom. In former days when it was proposed to burn atheists, charitable people used to suggest putting them in a madhouse instead: it would be nothing surprising nowadays were we to see this done and the doers applauding themselves, because, instead of persecuting for religion, they had adopted so humane and Christian a mode of treating these unfortunates, not without a silent satisfaction at their having thereby obtained their deserts.

usual, and they consequently do not understand those who have, and class all such with the wild and intemperate whom they are accustomed to look down upon. Now in addition to this fact which is general, we have only to suppose that a strong movement has set in towards the improvement of morals, and it is evident what we have to expect. In these days such a movement has set in; much has actually been effected in the way of increased regularity of conduct, and discouragement of excesses; and there is a philanthropic spirit abroad, for the exercise of which there is no more inviting field than the moral and prudential improvement of our fellow creatures. These tendencies of the times cause the public to be more disposed than at most former periods to prescribe general rules of conduct, and endeavour to make every one conform to the approved standard. And that standard, express or tacit, is to desire nothing strongly. Its ideal of character is to be without any marked character; to maim by compression, like a Chinese lady's foot, every part of human nature which stands out prominently, and tends to make the person markedly dissimilar in outline to commonplace humanity.

As is usually the case with ideals which exclude one-half of what is desirable, the present standard of approbation produces only an inferior imitation of the other half. Instead of great energies guided by vigorous reason, and strong feelings strongly controlled by a conscientious will, its result is weak feelings and weak energies, which therefore can be kept in outward conformity to rule without any strength either of will or of reason. Already energetic characters on any large scale are becoming merely traditional. There is now scarcely any outlet for energy in this country except business. The energy expended in this may still be regarded as considerable. What little is left from that employment is expended on some hobby; which may be a useful, even a philanthropic hobby, but is always some one thing, and generally a thing of small dimensions. The greatness of England is now all collective: individually small, we only appear capable of anything great by our habit of combining; and with this our moral and religious philanthropists are perfectly contented. But it was men of another stamp than this that made England what it has been; and men of another stamp will be needed to prevent its decline.

The despotism of custom is everywhere the standing hindrance to human advancement, being in unceasing antagonism to that disposition to aim at something better than customary, which is called, according to circumstances, the spirit of liberty, or that of progress or improvement. The spirit of improvement is not always a spirit of liberty, for it may aim at forcing improvements on an unwilling people, and the spirit of liberty, in so far as it resists such attempts, may ally itself locally and temporarily with the opponents of improvement, but the only unfailing and permanent source of improvement is liberty, since by it there are as many possible independent centres of improvement as there are individuals. The progressive principle, however, in either shape, whether as the love of liberty or of improvement, is antagonistic to the sway of Custom, involving at least emancipation from that yoke; and the contest between the two constitutes the chief interest of the history of mankind. The greater part of the world has, properly speaking, no history, because the despotism of Custom is complete. This is the case over the whole East. Custom is there, in all things, the final appeal; justice and right mean conformity to custom; the argument of custom no one, unless some tyrant intoxicated with power, thinks of resisting. And we see the result. Those nations must once have had originality; they did not start out of the ground populous, lettered, and versed in many of the arts of life, they made themselves all this, and were then the greatest and most powerful nations of the world. What are they now? The subjects or dependants of tribes whose forefathers wandered in the forests when theirs had magnificent palaces and gorgeous temples, but over whom custom exercised only a divided rule with liberty and progress. A people, it appears, may be progressive for a certain length of time, and then stop: when does it stop? When it ceases to possess individuality. If a similar change should befall the nations of Europe, it will not be in exactly the same shape: the despotism of custom with which these nations are threatened is not precisely stationariness. It proscribes singularity, but it does not preclude change, provided all change together. We have discarded the fixed costumes of our forefathers, every one must still dress like other people, but the fashion may change once or twice a year. We thus take care that when there is change it shall be for change's sake, and not from any idea of beauty or convenience; for the same idea of beauty or convenience would not strike all the world at the same moment, and be simultaneously thrown aside by all at another moment. But we are progressive as well as changeable: we continually make new inventions in mechanical things, and keep them until they are again superseded by better; we are eager for improvement in politics, in education, even in morals, though in this last our idea of improvement chiefly consists in persuading or forcing other people to be as good as ourselves. It is not progress that we object to; on the contrary, we flatter ourselves that we are the most progressive people who ever lived. It is individuality that we war against: we should think we had done wonders if we had made ourselves all alike; forgetting that the unlikeness of one person to another is generally the first thing which draws the attention of either to the imperfection of his own type, and the superiority of another, or the possibility, by combining the advantages of both, of producing something better than either. We have a warning example in China—a nation of much talent, and, in some respects, even wisdom, owing to the rare good fortune of having been provided at an early period with a particularly good set of customs, the work, in some measure, of men to whom even the most enlightened European must accord, under certain limitations, the title of sages and philosophers. They are remarkable, too, in the excellence of their apparatus for impressing, as far as possible, the best wisdom they possess upon every min in the community, and securing that those who have appropriated most of it shall occupy the posts of honour and power. Surely the people who did this have discovered the secret of human progressiveness, and must have kept themselves steadily at the head of the movement of the world. On the contrary, they have become stationary—have remained so for thousands of years; and if they are ever to be farther improved, it must be by foreigners. They have succeeded beyond all hope in what English philanthropists are so industriously working at—in making a people all alike, all governing their thoughts and conduct by the same maxims and rules; and these are the fruits. The modern regime of public opinion is, in an unorganized form, what the Chinese educational and political systems are in an organized, and unless individuality shall be able successfully to assert itself against this yoke, Europe, notwithstanding its noble antecedents and its professed Christianity, will tend to become another China.

What is it that has hitherto preserved Europe from this lot? What has made the European family of nations an improving, instead of a stationary portion of mankind? Not any superior excellence in them which, when it exists, exists as the effect, not as the cause; but their remarkable diversity of character and culture. Individuals, classes, nations, have been extremely unlike one another: they have struck out a great variety of paths, each leading to something valuable; and although at every period those who travelled in different paths have been intolerant of one another, and each would have thought it an excellent thing if all the rest could have been compelled to travel his road, their attempts to thwart each other's development have rarely had any permanent success, and each has in time endured to receive the good which the others have offered. Europe is, in my judgement, wholly indebted to this plurality of paths for its progressive and many-sided development. But it already begins to possess this benefit in a considerably less degree. It is decidedly advancing towards the Chinese ideal of making all people alike. M. de Tocqueville, in his last important work,* remarks how much more the Frenchmen of the present day resemble one another, than did those even of the last generation. The same remark might be made of Englishmen in a far greater degree. In a passage already quoted from Wilhelm von Humboldt, he points out two things as necessary conditions of human development, because necessary to render people unlike one another; namely, freedom, and variety of situations. The second of these two conditions is in this country every day diminishing. The circumstances which surround different classes and individuals, and shape their characters, are daily becoming more assimilated. Formerly, different ranks, different neighbourhoods, different trades and professions, lived in what might be called different worlds; at present, to a great degree in the same. Comparatively speaking, they now read the same things, listen to the same things, see the same things, go to the same places, have their hopes and fears directed to the same objects, have the same rights and liberties, and the same means of asserting them. Great as are the differences of position which remain, they are nothing to those which have ceased. And the assimilation is still proceeding. All the political changes of the age promote it, since they all tend to raise the low and to lower the high. Every extension of education promotes it, because education brings people under common influences, and gives them access to the general stock of facts and sentiments. Improvements in the means of communication promote it, by bringing the inhabitants of distant places into personal contact, and keeping up a rapid flow of changes of residence between one place and another. The increase of commerce and manufactures promotes it, by diffusing more widely the advantages of easy circumstances, and opening all objects of ambition, even the highest, to general competition, whereby the desire of rising becomes no longer the character of a particular class but of all classes. A more powerful agency than even all these, in bringing about a general similarity among mankind, is the complete establishment, in this and other free countries, of the ascendancy of public opinion in the State. As the various social eminences which enabled persons entrenched on them to disregard the opinion of the multitude, gradually become levelled; as the very idea of resisting the will of the public, when it is positively known that they have a will, disappears more and more from the minds of practical politicians; there ceases to be any social support for nonconformity—any substantive power in society, which, itself opposed to the ascendancy of numbers, is interested in taking under its protection opinions and tendencies at variance with those of the public.

   The combination of all these causes forms so great a mass of influences hostile to individuality, that it is not easy to see how it can stand its ground. It will do so with increasing difficulty, unless the intelligent part of the public can be made to feel its value—to see that it is good there should be differences, even though not for the better, even though, as it may appear to them, some should be for the worse. If the claims of individuality are ever to be asserted, the time is now, while much is still wanting to complete the enforced assimilation. It is only in the earlier stages that any stand can be successfully made against the encroachment. The demand that all other people shall resemble ourselves, grows by what it feeds on. If resistance waits till life is reduced *nearly* to one uniform type, all deviations from that type will come to be considered impious, immoral, even monstrous and contrary to nature. Mankind speedily become unable to conceive diversity, when they have been for some time unaccustomed to see it.

*[Alexis de Tocqueville (1805–1859), *The Old Régime and the French Revolution.* De Tocqueville was a Frenchman who wrote *Democracy in America,* an insightful analysis of American culture.]

SØREN KIERKEGAARD
1813–1855

Søren Aabye Kierkegaard was born in Copenhagen, Denmark, the youngest child of middle-aged parents. His father, Michael, had been an impoverished serf in a bleak area of northern Denmark. While still a boy, Michael had cursed God for the dreariness of his life and from that point on considered himself and his descendants to be under God's condemnation. The external events of Michael's life gave little indication of such a curse, however, as he worked his way to great wealth as a merchant in Copenhagen. Following the death of his first wife, and before the period of mourning was over, Michael was forced to marry his first wife's maid, Anne Lund, and five months later she bore the first of their five children.

Michael was already fifty-six and retired from business when Søren was born in 1813. Like James Mill, Michael educated Søren at home and also put his son through rigorous intellectual endeavors. But unlike his predecessor, Michael also communicated to his son a strong religious sentiment and deep, though perhaps warped, emotional feelings. Michael would often take Søren on "trips of fantasy" while conversing in the family library.

In 1830, at his father's urging, Kierkegaard entered the University of Copenhagen to study theology. While there, he encountered the work of Hegel and reacted strongly against it. Kierkegaard objected to the implicit optimism and the "swallowing up" of contradictions in Hegel's dialectic. But more important, Kierkegaard claimed that even though Hegel's "System" was an impressive philosophical *tour de force,* it did not relate to the lived existence of the individual—it did not give any guidance as to what a person should *do.* A famous entry from Kierkegaard's journal at this time is worth quoting at length:

What I really lack is to be clear in my mind *what I am to do,* not what I am to know, except in so far as a certain understanding must precede every action. The thing is to understand myself, to see what God really wishes *me* to do; the thing is to find a truth which is true *for me,* to find *the idea for which I can live and die.* What would be the use of discovering so-called objective truth, of working through all the systems of philosophy and of being able, if required, to review them all and show up the inconsistencies within each system;—what good would it do me to be able to develop a theory of the state and combine all the details into a single whole, and so construct a world in which I did not live, but only held up to the view of others;— what good would it do me to be able to explain the meaning of Christianity if it had *no* deeper significance *for me and for my life;*—what good would it do me if truth stood before me, cold and naked, not caring whether I recognised her or not, and producing in me a shudder of fear rather than a trusting devotion? I certainly do not deny that I still recognise an *imperative of understanding* and that through it one can work upon men, *but it must be taken up into my life,* and *that is* what I now recognise as *the most important thing.**

Kierkegaard did not find the answer for "what to do" in his studies in theology and soon began living what he would later call an "aesthetic" life as a rich merchant's son. He spent large sums of money on food, drink, and clothing. He frequented parties and appeared to be having a great time. But hedonistic indulgence did not really give an answer for "what to do" either, and he plunged into despair. Another entry from his journals makes this clear:

I have just returned from a party of which I was the life and soul; wit poured from my lips, everyone laughed and admired me—but I went away—and the dash should be as long as the earth's orbit ————————————————————————

———————— and wanted to shoot myself.**

On his son's twenty-fifth birthday, May 15, 1838, Michael revealed to Søren his own sexual sins as well as his understanding of God's condemnation of their family. Four days later, Søren Kierkegaard underwent a religious conversion and was reconciled to his father, who died shortly afterward. Kierkegaard now had an answer for "what to do"—he would live as a penitent seeking to "become a Christian." Kierkegaard finished his theological studies, prepared to become a Lutheran pastor, and became engaged to marry seventeen-year-old Regine Olsen.

But by 1841, Kierkegaard realized that he could never live the life of a Lutheran pastor and devoted husband. He came to believe that the Danish Lutheran church had made religion a matter of intellectual assent to certain objective truths and no longer deserved to be called "Christian." For the rest of his life, Kierkegaard would be an opponent of institutional Christianity. The decision to break his engagement to Regine Olsen was a torturous one, but one he believed he had to make. He decided that a "divine veto" had been cast against this marriage, that his role as penitent was incompatible with that of husband.

Kierkegaard spent the rest of his short life as a writer, publishing a number of books including *Either/Or* (1843), *Fear and Trembling* (1843), *Philosophical Fragments* (1844), *Stages on Life's Way* (1845), *Concluding Unscientific Post-*

---

*Søren Kierkegaard, *The Journals of Søren Kierkegaard,* edited and translated by Alexander Dru (London: Oxford University Press, 1938), p. 15 [entry from August 1, 1835].
**Ibid., p. 27 [entry from early spring, 1836].

script (1846), *The Sickness unto Death* (1849), *Training in Christianity* (1850), and *The Attack upon "Christendom"* (1854–1855). All but the last of these works were written under various pseudonyms, and virtually all of them included attacks on the prevailing Hegelian philosophy of his time. In 1855, while returning from the bank with the last of his considerable inheritance, Kierkegaard collapsed on the street and died soon thereafter.

*   *   *

Kierkegaard's biography is reflected in his philosophical quest to establish what it means to be an individual. In such works as *Either/Or, Stages on Life's Way,* and *Fear and Trembling,* he describes a process of self-actualization through three stages in life: the aesthetic, the ethical, and the religious. At the aesthetic stage, an individual's life centers on either hedonistic pleasure or abstract philosophical speculation. The hedonist lives for the immediate pleasures of the moment without concern for the future. The abstract intellectual (Hegel being the prime example) lives in a theoretical world removed from concrete existence. The hedonist reduces existence to immediate pleasure whereas the abstract speculator reduces existence to thought; but in both cases the aesthete has avoided the either/or decisions of real life, and authentic selfhood has not been achieved. The result, says Kierkegaard, is a life of boredom—and the pointless pursuit of diversions to alleviate such boredom. This was the life Kierkegaard himself lived in his early years at the university.

Those who move beyond the aesthetic to the ethical level choose to accept moral standards and attempt to do their duty. By choosing decisively and accepting responsibility for that choice, an individual's life becomes centralized and unified. For example, the seducing man operates on the aesthetic level where every woman he meets is merely a general source of momentary pleasure. He has no past, no future, only the present desire for fulfillment. He is not really a complete person because he is living life as a series of disconnected "nows." On the other hand, the man who has chosen to fulfill the duties of a faithful husband operates on the ethical level. He has a memory of the past and a hope for the future based on his commitments, which give an integrated wholeness to his present.

But even though universal moral standards can become personal when chosen by an individual, the ethical stage is not sufficient to bring a person to complete self-actualization. The ethical stage leads to a point at which one realizes that one cannot entirely fulfill the moral law, that one is sinful in the presence of God. Only in the religious stage, where one "leaps" to passionate commitment to God, is one totally free from meaninglessness and dread. In the religious stage, a person must be willing to give up everything—even abstract ethical universals—to God. In the selection reprinted here from *Fear and Trembling,* in the Howard and Edna Hong translation, Kierkegaard illustrates this movement from the ethical to the religious stage by contrasting the stories of Agamemnon and Abraham. Although both were called upon by a divinity to sacrifice a child, Agamemnon's sacrifice would serve a higher ethical purpose while Abraham's would not. In fact, Abraham was in the odd position of being *tempted* to do the ethical: to not murder/sacrifice Isaac. Yet Abraham had faith in God, rather than Agamemnon's resignation to the gods, and continued to believe that God would return his son to him. Abraham performed a "teleological [i.e., considering the end or goal] suspension of the ethical," giving up what was most dear to him, and by virtue of the absurd, God gave it all back. It is interesting to note that Kierkegaard wrote this work right after he had given up to God what was most dear to him: Regine Olsen. Apparently believing that God would give her back to him, Kierkegaard was shocked when she became engaged to another man.

In the selection from *Concluding Unscientific Postscript,* reprinted here in the Howard and Edna Hong translation, Kierkegaard argues that whereas a logical system is possible, an existential system is not. Hegel's entire systematic enterprise is misguided because it assumes a finality that lived existence never has. When it comes to the important issues of life, such as knowledge of God, no system, no set of objective truths will give any real guidance. According to Kierkegaard, only subjective truth, "An objective uncertainty, held fast through appropriation with the most passionate inwardness," can be the truth for an existing person. So whereas one can never have objective certainty that God exists, one can make it true in one's own life by committing oneself completely and living as if it were true.

Written in Danish and presenting a pessimistic view of objective reason that was out of touch with the spirit of his time, it is not surprising that Kierkegaard's works were ignored for decades. The horror of World War I, together with the work done by Martin Heidegger in philosophy and Karl Barth in theology, brought Kierkegaard's pessimistic assessment of objectivism to prominence. Today Kierkegaard is acknowledged as the "father of existentialism" and is studied widely.

*   *   *

For representative collections of Kierkegaard's writings, see *A Kierkegaard Anthology,* edited by Robert Bretall (New York: Modern Library, 1936) and Walter A. Kaufmann, ed., *Existentialism from Dostoevsky to Sartre* (New York: Meridian Books, 1956). For biographies of Kierkegaard, see Walter Lowrie, *Kierkegaard* (Oxford: Oxford University Press, 1938) for comprehensive coverage, and Walter Lowrie, *A Short Life of Kierkegaard* (Princeton, NJ: Princeton University Press, 1942) for a more succinct study. There are a number of general overviews of Kierkegaard's thought, including H. Diem, *Kierkegaard: An Introduction,* translated by David Green (Richmond, VA: John Knox Press, 1966); Josiah Thompson, *Kierkegaard* (New York: Knopf, 1973); Alastair Hannay, *Kierkegaard* (London: Routledge & Kegan Paul, 1982); Diogenes Allen, *Three Outsiders: Pascal, Kierkegaard, Simone Weil* (Cambridge, MA: Cowley, 1983); and Patrick Gardiner, *Kierkegaard* (Oxford: Oxford University Press, 1988). For studies of specific aspects of Kierkegaard's thought, see Louis K. Dupre, *Kierkegaard as Theologian* (New York: Sheed and Ward, 1964); Niels Thulstrup, *Kierkegaard's Relation to Hegel,* translated by George L. Stengren (Princeton, NJ: Princeton University Press, 1980); John W. Elrod, *Kierkegaard and Christendom* (Princeton, NJ: Princeton University Press, 1981); C. Stephen Evans, *Kierkegaard's "Fragments" and "Postscript": The Religious Philosophy of Johannes Climacus* (Atlantic Highlands, NJ: Humanities Press, 1983); and Merold Westphal, *Kierkegaard's Critique of Reason and Society* (Macon, GA: Mercer University Press, 1987). For collections of essays, see H.A. Johnson and N. Thulstrup, eds., *A Kierkegaard Critique* (Chicago: Henry Regnery, 1967); Jerry H. Gill, ed., *Essays on Kierkegaard* (Minneapolis, MN: Burgess, 1969); Josiah Thompson, ed., *Kierkegaard: A Collection of Critical Essays* (Garden City, NY: Anchor Books,

1972); and Harold Bloom, ed., *Søren Kierkegaard* (New York: Chelsea House, 1989).

FEAR AND TREMBLING (in part)

Is There a Teleological Suspension of the Ethical?

The ethical as such is the universal, and as the universal it applies to everyone, which from another angle means that it applies at all times. It rests immanent in itself, has nothing outside itself that is its ⟨*telos*⟩ [end, purpose] but is itself the ⟨*telos*⟩ for everything outside itself, and when the ethical has absorbed this into itself, it goes not further. The single individual, sensately and psychically qualified in immediacy, is the individual who has his ⟨*telos*⟩ in the universal, and it is his ethical task continually to express himself in this, to annul his singularity in order to become the universal. As soon as the single individual asserts himself in his singularity before the universal, he sins, and only by acknowledging this can he be reconciled again with the universal. Every time the single individual, after having entered the universal, feels an impulse to assert himself as the single individual, he is in a spiritual trial *[Anfægtelse]*, from which he can work himself only by repentantly surrendering as the single individual in the universal. If this is the highest that can be said of man and his existence, then the ethical is of the same nature as a person's eternal salvation, which is his ⟨*telos*⟩ forevermore and at all times, since it would be a contradiction for this to be capable of being surrendered (that is, teleologically suspended), because as soon as this is suspended it is relinquished, whereas that which is suspended is not relinquished but is preserved in the higher, which is its ⟨*telos*⟩.

If this is the case, then Hegel is right in "The Good and Conscience," where he qualifies man only as the individual and considers this qualification as a "moral form of evil" (see especially *The Philosophy of Right*), which must be annulled *[ophævet]* in the teleology of the moral in such a way that the single individual who remains in that stage either sins or is immersed in spiritual trial. But Hegel is wrong in speaking about faith; he is wrong in not protesting loudly and clearly against Abraham's enjoying honor and glory as a father of faith when he ought to be sent back to a lower court and shown up as a murderer.

Faith is namely this paradox that the single individual is higher than the universal—yet, please note, in such a way that the movement repeats itself, so that after having been in the universal he as the single individual isolates himself as higher than the universal. If this is not faith, then Abraham is lost, then faith has never existed in the world precisely because it has always existed. For if the ethical—that is, social morality—is the highest and if there is in a person no residual incommensurability in some way such that this incommensurability is not evil (i.e., the single individual, who is to be expressed in the universal), then no categories are needed other than what Greek philosophy had or what can be deduced from them by consistent thought. Hegel should not have concealed this, for, after all, he had studied Greek philosophy.

People who are profoundly lacking in learning and are given to clichés are frequently heard to say that a light shines over the Christian world, whereas a darkness enshrouds paganism. This kind of talk has always struck me as strange, inasmuch as every more thorough thinker, every more earnest artist still regenerates himself in the eternal youth of the Greeks. The explanation for such a statement is that one does not know what one should say but only that one must say something. It is quite right to say that paganism did not have faith, but if something is supposed to have been said thereby, then one must have a clearer understanding of what faith is, for otherwise one falls into such clichés. It is easy to explain all existence, faith along with it, without having a conception of what faith is, and the one who counts on being admired for such an explanation is not such a bad calculator, for it is as Boileau says: *Un sot trouve toujours un plus sot, qui l'admire* [One fool always finds a bigger fool, who admires him].

Faith is precisely the paradox that the single individual as the single individual is higher than the universal, is justified before it, not as inferior to it but as superior—yet in such a way, please note, that it is the single individual who, after being subordinate as the single individual to the universal, now by means of the universal becomes the single individual who as the single individual is superior, that the single individual as the single individual stands in an absolute relation to the absolute. This position cannot be mediated, for all mediation takes place only by virtue of the universal; it is and remains for

Wanderer Above the Mist, 1817–1918, by Caspar David Friedrich (1774–1840). "Faith is precisely the paradox that the single individual as the single individual is higher than the universal. . . . This position cannot be mediated . . . it is and remains for all eternity a paradox, impervious to thought." Kierkegaard, *Fear and Trembling.* (*Marburg/Art Resource*)

all eternity a paradox, impervious to thought. And yet faith is this paradox, or else (and I ask the reader to bear these consequences *in mente* [in mind] even though it would be too prolix for me to write them all down) or else faith has never existed simply because it has always existed, or else Abraham is lost.

It is certainly true that the single individual can easily confuse this paradox with spiritual trial *[Anfægtelse]*, but it ought not to be concealed for that reason. It is certainly true that many persons may be so constituted that they are repulsed by it, but faith ought not therefore to be made into something else to enable one to have it, but one ought rather to admit to not having it, while those who have faith ought to be prepared to set forth some characteristics whereby the paradox can be distinguished from a spiritual trial.

The story of Abraham contains just such a teleological suspension of the ethical. There is no dearth of keen minds and careful scholars who have found analogies to it. What their wisdom amounts to is the beautiful proposition that basically everything is the same. If one looks more closely, I doubt very much that anyone in the whole wide world will find one single analogy, except for a later one, which proves nothing if it is certain that Abraham represents faith and that it is manifested normatively in him, whose life not only is the most paradoxical that can be thought but is also so paradoxical that it simply cannot be thought. He acts by virtue of the absurd, for it is precisely the absurd that he as the single individual is higher than the universal. This paradox cannot be mediated, for as soon as Abraham begins to do so, he has to confess that he was in a spiritual trial, and if that is the case, he will never sacrifice Isaac, or if he did sacrifice Isaac, then in repentance he must come back to the universal. He gets Isaac back again by virtue of the absurd. Therefore, Abraham is at no time a tragic hero but is something entirely different, either a murderer or a man of faith. Abraham does not have the middle term that saves the tragic hero. This is why I can understand a tragic hero but cannot understand Abraham, even though in a certain demented sense I admire him more than all others.

In ethical terms, Abraham's relation to Isaac is quite simply this: the father shall love the son more than himself. But within its own confines the ethical has various gradations. We shall see whether this story contains any higher expression for the ethical that can ethically explain his behavior, can ethically justify his suspending the ethical obligation to the son, but without moving beyond the teleology of the ethical.

When an enterprise of concern to a whole nation is impeded, when such a project is halted by divine displeasure, when the angry deity sends a dead calm that mocks every effort, when the soothsayer carries out his sad task and announces that the deity demands a young girl as sacrifice—then the father must heroically bring this sacrifice. He must nobly conceal his agony, even though he could wish he were "the lowly man who dares to weep" and not the king who must behave in a kingly manner. Although the lonely agony penetrates his breast and there are only three persons in the whole nation who know his agony, soon the whole nation will be initiated into his agony and also into his deed, that for the welfare of all he will sacrifice her, his daughter, this lovely young girl. O bosom! O fair cheeks, flaxen hair (v, 687). And the daughter's tears will agitate him, and the father will turn away his face, but the hero must raise the knife. And when the news of it reaches the father's house, the beautiful Greek maidens will blush with enthusiasm, and if the daughter was engaged, her betrothed will not be angry but will be proud to share in the father's deed, for the girl belonged more tenderly to him than to the father.

When the valiant judge who in the hour of need saved Israel binds God and himself in one breath by the same promise, he will heroically transform the young maiden's jubilation, the beloved daughter's joy to sorrow, and all Israel will sorrow with her over her virginal youth. But every freeborn man will understand, every resolute woman will admire Jephthah, and every virgin in Israel will wish to behave as his daughter did, because what good would it be for Jephthah to win the victory by means of a promise if he did not keep it—would not the victory be taken away from the people again?

When a son forgets his duty, when the state entrusts the sword of judgment to the father, when the laws demand punishment from the father's hand, then the father must heroically forget that the guilty one is his son, he must nobly hide his agony, but no one in the nation, not even the son, will fail to admire the father, and every time the Roman laws are interpreted, it will be remembered that many interpreted them more learnedly but no one more magnificently than Brutus.

But if Agamemnon, while a favorable wind was taking the fleet under full sail to its destination, had dispatched that messenger who fetched Iphigenia to be sacrificed; if Jephthah, without being bound by any promise that decided the fate of the nation, had said to his daughter: Grieve now for two months over your brief youth, and then I will sacrifice you; if Brutus had had a righteous son and yet had summoned the lictors to put him to death—who would have understood them? If, on being asked why they did this, these three men had answered: It is an ordeal in which we are being tried [forsøges]— would they have been better understood?

When in the crucial moment Agamemnon, Jephthah, and Brutus heroically have overcome the agony, heroically have lost the beloved, and have only to complete the task externally, there will never be a noble soul in the world without tears of compassion for their agony, of admiration for their deed. But if in the crucial moment these three men were to append to the heroic courage with which they bore the agony the little phrase: But it will not happen anyway—who then would understand them? If they went on to explain: This we believe by virtue of the absurd—who would understand them any better, for who would not readily understand that it was absurd, but who would understand that one could then believe it?

The difference between the tragic hero and Abraham is very obvious. The tragic hero is still within the ethical. He allows an expression of the ethical to have its ⟨telos⟩ in a higher expression of the ethical; he scales down the ethical relation between father and son or daughter and father to a feeling that has its dialectic in its relation to the idea of moral conduct. Here there can be no question of a teleological suspension of the ethical itself.

Abraham's situation is different. By his act he transgressed the ethical altogether and had a higher ⟨telos⟩ outside it, in relation to which he suspended it. For I certainly would like to know how Abraham's act can be related to the universal, whether any point of contact between what Abraham did and the universal can be found other than that Abraham transgressed it. It is not to save a nation, not to uphold the idea of the state that Abraham does it; it is not to appease the angry gods. If it were a matter of the deity's being angry, then he was, after all, angry only with Abraham, and Abraham's act is totally unrelated to the universal, is a purely private endeavor. Therefore, while the tragic hero is great because of his moral virtue, Abraham is great because of a purely personal virtue. There is no higher expression for the ethical in Abraham's life than that the father shall love the son. The ethical in the sense of the moral is entirely beside the point. Insofar as the universal was present, it was cryptically in Isaac, hidden, so to speak, in Isaac's loins, and must cry out with Isaac's mouth: Do not do this, you are destroying everything.

Why, then, does Abraham do it? For God's sake and—the two are wholly identical—for his own sake. He does it for God's sake because God demands this proof of his faith; he does it for his own sake so that he can prove it. The unity of the two is altogether correctly expressed in the word already used to describe this relationship. It is an ordeal, a temptation. A temptation—but what does that mean? As a rule, what tempts a person is something that will hold him back from doing his duty, but here the temptation is the ethical itself, which would hold him back from doing God's will. But what is duty? Duty is simply the expression for God's will.

Here the necessity of a new category for the understanding of Abraham becomes apparent. Paganism does not know such a relationship to the divine. The tragic hero does not enter into any private relationship to the divine, but the ethical is the divine, and thus the paradox therein can be mediated in the universal.

Abraham cannot be mediated; in other words, he cannot speak. As soon as I speak, I express the universal, and if I do not do so, no one can understand me. As soon as Abraham wants to express himself in the universal, he must declare that his situation is a spiritual trial *[Anfægtelse]*, for he has no higher expression of the universal that ranks above the universal he violates.

Therefore, although Abraham arouses my admiration, he also appalls me. The person who denies himself and sacrifices himself because of duty gives up the finite in order to grasp the infinite and is adequately assured; the tragic hero gives up the certain for the even more certain, and the observer's eye views him with confidence. But the person who gives up the universal in order to grasp something even higher that is not the universal—what does he do? Is it possible that this can be anything other than a spiritual trial? And if it is possible, but the individual makes a mistake, what salvation is there for him? He suffers all the agony of the tragic hero, he shatters his joy in the world, he renounces everything, and perhaps at the same time he barricades himself from the sublime joy that was so precious to him that he would buy it at any price. The observer cannot understand him at all; neither can his eye rest upon him with confidence. Perhaps the believer's intention cannot be carried out at all, because it is inconceivable. Or if it could be done but the individual has misunderstood the deity— what salvation would there be for him? The tragic hero needs and demands tears, and where is the envious eye so arid that it could not weep with Agamemnon, but where is the soul so gone astray that it has the audacity to weep for Abraham? The tragic hero finishes his task at a specific moment in time, but as time passes he does what is no less significant: he visits the person encompassed by sorrow, who cannot breathe because of his anguished sighs, whose thoughts oppress him, heavy with tears. He appears to him, breaks the witchcraft of sorrow, loosens the bonds, evokes the tears, and the suffering one forgets his own sufferings in those of the tragic hero. One cannot weep over Abraham. One approaches him with a *horror religiosus*, as Israel approached Mount Sinai. What if he himself is distraught, what if he had made a mistake, this lonely man who climbs Mount Moriah, whose peak towers sky-high over the flatlands of Aulis, what if he is not a sleepwalker safely crossing the abyss while the one standing at the foot of the mountain looks up, shakes with anxiety, and then in his deference and horror does not even dare to call to him?—Thanks, once again thanks, to a man who, to a person overwhelmed by life's sorrows and left behind naked, reaches out the words, the leafage of language by which he can conceal his misery. Thanks to you, great Shakespeare, you who can say everything, everything, everything just as it is—and yet, why did you never articulate this torment? Did you perhaps reserve it for yourself, like the beloved's name that one cannot bear to have the world utter, for with his little secret that he cannot divulge the poet buys this power of the word to tell everybody else's dark secrets. A poet is not an apostle; he drives out devils only by the power of the devil.

But if the ethical is teleologically suspended in this manner, how does the single individual in whom it is suspended exist? He exists as the single individual in contrast to the universal. Does he sin, then, for from the point of view of the idea, this is the form of sin. Thus, even though the child does not sin, because it is not conscious of its existence as such, its existence, from the point of view of the idea, is nevertheless sin, and the ethical makes its claim upon it at all times. If it is denied that this form can be repeated in such a way that it is not sin, then judgment has fallen upon Abraham. How did Abraham exist? He had faith. This is the paradox by which he remains at the apex, the paradox that he cannot explain to anyone else, for the paradox is that he as the single individual places himself in an absolute relation to the absolute. Is he justified? Again, his justification is the paradoxical, for if he is, then he is justified not by virtue of being something universal but by virtue of being the single individual.

How does the single individual reassure himself that he is legitimate? It is a simple matter to level all existence to the idea of the state or the idea of a society. If this is done, it is also simple to mediate, for one never comes to the paradox that the single individual as the single individual is higher than the universal, something I can also express symbolically in a statement by Pythagoras to the effect that the odd number is more perfect than the even number. If occasionally there is any response at all these days with regard to the paradox, it is likely to be: One judges it by the result. Aware that he is a paradox who cannot be understood, a hero who has become a ⟨*skandalon*⟩ [offense] to his age will shout confidently to his contemporaries: The result will indeed prove that I was justified. This cry is rarely heard in our age, inasmuch as it does not produce heroes—this is its defect—and it likewise has the advantage that it produces few caricatures. When in our age we hear these words: It will be judged by the result—then we know at once with whom we have the honor of speaking. Those who talk this way are a numerous type whom I shall designate under the common name of assistant professors. With security in life, they live in their thoughts: they have a *permanent* position and a *secure* future in a well-organized state. They have hundreds, yes, even thousands of years between them and the earthquakes of existence; they are not afraid that such things can be repeated, for then what would the police and the newspapers say? Their life task is to judge the great men, judge them according to the result. Such behavior toward greatness betrays a strange mixture of arrogance and wretchedness—arrogance because they feel called to pass judgment, wretchedness because they feel that their lives are in no way allied with the lives of the great. Anyone with even a smattering *erectioris ingenii* [of nobility of nature] never becomes an utterly cold and clammy worm, and when he approaches greatness, he is never devoid of the thought that since the creation of the world it has been customary for the result to come last and that if one is truly going to learn something from greatness one must be particularly aware of the beginning. If the one who is to act wants to judge himself by the result, he will never begin. Although the result may give joy to the entire world, it cannot help the hero, for he would not know the result until the whole thing was over, and he would not become a hero by that but by making a beginning.

Moreover, in its dialectic the result (insofar as it is finitude's response to the infinite question) is altogether incongruous with the hero's existence. Or should Abraham's receiving Isaac by a *marvel* be able to prove that Abraham was justified in relating himself as the single individual to the universal? If Abraham actually had sacrificed Isaac, would he therefore have been less justified?

But we are curious about the result, just as we are curious about the way a book turns out. We do not want to know anything about the anxiety, the distress, the paradox. We carry on an esthetic flirtation with the result. It arrives just as unexpectedly but also just as effortlessly as a prize in a lottery, and when we have heard the result, we have built ourselves up. And yet no manacled robber of churches is so despicable a criminal as the one who plunders holiness in this way, and not even Judas, who sold his Lord for thirty pieces of silver, is more contemptible than someone who peddles greatness in this way.

It is against my very being to speak inhumanly about greatness, to make it a dim and nebulous far-distant shape or to let it be great but devoid of the emergence of the humanness without which it ceases to be great, for it is not what happens to me that makes me great but what I do, and certainly there is no one who believes that someone became great by winning the big lottery prize. A person might have been born in lowly circumstances, but I would still require him not to be so inhuman toward himself that he could imagine the king's castle only at a distance and ambiguously dream of its greatness, and destroy it at the same time he elevates it because he elevated it so basely. I require him to be man enough to tread confidently and with dignity there as well. He must not be so inhuman that he insolently violates everything by barging right off the street into the king's hall—he loses more thereby than the king. On the contrary, he should find a joy in observing every bidding of propriety with a happy and confident enthusiasm, which is precisely what makes him a free spirit. This is merely a metaphor, for that distinction is only a very imperfect expression of the distance of spirit. I require every person not to think so inhumanly of himself that he does not dare to enter those palaces where the memory of the chosen ones lives or even those where they themselves live. He is not to enter rudely and foist his affinity upon them. He is to be happy for every time he bows before them, but he is to be confident, free of spirit, and always more than a charwoman, for if he wants to be no more than that, he will never get in. And the very thing that is going to help him is the anxiety and distress in which the great were tried, for otherwise, if he has any backbone, they will only arouse his righteous envy. And anything that can be great only at a distance, that someone wants to make great with empty and hollow phrases—is destroyed by that very person.

Who was as great in the world as that favored woman, the mother of God, the Virgin Mary? And yet how do we speak of her? That she was the favored one among women does not make her great, and if it would not be so very odd for those who listen to be able to think just as inhumanly as those who speak, then every young girl might ask: Why am I not so favored? And if I had nothing else to say, I certainly would not dismiss such a question as stupid, because, viewed abstractly, vis-à-vis a favor, every person is just as entitled to it as the other. We leave out the distress, the anxiety, the paradox. My thoughts are as pure as anybody's, and he who can think this way surely has pure thoughts, and, if not, he can expect something horrible, for anyone who has once experienced these images cannot get rid of them again, and if he sins against them, they take a terrible revenge in a silent rage, which is more terrifying than the stridency of ten ravenous critics. To be sure, Mary bore the child wondrously, but she nevertheless did it "after the manner of women," and such a time is one of anxiety, distress, and paradox. The angel was indeed a ministering spirit, but he was not a meddlesome spirit who went to the other young maidens in Israel and said: Do not scorn Mary, the extraordinary is happening to her. The angel went only to Mary, and no one could understand her. Has any woman been as infringed upon as was Mary, and is it not true here also that the one whom God blesses he curses in the same breath? This is the spirit's view of Mary, and she is by no means—it is revolting to me to say it but even more so that people have inanely and unctuously made her out to be thus—she is by no means a lady idling in her finery and playing with a divine child. When, despite this, she said: Behold, I am the handmaid of the Lord—then she is great, and I believe it should not be difficult to explain why she became the mother of God. She needs worldly admiration as little as Abraham needs tears, for she was no heroine and he was no hero, but both of them became greater than these, not by being exempted in any way from the distress and the agony and the paradox, but became greater by means of these.

It is great when the poet in presenting his tragic hero for public admiration dares to say: Weep for him, for he deserves it. It is great to deserve the tears of those who deserve to shed tears. It is great that the poet dares to keep the crowd under restraint, dares to discipline men to examine themselves individually to see if they are worthy to weep for the hero, for the slop water of the snivellers is a debasement of the sacred.—But even greater than all this is the knight of faith's daring to say to the noble one who wants to weep for him: Do not weep for me, but weep for yourself.

We are touched, we look back to those beautiful times. Sweet sentimental longing leads us to the goal of our desire, to see Christ walking about in the promised land. We forget the anxiety, the distress, the paradox. Was it such a simple matter not to make a mistake? Was it not terrifying that this man walking around among the others was God? Was it not terrifying to sit down to eat with him? Was it such an easy matter to become an apostle? But the result, the eighteen centuries—that helps, that contributes to this mean deception whereby we deceive ourselves and others. I do not feel brave enough to wish to be contemporary with events like that, but I do not for that reason severely condemn those who made a mistake, nor do I depreciate those who saw what was right.

But I come back to Abraham. During the time before the result, either Abraham was a murderer every minute or we stand before a paradox that is higher than all mediations.

The story of Abraham contains, then, a teleological suspension of the ethical. As the single individual he became higher than the universal. This is the paradox, which cannot be mediated. How he entered into it is just as inexplicable as how he remains in it. If this is not Abraham's situation, then Abraham is not even a tragic hero but a murderer. It is thoughtless to want to go on calling him the father of faith, to speak of it to men who have an interest only in words. A person can become a tragic hero through his own strength—but not the knight of faith. When a person walks what is in one sense the hard road of the tragic hero, there are many who can give him advice, but he who walks the narrow road of faith has no one to advise him—no one understands him. Faith is a marvel, and yet no human being is excluded from it; for that which unites all human life is passion, and faith is a passion.

CONCLUDING UNSCIENTIFIC POSTSCRIPT (in part)

SECTION I, CHAPTER 2: POSSIBLE AND ACTUAL THESES BY LESSING

* * *

(A) A logical system can be given; (B) but a system of existence [Tilværelsens System] cannot be given.

(A) A logical system can be given.

α. If, however, a logical system is to be constructed, special care must be taken not to incorporate anything that is subject to the dialectic of existence, accordingly, anything that is *[er]* solely by existing *[være til]* or by having existed *[have været til]*, not something that is *[er]* simply by being *[være]*. It follows quite simply that Hegel's matchless and matchlessly admired invention—the importation of movement into logic (not to mention that in every other passage one misses even his own attempt to make one believe that it is there)—simply confuses logic.* It is indeed curious to make movement the basis in a sphere in which movement is inconceivable or to have movement explain logic, whereas logic cannot explain movement.

On this point, however, I am very happy to be able to refer to a man who thinks soundly and fortunately is educated by the Greeks (rare qualities in our age!); a man who has known how to extricate himself and his thought from every trailing, groveling relation to Hegel, from whose fame everyone usually seeks to profit, if in no other way, then by going further, that is, by having absorbed Hegel; a man who has preferred to be content with Aristotle and with himself—I mean Trendlenburg *(Logische Untersuchungen)*. One of his merits is that he comprehended movement as the inexplicable presupposition, as the common denominator in which being and thinking are united, and as their continued reciprocity. I cannot attempt here to show the relation of his conception to the Greeks, to Aristotelian thought, or to what, oddly enough, although in a popular

---

*The light-mindedness with which systematicians admit that Hegel has perhaps not been successful everywhere in importing movement into logic, much like the grocer who thinks that a few raisins do not matter when the purchase is large—his farcical docility is, of course, contempt for Hegel that not even his most vehement attacker has allowed himself. There have certainly been logical attempts prior to Hegel, but his method is everything. For him and for everyone who has intelligence enough to comprehend what it means to will something great, the absence of it at this or that point cannot be a trivial matter, as when a grocer and a customer bicker about whether there is a little underweight or overweight. Hegel himself has staked his whole reputation on the point of the method. But a method possesses the peculiar quality that, viewed abstractly, it is nothing at all, it is a method precisely in the process of being carried out; in being carried out it is a method, and where it is not carried out, it is not a method, and if there is no other method, there is no method at all. To turn Hegel into a rattlebrain must be reserved for his admirers; an attacker will always know how to honor him for having willed something great and having failed to achieve it.

sense only, bears a certain resemblance to his presentation: a small section in Plutarch's work on Isis and Osiris. It is by no means my view that Hegelian philosophy has not had a salutary influence on Trendlenburg, but it is fortunate that he has perceived that wanting to improve Hegel's structure, to go further etc., will not do (a mendacious approach by which many a botcher in our age arrogates Hegel's celebrity to himself and mendicantly fraternizes with him); on the other hand, it is fortunate that Trendlenburg, sober like a Greek thinker, without promising everything and without claiming to beatify all humankind, does indeed accomplish much and beatifies whoever would need his guidance in learning about the Greeks.

In a logical system, nothing may be incorporated that has a relation to existence, that is not indifferent to existence. The infinite advantage that the logical, by being the objective, possesses over all other thinking is in turn, subjectively viewed, restricted by its being a hypothesis, simply because it is indifferent to existence understood as actuality. This duplexity distinguishes the logical from the mathematical, which has no relation whatever toward or from existence *[Tilværelse]* but has only objectivity—not objectivity and the hypothetical as unity and contradiction in which it is negatively related to existence *[Existents]*.

The logical system must not be a mystification, a ventriloquism, in which the content of existence *[Tilværelse]* emerges cunningly and surreptitiously, where logical thought is startled and finds what the Herr Professor or the licentiate has had up his sleeve. Judging between the two can be done more sharply by answering the question: In what sense is a category an abbreviation of existence, whether logical thinking is abstract after existence or abstract without any relation to existence. I would like to treat this question a little more extensively elsewhere, and even if it is not adequately answered, it is always something to have inquired about it in this way.

β. The dialectic of the beginning must be clarified. The almost amusing thing about it, that the beginning is and then in turn is not, because it is the beginning—this true dialectical remark has long enough been like a game that has been played in Hegelian society.

The system, so it is said, begins with the immediate; some, failing to be dialectical, are even oratorical enough to speak of the most immediate of all, although the comparative reflection contained here might indeed become dangerous for the beginning.* The system begins with the immediate and therefore without presuppositions and therefore absolutely, that is, the beginning of the system is the absolute beginning. This is entirely correct and has indeed also been adequately admired. But why, then, before the system is begun, has that other equally important, definitely equally important, question not been clarified and its clear implications honored: *How does the system begin with the immediate, that is, does it begin with it immediately?* The answer to this must certainly be an unconditional no. If the system is assumed to be after existence (whereby a confusion with a system of existence is created), the system does indeed come afterward and consequently does not begin immediately with the immediate with which existence began, even though in another sense existence did not begin with it, because the immediate never is but is annulled when it is. The beginning of the system that begins with the immediate *is then itself achieved through reflection.*

---

*To show how would become too prolix here. Frequently it is not worth the trouble either, because, after a person has laboriously advanced an objection sharply, from a philosopher's rejoinder he discovers that his misunderstanding was not that he could not understand the idolized philosophy but rather that he had allowed himself to be persuaded to believe that the whole thing was supposed to be something—and not flabby thinking concealed by the most overbearing expressions.

Here is the difficulty, for if one does not let go of this one thought, deceptively or thoughtlessly or in breathless haste to have the system finished, this thought in all its simplicity is capable of deciding that there can be no system of existence and that a logical system must not boast of an absolute beginning, because such a beginning is just like pure being, a pure chimera.

In other words, if a beginning cannot be made immediately with the immediate (which would then be conceived as a fortuitous event or a miracle, that is, which would mean not to think), but this beginning must be achieved through reflection, then the question arises very simply (alas, if only I am not put in the doghouse on account of my simplicity, because everyone can understand my question—and consequently must feel ashamed of the questioner's popular knowledge): How do I bring to a halt the reflection set in motion in order to reach that beginning? Reflection has the notable quality of being infinite. But being infinite must in any case mean that it cannot stop of its own accord, because in stopping itself it indeed uses itself and can be stopped only in the same way as a sickness is cured if it is itself allowed to prescribe the remedy, that is, the sickness is promoted. Perhaps this infinity of reflection is the bad or spurious infinity. In that case, we are indeed almost finished, since the spurious infinity is reputedly something despicable that one must give up, the sooner the better. In that connection, may I not ask a question: How is it that Hegel and all Hegelians, who are generally supposed to be dialecticians, at this point become angry, yes, as angry as Germans? Or is "spurious" a dialectical qualification? From where does such a predicate enter logic? How do scorn and contempt and ways of frightening find a place as legitimate means of movement within logic, so that the absolute beginning is assumed by the individual because he is afraid of what his neighbors on all sides will think of him if he does not do it? Is not "spurious" an ethical category?*

What do I mean by speaking of the spurious infinity? I am charging the individual in question with not willing to stop the infinity of reflection. Am I requiring something of him, then? But on the other hand, in a genuinely speculative way, I assume that reflection stops of its own accord. Why, then, do I require something of him? And what do I require of him? I require a resolution. And in that I am right, for only in that way can reflection be stopped. But, on the other hand, it is never right for a philosopher to make sport of people and at one moment have reflection stop of its own accord in the absolute beginning and at the next moment taunt someone who has only one flaw, that he is obtuse enough to believe the first, taunt him so as to help him in this fashion to the absolute beginning, which then occurs in two ways. But if a resolution is required, presuppositionlessness is abandoned. The beginning can occur only when reflection is stopped, and reflection can be stopped only by something else, and this something else is something altogether different from the logical, since it is a resolution. Only when the beginning, at which point reflection comes to a halt, is a breakthrough, so that the absolute beginning itself breaks forth through the endlessly perpetuated reflection—only then is the beginning presuppositionless. But if it is a break whereby reflection is broken off in order that the beginning can emerge, then this beginning is not absolute, since it has occurred by a ⟨*metabasis eis allo genos*⟩ [shifting from one genus to another].

When a beginning with the immediate is achieved by reflection, the immediate must mean something different from what it usually does. Hegelian logicians have correctly discerned this, and therefore they define the immediate, with which logic begins, as follows: the most abstract remainder after an exhaustive abstraction. There is no ob-

---

*And if it is not that, it is in any case an esthetic category, as when Plutarch states that some have assumed one world because they feared that otherwise the result would be an unlimited and embarrassing infinity of worlds ⟨*euthus aoristou kai ksalepas apeirias hypolambanousas*⟩. (*De defectu oraculorum*, XXII.)

jection to this definition, but it is certainly objectionable that they do not respect what they themselves are saying, inasmuch as this definition indirectly states that there is no absolute beginning. "How is that?" I hear someone say. "When one has abstracted from everything, is there not then, etc.?" Indeed, *when* one has abstracted from everything. Let us be human beings. Like the act of reflection, this act of abstraction is infinite; so how do I bring it to a halt—and it is indeed first when . . . that . . . Let us even venture an imaginary construction in thought. Let that act of infinite abstraction be *in actu* [in actuality]; the beginning is not an act of abstraction but comes afterward. But then with what do I begin, now that there has been an abstraction from everything? Alas, at this point a Hegelian, deeply moved, perhaps would collapse on my chest and blissfully stammer: With nothing. And this is precisely what the system declares—that it begins with nothing. But I must pose my second question: How do I begin with this nothing? If, namely, the act of infinite abstraction is not the kind of trick of which two can very well be done at the same time, if, on the contrary, it is the most strenuous work that can be done—what then? Then all my strength will go into maintaining it. If I do not use all my strength, I do not abstract from everything. If, then, on this presupposition I make a beginning, I do not begin with nothing, simply because at the moment of beginning I did not abstract from everything. This means that if it is possible for a human being, thinking, to abstract from everything, it is impossible for him to do more, since this act, provided that it does not surpass human strength altogether, in any case completely exhausts it. To become tired of the act of abstraction and thus to manage to begin is only an explanation befitting grocers, who are not particular about a little irregularity.

The expression "to begin with nothing," even apart from its relation to the infinite act of abstraction, is itself deceptive. That is, to begin with nothing is neither more nor less than a new paraphrasing of the very dialectic of beginning. The beginning is and in turn is not, simply because it is the beginning, something that can also be expressed in this way: the beginning begins with nothing. It is merely a new expression, not a single step ahead. In the one instance, I only think a beginning *in abstracto;* in the other instance, I think the relation of the equally abstract beginning to a something with which a beginning is made. Now it is quite properly manifest that this something, indeed, the only something that corresponds to such a beginning, is nothing. But this is merely a tautological paraphrasing of the second thesis: the beginning is not. "The beginning is not" and "the beginning begins with nothing" are altogether identical theses, and I do not move from the spot.

What if, rather than speaking or dreaming of an absolute beginning, we speak of a leap? To want to be satisfied with a "mostly," an "as good as," a "one can almost say that," an "if you sleep on it until tomorrow, you may well say that" merely shows that one is related to Trop, who little by little went so far as to assume that having almost taken the bar examination was the same as having taken it. Everyone laughs at this, but when one chatters speculatively in the same manner in the realm of truth, in the shrine of science and scholarship, then it is good philosophy—genuine speculative philosophy. Lessing was no speculative philosopher; therefore he assumed the opposite, that an infinitely little distance makes the ditch infinitely broad, because the leap itself makes the ditch that broad.

It is very odd—the Hegelians, who in logic know that reflection is stopped by itself and that doubting everything flips over into its opposite by itself (a true sailor's yarn, that is, truly a sailor's yarn), know for daily use, however, when they are pleasant people, when they are like the rest of us (only more learned and gifted etc., something I shall always be willing to admit)—they know that reflection can be stopped only by a leap. Let us dwell on this point for a moment. If the individual does not stop reflection, he will be infinitized in reflection, that is, no decision is made.* By thus going astray in reflection, the individual really becomes objective, more and more he loses the decision of subjectivity and the return into himself. Yet it is assumed that reflection can stop itself objectively, whereas it is just the other way around; reflection cannot be stopped objectively, and when it is stopped subjectively, it does not stop of its own accord, but it is the subject who stops it.

For example, as soon as Rötscher (who in his book on Aristophanes does indeed understand the necessity of transition in the world-historical development, and who in the realm of logic must have understood the passage of reflection through itself to the absolute beginning) sets himself the task of interpreting Hamlet, he knows that reflection is stopped only by a resolution. He does not assume (shall I say "oddly enough"?), oddly enough, he does not assume that Hamlet finally arrived at the absolute beginning by continuing to reflect; but in logic he assumes (shall I say "oddly enough"?), oddly enough, there he most likely assumes that the passage of reflection through itself comes to a halt at the absolute beginning. This I do not understand, and it pains me not to understand it, because I have admiration for Rötscher's talent, for his classical education, for his esthetically sensitive and yet primitive conception of psychological phenomena.

What has been said here about a beginning in logic (that the same thing shows that there is no system of existence will be pursued in detail in *b*) is very plain and simple. I am almost embarrassed to say it or embarrassed to have to say it, embarrassed because of my situation—that a poor pamphlet writer, who would rather be worshiping on his knees before the system, should be constrained to say such a thing. What has been said could be stated in yet another way whereby it would perhaps make an impression on someone or other because the presentation would recall more specifically the scholarly disputes in the past. It would then become a question of the importance of the Hegelian phenomenology for the system, whether it is an introduction, whether it remains outside, and if it is an introduction, whether it is in turn incorporated in the system; further, whether Hegel may not even have the amazing merit of having written not only the system but two or even three systems, which always takes a matchless systematic head, and which nevertheless seems to be the case, since the system is completed more than once etc. Actually, all this has been said often enough, but frequently it has also been said in a confusing way. A large book has been written about it. First everything is said that Hegel has said, and thereafter consideration is given to this or that later addition, all of which merely diverts attention and shrouds in distracting prolixity what can be stated very briefly.

γ. In order to shed light on logic, it might be desirable to become oriented psychologically in the state of mind of someone who thinks the logical—what kind of dying to oneself is required for that purpose, and to what extent the imagination plays a part in it. The following is again another meager and very simple comment, but it may be quite true and not at all superfluous: a philosopher has gradually come to be such a marvelous creature that not even the most prodigal imagination has invented anything quite so fabulous. How, if at all, is the empirical *I* related to the pure *I-I*? Whoever wants to be a philosopher will certainly also want to be somewhat informed on this point and above all not want to become a ludicrous creature by being transmogrified—*eins, zwei, drei, kokolorum* [one, two, three, hocus pocus]—into speculative thought. If the person occupied with logical thought is also human enough not to forget that he is an existing individual, even if he has finished the system, the fantasticality and the charlatanry will gradually vanish. And even though it takes an eminently logical head to recast Hegel's logic, only sound common

---

*Perhaps the reader will recall that when the issue becomes objective, there is no question of an eternal happiness, because this lies precisely in subjectivity and in decision.

sense is needed for the person who at one time enthusiastically believed in the great thing Hegel claimed to have done and who demonstrated his enthusiasm by believing *[tro]* it, and his enthusiasm for Hegel by crediting *[tiltro]* him with it—and it takes only sound common sense to perceive that in many places Hegel behaved irresponsibly—not toward grocers, who believe only half of what a person says anyway, but toward enthusiastic youths who believed him. Even if such a young person was not exceptionally and splendidly endowed, yet when he has had the enthusiasm to believe the highest, as attributed to Hegel, when he has had the enthusiasm to despair over himself in a dubious moment in order not to abandon Hegel—when such a young person comes to himself again, he has a right to demand the nemesis of having laughter consume in Hegel what laughter may legitimately claim as its own. And such a young person has indeed vindicated Hegel in a way much different from that of many an adherent who in deceptive asides would now make Hegel everything, now a trifle.

(B) A system of existence cannot be given.

A system of existence *[Tilværelsens System]* cannot be given. Is there, then, not such a system? That is not at all the case. Neither is this implied in what has been said. Existence itself is a system—for God, but it cannot be a system for any existing *[bexisterende]* spirit. System and conclusiveness correspond to each other, but existence is the very opposite. Abstractly viewed, system and existence cannot be thought conjointly, because in order to think existence, systematic thought must think it as annulled and consequently not as existing. Existence is the spacing that holds apart; the systematic is the conclusiveness that combines.

Actually there now develops a deception, an illusion, which *Fragments* has attempted to point out. I must now refer to this work, namely, to the question of whether the past is more necessary than the future. That is, when an existence is a thing of the past, it is indeed finished, it is indeed concluded, and to that extent it is turned over to the systematic view. Quite so—but for whom? Whoever is himself existing cannot gain this conclusiveness outside existence, a conclusiveness that corresponds to the eternity into which the past has entered. Even if a good-natured thinker is so absentminded as to forget that he himself is existing, speculative thought and absentmindedness are still not quite the same thing. On the contrary, that he himself is existing implies the claim of existence upon him and that his existence, yes, if he is a great individual, that his existence at the present time may, as past, in turn have the validity of conclusiveness for a systematic thinker. But who, then, is this systematic thinker? Well, it is he who himself is outside existence and yet in existence, who in his eternity is forever concluded and yet includes existence within himself—it is God. So why the deception! Just because the world has lasted now for six thousand years, does existence therefore not have the very same claim upon the existing individual that it has always had, which is not that he in make-believe should be a contemplating spirit but that he in actuality should be an existing spirit. All understanding comes afterward. Whereas an individual existing now undeniably comes afterward in relation to the six thousand years that preceded, the curiously ironic consequence would emerge—if we assumed that he came to understand them systematically—that he would not come to understand himself as an existing being, because he himself would acquire no existence, because he himself would have nothing that should be understood afterward. It follows that such a thinker must be either the good Lord or a fantastical *quodlibet* [anything]. Certainly everyone will perceive the immorality in this, and certainly everyone will also perceive that what another author has observed regarding the Hegelian system is entirely in order: that through

Hegel a system, the absolute system, was brought to completion—without having an ethics. By all means, let us smile at the ethical-religious fantasies of the Middle Ages in asceticism and the like, but above all let us not forget that the speculative, farcical exaggeration of becoming an *I-I*—and then *qua* human being often such a philistine that no enthusiast would have cared to lead such a life—is equally ludicrous.

So let us ask very simply, as a Greek youth would ask his master (and if the lofty wisdom can explain everything else but cannot answer a simple question, one surely sees that the world is out of joint), about the impossibility of a system of existence: Who is supposed to write or finish such a system? Surely a human being, unless we are to resume the peculiar talk about a human being's becoming speculative thought, a subject-object. Consequently, a human being—and surely a living, that is, an existing, human being. Or if the speculative thought that produces the system is the joint effort of these various thinkers, in what final conclusion does this fellowship combine? How does it come to light? Surely through a human being? And how, in turn, do the individual thinkers relate themselves to this effort; what are the middle terms between the particular and the world-historical; and in turn what sort of being is the one who is stringing it all on the systematic thread? Is he a human being or is he speculative thought? But if he is a human being, then he is indeed existing. Now, all in all, there are two ways for an existing individual: either he can do everything to forget that he is existing and thereby manage to become comic (the comic contradiction of wanting to be what one is not, for example, that a human being wants to be a bird is no more comic than the contradiction of not wanting to be what one is, as *in casu* [in this case] an existing individual, just as in the use of language it is comic when someone forgets his name, which signifies not so much forgetting his name as the singularity of his nature), because existence possesses the remarkable quality that an existing person exists whether he wants to or not; or he can direct all his attention to his existing. It is from this side that an objection must first be made to modern speculative thought, that it has not a false presupposition but a comic presupposition, occasioned by its having forgotten in a kind of world-historical absentmindedness what it means to be a human being, not what it means to be human in general, for even speculators might be swayed to consider that sort of thing, but what it means that we, you and I and he, are human beings, each one on his own.

The existing individual who directs all his attention to the actuality that *he* is existing will approvingly look upon those words of Lessing about a continued striving as a beautiful saying, not as something that gained its author immortal fame, because the saying is so very simple, but as something every attentive person must certify. The existing individual who forgets that he is existing will become more and more absentminded, and just as people occasionally set down the fruits of their *otium* [leisure] in books, so we may expect the expected existential system as the fruit of his absentmindedness—well, not all of us, but only those who are as absentminded as he is. Whereas the Hegelian system in absentmindedness goes ahead and becomes a system of existence, and what is more, is finished—without having an ethics (the very home of existence), that other simpler philosophy, presented by an existing individual for existing individuals, is especially intent upon advancing the ethical.

As soon as it is remembered that philosophizing is not speaking fantastically to fantastical beings but speaking to existing individuals, consequently that a decision about whether a continued striving is somewhat inferior to systematic conclusiveness is not to be made fantastically *in abstracto,* but that the question is what existing beings have to be satisfied with insofar as they are existing—then the continued striving will be unique in not involving illusion. Even if a person has achieved the highest, the repetition by which he must indeed fill out his existence, if he is not to go backward (or become a fantastical being), will again be a continued striving, because here in turn the conclusiveness is moved ahead and postponed. This is just like the Platonic conception of love; it is a want, and not only does that person feel a want who craves something he does not have but also that person who desires the continued possession of what he has. In the system and in the fifth act of the drama, one has a positive conclusiveness speculatively-fantastically and esthetically-fantastically, but such a conclusiveness is only for fantastical beings.

The continued striving is the expression of the existing subject's ethical life-view. The continued striving must therefore not be understood metaphysically, but neither is there any individual who exists metaphysically. Thus through a misunderstanding a contrast could be drawn between systematic conclusiveness and the continued striving for truth. One might then be able, and perhaps has even tried, to bear in mind the Greek notion of continually wanting to be a learner. But that is only a misunderstanding in this sphere. On the contrary, ethically understood, the continued striving is the consciousness of being an existing individual, and the continued learning the expression of the perpetual actualization, which at no moment is finished as long as the subject is existing; the subject is aware of this and is therefore not deluded. But Greek philosophy had a continual relation to ethics. That was why continually wanting to be a learner was not regarded as a great discovery or the inspired undertaking of an exceptional individual, since it was neither more nor less than the understanding that one is existing and that to be conscious of this is no merit but to forget it is thoughtlessness.

So-called pantheistic systems have frequently been cited and attacked by saying that they cancel freedom and the distinction between good and evil. This is perhaps expressed just as definitely by saying that every such system fantastically volatilizes the concept *existence*. But this should be said not only of pantheistic systems, for it would have been better to show that every system must be pantheistic simply because of the conclusiveness. Existence must be annulled in the eternal before the system concludes itself. No existing remainder may be left behind, not even such a tiny little dingle-dangle as the existing Herr Professor who is writing the system. But the issue is not presented this way. No, the pantheistic systems are contested, partly with tumultuous aphorisms that again and again promise a new system, partly with a compilation that is supposed to be a system and has a separate paragraph in which it is declared that emphasis is placed on the concepts "existence" and "actuality." That such a paragraph mocks the entire system, that instead of being a paragraph in the system it is an absolute protest against the system, is of no consequence to busy systematic triflers. If the concept of existence is actually to be emphasized, this cannot be stated directly in a paragraph in a system, and all direct oaths and "the devil take me" only make the didacticizing upside-downness even more ludicrous. That existence is actually emphasized must be expressed in an essential form, and in relation to the illusiveness of existence this is an indirect form—that there is no system. Yet this must not in turn become a reassuring standardized formula, because the indirect expression will always be regenerated in the form. In committee deliberations, it is quite all right to include a dissenting vote, but a system that has a dissenting vote as a paragraph within it is a queer monstrosity. No wonder, then, that the system survives. It proudly ignores objections; and if it comes across a particular objection that appears to draw a little attention, the systematic entrepreneurs proceed to have a copyist make a copy of the objection, which is thereupon recorded in the system, and with the bookbinding the system is finished.

The systematic idea is subject-object, is the unity of thinking and being; existence, on the other hand, is precisely the separation. From this it by no means follows that existence is thoughtless, but existence has spaced and does space subject from object, thought from being. Objectively understood, thinking is pure thinking, which just as abstractly-objectively corresponds to its object, which in turn is therefore itself, and truth is the correspondence of thinking with itself. This objective thinking has no relation to the existing subjectivity, and while the difficult question always remains—namely, how the existing subject gains entrance into this objectivity in which subjectivity is pure abstract subjectivity (which again is an objective qualification and does not signify any existing human being)—it is certain that the existing subjectivity evaporates more and more. And finally, if it is possible that a human being can become such a thing and that all this is not something of which he at best can become cognizant through imagination, this existing subjectivity becomes a pure abstract co-knowledge *[Medviden]* in and knowledge of this pure relation between thinking and being, this pure identity, indeed this tautology, because here being does not mean that the thinking person is, but basically only that he is a thinker.

The existing subject, however, is existing, and so indeed is every human being. Yet let us not do the wrong of calling the objective tendency impious, pantheistic self-worship but rather view it as a venture in the comic, because the idea that from now on to the end of the world nothing should be said except what would suggest a further improvement in a nearly finished system is simply a systematic consequence for systematizers.

By beginning straightway with ethical categories against the objective tendency, one does wrong and fails to hit the mark, because one has nothing in common with the attacked. But by remaining within the metaphysical, one can employ the comic, which also is in the metaphysical sphere, in order to overtake such a transfigured professor. If a dancer could leap very high, we would admire him, but if he wanted to give the impression that he could fly—even though he could leap higher than any dancer had ever leapt before—let laughter overtake him. Leaping means to belong essentially to the earth and to respect the law of gravity so that the leap is merely the momentary, but flying means to be set free from telluric conditions, something that is reserved exclusively for winged creatures, perhaps also for inhabitants of the moon, perhaps—and perhaps that is also where the system will at long last find its true readers. To be a human being has been abolished, and every speculative thinker confuses himself with humankind, whereby he becomes something infinitely great and nothing at all. In absentmindedness, he confuses himself with humankind, just as the opposition press uses "we" and the skippers say "the devil take me." But having cursed for a long time, one finally returns to the direct statement, because all swearing cancels itself; and when one has learned that every urchin can say "we," one learns that it nevertheless means a little more to be *one;* and when one sees that every cellar dweller can play the game of being humankind, one finally perceives that to be simply and solely a human being means something more than playing party games this way. And one thing more—when a cellar dweller plays this game, everyone thinks it ludicrous; and yet it is just as ludicrous when the greatest human being does it. And in that regard one may laugh at him and, as is fitting, still have respect for his abilities, his learning, etc.

SECTION II, CHAPTER 2: SUBJECTIVE TRUTH, INWARDNESS; TRUTH IS SUBJECTIVITY

*   *   *

When the question about truth is asked objectively, truth is reflected upon objectively as an object to which the knower relates himself. What is reflected upon is not the relation but that what he relates himself to is the truth, the true. If only that to which he relates himself is the truth, the true, then the subject is in the truth. When the question about *truth is asked subjectively, the individual's relation is reflected upon subjectively. If only the how of this relation is in truth, the individual is in truth, even if he in this way were to relate himself to untruth.**

Let us take the knowledge of God as an example. Objectively, what is reflected upon is that this is the true God; subjectively, that the individual relates himself to a something in *such a way* that his relation is in truth a God-relation. Now, on which side is the truth? Alas, must we not at this point resort to mediation and say: It is on neither side; it is in the mediation? Superbly stated, if only someone could say how an existing person goes about being in mediation, because to be in mediation is to be finished; to exist is to become. An existing person cannot be in two places at the same time, cannot be subject-object. When he is closest to being in two places at the same time, he is in passion; but passion is only momentary, and passion is the highest pitch of subjectivity.

The existing person who chooses the objective way now enters upon all approximating deliberation intended to bring forth God objectively, which is not achieved in all eternity, because God is a subject and hence only for subjectivity in inwardness. The existing person who chooses the subjective way instantly comprehends the whole dialectical difficulty because he must use some time, perhaps a long time, to find God objectively. He comprehends this dialectical difficulty in all its pain, because he must resort to God at that very moment, because every moment in which he does not have God is wasted.** At that very moment he has God, not by virtue of any objective deliberation but by virtue of the infinite passion of inwardness. The objective person is not bothered by dialectical difficulties such as what it means to put a whole research period into finding God, since it is indeed possible that the researcher would die tomorrow, and if he goes on living, he cannot very well regard God as something to be taken along at his convenience, since God is something one takes along a *tout prix* [at any price], which, in passion's understanding, is the true relationship of inwardness with God.

It is at this point, dialectically so very difficult, that the road swings off for the person who knows what it means to think dialectically and, existing, to think dialectically, which is quite different from sitting as a fantastical being at a desk and writing about something one has never done oneself, quite different from writing *de omnibus dubitandum* and then as an existing person being just as credulous as the most sensate human being. It is here that the road swings off, and the change is this: whereas objective knowledge goes along leisurely on the long road of approximation, itself not actuated by passion, to subjective knowledge every delay is a deadly peril and the decision so infinitely important that it is immediately urgent, as if the opportunity had already passed by unused.

Now, if the problem is to calculate where there is more truth (and, as stated, simultaneously to be on both sides equally is not granted to an existing person but is only a beatifying delusion for a deluded *I-I*), whether on the side of the person who only objectively seeks the true God and the approximating truth of the God-idea or on the side of the person who is infinitely concerned that he in truth relate himself to God with the infinite passion of need—then there can be no doubt about the answer for anyone who is not totally botched by scholarship and science. If someone who lives in the midst of Christianity en-

---

*The reader will note that what is being discussed here is essential truth, or the truth that is related essentially to existence, and that it is specifically in order to clarify it as inwardness or as subjectivity that the contrast is pointed out.

**In this way God is indeed a postulate, but not in the loose sense in which it is ordinarily taken. Instead, it becomes clear that this is the only way an existing person enters into a relationship with God: when the dialectical contradiction brings passion to despair and assists him in grasping God with "the category of despair" (faith), so that the postulate, far from being the arbitrary, is in fact *necessary* defense [Nødværge], self defense; in this way God is not a postulate, but the existing person's postulating of God is—a necessity [Nødvendighed].

ters, with knowledge of the true idea of God, the house of God, the house of the true God, and prays, but prays in untruth, and if someone lives in an idolatrous land but prays with all the passion of infinity, although his eyes are resting upon the image of an idol—where, then, is there more truth? The one prays in truth to God although he is worshiping an idol; the other prays in untruth to the true God and is therefore in truth worshiping an idol.

If someone objectively inquires into immortality, and someone else stakes the passion of the infinite on the uncertainty—where, then, is there more truth, and who has more certainty? The one has once and for all entered upon an approximation that never ends, because the certainty of immortality is rooted in subjectivity; the other is immortal and therefore struggles by contending with the uncertainty.

Let us consider Socrates. These days everyone is dabbling in a few proofs or demonstrations—one has many, another fewer. But Socrates! He poses the question objectively, problematically: if there is an immortality. So, compared with one of the modern thinkers with the three demonstrations, was he a doubter? Not at all. He stakes his whole life on this "if"; he dares to die, and with the passion of the infinite he has so ordered his whole life that it might be acceptable—if there is an immortality. Is there any better demonstration for the immortality of the soul? But those who have the three demonstrations do not order their lives accordingly. If there is an immortality, it must be nauseated by their way of living—is there any better counter-demonstration to the three demonstrations? The "fragment" of uncertainty helped Socrates, because he himself helped with the passion of infinity. The three demonstrations are of no benefit whatever to those others, because they are and remain slugs and, failing to demonstrate anything else, have demonstrated it by their three demonstrations.

In the same way a girl has perhaps possessed all the sweetness of being in love through a weak hope of being loved by the beloved, because she herself staked everything on this weak hope; on the other hand, many a wedded matron, who more than once has submitted to the strongest expression of erotic love, has certainly had demonstrations and yet, strangely enough, has not possessed *quod erat demonstrandum* [that which was to be demonstrated]. The Socratic ignorance was thus the expression, firmly maintained with all the passion of inwardness, of the relation of the eternal truth to an existing person, and therefore it must remain for him a paradox as long as he exists. Yet it is possible that in the Socratic ignorance there was more truth in Socrates than in the objective truth of the entire system that flirts with the demands of the times and adapts itself to assistant professors.

Objectively the emphasis is on what is said; subjectively the emphasis is on how it is said. This distinction applies even esthetically and is specifically expressed when we say that in the mouth of this or that person something that is truth can become untruth. Particular attention should be paid to this distinction in our day, for if one were to express in a single sentence the difference between ancient times and our time, one would no doubt have to say: In ancient times there were only a few individuals who knew the truth; now everyone knows it, but inwardness has an inverse relation to it. Viewed esthetically, the contradiction that emerges when truth becomes untruth in this and that person's mouth is best interpreted comically. Ethically-religiously, the emphasis is again on: *how.* But this is not to be understood as manner, modulation of voice, oral delivery, etc., but it is to be understood as the relation of the existing person, in his very existence, to what is said. Objectively, the question is only about categories of thought; subjectively, about inwardness. At its maximum, this "how" is the passion of the infinite, and the passion of the infinite is the very truth. But the passion of the infinite is precisely subjectivity, and thus subjectivity is truth. From the objective point of view, there is no infinite decision, and thus it is objectively correct that the distinction between good and evil is canceled, along with the principle of contradiction, and thereby also the infinite distinction between truth and falsehood. Only in subjectivity is there decision, whereas wanting to become objective is untruth. The passion of the infinite, not its content, is the deciding factor, for its content is precisely itself. In this way the subjective "how" and subjectivity are the truth.

But precisely because the subject is existing, the "how" that is subjectively emphasized is dialectical also with regard to time. In the moment of the decision of passion, where the road swings off from objective knowledge, it looks as if the infinite decision were thereby finished. But at the same moment, the existing person is in the temporal realm, and the subjective "how" is transformed into a striving that is motivated and repeatedly refreshed by the decisive passion of the infinite, but it is nevertheless a striving.

When subjectivity is truth, the definition of truth must also contain in itself an expression of the antithesis to objectivity, a memento of that fork in the road, and this expression will at the same time indicate the resilience of the inwardness. Here is such a definition of truth: *An objective uncertainty, held fast through appropriation with the most passionate inwardness, is the truth,* the highest truth there is for an *existing* person. At the point where the road swings off (and where that is cannot be stated objectively, since it is precisely subjectivity), objective knowledge is suspended. Objectively he then has only uncertainty, but this is precisely what intensifies the infinite passion of inwardness, and truth is precisely the daring venture of choosing the objective uncertainty with the passion of the infinite. I observe nature in order to find God, and I do indeed see omnipotence and wisdom, but I also see much that troubles and disturbs. The *summa summarum* [sum total] of this is an objective uncertainty, but the inwardness is so very great, precisely because it grasps this objective uncertainty with all the passion of the infinite. In a mathematical proposition, for example, the objectivity is given, but therefore its truth is also an indifferent truth.

But the definition of truth stated above is a paraphrasing of faith. Without risk, no faith. Faith is the contradiction between the infinite passion of inwardness and the objective uncertainty. If I am able to apprehend God objectively, I do not have faith; but because I cannot do this, I must have faith. If I want to keep myself in faith, I must continually see to it that I hold fast the objective uncertainty, see to it that in the objective uncertainty I am "out on 70,000 fathoms of water" and still have faith.

The thesis that subjectivity, inwardness, is truth contains the Socratic wisdom, the undying merit of which is to have paid attention to the essential meaning of existing, of the knower's being an existing person. That is why, in his ignorance, Socrates was in the truth in the highest sense within paganism. To comprehend this, that the misfortune of speculative thought is simply that it forgets again and again that the knower is an existing person, can already be rather difficult in our objective age. "But to go beyond Socrates when one has not even comprehended the Socratic—that, at least, is not Socratic." See "The Moral" in *Fragments.*

Just as in *Fragments,* let us from this point try a category of thought that actually does go beyond. Whether it is true or false is of no concern to me, since I am only imaginatively constructing, but this much is required, that it be clear that the Socratic is presupposed in it, so that I at least do not end up behind Socrates again.

When subjectivity, inwardness, is truth, then truth, objectively defined, is a paradox; and that truth is objectively a paradox shows precisely that subjectivity is truth, since the objectivity does indeed thrust away, and the objectivity's repulsion, or the expression for the objectivity's repulsion, is the resilience and dynamometer of inwardness. The paradox is the objective uncertainty that is the expression for the passion of inwardness that is truth. So much for the Socratic. The eternal, essential truth, that is, the truth that is related essentially to the existing person by pertaining essentially to what it means to exist (viewed Socratically, all other knowledge is accidental, its degree and scope indifferent), is a paradox. Nevertheless the eternal, essential truth is itself not at all a paradox, but it is a paradox by being related to an existing person. Socratic ignorance is an expression of the objective uncertainty; the inwardness of the existing person is truth. In anticipation of what will be discussed later, the following comment is made here: Socratic ignorance is an analogue to the category of the absurd, except that there is even less objective certainty in the repulsion exerted by the absurd, since there is only the certainty that it is absurd, and for that very reason there is infinitely greater resilience in the inwardness. The Socratic inwardness in existing is an analogue to faith, except that the inwardness of faith, corresponding not to the repulsion exerted by ignorance but to the repulsion exerted by the absurd, is infinitely deeper.

Viewed Socratically, the eternal essential truth is not at all paradoxical in itself, but only by being related to an existing person. This is expressed in another Socratic thesis: that all knowing is a recollecting. This thesis is an intimation of the beginning of speculative thought, but for that very reason Socrates did not pursue it; essentially it became Platonic. This is where the road swings off, and Socrates essentially emphasizes existing, whereas Plato, forgetting this, loses himself in speculative thought. Socrates' infinite merit is precisely that of being an *existing* thinker, not a speculative thinker who forgets what it means to exist. To Socrates, therefore, the thesis that all knowing is a recollecting has, at the moment of parting and as a continually annulled possibility of speculating, a double significance: (1) that the knower is essentially *integer* [uncorrupted] and that for him there is no other dubiousness with regard to knowledge of the eternal truth than this, that he exists, a dubiousness so essential and decisive to him that it signifies that existing, the inward deepening in and through existing, is truth; (2) that existence in temporality has no decisive significance, because there is continually the possibility of taking oneself back into eternity by recollecting, even though this possibility is continually annulled because the inward deepening in existing fills up time.*

*This may be the proper place to elucidate a dubiousness in the design of *Fragments,* a dubiousness that was due to my not wanting immediately to make the matter as dialectically difficult as it is, because in our day terminologies and the like are so muddled that it is almost impossible to safeguard oneself against confusion. In order, if possible, to elucidate properly the difference between the Socratic (which was supposed to be the philosophical, the pagan philosophical position) and the category of imaginatively constructed thought, which actually goes beyond the Socratic, I carried the Socratic back to the thesis that all knowing is a recollecting. It is commonly accepted as such, and only for the person who with a very special interest devotes himself to the Socratic, always returning to the sources, only for him will it be important to distinguish between Socrates and Plato on this point. The thesis certainly belongs to both of them, but Socrates continually parts with it because he wants to exist. By holding Socrates to the thesis that all knowing is recollecting, one turns him into a speculative philosopher instead of what he was, an existing thinker who understood existing as the essential. The thesis that all knowing is recollecting belongs to speculative thought, and recollecting is immanence, and from the point of view of speculation and the eternal there is no paradox. The difficulty, however, is that no human being is speculation, but the speculating person is an existing human being, subject to the claims of existence. To forget this is no merit, but to hold this fast is indeed a merit and that is precisely what Socrates did. To emphasize existence, which contains within it the qualification of inwardness, is the Socratic, whereas the Platonic is to pursue recollection and immanence. Basically Socrates is thereby beyond all speculation, because he does not have a fantastical beginning where the speculating person changes clothes and then goes on and on and speculates, forgetting the most important thing, to exist. But precisely because Socrates is in this way beyond speculative thought, he acquires, when rightly depicted, a certain analogous likeness to what the imaginary construction set forth as that which truly goes beyond the Socratic: the truth as paradox is an analog to the paradox *sensu eminentiori* [in the more eminent sense]; the passion of inwardness in existing is then an analog to faith *sensu eminentiori.* That the difference is infinite nevertheless, that the designations in *Fragments* of that which truly goes beyond the Socratic are unchanged, I can easily show, but I was afraid to make complications by promptly using what seem to be the same designations, at least the same words, about the different things when the imaginary construction was to be presented as different from these. Now, I think there would be no objection to speaking of the paradox in connection with Socrates and faith, since it is quite correct to do so, provided that it is understood correctly. Besides, the ancient Greeks also use the word ⟨*pistis*⟩ [Faith], although by no means in the sense of the imaginary construction, and use it so as to make possible some very illuminating observations bearing upon its dissimilarity to faith *sensu eminentiori,* especially with reference to one of Aristotle's works where the term is employed.

The great merit of the Socratic was precisely to emphasize that the knower is an existing person and that to exist is the essential. To go beyond Socrates by failing to understand this is nothing but a mediocre merit. This we must keep *in mente* [in mind] and then see whether the formula cannot be changed in such a way that one actually does go beyond the Socratic.

So, then, subjectivity, inwardness, is truth. Is there a *more inward* expression for it? Yes, if the discussion about "Subjectivity, inwardness, is truth" begins in this way: "Subjectivity is untruth." But let us not be in a hurry. Speculative thought also says that subjectivity is untruth but says it in the very opposite direction, namely, that objectivity is truth. Speculative thought defines subjectivity negatively in the direction of objectivity. The other definition, however, puts barriers in its own way at the very moment it wants to begin, which makes the inwardness so much more inward. Viewed Socratically, subjectivity is untruth if it refuses to comprehend that subjectivity is truth but wants, for example, to be objective. Here, on the other hand, in wanting to begin to become truth by becoming subjective, subjectivity is in the predicament of being untruth. Thus the work goes backward, that is, backward in inwardness. The way is so far from being in the direction of the objective that the beginning only lies even deeper in subjectivity.

But the subject cannot be untruth eternally or be presupposed to have been untruth eternally; he must have become that in time or he becomes that in time. The Socratic paradox consisted in this, that the eternal truth was related to an existing person. But now existence has accentuated the existing person a second time; a change so essential has taken place in him that he in no way can take himself back into eternity by Socratically recollecting. To do this is to speculate; to be able to do this but, by grasping the inward deepening in existence, to annul the possibility of doing it is the Socratic. But now the difficulty is that what accompanied Socrates as an annulled possibility has become an impossibility. If speculating was already of dubious merit in connection with the Socratic, it is now only confusion.

The paradox emerges when the eternal truth and existing are placed together, but each time existing is accentuated, the paradox becomes clearer and clearer. Viewed Socratically, the knower was an existing person, but now the existing person is accentuated in such a way that existence has made an essential change in him.

Let us now call the individual's untruth *sin*. Viewed eternally, he cannot be in sin or be presupposed to have been eternally in sin. Therefore, by coming into existence (for the beginning was that subjectivity is untruth), he becomes a sinner. He is not born as a sinner in the sense that he is presupposed to be a sinner before he is born, but he is born in sin and as a sinner. Indeed, we could call this *hereditary sin*. But if existence has in this way obtained power over him, he is prevented from taking himself back into eternity through recollection. If it is already paradoxical that the eternal truth is related to an existing person, now it is absolutely paradoxical that it is related to such an existing person. But the more difficult it is made for him, recollecting, to take himself out of existence, the more inward his existing can become in existence; and when it is made impossible for him, when he is lodged in existence in such a way that the back door of recollection is forever closed, then the inwardness becomes the deepest. But let us never forget that the Socratic merit was precisely to emphasize that the knower is existing, because the more difficult the matter becomes, the more one is tempted to rush along the easy road of speculative thought, away from terrors and decisions, to fame, honor, a life of ease, etc. If even Socrates comprehended the dubiousness of taking himself speculatively out of existence back into eternity, when there was no dubiousness for the existing person except that he existed and, of course, that existing was the essential—now it is impossible. He must go forward; to go backward is impossible.

Subjectivity is truth. The paradox came into existence through the relating of the eternal, essential truth to the existing person. Let us now go further; let us assume that the eternal, essential truth is itself the paradox. How does the paradox emerge? By placing the eternal, essential truth together with existing. Consequently, if we place it together in the truth itself, the truth becomes a paradox. The eternal truth has come into existence in time. That is the paradox. If the subject just mentioned was prevented by sin from taking himself back into eternity, now he is not to concern himself with this, because now the eternal, essential truth is not behind him but has come in front of him by existing itself or by having existed, so that if the individual, existing, does not lay hold of the truth in existence, he will never have it.

Existence can never be accentuated more sharply than it has been here. The fraud of speculative thought in wanting to recollect itself out of existence has been made impossible. This is the only point to be comprehended here, and every speculation that insists on being speculation shows *eo ipso* [precisely thereby] that it has not comprehended this. The individual can thrust all this away and resort to speculation, but to accept it and then want to cancel it through speculation is impossible, because it is specifically designed to prevent speculation.

When the eternal truth relates itself to an existing person, it becomes the paradox. Through the objective uncertainty and ignorance, the paradox thrusts away in the inwardness of the existing person. But since the paradox is not in itself the paradox, it does not thrust away intensely enough, for without risk, no faith; the more risk, the more faith; the more objective reliability, the less inwardness (since inwardness is subjectivity); the less objective reliability, the deeper is the possible inwardness. When the paradox itself is the paradox, it thrusts away by virtue of the absurd, and the corresponding passion of inwardness is faith.

But subjectivity, inwardness, is truth; if not, we have forgotten the Socratic merit. But when the retreat out of existence into eternity by way of recollection has been made impossible, then, with the truth facing one as the paradox, in the anxiety of sin and its pain, with the tremendous risk of objectivity, there is no stronger expression for inwardness than—to have faith. But without risk, no faith, not even the Socratic faith, to say nothing of the kind we are discussing here.

When Socrates believed that God is, he held fast the objective uncertainty with the entire passion of inwardness, and faith is precisely in this contradiction, in this risk. Now it is otherwise. Instead of the objective uncertainty, there is here the certainty that, viewed objectively, it is the absurd, and this absurdity, held fast in the passion of inwardness, is faith. Compared with the earnestness of the absurd, the Socratic ignorance is like a witty jest, and compared with the strenuousness of faith, the Socratic existential inwardness resembles Greek nonchalance.

What, then, is the absurd? The absurd is that the eternal truth has come into existence in time, that God has come into existence, has been born, has grown up, etc., has come into existence exactly as an individual human being, indistinguishable from any other human being, inasmuch as all immediate recognizability is pre-Socratic paganism and from the Jewish point of view is idolatry. Every qualification of that which actually goes beyond the Socratic must essentially have a mark of standing in relation to the god's having come into existence, because faith, *sensu strictissimo* [in the strictest sense], as explicated in *Fragments,* refers to coming into existence. When Socrates believed that God is *[er til]*, he no doubt perceived that where the road swings off there is a road of objective approximation, for example, the observation of nature, world history, etc. His merit was precisely to shun this road, where the quantifying siren song spellbinds and tricks the existing person. In relation to the absurd, the objective approximation resembles the comedy *Misforstaaelse paa Misforstaaelse* [Misunderstanding upon Misunderstanding], which ordinarily is played by assistant professors and speculative thinkers.

It is by way of the objective repulsion that the absurd is the dynamometer of faith in inwardness. So, then, there is a man who wants to have faith; well, let the comedy begin. He wants to have faith, but he wants to assure himself with the aid of objective deliberation and approximation. What happens? With the aid of approximation, the absurd becomes something else; it becomes probable, it becomes more probable, it may become to a high degree and exceedingly probable. Now he is all set to believe it, and he dares to say of himself that he does not believe as shoemakers and tailors and simple folk do, but only after long deliberation. Now he is all set to believe it, but, lo and behold, now it has indeed become impossible to believe it. The almost probable, the probable, the to-a-high-degree and exceedingly probable—that he can almost know, or as good as know, to a higher degree and exceedingly almost *know*—but *believe* it, that cannot be done, for the absurd is precisely the object of faith and only that can be believed.

Or there is a man who says he has faith, but now he wants to make his faith clear to himself; he wants to understand himself in his faith. Now the comedy begins again. The object of faith becomes almost probable, it becomes as good as probable, it becomes probable, it becomes to a high degree and exceedingly probable. He has finished; he dares to say of himself that he does not believe as shoemakers and tailors or other simple folk do but that he has also understood himself in his believing. What wondrous understanding! On the contrary, he has learned to know something different about faith than he believed and has learned to know that he no longer has faith, since he almost knows, as good as knows, to a high degree and exceedingly almost knows.

Inasmuch as the absurd contains the element of coming into existence, the road of approximation will also be that which confuses the absurd fact of coming into existence, which is the object of faith, with a simple historical fact, and then seeks historical certainty for that which is absurd precisely because it contains the contradiction that something that can become historical only in direct opposition to all human understanding has become historical. This contradiction is the absurd, which can only be believed. If a historical certainty is obtained, one obtains merely the certainty that what is certain is not what is the point in question. A witness can testify that he has believed it and then testify that, far from being a historical certainty, it is in direct opposition to his understanding, but such a witness repels in the same sense as the absurd repels, and a witness who does not repel in this way is *eo ipso* a deceiver or a man who is talking about something altogether different; and such a witness can be of no help except in obtaining certainty about something altogether different. One hundred thousand individual witnesses, who by the special nature of their testimony (that they have believed the absurd) remain individual witnesses, do not become something else *en masse* so that the absurd becomes less absurd. Why? Because one hundred thousand people individually have believed that it was absurd? Quite the contrary, those one hundred thousand witnesses repel exactly as the absurd does.

But I do not need to develop this further here. In *Fragments* (especially where the difference between the follower at first hand and the follower at second hand is annulled) and in Part One of this book, I have with sufficient care shown that all approximation is futile, since the point is rather to do away with introductory observations, reliabilities, demonstrations from effects, and the whole mob of pawnbrokers and guarantors, in order to get the absurd clear—so that one can believe if one will—I merely say that this must be extremely strenuous.

If speculative thought wants to become involved in this and, as always, say: From the point of view of the eternal, the divine, the theocentric, there is no paradox—I shall not be able to decide whether the speculative thinker is right, because I am only a poor existing human being who neither eternally nor divinely nor theocentrically is able to observe the eternal but must be content with existing. This much, however, is certain, that with speculative thought everything goes backward, back past the Socratic, which at least comprehended that for an existing person existing is the essential; and much less has speculative thought taken the time to comprehend what it means to be *situated* in existence the way the existing person is in the imaginary construction.

The difference between the Socratic position and the position that goes beyond the Socratic is clear enough and is essentially the same as in *Fragments,* for in the latter nothing has changed, and in the former the matter has only been made somewhat more difficult, but nevertheless not more difficult than it is. It has also become somewhat more difficult because, whereas in *Fragments* I set forth the thought-category of the paradox only in an imaginary construction, here I have also latently made an attempt to make clear the necessity of the paradox, and even though the attempt is somewhat weak, it is still something different from speculatively canceling the paradox.

Christianity has itself proclaimed itself to be the eternal, essential truth that has come into existence in time; it has proclaimed itself as *the paradox* and has required the inwardness of faith with regard to what is an offense to the Jews, foolishness to the Greeks—and an absurdity to the understanding. It cannot be expressed more strongly that subjectivity is truth and that objectivity only thrusts away, precisely by virtue of the absurd, and it seems strange that Christianity should have come into the world in order to be explained, alas, as if it were itself puzzled about itself and therefore came into the world to seek out the wise man, the speculative thinker, who can aid with the explanation. It cannot be expressed more inwardly that subjectivity is truth than when subjectivity is at first untruth, and yet subjectivity is truth.

*   *   *

The direct relationship with God is simply paganism, and only when the break has taken place, only then can there be a true God-relationship. But this break is indeed the first act of inwardness oriented to the definition that truth is inwardness. Nature is certainly the work of God, but only the work is directly present, not God. With regard to the individual human being, is this not acting like an illusive author, who nowhere sets forth his result in block letters or provides it beforehand in a preface? And why is God illusive? Precisely because he is truth and in being illusive seeks to keep a person from untruth. The observer does not glide directly to the result but on his own must concern himself with finding it and thereby break the direct relation. But this break is the actual breakthrough of inwardness, an act of self-activity, the first designation of truth as inwardness.

Or is it not the case that God is so unnoticeable, so hidden yet present in his work, that a person might very well live on, marry, be respected and esteemed as husband, father, and captain of the popinjay shooting club, without discovering God in his work, without ever receiving any impression of the infinitude of the ethical, because he managed with an analogy to the speculative confusion of the ethical and the world-historical by managing with custom and tradition in the city where he lived? Just as a mother admonishes her child who is about to attend a party, "Now, mind your manners and watch the other polite children and behave as they do," so he, too, could live on and behave as he saw others behave. He would never do anything first and would never have any opinion unless he first knew that others had it, because "the others" would be his very first. On special occasions he would act like someone who does not know how to eat a course that is served at a banquet; he would reconnoiter until he saw how the others did it etc. Such a person could perhaps know ever so much, perhaps even know the system by rote; he could perhaps live in a Christian country, know how to bow his head every time God's name was mentioned, perhaps also see God in nature if he was in the company of others who saw God; in short, well, he could be a congenial party goer—and yet he would be deceived by the direct relation to truth, to the ethical, to God.

If one were to portray such a person in an imaginary construction, he would be a satire on what it is to be a human being. It is really the God-relationship that makes a human being a human being, but this is what he would lack. Yet no one would hesitate to consider him an actual human being (for the absence of inwardness is not seen directly), although he would be more like a puppet character that very deceptively imitates all the human externalities—would even have children with his wife. At the end of his life, one would have to say that one thing had escaped him: he had not become aware of God. If God could have permitted a direct relationship, he would certainly have become aware. If God had taken the form, for example, of a rare, enormously large green bird, with a red beak, that perched in a tree on the embankment and perhaps even whistled in an unprecedented manner—then our party going man would surely have had his eyes opened; for the first time in his life he would have been able to be the first.

All paganism consists in this, that God is related directly to a human being, as the remarkably striking to the amazed. But the spiritual relationship with God in truth, that is, inwardness, is first conditioned by the actual breakthrough of inward deepening that corresponds to the divine cunning that God has nothing remarkable, nothing at all remarkable, about him—indeed, he is so far from being remarkable that he is invisible, and thus one does not suspect that he is there *[er til]*, although his invisibility is in turn his omnipresence. But an omnipresent being is the very one who is seen everywhere, for example, as a police officer is—how illusive, then, that an omnipresent being is cognizable precisely by his being invisible,* simply and solely by this, because his very visibility would annul his omnipresence. This relation between omnipresence and invisibility is like the relation between mystery and revelation, that the mystery expresses that the revelation is revelation in the stricter sense, that the mystery is the one and only mark by which it can be known, since otherwise a revelation becomes something like a police officer's omnipresence.

If God *[Gud]* wants to reveal himself in human form and provide a direct relation by taking, for example, the form of a man who is twelve feet tall, then that imaginatively constructed party goer and captain of the popinjay shooting club will surely become aware. But since God is unwilling to deceive, the spiritual relation in truth specifically requires that there be nothing at all remarkable about his form; then the party goer must say: There is nothing to see, not the slightest. If the god *[Guden]* has nothing whatever that is remarkable about him, the party goer is perhaps deceived in not be-

---

*In order to indicate how illusive the rhetorical can be, I shall show here how one could perhaps produce an effect upon a listener rhetorically, even though what was said would be a dialectical retrogression. Suppose a pagan religious orator says that here on earth the god's temple is actually empty, but (and here the rhetorical begins) in heaven, where everything is more perfect, where water is air, and air is ether, there are also temples and shrines for the gods, but the difference is that the gods actually dwell in these temples—that the god actually dwells in the temple is dialectical retrogression, because his not dwelling in the temple is an expression for the spiritual relation to the invisible. But rhetorically it produces the effect.—Incidentally, I had in mind a specific passage by a Greek author, but I shall not quote him.

coming aware at all. But the god is without blame in this, and the actuality of this deception is continually also the possibility of the truth. But if the god has something remarkable about him, he deceives, inasmuch as a human being thus becomes aware of the untruth, and this awareness is also the impossibility of the truth.

In paganism, the direct relation is idolatry; in Christianity, everyone indeed knows that God cannot manifest himself in this way. But this knowledge is not inwardness at all, and in Christianity it can certainly happen with a rote knower that he becomes utterly "without God in the world," which was not the case in paganism, where there was still the untrue relation of idolatry. Idolatry is certainly a dismal substitute, but that the rubric "God" disappears completely is even more mistaken.

Accordingly, not even God relates himself directly to a derived spirit (and this is the wondrousness of creation: not to produce something that is nothing in relation to the Creator, but to produce something that is something and that in the true worship of God can use this something to become by itself nothing before God); even less can one human being relate himself in this way to another *in truth*. Nature, the totality of creation, is God's work, and yet God is not there, but within the individual human being there is a possibility (he is spirit according to his possibility) that in inwardness is awakened to a God-relationship, and then it is possible to see God everywhere. Compared with the spiritual relationship in inwardness, the sensate distinctions of the great, the amazing, the most crying-to-heaven superlatives of a southern nation are a retrogression to idolatry. Is it not as if an author wrote 166 folio volumes and the reader read and read, just as when someone observes and observes nature but does not discover that the meaning of this enormous work lies in the reader himself, because amazement at the many volumes and the five hundred lines to the page, which is similar to amazement at how immense nature is and how innumerable the animal species are, is not understanding.

With regard to the essential truth, a direct relation between spirit and spirit is unthinkable. If such a relation is assumed, it actually means that one party has ceased to be spirit, something that is not borne in mind by many a genius who both assists people *en masse* into the truth and is good-natured enough to think that applause, willingness to listen, signatures, etc. mean accepting the truth. Just as important as the truth, and of the two the even more important one, is the mode in which the truth is accepted, and it is of slight help if one gets millions to accept the truth if by the very mode of their acceptance they are transposed into untruth. And therefore all good-naturedness, all persuasion, all bargaining, all direct attraction with the aid of one's own person in consideration of one's suffering so much for the cause, of one's weeping over humankind, of one's being so enthusiastic, etc.—all such things are a misunderstanding, in relation to the truth a forgery by which, according to one's ability, one helps any number of people to acquire a semblance of truth.

KARL MARX
1818–1883

It is hard to think of a more influential—or more controversial—nineteenth-century thinker than Karl Marx. Not content simply to develop a theory, Marx sought fundamental change in social, economic, and political structures. As he put it, "The philosophers have only *interpreted* the world in various ways; the point is, to *change* it."

Marx was the third of nine children born to Heinrich and Henrietta Marx in the Rhineland town of Trier. His parents were of Jewish ancestry but had converted to Protestant Christianity to protect Heinrich's job as a government lawyer. In 1835, Karl went to the University of Bonn to study law. Hardly the model student, he spent much of his time drinking or writing love letters to his childhood sweetheart and then fiancée, Jenny von Westphalen. At his father's insistence, Marx transferred to the University of Berlin and began to focus on his studies. While there, he abandoned his legal training and began preparing for an academic career as a philosophy professor. He wrote a dissertation contrasting Democritus and Epicurus that was accepted by the University of Jena, and in 1841 Marx received his doctorate in philosophy.

But the leftist politics Marx had adopted while in Berlin made it impossible for him to obtain a university post, so in 1842 he took a position as editor of the *Rheinische Zeitung (Rhenish Gazette),* a liberal middle-class newspaper in Cologne. Marx was very successful as an editor—too successful for the government censors who suppressed the paper after an article by Marx on the poverty of the Mosel winemakers. Marx moved to Paris where he became coeditor of the new journal, the *Deutsch-Französische Jahrbücher (German-French Annals).*

With his future seeming secure, Marx finally felt free to marry his fiancée, Jenny, in 1843. But the *Jahrbücher* closed almost immediately and once again Marx was unemployed. Fortunately, at about the same time, Marx received a sizable settlement from the shareholders of the *Rheinishe Zeitung,* and he and his new bride were able to live comfortably. Freed from his editing duties, Marx wrote extensively on economic and political matters. He also met the man who was to be his lifelong friend, collaborator, and financial backer: Friedrich Engels (1820–1895). Engels came from a family of wealthy textile industrialists and was, himself, the manager of his family's Manchester, England, branch. Together Marx and Engels produced *The Holy Family* (1845), Marx's first published book, which criticized a number of their fellow leftists.

While pursuing his writing projects, Marx was politically active among German communists living in Paris—activity that led to his expulsion from France in 1845. Living for a time in Brussels, Marx produced *The German Ideology* (1846) and *The Poverty of Philosophy* (1847) while continuing his political involvement. In 1847, he attended the congress of the newly formed Communist League in London. He and Engels were commissioned to produce an easy-to-read pamphlet outlining the league's doctrines. The result was the immensely influential work the *Manifesto of the Communist Party* (1848).

Following another attempt at editing an opposition newspaper in Cologne— and another expulsion by the government—Marx eventually settled in London. The next two decades were a time of poverty and hardship for the Marx family due as much to financial mismanagement as to lack of income. (Marx reflected often on the irony of his extensive work on capital when he had so little talent for managing it personally.) Marx received some income as a correspondent for the *New York Tribune;* but for the rest of his life, his primary source of income was Engels's gifts. In London, Marx became a fixture in the reading room of the British Museum, where he pored over government records, histories, and the writings of other economists, gathering data to document his thought. There he wrote *Critique of Political Economy* (1859) and began his magnum opus, *Das Kapital (Capital;* 1867). He also continued his political involvement, becoming the leader of the International Working Men's Association. He worked with the International until factional strife, particularly conflict with the anarchist Mikhail Aleksandrovich Bakunin (1814–1876), led Marx to dismantle the organization in 1872.

It wasn't until Marx's final years that he managed to gain some financial stability and to live the life of a bourgeois Victorian gentleman. But these years also brought tragedy and hardship of a different kind. Marx developed boils over his entire body and used creosote, opium, and arsenic among other remedies in a futile attempt to effect a cure. His beloved Jenny died in 1881 and his eldest daughter two years later. Shortly thereafter, Marx developed bronchitis and died in 1883.

*   *   *

While a student in Berlin, Marx had come under the influence of Hegelian philosophy. Hegel had understood *history* as a progressive actualization of the Absolute, but he was somewhat ambiguous about the future. One group of followers, the Old Hegelians, argued in a reactionary way that this progressive actualization was now complete and that Christianity was the Absolute Religion, Hegelianism the Absolute Philosophy, and Prussia the Absolute State. Another group, the Young Hegelians, led by Bruno Bauer, argued that the dialectical movement of history was continuing. To move to the next stage in this historical dialectic, they sought to expose the contradictions of the existing order.

Although Marx accepted Hegel's dialectical understanding of history, he became convinced that Hegel's philosophy (and that of the Young Hegelians) devalued humanity by its emphasis on the Absolute. Marx then drew on the materialism espoused in Ludwig Feuerbach's work, *The Essence of Christianity* (1841). Feuerbach had argued that Hegel's philosophy was nothing more than rationalized religion, which asserted that humans were merely the "self-alienation," or loss of identity, of God. Instead, Feuerbach advocated an atheistic materialism that claimed that God was simply the self-alienation of humans. That is, all the divine characteristics were nothing more than idealized human characteristics objectified and projected onto an imagined deity.

In "The Critique of Hegel's Dialectic and General Philosophy," reprinted here (complete) from the Tom Bottomore translation of the *Economic and Philosophical Manuscripts of 1844,* Marx uses Feuerbach's work to present his criticism of Hegel. Marx expresses appreciation for Hegel's dialectical understanding of the "self-creation of man as a process" and points out that Hegel conceives of "objective man" as the result of "his own labor." But Hegel understood labor as being "abstract mental" labor, not the natural, embodied interaction with real objects that concerned Marx. On the other hand, whereas he appreciated Feuerbach's materialism, Marx held that his predecessor did not tie his criticism to historical development. As Marx wrote in *The German Ideology,* "As far as Feuerbach is a materialist he does not deal with history, and as far as he considers history he is not a materialist." Synthesizing the historical development of Hegel and the materialism of Feuerbach, Marx's theory has often been called "dialectical materialism" (though Marx himself did not use that term).

Marx also adapted Feuerbach's concept of alienation, applying it to political, social, and economic interactions. In the section on "Alienated Labor" from the *Economic and Philosophical Manuscripts of 1844,* given here (complete), Marx explains how a capitalist system results in alienation for the worker. The worker's labor is alien to the worker because it belongs to the capitalist. In return for the worker's labor, the capitalist pays the worker a wage—a wage that competition keeps at a subsistence level. Yet the worker must continue to labor in order to survive. This means the worker is now self-alienated since the life activity, the essence of the worker, becomes "only a means for his existence." But alienation is not limited to individuals. Because they have different interests, workers, as an economic class, are alienated from those who own the means of production. This, in turn, gives rise to class struggle because the interests of one class are always in opposition to the interests of other economic classes. Only by having communal ownership of the means of production, that is, by the abolition of private property, will such conflict be overcome. Only then will those who work control both the process and the product of their labor. The selection from *Manifesto of the Communist Party,* given here in the Samuel Moore translation, calls on the workers of the world to bring about such a revolutionary change in the modes of production.

Throughout his analysis of the human situation, Marx continually returns to the material forces of production, distribution, exchange, and consumption. Whereas previous thinkers had seen philosophy, art, religion, morality, science, and law as the foundation of society, Marx claims that these elements of "higher culture" are actually the superstructure. In the brief "Preface" to *A Contribution to the Critique of Political Economy,* reprinted here in the N.I. Stone translation, Marx explains that the real foundations of society are the productive forces and the relations of production.

* * *

For good selections of primary source writings, see *Karl Marx: Early Writings,* edited and translated by Tom Bottomore (London: C.A. Watts, 1963), and *The Marx-Engels Reader,* edited by Robert C. Tucker (New York: Norton, 1978). For a collection of writings by Marx's followers, see David McLellan, ed., *Marxism: Essential Writings* (Oxford: Oxford University Press, 1988). Isaiah Berlin's *Karl Marx: His Life and Environment* (1963; reprinted Oxford: Oxford University Press, 1978) is still considered by many to be the best general introduction to Marx's life and philosophy, whereas more recent studies include David McLellan, *Karl Marx: His Life and Thought* (New York: Harper & Row, 1973); David McLellan, *Karl Marx* (New York: Penguin Books, 1975); Peter Singer, *Marx* (Oxford: Oxford University Press, 1980); Allen W. Wood, *Karl Marx* (London: Routledge & Kegan Paul, 1981); and Jon Elster, *An Introduction to Karl Marx* (Cambridge: Cambridge University Press, 1986). The following are samples of the many recent studies in particular areas of Marx's thought: Nicholas Lash, *A Matter of Hope: A Theologian's Reflections on the Thought of Karl Marx* (Notre Dame, IN: University of Notre Dame Press, 1982); Nancy Sue Love, *Marx, Nietzsche, and Modernity* (New York: Columbia University Press, 1986); Harold Mah, *The End of Philosophy, The Origin of "Ideology" : Karl Marx and the Crisis of the Young Hegelians* (Berkeley: University of California Press, 1987); and Robert Meister, *Political Identity: Thinking Through Marx* (Cambridge, MA: Basil Blackwell, 1990). For an interesting criticism of Marx by one of his contemporaries, see M.A. Bakunin, *Bakunin on Anarchy: Selected Works by the Activist-Founder of World Anarchism,* edited and translated by Sam Dolgoff (New York: Knopf, 1972). For collections of critical essays, see Tom Bottomore, ed., *Modern Interpretations of Marx* (Oxford: Basil Blackwell, 1981); David McLellan, ed., *Marx: The First Hundred Years* (New York: St. Martin's Press, 1983); Terence Ball and James Farr, eds., *After Marx* (Cambridge: Cambridge University Press, 1984); and Terrell Carver, ed., *The Cambridge Companion to Marx* (Cambridge: Cambridge University Press, 1991).

ECONOMIC AND PHILOSOPHICAL MANUSCRIPTS (in part)

ALIENATED LABOUR

[XXII] We have begun from the presuppositions of political economy. We have accepted its terminology and its laws. We presupposed private property; the separation of labour, capital and land, as also of wages, profit and rent; the division of labour; competition; the concept of exchange value, etc. From political economy itself, in its own words, we have shown that the worker sinks to the level of a commodity, and to a most miserable commodity; that the misery of the worker increases with the power and volume of his production; that the necessary result of competition is the accumulation of capital in a few hands, and thus a restoration of monopoly in a more terrible form; and finally that the distinction between capitalist and landlord, and between agricultural labourer and industrial worker, must disappear, and the whole of society divide into the two classes of property *owners* and *propertyless* workers.

Political economy begins with the fact of private property; it does not explain it. It conceives the *material* process of private property, as this occurs in reality, in general and abstract formulas which then serve it as laws. It does not *comprehend* these laws; that is, it does not show how they arise out of the nature of private property. Political economy provides no explanation of the basis for the distinction of labour from capital, of capital from land. When, for example, the relation of wages to profits is defined, this is explained in terms of the interests of capitalists; in other words, what should be explained is assumed. Similarly, competition is referred to at every point and is explained in terms of external conditions. Political economy tells us nothing about the extent to which these external and apparently accidental conditions are simply the expression of a necessary development. We have seen how exchange itself seems an accidental fact. The only motive forces which political economy recognizes are *avarice* and the *war between the avaricious, competition.*

Just because political economy fails to understand the interconnexions within this movement it was possible to oppose the doctrine of competition to that of monopoly, the doctrine of freedom of the crafts to that of the guilds, the doctrine of the division of landed property to that of the great estates; for competition, freedom of crafts, and the division of landed property were conceived only as accidental consequences brought about by will and force, rather than as necessary, inevitable and natural consequences of monopoly, the guild system and feudal property.

Thus we have now to grasp the real connexion between this whole system of alienation—private property, acquisitiveness, the separation of labour, capital and land, exchange and competition, value and the devaluation of man, monopoly and competition—and the system of *money.*

Let us not begin our explanation, as does the economist, from a legendary primordial condition. Such a primordial condition does not explain anything; it merely removes the question into a grey and nebulous distance. It asserts as a fact or event what

Economic and Philosophical Manuscripts (1844), from *Karl Marx: Early Writings,* edited and translated by T.B. Bottomore (New York: McGraw-Hill, 1964). Reprinted by permission of McGraw-Hill.

it should deduce, namely, the necessary relation between two things; for example, between the division of labour and exchange. In the same way theology explains the origin of evil by the fall of man; that is, it asserts as a historical fact what it should explain.

We shall begin from a *contemporary* economic fact. The worker becomes poorer the more wealth he produces and the more his production increases in power and extent. The worker becomes an ever cheaper commodity the more goods he creates. The *devaluation* of the human world increases in direct relation with the *increase in value* of the world of things. Labour does not only create goods; it also produces itself and the worker as a *commodity,* and indeed in the same proportion as it produces goods.

This fact simply implies that the object produced by labour, its product, now stands opposed to it as an *alien being,* as a *power independent* of the producer. The product of labour is labour which has been embodied in an object and turned into a physical thing; this product is an *objectification* of labour. The performance of work is at the same time its objectification. The performance of work appears in the sphere of political economy as a *vitiation* of the worker, objectification as a *loss* and as *servitude to the object,* and appropriation as *alienation.*

So much does the performance of work appear as vitiation that the worker is vitiated to the point of starvation. So much does objectification appear as loss of the object that the worker is deprived of the most essential things not only of life but also of work. Labour itself becomes an object which he can acquire only by the greatest effort and with unpredictable interruptions. So much does the appropriation of the object appear as alienation that the more objects the worker produces the fewer he can possess and the more he falls under the domination of his product, of capital.

All these consequences follow from the fact that the worker is related to the *product of his labour* as to an *alien* object. For it is clear on this presupposition that the more the worker expends himself in work the more powerful becomes the world of objects which he creates in face of himself, the poorer he becomes in his inner life, and the less he belongs to himself. It is just the same as in religion. The more of himself man attributes to God the less he has left in himself. The worker puts his life into the object, and his life then belongs no longer to himself but to the object. The greater his activity, therefore, the less he possesses. What is embodied in the product of his labour is no longer his own. The greater this product is, therefore, the more he is diminished. The *alienation* of the worker in his product means not only that his labour becomes an object, assumes an *external* existence, but that it exists independently, *outside himself,* and alien to him, and that it stands opposed to him as an autonomous power. The life which he has given to the object sets itself against him as an alien and hostile force.

[XXIII] Let us now examine more closely the phenomenon of *objectification;* the worker's production and the *alienation* and *loss* of the object it produces, which is involved in it. The worker can create nothing without *nature,* without the *sensuous external world.* The latter is the material in which his labour is realized, in which it is active, out of which and through which it produces things.

But just as nature affords the *means of existence* of labour, in the sense that labour cannot *live* without objects upon which it can be exercised, so also it provides the *means of existence* in a narrower sense; namely the means of physical existence for the *worker* himself. Thus, the more the worker *appropriates* the external world of sensuous nature by his labour the more he deprives himself of *means of existence,* in two respects: first, that the sensuous external world becomes progressively less an object belonging to his labour or a means of existence of his labour, and second, that it becomes progressively less a means of existence in the direct sense, a means for the physical subsistence of the worker.

In both respects, therefore, the worker becomes a slave of the object; first, in that he receives an *object of work,* i.e. receives *work,* and second, in that he receives *means of subsistence.* Thus the object enables him to exist, first as a worker and second, as a *physical subject.* The culmination of this enslavement is that he can only maintain himself as a *physical subject* so far as he is a *worker,* and that it is only as a *physical subject* that he is a worker.

(The alienation of the worker in his object is expressed as follows in the laws of political economy: the more the worker produces the less he has to consume; the more value he creates the more worthless he becomes; the more refined his product the more crude and misshapen the worker; the more civilized the product the more barbarous the worker; the more powerful the work the more feeble the worker; the more the work manifests intelligence the more the worker declines in intelligence and becomes a slave of nature.)

Political economy conceals the alienation in the nature of labour in so far as it does not examine the direct relationship between the worker (work) and production. Labour certainly produces marvels for the rich but it produces privation for the worker. It produces palaces, but hovels for the worker. It produces beauty, but deformity for the worker. It replaces labour by machinery, but it casts some of the workers back into a barbarous kind of work and turns the others into machines. It produces intelligence, but also stupidity and cretinism for the workers.

The direct relationship of labour to its products is the relationship of the worker to the objects of his production. The relationship of property owners to the objects of production and to production itself is merely a *consequence* of this first relationship and confirms it. We shall consider this second aspect later.

Thus, when we ask what is the important relationship of labour, we are concerned with the relationship of the *worker* to production.

So far we have considered the alienation of the worker only from one aspect; namely, *his relationship with the products of his labour.* However, alienation appears not merely in the result but also in the *process* of *production,* within *productive activity* itself. How could the worker stand in an alien relationship to the product of his activity if he did not alienate himself in the act of production itself? The product is indeed only the *résumé* of activity, of production. Consequently, if the product of labour is alienation, production itself must be active alienation—the alienation of activity and the activity of alienation. The alienation of the object of labour merely summarizes the alienation in the work activity itself.

What constitutes the alienation of labour? First, that the work is *external* to the worker, that it is not part of his nature; and that, consequently, he does not fulfill himself in his work but denies himself, has a feeling of misery rather than wellbeing, does not develop freely his mental and physical energies but is physically exhausted and mentally debased. The worker, therefore, feels himself at home only during his leisure time, whereas at work he feels homeless. His work is not voluntary but imposed, *forced labour.* It is not the satisfaction of a need, but only a *means* for satisfying other needs. Its alien character is clearly shown by the fact that as soon as there is no physical or other compulsion it is avoided like the plague. External labour, labour in which man alienates himself, is a labour of self-sacrifice, of mortification. Finally, the external character of work for the worker is shown by the fact that it is not his own work but work for someone else, that in work he does not belong to himself but to another person.

Just as in religion the spontaneous activity of human fantasy, of the human brain and heart, reacts independently as an alien activity of gods or devils upon the individual, so the activity of the worker is not his own spontaneous activity. It is another's activity and a loss of his own spontaneity.

We arrive at the result that man (the worker) feels himself to be freely active only in his animal functions—eating, drinking and procreating, or at most also in his dwelling and in personal adornment—while in his human functions he is reduced to an animal. The animal becomes human and the human becomes animal.

Eating, drinking and procreating are of course also genuine human functions. But abstractly considered, apart from the environment of human activities, and turned into final and sole ends, they are animal functions.

We have now considered the act of alienation of practical human activity, labour, from two aspects: (1) the relationship of the worker to the *product of labour* as an alien object which dominates him. This relationship is at the same time the relationship to the sensuous external world, to natural objects, as an alien and hostile world; (2) the relationship of labour to the *act of production* within *labour.* This is the relationship of the worker to his own activity as something alien and not belonging to him, activity as suffering (passivity), strength as powerlessness, creation as emasculation, the *personal* physical and mental energy of the worker, his personal life (for what is life but activity?), as an activity which is directed against himself, independent of him and not belonging to him. This is *self-alienation* as against the above mentioned alienation of the *thing*.

[XXIV] We have now to infer a third characteristic of *alienated labour* from the two we have considered.

Man is a species-being not only in the sense that he makes the community (his own as well as those of other things) his object both practically and theoretically, but also (and this is simply another expression for the same thing) in the sense that he treats himself as the present, living species, as a *universal* and consequently free being.

Species-life, for man as for animals, has its physical basis in the fact that man (like animals) lives from inorganic nature, and since man is more universal than an animal so the range of inorganic nature from which he lives is more universal. Plants, animals, minerals, air, light, etc. constitute, from the theoretical aspect, a part of human consciousness as objects of natural science and art; they are man's spiritual inorganic nature, his intellectual means of life, which he must first prepare for enjoyment and perpetuation. So also, from the practical aspect, they form a part of human life and activity. In practice man lives only from these natural products, whether in the form of food, heating, clothing, housing, etc. The universality of man appears in practice in the universality which makes the whole of nature into his inorganic body: (1) as a direct means of life; and equally (2) as the material object and instrument of his life activity. Nature is the inorganic body of man; that is to say nature, excluding the human body itself. To say that man *lives* from nature means that nature is his *body* with which he must remain in a continuous interchange in order not to die. The statement that the physical and mental life of man, and nature, are interdependent means simply that nature is interdependent with itself, for man is a part of nature.

Since alienated labour: (1) alienates nature from man; and (2) alienates man from himself, from his own active function, his life activity; so it alienates him from the species. It makes *species-life* into a means of individual life. In the first place, it alienates species-life and individual life, and second, it turns the latter, as an abstraction, into the purpose of the former, also in its abstract and alienated form.

For labour, *life activity, productive life,* now appear to man only as *means* for the satisfaction of a need, the need to maintain his physical existence. Productive life is, however, species-life. It is life creating life. In the type of life activity resides the whole character of a species, its species character; and free, conscious activity is the species character of human beings. Life itself appears only as a *means of life.*

The animal is one with its life activity. It does not distinguish the activity from itself. It is *its activity*. But man makes his life activity itself an object of his will and consciousness. He has a conscious life activity. It is not a determination with which he is completely identified. Conscious life activity distinguishes man from the life activity of animals. Only for this reason is he a species-being. Or rather, he is only a self-conscious being, i.e. his own life is an object for him, because he is a species-being. Only for this reason is his activity free activity. Alienated labour reverses the relationship, in that man because he is a self-conscious being makes his life activity, his *being*, only a means for his *existence*.

The practical construction of an *objective world*, the *manipulation* of inorganic nature, is the confirmation of man as a conscious species-being, i.e. a being who treats the species as his own being or himself as a species-being. Of course, animals also produce. They construct nests, dwellings, as in the case of bees, beavers, ants, etc. But they only produce what is strictly necessary for themselves or their young. They produce only in a single direction, while man produces universally. They produce only under the compulsion of direct physical needs, while man produces when he is free from physical need and only truly produces in freedom from such need. Animals produce only themselves, while man reproduces the whole of nature. The products of animal production belong directly to their physical bodies, while man is free in face of his product. Animals construct only in accordance with the standards and needs of the species to which they belong, while man knows how to produce in accordance with the standards of every species and knows how to apply the appropriate standard to the object. Thus man constructs also in accordance with the laws of beauty.

It is just in his work upon the objective world that man really proves himself as a *species-being*. This production is his active species-life. By means of it nature appears as his work and his reality. The object of labour is, therefore, the *objectification of man's species-life;* for he no longer reproduces himself merely intellectually, as in consciousness, but actively and in a real sense, and he sees his own reflection in a world which he has constructed. While, therefore, alienated labour takes away the object of production from man, it also takes away his *species-life,* his real objectivity as a species being, and changes his advantage over animals into a disadvantage in so far as his inorganic body, nature, is taken from him.

Just as alienated labour transforms free and self-directed activity into a means, so it transforms the species-life of man into a means of physical existence.

Consciousness, which man has from his species, is transformed through alienation so that species-life becomes only a means for him. (3) Thus alienated labour turns the *species life of man,* and also nature as his mental species-property, into an *alien* being and into a *means* for his *individual existence*. It alienates from man his own body, external nature, his mental life and his *human* life. (4) A direct consequence of the alienation of man from the product of his labour, from his life activity and from his species-life, is that *man is alienated* from other *men*. When man confronts himself he also confronts *other* men. What is true of man's relationship to his work, to the product of his work and to himself, is also true of his relationship to other men, to their labour and to the objects of their labour.

In general, the statement that man is alienated from his species-life means that each man is alienated from others, and that each of the others is likewise alienated from human life.

Human alienation, and above all the relation of man to himself, is first realized and expressed in the relationship between each man and other men. Thus in the relationship of alienated labour every man regards other men according to the standards and relationships in which he finds himself placed as a worker.

[XXV] We began with an economic fact, the alienation of the worker and his production. We have expressed this fact in conceptual terms as *alienated labour,* and in analysing the concept we have merely analysed an economic fact.

Let us now examine further how this concept of alienated labour must express and reveal itself in reality. If the product of labour is alien to me and confronts me as an alien power, to whom does it belong? If my own activity does not belong to me but is an alien, forced activity, to whom does it belong? To a being *other* than myself. An who is this being? The *gods?* It is apparent in the earliest stages of advanced production, e.g. temple building, etc. in Egypt, India, Mexico, and in the service rendered to gods, that the product belonged to the gods. But the gods alone were never the lords of labour. And no more was *nature.* What a contradiction it would be if the more man subjugates nature by his labour, and the more the marvels of the gods are rendered superfluous by the marvels of industry, the more he should abstain from his joy in producing and his enjoyment of the product for love of these powers.

The *alien* being to whom labour and the product of labour belong, to whose service labour is devoted, and to whose enjoyment the product of labour goes, can only be *man* himself. If the product of labour does not belong to the worker, but confronts him as an alien power, this can only be because it belongs to *a man other than the worker.* If his activity is a torment to him it must be a source of enjoyment and pleasure to another. Not the gods, nor nature, but only man himself can be this alien power over men.

Consider the earlier statement that the relation of man to himself is first *realized, objectified,* through his relation to other men. If he is related to the product of his labour, his objectified labour, as to an *alien,* hostile, powerful and independent object, he is related in such a way that another alien, hostile, powerful and independent man is the lord of this object. If he is related to his own activity as to unfree activity, then he is related to it as activity in the service, and under the domination, coercion and yoke, of another man.

Every self-alienation of man, from himself and from nature, appears in the relation which he postulates between other men and himself and nature. Thus religious self-alienation is necessarily exemplified in the relation between laity and priest, or, since it is here a question of the spiritual world, between the laity and a mediator. In the real world of practice this self-alienation can only be expressed in the real, practical relation of man to his fellow men. The medium through which alienation occurs is itself a *practical* one. Through alienated labour, therefore, man not only produces his relation to the object and to the process of production as to alien and hostile men; he also produces the relation of other men to his production and his product, and the relation between himself and other men. Just as he creates his own production as a vitiation, a punishment, and his own product as a loss, as a product which does not belong to him, so he creates the domination of the non-producer over production and its product. As he alienates his own activity, so he bestows upon the stranger an activity which is not his own.

We have so far considered this relation only from the side of the worker, and later on we shall consider it also from the side of the non-worker.

Thus, through alienated labour the worker creates the relation of another man, who does not work and is outside the work process, to this labour. The relation of the worker to work also produces the relation of the capitalist (or whatever one likes to call the lord of labour) to work. *Private property* is, therefore, the product, the necessary result, of *alienated labour,* of the external relation of the worker to nature and to himself.

Private property is thus derived from the analysis of the concept of *alienated labour;* that is, alienated man, alienated labour, alienated life, and estranged man.

We have, of course, derived the concept of *alienated labour (alienated life)* from political economy, from an analysis of the *movement of private property*. But the analysis of this concept shows that although private property appears to be the basis and cause of alienated labour, it is rather a consequence of the latter, just as the gods are *fundamentally* not the cause but the product of confusions of human reason. At a later stage, however, there is a reciprocal influence.

Only in the final stage of the development of private property is its secret revealed, namely, that it is on one hand the *product* of alienated labour, and on the other hand the *means* by which labour is alienated, *the realization of this alienation*.

This elucidation throws light upon several unresolved controversies—

1. Political economy begins with labour as the real soul of production and then goes on to attribute nothing to labour and everything to private property. Proudhon, faced by this contradiction, has decided in favour of labour against private property. We perceive, however, that this apparent contradiction is the contradiction of *alienated labour* with itself and that political economy has merely formulated the laws of alienated labour.

   We also observe, therefore, that *wages* and *private property* are identical, for wages, like the product or object of labour, labour itself remunerated, are only a necessary consequence of the alienation of labour. In the wage system labour appears not as an end in itself but as the servant of wages. We shall develop this point later on and here only bring out some of the [XXVI] consequences.

   An enforced *increase in wages* (disregarding the other difficulties, and especially that such an anomaly could only be maintained by force) would be nothing more than a *better remuneration of slaves,* and would not restore, either to the worker or to the work, their human significance and worth.

   Even the *equality of incomes* which Proudhon demands would only change the relation of the present-day worker to his work into a relation of all men to work. Society would then be conceived as an abstract capitalist.

2. From the relation of alienated labour to private property it also follows that the emancipation of society from private property, from servitude, takes the political form of the *emancipation of the workers;* not in the sense that only the latter's emancipation is involved, but because this emancipation includes the emancipation of humanity as a whole. For all human servitude is involved in the relation of the worker to production, and all the types of servitude are only modifications or consequences of this relation.

As we have discovered the concept of *private property* by an *analysis* of the concept of *alienated labour,* so with the aid of these two factors we can evolve all the *categories* of political economy, and in every category, e.g. trade, competition, capital, money, we shall discover only a particular and developed expression of these fundamental elements.

However, before considering this structure let us attempt to solve two problems.

1. To determine the general nature of *private property* as it has resulted from alienated labour, in its relation to *genuine human and social property.*

2. We have taken as a fact and analysed the *alienation of labour.* How does it happen, we may ask, that *man alienates his labour?* How is this alienation founded in the nature of human development? We have already done much to solve the problem in so far as we have *transformed* the question concerning the *origin of private property* into a question about the relation between *alienated labour* and the process of development of mankind. For in speaking of private property one believes oneself to be dealing with something external to mankind. But in speaking of labour one deals directly with mankind itself. This new formulation of the problem already contains its solution.

ad (1) The general nature of private property and its relation to genuine human property.

We have resolved alienated labour into two parts, which mutually determine each other, or rather, which constitute two different expressions of one and the same relation. *Appropriation* appears as *alienation* and *alienation* as *appropriation,* alienation as genuine acceptance in the community.

We have considered one aspect, *alienated* labour, in its bearing upon the *worker* himself, i.e. *the relation of alienated labour to itself.* And we have found as the necessary consequence of this relation the *property* relation of the *non-worker* to the *worker* and to labour. *Private property* as the material, summarized expression of alienated labour includes both relations; *the relation of the worker to labour, to the product of his labour and to the non-worker,* and the relation of the *non-worker to the worker and to the product of the latter's labour.*

We have already seen that in relation to the worker, who *appropriates* nature by his labour, appropriation appears as alienation, self-activity as activity for another and of another, living as the sacrifice of life, and production of the object as loss of the object to an alien power, an alien man. Let us now consider the relation of this *alien* man to the worker, to labour, and to the object of labour.

It should be noted first that everything which appears to the worker as an *activity of alienation,* appears to the nonworker as a *condition of alienation.* Second, the *real, practical* attitude (as a state of mind) of the worker in production and to the product appears to the non-worker who confronts him as a *theoretical* attitude.

[XXVII] Third, the non-worker does everything against the worker which the latter does against himself, but he does not do against himself what he does against the worker.

Let us examine these three relationships more closely.*

* * *

CRITIQUE OF HEGEL'S DIALECTIC AND GENERAL PHILOSOPHY

This is perhaps an appropriate point at which to explain and substantiate what has been said, and to make some general comments upon Hegel's dialectic, especially as it is expounded in the *Phenomenology* and *Logic,* and upon its relation to the modern critical movement.

Modern German criticism was so much concerned with the past, and was so hampered by its involvement with its subject-matter, that it had a wholly uncritical attitude to the methods of criticism and completely ignored the partly formal, but in fact *essential* question—how do we now stand with regard to the Hegelian *dialectic?* This ignorance of the relationship of modern criticism to Hegel's general philosophy and his dialectic in particular was so great that critics such as Strauss and Bruno Bauer (the former in all his writings; the latter in his *Synoptiker,* where, in opposition to Strauss, he substitutes the "self-consciousness" of abstract man for the substance of "abstract na-

*[The manuscript breaks off unfinished at this point.]

ture," and even in *Das entdeckte Christentum*) were, at least implicitly, ensnared in Hegelian logic. Thus, for instance, in *Das entdeckte Christentum* it is argued: "As if self-consciousness in positing the world, that which is different, did not produce itself in producing its object; for it then annuls the difference between itself and what it has produced, since it exists only in this creation and movement, has its purpose only in this movement, etc." Or again: "They (the French materialists) could not see that the movement of the universe has only become real and unified in itself in so far as it is the movement of self-consciousness." These expressions not only do not differ from the Hegelian conception, but reproduce it textually.

[XII] How little these writers, in undertaking their criticism (Bauer in his *Synoptiker*), were aware of their relation to Hegel's dialectic, and how little such an awareness emerged from the criticism, is demonstrated by Bauer in his *Gute Sache der Freiheit* when, instead of replying to the indiscreet question put by Gruppe, "And now what is to be done with logic?," he transmits it to future critics.

Now that Feuerbach, in his "Thesen" in the *Anecdotis* and in greater detail in his *Philosophie der Zukunft,* has demolished the inner principle of the old dialectic and philosophy, the "Critical School," which was unable to do this itself but has seen it accomplished, has proclaimed itself the pure, decisive, absolute, and finally enlightened criticism, and in its spiritual pride has reduced the whole historical movement to the relation existing between itself and the rest of the world, which comes into the category of "the mass." It has reduced all dogmatic antitheses to the single dogmatic antithesis between its own cleverness and the stupidity of the world, between the critical Christ and mankind—"the rabble." At every moment of the day it has demonstrated its own excellence *vis-à-vis* the stupidity of the mass, and it has finally announced the critical *last judgment* by proclaiming that the day is at hand when the whole of fallen mankind will assemble before it and will be divided up into groups each of which will be handed its *testimonium paupertatis* (certificate of poverty). The Critical School has made public its superiority to all human feelings and to the world, above which it sits enthroned in sublime solitude, content to utter occasionally from its sarcastic lips the laughter of the Olympian gods. After all these entertaining antics of idealism (of Young Hegelianism) which is expiring in the form of criticism, the Critical School has not even now intimated that it was necessary to discuss critically its own source, the dialectic of Hegel; nor has it given any indication of its relation with the dialectic of Feuerbach. This is a procedure totally lacking in critical sense.

Feuerbach is the only person who has a *serious* and *critical* relation to Hegel's dialectic, who has made real discoveries in this field, and above all, who has vanquished the old philosophy. The magnitude of Feuerbach's achievement and the unassuming simplicity with which he presents his work to the world are in striking contrast with the behaviour of others.

Feuerbach's great achievement is—

1. to have shown that philosophy is nothing more than religion brought into thought and developed by thought, and that it is equally to be condemned as another form and mode of existence of human alienation;
2. to have founded *genuine materialism* and *positive science* by making the social relationship of "man to man" the basic principle of his theory;
3. to have opposed to the negation of the negation which claims to be the absolute positive, a self-subsistent principle positively founded on itself.

Feuerbach explains Hegel's dialectic, and at the same time justifies taking the positive phenomenon, that which is perceptible and indubitable, as the starting-point, in the following way.

Hegel begins from the alienation of substance (logically, from the infinite, the abstract universal) from the absolute and fixed abstraction; i.e. in ordinary language, from religion and theology. Secondly, he supersedes the infinite, and posits the real, the perceptible, the finite, and the particular. (Philosophy, supersession of religion and theology.) Thirdly, he then supersedes the positive and reestablishes the abstraction, the infinite. (Re-establishment of religion and theology.)

Thus Feuerbach conceives the negation of the negation as being *only* a contradiction within philosophy itself, which affirms theology (transcendence, etc.) after having superseded it, and thus affirms it in opposition to philosophy.

For the positing or self-affirmation and self-confirmation which is implied in the negation of the negation is regarded as a positing which is still uncertain, burdened with its contrary, doubtful of itself and thus incomplete, not demonstrated by its own existence, and implicit. [XIII] The positing which is perceptually indubitable and grounded upon itself is directly opposed to it.

In conceiving the negation of the negation, from the aspect of the positive relation inherent in it, as the only true positive, and from the aspect of the negative relation inherent in it, as the only true act and the self-confirming act of all being, Hegel has merely discovered an *abstract, logical* and *speculative* expression of the historical process, which is not yet the real history of man as a given subject, but only the history of the *act of creation,* of the *genesis of man.*

We shall explain both the abstract form of this process and the difference between the process as conceived by Hegel and by modern criticism, by Feuerbach in *Das Wesen des Christentums;* or rather, the critical form of this process which is still so uncritical in Hegel.

Let us examine Hegel's system. It is necessary to begin with the *Phenomenology,* because it is there that Hegel's philosophy was born and that its secret is to be found. [Marx's version of the table of contents from Hegel's *Phenomenology* which follows here has been deleted—F.B.]

*   *   *

Hegel's *Encyclopaedia* begins with logic, with *pure speculative thought,* and ends with *absolute knowledge,* the self-conscious and self-conceiving philosophical or absolute mind, i.e. the superhuman, abstract mind. The whole of the *Encyclopaedia* is nothing but the extended being of the philosophical mind, its self-objectification; and the philosophical mind is nothing but the alienated world-mind thinking within the bounds of its self-alienation, i.e. conceiving itself in an abstract manner. *Logic* is the *money* of the mind, the speculative *thought-value* of man and of nature, their essence indifferent to any real determinate character and thus unreal; *thought* which is *alienated* and abstract and ignores real nature and man. *The external character of this abstract thought . . . nature* as it exists for this abstract thought. Nature is external to it, loss of itself, and is only conceived as something external, as abstract thought, but alienated abstract thought. Finally, spirit, this thought which returns to its own origin and which, as anthropological, phenomenological, psychological, customary, artistic-religious spirit, is not valid for itself until it discovers itself and relates itself to itself as absolute knowledge in the absolute (i.e. abstract) spirit, and so receives its conscious and fitting existence. For its real mode of existence is *abstraction.*

Hegel commits a double error. The first appears most clearly in the *Phenomenology,* the birthplace of his philosophy. When Hegel conceives wealth, the power of the state, etc. as entities alienated from the human being, he conceives them only in their thought form. They are entities of thought and thus simply an alienation of *pure* (i.e. abstract) philosophical thought. The whole movement, therefore, ends in absolute knowledge. It is precisely abstract thought from which these objects are alienated, and which they confront with their presumptuous reality. The *philosopher,* himself an abstract form of alienated man, sets himself up as the *measure* of the alienated world. The whole *history of alienation,* and of the retraction of alienation, is, therefore, only the *history of the production* of abstract thought, i.e. of absolute, logical, speculative thought. *Estrangement,* which thus forms the real interest of this alienation and of the supersession of this alienation, is the opposition of *in itself* and *for itself,* of *consciousness* and *self-consciousness,* of *object* and *subject,* i.e. the opposition in thought itself between abstract thought and sensible reality or real sensuous existence. All other contradictions and movements are merely the *appearance,* the *cloak,* the *exoteric* form of these two opposites which are alone important and which constitute the *significance* of the other, profane contradictions. It is not the fact that the human being *objectifies* himself *inhumanly,* in opposition to himself, but that he *objectifies* himself by *distinction* from and in *opposition* to abstract thought, which constitutes alienation as it exists and as it has to be transcended.

[XVIII] The appropriation of man's objectified and alienated faculties is thus, in the first place, only an *appropriation* which occurs in *consciousness,* in *pure thought, i.e. in abstraction. It is the appropriation of these objects as* thoughts and as *movements of thought.* For this reason, despite its thoroughly negative and critical appearance, and despite the genuine criticism which it contains and which often anticipates later developments, there is already implicit in the *Phenomenology,* as a germ, as a potentiality and a secret, the uncritical positivism and uncritical idealism of Hegel's later works—the philosophical dissolution and restoration of the existing empirical world. *Secondly,* the vindication of the objective world for man (for example, the recognition that sense perception is not *abstract* sense perception but *human* sense perception, that religion, wealth, etc. are only the alienated reality of *human* objectification, of *human* faculties put to work, and are, therefore, a way to genuine *human* reality), this appropriation, or the insight into this process, appears in Hegel as the recognition of *sensuousness, religion,* state power, etc. as *mental* phenomena, for *mind* alone is the true essence of man, and the true form of mind is thinking mind, the logical, speculative mind. The *human character* of nature, of historically produced nature, of man's products, is shown by their being *products* of abstract mind, and thus phases of *mind, entities of thought.* The *Phenomenology is* a concealed, unclear and mystifying criticism, but in so far as it grasps the *alienation* of man (even though man appears only as mind) all the elements of criticism are contained in it, and are often *presented* and *worked out* in a manner which goes far beyond Hegel's own point of view. The sections devoted to the "unhappy consciousness," the "honest consciousness," the struggle between the "noble" and the "base" consciousness, etc., etc. contain the *critical* elements (though still in an alienated form) of whole areas such as religion, the state, civil life, etc. Just as the *entity,* the *object,* appears as an entity of thought, so also the *subject* is always *consciousness* or *self-consciousness;* or rather, the object appears only as abstract consciousness and man as *self-consciousness.* Thus the distinctive forms of alienation which are manifested are only different forms of consciousness and self-consciousness. Since abstract consciousness (the form in which the object is conceived) is in *itself* merely a distinctive moment of self-consciousness, the outcome of the movement is the identity of self-consciousness and consciousness—absolute knowledge—the movement of abstract thought not directed outwards but proceeding within itself; i.e. the dialectic of pure thought is the result.

[XXIII] The outstanding achievement of Hegel's *Phenomenology*—the dialectic of negativity as the moving and creating principle—is, first, that Hegel grasps the self-creation of man as a process, objectification as loss of the object, as alienation and tran-scendence of this alienation, and that he, therefore, grasps the nature of *labour,* and con-ceives objective man (true, because real man) as the result of his *own* labour. The *real, active* orientation of man to himself as a species-being, or the affirmation of himself as a real species-being (i.e. as a human being) is only possible so far as he really brings forth all his *species-powers* (which is only possible through the co-operative endeav-ours of mankind and as an outcome of history) and treats these powers as objects, which can only be done at first in the form of alienation.

We shall next show in detail Hegel's one-sidedness and limitations, as revealed in the final chapter of the *Phenomenology,* on absolute knowledge; a chapter which con-tains the concentrated spirit of the *Phenomenology,* its relation to the dialectic, and also Hegel's *consciousness* of both and of their interrelations.

For the present, let us make these preliminary observations: Hegel's standpoint is that of modern political economy. He conceives *labour* as the *essence,* the self-confirming essence of man; he observes only the positive side of labour, not its negative side. Labour is *man's coming to be for himself* within *alienation,* or as an alienated man. Labour as Hegel understands and recognizes it is *abstract mental labour.* Thus, that which above all constitutes the *essence* of philosophy, the *alienation of man knowing himself,* or *alienated* science *thinking* itself, Hegel grasps as its essence. Consequently, he is able to bring together the separate elements of earlier philosophy and to present his own as the philosophy. What other philosophers did, that is, to conceive separate ele-ments of nature and of human life as phases of self-consciousness and indeed of abstract self-consciousness, Hegel *knows* by doing philosophy; therefore, his science is absolute.

Let us now turn to our subject.

Absolute Knowledge. The Final Chapter of the "Phenomenology."

The main point is that the *object of consciousness* is nothing else but *self-consciousness,* that the object is only *objectified* self-consciousness, self-consciousness as an object. (Positing man = self-consciousness.)

It is necessary, therefore, to surmount the *object of consciousness. Objectivity* as such is regarded as an alienated human relationship which does not correspond with the *essence of man,* self-consciousness. The reappropriation of the objective essence of man, which was produced as something alien and determined by alienation, signifies the supersession not only of *alienation* but also of *objectivity;* that is, man is regarded as a *non-objective, spiritual* being.

The process of *overcoming the object of consciousness* is described by Hegel as follows: The *object* does not reveal itself only as *returning* into the Self (according to Hegel that is a *one-sided* conception of the movement, considering only one aspect). Man is equated with self. The Self, however, is only man conceived *abstractly* and pro-duced by abstraction. Man is self-referring. His eye, his ear, etc. are *self-referring;* every one of his faculties has this quality of *self*-reference. But it is entirely false to say on that account, "*Self-consciousness* has eyes, ears, faculties." Self-consciousness is rather a quality of human nature, of the human eye, etc.; human nature is not a quality of [XXIV] *self-consciousness.*

The Self, abstracted and determined for itself, is man as an *abstract egoist,* purely abstract *egoism* raised to the level of thought. (We shall return to this point later.)

For Hegel, *human life, man,* is equivalent to *self-consciousness.* All alienation of human life is, therefore, *nothing* but *alienation of self-consciousness.* The alienation of self-consciousness is not regarded as the *expression,* reflected in knowledge and thought, of the *real* alienation of human life. Instead, *actual* alienation, that which appears real, is in its *innermost* hidden nature (which philosophy first discloses) only the *phenomenal being* of the alienation of real human life, of *self-consciousness.* The science which comprehends this is therefore called *Phenomenology.* All reappropriation of alienated objective life appears, therefore, as an incorporation in self-consciousness. The person who takes possession of his being is only the self-consciousness which takes possession of objective being; the return of the object into the Self is, therefore, the reappropriation of the object.

Expressed in a *more comprehensive* way the *supersession of the object of consciousness* means: (1) that the object as such presents itself to consciousness as something disappearing; (2) that it is the alienation of self-consciousness which establishes "thinghood"; (3) that this alienation has *positive* as well as *negative* significance; (4) that it has this significance not only *for us* or in itself, but also *for self-consciousness itself;* (5) that for *self-consciousness* the negative of the object, its self-supersession, has *positive* significance, or self-consciousness *knows* thereby the nullity of the object in that self-consciousness alienates itself, for in this alienation it establishes *itself* as object or, for the sake of the indivisible unity of *being-for-itself,* establishes the object as itself; (6) that, on the other hand, this other "moment" is equally present, that self-consciousness has superseded and reabsorbed this alienation and objectivity, and is thus *at home* in its other being as such; (7) that this is the movement of consciousness, and consciousness is, therefore, the totality of its "moments"; (8) that similarly, consciousness must have related itself to the object in all its determinations, and have conceived it in terms of each of them. This totality of determinations makes the object *intrinsically* a *spiritual being,* and it becomes truly so for consciousness by the apprehension of every one of these determinations as the Self, or by what was called earlier the *spiritual* attitude towards them.

ad (1) That the object as such presents itself to consciousness as something disappearing is the above-mentioned *return of the object into the Self.*

ad (2) *The alienation of self-consciousness* establishes "*thinghood.*" Because man equals self-consciousness, his alienated objective being or "*thinghood*" is equivalent to *alienated self-consciousness,* and "thinghood" is established by this alienation. ("Thinghood" is that which is *an object for him,* and an object for him is really only that which is an essential object, consequently his *objective* essence. And since it is not the real *man,* nor *nature*—man being *human nature*—who becomes as such a subject, but only an abstraction of man, self-consciousness, "thinghood" can only be *alienated self-consciousness.*) It is quite understandable that a living, natural being endowed with objective (i.e. material) faculties should have *real natural objects* of its being, and equally that its self-alienation should be the establishment of a *real,* objective world, but in the form of *externality,* as a world which does not belong to, and dominates, its being. There is nothing incomprehensible or mysterious about this. The converse, rather, would be mysterious. But it is equally clear that a self-consciousness, i.e. its alienation, can only establish "*thinghood,*" i.e. only an abstract thing, a thing created by abstraction and not a real thing. It is [XXVI] clear, moreover, that "thinghood" is totally lacking in *independence,* in *being, vis-à-vis* self-consciousness; it is a mere *construct* established by self-consciousness. And what is established is not self-confirming; it is the confirmation of the act of establishing, which for an instant, but only for an instant, fixes its energy as a product and *apparently* confers upon it the role of an independent, real being.

When real, corporeal *man,* with his feet firmly planted on the solid ground, inhaling and exhaling all the powers of nature, *posits* his real objective faculties, as a result of his alienation, as alien objects, the *positing* is not the subject of this act but the subjectivity of *objective* faculties whose action must also, therefore, be *objective.* An objective being acts objectively, and it would not act objectively if objectivity were not part of its essential being. It creates and establishes *only objects, because* it is established by objects, and because it is fundamentally *natural*. In the act of establishing it does not descend from its "pure activity" to the *creation of objects; its objective* product simply confirms its *objective* activity, its activity as an objective, natural being.

We see here how consistent naturalism or humanism is distinguished from both idealism and materialism, and at the same time constitutes their unifying truth. We see also that only naturalism is able to comprehend the process of world history.

Man is directly a *natural being*. As a natural being, and as a living natural being he is, on the one hand, endowed with *natural powers* and *faculties,* which exist in him as tendencies and abilities, as *drives*. On the other hand, as a natural, embodied, sentient, objective being he is a *suffering,* conditioned and limited being, like animals and plants. The *objects* of his drives exist outside himself as *objects* independent of him, yet they are *objects* of his *needs,* essential *objects* which are indispensable to the exercise and confirmation of his faculties. The fact that man is an *embodied,* living, real, sentient, objective being with natural powers, means that he has *real, sensuous objects* as the objects of his being, or that he can only express his being in real, sensuous objects. *To be* objective, natural, sentient and at the same time to have object, nature and sense outside oneself, or to be oneself object, nature and sense for a third person, is the same thing. *Hunger* is a natural *need;* it requires, therefore, a *nature* outside itself, an *object* outside itself, in order to be satisfied and stilled. Hunger is the objective need of a body for an *object* which exists outside itself and which is essential for its integration and the expression of its nature. The sun is an *object,* a necessary and life-assuring object, for the plant, just as the plant is an object for the sun, an *expression* of the sun's life-giving power and *objective* essential powers.

A being which does not have its nature outside itself is not a *natural* being and does not share in the being of nature. A being which has no object outside itself is not an objective being. A being which is not itself an object for a third being has no being for its *object,* i.e. it is not objectively related and its being is not objective.

[XXVII] A non-objective being is a *non-being*. Suppose a being which neither is an object itself nor has an object. In the first place, such a being would be the *only* being; no other being would exist outside itself and it would be solitary and alone. For as soon as there exist objects outside myself, as soon as I am not *alone,* I am *another,* another *reality* from the object outside me. For this third object I am thus an *other reality* than itself, i.e. *its object*. To suppose a being which is not the object of another being would be to suppose that *no* objective being exists. As soon as I have an object, this object has me for its object. But a *non-objective* being is an unreal, non-sensuous, merely conceived being; i.e. a merely imagined being, an abstraction. To be *sensuous,* i.e. real, is to be an object of sense or *sensuous* object, and thus to have sensuous objects outside oneself, objects of one's sensations. To be sentient is to *suffer* (to experience).

Man as an objective sentient being is a *suffering* being, and since he feels his suffering, a *passionate* being. Passion is man's faculties striving to attain their object.

But man is not merely a natural being; he is a *human* natural being. He is a being for himself, and, therefore, a *species-being;* and as such he has to express and authenticate himself in being as well as in thought. Consequently, *human* objects are not natural objects as they present themselves directly, nor is *human sense,* as it is immediately and objectively given, *human* sensibility and human objectivity. Neither objective nature nor subjective nature is directly presented in a form adequate to the *human* being. And as everything natural must have its *origin* so *man* has his process of genesis, *history,* which is for him, however, a conscious process and thus one which is consciously self-transcending. (We shall return to this point later.)

Thirdly, since this establishment of "thinghood" is itself only an appearance, an act which contradicts the nature of pure activity, it has to be annulled again and "thinghood" has to be denied.

ad 3, 4, 5, 6. (3) This alienation of consciousness has not only a negative but also a positive significance, and (4) it has this positive significance not only for us or in itself, but for consciousness itself. (5) For *consciousness* the negation of the object, or its annulling of itself by that means, has positive significance; it *knows* the nullity of the object by the fact that it alienates *itself,* for in this alienation it *knows* itself as the object or, for the sake of the indivisible unit of *being-for-itself,* knows the object as itself. (6) On the other hand, this other "moment" is equally present, but consciousness has superseded and reabsorbed this alienation and objectivity and is thus *at home in its other being as such.*

We have already seen that the appropriation of alienated objective being, or the supersession of objectivity in the form of *alienation* (which has to develop from indifferent otherness to real antagonistic alienation), signifies for Hegel also, or primarily, the supersession of *objectivity,* since it is not the determinate character of the object but its *objective* character which is the scandal of alienation for self-consciousness. The object is therefore negative, self-annulling, a *nullity.* This nullity of the object has a positive significance because it knows this nullity, objective being, as its *self-alienation,* and knows that this nullity exists only through its self-alienation. . . .

The way in which consciousness is, and in which something is for it, is *knowing.* Knowing is its only act. Thus something comes to exist for consciousness so far as it *knows* this *something.* Knowing is its only objective relation. It knows, then, the nullity of the object (i.e. knows the nonexistence of the distinction between itself and the object, the non-existence of the object for it) because it knows the object as its *self-alienation.* That is to say, it knows itself (knows knowing as an object), because the object is only the semblance of an object, a deception, which is intrinsically nothing but knowing itself which has confronted itself with itself, has established in face of itself a *nullity,* a "something" which has no objective existence outside the knowing itself. Knowing knows that in relating itself to an object it is only *outside* itself, alienates itself, and that *it* only *appears* to itself as an object; or in other words, that that which appears to it as an object is only itself.

On the other hand, Hegel says, this other "moment" is present at the same time; namely, that consciousness has equally superseded and reabsorbed this alienation and objectivity, and consequently is at *home in its other being as such.*

In this discussion all the illusions of speculation are assembled.

First, consciousness—self-consciousness—is *at home in its other being as such.* It is, therefore—if we abstract from Hegel's abstraction and substitute the self-consciousness of man for self-consciousness—*at home in its other being as such.* This implies, first, that consciousness (knowing as knowing, thinking as thinking) claims to be directly the *other* of itself, the sensuous world, reality, life; it is thought overreaching itself in thought (Feuerbach). This aspect is contained in it, in so far as consciousness as mere consciousness is offended not by the alienated objectivity but by *objectivity* as such.

Secondly, it implies that self-conscious man, in so far as he has recognized and superseded the spiritual world (or the universal spiritual mode of existence of his world) then confirms it again in this alienated form and presents it as his true existence; he reestablishes it and claims to *be at home in his other being.* Thus, for example, after superseding religion, when he has recognized religion as a product of self-alienation, he then finds a confirmation of himself in *religion as religion. This is* the root of Hegel's false positivism, or of his merely *apparent* criticism; what Feuerbach calls the positing, negation and re-establishment of religion or theology, but which has to be conceived in a more general way. Thus reason is at home in unreason as such. Man, who has recognized that he leads an alienated life in law, politics, etc. leads his true human life in this alienated life as such. Self-affirmation, in contradiction with itself, with the knowledge and the nature of the object, is thus the true *knowledge* and *life*.

There can no longer be any question about Hegel's compromise with religion, the state, etc., for this falsehood is the falsehood of his whole argument.

[XXIX] If I *know* religion as *alienated* human self-consciousness what I know in it as religion is not my self-consciousness but my alienated self-consciousness confirmed in it. Thus my own self, and the self-consciousness which is its essence, is not confirmed in *religion* but in the *abolition* and *supersession* of religion.

In Hegel, therefore, the negation of the negation is not the confirmation of true being by the negation of illusory being. It is the confirmation of illusory being, or of self-alienating being in its denial; or the denial of this illusory being as an objective being existing outside man and independently of him, and its transformation into a subject.

The act of *supersession* plays a strange part in which denial and preservation, denial and affirmation, are linked together. Thus, for example, in Hegel's *Philosophy of Right, private right* superseded equals *morality,* morality superseded equals the *family,* the family superseded equals *civil society,* civil society superseded equals the *state,* and the state superseded equals *world history.* But in *actuality* private right, morality, the family, civil society, the state, etc. remain; only they have become "moments," modes of existence of man, which have no validity in isolation but which mutually dissolve and engender one another. *They are "moments" of the movement.*

In their actual existence this mobile nature is concealed. It is first revealed in thought, in philosophy; consequently, my true religious existence is my existence in the *philosophy of religion,* my true political existence is my existence in the *philosophy of right,* my true natural existence is my existence in the *philosophy of nature,* my true artistic existence is my existence in the *philosophy of art,* and my true human existence is my existence in *philosophy.* In the same way, the true existence of religion, the state, nature and art, is the *philosophy* of religion, of the state, of nature, and of art. But if the philosophy of religion is the only true existence of religion I am only truly religious as a *philosopher of religion,* and I deny actual religious sentiment and the actual *religious* man. At the same time, however, I *confirm* them, partly in my own existence or in the alien existence with which I confront them (for this *is* only their philosophical expression), and partly in their own original form, since they are for me the merely *apparent* other being, allegories, the lineaments of their own true existence (i.e. of my *philosophical* existence) concealed by sensuous draperies.

In the same way, *quality* superseded equals *quantity,* quantity superseded equals *measure,* measure superseded equals *being,* being superseded equals *phenomenal being,* phenomenal being superseded equals *actuality,* actuality superseded equals the *concept,* the concept superseded equals *objectivity,* objectivity superseded equals the *absolute* idea, the absolute idea superseded equals *nature,* nature superseded equals *subjective* spirit, subjective spirit superseded equals *ethical* objective spirit, *ethical* spirit superseded equals *art,* art superseded equals *religion,* and religion superseded equals *absolute knowledge.*

On the other hand, this supersession is supersession of an entity of thought; thus, private property as *thought* is superseded in the *thought* of morality. And since thought imagines itself to be, without mediation, the other aspect of itself, namely *sensuous reality,* and takes its own action for *real, sensuous action,* this supersession in thought, which leaves its object in existence in the real world, believes itself to have really overcome it. On the other hand, since the object has now become for it a "moment" of thought, it is regarded in its real existence as a confirmation of thought, of self-consciousness, of abstraction.

[XXX] From the one aspect the existent which Hegel *supersedes* in philosophy is not therefore the *actual* religion, state or nature, but religion itself as an object of knowledge, i.e. *dogmatics;* and similarly with *jurisprudence, political science* and *natural science.* From this aspect, therefore, he stands in opposition both to the actual being and to the direct, non-philosophical science (or the non-philosophical *concepts*) of this being. Thus he contradicts the conventional conceptions.

From the other aspect, the religious man, etc. can find in Hegel his ultimate confirmation.

We have now to consider the *positive* moments of Hegel's dialectic, within the condition of alienation.

(a) Supersession as an objective movement which reabsorbs alienation into itself. This is the insight, expressed within alienation, into the *appropriation* of the objective being through the supersession of its alienation. It is the alienated insight into the *real objectification* of man, into the real appropriation of his objective being by the destruction of the *alienated* character of the objective world, by the annulment of its alienated mode of existence. In the same way, atheism as the annulment of God is the emergence of theoretical humanism, and communism as the annulment of private property is the vindication of real human life as man's property. The latter is also the emergence of practical humanism, for atheism is humanism mediated to itself by the annulment of religion, while communism is humanism mediated to itself by the annulment of private property. It is only by the supersession of this mediation (which is, however, a necessary pre-condition) that the self-originating *positive* humanism can appear.

But atheism and communism are not flight or abstraction from, nor loss of, the objective world which men have created by the objectification of their faculties. They are not an impoverished return to unnatural, primitive simplicity. They are rather the first real emergence, the genuine actualization, of man's nature as something real.

Thus Hegel, in so far as he sees the positive significance of the self-referring negation (though in an alienated mode) conceives man's self-estrangement, alienation of being, loss of objectivity and reality, as self-discovery, change of nature, objectification and realization. In short, Hegel conceives labour as man's *act of self-creation* (though in abstract terms); he grasps man's relation to himself as an alien being and the emergence of *species-consciousness* and *species-life* as the demonstration of his alien being.

(b) But in Hegel, apart from, or rather as a consequence of, the inversion we have already described, this act of genesis appears, in the first place, as one which is merely *formal,* because it is abstract, and because human nature itself is treated as merely *abstract, thinking nature,* as self-consciousness.

Secondly, because the conception is *formal* and *abstract* the annulment of alienation becomes a confirmation of alienation. For Hegel, this movement of *self-creation* and *self-objectification* in the form of *self-estrangement* is the *absolute* and hence final *expression of human life,* which has its end in itself, is at peace with itself and at one with its own nature.

This movement, in its abstract [XXXI] form as dialectic, is regarded therefore as *truly human life,* and since it is nevertheless an abstraction, an alienation of human life, it is regarded as a divine process and thus as the *divine process* of mankind; it is a process which man's abstract, pure, absolute being, as distinguished from himself, traverses.

Thirdly, this process must have a bearer, a subject; but the subject first emerges as a result. This result, the subject knowing itself as absolute self-consciousness, is therefore *God, absolute spirit, the self-knowing and self-manifesting idea*. Real man and real nature become mere predicates, symbols of this concealed unreal man and unreal nature. Subject and predicate have, therefore, an inverted relation to each other; *a mystical subject-object,* or a *subjectivity reaching beyond the object,* the *absolute subject* as a process of self-alienation and of return from alienation into itself, and at the same time of reabsorption of this alienation, the *subject* as this process; pure, *unceasing* revolving within itself.

First, the formal and abstract conception of man's act of self-creation or self-objectification.

Since Hegel equates man with self-consciousness, the alienated object, the alienated real being of man, is simply *consciousness,* merely the thought of alienation, its abstract and hence vacuous and unreal expression, the *negation.* The annulment of alienation is also, therefore, merely an abstract and vacuous annulment of this empty abstraction, the *negation of the negation.* The replete, living, sensuous, concrete activity of self-objectification is, therefore, reduced to a mere abstraction, *absolute negativity,* an abstraction which is then crystallized as such and is conceived as an independent activity, as activity itself. Since this so-called negativity is merely the *abstract, vacuous* form of that real living act, its content can only be a formal content produced by abstraction from all content. They are, therefore, general, abstract *forms of abstraction* which refer to any content and are thus neutral towards, and valid for, any content; forms of thought, logical forms which are detached from *real* spirit and *real* nature. (We shall expound later the *logical* content of absolute negativity.)

Hegel's positive achievement in his speculative logic is to show that the *determinate concepts,* the universal *fixed thought-forms,* in their independence from nature and spirit, are a necessary result of the general alienation of human nature and also of human thought; and to depict them as a whole as moments in the process of abstraction. For example, being superseded is essence, essence superseded is concept, the concept superseded is . . . the absolute idea. But what is the absolute idea? It must supersede itself if it does not want to traverse the whole process of abstraction again from the beginning and to rest content with being a totality of abstractions or a self-comprehending abstraction. But the self-comprehending abstraction knows itself to be nothing; it must abandon itself, the abstraction, and so arrives at an entity which is its exact opposite, *nature.* The whole *Logic* is therefore, a demonstration that abstract thought is nothing for itself, that the absolute idea is nothing for itself, that only *nature* is something.

[XXXII] The absolute idea, the *abstract* idea which *"regarded* from the aspect of its unity with itself, is *intuition"* (Hegel's *Encyclopaedia,* 3rd ed., p. 222), and which "in its own absolute truth *resolves* to let the moment of its particularity or of initial determination and other-being, the *immediate idea,* as its reflection, *emerge freely from itself as nature"* (ibid.); this whole idea which behaves in such a strange and fanciful way and which has given the Hegelians such terrible headaches is throughout nothing but *abstraction,* i.e. the abstract thinker. It is abstraction which, made wise by experience and enlightened about its own truth, resolves under various (false and still abstract) conditions to *abandon* itself, and to establish its other being, the particular, the determinate, in place of its self-absorption, non-being, universality and indeterminateness; and which resolves to let nature, which it concealed within itself only as an abstraction, as an entity of thought, *emerge freely from itself.* That is, it decides to forsake abstraction and to observe nature free from abstraction. The abstract idea, which without mediation becomes *intuition,* is nothing but abstract thought which abandons itself and decides for *intuition.* This whole transition from logic to the philosophy of nature is simply the transition from *abstracting* to *intuiting,* a transition which is extremely difficult for the abstract thinker to accomplish and which he therefore describes in such strange terms. The *mystical feeling* which drives the philosopher from abstract thinking to intuition is *ennui,* the longing for a content.

(Man alienated from himself is also the thinker alienated from his *being,* i.e. from his natural and human life. His thoughts are consequently spirits existing outside nature and man. In his *Logic* Hegel has imprisoned all these spirits together, and has conceived each of them first as negation, i.e. as *alienation of human* thought, and secondly as negation of the negation, i.e. as the supersession of this alienation and as the real expression of human thought. But since this negation of the negation is itself still confined within the alienation, it is in part a restoration of these fixed spiritual forms in their alienation, in part an immobilization in the final act, the act of self-reference, as the true being of these spiritual forms.* Further, in so far as this abstraction conceives itself, and experiences an increasing weariness of itself, there appears in Hegel an abandonment of abstract thought which moves solely in the sphere of thought, devoid of eyes, ears, teeth, everything, and a resolve to recognize *nature* as being and to go over to intuition.)

[XXXIII] But *nature* too, taken abstractly, for itself, and rigidly separated from man, is *nothing* for man. It goes without saying that the abstract thinker who has committed himself to intuition, intuits nature abstractly. As nature lay enclosed in the thinker in a form which was obscure and mysterious even to himself, as absolute idea, as an entity of thought, so in truth, when he let it emerge from himself it was still only *abstract nature,* nature as an *entity of thought,* but now with the significance that it is the other-being of thought, is real, intuited nature, distinguished from abstract thought. Or, to speak in human language, the abstract thinker discovers from intuiting nature that the entities which he thought to create out of nothing, out of pure abstraction, to create in the divine dialectic as the pure products of thought endlessly shuttling back and forth in itself and never regarding external reality, are simply *abstractions* from *natural characteristics.* The whole of nature, therefore, reiterates to him the logical abstractions, but in a sensuous, external form. He *analyses* nature and these abstractions again. His intuition of nature is, therefore, simply the act of confirmation of his abstraction from the intuition of nature; his conscious re-enactment of the process of generating his abstraction. Thus, for example, Time equals Negativity which refers to itself (loc. cit., p. 238). In the natural form, superseded Movement as Matter corresponds to superseded Becoming as Being. In the *natural* form Light is *Reflection-in-itself.* Body as *Moon* and *Comet* is the natural form of the antithesis which, according to the *Logic,* is on the one hand the *positive grounded upon itself,* and on the other hand, the *negative grounded upon itself.* The Earth is the *natural* form of the logical *ground,* as the negative unity of the antithesis, etc.

---

*That is, Hegel substitutes the act of abstraction revolving within itself, for these fixed abstractions. In so doing, he has first of all the merit of having indicated the source of all these inappropriate concepts which originally belonged to different philosophies, and of having brought them together and established the comprehensive range of abstractions, instead of some particular abstraction, as the object of criticism. We shall see later why Hegel separates thought from the *subject.* It is already clear, however, that if man is not human the expression of his nature cannot be human, and consequently thought itself could not be conceived as an expression of man's nature, as the expression of a human and natural subject, with eyes, ears, etc. living in society, in the world, and in nature.

Nature as nature, i.e. so far as it is sensuously distinguished from that secret sense concealed within it, nature separated and distinguished from these abstractions is *nothing* (a *nullity demonstrating its nullity*), is *devoid of sense,* or has only the sense of an external thing which has been superseded.

"In the finite-*teleological* view is to be found the correct premise that nature does not contain within itself the absolute purpose" (loc. cit., p. 225). Its purpose is the confirmation of abstraction. "Nature has shown itself to be the idea in the *form* of *other-being.* Since the idea is in this form the negative of itself, or *external to itself,* nature is not just relatively external *vis-à-vis* this idea, but *externality* constitutes the form in which it exists as nature" (loc. cit., p. 227).

Externality should not be understood here as the *self-externalizing world of sense,* open to the light and to man's senses. It has to be taken here in the sense of alienation, as error, a defect, that which ought not to be. For that which is true is still the idea. Nature is merely the form of its other-being. And since abstract thought is *being,* that which is external to it is by its nature a merely *external thing.* The abstract thinker recognizes at the same time that *sensuousness, externality* in contrast to thought which shuttles back and forth *within itself,* is the essence of nature. But at the same time he expresses this antithesis is such a way that this *externality* of nature, and its *contrast* with thought, appears as a deficiency, and that nature distinguished from abstraction appears as a deficient being. [XXXIV] A being which is deficient, not simply for me or in my eyes, but in itself, has something outside itself which it lacks. That is to say, its being is something other than itself. For the abstract thinker, nature must therefore supersede itself, because it is already posited by him as a potentially *superseded* being.

"*For us,* spirit has *nature as its premise,* being the truth of nature and thereby its *absolute primus.* In this truth nature has *vanished,* and spirit has surrendered itself as the idea which has attained being-for-itself, whose *object,* as well as the *subject,* is the *concept.* This identity is *absolute negativity,* for whereas in nature the concept has its perfect external objectivity, here its alienation has been superseded and the concept has become identical with itself. It is this identity only so far as it is a return from nature" (loc. cit., p. 392).

"*Revelation,* as the *abstract* idea, is unmediated transition to, the *coming-to-be* of, nature; as the revelation of the spirit, which is free, it is the establishment of nature as *its own* world, an establishment which, as reflection, is simultaneously the *presupposition* of the world as independently existing nature. Revelation in conception is the creation of nature as spirit's own being, in which it acquires the *affirmation* and *truth* of its freedom." "*The absolute is spirit;* this is the highest definition of the absolute."

MANIFESTO OF THE COMMUNIST PARTY
(in part)

A spectre is haunting Europe—the spectre of Communism. All the powers of old Europe have entered into a holy alliance to exorcise this spectre: Pope and Czar, Metternich and Guizot, French Radicals and German police spies.

Where is the party in opposition that has not been decried as communistic by its opponents in power? Where the opposition that has not hurled back the branding reproach of Communism against the more advanced opposition parties, as well as against its reactionary adversaries?

Two things result from this fact:

I. Communism is already acknowledged by all European powers to be itself a power.

II. It is high time that Communists should openly, in the face of the whole world, publish their views, their aims, their tendencies, and meet this nursery tale of the spectre of Communism with a manifesto of the party itself.

To this end, Communists of various nationalities have assembled in London and sketched the following manifesto, to be published in the English, French, German, Italian, Flemish, and Danish languages.

CHAPTER I: BOURGEOIS AND PROLETARIANS*

The History of all hitherto existing society** is the history of class struggles.

Freeman and slave, patrician and plebeian, lord and serf, guild-master*** and journeyman, in a word, oppressor and oppressed stood in constant opposition to one another, carried on an uninterrupted, now hidden, now open fight, a fight that each time ended either in a revolutionary reconstitution of society at large, or in the common ruin of the contending classes.

In the earlier epochs of history we find almost everywhere a complicated arrangement of society into various orders, a manifold gradation of social rank. In ancient Rome we have patricians, knights, plebeians, slaves; in the Middle Ages, feudal lords, vassals, guild-masters, journeymen, apprentices, serfs; in almost all of these classes, again, subordinate gradations.

The modern bourgeois society that has sprouted from the ruins of feudal society has not done away with class antagonisms. It has but established new classes, new conditions of oppression, new forms of struggle in place of the old ones.

Our epoch, the epoch of the bourgeoisie, possesses, however, this distinctive feature: it has simplified the class antagonisms. Society as a whole is more and more splitting up into two great hostile camps, into two great classes directly facing each other— bourgeoisie and proletariat.

From the serfs of the Middle Ages sprang the chartered burghers of the earliest towns. From these burgesses the first elements of the bourgeoisie were developed.

---

*By *bourgeoisie* is meant the class of modern capitalists, owners of the means of social production, and employers of wage labor; by *proletariat*, the class of modern wage laborers who, having no means of production of their own, are reduced to selling their labor power in order to live.

**That is, all *written* history. In 1837, the pre-history of society, the social organization existing previous to recorded history, was all but unknown. Since then Haxthausen discovered common ownership of land in Russia; Maurer proved it to be the social foundation from which all Teutonic races started in history, and, by and by, village communities were found to be, or to have been, the primitive form of society everywhere from India to Ireland. The inner organization of this primitive communistic society was laid bare, in its typical form, by Morgan's crowning discovery of the true nature of the *gens* and its relation to the *tribe*. With the dissolution of these primeval communities society begins to be differentiated into separate and finally antagonistic classes. I have attempted to retrace this process of dissolution in *The Origin of the Family, Private Property and the State*.

***[Guild-master, that is, a full member of a guild, a master within, not a head of a guild.]

The discovery of America, the rounding of the Cape, opened up fresh ground for the rising bourgeoisie. The East Indian and Chinese markets, the colonization of America, trade with the colonies, the increase in the means of exchange and in commodities generally, gave to commerce, to navigation, to industry, an impulse never before known, and thereby, to the revolutionary element in the tottering feudal society, a rapid development.

The feudal system of industry, in which industrial production was monopolized by closed guilds, now no longer sufficed for the growing wants of the new markets. The manufacturing system took its place. The guild-masters were pushed aside by the manufacturing middle class; division of labor between the different corporate guilds vanished in the face of division of labor in each single workshop.

Meantime the markets kept ever growing, the demand ever rising. Even manufacture no longer sufficed. Thereupon, steam and machinery revolutionized industrial production. The place of manufacture was taken by the giant, modern industry, the place of the industrial middle class, by industrial millionaires—the leaders of whole industrial armies, the modern bourgeois.

Modern industry has established the world market, for which the discovery of America paved the way. This market has given an immense development to commerce, to navigation, to communication by land. This development has, in its turn, reacted on the extension of industry; and in proportion as industry, commerce, navigation, railways extended, in the same proportion the bourgeoisie developed, increased its capital, and pushed into the background every class handed down from the Middle Ages.

We see, therefore, how the modern bourgeoisie is itself the product of a long course of development, of a series of revolutions in the modes of production and of exchange.

Each step in the development of the bourgeoisie was accompanied by a corresponding political advance of that class. An oppressed class under the sway of the feudal nobility, it became an armed and self-governing association in the medieval commune:* here independent urban republic (as in Italy and Germany); there, taxable "third estate" of the monarchy (as in France); afterwards, in the period of manufacture proper, serving either the semi-feudal or the absolute monarchy as a counterpoise against the nobility, and, in fact, cornerstone of the great monarchies in general. The bourgeoisie has at last, since the establishment of modern industry and of the world market, conquered for itself, in the modern representative state, exclusive political sway. The executive of the modern state is but a committee for managing the common affairs of the whole bourgeoisie.

The bourgeoisie has played a most revolutionary role in history.

The bourgeoisie, wherever it has got the upper hand, has put an end to all feudal, patriarchal, idyllic relations. It has pitilessly torn asunder the motley feudal ties that bound man to his "natural superiors," and has left no other bond between man and man than naked self-interest, than callous "cash payment." It has drowned the most heavenly ecstasies of religious fervor, of chivalrous enthusiasm, of philistine sentimentalism, in the icy water of egotistical calculation. It has resolved personal worth into exchange value, and in place of the numberless indefeasible chartered freedoms has set up that single, unconscionable freedom—Free Trade. In one word, for exploitation, veiled by

---

*"Commune" was the name taken in France by the nascent towns even before they had conquered from their feudal lords and masters local self-government and political rights as the "Third Estate." Generally speaking, for the economic development of the bourgeoisie, England is here taken as the typical country; for its political development, France.

religious and political illusions, it has substituted naked, shameless, direct, brutal exploitation.

The bourgeoisie has stripped of its halo every occupation hitherto honored and looked up to with reverent awe. It has converted the physician, the lawyer, the priest, the poet, the man of science, into its paid wage laborers.

The bourgeoisie has torn away from the family its sentimental veil, and has reduced the family relation to a mere money relation.

The bourgeoisie has disclosed how it came to pass that the brutal display of vigor in the Middle Ages which reactionaries so much admire found its fitting complement in the most slothful indolence. It has been the first to show what man's activity can bring about. It has accomplished wonders far surpassing Egyptian pyramids, Roman aqueducts, and Gothic cathedrals; it has conducted expeditions that put in the shade all former migrations of nations and crusades.

The bourgeoisie cannot exist without constantly revolutionizing the instruments of production, and thereby the relations of production, and with them the whole relations of society. Conservation of the old modes of production in unaltered form was, on the contrary, the first condition of existence for all earlier industrial classes. Constant revolutionizing of production, uninterrupted disturbance of all social conditions, everlasting uncertainty and agitation distinguish the bourgeois epoch from all earlier ones. All fixed, fast-frozen relations with their train of ancient and venerable prejudices and opinions are swept away; all new-formed ones become antiquated before they can ossify. All that is solid melts in air, all that is holy is profaned, and man is at last compelled to face with sober senses his real conditions of life and his relations with his kind.

The need of a constantly expanding market for its products chases the bourgeoisie over the whole surface of the globe. It must nestle everywhere, settle everywhere, establish connections everywhere.

The bourgeoisie has through its exploitation of the world market given a cosmopolitan character to production and consumption in every country. To the great chagrin of reactionaries it has drawn from under the feet of industry the national ground on which it stood. All old-established national industries have been destroyed or are daily being destroyed. They are dislodged by new industries whose introduction becomes a life and death question for all civilized nations; by industries that no longer work up indigenous raw material, but raw material drawn from the remotest zones; industries whose products are consumed, not only at home, but in every quarter of the globe. In place of the old wants, satisfied by the production of the country, we find new wants, requiring for their satisfaction the products of distant lands and climes. In place of the old local and national seclusion and self-sufficiency we have intercourse in every direction, universal interdependence of nations. And as in material, so also in intellectual production. The intellectual creations of individual nations become common property. National one-sidedness and narrow-mindedness become more and more impossible, and from the numerous national and local literatures there arises a world literature.

The bourgeoisie, by the rapid improvement of all instruments of production, by the immensely facilitated means of communication, draws all nations, even the most barbarian, into civilization. The cheap prices of its commodities are the heavy artillery with which it batters down all Chinese walls, with which it forces the barbarians' intensely obstinate hatred of foreigners to capitulate. It compels all nations, on pain of extinction, to adopt the bourgeois mode of production; it compels them to introduce what it calls civilization into their midst, i.e., to become bourgeois themselves. In a word, it creates a world after its own image.

The bourgeoisie has subjected the country to the rule of the towns. It has created enormous cities, has greatly increased the urban population as compared with the rural, and has thus rescued a considerable part of the population from the idiocy of rural life. Just as it has made the country dependent on the towns, so it has made barbarian and semi-barbarian countries dependent on the civilized ones, nations of peasants on nations of bourgeois, the East on the West.

More and more the bourgeoisie keeps doing away with the scattered state of the population, of the means of production, and of property. It has agglomerated population, centralized means of production, and has concentrated property in a few hands. The necessary consequence of this was political centralization. Independent, or but loosely connected provinces, with separate interests, laws, governments and systems of taxation, became lumped together into one nation, with one government, one code of laws, one national class interest, one frontier and one customs tariff.

The bourgeoisie during its rule of scarce one hundred years has created more massive and more colossal productive forces than have all preceding generations together. Subjection of nature's forces to man, machinery, application of chemistry to industry and agriculture, steam-navigation, railways, electric telegraphs, clearing of whole continents for cultivation, canalization of rivers, whole populations conjured out of the ground—what earlier century had even a presentiment that such productive forces slumbered in the lap of social labor?

We see, then, that the means of production and of exchange which served as the foundation for the growth of the bourgeoisie were generated in feudal society. At a certain stage in the development of these means of production and of exchange, the conditions under which feudal society produced and exchanged, the feudal organization of agriculture and manufacturing industry, in a word, the feudal relations of property became no longer compatible with the already developed productive forces; they became so many fetters. They had to be burst asunder; they were burst asunder.

Into their place stepped free competition, accompanied by a social and political constitution adapted to it, and by the economic and political sway of the bourgeois class.

A similar movement is going on before our own eyes. Modern bourgeois society with its relations of production, of exchange and of property, a society that has conjured up such gigantic means of production and of exchange, is like the sorcerer who is no longer able to control the powers of the nether world whom he has called up by his spells. For many a decade past the history of industry and commerce is but the history of the revolt of modern productive forces against modern conditions of production, against the property relations that are the conditions for the existence of the bourgeoisie and of its rule. It is enough to mention the commercial crises that by their periodical return put the existence of the entire bourgeois society on trial, each time more threateningly. In these crises a great part not only of the existing products, but also of the previously created productive forces, are periodically destroyed. In these crises there breaks out an epidemic that, in all earlier epochs, would have seemed an absurdity—the epidemic of over-production. Society suddenly finds itself put back into a state of momentary barbarism; it appears as if a famine, a universal war of devastation had cut off the supply of every means of subsistence; industry and commerce seem to be destroyed. And why? Because there is too much civilization, too much means of subsistence, too much industry, too much commerce. The productive forces at the disposal of society no longer tend to further the development of the conditions of bourgeois property; on the contrary, they have become too powerful for these conditions, by which they are fettered, and no sooner do they overcome these fetters than they bring disorder into the whole of bourgeois society, endanger the existence of bourgeois property. The conditions of bourgeois society are too narrow to comprise the wealth created by them. And how does the bourgeoisie get over these crises? On the one hand by enforced destruction of a mass of productive forces; on the other, by the conquest of new markets and by the more thorough exploitation of the old ones. That is to say, by paving the way for more extensive and more destructive crises, and by diminishing the means whereby crises are prevented.

The weapons with which the bourgeoisie felled feudalism to the ground are now turned against the bourgeoisie itself.

But not only has the bourgeoisie forged the weapons that bring death to itself; it has also called into existence the men who are to wield those weapons—the modern working class, the proletarians.

In proportion as the bourgeoisie, i.e., capital, is developed, in the same proportion is the proletariat, the modern working class, developed—a class of laborers, who live only so long as they find work, and who find work only so long as their labor increases capital. These laborers, who must sell themselves piecemeal, are a commodity like every other article of commerce, and are consequently exposed to all the vicissitudes of competition, to all the fluctuations of the market.

Owing to the extensive use of machinery and to division of labor, the work of the proletarians has lost all individual character, and, consequently all charm for the workman. He becomes an appendage of the machine, and it is only the most simple, most monotonous, and most easily acquired knack that is required of him. Hence, the cost of production of a workman is restricted almost entirely to the means of subsistence that he requires for his maintenance and for the propagation of his race. But the price of a commodity, and therefore also of labor, is equal to its cost of production. In proportion, therefore, as the repulsiveness of the work increases, the wage decreases. Nay more, in proportion the burden of toil also increases, whether by prolongation of the working hours, by increase of the work exacted in a given time, or by increased speed of the machinery, etc.

Modern industry has converted the little workshop of the patriarchal master into the great factory of the industrial capitalist. Masses of laborers, crowded into the factory, are organized like soldiers. As privates of the industrial army they are placed under the command of a perfect hierarchy of officers and sergeants. Not only are they slaves of the bourgeois class and of the bourgeois state; they are daily and hourly enslaved by the machine, by the overseer, and, above all, by the individual bourgeois manufacturer himself. The more openly this despotism proclaims gain to be its end and aim, the more petty, the more hateful, and the more embittering it is.

The less the skill and exertion of strength implied in manual labor—in other words, the more modern industry develops—the more is the labor of men superseded by that of women. Differences of age and sex have no longer any distinctive social validity for the working class. All are instruments of labor, more or less expensive to use, according to their age and sex.

No sooner has the laborer received his wages in cash, for the moment escaping exploitation by the manufacturer, than he is set upon by the other portions of the bourgeoisie—the landlord, the shopkeeper, the pawnbroker, etc.

The lower strata of the middle class—the small tradespeople, shopkeepers, and retired tradesmen generally, the handicraftsmen and peasants—all these sink gradually into the proletariat, partly because their diminutive capital does not suffice for the scale on which modern industry is carried on and is swamped in the competition with the large capitalists, partly because their specialized skill is rendered worthless by new methods of production. Thus the proletariat is recruited from all classes of the population.

The proletariat goes through various stages of development. With its birth begins its struggle with the bourgeoisie. At first the contest is carried on by individual laborers, then by the workpeople of a factory, then by the operatives of one trade, in one locality, against the individual bourgeois who directly exploits them. They direct their attacks not against the bourgeois conditions of production, but against the instruments of production themselves; they destroy imported wares that compete with their labor, they smash machinery to pieces, they set factories ablaze, they seek to restore by force the vanished status of the workman of the Middle Ages.

At this stage the laborers still form an incoherent mass scattered over the whole country, and broken up by their mutual competition. If anywhere they unite to form more compact bodies, this is not yet the consequence of their own active union, but of the union of the bourgeoisie, which class, in order to attain its own political ends, is compelled to set the whole proletariat in motion, and is, moreover, still able to do so for a time. At this stage, therefore, the proletarians do not fight their enemies, but the enemies of their enemies, the remnants of absolute monarchy, the landowners, the nonindustrial bourgeois, the petty bourgeoisie. Thus the whole historical movement is concentrated in the hands of the bourgeoisie; every victory so obtained is a victory for the bourgeoisie.

But with the development of industry the proletariat not only increases in number; it becomes concentrated in greater masses, its strength grows, and it feels that strength more. The various interests and conditions of life within the ranks of the proletariat are more and more equalized, in proportion as machinery obliterates all distinctions of labor and nearly everywhere reduces wages to the same low level. The growing competition among the bourgeois and the resulting commercial crises make the wages of the workers ever more fluctuating. The unceasing improvement of machinery, ever more rapidly developing, makes their livelihood more and more precarious; the collisions between individual workmen and individual bourgeois take more and more the character of collisions between two classes. Thereupon the workers begin to form combinations (trade unions) against the bourgeoisie; they club together in order to keep up the rate of wages; they found permanent associations in order to make provision beforehand for these occasional revolts. Here and there the contest breaks out into riots.

Now and then the workers are victorious, but only for a time. The real fruit of their battles lies not in the immediate result but in the ever expanding union of the workers. This union is furthered by the improved means of communication which are created by modern industry, and which place the workers of different localities in contact with one another. It was just this contact that was needed to centralize the numerous local struggles, all of the same character, into one national struggle between classes. But every class struggle is a political struggle. And that union, which the burghers of the Middle Ages, with their miserable highways, required centuries to attain, the modern proletarians, thanks to railways achieve in a few years.

This organization of the proletarians into a class, and consequently into a political party, is continually being upset again by the competition between the workers themselves. But it ever rises up again, stronger, firmer, mightier. It compels legislative recognition of particular interests of the workers by taking advantage of the divisions among the bourgeoisie itself. Thus the Ten Hour bill in England was carried.

Altogether, collisions between the classes of the old society further the course of development of the proletariat in many ways. The bourgeoisie finds itself involved in a constant battle—at first with the aristocracy; later on, with those portions of the bourgeoisie itself whose interests have become antagonistic to the progress of industry; at all times with the bourgeoisie of foreign countries. In all these battles it sees itself compelled to appeal to the proletariat, to ask for its help, and thus to drag it into the political arena. The bourgeoisie itself, therefore, supplies the proletariat with its own elements of political and general education; in other words, it furnishes the proletariat with weapons for fighting the bourgeoisie.

Further, as we have already seen, entire sections of the ruling classes are, by the advance of industry, precipitated into the proletariat, or are at least threatened in their conditions of existence. These also supply the proletariat with fresh elements of enlightenment and progress.

Finally, in times when the class struggle nears the decisive hour, the process of dissolution going on within the ruling class, in fact within the whole range of old society, assumes such a violent, glaring character that a small section of the ruling class cuts itself adrift and joins the revolutionary class, the class that holds the future in its hands. Just as, therefore, at an earlier period a section of the nobility went over to the bourgeoisie, so now a portion of the bourgeoisie goes over to the proletariat, and in particular, a portion of the bourgeois ideologists who have raised themselves to the level of comprehending theoretically the historical movement as a whole.

Of all the classes that stand face to face with the bourgeoisie today, the proletariat alone is a really revolutionary class. The other classes decay and finally disappear in the face of modern industry; the proletariat is its special and essential product.

The lower middle class, the small manufacturer, the shopkeeper, the artisan, the peasant—all these fight against the bourgeoisie, to save from extinction their existence as fractions of the middle class. They are, therefore, not revolutionary but conservative. Nay more, they are reactionary, for they try to roll back the wheel of history. If by chance they are revolutionary they are so only in view of their impending transfer into the proletariat; they thus defend not their present but their future interests; they desert their own standpoint to adopt that of the proletariat.

The "dangerous class," the social scum *[Lumpenproletariat]*, that passively rotting mass thrown off by the lowest layers of old society, may here and there be swept into the movement by a proletarian revolution; its conditions of life, however, prepare it far more for the part of a bribed tool of reactionary intrigue.

The social conditions of the old society no longer exist for the proletariat. The proletarian is without property; his relation to his wife and children has no longer anything in common with bourgeois family relations; modern industrial labor, modern subjection to capital, the same in England as in France, in America as in Germany, has stripped him of every trace of national character. Law, morality, religion are to him so many bourgeois prejudices, behind which lurk in ambush just as many bourgeois interests.

All the preceding classes that got the upper hand sought to fortify their already acquired status by subjecting society at large to their conditions of appropriation. The proletarians cannot become masters of the productive forces of society except by abolishing their own previous mode of appropriation, and thereby also every other previous mode of appropriation. They have nothing of their own to secure and to fortify; their mission is to destroy all previous securities for, and insurances of, individual property.

All previous historical movements were movements of minorities, or in the interest of minorities. The proletarian movement is the self-conscious, independent movement of the immense majority, in the interest of the immense majority. The proletariat, the lowest stratum of our present society, cannot stir, cannot raise itself up, without the whole superincumbent strata of official society being sprung into the air.

Though not in substance, yet in form, the struggle of the proletariat with the bourgeoisie is at first a national struggle. The proletariat of each country must, of course, first of all settle matters with its own bourgeoisie.

In depicting the most general phases of the development of the proletariat we traced the more or less veiled civil war raging within existing society, up to the point where that war breaks out into open revolution, and where the violent overthrow of the bourgeoisie lays the foundation for the sway of the proletariat.

Hitherto, every form of society has been based, as we have already seen, on the antagonism of oppressing and oppressed classes. But in order to oppress a class certain conditions must be assured to it under which it can, at least, continue its slavish existence. The serf, in the period of serfdom, raised himself to membership in the commune, just as the petty bourgeois, under the yoke of feudal absolutism, managed to develop into a bourgeois. The modern laborer, on the contrary, instead of rising with the progress of industry, sinks deeper and deeper below the conditions of existence of his own class. He becomes a pauper, and pauperism develops more rapidly than population and wealth. And here it becomes evident that the bourgeoisie is unfit any longer to be the ruling class in society and to impose its conditions of existence upon society as an overriding law. It is unfit to rule because it is incompetent to assure an existence to its slave within his slavery, because it cannot help letting him sink into such a state that it has to feed him, instead of being fed by him. Society can no longer live under this bourgeoisie, in other words, its existence is no longer compatible with society.

The essential condition for the existence and sway of the bourgeois class is the formation and augmentation of capital; the condition for capital is wage labor. Wage labor rests exclusively on competition between the laborers. The advance of industry, whose involuntary promoter is the bourgeoisie, replaces the isolation of the laborers, due to competition, by their revolutionary combination, due to association. The development of modern industry, therefore, cuts from under its feet the very foundation on which the bourgeoisie produces and appropriates products. What the bourgeoisie, therefore, produces above all are its own grave-diggers. Its fall and the victory of the proletariat are equally inevitable.

*   *   *

[The specific measures called for by the Communist Party] will, of course, be different in different countries.

Nevertheless, in the most advanced countries the following will be pretty generally applicable:

1. Abolition of property in land and application of all rents of land to public purposes.
2. A heavy progressive or graduated income tax.
3. Abolition of all right of inheritance.
4. Confiscation of the property of all emigrants and rebels.
5. Centralization of credit in the hands of the state by means of a national bank with state capital and an exclusive monopoly.
6. Centralization of the means of communication and transport in the hands of the state.
7. Extension of factories and instruments of production owned by the state; the bringing into cultivation of waste lands, and the improvement of the soil generally in accordance with a common plan.
8. Equal obligation of all to work. Establishment of industrial armies, especially for agriculture.

9. Combination of agriculture with manufacturing industries; gradual abolition of the distinction between town and country by a more equable distribution of the population over the country.

10. Free education for all children in public schools. Abolition of child factory labor in its present form. Combination of education with industrial production, etc.

*   *   *

CHAPTER IV: POSITION OF THE COMMUNISTS IN RELATION TO THE VARIOUS EXISTING OPPOSITION PARTIES

Section II has made clear the relations of the Communists to the existing working class parties, such as the Chartists in England and the Agrarian Reformers in America.

The Communists fight for the attainment of the immediate aims, for the enforcement of the momentary interests of the working class; but in the movement of the present they also represent and take care of the future of that movement. In France the Communists ally themselves with the Social-Democrats* against the conservative and radical bourgeoisie, reserving, however, the right to take up a critical position in regard to phrases and illusions traditionally handed down from the great Revolution.

In Switzerland they support the Radicals without losing sight of the fact that this party consists of antagonistic elements, partly of Democratic Socialists, in the French sense, partly of radical bourgeois.

In Poland they support the party that insists on an agrarian revolution as the prime condition for national emancipation, that party which fomented the insurrection of Cracow in 1846.

In Germany they fight with the bourgeoisie whenever it acts in a revolutionary way, against the absolute monarchy, the feudal squirearchy, and the petty bourgeoisie.

But they never cease for a single instant to instil into the working class the clearest possible recognition of the hostile antagonism between bourgeoisie and proletariat, in order that the German workers may straightway use, as so many weapons against the bourgeoisie, the social and political conditions that the bourgeoisie must necessarily introduce along with its supremacy, and in order that, after the fall of the reactionary classes in Germany, the fight against the bourgeoisie itself may immediately begin.

The Communists turn their attention chiefly to Germany because that country is on the eve of a bourgeois revolution that is bound to be carried out under more advanced conditions of European civilization and with a much more developed proletariat than what existed in England in the seventeenth and in France in the eighteenth century, and because the bourgeois revolution in Germany will be but the prelude to an immediately following proletarian revolution.

In short, the Communists everywhere support every revolutionary movement against the existing social and political order of things.

---

*The party then represented in Parliament by Ledru-Rollin, in literature by Louis Blanc, in the daily press by the *Réforme*. The name of Social-Democracy signifies, with these its inventors, a section of the Democratic or Republican Party more or less tinged with Socialism.

"Capital and Labour," cartoon from *Punch* magazine, 1843. The cartoon shows
the suffering of the workers and their families that makes possible the
bourgeois capitalists' high life. It was in response to conditions such as this that
Marx and Engels wrote in *The Communist Manifesto* (1848), "The proletarians
have nothing to lose but their chains. They have a world to win. Workingmen
of all countries, unite!"(*Library of Congress*)

In all these movements they bring to the front as the leading question in each case
the property question, no matter what its degree of development at the time.

Finally, they labor everywhere for the union and agreement of the democratic parties of all countries.

The Communists disdain to conceal their views and aims. They openly declare
that their ends can be attained only by the forcible overthrow of all existing social conditions. Let the ruling classes tremble at a Communist revolution. The proletarians have
nothing to lose but their chains. They have a world to win.

Workingmen of all countries, unite!

A CONTRIBUTION TO THE CRITIQUE
OF POLITICAL ECONOMY (in part)

Author's Preface

*   *   *

In the social production which men carry on they enter into definite relations that are indispensable and independent of their will; these relations of production correspond to a definite stage of development of their material powers of production. The sum total of these relations of production constitutes the economic structure of society—the real foundation, on which rise legal and political superstructures and to which correspond definite forms of social consciousness. The mode of production in material life determines the general character of the social, political and spiritual processes of life. It is not the consciousness of men that determines their existence, but, on the contrary, their social existence determines their consciousness. At a certain stage of their development, the material forces of production in society come in conflict with the existing relations of production, or—what is but a legal expression for the same thing—with the property relations within which they had been at work before. From forms of development of the forces of production these relations turn into their fetters. Then comes the period of social revolution. With the change of the economic foundation the entire immense superstructure is more or less rapidly transformed. In considering such transformations the distinction should always be made between the material transformation of the economic conditions of production which can be determined with the precision of natural science, and the legal, political, religious, aesthetic or philosophic—in short ideological forms in which men become conscious of this conflict and fight it out. Just as our opinion of an individual is not based on what he thinks of himself, so can we not judge of such a period of transformation by its own consciousness; on the contrary, this consciousness must rather be explained from the contradictions of material life, from the existing conflict between the social forces of production and the relations of production. No social order ever disappears before all the productive forces, for which there is room in it, have been developed; and new higher relations of production never appear before the material conditions of their existence have matured in the womb of the old society. Therefore, mankind always takes up only such problems as it can solve; since, looking at the matter more closely, we will always find that the problem itself arises only when the material conditions necessary for its solution already exist or are at least in the process of formation. In broad outlines we can designate the Asiatic, the ancient, the feudal, and the modern bourgeois methods of production as so many epochs in the progress of the economic formation of society. The bourgeois relations of production are the last antagonistic form of the social process of production—antagonistic not in the sense of individual antagonism, but of one arising from conditions surrounding the life of individuals in society; at the same time the productive forces developing in the womb of bourgeois society create the material conditions for the solution of that antagonism. This social formation constitutes, therefore, the closing chapter of the prehistoric stage of human society.

Friedrich Nietzsche
1844–1900

Friedrich Wilhelm Nietzsche was born in Röcken, Prussia, in 1844. He was named in honor of the Prussian king, Friedrich Wilhelm IV, whose birthday, October 15, he shared. Nietzsche's father, Ludwig Nietzsche, was a Lutheran minister and his mother, Franziska Oehler Nietzsche, was the daughter of a Lutheran minister. When Nietzsche was only five years old, his father died from what was then called "softening of the brain," after a year of mental instability. The rest of Nietzsche's childhood was spent in a household of women, including his widowed mother, his sister, his anxiety-prone paternal grandmother, and two maiden aunts.

Following grade school, Nietzsche attended a famous boarding school at Pforta, where he did outstanding work. However, while there, Nietzsche suffered migraine headaches, which continued to afflict him until he experienced a mental breakdown in 1889. The medicine he took to relieve the headaches would upset his stomach and leave him nauseous. For much of his adult life, he would alternate between the extremes of headaches and nausea with only short periods of health in between.

In 1864, he enrolled at the University of Bonn to study theology and classical philology (linguistics), but he left within a year. By this time, he had given up whatever religious faith he had had and was no longer interested in theology. He then moved to the University of Leipzig to continue his studies in philology. His professor at Leipzig, Friedrich Ritschl, was so impressed with Nietzsche's work that he published some of his papers and later recommended him for a chair of classical philology at the University of Basel. In 1869, at the unusual age of only twenty-four, Nietzsche was given the chair as an associate professor. He had produced neither a doctoral dissertation nor the additional book normally required of an associate professor, but Leipzig immediately awarded him a doctorate without examination or thesis and within a year he was promoted to full professor at Basel.

In 1872, Nietzsche published his first book, *The Birth of Tragedy,* which included a laudatory section on Richard Wagner's music. Over the next four years, Nietzsche wrote four meditations (published collectively in English as *Thoughts Out of Season*), the last of which was another tribute to Wagner. During this period, Nietzsche and Wagner were close friends; and Nietzsche often visited Wagner's villa on Lake Lucerne. But by 1878, they had broken relations over Wagner's nationalism and anti-Semitism.

Nietzsche's health began to deteriorate, and he was forced to resign from the university in 1879. Over the next ten years, Nietzsche traveled and devoted all his remaining energy to writing, publishing such books as *The Gay Science* (1882), *Thus Spoke Zarathustra* (1883–1885), *Beyond Good and Evil* (1886), *On the Genealogy of Morality* (1887), and his final denunciation of his former friend, *The Case of Wagner* (1888).

By the end of 1888, Nietzsche was showing signs of oncoming madness, and in January 1889 he collapsed in the street in Turin, Italy, while hugging the neck of a horse. For the next eleven years until his death in 1900, he lived in the care of his mother and sister. Works that he had written in 1888, including *The Will to Power, Twilight of the Idols, The Anti-Christ,* and his outrageous autobiography *Ecco Homo* (which includes chapter headings such as "Why I Am So Clever"), were published after distorted editing by his sister. Only in the twentieth century have unedited versions of these works become available.

The cause of Nietzsche's insanity has been vigorously debated. Critics have held that his ideas caused it and claim to have found evidence of insanity in many of his writings. His sister romanticized that he went mad because Germany spurned him. More likely explanations are that he contracted syphilis during a rare sexual escapade while a young man or that he simply inherited a brain disease from his father.

*   *   *

Nietzsche's style of writing in epigrams, aphorisms, stories, poetry, and essays virtually defies an editor to systematically summarize his thought. Even though Nietzsche never sought to build a system, there are recurring, interwoven themes represented by the selections given here.

In *The Birth of Tragedy,* translated by Francis Golffing, Nietzsche presents a distinction between Apollonian and Dionysian tendencies in art. The Apollonian tendency (named for the Greek god of the sun, Apollo) represents the harmony and restraint exemplified by Greek sculpture and architecture. The Dionysian tendency (named for the Greek god of wine and revelry, Dionysos) represents wild abandonment as exemplified by the drunken sexual frenzies of the Dionysian cult festivals or the music of Beethoven's Ninth Symphony. Greek tragedy arises as a synthesis of Apollonian form and Dionysian urges. But Greek tragedy is in turn superseded by Greek rationalism as exemplified by Socrates: the theoretical man who optimistically sees knowledge as the panacea to the problems of life. What is needed now, Nietzsche argues, is a new synthesis of these Dionysian and Apollonian tendencies by an "artistic" Socrates. Such a Socratic figure would be a creative genius who would honestly face the harshness of life without losing a clear rational analytic perspective.

In order to produce new values, such a creative genius must be free from all constraints, including moral constraints that would limit creativity by imposing "universal" standards. In the first essay of *On the Genealogy of Morality,* given here in the Carol Diethe translation, Nietzsche shows how such a limiting morality developed as he distinguishes between "master morality" and "slave morality." Master morality is basically affirmative and defines itself on its own terms. In this morality, "good" means that which is noble, powerful, and beautiful, and which belongs to the highest rank; and "bad" signifies that which is base, low-minded, and unworthy of greatness. On the other hand, slave morality is basically negative and claims to find values "out there," ordained by God or some other transcedent law-giver. It is born out of resentment and identifies the "good" with such base sentiments as humility and pity. Instead of "bad," this morality uses the vindictive term "evil" to castigate all who would stand against it. Nietzsche claims that beginning with the Jews, and completed by the Christians, this slave morality had infected all of Europe with its life-denying poison. What is now needed is a "transvaluation of all values," which would move us "beyond good and evil."

In affirming the master morality, the creative genius must begin by proclaiming the death of God. With the death of God, slave morality—and all values dependent on some external law-giver—collapses and the individual is free to create self-defined values. By the "death of God," Nietzsche does not mean that there once was a diety who got old and passed away, nor that people no longer should live holy lives. Rather, Nietzsche claims that all *absolutes* have collapsed and there is no transcendent basis in any area—whether religion, philosophy, science, or politics—for making meaning out of life. The brief selection here from *Thus Spoke Zarathustra,* translated by Walter Kaufmann, is one of several passages in which Nietzsche announces the death of God.

In our selection from *Twilight of the Idols,* also translated by Walter Kaufmann, Nietzsche examines how philosophers have tried to find something transcendent, something permanent. Beginning with the Pre-Socratic thinker Parmenides, philosophers have been unwilling to accept the actual transitory world of "becoming." Instead they have denigrated this world, labeling it "apparent," and have in its place invented an immutable world of "being." But, as Nietzsche explains, "Any distinction between a 'true' and an 'apparent' world—whether in the Christian manner or in the manner of Kant . . . is only a suggestion of decadence, a symptom of the *decline of life.*"

The genius who can embrace "becoming," who acknowledges the death of all external values, could become an *Übermensch* ("overman" or "superman"). Such an overman would be a this-world antithesis to God and would affirm life without any resentment. The overman would be to humans as humans are to apes. But, most important, the overman would be one who acknowledges and celebrates the *will to power.*

According to Nietzsche, all human behavior can be understood in terms of the will to power and every relationship between persons is a power relationship. In master morality, the hero asserts the will to power by taking direct action. In slave morality, as explained in our final selection from Walter Kaufmann's translation of *The Anti-Christ,* the will to power is perverted into resentment in order to gain the imaginary powers of revenge and pity.

But the will to power can also be expressed *within* the person. That is, more than gaining power over others, the will to power can lead to power over the self. The overman will be the one who uses power in this way to "overcome his animal nature, organize the chaos of his passions, sublimate his impulses, and give style to his character,"* becoming completely free and self-created.

Ironically, despite his distaste for anti-Semitism and his emphasis on the *self*-overcoming aspects of the will to power, Nietzsche was hailed as a hero by the Nazis. They used his emphases on the master morality and the will to power as a justification for their atrocities. Nietzsche's sister, Elisabeth, married a German anti-Semite and in her old age eagerly received Adolph Hitler at the Nietzsche Archives. Yet despite its unfortunate association with the Nazis, Nietzsche's thought has continued to be influential, as his insights have been developed by existentialists, phenomenologists, psychoanalysts, poststructuralists, and deconstructionists, as well as poets and novelists.

*   *   *

A representative sampling of Neitzsche's thought can be found in *The Portable Nietzsche,* edited by Walter A. Kaufmann (New York: Viking Press, 1968). The best general introduction to Nietzsche's thought remains Walter A. Kaufmann, *Nietzsche: Philosopher, Psychologist, Antichrist* (Princeton, NJ: Princeton University Press, 1968). Recent overviews include Richard Schacht, *Nietzsche* (London: Routledge, 1983); Alexander Nehamas, *Nietzsche: Life as Literature* (Cambridge, MA: Harvard University Press, 1985); Graham Parke, *Composing the Soul* (Chicago: University of Chicago Press, 1994); John Richardson, *Nietzsche's System* (Oxford: Oxford University Press, 1995); and Michael Tanner, *Nietzsche* (Oxford: Oxford University Press, 1995). Ivo Frenzel, *Friedrich Nietzsche: An Illustrated Biography,* translated by Joachim Neugroschel (New York: Pegasus, 1967); and Sander L. Gilman, ed., *Conversations with Nietzsche: A Life in the Words of His Contemporaries,* translated by David J. Parent (New York: Oxford University Press, 1987), provide general biographies, whereas H.F. Peters, *Zarathustra's Sister: The Case of Elisabeth and Friedrich Nietzsche* (New York: Crown, 1977), presents a fascinating history of the expropriation of Nietzsche's thought in the service of German anti-Semitism. Walter A. Kaufmann, *Nietzsche, Heidegger, and Buber* (New York: McGraw-Hill, 1980), and Allan Megill, *Prophets of Extremity: Nietzsche, Heidegger, Foucault, Derrida* (Berkeley: University of California Press, 1985) show the connections between Nietzsche and other important thinkers. For collections of critical essays, see Robert C. Solomon, ed., *Nietzsche: A Collection of Critical Essays* (Garden City, NY: Anchor Doubleday, 1973); and Richard Schacht, ed., *Nietzsche, Genealogy, Morality: Essays on Nietzsche's On the Geneality of Morals* (Berkeley: University of California Press, 1994). Harold Bloom, ed., *Friedrich Nietzsche* (New York: Chelsea House, 1987). Finally, Robert C. Solomon and Kathleen M. Higgins, eds., *Reading Nietzsche* (New York: Oxford University Press, 1988) provide helpful introductory essays on several of Nietzsche's works.

---

*Walter Kaufmann, *Nietzsche: Philosopher, Psychologist, Antichrist* (Princeton, NJ: Princeton University Press, 1950), p. 316.

THE BIRTH OF TRAGEDY (in part)

I

Much will have been gained for esthetics once we have succeeded in apprehending directly—rather than merely *ascertaining*—that art owes its continuous evolution to the Apollonian-Dionysiac duality, even as the propagation of the species depends on the duality of the sexes, their constant conflicts and periodic acts of reconciliation. I have borrowed my adjectives from the Greeks, who developed their mystical doctrines of art through plausible *embodiments,* not through purely conceptual means. It is by those two art-sponsoring deities, Apollo and Dionysos, that we are made to recognize the tremendous split, as regards both origins and objectives, between the plastic, Apollonian arts and the non-visual art of music inspired by Dionysos. The two creative tendencies developed alongside one another, usually in fierce opposition, each by its taunts forcing the other to more energetic production, both perpetuating in a discordant concord that agon which the term art but feebly denominates: until at last, by the thaumaturgy of an Hellenic act of will, the pair accepted the yoke of marriage and, in this condition, begot Attic tragedy, which exhibits the salient features of both parents.

To reach a closer understanding of both these tendencies, let us begin by viewing them as the separate art realms of *dream* and *intoxication,* two physiological phenomena standing toward one another in much the same relationship as the Apollonian and Dionysiac. It was in a dream, according to Lucretius, that the marvelous gods and goddesses first presented themselves to the minds of men. That great sculptor, Phidias, beheld in a dream the entrancing bodies of more-than-human beings, and likewise, if anyone had asked the Greek poets about the mystery of poetic creation, they too would have referred him to dreams and instructed him much as Hans Sachs instructs us in *Die Meistersinger:*

> My friend, it is the poet's work
> Dreams to interpret and to mark.
> Believe me that man's true conceit
> In a dream becomes complete:
> All poetry we ever read
> Is but true dreams interpreted.

The fair illusion of the dream sphere, in the production of which every man proves himself an accomplished artist, is a precondition not only of all plastic art, but even, as we shall see presently, of a wide range of poetry. Here we enjoy an immediate apprehension of form, all shapes speak to us directly, nothing seems indifferent or redundant. Despite the high intensity with which these dream realities exist for us, we still have a residual sensation that they are illusions; at least such has been my experience—and the frequency, not to say normality, of the experience is borne out in many passages of the poets. Men of philosophical disposition are known for their constant premonition that our everyday reality, too, is an illusion, hiding another, totally different kind of reality. It was Schopenhauer who considered the ability to view at certain times all men and things as mere phantoms or dream images to be the true mark of philosophic talent. The person who is responsive to the stimuli of art behaves toward the reality of dream much the way the philosopher behaves toward the reality of existence: he observes exactly and enjoys his observations, for it is by these images that he interprets life, by these processes that he rehearses it. Nor is it by pleasant images only that such plausible connections are made: the whole divine comedy of life, including its somber aspects, its sudden balkings, impish accidents, anxious expectations, moves past him, not quite like a shadow play—for it is he himself, after all, who lives and suffers through these scenes—yet never without giving a fleeting sense of illusion; and I imagine that many persons have reassured themselves amidst the perils of dream by calling out, "It is a dream! I want it to go on." I have even heard of people spinning out the causality of one and the same dream over three or more successive nights. All these facts clearly bear witness that our innermost being, the common substratum of humanity, experiences dreams with deep delight and a sense of real necessity. This deep and happy sense of the necessity of dream experiences was expressed by the Greeks in the image of Apollo. Apollo is at once the god of all plastic powers and the soothsaying god. He who is etymologically the "lucent" one, the god of light, reigns also over the fair illusion of our inner world of fantasy. The perfection of these conditions in contrast to our imperfectly understood waking reality, as well as our profound awareness of nature's healing powers during the interval of sleep and dream, furnishes a symbolic analogue to the soothsaying faculty and quite generally to the arts, which make life possible and worth living. But the image of Apollo must incorporate that thin line which the dream image may not cross, under penalty of becoming pathological, of imposing itself on us as crass reality: a discreet limitation, a freedom from all extravagant urges, the sapient tranquillity of the plastic god. His eye must be sunlike, in keeping with his origin. Even at those moments when he is angry and ill-tempered there lies upon him the consecration of fair illusion. In an eccentric way one might say of Apollo what Schopenhauer says, in the first part of *The World as Will and Idea,* of man caught in the veil of Maya: "Even as on an immense, raging sea, assailed by huge wave crests, a man sits in a little rowboat trusting his frail craft, so, amidst the furious torments of this world, the individual sits tranquilly, supported by the *principium individuationis* and relying on it." One might say that the unshakable confidence in that principle has received its most magnificent expression in Apollo, and that Apollo himself may be regarded as the marvelous divine image of the *principium individuationis,* whose looks and gestures radiate the full delight, wisdom, and beauty of "illusion."

In the same context Schopenhauer has described for us the tremendous awe which seizes man when he suddenly begins to doubt the cognitive modes of experience, in other words, when in a given instance the law of causation seems to suspend itself. If we add to this awe the glorious transport which arises in man, even from the very depths of nature, at the shattering of the *principium individuationis,* then we are in a position to apprehend the essence of Dionysiac rapture, whose closest analogy is furnished by physical intoxication. Dionysiac stirrings arise either through the influence of those narcotic potions of which all primitive races speak in their hymns, or through the powerful approach of spring, which penetrates with joy the whole frame of nature. So stirred, the individual forgets himself completely. It is the Same Dionysiac power which in medieval Germany drove ever increasing crowds of people singing and dancing from place to place; we recognize in these St. John's and St. Vitus' dancers the bacchic choruses of the Greeks, who had their precursors in Asia Minor and as far back as Babylon and the orgiastic Sacaea. There are people who, either from lack of experience or out of sheer stupidity, turn away from such phenomena, and, strong in the sense of their own sanity, label them either mockingly or pityingly "endemic diseases." These benighted souls have no idea how cadaverous and ghostly their "sanity" appears as the intense throng of Dionysiac revelers sweeps past them.

Not only does the bond between man and man come to be forged once more by the magic of the Dionysiac rite, but nature itself, long alienated or subjugated, rises again to celebrate the reconciliation with her prodigal son, man. The earth offers its gifts voluntarily, and the savage beasts of mountain and desert approach in peace. The chariot of Dionysos is bedecked with flowers and garlands; panthers and tigers stride beneath his yoke. If one were to convert Beethoven's "Paean to Joy" into a painting, and refuse to curb the imagination when that multitude prostrates itself reverently in the dust, one might form some apprehension of Dionysiac ritual. Now the slave emerges as a freeman; all the rigid, hostile walls which either necessity or despotism has erected between men are shattered. Now that the gospel of universal harmony is sounded, each individual becomes not only reconciled to his fellow but actually at one with him—as though the veil of Maya had been torn apart and there remained only shreds floating before the vision of mystical Oneness. Man now expresses himself through song and

Starry Night, 1889, by Vincent Van Gogh (1853–1890). It is hard not to think of the paintings of Nietzsche's contemporary Vincent Van Gogh when reading Nietzsche's words: "If one were to convert Beethoven's 'Paean to Joy' into a painting, and refuse to curb the imagination when that multitude prostrates itself reverently in the dust, one might form some apprehension of Dionysiac ritual." (*Museum of Modern Art, New York*)

dance as the member of a higher community; he has forgotten how to walk, how to speak, and is on the brink of taking wing as he dances. Each of his gestures betokens enchantment; through him sounds a supernatural power, the same power which makes the animals speak and the earth render up milk and honey. He feels himself to be godlike and strides with the same elation and ecstasy as the gods he has seen in his dreams. No longer the *artist,* he has himself become a *work of art: the productive power of the whole universe is now manifest in his transport, to the glorious satisfaction of the primordial One. The finest clay, the most precious marble—man—is here kneaded and hewn, and the chisel blows of the Dionysiac world artist* are accompanied by the cry of the Eleusinian mystagogues: "Do you fall on your knees, multitudes, do you divine your creator?"

II

So far we have examined the Apollonian and Dionysiac states as the product of formative forces arising directly from nature without the mediation of the human artist. At this stage artistic urges are satisfied directly, on the one hand through the imagery of dreams, whose perfection is quite independent of the intellectual rank, the artistic development of the individual; on the other hand, through an ecstatic reality which once again takes no account of the individual and may even destroy him, or else redeem him through a mystical experience of the collective. In relation to these immediate creative conditions of nature every artist must appear as "imitator," either as the Apollonian dream artist or the Dionysiac ecstatic artist, or, finally (as in Greek tragedy, for example) as dream and ecstatic artist in one. We might picture to ourselves how the last of these, in a state of Dionysiac intoxication and mystical self-abrogation, wandering apart from the reveling throng, sinks upon the ground, and how there is then revealed to him his own condition—complete oneness with the essence of the universe—in a dream similitude.

Having set down these general premises and distinctions, we now turn to the Greeks in order to realize to what degree the formative forces of nature were developed in them. Such an inquiry will enable us to assess properly the relation of the Greek artist to his prototypes or, to use Aristotle's expression, his "imitation of nature." Of the dreams the Greeks dreamed it is not possible to speak with any certainty, despite the extant dream literature and the large number of dream anecdotes. But considering the incredible accuracy of their eyes, their keen and unabashed delight in colors, one can hardly be wrong in assuming that their dreams too showed a strict consequence of lines and contours, hues and groupings, a progression of scenes similar to their best bas-reliefs. The perfection of these dream scenes might almost tempt us to consider the dreaming Greek as a Homer and Homer as a dreaming Greek; which would be as though the modern man were to compare himself in his dreaming to Shakespeare.

Yet there is another point about which we do not have to conjecture at all: I mean the profound gap separating the Dionysiac Greeks from the Dionysiac barbarians. Throughout the range of ancient civilization (leaving the newer civilizations out of account for the moment) we find evidence of Dionysiac celebrations which stand to the Greek type in much the same relation as the bearded satyr, whose name and attributes are derived from the he-goat, stands to the god Dionysos. The central concern of such celebrations was, almost universally, a complete sexual promiscuity overriding every form of established tribal law; all the savage urges of the mind were unleashed on those occasions until they reached that paroxysm of lust and cruelty which has always struck me as the "witches' cauldron" *par excellence*. It would appear that the Greeks were for a while quite immune from these feverish excesses which must have reached them by every known land or sea route. What kept Greece safe was the proud, imposing image of Apollo, who in holding up the head of the Gorgon to those brutal and grotesque Dionysiac forces subdued them. Doric art has immortalized Apollo's majestic rejection of all license. But resistance became difficult, even impossible, as soon as similar urges began to break forth from the deep substratum of Hellenism itself. Soon the function of the Delphic god developed into something quite different and much more limited: all he could hope to accomplish now was to wrest the destructive weapon, by a timely gesture of pacification, from his opponent's hand. That act of pacification represents the most important event in the history of Greek ritual; every department of life now shows symptoms of a revolutionary change. The two great antagonists have been reconciled. Each feels obliged henceforth to keep to his bounds, each will honor the other by the bestowal of periodic gifts, while the cleavage remains fundamentally the same. And yet, if we examine what happened to the Dionysiac powers under the pressure of that treaty we notice a great difference: in the place of the Babylonian Sacaea, with their throwback of men to the condition of apes and tigers, we now see entirely new rites celebrated: rites of universal redemption, of glorious transfiguration. Only now has it become possible to speak of nature's celebrating an aesthetic triumph; only now has the abrogation of the principium individuationis become an aesthetic event. That terrible witches' brew concocted of lust and cruelty has lost all power under the new conditions. Yet the peculiar blending of emotions in the heart of the Dionysiac reveler—his ambiguity if you will—seems still to hark back (as the medicinal drug harks back to the deadly poison) to the days when the infliction of pain was experienced as joy while a sense of supreme triumph elicited cries of anguish from the heart. For now in every exuberant joy there is heard an undertone of terror, or else a wistful lament over an irrecoverable loss. It is as though in these Greek festivals a sentimental trait of nature were coming to the fore, as though nature were bemoaning the fact of her fragmentation, her decomposition into separate individuals. The chants and gestures of these revelers, so ambiguous in their motivation, represented an absolute *novum* in the world of the Homeric Greeks; their Dionysiac music, in especial, spread abroad terror and a deep shudder. It is true: music had long been familiar to the Greeks as an Apollonian art, as a regular beat like that of waves lapping the shore, a plastic rhythm expressly developed for the portrayal of Apollonian conditions. Apollo's music was a Doric architecture of sound—of barely hinted sounds such as are proper to the cithara. Those very elements which characterize Dionysiac music and, after it, music quite generally: the heart-shaking power of tone, the uniform stream of melody, the incomparable resources of harmony—all those elements had been carefully kept at a distance as being inconsonant with the Apollonian norm. In the Dionysiac dithyramb man is incited to strain his symbolic faculties to the utmost; something quite unheard of is now clamoring to be heard: the desire to tear asunder the veil of Maya, to sink back into the original oneness of nature; the desire to express the very essence of nature symbolically. Thus an entirely new set of symbols springs into being. First all the symbols pertaining to physical features: mouth, face, the spoken word, the dance movement which coordinates the limbs and bends them to its rhythm. Then suddenly all the rest of the symbolic forces—music and rhythm as such, dynamics, harmony—assert themselves with great energy. In order to comprehend this total emancipation of all the symbolic powers one must have reached the same measure of inner freedom those powers themselves were making manifest; which is to say that the votary of Dionysos could not be understood except by his own kind. It is not difficult to imagine the awed surprise with which the Apollonian Greek must have looked on him. And that surprise would be further increased as the latter realized, with a shudder, that all this was not so alien to him after all, that his Apollonian consciousness was but a thin veil hiding from him the whole Dionysiac realm.

III

In order to comprehend this we must take down the elaborate edifice of Apollonian culture stone by stone until we discover its foundations. At first the eye is struck by the marvelous shapes of the Olympian gods who stand upon its pediments, and whose exploits, in shining bas-relief, adorn its friezes. The fact that among them we find Apollo as one god among many, making no claim to a privileged position, should not mislead us. The same drive that found its most complete representation in Apollo generated the whole Olympian world, and in this sense we may consider Apollo the father of that world. But what was the radical need out of which that illustrious society of Olympian beings sprang?

Whoever approaches the Olympians with a different religion in his heart, seeking moral elevation, sanctity, spirituality, loving-kindness, will presently be forced to turn away from them in ill-humored disappointment. Nothing in these deities reminds us of asceticism, high intellect, or duty: we are confronted by luxuriant, triumphant *existence,* which deifies the good and the bad indifferently. And the beholder may find himself dismayed in the presence of such overflowing life and ask himself what potion these heady people must have drunk in order to behold, in whatever direction they looked, Helen laughing back at them, the beguiling image of their own existence. But we shall call out to this beholder, who has already turned his back: Don't go! Listen first to what the Greeks themselves have to say of this life, which spreads itself before you with such puzzling serenity. An old legend has it that King Midas hunted a long time in the woods for the wise Silenus, companion of Dionysos, without being able to catch him. When he had finally caught him the king asked him what he considered man's greatest good. The daemon remained sullen and uncommunicative until finally, forced by the king, he broke into a shrill laugh and spoke: "Ephemeral wretch, begotten by accident and toil, why do you force me to tell you what it would be your greatest boon not to hear? What would be best for you is quite beyond your reach: not to have been born, not to be, to be *nothing.* But the second best is to die soon."

What is the relation of the Olympian gods to this popular wisdom? It is that of the entranced vision of the martyr to his torment.

Now the Olympian magic mountain opens itself before us, showing us its very roots. The Greeks were keenly aware of the terrors and horrors of existence; in order to be able to live at all they had to place before them the shining fantasy of the Olympians. Their tremendous distrust of the titanic forces of nature: *Moira,* mercilessly enthroned beyond the knowable world; the vulture which fed upon the great philanthropist Prometheus; the terrible lot drawn by wise Oedipus; the curse on the house of Atreus which brought Orestes to the murder of his mother: that whole Panic philosophy, in short, with its mythic examples, by which the gloomy Etruscans perished, the Greeks conquered—or at least hid from view—again and again by means of this artificial Olympus. In order to live at all the Greeks had to construct these deities. The Apollonian need for beauty had to develop the Olympian hierarchy of joy by slow degrees from the original titanic hierarchy of terror, as roses are seen to break from a thorny thicket. How else could life have been borne by a race so hypersensitive, so emotionally intense, so equipped for suffering? The same drive which called art into being as a completion and consummation of existence, and as a guarantee of further existence, gave rise also to that Olympian realm which acted as a transfiguring mirror to the Hellenic will. The gods justified human life by living it themselves—the only satisfactory theodicy ever invented. To exist in the clear sunlight of such deities was now felt to be the highest good, and the only real grief suffered by Homeric man was inspired by the thought of leaving that sunlight, especially when the departure seemed imminent. Now it became possible to stand the wisdom of Silenus on its head and proclaim that it was the worst evil for man to die soon, and second worst for him to die at all. Such laments as arise now arise over short-lived Achilles, over the generations ephemeral as leaves, the decline of the heroic age. It is not unbecoming to even the greatest hero to yearn for an afterlife, though it be as a day laborer. So impetuously, during the Apollonian phase, does man's will desire to remain on earth, so identified does he become with existence, that even his lament turns to a song of praise.

It should have become apparent by now that the harmony with nature which we late-comers regard with such nostalgia, and for which Schiller has coined the cant term naive, is by no means a simple and inevitable condition to be found at the gateway to every culture, a kind of paradise. Such a belief could have been endorsed only by a period for which Rousseau's Emile was an artist and Homer just such an artist nurtured in the bosom of nature. Whenever we encounter "naïveté" in art, we are face to face with the ripest fruit of Apollonian culture—which must always triumph first over titans, kill monsters, and overcome the somber contemplation of actuality, the intense susceptibility to suffering, by means of illusions strenuously and zestfully entertained. But how rare are the instances of true naïveté, of that complete identification with the beauty of appearance! It is this achievement which makes Homer so magnificent—Homer, who, as a single individual, stood to Apollonian popular culture in the same relation as the individual dream artist to the oneiric capacity of a race and of nature generally. The naïveté of Homer must be viewed as a complete victory of Apollonian illusion. Nature often uses illusions of this sort in order to accomplish its secret purposes. The true goal is covered over by a phantasm. We stretch out our hands to the latter, while nature, aided by our deception, attains the former. In the case of the Greeks it was the will wishing to behold itself in the work of art, in the transcendence of genius; but in order so to behold itself its creatures had first to view themselves as glorious, to transpose themselves to a higher sphere, without having that sphere of pure contemplation either challenge them or upbraid them with insufficiency. It was in that sphere of beauty that the Greeks saw the Olympians as their mirror images; it was by means of that aesthetic mirror that the Greek will opposed suffering and the somber wisdom of suffering which always accompanies artisic talent. As a monument to its victory stands Homer, the naive artist.

*   *   *

XV

. . . The influence of Socrates (like a shadow cast by the evening sun, ever lengthening into the future) has prompted generation after generation to reconsider the foundations of its art—art taken in its deepest and broadest sense—and as that influence is eternal it also guarantees the eternity of artistic endeavor. But before people were able to realize that all art is intimately dependent on the Greeks from Homer to Socrates, they had necessarily toward the Greeks the same attitude that the Athenians had toward Socrates. Practically every era of Western civilization has at one time or another tried to liberate itself from the Greeks, in deep dissatisfaction because whatever they themselves achieved, seemingly quite original and sincerely admired, lost color and life when held against the Greek model and shrank to a botched copy, a caricature. Time and again a hearty anger has been felt against that presumptuous little nation which had the nerve to brand, for all time, whatever was not created on its own soil as "barbaric." Who are these people, whose historical splendor was ephemeral, their institutions ridiculously narrow, their mores dubious and sometimes objectionable, who yet pretend to the special place among the nations which genius claims among the crowd? None of the later detractors was fortunate enough to find the cup of hemlock with which such a being could be disposed of once and for all: all the poisons of envy, slander, and rage have proved insufficient to destroy that complacent magnificence. And so people have continued to be both ashamed and fearful of the Greeks—though now and again someone has come along who has acknowledged the full truth: that the Greeks are the chariot drivers of every subsequent culture, but that, almost always, chariot and horses are of too poor a quality for the drivers, who then make sport of driving the chariot into the abyss—which they themselves clear with the bold leap of Achilles.

In order to see Socrates as one of these charioteers, it is necessary only to view him as the prototype of an entirely new mode of existence. He is the great exemplar of that theoretical man whose significance and aims we must now attempt to understand. Like the artist, *theoretical* man takes infinite pleasure in all that exists and is thus saved from the practical ethics of pessimism, with its lynx eyes that shine only in the dark. But while the artist, having unveiled the truth garment by garment, remains with his gaze fixed on what is still hidden, theoretical man takes delight in the cast garments and finds his highest satisfaction in the unveiling process itself, which proves to him his own power. Science could not have developed as it has done if its sole concern had been that one naked goddess. For then the adepts of science would have felt like people trying to dig a hole through the earth, each of whom soon realizes that though he toil in lifelong labor he will excavate only an infinitesimal fraction of the great distance and that even this fraction will be covered over before his eyes by another's efforts, so that a third man would do well to find a new spot for his tunneling. Moreover, once it has been proved beyond question that the Antipodes can never be reached by such a direct method, what person in his right mind would want to go on digging—unless it were for the accidental benefit of striking some precious metal or hitting upon a law of nature? For this reason Lessing, most honest of theoretical men, dared to say that the search for truth was more important to him than truth itself and thereby revealed the innermost secret of inquiry, to the surprise and annoyance of his fellows. Yet, sure enough, alongside sporadic perceptions such as this one of Lessing's, which represented an act of honesty as well as high-spirited defiance, we find a type of deep-seated illusion, first manifested in Socrates: the illusion that thought, guided by the thread of causation, might plumb the farthest abysses of being and even *correct* it. This grand metaphysical illusion has become integral to the scientific endeavor and again and again leads science to those far limits of its inquiry where it becomes art—*which, in this mechanism, is what is really intended.*

If we examine Socrates in the light of this idea, he strikes us as the first who was able not only to live under the guidance of that instinctive scientific certainty but to die by it, which is much more difficult. For this reason the image of the dying Socrates—

mortal man freed by knowledge and argument from the fear of death—is the emblem which, hanging above the portal of every science, reminds the adept that his mission is to make existence appear intelligible and thereby justified. If arguments prove insufficient, the element of myth may be used to strengthen them—that myth which I have described as the necessary consequence, and ultimate intention, of all science.

Once we have fully realized how, after Socrates, the mystagogue of science, one school of philosophers after another came upon the scene and departed; how generation after generation of inquirers, spurred by an insatiable thirst for knowledge, explored every aspect of the universe; and how by that ecumenical concern a common net of knowledge was spread over the whole globe, affording glimpses into the workings of an entire solar system—once we have realized all this, and the monumental pyramid of present-day knowledge, we cannot help viewing Socrates as the vortex and turning point of Western civilization. For if we imagine that immense store of energy used, not for the purposes of knowledge, but for the practical, egotistical ends of individuals and nations, we may readily see the consequence: universal wars of extermination and constant migrations of peoples would have weakened man's instinctive zest for life to such an extent that, suicide having become a matter of course, duty might have commanded the son to kill his parents, the friend his friend, as among the Fiji islanders. We know that such wholesale slaughter prevails wherever art in some form or other—especially as religion or science—has not served as antidote to barbarism.

As against this practical pessimism, Socrates represents the archetype of the theoretical optimist, who, strong in the belief that nature can be fathomed, considers knowledge to be the true panacea and error to be radical evil. To Socratic man the one noble and truly human occupation was that of laying bare the workings of nature, of separating true knowledge from illusion and error. So it happened that ever since Socrates the mechanism of concepts, judgments, and syllogisms has come to be regarded as the highest exercise of man's powers, nature's most admirable gift. Socrates and his successors, down to our own day, have considered all moral and sentimental accomplishments—noble deeds, compassion, self-sacrifice, heroism, even that spiritual calm, so difficult of attainment, which the Apollonian Greek called *sophrosyne*—to be ultimately derived from the dialectic of knowledge, and therefore teachable. Whoever has tasted the delight of a Socratic perception, experienced how it moves to encompass the whole world of phenomena in ever widening circles, knows no sharper incentive to life than his desire to complete the conquest, to weave the net absolutely tight. To such a person the Platonic Socrates appears as the teacher of an entirely new form of "Greek serenity" and affirmation. This positive attitude toward existence must release itself in actions for the most part pedagogic, exercised upon noble youths, to the end of producing genius. But science, spurred on by its energetic notions, approaches irresistibly those outer limits where the optimism implicit in logic must collapse. For the periphery of science has an infinite number of points. Every noble and gifted man has, before reaching the mid-point of his career, come up against some point of the periphery that defied his understanding, quite apart from the fact that we have no way of knowing how the area of the circle is ever to be fully charted. When the inquirer, having pushed to the circumference, realizes how logic in that place curls about itself and bites its own tail, he is struck with a new kind of perception: a tragic perception, which requires, to make it tolerable, the remedy of art.

If we look about us today, with eyes refreshed and fortified by the spectacle of the Greeks, we shall see how the insatiable zest for knowledge, prefigured in Socrates, has been transformed into tragic resignation and the need for art; while, to be sure, on a lower level that same zest appears as hostile to all art and especially to the truly tragic,

Dionysiac art, as I have tried to show paradigmatically in the subversion of Aeschylean art by Socratism.

At this point we find ourselves, not without trepidation, knocking at the gates of present and future. Will this dialectic inversion lead to ever new configurations of genius, above all to that of Socrates as the practitioner of music? Will the all-encompassing net of art (whether under the name of religion or science) be woven ever more tightly and delicately? Or will it be torn to shreds by the restless and barbaric activities of our present day? Deeply concerned, yet not unhopeful, we stand aside for a little while as spectators privileged to witness these tremendous struggles and transitions. Alas, it is the spell inherent in such battles that he who watches them must also fight them.

*   *   *

XXV

Music and tragic myth are equally expressive of the Dionysiac talent of a nation and cannot be divorced from one another. Both have their origin in a realm of art which lies beyond the Apollonian; both shed their transfiguring light on a region in whose rapt harmony dissonance and the horror of existence fade away in enchantment. Confident of their supreme powers, they both toy with the sting of displeasure, and by their toying they both justify the existence of even the "worst possible world." Thus the Dionysiac element, as against the Apollonian, proves itself to be the eternal and original power of art, since it calls into being the entire world of phenomena. Yet in the midst of that world a new transfiguring light is needed to catch and hold in life the stream of individual forms. If we could imagine an incarnation of dissonance—and what is man if not that?—that dissonance, in order to endure life, would need a marvelous illusion to cover it with a veil of beauty. This is the proper artistic intention of Apollo, in whose name are gathered together all those countless illusions of fair semblance which at any moment make life worth living and whet our appetite for the next moment.

But only so much of the Dionysiac substratum of the universe may enter an individual consciousness as can be dealt with by that Apollonian transfiguration; so that these two prime agencies must develop in strict proportion, conformable to the laws of eternal justice. Whenever the Dionysiac forces become too obstreperous, as is the case today, we are safe in assuming that Apollo is close at hand, though wrapped in a cloud, and that the rich effects of his beauty will be witnessed by a later generation.

The reader may intuit these effects if he has ever, though only in a dream, been carried back to the ancient Hellenic way of life. Walking beneath high Ionic peristyles, looking toward a horizon defined by pure and noble lines, seeing on either hand the glorified reflections of his shape in gleaming marble and all about him men moving solemnly or delicately, with harmonious sounds and rhythmic gestures: would he not then, overwhelmed by this steady stream of beauty, be forced to raise his hands to Apollo and call out: "Blessed Greeks! how great must be your Dionysos, if the Delic god thinks such enchantments necessary to cure you of your dithyrambic madness!" To one so moved, an ancient Athenian with the august countenance of Aeschylus might reply: "But you should add, extraordinary stranger, what suffering must this race have endured in order to achieve such beauty! Now come with me to the tragedy and let us sacrifice in the temple of both gods."

ON THE GENEALOGY OF MORALITY
(in part)

"GOOD AND EVIL," "GOOD AND BAD"

1

—These English psychologists, who have to be thanked for having made the only attempts so far to write a history of the emergence of morality,—provide us with a small riddle in the form of themselves; in fact, I admit that as living riddles they have a significant advantage over their books—*they are actually interesting!* These English psychologists—just what do they want? You always find them at the same task, whether they want to or not, pushing the *partie honteuse* of our inner world to the foreground, and looking for what is really effective, guiding and decisive for our development where man's intellectual pride would least wish to find it (for example, in the *vis inertiae* of habit, or in forgetfulness, or in a blind and random coupling of ideas, or in something purely passive, automatic, reflexive, molecular and thoroughly stupid)—what is it that actually drives these psychologists in precisely *this* direction all the time? Is it a secret, malicious, mean instinct to belittle man, which is perhaps unacknowledged? Or perhaps a pessimistic suspicion, the mistrust of disillusioned, surly idealists who have turned poisonous and green? Or a certain subterranean animosity and *rancune* towards Christianity (and Plato), which has perhaps not even passed the threshold of the consciousness? Or even a lewd taste for the strange, for the painful paradox, for the dubious and nonsensical in life? Or finally—a bit of everything, a bit of meanness, a bit of gloominess, a bit of anti-Christianity, a bit of a thrill and need for pepper? . . . But people tell me that they are just old, cold, boring frogs crawling round men and hopping into them as if they were in their element, namely a *swamp*. I am resistant to hearing this and, indeed, I do not believe it; and if it is permissible to wish where it is impossible to know, I sincerely hope that the reverse is true,—that these analysts holding a microscope to the soul are actually brave, generous and proud animals, who know how to control their own pleasure and pain and have been taught to sacrifice desirability to truth, every truth, even a plain, bitter, ugly, foul, unchristian, immoral truth . . . Because there are such truths.

2

So you have to respect the good spirits which preside in these historians of morality! But it is unfortunately a fact that *historical spirit* itself is lacking in them, they have been left in the lurch by all the good spirits of history itself! As is now established philo-

On the Genealogy of Morality, first essay: "Good and Evil," "Good and Bad" (complete), translated by Carol Diethe from Friedrich Nietzsche, *On the Genealogy of Morality,* edited by Keith Ansell-Pearson (Cambridge: Cambridge University Press, 1994). Reprinted by permission of Cambridge University Press.

sophical practice, they all think in a way that is *essentially* unhistorical; this can't be doubted. The idiocy of their moral genealogy is revealed at the outset when it is a question of conveying the descent of the concept and judgment of "good." "Originally"—they decree—"unegoistic acts were praised and called good by their recipients, in other words, by the people to whom they were *useful;* later, everyone *forgot* the origin of the praise and because such acts had always been *routinely* praised as good, people began also to experience them as good—as if they were something good *as such*." We can see at once: this first deduction contains all the typical traits of idiosyncratic English psychologists, we have "usefulness," "forgetting," "routine" and finally "error," all as the basis of a respect for values of which the higher man has hitherto been proud, as though it were a sort of general privilege of mankind. This pride *must be* humbled, this valuation devalued: has that been achieved? . . . Now for me, it is obvious that the real breeding-ground for the concept "good" has been sought and located in the wrong place by this theory: the judgment "good" does *not* emanate from those to whom goodness is shown! Instead it has been "the good" themselves, meaning the noble, the mighty, the high-placed and the high-minded, who saw and judged themselves and their actions as good, I mean first-rate, in contrast to everything lowly, low-minded, common and plebeian. It was from this *pathos of distance* that they first claimed the right to create values and give these values names: usefulness was none of their concern! The standpoint of usefulness is as alien and inappropriate as it can be to such a heated eruption of the highest rank-ordering and rank-defining value judgments: this is the point where feeling reaches the opposite of the low temperatures needed for any calculation of prudence or reckoning of usefulness,—and not just for once, for one exceptional moment, but permanently. The pathos of nobility and distance, as I said, the continuing and predominant feeling of complete and fundamental superiority of a higher ruling kind in relation to a lower kind, to those "below"—that is the origin of the antithesis "good" and "bad." (The seigneurial privilege of giving names even allows us to conceive of the origin of language itself as a manifestation of the power of the rulers: they say "this is so and so," they set their seal on everything and every occurrence with a sound and thereby take possession of it, as it were.) It is because of this origin that the word "good" is *not* absolutely necessarily attached to "unegoistic" actions: as the superstition of these moral genealogists would have it. On the contrary, it is only with a *decline* of aristocratic value-judgments that this whole antithesis between "egoistic" and "unegoistic" forces itself more and more on man's conscience,—it is, to use my language, the *herd instinct* which, with that, finally gets its word in (and makes *words*). And even then it takes long enough for this instinct to become sufficiently dominant for the valuation of moral values to become enmeshed and embedded in the antithesis (as is the case in contemporary Europe, for example: the prejudice which takes "moral," "unegoistic" and *"desinteresse"* as equivalent terms already rules with the power of a "fixed idea" and mental illness).

3

But secondly: quite apart from the fact that that hypothesis about the descent of the value judgment "good" is historically untenable, it also suffers from an inner psychological contradiction. The usefulness of unegoistic behaviour is supposed to be the origin of the esteem in which it is held, and this origin is supposed to have been *forgot-*

ten:—but how was such forgetting *possible?* Did the usefulness of such behaviour suddenly cease at some point? The opposite is the case: it is that this usefulness has been a permanent part of our everyday experience, something, then, which has been constantly stressed anew; consequently, instead of fading from consciousness, instead of becoming forgettable, it must have impressed itself on consciousness with ever greater clarity. How much more sensible is the opposite theory (that doesn't make it any more true—), which is held, for example, by Herbert Spencer: he judges the concept "good" as essentially the same as "useful," "practical," so that in their judgments "good" and "bad," people sum up and sanction their *unforgotten, unforgettable* experiences of what is useful-practical, harmful impractical. According to this theory, good is what has always shown itself to be useful: so it can claim validity as "valuable in the highest degree," as "valuable as such." This route towards an explanation is wrong, as I said, but at least the explanation in itself is rational and psychologically tenable.

4

—I was given a pointer in the *right* direction by the question as to what the terms for "good," as used in different languages, mean from the etymological point of view: then I found that they all led me back to the *same conceptual transformation,*— that everywhere, "noble," "aristocratic" in social terms is the basic concept from which, necessarily, "good" in the sense of "spiritually noble," "aristocratic," of "spiritually highminded," "spiritually privileged" developed: a development which always runs parallel with that other one which ultimately transfers "common," "plebeian," "low" into the concept "bad." The best example for the latter is the German word *"schlecht"* (bad) itself which is identical with *"schlicht"* (plain, simple)—compare *"schlechtweg"* (plainly), *"schlechterdings"* (simply)—which originally referred to the simple, the common man with no derogatory implication, but simply in contrast to the nobility. Round about the time of the Thirty Years War, late enough, then, this meaning shifted into its current usage. To me, this seems an *essential* insight into moral genealogy; that it has been discovered so late is due to the obstructing influence which the democratic bias within the modern world exercises over all questions of descent. And this is the case in the apparently most objective of fields, natural science and physiology, which I shall just allude to here. The havoc this prejudice can wreak, once it is unbridled to the point of hatred, particularly for morality and history, can be seen in the famous case of Buckle; the *plebeianism* of the modern spirit, which began in England, broke out there once again on its native soil as violently as a volcano of mud and with that salted, overloud, vulgar loquacity with which all volcanoes have spoken up till now.—

5

With regard to *our* problem, which can justifiably be called a *quiet* problem and which fastidiously addresses itself to only a few ears, it is of no little interest to discover that, in these words and roots which denote "good," we can often detect the main nuance which made the noble feel they were men of higher rank. True, in most cases they might give themselves names which simply show superiority of power (such as "the mighty," "the masters," "the commanders") or the most visible sign of this superiority, such as "the rich," "the propertied" (that is the meaning of *arya;* and the equivalent in Iranian and Slavic). But the names also show a *typical character trait:* and this is what concerns us here. For example, they call themselves "the truthful": led by the Greek aristocracy, whose mouthpiece is the Megarian poet Theognis. The word used specifically for this purpose, ⟨*esthlos*⟩*, means, according to its root, one who *is,* who has reality, who really exists and is true; then, with a subjective transformation, it becomes the slogan and catch-phrase of the aristocracy and is completely assimilated with the sense of "aristocratic," in contrast to the *deceitful* common man, as taken and shown by Theognis,—until, finally, with the decline of the aristocracy, the word remains as a term for spiritual *noblesse,* and, as it were, ripens and sweetens. Cowardice is underlined in the word ⟨*kakos*⟩ [weak, ugly, cowardly, worthless] and in ⟨*deilos*⟩ [cowardly (and thus despicable)] (the plebeian in contrast to the ⟨*agathos*⟩: perhaps this gives a clue as to where we should look for the etymological derivation of the ambiguous term ⟨*agathos*⟩ [capable, useful, good]. In the Latin word *malus* [bad, evil] (to which I juxtapose ⟨*melas*⟩ [dark, black]) the common man could be characterized as the dark-skinned and especially the dark-haired man ("hic niger est—")**, as the pre-Aryan occupant of Italian soil who could most easily be distinguished from the blond race which had become dominant, namely the Aryan conquering race, by its colour; at any rate, I have found exactly the same with Gaelic peoples,—fin (for example in Fin-gal), the word designating the aristocracy and finally the good, noble, pure, was originally a blond person in contrast to the dark-skinned, dark-haired native inhabitants. By the way, the Celts were a completely blond race; it is wrong to connect those traces of an essentially dark-haired population, which can be seen on carefully prepared ethnological maps in Germany, with any Celtic descent and mixing of blood in such a connection, as Virchow does: it is more a case of the *pre-Aryan* population of Germany emerging at these points. (The same holds good for virtually the whole of Europe: to all intents and purposes the subject race has ended up by regaining the upper hand in skin colour, shortness of forehead and perhaps even in intellectual and social instincts: who can give any guarantee that modern democracy, the even more modern anarchism, and indeed that predilection for the "commune," the most primitive form of social structure which is common to all Europe's socialists, are not in essence a huge *counter-attack*— and that the conquering *master race,* that of the Aryans, is not physiologically being defeated as well? . . .) I think I can interpret the Latin *bonus* [good] as "the 'warrior'": providing I am correct in tracing *bonus* back to an older *duonus* (compare *bellum**** = *duellum* = *duen-lum,* which seems to me to contain that *duonus*). Therefore *bonus* as a man of war, of division *(duo),* as warrior: one can see what made up a man's "goodness" in ancient Rome. Take our German *"gut"*: does it not mean "the godlike man," the man "of godlike race"? And is it not identical with the popular (originally noble), name of the Goths. The grounds for this supposition will not be gone into here.

---

*[This word seems originally to have meant "genuine, real"; it later becomes one of the most commonly used words for "noble."]

**["That man is a dangerous character," literally "He is black." (Horace, *Satires* I, 85.)]

***[Both "bellum" and "duellum" mean "war" in Latin.]

6

If the highest caste is at the same time the *clerical* caste and therefore chooses a title for its overall description which calls its priestly function to mind, this does not yet constitute an exception to the rule that the concept of political superiority always resolves itself into the concept of psychological superiority (although this may be the occasion giving rise to exceptions). This is an example of the first juxtaposition of "pure" and "impure" as signs of different estates; and later "good" and "bad" develop in a direction which no longer refers to social standing. In addition, people should be wary of taking these terms "pure" and "impure" too seriously, too far or even symbolically: all ancient man's concepts were originally understood—to a degree we can scarcely imagine—as crude, coarse, detached, narrow, direct and in particular *unsymbolic*. From the outset the "pure man" was just a man who washed, avoided certain foods which cause skin complaints, did not sleep with the filthy women from the lower orders and had a horror of blood,—nothing more, not much more! And yet the very nature of an essentially priestly aristocracy shows how contradictory valuations could become dangerously internalized and sharpened, precisely in such an aristocracy at an early stage; and in fact clefts were finally driven between man and man which even an Achilles of free-thinking would shudder to cross. From the very beginning there has been something *unhealthy* about these priestly aristocracies and in the customs dominant there, which are turned away from action and which are partly brooding and partly emotionally explosive, resulting in the almost inevitable bowel complaints and neurasthenia which have plagued the clergy down the ages; but as for the remedy they themselves found for their sickness,—surely one must say that its after-effects have shown it to be a hundred times more dangerous than the disease it was meant to cure? People are still ill from the after-effects of these priestly quack-cures! For example, think of certain diets (avoidance of meat), of fasting, sexual abstinence, the flight "into the desert" (Wier-Mitchell's bed-rest, admittedly without the subsequent overfeeding and weight-gain which constitute the most effective antidote to all hysteria brought on by the ascetic ideal): think, too, of the whole metaphysics of the clergy, which is antagonistic towards the senses, making men lazy and refined, think, too, of their Fakir-like and Brahmin-like self-hypnotizing—Brahminism as crystal ball and fixed idea—and the final, all-too-comprehensible general disenchantment with its radical cure, *nothingness* (or God:—the yearning for a *unio mystica* with God is the Buddhist yearning for nothingness, Nirvâna—and no more!) Priests make *everything* more dangerous, not just medicaments and healing arts but pride, revenge, acumen, debauchery, love, lust for power, virtue, sickness;—in any case, with some justification one could add that man first became an *interesting animal* on the foundation of this *essentially dangerous* form of human existence, the priest, and that the human soul became *deep* in the higher sense and turned *evil* for the first time—and of course, these are the two basic forms of man's superiority, hitherto, over other animals! . . .

7

—You will have already guessed how easy it was for the priestly method of valuation to split off from the chivalric-aristocratic method and then to develop further into the opposite of the latter; this receives a special impetus when the priestly caste and warrior caste confront one another in jealousy and cannot agree on the prize of war. The chivalric-aristocratic value-judgments are based on a powerful physicality, a blossoming, rich, even effervescent good health which includes the things needed to maintain it, war, adventure, hunting, dancing, jousting and everything else that contains strong, free, happy action. The priestly-aristocratic method of valuation—as we have seen—has different criteria: woe betide it when it comes to war! As we know, priests make the most *evil enemies*—but why? Because they are the most powerless. Out of this powerlessness, their hate swells into something huge and uncanny to a most intellectual and poisonous level. The greatest haters in world history, and the most intelligent *[die geistreichsten Hasser]*, have always been priests:—nobody else's intelligence *[Geist]* stands a chance against the intelligence *[Geist]* of priestly revenge.*) The history of mankind would be far too stupid a thing if it had not had the intellect *[Geist]* of the powerless injected into it:—let us take the best example straight away. Nothing which has been done on earth against "the noble," "the mighty," "the masters" and "the rulers," is worth mentioning compared with what *the Jews* have done against them: the Jews, that priestly people, which in the last resort was able to gain satisfaction from its enemies and conquerors only through a radical revaluation of their values, that is, through an act of the most deliberate revenge. Only this was fitting for a priestly people with the most entrenched priestly vengefulness. It was the Jews who, rejecting the aristocratic value equation (good = noble = powerful = beautiful = happy = blessed) ventured, with awe-inspiring consistency, to bring about a reversal and held it in the teeth of their unfathomable hatred (the hatred of the powerless), saying, "Only those who suffer are good, only the poor, the powerless, the lowly are good; the suffering, the deprived, the sick, the ugly, are the only pious people, the only ones saved, salvation is for them alone, whereas you rich, the noble and powerful, you are eternally wicked, cruel, lustful, insatiate, godless, you will also be eternally wretched, cursed and damned!" . . . We know who became heir to this Jewish revaluation . . . With regard to the huge and incalculably disastrous initiative taken by the Jews with this most fundamental of all declarations of war, I recall the words I wrote on another occasion *[Beyond Good and Evil]*—namely, that *the slaves' revolt in morality* begins with the Jews: a revolt which has two thousand years of history behind it and which has only been lost sight of because—it was victorious . . .

8

—But you don't understand that? You don't have eyes for something which needed two millennia to achieve victory? . . . There is nothing surprising about that: all *long* things are difficult to see, to see round. But *that* is what happened: from the trunk of the tree of revenge and hatred, Jewish hatred—the deepest and most sublime, indeed a hatred which created ideals and changed values, the like of which has never been seen on earth—there grew something just as incomparable, a *new love,* the deepest and most sublime kind of love: and what other trunk could it have grown out of? . . . But don't make the mistake of thinking that it had grown forth, as a denial of the thirst for re-

*[The German term *Geist* and its derivatives are generally rendered by "spirit" and its derivatives, but can also, as in this sentence, be translated as "intelligence" and, as elsewhere, "mind," "intellectual," etc.—translator's note.]

venge, as the opposite of Jewish hatred! No, the reverse is true! This love grew out of the hatred, as its crown, as the triumphant crown expanding ever wider in the purest brightness and radiance of the sun, the crown which, as it were, in the realm of light and height, was pursuing the aims of that hatred, victory, spoils, seduction with the same urgency with which the roots of that hatred were burrowing ever more thoroughly and greedily into everything that was deep and evil. This Jesus of Nazareth, as the embodiment of the gospel of love, this "redeemer" bringing salvation and victory to the poor, the sick, to sinners—was he not seduction in its most sinister and irresistible form, seduction and the circuitous route to just those very *Jewish* values and innovative ideals? Did Israel not reach the pinnacle of her sublime vengefulness via this very "redeemer," this apparent opponent of and disperser of Israel? Is it not part of a secret black art of a truly *great* politics of revenge, a far-sighted, subterranean revenge, slow to grip and calculating, that Israel had to denounce her actual instrument of revenge before all the world as a mortal enemy and nail him to the cross so that "all the world," namely all Israel's enemies, could safely nibble at this bait? And could anyone, on the other hand, using all the ingenuity of his intellect, think up a more *dangerous* bait? Something to equal the enticing, intoxicating, benumbing, corrupting power of that symbol of the "holy cross," to equal that horrible paradox of a "God on the Cross," to equal that mystery of an unthinkable final act of extreme cruelty and self crucifixion of God for the *salvation of mankind?* . . . At least it is certain that *sub hoc signo** Israel, with its revenge and revaluation of all former values, has triumphed repeatedly over all other ideals, all *nobler* ideals.—

9

—"But why do you talk about *nobler* ideals! Let's bow to the facts: the people have won—or 'the slaves', the 'plebeians,' 'the herd,' or whatever you want to call them—if the Jews made this come about, good for them! No people ever had a more world-historic mission. 'The Masters' are deposed; the morality of the common people has triumphed. You might take this victory for blood-poisoning (it did mix the races up)—I do not deny it; but undoubtedly this intoxication has *succeeded*. The 'salvation' of the human race (I mean, from 'the Masters') is well on course; everything is being made appreciably Jewish, Christian or plebeian (never mind the words!). The passage of this poison through the whole body of mankind seems unstoppable, even though its tempo and pace, from now on, might tend to be slower, softer, quieter, calmer—there is no hurry . . . With this in view, does the church still have a vital role, indeed, does it have a right to exist? Or could one do without it? *Quaeritur* [That is the question]. It seems that the Church rather slows down and blocks the passage of poison instead of accelerating it? Well, that might be what makes it useful . . . Certainly it is by now crude and boorish, something which is repugnant to a more tender intellect, to a truly modern taste. Should not the church at least try to be more refined? . . . Nowadays it alienates, more than it seduces . . . Who amongst us would be a freethinker if it were not for the Church? We loathe the Church, *not* its poison . . . Apart from the Church, we too love

---

*[The Emperor Constantine once had a vision of a cross with the attached legend: "By this, conquer." This phrase was eventually transformed into the Latin: "In hoc signo vinces" ("In this sign you will conquer"). "Sub hoc signo" ("Under this sign) is presumably to be understood as a variant of "In hoc signo."]

the poison . . ."–This is the epilogue by a "free-thinker" to my speech, an honest animal as he clearly shows himself to be, and moreover a democrat; he had listened to me up to that point, and could not stand listening to my silence. As a matter of fact, there is much for me to keep silent about at this point.—

10

The beginning of the slaves' revolt in morality occurs when *ressentiment* itself turns creative and gives birth to values: the *ressentiment* of those beings who, being denied the proper response of action, compensate for it only with imaginary revenge. Whereas all noble morality grows out of a triumphant saying "yes" to itself, slave morality says "no" on principle to everything that is "outside," "other," "non-self": and *this* "no" is its creative deed. This reversal of the evaluating glance—this *inevitable* orientation to the outside instead of back onto itself—is a feature of *ressentiment:* in order to come about, slave morality first has to have an opposing, external world, it needs, physiologically speaking, external stimuli in order to act at all,—its action is basically a reaction. The opposite is the case with the noble method of valuation: this acts and grows spontaneously, seeking out its opposite only so that it can say "yes" to itself even more thankfully and exultantly,—its negative concept "low," "common," "bad" is only a pale contrast created after the event compared to its positive basic concept, saturated with life and passion, "We the noble, the good, the beautiful and the happy!" When the noble method of valuation makes a mistake and sins against reality, this happens in relation to the sphere with which it is *not* sufficiently familiar, a true knowledge of which it has indeed rigidly resisted: in some circumstances, it misjudges the sphere it despises, that of the common man, the rabble; on the other hand, we should bear in mind that the distortion which results from the feeling of contempt, disdain and superciliousness, always assuming that the image of the despised person is *distorted,* remains far behind the distortion with which the entrenched hatred and revenge of the powerless man attacks his opponent—in effigy of course. Indeed, contempt has too much negligence, nonchalance, complacency and impatience, even too much personal cheerfulness mixed into it, for it to be in a position to transform its object into a real caricature and monster. Nor should one fail to hear the almost kindly nuances which the Greek nobility, for example, places in all words which it uses to distinguish itself from the rabble; a sort of sympathy, consideration and indulgence incessantly permeates and sugars them, with the result that nearly all words referring to the common man remain as expressions for "unhappy," "pitiable" (compare ⟨*deilos*⟩ [timid, fearful], ⟨*deilaios*⟩ [timidity], ⟨*ponêros*⟩ [bad, wicked, slothful], ⟨*moxthâros*⟩ [wearisome labor, toil], the last two actually designating the common man as slave worker and beast of burden)—and on the other hand, "bad," "low" and "unhappy" have never ceased to reverberate in the Greek ear in a tone in which "unhappy" predominates: this is a legacy of the old, nobler, aristocratic method of valuation, which does not deny itself even in contempt (philologists will remember the sense in which ⟨*oizuros*⟩ [to have pain], ⟨*anolbos*⟩ [not prosperous, unfortunate], ⟨*tlêmon*⟩ [one who endures or suffers], ⟨*dustuxein*⟩ [one who has bad luck], ⟨*tsumphora*⟩ [accident, misfortune] are used). The "well-born" felt they were "the happy"; they did not need first of all to construct their happiness artificially by looking at their enemies, or in some cases by talking themselves into it, *lying themselves into it* (as all men of *ressentiment* are wont to do); and also, as complete men bursting with strength and therefore *necessarily* active, they knew they must not separate happiness from action,—being active is by necessity counted as part of happiness (this is the etymological derivation of ⟨*eu prattein*⟩ [do well]—all very much the opposite of "happiness" at the level of the powerless, the oppressed, and those rankled with poisonous and hostile feelings, for whom it manifests itself as essentially a narcotic, an anaesthetic, rest, peace, "sabbath," relaxation of the mind and stretching of the limbs, in short as something *passive*. While the noble man is confident and frank with himself (⟨*gennaios*⟩, "of noble birth," underlines the nuance "upright" and probably "naive" as well), the man of *ressentiment* is neither upright nor naive, nor honest and straight with himself. His soul *squints;* his mind loves dark corners, secret paths and back-doors, everything secretive appeals to him as being *his* world, *his* security, *his* comfort; he knows all about keeping quiet, not forgetting, waiting, temporarily humbling and abasing himself. A race of such men of *ressentiment* will inevitably end up *cleverer* than any noble race, and will respect cleverness to a quite different degree as well: namely, as a condition of existence of the first rank, whilst the cleverness of noble men can easily have a subtle aftertaste of luxury and refinement about it:—precisely because in this area, it is nowhere near as important as the complete certainty of function of the governing *unconscious* instincts, nor indeed as important as a certain lack of cleverness, such as a daring charge at danger or at the enemy, or those frenzied sudden fits of anger, love, reverence, gratitude and revenge by which noble souls down the ages have recognized one another. When *ressentiment* does occur in the noble man himself, it is consumed and exhausted in an immediate reaction, and therefore it does not *poison,* on the other hand, it does not occur at all in countless cases where it is unavoidable for all who are weak and powerless. To be unable to take his enemies, his misfortunes and even his *misdeeds* seriously for long—that is the sign of strong, rounded natures with a superabundance of a power which is flexible, formative, healing and can make one forget (a good example from the modern world is Mirabeau, who had no recall for the insults and slights directed at him and who could not forgive, simply because he—forgot.) A man like this shakes from him, with one shrug, many worms which would have burrowed into another man; here and here alone is it possible, assuming that this is possible at all on earth truly to "*love* your neighbour" [Matt. 5:43]. How much respect a noble man has for his enemies!—and a respect of that sort is a bridge to love . . . For he insists on having his enemy to himself, as a mark of distinction, indeed he will tolerate as enemies none other than such as have nothing to be despised and a *great deal* to be honoured! Against this, imagine "the enemy" as conceived of by the man of *ressentiment*—and here we have his deed, his creation: he has conceived of the "evil enemy," *"the evil one"* as a basic idea to which he now thinks up a copy and counterpart, the "good one"—himself! . . .

11

Exactly the opposite is true of the noble man who conceives of the basic idea "good" by himself, in advance and spontaneously, and only then creates a notion of "bad"! This "bad" of noble origin and that "evil" from the cauldron of unassuaged hatred—the first is an afterthought, an aside, a complementary colour, whilst the other is the original, the beginning, the actual *deed* in the conception of slave morality—how different are the two words "bad" and "evil," although both seem to be the opposite for the same concept, "good"! But it is not the same concept "good"; on the contrary, one should ask who is actually evil in the sense of the morality of *ressentiment*. The stern reply is: *precisely* the "good" person of the other morality, the noble, powerful, dominating man, but re-touched, re-interpreted and reviewed through the poisonous eye of *ressentiment*. Here there is one point which we would be the last to deny: anyone who came to know these "good men" as enemies came to know nothing but *"evil enemies,"* the same people who are so strongly held in check by custom, respect, habit, gratitude and even more through spying on one another and through peer-group jealousy, who, on the other hand, behave towards one another by showing such resourcefulness in consideration, self-control, delicacy, loyalty, pride and friendship,—they are not much better than uncaged beasts of prey in the world outside where the strange, the foreign, begin. There they enjoy freedom from every social constraint, in the wilderness they compensate for the tension which is caused by being closed in and fenced in by the peace of the community for so long, they *return* to the innocent conscience of the wild beast, as exultant monsters, who perhaps go away having committed a hideous succession of murder, arson, rape and torture, in a mood of bravado and spiritual equilibrium as though they had simply played a student's prank, convinced that poets will now have something to sing about and celebrate for quite some time. At the centre of all these noble races we cannot fail to see the blond beast of prey, the magnificent *blond beast* avidly prowling round for spoil and victory; this hidden centre needs release from time to time, the beast must out again, must return to the wild:—Roman, Arabian, Germanic, Japanese nobility, Homeric heroes, Scandinavian Vikings—in this requirement they are all alike. It was the noble races which left the concept of "barbarian" in their traces wherever they went; even their highest culture betrays the fact that they were conscious of this and indeed proud of it (for example, when Pericles, in that famous funeral oration, tells his Athenians, "Our daring has forced a path to every land and sea, erecting timeless memorials to itself everywhere for good *and ill"* [Thucydides II.39ff.]). This "daring" of the noble races, mad, absurd and sudden in the way it manifests itself, the unpredictability and even the improbability of their undertakings—Pericles singles out the ⟨*hrathumia*⟩ of the Athenians for praise—their unconcern and scorn for safety, body, life, comfort, their shocking cheerfulness, and depth of delight in all destruction, in all the debauches of victory and cruelty—all this, for those who suffered under it, was summed up in the image of the "barbarian," the "evil enemy," perhaps the "Goth" or the "Vandal." The deep and icy mistrust which the German arouses as soon as he comes to power, which we see again even today—is still the aftermath of that inextinguishable horror with which Europe viewed the raging of the blond Germanic beast for centuries (although between the old Germanic peoples and us Germans there is scarcely an idea in common, let alone a blood relationship). I once remarked on Hesiod's dilemma when he thought up the series of cultural eras and tried to express them in gold, silver and iron: he could find no other solution to the contradiction presented to him by the magnificent but at the same time so shockingly violent world of Homer than to make two eras out of one, which he now placed one behind the other—first the era of heroes and demigods from Troy and Thebes, as that world which remained in the memory of the noble races which had their ancestors in it; then the iron era, as that same world appeared to the descendants of the downtrodden, robbed, ill-treated, and those carried off and sold: as an era of iron, hard, as I said, cold, cruel, lacking feeling and conscience, crushing everything and coating it with blood. Assuming that what is at any rate believed as "truth" were indeed true, that it is the *meaning of all culture* to breed a tame and civilized animal, a *household pet,* out of the beast of prey "man," then one would undoubtedly have to view all instinctive reaction and instinctive ressentiment, by means of which the noble races and their ideals were finally wrecked and overpowered, as the actual *instruments of culture;* which, however, is not to say that the *bearers* of these instincts were themselves representatives of the culture. Instead, the opposite would be not only probable—no! it is *visible* today! These bearers of oppressive, vindictive instincts, the descendants of all European and non-European slavery, in particular of all pre-Aryan population—represent the *decline* of mankind! These "instruments of culture" are a disgrace to man, more a grounds for suspicion of, or an argument against, "culture" in general! We may be quite justified in retaining our fear of the blond beast at the centre of every noble race and remain on our guard: but who would not, a hundred times over, prefer to fear if he can admire at the same time, rather than not fear, but thereby permanently retain the disgusting spectacle of the failed, the stunted, the wasted away and the poisoned? And is that not our fate? What constitutes *our* aversion to "man" today?—for we *suffer* from man, no doubt about that.—*Not* fear; rather, the fact that we have nothing to fear from man; that "man" is first and foremost a teeming mass of worms; that the "tame man," who is incurably mediocre and unedifying, has already learnt to view himself as the aim and pinnacle, the meaning of history, the "higher man";—yes, the fact that he has a certain right to feel like that in so far as he feels distanced from the superabundance of failed, sickly, tired and exhausted people of whom today's Europe is beginning to reek, and in so far as he is at least relatively successful, at least still capable of living, at least saying "yes" to life . . .

12

—At this juncture I cannot suppress a sigh and one last hope. What do I find absolutely intolerable? Something which I just cannot cope alone with and which suffocates me and makes me feel faint? Bad air! Bad air! That something failed comes near me, that I have to smell the bowels of a failed soul! . . . Apart from that, what cannot be borne in the way of need, deprivation, bad weather, disease, toil, solitude? Basically we can cope with everything else, born as we are to an underground and battling existence; again and again we keep coming up to the light, again and again we experience our golden hour of victory,—and then there we stand, the way we were born, unbreakable, tense, ready for new, more difficult and distant things, like a bow which is merely stretched tauter by affliction.—But from time to time grant me—assuming that there are divine benefactresses beyond good and evil—a glimpse, grant me just one glimpse of something perfect, completely finished, happy, powerful, triumphant, which still leaves something to fear! A glimpse of a man who justifies man *himself,* a stroke of luck, an instance of a man who makes up for and redeems man, and enables us to retain our *faith in mankind!* . . . For the matter stands like so: the stunting and levelling of European man conceals *our* greatest danger, because the sight of this makes us tired . . . Today we see nothing that wants to expand, we suspect that things will just continue to decline, getting thinner, better-natured, cleverer, more comfortable, more mediocre, more indifferent, more Chinese, more Christian—no doubt about it, man is getting "better" all the time . . . Right here is where the destiny of Europe lies—in losing our fear of man we have also lost our love for him, our respect for him, our hope in him and even our will to be man. The sight of man now makes us tired—what is nihilism today if it is not *that?* . . . We are tired of *man* . . .

13

—But let us return: the problem of the *other* origin of "good," of good as thought up by the man of *ressentiment,* demands its solution. There is nothing strange about the fact that lambs bear a grudge towards large birds of prey: but that is no reason to blame the large birds of prey for carrying off the little lambs. And if the lambs say to each other, "These birds of prey are evil; and whoever is least like a bird of prey and most like its opposite, a lamb,—is good, isn't he?," then there is no reason to raise objections to this setting-up of an ideal beyond the fact that the birds of prey will view it somewhat derisively, and will perhaps say, "We don't bear any grudge at all towards these good lambs, in fact we love them, nothing is tastier than a tender lamb."—It is just as absurd to ask strength *not* to express itself as strength, not to be a desire to overthrow, crush, become master, to be a thirst for enemies, resistance and triumphs, as it is to ask weakness to express itself as strength. A quantum of force is just such a quantum of drive, will, action, in fact it is nothing but this driving, willing and acting, and only the seduction of language (and the fundamental errors of reason petrified within it), which construes and misconstrues all actions as conditional upon an agency, a "subject," can make it appear otherwise. And just as the common people separates lightning from its flash and takes the latter to be a *deed,* something performed by a subject, which is called lightning, popular morality separates strength from the manifestations of strength, as though there were an indifferent substratum behind the strong person which had the *freedom* to manifest strength or not. But there is no such substratum; there is no "being" behind the deed, its effect and what becomes of it; "the doer" is invented as an afterthought,—the doing is everything. Basically, the common people double a deed; when they see lightning, they make a doing-a-deed out of it: they posit the same event, first as cause and then as its effect. The scientists do no better when they say "force moves, force causes" and such like,—all our science, in spite of its coolness and freedom from emotion, still stands exposed to the seduction of language and has not ridded itself of the changelings foisted upon it, the "subjects" (the atom is, for example, just such a changeling, likewise the Kantian "thing-in-itself"): no wonder, then, if the entrenched, secretly smouldering emotions of revenge and hatred put this belief to their own use and, in fact, do not defend any belief more passionately than that *the strong are free* to be weak, and the birds of prey are free to be lambs:—in this way, they gain the right to make the birds of prey *responsible* for being birds of prey . . . When the oppressed, the downtrodden, the violated say to each other with the vindictive cunning of powerlessness: "Let us be different from evil people, let us be good! And a good person is anyone who does not rape, does not harm anyone, who does not attack, does not retaliate, who leaves the taking of revenge to God, who keeps hidden as we do, avoids all evil and asks little from life in general, like us who are patient, humble and upright"—this means, if heard coolly and impartially, nothing more than "We weak people are just weak; it is good to do nothing *for which we are not strong enough*"—but this grim state of affairs, this cleverness of the lowest rank which even insects possess (which play dead, in order not to "do too much" when in great danger), has, thanks to the counterfeiting and self-deception of powerlessness, clothed itself in the finery of self-denying, quiet, patient virtue, as though the weakness of the weak were itself—I mean its *essence,* its effect, its whole unique, unavoidable, irredeemable reality—a voluntary achievement, something wanted, chosen, a *deed,* an *accomplishment*. This type of man *needs* to believe in an unbiased "subject" with freedom of choice, because he has an instinct of self-preservation and self-affirmation in which every lie is sanctified. The reason the subject (or, as we more colloquially say, *the soul*) has been, until now, the best doctrine on earth, is perhaps because it facilitated that sublime self-deception whereby the majority of the dying, the weak and the oppressed of every kind could construe weakness itself as freedom, and their particular mode of existence as an *accomplishment.*

14

—Would anyone like to have a little look down into the secret of how *ideals are fabricated* on this earth? Who has enough pluck? . . . Come on! Here we have a clear glimpse into this dark workshop. Just wait one moment, Mr Nosy Daredevil: your eyes will have to become used to this false, shimmering light . . . There! That's enough! Now you can speak! What's happening down there? Tell me what you see, you with your most dangerous curiosity—now *I* am the one who's listening.

—"I cannot see anything but I can hear all the better. There is a guarded, malicious little rumour-mongering and whispering from every nook and cranny. I think people are telling lies; a sugary mildness clings to every sound. Lies are turning weakness into an *accomplishment,* no doubt about it—it's just as you said."

—Go on!

—"and impotence which doesn't retaliate is being turned into 'goodness'; timid baseness is being turned into 'humility'; submission to people one hates is being turned into 'obedience' (actually towards someone who, they say, orders this submission—they call him God). The inoffensiveness of the weakling, the very cowardice with which he is richly endowed, his standing-by-the-door, his inevitable position of having to wait, are all given good names such as 'patience,' which is also called *the* virtue; not-being-able-to-take revenge is called not-wanting-to-take-revenge, it might even be forgiveness ('for they know not what they do [Luke 23:34]—but we know what they are doing!'). They are also talking about 'loving your enemy' and sweating while they do it."

—Go on!

—"They are miserable, without a doubt, all these rumour-mongers and clandestine forgers, even if they do crouch close together for warmth—but they tell me that their misery means they are God's chosen and select, after all, people beat the dogs they love best; perhaps this misery is just a preparation, a test, a training, it might be even more than that—something which will one day be balanced up and paid back with enormous interest in gold, no! in happiness. They call that 'bliss.'"

—Go on!

—"They are now informing me that not only are they better than the powerful, the masters of the world whose spittle they have to lick (*not* from fear, not at all from fear! but because God orders them to honour those in authority [Rom. 13:1])—not only are they better, but they have a 'better time,' or at least will have a better time one day. But enough! enough! I can't bear it any longer. Bad air! Bad air! This workshop where *ideals are fabricated*—it seems to me just to stink of lies."

—No! Wait a moment! You haven't said anything yet about the masterpieces of those black magicians who can turn anything black into whiteness, milk and innocence:—haven't you noticed their perfect *raffinement,* their boldest, subtlest, most ingenious and mendacious stunt? Pay attention! These cellar rats full of revenge and hatred—what do they turn revenge and hatred into? Have you ever heard these words? Would you suspect, if you just went by what they said, that the men around you were nothing but men of *ressentiment?* . . .

—"I understand, I'll open my ears once more (oh! oh! oh! and *hold* my nose). Now, at last, I can hear what they have been saying so often: 'We good people—*we are the just*'—what they are demanding is not called retribution, but 'the triumph of *justice*'; what they hate is not their enemy, oh no! they hate *'injustice,'* 'godlessness'; what they believe and hope for is not the prospect of revenge, the delirium of sweet revenge (—Homer early on dubbed it "'sweeter than honey'"), but the victory of God, the *just* God, over the Godless; all that remains for them to love on earth are not their brothers in hate but their 'brothers in love,' as they say, all good and just people on earth."

—And what do they call that which serves as a consolation for all the sufferings of the world—their phantasmagoria of anticipated future bliss?

—"What? Do I hear correctly? They call it 'the last judgment,' the coming of *their* kingdom, the 'kingdom of God'—but *in the meantime* they live 'in faith,' 'in love,' 'in hope.'"

—Enough! Enough!

15

Faith in what? Love of what? Hope for what?—These weaklings—in fact *they,* too, want to be the powerful one day, this is beyond doubt, one day *their* "kingdom" will come too—"the kingdom of God" *simpliciter* is their name for it, as I said: they are so humble about everything! Just to experience *that,* you need to live long, well beyond death,—yes, you need eternal life in order to be able to gain eternal recompense in "the kingdom of God" for that life on earth "in faith," "in love," "in hope." Recompense for what? Recompense through what . . . It seems to me that Dante made a gross error when, with awe-inspiring naivete he placed the inscription over the gateway to his hell: "Eternal love created me as well":—at any rate, this inscription would have a better claim to stand over the gateway to Christian Paradise and its "eternal bliss": "Eternal *hate* created me as well" assuming that a true statement can be placed above the gateway to a lie! For what is the bliss of this Paradise? . . . We might have guessed already; but it is better to be expressly shown it by no less an authority in such matters than Thomas Aquinas, the great teacher and saint. "The blessed in the heavenly kingdom," he says as meekly as a lamb, "will see the torment of the damned *so that they may even more thoroughly enjoy their blessedness*."* Or, if you want it even more forcefully, for example from the mouth of a triumphant Church Father [Tertullian] who advised his Christians against the cruel voluptuousness of the public spectacles—but why? "Faith offers us much more"—he says, *De Spectaculis.* Chs. 29ff—"something *much stronger,* thanks to salvation, quite other joys are at our command; instead of athletes we have our martyrs; we want blood, well then, we have the blood of Christ . . . But think what awaits us on the day of his second coming, of his triumph!"—and then the enraptured visionary goes on: "But there are yet other spectacles: that final and everlasting day of judgement, that day that was not expected and was even laughed at by the nations, when the whole old world and all it gave birth to are consumed in one fire. What an ample breadth of sights there will be then! *At which one shall I gaze in wonder? At which shall I laugh? At which rejoice? At which exult,* when I see so many great *kings* who were proclaimed to have been taken up into

---

*[This passage is given in Latin by Nietzsche.]

heaven, groaning in the deepest darkness together with those who claimed to have witnessed their apotheosis and with Jove himself. And when I see those [provincial] governors, persecutors of the Lord's name, melting in flames more savage than those with which they insolently raged against Christians! When I see those wise philosophers who persuaded their disciples that nothing was of any concern to god and who affirmed to them either that we have no souls or that our souls will not return to their original bodies! Now they are ashamed before those disciples, as they are burned together with them. Also the poets trembling before the tribunal not of Minos or of Radamanthus, but of the unexpected Christ! Then the tragic actors will be easier to hear because they will be in better voice [i.e. screaming even louder] in their own tragedy. Then the actors of pantomime will be easy to recognize, being much more nimble than usual because of the fire. Then the charioteer will be on view, all red in a wheel of flame and the athletes, thrown not in the gymnasia but into the fire. Unless even then I don't want to see them alive, preferring to cast an *insatiable* gaze on those who raged against the Lord. "This is he," I will say, "that son of a carpenter or prostitute [Nietzsche adds:] (Tertullian refers to the Jews from now on, as is shown by what follows and in particular by this well-known description of the mother of Jesus from the Talmud) that destroyer of the Sabbath, that Samaritan, that man who had a devil. He it is whom you bought from Judas, who was beaten with a reed and with fists, who was defiled with spit and had gall and vinegar to drink. He it is whom his disciples secretly took away so that it might be said that he had risen again, or whom the gardener removed so that his lettuces would not be harmed by the crowd of visitors." What praetor or consul or quaestor or priest will grant you from his largesse the chance of seeing and *exulting in such things?* And yet to some extent we have such things already *through faith,* made present in the imagining spirit. Furthermore what sorts of things are those which the eye has not seen nor the ear heard, and which have not come into the human heart? (I Cor. 2:9) I believe that they are more pleasing than the circus or both of the enclosures [first and fourth rank of seats, or, according to others, the comic and the tragic stages] or than any race-track."*

(*Per fidem* [By my faith]: that is what is written.)

16

Let us draw to a close. The two *opposing* values "good and bad," "good and evil" have fought a terrible battle for thousands of years on earth; and although the latter has been dominant for a long time, there is still no lack of places where the battle remains undecided. You could even say that, in the meantime, it has reached ever greater heights but at the same time has become ever deeper and more intellectual: so that there is, today, perhaps no more distinguishing feature of the *"higher nature,"* the intellectual nature, than to be divided in this sense and really and truly a battle ground for these opposites. The symbol of this fight, written in a script which has hitherto remained legible throughout human history, is "Rome against Judea, Judea against Rome":—up to now there has been no greater event than *this* battle, *this* question, *this* contradiction of mortal enemies. Rome saw the Jew as something contrary to nature, as though he were its polar opposite, a monster; in Rome, the Jew was looked upon as *convicted* of hatred against the whole of mankind: rightly, if one is right in linking the well being and future of the human race

*[This passage is given in Latin by Nietzsche.]

with the unconditional rule of aristocratic values, Roman values. What, on the other hand, did the Jews feel about Rome? We can guess from a thousand indicators; but it is enough to call once more to mind the Apocalypse of John, the wildest of all outbursts ever written which revenge has on its conscience. (By the way, we must not underestimate the profound consistency of Christian instinct in inscribing this book of hate to the disciple of love, the very same to whom it attributed that passionately ecstatic gospel—: there is some truth in this, however much literary counterfeiting might have been necessary to the purpose.) So the Romans were the strong and noble, stronger and nobler than anybody hitherto who had lived or been dreamt of on earth; their every relic and inscription brings delight, provided one can guess *what* it is that is doing the writing there. By contrast, the Jews were a priestly nation of *ressentiment par excellence,* possessing an unparalleled genius for popular morality: compare peoples with similar talents, such as the Chinese or the Germans, with the Jews, and you will realize who are first rate and who are fifth. Which of them has *prevailed* for the time being, Rome or Judea? But there is no trace of doubt: just consider whom you bow down to in Rome itself; today, as though to the embodiment of the highest values and not just in Rome, but over nearly half the earth, everywhere where man has become tame or wants to become tame, to *three Jews,* as we know, and *one Jewess* (to Jesus of Nazareth, Peter the Fisherman, Paul the Carpet-Weaver and the mother of Jesus mentioned first, whose name was Mary). This is very remarkable: without a doubt Rome has been defeated. However, in the Renaissance there was a brilliant, uncanny reawakening of the classical ideal, of the noble method of valuing everything: Rome itself woke up, as though from suspended animation, under the pressure of the new, Judaic Rome built over it, which looked like an ecumenical synagogue and was called "Church": but Judea triumphed again at once, thanks to that basically proletarian (German and English) *ressentiment*-movement which people called the Reformation, including its inevitable consequence, the restoration of the church,—as well as the restoration of the ancient, tomb-like silence of classical Rome. In an even more decisive and profound sense than then, Judea once again triumphed over the classical ideal with the French Revolution: the last political nobility in Europe, that of the *French* seventeenth and eighteenth centuries, collapsed under the *ressentiment*-instincts of the rabble,—the world had never heard greater rejoicing and more uproarious enthusiasm! True, the most dreadful and unexpected thing happened in the middle: the ancient ideal itself appeared *bodily* and with unheard-of splendour before the eye and conscience of mankind, and once again, stronger, simpler and more penetrating than ever, in answer to the old, mendacious *ressentiment* slogan of *priority for the majority,* of man's will to baseness, abasement, levelling, decline and decay, there rang out the terrible and enchanting counter-slogan: *priority for the few!* Like a last signpost to the *other* path, Napoleon appeared as a man more unique and late-born for his times than ever a man had been before, and in him, the problem of the *noble ideal itself* was made flesh—just think *what* a problem that is: Napoleon, this synthesis of monster *[Unmensch]* and *Übermensch* . . .

17

—Was it over after that? Was that greatest among all conflicts of ideals placed *ad acta* for ever? Or just postponed, postponed indefinitely? . . . Won't there have to be an even more terrible flaring up of the old flame, one prepared much longer in advance? And more: shouldn't one desire *that* with all one's strength? or will it, even? or even promote it? . . . Whoever, like my readers, now starts to ponder these points and reflect further, will have difficulty coming to a speedy conclusion,—reason enough, then, for me to come to a conclusion myself, assuming that it has been sufficiently clear for some time what I want, what I *actually* want with that dangerous slogan which is written on the spine of my last book, *Beyond Good and Evil* . . . at least this does *not* mean "Beyond Good and Bad."—

Note

I take the opportunity presented to me by this essay, of publicly and formally expressing a wish which I have only expressed in occasional conversations with scholars up till now: that is that some Faculty of Philosophy should do the great service of promoting the study of *the history of morality* by means of a series of academic prize essays:— perhaps this book might serve to give a powerful impetus in such a direction. With regard to such a possibility, I raise the following question for consideration: it merits the attention of philologists and historians as well as those who are actually philosophers by profession:

> *"What signposts does linguistics, especially the study of etymology, give to the history of the evolution of moral concepts?"*

—On the other hand, it is just as essential to win the support of physiologists and doctors for these problems (on the *value* of all previous valuations): we can leave it to the professional philosophers to act as advocates and mediators in this, once they have completely succeeded in transforming the originally so reserved and suspicious relationship between philosophy, physiology and medicine into the most cordial and fruitful exchange. Indeed, every table of values, every "thou shalt" known to history or the study of ethnology, needs first and foremost a *physiological* elucidation and interpretation, rather than a psychological one; and all of them await critical study from medical science. The question: what is this or that table of values and "morals" *worth?* needs to be asked from different angles; in particular, the question "value for *what?*" cannot be examined too finely. Something, for example, which obviously had value with regard to the longest possible life-span of a race (or to the improvement of its abilities to adapt to a particular climate, or to maintaining the greatest number) would not have anything like the same value if it was a question of developing a stronger type. The good of the majority and the good of the minority are conflicting moral stand-points: we leave it to the naivety of English biologists to view the first as higher in value as *such* . . . *All* sciences must, from now on, prepare the way for the future work of the philosopher: this work being understood to mean that the philosopher has to solve the *problem of values* and that he has to decide on the *hierarchy of values*.

THUS SPOKE ZARATHUSTRA (in part)

ZARATHUSTRA'S PROLOGUE

[1] When Zarathustra was thirty years old he left his home and the lake of his home and went into the mountains. Here he enjoyed his spirit and his solitude, and for ten years did not tire of it. But at last a change came over his heart, and one morning he rose with the dawn, stepped before the sun, and spoke to it thus:

"You great star, what would your happiness be had you not those for whom you shine?

"For ten years you have climbed to my cave: you would have tired of your light and of the journey had it not been for me and my eagle and my serpent.

"But we waited for you every morning, took your overflow from you, and blessed you for it.

"Behold, I am weary of my wisdom, like a bee that has gathered too much honey; I need hands outstretched to receive it.

"I would give away and distribute, until the wise among men find joy once again in their folly, and the poor in their riches.

"For that I must descend to the depths, as you do in the evening when you go behind the sea and still bring light to the underworld, you over rich star.

"Like you, I must go *under*—go down, as is said by man, to whom I want to descend.

"So bless me then, you quiet eye that can look even upon an all-too-great happiness without envy!

"Bless the cup that wants to overflow, that the water may flow from it golden and carry everywhere the reflection of your delight.

"Behold, this cup wants to become empty again, and Zarathustra wants to become man again."

Thus Zarathustra began to go under.

[2] Zarathustra descended alone from the mountains, encountering no one. But when he came into the forest, all at once there stood before him an old man who had left his holy cottage to look for roots in the woods. And thus spoke the old man to Zarathustra:

"No stranger to me is this wanderer: many years ago he passed this way. Zarathustra he was called, but he has changed. At that time you carried your ashes to the mountains; would you now carry your fire into the valleys? Do you not fear to be punished as an arsonist?

"Yes, I recognize Zarathustra. His eyes are pure, and around his mouth there hides no disgust. Does he not walk like a dancer?

"Zarathustra has changed, Zarathustra has become a child, Zarathustra is an awakened one; what do you now want among the sleepers? You lived in your solitude as in the sea, and the sea carried you. Alas, would you now climb ashore? Alas, would you again drag your own body?"

Zarathustra answered: "I love man."

"Why," asked the saint, "did I go into the forest and the desert? Was it not because I loved man all-too-much? Now I love God; man I love not. Man is for me too imperfect a thing. Love of man would kill me."

Zarathustra answered: "Did I speak of love? I bring men a gift."

"Give them nothing!" said the saint. "Rather, take part of their load and help them to bear it—that will be best for them, if only it does you good! And if you want to give them something, give no more than alms, and let them beg for that!"

"No," answered Zarathustra. "I give no alms. For that I am not poor enough."

The saint laughed at Zarathustra and spoke thus: "Then see to it that they accept your treasures. They are suspicious of hermits and do not believe that we come with gifts. Our steps sound too lonely through the streets. And what if at night, in their beds, they hear a man walk by long before the sun has risen—they probably ask themselves, Where is the thief going?

"Do not go to man. Stay in the forest! Go rather even to the animals! Why do you not want to be as I am—a bear among bears, a bird among birds?"

"And what is the saint doing in the forest?" asked Zarathustra.

The saint answered: "I make songs and sing them; and when I make songs, I laugh, cry, and hum: thus I praise God. With singing, crying, laughing, and humming, I praise the god who is my god. But what do you bring us as a gift?"

When Zarathustra had heard these words he bade the saint farewell and said: "What could I have to give you? But let me go quickly lest I take something from you!" And thus they separated, the old one and the man, laughing as two boys laugh.

But when Zarathustra was alone he spoke thus to his heart: "Could it be possible? This old saint in the forest has not yet heard anything of this, that God is *dead!*"

[3]   When Zarathustra came into the next town, which lies on the edge of the forest, he found many people gathered together in the market place; for it had been promised that there would be a tightrope walker. And Zarathustra spoke thus to the people:

"*I teach you the overman.* Man is something that shall be overcome. What have you done to overcome him?

"All beings so far have created something beyond themselves; and do you want to be the ebb of this great flood and even go back to the beasts rather than overcome man? What is the ape to man? A laughingstock or a painful embarrassment. And man shall be just that for the overman: a laughingstock or a painful embarrassment. You have made your way from worm to man, and much in you is still worm. Once you were apes, and even now, too, man is more ape than any ape.

"Whoever is the wisest among you is also a mere conflict and cross between plant and ghost. But do I bid you become ghosts or plants?

"Behold, I teach you the overman. The overman is the meaning of the earth. Let your will say: the overman *shall be* the meaning of the earth! I beseech you, my brothers, *remain faithful to the earth,* and do not believe those who speak to you of otherworldly hopes! Poison-mixers are they, whether they know it or not. Despisers of life are they, decaying and poisoned themselves, of whom the earth is weary: so let them go.

"Once the sin against God was the greatest sin; but God died, and these sinners died with him. To sin against the earth is now the most dreadful thing, and to esteem the entrails of the unknowable higher than the meaning of the earth.

"Once the soul looked contemptuously upon the body, and then this contempt was the highest: she wanted the body meager, ghastly, and starved. Thus she hoped to escape it and the earth. Oh, this soul herself was still meager, ghastly, and starved: and cruelty was the lust of this soul. But you, too, my brothers, tell me: what does your body proclaim of your soul? Is not your soul poverty and filth and wretched contentment?

"Verily, a polluted stream is man. One must be a sea to be able to receive a polluted stream without becoming unclean. Behold, I teach you the overman: he is this sea; in him your great contempt can go under.

"What is the greatest experience you can have? It is the hour of the great contempt. The hour in which your happiness, too, arouses your disgust, and even your reason and your virtue.

"The hour when you say, 'What matters my happiness? It is poverty and filth and wretched contentment. But my happiness ought to justify existence itself.'

"The hour when you say, 'What matters my reason? Does it crave knowledge as the lion his food? It is poverty and filth and wretched contentment.'

"The hour when you say, 'What matters my virtue? As yet it has not made me rage. How weary I am of my good and my evil! All that is poverty and filth and wretched contentment.'

"The hour when you say, 'What matters my justice? I do not see that I am flames and fuel. But the just are flames and fuel.'

"The hour when you say, 'What matters my pity? Is not pity the cross on which he is nailed who loves man? But my pity is no crucifixion.'

"Have you yet spoken thus? Have you yet cried thus? Oh, that I might have heard you cry thus!

"Not your sin but your thrift cries to heaven; your meanness even in your sin cries to heaven.

"Where is the lightning to lick you with its tongue? Where is the frenzy with which you should be inoculated?

"Behold, I teach you the overman: he is this lightning, he is this frenzy."

When Zarathustra had spoken thus, one of the people cried: "Now we have heard enough about the tightrope walker; now let us see him tool." And all the people laughed at Zarathustra. But the tightrope walker, believing that the word concerned him, began his performance.

TWILIGHT OF THE IDOLS (in part)

"REASON" IN PHILOSOPHY

[1] You ask me which of the philosophers' traits are really idiosyncrasies? For example, their lack of historical sense, their hatred of the very idea of becoming, their Egypticism. They think that they show their *respect* for a subject when they de-historicize it, *sub specie aeterni*—when they turn it into a mummy. All that philosophers have handled for thousands of years have been concept-mummies; nothing real escaped their grasp alive. When these honorable idolators of concepts worship something, they kill it and stuff it; they threaten the life of everything they worship. Death, change, old

age, as well as procreation and growth, are to their minds objections—even refutations. Whatever has being does not become; whatever becomes does not have being. Now they all believe, desperately even, in what has being. But since they never grasp it, they seek for reasons why it is kept from them. "There must be mere appearance, there must be some deception which prevents us from perceiving that which has being: where is the deceiver?"

"We have found him," they cry ecstatically; "it is the senses! These senses, which are so immoral in other ways too, deceive us concerning the *true* world. Moral: let us free ourselves from the deception of the senses, from becoming, from history, from lies; history is nothing but faith in the senses, faith in lies. Moral: let us say No to all who have faith in the senses, to all the rest of mankind; they are all 'mob.' Let us be philosophers! Let us be mummies! Let us represent monotono-theism by adopting the expression of a gravedigger! And above all, away with the body, this wretched *idée fixe* of the senses, disfigured by all the fallacies of logic, refuted, even impossible, although it is impudent enough to behave as if it were real!"

[2] With the highest respect, I except the name of *Heraclitus*. When the rest of the philosophic folk rejected the testimony of the senses because they showed multiplicity and change, he rejected their testimony because they showed things as if they had permanence and unity. Heraclitus too did the senses an injustice. They lie neither in the way the Eleatics believed, nor as he believed—they do not lie at all. What we *make* of their testimony, that alone introduces lies; for example, the lie of unity, the lie of thinghood, of substance, of permanence. "Reason" is the cause of our falsification of the testimony of the senses. Insofar as the senses show becoming, passing away, and change, they do not lie. But Heraclitus will remain eternally right with his assertion that being is an empty fiction. The "apparent" world is the only one: the "true" world is merely added by a lie.

[3] And what magnificent instruments of observation we possess in our senses! This nose, for example, of which no philosopher has yet spoken with reverence and gratitude, is actually the most delicate instrument so far at our disposal: it is able to detect minimal differences of motion which even a spectroscope cannot detect. Today we possess science precisely to the extent to which we have decided to *accept* the testimony of the senses—to the extent to which we sharpen them further, arm them, and have learned to think them through. The rest is miscarriage and not-yet-science-in other words, metaphysics, theology, psychology, epistemology—or formal science, a doctrine of signs, such as logic and that applied logic which is called mathematics. In them reality is not encountered at all, not even as a problem—no more than the question of the value of such a sign-convention as logic.

[4] The other idiosyncrasy of the philosophers is no less dangerous; it consists in confusing the last and the first. They place that which comes at the end—unfortunately! for it ought not to come at all!—namely, the "highest concepts," which means the most general, the emptiest concepts, the last smoke of evaporating reality, in the beginning, *as* the beginning. This again is nothing but their way of showing reverence: the higher *may* not grow out of the lower, may not have grown at all. Moral: whatever is of the first rank must be *causa sui* [self-caused]. Origin out of something else is considered an objection, a questioning of value. All the highest values are of the first rank; all the highest concepts, that which has being, the unconditional, the good, the true, the perfect— all these cannot have become and must therefore be *causa sui*. All these, moreover, cannot be unlike each other or in contradiction to each other. Thus they arrive at their stupendous concept, "God." That which is last, thinnest, and emptiest is put first, as *the* cause, as *ens realissimum* [the most real being]. Why did mankind have to take seriously the brain afflictions of sick web-spinners? They have paid dearly for it!

[5] At long last, let us contrast the very different manner in which we conceive the problem of error and appearance. (I say "we" for politeness' sake.) Formerly, alteration, change, any becoming at all, were taken as proof of mere appearance, as an indication that there must be something which led us astray. Today, conversely, precisely insofar as the prejudice of reason forces us to posit unity, identity, permanence, substance, cause, thinghood, being, we see ourselves somehow caught in error, compelled into error. So certain are we, on the basis of rigorous examination, that this is where the error lies.

It is no different in this case than with the movement of the sun: there our eye is the constant advocate of error, here it is our language. In its origin language belongs in the age of the most rudimentary form of psychology. We enter a realm of crude fetishism when we summon before consciousness the basic presuppositions of the metaphysics of language, in plain talk, the presuppositions of reason. Everywhere it sees a doer and doing; it believes in will as *the* cause; it believes in the ego, in the ego as being, in the ego as substance, and it projects this faith in the ego-substance upon all things-only thereby does it first *create* the concept of "thing." Everywhere "being" is projected by thought, pushed underneath, as the cause; the concept of being follows, and is a derivative of, the concept of ego. In the beginning there is that great calamity of an error that the will is something which is effective, that will is a capacity. Today we know that it is only a word.

Very much later, in a world which was in a thousand ways more enlightened, philosophers, to their great surprise, became aware of the sureness, the subjective certainty, in our handling of the categories of reason: they concluded that these categories could not be derived from anything empirical—for everything empirical plainly contradicted them. Whence, then, were they derived?

And in India, as in Greece, the same mistake was made: "We must once have been at home in a higher world (instead of a very much lower one, which would have been the truth); we must have been divine, for we have reason!" Indeed, nothing has yet possessed a more naive power of persuasion than the error concerning being, as it has been formulated by the Eleatics, for example. After all, every word we say and every sentence speak in its favor. Even the opponents of the Eleatics still succumbed to the seduction of their concept of being: Democritus, among others, when he invented his atom. "Reason" in language—oh, what an old deceptive female she is! I am afraid we are not rid of God because we still have faith in grammar.

[6] It will be appreciated if I condense so essential and so new an insight into four theses. In that way I facilitate comprehension; in that way I provoke contradiction.

First proposition. The reasons for which "this" world has been characterized as "apparent" are the very reasons which indicate its reality; any other kind of reality is absolutely indemonstrable.

Second proposition. The criteria which have been bestowed on the "true being" of things are the criteria of not-being, of *naught;* the "true world" has been constructed out of contradiction to the actual world: indeed an apparent world, insofar as it is merely a moral-optical illusion.

Third proposition. To invent fables about a world "other" than this one has no meaning at all, unless an instinct of slander, detraction, and suspicion against life has gained the upper hand in us: in that case, we avenge ourselves against life with a phantasmagoria of "another," a "better" life.

Fourth proposition. Any distinction between a "true" and an "apparent" world—whether in the Christian manner or in the manner of Kant (in the end, an underhanded Christian)—is only a suggestion of decadence, a symptom of the *decline of life*. That the artist esteems appearance higher than reality is no objection to this proposition. For "appearance" in this case means reality *once more,* only by way of selection, reinforcement, and correction. The tragic artist is no pessimist: he is precisely the one who says Yes to everything questionable, even to the terrible—he is *Dionysian.*

* * *

MORALITY AS ANTI-NATURE

[1] All passions have a phase when they are merely disastrous, when they drag down their victim with the weight of stupidity—and a later, very much later phase when they wed the spirit, when they "spiritualize" themselves. Formerly, in view of the element of stupidity in passion, war was declared on passion itself, its destruction was plotted; all the old moral monsters are agreed on this: *il faut tuer les passions* [one must kill the passions]. The most famous formula for this is to be found in the New Testament, in that Sermon on the Mount, where, incidentally, things are by no means looked at from a height. There it is said, for example, with particular reference to sexuality: "If thy eye offend thee, pluck it out." Fortunately, no Christian acts in accordance with this precept. *Destroying* the passions and cravings, merely as a preventive measure against their stupidity and the unpleasant consequences of this stupidity—today this itself strikes us as merely another acute form of stupidity. We no longer admire dentists who "pluck out" teeth so that they will not hurt any more.

To be fair, it should be admitted, however, that on the ground out of which Christianity grew, the concept of the *"spiritualization* of passion" could never have been formed. After all the first church, as is well known, fought against the "intelligent" in favor of the "poor in spirit." How could one expect from it an intelligent war against passion? The church fights passion with excision in every sense: its practice, its "cure," is *castratism.* It never asks: "How can one spiritualize, beautify, deify a craving?" It has at all times laid the stress of discipline on extirpation (of sensuality, of pride, of the lust to rule, of avarice, of vengefulness). But an attack on the roots of passion means an attack on the roots of life: the practice of the church *is hostile to life.*

[2] The same means in the fight against a craving—castration, extirpation—is instinctively chosen by those who are too weak-willed, too degenerate, to be able to impose moderation on themselves; by those who are so constituted that they require *La Trappe,* [The Trappist Order] to use a figure of speech, or (without any figure of speech) some kind of definitive declaration of hostility, a *cleft* between themselves and the passion. Radical means are indispensable only for the degenerate; the weakness of the will—or, to speak more definitely, the inability not to respond to a stimulus—is itself merely another form of degeneration. The radical hostility, the deadly hostility against sensuality, is always a symptom to reflect on: it entitles us to suppositions concerning the total state of one who is excessive in this manner.

This hostility, this hatred, by the way, reaches its climax only when such types lack even the firmness for this radical cure, for this renunciation of their "devil." One should survey the whole history of the priests and philosophers, including the artists: the most poisonous things against the senses have been said not by the impotent, nor by ascetics, but by the impossible ascetics, by those who really were in dire need of being ascetics.

[3] The spiritualization of sensuality is called *love:* it represents a great triumph over Christianity. Another triumph is our spiritualization of *hostility.* It consists in a profound appreciation of the value of having enemies: in short, it means acting and thinking in the opposite way from that which has been the rule. The church always wanted the destruction of its enemies; we, we immoralists and Antichristians, find our advantage in this, that the church exists. In the political realm too, hostility has now become more spiritual—much more sensible, much more thoughtful, much more *considerate.* Almost every party understands how it is in the interest of its own self-preservation that the opposition should not lose all strength; the same is true of power politics. A new creation in particular—the new *Reich,* for example—needs enemies more than friends: in opposition alone does it *feel* itself necessary, in opposition alone does it *become* necessary.

Our attitude to the "internal enemy" is no different: here too we have spiritualized hostility; here too we have come to appreciate its value. The price of fruitfulness is to be rich in internal opposition; one remains young only as long as the soul does not stretch itself and desire peace. Nothing has become more alien to us than that desideratum of former times, "peace of soul," the *Christian* desideratum; there is nothing we envy less than the moralistic cow and the fat happiness of the good conscience. One has renounced the *great* life when one renounces war.

In many cases, to be sure, "peace of soul" is merely a misunderstanding—something else, which lacks only a more honest name. Without further ado or prejudice, a few examples. "Peace of soul" can be, for one, the gentle radiation of a rich animality into the moral (or religious) sphere. Or the beginning of weariness, the first shadow of evening, of any kind of evening. Or a sign that the air is humid, that south winds are approaching. Or unrecognized gratitude for a good digestion (sometimes called "love of man"). Or the attainment of calm by a convalescent who feels a new relish in all things and waits. Or the state which follows a thorough satisfaction of our dominant passion, the well-being of a rare repletion. Or the senile weakness of our will, our cravings, our vices. Or laziness, persuaded by vanity to give itself moral airs. Or the emergence of certainty, even a dreadful certainty, after long tension and torture by uncertainty. Or the expression of maturity and mastery in the midst of doing, creating, working, and willing—calm breathing, *attained* "freedom of the will." *Twilight of the Idols*—who knows? perhaps also only a kind of "peace of soul."

[4] I reduce a principle to a formula. Every naturalism in morality—that is, every healthy morality—is dominated by an instinct of life; some commandment of life is fulfilled by a determinate canon of "shalt" and "shalt not"; some inhibition and hostile element on the path of life is thus removed. *Anti-natural* morality—that is, almost every morality which has so far been taught, revered, and preached—turns, conversely, *against* the instincts of life: it is *condemnation* of these instincts, now secret, now outspoken and impudent. When it says, "God looks at the heart," it says No to both the lowest and the highest desires of life, and posits God as the *enemy* of *life.* The saint in whom God delights is the ideal eunuch. Life has come to an end where the "kingdom of God" begins.

[5] Once one has comprehended the outrage of such a revolt against life as has become almost sacrosanct in Christian morality, one has, fortunately, also comprehended something else: the futility, apparentness, absurdity, and *mendaciousness* of such a revolt. A condemnation of life by the living remains in the end a mere symptom of a certain kind of life: the question whether it is justified or unjustified is not even raised thereby. One would require a position *outside* of life, and yet have to know it as well as one, as many, as all who have lived it, in order to be permitted even to touch the problem of the *value* of life: reasons enough to comprehend that this problem is for us an unapproachable problem. When we speak of values, we speak with the inspiration, with the way of

looking at things, which is part of life: life itself forces us to posit values; life itself values through us when we posit values. From this it follows that even that anti-natural morality which conceives of God as the counter-concept and condemnation of life is only a value judgment of life—but of what life? of what kind of life? I have already given the answer: of declining, weakened, weary, condemned life. Morality, as it has so far been understood—as it has in the end been formulated once more by Schopenhauer, as "negation of the will to life"—is; the very *instinct of decadence,* which makes an imperative of itself. It says: *"Perish!"* It is a condemnation pronounced by the condemned.

[6] Let us finally consider how naive it is altogether to say: "Man *ought* to be such and such!" Reality shows us an enchanting wealth of types, the abundance of a lavish play and change of forms—and some wretched loafer of a moralist comments: "No! Man ought to be different." He even knows what man should be like, this wretched bigot and prig: he paints himself on the wall and comments, *"Ecce homo!"* But even when the moralist addresses himself only to the single human being and says to him, "You ought to be such and such!" he does not cease to make himself ridiculous. The single human being is a piece of *fatum* from the front and from the rear, one law more, one necessity more for all that is yet to come and to be. To say to him, "Change yourself!" is to demand that everything be changed, even retroactively. And indeed there have been consistent moralists who wanted man to be different, that is, virtuous— they wanted him remade in their own image as a prig: to that end, they *negated* the world! No small madness! No modest kind of immodesty!

Morality, insofar as it *condemns* for its own sake, and not out of regard for the concerns, considerations, and contrivances of life, is a specific error with which one ought to have no pity—an *idiosyncrasy of degenerates* which has caused immeasurable harm.

We others, we immoralists, have, conversely, made room in our hearts for every kind of understanding, comprehending, and *approving.* We do not easily negate; we make it a point of honor to be *affirmers.* More and more, our eyes have opened to that economy which needs and knows how to utilize all that the holy witlessness of the priest, of the *diseased* reason in the priest, rejects—that economy in the law of life which finds an advantage even in the disgusting species of the prigs, the priests, the virtuous. *What* advantage? But we ourselves, we immoralists, are the answer.

THE ANTI-CHRIST (in part)

PREFACE: REVALUATION OF ALL VALUES

This book belongs to the very few. Perhaps not one of them is even living yet. Maybe they will be the readers who understand my *Zarathustra:* how *could* I mistake myself for one of those for whom there are ears even now? Only the day after tomorrow belongs to me. Some are born posthumously.

The conditions under which I am understood, and then of *necessity*—I know them only too well. One must be honest in matters of the spirit to the point of hardness before one can even endure my seriousness and my passion. One must be skilled in living on mountains—seeing the wretched ephemeral babble of politics and national self-seeking, *beneath* oneself. One must have become indifferent; one must never ask if the truth is useful or if it may prove our undoing. The predilection of strength for questions for which no one today has the courage; the courage for the *forbidden;* the predestination to the labyrinth. An experience of seven solitudes. New ears for new music. New eyes for what is most distant. A new conscience for truths that I have so far remained mute. And the will to the economy of the great style: keeping our strength, our *enthusiasm* in harness. Reverence for oneself; love of oneself; unconditional freedom before oneself.

Well then! Such men alone are my readers, my right readers, my predestined readers: what matter the *rest?* The rest—that is merely mankind. One must be above mankind in strength, in *loftiness* of soul—in contempt.

FIRST BOOK: ATTEMPT AT A CRITIQUE OF CHRISTIANITY

1. Let us face ourselves. We are Hyperboreans; we know very well how far off we live. "Neither by land nor by sea will you find the way to the Hyperboreans"—Pindar already knew this about us. Beyond the north, ice, and death—*our* life, *our* happiness. We have discovered happiness, we know the way, we have found the exit out of the labyrinth of thousands of years. Who else has found it? Modern man perhaps? "I have got lost; I am everything that has got lost," sighs modern man.

This modernity was our sickness: lazy peace, cowardly compromise, the whole virtuous uncleanliness of the modern Yes and No. This tolerance and *largeur* of the heart, which "forgives" all because it "understands" all, is *sirocco* for us. Rather live in the ice than among modern virtues and other south winds! We were intrepid enough, we spared neither ourselves nor others; but for a long time we did not know where to turn with our intrepidity. We became gloomy, we were called fatalists. *Our fatum*—the abundance, the tension, the damming of strength. We thirsted for lightning and deeds and were most remote from the happiness of the weakling, "resignation." In our atmosphere was a thunderstorm; the nature we are became dark—*for we saw no way.* Formula for our happiness: a Yes, a No, a straight line, a goal.

2. What is good? Everything that heightens the feeling of power in man, the will to power, power itself.

What is bad? Everything that is born of weakness.

What is happiness? The feeling that power is *growing,* that resistance is overcome.

Not contentedness but more power; not peace but war; not virtue but fitness (Renaissance virtue, *virtù,* virtue that is moraline*-free).

The weak and the failures shall perish: first principle of our love of man. And they shall even be given every possible assistance.

What is more harmful than any vice? Active pity for all the failures and all the weak: Christianity.

---

*The coinage of a man who neither smoked nor drank coffee.

3. The problem I thus pose is not what shall succeed mankind in the sequence of living beings (man is an *end*), but what type of man shall be *bred,* shall be *willed,* for being higher in value, worthier of life, more certain of a future.

Even in the past this higher type has appeared often—but as a fortunate accident, as an exception, never as something *willed.* In fact, this has been the type most dreaded—almost *the* dreadful—and from dread the opposite type was willed, bred, and *attained:* the domestic animal, the herd animal, the sick human animal—the Christian.

4. Mankind does *not* represent a development toward something better or stronger or higher in the sense accepted today. "Progress" is merely a modern idea, that is, a false idea. The European of today is vastly inferior in value to the European of the Renaissance: further development is altogether *not* according to any necessity in the direction of elevation, enhancement, or strength.

In another sense, success in individual cases is constantly encountered in the most widely different places and cultures: here we really do find a *higher type,* which is, in relation to mankind as a whole, a kind of overman. Such fortunate accidents of great success have always been possible and will perhaps always be possible. And even whole families, tribes, or peoples may occasionally represent such a *bull's-eye.*

5. Christianity should not be beautified and embellished: it has waged deadly war against this higher type of man; it has placed all the basic instincts of this type under the ban; and out of these instincts it has distilled evil and the Evil One: the strong man as the typically reprehensible man, the "reprobate." Christianity has sided with all that is weak and base, with all failures; it has made an ideal of whatever *contradicts* the instinct of the strong life to preserve itself; it has corrupted the reason even of those strongest in spirit by teaching men to consider the supreme values of the spirit as something sinful, as something that leads into error—as temptations. The most pitiful example: the corruption of Pascal, who believed in the corruption of his reason through original sin when it had in fact been corrupted only by his Christianity.

6. It is a painful, horrible spectacle that has dawned on me: I have drawn back the curtain from the *corruption* of man. In my mouth, this word is at least free from one suspicion: that it might involve a moral accusation of man. It is meant—let me emphasize this once more—*moraline-free.* So much so that I experience this corruption most strongly precisely where men have so far aspired most deliberately to "virtue" and "godliness." I understand corruption, as you will guess, in the sense of decadence: it is my contention that all the values in which mankind now sums up its supreme desiderata are *decadence-values.*

I call an animal, a species, or an individual corrupt when it loses its instincts, when it chooses, when it prefers, what is disadvantageous for it. A history of "lofty sentiments," of the "ideals of mankind"—and it is possible that I shall have to write it— would almost explain too *why* man is so corrupt. Life itself is to my mind the instinct for growth, for durability, for an accumulation of forces, for *power:* where the will to power is lacking there is decline. It is my contention that all the supreme values of mankind *lack* this will—that the values which are symptomatic of decline, *nihilistic* values, are lording it under the holiest name.

7. Christianity is called the religion of *pity.* Pity stands opposed to the tonic emotions which heighten our vitality: it has a depressing effect. We are deprived of strength when we feel pity. That loss of strength which suffering as such inflicts on life is still further increased and multiplied by pity. Pity makes suffering contagious. Under certain circumstances, it may engender a total loss of life and vitality out of all proportion to the magnitude of the cause (as in the case of the death of the Nazarene). That is the first consideration, but there is a more important one.

Suppose we measure pity by the value of the reactions it usually produces; then its perilous nature appears in an even brighter light. Quite in general, pity crosses the law of development, which is the law of *selection*. It preserves what is ripe for destruction; it defends those who have been disinherited and condemned by life; and by the abundance of the failures of all kinds which it keeps alive, it gives life itself a gloomy and questionable aspect.

Some have dared to call pity a virtue (in every *noble* ethic it is considered a weakness); and as if this were not enough, it has been made *the* virtue, the basis and source of all virtues. To be sure—one should always keep this in mind—this was done by a philosophy that was nihilistic and had inscribed the *negation of life* upon its shield. Schopenhauer was consistent enough: pity negates life and renders it *more deserving of negation*.

Pity is the *practice* of nihilism. To repeat: this depressive and contagious instinct crosses those instincts which aim at the preservation of life and at the enhancement of its value. It multiplies misery and conserves all that is miserable, and is thus a prime instrument of the advancement of decadence: pity persuades men to *nothingness!* Of course, one does not say "nothingness" but "beyond" or "God," or "*true* life," or Nirvana, salvation, blessedness.

This innocent rhetoric from the realm of the religious-moral idiosyncrasy appears much less innocent as soon as we realize which tendency it is that here shrouds itself in sublime words: *hostility against life*. Schopenhauer was hostile to life; therefore pity became a virtue for him.

Aristotle, as is well known, considered pity a pathological and dangerous condition, which one would be well advised to attack now and then with a purge: he understood tragedy as a purge. From the standpoint of the instinct of life, a remedy certainly seems necessary for such a pathological and dangerous accumulation of pity as it is represented by the case of Schopenhauer (and unfortunately by our entire literary and artistic decadence from St. Petersburg to Paris, from Tolstoy to Wagner)—to puncture it and make it *burst*.

In our whole unhealthy modernity there is nothing more unhealthy than Christian pity. To be physicians *here,* to be inexorable here, to wield the scalpel *here*—that is *our* part, that is *our* love of man, that is how we are philosophers, we *Hyperboreans*.

*   *   *

62. With this I am at the end and I pronounce my judgment. I *condemn* Christianity. I raise against the Christian church the most terrible of all accusations that any accuser ever uttered. It is to me the highest of all conceivable corruptions. It has had the will to the last corruption that is even possible. The Christian church has left nothing untouched by its corruption; it has turned every value into an un-value, every truth into a lie, every integrity into a vileness of the soul. Let anyone dare to speak to me of its "humanitarian" blessings! To *abolish* any distress ran counter to its deepest advantages: it lived on distress, it *created* distress to eternalize *itself*.

The worm of sin, for example: with this distress the church first enriched mankind. The "equality of souls before God," this falsehood, this *pretext* for the rancor of all the base-minded, this explosive of a concept which eventually became revolution, modern idea, and the principle of decline of the whole order of society—is *Christian* dynamite. "Humanitarian" blessings of Christianity! To breed out of *humanitas* a self-contradiction, an art of self-violation, a will to lie at any price, a repugnance, a contempt for all good and honest instincts! Those are some of the blessings of Christianity!

Parasitism as the *only* practice of the church; with its ideal of anemia, of "holiness," draining all blood, all love, all hope for life; the beyond as the will to negate every reality; the cross as the mark of recognition for the most subterranean conspiracy that ever existed—against health, beauty, whatever has turned out well, courage, spirit, *graciousness* of the soul, *against life itself*.

This eternal indictment of Christianity I will write on all walls, wherever there are walls—I have letters to make even the blind see.

I call Christianity the one great curse, the one great innermost corruption, the one great instinct of revenge, for which no means is poisonous, stealthy, subterranean, *small* enough—I call it the one immortal blemish of mankind.

And time is reckoned from the *dies nefastus* with which this calamity began—after the *first* day of Christianity! *Why not rather after its last day? After today?* Revaluation of all values!

αναγκη δη στῆναι.
There must be a stop at some point.

Aristotle, *Metaphysics,* 1070a4